Apollo
Crossword
Puzzle Dictionary

Apollo
Crossword
Puzzle Dictionary

By Andrew Swanfeldt

THOMAS Y. CROWELL, PUBLISHERS
ESTABLISHED 1834
NEW YORK

FOREWORD

THE solving of crossword puzzles has for years been a popular hobby. The solutions require enough concentration to be diverting, and as an avocation they may be taken seriously or lightly. Frequently, however, the task of locating odd words becomes a labor rather than a pleasure. Thus the whole value of a few minutes' relaxation may be lost in an hour's discouraging search for an annoying word. To eliminate such an annoyance, this dictionary was compiled. More than 200,000 of the worst "sticklers" known to the puzzle makers are here in an easy-to-find form.

The listing of words in this book differs radically from the method used in other reference books and dictionaries. The construction of the puzzles themselves has dictated the arrangement of the compilation. Definitions are listed first and the applicable answer words follow. This is the reverse of standard dictionary practice, but experience has proved it the most practical method of helping both the novice and the expert to solve and build puzzles with less effort and more pleasure.

The compiling of this book is the result of years of experience in the actual working of crossword puzzles and the filing away of "posers" for future reference and confirmation. This experience, plus the constructive suggestions and criticisms from a host of friends, provides the material from which the book is made.

To all those whose contributions of words and work have helped to bring about this dictionary, my sincere thanks!

ANDREW SWANFELDT

Apollo
Crossword
Puzzle Dictionary

A

Aaron's associate–Hur
Aaron's burial place–Hor
Aaron's sister–Miriam
Abakan River group (one of)–Sagai
abalone (Eng.)–ormer
abandon – desert, discard, forswear, leave, quit, relinquish, remit, renounce, resign, surrender, vacate
abandoned–derelict, desolated, forsaken, left
abandoner of cause–deserter
abase–bemean, degrade, demean, depose, disgrace, dishonor, humble, lessen, lower, mortify, reduce, shame
abashed – ashamed, confounded, discomfited, disconcerted, humiliated, mortified, shamed, sheepish
abate–abolish, lessen, slacken, subside, wane
abate for a time–lull
abatement (coll.)–letup
abattoir–slaughterhouse
abbess (spiritual mother)–amma
abbey's head–abbot
abbot (Celtic)–coarb
abbot (Celtic monastery)–coarb
abbreviate – abridge, contract, curtail, epitomize, shorten
abbreviation (mental)–lapse
abdicate–demit, depose, disclaim, disinherit, disown, relinquish, renounce, resign
abdomen–paunch
abed–retired, sick
abet–advocate, aid, assist, back, connive, countenance, encourage, foment, help, incite, instigate, sec-

ond, succor, support, sustain, uphold
abhor–abominate, execrate, hate, loathe
abhorrence–disliking, hatred, odium
abide–await, delay, dwell, endure, live, pause, remain, reside, tarry, wait
abiding–continuing, lasting, resident
abies–firs
abigail–maid
ability–aptitude, caliber, capability, competence, efficiency, faculty, force, power, proficiency, qualification, skill, strength, sufficiency, talent
ability (creative)–genius
ability (innate)–talent
ability (special)–talent
ability to act–power
ability to bear pain or hardship–endurance
abject–beggarly, cringing, ignoble, mean, miserable, slavish, supine, vile
abject one–abaser
abjure–deny, disavow, forswear, recant, reject, renounce, repudiate
able–can, capable, clever, competent, effective, efficient, fit, fitted, powerful, proficient, qualified, skillful, vigorous
able to pay–solvent
able to read and write–literate
abnormal–aberrant, eccentric, exceptional, extraordinary, unnatural, unusual
abnormally white–albino
aboard–across, athwart, onto
abode–dar, delay, dwelling, foreshow, habitation, house, omen, prognostication

abode (humble)–cot
abode (natural)–habitat
abode (small)–cell
abode of dead–Hades, Sheol
abode of gods–Olympus
abolish – abrogate, annul, cancel, countermand, invalidate, nullify, quash, recall, rescind, reverse, revoke, vacate
abominable–detestable, execrable, hateful, loathsome, odious, vile
abominable (coll.)–beastly
abominate – abhor, hate, loathe
abomination – aversion, crime, disgust, loathsomeness, odiousness, repugnance
aboriginal–first, indigenous, native, original, primitive
aborigine–Indian, native, savage
abortion – failure, miscarriage, misconception, monstrosity
abound – exuberate, overflow, plentiful, teem
abounding – overflowing, plenteous, rife, teeming
abounding in forests–sylvan
abounding in pepper grass–cressy
abounding to excess–superabundant
abounding with blossoms–flowery
abounding with snow–nival
about–anent, around, concerning, of, on
about (prefix)–amb
above–beyond, on, over, upon
above (poetic)–oer
above (prefix)–super, supra, sur
abrade–excoriate, fret, gall, grate, raw, rub, scrape
abrading tool–file

Abraham's birthplace–Ur

Abraham's father–Terah

Abraham's grandson–Esau

Abraham's nephew–Lot

Abraham's son–Isaac, Ishmael, Medan

Abraham's wife–Sara, Sarah, Sarai

abrasion–attrition, gall

abrasive–corundum, emery

abreast–alongside, beside, even

abrege–abridgement, epitome

abri–cavity, dugout, shed, shelter

abridge – abbreviate, abstract, condense, curtail, diminish, epitomize, rasee, razee, retrench, shorten

abridge (var.)–rasee, razee

abridged statement – summary

abridgement–abstract, compend, compendium, deprivation, digest, diminution, epitome, lessening, reduction, synopsis

abroad–forth

abrogate–abolish, annul, cancel, repeal, rescind, revoke

abrupt–blunt, brusque, curt, disconnected, headlong, impetuous, perpendicular, precipitate, quick, rough, sharp, sheer, unexpected, vertical

abruptly–suddenly

Absalom captain of host–Amasa

Absalom host's captain–Amasa

Absalom's father–David

abscond – decamp, desert, eloine, elope

absence–deficiency, nonappearance, nonattendance, want

absence of mention–silence

absence of pain–anodynia

absence of pigment–alphosis

absence of self-assertion–modesty

absence without leave–A. W. O. L.

absent–absorbed, abstracted, away, dreaming, engrossed, lost, musing, nonattendant, off, preoccupied

absent-minded–distrait

absent without leave–A. W. O. L., truant

absolute–arbitrary, categorical, certain, dead, downright, peremptory, sheer, total, unconditional, utter

absolute dominion–empery, emperies (pl.)

absolute independence–alod

absolute superlative–elative

absolutely–entirely, positively, stark, thoroughly, unequivocally, utterly

absolutely (not)–conditionally

absolutely sure–positive

absolution–exculpation, forgiveness, pardon, remission

absolution given and confession received–shrive

absolves–acquits, discharges, exonerates, forgives, frees, remits, shrives

absorb–assimilate, drink, engross, imbibe

absorbed–buried, deep, incorporated, intent, lost, plunged, rapt, sunk

absorber (shock)–snubber

abstain–forbear, refrain, restrain, withhold

abstain from–eschew

abstemious–abstinent, moderate, sober, temperate

abstract–argument, compendium, deduct, remove, summary, withdraw

abstract being (existence)–ens, entia (pl.)

abstract being (Latin)–esse

abstract of account–statement

abstract of main points in course of study–syllabus

abstruse–acroamatic, acroatic, concealed, deep, eso-

teric, hidden, incomprehensible, obscure, profound, recondite

absurd–asinine, inept, irrational, nonsensical, ridiculous, silly, unreasonable

absurd (unbecoming)–inept

absurdity–nonsense

abundance–affluence, copiousness, exuberance, opulence, overflow, plenteousness, riches

abundance (great)–galore

abundance (suffix denoting)–ose

abundant–abounding, ample, galore, plentiful, plenty, profuse, rich, rife, teem

abundant (most)–rifest

abundant (not)–lenten

abuse–berate, contumely, harm, injure, insult, malign, maltreat, maul, opprobrium, rate, revile, scold, scurrility, traduce, upbraid

abuse (slang)–maul

abut–adjoin, border, join, touch

abutments (pilaster-like)–alettes

abysmal–bottomless, deep, profound, unending

abyss–chasm, deep, engulf, gulf, pit, void

Abyssinian bananas–ensetes

Abyssinian capital – Addis Ababa

Abyssinian city–Addis Ababa (c.), Adowa, Ankober, Antalo, Axum, Gambela, Gondar, Gore, Harrar, Magdala

Abyssinian coin – amole (salt), ashrafi (ac.), besa (cop.), dollar (s.), girsh (s.), Levant dollar (s.), Maria Theresa dollar (s.), Menelik dollar (s.), piaster (base s.), Talari (s.)

Abyssinian district–Harar

Abyssinian divisions–Amhara, Shoa, Tigre

Abyssinian Hamite tribe–Afar

Abyssinian lake–Dembea, Tsana, Tzana

Abyssinian lyre–kissar

Abyssinian measure–farsakh, farsang, kuba, sinjer, sinzer, tat

Abyssinian mountain–Ras Dashan

Abyssinian native (negro)–Ethiop

Abyssinian prince–Ras

Abyssinian river–Albai, Tacazze

Abyssinian ruler's title–Negus

Abyssinian sovereign title–Negus

Abyssinian title–Ras

Abyssinian weight–alada, artal, farasula, kasm, mocha, mutagalla, natr, neter, oket, ratel, rotl, wakea, wogiet

academic–scholarly, scholastic

academy–college, institution, school, society, university

academy (near Athens)–garden, grove

academy (riding)–manege

accede–acquiesce, agree, attain, comply, concur, conform, consent, enter, grant, yield

accelerated–advanced, dispatched, expedited, forwarded, furthered, sped

acceleration of one velo per second–celo

accelerator–speeder, throttle

accent–accentuate, emphasis, emphasize, mark, pitch, stress, tone

accent (Scotch peculiar rough)–birr

accent mark–breve

accept–adopt, approve, embrace, receive, take

accept as equal to one's own –nostrificate

accept as one's own–adopt

acceptable–agreeable, allowable, comfortable, pleasant, satisfactory, welcome

accepted–conventional, orthodox, popular, standard

accepted as true–credited

accepted widely–prevalent

access–accessibility, accost, admission, admittance, approach, entree

accessible–attainable, getatable, handy, obtainable, open, procurable, reachable

accession–addition, enlargement, increase, reinforcement

accessory–abettor, accompanying, appurtenant, auxiliary, contributary, subservient, subsidiary, supplementary

accessory condition–circumstance

accident–calamity, casualty, catastrophe, chance, disaster, mischance, misfortune, mishap

accident (fatal)–casualty

acclaim–applaud, applause, praise

acclaim (spontaneous, popular)–ovation

acclamation–cry, shout

acclimatize–naturalize, season

acclivity–declivity, hill

accommodate–adapt, conform, fit, lend, oblige

accommodation–loan

accompanier (minstrel's)–harpist

accompaniment – descant, obligato

accompany–attend, conduct, convoy, escort, see, squire

accomplice–abettor, accessory, ally, assistant, associate, confederate, pal

accomplish–achieve, attain, compass, consummate, contrive, do, effect, engineer, equip, execute, furnish, manage, negotiate, operate, perfect, realize, win, work

accomplished–did, done

accomplished (arch.) – beseen

accomplished in an unobserved manner–stolen

accomplished with fatigue–toilsome

accomplishment – attainment, completion, deed, feat, fulfillment, performance, proficiency

accord–accede, agreement, comport, concurrence, harmonize

accordant – agreeable, attuned, consistent, correspondent, harmonious

according to–ala

according to a chronology–datal

according to fact–true

according to fashion–alamode

according to style (Fr.)–alamode

accost–access, address, approach, greet, hail, halloo

account–explanation, narration, recital, recitation, record, rehearsal, sake, score, tale

account (autobiographical of one's experience)–memoirs

account (particularized)–recital

account deemed worthy of record–memoir

account of (abbr.)–ao

accountability–detail

accountable–amenable, answerable, liable, responsible

accountant–calculator, reckoner

accounted–reputed

accouter–see accoutre

accouterments–attire, dress, equipment, trapping

accoutre–array, attire, equip, provide

accoy–daunt, soothe, subdue, tame

accredit–approve, ascribe, confirm, sanction

accrete–add

accretion–addition, adhesion, gain

accretion (corrosive)–rust

accrue–arise, grow, mature, redound
accrues (law)–accresces
accumulate – aggregate, amass, collect, garner, gather, heap, hoard, mass, muster, save, store
accumulation–store
accumulation in blood (causing toxic condition) –uremia
accumulation of odd bits of information–serendipity
accumulation of resources–fund
accuracy–correctness, exactness, nicety, precision
accurate – close, correct, faithful, just, nice, particular, precise, proper, strict, true
accurate (strictly)–precise, prim
accursed – anathematized, cursed, damned, detestable, doomed, execrated
accusation–attack, charge, denunciation, impeachment, indictment, taxing
accusation (malicious)–calumny
accuse – arraign, attack, blame, censure, charge, criminate, denounce, impeach, indict, recriminate, tax
accuser–complainant, libelant, plaintiff, prosecutor
accustom–acclimate, addict, enure, habituate, inure, train, use, wont
accustom to (var.)–enure
accustomed–customary, usual, used, wont
accustomed to sit much–sedentary
acerbity–acrimony, asperity, bitterness, harshness, severity, tartness
acetaldehyde–ethanal
acetic acid radical–acetyl
acetic acid salt–acetate
acetic compound–acetin
acetous–acid, sour
acetylenes–ethines
ache–pain, pang, twinge

achene (one called)–utricle
achieve–accomplish, attain, compass, complete, conclude, consummate, contrive, do, effect, fulfill, gain, get, realize, win
achievement–career, feat, fosterage
achievement (best)–record
achievement (single)–oner
Achilles' father–Peleus
Achilles' vulnerable part–heel
acid–acrid, acrimonious, biting, keen, sour
acid (bleaching)–oxalic
acid (boric salt)–borate
acid (for converting hides)–tannin
acid (grape)–racemic
acid (hydrobromic)–bromide
acid (kind of)–aconic, boric, malic, mucic, terebic
acid (protein, typical) – amino
acid (pyrogallic)–pyrol
acid (salt of arabic)–arabate
acid (salt of tannic)–tannate
acid (stearic)–stearin
acid berry–currant
acid condiment–vinegar
acid formed from carone–caronic
acid forming–acidific
acid found in grapes (pert. to)–racemic
acid fruit–lemon, lime
acid neutralizer–alkalizer
acidity–acor, verjuice
acidity (stomach)–acor
acknowledge – accede, accept, allow, answer, assent, avow, concede, confess, grant, own, thank, yield
acknowledge openly–avow
acknowledge with regret–apologize
acknowledgment of an offense–apology
acknowledgment of taking goods (law)–avowry
acme–apex, climax, culmination, top, zenith
acorn (naut.)–mast

acquaint–advise, apprise, inform
acquaintance – companion, familiar, familiarity, fellowship, friend, intimacy, intimate, knowledge
acquaintance with facts–knowledge
acquiesce–accede, agree, assent, comply, concur, conform, consent, submit, yield
acquire–adopt, attain, cultivate, earn, effect, gain, get, learn, obtain, procure, reap, receive, secure, win
acquire beforehand – preempt
acquire by service–earn
acquire feathers before flight–fledge
acquire knowledge–learn
acquit–absolve, clear, exculpate, exonerate, free, release
acquittal – clearance, clearing, discharge, exculpation, freeing, release
acquittance–quietus
acre (quarter)–rood, snood
acrid–acid, acidulous, biting, caustic, pungent, rough, sharp, sour, virulent
acrimony–astringency, crabbedness, pungency, roughness, rudeness, sourness, virus
acrobat–contortionist, gymnast, ropedancer, tumbler
acrobat (aerial)–risley
across–athwart, over
across (prefix)–dia, tran
acrostic–crosswise, erratic
act–actus, behave, comport, deed, demean, do, law, play, skit, stunt
act (criminal)–villainy
act (detestable)–abomination
act (illegal)–crime
act (outstanding)–feat
act (plan of beforehand)–premeditation
act (to)–emote

act (vaudeville)–turn
act (wrongful)–tort
act against–oppose
act arrogantly–presume
act as agent–represent
act furiously–rage
act impertinent–sass
act improperly–misdeal
act of bringing up to date–revision
act of charging with gas–aeration
act of coming back to former condition–reversion
act of controlling–predomination
act of conveying–conduction
act of cutting–kerf
act of cutting off–elision
act of devoting to sacred use –consecration
act of embodiment–incorporation
act of encouraging–fosterage
act of endearment–caress, kiss
act of flowing in–influx
act of grace (good will)–favor
act of granting back–recession
act of holding–retention, tenure
act of holding back–retention
act of inserting extraneous matter–interpolation
act of kindness–benefit, favor
act of leaving–egress
act of linking together–concatenation
act of opening engine's exhaust port–prerelease
act of placing (resting)–reposal
act of praise–commendation
act of producing falsely–forgery
act of putting in motion or exertion–arousal
act of respect–courtesy, curtsy, homage

act of restraining–determent
act of rubbing together–attrition
act of self-examination–introspection
act of sharing–participation
act of solving–solution
act of taking for one's own–adopt
act of taking private property for public use–expropriation
act of telling–relation
act of throwing person or things out of window–defenestration
act of witnessing–attestation
act of working together–collaboration
act of worship–devotion
act out of sorts–mope
act pompously–pontificate
act upon–affect
act wildly–rave
acted enigma–charade
acted in opposition of–counteracted
acting–execution, impersonation, operating, performance, serving
acting from sense of right–conscientious
acting with great force–vehement
action–act, deed, doing
action (at law)–re, res
action (court)–lawsuit
action (evil)–misdeed
action (expressive)–gesture
action (fixed mode of)–habit
action (legal)–suit
action (regular course of)–routine
action (right)–duty
action (secret)–stealth
action (slow in)–deliberate
action (surprise)–coup de main
action (to recover goods)–replevin
action (to recover personal property)–replevin, trover
active–agile, alert, animat-

ed, assiduous, brisk, dapper, industrious, kinetic, nimble, prompt, quick, ready, smart, spirited, sprightly, spry, vigorous
active (make)–energized
active (not)–dormant, inoperative, static
active cause–agent
active in business – pragmatic
activity–agility, briskness, bustle, gog, nimbleness, quickness, stir, vigor
activity (animated)–pep
activity (center of)–focus
activity (in)–about
activity (lack of)–stagnation
activity (Scot.)–vir
activity (unnecessary)–ado
actor–agent, doer, entertainer, mime, mummer, performer, personator, player, portrayer, protagonist, thespian, trooper
actor (chief)–hero, protagonist, star
actor (famous) – Edwin Booth, John Wilkes Booth, William Faversham, Otis Skinner, Edward Sothern, Fredrick Ward, David Warfield
actor (Irish)–aisteoir
actor (kind of)–comedian, comedien, comedienne (fem.), pantomimic, pantomimist, tragedian, tragedienne (fem.)
actor (poor, slang)–ham
actor (present day)–Lunt
actor (second rate)–barnstormer
actor's last word–cue
actress (famous)–Maude Adams (Maude Kiskadden), Blanche Bates, Sarah Bernhardt (Rosine Benard), Julia Marlowe, Mme. Modjeska, Mme. Rejane (Gabrielle Charlotte), Eleanor Robson, Lillian Russell, Fritzi Scheff
actual–factual, genuine, positive, practical, real, sub-

stantial, tangible, true, veritable
actual being (Lat.)–esse
actual happening–fact
actuality–fact, reality, realness, substantiality, verity
actually–truly
actuate – animate, arouse, egg, impel, induce, move, rouse
acumen–acuteness, discernment, discrimination, keenness, perspicacity, sagacity, sharpness, shrewdness
acute – discriminating, ingenious, keen, perspicacious, sharp, subtle, tart
ad (form of the prefix)–ap
adage–axiom, dict, maxim, motto, proverb, saw, saying, truism
adamant–hard, loadstone, obdurate
Adam's ale (coll.)–water
Adam's-flannel–mullein
Adam's grandson–Enos
Adam's son–Abel, Cain, Seth
Adam's son (third)–Seth
Adam's wine (coll.)–water
adapt–accommodate, adjust, arrange, comply, fit, harmonize, suit
adapt to foreign environment–acclimate
adaptable – accommodative, conformable, pliable, tractable
adaptation–accommodation, arrangement, qualification
adapted for cutting–incisor
add–accrete, affix, annex, append, attach, compute, plus, subjoin, tot
add scant amounts–eke
add to laboriously–eke
add up–sum, tot, total
add zest to–spice
adda–skink
added–extra, joined, supplementary, united
added to–plus
addict–habituate, hophead
addicted–accustomed, at-

tached, devoted, habituated, inclined, prone
addicted to pillaging–predatory
Addison's signature (in *The Spectator*)–Clio
addition–adjunct, appendage, extension, joining, plus, uniting
addition (in)–addendum, addenda (pl.), plus, too
addition (subordinate)–appendage
addition (to a building)–ell, leanto, wing
addition (to a document)–addendum, addenda (pl.), rider
addition (to Latin service)–farse
addition (union)–amendment, annexation
additional–besides, else, extra, fresh, further, more, new, other
additional (an)–another
additional (in)–besides, else, extra, more
additional biological specimen–cotype
additional grant–bonus
address–accost, direct, discourse, eulogy, greet, hail, harangue, ingenuity, lecture, oration, readiness, salute, sermon, speech, tact, talk
address again–redirect
address lengthily–perorate
adds over and above–superadds
adduce–advance, allege, assign, cite, infer, name, present, quote
adept–conversant, expert, proficient, skilled, skillful, versed
adept (coll.)–dabster
adept in fine arts–artist
adequate–ample, commensurate, competent, due, enough, equal, equalize, full, proportionate, satisfactory, sufficient, suitable
adhere – accrete, cleave,

cling, cohere, glue, hold, stick
adhere (cause to)–paste
adhere (closely)–cling
adhere (Prov. Eng.)–cleg
adherence to duty–right
adherent – adhering, ally, clinging, disciple, follower, partisan, sequela, sequelae (pl.), sticking, supporter, upholder
adherent (of a belief)–dualist
adherent (strong)–partisan
adherent (unwelcome)–bur
adherent of (suffix)–ite, ites (pl.)
adherent of faction–partisan
adherent to crown–Tory
adhesive – cement, glue, mastic, mucilage, paste, sticky, tenacious
adhesiveness–tenacity
adhibit–administer, admit, affix, attach
adieu–farewell
adipic acid salt–adipate
adipose–fat, fatty
adit–access, admission, approach, drainage, entrance, entry, haulage, stulm
adjacent–abutting, bordering, close, conterminous, contiguous, juxtaposed, meeting, neighboring, nigh, touching
adject–add, annex, join
adjective–accessory, dependent
adjective (descriptive)–epithet
adjective (limiting)–the
adjective ending–ic
adjective forming suffix–ent
adjective suffix–ent, ial, ian, il, ile, ive
adjoin–abut, add, attach, unite
adjudge–assign, award, decree, ordain, try
adjudged unfit for use–condemned, IC
adjunct–accessory, added, addition, annexed, ap-

pendage, appendant, appurtenance, auxiliary
adjunct (natural)–apanage
adjuration–appeal, oath
adjure–ask, bid, bind, charge, command, swear
adjust–adapt, align, arrange, attune, coordinate, fix, frame, harmonize, justify, rectify, regulate, set, settle, suit, systematize, true
adjusted for certain speed–geared
adjuster–arranger, fitter
adjustment–adaptation, arrangement, disposition, fitting, rectification, regulation, settlement, suiting
adjutant – aide, assistant, auxiliary, helper
adjutant (the)–argala
adjutant bird–argala
adjutant stork–marabou
administer–conduct, distribute, execute, furnish, manage
administer corporal punishment–spank
administer extreme unction –anele
administer extreme unction (obs.)–enele
administration – conduct, dispensation, execution, regimen, regulation
administration of justice–judicature
administrative person–executive
administrator–director, dispenser, executor, manager, trustee
admiration–adoration, appreciation, esteem, liking, reverence, wonder
admire–approve, esteem, idolize, like, regard, revere
admission–access, entrance, entree, initiation
admission to citizenship–enfranchisement, naturalization

admit–adhibit, avow, concede, confess, enter, own
admittance–access, entrance, initiation, reception
admitted (newly)–initiate
admonish–caution, chide, exhort, rebuke, warn
admonisher–monitor
admonition–caution, reprehension, reproof, warning
ado–bustle, commotion, flurry, fuss, hurry, pother, stir
adolescent–lad
adopt – accept, assume, choose, embrace, espouse, father, mother, naturalize, receive, take, welcome
adopt by vote–resolve
adoption–assumption, espousal
adoption of cause (defense) –espousal
adore–esteem, honor, idolize, love, revere, worship
adorn – array, bedight, clothe, deck, decorate, drape, embellish, emblaze, garnish, grace, primp
adorn ostentatiously–prink
adorn richly–caparison
adorn with feathers–implume
adorn with gaudy ornaments–tinsel
adorn with jewels–bedeck, begem
adorned–clad, clothed, ornate, pranked, prinked
adorned (elaborately)–ornate
adorned (least)–barest
adorned in excess–ornate
adorned with gold and ivory–chryselephantine
adornment (cheap)–tinsel
adornment (Fr.)–decor
adornment (superficial) – tinsel
adornment (useless)–frill
Adriatic city–Venice
Adriatic island–Bua, Lagosta

Adriatic peninsula–Istria
Adriatic port–Pola, Trieste
Adriatic wind–bora
adrift–asea, floating, unanchored, unmoored
adroit–cunning, dexterous, expert, habile, ingenious, neat, ready, skillful
adroitness–address, dexterity, knack, tact
adulation–compliment, flattery, praise
adulator–praiser
adulterate–contaminate, corrupt, debase, defile
adulterated–counterfeit, impure, spurious
adust–burn, burnt, fiery, scorch, scorched
advance–boost, gain, loan, nose, process, progress, promote, promotion, raise, rise
advance (in)–ahead
advance guard–van
advance in years–age
advance violently–dash
advanced (most)–foremost
advanced course of study–seminar
advanced equally–abreast
advancement (great moral and intellectual)–enlightenment
advantage–behalf, behoof, benefit, boot, interest, odds, start, stead
advantage (slang)–edge
advantageous – auspicious, encouraging, expedient, favorable
adventitious – episodic, extrinsic, fortuitous, incidental
adventure–undertaking, enterprise, venture
adventure (an)–gest
adventure (prankish)–escapade
adventure story (coll.)–yarn
adventurer–enterpriser
adventurous tale–gest
adverbial ending–ly
adversary – competitor, enemy, foe, foeman, opponent

adverse – conflicting, contrary, disinclined, ill, loath, opposed, opposing, reluctant, unfavorable

adverse (entirely or directly)–diametric

adversity–distress, ill, misery, misfortune, suffering

advert–allude, recur, refer, return

advertise–notify, announce, proclaim, promulgate, publish, publicize

advertisement – ad, Neon, sign

advertising (radio) – commercial, plug

advice–admonition, consultation, counsel, deliberation, exhortation, instruction, opinion, recommendation, suggestion

advice (arch.)–rede

advice (old form)–avis

advice not to (contr.)–don't

advisable–befitting, desirable, expedient, proper, prudent

advise–admonish, acquaint, apprise, coach, counsel

advise (arch.)–rede

adviser – admonisher, appriser, counselor, monitor, nestor

adviser (woman)–egeria

advisers (body of)–cabinet

advocate–backer, champion, defend, endorse, espouse, paraclete, pro, proponent, urge

advocate of simple life – simplicitarian

advocate of the newest–neo

advocate of the novel–neo

advocated by argument–pleaded

advocator of doctrine or cause–apostle

Aeetes' daughter–Medea

Aegean Island–Chios, Mitylene, Nikaria, Samos

Aegean Island inhabitants (anc.)–Leleges

Aegean Sea Gulf–Saros

Aegean Sea Island–Ios, Nio, Samos, Scio

Aegean seaport–Enos

Aegean Sea rock–Aex

Aello–harpy

Aeneid's hero–Aeneas

aequor–plane, sea, surface

aequoreal–marine, oceanic

aerage–ventilation

aerate–aerify, inflate, ventilate

aerial–aeric, airy

aerial jouster–aviator

aerie–brood, nest

aeriform–gaseous

aeriform fluid–gas

aeronautics (pert. to)–aero

Aeson's son–Jason

Aeta (var.)–Ita

affability towards inferiors–condescension

affable–accessible, benign, civil, complaisant, gracious

affair – circumstance, concern, duel, fight, matter, proceeding, thing, transaction

affair of chance–lottery

affairs (human)–life

affect–assume, concern, frequent, haunt, influence, melt, move, operate, pretend, simulate, soften

affect emotionally–thrill

affect with overcrowding–congested

affectations – airs, mannerisms, mince, poses, pretenses

affected–ailed, airy, fallal, pretended, stilted

affected by age–senile

affected harshly–rasped

affected sentimentality – lackadaisicalness

affected with incomplete paralysis–paretic

affected with love or amorous fancy–smit, smitten

affected with partial paralysis–paretic

affected with wonder–marvel

affectedly sentimental–gushing

affectedly shy or modest–coy, demure, mim

affecting sense of taste–sapid

affection–attachment, fondness, love, tenderness

affection (ardent)–love

affection (nervous spasmodic)–tetanus

affection (paternal)–storge

affection (throat, inflammatory)–angina

affection of the muscles–crick

affectionate – ardent, attached, devoted, earnest, fond, loving, parental, warm

affector of devotion–pietist

affector of superiority–prig

affects pleasurably–regales

affiance – betroth, confidence, faith, pledge, promise, reliance, trust

affiant–affidavit, deponent

affiche–advertised, paraded, posted

affidavit–oath, statement

affinity–attraction, family, kin, kindred, liking

affirm–allege, assert, attest, aver, avouch, avow, declare, predicate, profess, pronounce, swear, testify

affirm (earnestly)–assever

affirm (positively)–avouch

affirmation–assertion, oath, ratification, vow

affirmation (solemn)–oath

affirmation by denial of opposite–litotes

affirmative–aye, declarative, predicative, yea, yes

affirmatory–assertional

affix–add, annex, append, attach, connect, subjoin

affix firmly–anchor

affix signature to–sign

affixed to–entitled

afflict – chasten, distress, grieve, harass, hurt, oppress, pain, torment, trouble, vex, wound

afflict with grief–lacerate

afflicted – ailed, depressed, sad, troubled

afflicted (grievously)–smitten

affliction–adversity, calamity, distress, grief, hardship, misery, misfortune, pain, trouble, woe, wretchedness

afflictive–severe

affluence–abundance, opulence, plenitude, plenty, riches, wealth

affluent–abundant, copious, fat, opulent, plenteous, rich, wealthy

afford–confer, furnish, give, grant, lend, yield

affording observation–attentional

affording testimony–evidential

affray–assault, brawl, contest, disturbance, encounter, feud, fight, melee, quarrel, riot, scuffle, tumult

affright–alarm, appall, dismay, scare, startle, terrify

affront–abuse, defy, illtreat, indignity, insult, irritate, nettle, offend, outrage, provoke

Afghan carpet (fine)–Herat

Afghan coin–abbasi (s.), afghani (s.), amania (g.), kabuli rupee (s.), pul (cop.)

Afghan fox–corsac

Afghan prince–ameer, amir, emeer, emir

Afghanistan city–Cabul (c.), Kabul, Kandahar, Ghuzni, Herat

Afghanistan mountain – Himalayas, Hindu Kush, Sulaiman

Afghanistan pony (hardy mountain)–yaboo, yabu

Afghanistan river–Archandab, Cabul, Hari Rud, Helmund, Indus

Afghanistan sovereign – ameer, amir, emeer, emir

Afghanistan tribe–Ulus

afire (Eng. dial.)–alow

aforethought – premediated, premeditation, prepense

afraid – alarmed, anxious, cowardly, fainthearted,

pusillanimous, scared, shrinking, terrified

afraid (dial.)–afeard

afraid (Scot.)–rad

afreet–demon, giant, jinni

afresh–again, anew, denovo

Africa (old name)–Libya

Africa (poetic)–Afric

Africa East Coast soldier (native, in European power's service)–Askari

African – Moor, Negress, Negro

African (South, warlike)–Suto

African animal (river seal-like)–ayu

African antelope – addax, bisa, bongo, eland, gnu, kob, koba, koodoo, kudu, oribi, oryx, tolo, tora

African antelope (large)–gnu, sassaby

African antelope (small)–oribi

African arrow poison–haya, inee

African ash (prickly)–artar

African baboon (large West)–mandrill

African bird–taha

African bird (weaver)–taha

African calabash tree (var.)–lalo

African carnivore–civet, ratel

African cataract–Victoria

African charm–grigri

African charm (var.)–greegree

African chief's residence–tata

African city–Oran, Tripoli, Tunis

African civet (ring-tailed palm)–nandine

African colony–Kenya

African colony (French)–Algeria

African country–Algeria

African country (grassy)–veldt

African country (north)–Arabia, Tunis

African desert–Igidi, Kalahari, Libyan, Sahara

African desert region (of shifting sand)–reg

African division–Abyssinia, Adrar, Algeria, Angola, Bechuanaland, Cameroons, Congo, Egypt, Eritrea, Fernando Po, Gold Coast, Guinea, Liberia, Madagascar, Natal, Nigeria, Nyassaland, Orange Free State, Rhodesia, Rio de Oro, Sahara, Senegambia, Somali, Somaliland, Sudan, Togoland, Transvaal, Tripoli, Tunis, Uganda, Union of South Africa

African enclosure (South)–kraal

African equine–zebra

African fat-yielding tree–shea

African fence enclosure (defense)–bomar

African finch–senegal

African flies–kivus, tsetses

African fox–asse, fennec

African fox (small)–asse

African gazelle–cora

African ground squirrel–xerus

African gulf–Aden

African harp (small)–nanga

African hemp (fibrous)–ife

African herb–ocra

African horse–barb

African horse disease–surra

African Hottentot–Nama

African insect (poisonous)–tsetse

African instrument–nanga

African instrument (stringed)–rebab

African instrument (xylophone-like)–balafo

African Islamatic sect–Almohades

African island–Ascension, Bourbon, Canaries, Cape Verde, Comoros, Fernando Po, Madagascar, Madeira, Mauritius, Prince's, Socotra, St. Helena, St. Thomas

African jackal (north)–diebs.

African kingdom–Ashanti

African lake–Albert Nyanza, Bangweulu, Chad, Mweru, Nyasa, Rudolf, Tanganyika, Tchad, Victoria Nyanza
African lake (shallow, saline)–shat, shot, shott
African language–Bantu
African lily–aloe
African lynx–caracal
African mammal–okapi, ratel, zebra
African mammal (ass-like)–zebra
African measure–Cape foot, mkono, morgen, muid, rood, rope, schepel, ton
African monkey – grivet, waag
African mountain – Atlas, Cameroon, Cathkin Peak, Drakenberg, Kenia, Kilimanjaro, Natal
African mountain pass–Nek
African native–ashantee, damara
African negrito–Aka, Akka, Bambute, Batwa
African Negro–Dahoman, Jur, Vai, Vei
African Negro (equatorial) –Bantu
African Negro society–Egbo
African palmyra (cultivated for nuts)–ronier
African peasant–kopi
African people (pygmy)–Afifi, Akka
African plant–calla
African polecat–zoril
African port–Dakar
African powdered leaf powder (soup)–lalo
African prickly ash–atar
African pygmy tribe–Afifi, Akka
African race–Arabs, Bantus, Bechuanas, Berbers, Bushmen, Copts, Danakil, Fulahs, Hamites, Hottentots, Kabyles, Kaffres, Negroes, Nubians, Semites, Somali, Swahili
African race (small)–Dokos
African region (central)–Sudan

African region (West Coast)–Guinea
African residence–tata
African rhinoceros–umhofo
African river–Congo, Gambia, Niger, Nile, Senegal, Tana, Zambesi
African river bed–donga
African rodent–ratel
African rosewood–mulompi
African ruminant–okapi
African savage–zulu
African seaport–Tunis
African seaport (fortified)–Oran
African (Lake Victoria) society member (cannibal secret)–Bachichi
African soldier–spahi
African sorcery–obi
African stockade–boma
African stork – marabou, simbil
African strap (rawhide)–riem
African town–Bardia
African tree–akee, cola, shea, siris
African tree (fat-yielding)–shea
African tree (timber)–baku
African tree (tropical)–artar, etua
African tree (West)–sassy
African tree genus–cola
African tribe (central migratory)–Bapindi
African tribe (southern)–Batonga
African tribesman–Bantu, Berber
African village–kraal
African weaver bird–taha
African weight–barrel, bundle, cental, ton
African worm (infesting eyes)–loa
aft–abaft, astern
after–later, past, since, subsequent
after a while–anon, later
afterbreast–metathorax
afterdate–postdate
after dinner–postprandial
after-dinner coffee – demitasse

afterhand–afterwards
aftermath – consequences, rowen
aftermost–hindmost, last
afterpiece (comic, romantic) –exode
aftersong–epode
aftersong (resembling an)–epodic
after wrist–metacarpus
agacant–exciting, provocative
agacella–antelope
agacerie–coquetry
again–afresh, anew, back, encore, freshly, newly
again (prefix)–re
against–anti, con, opposed, versus, vs
against (prefix)–anti
against the law–illegal
agallochum–aloes
Agamemnon's brother – Menelaus
Agamemnon's daughter – Electra
Agamemnon's father – Atreus
Agamemnon's son–Orestes
Agamemnon's wife – Clytemnestra
Agamemnon's wife's paramour–Aegisthus
agar carbohydrate–gelose
agasp–eager
agate–chalcedony, marble, pebble
agave–aloe
age–aeon, cycle, date, eon, epoch, era, generation, period, time
age (pert. to)–eral, eval
age (present geological)–neozoic
age (youthful)–teen
Age of Reason author–Paine
aged–elderly, old, senile
aged (obs.)–veared
agency–action, efficiency, instrumentality, intermediation, management, means, operation
agency (active)–dint
agency (caustic)–erodent
agency (cleaning) – borax, soap

agency (news)–AP, DNB, Domei (Jap.), INS, International, Reuters (Eng.), UP

agent–actor, aumildar, consignee, deputy, doer, emissary, envoy, factor, gobetween, instrument, intermediary, operative, operator, representative

agent (acting for another)–factor, proctor

agent (adhesive)–glue, paste

agent (assistive)–facilitator

agent (espionage)–spy

agent (military)–spy

agent (minifying)–lessener

agent (native employed by foreign establishment)–comprador

agent (native, of foreign firm)–comprador

agent (purchasing)–buyer

agent (secret, disguised)–emissary, spy

agents (hair-removing)–depilatories

ages (belonging to first)–primeval

ages (pert. to middle)–medieval

aggrandize–advance, augment, exalt, promote

aggravate – heighten, increase, intensify, magnify, nag, pester, taunt, tease, twit

aggregate – combination, compound, sum, total

aggregate fruit–etaerio

aggregate of plants in district–flora

aggregation – assemblage, collection, congeries, group

aggregation (small)–cluster, flock

aggression–attack, encroachment, injury, intrusion, invasion, offense, provocation

aggressive–assaulting, assertive, attacking, invasive, offensive, provoking

aggrieved (more)–sorer

agile–active, alert, brisk, lively, nimble, quick, spry

agilely–lissomely

aging–senescent

agitate–churn, discompose, discuss, disquiet, distract, disturb, jar, move, perturb, revolve, rile, rouse, shake, stir, trouble

agitate violently–churn

agitates air–fans

agitation – commotion, excitement, flutter, perturbation, shake, tumult, turmoil

ago–past, since

agog–eager, excited, vigilant

agonize – excruciate, rack, torture

agony–anguish, pain, pang, suffering, throe, torture

agree–accede, acquiesce, assent, bargain, coincide, comply, comport, concur, conform, consent, contract, engage, jibe, nice, promise, side, stipulate, submit

agree (coll.)–gee, jibe

agree in final sound–rhyme, rime

agreeable–acceptable, amiable, charming, compliant, desirable, dulcet, nice, pleasant, pleasing, suave

agreeable (more)–nicer

agreeableness–amiability

agreeably sociable–companionable

agreed on–concerted

agreeing (not)–dissent

agreeing in final sound – riming

agreement – accession, accord, accordment, assent, bargain, cartel, compact, consent, contract, covenant, entente, pact, rapport, stipulation, terms, treaty, unison

agreement (convention) – mise

agreement (general) – consensus

agreement (international)–pact, treaty

agreement (law) – stipulation

agreement (payment)–terms

agreement (prisoner exchange)–cartel

agreement (solemn)–covenant

agreement (written official) –cartel

agreement by treaty–concord

agricultural community – hamlet, thorp

agricultural establishment–farm, grove, orchard, ranch

agricultural machine–combine, header, reaper, seeder, thrasher, tractor

Agriculture (god of)–Faunus, Nabu, Nebo

Agriculture (goddess of) – Ops

agriculture technology – agrotechny

agriculturist (Southern) – planter

agrise – abhor, affright, dread, loathe, terrify

aground–ashore, stranded

aground by spring's highest tide–neaped

agrypnia–insomnia

agua–water

aguacate–avocado

aguamas–pinguin

ague–fever

ague tree–sassafras

Ahasuerus' chief minister–Haman

Ahaziah's sister–Jehosheba, Jehosobeath

ahead–advance, before, fore, forward, leading, on, onward

ahead (prefix)–pre

Ahian's father–Sacar

ahoy–avast

Ahriman angel–div

aid–abet, assist, befriend, help, relief, service, succor, support

aid (mountebank's)–zany

aid (printer's)–devil

aide (duelist's)–second

aim–aspire, end, goal, intent, intention, object, point, purpose

aim high–aspire

aimless–blind, chance, desultory, idle, purposeless, random, undirected, aimlessly–idle

aine–elder, senior

air – attitude, deportment, manner, mien, ventilate, wind

air (buoyant)–lilt

air (comb. form)–aer, aeri, aero

air (element of)–argo

air (musical)–aria, melody, solo, tune

air (operatic, sung on entrance)–sortita

air (pert. to)–aural

air (refreshing, coll.)–ozone

air (short)–arietta, ariette

air (upper)–aether, ether, stratosphere

air being (imaginary)–sylph

air clipper–liner

air-course pillar–pylon

aircraft (coll.)–aero

aircraft (forward end)–nose

aircraft carrier (Navy slang) –flattop

aircraft route–skyway

aircraftsman (Fr.)–AC, erk

aircraftsman (Fr. slang)–erk

air element–xenon

airfield–airport

airfield commander (French slang)–stationmaster

air-fleet arrangement–echelon

air force (Eng. abbr.)–RAF

airily–delicately, gaily, jauntily, lightly, thinly

airiness–aeriality, delicacy, jauntiness, sprightliness

airline (abbr.)–TWA, UAL

air navigation (pert. to)–aeronautic

air nozzle (blast furnace)–tuyere

air passage–ventiduct

airplane–aeri, aero

airplane (French)–avion

airplane (kind of)–biplane, helicopter, monoplane, Taube

airplane (motorless)–glider

airplane (part of)–aileron

airplane course marker–pylon

airplane inventor–Wright

airplane manufacturer–Boeing, Consolidated, Curtiss, Douglas, Lockheed, Martin, Ryan, Timms, Vega, Vultee, Wright

airplane wing framework–cabane

airport–airfield

air propeller–fan

air-race marker–pylon

air-raid alarm (Eng.)–flap

airs (single voice, Italian)–soli

airship–aeronat, balloon, biplane, blimp, dirigible, monoplane

airship (coll.)–aero

airship (small dirigible)–blimp

airship fin (vertical)–keel

air stone–aerolite

airtight–hermetic

air vehicle (coll.)–aero

air vesicle in algae–aerocyst

air weapon (Ger.) – Luftwaffe

airy–aerial, airlike, delicate, flippant, insubstantial, light

aiseweed–goutweed

aisteori (Irish)–actor

ait–eyot, isle, islet

ait (Irish)–oat

aitu–demon, god, spirit

aizle–ember, spark

ajenjo–absinthe

ajonjoli–sesame

akin–allied, consanguineous, related, sib

akin (closely)–correlated

ala–wing, winglike

Alabama city – Anniston, Selma

Alabama county–Etowah

Alabama state flower–goldenrod

alabaster–gypsum

alack–alas

alackaday–alas

alacrity – briskness, eagerness, promptitude, readiness, sprightliness, willingness

Aladdin's Lamp spirit–genie, genii (pl.), jinni, jinn (pl.)

aladiable–deviled, seasoned

alameda–promenade, walk

alamode–fashion, fashionably, mood

alarm–affright, arouse, consternation, dismay, fear, fright, frighten, scare, startle, terrify, terror, tocsin, trepidation

alarm (overmastering)–terror

alarm (real or threatened attack)–alert

alarm (war, Eng. slang)–flap

alarm signal–alert

alarmist–pessimist, scaremonger, terrorist

alas–ay

alas (Irish, var.)–ohone

Alaskan boat (portable, made of skins)–bidarka, bidarkee

Alaskan codfish–wachna

Alaskan Eskimo–Aleut

Alaskan glacier–Muir

Alaskan highway–Alcan

Alaskan Indian–Auk

Alaskan Indian liquor–hoochinoo

Alaskan island–Aleutian, Adreanof

Alaskan island Indian–Aleut, Aleutic

Alaskan mountain–Ada

Alaskan outer garment–parka

Alaskan town–Fairbanks, Juneau, Nome, Sitka

Albanian capital–Tirana

Albanian city–Avlona, Berat, Chimara, Coritza, Durazzo, Durres, Elbasan, Elbasani, Koritza, Prevesa, Scutari, Tepeleni, Tirana, Tirane, Valona

Albanian coin–franc (s.), lek (ni.), qintar (br.)

Albanian king–Zog

Albanian lake – Ochrida, Scutria
Albanian river–Drin
Albanian soldier–palikar
albardine–esparto
albatross (sooty)–nelly
albé–album
albify–whiten
albornoz–burnoose, cloak
album–albe, register
albumen (seed)–endosperm
albuminoid–collagen, elastin, keratin, proteid
albumose in seralbumin–serose
alcazar–fortress, palace
alcazava–fortress
alcohol (class of solid, higher)–sterin, sterol
alcohol (fluid)–nerol
alcohol (suffix denoting)–ol
alcohol (vinyl)–ethenol
alcohol beverage–brandy, negus, rum, whisky
alcohol radical–amyl
alcoholic standard–proof
alcove–niche, recess
alcove (dining)–dinette
alder – chief, patriarch, prince, ruler
alder (yellow)–sagerose
alder tree (Scot.)–arn
ale (strong)–mum
ale tub–alevat
alee (opposite of)–aweather, stoss
alert–active, agile, awake, brisk, circumspect, lively, nimble, observant, prompt, ready, vigilant, wary, watchful
alert (less)–slower
Alexandrian bishop (early) –Athanasius
Alexandrian presbyter–Arius
Alexandrian theologian–Arius
alfa–esparto
alfalfa–lucerne
alforja–bag, pouch, saddlebag, wallet
alga (algae, pl.)–seaweed
Algerian capital–Oran
Algerian cavalryman–spahee, spahi

Algerian city–Algiers, Bona, Constantine, Oran, Tlemcen
Algerian departments–Algiers, Constantine, Oran
Algerian governor–dey
Algerian grass–esparto
Algerian half bushel–tarris
Algerian measure–pik, pik halebi, rebis, tarri, termin
Algerian monastery–ribat
Algerian mountain–Atlas
Algerian name (old)–Numidia
Algerian race–Arabs, Berbers, Kabyles
Algerian river–Shelif
Algerian ruler–bey, dey
Algerian seaport – Oran, Orel
Algerian soldier–she, spahee, spahi
Algerian vessel–xebec
Algonquin–Arapaho
Algonquin Indian–Cree, Ottawa, Sac
Algonquin Indian (Montana)–Blackfoot
Algonquin spirit–Manitou
Algonquin tribe–Miami
Ali Baba's key word–sesame
Alice in Wonderland author–Carroll
Alice in Wonderland beast (vocal)–walrus
Alice in Wonderland character–Mad Hatter
alien–foreigner, stranger
alienate–devest, disunite, estrange, separate, wean
alienation–estrangement
alight–descend, dismount, lodge, perch, rest, settle, stop
align–range
alike–duplicate, identical, like, same, similar
aliment–nutriment, sustenance, food, pabulum, broma
aliped–bat
alipin–slave
alive–brisk, lively, sprightly
alizarin (crude)–azale
alkaline remedy–antacid

alkaloid–eserin
alkaloid (calabar bean)–eserin, eserine
alkaloid (chief of calabar bean)–physostigmine
alkaloid (cusco bark)–aricine
alkaloid (in coffee)–caffein
alkaloid (liquid)–conine
alkaloid (myotic)–eserin, eserine
alkaloid (putrefactive)–ptomain, ptomaine
alkaloid (white crystalline) –emetine
all–completely, entire, every, wholly
all (comb. form)–pan
all apart (obs.)–apieces
all inclusive–entire
all pins down with one ball –strike
all reaching–universal
all right (slang)–hunky, hunky dory
all that could be desired– ideal
all there–same
allay–abate, alleviate, appease, check, compose, relieve, repress, slake, soothe, subdue
allee–aisle, avenue, mall, passage, walk
allege–adduce, advance, affirm, ascribe, assert, assign, attribute, aver, cite, declare, maintain, offer, plead, present, profess, propose, quote
allegiance–constancy, devotion, fealty, fidelity, homage, loyalty
allegiance violation–treachery
allegorical story (teaching truth)–parable
alleviate–abate, allay, assuage, compose, ease, extenuate, lessen, lighten, mitigate, moderate, pacify, palliate, quiet, relieve, soften, solace, soothe, tranquilize
alley–byway, lane, mall, path, way

alley (back)–slum
alley (blind)–cul de sac
alley or lane (narrow, Eng. dial.)–tewer
alliance–agnation, association, combination, compact, covenant, entente, fusion, league, pact, union
alliance (between nations)–entente
alliance for joint action–coalition
allied–akin, kindred, related, united
allied by blood–cognate
allied closely–germane
alligator (American tropical)–cayman
alligator pear–avocado
allocate–allot, apportion, assign, distribute, mete
allocation–collocation
allot–appoint, apportion, appropriate, assign, design, destine, dole, fix, grant, intend, mete, ordain, portion out, prescribe, ration, select, specify
allotment – apportionment, assignment, ration
allow–authorize, bear, concede, endure, let, permit, suffer, tolerate
allow as a reduction–rebate
allow to enter in advance (as steam)–preadmit
allow to pass–lapse
allow to pass in–intromit
allow to remain–leave
allowance–admitting, authorization, conceding, granting, permission, ration, sanction, stipend, tolerance
allowance (prince's)–appenage
allowance for packing–tare
allowance for past services–pension
allowance for shrinkage–scalage
allowance for waste–tret
allowance for weight of container–tare

allowed variance from specifications–tolerance
allowing for that–if
alloy–adulterate, brass, mix, pewter
alloy (aluminum)–duralumin
alloy (anc.)–asem
alloy (artificial gold)–asem
alloy (black metallic, of sulphur)–niello
alloy (cheap jewelry)–oroide
alloy (Chinese of zinc, nickel and copper)–packtong, paktong
alloy (copper)–oroide
alloy (copper and aluminum)–duralumin
alloy (copper and tin)–bronze
alloy (copper and zinc)–brass
alloy (deep metallic, black, of sulphur)–niello
alloy (gold and silver, artificial)–asem
alloy (gold colored)–oroide
alloy (gold-like)–oroide
alloy (like German silver)–packtong, paktong
alloy (metallic)–brass
alloy (of gold brilliancy)–doralium
alloy (silver)–billon
alloy (tin and copper, resembling gold)–oroide
alloy of copper (black)–niello
alloy of copper and white metal–oroide
alloy of copper and zinc–brass
alloy of mercury–amalgam
alloy of tin and lead–pewter
alloy used for tea canisters–calin
allseed (genus of)–radiola
allspice tree–pimento
alltud–alien, foreigner, slave
allude–hint, indicate, insinuate, intimate, mention, point, refer, relate, suggest
allure–attract, decoy, entice, entrap, inveigle, invite,

lead, lure, persuade, prevail, snare, tempt, tole, win
allurement–attraction, bait, bribe, enticement, lure, temptation
allusion–hint, reference
allusion (derisive)–twit
allusion (derogatory)–innuendo
alluvial deposit–delta
alluvial fan–delta
alluvial matter–geest
ally – adherent, associate, confederate, friend, kinsman, pal, partner, relative
alma–cherishing, nourishing, soul, spirit
almacen–magazine, shop, warehouse
almanac–calendar
almighty – irresistible, omnipotent
almost–nearly, nigh
almost beyond hope–desperate
alms–charity, dole, philanthropy
alms (Scot.)–aumous
alms box–arca
alms dispenser–almoner
aloe fiber (American)–pita
aloes (compound from)–aloin
aloft (opposite of)–alow
alone–companionless, desolate, isolated, separate, solely, solitary, solo, unaccompanied
alone (stage direction)–solus
along–on, via
along side–aboard, by
aloofness–indifference
aloud–oral
alp–bullfinch, demon, nightmare, witch
alpeen (Irish)–cudgel
alphabet–ABC's
alphabet character (early)–rune
alphabetical character (Teutonic)–rune
alphabetical characters–letters

alphabetical list–catalog, catalogue
Alpine dance–gavot
Alpine dog's succor–brandy
Alpine goat–ibex
Alpine herdsman–senn
Alpine province (West Austria)–Tirol, Tyrol
Alpine shelter–hospice
Alpine wind–foehn
Alps (division of)–Lepontine
Alps plant–edelweiss
Alps tunnel (pass)–Simplon
already (contr.)–een
already spoken of–said
also–and, further, more, moreover, similarly, too, yet
also (arch.)–eke
also (Latin)–et
also called–alias
altar (procession of Corpus Christi)–reposoir
altar (the)–ara
altar (top of)–mensa
altar boy–acolyte
altar cover–dossal, dossel
altar curtain costor
altar end of church–apse
altar hangings (rich, back of)–dorsals
altar ledge (in back of)–retable
altar piece (decorated)–predella
altar screen–reredos
altar slab–mensa
alter – amend, castrate, change, emend, geld, reset, revise
alteration–change, interpolation, modification
altercation–controversy, dispute, fight, tiff, wrangle
altered brand of stolen cattle–duffed
altered repeatedly–varied
alternate–interchange, reciprocate, rotate, seesaw, substitute, vary
alternate writing–boustrophedon
alternately–else
alternative–choice, election, option, or, preference

alternative (choice)–dilemma, perplexing
alt horn (alto horn)–alto
although–when
altitude–elevation, height
altogether–quite
alum rock–alunite
aluminum (calcium silicate)–epidote
aluminum alloy–doralium
aluminum discoverers–Davy and Wohler
aluminum oxide–alumina
aluminum sulphate–alum
alumni–grads, graduates, pupils
alumnus–grad, graduate, pupil
alure–ambulatory, gallery, passage
alveary–beehive
alveolar plasma – trophoplasm
always–ay, aye, constantly, continually, eternally, ever, everlastingly, evermore, forever, invariably, perpetually, uniformly
always (contr.)–eer
always (Latin)–semper
always (poetic)–eer
am obliged–must
ama–amula
amabile–agreeable, gentle, tender
amability–lovableness
amah–nurse, servant
Amalekite king–Agag
amalgamate–blend, coalesce, combine, consolidate, join, merge, mix, unite
amalgamation–merger
amant–lover
amanuensis–secretary
Amaryllis – shepherdess, sweetheart
amaryllis (kind of)–agave
amaryllis family (genus of)–agave
amass–accumulate, collect, gather, hoard, save, store
amass (secretly)–hoard
amate–daunt, dishearten, subdue
amateur–beginner, dabbler,

dilettante, fancier, nonprofessional
amateur (superficial)–dilettant, dilettante
amateurish–inapt
amatory–amorous, erotic, fond, loving, philter, tender
amaze–astonish, astound, awe, bewilder, confound, stupefy, surprise
amazement–alarm, awe, bewilderment, consternation, perplexity, surprise, wonder
Amazon ant (jungle fire)–aracara
Amazon cetacean–inia
Amazon mouth–Para
Amazon rain forest–selva
Amazon river estuary–Para
Amazon tributary–Napo
ambary (the)–da
ambassador–envoy, intermediary, legate, messenger, minister, representative
amber–electrum
ambiguous–double, dubious, indefinite, indeterminate, indistinct, mistakable, questionable, unsettled
ambition–aspiration, goal
ambitious (to be)–aspire
ambush–ambuscade, trap
ameliorate–better, ease, improve, mend
amelioration – betterment, improvement
amend–atone, convert, correct, redress, reform, reparation
amend (dial.)–beete
amendment–addition, correction, improvement, reformation, rider
amendment (to bill)–rider
amends for loss–redress
amerce–fine, mulct, punish
American aborigine–Amerind
American actor–Barrymore, Booth, Drew, Muni, Sothern, Ward

American admiral – Evans, Sims

American air force (volunteer in China)–AVG, Flying Tigers

American aloe fiber–pita

American Arctic explorer–Peary

American author – Ade, Ames, Pyle, Roe

American author and artist –Pyle

American bear (black)–musquaw

American bighorn–argali

American bird (oscine)–tanager

American black snake–racer

American black vulture–urubu

American bovine–bison

American buffalo–bison

American capitalist–Astor

American caricaturist–Nast

American carnivore–puma

American cat–puma

American cat (spotted)–ocelot

American cataract–Niagara

American century plant–aloe

American child (native)–papoose

American college president –Ames

American commodore–Porter

American conference–powwow

American continent discoverer–Cabot

American deer (large)–wapiti

American Delaware Indians –Lenapes

American diva–Melba

American divine–Olin, Randall

American dramatist–Crothers

American dwarf palm (genus of)–sabal

American educator–Hume, Mann

American electrician–Tesla

American elk–wapiti

American engineer (Mississippi River bridge)–Eads

American explorer–Byrd, Clark, Peary

American explorer (1774–1809)–Lewis

American feline (wild)–ocelot

American fiber (tropical)–istle

American general–Grant, Lee, Lyman, Lyon

American general (Revolutionary)–Sumter

American geologist–Dana

American grass (coarse forage)–gama

American gum tree–tupelo

American humorist–Ade, Clemens, Lardner, Neal, Nye, Rogers, Mark Twain

American Indian–Amerind, Chippewa, Cree, Erie, Hopi, Iowa, Kansa, Kaw, Muskhogean, Onondaga, Osage, Oto, Otoe, Piman, Piute, Red, Sac, Tano, Ute

American Indian (most cultured)–Cherokee

American Indian chief–sachem

American Indian myth (daughter of moon)–Nokomis

American Indian tribes (group)–Ges

American Indian warrior–brave

American inventor–Hoe

American inventor of color photography–Ives

American-Japanese children (second generation)–Nisei

American-Japanese children (second generation, educated in Japan)–Kibbei

American jockey–Sande

American journalist–Block, Lorimer

American journalist and diplomat–Reid

American jurist–Ide, Lamar

American lawyer and senator–Frye

American leopard–ocelot

American librarian–Poole

American linden–lin

American marsupial–opossum

American marsupial (coll.)–possum

American mathematician–Nathaniel Bowditch

American merganser–tweezer

American mink–vison

American moth (large)–io

American musical composer –Foote

American national tree–Sequoia

American naturalist (1823–1887)–Baird

American naval officer–Decatur, Lawrence

American novelist–Poole, Simms

American officer (naval)–Decatur, Lawrence

American operatic soprano–Eames

American ostrich–rhea

American oyster catcher–pilwillet

American painter–Sargent

American painter and etcher–Sloan

American painter (portrait) –Peale, Stuart

American patriot–Otis, Revere

American philanthropist–Riis

American pioneer–Boone

American pirate (reputed)–Kidd

American plant (tropical)–guaco

American poet–Ade, Hassam, Lanier, Osgood, Poe, Riley, Saxe

American poet (humorous)–Saxe

American poet and critic–Stedman

American poet and journalist–Alsop

American politician–Platt

American producer (theatrical)–Belasco
American quail–colin
American rail (short-billed)–sora
American railroad magnate–Rea
American red cedar–savin
American reformer–Neal Dow
American Revolutionary general–Sumter
American Revolutionary soldier–Allen
American sable–marten
American sculptor–Mead
American senator and lawyer–Frye
American settler (early)–Puritan
American shrub–wahoo
American shrub (tropical)–majo, majoe
American soldier (Revolutionary)–Allen
American squirrel (flying)–assapan
American squirrel (red)–chickaree
American theatrical manager–Daly
American tree–catalpa, lin
American tree (gum)–tupelo
American tree (tropical fruit)–papaw, pawpaw, sweetsop
American tree (tropical soft wood)–balsa
American tropical cactus–bleo
American tropical herb–samphire
American tropical plant genus–canna
American tropical shrub–guava
American tropical tree–papaw, pawpaw, sweetsop
American tropical tree (fruit)–sapota
American Unitarian divine–Weiss
American vulture–condor
American widgeon–zuisan

American woodchuck – shrups
American writer–Alger, Dana, Harte
Americans (Mexican name for)–gringos
Amerind Ute
Amerind memorial post–xat
Amerind sib symbol–totem, xat
Amerindic child–papoose
Amerinds (extinct)–Eries
Amfortas' father–Titurel
ami–friend, lover
amiable–agreeable, charming, friendly, kindly, lovable, pleasing
amicable–friendly, harmonious, kind, peaceable
amid–among, amongst, in
amigo (Mexican)–friend
amine (corn)–bal
amino compound (double)–diamide, diamin
amiss–astray, erroneously, fault, faultily, ill, improper, mistake, wrong
amity–friendliness, friendship, harmony, peace
amma–abbess
ammonia (volatile preparation)–hartshorn
ammonia compound–amid, amide, amin, amine
ammonia derivative–amid, amide, amin, amine
ammunition–arms, bombs, bullets, grenades, shells
ammunition box–bandolier
ammunition chest–caisson
ammunition for machine guns (Eng.)–ammo
among–amid, amidst, between, in, mid
among nations–international
Amorc member–Rosicrucian
amorous – ardent, erotic, fond, loving, passionate, tender
amorphous–formless, shapeless, uncrystallized
amorphous exudation–resin
amorphous silica (form of)–opal
amorphous substance–resin

amort–dejected, inanimate, lifeless, spiritless
amount–lot, store, sum, total
amount (certain)–quantum
amount (determinate)–unit
amount (fair)–chunk
amount (fixed) rate
amount (indefinite)–any, some
amount (least possible)–grain, minimum
amount (relative)–degree
amount (small)–modicum, morsel
amount (smallest)–least
amount drawn in–intake
amount of medicine–dosage, dose
amounted to–all
amounted to mean–averaged
amounts (enormous)–reams
amounts realized–proceeds, take
amounts to–totals
ampere–Weber
amphibian (leaping tailless)–frog, toad
amphibian (order of)–anura
amphibian (tailless)–frog, toad
amphibian (young)–tadpole
amphibian mammal–otter
amphibian order–aglossa
amphibious animal–otter
amphibole (fibrous green)–oralite
amphibole (variety of)–edenite
amphibole (variety of aluminous)–edenite
Amphion's wife–Niobe
amphitheater–arena
amphora–jar, vase
ample–abundant, bountiful, capacious, extensive, full, large, liberal, munificent, plenteous, plentiful, rich, unstinted, wide
amplify–dilate, enlarge, exaggerate, increase, overstress, widen
amplify (unduly)–pad
amulet–charm, periapt, protection, talisman

amuse–beguile, divert, entertain, exhilarate, gratify, please, recreate, tickle

amusement–avocation, diversion, divertisement, entertainment, fun, pastime, play, recreation, relaxation, sport

amusement place (public)–casino, midway, park, theater

amusing remark (coll.)–gag

anaconda–boa, snake

Anak's father–Arba

analogous–correlative, correspondent, like, similar

analogue–correlative, equivalent, parallel

analogy–resemblance, similarity, similitude

analyze–assay, parse

analyze grammatically – parse

anarch–red

anarchist–antisocial, red, socialist

anathematize–ban, curse

Anatolian rug (similar to Konia)–Tuzla

anatomical tissue–tela

anatomize–dissect

Anaximander's first principle–Apeiron

ancestor–elder, forebear, forefather, forerunner, parent, predecessor, progenitor, sire

ancestor (common)–Adam

ancestor (remote)–Atavus

ancestor of Pharaoh–Ra

ancestral–aval, avital, hereditary, patrimonial

ancestry–antecedents, lineage, lineal

ancestry (in direct line)–lineal

ancestry (not in direct line)–unlineal

anchor–fasten, fix, hook, moor, secure, stop

anchor (bill of)–pee

anchor (part of)–palm

anchor (point of)–pee

anchor (small) – grapnel, kedge

anchor (small with flukes)–grapnel

anchor a vessel–moor

anchor bill–pee

anchor hoisting apparatus–capstan

anchor holster–cat

anchor part–arm, palm, pee

anchor ring–tore, toroid

anchor-shaped–ankyroid

anchor tackle–cat

anchoret–anchorite, eremite, hermit, recluse

anchovy–herring

anchovy sauce–alec

ancient–aged, antiquated, early, historic, hoary, obsolete, old, olden, primeval, primitive, pristine

ancient (Scot.)–auld

ancient chariot–essed

ancient city–Tyre

ancient coin (weight)–shekel

ancient country–Aram

ancient drink (honey and mulberry)–morat

ancient Greek city–Elis

ancient language–Latin, Pali

ancient measure–span

ancient overseer–reeve

ancient people–Medes

ancient race–Medes

ancient Semitic idols–Baal, Baalism

ancient site–ruin

ancient stone tool–celt, eolith

ancient Tartar (Tatar)–Hun

ancient tower–Babel

ancient weapon–lance, sling, spear

ancient wine vessel–ama, amula

and–also

and (Fr.)–et

and (Latin)–et

and (obs., var.)–ant

and not–nor

and ten (suffix)–teen

Andean beast of burden–llama

Andean camel–llama

andiron–dog, firedog

andrite (variety of)–aplome

android–automaton, robot

anecdote–narrative, story, tale

anecdotes–ana

anemone (sea)–actinia

anent–about, concerning, on, re

anesthetic – chloroform, ether, gas

anesthetic (local)–cocaine, menthol

anew–afresh, again, denovo, newly, recently

angel–cherub, seraph

angel (biblical)–Raphael

angel (kind of)–seraph

angel (Spanish)–seraf

angel of light–cherub

Angel of the House author–Patmore

angelic–beneficent, cherubic, heavenly, saintly

angelica (wild)–jellica

Angelican Church psalm (opening communion)–introit

angelina–angelic, lovely

angeline–surinamine

anger–affliction, choler, dander, displeasure, dudgeon, emotion, enrage, exasperation, indignation, ire, irritation, offend, passion, rage, resentment, temper, trouble, vexation, wrath

anger (coll.)–rile

anger (old word meaning)–arrs

angered–incensed, irate, wroth

angered (easily)–irascible

angle–coin, corner, nook

angle (fortification projecting)–bastion

angle (geometric)–incidence

angle (reentrant)–in

angle (right)–ell

angle (shoulder of bastion)–epaule

angle (to)–fish

angle of keel and bowsprit–steeve

angler's basket–creel

Anglian kingdom–Deira

Anglo-Egyptian commander-in-chief–Sirdar
Anglo-Egyptian Sudan capital–Khartum
Anglo-Indian (wealthy)–nabob
Anglo-Indian heiress – begum
Anglo-Indian measure–ser
Anglo-Indian officials (revenue)–dessayes
Anglo-Indian peasant–ryot
Anglo-Indian weight–ser, tola
Anglo-Saxon assembly–gemot, gemote
Anglo-Saxon coin–ora
Anglo-Saxon consonant–eth
Anglo-Saxon court–gemot, gemote, leet
Anglo-Saxon freeman–thane
Anglo-Saxon god–Ing
Anglo-Saxon king (founder of Roman school)–Ine
Anglo-Saxon king's attendant–thane
Anglo-Saxon king's council –witan
Anglo-Saxon landholder–thane
Anglo-Saxon letter–edh
Anglo-Saxon meeting–gemot, gemote
Anglo-Saxon money–ora
Anglo-Saxon nobleman–earl
Anglo-Saxon silver coin–sceat
Anglo-Saxon slave–esne
Anglo-Saxon title–thane
Anglo-Saxon village–Ham
Anglo-Saxon warrior–thane
Angola capital (Africa)–Loanda
Angola city–Benguela, Loanda (c.), Mossamedes
Angola coin–angolar (s.), macuta (c.)
Angola monetary unit–angolar
Angola river–Coanza, Kunene, Kwanza
angora goat hair–mohair
angora wool–mohair
angry–enraged, irascible, irate, ireful, irked, mad, passionate, sore, wrath

angry (old word)–grame
angry at–resent
anguish–agony, distress, dolor, pang, torment, torture
angular–abrupt, cornered, edgy, sharp
animadversion aspersion, censure, comment, condemnation, reproach
animadvert–censure, comment, criticize, remark
animal – anteater, beast, brute, creature, panda
animal (African river, seal-like)–ayu
animal (aliped)–bat
animal (allied to giraffe)–okapi
animal (allied to hedgehog)–tenrec
animal (allied to mink)–weasel
animal (allied to raccoon)–coati
animal (amphibian)–frog, toad
animal (aquatic) – fish, polyp, seal, whale
animal (aquatic, herbivorous)–manatee
animal (back hanging down)–ai
animal (badger-like)–ratel
animal (Biblical, wild horned)–reem
animal (body of)–soma
animal (camel-like)–guanaco
animal (carnivorous)–civet, genet, genette, lion, tiger, weasel
animal (cat family)–cheetah, jaguar, pard, tiger
animal (cervidae family)–deer
animal (civet-like)–genet, genette
animal (crawling)–worm
animal (cross-bred)–hinny, hybrid, mule
animal (developed individual of a compound)–zoon
animal (draft) – elephant, horse, mule, ox, oxen (pl.)
animal (dwarf)–runt

animal (East, bovine)–zebu
animal (East, domesticated) –zebu
animal (Egyptian, common) –adda
animal (elephant-like extinct)–mastodon
animal (elk like)–moose
animal (equine)–zebra
animal (fabulous)–dragon
animal (fabulous horse-like) –unicorn
animal (fabulous, one-horned)–unicorn
animal (fabulous, sea)–rosmarine
animal (feigning death when caught)–opossum, possum
animal (feline)–cat, cheetah, jaguar, pard, tiger
animal (female, feathered)–hen
animal (fin-footed) – pinniped
animal (fleet) – antelope, deer, hare
animal (flesh-eating)–carnivore
animal (footless) – apod, apoda
animal (French, small)–toto
animal (full-grown, castrated)–seg, segg
animal (fur-bearing)–badger, ermine, genet, genette, mink, otter, sheep, skunk, squirrel
animal (genus mephitis)–polecat
animal (giraffe-like)–okapi
animal (graceful, speedy)–antelope
animal (hairless)–pelon
animal (having legs used as oars)–remiped
animal (having one foot or leg)–uniped
animal (headless, fabulous) –acephal
animal (hibernating)–bear, sleeper
animal (hornless)–pollard
animal (hunted) – game, prey

animal (hybrid) – hinny, mule
animal (identified with kings)–ermine
animal (imaginary, invented by Lewis Carroll)–snark
animal (Indian, ox-like)–zebu
animal (invertebrate) – insect, mollusk
animal (invertebrate, marine)–polyps, sponge
animal (leaping)–frog, toad
animal (lost)–estray, stray
animal (lower)–beast, brute
animal (lumbering)–bear, bruin
animal (Madagascar, nocturnal)–ayeaye
animal (male)–bull, jack, mas, stag, stallion, tom
animal (many-celled aquatic)–rotifer, rotifera
animal (many-footed)–multiped
animal (many-footed and -jointed)–centipede
animal (marine)–jellyfish, orc, polyp
animal (marine, minute)–coral
animal (microscopic)–ameba, amebic, amoeba, amoebic
animal (mink-like)–weasel
animal (minute)–acarid, animalcule
animal (monkey-like)–lemur, loris
animal (musteloid)–ratel
animal (nocturnal)–coon, lemur
animal (one-celled)–ameba, amoeba, monad, protozoa, protozoan
animal (one-horned)–unicorn
animal (one-horned, horse-like)–unicorn
animal (ovine)–sheep
animal (pet)–cade
animal (porcine)–hog, pig
animal (porcine, wild)–boar
animal (pouched)–marsupial

animal (prehistoric, huge) –dinosaur
animal (raccoon-like)–coati
animal (revered)–totem
animal (ruminant) – antelope, camel, cow, deer, goat, sheep
animal (sea)–inia, orc
animal (simplest form of)–ameba, amoeba, protozoan
animal (single-celled)–monad, protozoa, protozoan, rhizopoda
animal (skunk-like)–zoril
animal (small)–animalcule
animal (small pack)–burro
animal (small, preying)–weasel
animal (small, six legs)–insect
animal (spined)–vertebrate
animal (spotted, arch.)–pard
animal (thick-skinned)–elephant, pachyderm
animal (timid)–hare
animal (tropical, pig-like)–peccary
animal (two-footed)–biped
animal (ursine)–bear
animal (valuable, stray)–estray
animal (voracious)–pig
animal (vulpine)–fox
animal (weasel-like, fish feeding)–otter
animal (web-footed)–otter
animal (whose fur is called nutria)–coypu
animal (wild) – antelope, bear, boar, deer, jaguar, lion, lynx, onager, polecat, puma, seladang, tiger
animal (winged)–bird
animal (wing-footed) – aliped
animal (worshiped)–totem
animal (young, wild)–bruin, cub, lionet
animal abode–habitat, menagerie, zoo
animal allied to zebra–quagga
animal and plant life–bios
animal backbone–chine
animal class–genera

animal coat–pelage
animal covering–fur, hair, hide, pelage, wool
animal covering (fur)–pelage
animal disease (epidemic)–epizootic
animal doctor–vet
animal fat–adeps, lard, suet
animal group–drove, herd
animal hair (fur, wool)–pelage
animal handler–tamer
animal inclosure – cage, coop, corral, cote, hutch, kraal, pasture, pen, stall, sty, yard
animal jelly–gelatine
animal life (God of)–Faunus
animal life (lowest, simple form)–ameba, amoeba
animal life (pert. to)–zoologic
animal location (natural)–habitat
animal pouch–sac
animal race–breed
animal skin disease–mange
animal starch–glycogen
animal stomach – craw, maw, rumen
animal stomach (first)–rumen
animal stomach (fourth)–abomasum, read, reed
animal stomach (second)–reticulum
animal stomach (third)–omasum
animal symbol–totem
animal tender–herder, husbandman
animal tissues (decay of)–caries
animal trail–spoor
animal whose fur is called nutria–coypu
animalcule (wheel)–rotifer
animals (class of)–mammal
animals (one-celled)–amebae, amebas, amoebae, protozoas
animals living within other animals–entozoa
animals of region–fauna

animal's back–nota
animal's backbone–chine
animal's body–soma
animal's coat–pelage
animal's father–sire
animal's hind leg (lower part)–crus
animal's home–den
animal's mother–dam
animal's nose–snout
animate – alive, arouse, cheer, energize, enliven, ensoul, exhilarate, fire, imbue, inspire, live, liven, move, spirit, vitalize, vivify
animate (able to)–sthenic
animated–active, living
animating spirit–animus
animation–airiness, ardor, buoyancy, earnestness, energy, enthusiasm, liveliness, spirit, sprightliness, vivacity
animation (slang)–pep
animation (spirit)–dash, pep
animation (suspended)–torpor
animosity–acharnement, antagonism, enmity, hatred, hostility, opposition, spite
animous (animose)–hot, resolute, vehement
animus–disposition, inclination, intention, mind, temper, will
anisic acid salt–anigate
ankle–talus, tali (pl.), tarsus, tarsi (pl.)
ankle (pert. to)–tarsal
ankle bone–astragal, talus, tali (pl.)
ankle covering–gaiter
ankle ornament–anklet
ankylostoma–lockjaw
annalist–historian, writer
Annam city–Haoi, Hue (c.)
Annam coast tribe–Moi
Annam division – Cochin China, Tonquin
Annam group of tribes–Moi
Annam measure–chai vai, con, gon, ly, mau, ngu, phan, quo, sao, shita, tao, tat, that, thouc, troung

Annam river–Songka
Annam weight–binh, can, dong, ta
Annamese savage–Moi
Annamite game (gambling) –baquan
annatto–achiote
anneal–temper, toughen
annelid (whitish, marine)–lurg
annelids (species of fresh water)–naid
annex–add, affix, append, attach, join, subjoin
annihilate – destroy, extinguish, extirpate, obliterate
annihilation – destruction, extermination
anniversary (tenth)–decennial
anniversary (wedding) – see wedding anniversaries
annotate–gloss, note
announce–bid, declare, herald, proclaim, promulgate
announce (publicly)–advertise, broadcast
announce acceptance of Roman inheritance–cern
announce ownership–claim
announced by decree–edictal
announcement – advertisement, declaration, notice, notification, proclamation
announcement (authoritative)–decree, edict, fiat, proclamation
announcer (court)–crier
announcer (public)–crier
announcer of coming events –harbinger
annoy–bore, bother, displease, disturb, harass, harry, inconvenience, irk, irritate, molest, nag, offensive, pest, pester, rile, tease, troublesome, vex
annoy out of petty malice–spite
annoyance–bore, inconvenience, molestation, nuisance, pest, vexation

annual–etesian, publication
annual (tall)–ocra
annual income (Fr.)–rentes
annual periodic–etesian
annually–yearly
annually periodic (as winds) –etesian, monsoon
annuity (life)–tontine
annul–abolish, abrogate, annihilate, avoid, blank, cancel, derogate, invalidate, nullify, obliterate, quash, repeal, revoke, undo, void
annulet (her.)–vire
annulment – abolition, erasure, invalidation
annuls again–reabrogates
anodyne–antalgic, narcotic, opiate
anoesia–idiocy
anoint–anele, oil, smear
anomalous – dissimilar, exceptional, irregular, unconformable, unusual
anon–later, soon
anonymous – nameless, unavowed, unknown
another–second
another time–again
answer–defense, rejoinder, reply, respond, response, retort, serve, solution
answer (authoritative)–oracle
answer (witty)–repartee
answer the purpose–avail, do, serve
answerable–amenable, liable, responsible
ant–emmet, formicid, formicidae (pl.), pismire
ant (destructive)–termite
ant (nonworker)–drone
ant (Philippine white)–anai, anay
ant (white)–anai, anay, termite
ant (worker)–ergate
ant poison – formicicide, formicide
antagonism (open)–hostility, war
antagonist – adversary, enemy, foe, opponent

Antarctic bird – penguin, skua
Antarctic sea–Ross
Antarctic seal – Ross seal, Ross's
ante–pay, stake
anteater–manis
anteater (scaly)–pangolin
antecedent–fore, foregoing, former, precedent, preceding, previous, prior
antecedent proposition – premis, premise
antecedents–past
antecedents (necessary)–prerequisites
antechamber (small)–lobby, vestibule
antedate–predate
antelope–serow
antelope (European high mountain)–chamois
antelope (goat)–goral, serow
antelope (harnessed)–guib
antelope (kind of)–cabree, gnu, roan
antelope (large)–aste, eland, nilgau, nilgai, nilgais (pl.)
antelope (pied)–bontebok
antelope (royal)–ipete
antelope (sheep-like)–saiga
antelope (short-maned)–nilgau
antelope (South African)–eland, peele, rhebok
antelope (Tibetan)–sus
antelope (tiger-like)–agacella
antelope-like–bovid
antenna–aerial, feeler, horn
antenna (club-shaped end of insect's)–clava
antenna (radio)–aerial
anterior–foregoing, preceding, previous, prior
anteroom – antechamber, hall, lobby, vestibule
anthazoan–coral, polyp
anthem – motet, offertory, responsory
anthill–formicary
anthozoan (tentacled) – anemone
anthropoid–ape, chimpan-

zee, gibbon, gorilla, lar, orangutan
anthropoidea – apes, chimpanzees, gibbons, gorillas, lars, orangutans
antiaircraft fire–flak
antiaircraft guns–archies
antiaircraft pieces – pompoms
antic–caper, monkey-shine, prank, stunt
antic (coll.)–dido
anticipate–foresee, forestall, hope, obviate, prevent
anticipate with misgiving–dread
anticipated with foreboding–dread
anticipation – expectation, foresight, foretaste, forethought, preoccupation, presentiment
anticipation (expectant) – hope
anticipative–proleptic
anticipator – foreseer, seer, seeress
anticipatory–foreseeing
anticlimax–bathos
antidote–preventive, remedy
Antillean Indian god–Zeme
antimony (powdered)–kohl
Antioch proselyte – Nicolas
antipathy–abhorrence, antagonism, aversion, detestation, disinclination, dislike, disrelish, hostility, loathing, nausea, reluctance, repugnance
antiquated–aged, obsolete, passe, superannuated, voided
antique–ancient, old, outmoded, relic, venerable
antique milepost–stela, stelae (pl.), stele, steles (pl.)
antiquity–monument, relic, yore
antiquity (poetic)–eld
antiseptic – amido, amin, amine, amino, aminol, aristol, creosote, iodine, salol
antiseptic solution–eusol, iodine, phenol

antispasmodic (deadly carrot)–asadulcis
antithesis–Antipodes
antithesis of realism–idealism
antitoxic substance–serum
antitoxin–serum, sera (pl.)
antler (underbranched, Fr.) –dague
antler (young deer's underbranched)–dag
Antony and Cleopatra characters–Eros, Iras
antonym of former–latter
antrum–cavern, cavity, sinus
anurans (genus of)–rana
Anu's consort–Anat
Anu's partner–Anat
anvil (ear)–incus, incudes (pl.)
anvil (small)–teest
anvil (tinsmith's)–teest
anvil bone–incus, incudes (pl.)
anvil horn–beak
anxiety–apprehension, care, concern, dread, fear, foreboding, misgiving, solicitude, uneasiness, worry
anxiety (to free from)–reassure
anxiety as to outcome–suspense
anxious–concerned, disquieted, disturbed, eager, impatient, uneasy, unquiet, watchful
anxious (to be)–cark, eager
any–some
any (dial.)–ary
any (dial., var.)–oni
anybody–one
anyone of mixed blood–half-breed, metis (masc.), metisse (fem.), octoroon
anything causing condensation–alembic
anything exactly opposite–antipode
anything fantastic–caprice
anything having spiral form –helix
anything of least possible value–plack

anything of unusual speed–racer

anything of value–asset

anything remote (pert. to)–forane

anything small–tot

anything strictly true–fact

anything terrifying without danger–scarecrow

anything that exists–entity

anything that grows and bears green leaves in a forest–vert

anything that heals–balsam

anything very puzzling–crux

anything very small–minim

anything worthless–rap

aoudad–sheep

apa–wallaba

Apache Indian chief–Geronimo

Apache state–Arizona

Apache woman's jacket (deerskin)–bietle

Apache Yuma–Tulkepaia

apaid–paid, pleased, satisfied

apart–aloof, aside, asunder, separate

apart (prefix)–dis, se

apartment–flat, suite, tenement

apathetic–dull, indifferent, passive, phlegmatic

apathetically–indifference

apathy–indifference, insensibility, sluggishness, stoicism, supineness, torpor, unconcern, unfeelingness

apathy (spiritual in monasteries)–acedia

ape–dupe, emulate, fool, imitate, imitator, mimic, orang, parrot, simian

ape (anthropoid)–lar, orang

ape (dog-headed)–aani

ape (kind of)–lar, orang, orangoutang, outang

ape (largest)–gorilla

ape (long tailed)–kra

ape (men)–alali

ape (nocturnal)–lemur

ape (white hand and foot)–alali

aperture–chasm, cleft, fissure, gap, hole, leak, opening, orifice, pore, rima, rimae (pl.), window

aperture (in helmet)–vue

aperture (leaf)–stoma, stomata (pl.)

aperture (narrow)–slit, slot

aperture (small)–vent

aperture vignette–mask

apex–acme, cusp, height, point, summit, tip, top

apex (rounded and notched)–retuse

apex ornament–finial

Aphareus' son–Idas

aphorism–adage, apothegm, axiom, maxim, proverb, saw

aphoristic–gnomic

Aphrodite priestess–Hero

Aphrodite's consort (lover)–Ares

Aphrodite's son–Eros

apodes (order of)–eels, morays

apogee–apex, culmination

apograph–copy, transcript

apoidea–apina

Apollo's birthplace–Delos

Apollo's father–Zeus

Apollo's mother–Leto

Apollo's oracle–Delphi

Apollo's son–Hymen, Linos, Linus

Apollo's twin sister–Artemis

apologetic–sorry

apologue–fable

apology – acknowledgment, explanation, justification, plea, vindication

apoop–astern

apoplexy–stroke

apoplexy (plant)–esca

apostate – pervert, recreant, renegade, turncoat

apostle–Andrew, Bartholomew, James, John, Judas, Jude, Matthew, Matthias, Paul, Peter, Philip, Simon, Thomas

apostle (Biblical to gentiles)–Paul

apostle (pert. to)–petrine

Apostle of Rome–Neri

apothecary–druggist

apothecary weight (international)–dram, grain, pound, scruple

apothegm – adage, axiom, dict, maxim, saw, saying

apotheosize–deify, glorify

appall–dismay, enfeeble, reduce, weaken

appalling–awesome, awful, fearful, terrific

appalto–monopoly

appanage–adjunct, appurtenance, perquisite, prerogative

apparatus – equipment, instrument, machine

apparatus (anchor-hoisting)–capstan

apparatus (distillation) – alembic

apparatus (dyeing)–ager

apparatus (for determining acidity of solutions)–acidimeter

apparatus (heating)–boiler, etna, furnace, heater, radiator, stove

apparatus (hoisting) – derrick, jack, lever, lewis, pry

apparatus (Oriental smoking)–nargile

apparatus (registering)–recorder

apparatus (ship's lifting)–capstan, davit

apparatus (steering)–helm, rudder, tiller, wheel

apparatus (tobacco leaf moistening)–caser

apparatus (used for illustrating planetary motion)–orrery, orreries (pl.)

apparatus (water-raising)–noria, pump, siphon

apparel–attire, clothes, clothing, costume, dress, garb, garment, gear, habiliments, raiment, vesture, wear

apparent–certain, clear, distinct, evident, indubitable, manifest, notorious, obvious, overt, patent, plain, seeming, visible

apparent displacement of an object–parallax
apparent enlargement of an object by optical instrument–magnification
apparently but not actually fair–specious
apparently right–specious
apparition–eidolon, ghost, phantasm, phantom, phenomenon, revenant, shade, specter, spectre, spirit, spook, sprite, wraith
apparition (frightful)–hobgoblin
appeal – application, call, plea, request, suit
appeal for–seek
appealable–invocable
appealing–agreeable, imploring, nice, pleasant
appealing to reason–cogent
appear–arrive, emerge, seem
appear obscure–darkle
appear suddenly–loom
appearance–air, aspect, disclosure, form, guise, look, manifestation, manner, mien, ostent, semblance
appearance (book, general) –format
appearance (external) – guise, mien
appearance (first) – debut, premiere
appearance (frontal)–facade
appearance (personal)–presence
appearance (surface)–patina
appearance (watered) – moire
appearance (white)–pallid
appease–atone, calm, conciliate, content, pacify, placate, quiet
appease (Scot.)–mease, mees
appellation – denomination, name, nomenclature, title
appellation (familiar)–nickname
appellation of Athena–Alea, Pallas
append–add, affix, annex, attach, hang, subjoin

appendage – accessory, adjunct, appurtenance, arm, flap, tab, tag, tail
appendage (barbed)–awn
appendage (caudal)–tail
appendage (fleshy)–palpi
appendage (foliage leaf)–ligula
appendage (grass)–awn
appendage (having a rounded)–lobate
appendage (horn-like)–ceras, cerata (pl.)
appendage (leaf-like, beneath flower)–bract
appendage (rounded)–lobe
appendix–addendum, supplement
appendix to will–codicil
appertain–pertain, relate
appetite – craving, desire, hunger, longing, passion
appetite (with huge)–gargantuan
appetite satisfier–sater
appetizer–aperitif, canape
applaud–acclaim, approve, cheer, clap, commend, compliment, extol, praise
applaud (slang)–root
applause–acclaim, acclamation, clap, eclat, plaudits, praise
apple (American variety)–Roxbury
apple (custard)–anona
apple (kind of)–crab, Jonathan, pippin, russet, winesap
apple (love)–tomato
apple (May)–mandrake
apple (old variety)–rennet
apple (rosy-red)–spy
apple (small, immature)–codlin, codling
apple (small, sour)–crab
apple acid (pert. to)–malic
apple goddess (golden, throwing)–Eris
apple juice–cider
apple juice (pert. to)–malic
apple-like fruit–pome
apple of the eye–pupil
apple seed–pip
apple trees (genus of)–malus

apples (crushed)–pomace
apples (old English)–rennets
apples (pert. to) – malic, malto
appliance–application, device, instrument
appliance (dental)–dam
applicable–apposite, appropriate, compliant, fit, pertinent, pliable, relative, relevant
application–effort, use
application (external, to beautify skin)–cosmetic
application (hot)–stupe
application (medicinal)–plaster
application (persevering)–diligence
application (soothing)–balm
application for assistance–recourse
apply–appose, devote, use
apply habitually–addict
apply heat to–warm
apply remedies to–treat
appoggiatura–gracenote
appoint–assign, decree, detail, name, ordain, prescribe
appoint (to)–crest, ordain
appoint as agent–depute
appoint for particular service–delegate, depute, deputize, detail
appointed–destined
appointed lot–fate
appointed to arrive–due
appointment – command, date, designation, direction, engagement, equipment, establishment, order, tryst
appointment (coll.)–date
appointment (Scot.)–steven
appointment for a meeting –tryst
apportion (to)–allocate, allot, assign, deal, dele, distribute, divide, lot, mete, share
apportioner (water in ditches)–divisor
apposer – examiner, questioner

apposite – appropriate, apt, pertinent, relevant

appraise–assay, commend, estimate, evaluate, evalue, gage, praise, rate, value

appraise carefully–evaluate

appraiser (tax) – assessor, lister

appreciable–any

appreciate – advance, approve, esteem, estimate, feel, increase, realize, value

appreciate fully–realize

appreciation–appraisal, estimation, recognition

appreciation of right–tact

apprehend–anticipate, arrest, capture, comprehend, conceive, grasp, imagine, perceive, realize, see, take, understand

apprehended (by mind)–perceived

apprehended (through sense)–sensate

apprehend as true–know

apprehender–captor

apprehension–anxiety, concern, distrust, dread, fear, premonition, presage, solicitude, suspicion, uneasiness

apprehensive – cognizant, conscious, knowing, nervous

apprise (apprize)–acquaint advise, inform

apprised–aware

approach – access, accost, come, near, verge

approach (ocean, convenient)–seagate

approach closely–near

approach stealthily–stalk

approbation – admiration, commendation, praise

appropriate–akin, allot, apt, condign, deserved, fit, germane, pertinent, proper, related, relevant, take, worthy

appropriate another's writings–pirate, plagiarize

appropriate for song–lyrical

appropriately–duly

appropriateness (nice)–elegance

approval – approbation, assent, endorsement, sanction, support

approve – applaud, countenance, endorse, indorse, OK, okay, sanction

approve of–accept

approximate–approach, near

approximate accuracy–circa

approximate situation – whereabouts

approximately–about

approximately (about a certain date)–circa

appui–prop, stay, support

appurtenance–accessory, adjunct, appendage, belonging

aprendiz–apprentice

apricot cordial–perisco, periscot

apricot vine–maypop

apricots (salted, So. Africa) –mebos, meebos

apron–pinafore

apron (coarse, Scot.)–brat

apron (fisherman's, large leather) barvel, barvell

apron (mason's)–lambskin

apropos – apt, opportunely, pat, pertinent, relevant, seasonable

apt – capable, competent, dexterous, disposed, inclined, likely, pat, prone, qualified, suitable

apt saying–mot

apt to believe (rare)–credent

aptitude–ability, appropriateness, art, fitness, flair, genius, gift, suitableness, talent

aptly – pertinently, readily, suitably

aqua–water

aquamarine–beryl

aquatic bird–duck, goose, swan

aquatic carnivore–otter

aquatic rodent–beaver

aquatic salamander–newt

aquatic switchback–chute

aqueous influx–tide

aquila–eagle

aquosity–moisture, wateriness

ara–macaw

Arab–Saracen, Semite

Arab (French street)–gamin

Arab beverage (sour milk) –leban, lebban

Arab chief–sheik

Arab drink (acidulated, fermented)–bosa, boza, bozah

Arab faction (Medina in Mohammedan's time)–Aus

Arab horse (race related to) –Turk

Arab nomad–Saracen

Arab shoulder cloth (white) –cabaan, caban

Arab tribe–Diendel

Arab's ideal state of bliss–kaif

Arab's woolen cloth used as outer garment–haik

Arabia (poetic)–Araby

Arabian antelope–addax

Arabian beverage–leban

Arabian bird–phoenix

Arabian caliph (fourth)–Ali

Arabian camel's-hair cloth–aba

Arabian chieftain – ameer, amir, emeer, emir

Arabian cities–Aden, Hail, Mecca, Medina, Mocha, Muscat, Oneizah, Riad, Sana

Arabian coin–commassee (base s.), riyal (s.)

Arabian coin (gold)–dinar

Arabian commander–ameer, amir, emeer, emir

Arabian cosmetic–kohl

Arabian country–Sheba

Arabian demon–afreet, afrit, genie, genii (pl.), jinnee, jinni, jinn (pl.)

Arabian desert–Ahkaf, Dehna, Nefud, Syrian

Arabian devil–afreet, afrit, genie, genii (pl.), jinnee, jinni, jinn (pl.)

Arabian dhow–sambuk

Arabian district–yemen

Arabian division–El Hasa, El Hedjaz, El Nejd, El

Tehama, El Yemen, Hadramaut, Mahara, Mecca, Medinah, Oman, Sinai, Suez
Arabian dress–aba
Arabian fable author–Lokman
Arabian father (term for)–abba, abou, abu, bu
Arabian garment–aba, haik
Arabian garment (cloaklike)–burnoose, burnous
Arabian gazelle–ariel, cora
Arabian goat leather–mocha
Arabian gulf–Aden
Arabian horses (mixed breed)–kadischi
Arabian jasmine–bela
Arabian judge–cadi
Arabian letter–ta
Arabian measure–achir, artaba, assbaa, barid, cabda, cafiz, caphite, covid, covido, cuddy, den, farsakh, farsang, feddan, ferk, foot, gariba, ghalva, kiladja, kist, makuk, marhale, mille, nusfiah, qasab, saa, teman, woibe, zudda
Arabian measure (old dry)–saa
Arabian Merchant of Bagdad–Sindbad
Arabian military commander–ameer, amir, emeer, emir
Arabian money (wire)–lari
Arabian mountain–Horeb, Nebo, Sinai
Arabian Nights' bird–roc
Arabian Nights' character–Ali, Amina
Arabian Nights' character (wife of Sidi)–Amine
Arabian Nights' dervish–Agib
Arabian Nights' Merchant of Bagdad–Sindbad
Arabian Nights' youth–Aladdin
Arabian nomad–Saracen
Arabian peninsula–Sinai
Arabian people (one of)–Irad

Arabian plant (narcotic)–kat
Arabian port–Aden
Arabian romance–antar
Arabian satan–Eblis
Arabian seaport–Aden
Arabian shrub–kat
Arabian state (independent)–Oman
Arabian state (N.E.)–Oman
Arabian sultanate–Oman
Arabian tambourine–taar
Arabian tree shrub (for tea)–kat
Arabian vessel (lateen sail)–dhow
Arabian vessel (small coasting)–boutre
Arabian weight–artal, artel, bahar, bokard, cheki, dirhem, farsalah, kella, miskal, nasch, nevat, ocque, oukia, ratel, rotl, toman, tomand, vakia
Arabian winds (high, dry)–simoom, simoon
Arabian word for father–abba, abou, abu, bu
Arabic letter–kaf
Arabic letter (first of alphabet)–alif
Arabic literature student–Arabist
Arabic surname (father)–Abu
aracanga–macaw
araceous–aroid
arachnid – ally, scorpion, spider
arachnid (minute)–mite
arachnida–acera
Aramaic dialect (Eastern)–Syriac
Aramaic language–Samaritan
Aramean deity (worshipped at Damascus)–Rimmon
Aran Isles moccasin or sandal (untanned cowhide)–pampootee, pampootie
araneous–cobweblike, delicate, thin
araphorostic–seamless
arapunga–bellbird, campanero
arara–macaw

aration–plowing, tillage
Arawakan Indian of Brazil–Araua, Guana
arbeit–research, work
arbiter–arbitrator, judge, referee, umpire
arbitrary–absolute, autocratic, discretionary, highhanded
arbitrate–decide, determine, mediate
arbitrator–arbiter, judge, referee, umpire
arbor–bower, latticework, pergola
arbor (architectural)–pergola
arc–bow, radian
arcs used in astronomy and surveying–azimuths
arca–box, chest, paten, reliquary
Arcadia (poetic)–Arcady
Arcadian character (Sidney's)–Musidorus
Arcadian huntress (legendary)–Atalanta
Arcadian princess–Auge
Arcadian town (anc.)–Alea
Arcadian woodland spirit–Pan
arch–chief, cunning, eminent, greatest, mischievous, principal, roguish, sly
arch (kind of)–ogee
arch (pointed)–ogee, ogive
arch enemy of man–devil, Satan
arch fiend–devil, Satan
arch resting point on support–springer
arch solid–voussoir
arch stone (top)–keystone
arch top piece–keystone
archaic–antiquated, obsolete, old
archangel–Michael
archangel (Oriental)–Uriel
archbishop–prelate, primate
archer (famous outlaw)–Clim
archer's target center–clout
archetype–idea, model, prototype

archipelago (Pacific Ocean)–
Malay
architect's lodge (order)–
Doric, Ionic
architectural–tectonic
architectural base–plinth
architectural decorations
(droop-like)–guttae, gut-
ta (sing.)
architectural ornament–bez-
ant
architectural pier–anta
architectural screen–spier
architectural space (triangular)–pediment
architectural style–Doric,
English, Gothic, Greek,
Ionic, Mediterranean,
Renaissance, Spanish,
Tudor
archive – annals, chronicles,
record, registers
archway (memorial, bear-
ing record of heroes)–pai-
loo, pailou, pailow
Arctic–polar
Arctic bird–auk
Arctic current–Labrador
Arctic falcon–gyrfalcon
Arctic islander–Aleut
Arctic penguin–auk
Arctic race–Eskimo
Arctic sea–Barents
Arctic sea animal–narwhale
ardent–affectionate, avid,
eager, fervent, fervid,
flaming, glowing, hot, intense, keen, passionate,
vehement, warm, zeal-
ous
ardent (not)–cool, tepid
ardent affection–love
ardent desire–thirst
ardently–eagerly, intensive-
ly, vehemently
ardor–eagerness, enthusi-
asm, elan, fervor, fire,
heat, spirit, zeal
ardor (artistic)–verve
ardor (French)–fougue
arduous–difficult, exhausting, hard, laborious, onerous, strenuous, toilsome
arduous duty–chore, task
ardurous–ardent, burning
are not (contraction)–nar

area–extent, locus, loci (pl.),
range, region, space, zone
area (aqueous landlocked)–
sea
area (drainage)–basin
area (enclosed)–sept
area (involving)–spatial
area (military)–objective,
sector
area (pert. to)–areal
area (plumed eye, of owls)–
disc
area (small surrounding)–
areola, areolae (pl.)
area of extent–compass
arena–amphitheater, circus,
cockpit, ring
arena (athletic)–stadium,
stadia (pl.)
arena (circular tent en-
closed)–circus
arena (curling)–rink
arena (skating)–rink
arenose–sandy
Ares–Mars
Ares' sister–Eris
argala–marabou
argan–hypochondriac
argent–shining, silver, silvery, white
Argentine city–Bahia, Blan-
ca, Buenos Aires (c.), Bur-
ras, Cordoba, Jujuy, La-
nus, La Plata, La Rioja,
Mendoza, Rosario, Salta,
Santa Fe, Tucuman
Argentine coin–argentino
(g.), centavo (br.), peso
(s.)
Argentine cowboy–gaucho
Argentine dance–tango
Argentine estuary–Plata
Argentine measure–baril,
braza, cuadra, fanega,
frasco, galon, last, lastre,
league, legua, line, linea,
manzana, tonelada, vara
Argentine plains (treeless)–
pampas
Argentine port (river)–Ro-
sario
Argentine president–Rosas
Argentine province–Cata-
marca, Chaco, Cordova,
Corrientes, Entre Rios,
Formosa, Jujuy, Men-

doza, Pampa, Patagonia,
Rioja, Salta, San Juan,
San Luis, Santa Fe, San-
tiago, Tacuman
Argentine river–Colorado,
Negro, Paraguay, Para-
na, Picomayo, Plata, Rio
Grande, Salado, Vermejo
Argentine tree (beautiful
timber)–timbo
Argentine tree (timber)–
tala
Argentine weight–grano,
last, libra, tonelada, quintal
argillaceous–clayey, slaty
argol–tartar
Argolis valley (Greece)–
Nemea
Argonaut (the)–Jason
Argos king (twelfth)–Abas
Argos princess–Danae
argosy–ship, vessel
argot–cant, dialect, jargon,
lingo, slang
argued–controverted, de-
bated, discussed, disput-
ed, evinced, expostulated,
meaned, mooted, ratioci-
nated, reasoned, remon-
strated
argued (coll.)–pled
arguer (fallacious)–sophist
argues for and against–
moots
argument–debate, plea, ratiocination, reason
argument (angry)–spar
argument (carping)–cavil
argument (false)–sophism
argument (frivolous)–cavil
argument (negative)–con
argument (opposing)–con
argument (unsound)–fal-
lacy
argument in favor of–pro
argument starting point–
premise
argumentation–debate, discussion, dispute
argumentative–disputatious,
indicative, presumptive
argumentive–dialectic
argute – acute, sagacious,
shrewd, subtle
aria–air, melody, solo, tune

aria (short)–arietta, ariette
Arianrhod's son–Dylan
arid–barren, dry, jejune, parched
arid division of Austral zone (pert. to)–Sonoran
Aries–Ram
aright – directly, straight, straightway
aril – appendage, coating, covering
aril (false)–arillode
arise–ascend, begin, emanate, issue, mount, originate, spring
aristocracy–elite, nobles, patriciate
aristocrat–aristos, noble, patrician
aristocratic–noble, patrician
aristocratic (more, slang) – tonier
arithmetic (generalized)–algebra
arithmetic problem–sums
arithmetical equation–operand
Arius (follower of)–Arian
Arius (pert. to)–Arian
Arizona city–Yuma
Arizona gourd–calabazilla
Arizona Indian–Pima
Arizona river–Gila
ark's builder–Noah, Noe
ark's resting place–Ararat
arm–branch, equip, forearm, limb, projection
arm (cross guard of sword)–quillon
arm (narrow, sea)–firth
arm (projection from moving part)–tappet
arm (side)–pistol, revolver, saber, sword
arm (sun dial)–gnomon
arm bone–humerus, radius, ulna
arm hole (garment)–scye
arm joint–ares, elbow
arm muscle–triceps
arm of sea–bayou, estuary, firth, gulf, meer, mere
armada–fleet, squadron
armadillo–apar, apara, peba, peludo, poyou, tatou, tatu

armadillo (giant)–peludo, tatou, tatu
armadillo (mule)–mulita
armadillo (nine-banded)–peba
armadillo (six-banded)–peludo, poyou
armadillo (small)–peba
armadillo (small, hairy)–quirquincho
armadillo (South American burrowing)–pichiciago
armadillo (the peba)–cachicama
armadillo (three-banded)–apar, apara
armed force–cohort
armed forces (attacking city)–besiegers
armed hostilities–war
armed vessel–carrack, destroyer, sub, submarine
Armenian cap–calpac
Armenian city–Erzerum
Armenian cumin–caraway
Armenian devil worshipers–Yezidis
Armenian lake–Urumiyah, Van
Armenian mountain–Ararat, Taurus
Armenian people (highland)–Gomer
Armenian river–Aras, Araxes, Cyrus, Euphrates, Halys, Kizil-Trmak, Kur, Tigris
Armenian worshipers (devil)–Yezidis
armistice–truce
armoire–clothespress, cupboard, wardrobe
armor (armour)–mail, panoply
armor (close-fitting, body-anc.)–cuirass
armor (defensive) – egis, plate, shield
armor (leg)–greave
armor (leg, med.)–jambeau
armor (part of horse)–testiere
armor (piece of, anc.)–lorica
armor (plate of thigh)–cuish
armor (shoulder)–epauliere
armor (thigh)–tuille

armor (war horse)–testiere
armor bearer – armiger, squire
armor bearer (knight's)–esquire
armor plate (protective)–tasset
armor shoulder guard–ailette
armor skirt (medieval)–tace, tasse, tasset
armor splint (steel)–tace, tasse
armored–ironclad, mailclad, mailed, panoplied
armpit–ala, axilla, axillae (pl.)
armpit (pert. to)–axillar
arms bent outward (hands on hips)–akimbo
army–forces, horde, host, troops
army (section of)–brigade, company, corps, division, platoon, regiment, squad
army assault–onset
army automobile–jeep
army camp officer (head)–commandant
army commission given higher rank, but no higher pay–brevet
army follower–sutler
army front–van
army meal–mess
army meal (slang)–chow
army squad car (little)–jeep
army trader–sutler
army unit–brigade, company, corps, division, platoon, regiment, squad, troop
aroid (edible)–taro
aroma–fragrance, flavor, odor, perfume, scent, smell
aromatic–fragrant, odorous, redolent
aromatic gum–myrrh
aromatic herb–clary
aromatic plant–lavender, nard, savories
aromatic seed–anise, aniseed
aromatic seed kernels–nutmegs
aromatic spice–mace

aromatic stimulant–sassafras
aromatic substance–balsam
aromatic wood–cedar
aromo–huisache
arose–ascend, stood
around–about
around (prefix)–peri
around an axis–axiate
arouse–agitate, awaken, excite, fire, foment, incite, kindle, raise, rouse, stir, spur, wake
arouse (coll.)–roust
arouse into action–awaken, excite, rally
arpa–harp
arpeggio–division, flourish, roulade
arpent–acre
arpenteur–surveyor
arraign–accuse, charge, denounce, impeach, indict
arrange–adapt, adjust, alphabetize, besee, catalog, catalogue, cite, classify, dispose, distribute, frame, plan, range, sort, systematize
arrange beforehand–organize, plan, prepare
arrange fastidiously–preen
arrange for beforehand–bespeak
arrange harmoniously–gradate
arrange in a table–tabulate
arrange in degrees–grade
arrange in folds–drape
arrange in layers (horizontally)–tier
arrange in order–catalog, catalogue, file
arrange in series–seriate
arrange in succession–seriate
arrange in thin layers–laminate
arrange mutually–concert
arrange settlement–negotiate
arranged alternately–paly
arranged as to duration–timed
arranged in fives–quinate
arranged in flower clusters–paniculate

arranged in grades–ranked
arranged in spikes–caramel
arranged in steps or groups–staggered
arranged in threes–ternate
arranged like rays–radial
arrangement–disposal, disposition, distribution, order, preparation, setup
arrangement (harmonious)–proportionality
arrangement (methodical)–system
arrangement (orderly)–rank, series, syntax, system
arrangement (step-like of body of troops)–echelon
arrangement of air fleet–echelon
arrangement of sails–rig
arrangement of troops–echelon
arrangement of works of watch or clock–caliper
array–align, arrange, clothe, deck, dispose, dress, robe, arrayed–dressed, drest
arrear–backward, behind
arrest–apprehend, check, delay, detain, hinder, hold, obstruct, restrain, seize, stop
arrest in passage–intercept
arrival – advent, coming, reaching
arrival (anc.)–comer
arrive–come
arrogance–conceit, disdain, haughtiness, hauteur, insolence, pride
arrogant–audacious, bold, contemptuous, contumelious, disdainful, domineering, forward, impertinent, impudent, lofty, lordly, masterful, overbearing, overweening, presuming, proud, uppish
arrogant manner–hauteur
arrogantly–loftily
arrogate–usurp
arrow–dart, reed, shaft
arrow (feathered to rotate)–vire
arrow (pert. to)–sagittal

arrow (poisoned)–sumpit
arrow case–quiver
arrow end (butt)–nock
arrowhead (shaped like)–sagittate
arrow maker–fletcher
arrow point–barb, neb
arrow poison–curare, inee, urali, uralis
arrowroot (Bermuda)–ararao, araru
arrowroot family–marantaceae
arrow stone–belemnite
arroyo–brook, creek, watercourse
arroyuelo–brooklet, rill
arroz (Span.)–rice
arse–buttocks, posteriors, rump
arsenate (hydrous zinc)–adamite
arsenate (red manganese)–sarkinite
arsenate of copper–erinite
arsenic trisulphide – orpiment
arsenopyrite (cobaltiferous)–danaite
art–adroitness, aptitude, artifice, business, calling, contrivance, cunning, dexterity, duplicity, ingenuity, knack, profession, readiness, science, skill, trade, wile
art (an)–science
art (mystic)–cabala
art (of government)–politics
art (realistic)–genre
art (shooting with bow)–archery
art curiosity–curio
art fancier–dilettante
art feature–motif
art gallery–salon
art of assaying–docimasy
art of decorating metal (black inlay)–niello
art of discourse–rhetoric
art of government–politics
art of Hermes–alchemy
art of horsemanship–manege
art of imitation–mimicry

art of improving memory–mnemonics

art of ivory carving–toreutics

art of rhyming–poesy

art of self-defense–boxing, fencing, fighting, jiujitsu, jiujutsu, jujitsu, jujutsu

art of transmuting base metal to gold–alchemy

art style–genre

art votary–aesthete, esthete

Artemis–Diana

Artemis' brother (twin)–Apollo

Artemis' mother–Leto

artery–ligament, trachea, windpipe

artery (great)–aorta, aortae (pl.)

artery (innominate)–anonyma

artery pulsation–ictus

artful–adroit, crooked, cunning, deceitful, designing, dexterous, politic, skillful, sly, stealthy, tricky, wily

artfulness–artifice, finesse, refinement, skill, stratagem, subtlety

arthron–articulation, joint

arthropod–insect

Arthurian legend character–Elaine

Arthurian wizard–Merlin

Arthur's abode (ocean island)–Avalon

article–an, clause, composition, condition, item, stipulation, term, the, thing, treaty

article (arch.)–ye

article (cheap merchandise)–camelot

article (Fr.)–la, le, les, un, une

article (leading)–editorial

article (newspaper)–item

article (plaited)–mat

article (prominent publication)–feature

article (rare)–antique, curio, relic

article (Span.)–el, las, los, un, una

article (treating of specific topic)–treatise

article of apparel–gaiter, tunic

article of faith–tenet

article of food–tripe

article of personal property–chattel

articles of attire (new and striking)–creations

articles of belief–creed, tenet

articles of virtu–curio

articulated joint–hinge

articulation–suture

artifice–blind, cheat, contrivance, deceit, dodge, evasion, expedient, finesse, fraud, imposition, imposture, intrigue, machination, plot, ruse, shift, sleight, stratagem, trick, trickery, wile

artificer–artisan, carpenter, coppersmith, craftsman, farrier, goldsmith, mechanic, silversmith, workman

artificer (metal)–smith

artificial–adulterated, bastard, counterfeit, fabulous, factitious, false, falsetto, fictitious, forged, imaginary, sham, spurious, suppositious, unnatural

artificial (not)–authentic, natural, real

artificial butter–oleo, oleomargarine

artificial channel – canal, flume, gat, sluice

artificial channel (Eng.)–leat

artificial gum–dextrin

artificial language–Esperanto, ido, ro, Volapuk

artificial likeness–imitation

artificial silk–rayon

artificial surface–rink

artificially sprouted grain–malt

artillery emplacement–battery

artillery fire (burst of)–rafale

artillery fire (round of)–salvo

artilleryman – cannoneer, gunner

artilleryman (obs.)–topechee

artillery salute–salvo

artiodactyla–antelope, artiad, camel, deer, giraffe, goat, hippopotamus, ox, pig, sheep

artisan – artist, mechanic, workman

artist–artisan, painter

artist (beast sculptor)–animalist

artist (modern)–Sarg

artist (sleight-of-hand) – mage, magician, magus

artist's atelier–studio

artist's equipment (part of)–easel, palette

artist's workshop–atelier, studio

artiste–actor, dancer, performer, singer

artistic ardor–verve

artistic dance–ballet

artistic enthusiasm–spirit, verve

artistic quality–virtue

artistic symbol of dead–orant

artistic temperament – caprice, disposition, emotion

artistically finished–ornate

artless–candid, frank, ingenuous, naif, naive, open, simple, unaffected, undesigning, unsophisticated

artlessly–rustically

artlessness–naivete

aru–indeed, really

arui–aoudad

arum family–araceae

arundineous–reedy

arupa–formless

arx–citadel

Aryan (anc.)–Mede

Aryan deity–Agni

Aryan fire god–Agni

Aryan invader of Great Britain (anc.)–Pict

as–because, qua, while

as far as–to

as it is written (music)–sta

as it stands (music)–sta
as stated–so
As You Like It character–
  Celia
asa–healer, physician
Asa's son–Jehoshaphat
asado (Span.)–roasted
asarabacca root compound–
  asarone
asaron (impure)–asarite
ascend–arise, aspire, climb,
  mount, rise, scale, soar,
  tower
ascend with difficulty–clamber
ascendancy (ascendency)–
  authority, control, dominion, domination, influ-
  ence, predominance, preponderance, sovereignty,
  supremacy, sway
ascendancy (based on recognition of power)–prestige
ascended–risen, rose, uprose
ascending–anodal, anodic,
  orient
ascending signs – Aries,
  Aquarius, Capricorn,
  Gemini, Pisces, Taurus
ascenseur–elevator
ascension–ascent, distillation, rise, rising
ascertain–learn
ascertain duration–time
ascertain the bearing of–orient
ascertained by a line–lineal
ascertained the time of–dated
ascetic–abstemious, austere,
  hermit, stoic, strict, yoga,
  yogi
ascetic (Hindu)–yati
ascribable–attributive, due
ascribe–accredit, assign, attribute, impute, refer
ash (American mountain)–
  rowan, rowen
ash (soda)–alkali
ash box–dust bin
ash receptacle–urn
Asher (New Testament
  spelling)–Aser
ashes–embers
ashes (melted mass of)–
  clinkers

ashes (Scot.)–ase
ashes (seaweed)–kelp
ashweed–goutweed
asialia–aptyalism
Asia Minor animal (small)–
  daman
Asia Minor city–Aintab,
  Sardis
Asia Minor city (anc.)–Teos,
  Troy
Asia Minor colony–Eolis
Asia Minor colony (Greek)–
  Ionia
Asia Minor country–Eolis
Asia Minor district (anc.)–
  Ionia, Troad, Troas
Asia Minor mountain–Ida
Asia Minor muskmelon–
  casaba
Asia Minor region (anc.)–
  Aria
Asia Minor river–Monderez
Asia Minor sea–Aegean
Asia Minor seaport (anc.)–
  Issus
Asia Minor town (anc.)–Is-
  sus
Asian–Arabian, Chinese,
  Japanese, Korean, Mon-
  golian, Syrian
Asian (eastern) people–Se-
  res
Asiatic–Armenian, Nepal,
  pika, Tai, Tartar, Tatar,
  tataric
Asiatic (barbarous)–Hun
Asiatic (pert. to old)–Chal-
  dean
Asiatic animal–panda
Asiatic antelope (goat)–se-
  row
Asiatic ass (wild)–onager
Asiatic bird–brambling, dot-
  terel, mina
Asiatic bird (southern)–pit-
  ta
Asiatic carnivore–panda
Asiatic Christian–Uniat
Asiatic city–Bagdad
Asiatic country–Anam, As-
  sam, Iran, Iraq, Japan,
  Korea, Nepal, Nepaul,
  Siam, Siberia, Syria, Tib-
  et, Thailand
Asiatic country (anc.)–Ac-
  cad, Syria

Asiatic country (desert)–
  Arabia
Asiatic country (poetic)–
  Ind, Arabe
Asiatic country (southern)–
  Accad
Asiatic country native–Hin-
  du
Asiatic countries–East, Ori-
  ent
Asiatic deer–axis, roe
Asiatic desert–Gobi
Asiatic disease–cholera
Asiatic district–Tartary
Asiatic fiber–ramie
Asiatic gazelle–ahu
Asiatic goat antelope–goral,
  serow
Asiatic grass–coix
Asiatic greeting – salaam,
  salam
Asiatic group of tribes–tai
Asiatic herb–hemp
Asiatic island–Borneo, Cele-
  bes, Ceylon, Cyprus, For-
  mosa, Japanese, Java, Lu-
  zon, Malay, Mindanao,
  Philippines, Sakhalin, Su-
  matra, Wrangell
Asiatic jay (long-tailed,
  crested)–sirgang
Asiatic kingdom–Irak, Iraq,
  Nepal, Siam, Thailand
Asiatic kingdom (south-
  west)–Irak, Iraq
Asiatic kingdom member–
  Siamese, Thai
Asiatic lake–Tai, Tami
Asiatic lemur–loris, macaco
Asiatic lynx–caracal
Asiatic mammal (deer-like)
  –chevrotain
Asiatic market place–bazaar
Asiatic measure (of length)
  –mou
Asiatic millet–dari
Asiatic mixed tribe–Tatar
Asiatic mongoose (crab-eat-
  ing)–urva
Asiatic monkshood–atis
Asiatic mountain–Altai, Ev-
  erest, Himalayas, Hindu-
  Kush, Kanchinjinga, Sa-
  yan
Asiatic mountain (pert. to)
  –altaic

Asiatic mountain sheep–argali

Asiatic nation (old)–Sumer

Asiatic native–Arab, Chinese, Japanese, Korean, Mongolian, Syrian

Asiatic nomad–Arab

Asiatic oil plant–odal

Asiatic orchids (genus of)–aerides

Asiatic ox–yak

Asiatic palm–areca, nipa

Asiatic palm (species of)–ti

Asiatic palm (tropical)–areca, calami

Asiatic partridge (sand)–seesee

Asiatic peninsula – Arabia, Corea, Kamchatka, Korea

Asiatic people–Seres, Seric

Asiatic people (anc.)–Seres

Asiatic periodic wind–monsoon

Asiatic plague–cholera

Asiatic plant–odal

Asiatic plant (edible)–betel

Asiatic plant (shrubbery)–betel

Asiatic plantigrade animal–panda

Asiatic poplar tree–carab

Asiatic port–Macao

Asiatic race (member of barbarous)–Hun

Asiatic race (one of)–Malay

Asiatic region (anc.)–Aria

Asiatic river–Amoor, Amur, Branma, Eelee, Euphrates, Ganges, Hoang-Ho, Ili, Indus, Irawaddy, Lena, Ob, Obi, Putra, Tigris, Yalu, Yalua, Yang-Tse, Yenisei

Asiatic rodent (rabbit-like)–pika

Asiatic Roman province official (priestly)–Asiarch

Asiatic sand storm (central)–tebbad

Asiatic sea–Azof, Caspian

Asiatic sea (central inland)–Aral

Asiatic sheep (large wild)–argali

Asiatic shrub–tea

Asiatic snow storm–buran

Asiatic squirrel (small, flying)–polatouche

Asiatic squirrel (southern)–jelerang

Asiatic tea (rolled)–cha

Asiatic tree – asak, asok, asoka, dita, rata, siris

Asiatic tree (poplar)–carab

Asiatic tree (sap used as colic remedy)–asak

Asiatic tribe–Tai

Asiatic tribesman (mixed)–Tartar, Tatar

Asiatic Turkey city–Adana

Asiatic vine–akebi

Asiatic weapon (short sword)–adaga

Asiatic weight–tael

Asiatic wind (periodic)–monsoon

aside–alongside, apart, beside

asinego–ass, fool

ask–beg, beseech, entreat, implore, inquire, interrogate, invite, petition, query, queries (pl.), question, request, solicit

ask (Scot.)–spere

ask advice of–consult

ask for–solicit

ask on religious grounds–obsecrate

askance–crooked, obliquely, sideways

askew – amiss, askance, asquint, awry, crooked, distorted, obliquely

askew (Scot.)–agley

aslant–athwart, atilt, obliquely

asleep–dormant, motionless, unruffled

Asoka's India empire (anc.)–Patna

asp head dress (sacred)–urateus

aspect–angle, appearance, guise, look, mien, phase, side, view, visage

aspect (fierce, forbidding)–grim

aspect (frowning, obs.)–glum

aspect (general)–facies

aspect (pleasing, of nature)–scenery

aspect (showing worst state of)–seaminess

aspect of a situation–phase

aspect of two planets in relation to Zodiac–decil

aspen – poplar, quaking, quivering, tremulous

asperge–asparagus, aspergillum, sprinkle

asperity–acerbity, acrimony, moroseness

asperse–besmirch, bespatter, blacken, calumniate, decry, defame, discredit, malign, slander, traduce, vilify

asperse with calumny–bespatter

aspersion – calumniating, calumniation, calumny, defamation, sprinkling

aspersion (indirect)–innuendo

asphalt–bitumen

aspiration – aim, ambition, exhalation, hope, ideal, inspiration

aspire–ascend, long, rise, soar, tower

ass–dolt, fool

ass (wild)–onager

assail–attack, beset

assail with small missiles–pelt, stone

Assam inhabitant–Ahom

Assam mongoloid–Garo

Assam silkworm–eri, eria

Assam tribe (Eastern)–Ao

Assamese hill dweller–Aka

assassin–bravo, cuttle, murderer, ruffian, thug

assassin (var.)–thag

assassin of kings–regicide

assassinate – kill, murder, slay

assault–assail, attack, descent, incursion, invasion, onset, storm

assault (army)–onset

assault (reprisal)–counterattack

assay–attempt, endeavor, test, trial, try

assayer's cup–cupel

assaying (art of)–docimasy
assemblage (cattle)–drove, herd
assemblage (disorderly)–rout
assemblage (fashionable)–salon
assemblage (splendid)–galaxy
assemblage of tents–camp, encampment
assemble–amass, assail, collect, congregate, convoke, couple, gather, mass, meet, muster, piece, rally, recruit, unite
assembly–collection, company, concourse, congregation, convention, convocation, council, gathering, group, meeting, synod
assembly (Anglo-Saxon)–gemot
assembly (close)–conclave
assembly (demonology, midnight)–sabbat
assembly (legislative, Ger.)–landtag
assembly (popular)–agora
assembly (public)–diet, forum
assembly (religious)–congregation
assembly (secret)–conclave
assembly officer (presiding)–moderator
assent–accede, accord, acquiesce, acquiescence, agree, amen, aye, compliance, concur, consent, yea, yes
assent (compelling)–cogent, conclusive, persuasive, telling
assert–advocate, affirm, allege, asseverate, aver, claim, declare, plead, protest, say, state, support, uphold
assert (positively)–avouch
assert as fact–posit
assert as true–posit
assert to be true–allege
assertion–affirmation, declaration, maintenance, statement, vindication

assertion (boastful)–vaunt
assertion of right–claim
assertiveness (pedantic)–pragmatism
assertor–affirmer, defender, supporter, vindicator
assess–charge, levy, tax, value
assessment–fee, levy, scot, surtax, tax, valuation
assessment (old Eng. law)–tac
assessment (percentage of)–ratal
assessment (pert. to)–ratal
assessor–rater
asset–property, resource
asseverate–affirm, allege, aver, declare, protest, say, state
asseveration–affirmation, assertion, declaration, vow
asseveration (solemn)–oath
assiduity–diligence
assiduous–active, busy, diligent, indefatigable, intense, laborious, persevering, sedulous, unintermitted, unwearied
assign–adjudge, allocate, appropriate, ascribe, attribute, delegate, detail, cede, transfer
assign as one's portion–allot
assign roles to actors–cast
assign to–refer
assigned–allotted, ascribed, designated
assigned task–stint
assignment–allegement, allotment, task, transfer
assimilates–absorbs, adapts, digests
assist–abet, aid, avail, back, befriend, boost, favor, help, prompt, relieve, second, succor, support, sustain
assistance–aid, furtherance, help, succor, support
assistant–abettor, aide, attendant, auxiliary, helper
assistant (magician's)–famulus
assistant (military)–aide
assistants (body of)–staff

assisting the memory–mnemonic
assize–appoint, assess, fix, rate, value
associate–accomplice, ally, colleague, comrade, consort, friend, mingle, mix, pal, partner
associate (familiarly)–hobnob
associate for common advantage–partner
associated–banded, joined, united
Associated Press (abbr.)–AP
associates–kith
association–alliance, body, combination, company, club, fellowship, league, society
association (debating, literary)–lyceum
association (mutual)–interrelation
association (Russian laborers')–artel
association (secret)–cabal
association (trade, abbr.)–NAM
association for literary improvement–lyceum
association for supplying publishing material–syndicate
assort–classify, distribute, separate
assortment–set
assuage–allay, alleviate, appease, calm, comfort, ease, lessen, mitigate, pacify, relieve, solace, soothe
assuaging–balmy
assuasive–mitigating, soothing, tranquilizing
assume–affect, betake, counterfeit, don, premise, pretend, sham, simulate, take
assume character of another–impersonate
assume different form–protean
assume tentatively–suppose
assume without proof–hypothetical

assumed–fictional, hypothetical, presumptive, presupposed, supposititious

assumes presumptuously–arrogated

assuming–arrogant, assumptive, lofty, presuming, presumptuous, pretentious, superior

assuming different form–protean

assumption – presupposition, supposition

assurance–aplomb, cocksureness, confidence, coolness, impudence, insurance, trust

assurance of manner–aplomb

assure–assert, asseverate, aver, avouch, convince, declare, embolden, encourage, guarantee, insure, persuade, protest, reassure, vouch

assured anticipation–trust

Assyria (old name)–Assur

Assyrian capital–Nineveh

Assyrian city–Al Sur, Arbela, Asshur, Assur, Calah, Dur Sargon, Kalakh, Nineveh

Assyrian deity (anc. chief)–Ashshur, Ashur, Asshur, Asur

Assyrian god–Adad, Nebo

Assyrian god (hunting)–Ninip

Assyrian god (moon)–Sin

Assyrian god (sun)–Shamas

Assyrian god (war)–Nergal

Assyrian goddess–Istar

Assyrian king–Pul

Assyrian king (legendary)–Belus

Assyrian measure–artaba, cane, foot, gariba, ghalva, makuk, mansion, qasab

astart–befall, escape, shun

aster–oxeye, star

aster family–carduaceae

asterisk–star

asterisk (small)–starlet

astern–abaft, aft, baft, behind

asteroid – Astrea, Ceres,

Egeria, Eunomia, Flora, Fortuna, Hebe, Hygeia, Irene, Iris, Juno, Lutetia, Massalia, Melpomene, Metis, Pallas, Parthenope, planetoid, Psyche, starlike, Thetis, Vesta, Victoria

asteroid (discovered in 1850)–Egeria

asteroid (433rd)–Eros

asthmatic–pursy, wheezy

astipulate–agree, assent, exstipulate

astir–about, active, moving, up

astite (obs.)–immediately, quickly

Astolat's lily maid–Elaine

astonishes–amazes, appals, astounds, overwhelms, surprises

astound–amaze, appal, astonish, shock, stun, stupefy, surprise

astraddle–astride

astral – sidereal, starlike, starry, stellar

astray–afield, amiss, erring, mistaken, wrong

astrict–confine, constipate, constrain, constrict, limit, restrict

astride–astraddle

astringent–acerb, alum, austere, constrictive, sour, stern, styptic

astringent (antiseptic)–argentamine

astringent (used in rhinitis) –salumin

astringent extract–catechu

astringent mineral salt–alum

astringent salt–alum

astrologer–astronomer, stargazer

astronomical–uranian, uranic

astronomical measurement–azimuth

astronomical year book–almanac

astronomy orbit (point)–apsis

astute–cunning, discrimi-

nating, keen, shrewd, skilled, smart

asylum–home, jail, retreat, sanctuary

at a distance–yonder

at all–ava, ever

at all (Scot.)–ava

at any time–ever

at any time (poetic)–eer

at ease–relaxed

at hand–near, nigh, present

at highest point–zenith

at last–ultimately

at no time (contr.)–neer

at no time hereafter–nevermore

at odds–out

at present–now

at rest–ease, relaxed

at that time–then

at the back–abaff, abaft, aft, arear, astern, postern

at the middle–central, centric

at the same time–meanwhile

at the tip–apical

at this–hereat

at this time–yet

atabal–drum, kettledrum, tabor

atacamite (powdered)–arsenillo

atalaya–watchtower

atap–nipa

atavistic–reversional

ate–dined, fared, supped

ate away (bit by bit)–gnawed

ate sparingly–dieted

atelier–studio, workshop

ates–sweetsop

Athamas' son – Learchus, Phrixos, Phrixus

Athamas' wife–Ino

athanasia – deathlessness, immortality

athanor–furnace

Athapascan Indian–Dene

atheist–infidel

Athena (name of)–Pallas

Athena priestess–Auge

Athena victory giving–nike

Athenian appellation–alea

Athenian assembly (popular)–pnyx

Athenian festival–aeora
Athenian general–Xenophon
Athenian historian–Xenophon
Athenian lawgiver–Draco, Solon
Athenian nickname–Alea
Athenian platform (rock cut assembly)–bema
Athenian statesman–Pericles
Athenian statesman (called "The Just")–Aristides
Athenian title–alea
Athens (pert. to)–Attic
Athens' citadel–Acropolis
Athens' king–Pandion
Athens of America–Boston
Athens of Ireland–Belfast, Cork
Athens of Switzerland–Zurich
Athens of the North–Edinburgh
Athens of the West–Cordoba
Athens' port–Piraeus
Athens' potter's quarter–Ceramicus
Athens' resident (alien, anc.)–metic
Athens' rival (anc.)–Sparta
athlete (paid)–pro
athlete (unprofessional)–amateur
athlete's covered portico–xyst
athletic–muscular, robust, strong, vigorous
athletic arena – stadium, stadia (pl.)
athletic balancer–acrobat
athletic star–ace
athwart–across, aslant
atimon–muskmelon
atlantal–anterior, cephalic
Atlantic fish (tropical)–salema
Atlantic island – Canary, Cuba, Iceland
Atlantic Ocean–pond
Atlantic sisters–Pleiades
atmosphere–air, ether
atmosphere (noxious)–miasma

atmospheric disturbance–static, storm
atole–gruel, porridge
atom–ace, jot, monad, particle, whit
atom (consisting of one)–monatomic
atom component–ion
atom having valences of eight–octad
atomic–minute, tiny
atomize–spray
atomy–atom, mote, skeleton
atonement–penance, propitiation, reparation
atones for–redeems
Atreus' brother–Thyestes
Atreus' father–Pelops
Atreus' half brother–Chrysippus
Atreus' mother–Hippodamia
Atreus' son–Agamemnon, Menelaus
atrip–aweigh
atrocious–abominable, cruel, flagrant, heinous, wicked
atrociousness – schrecklichkeit
atrophy–emaciation, tabes
attached–added, affixed, annexed, appended, connected, devoted, fixed, glued, hitched, joined, pasted, subjoined, tagged, united
attached (devotedly)–fond
attached directly at base–sessile
attached directly to stem–sessile
attached firmly–cemented, welded
attached to–annexed
attached to the soil–predial
attachment–adherence, affection, love
attachment (Arabic culture)–Arabism
attack–assail, assault, beset, charge, offense, onrush, onset, sally, sortie
attack (false)–feint
attack (forefront) – spear head

attack (sharp)–pang
attack (sudden)–descent, raid
attack by waiting–siege
attack on all sides–beset
attacks (one who)–aggressor
attain–accede, obtain, reach, win
attain recognition–arrive
attain success–arrive, win
attainment – accomplishment, acquirement, arrival
attempt–assay, attack, dare, effort, endeavor, essay, onset, trial, try, undertake, venture
attempt (slang)–stab
attempt to gain possession (continued)–siege
attend–accompany, conduct, escort, follow, hearken, ho, listen, nurse, serve, treat, visit, wait
attend to–see
attendance–presence
attendant–associate, attending, companion, concomitant, escort, follower, ministering, subsequent
attendant (boy)–page
attendant (court) – staff, staves (pl.)
attendant (hospital)–orderly
attendant (of sick)–nurse
attendant (riding master)–creat
attendant (Scot.)–gillie
attendants–maids, porters, retinue, ushers, waiters
attendants (train of)–cortege, retinue, suite
attention–care, ear, heed, intentness, notice, observance
attention (careful)–heed
attention (exclusive)–concentration
attention (favorable)–ear
attention (without)–carelessly
attentive – circumspect, courteous, heedful, mindful, observant, watchful
attentively occupied–intent

attenuation–emaciation, rarefaction, thinness
atter–poison, venom
attern–venomous
attery–malignant, poisonous, purulent
attest–certify, evidence, invoke, testify, vouch
attestation (solemn)–oath
attic–garret, loft
attic bird–nightingale
Attic muse–Xenophon
Attica aliens (anc.)–metics
Attica king (legendary)–Ogyges, Ogygos
Attica resident (noncitizen)–metic
Attica township–Deme
Attica valley–Icaria
Attila follower–Hun
Attila's hordes (one of)–Hun
Attilinae (one of)–Attiline
attire–apparel, array, clothe, dress, enrobe, garb, habiliment, toilet
attire (clerical)–cloth
attire (mean)–rags
attire (shining)–sheen
attire (unceremonious)–negligee, slacks
attitude–air, bearing, feeling, pose, position, posture, set, stand
attitude of reverence–genuflection, genuflexion, kneel
attorney–lawyer, solicitor
attorney's fee–retainer
attract–draw, entice, influence, lure, tempt
attracted (naturally)–gravitude
attraction–charm, looks, lure
attraction (side show)–freak
attraction (strong)–penchant
attractive–alluring, engaging, taking
attractive (very)–cute, winsome
attrap–adorn, array, ensnare, entrap
attributable–due
attribute–ascribe, characteristic, impute, owe, pecu-

liarity, property, quality, refer
attribute (essential)–property
attribute to–ascribe
attrist–sadden
attrite–worn
attrition–abrasion, contrition, friction
atweel (Scot.)–surely, truly
atwin–apart, asunder
auberge–inn
aubergiste–innkeeper
auction–sale
audace–bold, spirited
audacious – adventurous, barefaced, bold, impertinence, impudence, insolence, presumption, sauciness
audacity–assurance, courage, effrontery, hardihood, impertinence, impudence, insolence, nerve, presumption, sauciness, shamelessness, temerity
audacity (coll.)–cheek
audible–aloud
audible (barely)–faint
audible respiration–sigh
audibly–aloud
audience–ear, hearing, interview
auditor–accountant, bookkeeper, hearer, listener
auditory–audience, otic
auger–gimlet, wimble
auger edge–lip
aught–anything, valiant, worthy
augment–add, amplify, eke, enhance, enlarge, increase
augmentation–eking, increase
augur–bode, forebode, foretell, forewarn, omen, portend, predict, prognosticate, prophesy, signify
augurer–seer
augury–ceremony, omen, portent, prognostic, rite
august–awful, dignified, grand, imposing, magnificent, noble, solemn, stately

August (first day of)–Lammas
August meteors–Perseids
auk (razor-billed–Scot.)–falk
auk (short-billed)–rotch
auks (genus of)–alle
auks (razor-billed)–murres
aula–emblic, hall, room
aumail–enamel
aumous (Scot.)–alms
aural–otic
aureola–glory, halo, nimbus
aureole–halo
auricle–ear, pinna
auricle (heart)–atrium, atria (pl.)
auricular–otic
auriculate–eared
auriferous–golden
aurochs–tur, urus
aurora–eos
auroral–eoan, radiant, rosy
auspices–egis
auspicious–opportune, propitious
Aussie–Australia, Australian
Aussie ratite–emu
austere–ascetic, hard, harsh, rigid, severe, stern, strict
Australian (arboreal carnivorous)–dasyure
Australian aborigines' cry (peculiar)–cooee
Australian aborigines' weapon–liangle
Australian animal–wombat
Australian animal (arboreal)–koala
Australian anteater–echidna
Australian apple tree–emu
Australian badger–wombat
Australian bag (small)–dilli
Australian bear–koala, coala (var.)
Australian beefwood–belar
Australian beverage–kava
Australian bird–bustard, cassowary, emu, emue, friarbird, leipoa, lorikeet, lory, lyrebird, pardalote, platypus, roa
Australian bird (large)–emu
Australian bird (named for its cry)–morepork

Australian bird (owl)–boobook

Australian cake (rough, sweetened with currents) –brownie

Australian city–Adelaide, Brisbane, Melbourne, Perth, Sydney

Australian cockatoo–arara

Australian commonwealth (island state)–Tasmania

Australian crawfish–yabby

Australian cycad–banga

Australian division–Australia, Federal Capital Territory, New South Wales, Northern Territory, Queensland, Tasmania, Victoria

Australian dog (wild)–dingo

Australian eucalypt–mallee

Australian hut–miamia

Australian kiwi–roa

Australian lake–Amadeus, Eyre, Gairdner, Torrens

Australian mahogany–gunnung, jarrah

Australian mammal–koala, tait

Australian marsupial–kangaroo, tait, wombat

Australian missile–boomerang

Australian mountain–Kosciusko, Townsend

Australian mountain range–Darling, Flinders, Gawler

Australian parakeet–rosella

Australian parakeet (crested)–corella

Australian parakeet (grass)–budgerigar, budgie

Australian parrot–lory, lories (pl.)

Australian pepper (shrubby)–ava, ava-ava, arva, kava, kava-kava, yava

Australian petrel–titi

Australian phalanger (flying)–ariel

Australian pine tree–kauri, kaury

Australian plant–warratau

Australian plant secretion (sweet)–laap, laarp, lerp

Australian pompano–dart

Australian rifleman–yager

Australian river–Ashburton, Barcoo, Brisbane, Burdekin, Clarence, Darling, De Grey, Fitzroy, Flinders, Gascoyne, Hunter, Lachlan, Mitchell, Murchison, Murray, Murrumidgee, Swan, Victoria

Australian shark (large)–mako

Australian sheep dog–kelpie

Australian shrub (genus of) –alstonia

Australian shrub secretion–lerp

Australian snake–elapid

Australian soldier–digger

Australian state–Victoria

Australian thicket (brushwood)–mallee

Australian throwing stick–boomerang

Australian tree–belar, ironbark, jarrah, marara

Australian tree (beefwood)–belah, belar

Australian tree (timber)–penda, toon

Australian tree (with milky juice which blinds eyes)–alipata

Australian tree fruit–nonda

Australian tulip–waratah

Australian war club–waddy

Australian wattle–boobialla

Australian weight (former)–saum

Australian wild dog–dingo

Australian wild horse–brumbee

Australian wombat–koala

Australian wood (used for turner's work)–emu

Austrian and German union (political)–Anschluss

Austrian botanist–Mendel

Austrian capital–Vienna

Austrian city–Gratz, Graz, Linz, Salzburg, Vienna, Wien

Austrian coin–ducat (g.), florin (s.), groschen (br.),

heller (br.), krone (s.), schilling (s.)

Austrian coin (old)–heller

Austrian composer–Mozart

Austrian measure–achtel, becher, dreiling, fass, fuss, futtermassel, halbe, joch, klatter, linie, mass, melle, metze, muth, muthmassel, pfiff, punkt, seidel, viertel, yoke

Austrian name (prefix)–Von

Austrian nobleman–Ritter

Austrian nobility order (lowest)–Ritter

Austrian province–Bohemia, Bukowina, Carinthia, Carniola, Dalmatia, Galicia, Gorz, Gradisca, Istria, Moravia, Salzburg, Selesia, Styria, Tirol, Triest, Tyrol, Vorarlberg

Austrian river – Danube, Elbe, Enns, Inn, Isar, Moldau

Austrian weight–centner, denat, karch, marc, pfennig, pfund, quentchen, saum, stein, unze, vierling

autarch–autocrat, despot

authentic – authoritative, credible, genuine, pure, reliable, true, trustworthy, valid

authenticate – attestation, confirm

authenticate (officially)–attest

author–begetter, compiler, composer, creator, inventor, maker, originator, parent, penman, producer, writer

author (contemporary)–Milne

author's words (original)–text

authoritative –commanding, determinative, imperious, official

authoritative command–decree, fiat

authoritative example–precedent

authoritative rule–law
authoritative ruler–dictator
authoritative statement–dictum
authority–command, competency, dominion, influence, jurisdiction, power
authority (infallible)–oracle
authority (ruling)–regent
authorize–commission, delegate, empower, endorse, entitle, license, permit, ratify, sanction
authorized (law)–able
authorless–anonymous
autobiographical account (of one's experience)–memoirs
autochthonous – aboriginal, indigenous, native
autocracy–absolutism, despotism, monarchy
autocrat–czar, despot, mogul, monarch, sovereign, tzar
autograph–signature
automatic–machine, mechanical, spontaneous
automatic pistol (slang)–gat
automaton–golem, machine, robot
automobile (army, small)–jeep
automobile engine–motor
automobile engine part–magneto
autumn–fall, mature
auxiliary–accessory, additional, aiding, ancillary, assistant, cooperating, helping, secondary, subordinate, subservient, subsidiary, supporting
auxiliary verb–had, has, may, was
auxiliary verb (denoting future tense)–shall, will
auxiliary verb (old)–hast
avail–benefit, profit, service, use, utility
avail (to)–go, use
available – convenient, handy, obtainable, ready, usable
available (to become)–enure
avalanche–slide

avania–impost, tax
avarice–covetousness, cupidity, greed, greediness
avarice (spirit of)–Mammon
avaricious–close, covetous, grasping, greedy, miserly, niggardly, parsimonious, penurious, rapacious
avariciousness–rapacity
avatar–embodiment, epiphany, incarnation
avaunt–advance, begone, boast, depart, vaunt
ave–farewell, hail
avenaceous–oaten
avenge–requite, retaliate, vindicate
avenging goddess–Ate
avenue–opening, passageway, road, street
avenue (covered)–arcade
avenue (Fr.)–rue
aver–affirm, assert, asseverate, declare, protest, say, state
average–go, mean, normal, par
averse–loathe, reluctant, unwilling
aversion–antipathy, disgust, dislike, hate, odium, repugnance
aversion to society–anthropophobia
aversionist of wine–oenophobist
avert–evade, prevent
avestruz–rhea
aviary–birdhouse, enclosure, house, ornithon
aviation–aeronautics, airplaning, flying
aviation maneuver–Immelmann
aviator–ace, airman, flier, flyer, pilot
aviator (first)–Icarus
aviator (mythical)–Icarus
aviator's signal–Roger
avid–eager, greedy
avidity–cupidity, eagerness, greediness
avile–abase, debase, depreciate, vilify
avion (Fr.)–airplane

avoid–dodge, elude, escape, eschew, evade, shun
avoid as hurtful–eschew
avoidable (not)–unescapable
avoidance–emptying, evasion, removal, vacating, withdrawal
avoiding society–asocial
avoirdupois weight–dram, hundredweight, long hundredweight, long ton, ounce, pound, ton
avow–acknowledge, admit, confess, own, profess
awa (Scot.)–away
awabi–abalone
awaft–adrift, afloat, wafted
await–abide, ambush, bide, heed, pend, tarry, wait, watch
await settlement–pend
awake–alert, arouse, attentive, conscious, excite, waking
Awake and Sing author–Odets
awaken–arouse, excite
award–allot, meed, mete
award (historic word)–addeem
aware–apprised, cognizant, conscious, intelligent
aware (to be)–know, wot
away–abroad, absent, aside, fro, gone, off, out
away (prefix)–aph, apo
away (Scot.)–awa
away from–absent, out
away from center of body–distal
away from the mouth–aborad, aboral
awe–cow, dread, fear, terror, reverence
awe inspiring–awful, eerie, eery, ghostly
aweather (opposite of)–alee
aweigh–atrip
awesome–appalling, awful, eerie, eery, unearthly, weird
awful–appalling, awesome, dread, dreadful, fearful, shocking, terrible
awing–flying, fluttering
awk–clumsy, odd, perverse

awkward–blundering, bungling, clownish, clumsy, gawky, graceless, inapt, inelegant, inept, lubberly, lumbering, maladroit, ponderous, ungainly, ungraceful
awkward fellow–galoot
awl (Scot.)–elsen
awl (shoemaker's, Scot.)–elsin
awn–arista, aristae (pl.), barb, beard
awns (having)–eared
awning–canopy, velarium, velum
awning line fastening–earing

awry–agee, askew, asquint, crooked, distorted, oblique
awry (Scot.)–agley
ax–adz, adze
ax (small)–hatchet
ax blade–bit
ax butt–poll
ax handle–helve
ax-shaped implement (prehistoric)–celt
axial portion (of animal)–suma
axilla–ala, armpit
axillary–alar
axiom–adage, aphorism, apothegm, byword, dictum, maxim, motto, precept, proverb, saw, saying

axiomatically–sententiously
axis (pert. to)–axal, axial
axis (small)–spindle
axle–pin, spindle
axle (pert. to)–axile
axweed–goutweed
ayah–maid, nursemaid
aye – always, continually, ever
aye (an)–pro, yes
Azerbaijan city–Baku, Elizavetpol, Yelisavetpol
Azores port (chief)–Horta
Aztec emperor–Montezuma
Aztec myth–nana
Aztec stone–chalchihuitl
azure–blue, cerulean
azure-like blue–bice

B

baa–bleat
baahling–lamb
Baal–deity
baal (bail, bale)–no, not
baba–baby, child
babacoote–lemur
babble–blather, chat, chatter, gossip, prate, prattle
babbo (coll.)–daddy, father
babel–tumult
baboon–ape, papa
baboon (female)–babuina
babushka (Russ.)–grandmother
baby carriage–gocart, perambulator, pram
baby outfit–layette
baby shoes–bootees
babyish–childish, puerile, simple
Babylonian abode of the dead–Aralu
Babylonian cycle (lunar)–saros
Babylonian deity–Anu, Apsu, Aya, Bel, Ea, Enlil, Etana, Hea, Hes, Ira
Babylonian deity (of alcoholic drink)–Siris
Babylonian deity (primitive)–Alala, Alalu

Babylonian divinity–Hea
Babylonian era–sumer
Babylonian god–Adad, Bel, Ea, Irra, Ler
Babylonian god (earth)–Dagan
Babylonian god (of pestilence)–Irra
Babylonian god (sky)–Anu
Babylonian god (storm)–Zu
Babylonian god (war)–Bel, Ira, Irra, Nergal
Babylonian god (water)–Ea
Babylonian god (wind storm)–Adad
Babylonian goddess–Bau, Belit, Mylitta
Babylonian goddess (most ancient)–Belit, Beltis
Babylonian goddess (of the deep)–Nina
Babylonian hero (myth.) – Etana
Babylonian hero (nature myth.)–Adapa
Babylonian king–Nebuchadnezzar, Nebuchadrezzar
Babylonian kingdom (East, arch.)–Elam
Babylonian kingdom dweller–Elamite

Babylonian language–Accad
Babylonian mountain–Ararat
Babylonian native (Biblical) –Elamite
Babylonian numeral (sixty, sixties)–sar, saros
Babylonian people (anc. North Eastern)–Elamite
Babylonian regions (infernal)–Aralu
Babylonian sea–Nina
Babylonian war god–Irra
bacach–beggar, cripple
bacalao–codfish
bacalao bird – guillemot, murre
Bacardi–rum
bacca–berry
baccalaureate degree–BA
baccarat (variety of)–chemin-de-fer
Bacchanal's cry–evoe
bacchante–maenad
bache (Eng. dial.)–rivulet, stream, vale
bachelor–garcon
bachelor (confirmed) – celibate
back–abet, aid, dorsum, encourage, finance, fro,

hind, nape, posterior, rear, second, stern, support, sustain, uphold
back (animal's)–tergum, terga (pl.)
back (insect's)–nota
back (lower part of)–loin
back (pert. to)–dorsal, lumbar, tergal
back (pert. to lower)–lumbar
back (prefix)–re
back (zool.)–notum
back of hand–opisthenar
back of neck–nape
back pain–notalgia
backbone–spine, stamina
backbone (animal)–chine
backbone (pert. to)–spinal
backbone (small)–spinule
backboned–firm, resolute, vertebrate
background–distance, education, rear, setting, training
backward–arear, averse, back, bashful, dull, hesitating, loath, rearward, recessive, regressive, reluctant, retrograde, retrogressive, retrospective, reverse, stupid, unwilling
backward (prefix)–retro
backward movement–retrogression
backward projecting point–barb
backwater–bayou, ebb
backwort–comfrey
bacon (lower end of side)–gammon
bacon (slice)–rasher
bacon strips inserted–larded
bacteria–aerobes, aerobia, germ
bacteria (free from harmful)–aseptic
bacteria (grown only in oxygen)–aerobia
bacteria (requiring free oxygen)–aerobe, aerobia (pl.), aerobium, aerobes (pl.)
bacteria (rod-shaped)–bacillus, bacilli (pl.)
bacteriologist's culture–agar

bacteriologist's wire–oese
bad–corrupt, criminal, depraved, evil, fell, inferior, inopportune, nasty, poor, rotten, sinful, spoiled, tainted, unmoral, unsound, unsuitable, vicious, vile, wicked, wrong
bad (Chinook jargon)–cultus
bad (notoriously)–arrant
bad (prefix)–mal
bad blood–bitterness, resentment
bad character (Fr.)–drole
bad luck–deuce
bad luck (cause of, coll.)–hoodoo
badge–emblem, mark, pin, sign, symbol, token
badge (honorary order)–plaque
badge (policeman's)–buzzer, shield, star
badger–bandicoot, bother, das, harass, hawker, heckle, huckster, nag, pester, wombat
badger (honey)–ratel
badger-like animal–ratel
Badger State–Wisconsin
badinage–banter, fool, joker, raillery, simpleton
badly–faultily, ill, imperfectly, poorly, sick, unskillfully, unwell, viciously, wickedly
baff–beat, blow, strike, worthless
baffle–balk, defeat, elude, evade, foil, frustrate, thwart
baft–abaft, astern
bag–grip, net, portmanteau, pot, pouch, purse, reticule, sac, sack, satchel
bag (chatelaine)–etui, etwee
bag (leather)–budge
bag (membranous, bot.)–ascus, asci (pl.)
bag (ornamental powder)–sachet
bag (overnight)–sacdenuit
bag (perfume)–sachet
bag (powder)–sachet
bag (provision)–haversack

bag (saddle)–pannier
bag (scent)–sachet
bag (small)–poke, reticule, sachet
bag (traveling)–gladstone, grip, suitcase, valise
bagatelle–trifle
Bagdad capital–Irak
Bagdad kingdom–Irak
Bagdad merchant (Arabian Nights)–Sindbad
bagpipe (flute pipe)–chanter
bagpipe (play the)–doodle
bagpipe horn–drone
bagpipe player–piper
bagpipe tune–port
bah–faugh, foh
Bahama native (coll.)–conch
bahay (Phil. Is.)–house
bahi (gypsy)–fortune
bahia (Span.)–bay
bail–bucket, dip, guarantee, handle, hoop, lade, ladle, lave, ring, secure, surety, throw
bailiff–agent, deputy, officer, overseer, reeve, sheriff, staff, staves (pl.), steward, understeward
bailiff (old English)–reeve
bain–direct, forward, limber, lithe, near, ready, short, supple, willing
bairn–child
bait–badger, enticement, fulcrum, harass, lure, persecute, temptation, torment
bait (artificial)–hackle
bait dropped lightly–dap, dib
bakal–shopkeeper, tradesman
bake–anneal, dry, harden
baken–beacon, buoy, landmark
baker's dozen–thirteen
baker's implement (spadelike)–peel
baker's sheet–pan
baker's shovel–peel
baking (a)–batch
baking dish–ramekin
baking ingredient–soda, yeast

baking soda–saleratus

Bakongo goddess–Nyambe, Nzambi

balance–adjust, composure, counterpoise, equalize, equilibrium, equipoise, even, neutralize, offset, poise, rest, sanity, scale, serenity, weigh

balanced (evenly)–equal

balancer (athletic)–acrobat, gymnast

balat (Phil. Is.)–bark, leather, shell, skin

balate–trepang

balatron–buffoon

balcony (arena of theater)–podium

bald–crude, epilose, naked, plain, simple, unvarnished

Balder's wife–Nanna

bale–bundle, package

bale (covered with hide)–seroon

bale made of skins–seroon

Balearic Islands–Cabrera, Formentera, Ivza, Majorca, Minorca

Balearic Islands measure–barcella, misura, palmo, quarta, quarte, quartera, quartin

Balearic Islands weight–artal, artel, cargo, corta, libra, mayor, quartano, ratel, rotel

baleful–bad, pernicious

balk–baffle, check, disappoint, foil, frustrate, thwart

balk (Scot.)–reets

Balkan coin–novcic (cop.)

Balkan guerrilla–Serb

Balkan kingdom (former)–Serbia, Servia

balker–huer

ball–dance, globe, orb, sphere

ball (Fr.)–bal

ball (little)–pellet

ball (lofted)–fly, lob

ball (minced fried fish or meat)–rissole

ball (ornamental, small)–bead

ball (straight batted)–liner

ball game–pelota

ball game (old)–cat

ball of thread or yarn–clew, clue

ballad–derries, lay, song

ballast (a ship)–saburrate

ballast (pig iron)–kentledge

ballet (Delibes)–Naila

ballister (part of)–newel

balloon–aerostat, bag, blimp, gasbag

balloon barrage (Fr. slang)–rat-trap

balloon basket–car, nacelle

ballot–bale, vote

balloting–election

balmy–aromatic, assuaging, daffy, fragrant, healing, insane, mild, odoriferous, refreshing, soothing, spicy

balmy (slang)–daffy, insane, sleep

balsam–riga, tolu

balsam (fragrant)–tolu

balsam (South America)–tolu

Baltic barge (flatbottomed)–praam

Baltic city–Danzig

Baltic island–Oesel

Baltic port–Reval, Riga

Baltic river–Oder

Baltic Sea gulf–Riga

Baltic Sea island–Alsen

balustrade–railing

bam–cheat, hoax, sham

bambino–baby, child

bamboo-like grass–reed

bamboo sprouts (pickled)–achar

bamboo stems–cane

bamboo sugar–tabasheer

bamboozle–cajole, deceive, hoax, humbug, mystify, perplex

ban–curse, taboo

ban (authoritative)–veto

banal–commonplace, flat, stale, trite

banana–musa, plantain

banana family–musace.e

banana leaf–frond

band–bandy, belt, cohort,

company, copula, crew, strap, stripe, tribe

band (across sun spot)–bridge

band (arm)–cohort

band (armed)–posse

band (armor, horizontal, forming short skirt)–tonlet

band (around waist)–cummerbund, kummerbund

band (circular)–hoop, ring

band (decorative)–cornice

band (decorative garment fastening, Fr.)–patte

band (horizontal, across shield)–fess

band (in brain)–ligula

band (narrow)–stria, striae (pl.)

band (of silk)–sash

band (society)–Bund

band (tissue connecting)–ligament

band (trimming)–braid

bandage–ligate, ligature, sling, spica, swathe, tape

bandage (adhesive)–tape

bandaged–taped

banded adder–krait

bandhook–rifle

bandicoot–rat

bandido–bandit

bandit–bandido, brigand, highwayman, ladrone, marauder, outlaw, picaroon, robber, thief

bandleader–choragus, choragi (pl.), conductor, maestro

bando–edict, proclamation

bandolero – highwayman, robber

bandy–carriage, cart, exchange, reciprocate

bane–curse, harm, injury, kill, murderer, pest, poison, ruin, slayer, woe

baneful–harmful, ill, pernicious

bang–beat, drub, slam, thrash, thump

bangster–braggart, bully, victor, winner

Bani's son–Amzi, Uel

banish–ban, deport, dismiss,

dispel, exclude, exile, expatriate, expel, ostracize, oust, outlaw, proscribe, relegate

banish to background–relegate

banishment–dismissal, exile, expatriation

banister–baluster, balustrade

bank–brink, deposit, edge, marge, margin, shore, strand

bank (arch.)–rivage

bank (sloping earth)–terrace

bank (stream)–riverside

bank (stretch of paved and strengthened)–quay

bank aide–teller

banker's aversion (pet)–examiner

banner–ensign, exemplary, fane, flag, foremost, leading, pennant, standard, surpassing

banquet–feast, repast

bantam car (army, slang)–jeep

bantay–guard, sentinel

banteng–tsine

banter–badinage, chaff, delude, deride, mock, persiflage, raillery, ridicule, satire, trick, wheedle

banting period–fast

bantling–bastard, child, infant

Bantu language–ila

Bantu people–Duala

Bantu prefix (indicating language)–ki

baobab tree leaves (powdered)–lalo

baptism of fire (Germ.)–feuertaufe

baptismal vessel–font, piscina

baptismal water–laver

baptizing font–piscina

bar–barricade, barrier, block, cake, dam, exclude, hindrance, impediment, obstacle, obstruct, obstruction, preclude, prevent, rail, rod, saloon

bar (acrobat's)–trapeze

bar (by one's own act)–estop

bar (for slacking loom thread)–easer

bar (knock down, soap frame)–sess

bar (mechanical)–lever

bar (metal, for tamping)–stemmer

bar (mining steel)–moil

bar (notched door knocker)–risp

bar (of cast metal)–ingot

bar (of metal)–ingot, rail

bar (of soap frame)–sess

bar (of wood)–rail

bar (supporting)–fid

bar (toothed)–rack

bar (turning on a fulcrum)–lever

bar (typewriter)–spacer

bar (upright, forming principal support)–stanchion

bar (wheel)–axle

bar legally–estop

bar on escutcheon–fess

bar out–preclude, prevent

bar to which singletree is attached–doubletree

bar to which tugs of harness are attached–singletree

bar used in shipbuilding–set iron

barb of feather–pinnula

barb of feather (large)–harl

barbarian–hun, Philistine, rude, savage, uncivilized, unlettered, untutored

barbaric–cruel, gothic, primitive, uncivilized

barbarism–savagism, solecism

barbarous–brutal, fell, ignorant, uncultivated

Barbary state–Algiers, Tunis

barber–shaver, tonsorialist, tonsure

Barber of Seville heroine–Rosina

Barcelona street–rambla

bard–minstrel, musician, poet

bard (early)–scop

bare–bald, defenseless, denude, desolate, expose, mere, nude, strip, unarmed

bare (obs.)–nud

barefaced–audacious, impudent, shameless, undisguised

barely–hardly, insufficiently, merely, nakedly, nudely, only, poorly, scantily, scarcely

barely audible–faint

bargain–barter, chaffer, contract, deal, dicker, engagement, haggle, negotiate, purchase, sell, stipulation

bargain (secret)–deal

bargain hard–prig

bargainer (shrewd)–chiseler, shaver

barge–ark, berate, raft, rebuke, scold, scow

barge (chieftain's)–birling, birlinn

barge (flat-bottomed, Norwegian)–praam, praham, pram

barge (heavy)–hoy

barge charge (for use of)–lighterage

bargeman–bargee

bargh–hill, ridge

bari–cottage, hut

barium sulphate–barite

bark–bay, husk, rind, skin

bark (aromatic tree)–canella

bark (aromatic, used as condiments)–canella

bark (deep-sounding)–bay

bark (fibrous, inner tree)–bast

bark (mulberry)–tapa

bark (oak, rough part)–crut

bark (outer)–ross

bark (perennial plant)–cortex

bark (root, for tea making)–sassafras

bark (shrill)–yap, yelp

bark at–bay

bark-like–cortical

bark of tree (exterior)–ross

bark of tree (outer)–periderm

bark of tree (used for cloth)–tapa

bark of tree (used for tanning)–alder

barkeeper–tapster

barker–spieler
barking deer–muntjac
barkle–cake, incrust
barley (Scot.)–bere
barlow–jackknife
barm–ferment, froth, yeast
barn (cow)–byre
barn (upper floor of) loft
barn storage place–bay, loft, mow
Barnaby Rudge character–Varden
barnacle plate (dorsal)–tergum, terga (pl.)
barometer (kind of)–aneroid, glass
barometer (liquidless)–aneroid
barometer line–isobar
baronet–sir
baronet (abbr.)–Bart., Bt.
baronet's title–Sir
barong–knife, sword
barony–dignity, domain, rank
Barotse (old name)–Aalui
barrack–casern, caserne
barracks (garrison town)–casern, caserne
barracks (slave)–barracoon
barraclade–blanket
barracuda–sennet, spet
barracuda (small)–spet
barrage–cannonade
barrage (balloon, Fr. slang)–rat-trap
barranca–bank, bluff, ravine
barras–galipot
barrator–bully, fighter, rowdy
barrel–cask, keg
barrel (herring)–cade
barrel (side piece of)–stave
barrel (small)–cask, keg, kilderkin, rundlet, runlet
barrel (small herring)–cade
barrel (to)–cooper
barrelful of fresh herring–cran
barrel maker–cooper
barrel raising device–parbuckle
barrel stopper–bung
barren–arid, bare, desert, dull, effete, empty, infertile, meager, sterile, stupid, unfruitful, unproductive, unprofitable
barren (Span.)–steril
barren oak–blackjack
barren privet–alatern, houseleek
barricade–bar, block, close, obstruct, stop
barricade (of felled trees)–abatis
barrico–cask, keg
barrier–bar, dam, fence, fortress, hedge, obstruction, railing, restraint, stockade, wall, weir
barrier (artificial race)–hurdle
barrier (enclosing)–fence, wall
barrier (huge)–Alp
barrier (in stream)–dam, weir
barrier (movable fence)–bar, gate
barrier (of bushes)–hedge
barrier (protective)–parapet
barrier (swinging)–door, gate
barrikin (Eng. slang)–gibberish, jargon
barrister–attorney, lawyer
barroom–saloon
barroom (Span.)–cantina
barrow – hill, hod, hog, mound, mountain, tumuli
barry–barracuda
bartender–tapster
barter–exchange, sell, swap, trade, traffic, truck
baru–majagua
bas-relief (small)–plaquette
base–abject, basis, bed, contemptible, degraded, despicable, dishonorable, evil, foul, foundation, infamous, low, pedestal, petty, podium, root, shameful, sordid, villainous, worthless
base (dye)–aniline
base (in certain games)–den
base (in quality)–leaden
base (military)–depot
base (morally)–mean, vile
base (nitrogenous)–alkaloid
base (pier)–socle
base (soft powder)–talc
base (statue)–plinth
base of leaf–axil
baseball (manner of striking)–bunt
baseball association (abbr.)–A.L., N.L.
baseball catcher–backstop
baseball term–apple, bag, ball, bat, batter, bean, beat, benched, bingle, box, bull pen, bunt, burn, clout, clutch, cocked, count, curve, deck, delivery, dish, double, drive, error, fan, field, fielder, first, floater, fly, forced, forked, foul, fungo, groove, grounded, hassock, heave, high, hit, hitter, hole, home, homer, hot corner, inside, keystone, killing, liner, lob, low, middle, miss, mound, nothing, out, outside, pill, pitch, pitcher, plate, popout, pop-up, powdered, punch, rubber, run, runner, sack, score, screen, second, series, shelled, side-arm, single, slide, stance, strike, string, swing, target, third, toes, tools, toss, triple, walk, wide, windup
based on experience–empiric, empirical
based on number nine – nonary
based on number six–senary
based upon observation–empiric
basely–dishonorably, illegitimately, shamefully
basely purchasable–venal
baser–meaner
baserunner's goal – home, plate
bash (coll.)–lam
bashful–coy, diffident, modest, retiring, shy, timid, verecund
bashful (old word)–helo
basic (opposed to)–acidic

basically–essentially, funda-
mentally
basin–font, valley
basin (large)–laver, tank
basin (ornamental)–cuvette
basin (temple)–laver
basin (wash, with necessary
fittings)–lavabo
basis of argument–premise
basis of reasoning–premise
bask–sun
basket–gabion, hanaper,
panier, pannier
basket (angler's)–creel
basket (balloon)–car, nacelle
basket (coal mine)–corf
basket (covered)–ped
basket (fig)–cabas, tapnet
basket (fire-holding)–cresset, grate
basket (fish)–creel
basket (fish-catching)–pot
basket (fish-measuring)–pad
basket (fishing)–slath
basket (hop picker's)–bin
basket (large food)–hamper
basket (Scot.)–corf
basket (Scot., of rude straw)
–rusky
basket (small)–hanaper
basket (small wicker, used
in Spanish game of pelota)
–cesta
basket (starting foundation
of)–slath
basket (wicker, fish-catching)–pot
basket (wicker provision)–
hamper, panier, pannier
basket (with handles)–caul,
cawl
basket (wood slat)–caul,
cawl, trug
basket-ball team–five
basket twigs–wattles
basket work filling–slewing
Basque cap–beret
Basque game–pelota
bast–fiber
baste–lard, sew, stitch
bastion (shoulder)–epaule
bastion shoulder angle–
epaule
bat–aliped, chiroptera, club,
racket, vampire

bat (brown)–pipistrel, pipi-
strelle
bath (pert. to)–balneal
bath (photographic)–developer, toner
bath (sitz)–bidet
bath (warm)–therm, ther-
mae (pl.), therme
bath house–cabana
bathe–bask, immerse, lave,
permeate, pervade, wash
baton–baston, cudgel, scepter, staff, stick, truncheon,
wand
baton (king's)–scepter, sceptre
batrachians (genus of)–pipa
batsman–hitter, striker
batter–hitter, ram, striker
battery terminal – anode,
electrode
battle–action, affray, brush,
conflict, engagement,
fight, fray, skirmish
battle (Hundred Year War)
–Cressy
battle formation (harrow-
like)–herse
battle line–front
battle with lances–joust, tilt
battologize–iterate, repeat
bauble–gaud, gewgaw, plaything, toy
bauxite (derivative of)–
aluminum
bavardage–prattle, twaddle
Bavarian (Ger.) capital–
Munich
Bavarian city–Augsburg,
Munich, Nurnberg, Ratis-
bon, Regensburg, Wurz-
burg
Bavarian division–Aschaf-
fenburg, Franconia, Neu-
burg, Palatinate, Regens-
burg, Schwaben
Bavarian lake–Ammer-See,
Chiem-See, Starnberg-
See, Wurm-See
Bavarian measure–dreis-
siger, fass, fuss, juchert,
linie, massel, metze, morgen, rute, ruthe, tagwerk
Bavarian mountain–Vosges,
Watzmann, Zugspitze
Bavarian river – Altmuhl,

Eger, Iller, Inn, Isar,
Lech, Nab, Regen, Wor-
nitz
Bavarian weight – gran,
quentchen
bay–bight, cove, howl, inlet,
ria, roan, sinus, ululate
bay (small)–cove
bay (Span.)–bahia
bay bird–curlew, godwit,
plover, snipe
bay camphor–laurin
bay fruit compound–laurin
bay tree–laurel
bay window–oriel
bayacura root–biacura
bazaar (bazar)–canteen, fair,
market
baze–abash, stupefy
be (part of)–been
be afraid–fear
be chief feature of–domi-
nate
be compelled–must
be contiguous–abut
be dull and spiritless–mope
be enough–do, suffice
be imminent–impend
be in contact with–touch
be in harmony–chord
be in process of decision–
pend
be in store for–acts, awaits
be indignant at–resent
be interested–care
be made up of–consist
be master of–possess
be mistaken (to)–err
be obedient–behave, con-
form
be of consequence–matter
be of the opinion–feel
be of use–avail
be off one's guard–nap
be over fond of–dote
be quiet–sh
be sick–ail
be silent (Latin)–tace
be situated–lie
be sorry for–regret, repent
be still–sh, tut
be sufficient–do
be suitable to–become, befit
be the matter with–ail
be the outcome–eventuate
be undecided–pend

be ungainly in appearance–slouch, unkempt

beach–place, praya, shore, strand

beacon – light, lighthouse, seamark, signal, watch tower

beacon light–cresset

beadle–bailiff, crier, macer, messenger, servitor, summoner, usher

beads (rosary)–aves

beads (string of)–necklace

beads used as money by Indians–sewan

beak–bill, lora, neb, nib

beak (Eng. slang)–magistrate, stipendiary

beak (Eton)–master

beak (part of)–lora

beaker–cup

beam–emit, girder, radiate, rafter, ray, support, timber

beam (cross)–trave

beam (floor framing)–trimmer

beam (Scot.)–sile

beams (construction of horizontal)–trabeate

bean (Calabar)–esserine

bean (climbing)–lima

bean (cluster)–guar

bean (kind of)–calabar, castor, lima, navy, soy, string

bean (locust)–carob

bean (lubricant)–ben

bean (poisonous)–calabar, loco

bean eye–hilum, hila (pl.)

beanery (U.S. slang)–restaurant

bear–bring, bruin, carry, endure, grizzly, tote, ursa

bear (female)–ursa

bear (Latin)–ursa

bear (young)–cub

bear bane–wolfsbane

bear bush–inkberry

bear cat–binturong

bear cat (red)–panda

bear-like–ursine

bear malice–resent

bear-shaped–ursiform

bear with effort–lug

bear's ear–auricula

bears fruit–teems

beard – goatee, Vandyke, whiskers

beard (chin)–goatee

beard of grain–arista, aristae (pl.), arris, awn

bearded–whiskered

bearded (as grain)–aristate, awned

bearer–carrier, pallbearer, porter

bearer (official staff)–macer

bearer (shield)–escudero

bearer (staff)–macer

bearing–behavior, carriage, conduct, demeanor, deportment, direction, influence, manner, mien, port, producing, relation, tendency, yielding

bearing (body)–posture

bearing (fine)–belair

bearing (heraldic) – ente, orle, pheon

bearing (stately)–dignity

bearing skin–cutigeral

bearing weapons–armed

beast–animal, brute, cattle, horse

beast (castrated)–spado

beast (desert)–camel

beast (fabulous)–dragon

beast (Fr.)–bete

beast (pert. to)–leonine

beast (spotted)–pard

beast fly–gadfly

beast of burden–ass, burro, donkey, llama, mule, ox, yak

beast sculptor–animalist

beast's stomach–maw

beastly–abominable, animal, bestial, disgusting, gross, inhuman

beat–bang, baste, belabor, cane, conquer, cudgel, defeat, drub, flog, larrup, lash, maul, overcome, pound, pulsate, pummel, scoop, strike, swinge, taw, thrash, thresh, throb, thump, tund, vanquish

beat (coll.)–bash, lace, lam, larrup, lash, wap

beat (incessantly)–pelt

beat (thoroughly)–trounce

beat (to traverse)–patrol

beat (with cudgel)–lambskin

beat back–repulse

beaten together smoothly–creamed

beaten way–path

beater–caner, lacer, rab, thresher

beater (mortar)–rab

beatified–blessed, sainted

beating (rhythmic)–pulse

beatitude–happiness, joy

beau–admirer, courter, escort, spark

beautifier–beautician, decorator

beautiful–bonny, charming, comely, elegant, exquisite, fair, graceful, handsome, lovely, poetic, pretty

beautiful (slang)–stunning

beautify–adorn, deck, embellish, grace

beauty–belle, charm, grace, loveliness, pulchritude

beauty (radiant)–glory

beauty (reigning)–belle

beauty of form or movement–grace

beaux–admirers,• courters, escorts, sparks

beaver–castor, hat

beaver cloth–kersey

beaver eater–wolverine

beaver skin–plew

Beaver State–Oregon

became–got, grew

became available–enured

became calm–quiesced

became shallow–shoaled

became visible–emerged

because–as, for, since, so

because of that–thereby

bechance–befall, chance

beche-de-mer–trepang

beck–bidding, bow, curtsy, gesture, nod, salutation, signal

becken–cymbals

beckoning (a)–waft

beclap–ensnare, grab

becloud–bedim, darken, overcast

become–beseem, fit, get, grace, grow, suit, wax

become buoyant–levitate
become cheesy–caseate
become coldly formal–freeze
become covered with fungus –mildew
become depressed–despond
become different–change, vary
become dull through inactivity–rust, tarnish
become exhausted–fag, peter
become frayed–fag
become gray–age
become imperceptible–die, fade
become insipid–pall
become less favorable–worsen
become less severe–ease, relent
become liable to–encur, incur, owe
become moist–eve
become more genial–thaw
become morose–sour
become operative–enure, inure
become oxidized–rust
become separated from others–straggle
become slower (music, abbr.)–rit
become sour–tart
become spent–petering
become sullen–sulk
become useful (of service)–enure, inure
become visible–appear
become void–lapse
become weakened by inaction–rust
become weary–tire
become white–blanch
become whole–integrate
become widely known–eclat
become withered–sere
becomes a certain color–purples, reddens
becomes aware–learns
becoming–appropriate, befitting, decorous, decorum, fit, suitable
becoming magnetized in direction of field–paramagnetic
becousined–akin, related

becscie–merganser
becuna–barracuda
bed–berth, bunk, cot, couch, pallet
bed (bunkhouse)–bunk
bed (feather)–tye
bed (portable)–litter, stretcher
bed (railroad car)–berth
bed (river)–channel
bed canopy–ciel, tester
bed coverlet–counterpane, quilt, spread
bed of coal (thin, mixed with pyrites)–brat
bed of straw–pallet
bed quilt–comforter, counterpane
bed stay–slat
bedaub–bedizen, belaud, besmear, ornament, smear, soil
bedeck–adorn, array, gem, grace, ornament, trat
bedeck with finery–prink
bedim–becloud, cloud, fog
Bedouin–Arab, Moor, nomad
Bedouin's handkerchief cord (of goat's hair)–agal
bee–apis
bee (combining form)–api
bee (drone)–dor
bee butt–beehive
beehive–butt, scap, skep
beehive (straw)–scap, skep
beekeeper–apiculturist
bees (genus of)–apia, apis
bees (males)–drones
bees (pert. to)–apian
bees (U.S. dial.)–yeast
bees' wax acid (fatty)–cerotic
beechnuts–masts
beef (cut of)–aitchbone, chine, quarter, rattleran, roast, side, steak
beef (slang)–complain, rage
beef (spiced, smoked)–pastroma
beer–ale
beer (light)–lager
beer (malt)–porter
beer (stored for months before use)–lager
beer cask–butt

beer glass–schooner, stein
beet (genus of)–beta
beet (kind of)–chard, mangel, sugar
Beethoven's birthplace – Bonn
beetle–bat, beat, bug, dor, drive, pestle, prionid, ram, scarab
beetle (bark)–borer
beetle (bright-colored)–ladybug
beetle (buzzing)–dor
beetle (click)–elater
beetle (destructive)–weevil
beetle (dung) – sharnbud, sharnbug
beetle (ground)–amara
beetle (June)–chafer, dor, dorr
beetle (small red)–ladybug
beetle (snapping) – elater, skipjack
beetle (tapering)–elater
beetle (var.)–dorr
beetle head – blockhead, plover
beetle headed–blockheaded, stupid
beetles (family of)–elateridae
beetles (genus of)–sitaris
beetles (genus of ground)–amara
beetlenut palm–areca
befall–betide, come, hap, happen
befile–defile, soil
befit–become, beseem, suit
befitting–becoming, decorous, fit, fitting, proper, suitable
befitting (professionally)–ethical
befitting a son or daughter–filial
befogged–unclear
before–beforehand, ere, forward, heretofore, hitherto, prior
before (in time, place)–anterior
before (naut.)–afore
before (poetic)–ere
before (prefix)–ante, pro
before all others–ahead, first

before birth–prenatal
before long–soon
before mentioned–said, such
before this – ere, erenow, since
before this time–erenow
befoul–bemire, entangle, soil
befriend–abet, aid, assist, benefit, countenance, favor, foster, help, succor, support, sustain
befuddle–addle, asea, becloud, confuse, muddle
befurred (royally)–ermined
beg–beseech, cadge, crave, entreat, implore, importune, petition, plead, pray, solicit, supplicate, woo
beg (earnestly)–importune
began–commenced, entered, inaugurated, initiated, opened, started
began (arch.)–gan
beget–breed, engender, father, procreate, sire
begetters–parents
beggar–almsman, impoverish, mendicant, panhandler, pauper, suppliant
beggar (slang)–panhandler
beggarly–bankrupt, contemptible, indigent, mean
beggar's speech (whining)–cant
beggary–destitution, indigence, pauperism, want
begin–attack, enter, inaugurate, initiate, institute, introduce, open, originate, start
begin again–renew, resume
beginner–amateur, dub, entrant, neophyte, novice, tiro, tyro
beginning–birth, commencement, debut, foundation, genesis, inception, initiation, onset, opening, origin, outset, root, start, threshold
beginning (fresh)–restart
beginning of social career–debut
beginning to be green–virescent

beginning to exist–start
beginning with–from
begone – aroint, avaunt, away, out, scat
begrimed–soiled
begrudge–envy
beguile–cozen, deceive, deception, disappointment, ensnare, entertain, lure, mislead, trick
begunk–jilt, trick
behalf–advantage, affair, benefit, defense, interest, matter, part, sake, side, stead, support
behalf of (in)–for
behave–act, bear, carry, conduct, demean, deport, manage
behave atavistically–revert
behave morosely–sulk
behavior–action, air, bearing, comportment, conduct, demeanor, deportment, manner, mien
behavior (foolish)–simple
behavior (good)–decorum
behavior (riotous)–rampage
behavior (violent)–rampage
behavior (wicked)–wrongdoing
behead–decapitate, decollate, guillotine
beheld–saw
behest–command, injunction, mandate
behind–abaft, abaft, aft, after, arear, astern, later, posterior, rump
behind (naut.)–abaft, aft
behind (Scot.)–ahind
behind a vessel–astern
behind the curtain–backstage
behold–descry, discern, lo, look, maintain, regard, retain, scan, see, witness
behold (Latin)–ecce
behold (old word)–isee
beholder–looker-on, observer, onlooker, spectator, witness
beige–ecru
beige color (Fr.)–grege
being–actuality, creature, ens, entia, entity, essence,

existence, existent, human, mortal, presence, reality, self, subsistence
being (abstract sense)–ens, entia (pl.), esse
being (actual, Latin)–esse
being (celestial)–angel, cherub, seraph
being (conscious)–ego
being (diminutive)–gnome
being (divine)–deva
being (ethereal)–sylph
being (fabulous myth)–centaur
being (fairy-like)–pixy
being (human)–Adamite
being (hypothetical)–ens, entia (pl.)
being (imaginary)–fairy
being (intrinsic)–essence
being (Latin)–esse
being (living)–animal
being (phantom)–fairy
being (real)–entity
being (spiritual)–seraph
being (supernatural, half man and half bird)–Garuda
Being (Supreme)–Creator
being at right angles to the plane of horizon–perpendicular
being in abstract--ens, entia (pl.)
being that on which a matter turns–pivotal
beken–commend, deliver, entrust
beknow–acknowledge, confess, recognize
belabor (belabour)–assail, beat, drub, ply, thwack
belamour–flower, ladylove, lover
belated (obs.)–lated
belay–beset, besiege, invest, waylay
beldam (beldame)–ancestor, fury, grandmother, hag, virago
beleaguer–beset, besiege, blockade, encompass, invest, surround
beleaguering–investing
beleaguerment–siege

Belgian and French river–Lys

Belgian capital–Brussels

Belgian city – Anderlecht, Ans, Antwerp, Brussels, Ciney, Gand, Ghent, Ixelles, Liege, Mechlin, Molenbeek, Schaerbeek

Belgian coin–belga (ac.), centime (cop.), franc (ni.)

Belgian commune–Ath

Belgian Congo river–Uele

Belgian Congo tribe (wartribe)–Batetla

Belgian endive–witloof

Belgian hare–leporide

Belgian horse (breed of draft)–Brabancon

Belgian king–Albert

Belgian marble–rance

Belgian measure–aune, boisseau, carat, last, perche, pied, vat

Belgian national anthem–Brabanconne

Belgian prince–Namur

Belgian province–Antwerp, Brabant, Flanders, Hainaut, Liege, Limburg, Luxemburg, Namur

Belgian queen (late)–Astrid

Belgian river–Dender, Dyle, Lys, Maas, Merse, Ourthe, Rupel, Sambre, Schelde, Scheldt, Yser

Belgian seaport–Ostend

Belgian town–Alost, Ana, Ans, Antwerp, Ath, Liege, Mons, Namur, Spa, Ypres

Belgian tribe (anc.)–Bellovaci

Belgian violinist–Ysaye

Belgian weight – carat, charge, chariot, esterlin, last, livre, pound

belie–belong, besiege, calumniate, defame, encompass, misrepresent, pertain, slander, surround

belief–assurance, conviction, credence, creed, faith, ism, opinion, persuasion, reliance, tenet

beliefs (set of)–credo

believe–accept, credit, trust

believe (arch.)–trow, ween

believe (poetic)–wis

Believe me if all those endearing young charms author–Moore

believer (self)–egoist

believer (suffix)–ist

believer in certain century system of thought–gnostic

believer in communication with departed spirits–spiritualist

believer in evil spirits–demonist

believer in facts–realist

believer in form of theism–deist

believer in God–theist

believer in God but not in revelation–deist

believer in personal God–deist

believer in predestination–particularist

believer in second coming of Christ–Adventist

believing–credent

belittle–decry, depreciate, detract, discredit, disparage, minimize

belive–forthwith, quickly, soon

bell–gong

bell (alarm)–tocsin

bell (evening)–curfew

bell (flat)–gong

bell (funeral)–knell

bell (kind of)–church, cow, electric, gong, hand, jingle, school, ship's

bell (warning)–tocsin

bell clapper–tongue

bell ear–cannon

bell-mouthed (Fr.)–evase

bell ringer–toller, toler (var.)

bell set (lowest of)–tenor

bell tower–belfry, campanile

bells (set of fixed, rung by striking rim with hammer)–carillon

bell's sound–ding, tinkle

bellicose–belligerent, pugnacious, warlike

belligerent–bellicose, choler-

ic, contentious, disputatious, hostile, irascible, litigious, pugnacious, quarrelsome, wrangling

belligerent international attitude–jingoist

belligerent's right to destroy property–angary

Bellini opera–Norma

bellow–bawl, clamor, cry, low, moo, roar, vociferate

bellware (Scot.)–kelp

bellweather–sheep

bellweed–knapweed

belong–pertain

belonging to–inherent, of

belonging to a dean–decanal

belonging to a pencil–desmic

belonging to art of dialing–gnomonic

belonging to first stages–incipient

belonging to new era, starting point–epochal

belonging to present time–current

belonging to real estate–predial

belonging to spring–vernal

belonging to summer–estival

belonging to the first stages–primeval

belonging to the nobility–titled

belonging to winter–hiemal

belongings (coll.)–traps

beloved–dear, precious

beloved disciple–John

below–beneath, under

below (Italian)–sotto

below (naut.)–alow

below (poetic)–neath

below key–flat

Bel's wife–Belit, Beltis

belt–band, beat, blow, cest, encircle, encompass, girdle, girth, mark, sash, stripe, surround, whack, zone

belt (conveyor)–apron

belt (endless conveyor)–apron

belt (green on Mars)–Libya

belt (worn over shoulder, supporting sword)–baldric

belt of calms–doldrums
belt pulley–drum, rigger
belted–encircled, girt
beltie (Scot.)–coot
Belus' daughter–Dido
Belus' father–Libya
Belus' son (legendary)–Ninus
Belus' sons–Aegyptus, Cepheus, Danaus, Phineus
bemoan–bewail, deplore, lament, pity, sympathize
bemuse – absorbed, daze, muddle, stupefy
ben–hill, mountain, peak
bench–banc, pew, seat, settee, stool
bench (judge's)–banc
bench (outdoor)–exedra
bench (workman's)–siege
bench board–switchboard
bench plane handle–tote
bend–bow, buckle, crook, curve, direct, flex, inflex, ply, retract, sag, stoop, turn
bend (abruptly)–kink
bend (small, her.)–cotises
bend (timber, downward)–sny
bend (timber, upward)–sny
bend down–stoop
bend downward–sag
bend in timber–sny
bend into shape–crimp
bend inward–introvert
bend low–crouch
bend out of line–refract
bend the knee–genuflect
bend upward (shipbuilding) –sny
bendlet (heraldry)–baton
beneath–below, under
beneath (naut.)–alow
beneath (Scot.)–aneth
benediction–blessing, prayer
benefaction–alms, boon, donation, gift, gratuity, present
benefactor–helper, patron
benefice (first fruit of)–annat, annate
beneficence–charity, kindness
beneficent gift–boon
beneficial – advantageous,

good, helpful, lucrative, profitable, remunerative, salutary, serviceable, useful, wholesome
beneficiary–donee, heirfeudatory, vassal
benefit–advance, avail, help, improve, profit, service, use
benefit (poetic)–vail
benevolent–altruistic, benign, benignant, charitable, generous, good, kind, liberal, munificent, philanthropic
Bengal (primitive)–Kol
Bengal (Ind.) capital–Calcutta
Bengal city–Calcutta, Madras, Rangoon
Bengal hemp–sunn
Bengal measure–chattack, cotta, cottah
Bengal negro–Ebo, Eboe
Bengal quince–bel, bhel
Bengal river boat–baulea, bauleah
Bengal root–cassumunar
Bengal tree–bola
Bengali gentlemen–baboo
benignant–beneficial, bland, favorable, genial, kind, liberal, propitious, salubrious
benignity – graciousness, mildness, salubrity
Benin negro–Ebo, Eboe
benison–beatitude, benediction, blessing
benjamin bush–spicebush
Benjamin's descendant–Aher
Benjamin's grandson–Iri
Benjamin's man (chief)–Ader
Benjamin's son–Rosh
bent–crooked, inclination, leaning, penchant, predisposition, prejudice, prepossession, stooped, trend, turn
bent (natural)–aptitude
bent to one side–wry
benthonic plant–enalid
benumb–deaden, nip, stupefy

benzene (derivative of)–phenol
benzine derivative (basis of) –phenyl
bequeath–bestow, demise, endow, leave
bequest–legacy
berate–chide, lash, nag, rail, reprove, scold, slate
beray–defile, befoul
berceau–arbor, bower, cradle
bere–clamor, gesture, roar
bereave–despoil, divest, rob
bereaved–reft
bereft–lorn
beret–biretta, cap, tam
bergstock–alpenstock
Berlin park (famous)–Tiergarten
Bermuda arrowroot–ararao, aruru
Bermuda barracuda–spet
Bermuda berry–soapberry
Bermuda catfish–coelho
Bernicia founder (Anglican chief)–Ida
berry–acinus, acini (pl.)
berry (acid)–currant
berry (aromatic, small)–cubeb
berry (hawthorn)–haw
berry (juice)–grape
berth–appointment, billet, bunk, situation
berthage–anchorage, moorage
beseech–beg, crave, entreat, implore, plead, pray, sue, supplicate
beseeching–begging, precative, supplicating
beset–blockade, siege, stud, surround
beset with hairs (long stiff)– barbate
beside–along, by
besides–else, moreover, too, yet
besiege – beleaguer, beset, surround
besmear – bedaub, daub, smear, soil
besom–broom
besought–beseeched, prayed
bespangle–star

bespatter–asperse, blot, spot, stain

besprinkle–dot, strew, stud

best–beat, finest, outstrip, overmatch

best (comb.)–arist

best (slang)–tops

best of their kind (slang)– aces, tops

bestial – brutal, depraved, filthy, inhuman, low, sensual, vile

bestow–accord, confer, give, grant, impart, present

bestow as due–award

bestow by will–demise

bestowal–disposal, gift

bestowal (formal)–presentation

bestowal of things earned– award

bestowed–allotted, awarded, gave, granted, presented

bestowed (as inalienable possession)–entailed

bestower–dealer

bestraddle–bestride

bestride–bestraddle, straddle

bet–pledge, stake, wager

bet (roulette)–bas

betake–grant, hie

betake out of way–aroint

bete–beast, foolish, silly, stupid

betel nut tree–areca

betel palm–areca

bethink–recollect, reflect, remember

Bethuel's son–Laban

betimes–early

betise–folly, silliness, stupidity

betoken–denote, indicate, mark, note, portend, presage, signify, symbolize

betray–sell

betray for a price–sell

betrayal–treason

betrayer–traitor

betrayer of trust–derelict

betraying–telltale

betroth–engage, plight

betrothal–affiance, engagement, espousal

betrothing–espousal

better–advance, amend, big-

ger, choicer, emend, greater, improve, improved, meliorate, preferable, promote, reform, safer, superior, top, wiser

betting adviser–tout

betting figures–odds

betting method–parlay

betting odds–price

between–among, betwixt

between (Fr.)–entre

between (prefix)–dia, inter, meta

between periods (law)– mesne

between two extremes– mesne

between two periods–mesne

bevel–slant

bevel corners–splay

beverage–ale, beer, coffee, drink, gin, grog, julep, lager, mead, negus, pop, porter, posset, rum, soda, tea, water, wine

beverage (alcoholic)–negus

beverage (hot, sweet, alcoholic)–negus

beverage (made from peppers)–kava

beverage (malted wheat)– zythem, zythum

beverage (mixed)–smash

beverage (nourishing)–cocoa

beverage (Oriental)–arrack

beverage (pepper)–kava

beverage (spiced)–aleberry

beverage-making utensil– teapot

beverage of port wine, oranges or lemons, and sugar–bishop

beverage of wine, lemon juice, etc.–negus

bevy–assembly, collection, company, flock, group

bewail–bemoan, deplore, grieve, keen, lament, rue

bewail (audibly)–moan

bewilder–addle, amaze, confound, confuse, daze, distract, embarrass, fog, mystify, perplex

bewilder with brilliance– dazzle

bewildered–asea, confused, lost, perplexed

bewilderment–awe, distraction, embarrassment, fog

bewitch–captivate, charm, enchant, entice, fascinate, hoodoo, hex

bewitching – captivating, charming, enchanting, fascinating, siren

bewith (Scot.)–makeshift, substitute

beyond–above, over, ultra, yonder

beyond (prefix)–para, sur

bezel (cut gem)–templates

bias–amiss, awry, bent, diagonal, oblique, prejudice, prepossess, slanting

biased–bent, bigoted, narrow, partial

bib–drink, sip, tipple, tucker

Bible (book of)–Amos, Apocryphal, Esther, Ezra, Genesis, Hosea, Job, Micah, Psalms, Tobit

Bible (cony of)–hyrax

Bible (Parsee's)–Avesta

Bible name–Acan, Obal

Bible part (abbr.)–O.T.

Bible words (spiritual meaning)–anagoge

Biblical–scriptural

Biblical angel–Raphael

Biblical character–Ader, Adna, Agee, Aher, Ahi, Ai, Alian, Anak, Antioch, Ar, Aram, Arie, Aroer, Ater, Aven, Cana, Elias, Elmodam, Enos, Ephai, Eran, Eri, Esau, Esrom, Hanes, Ir, Irad, Iri, Isaac, Koa, Lot, Nain, Ner, Neri, Ono, Oreb, Oren, Paul, Peleg, Pilate, Sodom, Tabitha, Vale

Biblical city–Ai, Aner, Aven, Joppa, Nain, Sidon

Biblical city (wicked)–Sodom

Biblical coin–talent

Biblical country – Aram, Bela, Edom, Elam, Gath, Moab, Nod, Samaria, Seba

Biblical hero–Noah

Biblical introduction–isagogics
Biblical judge–Elon
Biblical king–Asa, Evi, Iva, Og, Reba, Saul
Biblical kingdom–Chaldee
Biblical land native (near Babylon)–Elamite
Biblical liar–Ananias
Biblical man of valor–Iri
Biblical measure–span
Biblical mountain–Ararat, Ebal, Gilead, Heres, Horeb, Nebo, Olivet, Peor, Pisgah, Sina, Sinai
Biblical mountain (Arabia)–Horeb
Biblical name – Abadias, Abel, Acub, Adam, Ador, Amam, Aman, Anam, Anem, Aner, Ater, Azal, Bedan, Besai, Cain, Dura, Edec, Edes, Enos, Etam, Eve, Idithum, Iram, Iri, Ner, Omar, Ono, Oren, Peleg, Ramath, Sami, Sarah, Seth, Suba, Tarah, Toi, Ucal, Uri, Vania, Zina
Biblical ornament–urim
Biblical patriarch–Israel
Biblical people–Ammon, Amorite, Dodanim
Biblical place–Escora
Biblical plotter–Haman
Biblical precious stone–ligure
Biblical priest–Eli, Levite
Biblical prophet–Amos
Biblical purveyor of untruths (well known)–Ananias
Biblical region–Enon, Perea
Biblical region (gold-bearing)–Ophir
Biblical region (ruled by Og)–Bashan
Biblical sermon (poetic)–psalm
Biblical sorceress' home–Endor
Biblical stage direction–selah
Biblical term of reproach–raca
Biblical tower–Babel, Edar
Biblical town–Cana, Elon

Biblical weed–tare
Biblical witch's home–Endor
Biblical word–selah, shelah
bicker–altercation, contention, dispute, wrangle
bid–beg, entreat, offer, offered, order, pray
biddy–chicken, hen
bide–abide, await, endure, remain, stay, suffer, tarry, tolerate, wait
bield – boldness, comfort, confidence, courage, cozy, den, embolden, habitation, hearten, shelter, sheltered
bien (bein)–comfortable, fine, good, prosperous, snug, thriving
bifarious–ambiguous, twofold
biff–blow
bifold–double, twofold
bifurcation–branch, forking, wye
big–bulky, great, huge, large, massive
big (marvelously)–tremendous
Big Bend State–Tennessee
big bug–bigwig
big coat–greatcoat, overcoat
big house–penitentiary
bight–angle, bend, corner, hollow, loop, noose
bigoted–intolerant, narrow, prejudiced
bigoted person–prude
bigotry–intolerance
bigotry (one who is free from)–tolerationist
bijou–jewel, trinket
bilbie (Scot.)–refuge, shelter
bilingual–diglot
biliousness–choler
bilk–cheat, cozen, deceive, defraud, delude, do, fleece, hoax, illude, sell, swindle
bill–beak, billhook, mattock, neb, pickax
bill (anchor)–pee
bill (five-dollar)–Vee
bill hook–snagger

bill of fare–card, carte, menu
bill payer–finn
bill poster–sticker
billet–appointment, bar, berth, coalfish, document, log, note, notice, polack, position, quarters, strap
billiard shot–carom, masse
billiard stroke–carom, masse
billow–sea, surge, swell, wave
billowy–surging, swelling, undulating, wavy
bin–box, crib, frame, manger, pungi, vina
bin (fish-salting)–kench
bin (storage)–crib, elevator, granary, loft, mow
binary–double, dual
binary oxygen compound–oxide
bind–confine, gird, hold, jam, stick, tape, tie
bind (legally or morally)–obligate
bind by promise–engage
bind closely–ally, tie
bind to secrecy–tile
bind up–gird, truss
bind with fetters–gyve
bind with ribbons–tape
binding–astringent, restraining, restrictive, stringent, tape, valid
binding (limp)–yapp
binding custom–law
binds–lashes, ligates, obligates, seal, seel, ties, trices, trusses
binds tightly–frap
binge–carousal, spree
bingo–brandy, lotto, tango
biographical fragments–anecdotes
biography–history, life
biography (Fr.)–memoire
biography (short)–lifelet
biological classes–genera
biological determiner–gene
biological divisions–genera, genus, species
biose–disaccharide
biotite (variety of)–anomite
biplane (small)–Spad
birch family–betulaceae
birch man–schoolmaster

birch tar–daggett
bird–kite, oriole, ortolan, peacock, pewee, pheasant, pie, plover, redwing, shrike, starling, waxwing
bird (adjutant)–argala
bird (American)–sora, tanager
bird (American large)–turkey
bird (Antarctic)–penguin, skua
bird (aquatic)–grebe, gull, small, swan
bird (aquatic, long-necked) –swan
bird (Asiatic)–brambling, dotterel
bird (Australian) – arara, bustard, cassowary, coachwhip, emu, friarbird, leipoa, lorikeet, lory, lyrebird, pardalote, platypus
bird (Australian owl)–boobook
bird (black)–ani, crow, daw, jackdaw, pie, raven
bird (brilliant plumage)–oriole, tanager, tody
bird (brilliant tropical)–jacamar, jalap, trogon
bird (California humming) –calliope
bird (Central American)–jacamar, puffbird
bird (corvine)–crow
bird (corvoid)–magpie
bird (crow family)–daw, jackdaw, jay
bird (crow-like)–pie
bird (cuculoid)–ani
bird (diurnal, large)–eagle
bird (diving)–auk, grebe, loon
bird (duck family)–smew
bird (duck-like)–coot
bird (edible, sea)–cahow
bird (European) – avocet, avoset, bittern, brambling, dotterel, gallinule, garga3ney, gaylag, godwit, goldfinch, kestrel, kite, lammergeyer, lammergeir, lammergeier, starling, starnel, tarin

bird (European, black)–merle
bird (European grouse)–capercaillie, capercailzie
bird (European, large land) –bustard
bird (extinct)–dodo, moa
bird (fabulous)–roc
bird (fabulous, providing money)–offbird
bird (female, large)–peahen
bird (finch-like)–tanager
bird (fish-catching)–cormorant
bird (flightless)–moa, penguin
bird (flightless extinct)–moa
bird (flying backward)–swallow
bird (food)–capon
bird (frigate)–ioa
bird (gallinaceous)–peacock
bird (game)–grouse, pheasant, quail, snipe
bird (golden)–oriole
bird (grallatorial)–wader
bird (gull family)–tern
bird (Hawaiian)–ava, iiwi, ioa, iwa, oo, ooaa
bird (Hawaiian frigate)–ioa
bird (Hawaiian, indigenous raptorial)–io
bird (hawk family)–elanet, kite
bird (heron family)–bittern
bird (huge, mythical)–roc
bird (humming)–colibri
bird (humming, large)–carib
bird (humming, topaz)–ava, aves (pl.)
bird (India weaver)–baya
bird (insectivorous)–owl, vireo
bird (jay family)–magpie
bird (jay, Scot.)–gae
bird (lamellirostral)–goose, geese (pl.)
bird (large)–eagle, emu, ostrich, pelican, seriema
bird (large, ratite) – emu, emeu
bird (large sea)–gannet, solan
bird (large shore)–willet

bird (large, webfooted)–goose, geese (pl.)
bird (largest known)–ostrich
bird (lark-like)–pipit
bird (Latin)–avis
bird (legendary)–roc
bird (little brown)–wren
bird (long-billed)–pelican, snipe
bird (long-legged)–avocet, avoset, io, sora, stilt
bird (long-legged, web footed)–avocet, avoset
bird (long-necked)–crane, goose, ostrich, stork, swan
bird (long-winged, sea)–petrel
bird (loon-like)–grebe
bird (loon-like, swimming)–grebe
bird (male)–cock, gander, rooster
bird (male, large)–peacock
bird (marsh)–snipe, sora
bird (Mexico)–jacamar, jacana, towhee
bird (mythical, large)–roc
bird (nestling, unfledged)–eyas
bird (New Zealand)–apteryx, kaka, kakapo, kea, kulu, morepork, notornis, ruru, titi, weka
bird (nocturnal)–owl, owlet
bird (nonexistent)–dodo
bird (North American)–bufflehead, cardinal, fulmar, grackle, killdeer, kingrail
bird (North Atlantic sea)–gannet, puffin
bird (North Pacific sea)–puffin
bird (North Sea, diving)–auk
bird (Northern)–auk, loon
bird (Numidian crane)–demoiselle
bird (of prey)–accipeter, eagle, elanet, elant, goshawk, kite
bird (of rail family)–coot
bird (old world)–clee

bird (oldest known)–archaeopteryx
bird (omnivorous)–crow
bird (oscine)–oriole
bird (oscine, finch family)–tanager
bird (ostrich-like)–emeu, emu, moa
bird (parson)–poe, tue, tui
bird (passerine)–chatterer, finch, sparrow
bird (pelican-like)–solan
bird (Persian song)–bulbul
bird (petrel family)–fulmar
bird (phoebe)–pewee
bird (plain, beach and upland)–plover
bird (plover-like)–drome
bird (predaceous sea)–yager
bird (predatory)–owl
bird (rapacious)–cormorant
bird (ratite, large)–emeu, emu
bird (reed)–bobolink
bird (sacred)–ibis
bird (Scot.)–gae
bird (sea)–gannet, puffin, solan
bird (sea, large)–solan
bird (sea, of auk family)–puffin
bird (second largest known)–emu
bird (shore)–avocet, curlew, rail, ree, snipe, sora, stilt, willet
bird (Sindbad's)–roc
bird (singing)–canary, lark, linnet, mocker, mocking, oriole, oscine, redstart, robin, thrush, veery, vireo, wren
bird (small)–creeper, pipit, sparrow, starling, tit, tody, todies (pl.), tomtit, vireo, wheater, wren
bird (small, singing)–pipit, titlark
bird (snipe family)–curlew
bird (South American)–barbet, bellbird, boatbill, chaja, guacharo, guan, myna, mynah, oilbird, puffbird
bird (South American hawk)–caracara

bird (South Pole)–penguin, skua
bird (starling-like)–grackle
bird (stitch)–ihi
bird (suitcase bill)–pelican
bird (swallow-like)–swift
bird (sweet-singing)–thrush
bird (talking)–myna, mynah, parrot
bird (that builds no nest)–cuckoo
bird (that flies backward)–humming
bird (the)–ava, aves (pl.)
bird (thrush family)–shama
bird (topaz humming)–ani, ava, aves (pl.)
bird (tropical)–ani, tody, trogon
bird (tropical, black)–ani
bird (tropical, brilliant)–jacamar, jalap, trogon
bird (unfledged)–eyas, nestling
bird (voracious, aquatic)–cormorant
bird (wading)–crane, heron, ibis, jacana, rail, stork
bird (water)–coot, loon
bird (weaver)–baya
bird (web-footed)–drake, duck, gander, goose
bird (West Indies, tiny)–tody
bird (which can walk on aquatic plants)–jacana
bird (which can sing while flying and flip tail while running)–pipit
bird (white-tailed)–ern
bird (wing process)–alula
bird (woodcock)–pewee
bird (yellowish)–oriole
bird (young)–birdikin, eya, nestling
bird cage–aviary, paddock
bird clapper–scarecrow
bird class–aves
bird egg collector–oologist
bird eggs (study of)–oology
bird eye–cuckoo flower
birdhouse–aviary
birdhouse keeper–aviarist
bird jaw (part of)–mala
bird loving–ornithophilous

birdman–airman, aviator, ornithologist
bird named from its cry–morepork
bird of Arabian Nights–roc
bird of heron family–bittern
bird of Jove–eagle
bird of Juno–peacock
bird of Minerva–owl
bird of prey–eagle, hawk, owl, vulture
bird of prey (young)–eaglet, owlet
bird of wonder–phoenix
bird related to crow–oriole
bird wing–pinion
bird wing part–alula
birds (as a class)–aves
birds (collectively)–fowl
birds (emu-like)–cassowaries
birds (genus)–anser, elanus, sula
birds (genus of, including emus, moras, cassowaries, ostriches)–ratitae
birds (large, web-footed)–geese
birds (old order)–rasores
birds (pert. to)–avine, ornithic
birds (swimming)–natatores
birds (the)–aves
bird's beak–bill, lora, neb, nib, rostra
bird's comb-like eye process–pecten, pectines (pl.)
bird's head (top of)–pileum
bird's head part–lores
bird's tarsal joint–knee
birds that scratch for their food–rasores
birl (Scot.)–rattle
birma–calaba
birse–irritation, temper
birth–beginning, descent, extraction, lineage, nativity, origin
birth (by)–nee
birth (new) – Renaissance, renascence
birth (pert. to)–natal
birth flower – carnation (Jan.); primrose (Feb.); violet (Mar.); daisy (Apr.); lily of the valley (May); rose (June); sweet

pea (July); gladiolus
(Aug.); aster (Sept.);
dahlia (Oct.); chrysanthe-
mum (Nov.); holly, poin-
settia (Dec.)
birthmark–naeve, naevus,
nevus
birthmark (pert. to)–nae-
void
birthright–heritage
birth seniority (pert. to)–
primogenitive
birth stone (day)–diamond,
topaz (Sun.); crystal, pearl
(Mon.); emerald, ruby
(Tues.); amethyst, load-
stone (Wed.); carnelian,
sapphire (Thurs.); cat's
eye, emerald (Fri.); dia-
mond, turquoise (Sat.)
birth stone (month)–garnet
(Jan.); amethyst (Feb.);
bloodstone, jasper (Mar.);
diamond, sapphire
(Apr.); emerald (May);
agate (June); turquoise
(July); carnelian (Aug.);
chrysolite (Sept.); beryl
(Oct.); topaz (Nov.);
ruby (Dec.)
bis–duplicate, encore, repetition, replica
biscuit–bun, rusk
biscuit (Spanish-American)–
panal
biscuit (sweet, of flour, sugar, marmalade, eggs)–
biscotin
biscuit (the color)–doe
biscuit (thin hard)–cracker
bisect–cross, divide, fork
bishop–director, inspector,
overseer, pontiff, prelate,
superintendent
bishop's cap–miterwort
bishop's crown–miter, mitre
bishop's hat–miter, mitre
bishop's headdress (pert. to)
–mitral
bishop's office–see
bishop's revenue (first year)
–annat, annate
bishop's staff–crosier
bishop's staves (pastoral)–
baculi, baculus (sing.)
bishop's throne–apse

bishop's throne (official)–
see
bishop's vestment–dalmatic
bishop's vestment (distinctive)–omophorion
bismar–steelyard
bismer – reproach, scorn,
shame
bison (European)–aurochs
bishopric–diocese, Episcopa-
cy, episcopate, see
bit–mite, morsel, piece,
scrap, smidge, smidgen
bit (bridle, jointed)–snaffle
bit (horse's curb)–pelham
bit (Irish)–traneen
bit (least)–jot
bit (small)–snip
bit (worthless)–ort
bite–cut, gnaw, hold, morsel, nibble, nip, pierce,
smart, sting
bite (insect)–sting
bite impatiently–champ
bite off–gnaw
bite smartly–knap
biting–acrid, caustic, cutting, mordant, nipping,
poignant, pungent, sar-
castic, sharp, trenchant
biting dragon–tarragon
bito (the)–hajilij
bitten–satirical, stung
bitter–acerb, acid, acrid, acrimonious, cutting, irate,
keen, pungent, severe,
sharp, stinging
bitter apple–colocynth
bitter cucumber–colocynth
bitter earth–manesia
bitter gentian–baldmoney
bitter gourd–colocynth
bitter grass–colicroot
bitter herb–aloe, centaury,
rue, turtlehead
bitter hickory–bitternut
bitter oak–cerris
bitter plant–colicroot, rue
bitter root (herb)–rue
bitter spar–dolomite
bitter vetch–ers
bitter white substance–linin
bitter wintergreen–pipsissewa
bitterly severe–scathing
bitterness–poignancy

bitterness (extreme)–rancor,
virulence
bivalve–clam, cockle, mollusk, mussel, oyster, scallop, spat
bivalve (large)–pinna
bivalve mollusks (genus of)–
anomia
bivocal–diphthong
bivouac–camp, encamp, en-
campment
bivouacked–encamped
biwa (Japanese)–loquat
bizarre in design–antic
bizarre–dedal, extravagant,
fanciful, fantastic, odd,
outre
Bizet's opera–Carmen
blab–chatter, reveal, taletell-
ing, tattle, telltale
blabber–babble, blab, chatter
black–atrocious, calamitous,
cruel, dark, dismal, ebon,
ebony, forbidding, foul,
gloomy, hateful, inky,
jet, melanic, mournful,
murky, pitchy, sable, tar,
unclean
black (very)–ebon
black (prefix)–atra
black (jet)–ebon, raven
black (Fr.)–noire
black amber–labdanum
blackamoor–negress, negro
black and blue–livid
black and glossy–raven
black and white (mixture)–
gray
black art–alchemy, conjuration, magic, necromancy,
wizardry
blackberry (variety of)–dew-
berry
blackbird–ani, crow, daw,
jackdaw, pie, raven
blackbird (European)–am-
sel, merl, merle
blackbird (tropical)–ani
blackbird (var.)–ousel
black blooded–atrabilious,
melancholy, moody
black bully–sapodilla
black coat–clergyman
black cod–beshow
blackdamp–chokedamp
black diamond–coal

black dot–dartrose
black earth – chernozem, mold
black elder–hackberry
black face–actor, minstrel, sheep
black fiber–kittul
blackfin–cisco
blackfin snapper–sesis
blackfish–tautog
black gang–stokers
black grunt–tripletail
blackguard–gamin, scoundrel, scullion, vagrant
black haw–hawthorn, sheepberry, sloe
black hole–cell, dungeon, solitary
black larch–tamarac
blackleg – gambler, scab, strikebreaker, swindler
blackmail–coerce, extort
blackmailer (coll.)–leecher
Blackmore heroine–Lorna Doone
blackout (Eng. slang)–scrounge
black sea bass–jewfish
Black Sea peninsula–Crimea
Black Sea seaport–Batum
blacksmith–smith, smithy
blacksmith's helper–striker
black snake–racer, whip
blackthorn (fruit of)–sloe
black vulture–urubu
Black Water State–Nebraska
black widow spider–pokomoo
black wort–comfrey
blacken–besmirch, calumniate, defame, ink, malign, slander, sully, tar, traduce, vilify
blackened–sooty
blackish–swart, swarthy, swarty
blade–blood, edge, gallant, leaf, spark, spear
blade (fencing)–epee, foil
blade (shoulder)–scapula, scapulae (pl.)
blade (skate)–bat
blade (tapering)–spire
blade (windmill) – edge, vane
blade bone–scapula

blade of grass (Anglo-Irish) –traneen
blae–bleak, livid, sunless, unbleached
blaeberry–billberry
blaff–bang, thump
blague–claptrap, humbug, raillery
blain–blister, bulla, inflame, pustule, sore, swelling
blair–battlefield
blake–colorless, pale, wan
blame–accuse, censure, condemnation, criticism, reprehension, reproach, reprobation, reproof, revile, shend
blameless–innocent
blameworthy–culpable, reprehensible
blanch (by exclusion of sunlight)–etiolate
blanched – chalked, pale, whitened
bland–oily, suave
blandish–cajole, flatter
blank–empty, fruitless, void
blank book–album, tablet
blank type (for spacing)–quad
blanket (bushman's)–bluey
blanket (coarse)–cotta
blanket (homespun, woolen, without nap)–barraclade
blanket (horse)–manta
blanket (knitted)–afghan
blanket slipper–neap
blare (horn)–fanfare, tantara, tantarara
blare (of trumpet)–fanfare, tantara, tantarara
blarney–flattery, wheedle
blart–bellow, blab, bleat, roar
blasé–bored, indifferent, sated, surfeited
blaspheme–abuse, calumniate, curse, revile
blasphemy–anathema, cursing, execration, impiety, imprecation, irreverance, malediction, profanity, sacrilege, swearing
blast–detonation, explosion, gust, wind
blast (horn)–toot

blast of wind–gust
blasting explosive–nitramite
blasting oil–nitroglycerine
blatant–brawling, clamorous, noisy, vociferous
blate–bashful, blab, blunt, diffident, dull, prate, sheepish, slow, spiritless, timid
blaubok–antelope, etaac
blaw–blow, boast, brag
blaze – bonfire, firebrand, flame, torch
blaze brightly–flare
blazer–jacket
blazon–adorn, deck, embellish
blazoning arms science–heraldry
bleach–decolor, etiolate, sun, whiten
bleaching vat–keeve, keir
bleak–cheerless, cold, depressing, desolate, dreary, frigid, pale, pallid, raw
bleaker and colder–rawer
bleat–baa
blemish–blur, breach, defacement, deficiency, deformity, dent, disfigurement, failing, fault, fissure, imperfection, macula, macule, mar, scar, spot, stigma, sully, taint
blemish (in wood)–mote
blemish (left by wound)–cicatrice, cicatrix, scar
blench–bleach, flinch, quail, shrink, stratagem, trick, whiten, wile
blend–amalgamate, coalesce, commingle, fuse, harmonize, merge, mingle, mix
blend (imperceptibly)–merge
blend into one–confluent
blended–fondu, merged, mingled, mixed
bless–beatify, bensh, consecrate, hallow
blessedness–beatitude, bliss, felicity
blessing–benediction, benison, boon
blew gently–breezed

blight–blast, destroy, nip, smut, wither

blimp–airship, balloon

blind–ambush, benighted, jalousie, purblind, screen, seel, senseless, shutter, sightless

blind (part of)–slat

blind fear–panic

blind in one eye (Eng.)–peed

blind staggers–gid

blind worm–orvet

blindness (day)–hemeralopia

blindness (partial or incomplete)–meropia

bliss–beatitude, blessedness, Eden, felicity, happiness, joy, rapture

blissful–beatified, blessed, Edenic, glorified, holy

blissful (sweetly)–elysian

blissful region–Eden, Utopia

blissfulness–felicity

blister–bleb, bulge, scorch, vesicatory, vesicle

blistered–vesicated

blithe–jocular

blithe song–lilt

blitzkrieg (Eng. slang)–blitzflu

bloated–cured, distended, pompous, sodden

blob–bleb, blister, bubble, pimple, pustule

block–bar, barricade, check, hamper, hinder, impede, obstruct, oppose, outline, parry, shape, stop

block (architectural) – mutule

block (architectural, tooth-like)–dentil

block (bearing) – clamp, cleat

block (blacksmith's)–anvil

block (coal, large, ready for mining, Eng.)–jud

block (electrically insulated) –taplet

block (English sandstone on chalk downs)–sarsen

block (hawser)–bitt

block (ice)–serac

block (iron for forging)–anvil

block (iron stamp)–vol

block (printing metal)–quad

block (sandstone, large) – sarsen

block (solid)–cube

block (square, in cornices)–dentil

block (type metal)–quad

block (wooden)–nog

block illegally (football) – clip

block of glacial ice–serac

blockade – beset, dam, obstruct, siege

blocked (coll.)–stumped

blockhead–dolt, oaf

blockhead (arch.)–mome

blockhead board–doll

bloke (slang)–chap, fellow, man, personage

blonde (blond)–fair, light

blood – gore, lineage, race, stock

blood (of the)–hemic

blood (person of mixed) – mestee, mestizo, mulatto, mulatta (fem.), mustee

blood (pert. to) – haemal, hemic

blood and thunder – melodrama, uproar, violence

blood condition – uraemia, uremia

blood constituent (fluid) – serum

blood disease (with excessive leucocytes or white corpuscles) – leucaemia, leucemia, leukaemia, leukemia

blood dust–hemoconia

blood fluid–plasma

blood horse–thoroughbred

blood in urine (presence of) –melituria

blood money (feud avoiding)–cro

blood of gods–ichor, icor

blood pudding–sausage

blood relation–kinsman, sib

blood relationship–consanguinity

blood slackening–statis

blood strain–family, race, stock

blood sucker–leech

blood vessel–artery, vein

bloody–bloodstained, bloodthirsty, cruel, ensanguined, gory, murderous

bloody back – redcoat, soldier

bloody bones – hobgoblin, specter

bloody urine–hematuria

bloom (fragrant)–rose

bloomer – blunder, error, failure

bloomery – forge, furnace, hearth

blooming–flowering, roseate

blossom–bell, bloom, blow, flourish, flower, prosper

blossom (small)–floweret

blossom keel–carina, carinae (pl.)

blossoming time – efflorescence

blot–blur, erase, expunge, smear, smutch, spot, stain, sully, tarnish

blot out–cancel

blotch–blemish, dab, patch, stain, stigma

blotched–mottled, smeared

blouse (bushman's)–bluey

blow–calamity, clout, disaster, knock, pant, rap, shock, slap

blow (fitfully, with violence and noise)–bluster

blow (gentle)–dab, tap

blow (heavy)–bump

blow (heavy, coll.)–clout

blow (heavy, slang)–oner

blow (mock)–feint

blow (resounding, coll.)–wallop

blow (severe, Scot.)–devel

blow (sharp)–slap

blow (with cudgel)–lambskin

blow cement on sculpture–kibosh

blow hard–braggart

blow in–appear, arrive

blow off–braggart, climax, culmination

blow the gaff (naut.)–betray
blow up – explosion, outburst
blowen–strumpet, wench
blower (stove)–sacheverell
blowzy–disheveled, dowdy, frowzy, slatternly
blub–puffed, swell, swollen
blubbery – fat, gelatinous, obese, protuberant, quivering, swollen
bludgeon–bat, billy, club, stick
blue–azure, perse
blue (azure-like)–bice, perse
blue (grayish)–perse
Bluebeard's wife (last)–Fatima
blue blood–aristocrat, noble
blue boneset–mistflower
bluebonnet–Scot, Scotsman
bluecap–Scot, bluebonnet
blue catalpa–paulownia
blue color–lobelia
blue colorant–anil
blue dandelion–chicory
blue dye–woad
blue earth–kimberlite
bluefish (young)–snapper
bluegill–sunfish
bluegrass (genus of)–poa
bluegrass (Kentucky)–poa
Bluegrass State–Kentucky
blue-green–bice
blue-green (genus of)–gloeocapsa
Blue Grotto (site of)–Capri, Italy
blue ground–kimberlite
blue gull–nilgai
blue gum–eucalyptus
blue huckleberry – tangleberry
blue jaundice–cyanosis
blue Joe–bluegill
blue John–milk
bluejoint–redtop
Blue Law State–Connecticut
blue malachite–azurite
bluenose–Nova Scotian
blue-pencil–edit
blue pigment–bice, smalt
blue point–oyster
blueprint–cyanotype
blue rocket–monkshood
blue-sailors–chicory

blue sheep–bharal
blue spar–lazulite
blue stuff–kimberlite
bluer–anil
bluff–bank, blinder, blinker, cliff, crusty, impolite, rude, short, uncivil
Bluff King Hal–Henry
bluish gray–caesious, slate
bluish purple–violet
bluish white pigment–zinc
blunder–err, error, mistake
blunt (as the mind)–hackney
blunt–brusque, deaden, dull, obtund, obtuse, stupid, unsharp
blur–blear, blot, cloud, dim, disfigure, obscure, spot
blurb–advertisement, brief, commendation, notice
blurt out–bolt
blush–color, mantle, redden
blushing–flushing, roseate, ruddy
bluster–boasting, bullying, confusion, noise, rant, rodomontade, roister, swaggering, tumult, turbulence
bluster (Eng.)–swank
blusterer – bully, roisterer, swaggerer
bo (boe)–hobo, tramp
bo (boh) – captain, chief, leader
bo (U.S. slang)–buddy, fellow, man
boa–scarf, snake
boa (ringed) – aboma, abomas (pl.)
boar (wild)–sanglier
board–deal, plank
board (blockhead)–doll
board (heavy)–plank
board (long, narrow)–lath, slat
board (spring)–alcalde
boast–bluster, brag, braggart, crow, flourish, prate, swagger, vapor, vaunt
boaster – braggart, crower, gascon
boaster (of country's preparedness)–jingo
boaster (of learning)–pedant

boasting–quacky, vainglory, vaunting
boat–barge, bateau, bateaux (pl.), brig, canoe, craft, cutter, dinghy, dingy, gig, junk, ketch, liner, pinnace, scooter, scow, ship, skiff, skift, vessel, watercraft, xebec
boat (Alaska, portable, made of skins)–bidarka, bidarkee
boat (Briton, anc.)–coracle
boat (Canadian flatbottom)–bateau, bateaux (pl.)
boat (clumsy)–ark, barge, scow
boat (dispatch)–aviso, packet
boat (Dnieper River)–baidak
boat (English raiding)–commando
boat (fire)–palander
boat (fishing) – seiner, trawler, trow
boat (fishing, six-oared) – sexern
boat (flatbottom) – ark, barge, bateau, bateaux (pl.), praam, praham, pram, punt, scow
boat (flatbottom, ferry)–bac
boat (freight)–barge, scow
boat (flying) – amphibian, seaplane
boat (harbor)–tug
boat (jolly)–yawl
boat (Levantine)–saic
boat (medieval)–caravel
boat (motor)–palander
boat (navy, named after cities)–cruiser
boat (Nile house)–dahabeah
boat (part of)–beam, bow, bridge, gunnel, gunwale, hold, keel, prow, stern, thwart
boat (passenger)–ferry, liner
boat (power)–cruiser, putput, speed
boat (propel with long stick)–poled
boat (propel with one oar at rear)–scull
boat (propelled by three rowers)–randan

boat (river)–ark, barge, tug

boat (river, flatbottomed)–barge

boat (roomy, flatbottomed) –barge

boat (row, flatbottomed) – dory

boat (row, small)–canoe, cog, skiff, skift

boat (royal)–barge

boat (ship's)–dingey, dinghy, dingy, pinnace, tender

boat (small)–canoe, coracle, dory, skiff, skift

boat (steel cargo)–tanker

boat (three or four oarsmen) –randan

boat (undersea)–sub, submarine, submersible

boat (U.S. raiding)–ranger

boat (Venetian)–gondola

boat captain (East)–rais

boat carrying charge–boatage

boat man (Ganges)–dandy

boat man (river)–barger

boat man (Venetian)–gondolier

boat ride–row, sail

boat rope–hawser, painter

boat side (upper edge)–gunnel, gunwale

boat song–Barcarole, chantey, chanty, shantey, shanty

boat trip–cruise, row, sail

boat's lowest deck–orlop

boat's lowest part–keel

boatswain–bosun

boatswain (Lascar crew) – serang

bob–cheat, cut, delude, filch, flout, haircut, jeer, jest, mock, taunt, trick

bobac–marmot

bobber – bobfly, deadhead, dropper, float

bobbin–cylinder, pin, pirn, reel, spool

bobble a bait–dib

bobby–peeler, policeman

bobsled–ripper

bobtails (Scot.)–strunts

bobwhite–colin, quail

Boche (slang)–German

bodach – bugaboo, churl, clown

bodacious–audacious, bold, reckless

bode – forebode, foreshow, foretell, portend, presage

bodega – storeroom, winecellar, wineshop

boden – accoutered, furnished

bodge–botch, patch

bodice–corsage, waist

bodies (intervening) – mediums

bodies (legislative)–senates

bodies (nonclerical)–laities

bodies (single-celled)–spores

bodies at rest (pert. to)–static

bodies of church buildings–naves

bodies politic–weals

bodily–carnal, corporal, corporeal, fleshy, material, physical, somatic

bodily contour–form, shape

bodily motion (pert. to)–gestic

boding – foreboding, ominous, prediction, prognostic

bodkin – dagger, eyeleteer, needle, poniard, stiletto

bodword – commandment, message, prediction, premonition

body–bulk, carcass, corpse, majority, mass, substance

body (celestial)–planet

body (clock-regulating) – pendulum

body (deliberative)–senate

body (flying)–meteor

body (globular, small)–pill

body (heavenly) – comet, luna, star, sun

body (motion of)–gesture

body (pert. to)–somal

body (petrified)–fossil

body (politic)–community

body (political)–cabinet

body (proteid)–albumin

body (reproductive of fern or fungus)–spore

body (spherical)–ball, globe, orb

body (suspended swinging) –pendulum

body (the)–deha

body (transparent, used in refraction experiment)–prism

body (wagon)–buck

body corporate (law)–corporation

body fallen to earth from outer space–meteorite

bodyguard–lifeguard, retinue

body height–stature

body joint–elbow, hip

body of advisers–cabinet

body of animal–soma

body of armed men (with authority)–posse

body of assistants–staff

body of household help–servantry

body of information (condensed)–digest

body of land (pert. to)–continental

body of law–code

body of men speaking same language–langue

body of paid applauders–cleaque

body of persons (organized) –corps, posse

body of persons employed–personnel

body of self-luminous gas–nebula

body of ship–hull

body of singers–chorus

body of soldiers–brigade, company, corps, division, file, platoon, squad, troop

body of troop arrangement–echelon

body of troops–corps

body of water–bay, lagoon, lake, ocean, pond, pool, reservoir, sea

body plasma–somatoplasm

body section (main)–torso

body servant–maid, valet

Boeotia king (legendary)–Ogyges, Ogygos

Boer general–Botha

Boer language–Taal

bog–bold, bug, fen, forward,

marsh, mire, moor, morass, moss, ooze, quagmire, saucy, sink
bog down–mire, stall
bogey–bugbear, devil, goblin
boggle – bungle, hesitate, shrink, start
bogglebo–hobgoblin, scarecrow, specter
bogle–bogy, bugbear, goblin, phantom, scarecrow, specter
bogus–fictitious, sham, spurious
bogy – bugbear, hobgoblin, specter
bohawn–cabin, cottage, hut
Bohemian capital – Prague, Praha
Bohemian city–Aussig, Budweis, Eger, Prague, Praha, Pilsen, Reichenberg, Teplitz
Bohemian dance–redowa
Bohemian measure–merice, stopa
Bohemian mineral (brown) –egeran
Bohemian reformer (religious)–Huss
Bohemian river–Elbe, Iser, Moldau
boil–seethe, steam, stew, sty, stye
boil (on eyelid)–sty, stye
boil (to)–buck
boil slowly–stew
boiler tube scaler–sooter
boiling–ebullient, seething
bois (Fr.)–wood
boist (Eng.)–bed, shelter, sofa
boisterous–clamorous, furious, loud, noisy, roaring, rough, tumultuous
bokom–sapanwood
bola–majagua, weapon
bolar–clayey
bold – audacious, brazen, daring, dashing, dauntless, fearless, forward, intrepid, pert, presumptuous, rash, valiant
boldness–assurance, audacity, bravery, brazenness,

confidence, courage, dauntlessness, hardihood, intrepidity, temerity
bolero–dance, jacket
boliche–inn
Bolivian capital–Sucre
Bolivian city – Chuquisaca, Cochabamba, La Paz (c.) Oruro, Potosi, Sucre
Bolivian coin–boliviano (ac., s.), centavo (br.), tomin (s.)
Bolivian Indian–Iten, Moxo, Uro
Bolivian lake–Aullugas, Desaguadero, Titicaca
Bolivian measure–celemin, league
Bolivian mountain – Andes, Illimani, Sajama, Sorata
Bolivian mutton (dried) – chalone
Bolivian river–Beni, Cordillera, Mamore, Paraguay, Pilcomayo, San Miguel
Bolivian weight–libra, marco
bolk (boke)–belch, vomit
bolo – defeatist, knife, machete, pacifist
Bolshevist leader–Lenin
bolster–cushion, pad, pillow
bolt–arrow, dart, decamp, flee, lightning, pintle, rivet, separate, sift, thunderbolt
bolt (lock projection)–nab
bolt (sliding machine) – pawl
bomb – grenade, projectile, shell
bomb (aerial, slang)–egg
bomb (depth)–ashcan
bomb (small paper)–petard
bomb (worthless)–dud
bomb guide–fin
bomb treatment–jet
bombard–shell
bombard fiercely–strafe
bombardier – artilleryman, gunner
bombardment (heavy) – strafe
bombardment (short intensive)–refale
bombast–boasting, fustian,

rage, rant, rave, rodomontade, turgidity
bombastic–tumid, pompous, grandiloquent, stilted
bombastic talk–rant
Bombay arrowroot–tikor
Bombay hemp – ambary, sunn
Bombay state–Edar
bombers (German dive) – stukas
bombproof chamber – casement
bombyx–eri, eria, silkworm
bonair–complaisant, courteous, gentle
bonamano–gratuity, tip
bon ami – friend, lover, sweetheart
Bonanza State–Montana
bonbon – candy, caramel, cream, sugarplum
bond–association, captivity, chain, contract, fetter, league, tie, yoke
bond between group members–nexus
bondman–esne, serf, servant, slave, vassal
bondman (Spartan)–helot
bone – humerus, os, ossa (pl.), rib, ulna
bone (ankle)–astragal, talus, tali (pl.)
bone (anvil)–incus, incudes (pl.)
bone (arm) – humerus, radius, ulna, ulnae (pl.)
bone (breast)–sternum
bone (cheek)–malar
bone (collar)–clavicle
bone (elbow) – ulna, ulnae (pl.)
bone (fish gill cover)–opercle
bone (flank)–ilium, ilia (pl.)
bone (foot)–metatarsus, tarsus
bone (forearm)–ulna, ulnae (pl.)
bone (hip)–ilium, ilia (pl.)
bone (hip, upper) – ilium, ilia (pl.)
bone (innomiate)–hip
bone (knee)–patella
bone (Latin)–os, ossa (pl.)

bone (leg)–femur, femora (pl.), femura, fibula, ilium, ilia (pl.), tibia
bone (little)–osselet
bone (nodular tendon)–sesamoid
bone (pelvis) – ilium, ilia (pl.), ischium, pubes
bone (shin)–tibia
bone (shoulder)–scapula
bone (skull)–vomer
bone (thigh) – femur, femura, ilium, ilia (pl.)
bone (thin plate of, covering inner ear)–tegmen
bone (vertebral column posterior)–pygostyle
bone (wrist)–carpus, carpi (pl.), ulna
bone cartilage–ossein
bonefish–ladyfish
bone house–coffin, ossuary
bone juncture–suture
bone-like–osteal
bone oil compound–animin
bone shaker–bicycle, jeep
bones (marrow of)–medulla
Bonhomme (Richard, his opponent)–Serapis
bonita (bonito)–atu, atualo, nice, pretty
bonne–maidservant, nursemaid
bonnet (close-fitting)–toque
bonnet brim (women's) – poke
bonnibel–handsome
bonnie – beautiful, handsome, healthy, plump, pretty
bonny–beautiful, handsome, healthy, plump, pretty
Bontoc town division–Ato
bony–osseous, osteal
boo–hoot
boobook–owl
booby–dunce, simpleton
booby hatch–jail, asylum
boohoo–hoot, sailfish, shout, sob, weep
book–canto, liber, volume
book (account)–day, journal, ledger
book (best-selling)–Bible
book (blank)–album, tablet

book (commendatory notice in)–blurb
book (division of)–chapter
book (elementary reading)–primer
book (essential in U.S. courtroom)–Bible
book (handsomely printed)–Aldine
book (large)–tome
book (make-up of)–format
book (mass)–missal
book (memorandum) – agenda
book (not bearing author's name) – anonyme, anonym
book (of Bible)–Amos, Esther, Exodus, Ezra, Micah, Nahum, Psalms, Revelation
book (of fiction)–novel
book (of hours) – Hora, Horae (pl.)
book (of maps)–atlas
book (of psalms)–Psalter
book (of rubrics)–Ordo
book (popular type)–mystery
book (printed and stitched)–brochure
book (religious service)–diurnal
book (sacred)–Psalter
book (small)–manual
book appearance (general)–format
bookbinder–bibliopegist
bookbinding leather–roan
book collector–bibliomaniac
book cover (front)–recto
book cover ornamenting – tooling
book given to under graduates as prize–detur
bookkeeping term – entry, post
book lover–bibliophile
book of Apocrypha–Tobit
book of Bible (Apocryphal)–Esdras
book page–folio
book palm–taliera, tara
book style–format
books (destroyer of)–biblioclast

books (lover of)–bibliophile
books (one versed in knowledge of)–bibliognost
books (production of)–bibliogony
books (seller of)–bibliopole
books (stealer of) – biblioklept, bibliokleptomaniac
books (with sheets fourth size of printing paper)–quartos
books (worshiper of)–bibliolater
books (writer of)–bibliographer
bool–bend, curvature
boom–spar
boom (ship's large fore)–bowsprit
boomerang–rebound
boon–blessing, present
boor–barbarian, cad, cauboge, churl, clodhopper, clown, husbandman, lout, oaf, peasant, rustic
boorish–awkward, clumsy, crabbed, lubberly, rude, rustic, sullen, surly, ungainly
boose–crib, stall
boost–assistance, commendation, increase, lift, plug, push, raise
boot (bird) – ocrea, ocreae (pl.)
boot (Eskimo)–kamik
boot (fishing)–wader
boot (half) – buskin, pac, pack
boot (heavy felt, half)–pac, pack
boot (high, worn by actor)–buskin
boot (high-water)–wader
boot (logger's)–pac, pack
boot (riding)–jemmy
boot (sealskin)–kamik
boot (top, 19th century)–Napoleon
booth–loge, stall
Booth Tarkington hero (boy)–Penrod
booty–loot, pillage, plunder, prey, prize, spoil
booty (slang)–swag
booty carriers (arch.)–reaves

boquet (bouquet) – aroma,
cigar, corsage, nosegay
borak–banter, chaff, ridicule
borax (native)–tincal
Bordeaux wine–claret
border–abut, adjoin, bound,
boundary, brink, confine,
edge, flank, fringe, frontier, hem, limit, line,
marge, margin, neighbor,
periphery, rim, skirt,
touch, verge
border (ornamental, around
main design of stamps)–
tressure
border (picture)–mat, orle
border (Scot.)–rund
border (shield)–bordure
border (wall)–dado
border (woven)–selvage
border of lace (loop)–picot
border on–abut
bore – carried, drill, irk,
penetrate, pierce, tire, tol-
erated, tunnel, weary
bore (obs.)–aigre, eagre
bore (size of)–calibre
bore (tidal)–eagre
Boreas' son–Calais
boredom–ennui, tedium
boric acid salt–borate
boring – dry, penetrating,
piercing, tedious, tire-
some, tiring
boring tool–auger, awl, bit,
gimlet, reamer
born–nee
born (well)–eugenic
born after death of father–
posthumous
born in the country–rurige-
nous
borne–limited, narrow, rode
borne by the wind–eolian
Borneo ape–orang
Borneo city–Bruni
Borneo mountain – Kini-
Balu
Borneo native–Dyak
Borneo pepper plant (in-
toxicating)–ara
Borneo Philippine sea–Sulu
Borneo pirates–bajau
Borneo protectorate (British)–Sarawak
Borneo river–Bruni

Borneo seacoast inhabitant–
Iban
Borneo tree (antproof timber)–billian
Borneo tribe–Dusuns
Borneo weight–chapah, para
boron (pert. to)–boric
boron combined with posi-
tive element–boride
borough–burg, burgh
borrel–auger, rough, rude,
unlearned
bosky–bushy, fuddled, in-
toxicated, tipsy, woody
Bosnia (Slavic) native–Croat
boss – director, foreman,
manage, master, stud,
superintendent
boss (shield)–umbo
bosthoon–boor, clout, dolt,
switch
botanic bag–ascus, asci (pl.)
botanical cell (structural
unit)–energid
botch–bungle, mess
botcher–clouter
both–two
both sexes (pert. to)–epicene
bother – ado, ail, annoy,
badger, disturbance, fuss,
irritate, molest, nag,
pother, tease, trouble
bothersome–molesting
bottle–cruet, flask
bottle (corrosive liquid) –
carboy
bottle (flat)–flask
bottle (glass ointment)–ampulla
bottle (glass table)–carafe
bottle (globular, large)–carboy
bottle (hot-water)–pig
bottle (leather)–matara
bottle (liquor, made of
skins)–borachio
bottle (oil, ointment)–aryballos, aryballus
bottle (ornamental) – de-
canter
bottle (small)–ampoule, ampul, phial, vial
bottle (tosspot's)–flagon
bottle (water)–carafe
bottle sealer–capper

bottom – base, bed, floor,
ground, root
bottom (coal car tilting)–
hopper
bottom (to lower)–deepen
bottom surface–bed, floor
bottomless – abysmal, baseless, unfathomable
bough – branch, offshoot,
shoot, spray, sprig, twig
bought back–redeemed
bounce – carom, leap, re-
bound, ricochet
bouncer–boaster, bully, liar,
whopper
bound–ambit, barrier, border, bounce, bourne, con-
fine, hurdle, jump, leap,
precinct, rebound, se-
cured, skip, spring, taped,
termination, tied, trussed,
vault, verge
bound (to)–delimit, limit
bound to secrecy–tiled
boundary–bourn, edge, end,
limit, march, meer, meta,
perimeter, rim, term,
terminus, termination,
verge
boundary (comb. form)–ori
boundary (extreme)–utmost
boundary (lateral)–side
boundary (line of figure enclosed by curve)–circum-
ference
boundary (outer)–perimeter
boundary (outer, of plane
figure)–perimeter
boundary lines – fences,
meres, metes
boundary marks – fences,
meres, metes
bounder–cad
boundless–illimitable, unconfined, unlimited, vast
bounteous–ample, freely, liberal, munificent, plenti-
ful
bountiful–abundant, boun-
teous, generous, liberal,
munificent, plentiful
bounty–beneficence, gratuity, largess, liberality, premium, reward, subsidy
bouquets – aromas, cigars,

compliments, corsages, nosegays

bourasque–storm, tempest

bourd – fun, jest, mock, mockery

bourn (bourne) – bound, boundary, brook, limit, rivulet, stream

bourock – cluster, crowd, heap, hut, mound

bourre–stuffed, wadded

bouse–beaker, carouse, cup, drink

bouser–boozer, toper

bousy–boozy, drunken, sotted

bout–attempt, conflict, contest, fracas, go, set-to, trial

bout (coll.)–set-to

bovine–bison, bull, cow, ox, oxlike, taurine

bovine (male)–bull, steer

bovine animal–neat

bow–arch, assent, curve, incline, knot, nod, node, rainbow, stoop, submit, yield

bow of promise–rainbow

bow of ship–prow

bowed–bent, curved, kneed

bower–arbor

bower (garden)–alcove

bower bird's playhouse–run

bower woman – chambermaid

bowfin–amia, mudfish

bowfins (genus of)–amia

Bowie State–Arkansas

bowk – bucket, pail, soak, steep

bowkail–cabbage

bowl–basin

bowl (wooden)–kitty

bowl (wooden, maple sap holding)–rogan

bowler–derby, kegler

bowling game–tenpins

bowling piece–ninepin

bowling pin–ninepin

bowling place–alley

bowling score–spare, strike

bowman–archer

bowsprit elevation from horizontal–steeve

box–buffet, case, chest, cist, crate, cuff, spar, stall

box (alms)–arca

box (ammunition)–bandolier, caisson

box (live fish, floating)–car

box (resistance)–rheostat

box (shallow)–tray

box (small French vanity)–dorine

box (strong) – chest, safe, vault

box (theater)–loge

box (tin lid)–caddy

box (treasure)–arca

box family–buxaceae

box for money offerings–arca

box sleigh–pung

boxer's hand covering (anc.) –cestus

boxes (set of lacquered)–inro

boxful–cageful

boxing contest (coll.)–setto

boy–child, garcon, gossoon, knave, lad, page, rascal, rogue, varlet, youth

boy (errand)–messenger, page

boy (farmer)–herder

boy (Latin)–puer

boy (liveried)–page

boy (roguish)–urchin

boy (small)–bo, tad

boy (Span.)–nino

boy (street)–Arab, gamin, tad

boy (young)–lad, tad

boy friend–beau, beaux (pl.), sweetheart

boy's book writer–Alger, Henty

boy's organization member –Scout

bozo–fellow

brabagious–cantankerous

brace–couple, leg, pair, reinforce, stay, stiffen, stimulate, strengthen, support

brace (between joists)–strut

brace (Scot.)–mantelpiece

brace (temporary)–spale

bracing–crisp, invigorating, strengthening, tonic

bracket (light, supporting)–electrolier

bracket (wall)–corbel

bracket candlestick (var.)–sconce

brackish–distasteful, nauseous, salty

bract (chaff-like)–palea

bract (floret)–palea

bract (inclosing a flower)–spathe

bract (upper grass)–palet

brad–nail, sprig

brad (headless, small)–sprig

brae–bank, hill, hillside, slope, valley

brag–boast, crow, gasconade, vaunt

braggart–boaster, crower, fanfaron, boaster

Brahman (learned)–pundit

Brahman (versed in Sanskrit)–pundit

Brahman title–aya

Brahminical institute of laws, letters, and teachings–Sastra, Shastra

braid–cue, entwine, interlace, plait, pleat, tress, weave

braid (gold and silver)–orris

braid (kind of)–lacet

braid (ornamental)–gimp, lace

braid (Russian)–soutache

braid (trimming)–soutache

braid of hair–cue, plait, queue

braided–cued, plaited, tress

braided cord–sennit

brain–mind

brain (obs.)–furious, mad

brain (white matter of)–alba

brain box–pan

brain canal–iter

brain covering lines–ripas

brain membrane–tela

brain operating instrument–trepan, trephine

brain part–aula, aulae (pl.), cerebrum

brain passage–iter

brain tumor–glioma

brains (Latin)–cerebra

brake–bridle, cage, curb, dilemma, snare, trap

brakeman (coll., U. S.)–brakie

Bram Stoker's novel–Dracula

Bran's father–Llyr

branch–arm, department, diverge, divide, fork, limb, offshoot, ramify, ramus, rami (pl.), shoot, sprig, twig, vimen

branch (flexible, used as band)–withe

branch (growing out)–ramal

branch (long, flexible, slender)–vimen

branch (slender)–stolon

branch (small)–spray, twig

branch (trailing)–stolon

branch diverging point (from stem)–axil

branch herring–alewife

branch-like–ramose, ramous

branch of flowers–spray

branch of knowledge (humorous)–ology

branch of mechanics–statics

branch off–fork

branched–forky, ramose

branches–rami, ramus (sing.)

branches (pert. to)–ramous

branches of learning–arts

branching–ramose

branchiopod (appendage)–endite

brand–label, sear, stamp, stigma, trademark

brand (sheep, Eng. dial.)–smit

brand iron–gridiron, trivet

brandish–flaunt, flourish, flutter, shake, swing, wave

brandy (mastic)–raki

brandy (Span.)–aguardiente

brandy and soda–peg

brant (common)–quink

brass – cash, impudence, money

brass (first, numis.)–sesterce

brass (skilled worker in)–brasier

brass (variety of)–platen

brass hat (army slang)–general

brasserie (French)–brewery, saloon

brassy–aerose, bold, brazen, impudent

brat–apron, bib, cloak, clothing, film, garment, imp, mantle, scum

brave–bold, courageous, daring, dauntless, fearless, gallant, game, heroic, intrepid, manly, stout, stouthearted, valiant, valorous

brave (be)–bedare

brave (heroically)–spartan

brave and noble–manly

brave man–hero

bravery–bravado, bravura, courage, valor

brawl–affray, altercation, dispute, fight, fracas, riot, row, scold, shindy, quarrel, uproar, wrangle

brawny–fleshy, powerful, robust, sinewy, stalwart, strong, sturdy

bray–pestle

braying tool–pestle

brazen–bold, brass, brassy, harsh, impudent, insolent, metallic, shameless

Brazil nut–niggertoe

Brazilian ant (powerful, stinging)–tucandera

Brazilian bird–ara, darter

Brazilian bird (large)–seriema

Brazilian city–Bahia, Campinas, Ceara, Manaos, Para, Pernambuco, Porto Alegre, Rio, Rio de Janeiro, Santos, Sao Paulo

Brazilian clover–alfalfa, lucern

Brazilian coin–conto (ac.), cruzeiro (ac., g.), milreis (g., pap.), milreis (alum., br.), reis (ac.)

Brazilian coin–rial

Brazilian crab (land)–horseman

Brazilian cuckoo–ani

Brazilian dance–maxixe

Brazilian drink–assai

Brazilian estuary–Para

Brazilian Indian–Acroa, Anta, Arara, Carib

Brazilian Indian (Arawakan)–Araua, Guana

Brazilian Indian (Paru River)–Araquaju

Brazilian Indian (Xingu River)–Arara

Brazilian macaw–ara, arara, ira, maracan

Brazilian mammal–tapir

Brazilian measure–alqueire, alquier, braca, canada, covado, cuarta, fanga, garrafa, league, legoa, milha, moio, palmo, passo, pe, pipa, pollegada, quartilho, quarto, sack, tarefa, tonel, vara

Brazilian money–ree, rei

Brazilian money of account–rei

Brazilian monkey–miriki

Brazilian mountain–Maririme, Organ, Serra do Mar, Serra dos Orgaos

Brazilian Negro–Mina

Brazilian night heron–soco

Brazilian palm–assai, jara

Brazilian parrot–ara, arara, tiriba

Brazilian plant–ayapana, yaje

Brazilian plant (used for rope)–caroa

Brazilian red–roset

Brazilian river–Amazon, Apa, Jurua, Madeira, Negro, Orinoco, Paraguay, Parana, Purus, San Francisco, Tapajos, Tocantins, Xingu

Brazilian rubber tree–seringa

Brazilian seaport–Bahia, Natal, Para, Rio

Brazilian state–Bahia, Ceara, Para, Parana

Brazilian tapir–anta

Brazilian tree–anda, dal

Brazilian tree (pea family)–araroba

Brazilian tree (rubber-producing)–seringa

Brazilian tree (yielding medicinal oil)–anda

Brazilian unit–rei

Brazilian walnut–embuia

Brazilian weight–arratel, arroba, bag, libra, oitava, onca, quilate, quintal, tonelada

breach–chasm, cleft, dispute, disruption, gap, infraction, infringement, misunderstanding, quarrel, rent, rift

bread (boiled)–panada

bread (browned)–toast

bread (corn)–pone

bread (crisp)–rusk

bread (heated)–toady

bread (loaf of)–miche

bread (mass of)–loaf

bread (pert. to)–panary

bread (ship's stores)–rusk

bread (small piece of toasted)–sippet

bread and butter–toadflax, greenbrier, boyish, girlish, juvenile

bread and cheese–sorrel

bread and milk dish–panada

breadbasket (slang)–stomach

bread crumbs boiled in milk and flavored–panada

bread crust–rind

bread plate (Eucharistic)–paten

breadth of planking–strake

breadwinner–earner, worker

break–blank, blunder, burst, cleft, dash, disrupt, hiatus, interval, lacuna, lapse, rent, rift, rush, shatter, slip, smash, snap, stop

break (arch.)–knap

break (rhythmic, in line of poetry)–caesura, cesura

break a flag–lower

break asunder–disrupt

break away–disappear, disengage, dissolve

break of day–morn, morning, sunup

break out suddenly–erupt

break rules–disobey

break without warning–snap

breaker – comber, roller, wave

breaking down–cataclasm

breaking forth–eruptive

breaking out–eruption

breaking waves–surf

breakup–dispersion, disruption, dissolution, spall

breakwater–mole, pier

breast–bosom

breastbone–sternum

breastbone (flat)–ratite

breastbone (pert. to)–sternal

breast-like–mastoid

breastplate (crescent-shaped)–gorget

breastplate (horse's medieval armor)–peitrel, peytrel, poitrail, poitrel

breastworks–parapet

breath–breeze, odor, pneuma, scent, smell

breathe–emanate, exhale, respire

breathe (convulsively)–gasp

breathe (heavily)–pant

breathe hard–pant

breathe one's last–die, expire

breathe spasmodically–sigh

breathing–alive, respiration, ventilation

breathing (adventitious)–rale

breathing (smooth)–lene

breathing arrangement (in plants)–stoma

breathing orifice–spiracle

breathing place–caesura, pause, vent

breathing rapidly–panting

breck–blemish, breach, gap

bred–board, lid, reared, tablet

brede–boil, braid, broaden, embroidery, extend, overspread, plait, roast, toast

bree–brow, commotion, disturbance, eyebrow, eyelash, eyelid, scare, terrify

breeches (coll.)–pantaloons, trousers

breeches (cowboy's)–chaps

breeches (riding)–jodhpur

breed–beget, class, engender, ilk, kind, nourish, produce, propagate, race, raise, rear, sort

breed (of mixed)–mongrel, mulatto, mulatta (fem.), quadroon

breed of cat–manx, Persian

breed of cattle–Devon, Durham, Guernsey, Hereford, Holstein, Jersey, Longhorn

breed of dogs–Spitz

breed of men–caste, race

breeding–deportment, education, instruction, training

breeding place–nidus, nidi (pl.)

breeze (gentle)–aura, aurae (pl.), zephyr

breeze (soft, gentle)–zephyr

breezes (gentle, Latin)–aurae, aura (sing.)

breezy–airy, brisk, fresh, vivacious

brevity–conciseness, shortness, succinctness, terseness

brew–ale, concoct, contrive, foment, hatch, plot

brewer (female)–brewster

brewer's yeast–barm

brewing vessel–teapot

brey–barnacle

bribe–sop

bribe money–boodle

bric-a-brac (piece of)–curio

bric-a-brac cabinet–atagere, etagere, whatnot

brick–stone, tile

brick (inner end of projecting)–tailing

brick (malting floor)–pament, pamment

brick (sun-baked)–adobe

brick (sun-dried)–bat

brick (tray of)–hod

brick-carrying device–hod

brick kiln–clamp

brick-making tool–lute

bride's portion (var.)–dowery

bridge–span

bridge (narrow)–viaduct

bridge (part of)–span

bridge (stringed instrument)–magas

bridge (supporting part)–truss

bridge bird–phoebe

bridge lever–bascule

Bridge of Paradise (Moslem tradition)–Alsirat

bridge score–slam

bridge strategy–finesse

bridge term–pass, renege, revoke, slam

bridle–govern, halter, master, repress, restrain, simper, subdue, suppress

bridle bit (jointed)–snaffle

bridle part–bit

bridle port–porthole

bridle strap–rein

brief–curt, compendious, compendium, concise, condensed, ephemeral, fleeting, short, short-lived, summary, terse, transitory

brief and compact–concise

brief interval of rest–respite

brier (briar)–thorn

brig–boat, guardhouse, vessel

brigand–bandit, highwayman, ladrone, picaroon, pirate, robber, thief

Brigham Young college seat –Logan (Utah)

bright–beamy, brilliant, clever, effulgent, flashing, gay, gleaming, glistening, glittering, lucid, lustrous, nitid, radiant, refulgent, resplendent, rosy, shining, sparkling, splendid, sunny, witty

bright (dazzling)–garish

bright (very)–vivid

bright and cheerful–sunny

bright-colored flowering plant–phlox

bright outlook–rosy

bright saying–mot

brighten–engild, enliven, light

brightest–rosiest

brightness–brilliance, clearness, luster, sheen, splendor

brilliancy–eclat, glitter, glory, lustrous, splendor

brilliancy of achievement–eclat

brilliant–bright, glittering, refulgent, sparkling, vivid

brilliant (transiently)–meteoric

brilliant circle (group)–galaxy

brim–border, brink, edge, lip, marge, margin, rim

brim (the)–lip

brim (women's bonnet)–poke

brineness–saltness

bring–bear, carry, convey, fetch, transport

bring about–consummate, effect, instigate

bring back–restore, retrieve, return, revive

bring charge against–delate

bring forth (as logical consequent)–educe

bring forth (Scot.)–ean

bring forth (to)–ean

bring forth young lambs–ean, yean

bring forward–adduce, cite

bring in (to)–usher

bring in proof–adduce

bring into a row–align, aline

bring into being–create, raise

bring into bondage–enslave

bring into consonance – homologate

bring into court (to answer a charge)–arraign

bring into harmony–attune

bring into harmony again–retune

bring into position–align, aline

bring into union–correlate

bring into vigorous action–exert

bring legal action–sue

bring near–appose

bring or place near–appose

bring out–educe

bring out clearly–emphasize, stress

bring to–resuscitate

bring to a close–end, finish

bring to earth–land

bring to light–disclose, discover, reveal, unearth

bring to memory–remind

bring to mind–recall

bring to naught–dash

bring to nothing–frustrate

bring to pass–accomplish

bring to perfection–ripen

bring to ruin–undo

bring to standstill–stalemate

bring to want–beggar

bring together again (after separation)–reunite

bring under–restrain, subdue

bring up–educate, raise, rear, vomit

bring upon one's self–incur

bringer of good luck–horseshoe, rabbit foot

bringer of ill luck–Jonah

bringing forward–adducent

bringing to a standstill–stalling

bringing up–bearing, rearing

brink–border, edge, lip, marge, margin, verge

briny–saline, salt

brisk–agile, alert, alive, animated, energetic, fast, fresh, gay, nimble, quick, snappy, sprightly, spry, stimulating, vivacious

brisk (dial.)–peart

briskly (dial.)–peartly

briss (Eng. dial.)–dust

bristle–hair, seta, setae (pl.)

bristle (needle-like)–acicula

bristle (pert. to)–setal

bristle (placed beneath skin) –seton

bristle (surgical)–seton

bristle-like–setal, setiform

bristles (comb. form)–seti

bristly–hispid, setal, setose, thorny

Bristol fashion–shipshape

Bristol priest (fictitious)–Thomas Rowley

Britain (early inhabitant of) –Pict

Britain (old name)–Albion

Britain chariot (two-wheeled)–essede

Britain people (anc.)–Silures

British–*see also* English
British airplane–Nighthawk, Spitfire, Tomahawk
British author–Shute
British base (Red Sea gateway)–Aden
British battleship–Anson, Howe
British buccaneer–Morgan
British cavalry (volunteer)–yeomanry
British coin–shilling
British colony (Arabian)–Aden
British dynasty's house (ancestral)–este
British East Africa coincent (br.)
British Empire in India (founder of)–Clive
British flying force–RAF
British foreign minister–Eden
British general–Gage
British governor (St. Helena)–Lowe
British government newspaper (official)–Gazette
British gun carrier–bren
British India city–Agra, Benares
British India money of account–anna
British India province–Assam
British India province (N. E.)–Bengal
British island (Mediterranean)–Malta
British island (West Indies)–Bahama
British isle–Ireland, Man, Wight
British king – Arthur, George, Henry
British king (legendary)–Lud
British king (myth)–Bran
British legislator–commoner
British Lion's den–London
British major–John Andre
British man-of-war–galatea
British measure – acre, barleycorn, barn, gallon, barrel, bodge, boll, bovate,

bushel, carat, carucate, chain, chaldron, comb, coomb, cran, cranne, cubit, digit, ell, fathom, firkin, float, floor, fluid ounce, foot, furlong, gallon, gill, goad, hand, hogshead, hutch, inch, jugrum, kilderkin, last, league, line, mile, mimim, ounce, oxgang, palm, peck, perch, pin, pint, pipe, point, pole, pool, pottle, prime, puncheon, quadrant, quart, quarten, quarter, rod, rood, rundlet, runlet, sack, shaftment, shaftmont, skein, span, spindle, stack, standard, strike, sulung, tablespoonful, teaspoonful, tertian, thread, tierce, ton, trug, truss, tun, vat, virgate, winchester, yard, yoke
British monetary unit–guinea
British National art gallery (founder of)–Tate
British national emblem–lion
British navy canvas (coarse)–poldavy
British oak–robur
British Pacific island–Gardner, Nive
British peninsula (Arabian)–Aden
British physicist–Boyle
British pirate–Kidd
British plane (fighter)–Nighthawk, Spitfire, Tomahawk
British poet laureate–Tate
British political party member–Labourite
British priest (early)–druid
British prime minister–Churchill
British prison–gaol
British protectorate (African)–Ashenti
British rear admiral (former)–Sturdee
British sea fish–dragonet
British sea hero–Nelson

British sixpence (slang)–sprat
British soldier–redcoat
British stronghold–Malta
British subdivision–shire
British subject–Scot
British tavern (slang)–pub
British territory (West Africa)–Nigeria
British war minister–Eden
British weight–stone
British woman's title–dame
Briton (anc.)–Celt
Briton (one of an order of ancient)–druid
Briton's boat (anc.)–coracle
Briton's war chariot–covinus
Brittany native–Breton
brittle–brash, breakable, candy, crisp, feeble, fragile, frail, frangible, infirm, slight, weak
brittle rock–shale
brittle silver ore–stephanite
broad–ample, expansive, large, roomy, thick, tolerant, wide
broad and flat–splat
broad footed–platypod
broad hearted – generous, magnanimous
broad minded–liberal, tolerant
broad scarf–shawl
broad thin piece–sheet
broadcasted by telephone–piped
broadcasts scenes–televises
broaden–dilate, widen
brocade (medieval)–baudekin
brochan–porridge
brod–awl, goad, poke, sprout, thorn, urge
brode (brodee) – embroidered
brodyaga–vagabond, vagrant
brogan–shoe
brogger–broker, jobber
brogue–dialect, fraud, shoe, trick
broil–affray, altercation, conflict, contention, contest, discord, dispute, dis-

sension, fray, grill, quarrel
broil in covered kettle or pan–braise, braize
broil on gridiron–grill
broke–bankrupt, insolvent
broke in pieces–staved
broke with violence–crashed
broken – bankrupt, burst, crushed, dispersed, intermittent, ruptured, shaken, shattered, subdued, tamed, weakened
broken open–sprung
broken pottery – shard, sheard, sherd
broker (ticket)–scalper
brokerage–agio, commission, fee
bromide–trite
bromide potash compound–tolane
brontolite–aerolite
bronze (gilded)–ormolu
bronze (Roman)–aes
bronze film (green)–patina
bronze in sun–tan
brooch–bar, boss, clasp, morse, ouch, pin, shield
brood–clutch, covey, fry, hatch, incubate, mope, nye, offspring, race
brood (pheasant)–nid, nide, nye
brood bud–bulbil, soredium
brood cell–gonidium
brood of young fish–fry
brood over–hover
brook–bear, bourn, burn, creek, endure, rill, rivulet, run, runlet
brook (little)–rillet
brook (Span.)–arroyo
brooklet–runnel
brooklet (Span.)–arroyuelo
broom–besom
broom (butcher's)–bruscus
broom (plant)–spart
broth–soup
broth (in which beef is boiled)–brewis
broth (thick, var.)–potage
brother–fra
brotherhood – association, confraternity, fellowship, fraternity, lodge, sodality

brotherly–affectionate, kind, tender
brothers (Mormon, early)–Danites
brought about–caused, did
brought about (as by magic) –conjured
brought forward for consideration–adduced
brought into a country–imported, migrated
brought into being–created
brought into exact position–aligned, alined, leveled, plumbed, trued
brought out–educed
brought to a standstill–stalemated
brought to naught–undid
brought together–compiled
brought up–bred, reared
brought up (by hand)–cade
brow of steep hill (Scot.)–snab
brown–dun, tawny, toast
brown (grayish)–dun
brown (reddish)–auburn, bay, russet, sorrel
brown Bess–musket
brown Betty–coneflower, pudding
brown color (rich)–sepia
brown daisy–coneflower
brown ebony–coffeewood, wamara
brown fur–nutria
brown pigment–umber
browned by frying in deep fat–rissole
Brownian movement–pedesis
brownie–cake (Aust.), elf, goblin, nis, sandpiper
brownie (Scot. folklore)–uruisg, urisk
brownie (Scandinavian)–nis, nisse
brownish–russet, umber
brownish-purple color–puce
brownish-red coal tar–eosin
brownish yellow–sallow
browse–graze
bruckle–begrime, brittle, changeable, dirty, frail, inconstant
bruin–bear

bruise–batter, contusion, pound, pulverize, triturate
bruise (to)–contuse
bruise by a blow–bash, contuse
bruise by hard usage–batter
bruiser–boxer, pugilist
bruit–clamor, din, fame, noise, report, rumor
brujeria (Span.)–magic, witchcraft
brujo (Span.)–sorcerer
brulyie–broil, disturbance
Brunnehilde's father–Woden, Wotan
Brunhild's husband–Gunther
brush–broom, comb, encounter, sweep, undergrowth
brush (bee's pollen)–scopa, scopae (pl.)
brush (of twigs)–besom
brush (prickly)–briar
brush (whitewash)–limer
brush bird–scrubbird
brush lightly–stroke
brush wolf–coyote
brusk – abrupt, blunt, brusque, curt, short
brusque – abrupt, bluff, blunt, brusk, curt, short
brute–animal, beast, beastly, bestial, brutish, gross, rough, uncivilized, unpolished
brutish–barbarous, bestial, brutal, carnal, cruel, fierce, gross, inhuman, insensate, insensible, irrational, rude, savage, stolid, stupid, unfeeling
bryophyte cultivating places –mosseries
bryophytes–liverworts, mosses
Brythonic god (of waves)–Dylan
Brythonic god (sea)–Ler
Brythonic goddess–Arianrhod, Rhiannon
Brython's god–Bran, Dea
bubble–bead, bleb, globule
bubble (before blowpipe)–intumesce

bubble in glass (small)–seed
bubble through heat action–boil
bubble up–boil, effervesce
buccaneer–corsair, freebooter, pirate
buck (Indian black)–sasin
bucks, in their fourth year–sores
bucket–pail
bucket (boat-water scooping)–bailer
bucket (Latin)–situla, situlae (pl.)
bucket (old word for)–skeel
bucket handle–bail
buckthorn–rhamn
buckwheat tree–teetee, titi
bucolic–local, pastoral, rural, rustic
bucolic (a)–eclogue
bud–blossom, germ, germinate, shoot, sprout
bud (brood on thallus of lichens)–soredium, soredia (pl.)
bud (large underground)–bulb
bud (society) – debutant, debutante
bud (society, coll.)–deb
bud of plant–cion, scion
buds (pickled flower)–capers
Buddha (Chinese for)–Fo, Foh
Buddha (the)–Fo
Buddha spirit of evil and enemy–Mara
Buddha's mother–Maya
Buddhism (center)–Lassa
Buddhism (noninjury of animal life)–ahimsa
Buddhist (retribution)–Karma
Buddhist church (Japan)–Tera
Buddhist column–lat
Buddhist festival (Japan)–bon
Buddhist friar – bhikku, bhikshu
Buddhist gate–torii
Buddhist language (sacred)–Pali
Buddhist mendicant–bhikku, bhikshu

Buddhist monastery (Japan)–Tera
Buddhist monk – Arhat, bhikku, bhikshu, bo, lama, talapoin
Buddhist pillar–lat
Buddhist priest–bo, lama
Buddhist rock temple–rath, ratha
Buddhist sacred language–Pali
Buddhist saint–Arhat
Buddhist scripture language–Pali
Buddhist shrine–tope
Buddhist shrine (relic)–stupa
Buddhist shrine building (round, cupola-topped)–tope
Buddhist shrine tower–stupa
Buddhist temple gateway–toran, torana
Buddhist temple pillar–lat
buddy–companion, mate, pal, tentmate
budge–austere, brisk, fur, jocund, movement, nervousness, pompous, stiff, stir, solemn
budget–pouch, wallet
Buenos Aires bourse–bolsa
buffalo–bamboozle, bison, overawe
buffalo (India, wild)–arna, arnee, arni
buffalo (large horned)–arna, arnee, arni
buffalo (Malay)–carabao
buffalo (Malay, wild)–seladang
buffalo (small)–timarau, timerau
buffalo (water)–carabao
buffalo (wild)–arna, arnee, arni
buffalo gourd–calabazilla
buffalo jack–jurel
buffalo tree–rabbitwood
buffet–beat, box, cuff, cupboard, sideboard, slap, strike
buffoon–clown, droll, fool, jester, mime, mimer, mummer, ridicule, zany
buffoon (female)–mima

bug–beetle, bogy, bugbear, insect
bug (lightning)–firefly
bug (needle)–ranatra
bug (pill)–slater
bugaboo–goblin, hobgoblin, ogre, scarecrow, specter
bugaboo (golfer's)–hook, slice, trap
bugan–ghost, hobgoblin, spirit
bugbear–bogy, bugaboo
buggy–caboose, demented, foolish, stanhope
bug house–asylum, insane
bug juice–liquor, whisky
bugle (yellow)–iva
bugle call–sennet
bugle call (Fr.)–alerte
bugle call (morning)–reveille
bugle call (night)–taps
bugle note–mot
build – construct, erect, found, frame, rear
build up morally (to)–edify
building–apartment, dwelling, edifice, factory, storehouse, structure, tenement
building (dilapidated)–rookery
building (exhibition)–museum
building (farm)–barn, crib, shed
building (high)–tower
building (medieval)–castle
building (projecting part)–apse, ell, wing
building (public)–casino, theater
building (round)–rotunda
building (sacred)–cathedral, church, fane, mosque, pantheon, temple
building (stately)–castle, edifice
building (stone in great mosque at Mecca)–caaba, kaaba, kaabeh
building (subordinate)–annex
building (subsidiary)–annex, lean-to
building (tall, slender)–tower

building addition–annex, apse, ell, lean-to, wing
building diagram–plan
building front–facade, face
building interior (pert. to)–indoor
building space (open)–area
built–constructed, erected, formed, made, shaped
built up (chemically)–synthetic
bulb–root
bulb (edible)–onion
bulb (small)–corm
bulb (solid)–corm
bulbous vegetable–onion
Bulgarian capital–Sofia
Bulgarian city–Bleven, Burgas, Plevna, Plovdiv, Rustchuk, Shumen, Shumla, Silistria, Sistova, Sliven, Slivno, Sofia (c.), Stara, Tirnova, Varna, Widdin, Zagora
Bulgarian coin – lev (ni., cop.), leva (pl.), lew (ni., cop.), stotinka (ac.)
Bulgarian king–Boris
Bulgarian measure – krine, lekha, oka, oke
Bulgarian monetary unit (gold)–leva
Bulgarian river – Danube, Marica, Maritsa, Struma
Bulgarian ruler–Boris, tsar
Bulgarian weight–oka, oke, tovar
bulge–flask, hump, pouch, projection, wallet
bulging (convex)–bowed
bulging (regularly)–convex
bulk – bigness, dimension, largeness, mass, massiveness, size, volume
bulky–clumsy, massive, ponderous, unwielding
bulky (Eng. slang)–policeman
bulky object of person–hulk
bull (sacred)–apis
bull (Scot., young)–stot
bull beggar–bogy, bugbear
bull bird–rotche
bulldozer–bully, machine, grader
bullfighter–capeador, mata-

dor, matadore, picador, toreador, torero
bullfighter (mounted)–toreador
bullfighter (on foot)–torero
bullfighter (one who excites animal)–picador
bullfighter (one who kills)–matador
bullfighter (one who uses cape to distract or excite)–capeador
bullfinch–nope, olp
bullfinch (prov. Eng.)–nope
bull-like–taurine
Bull Run hero–Lee
bullet–missile, pellet, slug
bullet (kind of)–tracer
bullet diameter–caliber
bullock (young)–steer
bully – browbeat, bulldoze, bulldozer, hector, intimidate
bully tree gum–balata
bulrush–tule
bulrush (California)–tule
bulwark–rampart, sconce
bulwark (defense)–rampart
bum trap–bailiff
bumpkin – cauboge, clod, gawk, lout, yokel
bunch–bundle, cluster
bunch (small)–wisp
bunch (tangled)–mop
bunch of grapes–bob
bunch of small flexible parts–tufts
bunder–harbor, pier, quay
bundle–bale, bunch, hank, pack, package, packet, parcel, sheaf
bundle (Irish)–pahil
bundle (portion of vascular, made of woody tissue)–xylem
bundle (small)–packet, parcel, wisp
bundle (swagman's)–bluey
bundle maker–baler
bundle of sticks–fagot
bundle of wood–fagot
bung – plug, spile, stopper, stopple, tampeon, tampion, tampoon
bung (Eng. slang) – falsehood

bungle–botch, blunder, err, muff
bungling–awkward, clumsy, unskilled
bunk–berth
bunker–bin
bunting–etamine
bunting (old world)–ortolan
buoy–float, marker
buoy (to mark trawling place)–dan
buoy (wooden)–deadhead
buoyance (state of)–flotage
buoyant – cheerful, elastic, sanguine, vivacious
buoyant (most)–unelastic
buoyant air–lilt
bur–nut
burble – confuse, disorder, muddle, trouble
burbot–eelpout, ling
burbots (genus of)–lota
burden – cargo, clog, lade, load, onus, oppress, tax, weight
burden of care–cark
burdensome – cumbersome, heavy, onerous, weighty
bureau–chiffonier, department, dresser, office
burglar–thief
burglar (slang)–yegg
burglary–larceny, stealage, theft
burgle–rob
burgomaster–alcalde
burgoo–burgout, porridge, pudding
burial mound–barrow
burial place – catacomb, cemetery, graveyard, necropolis
burlesque–caricature, comic, jest, mimicry, mockery, overact, travesty
burlesque comedy–review
burlesque imitation–parody
burlesque serenade – chari vari
burls (in mahogany)–roe
burly–bulky, corpulent, excellent, imposing, large, noble, stately, stout
Burman–Lai
Burmese–Lai
Burmese capital (former)–Ava

Burmese city–Rangoon
Burmese dagger–dah
Burmese demon–nat
Burmese hill dweller–Lai
Burmese knife–dah
Burmese mongoloid tribe member–Lai
Burmese native (northeastern)–Wa
Burmese robber–dacoit
Burmese skirts–engis
Burmese spirit (wood)–nat
Burmese town–Paan
Burmese traveler's shed – zayat
Burmese tribe group – Tai, Thai
Burmese tribe member–Lai
Burmese viol (three-stringed)–turr
Burmese weight–tical
Burmese wood demon–nat
burn–char, cremate, parch, scald, scorch, sear, singe
burn brightly–glow
burn incense–cense
burn superficially–singe
burn-the-wind–blacksmith
burn up the road–speed
burn with rage–smoke
burner (chemist's)–Bunsen
burner (incense)–censer
burner (midnight oil)–lucubrator
burning – ablaze, afire, ardent, blaze, combustion, conflagration, cremating, fervid, fiery, fire, flame, flaming, glowing, inustion, shining
burning (a)–fire
burning (malicious)–arson
burning heat–ardor
burning mountain–volcano
burning oil–kerosene
burning taste–acrid
burnish–glaze, polish
burns slightly–singes
burnt work–pyrography
burr in wood–gnar, knar, knurl
burro–ass, donkey
burrow – dig, hole, mine, shelter, tunnel
burst–erupt, explode, outbreak, rend, ruptured

burst asunder–disrupted
burst forth–eruct, erupt
burst of artillery fire (Fr.)–rafale
burst of cheers–salvo
bury – conceal, cover, entomb, inter, inurn, overwhelm, repress
bush–shrub
bush (hop)–ake, akeake
bushel (Scot.)–fou
bushing (long)–sleeve
bushing (machine)–sleeve
bushman–rustic, woodsman, San (pl.)
bushman's blanket–bluey
bushman's blouse–bluey
bushman's shirt–bluey
bushmaster–snake
bushy clump–tod
business–affair, concern, industry, matter, trade
business (place of) – mart, office, shop, shoppe, store
business (timber selling and cutting)–logging
business (troublesome)–ado
business custom–patronage
business exchange–bolsa
business getters–ads, drummers, salesmen, solicitors
business man (powerful)–tycoon
business management – intendence
business program–agenda
bustards (genus of)–otis
bustle–ado, agitation, commotion, fuss, stir, todo, tumult
bustle about–mull
busy – assiduous, attentive, diligent, employed, engaged, industrious, laborious, occupied, sedulous
busybody–meddler
but–mere
but (in music)–ma
butcher–slaughter, slay
butcher's tool–cleaver, knife, steel
butchery–carnage, massacre, murder, slaughter
butt–cart, flatfish, flounder, hinge, joint, jut, parapet,

pit, project, ram, run, target, thrust
butt (ax)–poll
butt of joke–it
butter (artificial)–margarin, magarine, oleomargarin
butter (roll of)–pat
butter (semi-fluid)–ghee
butter (small lump of)–pat
butter substitute–oleo, oleomargarin, oleomargarine, suine
buttercup fruit–achene
butterflies (expert on)–lepidopterist
butterflies (genus of) – lycaena
butterfly–io, satyr
butterfly (peacock)–io
butterfly larva (worm-like, elongated)–caterpillar
butterfly lily–sego
button (detachable)–stud
button (ornamental shirt)–stud
buttress–prop
buttress (against mole wall, arch.)–pile
buy back–redeem
buy freedom for–ransom
buyer–customer, purchaser, shopper
buzz–hum, rom
buzzard (honey)–pern
buzzard (turkey)–aura
by–ago, at, past, per
by birth–nee
by means of–per
by mouth–oral
by-product of smelting–slag
by reason–hereat
by slow stages–gradual
by the side of–beside, next
by this–hereby
by virtue of being–qua
by way of–via
by way of contemplation–retrospectively
by word of mouth–parol
bygone–olden, past
bypath–lane
Byron hero–Lara
bysen–example, pattern
byspell–parable, proverb
byway–alley, lane, path
Byzantine scepter–ferula

C

caama–asse, hartebeest

cabal – conspiracy, faction, intrigue, junto, party, plot, secret, tradition

caballero – cavalier, gentleman, knight

caballo–horse

cabbage – appropriate, cab, crib, pilfer, purloin

cabbage (curly leaf)–savoy

cabbage (genus of)–cos

cabbage (hardy)–kale

cabbage (headless)–kale

cabbage (variety of) – cole, colewort, kale, kohlrabi, savoy

cabbage (young)–colewort

cabbage broth–kale

cabbage daisy–globeflower

cabbage family–brassicaceae

cabbage salad–slaw

cabbage seed–colza

cabbage tree–angelin

cabby–cabman, dirty, sticky

caber–beam, pole, rafter

cabin–booth, coach, hovel, hut, shed

cabin bed (naut.)–berth

cabin car–caboose

cabinet – bahut, box, case, cupboard

cabinet (bric-a-brac) – atagere, etagere, whatnot

cabinet (liquor bottle)–cellaret

cabinet (open-shelved)–atagere, etagere, whatnot

cable (chain)–boom

cable (suspended for transporting materials)–ropeway

cable (telegraph)–wire

cable holder (naut.)–wildcat

cable lifter (naut.)–wildcat

cable post–bitt

cabling (arch.)–rudenture

cabochon–stone

caboodle–collection, kit, lot

caboose–galley

cabotin–actor, charlatan

cabree–pronghorn

cacao seeds (dry powder)–broma

cacao shell extract–martol

cachaca–rum

cache–hide, store, storehouse

cachet–seal, stamp

cachexia (cachexy)–malnutrition, wasting

cachoeira – cataract, waterfall

cachot–dungeon

cackle–babble, cank, chatter, clack, gabble, laugh

cacophonous – discordant, dissonant, jangling, raucous, strident, unmelodious

cactus (spineless)–mescal

cactus (spiny, tree-like) – cholla

cactus family plant–mescal

cadaver–corpse

cadaver (coll.)–stiff

cadaverous–gaunt, ghastly, haggard, pale

caddis worm–cadew

caddle–annoy, confuse, confusion, disarray, embarrassment, fuss, tease, trouble, worry

Caddoan Indian–Adai, Andarko, Eyeish, Hainai, Ioni, Nachitoch

caddow–coverlet, jackdaw, quilt

caddy–box, can, chest

cade–barrel, cask, indulged, keg, petted

cadence–lilt, rhythm

cadence (half) – demi-cadence

cadge–beg, hawk, peddle, sponge

cadger – carrier, dealer, hawker, huckster, packman, sponger

cadgy – cheerful, lustful, mirthful, wanton

Cadmus (pert. to)–Cadmean

Cadmus' daughter–Agave, Autonoe, Ino, Semele

Cadmus' father–Agenor

Cadmus' sister–Europa

Cadmus' wife–Harmonia

cadre – frame, framework, scheme

caduceus (caducei, pl.)–scepter, sceptre, staff, wand

caen stone–limestone

Caesar fiber (weed) – aramina

Caesar river (famed, he crossed)–Rubicon

Caesar's capital–Roma

Caesar's compatriots – Romans

Caesar's death city–Nolo

Caesar's fatal day–Ides

Caesar's native language – Latin

Caesar's sister–Atia

caesura – break, interval, pause

cafard–bigot, blues, depression, humbug, hypocrite

caffeine–theine

cafila–caravan

cag–insult, keg, offend

cage (hauling)–mew

cage (hawk's)–mew

Cain's brother–Abel, Pur

Cain's descendant–Lamech

caisson–box, chamber, chest, wagon

caitiff – base, captive, cowardly, despicable, mean, wicked, wretched

cajole – blandish, coax, delude, flatter, jolly, wheedle

cake – bake, block, crust, harden, lump, mass, solidify

cake (circular)–wafer

cake (corn)–pone

cake (custard)–eclair

cake (flat)–placent, placenta

cake (fourth part of thin)–farl, farle

cake (fried)–cruller

cake (frosted)–eclair

cake (kind of)–cimbal, ratafia, scone

cake (rich)–torte

cake (Scot., griddle)–bannock
cake (seed)–wig, wigg
cake (small, Eng.)–batty
cake (sweet, small)–bun
cake (tea)–scone
cake (thin)–scone, wafer
cake (thin, unleavened) – tortilla
cakes (corn)–pones
Calabar bean–eserine
calabash–gourd
calaboose–jail, prison
calamitous – adverse, afflictive, baleful, deplorable, dire, disastrous, distressful, evil, grievous, sad, tragic, tragical, unfortunate, woeful
calamity – adversity, affliction, blow, direfulness, disaster, distress, evil, fatality, ruin, unhappiness, wrack, wretchedness
calamity (sudden) – blow, catastrophe
calcaneum–heel
calcar–furnace, oven
calcareous deposit (travertine)–tufa
calcareous earth–marl
calcareous sinter–travertine
calcareous skeleton of anthozoan–coral
calcareous spar–calcite
calcitrant–recalcitrant, stubborn
calcium oxide–quicklime
calcium phosphate-fluoride–apatite
calcium sulphide–hepar
calcium sulphite–antichlor, antiseptic, disinfectant
calculate–aim, compute, determine, enumerate, estimate, figure, frame, number, rate, reckon, tell
calculating frame–abacus
Calcutta hemp–jute
caldron (cauldron) – boiler, kettle, pot, vat
Caledonia (New) bird–kagu
Caledonian–Scot, Scotsman
Caledonian (anc.)–Pict
calefy–heated, warm

calendar–almanac
calenture–ardor, fever, glow, passion, sunstroke
calepin–dictionary, lexicon
calf (motherless) – dogie, dogy
calf of leg (pert. to)–sural
calf's flesh–veal
calf's sweetbread–ris de veau
calfskin–kip
calfskin (untanned)–kip
Caliban's mother (witch) – Sycorax
caliber (calibre) – ability, bore, capacity, diameter
calico (East India)–sallo, salloo
calico block printing (stir up colors)–teer
calico horse–pinto
calico printing (in areas)–topical
calid–burning, hot, warm
Calif (fourth)–Ali
California (discoverer of Lower)–Cortez
California and Nevada lake –Tahoe
California big trees (English name)–Wellingtonia
California bird (humming) –calliope
California buckthorn–coffeeberry
California bulrush – sedge, tule
California fruit (cultivated) –kumquat
California Indian–Seri
California laurel – cajeput, cajuput
California mountain–Dana, Helena, Lowe, Shasta, Whitney
California oak–encina
California observatory–Lick, Mt. Wilson, Palomar
California river – Feather, Kern, King, Sacramento, Salinas, Russian
California rockfish – reina, rena
California shrub – manzanita, salal
California State motto–Eureka

California town–Asti, Fresno, Napa, Tracy
California tree (coniferous, tall)–torrey
California trees (English name)–Wellingtonia
caliph (calif) – Abu Bekr, Ali, caliphate, Imam, Omar, Othman
Caliph (fourth)–Ali
Caliph Ali's descendants – Alides
calk (calque)–copy
calk (sailor's slang)–sleep
call–appoint, assemble, collect, convene, convoke, cry, denominate, dub, muster, name, nominate, shout, style, summon, term, waken
call (brilliant trumpet)–fanfare
call (cattle)–sook
call (distress)–S.O.S.
call (drum, to arms)–rappel
call (elephant's)–trumpet
call (hog)–sook
call (naut.)–ahoy
call (sportsman's)–soho
call (stage trumpet, obs.)–sennet
call (trumpet)–fanfare, sennet
call attention to–remind
call back–recall, retract, revoke
call back to mind–recollect, remember
call by wrong name–misname
call down – invoke, reprimand
call down evil upon–execrate
call forth – elicit, evocate, evoke
call in question–challenge, impeach, impugn
call of triumph–aha
call out–evoke
call to action–rouse
call to arms–alarm, muster
call to attention–hip
call to mind–cite, recall, remember
call together–convoke, summon

callan (callant)–chap, customer, fellow
calle–street
called – named, termed, ycleped, yclept
called for–demanded
caller–visitor
callet–gossip, prostitute, rail, scold, trull, virago
callid–crafty, cunning
calligrapher – copyist, engrosser, penman
calling–business, career, circumstances, condition, employment, metier, occupation, outcry, profession, pursuit, summons, trade, undertaking, vocation
calling (special)–metier
calling hare–pika
calling out (old word)–gred
callous (to make)–sear
calloused–hardened, horny, indurated, obdurate, pachydermatous, unfeeling
callow–crude, green, immature, unformed, unsophisticated
calm – allay, appease, collected, compose, cool, dill, dispassionate, fair, imperturbable, peace, peaceful, phlegmatic, placate, placid, quiet, restful, sedate, serene, smooth, sober, soothe, steady, still, tranquil, undisturbed, unruffled
calm (Scot.)–mease, mees
calm (temporary)–lull
calmest–mildest
calmness–calm, equanimity, impassiveness, lull, peacefulness, placidity, poise, repose
calor – dolor, heat, rubor, tumor
caloric–heat
calorie (calory)–therm
calorie (great)–therm
calumniate–accuse, asperse, belie, libel, revile, slander, slur
calumniator–traducer
calumnious – abusive, de-

famatory, libelous, opprobrious
calumny–detraction, slander
Calvinism (where was taught)–Geneva
calyx (division of)–sepal
calyx (helmet-shaped part of)–galea
calyx leaf–sepal
calyx of flower–perianth
cam – askew, awry, crookedly, perverse, twisted
camalig–hut, storehouse
Cambodian religious spirit (dead friend)–Arac
came by–got
came into operation–pelota
came into view–appeared, emerged, loomed
came out into view – appeared, emerged, loomed
came to a halt – rested, stopped
came to rest–lit, sat
came together–bumped, collided, converged, joined, met
came upon–met
camel (Andean)–llama
camel (female)–naga
camel family animal–guanaco
camel's hair garment–aba
camel's hair shawl – Cashmere
camel's keeper (Israel)–obil
camel's thorn shrub (Arabic)–alhaj
camelopard–giraffe
Camelot's magician–Merlin
cameo stone–onyx
camera (part of) – finder, lens, shutter
cameriera – chambermaid, maid
cameriere–valet, waiter
Cameroon inhabitant–Sara
Cameroon Negro tribe–Abo
camino–journey, path, trail
camlet (angora goat, fine)–mohair
camp (soldier's, Anglo-Ind.) –campoo
camphor (Asarum)–asarone
camphorated tincture of opium–paregoric

camping places–etapes
campus (college)–quad
can–able, capable, competent
can (large oil)–oiler
can (slang)–discharge, dismiss, fire, jail
Canadian (slang)–Canuck
Canadian boat (flatbottomed)–bateau, bateaux (pl.)
Canadian capital–Ottawa
Canadian city – Banff, Calgary, Carstairs, Edmonton, Levis, Montreal, Ottawa (c.), Regina, Toronto, Vancouver, Victoria, Winnipeg
Canadian fur company employee–voyageur
Canadian gannet–margot
Canadian land tenure–roture
Canadian lynx–pishu
Canadian measure–chainon, minot, perch, pied, point, ton
Canadian mountain – Cascade, Gold, Laurentian, Logan, Notre Dame, Rockies, Shickshock, St. Elias
Canadian peninsula–Gaspe
Canadian poplar–liard
Canadian porcupine – cawquaw, urson
Canadian province–Alberta, British Columbia, Manitoba, New Brunswick, Northwest Territory, Nova Scotia, Ontario, Prince Edward Island, Quebec, Saskatchewan, Sorel, Yukon
Canadian province (abbr.)– Alta
Canadian river – Albany, Athabasca, Back, Churchill, Coppermine, Fraser, Gatineau, Great Bear, Great Fish, Great Slave, Mackenzie, Nelson, Ottawa, Peace, Richelieu, Saguenay, Saskatchewan, Skeena, St. Lawrence, St. Maurice, Stickeen, Trent

Canadian squaw–mahala
Canadian vehicle (two-wheeled)–calash, caleche
Canadian vest (woolen) – linder
Canadian weight–bag, cental, ton
canal – acequia, channel, drain, duct, pipe, tube, watercourse, waterspout
canal (brain)–iter
canal (natural passage) – meatus
canal connecting North Sea and Baltic Sea–Kiel
canal footpath–towpath
Canal Zone dam, locks, and town-Gatun
Canal Zone lake–Gatun
canard–hoax
Canary Island–Allegranza, Ferro, Fuerteventura, Gomero, Graciosa, Grand, Inferno, Lanzarote, Lobos, Palma, Roca, Rocca, Sta. Clara, Teneriffe
Canary Island city–Laguna, Santa Cruz (c.)
Canary Island commune - Icod
Canary Island measure - fanegada
Canary Island mountain–El Cumbre, Gran Canaria, Teneriffe
cancel–abolish, annul, blot, dele, delete, destroy, erase, obliterate, omit, recall, retract, revoke
cancion–lyric, song
Candia–Crete
candid–fair, frank, guileless, impartial, open, sincere, straightforward
candidate - applicant, aspirant
candidate (one who runs)–ran
candidate (winning)–electee
candidates (list of)–slate
candle–dip, taper
candle (desert) - ocatillo, ocotillo
candle (slender, wax, Fr.)–cierge
candle (small)–taper

candle (wax)–taper
candleholder – candlestick, sconce
candlelight – nightfall, twilight
candlelighter–acolyte, spill
candlenut tree–ama
candle receptacle–chandlery
candlestick (bracket)–sconce
candlestick (branched) – jesse
candlestick (church, large, branched)–jesse
candlestick (flat)–sconce
candlestick (hanging from ceiling)–chandelier
candlestick (large decorated)–flambeau
candlestick (large, ornamental)–candelabra
candlewick (charred part)–snuff
candor - frankness, outspokenness, unreserve
candy (made of nuts and sugar)–nougat
candy (on stick)–lollipop
candy (pulled sugar)–penide
candytuft–iberis
cane–beat, rod, staff, stick
cane (sugar, refuse)–bagasse
cane sugar–sucrose
cangle – dispute, quarrel, wrangle
canine–cur, dog, pup
canine (large) – mastiff, Newfoundland
canine (nondescript)–cur
canine tooth–laniary
cannibalism–anthropophagy
cannon (short)–mortar
cannon fire–barrage
cannon handle–anse
cannon muzzle plug–tampion
cannon part–rimbase
cannon part (forward) – chase
cannon shot (small)–grape
canoe–kayak, kiak, proa
canoe (bark)–cascara
canoe (crude)–dugout
canoe (dugout) - corial, pirogue, piroque (var.)
canoe (Hawaiian short broad)–waapa

canoe (large)–bungo
canoe (long dugout)–pambanmanche
canoe (Malayan outrigger)–proa
canoe (seagoing)–pahi
canoe (swift sailing)-proa
canoe (war)–proa
canon - code, constitution, decision, decree, law, model, regulation, rule
canon (enigmatical)–nodus
canonical hour–sext
canonized person–saint
canopy–cope, dais, tester
canopy (altar)–ciborium
canopy (bed)–ceil, tester
canopy (flat)–tester
canorous - euphoniously, melodious, sonorous
cant–argot, careen, chant, intonation, intone, jargon, lingo, pretense, sanctimoniousness, sing, slang, slope, snivel, tilt, tip
cant (popular)–slang
cant (slang)–jargon
cantabank–singer
cantankerous - contentious, crossgrained, malicious, perverse
cantata (idyllic or rustic)–pastoral, pastorale
cantata (pastoral)–serenata
cantata (sacred)–motet
cantation–enchantment, incantation, singing
canted (naut.)–alist
canter (easily)–lope
Canterbury archbishop - Cranmer
Canterbury archbishop (medieval)–Anselm
Canterbury gallop–aubin
canticle–hymn, ode, song
canticle (church)–Te Deum, venite
canticle (scripture)–ode
cantilena–graceful, legato
cantina–bag, canteen, pocket, pommel, saloon
cantle–corner, cornerpiece, nook, segment
canto–song, verse
cantor - leader, precentor, singer, soloist

cantoria–balcony, gallery
cantrip–charm, spell, trick
canty – cheerful, lively, sprightly
Canuck–Canadian
canvas–duck
canvas (covered with tar)–tarpaulin
canvas (waterproof)–tarpaulin
canvass–campaign, consider, examine, poll, solicit, study
canvass for votes–electioneer
canyon–chasm, gorge, gulch, ravine
canyon (mouth of)–abra
caoba – mahogany, muskwood
caoutchouc–rubber
caoutchouc (shrub-yielding)–ule
caoutchouc (source of)–ule
caoutchouc tree–rubber, ule
cap – beret, bonnet, coif, cover, dome, fez, hood, lid, taj, tam, tip, top
cap (blue)–Scot
cap (close-fitting)–coif
cap (dervish's)–atef, taj
cap (ecclesiastical, skull) – callot, calotte
cap (fur, tall round)–shtreimel
cap (ignition)–fuze
cap (knee)–patella
cap (military)–kepi, shako
cap (Oriental)–calpack
cap (priestly)–biretta, baret (var.)
cap (round, woolen)–boina
cap (Scot.)–tam, tamoshanter
cap (skull, felt)–pileus
cap covering (light cloth)–havelock
capa–cloak, mantle
capability–capacity
capability (power)–potency
capability of multiplying sounds–polyphony
capable – able, adept, apt, can, competent, expert, proficient, skilled
capable (most)–best

capable of being corrupted–taintable
capable of being cut–sectile
capable of being defended–tenable
capable of being definitely ascertained–determinable
capable of being drawn into wire–ductile, tensile
capable of being expressed–effable
capable of being extended–tensile
capable of being heard–audible
capable of being helped–tenable
capable of being maintained–tenable
capable of being proved–demonstrability, testable
capable of being regulated–controllable
capable of being separated–divisible
capable of being thrown–missile
capable of being touched–tangible
capable of being warded off–avertable, avertible
capable of carrying–portative
capable of combining with three molecules of monobasic acid–triacid
capable of cultivation–arable
capable of cutting wood (as an insect)–xylotomous
capable of extension–tensile
capable of flying–volant
capable of listening to reason–pervious
capable of living–viable
capable of living harmoniously–compatible
capable of resisting great strain–tough
capable of suffering–passible
capacious–ample, broad, considerable, extensive, full, large, roomy, spacious, wide
capacity–aptitude, capability, content, faculty, fit-

ness, power, skill, space, strength, talent
capacity for thought–intellect
capataz–boss, foreman
cape–cloak, headland, mantle, ness, point, ras
cape (clerical)–amice
cape (crocheted or knitted)–sontag
cape (ecclesiastical)–cappa
cape (headland)–ness, point
cape (hooded)–amice
cape (knitted)–sontag
cape (lace)–collaret, fichu
cape (papal, short)–orale
cape (woman's long fur)–pelerine
Cape anteater–aardvark
Cape armadillo–pangolin
Cape Cod turkey (humorous)–codfish
Cape Dutch–Afrikaans
Cape elk–eland
Cape gooseberry–poha
Cape lancewood–assagai
Cape merchant–supercargo
Cape of Good Hope discoverer–Diaz
Cape polecat–zoril
Cape Province negroid–Pondo, Xosa
Cape ruby–garnet, pyrope
Cape sheep–albatross
Cape Verde island–Sal
Cape Verde island native–Brava
Cape Verde Negro–Serer
caper–antic, dance, dido, frisk, frolic, gambol, prance, prank, romp
caper (coll.)–dido
caper about–cavort
caper family–capparidaceae
capercaillie–grouse
capercaillie grouse courtship performance–lek
capias (law)–process, writ
capillus–hair
capilotade–ragout, stew
capistrate–cowled, hooded
capital–chief, leading, main, major, paramount, preeminent, principal, prominent, rare, serious, vital, weighty

capital (anc.)–Roma

capital impairment–depletion

capital punishment–electrocution, hanging

capitalist–investor

capitano – captain, chief, headman

capitulate–fall, surrender

capocchia–fool, simpleton

caporal–overseer, tobacco

capot–cloak, overcoat, mantle

capped–crested, pileate

caprate–rutate

capric acid salt–rutate

caprice – crochet, fancy, freak, humor, inconsistent, kink, mood, quirk, vagary, whim, whimsey, whimsy

capricious–arbitrary, crotchety, erratic, fanciful, fantastic, fickle, fitful, humorous, inconstant, moody, unsteady, wayward

Capricorn–Goat

capsicum (fruit of)–chile

capstan bar–lever

capsule (flat form)–wafer

capsule (spore)–ascus, asci (pl.)

captain–chief, commander, headman, leader, master, skipper

captain (curling)–skip

captain of Hosts of Absalom –Amasa

captain's boat–gig

captious–carping, caviling, critical, faultfinding, hypercritical, severe

captious objection–cavil

captivate–bewitch, capture, charm, enamor, enamour, enchant, enrapture, enthrall, fascinate, infatuate, ravish, transport

captive–enamor, prisoner

captivity–confinement, duress, imprisonment, serfdom, servitude, slavery, subjection, thralldom

captor–catcher, taker

capture–apprehension, ar-

rest, bag, collar, detention, nab, seizure, take

capture again–retake, rewin

capture by force–raven

capuche–cowl, hood

Capuchin monkey–sai

car (army bantam, slang)–jeep

car (army command, slang) –jeep

car (drawn behind another) –trailer

car (mine)–tram

car (Scot.)–awkward, left-handed, perverse, sinister, wrong

car (sleeping)–Pullman

car (train, or crew)–caboose

car barn–depot

carabao–buffalo

caracol–snailflower

caract–charm, symbol

carafe–bottle

carafon–decanter

carapace–lorica

caravan station–serai

caravansary–hostelry, hotel, imaret, inn, serai, serais (pl.)

caravansary (Eastern)–serai

carbohydrate (common)–starch, sugar

carbohydrate (soluble, gummy)–dextrin

carbon (native, hexagonal crystals)–graphite

carbon (partially burned)–soot

carbon point (arc lamp)–crayon

carbonate (sodium)–salsoda

carbonate (sodium native)–natron

carbonate (white crystalline sodium)–trona

carborundum–abrasive

carcass–body, corpse

carcass (whale)–kreng

carcle–yodel

carcoon–clerk

card–menu, program

card (blank, wild, in card game)–mistigri, mistigris

card (old playing)–tarot

card as wool–rove

card combination (faro)–cathop

card drawn after top card (faro)–loser

card game–bank, cassino, cayenne, contract, cribbage, ecarte, faro, loo, masset, monte, ombre, pam, pedro, piquet, pitch, poker, rounce, rummy, skat, solitaire, solo, waist, whist

card game (Fr.)–baccara, baccarat

card game (like Napoleon)–pam

card game (old)–comet, hoc, loo, omber, pam, penneech, penneeck

card game (Spanish origin) –omber, ombre

card game (three-handed)–skat

card game (var.)–lus

card game bid–misere, slam

card of admission (free)–pass

card player (who cuts)–pone

card wool–comb, tum

card wool (preliminary)–toom

cards (three of same denomination)–tricon

cardinal number–eleven, primary, ten

cardinal point–east, north, south, west

Cardinal Wolsey's birthplace –Ipswich

cardinal's office–hat

cardinal's rank–hat

care–anxiety, cherish, concern, desire, fret, mind, solicitude, tend, wish, worry

care for–mind, nurse, relish, tend

careen–heel, keel, list, tip

career–vocation

career entrance–debut

careful–advertent, cautious, chary, circumspect, considerate, discreet, exact, gingerly, guarded, heedful, meticulous, painstaking, prudent, punctilious,

scrupulous, thoughtful, vigilant, wary
careful observer–student
carefully–painstaking
carefully wrought production–elaboration
carefulness–prudence
careless–heedless, inadvertent, inconsiderate, lax, negligent, nonchalant, remiss, slipshod, thoughtless, unheeding, unthinking
careless (culpably)–negligent
careless (utterly)–reckless
caress–bill, coddle, cosset, fondle, pat, pet, stroke
caressing–endearing, fondling
cargo discarded–jetsam
cargo stower–stevedore
Cariban Indian–Akawais, Aparais, Arara, Arecunas, Bakairis, Caribs, Chaymas, Cumanagotos, Macusis, Maquiritares, Oyanas, Tamanacos, Trios, Woyaways, Yaos
Caribbean bird–tody, todies (pl.)
caribou–reindeer
caricature–burlesque, cartoon, overdo, parody, travesty
caricature of a poem–parody
caricaturist (19th century)–Nast
carillon–bells, chimes
cark–burden, care, charge, heed, load, pains
carlot–boor, churl
Carmelite–friar, monk
carmen–incantation, poem, song
carmine–crimson, scarlet
carnage–butchery, massacre, slaughter
carnal–bodily, corporeal, earthly, fleshy, lewd
carnation–pink
carnation (yellow or white, with red band)–picotee
carnelian–sard
carnival–festival, merrymaking, revelry

carnivore–bear, cat, dog, lion, puma, seal, tiger
carnivore (civet-like)–genet, ichneumon
carnivore (female, rare)–bearess
carnivore (marine)–otter
carnivore (musteline)–marten, pekan
carnivore (nocturnal)–ratel
carnivore (old world)–genet
carnivore (plantigrade)–panda
carnivore (small)–genet
carnivore (weasel-like)–sable
carnivore (web-footed)–otter
carnivorous animal–bear, cat, civet, dog, lion, puma, seal, tiger, weasel
carnivorous mammal–lion, panda
carnivorous quadruped–badger
carol–lay, Noel, sing, song
caroled–sang
caroler–singer, yodler, yodlist
Caroline island–Yap
carom–bounce, ricochet
carousal–banquet, frolic, lark, orgy, revel, romp, shindy, spree, wassail
carouse–house, revel
carpellate strobiles–cones
carpels (coalescent mass of)–sorema
carpenter – cabinetmaker, framer, joiner
carpenter's machine–lathe, planer, shaper
carpenter's square–norma
carpenter's tool–hammer, level, plane, saw, square
carpet–mat, tapis
carpet design–medallion
carriage–air, bearing, demeanor, deportment, mien, shay
carriage (elevator)–car
carriage (four-wheeled)–omnibus
carriage (four-wheeled, covered)–landau

carriage (light)–dennet, gig, shay
carriage (light, four-wheeled)–phaeton, rockaway, surrey
carriage (light, low-wheeled)–calash, caleche
carriage (light, two-wheeled)–chaise, cisium, shay
carriage (Russian)–droshky
carriage (Russian, four-wheeled)–tarantas
carriage (small)–landaulet
carriage (small, one-horse)–cariole, dennet
carriage (two-wheeled)–carromata, chaise, gig, hansom, sulky, tilbury
carriage (two-wheeled, one-horse)–trap
carriage (type of)–phaeton
carried – borne, carted, lugged, toted, transported
carried away with delight–entranced
carried on–waged
carrier–bearer, drayman, messenger, porter, teamster
carrier (plague)–rat
carrier (staff)–macer
carriers of booty (arch.)–reaves
carries over–tides
carries with difficulty–lugs
carrion–carcass, corpse, corrupt, loathsome, rotten, vile
carrion buzzard–vulture
carrion fungus–stinkhorn
carrot (deadly)–drias
carrot family–ammaicea
carrots (glazed, in consommé)–nivernaise
carry–bear, bring, cart, convey, lug, take, tote, transfer, transmit, transport
carry across water–ferry
carry away–remove
carry away (as property)–eloign, eloin
carry into effect–effect, execute, perform
carry off booty (arch.)–reave

carry on–conduct, manage, prosecute, wage

carry on wind–waft

carry out–enrapture, execute, perform, ravish

carry the day–prevail, win

carry through–complete, sustain, transact

cart–carry, convey, dray, wagon

cart (farmer's)–morfrey, morphrey

cart (having wheels and seat for driver)–sulky

cart (Oriental)–araba

cart (racing)–sulky

cart (Russian)–telega

cart (two-wheeled)–sulky, tumbril

cart (two-wheeled, passenger)–reckla

cart horse (Scot. dial.)–cartaver

cart rope (short, Scot.)–wanty

cartage–drayage

carter–teamster

cartload–fother

carts (collectively)–wagonage

carte–chart, diagram, map, menu

cartel–agreement, challenge, defy, letter

Carthage (pert. to)–Punic

Carthaginian–Punic

Carthaginian citadel (anc.)–Bursa, Byrsa

Carthaginian foe–Cato

Carthaginian general–Hanno

Carthaginian language (anc.)–Punic

Carthaginian magistrate (chief)–Suffete

Carthaginian queen–Dido

cartilage (ossified)–bone

cartograph–chart, map

cartoonist (well-known)–Ding, Disney

carval–hymn

carve–cut, engrave, grave, hew

carved stone–cameo

carvel–jellyfish

carvene–dextrolimonene

carver of "The Thinker"–Rodin

carving (art of)–sculptor

carving (incised)–intaglio

casalty–casual, fickle, infirm, insecure, shaky, uncertain, unreliable

cascade–waterfall

case–box, cabinet, covering, cupboard, event, folio, instance, sheath

case (arrow)–quiver

case (cigar)–humidor

case (egg)–outheca

case (egg, zool.)–ovisac

case (fancy, for small articles)–etui, etwee

case (for sanctified relics)–apse

case (girdle)–inro

case (grammatical) – ablative, dative, nominative

case (grammatical, of direct address)–vocative

case (jewel)–tye

case (needle, etc.)–etui, etwee

case (paper)–binder, file, folio

case (pert. to)–casal

case (pistol)–holster

case (portable)–etui, etwee

case (rough seed)–burr

case (sheet music)–folio

case (slip for holding books)–forel

case (small)–etui, etwee

case (spore)–ascus, asci (pl.)

case (surgeon's instrument)–tweezer

case (wooden bed)–bunk

case divinity–casuistry

case history–record

case oil–kerosene

cases (explosive) – firecracker, petard

cash–capital, coin, currency, funds, money, specie

cash (U.S. slang)–kale, spondulics, spondulix

cashier–cassere, casseir, discharge, dismiss

casing (shell)–gaine

cask–barrel, bareca, butt, casket, casque, keg, tierce, tub, tun

cask (beer)–butt

cask (large)–tierce, tun

cask (liquid measure, abbr.)–TCS

cask (oil, stowed at ends of tiers, in whaling)–rier

cask (protuberant part)–bilge

cask (small)–keg, tub

cask (small, naut.)–bareca, bareka

cask (small oil)–rier

cask (whale oil)–rier

cask (wine)–tun

cask (wine, large)–pipe

cask part–stave

cask stave–lag

casket–box, cassette, chest, cist, coffer, coffin, tomb

casket (jewel)–tye

cassare–abate, annul, quash

cassava product–manioc

cassava root food–tapioca

cassena–yaupon

cassia (kind of)–senna

cassie–huisache

cassina–yaupon

cast–fling, heave, hurl, pitch, shed, sling, throw, toss

cast aside–discard, jilt, junk, reject, scrap, shed

cast away–dismiss, reject

cast down–abase, deject, demolish, depress, destroy, dispirit

cast lots (to)–cavel

cast off–molt, shed, unmoor, untie

cast out–eject

cast sidelong glances–leer

cast up–add, compute, reckon

castaway–derelict, outcast, reject, reprobate, shipwreck, stranded

castback–reversion

caste–breed, class, lineage, race, stock

caste (dairymen)–ahir

caste (priestly)–magi

caste of Hindu merchants–banian, banyan

caster–cruet, roller, vial, wheel

castigate–chastise, correct,

emend, punish, reprove, revise, strafe
castillo–castle, fort
casting (form for)–mold
casting (rough)–pig
castle–citadel, fort, fortification, fortress, rook, stronghold
castle tower–keep
castor oil bean protein–ricin
castor silk–eri, eria
Castor's brother (twin)–Pollux
Castor's mother–Leda
castrate–emasculate, eunuch, geld, prune, spay
castrated–gibbed
casual–chance, contingent, fortuitous, incidental, indifferent, occasional, random, stray, unforeseen, unpremeditated
casual observation–remark
casualities (unfortunate)–accidents
casualty–accident, chance, contingency, disaster, mischance, misfortune, mishap
casus–event, occasion
cat – grimalkin, leopard, lynx, puma, tiger, wildcat
cat (animal of family)–cheetah
cat (any)–felid
cat (breed of)–Angora, Maltese, Manx, Persian
cat (civet)–rasse
cat (genus of)–felis
cat (kind of)–alley, Angora, Maltese, Manx, Persian
cat (leopard-like) – ocelot, ounce
cat (musk)–civet
cat (old female)–grimalkin
cat (Pampas)–pajero
cat (spotted)–ocelot
cat (wild)–catamount, eyra, ocelot, serval
cat's cradle–ribwort
cat's cradle game (Hawaiian)–hei
cat's cry–mew, miaou, miaow, miau, miaul
cat's paw–dupe, tool
catalepsy–trance

catalogue–enumeration, index, list, record, schedule
catamaran–float, raft
catapult (military, anc.)–onager
cataract–cachoeira, waterfall
cataria–catnip
catarrh–pose
catarrh cure–cubeb
catasta – scaffold, stage, stocks
catastrophe – denouement, disaster
catastrophe (overwhelming)–cataclysm, disaster
catastrophic – cataclysmatic
catch–attract, capture, draw, engage, entrap, hold, hook, intercept, nab, overtake, snare, trap
catch (clock control)–detent
catch (naut.)–ketch
catch in trap–ensnare
catch sight of–descry, espy
catch suddenly (coll.)–nab
catch up with–overtake
catchword–cue, phrase, slogan
cate–dainties, delicacies, provisions, viands
catechu (product similar to)–kino
categorical–absolute, direct, explicit, unqualified
category–class, denomination, division, family, genre, genus, specie
catena–chain
catena (small)–chainlet
cater–pander, serve
cater to degrading or base desires–pander
caterpillar–erucae
caterpillar (South African)–risper
catface–scar
catfish–hassar
catfish (electric)–raad
cathedral–fane
cathedral chapter (member of)–capitular
cathedral church–dom
cathedral passage (to transept)–slype
cathode–electrode

catholic – ecumenical, general, universal
cation–ion
catkin–ament, amenta (pl.)
catlike – feline, noiseless, stealthy
catmint–catnep, catnip, nep
catnip–catnep, nep
Catoism–austerity, harshness
catstep–corbiestep
cattail–ament, catkin
cattail (narrow-leaved)–reree
cattail (used by Maoris for roof thatching)–raupo
cattail family–typhaceae
cattle–asses, goats, horses, kine, mules, neat, sheep, swine
cattle (breed of)–Devon, Durham, Guernsey, Hereford, Holstein, Jersey, Longhorn
cattle (breed of dwarf)–Niata
cattle (collection of)–drove, herd
cattle (dwarf)–niatas
cattle (dwarf, var.)–nata
cattle (Irish, small, black)–Kerries
cattle assemblage – drove, herd
cattle dealer–drover
cattle driver–drover
cattle herder–cowboy
cattle plague–rinderpest
cattle stealer–abigeus
cattle thief–rustler
catwort–catnip
cauboge–boor, bumpkin
Caucasian and Negro blooded person–mulatto, mulatta (fem.)
Caucasian goat–tur
Caucasian language (north)–Avar
Caucasian race (member of)–Arya, Semite
Caucasian tribe–Pshav
Caucasian wild goat–tur
Caucasus dialect–andi
Caucasus Georgian–Svan
cauch–mess
cauchemar–nightmare

caudal appendage–tail
caught–cornered, treed (*see* catch)
caught sight of–descried
cauk–chalk, limestone
caulked (slightly, naut.)–chinsed
cause–agent, breed, create, induce, motive, occasion, originate, produce, provoke, reason
cause (most efficient)–mainspring
cause it to be done (Lat.)–fieri facias
cause mental irritation–rankle
cause of ruin–bane
cause of suffering–painful
cause to be loved–endear
cause to be taken–send
cause to burst forth–erupt
cause to buy high and sell low–whipsaw
cause to coagulate–curd
cause to contract unevenly–pucker
cause to fall–overthrow
cause to float gently–waft
cause to go–send
cause to heel over–careen
cause to move faster–accelerate
cause to remember–remind
cause to revolve–trundle
cause to revolve (Scot.)–tirl
cause to shake–jar
cause to stand–erect
cause to stand out–emboss
cause to stick–mire
cause to take opposite place–counterchange
cause to take root–radicate
caused by animal food–creatic
caused by earthquake–seismal, seismic
causerie–chat, conversation, discussion, talk
causes to face East–Orients
causeway–dike
causey–bank, dam, mound
causing destruction–fatal
causing emotion–emotive
causing feeling–emotive

causing forgetfulness – nepenthean
causing laughter–risorial
causing motion–motile
causing pain–bitter
causing privation–privative
caustic–acrid, biting, bitter, cutting, erodent, mordant, pungent, satirical, severe, sharp, stinging, tart
caustic agent–erodent
caustic exposure to ridicule–satire
caustic solution (alkali)–lye
cautelous–cautious, crafty, deceitful, prudent, wary, wily
cauterize–burn, sear
cautery–burning, searer, searing
caution–admonition, advice, anxiety, care, caveat, chariness, circumspection, forecast, forethought, heed, providence, prudence, vigilance, warn, warning, watchfulness
cautious–careful, chary, circumspect, fabian, prudent, wary
cautious (more)–warier
cautious of danger–wary
cautiously–gingerly
cavalcade–march, procession, raid, ride
cavalier – escort, gallant, knight, rider, soldier
Cavalleria Rusticana heroine –Lola
cavalry–horsemen, horses, knighthood
cavalry horse (light)–lancer
cavalry man – dragoon, lancer, trooper
cavalry soldier–dragoon, lancer, trooper
cavalry unit–troop
cavalry weapon–lance, saber
cave–cavern, den, grotto, speos
cave (animal's)–lair
cave (arch.)–antre
cavern–cave, den, grot, grotto
caviar–roe

caviar (sort of)–garum
cavil–cark, carp, criticise, criticize, haggle, marl, quibble
caviler–critic
cavities – antra, antrum (sing.), aulae, aula (sing.)
cavities in bedrock–geodes
cavity–antrum, antra (pl.), hole, pit, sac, sinus
cavity (anatomy)–fossa, fossae (pl.)
cavity (auricular)–atrium, atria (pl.)
cavity (biol.)–lumen
cavity (bone)–antrum, antra (pl.)
cavity (crystal-lined, stone)–geode
cavity (ear, spiral)–cochlea
cavity (gun)–bore
cavity (heart)–atrium, atria (pl.)
cavity (lode, small, unfilled) –vug, vugg, vugh
cavity (sac-like)–bursa
cavity (small)–areole
cavity (small, unfilled in mineral)–vug, vugg, vugh
cavity lined with crystal (pert. to)–geodic
cavity side–wall
cavort–caper, curvet, gambol, prance
cavy–agouti, capybara, guinea pig, paca, rodent
cay–inlet, key
cease–desist, discontinue, end, intermit, pause, quit, refrain, stop
cease (naut.)–avast
cease voluntarily from introducing evidence (law) –rest
ceased from work–rested
ceaseless–incessant, unceasing
ceases to please–palls
ceasing of liability–cesser
Cebine monkey–sai
Cebu hemp–manila
cecidium–gall
cecils–croquettes
cecity–blindness
Cecrops' daughter–Aglauros, Herse

cedar (American red)–savin
cedar (red)–savin, savine
cedar camphor–cedrol
cedar green–cedre
cedar moss–hornwort
cede–grant, surrender, yield
cedrate (cedrat)–citron
cedula–schedule
ceil–line, overlay, wainscot
ceiling–covering, curtain, lining, screen
ceiling (mine)–astel
ceiling (semicircular room)–semidome
ceiling covering–calcimine, kalsomine
Celebes bovine–anoa
Celebes ox–anoa
Celebes oxen (like)–anoine
Celebes pagan people–toradja, toraja
celebrate – commemorate, keep, observe, revel, solemnize
celebrated in poetry–sing
celebrated–distingue, distinguished, famous, feasted, illustrious, noted, observed, renowned, solemnized
celebration–fete
celebration (memorial)–commemoration
celebrity–celebration, fame, renown, solemnization
celerity–haste, quickness, speed, swiftness, velocity
celerity (with)–rapidly
celery (wild form)–smallage
celery family–ammiaceae
celestial–Chinese, ethereal, heavenly, uranic
celestial beings–angels, cherubs, seraphs
celestial body–comet, nebula, planet, star
celestial body of self-luminous gas–nebula
celestial visitor–comet
celibate–bachelor, single, spinster, unmarried
cell–cytode
cell (church)–crypt
cell (honeycomb)–alveola, alveolus, alveoli (pl.)
cell (nerve)–neurone

cell (nucleated egg)–ovum, ova (pl.)
cell (plant seed)–cyst
cell (thread)–cnida, cnidae (pl.)
cell (underground)–dungeon
cell structural unit–energid
cella–naos
cellulose (elastic)–rayon
celosia (feathered)–heatherdell
Celt–Gael
Celtic dialect–Manx
Celtic divinity–Taranis
Celtic foot soldier–kern
Celtic god (sea)–Ler, Llyr
Celtic head of family–coarb
Celtic language–Erse, Gaelic, Irish
Celtic minstrel–bard
Celtic neptune–Ler, Leir (var.)
Celtic peasant–kern
Celtic priest (anc.)–Druid
Celtic sea god–Ler, Llyr
Celts (pert. to)–Erse
celure–canopy, hanging
cembalo–dulcimer
cement–cohere, glue, mortar, stick, unite
cement (infusible substance)–lute
cement (metal)–solder
cement (pasty)–mastic
cement (quick-drying) – mastic
cement window glass–putty, putties (pl.)
cemetery–catacomb, graveyard, necropolis
cenobite–essene
censorious–captious, severe
censurable–blamable, reprehensible
censure–accuse, blame, chasten, condemn, inveigh, reprehension, reprimand, reproach, reprove, slate
censure (harshly)–flay
censured (not)–unblamed
census taker–enumerator
cent (one-tenth of)–mill
centaur (bull's head)–bucentaur

centaur (killed by Hercules)–Nessus
Centennial State–Colorado
center–cor, core, heart, hub, middle, midst
center (shipping)–seaport
center of archery target–clout
center of interest–focus, foci (pl.)
center of nervous system–brain
center of sail–bunt
center of target–eye
centerpiece (table decoration)–epergne
central–basic, capital, equidistant, focal, middle, pivotal, primary, prime
Central American bird–jacamar, puffbird
Central American boat (fishing)–cayuco
Central American canoe (long, flatbottom)–pitpan
Central American capital–Belize
Central American city–Panama
Central American country–Panama
Central American dugout (for fishing)–cayuco
Central American Indian–Carib, Maya
Central American measure–cantaro
Central American monkey (howling)–mono
Central American republic–Costa Rica, Guatemala, Honduras, Nicaragua, Panama, Salvador
Central American rodent–paca
Central American snake (largest, venomous) – bushmaster
Central American stockade–boma
Central American tree–ebo, eboe
Central American tree (large, evergreen)–sapodilla

Central American tree (rubber)–ule
Central American tree (timber)–amate
Central American village–boma
Central American weight–libra
Central Asia blizzard–buran
Central Asia dung (dry camel, cattle, sheep, etc.)–argal, argol, argul
Central Asia gazelle–ahu
Central Asia river–Ili
Central Asia wild horse–tarpan
central cylinder (stem and roots)–stele
Central European–Serb
central line (pert. to)–axile
central mass (pert. to)–nuclear
central part–core, focal, solar
central part (denoting)–mid
central point–focus, foci (pl.)
central point (of matter)–nucleus
central point (pert. to)–focal
central square–agora
Central State–Kansas
centric–central, cylindrical, middle, terete
century–age
century plant–agave, aloe
century plant fiber–pita
ceorl–churl, freeman, villein
cepa–onion
cephalopod (eight-armed)–octopus
ceramics–pottery, tiles
ceratoid–hornlike, horn-shaped, horny
cere–anoint, wax, wrap
cereal–corn, maize, oats, rice, rye, spelt, wheat
cereal (coarse)–bran
cereal coating–bran
cereal grass–barley, grain, oat, ragi, rye, wheat
cereal grass disease–smut
cereal plants–grain
cereal spike–ear
ceremonial – conventional, formal, precise, prim, punctilious, stiff, studied
ceremonial post–totem

ceremonial splendor–pageantry
ceremonious–formal, precise
ceremony – observance, pomp, rite, ritual, show, solemnity
certain–confident, incontrovertible, indubious, plain, positive, sure, undeniable, undoubted, undoubting, unquestionable
certainly–amen
certainty–assurance, inevitability, pledge, surety
certificate (medical, for ill student)–aegrotat
certificate (money owed)–debenture
certificate (sanctioning vessel's cargo)–navicert
certificates (stock)–scrip
certification – attestation, proof
certify–attest, verify
certify under oath–attest
certifying clause of an affidavit–jurat
cervine–deerlike
cess–assess, bog, cede, surrender, tax, yield
cessation – discontinuance, intermission, interruption, interval, letup, lull, pause, recess, remission, respite, rest, stay, surcease
cessation (temporary)–interruption
cessation (temporary, of storm, or wind)–lull
cessation of arms–armistice, truce
cessation of being–desition
cetacea–dolphins, grampus, orc, orca, porpoises, whales
cetacean (blind)–susu
cetacean (dolphin-like)–inia
cetaceans (genus of dolphin-like)–inia
cete–cetacea, whale
cetus star–Mira
Ceylon canoe (sailing)–balsa
Ceylon capital–Colombo
Ceylon city–Colombo
Ceylon coin–cent (cop.)

Ceylon fishing boat–dhoni, done, doney, doni
Ceylon garment–sarong
Ceylon gooseberry–ketembilla
Ceylon Isle (anc. Greek name)–Taprobane
Ceylon monkey–rillow
Ceylon monkey (toque)–rilawa
Ceylon moss – agar-agar, alga, gulaman
Ceylon moss substance–agar
Ceylon oak–kusam
Ceylon palm–talipot
Ceylon people (one of)–Vedda
Ceylon rat–bandicoot
Ceylon rose–oleander
Ceylon sea moss substance–agar, agar-agar
Ceylon seaport–Galle
Ceylon tea–pekoe
Ceylon trading craft–dhoni, done, doney, doni
Ceylon tree–doon, tala
Ceylon vessel (coastal)–dhoni, done, doney, doni
chack–bite, clack, snack, snap, wheatear
chaetopod larva–atrocha
chafe–abrade, annoy, banter, excite, fret, gall, grind, harass, inflame, irk, rub, vex
chaff–banter, glume, husks, raillery, ridicule, straw, tailing
chaff (like bract)–palea
chaff (Scot.)–caff
chaff (wheat)–bran
chaffer–bargain, buying, haggle, market, selling, traffic
chafing dish–cresset
chagrin – mortification, troubles, vexation
chain–bind, bond, catena, fasten, fetter, secure, tether
chain (endless)–creeper
chain (large, strong)–cable
chain (mountain)–range, Rocky, Sierras
chain (neck, twisted)–torc
chain (obs.)–tew

chain (of circumstances)–catena

chain cable–boom

chain grab (naut.)–wildcat

chain-like–catenate

chain of fortifications–contravallation

chain of rocks (near surface) reef

chain reasoning–sorites

chain syllogism–sorites

chair–seat

chair (back of)–splat

chair (easy)–morris, rocker

chair (middle part of back) –splats

chair (portable)–sedan

chair (regal)–throne

chair cover–tidy

chair of state–throne

chairman of town meeting–moderator

chairman's mallet–gavel

chairwarmer–loafer

chalcedony–agate, carnelian, chrysoprase, onyx, opal

chalcedony (dark red)–sard

chalcedony (green)–jasper

chalcedony (kind of)–agate, carnelian, chrysoprase, onyx, opal, sard

chalcedony (yellow variety) –opaline

chalcedony in parallel layers –onyx

Chaldean city–Ur

Chaldean measure–artaba, cane, foot, gariba, ghalva, makuk, mansion, qasab

chalice–ama, cup, goblet, grail

chalice (broad)–grail

chalice cover–pall

chalk–account, blanch, bleach, crayon, credit, pale, reckoning, score, tick, whiten

chalker–milkman

challenge–accusation, claim, controvert, dare, defy, demand, gage, query, reproach

chamber–bedroom, hall, room

chamber (annealing)–leer

chamber (bombproof)–casemate

chamber (earthen)–cave

chamber (harem)–oda

chamber (heart)–auricle, ventricle

chamber (king's private audience)–camarilla

chamber (Pueblo ceremonial)–Kiva

chamber (small)–loculus

chambers (solicitor's)–inns

champagne (Edwardian slang)–boy

champion – combatant, fighter, unexcelled

champion (Christian legendary)–Cid

champion (distinguished)–Paladin

champleve–enamel

chance–die, fate, hap, happen, lot, probability, risk

chance (by)–haply

chance (even)–tossup

chancel (inner part of early church)–bema

chancel seat–sedile, sedilia (pl.)

chancery petitioner–relator

chances of success–odds

chandler–candlestick, chandelier

change–alter, amend, break, convert, diversification, diversity, metamorphosis, mutate, shift, transfer, transmute, turn, vary, veer

change (music)–muta

change color–blush, dye, redden

change for the better–revise

changes from past evil–repent

change in course–sheer, veer

change of direction–veer

change of life–menopause

change of order–rearrangement

change or pervert (misleading)–garble

change order of–transpose

change the form of–transhape, transshape

changeable–capricious, er-

ratic, fickle, inconstant, mobile, mutable, protean, unsettled, unstable, variable, volatile

changeable in form–metabolic

changed – metamorphosis, mutate

changed state–transmutation

changed the seating–reseated

changed within limits–ranged, varied

changeling–idiot, imbecile, oaf, renegade, simpleton, turncoat, waverer

changes (plant formation)–seres

changes place–moves

changing pattern and color –kaleidoscopic

channel–canal, ditch, drain, flute, groove, gutter, river, vein

channel (artificial)–canal, drainer, gat, sluice

channel (artificial, Eng.)–leat

channel (bodily)–cava

channel (Eng., arch.)–leat

channel (from shore inland) –gat

channel (great)–artery

channel (inclined, water)–flume

channel (metal, pouring into mold)–gate

channel (river)–alveus, alvei (pl.), bed

channel (ship's)–gat

channel (shore to island)–gat

channel (water, below mill wheel)–tailrace

channel in which tide sets–tideway

Channel Island–Guernsey

Channel Islands measure–cabot, cade

channer–grumble, mutter, scold

chant–intone, sing, warble

chanter–cantor, chorister, singer, songster

chanter (rare)–entoner

chanteuse–singer
chanticleer–cock, rooster
chantier–hut, shanty
chaos–abyss, chasm, confusion, disorder, gulf
Chaos' daughter–Nyx
Chaos' son–Erebus
chap–barter, boy, buy, buyer, chapman, chink, cleft, crack, customer, fellow, man, trade, youth
chap (queer, slang)–galoot
chapeau–beret, hat
chapel–cape, cloak, cope, cowl, hood, reliquary
chapel (monumental, church)–sacellum
chapel (private)–oratory
chapel (seaman's)–bethel
chaperon (Span.)–duenna
chaplet–anadem, garland, necklace, wreath
chappow–foray, raid
chapter (cathedral, member of)–capitular
chapter member–capitular
chapter of Koran–Sura
chaptrel–impost
char–burn, scorch
character–disposition, mark, nature, role, sign, symbol
character (alphabetical)–letter
character (Arthurian legend)–Elaine
character (assumed)–role
character (bad, Fr.)–drole
character (chief)–hero, star
character (fairie queen)–Una, Amoret
character (fundamental)–nature
character (hebraic)–Tav
character (intrinsic)–nature
character (musical)–bar, clef, rest
character (musical, anc.)–neume
character (real)–essence
character (to impart)–tone
character of people (distinguishing)–ethos
characteristic–attribute, distinctive, feature, impress, lineament, mark, peculiar, quality, symbolic, trait, typical
characteristic (peculiar or individual)–idiopathy
characteristic of descent–racial
characteristic spirit (of people or community)–ethos
characteristically – distinctively
characteristics (distinguishing)–stripes
characterization – representation, role
characterize–delineate, designate, engrave, imprint, inscribe, represent
characterized by cruelty–neronic
characterized by exact thinking–ratiocinative
characterized by melody–ariose
characterized by pompous style–grandiloquent
characterized by precautions for exclusion of bacteria–aseptic
characterized by severe abstinence–ascetic
characterizing man–human
characterless–inane
charcoal – blacken, boneblack
charge–accusation, accuse, allege, arraignment, assault, attack, bill, command, concern, cost, custody, debit, expense, fee, impute, injunction, instruction, keeping, load, management, mandate, onset, onus, order, rate, responsibility, ward
charge (customary)–dues
charge (depth)–mine
charge (hauling)–towage, drayage, cartage
charge (railway freight)–haulage
charge again–reload
charge against property–lien
charge for use of road–toll
charge paid in addition to freight–primage

charge with a crime–accuse, impeach, indict
charge with crime–incriminate
charge with debt–debit
charge with fault–accuse
charge with gas–aerate
charge with offense–accuse
charged with electricity–live
charged with high emotion –tense
charger–accuser, horse, steed
charges (law)–costs, fees, retainers
charges (legal)–dues, fees
charily–carefully, cautiously, frugally
chariness–caution, frugality, heedfulness, sparingness
chariot–car, cart, vehicle, wagon
chariot (anc., two-horse)–biga
chariot (anc., two-wheeled, Roman)–essed, esseda, essede
chariot (poetic)–wain
chariot (war)–essed, esseda, essede
charitable–beneficient, benevolent, compassionate, forgiving, indulgent, kind, kindly, lenient, liberal, philanthropic
charity–alms, beneficence, benevolence, dole, largess, lenience, liberality, philanthropy, tenderness
charity (model of)–Samaritan
charity dispenser (official)–almoner
charlatan – faker, impostor, mountebank, pretender, quack
charlatan (medical)–medicaster
charlatanic–empiric, empirical, pretentious, quackish
Charlemagne (peer of)–Paladin
Charles I coin–carolus, caroli (pl.)
charlet–custard
charm – agreeable, allure,

amulet, attraction, beguile, captivate, conjuration, delight, enamor, enamour, enchant, entice, entrance, fascinate, glamour, grace, obi, spell

charm (beetle-like)–scarab

charming–winsome

chart–map, plot

charter–hire

chary–frugal, skimpy

Charybdis whirlpool rock–Scylla

chase–follow, hunt, ornament, pursue, pursuit

chased away–driven, routed

chased up a tree–trunk

chasm–abyss, breach, canyon, crevasse, fissure, gap, gulf, hiatus, rift

chasse–dismiss, reliquary, shrine

chasseur–hunter, huntsman

chaste–continent, immaculate, innocent, undefiled, virtuous

chasten–discipline, punish, rate, refine, smote

chastise–amend, correct, punish, rebuke, reprove, scold

chastisement – discipline, punishment

chastity–purity, virtue

chat–babble, chatter, gabble, gibber, jabber, prate, prattle

chat (friendly)–coze

Chateaubriand's novel–Atala

chatelaine–clasp, etui, hook, pin, purse, watch

chattel–goods, livestock, money, principal, property

chattel (distraint of)–naam

chattels (portable)–goods, wares

chatter–clack, gab, jabber, prate, prattle

chatterbox–mag, piet

Chaucer's Canterbury Tales inn–Tabard

Chaucer's Knight's Tale character–Palamon

cheap sport (slang)–piker

cheaper–depreciated, inferior

cheaply splendid–tinny

cheat–artifice, bamboozle, bilk, cozen, deceit, deceive, defraud, delude, delusion, do, fake, finesse, fleece, fob, guile, gull, hinder, hoax, humbug, illude, liar, overreach, rook, sell, sharper, stratagem, swindle, victimize

cheat (coll.)–bam

check–balk, bridle, curb, damp, delay, impede, inhibit, limit, nip, oppose, rebuff, rein, repel, repress, stem, stop, tally

check (coll.)–tab

check (sharply)–nip

check development of–stunt

check to effect of poison–antidote

checked by fear or danger–daunted

checker opening–dyke

checker pattern squares–panes

checkered–diversified, plaid, tesserated, variegated

checkered cloth–tartan

checkers (game of)–drafts, draughts

checkers (in Holland)–damrod

checkerwork inlay–mosaic

checking device–detent, register

cheek (coll.)–gall, nerve

cheek (pert. to)–malar

cheek (the)–gena

cheekbone–malar

cheer–animate, applaud, console, elate, encourage, exhilarate, gladden, hearten, hurrah, huzza, huzzah, inspirit, jollity, merriment, rah, refresh, vivacity, yell

cheer (burst of)–salvo

cheer (var.)–hurra

cheer up–solace

cheerful–blithe, contented, genial, hearty, lightsome, rosy

cheerful (coll.)–peart

cheerful (Scot.)–gleg

cheerful song–lilt

cheerfulness–cheer, exhilaration, gaiety, gladness, glee, hilarity, jollity, joy, merriment, mirth

cheerless–cold, dejected, disconsolate, dismal, dispiriting, dreary, forlorn, gloomy, melancholy, sad

cheerless (poetic)–drear

cheery – bright, cheerful, cheering, gay, gaysome, lively

cheese (cream)–brie

cheese (Fr.)–brie

cheese (kind of)–American, barrie, brie, camembert, cheddar, cream, edam, jack, Swiss

cheese (Normandy, small)–angelot

cheese (pressed)–edam

cheese (whey)–zieger, ziga

cheese dish–rarebit, souffle

chelonian–tortoise, turtle

chemical–acid

chemical (used in photography)–toner

chemical analysis–assay

chemical compound–amide, ester, imine, metamer

chemical compound (hypothetical)–penthiophene

chemical compound (white, colorless)–purin

chemical compounds (series of)–toluid

chemical products of organs–hormones

chemical salt–sal

chemical strength standard–titer

chemical substance–linin

chemical suffix–ac, ane, ene, ile, ine, ol, ole, ose, osan

chemical symbol–see element (chemical)

chemical vessel–aludel

chemical washing–eluate

chemist's pot (vessel, pear-shaped)–aludel

chemist's shop–drugstore

cherish–caress, comfort, encourage, entertain, faddle, fondle, foster, hug, nour-

ish, nurture, pet, support, treasure
cherish as sacred–enshrine
cherished–dear, faddled
cherries (kind of)–bigarreau
cherries (sour)–egriots
cherry–oxheart
cherry (dark red)–morello
cherry (wild black, source of maraschino)–marasca
cherry-colored–cerise
cherry finch–hawfinch
cherry holly–islay
cherry orange–kumquat
Chesapeake Cape–Charles
chess draw game–stalemate
chess king position (when unable to move safely)–stalemate
chess move–gambit
chess opening–debut, gambit
chess piece–bishop, castle, king, man, queen, rook
chest–bahut, box, breast, cist, coffer, coffin
chest (ammunition)–caisson
chest (sacred)–arca, ark
chest (sepulchral terra cotta) –larnax
chest (small)–cajeta
chest front–breast
Chester, England (pert. to)– Cestrian
chesterfield–davenport, divan, overcoat, sofa
chestnut–joke, rata
chestnut (horse)–buckeye
chestnut (water)–trapa
chestnut and gray colored– roan
chestnut bay–roan
chetif–mean, miserable, paltry, sordid
chevalier–cavalier, gallant, horseman, knight
chevron–beam, glove, rafter
chevron (army slang)– gravystain
chevron (soldier slang)– stripe
chevrotain–deerlet, napu
chevy–chase, flight, hunt
chew–bite, cud, gnaw, masticate, munch, quid
chew deliberately–munch

chiaus–cheat, messenger, sergeant, swindler
chib–language, tongue
chic–smart, stylish, trig, trim
chick pea–chich, cicer, garvanzo, gram
chicken–broiler, chick, cock, fowl, hen, poult, pullet, rooster
chicken (large, roasting)– capon
chicken (male)–capon, cock, rooster
chicken (young)–cockerel, deedy, poult, pullet
chickenhearted – cowardly, timid
chicken plover–turnstone
chicory family–cichoriaceae
chicory-like herb–endive
chide–berate, blame, censure, rate, rebuke, reproach, reprove, scold
chief–aga, agha, arch, first, head, leader, main, major, principal, prominent, primal, rais, reis
chief (American Indian)– sachem
chief (American Indian tribe)–Sagamore
chief (Chinook jargon)– tyee
chief (Cossack)–ataman, hetman
chief (Oriental)–kahn
chief (school, Scot.)–dux
chief actor–hero, protagonist, star
chief character–hero, lead, star
chief executive officer–governor, mayor, president
chief of jinns (myth.)–eblis
chief of the fairies–Puck
chief part–pith
chiffonier – cabinet, commode
child–baby, fetus, infant
child (foster)–stepson
child (foster, obs.)–nurry
child (homeless)–waif
child (lively)–tike, tyke
child (mischievous) – imp, tike, tyke

child (mulatto's and white's)–quadroon
child (parentless)–orphan
child (perverse)–imp
child (Scot.)–bairn, bairnly
child (sent out of London)– evacuee, vackie (slang)
child (small)–tad, tot
child (sportive)–elfin
child (Tagalog)–bata
child (winged)–cherub
child (young)–baby, infant, nestler
child study–pedology, paedology
child's cry–snivel
child's game (Eng.)–tig
childish – kiddish, kidlike, kittenish, naive, puerile, silly, simple, unmanly
childish (coll.)–kittenish
children (mischievous)– imps, tikes, tykes
children (precocious)–brats
children (rude)–brats
children (stray)–waifs
children (Tagalog)–Anacs, batas
Children of God–elect
children's disease (science of)–pediatrics, paediatrics
children's tender–nursemaid
Chilean and Peruvian wind (southerly)–sures
Chilean city–Arauco, Caldera, Cobija, Concepcion, Copiapo, Coquimbo, Santiago (c.), Serena, Valdivia, Valparaiso
Chilean clover–alfalfa
Chilean coin–condor (g.), libra (g.), peso (s.)
Chilean coin (gold, former) –escudo
Chilean desert–Atacama
Chilean Indian–Ona
Chilean measure–cuadra, fanega, legua, linea, vara
Chilean mineralogist–Domeyko
Chilean mountains–Andes
Chilean proletariat–roto
Chilean province – Atacama
Chilean river–Biobio, Chuapa, Illapel, Itata, Loa, Lontue, Maule, Valdivia

Chilean (north) river–Loa
Chilean rodent–chinchilla
Chilean seaport–Arica
Chilean shrub–pepino
Chilean tree (timber)–pelu, rauli
Chilean weight–grano, libra, quintal
Chilean workman–rotos
chill–ague, cold, coldness, ice
chimed–pealed, rang
chimerical – delusive, fanciful, fantastic, imaginary, unfounded, vain
chimes–bells
chimney–flue, smokestack, stack
chimney corner–inglenook
chimney part–flue
chin (anat.)–mentum, menta (pl.)
china–crockery, earthenware, pottery
China (old name)–Cathay
china (translucent)–porcelain
China Sea island–Hainan
chine – backbone, back, chink, cleave, crack, crest, crevice, fissure, ridge, spine
Chinese–Sangley, sinic, sinico
Chinese (comb. form used to denote)–Sino
Chinese (prefix)–sinic, sino
Chinese (slang)–Chink
Chinese aboriginal people–Miao, Miaotse, Miaotze
Chinese alloy (nickel, zinc, and copper)–packtong, paktong
Chinese bean–cowpea, soy
Chinese boat (small)–sampan
Chinese Buddha (name of)–Fo, Foh
Chinese cabbage–pakchoi
Chinese capital–Nanking
Chinese canton–Hsein
Chinese card game–fantan, lu
Chinese Christian God–Shen
Chinese city–Amoy, Canton,

Changchau, Changsha, Chaochau, Chengte, Chengtu, Chingkiang, Chingtu, Chinkiang, Chungking, Fachan, Fancheng, Fatshan, Foochow, Fuchau, Hangchau, Hangchow, Hankau, Hankow, Hanyang, Huchau, Jehol, Kaifeng, Kalgan, Kiaochau, Kingtechen, Lanchau, Lienkiang, Macao, Macau, Nanchang, Nankin, Nanking, Ningpo, Paoting, Pekin, Shanghai, Shaohing, Siangtan, Suchau, Swatow, Taiyuen, Tengchau, Tientsin, Tsin, Tsinan, Tungchau, Tunghwan, Tunkuan, Wenchau, Wuchang, Wuhu, Yanphing, Yenping, Yunnan
Chinese city (walled)–Peking
Chinese civet–rasse
Chinese clay–kaolin
Chinese cloth (firm-textured)–nankeen, nankin
Chinese cloth stiffening gelatin–haitsai
Chinese coin – candareen (ac.), cash (cop.), cent (cop.), dollar (s.), Haikwantael (ac.), Kupingtael (ac.), le, tael (s.), tiao (ac.), tsien, yuan (s.)
Chinese coin (early bronze)–pu
Chinese council (government)–Yuan
Chinese deer–elaphure
Chinese department subdivision–Hsien
Chinese dependency–Tibet
Chinese dialect–Wu
Chinese division of aboriginals–Miao, Miaotse, Miaotze
Chinese dog–chow
Chinese dragon–chilin
Chinese drink (alcoholic)–samshu
Chinese duck eggs (preserved in brine)–pidan

Chinese dynasty–Chou, Fo, Han, Hsia, Ming, Sui, Tsin
Chinese figure (small, grotesque)–magot
Chinese fish sauce–soy
Chinese flute–che
Chinese flute (old)–tche
Chinese foreign minister–Quo
Chinese fruit–litchi
Chinese game (gambling)–fantan
Chinese gelatine–agar-agar
Chinese ginger–galingale
Chinese god–Shen
Chinese gong–tamtam
Chinese gooseberry–carambola
Chinese guerrilla war cry–Chee li
Chinese herb–tea
Chinese houseboat–tanka
Chinese idol–joss
Chinese image–joss
Chinese island–Amoy, Formosa, Hainan
Chinese ingots (silver, used for money)–sycee
Chinese insect (wax)–pela
Chinese instrument (anc.)–kin
Chinese isinglass–agar, agar-agar
Chinese jute–chingma
Chinese laborer–coolie
Chinese lake–Tung-ting
Chinese lemon–citron
Chinese magistrate–mandarin
Chinese mandarin residence–yamen
Chinese material for tea canister–calin
Chinese measure–chang, chih, ching, fang, fen, ho, hu, kish, ko, kung chih, kung ching, kung fen, kung ho, kung li, kung mu, kung sheng, kung shih, li, mu, pu, quei, sheng, shih, shing, ta, to, tou, tsun, tu, yin
Chinese measure (distance)–li
Chinese measure (road)–tu

Chinese mile–li
Chinese monetary unit–tael
Chinese money–mo, tsien
Chinese money of account–tiao
Chinese mongol–hu
Chinese mountain–Alashan, Funiu-shan, Inshan, Kuen-lun, Kuliang, Pu-ling, Ta-yu-ling, Tsing-Ling, Tsins
Chinese native–coolie
Chinese noodles–mein
Chinese orange–kumquat
Chinese ounce–tael
Chinese ox–zebu
Chinese pagoda–taa, taag
Chinese paradise (Bud-dhism)–Chingtu
Chinese parasol tree–aogiri
Chinese peony–moutan
Chinese people (aboriginal) –Miao, Miaotse, Miaotze
Chinese philosopher–Confu-cius
Chinese plant (bushy)–udo
Chinese plant (medicine root)–ginseng
Chinese porcelain glaze–eel-skin
Chinese porgy–tai
Chinese prefecture–fu
Chinese province–Amur, Chekiang, Chili, Fokien, Fukien, Honan, Hunan, Hupeh, Kansu, Kiangsi, Kiangsu, Kwangtung, Kwangsi, Kweichau, Manchuria, Nganhui, Shansi, Shantung, Shensi, Szechuen, Yunnan
Chinese public officer–man-darin
Chinese puzzle–tangram
Chinese race–Soyot
Chinese river–Hoang-ho, Hwang, Ili, Min, Pei, Pei-ho, Pie-ho, Si-kiang, Si, Tarim, Wei, Yang-tse-kiang
Chinese river (fukim)–Min
Chinese river boat–sampan
Chinese rolled tea–cha
Chinese roller–sirgang
Chinese salutation–kowtow
Chinese seaport – Amy,

Canton, Foochow, Han-kow, Hong Kong, Ning-po, Shanghai, Swatow, Tientsin
Chinese secret society–Tong
Chinese sedge (with edible tubers)–mati
Chinese shrub–ramie, tea
Chinese silk–Pekin
Chinese silk plant–ramie
Chinese silkworm–sina
Chinese silver ingots–sycee
Chinese skiff–sampan
Chinese society–Tong
Chinese spring festival–Ching Ming
Chinese squash–cushaw
Chinese state (old)–Tsao
Chinese states (feudal)–Wei
Chinese stocks–cangue
Chinese sugar cane–sorgo
Chinese Tartar tribe (anc.)–Toda
Chinese tea (green)–Emesa, Hyson
Chinese tea (rolled)–cha
Chinese teas–tias
Chinese tower-like building –pagoda
Chinese toy (made of seven pieces of thin material)–tangram
Chinese trader (Philippine) –Sangley
Chinese treaty port–Amoy
Chinese tree (cultivated)–kinkan
Chinese tribe (southern)–Shan
Chinese-Turkish carpet or rug–Samarkand
Chinese unit of area–ching
Chinese unit of measure–tsun
Chinese vegetable–udo
Chinese vessel–sampan
Chinese wax–cere, pela
Chinese wax insects–pelas
Chinese weight–candareen, catty, chee, chien, chin, fen, haikwan tael, hao, kin, kung chin, kung fen, kung li, kung ssu, kung tun, kuping tael, li, liang, mace, picul, shih, ssu, tael, tan, yin

Chinese weight (var.)–tsien
Chinese weight unit–ssu
Chinese wood oil–tung
Chinese wormwood (used as counterirritant)–moxa
chink–cleft, crack, cranny, fissure, rent
Chink (slang)–Chinese
chinklike–rimal
chinky–rimose
chinny–talkative
Chinook chief–Tyee
Chinook State–Washington
chip–chisel, cut, flake, hew
chip stone–nig
chipmunk–hackee
chipped and not polished–paleolithic
chipper–babble, cheerful, chirp, chirrup, lively, twitter
chirognomy–palmistry
chirography – engrossing, handwriting, script
chiroptera (one of)–bat
chirotonsor–barber
chirp–chirrup, peep, tweet, twitter
chirp (as chickens)–pip
chirrup–chirp, tweet
chisel–cut, engrave, gouge, pare
chisel (Cornish mine)–peeker
chisel (mine)–gad
chisel (prehistoric)–celt
chisel (primitive)–celt
chisel (slang)–cheat
chisel (stonemason's)–drove
chisel (toothed)–jagger
chisel (wheelwright's cor-ner)–bruzz
chitarra–guitar
chivalrous–gallant, gentle, knightly, valiant
chloride (mercurous)–calo-mel
chlorine (symbol for)–Cl
chloroform ingredient–ace-tone
chocolate (powder used in making)–pinole
chocolate corn–durra
chocolate family–sterculi-aceae
chocolate tree–cacao

choice–best, dainty, election, preference, prime, rare, selection, uncommon

choice (alternative)–dilemma, perplexing

choice morsel–tidbit

choice part–elite, marrow

choicer–better

choicy–choosy, fastidious

choir leader–cantor

choirmaster–precentor

choir member–chorister

choir singer (male)–songman

choke–check, hinder, impede, obstruct, repress, strangle, throttle

choke back–repress, smother, stifle, suppress

choke coil–reactor

choler–anger, ire, rage

choleric–angry, bilious, enraged, iracund, irascible, wrathful

choose–cull, elect, opt, pick, prefer, select

choose (poetic)–opt

choose rather–prefer

choosing–eclectic

chop–cut, hack, hew, jowl, mince

chop (eye of)–noisette

chop (pork)–griskin

chop into small pieces–mince

chop off–amputate, drib, lop, prune

chord (four-toned) – tetrad

chord (three-toned)–triad

chord composition–cantata

chords (succession of)–cadence

chore–task

chorister–choirboy, singer

chorten–reliquary, stupa

chorus (small)–octette

chorus girl (slang)–chorine

chorus leader – choragus, choragi (pl.), conductor

chose one or other (by vote) –opted

chosen–elect, elected

Chosen (old name)–Corea, Korea

Chosen city–Pingyang, Seoul

Chosen native–Corean, Korean

chosen ones–elite

chosen people–Israelites

Christ's thorn–nabk

Christian (Eastern, in communion with Roman church)–Uniat

Christian (Oriental, under Rome jurisdiction)–Uniat

Christian era (abbr.)–A.D., B.C.

Christian feast (early love)–agape

Christian festival–Christmas

Christian martyr (first)–Stephen

Christian sect (heretical)–Docetae

Christian service (held at midnight and daybreak)–nocturn

Christian worship (against) –antireligious

Christmas carol–Noel

Christmas Carol character–Tim

Christmas decoration–holly

Christmas midnight mass supper–reveillon

Christmas plant (evergreen) –mistletoe

Christmas rose–hellebore

Christmas song–carol, Noel

chromium group element–molybdenum, tungsten, uranium

chronic – confirmed, constant, continuous, inveterate

chronic invalidism–valetudinarianism

chronicle–account, annal, archive, history, narrative, record, register, sard

chronicler of events–compiler, historian, recorder, writer

chronology (according to)–datal

chronometer–clock, timepiece

chrysalis–pupa, pupae (pl.)

chub–dace, dolt, fallfish, fool, hornyhead, lout, shiner, squawfish

chubby–plump

chuck–jerk, throw, toss

chuckled (gleefully)–chortled

chuff–boor, conceited, cross, chubby, churl, elated, fat, proud, rustic, sulky, surly

chum–associate, bait, companion, crony, pal, roommate

chum (coll.)–pard

chump–block, endpiece

chunk–gob, throw

chunk (of metal)–slug

chunk (small)–dab, pat, wad

chunky – lumpy, plump, thickset

church (cathedral)–dom

church (dominion of)–sacerdotium

church (kind of)–basilica

church (monastery)–abbey, minster

church (Roman cathedral)–lateran

church (Scot.)–kirk

church (small)–chapel, templet

church altar end–apse

church bell axle bearing–cod

church bench–pew, pue

church bodies – canons, naves, synods

church building bodies–naves

church canticle–venite

church council (previous to) –antenicene

church councils–canons, naves, synods

church dignitary–prelate

church feast (octave of)–utas

church festival–Easter

church holiday (August)–Lammas

church member–communicant

church morning service–matin

church officer–beadle, deacon, dean, divine, elder, moderator, prelate, reverend, sexton, vicar, warden

church officer (Eng.)–beadle

church officer (under)–sexton

church official–priest

church part–apse, clerestory, nave, transept

church pulpit (anc.)–ambo

church reader–lector

church seat–pew, pue, sedile, sedilia (pl.)

church service–mass

church service part–introit

church sexton–verger

church sitting–pew, pue, sedile, sedilia (pl.)

church stipend–prebend

church vault–crypt

church vestry room–sacristy

church wing–aisle

churl–boor, bondman, cad, countryman, freeman, peasant, rustic, serf, villain, villein

churlish–boorish, crabbed, knavish, mean, rough, sullen, surly, violent, vulgar

churn (Scot.)–kirn

churn part (beating)–dasher

chute–flume, slide, trough, tube

ciborium – canopy, coffer, vessel

cicada–locust

cicatrice–scar

cicatrix–scab, scar

cider (pear)–perry

cigar (ends cut square)–cheroot

cigar (kind of)–cheroot, colorado, claro, stogie

cigar (large cylindrical)–londres

cigar (light-colored, mild)–claro

cigar (little)–cigarillo

cigar (long slender, inferior)–toby

cigar (long, thin)–panetela

cigar (small)–concha

cigarette (coll.)–fag

cigarette (marijuana)–reefer

cigarfish–scad

Cilician seaport (anc.)–Issus

cilium–eyelash, lash

cinch–girth, grip

cinders–ash, dross, slag

cingle–belt, girdle, girth

cinnabar (derivative of mercury)–quicksilver

cinnamic acid derivative–sinapic

cinnamon (coarse variety)–cassia

cinnamon tree–cassia

cipher–zero

Circassian king–Sacripant

Circe's father–Helios

Circe's sister–Medea

circle–circuit, circumference, compass, encompass, girdle, halo, loop, orb, revolve, rigol, ring

circle (celestial sphere)–colure

circle (eighth part of)–octant

circle (geographical)–tropic

circle (Japanese)–maru

circle (longest chord)–diameter

circle (luminous)–corona

circle (of metal)–hoop, rim

circle (of wood)–hoop

circle (part of)–arc, sector

circle (semidiameter of)–radius, radii (pl.)

circle of altitude–almucantar

circle of light–halo

circle of persons–cordon

circlets of light–aureolae

circuit – ambit, compass, cycle, gyre, lap, loop, orb, tour

circuit (auxiliary)–relay

circuit court–eyre

circuitous–crooked, curved, deceitful, deviating, disingenuous, flexuous, labyrinthine, mazy, rambling, serpentine, twisted, underhand, vagrant, wandering, winding

circular–annular, circuitous, indirect, orbicular, ringed, round, roundabout

circular and flat–discoid

circular inclosure–lis

circular indicator–dial

circulate–diffuse, disseminate, propagate, spread

circulated (publicly) – reported

circumference–bound, circuit, girt, girth, perimeter, periphery

circumference (half)–semicircle

circumscribe–define, encircle, enclose, encompass, environ, fence, limit, restrict

circumspect–careful, cautious, discreet, prudent, wary

circumspection–caution, deliberation, prudence, thoughtfulness, wariness, watchfulness

circumstance – condition, event, fact, item, occurrence, particular, position, state

circumstance (modifying)–condition

circumstances (essential)–merits

circumstantial–detailed, exact, precise

circus–arena

cirque–circle, circlet, corrie

cirque (geol.)–CWM

cist–box, chamber, chest, cistvaen

cistern–back, cuvette, reservoir, sac, tank, tub, vat, well

citadel–fastness, fort, fortification, fortress, stronghold, tower

citadel (Roman, anc.)–arx, arces (pl.)

citadel (Texas)–Alamo

citation–notice, summons

cite–adduce, extract, quote, repeat

cite as proof–adduce

citizen–cit, civilian, inhabitant, native, townsman

citizens of ancient empire–Roman

citizenship (admission to)–enfranchisement

citron–cedrat

citrus fruit–grapefruit, lemon, lime, orange

city–municipality, town

city (anc., noted for hanging gardens)–Babylon
city (chief)–metropolis
city (League of Nations)–Geneva
city (pert. to)–civic, urban
city division–district, precinct, ward
City of Bells–Strasbourg
City of Bridges–Bruges
City of Brotherly Love–Philadelphia
City of Churches–Brooklyn
City of David–Jerusalem
city of dead–cemetery
City of Hundred Towers–Pavia
City of Lilies–Florence
City of Masts–London
City of Rams–Canton
City of Saints–Montreal
civet–rasse
civet (Chinese)–rasse
civet (East Indian palm)–musang
civet-like animal–genet
civet-like carnivore–genet
civic–urban
civic corruption–graft
civil–affable, complaisant, condescending, courteous, courtly, discreet, elegant, gracious, obliging, polished, polite, respectful, suave, urbane, well-bred
civil injury–tort
civil offense–stellionate
civil powers–states
civil strife–stasis
Civil War campaign–Peninsular
Civil War commander (Ohio Army)–Buell
Civil War major general–Emory
Civil War battle site (second great)–Shiloh
civil wrong–tort
civilian dress–mufti
civility–affability, amenity, courtesy
civilization–cultivation, culture, refinement
civilization (Ger.)–kultur
civilize–cultivate, humanize, polish, urbanize

clad – arrayed, clothed, decked, dressed, drest
cladome (branch of)–cladus
cladose–branched, ramose
claim–assert, demand, lien, maintain, name, pretence, pretense, proclaim, profess, title
claim (justifiable)–case
claim (legal)–lien
claim (legal, India)–hak, hakh
claim as existent or true–postulate
claim to attention–pretension
claimant–pretender
clairvoyance–divination, insight, penetration, sagacity
clairvoyant–sagacious, seeress
clam (razor)–solen
clambering–scaling
clammy–damp, dank, moist, soft, sticky
clamor–din, hue, hullabaloo, noise, uproar
clamor against–decry
clamorous–blatant, brawling, loud, noisy, turbulent, vociferous
clamp–vise
clamping device–vise
clams (genus of) mya
clan–clique, cult, party, sept, set, society, tribe
clan (pert. to)–tribal
clan quarrel–feud
clandestine – concealed, fraudulent, furtive, secret, sly, stealthy, surreptitious, underhand
clangor–din
clarify–purify, refine, render
clarinet part–birn
clarion–trumpet
clash–collide, collision, conflict
clasp–agraffe, embrace, fasten, grasp
clasp (lock)–hasp
clasp (ornamental)–chatelaine
clasp (priest's garment)–morse

class–catalog, catalogue, category, genus, genera (pl.), genre, genra (pl.), grade, rank
class (biological)–genus, genera (pl.)
class (broad, general)–genus, genera (pl.)
class (educated)–intelligentsia
class (hereditary)–caste
class (learned)–literati
class (member of graduating)–senior
class (of animals)–mammal
class (social)–caste, estate, tribe
classical–academic, attic
classification–category, genus, genera (pl.), genre, genra (pl.), grade, rank
classification (biological)–genus, genera (pl.)
classification (method of)–system
classification between variety and genus–species
classified – assorted, arranged, catalogued, graded, labeled, ranged, ranked, rated, sorted, typed
classify–aggroup, assort, arrange, catalogue, grade, label, range, rank, rate, sort, type
clatter–babble, chatter, din, gabble, jar, rattle
clause (added)–rider
claw–hand, nail, talon
claw (bird of prey)–talon
claw (lobster)–chela, chelae (pl.), nipper
clay (baked)–tile
clay (colored, earthy)–bole
clay (fired)–tile
clay (kind of)–marl
clay (made of)–fictile
clay (pale, yellowish)–loess
clay (piece of baked)–tile
clay (potter's)–argil
clay (white)–kaolin
clay and sand mixture–loam
claybrained–dull, stupid
clay-cold–inanimate, lifeless

clay-covered–lutose
clay layer in coal–sloam
clayey–bolar, marly
clean–cleanse, dust, launder, swab, wash
clean (by wiping)–absterge
cleaned thoroughly–renovated
cleaned up (in army)–policed
cleaner–wiper
cleaner (gun barrel)–ramrod
cleanest–purest
cleaning implement–broom, mop, ramrod, sweeper
cleanliness–purity
cleanse–brush, clean, deterge, purge, renovate, scrub, wash
cleanse by rubbing–scrape
cleanse of impurities–refine
cleansed well–berinsed
cleansed with water (arch.) –washen
cleanses (dial.)–feys
cleansing–acquittal, bath, detergent, purification
cleansing agent–borax, soap
clear–absolve, apparent, brighten, clean, cloudless, crystal, exonerate, extricate, free, gain, lighten, limpid, lucid, net, over, plain, pure, purify, rid
clear (not)–cloudy, foggy, hazy, misty
clear (prefix, biol.)–delo
clear (strikingly)–graphic
clear cut–concise, distinct, incisive
clear of accusations–absolve, acquit, exonerate
clear of ground (as an anchor)–atrip
clear of obscurity–explain
clear sighted–perspicacious
clear up–solve
clear yellow light–amber
clearing for cultivation–twaite
clearing in woods–glade
clearly and vividly told–graphical
clearly defined–determinate
clearly marked out–defined

clearness–distinctness, limpidity
cleat–bitt, kevel
cleat (belaying)–kevel
cleavage–fission, partition, separation
cleave–adhere, clave, cling, clove, crack, cut, divide, part, pierce, rend, rive, separate, sever, shear, split, tear
cleave asunder–sever
cleche–urde, urdee
clee–claw, hoof, redshank
cleek–clutch, pluck, seize, snatch
clef (treble)–gee
cleft–chasm, chink, crack, cranny, crevice, fissure, gap, recess, reft, rift, riven, split
cleft (biology)–rima
cleft-like–rimal
cleg–gadfly, horsefly
clemency–compassion, indulgence, kindness, leniency, lenity, mercy, mildness, quarter
clement–lenient, mild
clench – clutch, fist, grasp, grip, grit, interlock
Cleopatra and Antony character–Eros, Iras
Cleopatra's attendant–Iras
Cleopatra's lover–Marc Antony
Cleopatra's river–Nile
clergy (body of)–pulpit
clergyman–cleric, curate, minister, pastor, preacher, presbyter, vicar
clergyman (high)–prelate
clergyman (parish)–divine, minister, pastor, rector
clergyman (pastoral)–dean
clergyman's hood (anc.)–amice
clergyman's residence – manse, parsonage
clergyman's title–Reverend
clergyman's title (abbr.)–Rev.
clergywoman–nun, priestess, religieuse
cleric–abbe, clerk, deacon
cleric (high)–prelate

clerical–ministerial
clerical attire–cloth
clerical cape–amice
clerical collar–rabat
clerical garment–amice
clerical hat–biretta
clerical scarf–stole
clerical title–abba, abbe
clerical vestment–alb, stole
clerk–clergyman, cleric, ecclesiastic, hermit, monk, nun
clerkly–learned, scholarly, scribal
cleronomy–heritage, inheritance
clever–able, apt, astute, cute, deft, dexterous, expert, ingenious, parlous, skillful, slick, smart, talented
clever (dangerously)–parlous
clever phrase (remark)–mot
clever remark–mot
cleverness – adroitness, astuteness, ingenuity, tact
clew–ball, globe, key
click beetle–elater
cliff–precipice
cliff (broken)–crag
cliff (high)–precipice
cliffs (bold)–palisade
climax–acme, cap, culmination, near, shut, tight
climb–ascend, scale, shin
climb (as a plant)–gad
climb (Scot.)–speel
climb (with difficulty)–clamber
climb high slope–scale
climb on all fours–clamber
climbing pepper–betel
climbing plant–bine, liana, liane, vine
climbing stem–bine
clime–climate, realm, region, tract
clinch–bind, conclude, confirm, establish, grapple, grasp, grip, seal, secure
cling–adhere, cohere, stick
clip–bob, dock, lop, mow, prune, scissor, shear, shorten, snip, trim
clip closely–shear
clipped–shorn

clipper–shearer
clipper (air)–liner
clique–coterie, set
clit–close, heavy, sticky
cloak–disguise, dissemble, manta, mantua, manteau, mantle, mask, pall, robe, screen, serape, shield, wrap
cloak (hooded)–capote
cloak (long)–capote
cloak (long, close-fitting)–newmarket
cloak (long, sleeveless)–paenula
cloak (loose)–cape, paletot, rochet
cloak (Roman, cape-like)–sagum
cloak (short)–cape, grego
cloak (short-sleeved)–jelab, jellab
cloak (sleeveless)–cape
cloak (wolfskin, lined)–witzchoura
cloak (woman's cape-like)–dolman
cloam – crockery, earthenware
clock–time
clock (anc.)–clepsydra
clock (in form of ship)–nef
clock (ship form)–nef
clock (time)–recorder
clock face–dial
clock part (striking mechanism)–detent
clock regulating body–pendulum
clockwise – deasil, deiseal, dessil
clockworks arrangement–caliper
clog–choke, encumber, hamper, impede, obstruct, pattern, restrain, stop
clog with mud–daggle
clogwyn–cliff, precipice
cloister–abbey, convent, friary, hermitage, monastery, nunnery, priory, stoa
cloistered–recluse, sequestered
close–by, complete, conclude, dense, end, ex-

treme, extremity, finis, finish, near, nigh, occlude, period, seal, shut, slam, terminate, termination
close (comb. form)–steno
close (poetic)–anear
close by (poetic)–anear
close firmly–bar, batten, seal
close-fitting–snug, tight
close tightly–clench, enseal, seal
close to–near, nigh
close up tightly–cement, enseal, seal
closed (half)–mid
closefisted–niggardly, stingy
closely allied–germane
closely familiar–chummy, intimate
closeness–compactness, conciseness, fidelity, intimacy, literalness, narrowness, nearness, oppressiveness, secrecy, stinginess, strictness, tightness
closet–cabinet, cuddy, cupboard
closet (clothes)–wardrobe
closet (small)–cupboard, locker
closing device–lock, zipper
clot–coagulate, coagulum, concrete, mass, thicken
cloth–rag, satinet
cloth (ailette cover)–carda
cloth (bark)–tapa
cloth (checkered woolen)–tartan
cloth (coarse cotton)–manta, surat
cloth (coarse, for rugs, etc.)–rugging
cloth (coarse linen)–dowlas
cloth (communion)–corporal, corporale
cloth (cotton)–calico, denim, jeans, khaki, percale, surat
cloth (cotton, bluish color)–bluet
cloth (cotton, ordinary)–manta
cloth (cotton sheeting or drilling)–manta

cloth (durable cotton)–nankin
cloth (fine-textured)–silk
cloth (gold)–samite
cloth (grave)–cerements
cloth (gunny)–tat
cloth (India gunny)–tat
cloth (kind of)–baracan, barracan, crash, huckaback, jane, nankeen
cloth (levant)–baracan, barracan
cloth (linen)–cambric
cloth (linen, stout)–brin
cloth (modern kind)–acetate
cloth (narrow)–tape
cloth (piece of)–clout
cloth (plaid)–tartan
cloth (roll of)–bolt
cloth (silk, interwoven with gold)–samite
cloth (stiff)–crinoline
cloth (striped)–ray
cloth (striped cotton)–bezan, express
cloth (strong)–canvas, duck
cloth (unwoven)–felt
cloth (upholstery)–terry
cloth (woolen) – flannel, frieze, melton, taminy, tamis
cloth (woolen, checkered)–tartan
cloth (woolen, coarse)–baize
cloth (woolen, naplike)–duffel
cloth (worsted)–serge, tamine
cloth dealer–draper, mercer
cloth finisher–beetler
cloth measure (old)–ell
cloth piece–bolt
cloth ridge–wale
cloth strainer–tamis
cloth stretching machine–tenter
cloth treating device (steam)–ager
clothe–accouter, array, dress, endue, enrobe, garb, indue, invest, robe, vest
clothe with authority–vest
clothed–habited
clothes – apparel, attire, clothing, costume, garb,

garments, habiliments, habit, raiment, wear
clothes (coll.)–duds
clothes drying frame–airer
clothes moth–tinea
clothes press–chest, wardrobe
clothes presser–sadiron
clothing–attire, clothes, covering, dress, duds, garb, garments, raiment, togs
clothing spy (slang)–keek
cloud – blacken, damage, darken, defame, fog, nubia, obscure, overcast, shadow, stain, sully, taint, tarnish
cloud (dark)–nimbus
cloud (destructive funnel-shaped)–tornado
cloud (fast-flying)–scud
cloud (high, white, filmy)–cirrus, cirri (pl.)
cloud (kind of)–cumulus
cloud (thin, broken)–rack
cloud (tufted form of)–cirrus
cloud (type of)–cumulus
cloud built–airy, imaginary, unsubstantial
cloud form–nimbus
cloud formation (kind of)–stratus, strati (pl.)
cloud-like–nebular
cloud-like object in sky–nebula
cloud of pulverized earth–dust
cloud of smoke (aromatic)–fume
cloud resting on earth's surface–fog
clouds (flying)–rack
clouds (morning)–velo
cloudy–cloud-like, confused, dark, dim, foggy, gloomy, indistinct, lackluster, lowery, misty, nebular, obscure, overcast, shady, vaporous
clout–bandage, blow, handkerchief, hit, mend, patch
clove–cleft, gap, ravine
clover–medic, trefoil
clover (species of)–melilot
clover (Swedish)–alsike

clover (sweet)–lotus
clover-like plant–melilot
clown–boor, buffoon, countryman, fool, harlequin, jester, lout, mime, mimer, mome, oaf, rustic, zany
clownish–awkward, clumsy, coarse, ill-bred, rough, rude, rustic, uncivil, ungainly, untutored
clownish fellow–lout
clown's spikenard–cinnamonroot
clown's woundwort–clownheal
cloy–glut, pall, sate, satiate, satisfy, surfeit
club–association, bat, beat, bludgeon, clout, cudgel, hit, join, mace, staff, unite
club (actor's famous)–Friars
club (ancient)–mace
club (heavy weapon)–mace
club (medieval)–mace
club (policeman's)–billy, espantoon
club (throwing)–boomerang
club (war)–mace
club (woman's)–Ebell, Sorosis
clubfooted–taliped, talipedic
club grass–cattail
club officer–steward
club-shaped–clavate
clue–key, tip
clump – bunch, cluster, group, heap, lump, patch, thicket, tuft
clump (bushy)–tod
clumsy–awkward, gawky, inappropriate, inept, misshapen, unhandy, unwieldy
clumsy (obs.)–awk
clumsy fellow–gawk
clumsy person – bungler, staup
cluster – bunch, clump, group, tuft
cluster (flower)–cyme
cluster (flower-like)–rosette
cluster (fruit)–grapes
cluster (plant)–tuft
cluster bean–guar
cluster cup (of rust fungi)–aecium, aecia (pl.)

cluster of fibers–nep
cluster of fibers in wool staple–nep
cluster of grapes (obs.)–racemation
cluster of spore cases–sorus, sori (pl.)
clusters (arranged in)–racemose
clustery–racemose
clutch–catch, clasp, clench, cletch, grasp, grip, nab, seize, snatch
clutched–clipt
clutches at wildly–claws, grips, paws
clyster–enema
Clytemnestra's mother – Leda
cnemis–shin, tibia
cnicin–thistle
cnicus–thistle
cnida–nematocyst, nettle
coach–car, carriage, direct, instruct, instructor, prepare, preparer, prime, stage, train, tutor
coach (fast)–flier
coach (four-in-hand)–tally-ho
coach dog–Dalmatian
coachman–driver, jehu
coagulate–clot, congeal, curdle, jel
coagulator (milk)–rennet
coagulum–clot, curd
coal (hot)–cinder, ember
coal (impurities in)–clinkers
coal (kind of)–anthracite, bituminous, cannel, coke
coal (large, block, ready for mining, Eng.)–jud
coal (lighted)–ember
coal (partly burned)–cinder, clinker
coal (size of)–broken, buckwheat, chestnut, egg, lump, nut, pea, slack, stove
coal (soft, Eng. dial.)–dant
coal bed–seam
coalbin–bunker
coal car bottom (tilting)–hopper
coal constituent–carbon
coal dust–smut

coalfish (Scot.)–sey
coalfish (young)–parr
coal goose–cormorant
coalheugh (Scot.)–coalpit
coal mine accessory–breaker
coal mine debris (abandoned)–thursts
coal mine shaft–pit
coal miner–collier
coal oil–kerosene
coal tar (brownish red)–eosin
coal tar product–phenol
coal tunnel–adit
coal waste (anthracite)–culm
coals–embers
coals of fire (dial.)–gleds
coalesce–mingle, unite
coalescence – combination, unification, union
coalition–alliance, combination, confederacy, confederation, conjunction, fusion, league, merger, trust, union
coarse–broad, dank, earthy, gross, immodest, impure, indecent, lewd, low, obscene, offensive, ribald, rude, sensual, unchaste, vile, vulgar
coarse grain–meal
coarse grass–reed, sedge, quitch
coarse hominy–samp
coarse part–dregs
coarse rustic–boor
coast–seaboard, seashore, seaside, shore
coast (arch.)–rivage
coast live oak–encina
coast navigation (trade)–cabotage
coastal projection–cape, ness
coat–bark, cover, husk, incrust, layer, mantle, membrane, overlay, tegument, veneer
coat (animal's)–pelage
coat (auto, old fashioned)–duster
coat (eye, inner)–retina
coat (fur)–pelage
coat (heavy, short, double-breasted)–mackinaw

coat (hooded)–capote
coat (long)–paletot
coat (long, close-fitting)–newmarket
coat (long, loose)–cassock
coat (mammal)–pelage
coat (part of)–collar, cuff, lapel
coat (protective)–armor
coat (rough)–shag
coat (seed)–aril
coat (short)–pea, reefer
coat (sleeveless)–aba
coat (tailed, tapered)–cutaway
coat (waterproof)–gossamer, slicker
coat (woman's double-breasted)–redingote
coat fastener–frog
coat neck part–george
coat of arms–crest
coat of mail–byrnie, hauberk
coat part (neck)–george
coat with alloy (tin and lead)–terne
coat with color–paint
coat with icing–glace
coat with metal–plate
coat with tin and lead–terne
coat with vitreous composition–enamel
coating (cereal)–bran
coating (grain)–bran
coating (light)–film
coating (seed, external, hard)–testa
coating (seed, internal)–tegman
coating (teeth)–enamel
coating (thin)–crust, film, veneer
coating (vitreous)–enamel
coax–beg, beguile, cajole, entice, flatter, implore, inveigle, persuade, tease, wheedle
cob–basket, beating, block, blow, breakwater, chief, dumpling, horse, leader, loaf, mole, muffin, pier, spider
cob swan–male
cobaltiferous arsenophyrite–danaite
cobber–chum, mate, pal

cobbler–botcher, shoemaker, soler
cobbra–head, skull
cobby–headstrong, hearty, lively, stocky, stout
cobra–asp
cobweb–net
cobweb (dial.)–wevet
cocaine (slang)–snow
cocco–taro
Cochin coin–puttan (s.)
cock–faucet, leader, pile, rooster, strut, swagger, tap, valve
cock (gun)–nab
cock (sage)–grouse
cock (water)–kora
cock (without spurs) – muckna
cockade–knot, rosette
Cockade State–Maryland
cockatoo–ara, parrot
cockatoo (palm)–arara
cockle–boat, kiln, mollusk, oast
cockpit–arena
cockpit (airplane)–cabin
cockroaches (genus of)–blatta
cocktail (of gin, vermouth, and orange juice)–bronx
coco plum–icaco
coco root–taro
cocoa (oilless)–broma
cocoanut fiber–coir, kyar
cocoanut husk fiber–coir
cocoanut kernel (dried)–copra
cocoanut meat (dried, commercial)–copra
cocoon (silkworm)–clew
cod (baby)–scrod
cod family (pert. to)–gadoid
cod-like fish–bib, ling
coddle–baby, caress, fondle, pamper, pet
code of good conduct–decorum
code of law–codex, salic
codfish–bacaloa
codfish (genus of)–gadus
codfish (Span.)–bacalao
codfish (young, boiled)–scrod
codfishing vessel–banker

coelenterate (having cylindrical body)–polyp

coerce–compel, curb, enforce, repress

coerce (by intimidation)–terrorize

coercion–duress, force

coffee (navy slang)–mud

coffee (variety of)–Bogota, Brazil, Java, Maracaibo, Medellin, Milds, Mocha, Rio, Santos, Sumatra

coffee and tea constituent–caffeine

coffee bean–nib

coffee container–canister

coffee house–cafe

coffee receptacle–canister

coffer–casket, chest, trunk

coffin–basket, bier, case, casket, casing, chest, crust, mold

coffin litter–bier

coffin support–bier

cog–cheat, cozen, deceive, deception, gear, tooth, wheedle

cogent–conclusive, convincing, persuasive, potent, strong, telling

cogitate–mull, muse, think

cognizance – apprehension, heed, ken, knowledge, notice

cognizant – aware, intelligent, sensible

cognomen – appellation, name, nickname, surname

cogwheel–gear

cohere–adhere, cleave, cling, stick

coherence–cohesion, connected, connectedness, consistency

coherent and concise (precisely)–serried

coil–curl, loop, spiral, twine, twist

coil (coll.)–querl

coil into ball–clew, clue

coiled–tortile

coin–cash, dime, mint, money, specie, stamp

coin (Americana, issued 1717-1733)–rosa

coin (Biblical)–talent

coin (Charles I reign)–carolus, caroli (pl.)

coin (copper)–cent

coin (debased)–rap

coin (Eng., old)–groat

coin (Eur., anc.)–ducat

coin (gold)–eagle

coin (gold, anc.)–rial

coin (gold, Persian, old)–daric

coin (imperfectly minted)–brockage

coin (old, Eur.)–ducat

coin (reverse side)–tails

coin (silver, old)–tester

coin (small, coll.)–rap

coin (U.S. gold)–eagle

coin of trifling value–rap

coincide–agree

coiner–counterfeiter, fabricator, inventor

coiner of new words–neologist

coins (pert. to)–numismatical

coins (rolled in paper)–rouleau

coins (small)–change, chickenfeed

coin's date space–exergue

colander–sieve, strainer

colate–filter, strain

Colchis king–Aeetes

cold–chilled, icy, indifferent, passionless, unemotional, unheated

cold (arch.)–frore

cold (in the head)–pose

cold (moderately)–cool

cold (poetic)–gelid

cold (very)–frosty, gelid

cold and damp–dank, raw

cold feet–cowardice

cold in the head–coryza

cold or frozen (arch.)–frore, froren

colder and bleaker–rawer

coleopterous insect–beetle

coliseum–stadium, theater

coll–clip, embrace, hug, poll, prune

collaborate–aid

collapse–cave, cavein, downfall, failure, prostration, slump

collapse by removing air–deflate

collar (clerical)–rabat

collar (horse, Scot.)–bargham

collar (lace)–bertha

collar (plaited)–ruff

collar (priest's)–rabat

collar (quilled lace)–ruche

collar (turned down)–rabato

collar (wheel-shaped)–ruff

collarbone–clavicle

collar cell–choanocyte

collared monads–choanoflagellata

collate–compare, examine

collateral–subordinate

collation–address, collection, comparison, conference, consultation, contribution, meal, reading, repast, sermon, treatise

collation (light)–tea

colleague–associate, confrere, partner

collect–accumulate, aggregate, amass, compile, congregate, garner, gather, levy, muster, prayer, raise, sheave

collect food–forage

collect on repertory–sorite

collect piece by piece–glean

collection–aggregate, ana, assemblage, assembly, bag, congeries, gathering, group, hoard, olio, set, store

collection (complete)–set

collection (miscellaneous)–olio

collection (vast)–cloud

collection (wild animal)–menagerie, zoo

collection of anecdotes–ana

collection of bubbles–foam

collection of curiosities–museum

collection of documents–dossier

collection of facts–ana, data

collection of four–tetrad

collection of game–bag

collection of Hindu sacred literature–veda

collection of living pine trees–pinetum
collection of papers–dossier
collection of poems–anthology, sylva
collection of sayings–ana
collection of twenty-four–quire
collection of type–font
collective fruit–syncarp
collective writing–literature
collector (book)–bibliomaniac
colleen–girl, maiden
college–academy, school, university
college (Midwestern)–Coe
college (Moslem religious)–ulema
college campus–quad
college course (special)–seminar
college court–quad
college dance–prom
college degree–BA
college graduate–alumnus, alumni (pl.), bachelor
college half year–semester
college official–beadle, bursar, dean, prexy, proctor, regent
college song–glee
college student–freshman, sophomore, soph, junior, senior
college student organization –frat, fraternity, sorority
college year term–semester
collegian–coed
collide with–hit, ram
collier's lung–anthracosis
collieshangie (Scot.) – disturbance, quarrel, row, squabble
collision–clash, clashing, crash, encounter, opposition
collision (in a)–afoul
colloquy – conference, discourse, talk
Cologne king – Balthasar, Gaspar, Melchior
Colombian city–Barranquilla, Bogota (c.), Bucaramanga, Cartagena, Medellin

Colombian coin–centavo (cop., ni.), condor (g.), peseta (s.), peso (s.), real (s.)
Colombian mahogany–albarco
Colombian measure–celemin, vara
Colombian port–Barranquilla, Cartagena, Santa Marta
Colombian river – Atrato, Cuaca, Guaviara, Magdalena, Putumay, Yapura
Colombian weight–bag, carga, libra, quilate, quintal, saco
colonel (after whom drink was named)–Negus
coloni (Latin)–liti
colonial teak–flindosa
colonist–emigrant, pioneer, settler
colonize–establish, gather, settle
colonizer–oecist, settler
colonnade–pcristyle, stoa
colonus (Latin)–litus, liti (pl.)
colony–community, dependency, settlement
colony of bees–swarm
colophony–resin, rosin
color–amber, carmine, cerise, cherry, coral, dye, hue, lavender, maroon, orchid, paint, roan, sandy, sepia, shade, stain, tinge, tint
color (achromatic)–black, gray, white
color (antique red)–canna
color (beige, Fr.)–grege, greige
color (blue)–lobelia
color (bluish green-blue)–beryl
color (brown)–sedge
color (chestnut and gray)–roan
color (chromatic)–brown, green, pink, purple, red
color (dark brown)–bister
color (deep purple)–modena
color (delicate, var.)–tint
color (dull)–dun

color (dull in)–terne
color (full of)–chromatic
color (garden mignonette)–reseda
color (grayish green)–reseda
color (healthy)–tan
color (leaden)–gray
color (light blue)–gray
color (light, kind of)–tint
color (lilac)–mauve
color (line of)–streak
color (malachite)–bice
color (mat white)–alabaster
color (mole)–taupe
color (neutral)–black, gray, white
color (nutria)–greige, grege
color (pale)–pastel
color (pale purplish)–lavender
color (pale yellow)–flaxen, lemon
color (partly)–piebald
color (red-yellow)–aloma
color (reddish brown)–sorrel
color (secondary)–green, orange, purple
color (shade of difference)–nuance
color (tone)–timbre
color (unhealthy)–sallow
color (varieties of)–tints
color (Venetian red)–siena
color (yellowish red)–lava
color (wool)–beige
color graduation–shade
color organ–clavilux
color photography inventor (American)–Ives
color quality–tone
color slightly–tinge
color twine–anamite
color value–tone
color with rouge–raddle
Colorado county–Dolores, Otero
Colorado Indian–Arapahoe, Ute
Colorado mountain–Evans, Owen, Pikes Peak, Rosalie
Colorado mountain range–Raton
Colorado town – Denver, Manassa, Manitou

Colorado tributary–Gila
colorant (blue)–anil
colored partly–pied
colored "Uncle" (fictional)–
 Remus, Tom
coloring (slight)–tinge
coloring material (deep
 blue)–smalt
coloring matter–pigment
coloring matter (fustic)–
 morin
coloring matter (green, of
 plants)–chlorophyll, clorofil
coloring matter (reddish)–
 eosin
colorist–dyer
colorless – achromatic,
 blanched, blank, drab,
 dull, hueless, pale, pallid,
 uninteresting
colorless corpuscle–leucocyte
colors (pert. to)–chromatic
colors (rainbow-like)–iridescence
colors (stir in calico printing)–teers
colossal – gigantic, huge,
 large, monstrous
colt–foal
colt (female)–filly
Columbus' birthplace–Gen-
 oa
Columbus' caravel–Nina
Columbus' companion and
 discoverer of Venezuela–
 Ojeda
Columbus' ship–Nina, Pinta
column–pillar, shaft, stela,
 stelae (pl.), stele, steles
 (pl.)
column (balustrade, small)–
 baluster
column (shaft of)–shank
column (small)–stela, stelae
 (pl.), stele, steles (pl.)
column (upright)–shaft
column member (upper-
 most)–capital
column shaft–scape
columnar (rare)–stelene
columned–pillared, tabulated
coma (last degree)–carus
comatose–drowsy, lethargic

comb (as a horse)–curry
comb (as wool)–card, tease
comb (comb. form)–cten
comb jelly–ctenophore
comb-like–pectinal
combmaker's file–carlet
comb rat–gundi
comb-shaped–pectinate
combat–antagonize, argu-
 ment, battle, conflict, contention, contest, duel,
 fight, fray, oppose, repel,
 scuffle, strife, tilt, war,
 withstand
combat (between knights on
 horseback)–joust
combat (formal)–duel
combat code–duello
combatant–battler, contestant, dueler, fighter
combative–agonistic, belligerent, militant, pugna-
 cious
combination – camarilla,
 clique, coalition, com-
 bine, confederacy, ensemble, faction, gang, incorporation, league, merger,
 party, synthesis, trust, union
combination (trade)–merg-
 er, union
combination for common
 purpose–alliance, pact,
 pool
combination of natural
 views–scenery
combination of synthesis–
 incorporation
combine–add, join, ma-
 chine, merge, mingle,
 pool, unite
combine into a whole–incorporate
combined into one body–
 coalesced
comble–acme, heap, load,
 summit
combustion–agitation, conflagration, confusion, cremation, fire, inflamma-
 tion, tumult
combustion remnant–ash
come–approach, arrive
come across–contribute, pay
come back–answer, rebound,

recovery, repartee, retort,
 return
come between–intervene
come by–acquire, gain, get,
 inherit, obtain
come by way of advantage–
 accrue
come forth–appear, emerge,
 issue
come in–arrive, enter
come in without invitation–
 crash, intrude
come into operation–enure,
 inure
come into possession–accede
come into view–appear,
 emerge
come out–appear, emerge,
 extend, protrude
come out of the water–
 emerge, emerse
come to a point–taper
come to pass–befall, betide,
 happen, occur
come together – assemble,
 clash, collide, converge,
 join, meet
come together (as bones)–
 knit
come to light–develop
come to maturity–ripen
come to rest–light, settle, sit
come up to–advance, equal,
 match, toe
comedian (radio)–Amos,
 Andy
comedian (well-known)–Al-
 len, Baker, Benny, Can-
 tor, Chaplin, Durante,
 Hope, Skelton
comedy (burlesque)–revue
comedy (exaggerated)–farce
comedy (low)–slapstick
comedy (musical)–revue
comeling–immigrant, new-
 comer, sojourner
comely–agreeable, beautiful,
 fair, handsome, person-
 able, pleasing
comes together (for public
 purposes)–convenes
comet (part of)–coma
comet tail–streamer
comfort–animate, cheer,
 confirm, console, ease, enliven, inspirit, reassure,

refresh, relieve, solace, soothe, strengthen, support, sustain

comfortable–consolatory, encouraging, snug

comforter–quilt, scarf

comfortless–cheerless, desolate, forlorn, inconsolable

comical–droll, funny, humorous, laughable, ludicrous, quizzical, whimsical, witty

coming–approaching, future

coming after something else –latter

coming dimly into view–looming

coming from side–lateral

coming into being of anything–genesis

coming into existence–nascent

comity–amenity, civility, courtesy, suavity, urbanity

command–authority, bade, behest, bid, charge, check, compel, control, decree, dictate, direct, edict, enjoin, exact, fiat, govern, hest, mandate, order, power, prescribe, restrain, sway, ukase

command (arch.)–hest

command (authoritative)–decree, fiat

command (nautical)–avast

command (plowman's)–gee, haw

command car (army slang)–jeep

commander–chief, leader

commander (airfield, Fr. slang)–stationmaster

commander (Oriental)–ameer, amir, emeer, emir, ras

commander of army (chief) –generalissimo

commander in chief–generalissimo

commanding – authoritative, dominant, imperative, imperious

commandment–law, precept

commandments (ten)–Decalogue

commando members–raiders

commemorate–celebrate

commence–begin, initiate, open, originate, start

commenced (arch.)–gan

commenced (poetic)–gan

commencement–inchoation

commencing–nascent

commend–approve, commit, compliment, deliver, entrust, recommend, resign

commend (sanction)–approve

commend to favor–ingratiate

commendatory notice (in book)–blurb

comment–criticism, postil, remark

comment (brief, explanatory)–mote

comments (to furnish)–annotate

commerce–trade, traffic

commis–agent, clerk, deputy

commiserate–condole, pity, sympathize

commiseration– compassion, pity

commission – authority, board, constitute, delegate, depute, empower, mandate, office, ordain, trust, warrant

commission (military)–brevet

commission to act in one's place–depute

commissioned–breveted

commissioner–delegate, envoy

commit–confide, consign, entrust, refer, relegate, remand, perpetrate

commit to memory–con

commode–cap, chest, chiffonier

commodious–ample, capacious, fit, proper, suitable

commodities–articles, goods, wares

commodities (chief)–staples

common–cheap, commonplace, customary, familiar, frequent, general, mediocre, mutual, ordinary, plebeian, popular, stale, trite, universal, usual

common ancestor–Adam

common funds–pool

common gender (of)–epicene

common gull–mew

common informer–delator

common people–demos

common people (pert. to)–demotic

commonly accepted–vulgate

commonly thought or supposed–putative

commonplace–banal, humdrum, ordinary, platitude, prosaic, trite, truism

commonplace remark–platitude

commonplaceness (tedious) –humdrum

commonwealth–state, Kentucky, Massachusetts, Pennsylvania, Virginia

commonwealth (Greek)–demos

commorth – entertainment, shower

commotion–ado, confusion, fracas, fray, perturbation, riot, stir, to do, tumult, turmoil, whir

commotion (sudden)–flurry

communicant–member

communicate–bestow, impart

communicate by telepathy–telepath

communication – communique, intercourse, letter, message

communication (form of)–radio

communication (orally)–accroamatic

communication medium–organ

communicator by supernatural agency–revelator

communion – agreement, church, concord, converse, denomination, intercourse, participation, share

communion cloth–corporal

communion plate–paten

communion psalm (opening, in Anglican church)–introit

communion table–altar

communion vessel–pyx

communique – communication, message

communism (variety of)–Leninism

communist–socialist

communist Cabet follower–Icarian

compact–alliance, compendious, compressed, concise, condensed, conspiracy, contract, dense, plot, sententious, snug, solid, succinct, terse, tight, trim, vanity

compacted into rows–serried

companion–associate, compeer, comrade, consort, crony, fellow, mate, pal

companion (boon)–pal

companion (coll.)–pal

companionship–society

company–band, bevy, body, circle, cohort, concourse, crew, crowd, flock, gang, gathering, group, host, party, set, throng, troop, troupe

company (seamen on ship, var.)–crue

company of people–crew, gang

company of players–eleven, five, team, troupe

company of riders–cavalcade, troop

company of ships–armada, fleet

company of soldiers (in close rank)–phalanx

company of travelers–caravan, tourists

comparative – compeer, equal, relative, rival

comparative conjunction–than

comparatively short–curtate

compare–collate, contrast, liken

compare (as texts)–collate

compare critically–collate, examine

compared with (as)–than

comparison–metaphor, parable, simile

comparison (in, with)–to

compartment–alcove, stall

compartment (large)–bin

compass–area, divider, extent, range

compass (kind of)–solar

compass (to)–attain

compass housing–binnacle

compass ink leg–pen

compass part–needle

compassion– commiseration, condolence, mercy, pity, sympathy

compassion (arch.)–ruth

compassion (lack of)–unsympathetic

compassionate – clement, merciful, pitiful, sympathizing, tender

compassionately–mercifully, sympathetically

compatible – accordant, agreeable, congruous, consistent, harmonious, suitable

compeer–companion, equal, match, mate, peer

compel–actuate, coerce, constrain, drive, force, incite, influence, instigate, oblige, require, urge

compel submission (by violent measures)–dragoon

compelled (be)–must

compelled (is)–has

compelling assent–cogent

compendious – abridged, brief, concise, condensed, short, succinct, summarized

compendium – abbreviation, abridgement, abstract, brief, comprisal, contraction, digest, epitome, medulla, syllabus, synopsis

compensate–indemnify, pay, redress, repay, requite, reward

compensation–bonus, indemnification, pay, requital, reward, salary, satisfaction, wages

compensation (meager)–pittance

compensation (wages)–emolument

compensation for services–salary, stipend, wages

compensation paid lord for killing man – manbot, manbote

compete–contend, contest, cope, vie

competence–capability, capacity, efficiency, proficiency, qualification, skill, suitability

competency–independence

competent–able, adequate, apt, can, capable, fit, qualified, sufficient, suitable

competition–contest, emulation, rivalry

competitor–contestant, rival

compilation–cento, digest

compile–add, amass, edit

compiler (English Thesaurus)–Roget

complacent (stupidity)–fatuous

complacent (unctuously)–smug

complain–bewail, carp, deplore, grieve, grouse, grumble, kick, protest, repine

complain (peevishly)–pule, whine, yammer

complainant–repiner

complainer–puler

complaining–querulous

complaint–ailment, disease, disorder, grievance, illness, lament, lamentation, malady, murmuring, protest, repining, wail

complaisance–amenity, civility, courtesy, suavity, urbanity

complaisant–affable, civil, compliant, courteous, gracious, obliging, polite complement–adjunct, crew, supplement

complement of hook–eye

complete–absolute, accomplish, achieve, all, conclude, consummate, dead, effect, effectuate, end, entire, fill, full, germane, intact, realize, terminate, total, unqualified, utter, whole

complete (in all parts)–entire

complete (full)–plenary

complete agreement–unison

complete and particularized –detailed

complete collection–set

complete shadow–umbra

completed–done, over

completed (poetic)–oer

completely–all, entirely, fully, quite, Scot, solidly, stark, totally, utterly

completely efficient–effectual

completeness (in general)– entelechy

complex–complicated, entangled, interlaced, intricate, involved, knotty, mazy, perplexed, twisted

compliance – acquiescence, assent, concession, consent, obedience, submission

compliance (non, obstinate) –recalcitrancy

compliant–complaisant, obedient, submissive

complicated–complex, difficult, embarrassed, intricate, involved, snarled, tangled

complicated (least)–simplest

complication–nodus

complication (in a drama)– node

compliment–adulate, adulation, blandishment, commend, commendation, encomium, flatter, flattery, obsequiousness, praise, servility, sycophancy

complimentary ticket–comp, pass

comply–accede, accord, acquiesce, agree, assent, conform, obey, submit, yield

comply with–observe

compone–arrange, compose, compound, settle

component–constituent, element, ingredient

component (chief)–basis

component of an atom–ion

comport–act, behave, behavior, correspond, deportment

comportable – consistent, suitable, tolerable

compose–compound, fashion, form, make, order, pen, tranquilize

composed–calm, collected, cool, quiet, sedate, sober, tranquil, wrote

composed of–consist

composed of flat plates– lamellate

composed of heaths–ericetal

composed of lobes–lobate

composed of rocks–rupestrian

composed of small flowers– floscular

composer–author, compositor, typesetter

composer (famous)–Foster, Igor Stravinski

composition – constitution, construction, formation, make-up, theme

composition (amorous)– erotic

composition (choral)–cantata

composition (division of a literary)–paragraph

composition (glassy)–enamel

composition (instrumental) –sonata

composition (ironic)–satire

composition (literary)–cento, essay, thesis, treatise

composition (metrical)–poesy

composition (musical)–concerto, duet, glee, op, opus, rondo, solo, sonata, trio

composition (nine-voiced)– nonet

composition (of selected works)–cento

composition (orchestral)– symphony

composition (patchwork)– cento

composition (piano)–sonata

composition (religious)–anthem, motet

composition (sacred)–cantata, motet, oratorio

composition (sacred choral) –anthem

composition (sacred musical)–motet, oratorio

composition (unmetrical)– prose

composition (vocal)–aria, song

composition (written)–essay

composition (written, abbr.) –MS

composition for one – soli, solo

composition for seven–septet

composition for two (Italian)–duetino, duetini (pl.), duetto, duetti (pl.)

composition formed by selections–cento

composition made up of selections–cento

composition of parts, forming a whole–synthesis

composition to be acted– drama

compositions–opera

composure–calmness, equanimity, repose, sedateness, tranquility

compound–combine, commixture, composite, ester, mix, unite

compound (ammonia)– amid, amide, amin, amine

compound (amorphous)– phenose

compound (bay fruit)–laurin

compound (binary of oxygen, with an element or radical)–oxid, oxide

compound (bitter crystalline)–aloin

compound (bone oil)–animin

compound (bromide potash)–tolane

compound (chemical)–amide, azo, ester, imid, imine, metamer, osone

compound (containing double bonds)–triene

compound (disinfectant)–phenol

compound (double amino)–diamide, diamin

compound (ether)–ester

compound (hydrogen)–acid, amine

compound (hypnotic)–trional

compound (imidogen)–imid

compound (iodine)–iodide

compound (medicinal)–bromide

compound (metallic)–ore

compound (oil and resin)–oleoresin

compound (oily liquid)–olein

compound (one of large)–azola

compound (organic)–ketone

compound (selenium)–selenid

compound (sweetish)–phenose

compound (white alkaline)–soda

compound containing two hydroxyl groups–diols

compound from aloes–aloin

compound of elements–bromide

compound of hydrogen and nitrogen–ammonia

compound of iodine–iodide

compound of sodium–soda

compound tincture (medicinal)–elixir

compound with same elements as another but different properties–metamer

comprehend–conceive, em-

body, enclose, grasp, imagine, involve, know, see, sense, understand

comprehensible – comprised, conceivable, included, intelligible

comprehensible (readily)–exoteric

comprehensive – compendious, extensive, full, generic, large, wide

compress – astringe, condense, press, squeeze

compress (surgical)–stupe

comprise–contain, embrace, enclose, imply, involve

comprising a pair–twosome

compt–neat, polished, spruce

compulsion–duress, force

compulsory–imperative, obligatory

compunction – regret, remorse

computation–account, estimate, numeration, reckoning

computation (erroneous)–misreckoning

compute–calculate, count, enumerate, estimate, figure, number, reckon

comrade–associate, buddy, companion, fellow, mate, pal, peer

comrade (coll.)–pal

comrade in arms–ally

comte–count

comtesse–countess

con–cheat, deceive, know, learn, peruse, steer, study, swindle, understand

conceal – bescreen, cloak, cover, dern, derne, hide, mask, screen, secrete, veil

conceal (law)–eloin

conceal by false appearance–disguise

concealed–covered, covert, disguised, insidious, latent, perdue

concealed (by a mask)–larvate, larvated

concede–accord, acknowledge, admit, allow, grant, own, surrender, yield

conceit – caprice, egotism,

fancy, idea, tympany, vagary

conceited – arrogant, egotistic, egotistical, opinionated, proud, vain

conceited person–prig

conceited silly man–coxcomb

conceive–fancy, ideate, imagine, realize, suppose, suspect, think

conceive thoughts–ideate

conceived as possible–dreamed

concentrate–center, compact, condense, consolidate, focus, intensify, mass

concept – idea, opinion, thought

concept (ultimate)–category

conception – apprehension, comprehension, conceit, idea, notion

concern–affair, affect, care, interest, matter, pertain, sake, worry

concerning–about, anent, anenst, for, of, on, re, upon

concerning a title–titular

concerning the ear–otic

concert by single performer–recital

concerted (not)–solo

concession–acquiescence, assent, cession, compliance, favor

concierge–doorkeeper, warden

conciliate–appease, mollify, pacify, propitiate, reconcile

conciliatory–irenic, irenical, mollifying, propitiating

conciliatory bribe–sop

concise–compendious, comprehensive, crisp, curt, laconic, neat, pithy, pointed, pregnant, sententious, succinct, summary, terse

concise (rudely)–curt

concise and coherent (precisely)–serried

concise statement or summary–precis

conclude–arrange, close, deduce, determine, end, endeth, finish, infer, settle, terminate

conclusion–close, deduction, decision, determination, end, epilogue, finale, finis, finish, inference, last, result

conclusion arrived at through critical perception–diagnosis

conclusive–convincing, decisive, final, irrefutable, ultimate, unanswerable, valid

conclusively–definitely, determinately

concoct–assimilate, brew, digest, perfect, prepare

concoction – combination, compound, device, fabrication, invention, mixture, plan, plot

concocts–composes, devises, fabricates

concomitant–accessory, attendant, concurrent, coincident, co-operant, synchronous

concord – agreement, harmony, peace, unison

concordant–agreeing, consonant, correspondent, harmonic, harmonious

concrete (kind of)–beton

concrete (of lime, sand and cement)–beton

concretion (shelly, used as gem)–pearl

concretion found in mollusk shell–pearl

concur–accede, acquiesce, agree, approve, assent, combine, consent, unite

concurrence–adherence, coincidence, concourse, conjunction, union

concurrent – accompanying, associated, coincident, meeting, synchronous, united, uniting

condemn–adjudge, blame, censure, doom, sentence

condemn to punishment–sentence

condensation (atmospheric) –dew

condense–abridge, combine, compact, compress, concentrate, consolidate, constrict, contract, diminish, harden, lessen, narrow, reduce, solidify, squeeze, thicken, unite

condense by attraction to a solid surface–absorb

condensed publication–tabloid

condenser (flame of lamp)–cric

condescend–concede, deign, descend, stoop, submit, vouchsafe

condign – adequate, deserved, fit, severe, suitable, worthy

condiment–mace, mustard, pepper, relish, sage, salt, seasoning, vinegar

condiment (aromatic)–spice

condiment (spiced)–catsup, ketchup

condiment (spiced highly)–curry

condiment (vegetable)–spice

condite–pickled, preserved, seasoned

condition – case, circumstance, estate, fettle, if, limitation, plight, predicament, proviso, requisite, situation, stage, state, station, status, term

condition (flushed)–rosiness

condition (habitual)–tenor

condition (hypnotic)–trance

condition (miserable, unkempt)–squalor

condition (murky) – fog, haze

condition (proper, slang)–kilter

condition (supposition)–if

condition (thriving)–fettle

condition made–premise

condition of living–state

condition of stupor–narcose

conditional stipulation–proviso

conditionally–provided, provisionally

conditions (favorable)–odds

condog–agree, concur

condone – excuse, forgive, pardon .

condor–vulture

conduce–contribute, effect, redound, tend

conduct–action, bearing, behavior, comport, control, convoy, demeanor, deportment, direct, escort, govern, guide, lead, manage, mien, operate, regulate, rule, run, superintend, supervise

conduct (breach of)–guilty

conduct (pert. to)–moral

conduct a cause–plead

conduct one's self–behave, comport, demean

conductor–escort, director, guide, leader, manager, operator

conductor (great)–maestro

conductor by which electric current leaves–cathode

conduit–aqueduct, canal, channel, main, pipe, sewer, tube

conduit (side)–lateral

cone (pine)–strobile

cone (silver amalgam, prepared for smelting)–pina

cone-bearing tree–conifer, larch, larches (pl.)

cone-like–pineal

cone of silver amalgam–pina

cone-shaped–conic, conical, pineal

confabulate–chat, prattle

confection–bittersweet, caramel, comfit, preserve, sweetmeat

confection (soft, molded)–fondant

confederacy–alliance, association, coalition, combination, covenant, federation, league, union

confederacy of merchants–hanse

Confederacy president–Davis

confederate–abetter, abettor,

accessory, accomplice, ally, assistant, associate

confederate (coll.)–pal, reb

Confederate brigadier general–Morgan

confederation–alliance, compact, league

confer–advise, bestow, collate, commune, consult, counsel, give, invest, parley

confer knighthood upon–dub

confer on exchange of prisoners–parley

conference – consultation, council, discussion, interview, palaver, parley, pow-wow, trust

conference (secret)–huddle

conferred title upon–ennobled

confess–acknowledge, admit, avow, own

confession–admission, acknowledgement, avowal, creed, profession, shrift

confession of faith–creed, credo

confession received and absolution given–shrive

confetti–bonbons, confections, sweetmeats

confide–commit, rely, trust

confidence–assurance, credence, effrontery, faith, impertinence, impudence, morale, sureness

confidence (lacking in one's self)–diffident

confidence (to restore)–reassure

confidence game–bunco

confident–assured, hopeful, reliant, sanguine, secure, smug, sure

confidential–auricular, esoteric, intimate, private, privy, secret

confiding–reliable, trustful, trustworthy

configuration–contour, form, shape

confine–cage, circumscribe, compass, coop, hem, immure, incarcerate, intern,

limit, lock, mew, pen, restrain, stint, tie

confine by bars–cage, jail

confine in a hovel–sty

confine to a locality–intern

confine to a particular place–local

confined–caged, impended, impounded, interned, limited, pent

confined (not)–free, loose

confined in narrow habitation–cribbed

confined to a particular locality–endemic

confined to select circle–esoteric

confinement – accouchement, childbirth, restraint

confinement (solitary)–incommunicado

confirm–approve, assure, attest, corroborate, fortify, prove, ratify, sanction, seal, settle, substantiate, sustain, validate, verify

confirmed–inveterate, ratified

confiscate–appropriate, seize

conflagration–fever, fire, inflammation

conflict–battle, bout, clash, combat, competition, contend, contention, contest, duel, encounter, fight, oppose, strife, struggle, war

conflict (interlude in)–truce

conflict (military)–action

confluence – assimilation, junction, meeting

conform – accommodate, adapt, adjust, compose, fit, go, obey, reconcile, settle, suit

conform in conduct–lean

conform to shape–fit

conformances to the law–dharmas

conforming in action–parallel

conformist–complier, yielder

conformity–agreement, congruity, harmony

conformity to law–legality

confound–abash, amaze, astonish, astound, baffle, be-

wilder, dumbfound, embarrass, intermingle, mix

confront–encounter, face, meet, oppose

confronted (insolently)–nosed

confuse–abash, addle, baffle, befuddle, bewilder, disarrange, discompose, disconcert, disorder, distract, flurry, fluster, jumble, maze, mix, muddle, upset

confused (completely)–chaotic

confused in action–deranged

confused mixture–farrago

confused struggle–scuffle

confusion–abashment, agitation, bewilderment, chaos, derangement, din, disarray, disorder, jumble, mess, perplexity, pother, turmoil

confute–deny, expose, refute

conge–bow, curtsy, passport, permission

congeal–freeze, ice

congeal into hoarfrost–rime

congenial–boon, compatible, kindred, sympathetic

congeniality–compatibility

congenital–connate, constitutional, innate, natural

conger–cucumber, eel

congeries–aggregation, collection, heap

congestion – accumulation, gathering, heap, jam, stoppage

Congo tributary–Ubangi

congratulate–felicitate

congregate–assemble, collect, gather, group, herd, mass, meet, muster, troop

congregation–assembly, collection, gathering, mass

congregation (one of)–hearer

Congregation of Jesus and Mary–Eudist

congress–assembly, conclave, convention, convocation, council, diet, legislature, meeting, parliament

congressional edifice–capitol

conic sections–parabolas
conifer–cedar, pine
coniferous–piny
coniferous tree–cedar, larch, pine
conjecture – aim, divine, guess, imagine, opine, presume, supposal, suppose, surmise, suspect, think
conjoint–correlative
conjugal–connubial, matrimonial
conjugate point (a)–acnode
conjunct–combined, conjoined, united
conjunction–and, as, but, if, nor, or, since, than; association, combination, union
conjunction (comparative)–than
conjunction (Fr.)–et
conjunction (Latin)–et
conjure–adjure, enjoin, entreat, invoke, juggle, pray, supplicate
conjured up–exorcised
conjurer–juggler, mage, magician, voodoo
conk–decay, head, nose
connach–spoil, waste
Connacht king–Ailill
connate–akin, allied, cognate, congenial
connect–associate, attach, fasten, join, link, relate, unite
connect with short dash–hyphenate
connected (grown together)–adnates
connected (logically)–coherent
connected order–series
connected systematically–correlated
connected with a purpose–telic
Connecticut (island south of, abbr.)–L.I.
Connecticut city–Darien, Meriden
Connecticut school (former collegiate)–Yale
Connecticut town–Avon

connecting band of tissue–ligament
connecting cell–heterocyst
connection–alliance, association, coherence, commerce, communication, conjunction, continuity, family, intercourse, junction, kinship, nexus, relationship, relevance, union
connection (U-shaped) – clevis
connection (with outer world)–senses
connective (negative)–nor
conner–examiner, inspector, peruser, tester
connex–bond, tie
connoisseur–gourmand
connoisseur (eating and drinking)–gourmet
connoisseur (jewel)–lapidarist
connotation–denotation
connotation of a term–intent
connubial–marital, matrimonial
conquer–beat, best, crush, defeat, discomfit, humble, master, overcome, overpower, overthrow, reduce, subdue, subject, subjugate, surmount, vanquish, win
conqueror–hero, victor
conquest–mastery, triumph, victory
conquest (to enter)–invade
consanguineous–akin
consanguinity–affinity
consanguinity (Mohammedan law)–nasab
conscience smitten–contrite
conscientious–dutiful, faithful, punctilious, scrupulous
conscientious objections – scruples
conscious–aware, cognizant, feeling, sensible, sentient
consciousness (active)–attention
consecrate – anoint, bless, dedicate, devote, hallow
consecrate again–rededicate

consecrated–blest, devoted, hallowed, votive
consecrated (something)–sacrum
consecrated by vow–votary, votive
consecration (relating to)–dedicatory
consent–accede, accord, acquiesce, agree, approval, assent, compliance, concur, permission, yield
consequence – effect, end, event, inference, outcome, result
consequence (in, of)–pursuant
consequently–consecutively, hence, so, subsequently, therefore
conservative–staid, Tory
conserve–defend, guard, maintain, protect, save, secure, shield, sustain, uphold; preserves, sweetmeat
conserve (grape)–uvate
conserve (sweet)–jam
consider–cogitate, contemplate, deem, deliberate, esteem, heed, meditate, muse, ponder, rate, reflect, regard, revolve, ruminate, see, weigh
consider as good approve
considerable – important, large, notable, noteworthy, remarkable
considerable number–several
considerate – deliberate, gentle, heedful, kind, prudent, reflective, serious, thoughtful
consideration – attention, cogitation, consequence, deference, deliberation, esteem, examination, importance, incentive, inducement, influence, meditation, reflection, regard, reputation, rumination, study
consideration (personal)–self

consideration (practical)–attention

considered (can be)–debatable

considered apart from object –abstract

considering–since

consign–commit, deliver, remand, resign

consign to inferior position–relegate

consign to ruin–doom

consist of–comprise, comprize, contain, embrace, enclose, imply, involve

consist with–suit

consistent in point of reasoning–logical

consisting of cavities–cellulose

consisting of one atom–monomatic

consisting of pages–paginal

consisting of smaller particles–finer

consisting of thin layers–laminate

consisting of three measures –trimeter

consisting of two parts–binary

consolation–comfort, solace

console–alleviate, bracket, cabinet, cheer, comfort, desk, encourage, solace, soothe, support, sustain, table

consolidate–coalesce, combine, compact, compress, knit, mass, solidify, strengthen, unify, unite

consommé–soup

consonance – agreeableness, agreement, congruity, consistency, harmony, suitableness, unison

consonant–accordant, compatible, congruous, consistent, palatal

consonant (unaspirated)–lene

consonant (kind of)–palatal

consonant (smooth)–lenis

consonant (voiceless)–spirate, lene

consonous–symphonious

consort–associate, colleague, companion, husband, mate, partner, spouse, wife

consort (of Hindu deity)–Sakti

conspicuous–celebrated, famous, glaring, illustrious, outstanding, prominent

conspiracy–cabal, intrigue, machination, plot, scheme

conspire–collude, confederate, plot, scheme, unite

conspire together–complot

constable–keeper, policeman, staff, staves (pl.), warden

constabulary–police

constancy–adherence, allegiance, ardor, attachment, continual, devotedness, devotion, eagerness, earnestness, faith, faithfulness, fealty, fidelity, honesty, integrity, loyalty, steadfastness, truth, zeal

constant–continual, faithful, firm, fixed, invariable, invariant, perpetual, persistent, regular, resolute, steadfast, true, uniform

constant irritating desire–itch

Constantinople foreign quarter–Pera

constellation – Andromeda, Aquarius, Ara, Argo, Aries, Asterism, Bootes, Cancer, Capricornus, Car, Cepheus, Cetus, Dipper, Draco, Gemini, Leo, Libra, Lyre, Malus, Orion, Pegasus, Ram, Sagittarius, Scorpio, Sept, Septi, Taurus, Ursa, Vega, Virgo

constellation (Aries)–Ram

constellation (brightest star in)–Cora

constellation (either of two) –Ursa

constellation (northern) – Car, Draco, Leo, Lyra

constellation (southern)–Ara, Argo, Scorpio

constellation of Argo division–Vela

constellation of bears–Ursa

constellation on the equator –Orion

constellation star (in Aquila)–Deneb

consternation – alarm, amazement, fear, fright, horror, panic, trepidity

constituent – component, elector, element, factor, ingredient, matter, voter

constituent (necessary)–essence

constituent of blood serum–opsonin

constituent of claws, feathers, hair, horns, nails, wool–keratin

constituent of coal–carbon

constituent of earth's crust–odin

constituent of oil of cloves (chief)–eugenol

constituent of tea and coffee –caffeine

constituent part–element

constitute a whole (to help) –complementary

constitution–custom, enactment, institution, law, ordinance

Constitution State – Connecticut

constitutional right – franchise

constitutional vigor–nerve

constrain–check, compel, curb, drive, force, impel, necessitate, oblige, press, urge

constrained by sense of duty –obligated

constrains to go along–hales

constraint–bond, coercion, compulsion, confinement, force, pressure, reserve, stiffness, stress

constrict–bind, condense, contract, cramp, shrink, squeeze, tie, tighten

constriction of breathing tube–strangulation

construct–build, compose,

erect, fabricate, frame, make, originate, rear
constructive–creative, implicit, virtual
constructive metabolism–anabolism
constructor – acequiador, builder, contractor
construe–interpret, translate
consuetude – custom, habit, usage
consular officer's written authorization–exequator
consult together–confer
consultants–confreres
consultation–conference, deliberation, discussion, interview
consume–absorb, burn, devour, dissipate, eat, spend, squander, use
consumed (Hawaiian)–pau
consummate–achieve, complete, finish, ideal, perfect
contact–junction, meeting, touch, touching, union
contact (forcible)–impact
contact (three point of two branches of a curve)–oscnode
contact with (be in)–against, touch
contain–comprehend, comprise, cover, embody, embrace, have, hold, include, keep, retain, subsume
contained in the text–textual
container–bag, basket, bottle, box, can, capsule, carton, case, crate, cruet, decanter, ewer, jug, pan, pot, sack, tin, urn, vase
container (coffee and tea)–canister
container (drug)–capsule
container (large)–bin, cistern, crib, tub, vat
container (large glass, acid)–carboy
container (millinery)–bandbox, hatbox
container (prickly seed)–bur
container (seed)–bur, loment, pod
container (woven)–basket, hamper, hanaper

containing air–pneumatic
containing antimony–stibiate
containing boron–boracic, boric
containing carbon–carboniferous
containing cerium–ceric
containing copper–cupric
containing fire–igneous
containing gold–auric, dore
containing iron–ferric
containing maxims–gnomicar
containing no liquid–aneroid
containing orifices–porous
containing potash and soda –alkalic
containing pure spirit–alcoholic
containing rough, hard particles–gritty
containing saltpeter–nitrous
containing seedlike parts–acinous
containing silver–lunar
containing slag–drossy
containing ten–denar, denary
containing tin (chem.)–stanic
contaminate–befoul, corrupt, debauch, desecrate, dishonor, infect, poison, pollute, slur, soil, stain, sully, taint, vitiate
contaminated (least)–purest
contemn–despise, disdain, scorn, spurn
contemplate – consider, deign, meditate, muse, plan, ponder, propose, scan, study, view
contemplative – meditative, pensive, sedate
contempt–contumely, derision, disdain
contempt (rare)–despect
contemptible–abject, base, beggarly, cheap, despicable, groveling, inferior, insignificant, low, sordid, sorry, worthless
contemptibleness - despicability

contemptuous – contumelious, disdainful, haughty, insolent, scornful, supercilious
contemptuously (treat)–flout
contend–argue, assert, compete, contest, contrive, cope, fight, grapple, maintain, militate, quarrel, race, strive, vie
contend with on even footing–cope
content–gratify, please, satisfy, suffice
contention–combat, competition, conflict, debate, disagreement, dissension, emulation, feud, litigation, quarrel, rivalry, strife, struggle, variance, war
contention (violent)–strife
contentious–belligerent, dissentious, litigious, peevish, perverse, pugnacious, wrangling
contentment–bliss, gratification, pleasure, satisfaction
conterminous–adjacent, adjoining, next, proximal
contest–altercation, argue, argument, bout, competition, cope, debate, emulation, game, litigate, race, strife, struggle, sue, tilt, trial, vie
contest (boxing, coll.)–setto
contest (draw)–stalemate
contest (fitness)–tryout
contest (log birling)–roleo
contest (recreational)–game
contest (short, vigorous)–set-to
contest (slight)–skirmish
contest (undecided)–draw
contestant–contender
contestant for office–candidate
contiguous–adjacent, adjoining, immediate, near, neighboring, next, proximate, touching
continent (prehistoric)–Atlantis
continent (the)–mainland

contingency–accident, case, casualty, chance

contingent–accidental, casual, dependent, fortuitous, provisional

contingent upon–depends

continual–ceaseless, connected, constant, continued, endless, enduring, eternal, everlasting, imperishable, incessant, invariable, perennial, permanent, perpetual, regular, unceasing, undying, uniform, unintermitted, uninterrupted, unremitting

continually–constantly, ever, unceasingly

continuance–duration

continuation – continuity, prolongation, propagation, sequel

continue–abide, last, persevere, proceed, remain, resume, stay

continue doggedly–persist

continued striving–persevered

continuing–still

continuing long time–chronic

continuous–chronic, continued, endless, unbroken, uninterrupted

continuous outflow–drain

contorted–bent, deformed, distorted, perverted, twisted, wrested, wry

contour – configuration, curve, figure, form, graph, line, outline, profile

contra–against, contrariwise, contrary, offset

contraband – illegal, illicit, unlawful

contract–agreement, arrangement, bargain, cartel, compact, constrict, convention, covenant, engage, incur, indenture, knit, lease, pact, pledge, promise, reduce, shrink, straighten, understanding

contracting into wrinkles–shriveling

contraction (heart)–systole

contraction (involuntary muscular)–spasm

contraction (muscular)–tic

contraction (poetic)–tis

contraction in terms–bull

contrada – quarter, street, ward, way

contradict–belie, deny, gainsay, impugn, negate, oppose, rebut, refute

contradiction (seeming)–paradox

contradictory – inconsistent, opposite

contradictory (not)–consistent

contrary – adverse, antagonistic, counter, discordant, inimical, opposed, opposite, repugnant, reverse

contrary (on the)–rather

contrary minded–averse

contrary to conventional doctrine–unorthodox

contrary to happiness–ill

contrast–compare, opposite

contravene–defy, disregard, infringe, thwart, violate

contribute–conduce, donate, give

contribution–donation, payment, scot

contrite–humble, penitent, repentant, sorrowful

contrition–attrition, compunction, humiliation, penitence

contrivance–design, device, invention, machine, project, shift

contrivance (human)–art

contrivance (temporary)–makeshift

contrive–design, devise, fabricate, fashion, frame, hatch, invent, manage, plan, plot, project, scheme, weave

control–check, conduct, direct, direction, dominate, govern, gripe, guide, hold, manage, management, preside, regimen,

regulate, regulation, rein, restrain, rule, subdue, wield

control (full)–mastery

controller (motor speed)–rheocrat

controlling power–dominator

controversial – disputatious, eristic, eristical, polemic, polemical

controversialist–eristic

controversy–altercation, argument, contention, debate, disagreement, disputation, dispute, wrangle

controvert–deny, dispute, oppose

contumacious – headstrong, insubordinate, intractable, mutinous, perverse, rebellious, refractory, riotous, seditious, unruly, unyielding

contumacy–obstinacy, perverseness, stubbornness

contusion–bruise, injury

conundrum–enigma, riddle

convalesce–recover, recuperate

convene–assemble, congregate, meet, sit, unite

convenience–leisure

convenient – accessible, adapted, agreeable, commodious, fitted, handy, ready, suitable, suited

convent–cloister

convent head–abbess, abbot

convent reception room–parlatory

convention–assemblage, assembly, custom, gathering, meeting, usage

convention (long established)–tradition

conventional–accepted, ceremonial, correct, customary, modish, usual

conventional type–iconic

converge on a single point–focus

conversant – acquainted, adept, expert, familiar, practiced, proficient, skilled, versed conversation–chat, communion, conference, dialogue, discourse, interlocution, talk

conversation of three people (rare)–trialog

conversationalist–talker

converse–association, chat, communion, convert, discourse, intercourse, obverse, reverse, talk

converse (intimately)–commune

conversion (mutual)–interconversion

conversion into steel–acieration

convert–change, neophyte, proselyte, regenerate, transform

convert into aeriform fluid–gasify

convert into electric particles–ionize

convert into money–cash, liquidate, mint

convert into ordinary language–decode

convert into soap–saponify

convert into steam–evaporate

convert into steel–acierate

converted into silica–silicified

convertible–equivalent, interchangeable, reciprocal, synonymous

convex–curved, rounded

convex (bulging)–bowed

convex molding–torus

convexity–bulge, curve

convey–carry, communicate, convoy, deed, impart, import, pass, send, transfer, transmit, transport

convey (by lease)–demise

convey beyond jurisdiction (law)–eloin

convey legally–bequeath, deed, devise, dispone, grant

convey to nearer place–bring

conveyance–auto, automobile, bus, car, carriage, rattler, sled, taxi, train, tram

conveyance of an estate–demise

conveying ideas–notional

conveying outward–exodic

conveyor of property–alienor

convict–criminal, culprit, felon, lifer, malefactor, prisoner

convict (given special liberties)–trusty

convince–assure, confute, overcome, overpower, persuade, subdue

convincing–cogent, conclusive, persuasive, potent, telling

convincing evidence–proof

convivial–festive, gay, jovial, social

convocation–assembly, congregation, congress, convention, council, diet, meeting, synod

convoke–assemble, call, convene, summon

convoy–accompany, attend, conduct, escort, guide

convulse–agitate, disturb, shake

convulsion–agitation, disturbance, paroxysm, spasm, uproar

convulsive breath–gasp

cony–daman, ganam, rabbit

cony (Old Testament)–daman

cony (South African)–das

cony catcher–cheat, sharper, swindler

cony of the Bible–hyrax

coo (Scot.)–curr

coof–blockhead, dolt, lout

cooja–goglet

cook (partially)–parboil

cook with dry heat–bake, roast

cooked meat savors–nidors

cookies (crisp)–snaps

cookies (ginger)–snaps

cooking device–etna, griddle, plate, stove

cooking mixture–batter

cooking pot–olla

cool–calm, careless, chilly, collected, composed, fan, ice, imperturbable, nonchalant, sedate, tranquil, unconcerned, unmoved, unruffled

cool (to)–chill, fan, ice, mitigate, temper

cool to low point–freeze, ice

cooled lava–aa

cooler–jail, lockup, prison, refrigerant

cooler (water)–icer, olla

coolness–aplomb

coop–cage, confine, enclosure, pen

co-operate–agree, combine, concur, conduce, conspire, contribute, tend

co-operate secretly–connive

cootie–louse

copal (soft variety)–anime

copies (manuscript)–scribes

copious–abundant, ample, exuberant, full, overflowing, plenteous, plentiful, profuse, rich

copious flow–river

copper–cent, penny, policeman

copper (Roman)–aes

copper alloy–oroide

copper and tin alloy–bronze, oroide, pewter

copper and zinc alloy–brass

copper arsenate–erinite

copper film (green)–patina

copper kettle (anc.)–lebes

copper nickel–niccolite

copper sulpharsenate–enargite

copper sulphide (for coloring glass)–ferretto

Copperfield's (David) wife (first)–Dora

Copperfield's (David) wife (second)–Agnes

coppice–brushwood, copse, grove, growth, thicket, underwood

Coptic church titles (ecclesiastical)–Anbas

copy–ape, duplicate, imitate, imitation, reprint, reproduction, tracing, transcribe, transcript

copy (corrected)–revision
copy (exact, true)–estreat
copy (expert, law)–estreat
copy actions–ape
copy from original–ectype
copy made through thin paper–tracing
copy of document (original) –protocol
copyread–edit
coquet (male)–flirt
coquette (female)–flirt
coquettish–coy
coquin–knave, rascal, rogue
coral–millepore, polyps, red
coral (porous wall)–porite
coral division–aporosa
coral formation–palus, pali (pl.)
coral island–atoll, key
coral isle (ring-shaped)– atoll
coral reef–key
coral reef worm–palolo
coral ridge–reef
cord–line, rope, string
cord (braided)–sennit
cord (candlenut bark)–aea
cord (cloth-covered)–welt
cord (for drawing together) –lace
cord (Hawaiian)–aea
cord (spinal)–medulla
cord (twisted)–torsade
cordage (braided, for hat making)–sennit
cordage system installed on vessel–rigging
corded fabric–poplin, rep
cordelle–haul, tow, towline, towrope
cordial–anisette, ardent, elixir, genial, hearty, real, kummel, sincere, vigorous, unfeigned, warm, zealous
cordial (apricot)–periscot
cordial (kind of)–anisette
cordial (raspberry)–shrub
core–center, heart, hub, kernel, nub, nucleus, nut, substance
core (metal-object fashioning)–ame
core (prehistoric, shaping)– ame

core (used in forming a hollow metal object, anc.)– ame
Corinthian king–Polybus
corium–derm, derma
cork–bobber, float, plug, stopper, stopple
cork (pert. to)–suberic
cork (thin flat, for stopping wide-mouthed bottle)– shive
cormorant–bird, ravenous, voracious
cormorant (crested)–shag
cormorant (red-faced)–urile
cormorant (young)–shaglet
corn–salt
corn (ground)–grist
corn (hulled)–samp
corn belt state–Dakota, Illinois, Indiana, Iowa, Kansas, Missouri, Minnesota, Nebraska, Ohio
cornbinks–bluebottle
corn bread–pone
corncake–pone
corncracker–Kentuckian
Corncracker State – Kentucky
corndodger–pone
corn meal (fried)–hoecake
corn meal mush–atole
corn porridge–samp
cornstalk scale (outside)– shive
corner–angle, cantle, coign, coigne, in, nook, trap, tree
corner (projecting)–coign, coigne
cornered (sharp)–angular
cornet–horn
cornet (signal on)–sennet
cornice–eave
cornice (part of)–drip
Cornish prefix, signifying town–tre
cornucopia–horn
Cornwall mine–bal
corolla (helmet-shaped part of)–galea
corolla (leaf of)–petal
corolla (part of)–petal
corolla of flower–perianth
corollary (geometrical)– porism

corona–aureole, cigar, circlet, crown, garland
coroner (sheriff's deputy)– elisor
coronet–anadem, crown, diadem, tiara
corporal–bodily
corporal punishment–spanking, whipping
corporation–body
corporeal–bodily, material, physical, somal
corps (Ger.)–korps
corpse–body, cadaver
corpulence–fatness, fleshiness, obesity
corpulence (to reduce)–bant
corpulent–bulky, fat, obese, stout
corpuscle (red blood in anemia)–poikilocyte
corpuscles (lack of red)–anemia
corral–enclosure, pen
corral (cattle)–atajo
correct–accurate, amend, better, chasten, conventional, definite, edit, emend, faultless, improve, particular, perfect, proper, punctilious, rectify, reform, regular, remedy, right, rigorous, scrupulous, strict, true
correct (slang)–O.K., okay
correct a manuscript–edit
correct by punishment– chasten
correct copy–revise
correction – amendment, change, chastisement, punishment, rebuke, rectification, revisal
correctly–properly, rightly, truthfully
correctly tuned–keyed
corrector of evils, abuses–reformer
correlative–nor, reciprocal
correlative of either–or
correspond–accord, agree, analogous, comport, fit, harmonize, match, suit
correspond in sound–assonate

corresponding in certain respects–analogous

corresponding in structure–homologic

corresponding part – analogue

corresponds exactly–coincides

corresponds to–parallels

corridor–gallery, hall, passageway

corrige–correct, punish

corrigible–amended, correctable, reformed

corroborate–confirm, establish, prove, roborate, substantiate

corrode–bite, consume, eat, erode, gnaw, rust, waste

corrosive–erodent, mordant

corrugate–crimp, crinkle, crumpled, furrowed, wrinkled

corrupt–adulterated, contaminated, crooked, defiled, deprave, dishonest, polluted, putrefy, putrid, rot, rotten, taint, venal, vitiate

corruption – adulteration, contamination, debasement, defilement, depravation, pollution, putrescence, taint

corruption of English language–pidgin

corsage–bodice, boquet, bouquet, waist

corsair–pirate, privateer

Corsica feud–vendetta

cortege–parade, procession, retinue

cortex–bark, rind

corundum–abrasive, emery

corundum (dark granular)–emeru

coruscate–gleam, radiate, scintillate, shine, sparkle

cosmetic–cream, henna, lipstick, mascara, paint, rouge

cosmic order (Vedic religion)–rita

Cossack–ataman, hetman, tartar, tatar

Cossack captain–Sotnik

Cossack chief–ataman, hetman

Cossack whip–knout

cosset–caress, cuddle, fondle, lamb, pamper, pet

cossette–chip

cossid–messenger

cost–deprivation, detriment, expenditure, expense, loss, outlay, price, rental, suffering

costa–rib

Costa Rican city–Alajuela, Heredia, San Jose (c.)

Costa Rican coin–centimo (cop., ni.), colon (s.)

Costa Rican measure–caballeria, cajuela, fanega, manzana, tercia

Costa Rican mountain–Blanco, Chirripo

Costa Rican port–Porto Limon, Punta Arenas

Costa Rican weight–bag, caja

costate–ribbed

costermonger–hawker, peddler

costly–dear, expensive, extravagant, high-priced, rich, splendid

costmary plant–alecost

costume–attire, clothing, dress, garb, habit, raiment

cot–bed, bedstead, boat, charpoy, clique, coop, cote, cottage, house, hut, pen, set, shelter

cote–coop, cottage, house, hut

coterie–clique, set

cothamore–greatcoat

cotta–blanket, surplice

cottage–cot, house, hut, shed, shelter

cottage (suburban)–villa

cottager (peasant)–cottar

cotton (hard twisted)–lisle

cotton (raw, fine grade)–bayal

cotton (twisted roll of)–slub

cotton (waste)–noil

cotton cloth–calico, denim, jeans, percale

cotton cloth (twill)–janes

cotton extraction–bolly

cotton fabric (fine)–madras

cotton fiber–lint, staple

cotton gin inventor–Eli Whitney

cotton knot–nep

cotton seeding machine–gin

cotton spinning machine–mule

Cotton State–Alabama

cotton sugar–raffinose

couch–bed, cot, divan, lair, pallet, sofa

couch (with shafts)–litter, stretcher

cougar–catamount, panther, puma

cough (a)–tussis

cough (pert. to)–tussive

council – assembly, cabal, consultation, senate, synod

council (arch.)–rede

council (church)–synod

council (deliberate)–synod

council (ecclesiastical)–synod

council (pert. to)–cameral

council (secret)–conclave

council (supreme)–senate

council table cover–tapis

counsel–advice, advise, instruction, recommend, rede

counsel (arch.)–rede

counsel (professional)–advice

counselor (counsellor)–adviser, advisor, attorney, counsel, lawyer, mentor, nestor, sage

counselor (wise)–nestor

counselor-at-law–barrister

count–calculate, compute, enumerate, number, reckon, rely, tale, tell

Count of Monte Cristo hero –Dantes

count over–enumerate

countenance – abet, aid, brow, endorse, face, sanction, support, visage

counter–adverse, chip, computer, contrary

counteract–antidote, neutralize, nullify

counterfeit – artificial, as-

sume, fake, false, ficti-
tious, forge, forged, forgery, imitate, mock,
sham, spurious
counterfeiter–coiner
counterfeiting (act of)–falsification
counterfoil–stub
counterirritant–arnica
counterirritant (surgical)–
seton
countermand–abolish, an-
nul, cancel, counteract,
forbid, frustrate, prohibit,
recall, reverse, revoke
counterpane–coverlet, quilt
counterpart – complement,
copy, double, duplicate,
like, parallel, twin
counterpoise – compensate,
counteract, counterbal-
ance, equalize, offset
countersign–password, sign,
signal, signature, watch-
word
countersink–chamfer, ream
countless–incalculable, infinite, numberless
countrified–rural
country – commonwealth,
land, nation, state, territory
country (anc.)–Aram, Elis
country (conquered by Caesar)–Gaul
country (mythical)–Oz
country (open)–weald
country (pert. to)–agrestic,
pastoral, rural
country (settled)–colony
country (the, law)–pais
country gallant–swain
country gooseberry–bilimbi
country house (small)–ca-
sino
country inhabitant (oldest)
–aborigine
country jake–rustic, yokel
countryman – compatriot,
peasant, rustic, yokel
countryman (coll.)–hayseed,
rube
country place–seat, villa
country walnut–candlenut
county (Eng.)–shire
county (Louisiana)–parish

coup–barter, buy, capsize,
overturn, strike, traffic,
upset
coup-cart (Scot.)–dumpcart
couple–brace, bracket, duo,
dyad, join, link, marry,
mate, pair, team, tie,
twin, two, unite, yoke
couple (oxen)–yoke
couple together–bracket
coupled–braced, gemel,
joined, linked, married,
mated, paired, teamed,
united
courage–audacity, boldness,
bravery, daring, daunt-
lessness, fearlessness,
firmness, fortitude, gal-
lantry, grit, hardihood,
heart, heroism, intrepid-
ity, mettle, pluck, prow-
ess, sand, valor
courage (coll.)–sand
courage (passive)–fortitude
courage (to give)–embolden
courage (unyielding)–grit
courageous – adventurous,
bold, brave, daring, en-
terprising, fearless, gallant, game, hardy, heroic,
intrepid, manly, spartan,
stout, valiant, valorous
courageous (slang)–spunky
courant–caper, gazette, letter, messenger, newspa-
per, romp
courier–attendant, horse-
man, messenger
courier (military)–estafet
course–career, line, manner,
method, mode, path,
road, route, series, stream,
succession
course (direct)–beeline
course (fixed)–rote, route,
routine
course (general)–trend
course (regular)–regimen,
rote, route, routine
course (roundabout)–detour,
indirection
course (settled)–tenor
course (special college)–
seminar
course (straight)–beeline
course (swift)–career

course (take roundabout)–
detour
course (traveled)–route
course of achievement–ca-
reer
course of action–procedure
course of action (regular)–
routine
course of action (settled)–
habit
course of conduct–career
course of eating–diet
course of instruction–lessons
course of procedure–rule
course of public life–career
course of thought–tenor
course of travel–route
courser – charger, horse,
steed
court – quadrangle, spark,
tribunal, woo
court (circuit)–eyre
court (ecclesiastical)–rota
court (Eng., old)–eyre
court (inner)–patio
court (old)–leet
court (open)–area
court (papal)–curia, see
court (pert. to)–aulic, judiciary
court (sunken)–area
court advocate–pleader
court announcer–crier
court attendant–staff, staves
(pl.)
court bred–courtly, polished
court crier's call–oyes
court excuse for nonappearance–essoin
court game–badminton, tennis
court hearing–oyer
court holding (Eng. law)–
soc
court influencing (attempt
at)–embraceor
court minutes–acta, actum
(sing.)
court of attachments–wood-
mote
court of circuit judges–eyre
court of equity–chancery
court order–writ
court order (mandatory on
paper)–writ
court proceedings–trial

court session–assize
court sitting–session
court writ–capias
courteous–attentive, civil, gallant, gentle, gracious, polite, urbane
courtesy–affability, complaisance, courteousness, elegance, politeness, refinement, urbanity
courtly–aulic, civil, dignified, stately
courtyard–patio
cousin (short for)–coz
covenant–agreement, bargain, bond, compact, contract, engage, promise, stipulate, testament, undertaking
cover–cap, coat, drape, hatch, hide, lid, mantle, mask, overlay, overspread, pave, roof, screen, shelter, shield, span, veil
cover (chalice)–pall
cover (council table)–tapis
cover (mattress)–tick
cover (passageway)–canopy, caponier
cover inside–ceil, line
cover the face–mask
cover the top of–cap
cover thoroughly–becap
cover up–bury, camouflage, conceal, inter, submerge
cover with a sheath–glove
cover with alloy–terne
cover with cloth–drape
cover with cork–corticate
cover with crumbs–bread
cover with gold–gild, plate
cover with grass–sod
cover with jewels–begem
cover with leaves–enleaf
cover with mud–bespatter
cover with pitch–tar
cover with plaster–parget
cover with straw–thatch
cover with thin sheets–sheathe
cover with turf–sod
cover with water–flood, irrigate
cover with wax–cere
cover with white liquid preparation–limewash

covered (surrounded with solids)–encased
covered with dots–stippled
covered with fungi–moldy
covered with granular rock–sanded
covered with green herbage–grassy
covered with hair–pilar
covered with hairs–vilous
covered with layers (as of onions)–tunicated
covered with low tufted plants–mossed
covered with powdered earth–dusty
covered with protuberances–humpy
covered with sharp-pointed growth–spinate
covered with small, hair-like process–ciliate
covered with trees–forested
covered with vines–ivied
covered with water–awash
covering – roof, screen, shroud, wrapper
covering (ceiling)–calcimine, kalsomine
covering (dark)–pall
covering (defensive)–armor
covering (ear)–earcap, earmuff
covering (eye)–eyelid
covering (floor) – carpet, linoleum, mat, oilcloth, rug, tile
covering (hard thin)–shard
covering (head)–beret, bonnet, cap, chapeau, chapeaux (pl.), fascinator, hair, hat, hood, peruke, scalp, snood, toupee, wig
covering (leg joint)–kneelet
covering (nutmeg, dried)–mace
covering (outer)–armor, crust, hull, integument, jacket, tegument, testa, testae (pl.),
covering (protective)–apron, armor, lorica, shell
covering (seed, outer)–testa, testae (pl.)
covering (thin)–film

covering (wall)–calcimine, kalsomine
covering for apex of sharp-pointed roof–epi
covering for hands (anc., Roman boxer's)–cestus, cesti (pl.)
covering for woman's head (net work)–caul, cawl
covering of fruits–pericarp
coverlet–afghan, counterpane, quilt
covert–concealed, covered, den, disguised, hidden, insidious, lair, lie, private, secret, sheltered
covet–crave, desire, envy
covetousness–avarice
covey–bevy, brood, company, flock, hatch
cow–abash, awe, daunt, frighten, overawe, terrify
cow (genus of)–bos
cow (horned) – moulleen, mulley, pollard
cow (sea)–dungong, hippopotamus, manatee, serenian, walrus
cow (small)–garvey
cow (young)–heifer
cow basil–cowherb
cow house–byre, vaccary
cow pasture–vaccary
cow pilot–chirivita
cow tethering piece (of wood)–baikie
coward–caitiff, craven, dastard, poltroon, recreant, sneak
coward (arrant)–poltroon
coward (base)–craven
cowardly–craven, dastardly, poltroon, pusillanimous, recreant
cowboy–herder, puncher, roper
cowboy's breeches–chaps
cowcatcher (locomotive)–pilot
cowed–browbeaten
cower–cringe, crouch, fawn, quail
cowfish–toro
cowl–hood
cows–cattle, kine
cow's chewed food–cud

cow's cud–rumen
cow's low–moo
coxcomb–cleat, dude, fool, fop
coxcomb (chattering)–popinjay
coy–arch, bashful, demure, shy
coyness (assumed)–prudery
Coyote State–South Dakota
coypu fur–nutria
cozen–cheat, deceive, defraud
cozy–chatty, comfortable, contented, easy, familiar, snug, sociable, talkative
crab–crustacean, fiddler
crab (purse)–ayuyu
crab (spider)–maian
crabbed–cross, crusty, fractious, morose, peevish
crab's claw–nipper
crachoir–cuspidor, spittoon
crack–break, chap, chink, clap, cleave, crackle, cranny, fissure, fracture, leak, rift, snap, split
crack (flesh, caused by cold) –kibe
cracker dish–panada
Cracker State–Georgia
crackle–crepitate, snap
crackling–crepitant, crepitate, snap
crackpot (slang)–lunatic
cracksman (coll.)–yegg
cradle (wicker)–bassinet
cradle book–incunabulum
Cradle of Liberty–Faneuil Hall
cradle song–berceuse, lullaby
craft–aptitude, art, dexterity, employment, occupation, skill, skillfulness, trade
craft (small supply)–tender
craftsman–artificer, artisan, artist, writer, workman
craftsman's aid–cad
crafty–artful, astute, cunning, deceitful, fraudulent, ingenious, Mephistophelean, shrewd, skillful, slim, sly, subtle, wily
crag–arete, tor

crag (projecting)–spur
craggy–clifty, knotty, rough, rugged
cram–crowd, drive, force, press, stuff
crame–booth, stall, tent
cramp–compress, stunt
cranberry (small)–sourberry
crane–derrick
crane (ship's)–davit
crane arm–gib
crane charge (for use of)–cranage
cranial nerve root–radix, radices (pl.)
cranium–skull
cranny–chink, cleft, corner, crevice, fissure, nook
crash–shatter, smash
crate–basket, case, hamper
crate (slang)–airplane, automobile
crater edge–lip
cravat–four-in-hand, neckcloth, necktie, teck, tie
crave–ask, beg, beseech, covet, desire, entreat, hanker, implore, long, request, seek, solicit, supplicate, yearn
craven–afraid, coward, cowardly, dastard, fainthearted, poltroon
craving – appetite, desire, longing, yearning
craving for unnatural food–pica
craw–maw
craw (bird's)–maw
crawl–creep, grovel
crayon picture–pastel
craze–crack, fad, fashion, madden, mania
crazed–amok, deranged, insane
crazy–amok, insane, damaged, unsound
crazy (arch.)–wood
crazy (Scot.)–dottle
crazy (slang)–loco, luny
crazy (Southwestern U.S.)–loco
cream (cookery)–creme
cream (the)–elite
cream of tartar (crude)–argol

crease–fold
create–build, cause, fashion, generate, invent, make, originate, produce
create a disturbance–riot
creation (fictive)–fantasy
creative ability–genius
creator–author, inventor, maker, originator, producer
creator of original works of arts–designer
creature–creation, dependent, minion
creature (civet-like)–genet
creature (elf-like)–peri
creature (evil, Scot.)–hellicat
creature (fabled, marine)–mermaid, merman
creature (fairy-like)–peri
creature (mangy or scabby) –ronyon
creature (minute, living)–animalcule
creature (sentient)–animal
creature (timid)–deer, sheep
creature (underground)–gnome
creature (winged, fabulous, two-legged)–wivern
creddock–turnstone
credence–confidence, credit, trust, trustworthiness
credential–certificate, testimonial, voucher
credible–believable, likely, plausible, probable
credit–accredit, believe, credence, trust
creditor (extortionate)–Shylock, usurer
creed–belief, confession, dogma, tenet
creed (Christian)–Apostle's, Nicene
creek–bay, bayou, brook, inlet, ria, rivulet, stream
creek (marshland)–slough, slue
creek (Scot.)–burn
creek (Span.)–arroyo
creek (tidal, Span.)–estero
creep furtively–prowl
creeper (trumpet)–tecoma
creeping–reptant, reptatorial

Cremona–Amati, violin
crena – cleft, indentation, notch, scallop
crepitate (likely to)–crackly
crescent–cusp, horn
crescent-like–bicorn
crescent moon point–cusp
crescent-shaped–bicorn, lunate, lune, semilunar
crescent-shaped breastplate–gorget
crescent-shaped marking–lunula
crest–crista, crown, height, peak, pinnacle, ridge, top
crest (acute mountain)–aret, arete
crest (rugged)–arete, tor
creta–chalk
Cretan flier–Icarus
Cretan king–Minos
Cretan king's daughter–Ariadne
Cretan monster (legendary)–minotaur
Cretan mountain–Ida
Cretan seaport–Candia, Canea
Crete–Candia
Crete Island (Greek) city–Candia, Canea, Hag, Heraclion, Kasteli, Khora, Kisamo, Malemi, Mallia, Meleme, Nikolaos, Palaiokhora, Retimo, Sphakion, Tympakion
cretin–idiot
crevice–chink, cranny, fissure
crew–band, company, gang, men
crew member–hand
crib–bin, manger
cribbage score–peg
cricket field (part of)–ons
cricket runs made on missed ball–byes
cricket term–off, yorker
cricket wicket sides–ons
cricket's sound–chirp
cried – lamented, wailed, wept
cried out–exclaimed
crier (plaintive)–wailer
cries (confusion of)–babel
cries loudly–bawls

crime–evil, iniquity, offense, sin, violation, wickedness, wrong
crime (goddess of)–Ate
crime (scene of)–venue
crime of crippling–mayhem
crime site–venue
Crimean city–Kerch
Crimean river–Alma
Crimean sea–Azof
criminal–blameworthy, disgraceful, felon, malefactor, reprehensible
criminal (coll.)–crook
criminal (incorrigible)–recidivist
criminal (mad)–desperado
criminal (obs.)–nocent
criminal (reckless)–desperado
criminal (slang)–yegg, yeggman
criminality–guilt, guiltiness
criminology (branch of)–penology
criminal's defense–alibi
criminal's sanctuary–alsatia
crimp–fold, plait, ruffle
cringe–cower, fawn, shrink, sneak, wince
crinoid (fossil)–crinite
crinose–hairy
cripple–disable, incapacitate, lame, maim, weaken
cripple (Scot.)–lamiter
crisis–criterion, emergency, juncture, peril
crisp–brittle, curly, friable, sharp, short
criterion–canon, measure, rule, standard, test
critic–censor, collator, connoisseur, faultfinder, judge, reviewer, slater
critic (captious)–momus
critic (caustic)–slater
critic (contemptible)–criticaster
critic (legal)–censor
critic (official press)–censor
critic (severe)–slater
critical–captious, carping, discriminating, edgy, exacting, faultfinding
critical juncture–crisis
critical standard–canon

criticism – animadversion, review
criticism (adverse)–animadversion, rap
criticism (disparaging)–roast
criticize–animadvert, carp, castigate, cavil, censure, comment, judge, review
criticize (coll.)–rap
criticize fiercely–slate
criticize harshly – flay, knock, pan
criticize severely–slate
Croatian governor's title–ban
crochet–fad, knit, knitting, tat
crockery–china, earthenware
crockery (fine)–china
crocodile (India)–gavial
crocodile (marsh)–goa
crocus (drug-yielding)–saffron
croft–cavern, crypt, field, hillock, vault
crone–hag
Cronus' father–Uranus
Cronus' mother–Gaea
Cronus' wife–Rhea
crony–chum, companion, pal
crook–bend, crosier, warp
crook (to, Scot. dial.)–camshachle
crooked–askance, askew, aslant, asquint, awry, bent, curved, deformed, dishonest, distorted, false, fraudulent, oblique, twisted, turning, wry
crooked (dial.)–agee
crooked (Scot.)–agley
crookedness of legs (med.)–rhaebosis, rhebosis
croon–bellow, boom, complain, hum, lament, wail, whine
crop–craw, harvest, maw, reap
crop (bird's)–craw
crop (farm, lucrative)–soya
crop (riding)–dick
croquet–roque
croquet (form of)–roquet
croquettes (minced meat,

bread crumbs, onions, anchovies, etc.)–cecils

cross–athwart, crucifix, fretful, intersect, irritable, oblique, peevish, pettish, petulant, rood, snappish, swastica, swastika, touchy, transverse, traverse

cross (four spots, white field, her.)–ermine, erminee

cross (her.)–patee, patonce, patte, pattee, paty

cross by wading–ford

cross resembling the Greek letter "T"–tau

cross rib (Gothic vault)–lierne

cross stroke of letter–cerif, serif

cross timber (Span. naut.)–bao

cross wires (in optical instrument)–reticle

crossbar (on which wheels turn)–axle

crossbar frame–grate

crossbarred–trabeculated

crossbeam–girder, trave

crossbow (anc.)–arbalest

crossbreed (hybrid)–husky

crossing–cheating, crossbreeding, ford, opposing, passage, traversing

crossing at acute angle–chiasma

crossline (fine at top and bottom of letter)–cerif, serif

crosspiece–crossarm, spar

crouch–bend, cower, cringe, squat, stoop

crouch from fear–cower

crow–rook

crow-like bird–daw, jackdaw

crow's cry–caw

crowbar–lever, pry

crowbar (burglar's short)–jimmy

crowbar (Eng. dial)–gablock

crowbar (short) – jemmy, jimmy

crowd–crush, drive, hasten, herd, host, jam, mob,

multitude, pack, press, push, serry, squeeze, swarm, three, throng, wedge

crowd (moving)–drove

crowd (unruly)–mob

crowded–compact, congested

crowded (botany)–stipate

crown–anadem, cap, chaplet, corona, coronet, crest, diadem, enthrone, fillet, garland, pate, peak, pinnacle, surmount, tiara, top, wreath

crown (Egyptian king's)–atef

crown (hat)–poll

crown (jeweled)–diadem

crown (kind of)–miter, mitre

crown (of head)–pate

crown (papal)–tiara

crown (pert. to)–coronal

crown (poetic)–tiar

crown (Pope's triple)–tiara

crown (shaven)–tonsure

crown (small, inferior)–coronet

crown (triple)–tiara

crown adherent–tory

crown again–recap

crowned–bounteous, brimful, consummated, coronated, invested, surmounted

crowned with roses (obs.)–rosated

crucible–pot

crucifix–rood

crucifix (small)–pax

crude–callow, crass, green, inexperienced, raw, savage, unpolished, unrefined

crudity–crassness, immature, roughness

cruel–brutal, fell, ferocious, hard, harsh, inhuman, merciless, savage, severe, truculent, unhuman, unkind

cruel treatment–severities

cruelty–brutality, remorselessness, ruthlessness

cruelty (lovers of)–sadists

cruet–ama, bottle, caster, vessel, vial

cruet (wine cup used in mass)–ampulla

cruety–sour, vinegarish

cruise–sail

cruller–friedcake

cruller (kind of)–olycook, olykoek

crumb–bit, fragment, little, piece

crumble (easily)–friable

crumble into small bits–molder, moulder

crumble to dust–molder, moulder

crumbs (bread, boiled in milk and flavored)–panada

crusade (for principle or belief)–jehad, jihad

Crusader's enemy–Saracen

crush–bruise, crash, crowd, jam, mash, smash

crush (grinding)–crunching

crushed–pressed, subdued, trod

crushers (ore)–dollies

crust (bread)–rind

crustacea (group of)–carida

crustacea larval stage–alima

crustacean–crab, isopod, lobster, shrimp

crustacean (lobster-like)–shrimp

crustacean (shrimp-like)–prawn

crustacean (small)–isopod

crustacean (small, marine)–barnacle

crustacean (ten-footed)–crab

crustacean limb appendage–endite

crutch–stile

crux–gist, nub, pith, point

cry – call, lamentation, scream, shriek, wail, weep, yell

cry (as a child)–snivel

cry (bacchanal's)–evoe

cry (cat's)–mew, miaou, miaow, miau, miaul

cry (crow's)–caw

cry (deer's)–bell

cry (elephant's)–barr, trumpet
cry (Fr.)–cri
cry (harsh)–squawk
cry (hoarse, harsh)–croak
cry (infant's weak)–mewl
cry (obs.)–cri
cry (old word)–gred
cry (plaintive)–pule
cry (rallying)–slogan
cry (rook's)–caw
cry (sharp)–scream, yell, yelp
cry (sheep's)–baa, bleat
cry (sorrowful)–alas
cry (vociferous)–hue
cry (waveringly)–bleat
cry (woeful)–alas
cry loudly–bellow, boohoo
cry of derision–hoot
cry of sorrow–ay
cry out–clamor, exclaim, proclaim, scream, shout, vociferate
cry out against–blame, censure, complain
cry out harshly–crake
cry out on–censure, denounce
crying–clamant, heinous, notorious
crying bird–limpkin
crying hare–pika
crying out (Scot.)–childbirth, confinement
cryprinoid fish–id
cryptic–enigmatic, hidden, hieroglyphic, mysterious, occult, secret
crystal–clear, crystalline, dial, lucid, pellucid, transparent
crystal (glassy greenish used in gems)–datolite
crystal (needle-like)–acicula
crystal (transparent diamond)–glassie
crystal (twin)–macle
crystal clear–pellucid
crystal gazer–seer
crystal gazing–scry
crystalline–pellucid, pure, transparent
crystalline chemical compound–oscin

crystalline compound (yellow)–anisil
crystalline mineral–apatite, elaterin, spar
crystalline salt – analgene, borax
crystallize–congeal
crystals (sugar)–candy
cub–bin, coop, crib, cupboard, pen, shed, stall
cub (or puppy)–whelp
Cuban asphalt (fine)–chapapote
Cuban beverage–pina
Cuban capital–Havana
Cuban cigars–Havanas
Cuban city – Camaguay, Cienfuego, Havana (c.), Matanzas, Puerto Principe, Santa Clara, Santiago
Cuban coin–centavo (cop., ni.), cuarenta (s.), peso (s.)
Cuban dance–rhumba, rumba
Cuban dollar (silver)–gourde
Cuban drink–pina
Cuban fish (fresh water, small food)–viajaca
Cuban hutia–pilori
Cuban measure–bocoy, caballeria, cordel, fanega, tarea, vara
Cuban mountain–Copper, Pico Turquinos
Cuban port–Havana, Matanzas, Puerto Principe, Santiago
Cuban province–Oriente
Cuban rum–bacardi
Cuban tobacco–capa
Cuban tobacco cigar–Havana
Cuban town–Guines
Cuban weapon–machete
Cuban weight–libra, tercio
cube–die, dice (pl.)
cube (marble)–tessera
cube (small glass)–tessellar, tessellae (pl.)
cube of marble used for mosaic work–tessera
cube spar–anhydrite
cubeb substance–cubebin

cubic–isometric
cubic decimeter–liter, litre
cubic meter–stere
cubic shape–cuboid
Cuchullin's wife – Eimer, Emer
cuckoo (Indian)–koel
cuckoo (keel-billed)–ani
cuckoo bird–ani, anis (pl.)
cuckoo-fool–wryneck
cuckoo owl–boobook
cuckoopint herb–arum
cuckoo's cap–monkshood
cucumber (Span.)–pepino
cucumber substance–elaterium
cud–rumen
cud (Scot.)–cudgel
cuddle–hug, nestle, pet, snuggle
cudgel–bat, beat, belabor, club, drub, stave, stick
cudgel (Irish)–alpeen
cue – braid, catchword, prompt, twist
cue of hair–pig
cuff–clout, handcuff, slap, strike
cuittle–coax, tickle, wheedle
cull–choose, pick, select, separate, sort
cullers of doctrine–eclectics
culmination–acme, apex, climax, noon, vertex, zenith
culpability–blame, fault, guilt
culpable–blameworthy, censurable, criminal, faulty, guilty, immoral, reprehensible
cultivate–disk, farm, grow, harrow, hoe, plough, plow, till
cultivated–grew, seeded, urban
cultivated land–arada, farm, tilth
cultivation–civilization, culture, culturing, husbandry, refinement, tillage
cultivator–harrow, tiller
culture–art, civilization, polish, refinement, tillage
culture media–agar

cultured–civilized, cultivated

cumin (derived from)–cumic

cummer–girl, godmother, kimmer, lass, midwife, woman

cummerbund–band, belt, sash

cumshaw–bonus, gratuity, present, thanks, tip

cunning–artful, cute, designing, dexterity, dextrous, foxy, ingenious, ingenuity, insidious, politic, sharp, shyness, skill, skillful, sly, stealthy, subtle, tricky, wile, wily

cunningly formed–daedal

cup–beaker, can, chalice

cup (anc. wine)–ama

cup (drinking)–ama, mug, stein, tass

cup (International tennis)–Davis

cup (pastry-filled)–dariole

cup (refining)–cupel

cup (sacred)–grail

cup (Scot.)–tass

cup (small)–noggin

cup (small, for refining precious stones)–test

cup (two-handled)–tig, tyg

cup (wine)–ama, goblet

cupbearer of the gods–Hebe

cupboard–armoire, buffet, closet, dresser, larder, pantry, sideboard

cupboard (old name)–ambry

Cupid–Amor, Eros, love

Cupid's alias–Amor

Cupid's dart–onegite

Cupid's mother–Venus

Cupid's title–Dan

cupidity–appetite, avarice, avidity, desire, greed, longing, lust

cupola–dome, furnace

cupolaed–domed

cups (cluster of rust fungi)–aecia, aecium (sing.)

cur–goldeneye, gurnard, mongrel

cura–curate, priest

curare–urare, urari

curate–abbe, clergyman

curb–arrest, bit, bridle, check, control, inhibit, limit, rein, repress, restrict

cure–heal, remedy, salt, smoke

cure (as meat)–smoke

cure all–balm, panacea, remedy

cure in sun–rizzar

cured grass–hay

curer (meat)–salter, smoker

curio repository–reliquary

curiosity (art)–curio

curiosity (small value)–gabion

curious–inquiring, inquisitive, intrusive, meddling, nosey, nosy, odd, prying, rare

curiously made–dedal

curl – convolution, crisp, lock, ringlet, spiral, tress, twist

curled and wrinkled–savoyed

curlew (Tahiti)–kioea

curling mark (aimed at)–tee

curly hair (like)–cirrose, cirrous

curmudgeon–churl, miser, niggard

currant (red)–rissel, risser, rizzar

currant (red, Scot.)–rizzar, rizzart

currency–greenbacks, money

currency (former paper)–scrip

current–eddy, prevailing, recent, stream, tide

current (rapid water)–race

current (swift)–race

current of air–draft

current regulator–rheometer

currier's cuttings (used for glue)–scrow

curry–dress

curry a horse–groom

curry favor (Australian)–smooge

cursed (arch.)–beshrewed

curses–anathemas, banes, bans, execrates, impreca-

tions, malisons, oaths, swears

cursory–desultory, disconnected, evanescent, fitful, hasty, irregular, passing, rambling, roving, unmethodical

curt–abrupt, brief, brusk, brusque, buff, concise, condensed, short, terse

curtail–abridge, clip, crop, diminish, dock, lessen, reduce, short, shorten

curtain–drape, mask, portiere, screen, shade, veil

curtain (altar)–coster

curtain (altar, side)–riddel

curtain (church)–riddel

curtain (designed for casement windows)–vitrage

curtsey (curtsy)–bow

curvature (convex)–camber

curvature (local, center)–evolute

curvature of legs (med.)–rhaebosis, rhebosis

curvature (zero) surface–plane

curve–arc, arch, bend, bow, crook, curvature, flexure, spiral

curve (geometrical)–ellipse, evolute, spiral

curve (helical)–spiral

curve (mathematical plane)–polar

curve (plane)–parabola

curve (reverse)–ess

curve (sharp)–ess, "S"

curve (type of)–lemniscate

curve cusp or stationary point–spinode

curve of projectile–parabola

curve segment–arc

curved–anchoral, arched, bent

curved glass–lens

curved in form of bow–arcuated

curved inward–adunc

curved ship's planking–sny

curves in and out–sinuated

curvet–bound, frisk, frolic, leap, prank

cusco bark alkaloid–aricine

cush–cow, money, sorghum

cushion–pad

cushion (filled with perfume)–sachet

cushion (knitted, foot)–brioche

cushion (lace weaving)–bott

cushion stuffing (wooly, vegetable)–baru

Cush's father–Ham

Cush's son–Nimrod

Cush's son (eldest)–Seba

custard–flan

custard (boiled, containing brayed pork)–charlet

custard apple–anona, pawpaw, sweetsop

custodian–bailee, curator, guard, guardian, keeper, protector, warden, warder

custodian (chief)–curator

custodian (house)–janitor

custodian (museum)–curator

custody–charge, trust

custom – fashion, habit, mode, practice, patronage, usage, use, wont

custom (binding)–law

custom (Latin)–mos

custom (temporary)–fad, vogue

custom with force of law (Latin)–mos

customarily–traditionally

customary–general, usual, wonted

customary method–habit

customer–buyer, patron, shopper

cut–affront, bob, canal, carve, chop, crop, curtail, dock, engraving, excision, fell, gash, hew, incision, indignity, lance, lop, make, mangle, mode, mow, nick, nip, notch, pare, plate, reap, sever, shear, shorn, slash, slish, slit, snip, split, strait, trim, vogue, whittle

cut (in terms with snick)–snee

cut (Scot.)–rit

cut (small)–piece, snick

cut (not)–unhewn

cut across–slice

cut and polish (as precious stones)–lapidate

cut at random–slash

cut away–severed

cut, beat, or knock down–fell

cut closely–crop, cropped, shave

cut down–abash, curtail, fell, felled, hew, humble, lessen, mow, pare, prostrate, razee, reduce, retrench

cut down decks of a ship–razee

cut down wood on land–clear, slash

cut expense–economize, pare

cut fine–mince

cut gear teeth on–ratch

cut in–interpose, interrupt, introduce

cut in small pieces–hash

cut in squares–dice

cut in two–bisect, halve

cut into–incised

cut into cubes–dice

cut into pieces–chop

cut into thin slices–shave

cut jaggedly–snag

cut lengthwise–slit

cut of beef–aitchbone, brisket, chine, cutlet, icebone, loin, roast, saddle, shoulder, steak

cut off–amputated, bobbed, clipped, deprive, disinherit, intercept, lopped, pared, severed

cut off (as a syllable)–elide

cut off (rare)–scind

cut off by bits–drib

cut off edges (as of coins)–nig

cut off from inconvenience–screen

cut off short–bob, crop

cut off tops–crop

cut on slant–bevel, bias, miter, mitre

cut one's teeth–teethe

cut out with die (as shoe-sole blank)–dink

cut short–arrest, check, clipt, crop, cropped, curtail, dock, lop

cut timber–lumber

cut to deep slope–scarp

cut up–carve

cut wildly (at random)–slash

cut with geometrical surfaces–faceted

cut with scissors–snip

cutaneous–dermal

cutaway–coat

cute–attractive, clever, sharp, shrewd

cuticle–integument, membrane, pellicle, skin

cuticle (plant)–cutin

cutter–incisor, sleigh, sloop

cutting – biting, chilling, piercing, sarcastic, satiric, secant, severe, sharp, tart

cutting diamond–bort

cutting edge–blade

cutting implement–knife, mower, razor, reaper, scythe, shears

cutting tool–adze, ax, axe, bit, chisel, razor

cutting tool (taplike)–hob

cutting wit–satire

cuttings (currier's used for glue)–scrow

cuttle–assassin, knife, ruffian, swaggerer, thug

cuttlebone–osselet

cuttlefish–sepia

cuttlefish (eight-armed)–octopus

cuttlefish protective fluid–ink

cyanogen (compound of)–cyanide

Cyclades Island–Delos, Melos, Nio, Tinos

cycle–aeon, age, bicycle, circuit, course, eon, era, period, revolution, tricycle

cycle (astronomical)–saros

cycle (cosmic)–eon

cycle in which eclipses reoccur–saros

cyclone–tornado

cyclopean–gigantic, huge, massive, vast

Cycnus' father–Ares

cygneous–swanlike

cygnet's mother–pen

cylinder–roll

cylinder (hollow)–pipe, tube

cylinder (hollow, of wicker work)–gabion
cylinder (printing)–rounce
cylinder (revolving)–roller
cylinder (threaded metal)–screw
cylinder (tissue in exogenous stems)–stele
cylinder enlargement–bulb
cylinder in cross section–terete
cylindrical–terete, terecial
cylindrical (tapering)–conic
cylindrical and hollow–tubular
cylindrical and smooth–terete
cylindrical body (hollow)–tube
cymba lobe–ptere
cymbal (metal)–tal
cymbal (Oriental)–zel
cymbal (U.S. slang)–doughnut

Cymric–Welsh
Cymric god (of the dead)–Pwyll
Cymric god (sun)–Lleu
cynic–misanthrope
cynic (bitter)–Timon
cynical–captious, currish, misanthropic, pessimistic, snarling
cyprinoid–ide
Cyprus capital–Nicosia
Cyprus city–Famagusta, Limasol, Nicosia (c.)
Cyprus coin–para (br.), piaster (br.)
Cyprus measure–cass, donum, gomari, kartos, kouza, oka, oke, medimno
Cyprus mountain–Troodos
Cyprus weight – kantar, moosa, oka, oke
cyst–box, chest, pouch, sac

Czar (former)–Ivan, Nicholas, Peter
Czechoslovakia (part of)–Bohemia
Czechoslovakian capital–Praha
Czechoslovakian city–Bratislava, Pilsen, Prague, Praha, Pressburg
Czechoslovakian coin–ducat (g.), heller (ac.), koruna (ni., br.)
Czechoslovakian land measure–lan
Czechoslovakian measure–loket
Czechoslovakian president (former)–Benes
Czechoslovakian river–Iser
Czechoslovakian river (between Germany)–Oder
Czechoslovakian state–Moravia
czigany–gypsy

D

dabble–dally, meddle, mess, paddle, potter, splash, tamper, trifle
dactylic hexameter–epos
daer–saer
daft–crazy, foolish, gay, giddy, idiotic, insane, wild
Dagda's son (Celtic myth.)–Aed
dagger–creese, dirk, kreese, kris, skean, snee, stiletto
dagger (broad two-edged)–anlace
dagger (old time)–snee
dagger (triangular blade)–poniard
daily–aday, diurnal, quotidian
daily food and drink–fare
dainties–cates
dainty–choice, delicate, elegant, exquisite, fastidious, nice, rare
dairymaid (Scot.)–dey
dairy markets–creameries
dairymen caste–ahir

daisy (kind of)–oxeye
daisy (Scot.)–gowan
dale–dell, spout, trough, vale, valley
dalliance–chat, fondling, gossip, play, talk, toy, trifle
dally–linger, toy, trifle
Dalmatia channel–Narenta
dam–block, check, choke, mother, obstruct, parent, restrain, stay, stem, stop, weir
damage–detriment, disserve, harm, hurt, impair, impairment, injury, loss, mar
damage (malicious)–sabotage
damage by shellfire–strafe
Damascus river–Abana, Abanah, Barada
dames (correlative of)–sires
damp – blunt, dampen, deaden, humid, moist, rainy, wet

damp and cold–dank, raw
Danaë's son–Perseus
dance–bal, ball, ballet, bolero, corant, courant, fandango, farandole, foxtrot, frisk, galop, gavot, hop, jig, minuet, pavan, polka, prom, reel, rhumba, rumba, schottish, schottishe, tango, waltz
dance (anc.)–corant, galop
dance (army post slang)–struggle
dance (artistic)–ballet
dance (Bohemian)–redowa
dance (Fr.)–bal
dance (graceful)–minuet
dance (Latin-American)–criolla
dance (lively)–bolero, galop, gavot, jig, polka, reel, rhumba, rumba
dance (modern)–shag
dance (nineteenth century)–tempete
dance (old English)–morris

dance (old fashioned)–loure

dance (old formal) – farandola, farandole, pavan, pavane

dance (pantomimic)–ballet

dance (round)–waltz

dance (slow graceful)–minuet

dance (square) – lanciers, quadrille

dance (stately)–pavan, pavane, paven, pavin

dance motion (pert. to)–gestic

dance movement–chasse, pirouette

dance movement (to right or left)–chassed

dance of death–macaber, macabre

dance step–chasse, glissade, pas

dancer (slang)–hoofer

dancer's disk–castanet

dancer's pole (rope)–poy

dances (pert. to)–terpsichorean

dancing (relating to)–gestic

dancing shoes–pumps

dancing whirl–pirouette

dandified–spruce

dandy–beau, dude, exquisite, fop, foppish

Dane (comb. form)–Dano

danger–hazard, jeopardy, peril, risk

danger (concealed)–pitfall

danger signal–alarm

dangerous–hazardous, parlous, perilous, precarious, risky

dangle–droop, hang, loll, lop

Danish coin–krone, ore

Danish composer (music)–Gade

Danish cony–das

Danish county–Aabenraa, Aalborg

Danish division–amt

Danish fiord (fjord)–Ise

Danish glottal stop–stod, stodtone

Danish island–Als, Faroe

Danish island (North Atlantic)–Faroe

Danish king (anc.)–Canute

Danish measure–alen

Danish money–ora

Danish order (member of)–ke

Danish seaport–Aarhus

Danish settlers (in Ireland)–Ostmen

Danish weight–lod

dank–damp, humid, moist, wet

danseuses–ballerinas

Danube town–Ulm

Danube tributary–Raab

Danzig coin–gulden (s.), pfennig (br.)

dap–dab, dib, dibble, dip

dapper–finical, neat, pert, spruce, trim

dappled – dotted, flecked, spotted

dapples–flecks

D.A.R. presiding officer–regent

dare–assume, brave, challenge, defy, face, undertake, venture

daring–bold, brave, manly, rash, venturesome

dark–abstruse, ambiguous, dim, ebon, faint, indistinct, mirky, murky, obscure, tenebrous, uncertain, vague

dark (densely)–cimmerian

dark-complexioned (Scot.)–dusky, swarth, swarthy

dark gray–taupe

dark-skinned – dusky, swarthy

dark spot produced by cutting off light–shadow

darken–blacken, dim, dull, eclipse, shadow, umber

darkness–blackness, dark, dimness, dusk, murk, shade, shadow

darling–favorite, minion, pet, sweet

darling (arch.)–lieve

darling (Irish)–acushla

darnel–grass, tare, weed

darns–mends, patches, repairs

dart–arrow, bound, flit, javelin, lance, leap, spring, start

dart (coll.)–scoot

dart (poetic)–elance

dart (repeatedly)–dartle

D'Artagnan's creator–Dumas

Darwinian–evolutionist

dash–ardor, confound, elan, gift, gratuity, overthrow, slam, smash, spatter

dash to pieces–crash

dash water against–swash

dastardly–cowardly, foul

data (datum, pl.)–facts

datary office–dataria

date–appointment, fruit

date (erroneous)–anachronistic

date syrup–dhebbus

dating from birth–natal

datum–fact

daub–plaster, smear

daubed–plastered, smeared, smeary

daughter (arch.)–bint

daughter (pert. to)–filial

daughter (younger, Fr.)–cadette

Daughter of Moon (American Indian myth)–Nokomis

daunt–awe, cow, dismay, overawe

davenport–chesterfield, divan, sofa

David Copperfield villain–Heep

David Copperfield's wife–Dora, Agnes

David's chief ruler–Ira

David's daughter–Tamar

David's father–Jesse

David's man (mighty)–Igal

David's ruler (chief)–Ira

David's son–Solomon

David's wife–Abigail

dawdle–lag, loiter, poke, potter, trifle

dawdle (Scot.)–toit

dawn–aurora, daybreak, morn, sunrise

dawn (comb. form)–eo

dawn (goddess of)–Aurora, Eos

dawn (pert. to)–eoan

dawn (prefix)–eo

day (early, poetic)–morn

day (god of)–Horus

day (Hebrew)–yom

day (var.)–daeg, dag, dagas, dagr, dags, dai, daig, degti, dei, nidagha

day before–eve

day blindness–hemeralopia

daybreak (poetic)–morn, sunup

daydream–reverie

day's march–etape

daytime performance–matinee

daze–benumb, bewilder, confuse, dazzle, dumbfound, fog, stun, stupefy, trance

dazzling–bewildering, brilliant, garish, gorgeous

dazzling light–glare

dead–apathetic, deceased, defunct, expired, flat, inactive, inert, lapsed, lifeless, motionless, spiritless, tedious, unexciting

dead language–Latin

Dead Sea city (shore)–Sodom

Dead Sea pass (south of)–Akrabbin

Dead Sea territory (east of)–Moab

deaden–damp, devitalize, dull, enfeeble, repress, weaken

deaden sound of–mute

deadens–obtunds, opiates

deadlock–stalemate, standstill

deadly–dire, fatal, internecine, lethal, mortal

deafen (to, Scot.)–deave

deal–administer, allot, dispense, distribute, dole, mede, parcel, portion, wine

deal (vigorously)–wrestle

deal in–sell

deal out sparingly–dole

deal with–cope

dealer (cattle) – drover, herder

dealer (cloth)–draper, mercer

dealer (retail) – grocer, tradesman

dealer (textile fabric)–mercer

dealer in wood–xylopolist

dealing–trading

dealing (shrewd)–chicanery

deals–sales

deals in–purveys, trades

dean–decan, dene, doyen, verger

Dean (gloomy)–Inge

dean of diplomatic corps–doyen

dearth – famine, poverty, scarcity

death – decease, demise, doom, quietus

Death (as deity)–Mors

death (eternal)–perdition

death (Fr.)–mort

death by hanging–halter, lynch

death by stoning–lapidate

death notice–obit, obituary, orbit

death rattle–rale

debacle–rout, stampede

debar–deny, estop, hinder, preclude, refuse

debark–disembark, land

debase–abase, adulterate, degrade, demean, depreciate, deteriorate, lower, reduce

debase (by mixture)–alloy

debasement–vitiation

debatable–controversial, disputable, moot

debate–argue, controvert, discuss, moot

debate (stoppage of)–cloture

debauch–contaminate, defile, mislead, taint

debilitated–feeble, infirm, sapped, seedy, weak

debit–charge

debonair (debonaire)–airy, jaunty

debris–attle, refuse, rubbish, rubble, trash

debris (abandoned coal mine)–thursts

debris (rock at base of cliff)–talus

debt–liability

debt (unpaid portion)–arrearage

debt acknowledgement–I.O.U., note

debutante–bud, deb

decade–ten

decadence–decay, deterioration

decamp–abscond, depart, vamose, vamoose

decan–dean

decay–decadence, decompose, deteriorate, deterioration, rot, spoil, waste, wither

decay (discolored by incipient)–doty

decay (tooth)–caries

decay of animal tissues–caries

decay of fruit (internal)–blet

decayed (wood)–doty

deceased–dead, defunct, departed

deceit–artifice, chicanery, craft, cunning, deception, dissimulation, duplicity, fraud, guile, guise, imposture, intrigue, mendacity, sophistry, subtlety, tergiversation, treachery, trickery, wiliness

deceit (free from)–ingenuousness

deceitful–false, fraudulent, guileful, insincere, machiavellian, treacherous, trickish, tricky

deceitfulness–duplicity

deceive – baffle, beguile, cheat, cog, cozen, delude, dupe, elude, flam, fool, gull, hoax, hoodwink, illude, lie, mislead, trick

deceive (coll., slang)–spoof

deceive (in love)–jilt

deceive (rare)–illude

deceived easily–gullible

decennium–decade

deception–artifice, cheat, deceit, deceived, fallacy, fraud, imposture, lie, misled

deception by mockery–hoax

deceptive–illusive, illusory

decide–arbitrate, determine,

elect, judge, opt, referee, settle
decide upon–elect
decimal repeating parts–repetends
decimal system base–ten
decimeter (cubic) liter, litro
decipher – decode, read, translate
decision – determination, grit, pluck, resolution
decision of character–determination
decisive–conclusive, critical, crucial
decisive moments–crises
deck (lowest)–orlop
deck (ship's)–main, poop, upper
deck (vessel's lowest)–orlop
deck forth–array
deck gutter–scupper
deck out–array
deck out with cheap finery–bedizen
declaim–declamation, denounce, orate, rant, rave
declaim (vehemently)–rant
declaration (formal)–pronouncement
declaration (official)–oracle, proclamation
declare–advertise, allege, assert, asseverate, aver, avow, blazon, bruit, herald, maintain, say, state
declare as beyond doubt–posit
declare chargeable with crime–indict
declare innocent–acquit
declare openly–avow
declarer of opposition–protester
declinations–descents
decline–droop, dwindle, ebb, fade, fail, fall, flag, refuse, reject, repel, repudiate, retrograde, set, sink, stoop, wane, weaken
decline (sudden, coll.)–slump
decline in excellency–decadence
declining–decadent
declivity–acclivity, scarp

declivous–prone
decocted–seethed
decoction–apozem, preparation
decompose–decay, frit, rot
decomposed element–anion
decorate–adorn, deck, ornament, trim
decorate (prominently)–emboss
decorated–ornate
decorating (art of, on metal inlaid in black design)–niello
decorating metal (black inlay)–niello
decoration (droop-like architectural)–gutta, guttae (pl.)
decoration (table centerpiece)–epergne
decorations–medals, ornaments
decorative band (hanging)–festoon
decorative inlay for cabinet-work–buhl
decorative piece (flat thin)–plaque
decorous–calm, composed, decent, demure, fitting, grave, modest, quiet, regular, sedate, seemly, serene, settled, staid, unruffled
decorous (stiffly)–prim
decorticate–excoriate, flay, husk, pare, peel, skin, strip
decoy–allure, bait, inveigle, lure, pigeon, stool, tempt
decoy (arch.)–tole
decrease–abate, decline, diminish, drop, dwindle, ebb, lessen, moderate, shrink, sink, slacken, subside, wane, waste
decree–act, command, decision, dictum, edict, enact, fiat, law, mandate, ordain, order, ordinance
decree (authoritative)–arret, edict
decree (ecclesiastical)–canon
decree (obs.)–rede
decree (official)–rescript

decree (Turkish)–irade
decree again–reordain
decree beforehand–destine
decree of porte–irade
decrepit–infirm, lame, senile, weak
decry–belittle, boo, condemn, degrade, depreciate, derogate, detract, discredit, disparage, lower, slur, underrate, undervalue
dedal–artistic, daedal, ingenious, intricate, skillful
dedicate–consecrate, devote, hallow
deduce–derive, elicit, infer
deduct–bate, remove, separate, subtract, take
deduct from bill–rebate
deduction–allowance, discount, illation, induction, inference, rebate
deduction (estate rent)–reprise
deduction (incidental obvious) corollary
deductively–inferentially
deed–act, action, actus, actum, acta (pl.), doing, feat
deed (arch.)–gest
deed (evil)–malefaction
deed (law)–fiat
deeds (tenure clause)–tenenda
deem–believe, judge, suppose
deemed–adjudged, considered, reputed
Deemster (the author of)–Caine
deep–low, profound
deep crimson–carmine
deepen–enhance, intensify, strengthen
deepen a channel–dredge
deeper–lower, profounder
deeply tinged–imbued
deer–caribou, elk, moose, roe
deer (female)–does, hinds
deer (large)–caribou, elk, moose, wapiti
deer (male)–buck, hart, stag
deer (red)–hart, roe, stag

deer (small Sumatra)–napu
deer (young)–fawn
deer antler (young un-branched)–dag
deer cry–bell
deer meat–venison
deer meat (sliced dried)–charqui, jerky
deer pathway–run
deer's antlers (branch of)–trestines
deface–damage, distort, injure, mar, ruin, scar, spoil
defamation–aspersion, calumny, disgrace, dishonor, libel, slander
defamation (oral)–slander
defamation (printed)–libel
defame–asperse, detract, libel, malign, slander, traduce, vilify
defame (to)–traduce
default–fail, failure, neglect
defeat–baffle, beat, best, conquer, disappoint, frustrate, lose, rout
defeat (utter)–derout
defeat utterly–rout
defeated at chess–checkmated, mated
defeatist (Eng.) – handsupper, handupper
defect–blemish, fault, flaw, imperfection, inadequacy, lack, want
defect (optic)–anopia, myopia
defective – bad, deficient, faulty, incomplete, lame
defective (vocal)–lisp
defective vision–anopia, myopia
defend–guard, preserve, protect, save, screen, secure, shelter, shield, watch
defendant–appellee
defendant's answer–plea
defendant's plea–nolo contendre
defense–bulwark, protection
defense (bulwark)–rampart
defense (castle, for shooting missiles)–machicolation
defense (former military)–abatis
defense (legal)–alibi

defense enclosure–boma
defense subdivision–sector
defenseless–unarmed
defensive–apologetic, shielding
defensive device–abatis
defensive slope–glacis
defensive work–fort, rampart
defer – adjourn, bow, postpone, procrastinate, protract, retard
defer action–wait
deference – complaisance, consideration, esteem, homage, honor, regard, submission
deference (to show)–bow
defiance (challenge)–gage
deficiency–dearth, insufficiency, lack, scarcity, shortage, want
deficiency of nervous energy –aneuria
deficient–defective, insufficient, lacking, scarce, short, wanting
deficient in quantity–meager, meagre
defier of lightning–Ajax
defile–befoul, corrupt, deprave, pollute, soil, sully, taint
defile (mountain)–gorge, pass
define–bound, boundary, decide, delimit, determine, fix, limit
definite–clear, explicit, fixed, limited, unmistakable
definite (prefix, biol.)–delo
definitely–conclusively, determinately
deflect–bend, deviate, divert, warp
defraud–bilk, cheat, cozen
defunct–dead, deceased, depart, die, finish
defy–beard, brave, dare, stump
degeneracy – debasement, degradation
degenerate–debase. degrade, deprave, deteriorate
degeneration (fatty)–adiposis

degradation–decline, ignominy, reduction, shame
degrade–abase, debase, demote, depose, dishonor, humble, humiliate
degree–extent, grade, order, point, rank, shade, stage, station, step
degree (college)–A.B., B.A., B.S., B.Sc., D.D., LL.B., LL.D., M.A., M.S., M.Sc., Ph.D.
degree (engineering)–C.E.
degree (farthest)–extreme
degree (greatest)–utmost
degree (small)–slightly
degree of combining power of element–valence
degree of progression–stage
degree of taxation–ratal
degrees (latitude)–parallels
dehorned (applied to cattle) –muley
dehydrate–desiccate, dry
deign–condescend
deigning (act of)–condescension
deities (woodland)–sileni, silenus (sing.)
Deity–El, God
deity (avenging)–Erinys
deity (avenging relentless)–Alastor
deity (Babylonian)–Bel, Ea
deity (death of sea)–Ran
deity (Egyptian)–Ammon, Amon, Ra
deity (Etruscan)–Lar
deity (field)–Faun
deity (fish egg)–Roe
deity (forest)–Aegipan
deity (hawk-eyed)–Ra
deity (hawk-headed)–Ra
deity (hearth)–Vesta
deity (heathen)–idol
deity (Hindu)–Siva
deity (household)–Lar, Penates
deity (inferior)–demigod
deity (Norse)–Ull
deity (of fields)–Faun
deity (of hearth)–Vesta
deity (of herds)–Faun
deity (of love)–Amor, Ares, Cupid. Eros
deity (Oriental)–Bel

deity (Philistine)–Dagon
deity (primeval)–Bitan
deity (rural)–Faun
deity (Semitic)–Baal
deity (sun)–Ra
deity (sylvan)–Pan, satyr
deity (Teutonic)–Er, Hel
deity (tutelary)–Numen
deity (two-faced)–Janus
deity (war)–Ares
deity (woodland) – Faun, Pan, satyr, silenus, sileni (pl.)
dejected–abased, alamort, amort, depressed, prostrate
dejection–melancholy, sadness
Delaware town – Chester, Lewes
delay–arrest, check, confine, detain, hinder, impede, obstruct, retard, stay, tarry, wait
delay (legal)–mora
delayed–belated
delayed (long)–late
delegate–appoint, assign, authorize, commission, consign, depute, entrust, legate, name, representative, send
delete–dele, eradicate, erase, expunge, obliterate
deleterious–destructive, detrimental, hurtful, injurious, noxious, pernicious, prejudiced
Delhi province district–Simla
deliberate–consider, intentional, leisurely, measured, ponder, premeditated, studied, slow, voluntary
deliberate diligently–pore
Delibes ballet–Naila
delicacies–cates
delicacy–caviar, exactness, fineness, fragility, niceness, nicety, precision, sensitivity, slightness, tact, tenuity
delicate–dainty, fine, fragile, queasy, tender, tenuous

delicate and fine–ethereal, lacy
delicate and thin–araneous
delicate skill–finesse
delicate variant of color–tint
delicately sensitive–nice
delicately small–mignon, petite
deliciously sweet–nectarine
delight–charm, delectate, divert, enchant, glee, joy, pleasure, regale
delight (to greatly)–enrapture
delight in–love, savor
delineate–draw, limn, line, map, trace
delineator–illustrator
deliquesce – dissolve, give, melt
delirious–deliriumed, frenzied, raves, raving
delirium – aberration, derangement, fury, hallucination, insanity, lunacy, madness
deliver–consign, ransom, redeem, render
deliver formally–present
deliver into another's charge –commit
deliver oratorically–declaim
deliver treacherously–betray
dell–dalles (pl.), dene, ravine, vale, valley
delude (to)–befool, beguile, deceive, dupe, elude, fool, frustrate, mislead
deluge – flood, inundate, overwhelm, submerge
delusion–deception, fantasm, hallucination, illusion, phantasm
delusive reasoning–fallacy
delve–dig, exhume, mine
demand–ask, claim, cry, require
demand (public)–cry
demand as due–claimed
demandable–due
demeanor–behavior, deportment, mien
demented – crazy, insane, luny, mad
demerit–desert
demigod–hero

demigod (sea)–Triton
demigod (sylvan)–Satyr
demigoddess–heroine
demise–decease, death, lease
demit–abdicate, relinquish, resign
demivolt (kind of Menage, var.)–repolon
demoded–passe
demolish – destroy, overthrow, rase, raze, ruin
demon–atua, devil, fiend, imp, nat, ogre, satan, villain
demon (Arabic myth.)–afreet
demon (fabled)–ogre
demon (female)–hag, lamia
demon (inferior)–imp
demon (nature)–genius, genii (pl.)
demoniac–fiendish
demonstrate–display, manifest, portray, prove, show
demonstrate by evidence–prove
demonstrative (excessively) –effusive
demur–delay, hesitate, linger, stay, tarry
demure – coy, decorous, grave, prim, staid
den–cave, lair, retreat
denial–deprivation, disaffirmance, disavowal, negation, refusal
denial (with or by)–negatively
denizen–inhabitant
denizen by birth–native
denizen of hell–hellion
Denmark city – Aalborg, Aarhuus, Copenhagen (c.), Elsinore, Frederiksberg, Helsingor, Horsens, Odense, Randers
Denmark coin–krone (s.), ore (br.)
Denmark county–Amt, Soro
Denmark downs (sterile)–Klitten
Denmark island–Als
Denmark island possession–Faroe, Greenland, Iceland, Santa Cruz, St. John, St. Thomas

Denmark king–Christian

Denmark measure–achtel, album, alen, carat, ell, favn, fjerding, fod, kande, korntonde, landmil, last, linje, mil, oltonde, ottingkar, paegel, paegl, pot, rode, skeppe, skieppe, tomme, tonde, tonde hartkorn, tonde land, viertel

Denmark river–Guden, Holm, Lonborg, Stor Asa

Denmark weight–bismerpund, carat, centner, es, kvint, last, lispound, lispund, lod, mark, ort, pound, pund, quint, quintin, ship pound, skibslast, skippund, toende, unze, vog

denomination–class, cult, name, sect, society

denote–express, indicate, mark, signify

denoting authorship–by

denoting case of noun–dative

denoting central part–mid

denoting equal pressure–isobaric

denoting final cause–telic

denoting final end–telic

denoting maiden name–nee

denoting purpose–telic

denounce – arraign, condemn, reprobate, upbraid

dense–close, compact, crass, solid, thick

density–compactness, dord

dent–batter, dint, indent, indentation, tooth

dental appliance–dam

dental filling–inlay

dentation–serra, serrae (pl.)

dentine–ivory

dentine (elephant's tusk)–ivory

denude–bare, scalp, strip

denunciation–threat

denunciation speech–filippic, philippic

deny–confute, contradict, contravene, controvert, debar, disclaim, dispute, gainsay, impugn, negate,

refuse, refute, renege, traverse

deodars–cedars

depart–demise, go, leave, quit, withdraw

depart (secretly)–abscond

depart (secretly, suddenly)–decamp

department of France–Var

department of knowledge–art

departure–deviation, exit, going, variation, withdrawal

depend–bank, count, hang, hinge, lean, rely, turn

depend on–illative

depend upon–hinge

dependable–reliable, trustworthy

dependent–client, clinging, subject

dependent (parasitical)–sponge, sponger

depending upon uncertain contingency–aleatory

depict–characterize, delineate, draw, limn, paint, picture, portray, represent

depicted (broken, her.)–rompu

depiction of beautiful–art

depilatory (orpiment, quicklime)–rusma

deplete–drain, empty, exhaust, impoverish, unload

deplore–bemoan, bewail, lament, moan, rue

depone–depose, testify

deportment–air, bearing, behavior, demeanor, manner, mien, port

depose–abase, degrade, reduce

deposit–lay, set

deposit (alluvial)–delta

deposit (anode)–anion

deposit (earthly, used as fertilizer)–marl

deposit (glacial)–eskar, esker

deposit (glacial mineral)–placer

deposit (metalliferous)–ore

deposit (mineral)–lode

deposit (ore in rocks)–lode

deposit (sedimentary)–gobi

deposit in wine cask–tartar

deposit of loam–loess, silt

deposit of mud–silt

deposits (earth)–alluvia

depot–station

depot (naval)–base

depraved–corrupt, evil, immoral, perverted, vicious, vile, vitiated, wicked

depravities (moral)–evils

depravity–corruption, wickedness

depravity (irreclaimable)–incorrigibility

depreciate–belittle, disparage, lessen, shrink, slump, undervalue

depreciate (suddenly)–slumped

depredator–robber, spoiler, thief

depress–dent, discourage, dispirit, enfeeble, lower, oppress, sadden

depress with fear–cow

depressed – disheartened, downcast, downhearted, low, sad

depressed at poles–oblate

depressing–chill, saddening, somber

depression–cavity, col, dent, despondency, dip, fall, humiliation, melancholy

depression (anatomy)–fossa

depression (between mountain peaks)–col

depression (bowl-shaped)–crater

depression (small)–dent

depression of spirits–gloom

depression worn by running water–gully, ravine

deprivation – bereavement, loss, privation, want

deprive–bereave, debar, despoil, dispossess, divest, remove, rob, strip

deprive by prior action–forestall

deprive of any necessary part–maim

deprive of combustible material (anc., chem.) – dephlogisticate deprive of natural qualities–denature

deprive of professional character–laicize

deprive of rank–depose

deprive of strength–unnerve

deprive of vigor–deaden, enervate, sap

deprived–barred, bereaved, bereft, despoiled, reft, removed, rob, robbed, stripped

deprived of authority–dethroned

depth–intensity, midst, profundity

depth (vast)–abyss

depth bomb–ashcan

depths (spiritual nature)–adyta

depute–appoint, assign, delegate, devote

deputy–agent, envoy, legate, substitute

deride–cheat, dupe, flout, geck, gibe, jeer, mock, ridicule, scorn, trick

derision–contempt, fleer, mockery, ridicule, scorn

derisive–scornful

derisive cry–hoot

derisive imitation–mimicry

derivative (ammonia)–amid, amide

derivative (bauxite)–aluminum

derivative (cinnabar mercury)–quicksilver

derivative (cinnamic acid)–sinapic

derivative (flax)–linin

derivative (morphine)–heroin

derivative (pine tar)–retene

derivative (quinoline)–analgen

derivative (silicon)–monox

derivative from coal tar–creosote

derivative of benzine–phenol

derivative of phenol–anol

derivative of pitchblende–radium, uranium

derived from apple–malic

derived from cumin–cumic

derived from fatty substance–adipic

derived from fruits–citric

derived from government–political

derived from milk–lactic

derived from oil–oleic

derived from oily substance–adipic

derived from sorrel–oxalic

derrick–crane, hoist

derrick (jib)–spar

dervish–fakir

dervish (var.)–fakeer

dervish's cap–atef, taj

descend–decline, fall, lower, sink

descendant–child, offspring, scion, son

descendants–progeny

descendants of Caliph Ali–Alides

descended–alit, declined, fell, lowered, sunk

descended from same mother–enate, enatic

descent–assault, attack, degradation, drop, extraction, incursion, invasion, lineage, slope

descent (characteristic of)–racial

descent (irresistible)–avalanche

descent (steep)–scarp

describe–characterize, delineate, depict, explain, express, narrate, picture, recount, relate, represent, outline, portray

describe (as a sentence)–parse

description (artist's of rustic life)–account, idylls, idyls

descriptive adjective–epithet

descry–behold, detect, discern, discover, reveal, see

Desdemona's husband–Othello

Desdemona's murderer–Othello

desecrate–abuse, profane, violate

desert–abandon, bolt, desolate, due, forsake, mer-

it, relinquish, wilderness, worth

desert (sandy, Spanish-American)–hornada

desert beast–camel

desert candle–ocatillo, ocotillo

desert dweller–Arab

desert hallucination–mirage

desert region of shifting sand–erg

desert ship–camel

desert shrub–alhagi

desert shrub (juniper-like)–retem

desert train–caravan

desert travelers (company of)–caravan

desert wind–sirocco

desert wind (hot)–simoon

deserter–renegade

deserter (coll.)–rat

deserter of faith–apostate

deserved–appropriate, condign, earned, merited, worthy

deserved ill (arch.)–die

deserving serious consideration–grave

desiccated–arid, dehydrated, dried, dry

design–aim, destine, end, idea, intent, layout, mean, object, outline, pattern, plan, propose, sketch

design (carpet)–medallion

design (composed of scattered objects)–seme

design (ornamental)–swastika

design (tessellated)–mosaic

design carved into gem–intaglio

design of one's initials–monogram

design of scattered objects–seme

design on fabrics (method of doing)–batik

designate–appoint, denominate, describe, entitle, indicate, name, style, title

designating satirical comedy–atellan

designation–name

designed with incision of

black alloy–nielled, nielloed

designer on metal, glass, etc. –etcher

designing beforehand–premeditating

designs (pricked in skin)–tattoos

desire–appetite, care, covet, crave, craving, hunger, passion, prefer, thirst, want, wish, yearn, yen

desire (ardent)–thirst

desire (coll.)–yen

desire (expectant)–hope

desire (strongly)–hope

desire (teasing)–itch

desire (ungovernable) – mania

desire (wrongfully)–covet

desire for liquid–thirst

desire greatly–aspire

desire with eagerness–aspire

desirous–ardent, covetous, eager, solicitous, spirited

desirous (strongly)–avid

desist–cease, discontinue, forbear, halt, ho, quit, stop

desk–desse (obs.), escritoire, lectern, secretary, table board

desk (reading)–lectern

desk (reading, large)–ambo

Desmanthus–Acuan

desolate–bleak, forsaken, lonely, lorn, ravage, ruin, sad, solitary

desolate (poetic)–drear

despair–desperation, despondency, hopelessness

despect (rare)–contempt

desperado–bravo, criminal, lawbreaker, ruffian

desperate–despairing, desponding, frantic, headlong, hopeless, mad, precipitate, rash

despicable – contemptible, contemptuous, miserable, vile, wretched

despise–contemn, detest, disdain, disregard, hate, scorn, scout, slight, spurn

despised by society–pariah

despiser–vilipender

despoil–bereave, depredate, deprive, divest, pillage, ravage, rifle, strip

despoil (arch.)–reave

despoiled (arch.)–reft

despondency–despair, desperation

despot–czar, tsar, tyrant

despotic–arbitrary, autocratic, tyrannical, tyrannous

despotic official (subordinate)–satrap

despotism–absolutism, autocracy, tyranny

dessert–fruit, ice cream, pastry, pie, pudding, sherbet, strudel, sweets

dessert (frozen)–ice, mousse

dessert (frozen, Fr.)–glace

destine–allot, devote, doom, fate, foreordain, intend, predestine, predetermine

destiny–doom, fate, fortune, lot, stars

destiny (arch.)–ure

destiny (goddess of)–Fate

destiny (Oriental)–Kismet

destitute–abandoned, bereft, devoid, forlorn, forsaken, lacking, needy

destitute of purpose–driftless

destitute of sensation–numb

destitute of teeth–edentate

destroy–annihilate, demolish, dismantle, end, erase, rase, raze, ruin, slay

destroy (gradually)–consume

destroy (utterly)–eradicate, exterminate, raze, ruin

destroy a considerable part of–decimate

destroy the force of–annul

destroy the self-possession of–abash

destroyed (obs.)–ruinated

destroyed by fire–burnt

destroyer (wanton)–hun, saboteur, vandal

destruction–desolation, devastation, downfall, extermination, extinction, extirpation, havoc, holocaust, loss, overthrow, ruin

destruction (general) – shambles

destruction of property (malicious)–sabotage

destructive–baleful, deadly, fatal, mortal, pernicious, ruinous

desuetude – discontinuance, disuse, obsolescence

desultory–aimless, cursory, discursive, hasty, idle, inconstant, rambling, roving, unsettled

detach–disengage, disjoin, disunite, separate, sever, withdraw

detachable paper–coupon, stub

detached–aloof, free, isolated, unconnected

detachment–aloofness, disjunction, isolation, separation, unconcern

detail–appoint, assign, enumerate, item, itemize, narrative, specify

detail (small)–minutia, minutiae (pl.)

detail of an account–item

details (minute)–particulars

detain–arrest, check, delay, keep, hold, restrain, stop, withhold

detain (in custody)–imprison

detect–descry, discern, discover, reveal, show, spy, uncover

detective–operative, sleuth, tracer

detective (coll.)–dick, gumshoe, spotter

detective (fictional)–Nick Carter, Sherlock Holmes, Philo Vance

detective (private)–investigator, spotter

detective story writer–A. Conan Doyle

detent–catch, click, dog, pawl

detention – delay, detainment, hindrance

deter–daunt, delay, discourage, hinder, prevent, restrain

deterge–cleanse, purge
detergent–cleanser, cleansing, purging, soap, solvent
deteriorate–degenerate, impair, wear
deteriorating–decadent
deterioration – debasement, decadence, decay, declension, decline, degeneration, degradation, perversion
determinate–arbitrary, definite, established, invariable, specific
determination – decision, firmness, judgment, limit, purpose, resolution, resolve, settlement, termination, will
determine–arbitrate, conclude, decide, delimit, end, resolve, settle, state
determine rate of–assess
determined–decided, mulish, obstinate, perverse, pigheaded, resolute, set, stubborn
determined (already)–foregone
determiner (biological)–gene
detest–abhor, abominate, hate, loathe
detestable–execrable, hateful, loathsome, odious
detestation – abhorrence, hate, loathing, odium
detonation–blast, explosion
detract–asperse, depreciate, derogate, disparage, subtract, traduce, vilify, withdraw
detraction–calumny, slander
detriment–damage, disadvantage, hurt, impediment, injury, loss
detrimental – deleterious, harmful, hurtful, pernicious
devastate–demolish, pillage, plunder, ravage, scourge, waste
devastation – destruction, havoc, ravage, ruin, waste
develop–appear, arise, expand, grow, mature, ripen, unfold
developed (prematurely)–precocious
developed individual of a compound animal–zoon
developer (photographic dry plate)–revelator
developing along a single line–uniaxial
development – elaboration, evolution, expansion, formation, growth, increase, unfolding
development (full)–maturity
development (unfolding)–evolution
develops in detail–elaborates
Devi's parent–Himavat
deviate–deflect, depart, digress, diverge, err, miss, swerve, vary, veer
deviate from course – sheer, slew, veer
deviate from the vertical–hade
deviates from type (suddenly)–mutates
deviation–aberrance, aberrant, digressing, diverging
deviation (from main subject)–digress
deviation (syntactical) syncsis
device–adjunct, appliance, compass, contrivance, design, expedient, gadget, instrument, shift, tool
device (bark-peeling)–stripper
device (barrel-raising)–parbuckle
device (brick-carrying)–hod
device (button-like)–stud
device (clamping)–vise
device (clearing ship's path of underwater mines)–otter
device (cloth-treating)–ager
device (distilling)–alembic
device (eccentric)–cam
device (energy expending measuring)–ergometer
device (equalizing, as a doubletree)–evener
device (explosive)–grenade, mine
device (fabric-stretching)–stenter
device (fanning)–punka, punkah
device (flying)–glider, kite
device (for aging cloth)–ager
device (for amplifying sound)–resonater
device (for binding)–binder, clamp
device (for charging with gas)–aerator
device (for controlling air current)–damper
device (for deadening music sound)–mute
device (for fastening ropes)–bitt, cleat
device (for hoisting casks)–parbuckle
device (for hoisting large stones)–lewis
device (for raising cylindrical burden)–parbuckle
device (for raising nap)–teasel, teasle, teazel, teazle
device (for securing ropes)–bitt, cleat
device (for separating into sizes)–grader
device (for squeezing superfluous water)–squeegee
device (for stopping motion)–brake
device (for transmitting force)–belt, gear
device (gripping)–pincers, vise
device (heating)–etna, stove
device (heraldic)–ente
device (hoisting) – crane, davit, derrick, elevator, garnet
device (hurling)–sling
device (illuminating)–flashlight, lamp, lantern
device (leveling)–gimbal
device (lifting)–crane, davit, derrick, elevator, garnet,

lever, pry, pump, tongs
device (light rays refract-
ing)–lens
device (maturing)–ager
device (measuring)–chain,
gage, gauge, meter, mi-
crometer, ruler, tape
device (milk deodorizing)–
aerator
device (mine sweeping)–
paravane
device (old military explosion)–petard
device (preventing reverse
motion)–dog, pawl
device (protective, for cruis-
ing in mined waters)–
paravane
device (reflecting light)–lens
device (rhetorical)–epano-
dos
device (ring-like, used in
textile mills)–poteye
device (rope holding, naut.)
–becket
device (silk thread testing)–
serimeter
device (slide fastening)–zipper
device (starting and stopping)–detents
device (steering)–helm, rudder, tiller, wheel
device (sudden expected)–
coup
device (telegraphy current
reversing)–spacer
device (timepiece governor)
–regulator
device (to give uniform impulse to balance)–remon-
toir
device (to regulate flow in
passage)–valve
device (unrefined)–gadget
device (watering)–hose, nozzle, pump, spray
device (wheel motion stopping)–brake, sprag
devil–annoy, demon, field,
fiend, haze, imp, satan,
tease, torment
Devil (leading)–Beelzebub
devil (little)–imp
devil (Mex., Span.)–Diablo
devil (printer's)–apprentice

devil (Scot.)–deil
devil (Span., Mex.)–Diablo
Devil (the)–Beelzebub
Devil's grandmother–Baba
devil's tree–dita
devilfish–manta
devilish–demoniac, demon-
ic, diabolical, fiendish,
hellish, infernal, satanic,
wicked
devise–appoint, arrange, array, bequeath, contrive,
distinguish, distribute, divide, frame
devoid–destitute, empty,
free, vacant, void
devoid of feeling–apathetic,
insensate
devoid of point of interest–
jejune
devote–address, apply, appropriate, consign, dedi-
cate, destine, resign
devote to agriculture–farm
devote to religious uses–hallow
devoted–addicted, dedicated, doomed, loyal
devoted to a nation–patriotic
devotedly attached–doting,
fond
devotee–fanatic, ist, monk,
nun, partisan, votary
devotee (eating)–epicure
devotion–ardor, attachment,
constancy, devotedness,
earnestness, piety, reli-
giousness
devotion (fervent)–adora-
tion
devotion (nine day)–Nove-
na
devotion (one who effects)–
pietist
devour–annihilate, con-
sume, eat, engulf, waste
devour (greedily)–engorge
devout–cordial, godly, holy,
pious, righteous, saintly,
warm
devoutness–piety
dew (congealed)–rime
dewy–roral, roric
dexterity–ability, address,
aptitude, aptness, art,

cleverness, deftness, ex-
pertness, facility, finesse,
knack, nimbleness, skill
dexterous–adept, adroit, apt,
artful, clever, deft, handy,
quick, ready, skillful
diabolical–demoniac, de-
monic, devilish, fiendish,
hellish, infernal, satanic,
wicked
diacritical mark–tilde
diacritical sign–tilde
diadem–anadem, coronet,
crown, fillet, headband,
tiara
diagnose–analyze
diagonal–bias
diagram (branched)–tree
diagram (building)–plan
diagram (Fr.)–epure
diagram (well-defined) –
graph
diagram of dots and lines–
graph
diagram representing suc-
cessive values or changing
values–graph
dialect–idiom, language,
lingo, patois, speech, vernacular
dialect (Aramaic)–Syriac
dialect (provincial)–patois
dialect (Sanskrit)–pali
dialect (Semitic)–geez
dialect (South African)–taal
dialectic pronunciation–burr
diameter–pi
diameter (bullet) – caliber,
calibre
diameter (half) – radius,
radii (pl.)
diamond (cutting)–bort
diamond (inferior)–bort
diamond (South Africa)–
jager
diamond cutting stone (cup)
–dop
diamond hard–adamant
diamond surface–facet
dianthus plant (genus of)–
pinks
diaphanous–transparent
diaphragm (pert. to)–phrenic
diary–journal, log, record,
register

diaskeuast – ascertainment, editor, prepare, revise, revisor

diatribe–philippic, screed

Diaz de Bivar's title–Cid

dib–dap

dice (throw of six) sise

Dickens' adult character–Uriah Heep

Dickens' character–Dora, Bill Sikes

Dickens' child character–Nell, Tim

Dickens' Dombey and Son character–Cuttle

Dickens' pen name–Boz

dictate–command, enjoin, prescribe, suggest

dictatorial–arrogant, authoritative, autocratic, categorical, dogmatic, domineering, lordly, magisterial, opinionated, oracular, peremptory, pompous, positive, pragmatic

diction–language, phraseology, style, vocabulary

dictionary–calepin, lexicon, wordbook

dictionary compiler–lexicographer

dictionary of names–onomasticon

did–acted, performed

didactic–instructive, preceptive

didactic discourse–homily

dido–antic, caper, trick

Dido's sister–Anna

die–decease, depart, expire, fade, perish

die (annular drainpipe making)–dod

die (engraved)–seal

die down–wane

die symbol–ace

diet (German states)–Landtag

differ–clash, disagree, dispute, vary

differed within limits–ranged

difference–dissimilarity, distinction, unlikeness

difference (minute)–shade

different–divergent, divers,

diverse, diversified, manifold, many, other, several, sundry, unlike, variant, variegated

different (not)–identical

different shapes (of)–variform

differentiates–contrasts

differently shaped–variform

difficult–arduous, hard, laborious, painful, spiny, troublesome

difficult prefix–dys

difficult to grasp–eely

difficulty – bar, barrier, check, clog, hindrance, impediment, nodus, obstacle, obstruction, plight, rub, scrape, strait

difficulty (perplexing)–crux, knot

difficulty (unexpected)–problem, snag

diffidence – apprehension, doubt, hesitation, humility

diffident–coy, reserved, retiring, shrinking, shy, timid

diffuse–disperse, expand, extend, publish, shed, strew

diffuse (as light)–radiate

diffused (thinly)–sparse

diffused throughout–pervade

diffusion between fluids separated by porous particles–osmosis

dig–delve, excavate, exhume, root, spade, unearth

dig from earth–mine

dig in ground–grub, mine

dig up–exhume, grub, unearth

digest–compendium

digestion (good)–eupepsil

digesting–digerent

digestive agent–pepsin

digestive ferment–maltase, rennin

digger (trench)–sapper

digit–finger, number, toe, unit

digit (manual)–thumb

digit (rudimentary)–dewclaw

dignified–graced, majestic, manly, sedate, staid

dignify–elevate, ennoble, exalt, honor

dignitary–clergyman, priest

dignitary (church)–prelate

dignitary (collegiate)–don

dignity–decorum, honor, majesty, nobility, rank, sedateness

dignity and prerogative of a certain nobleman–earldom

digraph–ligature, oe

digress–deviate, divagate, diverge, swerve, transgress

digression–deviation, episode, excursion, excursus

digression (rhetoric)–ecbole

dike–bank, levee, pond, pool

dilapidation–decay, disintegration, disrepair, ruin

dilate–distend, enlarge, expand, inflate, swell, widen

dilation of hollow organ–ectasia

dilatory–backward, behindhand, inactive, procrastinating, slow, sluggish

dilatory (shrewdly)–fabian

dilemma–predicament

dilettante–amateur

diligence–assiduity, attention, care, caution, constancy, earnestness, heed, heedfulness, sedulousness

diligent–active, assiduous, attentive, busy, industrious, laborious, sedulous

dill seed–anet

dillydally–lag, loiter, trifle, vacillate

dilute–rarefy, reduce, thin, weaken

diluted–attenuate

dim–bleak, blear, darken, darkish, indistinct, mysterious, obscure, overcast

dim by tears–blear

dim with water (as the eyes) –blear

dimension–breadth, circumference, height, length, measurement, size, thickness

diminish–abate, bate, decrease, dwindle, ebb, fade, lessen, lower, pare, peter, reduce, taper, wane

diminish front (military)–ploy

diminish toward a point–taper

diminution–abate, abatement, decrease, decrement, lessening

diminution (rhetorical)–litotes

diminutive–bantam, little, petite, small

diminutive ending–ettes, ie

diminutive suffix–el, ette, ule

diminutive value (suffix)–ole

din–clang, clatter, hubbub, noise, racket, rattle, uproar

dine–eat, sup

dingle–glen, jingle, ring, tinkle, valley

dining room–cenacle, refectory

dinner course–dessert, entree, salad, soup

dinosaur (carnivorous)–tyrannosaurus

dinosaur (kind of)–morosaurian

Dinsmore (Miss)–Elsie

diocese–district, jurisdiction, see

Dionysus' lover–Selene

Dionysus' mother–Semele

Dioscuri's sister–Helen

dioxide (hydrous uranium)–ianthinite

dip–immerse, plunge, submerge

dip and throw–bail

dip in water–rinse

dip into liquid (suddenly)–souse

dip out–bail, scoop

diplomacy–artfulness, dexterity, tact

diplomat–consul

diplomatic–tactful

diplomatic aide–attache

diplomatic corps head–doyen

diptera lobe (wing)–alula

dipthong (diphthong)–ae, oe

dire–deadly, dismal, dreadful, evil, fatal, horrible, terrible

dire want (in)–needy

direct–aim, bend, bid, con, conduct, head, instruct, lead, manage, order, refer, steer, straight, turn

direct for information–refer

direct proceedings–preside

direct steering of vessel–con

directed inward (as an angle)–reentrant

directed to remain after being marked for omission–stetted

directed upward–erect

direction–bent, care, command, course, east, guidance, inclination, management, north, oversight, route, south, superintendence, way, west

direction (general)–trend

direction (naut.)–avast, belay

direction (stage)–exeunt, exit, sennet

direction (straight)–linear

direction (violinist's to use bow)–arco

direction to perform (quick, lively)–allegro

directions (Scot.)–airt

directly adverse–diametric

directly opposite–antipodean

director–boss, leader, manager, producer, superintendent

director (gunfire)–aimer

director (helmsman's)–conner

direful–calamitous, dreadful, terrible, woeful

dirge–hearse

dirge (for the dead)–keen

dirigible (famous)–Roma

dirk–dagger, snee, sword

dirt–dust, earth, excrement,

filth, grime, muck, mud, refuse

dirty – bemire, clouded, filthy, foggy, foul, gusty, muddied, muddy, nasty, squalid, stormy, sullied

dirty (through neglect)–squalid

dirty pool–puddle

disable–cripple, incapacitate, maim, unfit, weaken

disaccharide–biose, maltose, saccharose, sucrose

disadvantage–damage, detriment, handicap, hurt, injury, out

disagreeable–cross, invidious, offensive, repugnant, unpleasant

disagreeably sharp–edgy

disagreed–conflicted, differed, dissented, quarreled, varied

disagreeing–divergent

disagreement–clash, contrariety, controversy, discord, discrepancy, dispute, dissension, dissent, diversity, misunderstanding, unlikeness, variance, wrangle

disagrees (one who) – dissenter

disappear–vanish

disappear (gradually) – dwindle, fade

disappear (like vapor)–evanesce

disappoint–baffle, balk, bilk, fail, fall, thwart

disappointment – failure, frustration, rue

disapprobation – condemnation, disapproval, odium

disapproval–booh, censure, disapprobation, hiss, veto

disapprove–condemn, deprecate

disarrange–disorder, disturb, unsettle

disarrange (coll.)–muss

disarray–confusion, dishabille, disorder, disorderly, unkempt

disaster–accident, calamity, evil, misadventure, mischance, misfortune, mishap

disaster (boding)–sinister

disavow–decline, deny, disclaim, refuse, retract

disbeliever (of accepted beliefs)–heretic

disbeliever in God–atheist

disburse–expend, defray, spend

disc (honorary)–medal

disc (numbered)–dial

discard–abandon, cashier, dismiss, forsake, omit, sluff

discard as worthless–scrap, shed, sluff

discern–behold, descry, detect, discover, espy, perceive, see

discernible–apparent, conspicuous, distinguishable, evident, manifest, perceptible, visible

discernible (hardly)–inconspicuous

discerning–acute, astute, discriminating, sage

discernment–acumen, astuteness, discrimination, eye, perception, perspicacity, sharpness, shrewdness

discernment (nice)–acumen, tact

discharge–acquittal, defray, dismissal, emit, exude, fire, payment, performance, release, shoot, speed

discharge (dishonorable)–bobtail, drumhead

discharge (simultaneous of firearms)–fusillade

discharge (to, obs.)–cass

discharge a debt–payment

disciple–apostle, follower, pupil, scholar, student

disciple (betrayer of Christ)–Judas

disciple (in India)–chela

disciplinarian–trainer

disciplinarian (strict military)–martinet

discipline–chasten, chastisement, culture, education, instruction, punishment, training

discipline (penitential)–penance

discipline (strict)–regimentation

disclaim–abjure, abnegate, deny, disavow, renounce, repudiate

disclose–bare, divulge, impart, reveal, tell, unveil, utter

disclosure (embarrassing)–expose

discolor–spot, stain, tarnish

discolor (arch.)–distain

discolored by incipient or partial decay–doty

discomfit–baffle, confuse, embarrass, frustrate, overthrow, rout, upset

discomfiture–confusion, disappointment, embarrassment, frustration, inconvenience

discomfort–annoyance, embarrassment, inconvenience

discompose – confuse, derange, disconcert, disturb, flurry, fluster, fret, ruffle, unsettle, upset

disconcert–abash, confuse, disarrange, discomfit, disturb, embarrass

disconcert (coll.)–feeze, rattle

disconcert (utterly)–abash, nonplus

disconnect–disunite, separate, sever, uncouple

disconnected–broken, desultory, disjointed, rambling, scattered

disconsolate–desolate, forlorn, gloomy, hopeless, inconsolable, melancholy, sad, sorrowful, woeful

discontent–displeasure, disquiet, dissatisfaction

discontented (to be)–repine, unrest

discontinue – cease, drop, end, stop

discord–cacophony, contention, difference, disagreement, dissension, dissonance, strife, variance

discord (goddess of)–Ate, Eris

discordant–contrary, disagreeing, harsh, incongruous, inconsistent, inharmonious, irreconcilable, jangling, jarring, quarrelsome

discordant and noisy–wacky, whacky

discordant sound–jangle

Discordia–Eris

discount–agio, allowance, rebate

discourage–damp, daunt, deject, depress, deter, dismay, dispirit

discourage through fear–deter

discourse–account, converse, dissertation, lecture, narrate, narrative, speak, talk, tell, treatise

discourse (didactic)–homily

discourse (dull and tedious in)–prosy

discourse (elaborate public)–oration

discourse (laudatory)–eulogy, panegyric

discourse (long)–screed

discourse (religious)–homily, sermon

discourse (unimaginative)–prose

discourse (written)–paper

discourteous–rude, uncivil

discover–ascertain, descry, detect, disclose, espy, find, invent, spy, uncover, unearth

discoverable (by examination)–scrutable

discoverer–informer, scout, spy

discoverer of America (reputed)–Eric

discoverer of electric light–Edison

discoverer of radium–Curie

discoverer of telegraph–Morse

discoverer of telephone–Bell

discoverer of vaccination–
Jenner
discredit–disgrace, dishonor,
disparage, disrepute, distrust, doubt, scandal
discredited by open censure
–decried
discreet–careful, cautious,
circumspect, civil, polite,
politic, prudent, wary
discrepancy–contrariety, disagreement, variance
discretion–discontinuity, disjunction, prudence, tact
discriminate – differentiate,
distinguish, secern
discriminating–choosey, nice
discrimination–acumen, discernment, distinction,
penetration, taste
discus–quoit
discuss–argue, debate, dispute, moot, parley, treat
discuss (casually)–mention
discuss price–bargain
disdain–arrogance, askance,
contemn, contempt, de-
spise, haughtiness, pride,
scorn
disease–ailment, infirmity,
malady
disease (bee)–amoeba
disease (blood with excessive
leucocytes, white corpus-
cles)–leucaemia, leucemia,
leukaemia, leukemia
disease (cattle, dial.)–hoose
disease (cereal grass)–ergot,
smut
disease (chicken)–pip
disease (contagious)–mea-
sles, mumps, pox
disease (deficiency, faulty
diet)–pellagra
disease (diver's)–bends
disease (eye)–conjunctivitis,
glaucoma, trachoma
disease (febrile)–malaria
disease (fungus)–mildew
disease (grapevine)–erinose
disease (Oriental common)–
beriberi
disease (parrot)–psittacosis
disease (plant)–ergot, smut
disease (rye)–ergot
disease (sheep)–coe, rot

disease (skin) – eczema,
hives, psora, tetter
disease (skin, chronic) –
psoriasis
disease (stonecutter's)–silicosis
disease (sugar cane)–sereh
disembark–alit, debark, land
disembodied spirit–soul
disembowel–eviscerate
disencumber–disburden, disengage, free, rid
disengage–clear, detach, dis-
embarrass, disencumber,
disentangle, extricate, liberate, loosen
disentangle–clear, comb, dis-
embarrass, disengage, ex-
tricate, loose, ravel, sleav,
sleave, sleeve, unravel
disfigure–blemish, deface,
injure, mangle, mar, mu-
tilate, scar
disgorge–discharge, eject, relinquish, vent, vomit
disgrace–attaint, degrade,
discredit, disesteem, disparagement, humiliate,
humiliation, ignominy,
odium, opprobrium, re-
proach, shame, stain
disguise–camouflage, covert,
dissemble, dissimulate,
feign, mask, masque, mas-
querade, pretend
disgust – abhorrence, aversion, loathing, nausea,
nauseate, repugnance
disgusting–nasty, offensive,
revolting, sickening
dish–tureen
dish (braised liver)–haslet
dish (chafing)–cresset
dish (gravy)–boat
dish (milk and egg)–custard,
omelet, omelette
dish (minced)–hash
dish (of green herbs, Fr.)–
salade
dish (of herbs)–salad
dish (of meat and vegeta-
bles)–ragout
dish (Oriental, of rice, etc.)
–pilau, pilaw
dish (saucer-like, anc.)–patera, paterae (pl.)

dish (seasoned)–ragout
dish (shallow, church service)–paten
dish (spiced, of game, Fr.)–
salmis
dish (table)–tureen
dishabille–negligee, undress
dishearten–appal, daunt, depress, deter, discourage,
dispirit
dishearten (arch.)–amate
disheartened (be much)–
despond, discouraged
dishes – chargers, cheats,
frustrates, nappies, ruins,
saucers, serves, tureens
disheveled–disarranged, disarrayed, disordered,
mussed, ruffled, tumbled,
unkempt, untidy
disheveled (coll.)–tousled
dishonor–defame, degrade,
disgrace, disparagement,
disrepute, infamy, igno-
miny, obloquy, opprobri-
um, reproach, shame
dishwasher (slang) – pearl
diver
dishwashing (army slang)–
bubble dancing
disinclination–aversion, disaffection, dislike, distaste,
repugnance
disinclined – averse, indisposed, reluctant, unwill-
ing
disinfect–sterilize
disinfectant–germicide, phenol
disintegrate–crumble, de-
compose
disintegrating–corrosive
disjoin–detach, disconnect,
dissociate, part, separate,
sever, sunder
disk–harrow
disk (commemorative)–
medal, medallion
disk (commemorative small)
–medalet
disk (heavy grinding)–millstone
disk (in lathe to hold material)–faceplate
disk (measuring)–dial

disk (musical)–record, recording
disk (perforated)–washer
disk (rotating)–wheel
disk (small flat perforated) –washer
disk (solar)–aten, aton
disk (thin metal)–paten
disk for pitching–quoit
dislike–antipathy, aversion, disaffection, disinclination, disrelish, distaste, mind
dislike (moved by)–averse
dislike (strongly)–antipathy, aversion, odium
disloyal–false, inconstant, perfidious, treacherous, unfaithful, untrue
dismal–black, calamitous, dark, doleful, dolorous, dreary, funeral, gloomy, joyless, lonesome, lugubrious, lurid, melancholy, ominous, sad, sorrowful, unfortunate, unhappy, wan
dismal failure (slang)–dud, flop
dismantle–deprive, destroy, divest, raze, strip, uncloak
dismay–affright, alarm, appall, apprehension, consternation, daunt, dejection, depression, discouragement, fear, fright, terror
dismiss–discharge, drop, eject
dismiss forcibly–exile
dismiss forcibly (slang)– bounce
dismiss from office (law)– amove, recall
dismiss from station (law)– amove
dismissal (unceremonious)– conge
dismounted–alit
disobedient – contumacious, forward, froward, intractable, mutinous, rebellious, wayward
disorder–confusion, disarrangement, disorganization, distemper, illness,

indisposition, malady, mess, revolution, sickness
disorder (arch.)–deray
disorder (mental)–craziness, paranoia, paranomia
disorder (nervous)–tic
disorder (utter)–chaos, confusion
disorder (violent)–riot
disordered (coll.)–mussy
disordered state–clutter
disorderly–confused, irregular, slipshod, ungovernable, unmanageable
disorderly flight–rout
disorganize–derange, disarrange, disorder, disrupt, upset
disown–renounce, repudiate
disparage–decry, degrade, depreciate, detract, dishonor, incongruity, lower, slight, slur
dispart–break, cleave, divide, open, rend, rive, separate, sever, split
dispassionate – collected, composed, cool, fair, moderate, serene, temperate, unruffled
dispatch–accelerate, accomplish, conclude, expedite, haste, hasten, kill, mail, post, send, slay, speed
dispatch boat–aviso, packet
dispatcher–orderer, trainman
dispel–disperse, dissipate, scatter
dispense–administer, deal, dole
dispensed with–spared
disperse–diffuse, dissipate, distribute, rout, scatter, sow, spread, strew
dispirit–cow, damp, daunt, deject, depress, dishearten, intimidate
displace–depose, discharge, mislay, misplace, remove, supersede
display–air, evince, exhibit, flaunt, manifestation, parade, pomp, setout, show, wear

display (spectacular)–pageant
display conspicuously–emblazon
display impudently–flaunt
display intense feeling–enthuse
display of temper (public)– scene
display ostentatiously–sport
display publicly–stage
displayer (erudition)–pedant
displaying of energy at a distance–telenergic
displease–anger, annoy, dissatisfy, irritate, offend, provoke, vex
displeasure–anger, disfavor, dislike, distaste, indignation, offense
dispose–adjust, arrange, bestow, distribute, give, mind, order, place, set, settle
disposed–prone
disposed to cling together– clannish
disposed to doubt–skeptical
disposition – arrangement, bent, bias, character, mood, nature, organization, temper, temperament, turn
disposition (natural)–temperament
disposition to please others– complaisantness
dispossessed – bereft, deprived, divested, ejected, ousted
disproof–refutation, refute
disprove (to)–rebut, refute
disprove (utterly)–explode
disproving conclusively–confuting
disputant – controversialist, polemic
disputation – controversy, conversation, discussion, polemic
disputatious–argumentative, contentious, controversial, polemic, quarrelsome
dispute–altercation, argument, bicker, brawl, broil, contest, controversy, de-

bate, feud, haggle, quarrel, squabble, wrangle

dispute (in)–moot

dispute pettily – haggle, naggle

disqualify–debar, incapacitate, indispose

disquiet–agitate, disturb, excite, fret, vex

disquisition–discussion, essay

disquixote–disillusion

disregard–ignore, neglect, slight

disreputable–base, discreditable, low, seamy, shameful

disrupt–rend, tear

dissemble–cloak, conceal, counterfeit, disguise, hide

disseminate–circulate, disperse, propagate, scatter, sow, spread

dissension – disagreement, friction

dissent–disagree, disagreement, nonagreement, nonconcurrence, nonconformity

dissent (signal of)–nay

dissenter–heretic, nonconformist, protestor, recusant

dissention–variance

dissertation–debate, discourse, discussion, essay, lecture, thesis, treatise

Dissertation on a Roast Pig (author of)–Charles Lamb

dissidence – disagreement, dissent

dissimilarity–difference, heterogeneousness, unlikeness

dissipate–consume, dispel, expend, scatter, shatter, spend, waste

dissolute–abandoned, debauched, lawless, lewd, licentious, rakish, reckless, unbridled, uncurbed, vicious, wanton, wild

dissolve–adjourn, decompose, disintegrate, disor-

ganize, fuse, liquefy, melt, solve

dissonant–contradictory, discordant, grating, harsh, inconsistent, inharmonious, jangling, jarring, unmelodious

dissuade–dehort, deter, discourage, disincline, divert

distain – defile, discolor, stain, tarnish

distain (arch.)–discolor

distance–aloofness, coldness, mileage, outstrip, range, remoteness, space, yardage

distance (short)–step

distance (small)–step

distance down–depth

distance north and south (pert. to)–latitudinal

distance runner–miler

distant–afar, far, remote, separated, yon, yonder

distant (more)–ulterior

distant (prefix)–tel, tele

distaste–aversion, disgust, disinclination, displeasure, disrelish, dissatisfaction

distaste (settled)–aversion

distasteful–disagreeable, disgusting, displeasing, hateful, loathsome, nauseous, offensive, unpalatable, unpleasant, unsavory

distemper–ailment, dilute, disease, illness, malady, sickness, soak, steep

distend–dilate, enlarge, expand, grow, inflate, spread, swell

distended–patulous

distillate (turpentine)–resin, rosin

distilled wood substance–tar

distilling device–alembic, retort

distinct–distinguished, fair, individual, separate, several

distinction–difference, rank, renown, reputation, variation

distinction (unfair)–discrimination

distinctions (academic)–honors

distinctive – characteristic, conspicuous, peculiar, prominent

distinctive mark–badge, cachet

distinctive quality–specialty, talent

distinctly–clearly, obviously

distinguish – differentiate, discern, discriminate, secern

distinguish accurately–discriminate

distinguished – celebrated, conspicuous, defined, eminent, extraordinary, famous, illustrious, laureate, noted, prominent, renowned

distort–contort, deform, screw, twist, warp, wrest

distort (to, Scot. dial.)–camshackle

distorted–awry, twisted

distortion of head to one side–loxia

distract–distraught, puzzle

distracted–frantic, mad

distraction–confusion, derangement, dissension, disturbance, diversion, frenzy, perplexity, tumult

distress–agony, anguish, annoy, danger, grief, grieve, harrow, necessity, pain, perplex, trouble, worry

distress call–S.O.S.

distribute–administer, allocate, allot, apportion, assign, deal, dispense, divide, dole, dot, prorate, share

distribution–allotment, apportionment, arrangement, dispensation, dispersion, disposal

distribution of favors–patronage

distributively–apiece, each, individually, respectively, separately, severally

distributor (illicit narcotic)–doper

district–canton, circuit, demesne, province, quarter, territory

district (political)–canton, ward

district (poor)–slum

distrust–doubt, mistrust

distrustfully askance

disturb–agitate, alarm, annoy, discompose, disorder, distract, interrupt, molest, perturb, roil, ruffle, upset, vex

disturb easily–emotional

disturb the peace–riot

disturbance–agitation, annoyance, brawl, clatter, confusion, derangement, hubbub, perturbation, tumult, turmoil, uproar

disturbance (atmospheric)–static

disturbance (coll.)–rumpus

disturber–agitator, troubler

disturbing–disconcerting

disunion–alienation, detachment, disconnection, disjunction, dissension, separation, severance

disunite – disjoin, divide, part, rip, separate, sever, sunder, unravel, untie

disuse–abandon, discard, discontinue, misuse

disuse (state of)–desuetude

ditch–canal, channel, fosse, gutter, moat, rut, trench

ditch (artificial)–canal, fosse

ditch (deep narrow)–sap

ditch (large, Eng. dial.)–rhine

ditch (protective)–moat

ditch (side next to parapet)–escarp

ditty–lay, poem, song

ditty (obs.)–dite

diurnal–daily

divan–chesterfield, davenport, settee, sofa

divan (Fr.)–canape

diver–pickpocket, submarine

diverge–divide

divers–cruel, different, evil, perverse, several, sundry, various

diver's disease–bends

diverse–different, distinct, separate, several, sundry, unlike, various

diversify–variate, variegate, vary

diversion–amusement, deflection, entertainment, game, hobby, pastime, play, recreation, sport

diversity–variety

divert–amuse, delight, distract, entertain, recreate

divert by appeal–dissuade

divest–dispossess, reft, strip, unclothe

divest of office–depose

divide–bifurcate, cleft, fork, lot, prorate, separate, sever, share, slice, space, split, sunder, part, watershed

divide by partitions–separate

divide in proportion–prorate

divide into a number of parts–multisect

divide into four parts–paly, quarter

divide into parts–bisect, dismember, halve

divide into regular steps–graduate

divide into seven parts–septinate

divide into small areas–areolate

divide into strata–layer

divide into two parts–bisect

divide transversely–crossect

divide with grain–split

divided (nearly at base)–partite

divided by partitions–septate

divided by scallop-like lines–ente

divided into small spaces–aerolate

dividing–graduating, secant, separating

dividing wall (partition)–septum, septa (pl.)

divination–augury, discernment, omen

divination by means of burning straws–sideromancy

divination of dreams–oneiromancy

divine–celestial, clergyman, Godlike, heavenly, minister, priest, superhuman, supernatural

divine being–deva

divine gifts–blessings

divine messenger–apostle

diving bird–auk, grebe, loon

divinity (Celtic)–taranis

divinity (female)–nymph

divinity (Gaelic)–Ler

division–allotment, cleavage, compartment, department, disconnection, disjunction, dismemberment, part, partition, schism, section, sector, share

division (administrative of a country)–diocese

division (French territorial)–arrondissement, commune, canton, department

division (geological)–era

division (of city)–block, precinct, ward

division (political)–borough, city, county, district, parish, state, ward

division (religious)–schism

division (zoogeographic primary)–eogaea

division between torrid and temperate zone–tropic

division into small areas–areolation

division of a shield–ente

division of an act–scene

division of long poem–canto

division of mankind–race

division of mankind (pert. to)–racial

division of plants–archichlamydeae

division of thread in weaving machine–beer

division of time–day, decade, minute, moment, month, second, week, year

divisor (opposite of)–multiple

divot–clod

divulge–communicate, discover, impart, publish, reveal, tell, uncover

dizziness–giddiness, vertigo
dizzy–crazy, foolish, stupid, swimming, unsteady, vertiginous
dizzy (be)–swim
do–act, answer, avail, perform, serve, suffice, suit
do (arch.)–dost
do (music)–ut
do away with–abolish, destroy, discontinue, kill, rid
do without–dispense, spare
docile–calm, gentle, tame, tractable
dock–clip, curtail, pier, shorten, wharf
dock worker–stevedore
doctor–healer, teacher, treat
doctor (animal)–vet, veterinarian, veterinary
doctor (hospital)–intern, interne
doctor's assistant–intern, interne
doctrine–article, credo, dogma, gospel, ism, maxim, opinion, position, precept, principle, rule, tenet
doctrine (disagreeing)–heresy
doctrine (distinctive)–ism
doctrine (esoteric)–cabala
doctrine (philosophy of C. S. Pierce)–pragmatism
doctrine (secret)–cabala, esoteric
doctrine of inevitable–fatalism
doctrine of selfishness–egoism
document–paper
document (addition to)–codicil, rider
document (legal)–deed, writ
document (provisional)–scrip
document (public)–archive
document (true copy of)–estreat
document file–dossier
document hamper–hanaper
dodge–artifice, cheat, deceive, duck, elude, escape, evade, expedient
doe–female

doe (second year)–teg
doer–actor, agent, attorney, author, factor, maker, manager, performer
does (old form)–doth
does without–spares
doff–divest, remove, strip, undress, vail
dog (coach)–Dalmatian
dog (coll.)–canine, cur
dog (Eskimo)–Husky
dog (extinct breed)–Talbot
dog (fire)–andiron
dog (genus of)–canis
dog (howling)–ululation
dog (hunting) – basset, pointer, retriever, setter
dog (large) – Dane, mastiff, Newfoundland
dog (Latin)–canis
dog (short-eared, her.) – alan, aland, alant
dog (small)–Pekinese, Pekingese, pomeranian, spaniel
dog (small, abbr.)–pom
dog (trained to decoy ducks)–toler
dog (wild)–dingo
dog house–kennel
dog rose fruit–hip
dog salmon–keta
dog star (var.)–sopt
dog's delight–bone
dog's upper lip part–flew
Doge's barge (Venetian)–Bucentaur
dogma–doctrine, tenet
dogma (pert. to)–levitical
dogmatic–assertive, dictatorial, magisterial, opinionated
dogmatic saying–dictum, dicta (pl.)
dogmatic statement–dictum, dicta (pl.)
dogmatism–pragmatism
dole–allotment, distribute, grief, mete, misfortune, sorrow
doleful – dolorous, drear, dreary, lugubrious, melancholy, mournful, rueful, sad
doll (rag)–moppet

dolphin–bottlenose, dorado, fish, inia, porpoise
dolphin (tropical)–inia
dolphin-like cetaceans (genus of)–inia
dolphin waxy solid separating from oil–sperm
dolt–ass, asse, blockhead, dullard, dunce, ignoramus, numskull, oaf
domain–demesne, dominion
domain (emperor's)–empire
domain (imperial)–empery, emperies (pl.), empire
domain (region)–empire, realm
Dombey and Sons (Dickens') character–Cuttle
dome–cupola
domestic establishment–menage
domesticate–domiciliate
domesticated–tamed
domicile–abode, dwelling, habitation, residence
domicile identification–doorplate
dominant–ascendant, chief, imperious, outweighing, overbalancing, paramount, pre-eminent, preponderant, principal, superior, supreme
dominate – predominate, reign, rule
dominating–bossy, regnant
domineer–boss, dominate, lord, predominate
domineer over–ride
domineering–haughty, imperious, lordly, masterful, overbearing
Dominican Republic measure–fanega, ona, tarea
dominion–authority, control, empire, jurisdiction, realm, rule, sway
dominion (absolute)–empery, emperies (pl.)
dominion (supreme)–empire
dominion of sacred things–hierarchy
Don Juan's mother–Inez
Don Quixote's steed–Rosinante

donate–bestow, give, present
done – baked, completed, cooked, ended, exhausted, finished, through
done by word of mouth–parol
done quickly without thought–snap
done solely for pay–mercenary
done with difficulty–labor
done without proper authority–surreptitious
donkey–ass, burro, neddy
donkey (wild)–onager
donna–lady, madam, mistress, wife, woman
donned–wore
donor–giver
doom–condemn, death, destine, destiny, destruction, fate, lot, ruin
doomed (Scot.)–fey
doomed to death–fey, sentenced
door–doorway, entranceway, gate, portal, postern, opening
doorframe–jamb
doorkeeper–tiler
doorknocker–rapper
doorway–entranceway, exit, opening, portal
dope (heroin)–hop, narcotic, nitroglycerin, opiate, opium
Dorian festival–carnea, carneia
doric frieze bottom–taenia
Doric frieze slabs (sculptured)–metopes
dormant–asleep, inactive, latent, quiescent, sleeping, torpid
dormer window–lucarne
dormeuse–carriage, coach, nightcap, seat
dormient–dormant, sleeping
dormouse–lerot, loir
dory (the John)–doree
dose–draft, potion
dot–clot, dowry, lump, period, speck, stipple
dot (fungus)–telia
dote–decay, dotage, dotard, imbecile, rot, stupor

dote on–adore
doting–fond
dotted–specked
dottle (Scot.)–crazy, silly
dotty–crazy, feeble
doty (as in timbers)–discolored
Douay Bible name–Aree
double–binary, counterpart, dual, duplicate, twin, twofold
double (prefix)–di
double (state of being)–duality
doublet (medieval quilted)–pourpoint
doubletree – crosspiece, spreader
doubling of a cord–loop
doubt–demur, hesitate, misgiving, mistrust, question, suspicion, uncertainty, waver
doubt (to)–dubitate, question
doubter–cynic, skeptic
doubtful–ambiguous, distrustful, dubious, equivocal, hesitating, problematical, questionable, uncertain, undecided, vacillating
douce–neat, pleasant, prudent, sedate, sober, sweet, tidy
dough–cash, money, paste
dough (fermenting)–leaven
doughnut–friedcake
doughnut (kind of)–cruller, simball
dour–gloomy, inflexible, obstinate, severe, stern
dove–color, culver, pigeon
dovefoot–geranium
dovekey (dovelike)–alle, auk, guillemot, rotche
dovelike–gentle, lovable, pure
dover–doze, drowse, stun
dowdish woman–frump
dowdy–shabby, slatternly, slovenly, untidy
dowel–pin, pintle
dower–dos, dowry, endow
down–fuzz
down (Fr.)–bas

down (poetic)–adown
down (prefix)–de
downcast–despondent, discouraged, dispirited, sad
downright – blunt, forthright, plain, positive, stark, unceremonious
downward (poetic)–adown
downward slope–declivity
downy–soft
downy surface–nap
dowry–dos, dot, dower, gift
dowry (pert. to)–dotal
doze–drowse, nap, nod
draft–dose, drink, potion
draft (bitter)–rue
draft (deep)–swig
draft (full-size architectural, Fr.)–epure
draft (small)–nip
draft (to)–conscript
draft of document (original)–protocol
draftsman–drawer
drag–draw, hale, haul, lug, pull, tow, trail, tug
drag loosely–trail
dragon (star of)–arc
drain–acequia, alberca, exhaust, lade, sewer, sump
drain (dial.)–dreen
drain (large, Eng. dial.)–rhine
drain (Scot., open)–siver
drainage area–basin
dram (short or small)–nip
drama (form of)–tragedy
drama (main action)–epitasis
drama (musical)–opera
dramatic – melodramatic, scenic, theatrical, wild
dramatic piece (short)–skit
dramatic representation–impersonation
drank heavily–toped
draught–dose, draft, potion
Dravidian–Andhra, Arava, Gondi, Kanarese, Khond, Kodagu, Kota, Kurukh, Malayalam, Malto, Oraon, Tamil, Teluga, Toda, Tulu
Dravidian ghost–Bhut
Dravidian language–same as Dravidian

draw–attract, delineate, drag, haul, limn, lug, pull, tow, tug

draw (finely, clearly)–etch

draw away–detract

draw back–retire

draw forth–educe, elicit

draw game (at chess)–stalemate

draw mark below–underline

draw near (to, obs.)–coast

draw off–abstract, extract, withdraw

draw off by atmospheric pressure–siphon

draw out–educe, elicit

draw out carefully–tweezer

draw over–remap, replat

draw through an eye–rove

draw tight–cinch, frap, stretch

draw together–lace

draw up the shoulders–shrug

drawer (secret)–till

drawing–attracting, draft, extracting, hauling, pulling

drawing or scrolling (absentminded)–doodling

drawing room–parlor

drawn to a slender thread–finespun

drayage–cartage, haulage

dread–affright, anxiety, apprehension, dismay, fear, horror, reverence, terror

dreadful–dire, fearful, formidable, frightful, hideous, horrible, horrid, terrible, terrific

dreadnaught (dreadnought) –battleship, fearless

dream–reverie, romance, vision

dream (day)–reverie

dream (Fr.)–reve

dreamer–idealist, visionary

dreaminess–languor

dreamy–imaginative, languid, poetic, soothing

dreamy tranquillity–kef

dreary–bleak, cheerless, depressing, dull, monotonous

dredge–scoop

dreg–excrement, feces, faeces (pl.), feculence, lees, refuse, sediment

dregs (wine)–marc

drench – douse, saturate, soak, souse

drenched with water–asoak, doused, soaked

dress–attire, clothe, garb, habiliment, preen, tog, toilet, trim

dress (loose morning)–negligee, peignor

dress (servant's)–livery

dress (style of, coll.)–getup

dress feathers–preen

dress flax–ted

dress gaudily–bedizen

dress goods (cotton)–calico, gingham

dress goods (thin)–tarlatan

dressmaker–modiste

dress out (tawdrily)–bedizen

dress stone–nidge, nig

dress stone with hammer–nidge, nig

dress style (coll.)–getup

dress trimming (kind of)–ruche

dress up (coll.)–primp

dressed – attired, clad, clothed, garbed, gowned

dressed (loosely)–discinct

dressed (sprucely)–smart

dresser–bureau, rober

dresser (ultrafastidious)–dude

dressing–attiring

dressing (downy linen for wounds)–lint

dressing for wounds–pledget

drew forth–educed

drew near–approached, hied

drew over harshly–scraped

drew together–laced

dried–dehydrated, desiccated, drained, wiped, wizened

dried grass–hay

dries up–parches, seres

driest–serest

drift–deviation, float, sag, tendency

drift sidewise–crescent

drifting with rise and fall of water–tiding

drill–bore, borer, exercise, practice, train

drill (percussion)–gad

drill into again–retap

drilling (carpet)–denim

drink–beverage, bouse, coffee, decoction, draft, grog, imbibe, lap, potion, quaff, rum, skink, tea, tope, vodka

drink (alcoholic liquor taken before meals)–aperitif

drink (farinaceous)–ptisan

drink (fermented)–mead

drink (fermented milk)–airan

drink (frozen)–frappe

drink (gin)–bumbo

drink (honey flavored with mulberry)–morat

drink (hot spirituous)–toddy

drink (long, coll.)–swig

drink (mild)–ade, pop, soda

drink (of the gods)–nectar

drink (of wine, water, and sugar)–negus

drink (Philippine fermented rice)–bubud

drink (rum)–bumbo

drink (Russian)–vodka

drink (sassafras bark)–saloop

drink (small)–dram, nip, peg

drink (soft)–ade, pop, soda

drink (spiced milk with liquor)–posset

drink (strong)–mead

drink (sweet, delicious)–nectar

drink (vinegar and diluted wine)–posca

drink (vinegar and water)–posca

drink (wine and vinegar)–posca

drink heavily–tope

drink of spirits–dram

drink slowly–sip

drink to health of–toast

drinker–drunkard, imbiber, toper

drinker (habitual)–sot, toper

drinking cup–mug, stein, tass

drinking salutation–prosit

drinking vessel–cup, glass, goblet, jorum, mug, schooner, stein, tankard

drip–trickle

drive–force, impel, press, propel, ride, urge

drive (coll.)–roust

drive (public)–esplanade

drive (Scot.)–caa

drive away–banish, chase, dispel, repel

drive back–repulse

drive frantic–bedevil

drive in–restaurant

drive in and down–tamp

drive nail at an angle–toe

drive obliquely–slice, toe

drive out–eradicate, exile, expel

drive slantingly (as a nail)–toe

drive to right (Phil. I.)–mano

drivel–drool, slaver, twaddle

driveler–doter, fool

driver–charioteer, coachman, engineer, jehu, propeller

driver (cattle)–drover

driver (elephant)–mahout

driver (fast)–jehu, speeder

driver (furious) – jehu, speeder

driver (pied)–smew

driving line–rein

drizzling–rainy

droll–comic, diverting, farcical, humorous, laughable, merry, odd, queer, ridiculous, waggish

drollery – buffoonery, farce, humor, jest, puppet, wit

dromedary–camel, camelus, delul, dromond

drone–bee, hum, humming, idler

drool–drivel, slaver

droop–flag, languish, loll, pine, sag, slouch, wilt

drooping–nutant

drooping of eyelid (paralytic)–ptosis

drooping on one side–alop

drop–abandon, bead, drip, droop, fall, lower, omit, relinquish, shed, stop

drop (lachrymal)–tear

drop (saline)–tear

drop (Scot.)–drib

drop (small globular)–bead

drop bait lightly in water–dap

drop slowly–sink

dropping glass for counting drops–stactometer

dropping vowel or syllable in pronouncing–elision

dropsical–edemic

dropsy–edema

dross–chaff, dregs, lees, refuse, scum, slag, sprue, waste

dross of iron–sinter

dross of metal–slag

drossy–slaggy

drove–flock

drover–dealer, driver

drowse–doze, nod

drowsiness–dullness, emit, oscitance, sleepiness, sluggishness

drowsy–logy, sleepy, somnolent, soporific

drudge–fag, moil, slave, toil

drudges–slavies

drug–alum, dope, dull, ipecac, ipecacuanha, jalop, numb, opium, salol, senna, stupefy, tonga

drug (bitter)–aloe, rue

drug (convulsion causing)–tetanic

drug (medical)–sulfapyridine

drug (sleeping)–narcotic, sedative

drug (synthetic for malaria treatment)–atebrin

drug container–capsule

drug of forgetfulness–nepenthe

drug used for neuralgia–tonga

drug yielding species of crocus–saffron

drugget–mat, rug

druggist–apothecary

drugstore–pharmacy

drum–tambor, tambour

drum (kettle)–atabal, attabal, timpani, timpano

drum (Oriental)–tamtam, tomtom

dry–arid, barren, dull, fruitless, insipid, parch, pointless, sere, sterile, tiresome, uninteresting, unprofitable, vapid, wipe

dry (as new-mown grass)–ted

dry (as wine)–brut, sec

duck–scaup

duck (expert diving)–smew

duck (genus of)–anas

duck (hooked bill)–merganser

duck (longtailed)–hareld

duck (male)–drake

duck (North Sea)–scooter

duck (pintail) – piketail, smee

duck (rare)–merse

duck (sea)–coot, eider, scaup, scooter, scoter

duck (with fine down)–eider

duck-on-the-rock player–tenter

duct – aqueduct, canal, main, passage, pipe, trachea, tube, vas, vasa (pl.)

duct (anatomy)–vas, vasa (pl.)

ductile–compliant, docile, facile, flexible, malleable, manageable, plastic, pliant, tensile, tractile

dude–coxcomb, dandy, fop

dudeen–pipe

due–directly, exactly, meed, owing

due to motion–kinetic

duel–combat, conflict, contest, fence, tilt

duelist's aide–second

duet–duo

duet (instrumental)–duo

dug–spaded

dug out–spaded

duke (Fr.)–duc

dukedom–duchy

dulcimer–cembalo

dull–apathetic, barren, blear, crass, dead, deaden, dis-

mal, drab, dreary, drowsy,
dry, inanimate, irksome,
leaden, monotonous, ob-
tuse, prosaic, prose, prosy,
saturnine, sleepy, somber,
tedious, tiresome, unim-
aginative, vapid
dull (to become)–pall
dull and heavy–logy
dull and tedious discourse–
prosy
dull color–dun
dull finish–mat, matte
dull noise–klop
dull with drink–Scottish
dullest–tamest
Dumas character–Aramis,
Athos
dumb–inarticulate, mute,
speechless
dummy (sword practice)–
pel
dun–tan
dupe–catspaw, cheat, deceive, gull, mislead,
sucker, trick
duplicate–double, copy,
counterpart, facsimile,
likeness, mislead, replica,
transcript
duplicate (law)–estreat
duplicated–dittoed, repeated
durable–constant, continuing, enduring, firm, lasting, permanent, persist-
ent, stable
durable (not)–fleeting
duration–age, continuance,
lifetime, span, time
duration (without beginning or end)–eternity
during–pending, time
during the time that–whilst
dusk–gloaming, gloom, twilight
dusky – dark, somber,
swarth, swarthy
dust (deposited on glacier)–
kryokonite
dust (flax)–pouce
dust (flour mill floating)–
stive
dust speck–mote
Dutch assembly (legislative)–Raad

Dutch cheese–edam
Dutch city–commune, Ede
Dutch coin–doit, guilder,
stiver
Dutch commune–Ede, Epe
Dutch East Indies capital–
Batavia
**Dutch East Indies home
guard**–stadswacht
Dutch East Indies island–
Muna
Dutch East Indies island
(west of Sumatra)–Nias
**Dutch East Indies news
agency**–Aneta
Dutch fishing boat–tode
Dutch geographer–Aa
Dutch Guiana toad–pipa,
pipal
Dutch island (Pacific)–Java
Dutch landholder–patroon
Dutch measure–aam, ahm,
aum, el, ell, roede
Dutch measure (liquid)–
ahm
Dutch measure (wine, old)–
aum
Dutch measures–see Neth-
erlands
Dutch meter–el
Dutch name for Germans
(coll.)–Moffen
Dutch news agency–Aneta
Dutch painter–Lis, Rem-
brandt
Dutch pottery–delf, delft
Dutch secret society–Geu-
zen
Dutch South African–Boer
**Dutch South African hill-
kop**
Dutch uncle–eme, oom
Dutch vessel (merchant)–
galliot
Dutch weight–aam, lood
Dutch weight–see Nether-
lands
Dutch woman's abortion–
sooterkin
Dutch woman's birth (false)
–sooterkin
dutiful–compliant, docile,
reverent, reverential, sub-
missive
duty–care, chore, devoir,

job, obligation, stint, tariff, task, tax
duty (feudal)–heriot
dwale–belladonna, opiate,
potion, soporific, wander
dwarf–elf, elves (pl.),
gnome, midge, midget,
pigmy, pygmy, runt,
stunt
dwarf (mischievous)–troll
dwell–abide, delay, linger,
live, lodge, pause, remain,
reside, stay, tarry
dwell on tediously–harp
dwell unduly upon–harp
dweller–inhabitant, resident, tenant
dweller (coast)–orarian
dweller (jungle) – beast,
monkey
dwelling–abidance, abode,
apartment, domicile, du-
plex, flat, habitation, hotel, house, residence, tenement
dwelling (mean)–hovel,
hut, shanty
dwelling (movable)–tent,
trailer
dwelling (Oriental)–dar
dwelling (pert. to)–residential
dwelling (rude)–hovel, hut,
shanty
dwelling (sea)–marine
dwelling (tree)–nest
dwelling place of dead
(Babylonian myth)–Ara-
lu
dwelling place of souls–Po
dwelling place of spirits–Po
dwells continuously–harp
dwells upon tediously–harps
dwindle–decrease, diminish,
melt, taper, wane
dyad–couple, pair, two
dye–anil, color, stain
dye (blue)–wad, wade,
woad
dye (indigo)–al, anil
dye (mulberry)–al
dye (poisonous red)–aurin
dye (red)–aal
dye (red aniline)–magenta
dye (reddish)–annatto
dye (reddish orange)–henna

dye (violet)–archil
dye compound–aniline, eosin
dye plant–madder
dye prepared from quercitron bark–flavin
dye used in coloring butter–anatta, anatto, annato, arnato
dye used in coloring cheese–anatta, anatto, annato, arnato
dyeing apparatus–ager

dyeing shrub (used in)–sumac
dyer–stainer
dyes (morindin)–aches
dyestuff–aal, aniline, eosin, toluene
dyestuff (blue)–woad
dyestuff (red)–aurin
dynamic–forceful, potent
dynamic (opposed to)–static
dynamite inventor–Nobel
dynamo–generator

dynamo (inserted in distributing system)–booster
dynamo part – armature, commutator, rotor
dynasty–dominion, lordship, race, sovereignty, succession
dynasty (Chinese)–Fo, Han, Isin, Ming, Yin
dynasty member (Eastern Caliph's)–Ommiad
dysentery remedy–sulfaguanidine

E

each–apiece
each (abbr.)–ea
each (without exception)–all, every
eager–agog, anxious, ardent, avid, burning, excited, greedy, intent, keen, sharp
eager (arch.)–yare
eagerness–alacrity, alertness, ardor, avidity, cupidity, enthusiasm, fervency, fervor, impatience, impetuousness, readiness, zeal
eagerness for action–elan
eagle–ern, erne
eagle (northern)–ern, erne
eagle (whitetailed) – ern, erne
eagle (without beak or tail, her.)–allerion
eagle brood–aerie
eagle's nest–aerie, aery, eire, eirie, eyrie, eyry
eaglestone–aetites, etite
ear–auricle, hear, listen, lug, spike
ear (comb. form)–oto
ear (elephant's)–taro
ear (inflammation of)–otitis
ear (inner part)–tragi
ear (Latin)–auris
ear (middle)–drum
ear (near)–parotid
ear (of a bell)–cannon
ear (part of)–helix

ear (pert. to)–aural, auricular, otic
earache–otalgia
earbob–earring
ear cover–earlap, muff
ear covering–earcap, earmuff
ear disease treatment–otiatria
eardrop–earring, pendant
ear inflammation–otitis
ear inflammation (pert. to)–otitic
earlike projection–lug
ear lobe–lug
ear meatus (external)–burr
ear of grain (Scot.)–ressum
earpick (sug.)–auriscalp
ear science–otology
ear shell–abalone
ear specialist–aurist
ear weed–oreweed
eared seal–otary
ears (having)–aurate
earlier–elder, former, sooner
earliest–soonest
earliest born–eldest
earliest tertiary period (pert. to)–Eocene, Miocene, Oligocene, Pliocene
early–betimes, premature, soon
early (poetic)–rath
early Dutch theologian and scholar (pert. to)–Erasmian

early school of philosophy (pert. to)–eleatic
early theologian (pert. to)–Arian
earn–deserve, gain, merit
earnest – ardent, grave, hearty, sedate, serious, sincere, sober, solemn, staid, thoughtful, zealous
earnest (profoundly)–intense
earnestly–intensely, seriously
earth–clay, ground, rock, soil, terra, world
earth (black swamp)–muck
earth (calcareous)–marl
earth (comb. form)–geo
earth (goddess of)–Erda, Ge, Semele, Ve
earth (Latin)–terra
earth (loose)–dirt, sand
earth (lump of)–clod
earth (mound of)–rideau
earth (pert. to)–geal, telluric, terra
earth (poetic)–marl
earth (prefix)–geo
earth (Scot.)–erd
earth (small ridge of)–rideau
earth (surface)–topsoil
earth bank–levee, terrace
earth center (having)–geocentric
earth center mountain–Meru

earth deposit–alluvium, alluvia (pl.), loess, marl, silt

earth formed by decay of rocks in place–geest

earth god (Egyptian)–Geb, Keb

earth goddess–Erda, Ge, Semele

earth's axis end (either)–pole

earth's satellite–moon

earth's surface imaginary line–agone

earthen vessel maker–ceramist, potter

earthenware–crock, crockery, stoneware

earthlike–earthly

earthly–temporal, terrene

earthly (pert. to)–terra, terrafirm, terrene, terrestrial

earthly fragment–shard

earthquake–temblor

earthquake (pert. to)–seismic

earthquake (Tag.)–lindol

earthwork (besieger's)–terrace

earthworm–annelid, ipomoea

ease–allay, alleviate, assuage, calm, comfort, content, disburden, enjoyment, mitigate, pacify, peace, quiet, relax, relaxation, relieve, repose, rest, solicitude, soothe, tranquilize, tranquillity

ease (at)–otiose

ease of evaporation–volatility

ease up–relent

easement–assistance, relief

easily – gently, readily, smoothly

easily broken–fragile, shelly

easily deceived–gullible

easily frightened–skittish

easily ignited (capable of being)–flammable, inflammable

easily imposed upon–credulous

easily managed–docile

easily moved–mobile

easily offended–sensitive

easily split–schistic

easily understood–lucid

East–Levant

East (near)–Levant

East African coin (Ger.)–pesa

East African hartebeest–tora

East African house (native, of dried mud)–tembes

East African native–Somal, Somali

East African Negro tribe–Sotik

East African region–Adal

East African tree–moli

East Indian animal (nocturnal)–tarsier

East Indian bark (medicinal)–niepa

East Indian bark (used in dyeing)–lodh

East Indian bead tree–nim

East Indian bird–shama

East Indian bird (weaver)–baya

East Indian boatswain–serang

East Indian boiled butter–ghee, ghi

East Indian Buddhist gateway–toran, torana

East Indian bulbul–kala

East Indian cattle (wild)–gaur

East Indian cavalryman–sowar

East Indian cedar–deodar

East Indian cereal grass–ragee, raggee, raggi, ragi, raggy

East Indian cheroot–lunkah

East Indian chief (native)–sirdar

East Indian civet–musang

East Indian coin–anna, pice, rupee

East Indian cotton tree–simal

East Indian dialect–Urdu

East Indian drink–nipa

East Indian fabric (gold and silver)–tash

East Indian fan (large)–punka

East Indian fan (suspended)–punka

East Indian grass–ragee, raggee, ragi, raggi, raggy

East Indian groom–syce

East Indian harbor master–shabandar, shabunder

East Indian harem–zenana

East Indian hat (light)–topee

East Indian hawk (crested)–bacha

East Indian helmet (light)–topee

East Indian herb–pia, sesame, til

East Indian instrument (musical)–vina

East Indian island (Dutch)–Adi, Nias

East Indian island (pert. to)–Malayan

East Indian juniper berries–abhol

East Indian kidney bean–mung

East Indian language–Urdu

East Indian light hat–topee

East Indian measure–bamboo, bouw, coyang, depa, depoh, gantang, kilan, kit, parah, rood, rope, takar, tjenkal, tomebak

East Indian measure (distance)–kos

East Indian Mohammedan language–Urdu

East Indian money–anna, lac, lakh, rupee

East Indian money of account–anna

East Indian mountain pass–ghat, ghaut

East Indian mulberry tree bark–tapa

East Indian native–Lascar

East Indian nurse–amah, ayah

East Indian ox–gaur

East Indian palm–nipa, palmyra, tal

East Indian palm juice–sura

East Indian pea (split)–dal

East Indian plant–rea, sesame, sola

East Indian plant (fiber)–jute

East Indian plant (fodder)–dal

East Indian plant (long tubers)–tikor

East Indian plant (red dye)–chay, choy

East Indian poet–Tagore

East Indian police station–tanna

East Indian pots (water)–lotas

East Indian princess–ranee, rani

East Indian quadruped (hog-like) – babiroussa, babirusa, babirussa

East Indian race–swat

East Indian robber–dacoit

East Indian rubber tree–saj

East Indian sailing vessel–dhoni, doni

East Indian sailor–Lascar

East Indian sardine–lile

East Indian sheep–sna

East Indian shrub–ak, mudar, odal

East Indian shrub (climbing)–soma

East Indian soldier–sepoy

East Indian split pea–dal

East Indian title–sahib

East Indian title of respect–aya, mian

East Indian tree–ach, alof, banyan, bel, eng, mee, moli, oodal, poon, saj, sal, siman, toon

East Indian tree (bead)–nim

East Indian tree (bean family)–sapan

East Indian tree (cotton)–simal

East Indian tree (large)–neem

East Indian tree (orange-like for oil)–bel

East Indian tree (timber)–eng, poon, saj, sal, uadal

East Indian vessel (coastal)–patamar

East Indian vessel (water)–lota

East Indian vines–odales, soma

East Indian viol–ruana

East Indian warrior–singh

East Indian water pot–lota, lotas (pl.)

East Indian weaver bird–baya

East Indian weight–bahar, buncal, candy, catty, chee, gantang, hoen, kimbang, kojang, kulack, picul, reaal, ser, soekoe, tael, tali, tiembang, tji, tola, wang

East Indian wild cattle (genus of)–gaurs

East Indian wood–eng

East Indies–see East Indian

East Turkestan people (members of)–Uigur

east wind–eurus

Eastern–Oriental

eastern Asiatic people–Seres

Eastern Caliph's dynasty member–Ommiad

Eastern caravansary–serai

Eastern church clergy–papas

Eastern country (poetic name)–Ind

eastern Mediterranean–Levant

Eastern potentate–ameer, amir, emeer, emir

Eastern title–aga

Eastern viper (venomous)–cerastes

easy – calm, comfortable, complaisant, gentle, light, manageable, natural, suave, unconcerned

easy (not)–hard, labored, laborious, toilsome

easy job–sinecure

eat–consume, devour, dine, erode, feed, gnaw, sup

eat (raw flesh)–omophagic

eat away–corrode, gnaw

eat between meals–bever

eat by regimen–diet

eat grass–graze

eat greedily–gobble

eatable–edible, esculent

eater (fastidious)–epicure

eats away (bit by bit)–gnaws

ebb–abate, decay, decline, decrease, neap, recede, re-

flux, retire, sink, subside, wane

ebb and flow–aestus, estus

ebbing–refluent, refluxing

ebbing and flowing–tidal

Eber's father–Joktan

ebullition–agitation, commotion, effervescence, excitement, ferment, fermentation

eccentric–erratic, erratical, idiosyncratical, odd, strange

eccentric (on shaft)–cam

eccentric piece–cam

eccentricity–aberration, idiosyncrasy, peculiarity, queerness, strangeness

ecclesiastic–abbe, clergyman, priest

ecclesiastical council–synod

ecclesiastical court–rota

ecclesiastical garment–alb

ecclesiastical living–benefice

ecclesiastical neckpiece–rabat

ecclesiastical ruler (chief)–hierarch

ecclesiastical scarf–orale

ecclesiastical service–matin

ecclesiastical skull cap–callote

ecclesiastical vestment–stole

eche–enlarge, grow, increase

echelon–arrangement, maneuver

echinoderm (armed)–starfish

echo–eco, resound, reverberate, revoice, ring

eciton–ant

eclipse–cloud, darken, extinguish, obscure, sully

economical–careful, chary, frugal, provident, saving, thrifty

economize–husband, save, scrimp, skimp, stint, utilize

ecstasy–bliss, emotion, enrapture, rapture, transport

ecstatic–enraptured, rapt, rapturous, rhapsodic

ectad–outward

ectad (opposite of)–entad

ecu–coin, shield

Ecuador city–Cuenca, Esmeraldas, Guayaquil, Quito (c.), Riobamba

Ecuador coin–centavo (br.), condor (g.), sucre (s.)

Ecuador island–Galapagos

Ecuador measure–cuadra, fanega

Ecuador money unit–sucre

Ecuador mountain–Antisana, Cayambe, Chimborazo, Cotacachi, Cotopaxi, Pichincha

Ecuador province–El Oro

Ecuador river–Esmeraldas, Guayas, Napo, Pastaza, Tigre

Ecuador weight–libra

ecumenical–catholic, cosmopolitan, liberal, tolerant, worldwide

edaphic–local

Edgar Allan Poe character–Lenore

edge–border, brim, brink, brow, lip, marge, rim, side, verge

edge (beveled)–splay

edge (crater)–lip

edge (poetic)–marge

edge (ragged)–jag

edge (sharp, architecture)–arris

edge (unplowed field)–rand

edge of woven fabric–selvage, selvedge

edged (scalloped)–crenate

edging–binding, border, hem

edging (crimped)–frill

edible–eatable, esculent

edible fungus–morel

edible mollusk–asi

edible parts of certain fruits –pulp

edible seaweed–agar, agar-agar, laver

edible seed–bean, pea

edible tuber (root)–beet, oca, taro, uva, yam

edict–act, arret, ban, command, decree, dictum, dicta (pl.), fiat, irade, order, ordinance

edification–instruction

edifice–building, church, palace, structure

edifice (congressional)–capitol

edifice (sacred)–church, tabernacle, temple

edifice (stately)–capitol, palace

edify–build, construct, establish, improve, instruct, organize, teach

Edina–Edinburgh

Edinburgh (poetic name)–Edina

Edison's middle name–Alva

edit–arrange, correct, direct, emend, prepare, redact, revise

editor's room–sanctum

Edom king–Hadad

Edomite's ancestor–Esau

educate–cultivate, develop, enlighten, indoctrinate, inform, instruct, rear, teach, train

educated–lettered, taught, trained

education–breeding, discipline, training

eel (kind of)–lamprey, moray, moreia, muraena, murene

eel (mud)–siren

eel (sand)–grig

eel (young)–elver

eel-like fish–conger, eelpout, lamprey, ling, opah

eel trap–eelpot

eerie–awesome, uncanny, unearthly, weird

efface–cancel, erase, expunge, obliterate

effacer–eraser

effect–accomplish, achieve, close, compass, complete, consequence, consummate, discharge, does, execute, fulfill, operate, outcome, perform, realize, result

effect (optical)–mirage

effect (striking)–eclat

effect of magic art–conjure

effect of past experience–mneme

effect of weight (have)–militate

effective–active, adequate, capable, competent, effectual, efficacious, efficient, telling

effeminate–epicene, feminine, tender, womanly

effervescing–ebullient

effete–barren, exhausted, spent

efficacious–effective, potent

efficacy–dint, efficiency, force, potency, virtue

efficiency–ability, capability, competence, effectiveness, efficaciousness, efficacy, power, proficiency, skill

efficient–able, capable, competent, effective

efficiently–efficaciously

effigy–image

effluvium (invisible)–aura

efflux–effusion, emanation, outflow

effodient–burrowing, fossorial

effort–application, assay, attempt, dint, endeavor, essay, exertion, labor, nisus, pains, strain, struggle, toil, trial, trouble, try

effort (sudden)–burst

effort (violent)–adit

effrontery–audacity, impudence, sauciness

effulgence–brightness, brilliance, glory, splendor

effusive–demonstrative, exuberant, gushing, rhapsodic

eft–lizard, newt

egest–excrete

egg–goad, incite, instigate, prod, urge; ovum, ova (pl.)

egg (comb. form)–oo, ovi

egg (small)–ovule

egg (white of)–albumen, glair

egg case (zool.)–ovisac

egg cell (nucleated)–ovum, ova (pl.)

egg on–goad, incite, urge

egg-shaped – ooid, ooidal, oval, ovate, ovoid

egg-shaped (biol.)–ooidal
egg white–albumen, glair
egg yolk (substance of)–lecithin
egg yolk (thickening made from)–liaison
eggs–ova, roe
eggs (feeding on)–ovivorous
egis–shield
ego–self
egress–issue, outlet, exit
Egyptian–Copt, Ptolemy
Egyptian (descended from ancient stock)–Coptic
Egyptian alloy (of gold and silver, anc.)–asem
Egyptian astral body–Ka
Egyptian beetle–scarab
Egyptian boat (flatbottom)–baris
Egyptian body (astral)–Ka
Egyptian bottle (water)–doruck
Egyptian bull (sacred)–apis
Egyptian cap–fez
Egyptian capital–Cairo
Egyptian Christian–Copt
Egyptian city–Abydos, Alexandria, Armant, Cairo, Tanis
Egyptian city (anc.)–No
Egyptian cobra–haje
Egyptian coin–girsh (ni.), millieme (br.), piaster (ni., br.), pound (g.)
Egyptian crown–atef
Egyptian dancing girl–Alma, Alme, Almeh
Egyptian deity – Amen, Amon, Amone, Ani, Aten, Bes, Ibis, Isis, Min. Ptah, Ra, Seb, Serapis. (See Egyptian god and goddess, subentries.)
Egyptian deity (anc.)–Ptah
Egyptian deity (of an)–serapic
Egyptian deity's crown–atef
Egyptian diadem (royal)–atef
Egyptian divinity (anc.)–Ptah
Egyptian Elysium–Aalu
Egyptian entertainer (fe-

male musical)–Alma, Alme, Almeh
Egyptian genus of body (religion)–Ka
Egyptian god – Amen, Amon, Bes, Geb, Keb, Min, Osiris, Ptah, Ra, Seb
Egyptian god (agriculture)–Osiris
Egyptian god (earth)–Geb, Keb, Seb
Egyptian god (hawk-headed)–Horus, Ment
Egyptian god (pleasure)–Bes
Egyptian god (ram-headed)–Amon
Egyptian god (sun)–Ra, Tem, Tum
Egyptian god (underworld)–Osiris
Egyptian goddess–Anta, Bast, Isis, Mut, Nut
Egyptian goddess (justice)–Maat
Egyptian goddess (motherhood)–Apet
Egyptian goddess (personifying lower world)–Anaka
Egyptian goddess (principal)–Isis
Egyptian goddess (truth)–Maat
Egyptian governor–Pasha
Egyptian jinnie (myth.)–amset
Egyptian khedive's estate–daira
Egyptian king–Ptolemy, Ran
Egyptian king (myth.)–Busiris
Egyptian kings (dynasty of)–Rameses
Egyptian king's crown–atef
Egyptian lake – Birket-el-Kurun, Menzaleh
Egyptian language (anc.)–Coptic
Egyptian lily (water)–lotus
Egyptian lizard–adda
Egyptian measure–abdat, apt, ardab, ardeb, artaba, aurure, choryos, cubit, daribah, dira baladi, dira

mimari, dra, draa, farde, fedan, feddan nasri, hen, kassabah, keedah, keleh, kerat kamel, kharouba, khet, kilah, malouah, nifs keddah, rob, robhah, roub, rouboun, sahme, schene, theb, toummah
Egyptian measure (of length)–dera, pic
Egyptian measure (of weight, var.)–ocha
Egyptian month (11th of vague year)–Apap
Egyptian mythology (the earth deified)–Seb
Egyptian native (anc. stock)–Copt
Egyptian oasis–Bahriyeh, Dakhel, Farafra, Khargeh, Siwa, Wah-el-Khargeh
Egyptian paper (writing, anc.)–papyrus
Egyptian peninsula–Sinai
Egyptian plant (aromatic seed)–cumin
Egyptian princess–An
Egyptian queen–Cleopatra
Egyptian queen (of the gods)–Sati
Egyptian race (anc.)–Copt
Egyptian rattle–sistrum
Egyptian reed–papyrus
Egyptian religion–Ka
Egyptian religion (astral body)–Da
Egyptian river–Nile
Egyptian ruler–Rameses
Egyptian ruler (anc.)–Pharaoh
Egyptian sacred beetle–scarab
Egyptian sacred bull–apis
Egyptian seaport–Suez
Egyptian seed vessel–ciborium
Egyptian singing girl–Alma, Alme, Almeh
Egyptian skink–adda
Egyptian solar disk–aten
Egyptian sore eyes–trachoma
Egyptian stone (which served as clue to hieroglyphics)–rosetta

Egyptian sun god–Ra, Tem, Tum

Egyptian symbolism (the eye)–uta

Egyptian title–atef, pasha

Egyptian title (anc.)–Pharaoh

Egyptian title (for father)–atee

Egyptian tomb (type of)–mastaba

Egyptian tomb cell–serdab

Egyptian tree (sycamore)–daroc

Egyptian water-raising device–sakieh, shadoof

Egyptian water well sweep–shadoof

Egyptian water wheel–sakieh, sakiyeh

Egyptian weight–artal, artel, deben, dera, drachma, hamlan, heml, kantar, kat, kerat, khar, oka, oke, okia, okieh, quintal, ratel, rotl, uckia

Egyptian weight (anc.)–ket

Egyptian writing (mode of, anc.)–hieroglyphics

Egyptian writing material (anc.)–papyrus

eight (comb. form)–octo

eight (group of)–octad, octet, octette

eight-sided–octagonal

eighth day after nones–ides

eighth order (math.)–octic

Eire–Erin

either (correlative of)–or

ejaculate–blurt, eject

eject–banish, discharge, emit, evict, expel, extrude, oust, void

eject (in a jet)–spout, spurt

ejection–eviction, ouster

eke (arch.)–also, enlarge, increase

eking–piecing

el (measurement by)–alnage

El Salvador coin–centavo (cop., ni.), colon (s.), peso (g.)

El Salvador measure–botella, cajuela, fanega, manzana, tercia, vara

El Salvador weight–caja

elaborate–develop, embellish, ornate, perfect, refine

elaborate (unduly)–superfine

elan–ardor, dash, spirit

elapse–expire, go, pass, slip

elasmobranch fish–ray

elastic–buoyant, resilient, springy, stretchy

elastic fluid–gas

elation–glee

Elbe tributary–Eger, Iser

elbow–ancon

elder–senior

elder (marsh)–iva

eldest (law)–eigne

eldritch (Scot.)–eerie, eery, uncanny, weird

elect–choose, select

electantly–forecast

elector–elisor, voter

electric current (type of, abbr.)–AC., DC.

electric current measure–ammeter

electric current path–circuit

electric generator–dynamo

electric inductance (unit of)–henry

electric intensity (unit of)–ampere

electric light (kind of)–arc, incandescent

electric motor part–commutator

electric path into conducting medium–electrode

electric pole (particle)–anode

electric pole (positive)–anode

electric potential–voltage

electric power unit–watt

electric resistance unit–ohm

electric terminal–electrode

electric unit–ampere, coulomb, farad, henry, ohm, rel, volt, watt

electric unit (capacity)–farad

electric unit (force)–volt

electric unit (inductance)–henry

electric unit (intensity)–ampere

electric unit (light)–volt, watt

electric unit (power)–watt

electric unit (pressure)–farad

electric unit (quantity)–es

electric unit (reluctance)–rel

electric unit (resistance)–ohm

electric unit (smallest positive)–proton

electric wave meter–ondometer

electrical conductor (resistance of)–ohmage

electrical energy units–joules

electrical measure–ampere, barad, coulomb, farad, henry, kilowatt, ohm, proton, rel, volt, watt

electrical substance–ion

electrical unit–ampere, coulomb, es, farad, henry, joule, ohm, rel, volt, watt

electrical unit (current)–ampere

electrical unit (intensity)–ampere

electrically charged particle–proton

electrician (modern)–Tesla

electricity (kind of)–static

electricity (odic force of)–elod

electricity (slang)–juice

electrified compound (particle)–ion

electrified particle–ion

electromagnetic unit–farad

electromotive force unit–volt

elegance–grace, polish, propriety, refinement

elegant–fastidious, graceful, handsome, polished, refined, tasteful, urbane

elegant (coll.)–dressy

elegantly–genteelly

element–component, metal

element (acid-resisting)–tantalum

element (bluish white)–zinc, zink (var.)

element (chem.)–actinium (Ac), alabamine (Ab), aluminum (Al), antimony (Sb), argon (A), arsenic (As), barium (Ba), beryllium (Be), bismuth (Bi),

boron (B), bromine (Br), cadmium (Cd), calcium (Ca), carbon (C), cerium (Ce), cesium (Cs), chlorine (Cl), chromium (Cr), cobalt (Co), columbium (Cb), copper (Cu), dysprosium (Dy), erbium (Er), Europium (Eu), fluorine (F), gadolinium (Gd), gallium (Ga), germanium (Ge), gold (Au), hafnium (Hf), helium (He), holmium (Ho), hydrogen (H), illinium (Il), indium (In), iodine (I), iridium (Ir), iron (Fe), krypton (Kr), lanthanum (La), lead (Pb), lithium (Li), lutecium (Lu), magnesium (Mg), manganese (Mn), masurium (Ma), Mercury (Hg), molybdenum (Mo), neodymium (Nd), neon (Ne), neoytterbium (Yb), nickel (Ni), niobium (Cb), nitrogen (N), osmium (Os), oxygen (O), palladium (Pd), phosphorous (P), platinum (Pt), polonium (Po), potassium (K), praseodymium (Pr), protoactinium (Pa), radium (Ra), radon (Rn), rhenium (Re), rhodium (Rh), rubidium (Rb), ruthenium (Ru), samarium (Sm), scandium (Sc), selenium (Se), silicon (Si), silver (Ag), sodium (Na), strontium (Sr), sulphur (S), tantalum (Ta), tellurium (Te), terbium (Tb), thallium (Tl), thorium (Th), thulium (Tm), tin (Sn), titanium (Ti), tungsten (W), uranium (U), vanadium (V), virginium (Vi), xenon (Xe), ytterbium (Yb), yttrium (Y), zinc (Zn), zirconium (Zr)
element (decomposed)–anion
element (essential)–sap

element (fundamental) – fundament, stamen
element (gaseous)–neon
element (heavy gaseous)–niton
element (metallic)–lead, samarium, tungsten, uranium
element (minute)–monad
element (natural)–mineral
element (of economic wealth)–commodity
element (poisonous)–arsenic
element (rare metallic)–cerium, erbium, yttrium
element (voiceless speech)–surd
element (water)–hydrogen
element combining directly with metal–halogen
element having same tabular position as another, but different in weight–isotope
element of speech (voiceless)–surd
elementary organism–monad
elementary reader–primer
elementary substance–metal
elements of air–argon
elephant–bull, tusker
elephant (extinct) – mammoth
elephant (female)–cow
elephant (male)–bull
elephant call–trumpet
elephant cry–barr
elephant dentin–ivory
elephant driver–mahout
elephant goad–ankus
elephant keeper–mahout
elephant saddle–howdah
elephant seat (for back)–howdah
elephant's ear–taro
elevate–advance, dignify, elate, exhilarate, lift, promote, raise, uplift
elevated–el, elated, exalted, lofty, risen
elevated (imaginative composition)–poem
elevated condition – eminence
elevating–aerating

elevation–exaltation, height
elevator (grain)–silo
elevator carriage–car
elf–fairy, fay, gnome, hob, imp, incubi, pixie, sprite, succubi
elf (grotesque)–goblin
elf (Iranic)–peri
elfish–elfin, elflike, elvish, impish, mischievous, tricksy
elfland–fairyland
elfwort–elecampane
Elgin marbles–sculptures
elicit–claim, deduce, demand, draw, educe, entice, exact, extort, extract, induce, wrest, wring
elicit (by persistent questioning)–pump
elide–annul, demolish, destroy, nullify, omit, suppress
eligible–fit, qualified, suitable, worthy
eliminate–exclude, excrete, expel, release, separate
elite gathering–galaxy
elk–deer, moose, sambar, wapiti
elk (American)–wapiti
elk (Indian)–sambar
ellipse–oval
elliptical–oval, ovate
elm (fruit of)–samara
elm (rock)–wahoo
elm (wing)–wahoo
elm family (pert. to)–ulmaceous
elms (genus of)–ulmus
elocution–eloquence, oratory
elocutionist–reader, reciter
eloge–encomium, eulogy
eloign–conceal, convey, remove
elongate–lengthen, remove, stretch
elongated–linear, long, slender, stretched
elope–abscond, decamp
eloquence–elocution, fluency, oratory
eloquence teacher (anc.)–rhetor
eloquent–expressive, meaningful, significant

else—or, other, otherwise

else (Scot.)—ens, ense

elt—knead

elucidate—clear, explain, interpret, lucid

elude—avoid, baffle, dodge, escape, evade, flee, foil, mock

elusive—baffling, eely, elusory, evasive, impalpable, subtle

elves—fairies, fays, gnomes, hobs, imps, sprites

Elysium—Eden

em (half)—en

emaciated – lean, peaked, wasted

emaciation (Latin progressive)—tabes

emaciation (radium)—niton

emanate—arise, flow, issue, proceed

emanation—aura, aurae (pl.), consequence, outcome

emanation (supposed)—aura, aurae (pl.)

emanation from medium—ectoplasm

emanation of radium—niton

emancipation – enfranchisement, freedom, release

embalmer—cerer, undertaker

embankment—bund, dike, levee, revet

embargo—blockade, impediment, prohibition, stoppage

embark—sail

embarrass—abash, complicate, confuse, discomfit, disconcert, dumfound, encumber, hamper, handicap, hinder, impede, nonplus, shame

embarrassment—abashment, discomfiture, entanglement, inconvenience, involvement, shame

embellish—adorn, beautify, bedeck, bedrape, deck, enrich, garnish, grace, ornament

embellishment – garniture, ornamentation

ember—ash, cinder, coal

embezzle—dissipate, peculate, squander, steal

embezzlement—theft

embitter—acerbate, envenom, exacerbate

emblazon—celebrate, display, exhibit, extol, glorify, laud

emblem—badge, device, figure, image, symbol, token, type

emblem of grief—rue

emblematic—symbolic, typal

embodiment – incarnation, personification

embolden—encourage, hearten, nerve

embosom—cherish, enclose, foster, surround

embrace—adopt, clasp, cling, comprise, contain, enfold, espouse, fold, grasp, hug, inarm, include, involve

embracing—inclusive

embroidery frame—taboret

embroil—commingle, disorder, distract, implicate, perplex, trouble

embrown—tan

emend—amend, correct, edit, improve, mend, rectify, revise

emender—reviser

emerald—beryl, color, smaragd

Emerald Isle—Erin

emerge—dip, issue, plunge

emerge into open spaces—debouch

emergency – crisis, crises (pl.), juncture, necessity, pinch, strait

emery—corundum

emeute—outbreak, tumult

emigrant—colonist, immigrant, settler, stranger

eminence—elevation, height, loftiness

eminence (commanding a plain, Fr.)—rideau

eminence (highest)—transcendency

eminent—arch, celebrated, distinguished, great, high, illustrious, lofty, marked,

noted, renowned, signal, towering

emissary—agent, scout, spy

emissive—exhalant

emit—discharge, distill, eject, exhale, exude, issue, shed, transmit

emit heat—glow

emit light—glow

emit play of colors—opalesce

emit rays—eradiate, radiate

emit smoke—reek

emit vapor—reek

emitting splendor—refulgent

emmet – ant, formicid, pismire

emolument – compensation, fees, profit, salary, wages

emotion—agitation, agony, disturbance, feeling, sentiment

emotion (highest wrought)—passion

emotion (indifferent)—stoic

emotion (intense)—passion

emotion of thankfulness—gratitude

emperor—monarch, sovereign, tsar

Emperor (great mogul)—Akbar

Emperor (of India)—King of England

Emperor Jones (author of)—O'Neill

emperor's domain—empire

emphasis—accent, salience, stress

emphasize—accent, accentuate, stress

emphatic—earnest, energetic, forcible, positive

empire—control, domain, dominion, reign, rule, sovereignty, state, sway

emplacement (artillery)—battery

employ—hire, use

employ (frugally)—spare

employ blandishment—coax

employ rarely—spare

employ subterfuge—chicane

employee (towboat)—tugman

employees—hands, help, men

employer (who assumes risk

and management)–entrepreneur

employing indirect words–periphrastic

employment–business, calling, occupation, profession, trade, use, vocation, work

emporium–bazaar, market, mart, store

empower–authorize, commission, delegate, enable, entitle

empower to act for another–deputize

empty–blank, deplete, drain, inane, jejune, vacant, vacate, vacuous, void, unburdened, unfilled, unoccupied

empty (obs.)–iler

empty space–blank, vacuum, void

Empusa (Greek myth.) – hobgoblin

empyrean–firmament, heavens

emulate–competition, rival, vie

emulated (successfully)–rivaled

emulsion–pap

enact–actuate, appoint, constitute, decree, pass

enactment (legislative)–statute

enamor–captivate, charm

encamp–tent

enchant–captivate, charm, enrapture, fascinate

enchantment–charm, fascination, incantation, magic, necromancy, sorcery, spell, witchcraft, witchery

enchantress–Circe, sorceress

enchantress (who turned admirers to swine)–Circe

encina–oak

encircle–belay, enclose, environ, inorb, ring, surround, wreathe

encircle (to)–orb

encircled–belted, enlaced, girded, girt, hooped, orbed, paled, ringed, surrounded, wreathed, zoned

enclasp–inclip

enclose–bound, encompass, envelop, fence, harness, hem, imprison, surround

enclose within alien territory–enclave

enclosed–encased, encaved, internal, pent

enclosure–cage, coop, corral, kraal, mew, pen, prison, yard

enclosure (cattle)–corral, kraal, poundage

enclosure (in cloister built against window on inside to serve as study)–carol

enclosure (salmon-catching)–yair, yare

enclosure (wire)–cage

encomium–eloge, eulogy, panegyric, praise

encompass–begird, encircle, enclose, include, environ, ring, surround

encompassing – circumambient

encore–bis

encounter–attack, breast, brush, conflict, engagement, fight, incur, meet, onset, skirmish

encounter (fistic)–bout, go

encountered (courageously)–braved

encourage–abet, advance, assure, cheer, comfort, console, countenance, embolden, exhort, foster, hearten, impel, inspire, inspirit, instigate, nerve, promote, stimulate, urge

encroach–impinge, infringe, intrude, invade, poach, trench, trespass

encroach upon–invade

encumber–burden, check, clog, embarrass, hamper, handicap, hinder, load, oppress, overburden, overload, retard, saddle

encumbrance – impediment, impedimenta (pl.)

end–amend, cease, close, conclude, determine, extremity, finale, finis, finish, intention, limit, omega, purpose, tail, terminate, tip

end (arrow butt)–nock

end (blunt)–stub

end (church altar)–apse

end (pipe flanged)–taft

end (sharp)–point

end (support for sail)–yardarm

end (the)–omega, thirty

end (tip of things)–neb

end (ultimate, Greek)–telos

end (upper)–head

end aimed at–goal

endamage–harm, injure

endanger–compromise, imperil, jeopardize

endearment–caress

endeavor–aim, attempt, essay, seek, strive, struggle, tempt, try

endeavor (strenuous)–effort

ending–termination

ending (participial)–ed

ending in point–acuminate

endless–boundless, continual, eternal, everlasting, incessant, interminable, perpetual, unceasing, undying, unending, uninterrupted

endless (arch.)–eterne

endless chain–creeper

endless duration–eternity

endoderm (blastomere forming)–entomere

endorsement (formula)–fiat

endorsement (passport)–visa, vise

endow–clothe, dow, dower, endue, enrich, furnish, indue, invest, vest

endow with power–energize

endowment (natural)–apanage

endowments–gifts, talents

endue–clothe, endow, invest

endurable–bearable, sufferable, supportable, tolerable

endurance–fortitude, patience, perseverance, resignation, stamina, sufferance, suffering

endure–abide, bear, bide, brook, continue, dree, last,

persist, remain, stand, suffer, tide, tolerate, wear, withstand
endured–stood
endures (Scot.)–drees
enduring–durable, lasting, patient
enemy–adversary, foe, foeman, opponent
enemy (man's arch)–devil, Satan
enemy (personal)–hater
energetic – active, forceful, forcible, strenuous
energy–force, nerve, potency, power, spirit, strength, vigor, vim
energy (coll.)–go, pep
energy (Hindu female) – Sakti
energy (lack of)–anergy
energy (potential)–edar, ergal
energy (unit of)–erg, ergon
energy put into a machine–intake
enervate–debilitate, enfeeble, sap, unnerve, weaken
enfeeble–attenuate, decrepit, enervate, numb, soften, weakened
enfilade–rake
enfold–clasp, cover, embrace, envelop, wrap
enfold (var.)–enrol
enforce–compel, constrain, execute
engage–betroth, embark, employ, enlist, entangle, hire, involve, lease, promise, rent
engage wholly–absorb
engaged – affianced, betrothed, bonded, busy, embedded, employed, entered, hired, involved, meshed, occupied, pledged, promised
engaged (mentally)–versant
engaged in–at
engaged in controversy–disputant
engagement – appointment, attachment, battle, betrothal, encounter, involvement

engagement (coll.)–date
engaging–attractive, sapid, taking
engaging in single combat–duelling
engender – beget, breed, cause, develop, excite, generate, occasion, procreate, propagate
engine–locomotive, motor
engine (hydraulic)–ram
engine (kind of)–Diesel, gas, gasoline, steam, turbine
engine (medieval military)–onager
engine (military)–onager, robinet
engine (self-propelling)–locomotive
engine at rear of train–helper, pusher
engineer–constructor, contrive, designer, manage, maneuver, plan
engineer (American, builder of Mississippi River bridge)–Eads
engineer (civil, abbr.)–C.E.
engineering degree–E.E.
enginous–crafty, ingenious
engirdle–encompass, gird, zone
engirt–encircle, engird, envelop
England (early invader of)–Pict
England (pert. to)–Anglican
England (royal house of)–Lancaster
English–see also British
English actor (Shakespearean)–Tree
English admiral–Nelson, Rodney, Vernon
English admiral (old grog)–Vernon
English air force–R.A.F.
English ancestral house–estate
English Antarctic explorer–Scott
English anthem–motet
English architect–Wren
English author–Opie
English author and traveler–Ligon

English aviators (Fr. slang)–rafs
English aviators (Royal Air Force)–R.A.F.
English bailiff (old)–reeve
English boat (raiding)–commando
English calaboose–gaol
English church caretaker–verger
English church officer–beadle
English city–Aston Manor, Barrow-in-Furness, Birkenhead, Birmingham, Blackburn, Bolton, Bootle, Bournemouth, Bradford, Brighton, Bristol, Burnley, Coventry, Croydon, Derby, Devonport, Dewsbury, Ely, Exe, Exeter, Gateshead, Grimsby, Halifax, Hanley, Hastings, Hornsey, Huddersfield, Hull, Leeds, Leicester, Leyton, Liverpool, London, Manchester, Middlesbrough, Newcastle - upon - Tyne, Newport, Northampton, Norwich, Nottingham, Oldham, Plymouth, Portsmouth, Preston, Reading, Rochdale, Rotherham, Saint Helens, Salford, Sheffield, Smethwick, Southampton, Southend-on-sea, Southshields, Stockport, Stoke-upon-Trent, Sunderland, Tottenham, Wallasey, Walsall, Walthamstow, Warrington, West Bromwich, West Ham, West Hartlepool, Wigan, Willesden, Wolverhampton, York
English city (cathedral)–Ely, Exe, Truro, York
English city (racing)–Epsom Downs
English clergyman–Inge
English coin–crown (s.), farthing (br.), florin (s.), fourpence (s.), guinea (ac.), half crown (s.), halfpenny (br.), pound (ac.), shilling (s.), six-

pence (s.), sovereign (g.), threepence (s.), twopence (s.)

English coin (old)–groat, rial, ryal, teston

English coin (16th century) –angel

English college–Eton, Oxford

English comedian–Toole

English composer (modern) –Delius

English composer (musical) –Arne, Elgar

English conquerors–Saxons

English conservative (political)–tory

English county–Devon, Dorset, Essex, Kent, shire

English county officer (anc.) –escheator

English court (early)–leet

English court (old manor)–leet

English dance (former)–morris

English dialect (rustic)–Doric

English diarist–Pepys

English district–Soho

English divine–Inge

English dramatist–Jonson, Peele, Reade, Rowe, Steele

English dramatist (of the Renaissance)–Peele

English dynasty–Stuart, Tudor

English electrician–Faraday

English engraver–Pye

English essayist–Elia, Lang

English etcher–Haden

English expeditionary force –B.E.F.

English fee paid (old, for weighing goods)–pesage

English festival (country)–Ales

English field (small)–croft

English financier (16th century)–Sir Thomas Gresham

English fishing vessel–coble

English flood–spate

English freeman (lowest ranking)–ceorl

English freeman (who was not a noble)–ceorl

English game–cricket, hob, soccer

English hammer (leaden)–madge

English hat (straw)–Dunstable

English heather–ling

English historian–Macaulay

English household land–casate

English inhabitant (early)–Saxon

English island–Anglesey, Farne, Holy, Holyhead, Isle of Wight, Lundy, Scilly, Sheppy, Thanet, Walney

English jurisdiction (early law)–soc

English king – Edward, George, Henry, James

English king (anc.)–Lear

English king (legendary)–Lud

English kingdom (old)–Sussex

English lake–Coniston, Derwent, Ullswater, Water, Windermere

English landed estate–manor

English law officials–benchers

English leave of absence (college)–exeat

English legal chooser–elisor

English legal system (anc.)–danelaw

English liberal–Whig

Englishman–Britisher, Briton

English man of fashion–Richard Nash

English manor court (old)–leet

English measure–*see* British

English measure (of length) –landyard

Englishmen (Fr. slang)–teatimes, titeems

English money (medieval)–ora

English money of account (early)–ora

English money unit–guinea

English monk (8th century) –beda

English mountain–Cumbrian, Pennine, Scawfell

English murderer (famous) –Aram

English musical composer–Elgar

English musician (1710–1778)–Arne

English nature-story writer–Seton

English navigator–Cook, Drake

English negative (former)–ne

English news agency–Reuter

English nobleman–milord

English north valley inhabitant–Dalesman

English novelist – Caine, Hume, Ouida

English officer's civil dress–mufti

English officials (law)–benchers

English painter–Poynter

English painter (portrait)–Opie

English patron saint–George

English payment (old)–tac

English philosopher–Spencer

English poet–Albion, Browning, Byron, Carew, Heber, Lang, Milton, Rowe

English policeman–bobby, peeler

English porcelain (fine) – spode

English positive evidence–constat

English prelate–Hurd

English pronunciation (dialectic)–brogue

English queen–Anne, Elizabeth, Mary, Matilda, Victoria

English racecourse–Ascot, Epsom Downs

English raiding troops–commandos

English reformer (1750–1814)–Spence

English region–Sussex

English Renaissance author –Steele

English Renaissance dramatist–George Peele

English rent (old)–tac

English resort–Bath

English river–Aire, Avon, Dee, Eden, Esk, Exe, Humber, Mersey, Ouse, Ribble, Severn, Tees, Thames, Trent, Tyne, Ure, Wash, Wear, Wye

English royal house–Lancaster

English royal house member –Yorkist

English rural merrymaking –ale

English saloon–pub

English sandstone blocks on chalk downs–sarsens

English school–Eton, Oxford

English seaport–Deal, Dover, Liverpool

English settler (early)–Angle

English settler (original)–Shagoon

English shock troops–commandos

English signal–sennet

English socialism (father of) –Owen

English sovereign–Edward, George, Henry, James

English statesman–Eden, Eton, Grey, Pitt

English statesman (17th century)–Trevor

English station (Sussex prehistoric)–Piltdown

English stolen article–mainour

English street car–tram

English subdivision–shire

English surgeon – Haden, Paget

English tax (old)–prest

English tax formerly laid on hearths–fumage

English territorial division–shire

English thesaurus compiler–Roget

English thicket–spinney

English title–dame

English toll (illegal former) –maletolt

English toll charge (weighing)–peisage, pesage

English tract (sandy)–dene

English trolley car–tram

English uplands–downs

English valley – Coquet, Eden, Tees, Tyne

English warplane–Boulton-Paul Defiant, Hurricane, Spitfire

English women's auxiliary air force–W.A.A.F.

English wren–tomtit

English writer–Hurd

English writer (boys' books) –Henty

engrave–carve, chase, impress, imprint, incise, rist, sculpture

engrave (by dots)–stipple

engrave with acid–etch

engraved die–seal

engraver–chaser

engraver's tool–burin

engraving – cut, etching, print

engraving (father of)–Pye

engraving on wood–xylograph

engross–absorb, engage

engross (completely)–absorb

engrossed–absorbed, intent

engrossed (wholly)–rapt

engulf–absorb, overwhelm, swallow, swamp, submerge

enhance–augment, elevate, enlarge, exalt, extol, greaten, increase, lift, magnify, raise

enigma–charade, conundrum, mystery, riddle

enigma (acted)–charade

enigmatic–clear, equivocal, evident, inexplicable, mystic, obvious, puzzling

enigmatical canon–nodus

enjoin – admonish, command, forbid, prohibit

enjoy–relish

enjoy genial influences (to)–bask

enjoyer of–user

enjoyment–delight, ease, felicity, fruition, gratification, happiness, pleasure, satisfaction, zest

enjoys–has

enlarge–amplify, augment, dilate, eke, exaggerate, expand, increase, spread, swell

enlargement – augmentation, expansion, extension

enlargement of gland–adema

enlighten–educate, enkindle, illuminate, instruct

enlist–enrol, enroll, enter, induct, join

enliven – animate, cheer, comfort, encourage, exhilarate, inspire, inspirit, invigorate, rouse, stimulate

enmity–animosity, antagonism, antipathy, aversion, feud, hostility, malevolence, malice, rancor, repugnance, war

enmity of heart–malice

ennead–nine

ennoble–exalt, honor, raise, uplift

ennui–bored, boredom, tedium

enormous–abnormal, colossal, excessive, gigantic, great, huge, immense, monstrous, prodigious, stupendous, vast

enormous amounts (dial.)–gobs, reams

Enos' father–Seth

enough–adequate, ample, satisfactory, sufficient

enough (poetic)–enow

enough (was)–sufficed

enounce–enunciate, pronounce, state, utter

enow–presently

enrage–anger, incense, inflame, infuriate, madden

enraptured–enravished, entranced

enravished–enraptured, rapt

enrich–adorn, lard, ornament

enrich with fat–lards

enroll–enlist, enter, induct, initiate, join, register, unfurl

ens (two)–em

ensconce – conceal, hide, settle

ensemble (decorative)–decor

ensemble (ornamental)–decor

ensemble of embellishment –decor

enshroud–swathe

ensign–banner, flag, gonfalon, officer, standard

ensign (in battle)–oriflamb, oriflamme

enslave–enthrall

ensnare–benet, catch, enmesh, entrap, innet, noose, trap, trapan, trepan, web

ensues–follows, results

ensuing–next

ensure–assure, guarantee, insure, secure, warrant

entad–inward

entad (opposite of)–ectad

ental–inner

ental (opposite of)–ectal

entangle–confuse, enlace, enmesh, involve, mat, mire, snarl

entangle (collision)–afoul

entanglement–knot, snarl

entanglement (military)–abatis

enter–enlist, enrol, enroll, initiate, inscribe, introduce, join, penetrate, record

enter legal objection–demur

enter militantly–invade

enter upon a career–incept

enter without permission–intrude

entered illegally–ringer

enterprise–attempt, essay, undertaking, venture

enterprise (zealous)–crusade

enterprising–bold, energetic

entertain–amuse, beguile, divert, fete, regale, treat

entertain (royally)–regale

entertainer–actor, dancer, magician, singer, speaker

entertainer (female)–hostess

entertainment – diversion, pastime, play, recreation, sport

entertainment (public, 18th century)–ridotto

entertainment (social)–musicale

entertainment and fair–kirmis

enthusiasm–animation, ardor, eagerness, elan, fervor, fire, verve, zeal, zest

enthusiasm (artistic)–verve

enthusiasm (contagious)–furor, furore

enthusiasm (excessive)–mania

enthusiasm (great)–furor, furore

enthusiast–bigot, devotee, fan, fanatic, rooter, zealot

enthusiastic–ardent, eager, nutty, rabid, zealous

entice–allure, attract, cajole, coax, decoy, incite, inveigle, lure, persuade, seduce

entice (dial.)–tole

entice (var.)–tole

enticed–sirened

enticement–allurement, attraction, inducement, inveiglement, persuasion, seduction, temptation

entire–all, complete, integrate, perfect, sound, total, undiminished, unimpaired, unqualified, utter, whole

entire man–ego

entirely–all, clean, completely, stark, totally, wholly

entirely adverse–diametric

entitled–call, denominate, designate, dub, empower, enable, name, qualify, term

entity–being, ens, existence, unit

entomb – bury, inhume, inter, inurn

entourage–associates, attendants, retinue, suite, train

entrails–bowels, guts, viscera

entrance–access, adit, admission, door, entry, gate, gateway, ingress, inlet, overpower, portal, threshold

entrance (Buddhist temple) –toran, torana

entrance (formal)–debut

entrance (hostile)–incursion

entrance (private)–postern

entranced–rapt

entrap–beguile, catch, decoy, ensnare, entangle, inveigle, net, noose, tangle

entreat–appeal, ask, beg, crave, implore, importune, petition, plead, pray, solicit, supplicate, woo

entreat earnestly–beseech

entreaty–importunity, invitation, petition, plea, request, solicitation, suit, supplication

entree–access, permission

entrench–encroach, invade, trespass

entrepot–warehouse

entrust–commit, confide, consign, delegate

entry–item

entwine – clasp, enlace, twine, twist, weave, wreathe

enumerate–calculate, compute, count, detail, estimate, recapitulate, reckon, rehearse, relate, tell

enumerate details–particularize

enumerated–calculated, catalog, catalogue, census, citation, computed, detailed, estimated, list, recapitulated, reckoned, rehearsed, related

enunciate–announce, articulate, declare, proclaim, pronounce, utter

enunciation – attestation, declaration, pronouncement, pronunciation, utterance

envelop–case, cover, enclose, envelope, enwrap, infold, integument, invest, sheath, shroud, wrapper

envelope (luminous, surrounding sun)–corona

envelope (prickly fruit)–bur

enveloping–around

envious–jealous

environ–encircle, encompass, envelop, involve, suburb, surround

environment–element, medium, media (pl.), milieu, setting

environment (natural)–element

envisage–confront, face

envisioned – dreamed, dreamt

envoy–ambassador, commissioner, legate, messenger

envoy (papal special mission)–ablegate

envy – askance, covet, grudge, jealousy

enwrap–engross, infold, roll

enzyme–amylase, diastase, pepsin, protease, rennin, urease

enzyme suffix–ase

eoan–auroral

eon–age, eternity

Eolus' wife–Cyane

ephah (one-tenth of)–omer

ephemeral–transient

Ephesus (goddess of)–Diana

Ephraim chief–Amasa

epi–finial

epic–epos, heroic, saga

epic poem–epopee, epos

epicure–connoisseur, glutton, gourmand, gourmet

epidemic–pest, pestilence, plague

epidemic (wildly)–pandemic

epidemic everywhere–pandemic

epidermis–cuticle

epigastrium–stomach

epigram–mot

Epirus city (seat of Greek oracle)–Dodona

Epirus native–Epirote

Episcopal parish head–rector

episode–digression, event, incident, story

epistle–letter, missive

epitaph–inscription

epithet–name

epitome–compendium, comprisal, comprizal, digest

epitomize–abstract, compress, condense, contract, curtail, diminish

epoch–age, day, era, period

epoch (pert. to)–eral

epochal–eral

epopee–epic, epos

equal–adequate, commensurate, compeer, emulate, equitable, equivalent, even, identical, just, match, par, peer, proportionate, same, tie

equal (comb. form)–iso, pari

equal (prefix)–iso

equality–equity, evenness, fairness, impartiality, par, parity, uniformity

equality (exact)–tie

equality of laws (rights)– isonomy

equalize–balance, equate, even

equalizer–evener

equally–alike, as, evenly, justly

equally (prefix)–equi

equally advanced–abreast

equanimity–calmness, composure, equability, evenness, poise, serenity, tranquility

equidistant lines–parallels

equilateral triangle–square

equilibrium–balance, poise

equine (young) – colt, foal, mare

equine animal–zebra

equip–endow, furnish, gear, rig

equip for action–arm

equipment–apparatus, gear, outfit, tackle

equipment (warrior's complete)–panoply

equipped (with protective covering)–armored

equipped (with windows)–fenestrated

equitable–fair, honest, impartial, just, reasonable, right, upright

equity–fairness, honesty, justice, rectitude, rights, uprightness

equivalence–par, relativity

equivocal–ambiguous, dubious, enigmatic, indeterminate, mysterious, obscure, perplexing, problematical, puzzling, uncertain

equivocate–dodge, evade, palter, prevaricate, quibble, shift, shuffle, trifle

equivocation–evasion, prevarication, quibbling, shuffling

era–age, date, epoch, period, time

era (Christian abbr.)–A.D., B.C.

eradicable–deleble, delible

eradicate–abolish, annihilate, dele, destroy, erase, exterminate, extirpate, remove, root, uproot, weed

eradicate hair – epilate

erase–arase, cancel, dele, efface, expunge, obliterate, relieve

Erastus' teaching (pert. to)– Erastian

ere–also, before, earlier, early, erewhile, formerly, previously, soon, sooner

ere long–anon, soon

erect–build, construct, perpendicular, rear, stand upright, vertical

erect (was)–stood

eremite–hermit, recluse

eremite's hut–cell

erenow–heretofore

erewhile–heretofore

Eri's home–Assam

Eridant (star in)–Keid

Eridanus (star in constellation of)–Azha

Erin–Eire, Ireland

Eritrean capital–Asmara

Eritrean coin–dollar (s.), tallero (s.)

Eritrean measure–cabaho, cubi, derah, entelam, ghebeta, messe, tanica

ermine–clothe, fur, stoat, stot, stote, weasel

ermine (European)–stoat

erode–corrode, eat, disintegrate, gnaw, wear

err–blunder, bungle, sin, slip, transgress

errand–journey, mission

errand boy–courier, messenger, page

errant–itinerant, journeying, wandering

erratic–eccentric, planetary, queer, strange, wandering

erroneous–false, mistaken, untrue

error–blunder, erratum, errata (pl.), falsity, lapse, mistake, slip

error (slight)–lapse

error of conduct–misstep

Erse–Gaelic

erst–also, earlier, earliest, first, former, once, sooner, soonest

eruditely–learnedly, scholarly, wisely

erudition–finish, knowledge, learning, letters, lore

erudition displayer–pedant

Esau–Edom

Esau's descendant–Edomite

Esau's grandson–Amalek

Esau's name (after sale of birthright)–Edom

escape – avolation, elude, evade, evasion, flee

escape (privately)–elope

escape discovery–elude

escape unintentionally–spill

escargot–snail

escarole–endive

escarp–scarp, slope

eschar–crust, scab, slough

eschara–altar

escheat–fall, forfeit, lapse, revert

eschewer–avoider, shunner

escolar–mackerel, palu

escort–accompany, attend, beau, chaperon, conduct, convoy, retinue, see, usher

escorted–squired

escorts (paid)–gigolos

escritoire–bureau, dresser, secretary

esculent–eatable, edible

escutcheon–shield

escutcheon (voided)–orle

escutcheon band (horizontal)–fess, fesse

eskar–os, osar

esker–os, osar

Eskimo–Ita

Eskimo boat–oomiac, oomiak, umiack, umiak

Eskimo boot (sealskin)–kamik

Eskimo canoe–cayak, kayak, umiak

Eskimo coat–parka

Eskimo coat (birdskin)–temiak

Eskimo dog–husky

Eskimo garment–parka

Eskimo hut–igloo, iglu

Eskimo knife (woman's)–ulu

Eskimo settlement–Etah

Eskimo tribe–Atkas, Ita

esne–slave

esophagus–gula, gular, gullet

esoteric–inner, recondite, secret

esoteric doctrine–cabala

espalier – epaulet, railing, trellis

Espanol–Spanish

especial–chief, peculiar, uncommon

Esperanto's offering–Ido

espionage–espy, spying

espionage agent–spy

esplanade – drive, praya, walk

espousal – adoption, ceremony, wedding

espouse–adopt, betroth, bind, defend, embrace, maintain, marry, mate, pledge, support, wed

esprit (de corps)–devotion, enthusiasm

espritfort–freethinker

espy–behold, detect, discover, see

esquire–escudero

essay–disquisition, dissertation, effort, endeavor, paper, theme, thesis, theses (pl.), tract, try

essay (scholastic) – thesis, theses (pl.)

essay (short Latin)–chria

essence–attar, being, element, gist, perfume, pith, principle, scent

essence (pert. to)–basic

essential–indispensable, inherent, necessary, needful, vital

essential oil of roses–atar, atta, attar, ottar, otto

essential part–gist, pith

essential part (be an)–inherent

essential point–crux

establish–base, build, confirm, erect, fix, found, ground, locate, ordain, originate, plant, preempt, prove, seat

establish (firmly)–fix, found, plant, seat

established–rested, staple

established the truth–verified

establishment (domestic)–menage

establishment (manufacturing)–factory, mill, plant

establishment of cordial relations–rapprochement

establishment of migrating plant in new habitat–ecesis

estate–manor, property

estate (feudal law)–fief

estate (landed)–demesne, manor

estate (limited)–entail

estate purchaser (Fr. and Can. law)–acquereur

estate rent deduction–reprise

esteem–adore, appraise, appreciate, dear, honor, regard, repute, respect, revere, value, venerate

esteem (greatly)–admire

esteem (high)–respect
esteem (public)–repute
esteem (self)–pride
ester (stearic acid)–stearate
ester of vinegar–acetate
esthetic (Jewish, anc.)–essene
Esthonia–*see* Estonia
estimable – admirable, worthy
estimate–appraise, assess, compute, gage, guess, judgment, opinion, prize, rank, rate, repute
estimate (to)–set
estimate too highly–overrate
estimation in which one is held–repute
estimator–rater
Estonian city–Reval
Estonian coin – estmark (pap.), kroon (s.), sent (ni.)
Estonian island–Oesel
Estonian measure–elle, faden, kulimet, liin, lofstelle, pang, sagene, sund, toll, tonnland, toop, tun, verchoc, verchok, verst, versta, verste
Estonian weight–lood, nael, puud
estop–bar, fill, impede, plug, prevent, prohibit, stop
estrange–alienate, disunite, wean
estreat–copy, duplicate, extract
estuary–firth, frith
eternal–ageless, boundless, endless, enduring, everlasting, immortal, immutable, imperishable, incessant, interminable, unceasing
eternal death–perdition
eternally (Maori)–ake
eternity–aeon, ages, eon
ether compound–ester
ether derived from anisic acid–anisol
ethereal–aerie, aery, celestial, delicate, fragile, heavenly, slender
ethereal (poetic)–aery

ethereal being–sylph
ethereal fluid–ichor, icor
ethereal fluid (supposed to flow in God's veins)–ichor, icor
ethereal salt–ester
ethical–moral
ethics–morals
ethics (treating relation of duty to pleasure)–hedonics
ethics (teacher of)–moralist
Ethiopian – blackamoor, hamite, Negro
Ethiopian ape (hairy)–gelada
Ethiopian battleground–Adowa
Ethiopian chief–ras
Ethiopian city–Adowa
Ethiopian coin (silver)–talari, talaro
Ethiopian commander–ras
Ethiopian country (southern)–Seba
Ethiopian emperor–Menelik
Ethiopian ex-ruler–Negus
Ethiopian governor–ras
Ethiopian lake–Tana
Ethiopian language–Afar
Ethiopian prince–ras
Ethiopian religion (pert. to)–Coptic
Ethiopian river–Omo
Ethiopian title–negus, ras
Ethiopian torah–tetel
Ethiopian vizier–ras
ethnic–heathen, pagan
ethnological group of Europe (member of oldest)–Iberian
etiquette–form, label, manners, propriety, ticket
etiquette (breach of)–solecism
Etruscan–Rasenna, Tursenoi, Tyrrheni
Etruscan deity–Lar, Lares (pl.)
Etruscan god–Lar, Lares (pl.)
Etruscan goddess–Uni
Eucharistic bread plate–paten
Eucharistic plate–paten

Eucharistic wafer vessel–ciborium
Eucharistic wine vessel–ama, amula
eulogist–encomiast, panegyrist
eulogize–celebrate, extol, glorify, laud, panegyrize, praise
eulogy–eloge, encomium, laudation, panegyric, praise
euphony–metre
Euphrates city–Ur
Euphrates tributary–Tigris
Eurasian–Armenian, Finn, Turanian, Urgian
Eurasian catnip–nepeta
Eurasian herb–yarrow
Eurasian herb (weedy)–gosmore
European–Dane, Finn, Lett, Pole, Serb, Slav, Swede, Welsh
European (anc.)–Goth
European (northern)–Lapp, Lett
European antelope (high mountain)–chamois
European barracuda–spet
European bass–brasse
European bat (brown)–serotime
European bird–avocet, avoset, bittern, brambling, dotterel, gallinule, garganey, gaylag, godwit, goldfinch, kite, lammergeier, lammergeir, lammergeyer, linnet, ortolan, starling, starnel, tarin
European bird (bunting)–ortolan
European bird (grouse)–capercaillie, capercailzie
European bird (used for food)–ortolan
European bison–aurochs
European blackbird–ani, merle, ousel, ouzel
European burbot–lote
European capital–Berlin, Lisbon, Oslo, Paris, Riga, Rome, Stockholm
European cavalryman–Hussar

European city–Berlin, Lisbon, Oslo, Paris, Pilsen, Posen, Riga, Rome, Stockholm, Vichy

European city (anc.)–Gaul

European clover–alsike

European coin (former gold)–ducat, pistole

European colony (anc.)–Eolis

European corvine bird–daw

European country–Belgium, Bulgaria, Denmark, Finland, France, Greece, Holland, Hungary, Italy, Latvia, Norway, Poland, Rumania, Spain

European country (anc.)–Elis, Etruria

European country (former)–Navarre

European deer (smallest)–roe

European dictator (late)–Lenin

European dictator's title (former)–Duce

European division of jurassic–lias

European dogfish–morgay

European dormouse–lerot, loir

European ermine–stoat

European evergreen tree–carob

European falcon–peregrine, sacer, saker, sakeret (male)

European falcon (small)–merlin

European finch–serin, terin

European fish–blay, boces, id, ide, lote, meagre

European fish (flat, large)–turbot

European fish (food)–gars

European fish (fresh water)–rudd

European fish (small)–dace

European flatfish–turbot

European goatsucker–evechurr, evejar

European great lavender–aspic

European gulf–Riga

European gull (common)–mew

European herb–barage, dill

European herring (small)–sprat

European hundredweight–centner

European island–Aland, Erin

European juniper–cade

European kingdom (med.)–Aragon

European kite–gled, glede

European language–Ugric

European lavender–aspic

European lime–teil

European measure (liquid)–aam, liter

European mint–horehound, hyssop

European mountain–Alps

European mountain ash–rowan, rowen

European mountainous district–Tirol, Tyrol

European native – Croat, Dane, Serb, Swede

European oak (with valuable wood)–durmast

European ox (wild extinct)–urus

European peninsula–Iberian

European perch (small)–ruffe

European pigeon (wild)–turtledove

European polecat–fitchew

European porgy–besugo

European rabbit–cony

European republic–Andorra, Andorre

European republic (former)–Hesse

European river–Bug, Danube, Elbe, Narenta, Po, Ruhr, Saar

European rodent (ratlike)–hamster

European sea (inland)–Aral

European shark–tope

European ship canal–Kiel

European starling–starnel

European swallow–marten

European thrush – mavis, ossel, ousel, ouzel

European thrush (song)–mavis

European tree (fruit)–sorb

European vacation ground–Tirol, Tyrol

European worm–sao

European wren–stag

Eurytus' daughter–Iole

evacuate–deprive, discharge, empty, excrete, exhaust, expel, vacate, void

evade–avoid, dodge, elude, escape, foil, parry, shirk, shun

evading (obs.)–illuding

evanesce–disappear, dissipate, empty, vanish

evanescent–fleeting, impermanent, transient, vanishing

evangelical–gospel

Evangeline's home–Acadia

evaporate–dehydrate, dry, vaporise, vaporize, vapourize

evasion–dodge, equivocation, shift, shuffling

evasive–deceitful, eely, elusive, elusory, shifty, sly

eve (herb)–iva

even–equable, equal, level, placid, regular, steady, suant, tie

even (poetic)–een

even if–although, tho

even tempered–sedate, staid

evener–equalizer, doubletree

evenglome–twilight

evenglow–twilight

evenhand – equal, equality, equilibrium, equity, equivalent

evening–sunset

evening frock–wrap

evening party–soiree

evening song–serenade, vesper

evening star–Hesper, Hesperus, Venus, Vesper

evenness–uniformity

evens (contraction)–eens

event–adventure, circumstance, consequence, episode, incident, occurrence, termination event (discreditable)–scandal

event (exciting)–drama

event (extraordinary)–phenomenon, phenomena (pl.)

event (first)–opener, premiere

event (marking turning point)–crisis, crises (pl.), criterion, decision, landmark

event (supernatural)–miracle

ever (contraction)–eer

evergreen (small)–mastic

evergreen shrub–heath, ilex jasmine, laurel, salal, savin, titi

evergreen shrub (genus of)–erica

evergreen shrub (small)–moss

evergreens (trees)–balsam, carobs, cedars, firs, larches, pines, yews

everlasting–continual, durable, endless, enduring, eternal, forever, incessant, infinite, lasting, perpetual, unceasing, unintermitted, uninterrupted, wearisome

everlasting (poetic)–etern, eterne

every–all, complete, each, entire

every (Scot.)–ilk, ilka

everyone–all, each

evict–expel, oust

evidence–argument, attest, circumstantiate, manifest, proof, support, testimony, token

evidence (convincing) – proof

evidence (positive, Eng.)–constat

evident–apparent, clear, indubitable, manifest, notorious, obvious, palpable, patent, plain, visible

evil–adverse, bad, baleful, corrupt, depraved, hurtful, ill, immoral, injurious, malevolent, perni-

cious, satanic, sinful, sinister, vicious, vile, wicked

evil (impending) – imminence

evil (incarnation of)–Satan

evil (occasioning)–malefic

evil (prefix)–mal

evil action–misdeed

evil deed–sin

evil omen–knell

evil spirit–demon

evil spirit (imaginary)–imp

evils (Latin)–mala

evince – display, exhibit, manifest, show

evirate–castrate, emasculate

evolution–development

evolution of living things–biogeny

evolve–deduce, derive, develop, disentangle, educe, unfold, unroll

ewer–jug, pitcher

exacerbate–embitter, irritate

exact–accurate, careful, correct, demand, elicit, literal, methodical, minute, nice, precise, regular, strict

exact by way of fine–estreat

exact money penalty–fine

exact opposite–antipode

exact satisfaction–avenge

exact thinking (mental process)–ratiocination

exact vengeance (retribution)–avenge

exacted by compulsion–levied

exacting–arduous, critical, severe

exacting exclusive devotion–jealous

exactly – accurately, due, nicely, precisely

exactly (coll.)–spang

exactly suitable–fit, pat

exaggerated–enlarged, increased, magnified, outre, overdone, overstated, romanced

exaggerated comedy–farce

exagitate–agitate, censure, discuss, harass

exalt–elevate, ennoble, extol, raise

exaltation of spirit–elation

exalted–dignified, elevated, extolled, grand, noble, refined, sublime

examination–audit, inquiry, inquisition, inspection, investigation, research, scrutiny, specimen, test, trial

examination (thorough)–investigation

examination (undecisive legal)–mistrial

examination of accounts–audit

examine–analyze, audit, collate, consider, debate, discuss, explore, inspect, interrogate, probe, quest, scan, test

examine (compare critically)–collate

examine by touch–palpate

examine carefully–ponder, pore, probe

examine critically–probe, sift

examine judicially–try

examine minutely–sift

examine officially before publication–censor

examiner–auditor, inspector

examiner (publication official)–censor

example–case, exemplification, illustration, instance, model, paradigm, precedent, sample, specimen

example (authoritative)–precedent

example (representative)–type

example (typical)–norm

example of conjugation declension–paradigm

exasperate–embitter, enrage, imbitter, irritate, nettle

excavate–dig, dredge, mine, stope

excavation–hole, mine, pit

excavation (mining)–stope

excavation (ore)–stope

exceed – eclipse, excel, outdo, overshoot, overstep, outstrip, outvie, pass, surpass, top, transcend

exceedingly–very

excel–cap, emulate, exceed, outdo, outgo, surpass, top
excellence–meed, merit, virtue
excellence (moral)–virtue
excellence (surpassing)–inimitability
excellence (work of acknowledged)–classic
excellent–admirable, best, capital, choice, exquisite, fine, first-rate, prime, select, transcendent, valuable, worthy
excellent (slang)–corking, super
excellent (strikingly)–stunning
except–bar, besides, but, eliminate, save
except that–only
excepting–only, save
exception–cavil, condition, dissent, objection
exception (take)–demur
exception (with the)–only
exceptional – extraordinary, outstanding, remarkable, unusual
excerpt–cite, extract, quote
excess–over, overage, plus, profuse, redundancy, superfluity
excess of solar month–epact
excess of solar over lunar month–epact
excessive–exorbitant, extravagant, extreme, immoderate, inordinate, intemperate, overly, overmuch, undue, unreasonable
excessive (wasteful)–extravagant
excessive fear–phobia
excessively–too, unduly
excessively demonstrative–effusive
exchange–barter, dealing, interchange, resale, rialto, substitute, swap, trade, traffic, transpose
exchange discount–agio
exchange for money–sell
exchange letters–correspond
exchange place – market, mart, shoppe, store

exchange premium–agio
exchanged–bandied
exchanged for money–sold
excise officer (slang)–revenuer
excite – animate, arouse, awaken, fire, impel, inflame, instigate, kindle, prompt, provoke, spur, stir, urge
excite to action–rouse
excite to activity–arouse
excite violently–electrify
excited – agitated, agog, aroused, elated, heated, stimulated, weakened
excited (highly)–fevered
excited (not easily)–stoical, stolid
excited suddenly–startled
excited with curiosity–agog
excitement–ado, agitation, commotion, disturbance, ferment, irritation, stimulation, stir
excitement (extreme)–fever
excitement (great)–furore
exciting–hectic
exciting (coll.)–parlous
exciting sympathy–piteous
exclamation–ah, aha, ahem, alackaday, alas, bah, boo, egad, fie, hey, hi, ho, la, lo, och, oh, phew, pshaw, rats, so, tut; interjection
exclamation (old fashioned) –la
exclamation of approval–ah, bravo
exclamation of contempt–foh, pish, pshaw
exclamation of disbelief–bah
exclamation of disgust–faugh, fie, foh, pah, pugh, ugh
exclamation of distress–ai
exclamation of doubt–humph
exclamation of impatience–phew, pshaw
exclamation of incredulity–ahem, indeed
exclamation of repugnance–ugh
exclamation of sorrow–alas, ay

exclamation of triumph–ah, aha
exclamation to check–tut
exclamation to mark time–hep
exclude–bar, debar, eject, eliminate, expel
exclude from church–excommunicate
exclusive–select
exclusive rights–concession, ex, patents
excoriate–abrade, flay, gall, strip
excrete–egest
excruciate–rack, torture
excursion – elimination, jaunt, journey, junket, outing, ramble, ride, row, sail, tour, trip
excursion (water)–row, sail
excusable–allowable, defensible, justifiable, justified, pardonable, venial
excuse–absolve, acquit, alibi, apology, condone, exonerate, extenuate, forgive, overlook, pardon, plea, pretext, remit
excuse (coll.)–alibi
excuse (palliate)–extenuate
excuse for nonappearance in court (law)–essoin
execute–accomplish, administer, complete, conduct, direct, effect, enforce, finish, manage, perform
execute quickly–summary
execution – achievement, hanging, performance, technic
execution writ–outre
executioner–hangman
executioner (notorious)–Jack Ketch
exegesis–explain, interpret
exegete–interpreter
exemplar–archetype, example, model, pattern
exemplary – commendable, laudable, praiseworthy
exemplify–illustrate
exempt–clear, excepted, excluded, free, privileged, release
exempt (an)–exon

exemption – dispensation, freedom, immunity

exercise–activity, display, drill, employ, exert, exhibition, ply, school, use

exercise (arch.)–ure

exercise (exhausting as in a race)–burster

exercise (mathematical)–problem

exercise (musical)–etude

exercise (practice)–drill

exercise (vigorous)–athletics, gymnastics

exercise control–preside

exercise oversight–preside

exertion–attempt, effort, endeavor, essay, trial

exhalation–aura, effluvium, emanation, evaporation, expiration, steam

exhale–emit, respire

exhale (to)–transpire

exhaust–consume, deplete, drain, emit, empty, fag, overdo, sap, spend, tire, weary

exhausted–emptied, spent

exhausted (poetic)–forspent

exhaustion (complete)–prostration

exhibit–air, disclose, display, evidence, evince, expose, fair, manifest, parade, reveal, show, stage, wear

exhibit (agricultural)–fair

exhibit (arch.)–shew

exhibit (with detail)–circumstantiate

exhibit changing colors–iridesce

exhibit malign pleasure–gloat

exhibiting refined taste–elegant

exhibition–display, exposition, fair, manifestation, show

exhibitor of knowledge–pedant

exhort–dehort, encourage, incite, urge

exhumed – delved, disinterred, dug

exies–fit, hysterics

exigency–emergency, junc-

ture, need, pressure, urgency

exigent–critical, pressing, urgent

exile–banish, banishment, deport, expatriate, expatriation, expulsion, outcast, outlawry, proscription, relegate

exist–am, are, be, is, live

existed–been, was, were

existence–actus, being, ens, esse, essence, extant, life, reality

existence (future)–hereafter

existence (in)–extant

existence (Latin)–esse

existent–alive

existing at same time–contemporaneous

existing between commonwealths–interstate

existing in name only–nominal, titular

exit–departure, door, egress, gate, going, outlet, vent

exitus–exodus, issue, outcome

exlex–outlaw

exodus–hegira

exonerate–absolve, acquit, clear, exculpate, relieve

exorbitant–excessive

exorbitant interest rate–usury

exordium–preface

exotic–alien, extraneous, foreign, strange

exotic (not)–native

expand–broaden, dilate, distend, enlarge, grow, open, sheet, spread, swell

expanse – extent, reach, spread, stretch, tract

expanse (broad)–main

expanse (vast)–desert, ocean

expanse of time (immeasurable)–eternity

expansion – development, dilatation, distention, growth, increase, spread

expansion (seed)–ala

expansion of muscle–dilator

expansive–broad, comprehensive, elastic, liberal,

sympathetic, unrestrained, wide

expatiate – descant, dilate, dwell, enlarge, widespread

expatriate–banish, exile, expel, outlaw

expect – anticipate, await, hope, wait

expectant desire–hope

expectation – anticipation, hope

expected–natural

expedient–advantageous, advisable, politic, profitable, resource, shift, wise

expedient (temporary)–stopgap

expedite–accelerate, dispatch, easy, facilitate, free, hasten, hurry, light, quicken, speed

expedition–excursion, haste, journey

expedition (hunting)–safari

expedition (military, to recover Holy Land)–Crusade

expel–banish, discharge, dispossess, eject, eliminate, evict, exile, oust

expend–disburse, consume, distribute, spend, use

expenditure – consumption, disbursement, expense, outgo, outlay

expense–consumption, cost, disbursement, outlay, price

expensive–costly, dear, extravagant, lavish, liberal

experience–feel, have, know, ordeal, see, suffer, undergo

experience (trying)–ordeal

experience again–relive

experience of intense suffering–calvary

experience pleasure in–enjoy

experience regret–repent

experienced–had, underwent

experiment–essay, test, trial, try

experimental–tentative

experimental workshop (coll.)–lab

expert–ace, adept, adroit, artistic, experienced, proficient, skillful

expert (great, slang)–oner

expert in sophistical reasoning–casuist

expert on business affairs–economist

expert on snakes–herpetologist

expiate–atone

expiation–propitiation

expire–die, perish

explain–define, elucidate, expound, interpret

explain beforehand–premise

explanation – clarification, description, explication, exposition

expletive–bosh, exclamation, gosh, oath

expletive (mild)–gee

expletive (old)–begad, egad

explicit–absolute, discriminating, exact, fixed, implicit, open, positive, precise, unambiguous, unconditional

explode–blast, detonate

explode in muffler–backfire

explode with sudden force–detonate

exploit–achievement, act, advantage, feat, gest

explore–examine, discover, search

explorer–discoverer, pioneer

explorer (water)–diver

explosion–blast, detonation, outburst, pop

explosive–dynamite, guncotton, niter, nitramite, nitroglycerin, powder, tittle, TNT, tonite, trinitrotoluene

explosive device–cap

explosive device (old)–petard

explosive noise–blast, pop, report

explosive projectile – cartridge, grenade, shell

explosive shell (handthrown)–grenade

explosively inclined–eruptive

expose–bare, disclose, exhibit, exposition, open, reveal, unearth, unmask

expose to discussion–air, ventilate

expose to moisture–ret

expose to scorn–pillory

exposition–exhibition, expose, exposure, fair

exposition (extended written)–treatise

expostulates–complains, orates, remonstrates

exposure–exposition

exposure (instantaneous) – snapshot

exposure to ridicule (caustic) –satire

express–declare, expound, intimate, speak, testify, voice

express censure–animadvert

express disapproval–deprecate

express gratitude–thank

express impatience–tut

express in words–phrase

express mental feeling–emote

express merriment–laugh

express one's self copiously–expatiate

express willingness–consent

expressed in numbers–dubitative

expressing emotion–emotive

expressing feeling–emotive

expressing negation–not

expressing numerically–evaluating

expressing past time–preterite

expressing pique–pouty

expressing veneration–reverent

expression – delineation, phrase, representation, show, statement, term

expression (authoritative)–oracle

expression (facial) – grin, scowl, smile

expression (mathematical of equality)–equation

expression (peculiar)–idiom

expression (peculiar to language)–idiom

expression (pithy)–phrase

expression (vocal)–utterance

expression of approval–applause, clap, ovation

expression of contempt–bah, hiss, pshaw, sneer

expression of disapproval–rebuke

expression of emotion–sigh

expression of gratitude–thanksgiving

expression of inquiry–eh

expression of opinion (formal)–vote

expression of scorn–fie

expression of weariness–sigh

expressionless–stony

expressive–emphatic, indicative, significant

expressive motion–gesture

expressive of command–imperative

expressive of regard (praise) –complimentary

expulsion–banishment, ejection, exile

expunction–erasure

expunge–cancel, dele, delete, efface, erase, obliterate

exquisite–dainty, delicious, matchless, perfect, rare, refined

exsanguine–anemic, bloodless

exsanguinity–anemia

extant–being, existent

extend–broaden, bulge, eke, go, increase, lengthen, lie, prolong, reach, run, spread, steal, stretch, widen

extend (to)–reach

extend a subscription–renew

extend down–deepen

extend forward–protrude

extend from center–radiate

extend over–reach, span

extend to the front–deploy

extend written exposition–treatise

extended–assured, broad, open, outstretched, valued

extended view–panorama

extending from center–radial

extension–area, augmentation, duration, enlargement, expansion, increase, scope

extension (trench)–sap

extension of time–respite, stay

extensive–broad, expanded, far-reaching, immense, large, titanic, vast, wholesale, wide, widespread

extent–area, breadth, dimension, expanse, range, reach, scope

extent (superficial)–areal

extent (wide)–expanse

extent for space–room

extent in front–frontage

extenuate–palliate

exterior – ectal, external, outer

exterior (anat.)–ectal

exterminate–abolish, annihilate, destroy, eradicate, expel, extirpate

extermination – destruction, eradication, expulsion

extern–exterior, external, extrinsic, outward

external–outer, outside

external (comb. form)–ecto

external (var.)–outre

external appearance–guise

extinct–dead, extinguished, quenched

extinct bird–dodo, moa

extinction – annihilation, death, destruction, quenching

extinguish – annul, choke, destroy, douse, quell, quench, suppress

extinguisher (fire)–pyrene, pyroleter

extirpate – dele, eradicate, erase, exterminate, expel, root

extol–applaud, celebrate, commend, elevate, exalt, glorify, laud, praise

extort–elicit, wrest, wring

extort by violence–wrest

extortion–exaction, oppression, overcharge, rapacity

extortioner – blackmailer, vampire

extra–accessory, added, additional, bye, over, spare, superior, surplus

extra (stage)–supe, super

extra part–spare

extra supply–reserve, reservoir, stock, store

extract–deduce, elicit, essence, excerpt, pull, withdraw

extract (cacao shell)–martol

extract (forcibly)–evulse

extract (from court records) –estreat

extracted from earth–dug, mined

extraction – essence, origin, parentage, stock, tincture, withdrawal

extracts (collection of literary)–anthology

extraneous–exotic, foreign, intrinsic

extraordinary – exceptional, irregular, odd, rare, remarkable, singular, unusual

extravagance – lavishness, recklessness, waste, wildness

extravagant – excessive, fanatic, fanatical, outre, prodigal, wasteful

extreme–conclusive, drastic, excessive, farthest, final, great, greatest, immoderate, intense, last, outermost, outward, radical, severe, sore, ultra, utmost

extreme fear–horror, panic, terror

extreme in degree–intense

extremely–so, very

extremely (Scot.)–unco

extremity–border, end, terminal, termination, tip, verge

extricate–disembroil, disengage, disentangle, free, liberate, loose

extricated oneself–wangle

extrication – disengagement, disentanglement

extrinsic–adventitious, extra-

neous, foreign, incidental, nonessential

exuberance–abundance, copiousness, excess, luxuriance, overflow, plenty, profusion, rankness, superabundance

exuberant – overflowing, plentiful, profuse, superabundant

exudation–secretion

exudation (amorphous)–resin, rosin

exudation (pine tree)–resin, rosin

exudation (tree)–gum, lac, pitch, resin, rosin, sap, tar

exude–discharge, emit, ooze, sweat

exult–elate, joy, jubilate, rejoice

exultation–jubilance

exulted – elated, prided, raved, vaunted

exults – glories, jubilates, leaps, springs

eye–observe, optic, watch

eye (amorously)–ogle

eye (Gaelic)–ee

eye (pert. to)–optic

eye (Scot.)–ee

eye (slang)–glim, peeper

eyeball hardening–glaucoma

eyebrow (Scot.)–bree, eebree

eye covering–eyelid

eye disease–conjunctivitis, glaucoma, trachoma

eyeglass–lens, monocle

eyeglass frame–bon

eyeglasses (coll.)–specs

eyelashes – cilia, cilium (sing.)

eye opener–drink, nip

eye part–areola, cornea, iris, pupil, retina

eye part (pert. to)–corneal

eyeshot–range, reach

eyesight–observation, sight, view

eye socket–orbit

eyetooth–cuspid

eyes (blind, as hawks in falconry)–seel

eyes (hollows of)–sockets

eyes (Scot.)–ees

eyot–ait, islet

F

fable–allegory, apolog, apologue, fiction, legend, parable
fable writer–Aesop
fabled monster – centaur, ogre
fables in slang author–Ade
fabric–beige, creton, cretonne, etoile, felt, rayon, serge, tulle
fabric (artificial silk-like)–rayon
fabric (bunting-like)–etamine
fabric (canvas-like)–wigan
fabric (corded)–poplin, rep
fabric (cotton)–calico, canvas, denim, drilling, duck, galatea, gingham, jean, leno, muslin, penang, percale, rumal, sheeting
fabric (cotton and wool)–satinet
fabric (cotton, fine)–madras
fabric (cotton, striped)–galatea
fabric (cotton worsted)–etamine
fabric (crimped) – crape, crepe
fabric (crinkled) – crape, crepe
fabric (figured)–arras
fabric (fine)–linen, mohair
fabric (fine cotton)–percale
fabric (fine, lustrous)–silk
fabric (fine, striped with silk)–sousi
fabric (fine thin)–dimity
fabric (flaw in)–rase
fabric (gauze-like)–barege
fabric (glossy)–sateen
fabric (glossy silk)–satin
fabric (glossy textile) – madras
fabric (goat hair)–aba
fabric (heavy)–denim
fabric (heavy silk)–samite
fabric (interwoven with gold)–samite
fabric (jute)–burlap
fabric (knitted)–tricot

fabric (light cotton)–scrim
fabric (light linen)–scrim
fabric (light open cotton)–leno
fabric (loose textured)–ratine
fabric (loosely woven dress)–etamine
fabric (made from remnants)–mungo
fabric (meshed)–net
fabric (mourning)–alma
fabric (napped woolen)–baize
fabric (narrow)–ribbon
fabric (narrow binding)–tape
fabric (ornamental)–lace
fabric (ornamental, arch.)–riband
fabric (plaid)–tartan
fabric (printed)–percale
fabric (printed cotton)–calico
fabric (ribbed)–corduroy, serge, whipcord
fabric (ribbed worsted)–whipcord
fabric (rough)–terry
fabric (satin)–pekin
fabric (sheer linen)–lawn
fabric (short napped)–ras
fabric (silk)–rumal, satin, surah
fabric (silk or woolen)–hernani
fabric (silken)–schappe
fabric (soft napped)–panne
fabric (soft silk)–charmeuse
fabric (soft velvety)–panne
fabric (stretchy)–elastic
fabric (striped)–aba
fabric (striped cotton)–galatea
fabric (textile)–rep
fabric (texture of)–woof
fabric (thin)–gauze
fabric (thin dress)–voile
fabric (thin undyed silk)–pongee
fabric (turkish towel-like)–agaric

fabric (twilled)–corduroy, serge, whipcord
fabric (twilled silk)–surah
fabric (upholstery) rep
fabric (velvet-like)–panne
fabric (waste material)–mungo
fabric (woolen)–baize, serge, tweed
fabric (woolen dress)–beige
fabric (woolen or silk)–hernani
fabric (worsted)–etamine
fabric (woven)–tissue, twill
fabric (woven wool)–tweed
fabricate–coin, construct, devise, fashion, form, make, manufacture, weave
fabrication – construction, falsehood, fiction, forging, invention, lie, untruth, web
fabulist–liar
fabulous–absurd, astonishing, feigned, fictitious, mythical
fabulous beast–dragon
fabulous bird–roc
façade–face, front
face–cover, countenance, dare, defy, front, line, meet, mug, obvert, oppose, phiz, phizog, physiognomy, visage
face (clock)–dial
face (coll.)–phiz, phizog, physiognomy
face (graduated)–dial
face (part of)–brow, cheek, chin, jaw, lip
face (wry)–grimace
face an embankment (with stones, etc.)–revet
face eastward–orientate
face of gem–facet
face of hewn stone–panel
face to face–afront, vis-a-vis
face value–par
face with concrete–revet
face with masonry–revet
face with stone slabs–revet
facet (brilliant small)–culet

facet (star)–pane
facetious (cleverly)–witty
facia–plate, tablet
facial artery–maxillary
facial ingredient–cream, powder, rouge
facile–affable, easy, gentle, lenient
facilitate–aid, assist, help
facility–address, adroitness, art, ease, easiness, eclat, expertness, furtherance, help, pliability, readiness, skill
facing–opposite, surface
facing (fireplace)–mantel
facing (thin)–veneer
facing direction glacier moves–stoss
facing inward–introrse
facing outward–extrorse
facsimile–copy, counterpart, duplicate, replica
fact–datum, data (pl.)
fact (assumed)–datum, data (pl.)
fact (conceded)–datum, data (pl.)
fact (fundamental)–keynote
fact (law)–fiat
fact (seemingly untrue)–paradox
fact admitted–datum, data (pl.)
fact collector–statist, statistician
facts–data, datum (sing.)
facts (slang)–lowdown
faction–bloc, cabal, clique, combination, junto, party, sect, side
factions (opposing)–sides
factious–demagogic, seditious
factitious–artificial, sham, unnatural
factor–agent, gene
factor (determining)–gene
factor (heredity)–gene
factor (maturing)–ager
factor (minor)–detail
factory–manufactory, mill, plant
faculties (intellectual)–wits
faculties of perception–senses

faculty–ability, aptitude, art, ease, gift, talent
faculty (particular)–talent
fad–craze, custom, fancy, fashion, hobby, rage, whim
faddist–monomaniac
fade–decline, dissolve, flat, insipid, pale, peter, wan, wilt, wither
fade out–decline, pale, peter, wan, wilt
faded–passe
Faerie Queene–Una
Faerie Queene author–Spenser
Faerie Queene character – Una
Faerie Queene hag–Ate
Faerie Queene spirit–Una
fag – cigarette, droop, drudge, fatigue, flag, jade, menial, tire, toil, weary
fagot–lop
fail–decline, ebb, exhaust, sink
fail (coll.)–flop, flunk
fail in duty–lapse
fail to hit–fan, miss
failed–eight-balled
failing (harmless)–foible
failure–bankruptcy, delinquency, fault, insolvency, lapse, loss, miss, suspension
failure (dismal)–flop
failure (flat)–dud, flop
failure (ridiculous)–fiasco
failure (slang)–dud, flop
faint–dim, feeble, indistinct, listless, pale, soft, swoon, timid
faint (old wording)–evanid
faint from heat (to be)–swelter
faintheartedness (sudden)–qualm
faintness (sudden)–syncope
fair–auspicious, bazaar, blond, blonde, comely, dispassionate, honest, impartial, just, mart, reasonable, unbiased, unprejudiced
fair (entertainment)–kermis
fair amount–chunk

fairies (world of)–faerie
fairy–elf, fay, peri, pixie, pixy, sprite
fairy (Irish, little)–leprechaun
fairy (Persian)–peri
fairy (tricky)–puck
fairy (wailing)–banshee
fairy-like–elfin
fairy queen–Mab, Una
fairy tale monster–ogre
faith–belief, confidence, credence, creed, troth, trust
faith (religious)–belief
faithful–constant, devoted, feal, leal, liege, loyal, pious, sincere, steadfast, steady, true, trusty, veracious
faithful (arch.)–feal
faithful (poetic)–leal
faithless–apostate, deceptive, disloyal, false, fickle, incredulous, mercurial, punic, shifting, skeptical, untrue
faker–cheat, fraud, peddler, pretender
fakir–dervish, mendicant, yogi
falcon–kestrel, peregrine
falcon (European) – peregrine, sacer
falcon (European, small)–merlin
falcon (old world, var.)–sacer
fall–commence, depreciate, descend, drop, perish, plummet, ruin, sink, slip, surrender, tumble
fall (as an obligation)–devolve
fall back–recede, retreat
fall back into former state–relapse
fall behind–lag
fall gradually–sag
fall in–agree, cave, concur, lapse, terminate
fall noisily–crash
fall short–lack
fall suddenly–drop, flop, plop
fallacious–crafty, deceitful, deceptive, delusive, fraud-

ulent, guileful, insidious, misleading, untrue, wily

fallacy–deceitfulness, deception, sophism, sophistry

falling and rising–surging, tidal

falling back–recession, retreat

falls in drops–dribbles, drips

falls in with–meets

falls into disuse–lapse

falls short–deficient, lacking, miss, shy

false–bogus, counterfeit, deceitful, deceptive, faithless, fictitious, incorrect, insincere, mendacious, paste, pretended, pseudo, sham, spurious, traitorous, untrue, untruthful

false god–idol

false fruit–pseudocarp

false jewelry–costume, paste, strass

false report–canard, rumor, rumour, slander

false show–tinsel

falsehood–fabrication, falsity, fiction, lie, ·mendacity, untruth

falsetto tenor singer–tenorino

falsifier–forger, liar

falsify – adulterate, belie, counterfeit, lie

Falstaff's follower–Nym

falter–hesitate, pause, stumble, totter, tremble, waver

fame–renown, repute

familiar–accustomed, customary, habitual, usual, well-known

familiar with–conversant, versed

familiarity–acquaintance, affability, fellowship, intimacy

family–clan, class, group, house, household, kin, kindred, race

family (super, comprising true bees)–apina

family of kings–dynasty

family of organ pipes–reeds

famous–celebrated, distinguished, eminent, nama-

ble, notable, noted, notorious, renowned

famous football coach–Dana Bibble, Bernie Bierman, Crowley, Howard Jones, Kriesler, Frank Leahy, Little, Knute Rockne, Clark Shaughnessy, Smith, Alonzo Stagg, Lon Stiner, Frank Thomas, Wallace Wade, Glenn (Pop) Warner, Yost, Bob Zupke

famous murderer–Aram

famous pirate–Kidd

famous prima donna–Patti

fan–admirer, devotee, enthusiast, spread, winnow

fan (alluvial)–delta

fan (coll.)–rooter

fan (swung from ceiling)–punka, punkah

fan-shaped–flabellate

fan stick (radiating)–brin

fanatic–bigot, crank, devotee, enthusiast

fanatical–crazy, enthusiastic, mad, rabid

fanatical partisan–zealot

fancied–dreamed, unreal

fanciful–bizarre, chimerical, fantastic, grotesque, imaginative, odd, queer, strange, visionary

fanciful idea–conceit

fancy–dream, fantasy, freak, humour, idea, ideate, imagination, megrim, notion, phantasy, vagary, ween

fancy (absurd)–chimera

fancy (passing)–fad

fancy (perverse)–crotchet

fancy (wild)–ween

fane–banner, church, elf, fairy, flag, pennant, temple, weathercock

fanning device–punka, punkah

fanon–banner, cape, orale

fantastic–bizarre, chimerical, extravagant, fanciful, freakish, grotesque, imaginative, odd, queer, rococo, visionary

fantastic (anything)–caprice

fantasy–apparition, dream, fancy, hallucination, phantom, romance, vision

far (prefix)–tel, tele

far off–distant, faraway, remote

faraway–abstracted, distant, dreamy, remote

farce–comedy, forcemeat, mime, stuff

fare–diet, expedition, going, passage, rate, table

fare sumptuously–regale

farewell–adieu, adios, aloha, ave, good-bye, leaving, parting, vale

farewell (formal)–conge

farinaceous–mealy

farinaceous food–barley, cereals, cornstarch, flour, grain, meal, oats, puddings, rye, sago, salep, spelt, wheat

farm–cultivate, grange

farm (large)–ranch

farm (large grazing)–rancho

farm (small)–croft

farm area–acreage

farm holding (peasant)–cotland

farn. laborer–hind

farm out–hire, let

farm steward–granger

farm tenant–cotter

farmer–cultivator, grower, rancher, tiller

farmer (rich, Russ.)–kulak

farmer (working on shares)–cropper, metayer

farmers (collectively)–yeomanry

faro (form of)–monte

faro combination of cards–cathop

Faroe Island district manager–foud

Faroe Island whirlwind–oe

far-reaching–deep, intense, profound

farrow–pig

farsighted – foresighted, provident, sagacious, shrewd

farther–remote

farthest–endmost, extreme

fascinate–allure, captivate, charm, enamor, enrapture, entrance

fascinating – attractive, charming, siren

Fascist hymn–Viovanezza

fashion–craze, create, compose, construct, fabricate, fad, feign, forge, frame, guise, invent, mode, model, rage, shape, style, vogue

fashion (Fr.)–ton

fashion (pert. to)–modal

fashion (prevailing)–fad, mode, style, ton

fashion (prevailing, Fr.)–ton

fashionable–a la mode, modish, smart, stylish

fashionable (ostentatiously)–dash

fashionable reception–salon

fashioned–formed, shaped

fashioned (artistically) – carved

fast–abiding, agile, enduring, expeditious, firm, fixed, fleet, hasty, lively, quick, rapid, speedy, staple, stationary, swift, unyielding

fast horse (U.S.)–pelter

fasten–affix, bind, clamp, clasp, clip, lace, lash, moor, nail, padlock, paste, pin, rivet, rope, seal, secure, tether, wire

fasten (as a rope)–belay

fasten (securely)–solder

fasten shut (firmly)–bar

fasten to–tagged, tie

fasten with metal strand–wire

fasten with two-pointed tack –staple

fastened–girded

fastener–bolt, button, clasp, hasp, nail, pin, rivet, snapper, zipper

fastener (long metal)--hatpin

fastener (threaded metal)–nut

fastening line–earing, hawser, painter

fastidious–critical, dainty, delicate, elegant, finical, meticulous, nice, overnice, particular

fat–adipose, lard, lipin, obese, oily, opulent, portly, profitable, stocky, stout, suet

fat (animal, used for candles)–tallow

fat (comb. form)–steat

fat (hard beef or mutton)–suet

fat (liquid part)–olein, oleine

fat (liquid part, var.)–elain, elaine

fat (natural)–ester

fat (solid part)–stearin

fat (tallow making)–suet

fat (tried out)–lard, suet

fat (wool, purified)–lanolin, lanoline

fat of swine (rendered)–lard

fatal–calamitous, deadly, destined, disastrous, fateful, lethal, mortal

fatally–mortally, ruinously

fate–chance, destiny, doom, downfall, fortune, kismet, lot

fated – decreed, destined, doomed

fated to die (Scot.)–fey

fateful–inevitable, momentous, portentous, predestined

Fates (one of)–Atropos, Clotho, Lachesis, Parca, Parcae

father–abba, acknowledge, confessor, dad, friar, generate, pa, padre, papa, priest, procreate, sire

father (in Arab)–aba, abba, abou, abu

father (in Egyptian)–atef

father (in French)–pere

father (in Latin)–pater

father (in Spanish)–padre

father (old wording)–abba

father (pert. to)–paternal

father and mother (pert. to) –parental

father of English learning–Beda

father of engraving–Pye

fathered–sired

fatherhood–paternity

fathom–delve, measure, penetrate, solve

fatigued–exhausted, spent, tired, wearied

fatty–adipose, greasy, suety

fatty degeneration–adiposis

fatty oil substance (derived from)–adipic

fatty or oily substance (pert. to)–adipic

fatuous–demented, foolish, idiotic, imbecile, inane, insensate, witless

faucet–spigot, tap

fault–blunder, defect, delinquency, demerit, error, failing, foible, frailty, imperfection, lapse, offense, peccadillo, slip

fault (trifle)–peccadillo

faultfinder–carper

faultfinding–captious, censorial, critical

faultiness–badness

faultless–blameless, correct, flawless, unimpeachable, perfect, pure

faultlessness–preciseness

faults (moral)–vices

faulty–amiss, blameworthy, blemished, culpable, defective, ill, imperfect, unfit

faun–satyr

Faust (author of)–Goethe

faux pas–error, mistake

faux pas (printer's)–pies

favor–assistance, bless, boon, favoritism, grace, patronage, patronize

favorable–approving, auspicious, benign, complaisant, friendly, gracious, kind, opportune, pleasing, popular, propitious, rosy

favorable (become less)–worsen

favoring–for, pro

favoring neither–neutral

favorite–darling, pet

favorite (servile)–minion

favoritism (favouritism)–bias, predilection

favoritism (shown to relatives)–nepotism

fawn–coax, cower, crawl, creep, cringe, deer, grovel, ingratiate, shrink, toady, truckle

fawning–maam, servile

fay–elf, fairy

feal–faithful, loyal

fealty–constancy, fidelity, homage, loyalty

fear–alarm, apprehend, consternation, dismay, dread, fright, horror, panic, reverence, terror, venerate

fear (excessive)–phobia

fear (extreme)–awe, dread, fright, horror, terror

fear (overpowering)–panic

fear (reverential)–awe

fear (sudden)–consternation

fear (unreasoning)–panic

fear of being closed in–claustrophobia

fear of cats–aelurophobia

fear of crossing street–dromophobia

fear of darkness–nyctophobia

fear of fire–pyrophobia

fear of great heights–acrophobia

fear of lightning–brontephobia, trophobia

fear of open spaces–agoraphobia

fear of poison–toxiphobia

fear of thunder–brontephobia

fearful–appalling, apprehensive, awful, distressing, dreadful, frightful, horrible, pavid, shocking, terrible, timid, timorous

fearful (comb. form)–dino

fearless–audacious, bold, brave, confident, courageous, daring, intrepid, undaunted

feast–banquet, carousal, festival, fete, meal, regale, repast, revel

feast (early Christian)–agape

feast of lots–Purim

feast of nativity–Christmas

Feast of Pentecost (Jewish religion)–Shabuoth

Feast of Tabernacles (Jewish)–Succoth

Feast of Weeks (Jewish religion)–Shabuoth

feasting–dining

feat – accomplishment, achievement, act, deed, exploit, performance

feat (coll.)–stunt

feather–adorn, clothe, deck, penna, pinna, plume

feather (as an arrow)–fletch

feather (contour)–penna, pluma, plumae (pl.)

feather (shaft of)–scape

feather (to)–fledge

feather barb–pinnula

feather key–spline

feather-like–pinnate

feathered vertebrate–bird

feathers–plumage

feathers (soft)–down

feathers (to shed)–molt, moult

feature–characteristic, countenance, face

feature (artistic)–motif

feature (distinguishing)–aspect, trait

feature (leading musical work)–motif

feature (objectionable)–drawback

feature (principal)–motif

feature (salient, of work of art)–motif

features (natural)–geography

fed up–bored, satiated, surfeited, wearied

fed up (to be, Eng. slang)–brown off

federation–alliance, league, union

fee–charge, rate, tip

fee (professional)–honorarium

feeble–debilitated, infirm, lame, puny, weak

feeble-minded–anile

feed–fodder, furnish, indulge, nourish, nurture, supply

feed for hire–agist

feed to fill–sate

feeding (forced)–gavage

feeding of sheep (in movable pens)–foldage

feeding of swine in forest (Eng. law)–pannage

feel–examine, explore, handle, perceive, sense, touch

feel (blindly)–grope

feel (hear, see)–perceive

feel dejection–repine

feel melancholy–grieve

feel one's way–grope

feel want of–desiderate, miss

feel worth of–appreciate

feeler–antenna, antennae (pl.), palp, palpi, tentacle

feeling–atmosphere, consciousness, emotion, experience, feel, opinion, passion, perception, sensibility, sentiment, tact, touch, view

feeling (hostile)–animus

feeling (hurt or vexation)–pique

feeling (ill)–animus

feeling (repression)–stoicism

feeling (without)–apathy, insensibility, marble, numbness

feeling indignant displeasure–resentful

feeling of apprehension (coll.)–creeps

feeling of disgust (Scot.)–ug

feeling of horror (coll.)–creeps

feeling of indisposition–discomfort, malaise

feeling one's way–groping

feeling pleasure–jocund

feelingless–apathy, insensible, unfeeling

feelings (to injure)–aggrieve

feet (pert. to)–pedal

feet (without)–apodal

feign–act, assume, counterfeit, dissemble, gammon, pretend, sham, simulate

feign ignorance–connive

feign illness–malinger

feign sickness (to get out of work)–malinger

feldspar (like)–syenitic
feldspar (resembling)–gneissy
felicia–happiness
felicitate–bless, congratulate
felicity–bliss, blissfulness, happiness, well-being
felidae (family of)–cat
feline–cat, cheetah, jaguar, leopard, lion, lynx, puma, sly, stealthy, tiger, tom, treacherous, wildcat
feline animal–pard
felis domestica–cat
fell–barbarious, beat, brutish, crashed, cruel, cut, down, ferocious, fierce, moor, savage, skin, tumbled
fell in drops–dripped
fell into disuse–lapsed
fell short–failed
fellow (awkward overgrown)–gawk
fellow (clumsy)–oaf
fellow (coll.)–chap, codger
fellow (contemptible)–cad
fellow (craven)–coward
fellow (dial.)–yawp
fellow (droll)–wag
fellow (droll, coll.)–card
fellow (ill-bred)–boor
fellow (little)–shaver
fellow (low)–cad
fellow (not jolly)–drip
fellow (queer old)–geezer
fellow (reckless)–daredevil
fellow (smart)–aleck
fellow (vulgar)–cad
fellow (vulgar humorous)–pleb
fellow of American Academy (abbr.)–AAS
fellowman–brother
fellowship–alliance, companionship, comradeship, friendliness, guild, membership, partnership
felon–convict, criminal, culprit, malefactor, villain
felony–baseness, crime, daring, deceit, sin, treachery, wickedness, wrath
felt one's way–groped
felt through senses–sensate

female figure (used as pillar)–Caryatid
female figurine–orant
female monster (frightful)–gorgon
female name–see feminine name
female ovine–ewe
female ruff (sandpiper)–ree, reeve
female saint (abbr.)–ste
female sandpiper–ree, reeve
female spirit–banshee
female warrior–Amazon
feminine–female, soft, tender
feminine leader–Catt
feminine name–Ada, Adelai, Adele, Agnes, Alice, Aline, Alma, Anita, Ann, Anna, Annie, Arabella, Betsy, Betty, Cecelia, Celia, Cora, Dona, Dora, Dorcas, Doris, Dot, Dotty, Dulce, Edith, Edla, Edna, Ella, Ellen, Elsie, Emaline, Ena, Ethel, Etta, Eva, Eve, Flora, Genie, Greta, Helen, Heloise, Honora, Ina, Inez, Irene, Irma, Jen, Jennie, Kate, Katy, Lena, Lil, Lila, Lois, Lora, Lou, Louisa, Louise, Lucia, Lula, Mae, Maria, May, Meg, Mildred, Mina, Molly, Nan, Nina, Nita, Nora, Norma, Olga, Pat, Rae, Reta, Rhoda, Rita, Sara, Sarah, Susan, Susanna, Una, Vera
fen–bog, marsh, moor, swale
fen water–suds
fence – duel, enclosure, hedge, wall
fence (iron)–rail, railing
fence (picket)–pale, paling
fence (solid)–wall
fence (sunken)–aha, ha-ha, haw-haw
fence (upright) – paling, picket
fencer–duelist, swordsman
fencing (redoubling attack of)–reprise
fencing hit–punto

fencing position–carte, octave, prime, quarte, quinte, seconde, septime, sixte, terce, tierce
fencing sword–epee, foil, rapier
fencing term–touche
fencing thrust–estocade
fencing thrust (quick return)–riposte
fencing weapon–epee, foil, rapier, sword
fend–defend, parry, resist, ward
fender–buffer, bumper, guard, shield, splashboard
fennel (horse)–seseli
fennel flowers (genus of)–nigella
feral–bestial, deadly, funereal, malignant, savage, unbroken, uncultivated, undomesticated, untamed, wild
ferine–wild
ferment–disorder, fever, turbulence, uproar, yeast
ferment (digestive)–maltase, rennin
fermentation–ebullition
fermented drink–mead
fermenting vat–gyle
fern (kind of)–maidenhair, polypody
fern (seedless)–sorus, sori (pl.)
fern genus–anemia
fern leaf–frond
fern-like–pteridophyte, pteroid
fern part (scaly)–ramentum, ramenta (pl.)
ferocious–acharne, barbarous, bloodthirsty, bloody, brutal, cruel, fell, fierce, grim, implacable, inhuman, malevolent, malignant, merciless, murderous, pitiless, rapacious, ravenous, relentless, remorseless, ruthless, sanguinary, savage, truculent, wild
ferret–polecat, tape, weasel
ferret (male)–hob
ferrotype–tintype

ferryman (Styx River)–Charon

fertile–abundant, exuberant, fruitful, plentiful, prolific, rank, rich, teeming

fertile spot–oasis, oases (pl.)

fertilize with lime–marl

fertilizer–alinit, guano, manure, marl, nitrate, pollen, superphosphate

fertilizer (valuable)–marl

fertilizer of clay and calcium–marl

fervency–ardor, eager, fiery, heat, impassioned, keen, passionate, vehement, warmth

fervent–ardent, eager, fervid, fiery, impassioned, intense, keen, passionate, vehement, warm

fervid–ardent, fervent, impassioned, tropic, vehement, zealous

fervor–ardor, rage, zeal

fester–pustule, rankle

festival–banquet, feast, festivity, fete, gala, holiday, revel

festival (Christian)–Christmas, Easter

festival (church)–Easter

festival (country)–ale

Festival of Passover–Seder

festive–convivial, gala, gay, joyous, mirthful, sportive

festivity–celebration, conviviality, gaiety, gala, jollity, joyfulness, merrymaking, mirth, revel

fetch–bring

fetching–alluring, attractive, fascinating, pleasing

fete–entertainment, fiesta

fetid–malodorous, noisome, olid, rank

fetish–charm, idol, obi, talisman, totem

fetter–band, bond, chain, gyve, hamper, iron, manacle, shackle

feud–affray, broil, contest, dispute, fief, fray, strife

feudal estate (law)–fief

feudal jurisdiction–soke

feudal lord–suzerain

feudal tenant–vassal

fever–temperature

fever (intermittent)–ague

fever (malarial)–ague

fever (marsh)–helodes

fever (referring to tropical)–calentural

feverish–excited, febrile, frantic, hectic, impassioned, overeager, restless

fiat–command, decision, decree, edict, sanction

fiber (aloe)–pita

fiber (American aloe)–pita

fiber (chemically produced)–nylon

fiber (cotton)–lint, staple

fiber (cotton-tree silky)–kapok

fiber (durable white)–sisal

fiber (fine soft)–istle

fiber (flannel)–nap

fiber (glossy textile)–rayon

fiber (kind of)–sisal

fiber (knotted)–nep

fiber (Mexican)–istle

fiber (nuclear network)–linin

fiber (peacock feather)–marl

fiber (plant)–istle

fiber (sensitive)–nerve

fiber (silky cotton-tree)–kapok

fiber (small)–fibrilla

fiber (waste, of silk or wool)–noil

fiber (white durable)–sisal

fiber (woody strong)–bast

fiber cluster–nep

fiber grass–istle, ramie

fiber plant–cotton, hemp, istle, manila, pita, ramie, sisal

fibers–strands

fibers in wool (clusters of)–nep

fibula–brooch, buckle, clasp, perone, safety pin

fickle–changeful, capricious, deceitful, faithless, false, irresolute, mobile, mutable, unsettled, unsteady, vacillating, variable, wavering

fickle (was)–veered

fiction–coinage, fabrication, false, falsehood, figment, forgery, invention, legend, romance

fictional detective–Nick Carter, Sherlock Holmes, Philo Vance

fictitious – artificial, false, feigned, imitative, pretended

fictitious (prefix)–pseudo

fidelity–allegiance, constancy, devotion, fealty, honesty, troth, truth, veracity

fidget–fuss, fusser, impatient, nervous, restless

fidget (slang)–fantod

fidgety–impatient, restive, restless, uneasy

fiducial–confident, firm, trusted, trustworthy

fiduciary–founded, held, holding, trust, trustee

fief–benefice, fee

field–acre, battlefield, campus, clearing, compass, diamond, gridiron, ground, lot, meadow, range, sphere

field (adjoining house)–croft

field (athletic) – arena, course, court, diamond, gridiron, oval, stadium

field (enclosed)–ager

field (god of)–Faun

field (grassy)–lea, mead, meadow

field (grassy, poetic)–mead

field (grazing)–pasture

field (pert. to)–agrarian

field (small)–croft

field edge (unplowed)–rand

field mouse–vole

field of action–arena, sphere

field of activities–terrain

field of blood–aceldama, akeldama, ager sanguinis

field of granular snow–neve

fiend–demon, devil, enemy, foe, Satan, wizard

fiendish–cruel, demoniac, demonic, diabolic, devilish, wicked

fierce–brutish, cruel, forbidding, furious, grim, im-

petuous, passionate, raging, savage, violent
fierceness (evincing)–truculent
fiery–ardent, burning, choleric, feverish, flaming, glowing, hot, impetuous, inflamed, irascible, mettlesome, parched, red, spirited, vehement, violent.
fiesta–festival, festivity, holiday
fifish–cranky, half-crazy
fig (brand of)–eleme, elemi
fig (Smyrna)–eleme, elemi
fig basket–cabas
fight–affray, battle, bout, brawl, combat, combativeness, conflict, contest, duel, fray, melee, mell, pugnacity, scrap, strife, strike, struggle, tilt, war
fight (coll.)–scrap
fight (general)–melee
fighter–battler, champion, combatant, duelist, scrapper, soldier, warrior
fighters (single combat)–duelists
fighting–belligerent, militant, pugnacious, warlike
figment–fiction, invention
figurative use of words–trope
figure–digit, form, number, numeral, outline, shape
figure (depiction of praying)–orant
figure (female in prayer)–orant
figure (five-sided plane)–pentagon
figure (four-sided)–quadrilateral
figure (geometrical)–cone, ellipse, lune, oblong, prism, rhomb, rhombus, triangle
figure (geometrical solid)–cone, parallelepipedon
figure (male supporting column)–Atlantes, telamon
figure (nine-sided)–nonagon
figure (oval)–ellipse
figure (praying)–orant

figure (praying female) – orant
figure (star-shaped)–pentacle
figure (symbolic)–emblem
figure (ten-sided)–decagon
figure (undraped)–nude
figure bound by two intersecting arcs of circles–lune
figure of comparison–simile
figure of equal angles–isagon, isogon
figure of man (arch.)–elamon
figure of speech–imagery, metaphor, simile, trope
figure of speech (rhetorical)–aporia
figure out–dope, solve
figured (slang)–doped
figures continually repeated in certain decimals–repetend
figures of discourse–orant
figurine (female)–orant
Fijian drug–tonga
filament–hair, thread
filament (dermal)–hair
filament (fine)–fiber, fibre, thread
filament (flax)–harl
filament (growing out of animal's skin)–hair
filament lamp–incandescent
filao–beefwood
filbert–corylus, hazel, nut
filch–pilfer, steal
file–rasp, rate
files (combmaking)–carlets, grailles, grails
filing–limation
Filipino–see Philippine
fill–glut, gorge, hold, occupy, permeate, suffuse
fill again–replenish
fill out–distend, enlarge, extend, pad
fill up or supply (dial.)–plenish
fille–daughter, girl
filled–replete, sated
filled to capacity–loaded, replete, S.R.O., sated, saturated
filled to repletion–saturated

filled with crevices–areolar
filled with interstices–areolar
fillet–anadem, band, ribbon, snood
fillet (bottom of frieze)–taenia
fillet (hair)–snood
fillet (heraldic)–orle
fillet (lady's)–miter
fillet (narrow)–orle
fillet (narrow woven)–ribbon, tape
fillet (top of pillar)–orle
fillet (worn in hair)–snood
filling (dental)–inlay
filly–colt, foal
film–haze, layer, pellicle, photograph, skin, veil
film (green on copper)–patina
film (of liquid impurities)–scum
filmy – clouded, cloudy, gauzy, misty
filter–drain, percolate, strain
filth–dirt, slut, squalor, vermin
filthy–dirty, foul, gross, impure, licentious, low, obscene, polluting, squalid, unclean, vile
filthy lucre (coll.)–money
fimbriate–fringed
fin (airship vertical)–keel
fin (under)–ventral
final–conclusive, decisive, definite, determinating, eventual, last, ultimate
final outcome–issue, upshot
final parts–shanks
finale–coda, close, conclusion, end, termination
finality–conclusiveness, decisiveness, termination
financial–fiscal, monetary, pecuniary, solvent
finch–serin, siskin
finch (beautifully colored)–pape
finch (black and white)–snowflake
finch (canary-like)–serin
finch (Eur.)–moro, terin
finch (house)–linnet
finch (small)–linnet, serin

finch (yellow, small)–serin
find–discover, locate
find direction–orient
find fault–carp, complain, criticise, criticize
find fault with–cavil
find guilty convict
find one's bearing–orient
find out–detect, discover
find position of–locate
find solution–solve
fine–absolute, amerce, dandy, elegant, fragile, good, handsome, penalty, pure, pulverized, rare, sharp, sheer, skillful, slight, superior, surpassing
fine and delicate–ethereal, lacy
fine for murder (Scot. law)–cro
fine sensitiveness–delicacy
finely–nicely
finery – beauty, elegance, gaud, lavishness
finesse–artifice, clearness, cunning, purity, refinement, serene, stratagem, subtlety, thinness
finger–handle, meddle, toy
finger (fore)–index
finger (little)–minimus
fingernail moon–lunule
fingerprint mark–arch, composite, loop, whorl
fingerstall–cot
finial (pagoda)–tee
finial of spire–epi
finical–dainty, dapper, delicate, fastidious, finicking, foppish, jaunty, meticulous, mincing, nice, overscrupulous, spruce, squeamish
finis–conclusion, end, goal
finish–close, complete, completion, conclude, consummate, end, perfection, surface, terminate
finish (dull)–mat, matte
finish (hard)–enamel
finished–climaxed, closed, completed, concluded, done, ended, over, perfected, polished, refined, stopped, terminated

finished (poetic)–oer
finished (roughly and imperfect)–rude
finished with shingle gloss–lustered
finisher (file)–ender
finite–conditioned, definable, limited, restricted, terminable
Finland–Suomi
Finn–Estonian, Lapp, Magyar, Ostyak, Samoyed, Ugric
Finn (anc.)–Avar
Finns–Suomi
Finnish city–Aba, Abo, Helsingfors
Finnish coin–markka (ni., br.), penni (ac.)
Finnish composer–Sibelius
Finnish division–Ijore
Finnish government–Abo
Finnish island–Aland
Finnish isthmus–Karelia
Finnish lake–Enare
Finnish measure–fathom, kannu, ottinger, sjomil, tunland, tunnland, tunna, verst
Finnish mile (sea)–sjomil
Finnish port–Abo
Finnish weight–skalpund
fire–detonate, explode, fever, flame, heat, ignite, illumine, incite, inflammation, inspire, kindle, light, shoot
fire (artillery, concentrated delivery of)–barrage
fire (large, destructive)–conflagration
firearm–gun, musket, piece, revolver, rifle
firearm (small antique)–demihag
firearms (simultaneous discharge of)–fusillade
fireback–reredos
fire basket–cresset, grate
firecracker–petard
firedog–andiron
fire-eater–fireman
fire extinguisher–pyrene, pyroleter
fire feeder–fueler, stoker
fire god–Vulcan

fire god (Vedic)–Angi
fireman–stoker
fireplace (open)–forge
fireplace (Scot.)–ingle
fireplace facing–mantel
fireplace part–hob
firewood (stick of)–billet
fireworks – fizgigs, girandoles, rockets
fireworks (resembling)–pyrotechnical
fireworks (scintillating)–sparklers
fire worshiper–Parsee, Parsi
fired–discharged, lit, shot
firing (willful)–arson
firm – compact, decided, dense, determined, faithful, fast, fixed, hard, immovable, rigid, secure, solid, sound, stable, stanch, staunch, steadfast, steady, stout, substantial, sure, tight, trig, unslipping, unyielding
firmament–heavens, sky
firmly implanted–rooted
firmness–constancy, immobility, indissolubility, solidity, stability, steadiness, tenacity
firn–neve
firs (genus of)–abies
first–earliest, foremost, highest, initial, leading, original, primal, primary, prime, primordial, principal
first appearance–debut, premiere
first beginning–origin
first born (law)–eigne
first Christian martyr–Stephen
first class–excellent, prime
first handwriting word–mene, tekel, upharsin
first performance–premiere
first principle–element
first rate–admirable, good, skookum
first sawing off log–slab
first stages–inchoate, rudimentary
firth–estuary
fiscal–financial

fish–angle, troll
fish (Alaska, large, food, between white fish and salmon)–inconnu
fish (allied to id)–orf
fish (American fresh water) –darter
fish (attaching self to other fish)–pega, remora
fish (bait)–killifish, killy
fish (barracuda, small)–spet
fish (black)–tautog
fish (brilliant colored)–opah
fish (California rock)–reina, rena
fish (carp family)–id, ide
fish (caviar yielding)–sterlet
fish (certain, pert. to)–teleost
fish (cigar)–scad
fish (cod family)–lote
fish (cyprinoid)–dace, id, ide
fish (dark blue, food)–wahoo
fish (devil)–manta
fish (edible)–tautog
fish (edible marine)–wrasse
fish (eel-like)–conger, eelpout, lamprey, ling, opah
fish (elasmo branch)–ray
fish (elongated)–eel
fish (Eur.)–id, ide, meagre
fish (Eur., small)–dace
fish (fabled, upholding universe)–mah
fish (flat)–dab, flounder, fluke, sole
fish (food)–bass, cod, eel, gar, hake, halibut, herring, mackerel, mullet, salmon, scup, shad, snapper, tile, trout, tuna
fish (fresh water)–dace, darter, sucker
fish (friar)–scad
fish (gadoid)–cod
fish (game)–bass, grayling, marlin, salmon, swordfish, tarpon, trout, tuna
fish (herring-like)–sprat
fish (horse mackerel)–tunny
fish (kind of)–alewife, barbel, bass, bream, carp, cat, chub, cod, dab, dace, eel, haddock, id, ide, ling, mero, mola, mullet, pike,

pilchard, porgy, pout, rena, roach, ruff, ruffe, sauger, scup, shad, shiner, skate, smelt, sole, spot, tomcod, trout, tuna, turbot, wrasse
fish (lancet)–serra
fish (land-traveling)–anabas
fish (large)–opah, tarpon, sennett
fish (large food)–sturgeon
fish (large food, Alaska, between white fish and salmon)–inconnu
fish (largest fresh water)–arapaima
fish (large game)–maskalonge, muskellunge, maskinonge
fish (large scaled)–escolar
fish (little)–id, ide, minnow, sprat
fish (marine)–angler, opah, tarpon, wrasse
fish (milk)–awa, sabalo
fish (mormyroid of Nile)–erse
fish (newly hatched brood of)–fry
fish (Nile)–saide
fish (ocean)–opah
fish (of cod family)–gadoid, ling
fish (one-horned)–monoceros
fish (parasitic)–remora
fish (peacock)–wrasse
fish (perch-like)–darter
fish (percoid)–perch
fish (pike-like)–gar, luce
fish (pilot)–romero
fish (regarded as upholding universe, myth.)–mah
fish (rock)–reina, rena
fish (salmonoid) – ayu, powan
fish (Samoan food)–sesele
fish (scombroid)–ceros
fish (shad-like)–alewife
fish (slender)–eel, runner
fish (small)–dace, id, ide, minnow, riggle, sardine, seahorse, shiner, sprat
fish (small bait)–killifish, killy
fish (small barracuda)–spet

fish (small food)–cunner
fish (small shell)–limpet
fish (sparoid)–sar, sargo, tai
fish (sparoid food)–porgy
fish (star)–asteria
fish (sucking)–remora
fish (synodontoid)–tirus
fish (teleost)–eel
fish (thick-scaled food)–scup
fish (toad)–sapo, slimer
fish (total haul)–mess
fish (tunny)–tuna
fish (unicorn)–unie
fish (upholding universe, fabled)–mah
fish (used for bait)–killifish, killy
fish (voracious)–barracuda, shark
fish (yielding superior caviar)–sterlet
fish (young)–fry
fish basket–creel
fish basket (Cornwall)–caul
fish by trolling–drail
fish-catching fence (of twigs)–weir
fish from moving boat–troll
fish gig–spear
fish hide (close fitting)–eelskin
fishhook (part of)–barb
fishhook gut–snell
fishhook line–snell
fish-like vertebrate–ray
fish limb–fin
fishline snell–snood
fish net–seine, trawl
fish organ (breathing)–gill
fish process (wing-like)–fin
fish roe–caviar
fish sauce–alec
fish spear–gig
fish tackle part–snell
fish through ice with gaff–chug
fish trap–eelpot, weir
fish with spearlike snout–gar
fisher (kind of)–eeler, seiner, trawler, troller
fisher (the)–Wejack
fisherman–angler, trawler, Izaak Walton
fishes (female, dial.)–rauns

fishing appurtenance–cork, float

fishing duck–merganser

fishing eagle–osprey

fishing fly (artificial)–sedge

fishing net–lam, seine

fishing vessel–seiner, smack, trawler

fishy–dull, extravagant, improbable, lusterless, suspicious, unreliable, vacant

fissate–divided, fissured

fissile rock–shale

fissure–chine, cleft, crack, crevice, gap, lode, rift, rima, seam, vein

fissure (biology)–rima

fissure (ore-filled)–lode

fissure (small)–crack, crevice

fissured–rimate

fissures (full of)–rimose

fit–able, adapt, adapted, appropriate, attack, fancy, outbreak, proper, qualified, stroke, suitable, suited, whim

fit (petulant)–tantrum

fit for cultivation–arable

fit into groove–dado

fit of fury–rage

fit of petulance–huff, tantrum

fit of resentment–pique

fit of temperament–mood

fit out–equipment, outfit

fit to can (as fruit)–preservable

fit together–dovetail, mesh, nest

fit together (as gears)–mesh

fit together closely (shipbuilding)–fay

fitful–capricious, convulsive, impulsive, intermittent, irregular, restless, spasmodic, unstable, variable

fitful (intermittent)–spasmodic

fitly–duly, suitably

fitness–decorum

fitter–abler

fitting–appropriate, apt, become, meet, pat, proper, seemly, suitable

fitting for use–adapting

five (comb. form)–penta

five-cornered (obs.)–pentagonous

five-dollar bill–fin, "V"

Five Nations (Indian confederacy)–Cayugas, Mohawks, Oneidas, Onondagas, Senecas

five-year period–lustrum, pentad

fix–anchor, cement, confirm, define, delimit, establish, fasten, imbed, limit, mend, moor, nail, peg, pin, repair, set, settle, stabilize

fix a price–charge

fix deeply–imbed, stamp

fix firmly–anchor, brace, cement, moor, set

fix in a situation–set

fix in steady attention–nail

fixed allowance–ration, remittance, stipend

fixed by choice–elective

fixed charge–rate

fixed element (attribute)–inhere

fixed mode of action–habit

fixed sound–toned

fixed star–Vega

fixes beforehand–predetermine

fizgig–fireworks, whirligig

flabby–feeble, flaccid, limp, weak, yielding

flabellate–fan-shaped

flabrum–fan, flabellum

flaccid–flabby, limp, yielding

flag–banner, colors, decline, fail, fane, flower, pennant, pennon, pine, sag, signal, standard, streamer

flag (cavalry)–standard

flag (lower or haul down)–strike

flag (military)–colors

flag (mounted troop)–guidon

flag (pirate)–Roger

flag (ribbon-like)–streamer

flag (small) – banderole, guidon

flag (small position marker)–fanion

flag (standard)–vexillum

flag (swallow-tailed)–burgee

flagging–languid, spiritless, weak

flagitious–criminal, flagrant, heinous, scandalous, wicked

flagon–bottle, stoup, vessel

flagrant – abandoned, atrocious, glaring, hateful, heinous, monstrous, nefarious, odious, outrageous, profligate, villainous, violent, wanton

flagstone layers–pavers

flail–beat, flog, thrash

flam–cajole, cheat, deception, falsehood, pretext, trick

flambeau (flambeaux, pl.)–torch

flamboyant–flamelike, florid, ornate, resplendent

flame–ardor, blaze, brightness, flare, glare, glow, leye, light

flame condenser (of lamp)–cric

flank bone–ilium, ilia (pl.)

flap–tab

flap (loose)–lappet

flap (side of saddle)–skirt

flare–flame, flicker, illuminate, light, outburst, signal, spread

flare (railroad)–fusee

flaring–dazzling, gaudy, glaring

flaring out widely (Fr.)–evase

flash–blaze, burst, glance, gleam, glimmer, glint, glisten, glitter, shimmer, spark, sparkle

flash out–glint

flashing–meteoric, snapping

flashy–gaudy, gay, showy, sporty

flashy ornaments–gauds

flask (earthenware ointment)–ampulla

flask (glass ointment)–ampulla

flask (leather, classical, arch.)–olpe

flask (oil, ointment)–aryballos, aryballus

flask (water-carrying)–canteen

flat–blunt, boring, decided, dreary, horizontal, insipid, level, plane, unbroken, uniform, vapid

flat (musical)–molle

flat and circular–discoid

flatboat–ark, barge, scow

flatboat (river)–ark

flat-breasted–ratite

flat failure–dud, flop

flatfish–dab, flounder, fluke, sand dab, sole

flat piece–slab

flat surface (pert. to)–areal

flatten–deject, depress, discourage, dishearten, dispirit, even, prostrate, smooth

flatten at poles–oblate

flatter–adulate, blarney, float, flutter, ingratiate

flatter (Australian)–smooge

flatter (servile manner)–adulate

flatterer–courtier

flattering–complimenting

flattering talk–palaver

flattery–blarney, cajolery, compliment, fawning, obsequiousness, palaver

flattery (fulsome)–adulation

flaunt–boast, brandish, display, parade, vaunt, wave

flavor–aroma, perfume, piquancy, sapor, savor, scent, season, tang, taste, zest

flavoring shrub–mint, sage

flavory–tasty

flaw–blemish, breach, cleft, defect, fracture, imperfection, rift

flaw in fabrics–rase

flawless–perfect, sound

flax (coarse broken)–tow

flax derivative–linin

flax refuse (Scot.)–pob

flaxen–tow

flaxen cloth–linen

flaxseed–linseed

flay–censure, excoriate, reprove, skin

fleam–lancet, millstream, stream

flection–bending, bent, flexion, turning

flee–abandon, disappear, fly, forsake, speed, vanish

flee (slang)–lam

fleece–despoil, flay, fleck, sheer, wool

fleece (poorest part)–abb

fleece (sheep, two-year-old)–teg

fleer–flout, gibe, jeer, mock, scoff, sneer, taunt

fleet–drift, evanescent, fast, flit, float, hasten, navy, sail, speedy, swift, swim, transitory

fleet (old wording)–evand

fleeting–evanescent, passing, transient

flesh–body, family, kin, meat, mortality, muscle, sensuality

fleshy–beefy, carnal, carnose, corpulent, fat, plump, pulpy, stout

fleshy fruit–berry, drupe, pear, pome

fleur-de-lis–iris, lis

flew (lightly and quickly)–flitted

flew high–soared

flew in an airplane–aviated

flexible–limber, limp, lissome, lithe, pliant, supple

flexible shoot–bine

flexible tube–hose

flexion of limbs (forcible)–anaclasis

flicker–flit, flutter, waver

flier–ace, airman, aviator, pilot

flight–exodus, flock, hegira, hop, migration, swarming

flight (disorderly)–rout

flight (sudden)–stampede

flight (wild headlong)–stampede

flight of steps (outdoor)–perron

flight of wild fowl–skein

flighty–barmy, capricious, fitful, foolish, freakish

flimflam–deception, decep-

tive, humbug, nonsense, nonsensical, swindle, trick, trifling

flimmer–flicker, glimmer

flimsy–feeble, frail, limp, paltry, shallow, sleazy, slimsy, superficial, unsubstantial, vain, weak

flinch–flense, game, recoil, shrink, start, wince

fling–hurl, shy, sling, throw, toss

flint–firestone

flint (impure form)–chert

flip–fillip, somersault, toss

flippant–fluent, glib

flipper–arm, fin, hand, paw

flirt–dally, mash, play, toss, toy, trifle

flirt (female)–coquette

flirt (male)–coquet, masher, philanderer, trifler

flit–flicker, flutter, hover

flitter–flicker, flutter, hover, rag, tatter

flittermouse–bat

float–balsa, hove, hover, raft, ride, sail, soar

float (gently)–waft

float (mill wheel)–ladle

floating–awash, natant

floating at random–adrift

floating in water–natant

floats aimlessly–drifts

flock – assemblage, bevy, company, covey, drove, flight, fold, herd, multitude, pack, shoal, swarm

flock (partridge)–covey

flock (walrus)–pod

flock of herons–sedge

flock of pheasants–nid, nide, nye

flocks (god of)–Pan

floe–berg

flog–beat, cane, cat, larrup, lash, strike, tan, wale, whip

flogging (sound, slang)–larrup

flood–deluge, excess, freshet, inundate, overflow, sea, spate, torrent

flood (Eng.)–spate

flood (pert. to)–diluwan

flood (tidal)–eagre

flood gate–sluice
floor–defeat, pave, silence, story
floor (mine gallery)–sill
floor plank (pontoon bridge) –chess
flora–plants
Florentine family (famous)– Medici
floret bract–palea
florid–figurative, flowery, ornate, rhetorical, rubicund, ruddy
Florida balsam–torchwood
Florida city–Miami, Palatka, Pensacola, Tampa
Florida county–Dade
Florida fish (game)–tarpon
Florida Indian–Seminole
Florida people (inferior white)–conchs
Florida region–Everglades
floss–sleave, waste
flotilla–fleet
flounce–flap, flounder, frill, struggle
flounder–dab, fluke, struggle, stumble, turbot
flounder (summer)–plaice
flour–farina, meal, powder, sprinkle
flour (coarse)–middlings
flour (mesquite bean)–pinole
flour (old word)–padar
flour (unbolted)–meal
flour and butter mixture (gravy)–roux
flour maker–miller
flourish–arpeggio, brandish, display, embellish, grow, ornament, ostentation, prosper, roulade, show, thrive
flourish at end of signature –paraph
flourishing–fat
flout–fleer, gibe, insult, jeer, mock, scoff, scout, sneer, taunt
flow–current, flutter, flux, glide, gush, issue, outpouring, pour, roll, run, stream, streaming, teem
flow (abundant)–afflux
flow (copious)–river

flow (copiously)–gush
flow (gushing)–jet
flow (steady)–stream
flow (tidal high rapid)–bore
flow along–lave
flow back–ebb, recede
flow off gradually–drain
flow out–issue, spill
flow through pores–exude
flowed in jets – gushed, spurted, spurtled
flower–aster, best, bloom, blossom, blow, bud, crocus, dahlia, develop, elite, essence, iris, ixia, orchid, pink, rose, tulip, unfold
flower (delicate pink)–rhodora
flower (delicate wild)–bluet
flower (external part)–calyx
flower (garden)–gladiolus
flower (obs.)–pense
flower (part of)–anther, bract, calyx, petal, stem, stamen, torus
flower (passion)–maypop
flower (prickly)–burr
flower (showy)–phlox
flower (spike of)–ament, spadix
flower (spring)–arbutus, hepatica, tulip
flower (the)–elite
flower (white)–gowan
flower (wild) – anemone, bluebell, daisy, innocence, lupine, sage
flower (wild delicate)–bluet
flower (wind)–anemone
flower (yellow)–gowan
flower band–wreath
flower bed (ornamented arrangement of)–parterre
flower bud (used in sauces) –caper
flower cluster (flat round)– umbel
flower cluster (flat-topped)– cyme
flower cluster (spherical)– glomerule
flower cluster leaf–bract
flower clusters–racemes
flower clusters (arranged in) –paniculate, racemose

flower leaf (modified in cluster)–bract
flower of society–elite, four hundred
flower part–bract, corolla
flower stalk–peduncle, petiole
flowering plant–arum, calla, canna, geranium, orpin, petunia
flowering plant (water)–lotos, lotus
flowering shrub–oleaster, syringa
flowerless plants–ferns, lichens
flowers (genus of)–rosa
flowers (goddess of)–Flora
flowers (pert. to)–floral
flowers (small bunch of)– nosegay
flowing–copious, cursive, fluent, fluxing, transitive
flowing from source–emanate
flowing oil well–gusher
flowing together–confluent
flows (tidal)–eagres
fluctuate–irresolute, oscillate, vacillate, vary, veer, vibrate, undetermined, undulate, unsteady, waver
flue–barb, chimney, fluke, tunnel
fluent–copious, eloquent, facile, flowing, fluid, glib, ready, smooth, talkative, voluble
fluent in speech–verbose, voluble
fluff–down, floss
fluffy–downy, fuzzy, soft
fluid–flowing, liquid, water, watery
fluid (animal, watery part)– serum
fluid (containing essential oils)–nerol
fluid (cuttlefish, protective) –ink
fluid (elastic)–gas
fluid (ethereal, in God's veins)–ichor, icor
fluid (lacteal)–milk
fluid (lighter than air)–ether
fluid (liver)–bile

fluid (medical)–serum, sera (pl.)
fluid (unctuous)–oil
fluidize by heat–fusile
fluke–fish, flounder
flume–sluice
flung–pelt, threw
flunk–fail
flunky–cookee, footman, servant
fluorite–fluor, flux
flurry–ado, agitation, bustle, fluster, flutter, gust, squall
flush–abundant, affluent, blush, lavish, prodigal, prosperous, redden, rosiness, thrill
flush with success–elate
flushes–reddens, roses
fluster–flurry, shake
flute–crimp
flute player–piper
flutter–agitation, confusion, disorder, flap, flit, hover, palpitate, ruffle, wave, waver
flutter (in a)–pitapat
flutter over–float, hover
flux–flowing, fuse, outflow, smalt
flux (soldering)–resin, rosin
flux (volatile)–smear
fly–disappear, flee, float, hop, insect, leap, melt, soar, spring, vanish, wing
fly (artificial, used in fishing)–sedge
fly (as clouds)–scud
fly (caddis)–cadew
fly (horse)–bot
fly (kind of)–bot, breeze, gadfly, gnat, horse, house, tsetse
fly (moth, wormlike)–caterpillar
fly (poisonous)–tsetse
fly (small)–gnat, midge
fly before the wind–scud
fly quickly–flit
flying–awing, floating, volant, waving
flying adder–dragonfly
flying boat–amphibian, seaplane
flying body–meteor

Flying Dutchman heroine–Senta
flying machine–aerostat, gyroplane, plane
fly's enemy (natural)–spider
foal–colt, filly
foam–froth, fume, scum, spume
foaming–spumous
fob–cheat, impose, ornament, pocket, trick
focus–center, concentrate, converge
focusing–concentrating
fodder–feed, forage, silage
fodder (winter)–hay, silage
fodder pit–silo
fodder stored in silos–silage
fodder storing place–haymow
foe–adverse, enemy, hostile, rival
fog–daze, haze, mist, nebula, stupor, vapor
fog (Scot.)–haar
fog (Sierra Nevada dense winter)–pogonip
foggy–beclouded, cloudy, confused, dense, dim, dull, hazy, misty, muddled, obscure, roky
foghorn–siren
fogle–handkerchief
foible–fault, imperfection, infirmity, weakness
foil–defeat, frustrate, repulse
foiled (coll.)–stumped
foird (Danish)–ise
fold–cote, crease, double, envelop, furl, infold, lap, loop, pen, plait, pleat, ply, rimple, ruga, tuck
fold (like fan)–plicate
fold (loose)–lappet
fold of skin (pendulous)–dewlap
folder–leaflet, pamphlet
foliage–leafage, leaves
folio (abbr.)–fo
folk (learned)–pedants
folk song (depressing)–blues
folklore genie–sandman
follow–after, ensue, imitate, next, practice, pursue, replace, result, shadow, suc-

ceed, supervene, supplant, tail
follow closely–dog, heel, supervene, tail
follow exactly–trace
follow persistently–dog, tail
follow secretly–shadow
follow slowly–draggle
follow the chase–hunt
follow up–welled
followed–came
followed (coll.) – dogged, tailed
followed behind–dogged, lagged, shadowed, tailed, trailed
followed by scent–nosed
followed order–obeyed
follower–adherent, dependent, devotee, disciple, ensuer, fan, henchman, ite, partisan, satellite, son, votary
follower (of certain religion)–Christian
follower (suffix)–lie
follower of–ite
follower of early theologian–Arian
follower of Falstaff–Nym
following–ensuing, next, sequent, suant, subsequent, succeeding, successive, trailing
following after one's death–posthumous
following exact words–literal
following laws of arithmetical algebra–scalor
following stories–sequels
follows hard upon–courses
folly–foolishness, imprudence, indiscretion, lewdness, lunacy, madness, silliness, wantonness
foment–abet, agitate, arouse, excite, incite, spur
fomentation – encouragement, excitation, instigation, stupes
fond–amorous, ardent, doting, enamored, loving, passionate
fond of (excessively)–uxorious

fond of (overly)–dote
fond of drink–bibulous
fond of the sea–thalassophilous
fonda–hotel, inn
fondle–blandish, caress, coddle, cosset, dandle, neck, pamper, pet
fondling–fool, ninny, pet, simpleton
fondly–affectionately, dearly, tenderly
fondness–affection, attachment, predilection, tenderness
font (baptizing)–piscina
food–aliment, bread, diet, fare, meat, nutriment, viands, victuals
food (cassava root)–tapioca
food (coll.)–chow, grub
food (condensed, used by Arctic explorers)–pemmican
food (cow's chewed)–cud
food (delicate)–cate
food (eating of dried)–xerophagia, xerophagy
food (large shell sea)–abalone
food (luxuriant, arch.)–cates
food (slang)–chow, eats, victuals
food (small bit of)–morsel
food (soft)–pap
food (solid)–meat
food (stock of)–foray
food (tapioca-like)–salep
food (taro root)–poi
food article–tripe
food constituent (essential to health)–vitamin
food dressing–sauce
food element (nutritious)–gluten
food for animals–forage
food for luring–bait, chum
food from heaven–manna
food of gods–ambrosia
food regime–diet
food sauce–condiment
food stuff (prepared grain)–cereal
food used by Northern explorers (dried)–pemmican
fool–buffoon, butt, dolt,

dupe, idiot, jester, moron, nizey, nizy, simpleton
fool (aged)–dotard
fooled (easily)–gullible
foolhardy–adventurous, rash
foolish – absurd, asinine, brainless, fatuous, harish, idiotic, imprudent, inane, irrational, ludicrous, mad, preposterous, raca, rash, senseless, silly, simple, stupid, witless
foolish behavior–simples
foolishness–absurdity, folly, levity
fool's gold–pyrite
fool's paradise–limbo
foot–paw, pes
foot (animal's)–hoof, paw
foot (metric)–anapest, dactyl, spondee
foot (part of)–instep, toe
foot (pert. to)–pedal
foot (poetic three syllables)–anapest
foot (prosodic)–spondee
foot (two long syllables)–spondee
football coach (famous)–Bible, Bierman, Crowley, Jones, Kriesler, Leahy, Little, Rockne, Shaughnessy, Smith, Stagg, Stiner, Thomas, Wade, Warner, Yost, Zuker, Zupke
football play–spinner
football score–down, goal, safety, touchback, touchdown
foot bone–metatarsus, tarsus
foot covering–boot, brogan, sandal, shoe, sock, stocking
footgear (kind of)–patten
foot lever–pedal, treadle
foot-like–pedate
foot-like part–pes
footman–varlet
foot part (horse's, between fetlock and hoof)–pastern
footpath–trail
footprint–trace, track
footrest–footstool, hassock, rail
footstool–hassock

footstool (overstuffed)–ottoman
foot syllable (accented)–arsis
foot traveler–wayfarer
footwear–boot, moccasin, sandal, shoe, slipper
footed (two)–bipedal
footless–apod, apoda, apodal, apode, clumsy, inapt, stupid
footless animals–apod, apoda, apode
fop–dandy, dude
foppish–dandyish, dapper, finical, spruce
for–pro
for example (abbr.)–e.g.
for fear that–lest
for instance–as
for nothing–gratis, gratuity, lagniappe, lanyap
for the most part–generally
forage–browse, mast, pasturage, ravage, spoil
forage herb–clover
foray–pillage, raid, ravage
foray (Scot.)–rade
forbade–interdicted
forbear–abstain, ancestor, avoid, desist, forefather, parent, refrain, shun, sire
forbearance–abstinence, lenity, mercy, mildness, patience, tolerance
forbearing–desisting, patient
forbid–ban, debar, disallow, impede, inhibit, interdict, preclude, prohibit, proscribe, taboo, tabu, veto
forbid (by authority)–prohibit
forbid lawyer to practice–disbar
forbiddance–ban, interdiction, proscription, veto
forbidden–taboo, tabu, tapu
forbidden (Jewish law)–tref
Forbidden City–Lhasa
forbidding – displeasing, fierce, grim, odious, offensive, unpleasant
forbode (forebode)–omen
forbore–spared
force–coerce, compel, compulsion, constrain, constraint, dint, drive, en-

ergy, extort, impel, impetus, make, necessitate, power, press, pressure, puissance, repel, vim, violence, vis

force (alleged)–od

force (armed)–army, posse

force (communicating) – driving

force (creative)–nature

force (hypothetical)–od

force (Latin)–vis

force (mesmeric)–od

force (moving)–agent

force (physical)–nerve

force (power)–dint, steam

force (unit of)–tonal

force (with full)–amain

force air through nose–snort

force air upon–blow

force into smaller space–compress

force of men (coll.)–posse

force units–dynes

forced – compulsory, constrained, involuntary, labored, reluctant

forced feeding–gavage

forceful–dynamic, effective, energetic, mighty, strong, vigorous

forces (aggregate of operating)–dynames

forces (impelling, Latin)–momenta

forces (military)–troops

forcible–cogent, compulsory, impressive, influential, mighty, potent, puissant, violent, weighty

forcibly–amain, vigorously

forcibly seized without right –usurp

ford–wade

fore–former, front, journey, prior, track, way

forebear–ancestor, forefather, parent, sire

forebear (pert. to)–ancestral

forebode–augur, betoken, foretell, predict, presage, prognostication

foreboding – apprehension, presagement, presentiment

foreboding (gloomy)–pessimistic

foreboding (uttered) – croaked

foreboding disaster or evil–sinister

forecast–bode, foreordain, foretell, foretoken, predetermine, predict, prediction, scheme

forecast of one's life–fortune

forecaster – meteorologist, seer

forecaster (racing)–dopester

forecasting the future–oracular

foreclose–debar, hinder, preclude, prevent

foredoom–destiny, predestine

foredoomed to death–fey

forefather–ancestor, elder, parent, sire

forefinger–index

foregather–assemble, convene, encounter, meet

forego–precede, refrain, renounce, waive

foregoing–above, antecedent, past

foregone–past, previous

foregone conclusion – certainty

forehead–brow, sinciput

forehead (pert. to)–metopig

foreign–adventitious, alien, distant, exotic, extraneous, extrinsic, outlandish, remote

foreign (comb. form)–xeno

foreign matter insertion–interpolation

foreign service residence–consulate

foreigners–aliens, outsiders, strangers, tramontanes, ultramontanes

foreknow–preconceive

foreland–headland, promontory

forelock–bang, linchpin

foreman–boss, leader, supervisor

foremost–first, leading, supreme

forensic – argumentative, rhetorical

foreordain–destine, predestinate, predetermine, preordain

foreordinates–predestinates

forepart–front

forerun–foreshadow, herald, introduce, prefigure, prelude

forerunner–augury, forefather, harbinger, herald, messenger, omen, precursor, progenitor, sign

foreshank–shin

foresight–prevision, prevoyance, providence

forest–timber, wold, wood, woodland

forest deity–Aegipan

forest fire locator–alidade

forest glade–camas

forest god–Pan

forest open space–glade

forest warden–ranger

forestall–anticipate, hinder, intercept, prevent

foretell–augur, forebode, forecast, portend, predict, presage, prognosticate, prophetic, prophesy

foretell (Scot.)–spae

forethought – anticipation, premeditation, provident, prudence

foretoken–omen, prognosticate

foretooth–biter, cutter

forever – ay, aye, always, ceaselessly, constantly, continually, endless, ever, everlastingly, interminably, invariably, perpetual, perpetually, unceasingly, unchangeably

forever (Maori)–ake

forewarning–portent

foreword–preamble, preface, proem

forfeit–lose, mulct, penalty

forfeiture–amercement, fine, mulct, penalty

forfend–avert, forbid, prevent, prohibit

forfex–shears

forficulate–forked, furcate

forgather–assemble, con-vene, encounter, meet

forge–counterfeit, falsify, feign, smithy, swinge

forge nozzle–tew

forge tool cooling trough–bosh

forgery–counterfeit, fabrica-tion, falsification, sham

forget–disregard, omit

forgetful–careless, heedless, inattentive, neglectful

forgetfulness–amnesia, am-nesty, Lethe, oblivion

forgive–condone, excuse, pardon, remit, spare

forgiveness–absolution, con-donation, pardon, remis-sion

forgiving–humane, merci-ful, placable, remissive

forgo–forfeit, forsake, leave, neglect, overlook, relin-quish

forhoo (Scot.)–abandon, de-spise

forked–bifid, bifurcated, branched, divided

forlorn–abandoned, abject, bereft, deserted, desolate, destitute, forsaken, friend-less, helpless, pitiable, reft

form–build, conceive, con-figuration, conformation, contour, create, figure, guise, invent, model, mold, outline, profile, shape

form (display)–rack

form (good)–chic

form (hollow)–shell

form (liturgical)–service

form (philosophy)–eidos

form (primitive)–prototype

form (shoe)–last, tree

form (wormlike, insect)–larva

form electric luminous glow –arc

form for displaying mer-chandise–rack

form into chain–catenate

form into head (as cabbage, Eng.)–loave

form mental conception–ideate

form molding with plaster–run

form of architecture (pert. to)–Doric

form of greeting–bow

form of music (simplest choral)–chant

form of speech–phrase

form request–petition

form thought (to)–ideate

form used in stamping–die

forms (carved)–statuary

formal–affected, ceremoni-al, exact, methodical, out-ward, precise, prim, sol-emn, starched, stiff, stilted, superficial

formal bestowal–presenta-tion

formalist in teaching–ped-ant

formalities (conventional)–etiquette

formality–ceremony, con-ventionality, precise, stiff

formally religious–Pharisaic

format–shape, size, style

formation (geologic)–ter-rain, terrane

formation (harrow-like battle)–herse

formation (sand)–dene, dune

formation of troops–line

formative–plastic

formed–decided, matured, settled

formed (spiral)–helix

formed a connecting link–mediated

formed an electric arc–arced

formed at foot of mountain –piedmont

formed by law–corporate

formed by lips–labial

formed by the sea–marine

formed into chain–catenate

formed into hardened mass–caked, congealed, frozen

formed into kind of fabric–knitted

formed like twisted chain–torquated

formed of small pieces (like mosaic)–tesseral

formed on earth's surface–epigene

former–antecedent, erst, late, old, once, whilom

former (prefix)–ex

former officer–AGA

former ruler–Tsar

former time–old, past

formerly–aforetime, erst, erstwhile, heretofore, nee, once, onetime, sometime, then

formerly (in distant past)–erst

formicary–anthill

formicidae–ants

formicids–ants, emmets

formidable–alarming, dread-ful, fearful, menacing, re-doubtable, terrible, threat-ening

formless–amorphous, arupa, chaotic, indeterminate, shapeless

Formosa city – Dai-Hoku, Taipei

formula–recipe

forsake – abandon, avoid, deny, depart, desert, leave, quit, refuse, reject, re-nounce, shun, surrender, withdraw

forsake of–after

forsaken–deserted, forlorn, lorn

forsaken (desolate)–lorn

forspeak – asperse, bewitch, curse, forbid, renounce

forswear–abjure, deny, per-jure, reject, renounce

fort–bulwark, castle

fort (inner wall)–escarp

fort (part of)–redan

forth–accomplish, forward, manage, onward, out, outward

forthwith – immediately, now

fortification–bastion, citadel, defense, fortress, ravelin, redan, stronghold, wall

fortification (of felled trees) –abatis

fortification (part of)–bar-bette, redan

fortification (salient angle)–redan

fortification (traverse)–parados

fortification angle (projecting)–bastion

fortified place (small)–redoubt

fortified shelter–pillbox

fortifies–arms, mans

fortify–arm, man, spike, strengthen

fortitude–bravery, courage, endurance, impregnability, resoluteness, resolution, strength

fortress–castle, citadel, keep

fortress (part of)–redan

fortress (projecting part)–bastion

fortress (small)–bastille, castlet

fortuitous–accidental

fortuity–accidence, chance

fortunate – favored, hap, happy, lucky, prosperous, successful

fortunate (old word)–edi

fortunate periods–ups

fortune–circumstances, destiny, doom, estate, fate, lot, luck, prosperity, success

fortune (gypsy)–bahi

43,560 square feet–acre

forward–abet, ahead, aid, along, audacious, bright, encourage, front, further, help, impudent, on, onward, pert, relay, send, ship, to

forward (piquantly)–saucy

forward part–front

foss (fosse)–canal, ditch, grave, pit, trench

fossil of tun shell–dolite

foster–cherish, cultivate, gratify, indulge, nurse, promote, rear

fought–battled, warred

foul–abusive, contaminate, defame, dirty, entangle, grimy, inauspicious, indecent, malign, noisome, obnoxious, obscene, profane, putrid, rotten, scur-

rilous, stinking, sully, unclean, unfavorable

found–attach, base, cast, endow, establish, fix, foundation, institute

found by keen and persevering search–ferreted

foundation–base, basis, bed, bedding, pedestal

foundation (horizontal)–sill

foundation (loose stone)–riprap

foundation (of a story) – basis, plot

foundation (to form)–underlie

founded–based, predicated

founded on experience–empiric, empirical

founded on imaginary perfection–Utopian

founded on observation–empiric

founded on tests–empirical

founder – dismay, dumbfounder, establisher, fail, miscarry, stumble

founder of British National Art Gallery–Tate

founder of Keystone State–Penn

foundling–nursling, oaf, orphan, waif

fountain – fountainhead, head, reservoir, well

fountain (anc., poetic)–aganippe

fountain nymph–naiad

four (group of)–tetrad

four (the number)–tetrad

fourflusher–pretender

433d asteroid–Eros

fourth estate–newspapers, press

fowl–bird, cock, hen, rooster

fowl (domestic)–Malay, Minorca

fowl (water)–coot

fowl (young)–chick

fowl part (edible)–giblet

fox–tod

fox (female)–vixen

fox (Fr.)–Reynard

fox (male)–stag

fox (name of)–renary, reynard

foxglove leaves (purple)–digitalis

fox's foot–pad

foyer–anteroom, entrance, greenroom, lobby

Fra Diavolo composer–Auber

fracas–brawl, disturbance, melee, set-to, uproar

frache–pan

fraction – fragment, part, piece, scrap

fractious – cross, irritable, peevish, perverse, snappish, ugly, unruly, waspish

fracture – breach, break, crack, rupture

fragile–brittle, frangible, infirm, slight, weak

fragment–bit, chip, fraction, groat, grot, morsel, ort, part, piece, scrap, shard, sherd, shred

fragment (arch.)–ort

fragment (biographical)–anecdote

fragment (earthen)–sherd

fragment (earthly)–shard

fragment (ice afloat)–brash

fragment (remaining)–relic

fragment (small) – flake, flinder

fragment left at meal–ort

fragment of an unfinished work of art–torso

fragment of earthen vessel–shard, sherd

fragrance–aroma, odor, perfume, redolence, smell

fragrant–ambrosial, aromatic, balmy, odoriferous, odorous, olent, redolent, spicy

fragrant ointment–balm

fragrant ointment of ancients–nard

fragrant wood–aloes, cedar

frail–basket, brittle, destructible, sickly, slimsy, weak

frailties (minor)–peccadillos

frailty–failing, imperfection, infirmity

frame–build, construct, fashion, prepare, sill

frame (clothes-drying)–airer
frame (crossbar)–grate
frame (embroidery)–taboret
frame (soapmaker's)–sess
frame (wooden canvas supporting)–easel
frame for carrying thatched straw–knape
frame for drying cloth–tenter
frame for drying skins–herse
frame for stretching–tenter
framed–panelled
framework–cadre, rack, sill, skeleton
framework (braced)–trestle
framework of regiment–cadre
franc piece (twenty)–louis
France (ancient)–Gaul
France (dept. of)–isere, nord, orne (var.)
France (pert. to)–Gallic
France (southern)–Midi
franchised–patented
Franciscan nuns–Clares
frank–artless, candid, direct, free, generous, honest, ingenuous, liberal, naive, open, plain, sincere, straightforward, unreserved, unsophisticated
Franklin's (Benjamin) nickname–Poor Richard
frankly–artlessly, candidly, ingenuously, liberally, openly, plainly, sincerely, undisguisedly, unreservedly, willingly
frankness–candor, openness
Franks (pert. to)–Gallic
Franks' king (752–768)–Pepin
frantic–desperate, distracted, distraught, frenzied, furious, mad
frapped–chill, cooled, freeze, frozen, iced
fraternal–brotherly
fraud–cheat, circumvention, craft, deceit, deception, defraud, fake, guile, imposition, imposture, roguery, sham, stratagem, subtlety, wile
fraudulent–cheating, coun-

terfeit, crafty, cunning, deceiving, deceptive, designing, fake, fallacious, guileful, insidious, quacky, spurious, treacherous, wily
fraudulent (slang)–snide
fraught – burden, cargo, freight, freighted, lade, laden, load
fraught with danger–perilous
fraught with destiny–fatal, fateful
fray–affray, apprehension, broil, combat, commotion, contest, dread, fright, melee, panic, ruction, terror, tumult
freak–caprice, checker, crochet, crotchet, fancy, monster, monstrosity, sport, streak, variegate, whim
freak (mad)–lune
freath–foam, froth, lather
freck–bold, desirous, eager, forward, frack, hale, lusty, ready, stout, strong
Frederick of Saxony (designating elder branch)–Ernestine
free–autonomous, clear, exempt, gratis, immune, inexact, liberate, loose, open, release, rid, unbound, unconfined, uncontrolled, unhampered, unimpeded, unrestrained, unrestricted
free from ambiguity–decided
free from bacteria (harmful)–aseptic
free from binding–loosen
free from danger–rescue
free from deduction–net
free from difficulty–extricate
free from doubt–resolve
free from extremes–equable
free from flesh or flesh juices–maigre
free from integuments–hull
free from irons–unfetter, unmanacle, unshackle

free from knots–enode
free from obstacles–open
free from pathogenic bacteria–sterile
free from pathogenic microorganisms–aseptic
free from restraint–loose, untie
free from self-consciousness –easy
free from slavery–emancipate, manumit
free from suspicion–absolve, acquit, clear, exculpate, exonerate, purge
free from sweetness–sec
free time–leisure, recess, rest
freebooter–filibuster, pillager, pirate
freed–delivered, emancipated, liberated, loosed, manumitted, released, rid, spared, untied
freed from moisture–dehydrated, dried
freedom–emancipation, exemption, independence, liberty, license, manumission
freedom abused–license
freedom from activity–recess, respite, rest
freedom of access–entree
freeholder (petty)–yeoman
freeing–disengaging
freely–abundantly, bounteously, bountiful, copiously, generously, largely, liberally, plenteously, plentifully, readily, spontaneously, unconditionally, unobstructedly, voluntarily, willingly
freeze–chilled, congeal, ice
freeze together again–regelate
freight–cargo, fraught, laden, lading, transport
freight boat–barge, freighter
freighted (filled)–fraught
French (of the)–des
French (very)–tres
French actress–Rosine Bernard, Bernhardt, Duse

French administrative officer–prefect

French African colony–Algeria

French African protectorate –Tunis, Tunisia, Tunisie

French aircraftsman–ac, erk (slang)

French Algerian soldier (infantryman)–turco

French "and"–et

French animal (young)–toto

French annual income–rente

French annuity–rente

French anthem (national)–Marseillaise

French article–la, le, les, un, une

French article (indefinite)–un

French artist–Dore

French author–Dumas, Hugo, Loti, Renan

French bacteriologist–Pasteur

French ball–bal

French bay–Biscay

French biplane–Spad

French bonds–renan, rentes

French-Canadian law (annual payment apart from rent)–cens

French capital–Paris, Vichy

French capital (Isere)–Grenoble

French card game–escarte

French carrying case–etui

French chalk–talc

French cheese–Brie

French chemist–Pasteur

French city–Aix, Amiens, Angers, Aries, Arles, Arras, Bareges, Bordeaux, Brest, Caen, Calais, Clermont, Dijon, Ferrand, Havre, Lemans, Levallois, Lille, Limoges, Lisle, Lyons, Marseille, Metz, Montpellier, Mulhouse, Nance, Nantes, Nesle, Nice, Nimes, Orleans, Paris, Perret, Reims, Rennes, Rheims, Roubaix, Rouen, Saint-Denis, Saint-Etienne, Seine, Sen-

lis, Sens, Strasbourg, Strassburg, Toulon, Toulouse, Tourcoing, Tours, Valence, Vichy

French city (cathedral)–Nantes, Rheims

French cleric–abbe

French coin–centime (cop.), franc (ac., pap.), franc (s.), Napoleon (g.), sou (ac.)

French coin (copper)–sou

French coin (obs.)–obole

French coin (old)–ecu, gros, obole, teston, testoon

French coin (old silver)–livre

French coin (silver, anc.)–teston, testoon

French colony–Soudan

French colony (Mediterranean)–Algeria

French commune–cenon

French company (abbr.)–cie

French composer–Bizet, Debussy, Gounod, Lalo, Ravel, Thome

French Congo region–Boali

French conjunction–et

French constitution granted by Louis XVIII–charte

French critic (literary)–Taine

French crown–ecu

French curate–abbe

French daffodil–polyanthus

French daisy–marguerite

French dance–bal, cancan

French decoction–tisane

French decree (authoritative)–arret

French department–Caen, Var

French department (former)–Alsace

French diplomat–Ronsard, Segur

French district (winemaking)–Medoc

French dramatist – Piron, Racine

French dugout–abri

French duke–duc

French ecclesiastic–abbe

French edict–arret

French ell (old)–aune

French eminence (commanding a plain)–rideau

French family (royal, medieval)–Valois

French fashion (prevailing) –ton

French for beast–bete

French for mountain peak–pic

French for summer–ete

French fortification–Maginot

French fortress (former)–Sedan

French fugitive (royalist)–emigre

French general–Kleber

French government bond–rente

French government grant–octroi

French government monopoly–regie

French governor (dept.)–prefect

French hackney coach–fiacre

French hairdresser–friseur

French hardtack–galette

French hat–beret, chapeau, chapeaux (pl.)

French hero (revolutionary) –Danton

French horse stable–ecurie

French husband–mari

French illustrator (painter) –Dore

French income (annual)–rente

French Indo-China city–Bin Dinh, Cholon, Hanoi, Kesho, Kwang-Chow-Wan, Pnom Penh, Saigon

French Indo-China coin–piaster (s.)

French Indo-China seaport–Saigon

French infantryman (Algerian)–Turco

French island–ile

French journalist (controversial)–Leon

French judgment (court)–arret

French king–Louis, roi

French king (early)–capet
French land measure (old)–arpent
French landscape painter–Corot
French language (troubadour)–Provencal
French literary critic–Taine
Frenchman–Gaul
Frenchman (slang)–frogeater, froggy
French marshal–Murat, Ney
French mask (silk half)–loups
French measure–arpen, arpent, aune, boisseau, carat, chopine, decillion, hemine, league, lieue, ligne, line, mile, mine, minot, muid, perch, perche, pied, pinte, point, poisson, pot, pouce, quartaut, quarte, quarteron, roquille, sack, septier, setier, toise, tonneau de mer, velt, velte
French measure (old)–aune
French mechanic (slang)–erk
French money–franc
French money (five-franc piece)–ecu
French monk–friar
French monk (arch.)–frere
French mountain–Alps, Auvergne, Cevennes, Cote d'Or, Jura, Mount Blanc, Plomd du Cantal, Puy de Dome, Puy de Sancy, Pyrenees, Vignemale, Vosges
French national anthem–Marseillaise
French nome–Elis
French novelist – Dumas, Hugo, Loti, Verne, Zola
French nursemaid–bonne
French official–Laval, Petain
French opera–Carmen
French ornaments–parure
French outcast–agote
French painter–Corot, Manet, Renoir
French painter (landscape)–Corot

French pantomime character–Pierrot
French party (moderate)–centrist
French patois (Louisiana)–creole
French patron saint–Martin
French paving block–dalle
French plane–avion
French plane (war)–Spad
French poem (anc.)–dit
French poem (short)–dit
French poet (dramatist)–Rostand
French poetess–Labe
French police–Surete
French polishing material–rabat
French porcelain industry (seat of)–Limoges
French preposition–de
French priest–abbe, pere
French pronoun–moi, tu
French prune–prunelle
French psychologist–Coue
French region (S.W.)–Lande
French relative–parents
French resort–Cannes
French resort (winter)–Pau
French restaurant–bistro
French retreat (underground)–abris
French revolutionary hero–Danton
French revolutionist–Marat
French river–Adour, Ain, Aisne, Allier, Ardeche, Ariege, Aude, Charente, Cher, Dordogne, Drome, Durance, Escaut, Eure, Gard, Garonne, Gers, Gironde, Indre, Isere, Loir, Loire, Loiret, Lot, Maine, Marne, Meuse, Moselle, Nantaise, Nievre, Oise, Rhone, Saar, Sambre, Saone, Scarpe, Scheldt, Seine, Seyre, Somme, Tarn, Veste, Vienne, Yonne
French river (between Belgium)–Lys
French river (between Switzerland)–Rhone

French river (in Flanders)–Yser
French royal family (medieval)–Valois
French ruff collar–rabat
French school–ecole
French school (secondary)–lycee
French sculptor–Rodin
French sea biscuit–galette
French seaport–Bordeaux, Brest, Caen, Calais, Dunkerque, Havre, Toulon
French securities–rentes
French shield (old)–targe
French shooting match–tir
French short story–conte
French soldier–poilu
French song (popular)–caira
French stable (horse)–ecurie
French statesman–Laval
French stock exchange–bourse
French story (medieval short)–lai
French summer–ete
French surgeon–Pare
French tapestry–arras
French "the"–la, le, les (pl.)
French title–duc
French town–Longwy
French town (fortified)–Verdun
French town (mfg.)–Agen
French tragedienne–Rachel
French underground retreat–abris
French verse (form of)–rondel
French verse form–ballade, rondel
French verse form (old)–alba, lai
French verse poem (old)–virelay
French weight–carat, esterlin, esterling, gros, livre, marc, once, pound, tonne, tonneau, uckia
French West African capital–Dakar
French West African city–Dakar
French West African colony–Dahomey

French wind (cold dry)–mistral
French wine–sauterne
French wine district–Medoc
French woman (bored)–ennuyee
French World War I song–Madelon
French writer–Loti
Frenchy–Gallic
frenzied–frantic, maddened
frenzy–delirium, frantic, furor, mad, madness, mania
frequent–common, current, familiar, habitual, haunt, often, persistent, usual
frequented places – dives, haunts, resorts
frequenter–habitue
frequently–oft, often, ofttimes
frequently (poetic)–oft
frere–brother, friar
fresh–florid, good, lively, new, ruddy, sound, strong, sweet, unfaded, unimpaired, untried, unused
fresh set–relay
fresh supply–relay
fresh-water fish–chub, dace, id, ide
fresh water fish (genus of)–anabas
fresh water porpoise–inia
freshen–refresh, renew, revive, sweeten
fresher–sweeter
freshet (British)–spate
freshman (slang)–frosh
freshness–verdancy
freshness (to lose)–droop, fade, flag, wane, wilt
fret–chafe, harass, plague, rub, strait, worry
fret (Scot.)–orp
fretful–captious, irascible, irritable, peevish, pettish, petulant, querulous, repine
friable (more)–mealier
friar–Augustinian, brother, Carmelite, fish, Franciscan, monk
friar (medieval)–Teresian

fried–sauteed
fried cake–cruller, doughnut
fried mincemeat ball–rissole
Friend–Quaker
friend–associate, attendant, chum, companion, comrade, kith
friend (coll.)–pal
friend (familiar)–crony, pal
friend (Fr.)–ami
friend (Span.)–amigo
Friend church founder–George Fox
friendly–amiable, amicable, cordial, favorable, kind, sib
friendship–affection, amity, attachment, relation
Friesian (rare)–friese, frisian
frieze–adorn, chase, decoration, embroider, trimming
frieze (Scot. homespun)–kelt
frieze band (bottom)–taenia
fright–alarm, awe, consternation, panic, scare, shock, terror
fright (sudden groundless)–panic
frighten–alarm, appal, cow, intimidate, scare, startle
frighten away–scare, shoo
frightened–afraid, eerie
frightened (easily)–skittish, timid
frightful–alarming, awful, dreadful, hideous, horrible, horrid, shocking, terrible, terrific
frightfulness– atrociousness, schrecklichkeit
frigid–cold, freezing, icy
frill–jabot, purl, ruche
frill (lace)–jabot
frill (neck)–jabot
fringe–border, edging, margin
fringe (membranous)–loma, lomata (pl.)
fringed–frimbriate
frisk–brisk, caper, disport, frolic, frolicsome, gambol, lively, search

frisky–frolicsome, gay, lively, playful, sportive
frisson–chill, quiver, shiver, shudder, thrill
frivolous – fatuous, giddy, petty, trivial, worthless
frock–dress, gown, jersey, mantle, tunic
frock (evening)–wrap
frog–anuran, rana
frog (horse's foot)–frush
frog (South America)–jakie
frog (young)–peeper
frog genus–anura, rana
frog-like–ranine
frog pond–ranarium, ranaria (pl.)
frog rearing place–ranarium
frogs (pert. to)–anuran, ranine
frogs (young tree)–peepers
frogs (zoological order of)–anura
frolic–caper, carousal, disport, frisk, gambol, lark, oray, ramp, romp, shindy, spree, wassail
frolicsome–frisky, gay, waggish
from–of
from (away, prefix)–apo
from (prefix)–de
from beginning to end–over, through
from head to foot–capapie
from the egg–abovo
front–afore, appearance, before, facade, face, fore, forefront, van
front (false)–blind
front (in)–aface
frontiersman–Boone, Carson
frost–foam, rime, yeast
frost (as glass)–mat
frosted cake–eclair
frosting–ice, icing
frosty–chill, cold, freezing, frigid, inimical, rimy
froth–foam, lume, scum, spume
froth (soapsuds)–lather
frothy–foamy, spumous
frow–froe, wife, woman
froward–cross, obstinate, peevish, perverse, petu-

lant, refractory, ungovernable, untoward, unyielding, wayward
frowl–guillemot
frown–glower, lower, scowl
frowsy–disordered, musty, slovenly, unkempt
froze–congealed
frozen–chilled, coldhearted, gelid, refrigerated, unsympathetic, unyielding
frozen (arch.)–frore
frugal–careful, chary, economical, parsimonious, provident, saving, sparing, thrifty, unwasteful
frugal (was)–stinted
frugality–economy, thrift
fruit–apple, azarole, cherry, drupe, fig, melon, olive, peach, pear, pome
fruit (acid)–lemon, lime
fruit (aggregate)–etaerio
fruit (American tropical tree)–sapota
fruit (apocarpous, as strawberries)–etaerio
fruit (apple-like)–pome
fruit (astringent)–sloe
fruit (blackthorn)–sloe
fruit (buttercup) – achene, achenium, akene
fruit (characteristic gourd)–pepo
fruit (citrus)–grape, lemon, lime, orange, tangerine
fruit (cooked in syrup)–compote
fruit (dog rose, false)–hip
fruit (edible)–huckleberry
fruit (edible, orange-sized)–genipaps
fruit (elm tree)–samara
fruit (false, of rose)–hip
fruit (fatty)–olive
fruit (fleshy)–drupe, melon, pear, pome, tomato
fruit (fleshy part)–sarcocarp
fruit (globose)–lime
fruit (gourd family)–pepo
fruit (horseradish tree)–ben
fruit (imperfect)–nubbin
fruit (indehiscent succulent) –uva
fruit (intermediate between peach and plum)–apricot

fruit (juice)–rob
fruit (mild acid)–guava
fruit (multiple)–cone
fruit (oblong-shaped yellow)–pawpaw
fruit (of gourd family, characteristic)–pepo
fruit (of strawberry family) –etaerio
fruit (of trees)–nut
fruit (of tropical vine)–gourd
fruit (one seed, small)–achene, akene, samara
fruit (palm tree)–date
fruit (pear-shaped citrus)–shaddock
fruit (plum-like)–sloe
fruit (pome)–apple, pear
fruit (pome-like, yellow)–azarole
fruit (pulp)–pap
fruit (pulpy)–uva
fruit (pulpy, small)–berry
fruit (red)–apple, cherry, plum
fruit (red, pitted)–cherry
fruit (rose bush)–hip
fruit (soft, fleshy)–drupe
fruit (stewed)–compote
fruit (stone)–drupe
fruit (stone-inclosing) – drupe
fruit (tropical) – banana, date, fig, guava, mango, papaw, papaya, pawpaw
fruit (valonia oaks, immature)–camata
fruit (winged)–samara
fruit (withered)–nubbin
fruit basket–pottel, pottle
fruit carpet–apocarp
fruit covering–pericarp
fruit dealer–fruiterer, fruiteress, greengrocer
fruit decay (internal)–blet
fruitgrower–palmologist
fruit jar rubber ring–lute
fruit of Jove–persimmon
fruit of paradise–grapefruit, pomelo
fruit preserve–compote
fruit seed–pip, pit
fruit stalk–peduncle
fruit stone–putamen
fruit stone (small)–pyrene

fruit substance producing jelly–pectin
fruitful–abundant, fertile, plenteous, prolific
fruitful soil (goddess of)–Demeter
fruitless–barren, ineffectual, profitless, useless, vain
frump–dowdy, flout, gossip, insult, irritate, mock, provoke, snub, sulk, vex
frustrate–baffle, balk, bilk, blight, block, checkmate, circumvent, confound, cross, disappoint, disconcert, elude, foil, nullify, outwit, thwart
frustrate by craft–outwit
frustration (complete)–fiasco
frustration of one's dreams–disillusionment
frustrator of plan–marplot
fry–brood, offspring, young
fry lightly (Fr.)–saute
fry lightly and quickly (in fat)–saute
frying pan–skillet, spider
fuddled (obs.)–fap
fuddler (coll.)–drunkard
fudge–candy, counterfeit, fake, humbug, makeshift, nonsense, substitute
Fuegian – Alikuluf, Ona, Yahgan
fuel–coal, coke, gas, oil, peat, petroleum
fugie–cock, coward
fugient–fleeing, retiring
fugitive–evanescent, exile, fleeing, fleeting, fugacious, refugee, roaming, strolling, uncertain, unstable, vagabond, volatile
fugue (learned and elaborate, It.)–ricercare
Fukien river (China)–Min
fulcrum–prop, support
fulcrum (oar)–thole
fulfill–accomplish, complete, finish, meet, satisfy
fulfill a task–execute
full–plenary, replete, sated
full bloom (as flowers)–anthesis
full control–mastery

full force (with)–amain
full of–ose
full of cracks–rimose
full of fissures–rimose
full of hollows–lacunose
full of love–amative
full of meaning–pithy
full of minute openings–porous
full of sand–arenose
full of short bends–kinky
full of small openings–lacunose, spaced
full of substance–meaty
full of thorns–briary
full of vigor–lusty
full of zest–racy
full, round, **resonant**–orotund
fullness–completeness, perfection, repletion, satiety
fullness (suffix)–ose
fully–abundantly, amply, clearly, distinctly, largely, maturely, perfectly, plenteously, plentifully, utterly, wholly
fulsome–abundant, copious, fat, full, overfed, overgrown, plump, suave
Fulton's folly–Clermont
fume–odor, rage, rant, reek, smoke
fun – amusement, merriment, sport
function–calling, duty, office, operate, operating, providence, role, service, use, work, working
function (afternoon)–tea
function (assumed)–role
function (social)–reception, tea
function (trigonometrical)–cosine, sine
fund–basis, bottom, foundation, groundwork
fundamental–basal, basic, basilar, elemental, elementary, essential, organic, primary, principle, radical, rudiment, vital
funds–money
funeral (pert. to)–exequial
funeral bell–knell
funeral ceremony–exequy

funeral hymn–dirge
funeral oration–eloge
funeral oration (panegyrical)–eloge
funeral pile–pyre
funeral procession–cortege, exequy
funeral song–dirge, elogie, elogy, nenia
funeral vase (like a)–**urnal**
funereal–feral
fungi–rusts
fungi (parasitic)–rust
fungi (stage in development of)–uredo
fungi growth–mildew
fungoid–fungus, trama
fungus – geaster, mildew, mold, mushroom, puffball, rust, smut, toadstool
fungus (edible) – morel, moril
fungus (edible, purple)–blewits
fungus (grain)–ergot
fungus (poisonous)–aminita
fungus (rye)–ergot
fungus (species of)–bunt
fungus (stem of)–stipe
fungus (subterranean edible)–truffle
fungus dots–telia
fungus growth–mold
fungus-like–agaric
funk–cowardice, flinch, fright, kick, odor, rage, shrink, spark, touchwood
funk hole (slang)–dugout
funnel (conveying)–hopper
funny–comic, comical, droll, laughable, odd, queer, strange
fur–ermine, pelage, sable
fur (animal's, called nutria)–coypu
fur (coypu)–nutria
fur (dark)–sable
fur (kind of)–ermine, fox, martin, miniver, mink, nutria, otter, sable, seal
fur (medieval)–miniver
fur (medieval, costly)–vair
fur (middle ages)–miniver
fur (thick soft)–mink
fur-bearing animal – fox,

genet, martin, otter, sable, seal
fur tippet–palatine
furs–peltry, pelts
furbish–burnish, clean, polish, renovate, rub, scour
furbish up–vamp
Furies (one of)–Alecto, Erinnys, Erinyes, Erinys, Megaera, Tisiphone
furious–angry, frenzied, impetuous, tumultuous, turbulent, vehement
furl–roll, wrap
furlong–stade, stadium
furlough–leave
furnace–kiln, oven
furnace (revolving wrought iron)–rotator
furnish–afford, appoint, endow, equip, indue, lend, provide, render, supply
furnish crew–man
furnish with funds–endow
furnish with inlaid work–panel
furnish with meals–board, cater
furnish with military equipment–accoutre
furnish with steep slope–escarp
furnish with tapestry–arrased
furnished–equipped, provided, supplied
furnisher–lender
furnishing–apparatus, fixtures, furniture
furniture (kind of)–Sheraton
furrow–groove, plow, rut, trench
furrowed (sinuously)–rivose
further–abet, advance, aid, more, promote, remoter, yet
furtherance – advancement, progress, promotion
furthermore–and, moreover
furtive–secret, sly, sneaky, stealthy
fury–ire, madness, rage, turbulence, violence, wrath

furze–gorse
fuse–anneal, blend, dissolve, melt, smelt, unite
fuse ore–smelt
fusible opaque substance–metal

fuss–ado, bustle, spat, todo, tumult
fuss (Scot.)–busle
fustian–bombastic, inflated, pompous, rant, tumid
fustic coloring matter–morin

futile–hopeless, idle, ineffectual, otiose, vain
futilely–otiosely
fyke–net
fylfot – saustica, svastika, swastica, swastika

G

gab–boast, chatter, deceive, lie, mock, mouth, prate, scoff, taste, tongue, utterance
gabardine–fabric
gabari (gabirit) – gauge, model, mold
gabbard (gabbart)–barge, lighter, scow, vessel
gabble–chat, chatter, jabber, talk
gabble (Scot.)–rai
gaberdine–coat, frock, gown, mantle, pinafore
gable (low)–pediment
gablock–crowbar, gaff, spur
gad–bar, billet, chisel, goad, ingot, roam, rod, rove, spear, staff, wander
Gad's son–Eri
Gad tribe chieftain–Ahi
gadabout–dogcart, gadding, roving
gadget–contrivance, device, jigger
gadwall–duck
Gael – Celt, Highlander, Kelt, Manx, Scot
Gaelic–Erse
Gaelic body of warriors–Fenians
Gaelic clan–Sept
Gaelic for John–Ian
Gaelic language–Erse
Gaelic sea god–Ler
Gaelic spirit–banshee
gaff–deceit, fleece, fraud, hoax, hook, prating, spear, spearhead, spur, talk, trick, trickery
gag–choke, closure, hoax, imposture, interpolation,

joke, obstruct, prevent, retch
gaiety (gayety)–glee, jollity, liveliness, merriment, mirth, sprightliness, vivacity
gain–attain, earn, get, increase, net, obtain, procure, profit
gain (ill-gotten)–lucre, pelf
gain (unworthy)–lucre, pelf
gain command of–master
gain in victory–prevail
gain over expense–clear, net, profit
gaining possession of goods by finding–trover
gainsay–contradict, controvert, deny, dispute, forbid, oppose
gait–amble, canter, gallop, lope, pace, run, strut, tread, trot, walk, way
gait (easy)–lope
gait (jogging)–trot
gait (springing)–gallop
gaiter–puttee, spat
gaiter (long, var.)–legging
gaiter (low)–spat
gaiters (Eng.)–spats
gaiters (wrapped around the legs)–puttees
gala–festival, festivity, fete, gaiety
galago–lemur
Galatea's lover–Acis
gale–gust, outburst, storm, wind
gale (violent)–hurricane
Galilean town–Cana
galipot–rosin
gall–bile, effrontery, fret,

impudence, irritate, rancor, vex
gallant–attentive, chivalrous, courteous, lover, noble, stately, suitor
gallant (country)–swain
gallantry–bravery, courage, intrepidity
galleon–carack, carrack, vessel
gallera–cockpit
gallery–ambulatory, audience, corridor, promenade, veranda
gallery (roofed, open)–loggia
gallery (spectator's)–dedans
galley – caravel, caravelle, carvel, cookroom, kitchen, tray
galley (anc.)–aesc
galley (kind of)–aesc, bireme, trireme, unireme
galley (one-banked oared)–unireme
galley (three-banked oared)–trireme
galley (two-banked oared)–bireme
galley rostrum (anc.)–beak
Gallic–French
gallop (easy)–canter
galloped–careened
gamble–bet, chance, game, hazard, risk, stake, uncertainty, wager
gambler–gamester, sharper
gambler (playing for the house)–shill
gambler's aide–capper
gambles–dices
gambling (pert. to)–aleatory

gambling game – bingo, craps, faro, keeno, keno, lotto, montebank, pitch, poker, policy, rondo, roulette, stuss

gambling game (Span.)–monte

gambol–caper, frisk

game–amusement, backgammon, billiards, cards, contest, dice, diversion, frolic, fun, lame, play, pool, polo, sport, tennis

game (backgammon-like)–pachisi

game (bowling)–tenpins

game (card)–contract, cribbage, ecarte, faro, loo, masset, monte, montebank, ombre, pam, pedro, pitch, poker, rounce, rummy, skat, solitaire, waist, whist

game (confidence)–bunco

game (court)–badminton, croquet, roque, tennis

game (finger-counting)–mora

game (gambling)–bingo, craps, faro, keeno, keno, lotto, monte, montebank, pitch, poker, policy, rondo, roulette, stuss

game (guessing, played with sticks and nails by New Mexican Indian)–canute

game (indoor)–gobang

game (jaialai)–pelota

game (lotto-like) – bingo, keeno

game (mental skill)–chess

game (movable disk)–checkers, chess, halma

game (New Mexico Indian guessing)–canute

game (outdoor)–badminton, croquet, polo, roque, tennis

game (parlor)–ticktacktoe

game (similar to handball)–fives

game (small)–birds

game collection–bag

game of checkers–draughts

game of rackets–badminton, tennis

game of skill–diabolo

game resembling ninepins–skittles

game stealer–poacher

gamecock spur–gaff

gamin–Arab, tad, urchin

gaming cube–die, dice (pl.)

gamut – compass, range, scale, series

gang–band, company, complement, crew, group, outfit, set

gang of workers–crew, shift

Ganges valley efflorescence (salty)–reh

gangster–criminal, hireling, thief, thug

gannet–solan

ganoid (genus of)–amia

gantlet–gauntlet, glove

gap–breach, break, hiatus, lacuna, opening, pass, space

gap (rare)–lacune

gap in hedge (var.)–muset

gap in ridge–col

gape–gaze, stare, yawn

gaping–agape, chappy

gaping (as two-lipped corolla)–ringent

garb–apparel, array, clothe, costume, habit, raiment

garbed – attired, clad, dressed, habited

garble–alloy, mangle, mutilate, pervert, sophisticate

garden – Eden, enclosure, outfield

garden (botanical tree)–arboretum, arboreta (pl.), arboretums (pl.)

garden (kind of)–botanical, truck

garden (kitchen, Scot.)–kailyard, kaleyard

garden (tree)–arboretum

garden (zoological)–tiergarten

garden dormouse–lerot

garden earth–dirt, soil

garden implement – hoe, mower, rake, scythe, sickle, trowel, weeder

garden mignonette color–reseda

garden plant–aster

garden plant (blue flowered) –harebell

garden plot–bed

Garfield's death place–Elberon

gargantuan–huge

garish–gaudy, showy

garland – anadem, corona, coronal, festoon, wreath

garland (head)–chaplet

garland (poetic)–anadem

garlic-like herb–shallots

garment–cloak, coat, dress, gown, raiment, robe, stole, vest

garment (clerical)–amice

garment (ecclesiastical, close fitting)–cassock

garment (knight's)–tabard

garment (light, over)–duster

garment (light, outer, arch.) –simar

garment (long loose)–stole

garment (long, outer)–pelisse

garment (loose light outer) –simar

garment (medieval)–tabard

garment (outer) – duster, overcoat, paletot, surcoat, wrap

garment (patchwork)–cento

garment (priestly)–ephod

garment (protective)–apron, coveralls, overalls, pinafore

garment (sleeveless)–aba, cape, vest

garment (thin, waterproof) –gossamer

garment (woman's loose)–cymar, simar

garment maker–dressmaker, tailor

garner–accumulate, collect, gather, reap

garnet (black kind)–melanite

garnet (green)–olivine

garnish–adorn, decorate, ornament

garnishment–lien, ornament

garret–attic, turret, watchtower

garrulous–loquacious, talkative, wordy

gas–hydrogen
gas (blue)–ozone
gas (body of self-luminous)–nebula
gas (colorless)–ozone
gas (colorless poisonous)–arsine
gas (component of air)–nitrogen
gas (constituent of illuminating)–ethane
gas (essential to life)–oxygen
gas (inflammable)–ethane
gas (inflammable marsh)–methane
gas (most poisonous)–arsine
gas (of air)–argon, neon, xenon
gas (oxygen)–ozone
gas (poisonous)–arsine
gascon–boaster, swashbuckler
gasconade – bluster, boast, brag
gaseous component–argon
gaseous compound–ethane
gaseous element–neon
gaseous hydrocarbon–ethane
gaseous product (of combustion, soot-charged)–smoke
gash–cut, gossip, incision, slash, tattle
gasp–pant
gasping–agasp
gastropod – mollusk, slug, snail, volute
gastropod (ear-shaped)–abalone
gastropod (volutid)–yet
gastropod mollusk–abalone, slug, snail, whelk
gastropods (genus of)–oliva
gat–channel, passage
gate–defile, door, hole, opening, pass, portal, valve
gate (back)–postern
gate (kind of)–turnstile
gate (Oriental)–dar
gatekeeper–warden
gate money–admission
gateway–portal
gateway (Indian)–toran, torana
gather–accumulate, assemble, brew, collect, compile, convene, convoke,

garner, glean, meet, reap, shirr
gather into close compass–furl
gather into folds–bunch, furl, pleat, shirr
gather money by hard work –scratch
gathered for public discussion–forum
gathered on thread–shirred
gathered together–amassed, baled, bundled, collected
gatherer–collector, miser
gatherer (news)–reporter
gathering–abscess, accumulation, assemblage, collection, contraction, meeting, swelling, troop
gathering (elite)–galaxy
gathering (social, for men)–smoker, stag
gathers into mass–conglomerates
gaucho (pampas)–cowboy, herdsman
gaucho hunting device–bolas
gaucho lariat–bolas
gaud–adorn, artifice, finery, flashy, fraud, gewgaw, jest, joke, ornament, paint, sport, trick, trinket
gaudy–cheap, flashy, flaunting, flimsy, garish, glaring, loud, meretricious, ostentatious, pretentious, showy, tawdry, tinsel, trinket
gaudy trifles–gewgaws
gaufre–waffle
gauge (gage) – estimate, judge, measure
gauge (rain)–udometer
gauge (wind)–anemometer
gauge pointer–arm
Gauls (anc.)–Remi
gaunt–bony, haggard, lank, lean, spare, thin
gauntest–sparest
gauntlet–glove
gauze–crape
gauzy light fabric–tissue
gave–contributed, donated, imparted
gave formally–presented
gave out–emitted, released

gave outlet to–vented
gave to–handed
gaw–drain, gape, trench
gawk–left, lout, stare
gawky–awkward, clownish, clumsy, foolish
gawn–pail, tub
gawny–gawk, simpleton
gay–airy, blithe, cheery, frolicsome, gaudy, glad, gleeful, jolly, jovial, joyful, joyous, lighthearted, lively, merry, riant, sportive, sprightly, vivacious
gay time–jamboree, lark, revel, spree
gayness–riancy
gazabo (gazebo)–blunder, rabbit, whopper
gaze–eye, gape, glare, gloat, glower, peer, regard, stare
gaze with greed–gloat
gazed abstractedly–mooned
gazed intently–pored
gazed with satisfaction–gloated
gazelle–ahu, cora
gazelle (common)–goa
gazelle (Tibetan)–goa
gazelle (West African)–kudu, mhorr, mohr, mohrs (pl.), oryx
gazer–starer
Ge's children (any of twelve)–Titan
gear–appliances, clothing, equip, equipment, garments, harness, rig, tools, trappings, vestments
geck–dupe, gull
gecko–lizard
gee–agree, coincide, evade
geese–ninnies
geese (genus of)–anser
geese (kind of)–solans
geese (snow)–chen
geese (wild)–brants
gekko–lizard
gelatinous precipitation–gel
gelatinous substance–agar
gem – aquamarine, beryl, jewel, muffin, stone
gem (artificial)–paste
gem (iridescent)–cat's-eye
gem (of imperfect brilliancy)–loupe

gem (purple)–amethyst
gem (rose red)–avena
gem (semiprecious)–garnet
gem carved in relief–cameo
gem cut to show six rays on dome–asteria
gem face–facet
gem having changeable luster–tigereye, tiger's-eye
gem making glass (lead)–strass
gem supporter–setting
gem surface–bezel, facet
gem weight–carat
gemel–coupled, doubled, paired, twin
gendarme–cavalryman, soldier
gender–sex
genealogical record–tree
genealogy–lineage, pedigree
geneat–tenant, vassal
general–catholic, common, universal
general (not)–limited, local, particular, personal, restricted, specific
general (universal)–catholic
general (who defeated Lee at Gettysburg)–Meade
general agreement–consensus, pact
general course–trend
general direction–trend
general drift of thought–tenor
general favor (in)–popular
general idea–motif
general rule of law–canon
general supplication–litany
general type–average
general view of subject–synopsis
generalize–broaden, extend, spread, widen
generate–breed, create, develop, engender
generation – age, descent, genealogy
generation (of later)–epigonous
generator (electric)–dynamo
generous–free, liberal, magnanimous, unstinted
genesis–beginning birth, origin, origination

genesis of anything (pert. to)–genic
genet–horse
genial–bland, cheerful, expansive, pleasant, warm
genie (folklore)–Sandman
genip tree wood–lana
genius–talent
genteel–polite
Gentiles (pert. to)–ethnic
gentle–bland, calm, clement, compassionate, docile, mild, moderate, subdued, peaceful, tame, tender, tractable, tranquil
gentleman–sir
gentleman (would be)–shoneen
gentleness of treatment–lenity
gently and dully–tamely
genuflect–kneel
genuine–authentic, frank, germane, pucka, pukka, pure, real, sincere, unadulterated, unalloyed, veritable
genuine (more)–pure
genuine (not)–tin
genus–class, kind, order, sort
genus homo–man
genus including chick-pea–cicer
genus including currants–ribes
genus of aconitum plant–atis
genus of African tree–cola
genus of all-seed herb–radiola
genus of amaryllis family–agave
genus of American bluebird–sialia
genus of American dwarf palm–sabal
genus of American plants–phlox
genus of annual grass–avena
genus of ants–eciton
genus of anurans–rana
genus of apes–simia
genus of apple trees–malus
genus of armadillos–glyptodon

genus of Asiatic herbs–rheum, torenia
genus of Asiatic orchids–aerides
genus of Asiatic palms–areca
genus of auks–alle
genus of Australian bird–baritah
genus of Australian shrub–alstonia, olearia
genus of batrachians–pipa
genus of bees–apia, apis
genus of beetles–sitaris
genus of beets–beta
genus of birds–anser, sula
genus of birds (including cassowaries, ostriches, emus, moas)–ratitae
genus of bitter-rooted herbs–aletris
genus of bivalve mollusks–anomia
genus of blue grass–poa
genus of blue green algae–gloeocapsa
genus of blue whale–sibbaldus
genus of bog herbs–abama
genus of bowfins–amia
genus of bugs (long-legged)–emesa
genus of burbots–lota
genus of bustards–otis
genus of cabbage–cos
genus of candytuft–iberis
genus of cat–felis
genus of cattle (wild and domestic)–bos
genus of cetaceans–inia
genus of clams–mya
genus of cows–bos
genus of crustaceans–estheria
genus of cultivated rye–secale
genus of currant–ribes
genus of dianthus plant–pinks
genus of dogs–canis
genus of dolphin-like cetaceans–inia
genus of ducks–anas
genus of ducks (fresh water)–aix
genus of East Indian fish–cybium

genus of East Indian wild cattle–gaurs
genus of elms–ulmus
genus of evergreen shrub–erica
genus of fennel flowers–nigella
genus of ferns–anemia
genus of firs–abies
genus of fishes–remora
genus of flowering grasses–stipa
genus of flowers–rosa
genus of foraging ants–eciton
genus of fossil fernlike plants–lesleya
genus of fresh water fish–anabas
genus of fresh water mussels –unio
genus of frogs–anura, rana
genus of gannet–sula
genus of ganoid–amia
genus of garden mignonette –reseda
genus of gastropods–oliva
genus of geese–anser, chen
genus of goats–capra
genus of gooseberry–ribes
genus of grass–avena, poa
genus of ground beetles–amara
genus of ground sloths – megatherium
genus of gulls–xema
genus of herbs–arum, cassia, cirsium, dondia, inula, psoralea
genus of herbs (mustard family)–isatis
genus of holly–ilex
genus of honeybee–apia, apis
genus of honeyberry tree–genipa
genus of horse–equus
genus of housefly–musca
genus of house mouse–mus
genus of ipecac–evea
genus of lemurs (Africa)–galago
genus of lichens–evernia
genus of lily family–bessera
genus of lizards–uta
genus of low green shrubs–erica

genus of mammals (large extinct)–glyptodon
genus of maple–acer
genus of maple-like trees–rulac
genus of marine animal–otaria
genus of marine fish (herbivorous)–girella
genus of marine gastropods–eburna, murex, terebra
genus of marsh herbs–caltha
genus of marten–mustela
genus of meadow saxifrage–seseli
genus of mephitis (animal of)–polecat
genus of Mexican plants–dion
genus of mice–mus
genus of moles–chrysochloris
genus of mollusks–eolis, leda
genus of mollusks (bivalve) –anomia
genus of moose–alces
genus of moth–tinea
genus of musk ox–ovibos
genus of New Zealand wren –xenicus
genus of North American herbs–solidago
genus of North American plants–phlox
genus of nuthatches (typical)–sitta
genus of oats–avena
genus of old-world lizards–agama
genus of old-world trees and shrubs–olax
genus of olive trees–olea
genus of orchids–listera, vanda
genus of palms–areca, assai, nipa, raphia, serenoa
genus of peacocks–pavo
genus of perennial grasses–elymus
genus of pickerel–esox
genus of pigs–sus
genus of plants–arum, canna, cola, datura, dion, syringa
genus of poplar–alamo
genus of porcupines (terrestrial)–hystrix

genus of porpoise–inia
genus of pungent herbs–asarum
genus of razor clams–solen
genus of rhizopods–ameba, amoeba
genus of rhubarb–rheum
genus of road runner–geococcyx
genus of rodents–mus
genus of rose–rosa
genus of sable and marten–mustela
genus of sac fungi–geoglossum
genus of seaweeds–alaria
genus of seed plants–striga
genus of shad–alosa
genus of sheep–ovis
genus of shelled arthropods –crustacea
genus of shrubs–azalea, itea, lantana, olea, rosa
genus of shrubs (rose family)–opulaster
genus of slugs–arion
genus of snails–mitra, triton
genus of snakes–ophidia
genus of South American trees–simaba
genus of spider crabs–maia
genus of spider monkeys–ateles
genus of spiders–agalena
genus of stars (feather)–antedon
genus of stick-like insect–emesa
genus of stonecup–sedum
genus of succulent plants–aloe
genus of sunfish–mola
genus of swan–cygnus, olor
genus of swine–sus
genus of tea plants–thea
genus of terns–sterna
genus of thistle-like plant–carlina
genus of ticks–argas
genus of trees–olea
genus of trees and shrubs–olax, rhus
genus of tropical American herbs and shrubs–evea, ruellia

genus of tropical American prickly herbs–loasa

genus of tropical Asiatic palms–nypa

genus of tropical herbs–evea, tacca

genus of tropical shrub–urena

genus of tropical trees–cola, helicteres, kola, ocotea

genus of tsetse fly–glossina

genus of turkey–meleagris

genus of twining vines–tamus

genus of ulnus tree–elm

genus of verbascum–mullein

genus of Virginia willow–itea

genus of voracious flies–asilus

genus of wasps–vespa

genus of water scorpion–nepa

genus of whale killer–orca

genus of whales–areta, cete

genus of white heron–egretta

genus of wolverene–gulo

genus of woody vines–hedera

genus of worms (terrestrial tricald planarian) – geoplana

geode–druse

geological division–era, trias

geological period–eocene

geological remains–fossils

geological strata–lias

geological time (antedating life)–azoic

geological zones (succession of)–assise

geometric angle–incidence

geometric curve – evolute, spiral

geometrical figure–cone, ellipse, gnomon, lune, oblong, prism, rhomb, triangle

geometrical ratio–pi

geometrical solid – cube, prism

geometrical surfaces–nappe, tores

geoponic–agricultural, agriculture, rural, rustic

Georgia city (Caucasus)–Kutais, Tiflis

Georgia city (U.S.)–Cordele, Macon

Georgian (Caucasus)–Svan

georgic–rural

Geraint's wife–Enid

germ–microbe

germ cell–ovum, ova (pl.)

germ plasm–id

German–Teuton

German (Fr. slang)–Boche

German Africa coin (former)–pesa

German air force–Luftwaffe

German airplane–Dornier, Heinkel, Junkers, Messerschmitt, Stuka

German airplane (bombing, old)–Gotha

German air post–Luftpost

German alphabet signs (old) –runes

German Alpine province–Bavaria

German-American pianist–Bauer

German and Austrian union (political)–Anschluss

German and Swiss lake – Constance

German armored troops–panzer

German article–das, der, die

German astrologer–Faust

German athlete–Turner

German author–Nicolai

German baptism of fire–feuertaufe

German biographer–Emil Ludwig

German bombers (dive)–Stukas

German botanical illustrator –Ehret

German canal–Kiel

German (Saxony) capital–Dresden

German capital–Berlin

German city–Aachen, Altona, Aue, Augsburg, Barmen, Berlin (c.), Bielefeld, Bochum, Bonn, Braunsberg, Bremer, Breslau, Brunswick, Cassel, Charlottenburg, Chem-

nitz, Cologne, Crefeld, Darmstadt, Dessau, Dortmund, Dresden, Duisburg, Dusseldorf, Ede, Elberfeld, Ems, Erfurt, Essen, Flensburg, Frankfort-on-Main, Frankfort-on-Oder, Freiburg, Furth, Gelsenkirchen, Gorlitz, Gotha, Hagen, Halle, Hamburg, Hanover, Hannover, Harburg, Heidelberg, Herne, Karlsruhe, Kassel, Kiel, Koln, Konigsberg, Krefeld, Leipzig, Lichtenberg, Liegnitz, Linden, Lubeck, Ludwigshafen, Magdeburg, Mainz, Mannheim-on-Ruhr, Mayence, Munchen, Munich, Munster, Nuremberg, Nurnberg, Oberhausen, Oder, Offenbach, Osnabruck, Pforzheim, Plauen, Potsdam, Remscheid, Rostock, Saarbrucken, Schoneberg, Spandau, Steglitz, Stettin, Stuttgart, Trier, Ulm, Wiesbaden, Wurzburg, Zwickau

German city (mfg.)–Essen

German coin–mark (s.), pfennig (br.), reichsmark (s.), reichspfennig (br.)

German coin (former)–kreutzer

German coin (gold)–kronen

German coin (old)–thaler

German commune–Aalen

German composer–Bach, Handel, Nicolai, Wagner

German composer (music)–Abt

German corps–korps

German cutlass (anc.)–tesack

German dance–allemande

German district–Baden

German district leader–gauleiter

German dive bomber–Stuka

German East Africa coin–heller (cop.), pesa (cop.), rupie (s.)

German East Africa coin (copper, former)–pesa

German explorer–Ehrenberg

German for substitute–ersatz

German for war–krieg

German Gestapo chief–Himmler

German gnome–kobold

German god (thunder)–Donar

German gun (big)–bertha

German gymnast–Turner

German hail–heil

German kingdom (former)–Hanover

German knight–ritter

German leader (local)–gauleiter

German lecturer–docent, dozent, privat docent, privat dozent

German measles–rubello

German measure–aam, carat, chaussee meile, eimer, kanne, kette, klafter, last, maass, masskanne, sack, scheffel, schoppen, stab, strich, stubchen

German measure (land)–imi

German mechanized unit–panzer

German metaphysician–Kant

German money–pfennig

German musician–Abt

German name (Dutch coll.)–Moffen

German name (prefix)–von

German naturalist–Ehrenberg

German news agency–D.N.B.

German nobleman–junker, younker

German novelist–Ebers

German orientalist–Rosen

German ox (wild long-horned)–urus

German parachute jumper–parachutist

German parliament–Reichstag

German philosopher–Kant, Lange

German physiologist–Hasse

German plane – Dornier, Heinkel, Junkers, Messerschmitt, Stuka

German poet–Elze, Goethe, Heine, Lessing

German police (secret)–Gestapo

German port–Bremen

German province (north)–Pomerania

German raider–Spee

German resort–Ems

German rifleman–Yager

German river–Eder, Elbe, Ems, Oder, Rhine, Ruhr, Saar, Spree, Ulm, Weser

German salutation–heil

German scholar (Shakespearean)–Elze

German sculptor–Begas

German secret police head–Himmler

German society – Bund, Turnverein

German soldier – boche, Fritz, Heine, Heinie

German song–lied

German state–Bavaria

German student gathering (social)–kommers, kommerse

German substitute–ersatz

German-Swiss lake – Constance

German sympathizers (spies, traitors)–Fifth Column

German teacher–docent, dozent, privat docent, privat dozent

German theologian–Bauer

German title–Herr

German tribal organization–gau

German tribesman (anc.)–Jute, Ostrogoth

German troops (armored)–panzer

German troops (Eng. slang)–Jerrys

German troops (mechanized)–panzer

German unit (mechanized)–panzer

German valley–Saar

German vital space–lebensraum

German vowel change–umlaut

German war–krieg

German war attack–blitzkrieg

German warfare (lightning)–blitzkrieg

German warplane–Dornier, Heinkel, Junkers, Messerschmitt, Stuka

German watering place–Baden

German weight–carat, centner, drachma, last, liespfund, lot, pfund, quentchen, quentlein, stein, vierling, zollpfund

German wheat–spelt

German world war rear admiral–Spee

German "yes"–ja

Germanic law (anc.)–Salic

Germanic people–Prussians

Germanic people (anc.)–Herminones, Hermiones, Quadi

Germanic people (one of)–Saxon

Germanic tribesman (anc.)–Saxon

germicide–antiseptic, iodin, iodine, phenol

germinate–beget, bud, develop, effloresce, sprout

gest (geste) – adventure, deed, exploit

gesticulate–gesture, motion

gesticulation–gesture, motion

gesture–act, behave, gesticulation, motion, perform

get–achieve, acquire, ascertain, attain, capture, contract, derive, determine, earn, gain, induce, learn, obtain, procure, receive, secure, take, win

get along–advance, fare, hurry, progress, prosper, succeed

getaway–depart, elope, escape, leave, scat, start

get back–recover, redeem

get better of–best
get by force–extort
get hold of by effort–obtain
get on–board, embark, fare
get out–elicit, escape, evacuate, reveal, scram
get ready–prepare
get rid of–eliminate
get to bottom of–fathom
get up–arise
get wrong idea of–miscomprehend
ghastly–cadaverous, deathly, frightful, grim, grisly, gruesome, hideous, lurid, pale, terrible, wan
ghastly pale–lurid
ghost–apparition, eidolon, lemur, lemures (pl.), phantasm, phantom, shade, specter, spectre, spirit, spook
ghostly–eerie, eery, spectral
ghoulish–eerie, eery
giant–afreet, gargantuan, huge, monster, monstrous, nozzle, ogre, prodigious, titan, tremendous
giant (buried under Mt. Etna)–Enceladus
giant (fictional)–Gargantua, ogre
giant (hundred-eyed)–Argus
giant (mythical one-eyed)–Cyclops
giant (Norse myth.)–Mimir
giant (of hundred eyes)–Argus
giant (of thousand arms)–Bana
giant (one-eyed, myth.)–Cyclops
giant (thousand-armed)–Bana
gibbed–castrated
gibber–boulder, chat, stone
gibbet–gallows, hang
gibbon–ape, hoolock, siamang, wou-wou
gibbon (Malayan)–lar
gibe–fleer, flout, jape, jeer, jibe, scoff, sneer, taunt
giddiness–dizziness, levity
gift–aptitude, aptness, bent, boon, contribution, dona-

tion, endowment, faculty, gratuity, knack, present, readiness, talent, token
gift (charitable)–alms
gift (corrupting)–bribe
gift (liberal)–largess, largesse
gifted–talented
gifts (divine)–blessings
gigantic–colossal, enormous, giant, huge, immense, large, mammoth, prodigious
giggle–snicker, teehee, tehee, titter
gilded–aural, aurate, aureate
gilded bronze–ormolu
gilding–gilt
Gilgamesh epic goddess–Aruru
gills (four)–pint
gimcrack–bauble, gewgaw, toy, trifle, trinket
gimlet–awl, wimble
gimlet hole–bore
gimp (upholstery)–orris
gin–artifice, contrivance, device, liquor, scheme, snare, trap, trick
gin (kind of)–sloe
ginger–pep
gingerly–carefully, charily, fastidiously, finically, guardedly, warily
gingham (with linen finish)–chambray
giraffe-like animal–okapi
girasol (girasole)–heliotrope, opal, sunflower
gird–belt, bind, enclose, environ, fasten, gibe, girdle, scoff, secure, sneer
girdle–belt, cest, cingle, circle, encircle, ring, sash
girdle bone–sphenethmoid
girdle case–inro
girl–damsel, female, lass, lassie, maiden, maidservant, roebuck, shiver, sweetheart, thrill, tingle
girl (arch.)–bint, damosel
girl (giddy frolicsome)–giglet, giglot
girl (impudent)–minx
girl (little)–sis, sissy, tot
girl (naive)–ingenue
girl (pert)–minx

girl (romping)–hoiden, hoyden, tomboy
girl (saucy)–minx
girl (wanton)–fillock
girl (young)–girleen, maiden
girl cupbearer–Hebe
girlish–artless, immature, sissy
girl's name–(see feminine name)
girt–besiege, encircled, fasten
girth–band, circumference, encircle, hoop, measure, strap
gist–meat, nub, pith, point
give–accord, administer, afford, bestow, confer, donate, grant, hand, impart, present, proffer, render, supply, vouchsafe, yield
give (Scot.)–gie
give a place to–situate
give again–relent, soften, yield
give another title to–rename
give approval–assent, consent
give attendance–minister, nurse, tend
give authority to–empower
give away–bestow, betray, disclose, grant, present, sacrifice, succumb, yield
give back–echo, recede, replace, restore, retire, retreat, return
give back (law)–remise
give birth to–calve, farrow, foal
give deep slope to–escarp
give ear–heed, listen
give expression to–voice
give extreme unction to (obs.)–enele
give forth–emit
give ground–retire, withdraw
give information–advertise, publish, report, tell
give liberally–largess, largesse
give like for like–retaliate
give meaning to–define

give medicine to–dose, prescribe

give name to–dub, title

give notice–apprise, warn

give off–cease, emit, exude, issue, publish, quit

give off fumes–reek

give one's self up–surrender

give one's self up to habit–addict

give one's word–promise

give out–circulate, deal, emit, exude, issue, print, publish, release

give right to–empower, entitle

give rise to–gender

give special prominence–feature, headline, star

give strength to–nerve

give title to–dub, name

give to charity contribute, dole, donate, endow

give up–abdicate, demit, quit, renounce, resign, sacrifice, vacate

give up (treacherously)–betray

give variety to–diversify

give wrong information–misinform

given–addicted, granted, inclined

given and received–reciprocal

given or done by word of mouth–oral

given to displaying feeling–demonstrative

given to experiment–empiric

given to meditation–contemplative

given to suspicion (abnormally)–querulent

gives completely–devotes

gives forth rays–eradiates

gives ground for expectation–promises

gives soft surface to leather–buffs

gives up wholly–devotes

giving–bestowing, conferring, yielding

giving (law)–dation

giving (liberal)–largess, largesse

giving forth sound–sonant

giving information–indicative

giving name to a country–eponymic

giving name to a people–eponymic

giving up–sacrificing, surrendering

glacial debris collected–moraine

glacial drift ridge–eskar, esker, kame, oesar, osar

glacial ice–serac

glacial ice block–serac

glacial ice pinnacles–seracs

glacial ice tower–serac

glacial mass–serac

glacial ridge (gravelly deposit of)–eskar, esker

glacial ridges–eskars, eskers, kames, oesar, os, osar

glacial sand–neve

glacial snow–neve

glacial snow fields–firms, neves

glacial term–stoss

glacier (small)–icecap

glacier direction (movement of)–stoss

glacier dust (deposited on)–kryokonite

glacier fissure–crevass

glacier fragment–serac

glacis–slope

glack–defile, fork, ravine, valley

glad–animated, animating, cheering, delighted, exhilarated, exhilarating, gratified, joyful, joyous, merry, pleasing

gladden–cheer, elate, gratify, please

gladdy–yellowhammer

glade–vale

glade (comb. form)–nemo

gladiator's salutation–ave

gladly–cheerfully, eagerly, fain, fitly, joyfully, lief, preferably, properly, willingly

gladsome–blithe, cheerful, cheerfully, glad, jocular, joyful, pleased

gladstone–bag, buggy, carriage, portmanteau

glamorous–alluring, charming, fascinating

glance (quick)–scry

glance (sidelong)–leer, skew

glancer–fender, ogler, skid

gland (large)–liver

gland (near kidney)–adrenal

gland (neck)–thyroid

gland (suprarenal)–paranephros

gland enlargement–adema

gland enlargement (morbid)–adenoma

gland-like–adenoid, adenose

gland secretion–hormone

glands (full of)–adenose

glaring–apparent, barefaced, clear, conspicuous, evident, flagrant, flaring, manifest, obvious, plain, staring, visible, vividly

glaring (not)–soft

glass (brown flecked with brass filings)–aventurine

glass (curved)–lens

glass (cylindrical)–bocal

glass (drinking) – goblet, tumbler

glass (dropping, for counting drops)–stactometer

glass (field)–binocle

glass (in making)–frit

glass (in state of fusion)–metal

glass (in tension)–metal

glass (large beer)–seidel

glass (lead for gem making)–strass

glass (liqueur)–pony

glass (mass of molten coming from furnace)–parison

glass (milky)–opaline

glass (opera)–binocle

glass (optical)–lens

glass (plate of)–slide

glass (refuse)–calx

glass (sheets of)–panes

glass (small)–pony

glass (small hard blowpipe analysis)–matrass

glass (translucent)–opaline

glass froth (hardened volcanic)–pumice

glass furnace floor–siege
glass furnace mouth–bocca
glass handling rod–puntee, punty
glass-like–vitric
glass used in paste gems–strass
glassmaker's oven–leer, lehr
glassmaking device–iron-man
glassmaking frames (iron between tables)–drossers
glassware oven–leer, lehr
glassworks stoker–teaser
glasswort–kali
glaze–coat, cover, enamel, incrust, overlay, veneer, vitrify
glaze (Chinese porcelain)–eelskin
glazer–burnisher, polisher
glazing machine–calender
gleam – coruscate, flash, glimmer, glint, ray, shine
gleam (tremendously) – shimmer
glean–collect, gather
glee–cheerfulness, delight, joy, merriment, mirth
gleek–cheat, deception, gibe, sneer, trick
gleet–filth, ooze, phlegm, slime, slimy
glen–dale, dell, depression, dingle, vale, valley
glib–castrate, easy, flippant, oily, slippery, smooth, talkative
glide–coast, sail, slide, slip, soar
glide away (dial.)–slither
glimmer – blink, flash, gleam, glitter
glisten – coruscate, flash, sparkle
glitter–glare, glisten, shine, sparkle
globe–ball, orb, sphere
globe (half)–hemisphere
globes (composed of)–lobate
globose–globular, spherical
globose fruits–limes
globular–beady, globose, orbicular, orbiculate
globular body (small)–bead
globule (liquid)–drop

globulous–globular, orbicular, spherical
gloom–cloud, cloudiness, darkness, dejection, depression, dimness, heaviness, melancholy, sadness
gloomy–cloudy, dark, darkening, darkling, depressed, disheartened, downcast, drear, eerie, foreboding, glum, lowery, moody, morose, obscure, pessimistic, sad, wan
gloomy dean–Inge
gloomy person–killjoy
glories–prides
glorification–apotheosis, festivity, jollification
glorify–bless, celebrate, elevate, exalt, extol, honor, laud, praise
glorious–celebrated, eminent, grand, renowned, splendid
glorious (India)–sri
glory–admiration, boast, distinction, eclat, effulgence, honor, praise
glory (old word)–tir
gloss–brightness, burnish, enamel, glow, luster, sheen, shine
gloss over–color, fard
glossy–luster, lustrous, polished, reflecting, shining, smooth
glossy (make)–sleek
glossy and smooth–sleek
glove–gauntlet, mitt, mitten
glove (hand-protecting) – gantlet, gauntlet
glove shape (unstitched)–trank
glow–flame, gleam, incandescence
glowing–ardent, candent
glucinum (symbol for)–Gl.
glucose (rice paste)–ame
glucoside (very sweet)–estevin
glue–fasten, fix, paste, sizing, stick
glum – dismal, gloomy, moody, sullen
glut–cloy, engorge, fill, gorge, overload, pamper,

plethora, sate, satiate, saturate, surfeit
gluten – adhesive, fibrin, glue, gum
glutinous–gluey, viscid
glutton–epicure, gormandizer, rascal, scoundrel, wretch
gluttonized – gormandized, overate
gnar (gnarr)–growl, snarl
gnarl–contort, growl, knot, snarl, tangle, twist
gnat (small)–midge
gnaw–bite, eat
gnawed – ate, corroded, erose, gnawd, gnew, wasted
gnawing–rodent
gnede – lacking, miserly, scanty, sparing
gnib (Scot.)–clever, ready, sharp
gnof (gnoff)–churl, lout
gnome–aphorism, bogie bogey, dwarf, goblin, kobold, maxim, saw, sprite
gnomon–stile, style
gnomon (sun dial)–stile, style
go–act, betake, diminish, eventuate, extend, journey, leave, move, result, retire, travel, wane, weaken, wend, withdraw, work
go (Scot.)–gae
go (secretly, suddenly)–decamp
go aboard a public carrier–embark, entrain
go ahead–continue, progress, proceed
go along–continue, proceed
go around–detour
go ashore–disembark, land
go astray–err
go at–attack, undertake
go at easy gait–amble, lope
go away–begone, exit, leave, scat, shoo
go back–ebb, regress, repass, return
go back (musical)–D.S.
go back on–abandon, betray, recede, retrace

go before–lead, precede
go between–interpose, mediate
go by again–repass
go down–decline, decrease, descend, deteriorate, founder, set, sink
go easily–amble
go forward–advance, progress
go furtively–steal
go on–continue, enter, proceed
go over again–backtrack, renew, retrace
go over and change–revise
go rounds of–patrol
go softly–tiptoe
go suddenly and swiftly–scoot
go up–arise, ascend, raise, rise
goa powder–araroba
goad–egg, impel, incentive, incite, inflame, irritate, prick, prod, stimulus, sting, spur, urge
goad (dial.)–brode
goad (elephant)–ankus
goad (horse training)–valet
goal–aim, base, bourn, bourne, destination, end, mark, object
goal (base runner's)–home
goal (far away)–thule
goal (former spelling)–gol
goal (in games)–basket, first, home, spare, strike
goal (supremely desirable)–Mecca
goat–ram, ruminant
goat (wild)–ibex
goat (young)–kid
goat-like–caprine
goat's-hair cloth–tibet
goblet–cup, glass
goblet (historical)–hanap
goblin–bogey, bogie, brownie, elf, gnome, kobold, sprite
goblin (dwarf)–gnome
God–Jehovah
god (Celtic sea)–Lar
god (chief of ancient Memphis)–Ptah
god (Cymric sun)–Lleu

god (Egyptian) – Amen, Amon, Bes, Dis, Geb, Horus, Keb, Min, Osiris, Ptah, Ra, Seb
god (Egyptian hawk-headed)–Horus
god (Egyptian ram-headed)–Amon
god (false)–idol
God (Hebrew name for)–El, Elohim
god (Hindu)–Deva
god (household)–Lar, Lares
god (Latin)–Dei, Des, Deus
god (Norse)–Er, Loke, Loki, Odin, Thor, Ull, Van, Ve, Wodin
god (pagan)–idol
god (Teutonic chief)–Aesir
God be with you (contraction)–good-bye
God blind me (British oath)–blimy
god of agriculture–Faunus
god of Brythons–Dea
god (of commerce)–Mercury
god of day–Horus
god of earth (Egyptian)–Geb, Keb, Seb
god of east wind–Eurus
god of fire–Vulcan
god of fire (Vedic)–Agni
god of flocks (Greek)–Pan
god of Hebrews–El
god of Hindu triad–Siva
god of household–Lar, Lares, Penate
god of love–Amor, Ares, Cupid, Eros
god of love (Roman)–Amor
god of Memphis–Ptah
god of Northmen–Aesir
god of poetry (myth.)–Bragi
god of Romans–Dis, Dia (pl.), Jupiter, Lar, Lares
god of Romans (supreme)–Jupiter
god of sea–Aegir
god of sea (classic)–Neptune, Proteus
god of sky (Babylonian)–Anu
god of sleep–Morpheus
god of southeast wind–Eurus

god of stone or wood–idol
god of storm (Babylonian)–Zu
god of storm (evil)–Zu
god of sun–Apollo, Ra, Re
god of sun (Egyptian)–Ra
god of thunder–Thor
god of Thursday (named for)–Thor
god of Tuesday (named for)–Tiu, Tyr
god of teutonic pantheon–As
god of underworld–Dis, Dia (pl.), Pluto
god of war–Mars
god of war (Babylonian)–Ira
god of war (Celtic)–Coel
god of war (Greek)–Ares
god of war (Norse)–Tyr
god of wealth–Plutus
god of Wednesday (named for)–Woden
god of wind–Aeolus, Eolus
god of wind and storm–Adad
god of wood–Silen, Silenus
god of wood or stone–idol
god of youth–Apollo
Godavari (west) capital (British India)–Elore
goddess–dea
goddess (ancient Italian)–Diana
goddess (Aphrodite's attendant)–Peitho
goddess (avenging)–Ate
goddess (cow-headed)–Isis
goddess (Etruscan)–Uni
goddess (golden-apple throwing)–Eris
goddess (gracious)–Eumenides
goddess (Italian, anc.)–Diana
goddess (Latin)–dea
goddess (Olympian)–Hera
goddess (three-headed)–Hecate
goddess (thunder-smitten)–Semele
goddess deceived by Zeus–Leda
goddess of agriculture–Demeter, Ops

goddess of crime–Ate
goddess of dawn–Aurora, Eos
goddess of destiny–Fate
goddess of discord–Ate, Eris
goddess of earth–Erda, Ge, Semele
goddess of Ephesus–Diana
goddess of Eskimos–Sedna
goddess of flowers–Flora
goddess of fruitful soil–Demeter
goddess of fruitfulness–Demeter
goddess of Gilgamesh epic–Aruru
goddess of grain–Ceres
goddess of harvest–Ceres, Ops
goddess of harvest (Italian)–Ops
goddess of Hawaiians–Pele
goddess of healing (Norse)–Eir
goddess of healing (Teutonic)–Eir
goddess of hearth–Vesta
goddess of hearth (Italian)–Ops
goddess of hunt–Diana
goddess of infatuation–Ate
goddess of Italians–Diana, Juno, Ops
goddess of justice (retributive)–Nemesis
goddess of Kilauea–Pele
goddess of love–Aphrodite, Venus
goddess of magic–Hecate
goddess of man's fate–Ker
goddess of marriage–Hera
goddess of maternity (Egyptian)–Apet
goddess of May–Maia
goddess of mischief–Ate, Eris
goddess of moon–Diana, Luna, Selena, Selene
goddess of nature–Nymph
goddess of night–Nox, Nyx
goddess of peace–Irene
goddess of poetry–Erato
goddess of rainbow–Iris
goddess of retributive justice–Nemesis

goddess of Romans–Annona, Caca, Ceres, Dea, Diana, Juno, Lua, Nox, Ops, Venus, Vesta
goddess of sea–Doris
goddess of seasons–Horae
goddess of truth–Maat
goddess of vegetables–Ceres
goddess of vegetation–Ceres
goddess of vengeance–Ara, Ate, Nemesis
goddess of victory (Greek)–Nike
goddess of war–Anath, Bella
goddess of wisdom–Athena, Minerva
goddess of witchcraft–Hecate
goddess of youth–Hebe
God-fearing–devout, pious, religious
godforsaken–desolate, neglected, wretched
god-horse–mantis
god-like–devout, divine, pious, religious
godliness–piety
godling (woodland, Gr. myth)–Selenus
godly–devout, pious, religious, righteous
godly person–saint
godmother–cummer, kimmer, sponsor
gods (Latin)–dei, di
gods (mother of)–Rhea
gods' abode–Olympus
God's children–elect
gods' cupbearer–Ganymede
gods' eternal vein fluid–ichor, icor
gods' ethereal vein fluid–ichor, icor
gods' food–ambrosia
gods' messenger–Hermes
gods' mother–Rhea
gods' twilight–Ragnarok
gods' vein fluid (ethereal)–ichor, icor
goes astray–err
goes at easy gallop–canters
goes back–recedes, retrogresses, reverts
goes before–antecedes, leads, precedes

goes before (in time)–antecedent
goes down–declines, descends, falls, lowers, sets, sinks
goes furtively–sneaks
goes into the country–rusticates
goes out–exits, issues
Goetae–thaumaturgists
Goethe drama–Faust
goffer–crimp, flute, plait
goggler–scad
going beyond others–ultra
going from better to worse–retrogressive
going in certain direction–headed
goiter (goitre)–struma
gold (containing)–dore
gold (fool's)–pyrite
gold (heraldry)–or
gold (mosaic)–ormolu
gold (pert. to)–auric
gold alloy (artificial)–asem
gold and silver alloy (artificial)–asem
gold and silver lace or braid–orris
Gold Coast language (chief)–Tshi
Gold Coast Negro–Ga
gold coin–eagle
gold-colored alloy–oroide
gold imitation (from brass)–ormolu
gold in mass–bullion
gold-like (rare)–aureate
gold-like alloy–oroide
golden–aureate, aureous, auric, blest, blonde, gilt, halcyon, precious
golden-apple throwing goddess–Eris
golden bird–oriole
golden-breasted trumpeter–agami
golden bronze–ormolu
golden colored–dore
Golden Fleece seeker–Jason
golden in color–aureate
golden oriole–pirol
goldfish (fancy breed)–shubunkin
goldsmith's melting pot–cruset

golf (hole made in one)–ace
golf (perfect)–par
golf club–baffy, brassie, brassy, cleek, driver, iron, mashie, mashy, midiron, niblick, putter, spoon, wood
golf club face–loft
golf hazard–bunker, trap
golf hole (unplayed)–bye
golf stroke–drive, hook, loft, putt, slice
golf term–birdie, bogey, bogie, divot, eagle, fore, gallery, green, hook, lie, par, slice, stimy, stroke, stymie, tee
golfer (famous)–Hagen
goliath–giant
Goliath's abode–Gath
Goliath's slayer–David
Gomuti palm (wooly material from leaves of)–bara
gone–left, lost, off, ruined
gone beyond recall–lost
gone beyond recovery–lost
gone by–ago, bygone, passed
gone by (poetic)–agone, oer
goober–peanut
good–able, auspicious, competent, expert, favorable, gain, gratifying, helpful, interest, nifty, pleasing, profit, profitable, salutary, satisfactory, sound, suitable, trained, valid
good (Fr.)–bon
good (indifferently)–mediocre
good (mighty, Chinook jargon)–skookum
good (prefix)–eu
good behavior–decorum
good-bye – addio, adew, adieu, adios, farewell, so-long
good-bye (coll.)–tata
good form–chic
good health–prosit
good-looking – beautiful, comely, fair, personable, pretty
good luck image–alraun
good news–evangel
good news message–evangel

good of its kind–pucka, pukka
good spirit–Eudaemon
good taste–unpretentious
goods (movable)–chattels
goods (surplus)–overages
goods cast overboard–jetsam
goods cast overboard (fastened to buoy)–lagan, lagend, ligan
goose (kind of)–brant, solan
goose (male)–gander
goose (the)–anser
gooseberry–fabes
Gopher State–Minnesota
gore–blood, dirt, dung, filth, mud, penetrate, pierce, slime, stab
gorge–canyon, defile, glut, overeat, sate, satiate, valley
gorge (Anglo-Ind.)–nullah
gorge (deep)–coulee, ravine
gorge (miniature)–gully
gorge (narrow)–defile
gorgeous–grand, magnificent, resplendent, showy
gorgon (beheaded by Perseus)–Medusa
gorgon (Greek myth.)–Euryale, Medusa, Stheno
gorillas–apes
gorse–furze, juniper
goshawk (male)–tercel
gospel (pert. to)–evangelic
gospel (the)–evangel
gospel (to proclaim)–preach
gossip – chatterer, clatter, gabble, quidnunc, tattle
gossip (dialectic)–norate
gossip (malicious)–cat
gossip (to)–norate
got–became, procured, received
got back–recovered
got rid of – discarded, ditched, eliminated, ousted, shed
got the better of (coll.)–bested
Gounod's opera–Faust
gourd–melon
gourd (characteristic of)–pepo, pepos
gourd fruit–pepo, pepos
gourd-like fruit–melon

gourmand–epicure, glutton
gourmet–connoisseur, epicure, gourmand
gout–arthrithiaisis
gout remedy–lycetol
govern – bridle, conduct, curb, direct, dominate, manage, preside, regulate, rein, rule, run, supervise
governess of convent–abbess
governest–rulest
government (autocratic)–Tsarism
government (bad)–misrule
government (deputed)–regency
government (form of)–polity
government (form of, administered in church)–hierarchy
government (highly centralized)–totalitarian
government (pert. to)–political
government (real in exile)–defacto
government (vicarious)–regency
government by a few–oligarchy
government by God–theonomy
government by seven people–heptarchy
government by ten people–decarchy
government by three people–triumvirate
government conduct (pert. to)–political
government foes–anarchists, reds
government grant–patent
government head–premier
government impost–tax
government levy–tax
government official (authoritative)–bureaucrat
government representative abroad–consul
governments (strong)–powers
governor–captain, control, director, magistrate, pilot, regent, regulator, ruler

governor (castle)–alcaid, alcaide

governor (colonial)–viceroy

gowk–cuckoo, fool, gawk, simpleton

gowl–defile, gap, howl, throat, whine, yell

gowl (Scot.)–howl, yell

gown–clothe, dress, frock, garment, invest, robe, toga

gown (dressing)–kimono

goyle–gully, hollow, ravine valley

gozell–gooseberry

gozzard–gooseherd

gra–fondness, liking, love, lover, sweetheart

grab–arrest, boat, capture, clutch, grasp, nab, seize

grace – become, bedeck, comeliness, easiness, elegance, mercy, polish, refinement

graceful–airy, appropriate, charming, comely, debonair, elegant, fitting, seemly

graceful dance–minuet

gracefully–gracile

Graces (mother of)–Aegle

gracile–slender, slight, thin

gracious–benign, courteous, favorable, generous, kind, suave

grad–alumnus, alumni (pl.)

gradation – degrees, scale, stages, steps

grade–assort, degree, even, graduate, level, order, rank, rate, sort

gradual–easy, gentle, leisurely, slow

gradual loss of short unaccented vowel at beginning of word–aphesis

gradually vanish–evanesce

graduate–alumnus, alumni (pl.)

graduate (college)–bachelor

graduated plate–dial

graft–boodle, dig, ditch, inarch, labor, spade, toil, trench, work

grafted (in heraldry)–ente

grain–corn, fiber, jot, maize, oats, particle, rice, rye, scrap, spark, trace, wheat

grain (artificially sprouted)–malt, steeped

grain (bundles of)–sheaves

grain (chaffy ground part)–bran, grit

grain (coarse)–meal

grain (coarsely ground)–meal

grain (goddess of)–Ceres

grain (ground)–flour, grist, meal

grain (pert. to)–oaten

grain (sacrificial, Latin)–ador

grain (shock of)–cop

grain (small)–granule

grain coating–bran

grain for grinding–grist

grain fungus–ergot

grain funnel–hopper

grain husks (threshed)–straw

grain mildew–rust

grain mill–quern

grain mill (hand-grinding, small)–quern

grain spike–ear

grain stalk (Scot.)–ressum

grain storage place–mow

grain warehouse–elevator

grammar (part of)–syntax

grammatical case–ablative, dative, genitive, nom, nominative, vocative

grammatical case of direct address–vocative

grammatical element (resolves into)–parses

grammatical form (pert. to)–tamas

grammatical sex distinction–gender

grammatical term–phrase, simile

grammolecular weight–mol

grampus–cetacean, orc, orca, whale

grand–epic, epical, famous, gorgeous, grandiose, great, magnificent, noble, splendid, sublime, superb

grand scale (on)–epic

grand slam–vole

grandchild (Scot.)–oe, oy, oye

grandee–nobleman

grandeur–augustness, elegance, greatness, immensity, majesty, vastness

grandeval–ancient

grandiloquent – bombastic, pompous, turgid

grandiose–bombastic, epic, flaunting, grand, turgid

grandmother (Devil's)–Baba

grandparental–aval

grandparents (pert. to)–aval

grange–farm, farmhouse, granary

granger–farmer

grank–groan, murmur

grant–accord, bestow, cede, concede, confer, give, lend, spare, transfer

grant (additional)–bonus

grant by will–demise

granting–ceding, conceding, if, lending

grantor by deed–remiser

granular–corn

granular snow–neve

granulate–crystallize

grape (black wine)–Clinton

grape (bunch of)–bob

grape (kind of)–Catawba, Concord, Delaware, Hamburg, Malaga, Malage, Mission, Muscat, Thompson, Tokay

grape (pomace of)–rape

grape (Scot.)–vulture

grape acid–racemic

grape conserve–uvate

grape curculio–weevil

grape family–vitaceae

grapefruit–pomelo, shaddock

grapefruit (evaporated)–ptisan, rape, sapa

grape juice (unfermented)–must, stum

grape juice substance deposited in wine casks–tartar

grape preserve–uvate

grape refuse (crushed)–marc

grapevine disease–erinose

graph–chart

graphic–picturesque, vivid
graphic representation – chart
graphic symbol–character
grasp – apprehend, clasp, clinch, clutch, grip, hold, seize, take
grasp (coll.)–see, understand
grasping–avid, avaricious, covetous, greedy
grass (Algerian)–esparto
grass (annual)–darnel
grass (bamboo-like)–reed
grass (barnacle)–eel
grass (blue)–poa
grass (cereal)–barley, grain, oat, ragi, rye, wheat
grass (coarse)–quitch, reed, sedge
grass (cured)–hay
grass (ditch)–enalid
grass (dry)–hay
grass (fiber)–ramie
grass (for making cordage, shoes, baskets, etc.)–esparto
grass (genus of)–avena, poa
grass (grazing)–eatage
grass (herbs)–timothy
grass (June)–poa
grass (kind of)–chess
grass (marsh)–sedge, spart
grass (mat)–nard
grass (pepper)–cress
grass (row of cut)–swath
grass (Spanish)–esparto
grass (tall coarse)–reed
grass (used in making baskets, shoes, cordage, etc.)–esparto
grass (wiry)–bent
grass (with deeply furrowed grain)–avena
grass appendage–awn
grasschat–whinchat
grass-cutting tool–mower, sickle, scythe
grasshopper–locust
grassland–field, lea, meadow, pasture, range
grassland (wide expanse)–prairie
grass leaves–blades
grass plot–lawn, meadow
grassweed–eelgrass

grassy field (poetic)–mead
grassy ground–sod
grassy plain–mead, meadow
grate–abrade, grid, grind, grit, rasp, scrape
grateful – appreciative, thankful
grateful thanks (beggar's phrase)–cumshaw
grater (large)–rasper
gratified–glad, pleased
gratify–appease, arride, delight, humor, indulge, pamper, please, requite, satisfy
gratify one's vanity–flatter
gratify unduly–pamper
gratifying–well
grating–grate, grid, grill, grille, latticework, strident
gratis–free
gratitude – thankfulness, thanks
gratuitous–baseless, groundless, needless, superfluous, unwarranted, wanton
gratuity–dole, fee, gift, present, tip
grave–earnest, momentous, sedate, sepulcher, serious, sermonic, sober, solemn, staid, tomb, urn
grave robber–ghoul, goul
gravecloth–cerement
gravel and stone (loose on earth's surface)–erratics
graven – engraved, sculptured
graver–burin
gravestone–marker, monument, stela, stele, steles (pl.), stelae (pl.)
gravity–earnestness, momentousness, sobriety, weightiness
gravy boat–sauceboat
gravy dish–boat
gray – achromatic, ashy, cheerless, dismal, dull, hoar, hoary, hueless, leaden, neutral
gray (comb. form)–polio
gray (dark)–taupe
gray (pale bluish)–pearl

gray matter (nerve tissue)–cinerea
gray white mineral–chromiumptrona
gray with age–hoar, hoary
gray back–louse
grayish–grizzled, slaty
grayish brown–dun
grayish green–reseda
grayish white–ashy
grayish white and lustrous–silvery
graze–browse, brush, drab, rase, scrape, shave, skim
grazing ground–meadow, pasture, range
grease–bribe, daub, fat, lubricate, smear, soil
grease (wool)–lanolin
greasy–oily, porky
greasy substance in sheep wool–suint
great–big, extreme, huge, large, vast
great (Fr.)–grande
great albacore–tunny
great arteries–aortae, aorta (sing.)
great-aunt–grandaunt
Great Barrier island–Otea
Great Britain fishing vessel–coble
Great Britain flood–spate
Great Britain inhabitant (prehistoric)–Pict
Great Britain subdivision–shire
great deal (coll.)–gobs, lots
Great Divide–Rockies
great dragon–cuckoopint
great excitement or enthusiasm–furore
Great Lake–Erie, Huron, Michigan, Ontario, Superior
great misfortune–calamity, catastrophe, disaster, holocaust
great misfortune (pert. to)–catastrophic
great mogul emperor–Akbar
great number–multitude
great part–bulk
great personage–mogul
great realm–empire

greatest–extreme, noblest, utmost

greatly–much, nobly

greatly (very)–far

greatly removed–afar, distant

greatness of soul – magnanimity

Grecia (Bib.)–Greece

Grecian–see Greek

Greece (ancient assembly)–agora

Greece (ancient division of) –deme, Thessaly

Greece (ancient name)–Hellas

greed–avarice, cupidity

greediness–voracity

greedy – avid, devouring, gluttonous, grasping, insatiable, rapacious, ravenous, stingy, voracious

greedy of gain–mercenary

Greek–Argive, Athenian, Eolian, Hellene, Ionian, Spartan

Greek (modern)–Romaic

Greek administrative unit–deme

Greek altar (anc.)–eschara

Greek architecture (oldest and simplest)–Doric

Greek architecture (oldest order)–Doric

Greek architecture (pert. to oldest)–Doric

Greek army prophet–Calchas

Greek art (a female worshiper)–Orant

Greek assembly (popular)–agora

Greek assembly (public)–pnyx

Greek biographer–Plutarch

Greek boats–caiques

Greek cape (southern)–Matapan

Greek capital (old)–Elis

Greek character (myth.)–Adonis, Atalanta, Icarus, Pandora

Greek church section (men's)–andron

Greek church sections (reserved)–bemata

Greek city–Alexandroupolis, Athens, Corinth, Drama, Edessa, Ioannina, Komotine, Larisa, Larissa, Salonica, Salonika, Sparta

Greek city (anc.)–Elis, Eolis, Sparta

Greek clasp–fibula

Greek coin–drachma (cop., ni.), lepton (br.), obol (br.)

Greek coin (anc.)–stater

Greek colony–Ionia

Greek commonalty–demos

Greek commune–deme

Greek contests (anc.)–agones

Greek councils (legislative) –boules

Greek counselor (anc.)–nestor

Greek country (anc.)–Elis

Greek country (old)–Epirus

Greek cupid–Eros

Greek deity–Ares, Eros

Greek deity (avenging)–Alastor

Greek deity (dethroned by Zeus)–Kronos

Greek deity (supreme)–Cronus

Greek deity (sylvan)–Satyr

Greek dialect–Doric, Eolic

Greek dirge–linos

Greek district–deme

Greek district (anc.)–Ionia

Greek district (mountain)–Arcadia

Greek division (anc.)–deme

Greek division (pert. to)–nomic

Greek divisions–deme, nomea, nomes

Greek dog–greyhound

Greek dramatist (comic)–Aristophanes

Greek epic–Iliad

Greek epic poet–Homer

Greek foot soldier–hoplite

Greek form signifying blood –hema

Greek free alien resident–metic

Greek Furies–Alecto, Erinyes, Erinys, Megaera, Tisiphone

Greek game festival–agon

Greek garment–tunic

Greek ghost–ker

Greek giant (hundred-armed)–Enceladus

Greek god–Apollo, Ares, Atlas, Zeus

Greek god of flocks–Pan

Greek god of love–Eros

Greek god of lower world–Hades

Greek god of manly youth–Apollo

Greek god of mockery and censure–Mamus

Greek god's vein fluid–ichor, icor

Greek goddess–Ara, Demeter, Hera, Niobe, Rhea

Greek goddess of agriculture–Demeter

Greek goddess of earth–Ge

Greek goddess of fate–Moera

Greek goddess of heaven–Hera

Greek goddess of magic–Hecate

Greek goddess of moon–Selena, Selene

Greek goddess of night–Leto, Nyx

Greek goddess of peace–Irene

Greek goddess of victory–Nike

Greek governor (anc.)–Eparch

Greek gravestone (anc.) – stela, stele, stelae (pl.), steles (pl.)

Greek hero–Theseus

Greek hero (legend)–Cecrops

Greek hero (myth.)–Ajax

Greek instrument (reed)–aulos

Greek island–Crete, Delos, Kos, Melos, Nio, Samos

Greek island (pert. to)–Delian

Greek judge (anc.)–dicast

Greek Juno–Hera

Greek lake–Copais

Greek lawgiver–solon

Greek letter (anc.)–san

Greek letter (early)–Digamma

Greek letters–(1) Alpha; (2) Beta; (3) Gamma; (4) Delta; (5) Epsilon; (6) Zeta; (7) Eta; (8) Theta; (9) Iota; (10) Kappa; (11) Lambda; (12) Mu; (13) Nu; (14) Xi; (15) Omicron; (16) Pi; (17) Rho; (18) Sigma; (19) Tau; (20) Upsilon; (21) Phi; (22) Chi; (23) Psi; (24) Omega

Greek man of brass who guarded Crete (myth.)–Talos

Greek marker (anc. stone)–stela, stele, steles (pl.), stelae (pl.)

Greek market place–agora, agorae (pl.)

Greek measure–acaena, amphora, bachel, bacile, baril, barile, bema, cados, choenix, chous, condylos, cotula, cubit, cyathos, daktylos, dekapode, diaulos, dichas, digit, dolichos, gramme, hekteus, hemiekton, hemina, koilon, maris, medimnos, medimnus, metreta, metretes, orgyia, oxybaphon, palaiste, palame, pechys, pik, pik halebi, plethron, plethrum, pous, pygon, schene, sithame, stadion, stadium, stathmos, stremma, xylon

Greek measure (anc.)–bema

Greek measure (length) – bema

Greek milepost–stela, stele, steles (pl.), stelae (pl.)

Greek money (anc.)–drachma

Greek monster–gorgon

Greek monuments of dead–stelae, steles, stela (sing.), stele (sing.)

Greek mother (turned to stone)–Niobe

Greek mountain – Cambunian, Cithaeron, Hymettus, Ida, Oeta, Olympus,

Ossa, Othrys, Parnassus, Parnes, Pentelicus, Pindus, Psiloriti, Taygetus, Tymphrestus, Typhrestus, Velukhii

Greek musical note (anc.)–nete

Greek musical symbols (anc.)–netes

Greek myth–Atlantes, Atlas, Creon, Medea, Niobe

Greek mythological character–Adonis, Icarus, Pandora, Tantalus

Greek mythological youth–Adonis

Greek nome–Arta, Cephalonia, Corfu, Cyclades, Elis, Euboea, Zante

Greek nymph–Oread

Greek object of worship (anc.) – Sacrum, Sacra (pl.)

Greek official–eparch

Greek old testament – Septuagint

Greek paradise–Elysium

Greek patriarch–Arius

Greek peninsula–Morea

Greek people–Demos

Greek people (anc.)–Ionian

Greek personification of fate –Ker

Greek philosopher–Aristotle, Plato

Greek philosopher (pert. to) –eleatic

Greek philosophy school – stoic

Greek physician (anc.)–Galen

Greek pitcher–ollae (pl.)

Greek platform (anc., speaking)–bema

Greek poet–Arion, Homer, Ion

Greek poet (lyre player)–Arion

Greek poet (lyric)–Pindar

Greek poetess (var.)–Sapho

Greek port–Corfu, Enos, Patras, Piraeus, Syra

Greek portico–stoa

Greek province–nome

Greek race (old)–Dorian

Greek religion ghost–Ker

Greek religious festival–Delia

Greek representation of female worshiper (anc.) – Orant

Greek river–Achelous, Alpheus, Arachtus, Arta, Aspropotamo, Basilipotamo, Eurotas, Peneus, Ruphia

Greek ruler–eparch

Greek sacred enclosure (anc.)–Sekos

Greek sage (early)–Thales

Greek scale note (anc.)–nete

Greek school of philosophy (pert. to)–elian

Greek sea–Aegean, Ionian

Greek sea god–Nereus

Greek seaport–Enos

Greek skeptic–Timon

Greek skirt (men's stiff white) fustanella, fustanelle

Greek slave–helot

Greek soldier (foot)–hoplite

Greek speech (set)–rhesis

Greek spirit (avenging) – Erinys

Greek spirit (evil)–Momus

Greek statesman–Aristides

Greek stone marker (anc.)–stela, stele, steles (pl.), stelae (pl.)

Greek tablet (old) – stela, stele, steles (pl.), stelae (pl.)

Greek temple–naos

Greek temple chamber–naos

Greek temple part–cella

Greek tense (denoting past time)–aorist

Greek territory (anc.)–Acarnania, Achaia, Aetolia, Arcadia, Argolis, Attica, Boeotia, Corinth, Elis, Epirus, Laconia, Locris, Megaris, Messenia, Phocis, Sparta, Thessaly

Greek territory (old)–deme

Greek theater–odeon, odeum, odea (pl.)

Greek theater hall – odeon, odeum, odea (pl.)

Greek town (anc.)–Actium, Elea, Nemea

Greek township–deme
Greek unit (administrative) –deme
Greek valley (Argolis)–Nemea
Greek valley (pert. to, anc.) –Nemean
Greek vowel–eta
Greek vowel (fourth)–iota
Greek war cry (anc.)–alala
Greek war god–Ares
Greek weight – chalcon, chalque, diobol, diobolon, drachma, dramme, kantar, litra, livre, mina, obole, obolos, obolus, oka, oke, pound, stater, talanton, talent, tetradrachma
Greek weight (old)–obolus
Greek worshiper (female, art, anc.)–Orant
green–mossy, unripe, untrained
green (cedar)–cedre
green (Fr.)–vert
green (of Ireland)–emerald
green (shade of) – apple, bottle, emerald, Nile, olive
Green Mountain Boys' leader–Allen
green quartz–prase
green rust–patina
green spot in a waste–oasis, oases (pl.)
greenhorn (South Africa)–ikona
greenish yellow–olive
Greenland Eskimo settlement–Etah
'Greenland fluoride (sodium aluminum)–cryolite, kryolite
Greenland flying base–Etah
Greenland settlement–Etah
greenness–verdancy
greet–accost, address, hail, salute
greet (with courtesy)–welcome
greeting–address, ave, hail, reception, salutation, saluting, welcome
gregarious–social
grego–cloak, greatcoat, jacket

grenier–attic
grew bitter–soured
grew larger – expanded, waxed
grey–see gray
griddle cake–crumpet
gridiron–griddle, grill
grief–anguish, care, distress, dolor, mishap, pain, ruth, sadness, sorrow, suffering, trial, woe
grief (emblem of)–rue
grief (poetic)–dolor
grieve – distress, lament, mourn, pain, rue, sorrow, wound
grieve (obs.)–erme
grievous–bitter, sore
grievously afflicted–smitten
griff (Eng. dial.)–glen, ravine
griffaun–hoe
griffe–griffin, mulatto
grig–annoy, cricket, dwarf, grasshopper, heather, irritate, tantalize
grike–chink, crevice, ravine
grill–griddle, gridiron
grill with condiments–devil
grim–dour, ferocious, forbidding, frightful, ghastly, grisly, hideous, horrid, inexorable, pitiless, ruthless, sour, stern, sullen
grim and ghastly–grisly
grimace–affectation, mock, mop, moue, mow, pretense, sham
grimace (arch.)–mow, mowe
grimalkin–cat
grime–dirt, smut, soot
grimful–cruel, dreadful
grin–smile
grind – bray, comminute, crush, pestle, polish, powder, pulverize, sharpen, whet
grind fine–powder, pulverize
grind teeth–gnash
grind to powder–bray
grind together–gnash
grind whale–blackfish
grinder–molar
grinding–burdensome, excruciating, grating, molar

grinding down (by friction) –attrition
grindle–bowfin, ditch, drain
gringo–American, Englishman, foreigner
grip – bag, clasp, clutch, ditch, drain, furrow, grasp, trench
grip (shoe)–cleat
gripe–clutch, graip, grapple, grasp, griffin, vulture
gripped tightly–clenched
griskin–chop, loin, steak
grisly–ghastly, grim
gristle–cartilage
grit–bravery, nerve, perseverance, sand
grivet–monkey, waag
groggery (Irish, selling illegal liquor)–shebeen
groggy–shaky, tipsy, tottering, unsteady, wavering
groom–assistant, curry, manservant, servant, shopboy, tidy
groom (India)–syce
groom (to)–dress
groove–channel, dado, furrow, rabbet, rut, scarf, stria, striae (pl.)
groove (architectural)–flute
groove (in upper lip)–philtrum
groove (made by cutting)–scarf
groove (minute)–stria, striae (pl.)
groove cut in one piece to hold edge of other–rabbet
grooved–fluted, striate
grooved lead strips for fastening lead glass–cames
groped–felt
grosbeak–hawfinch
groser–gooseberry
gross – big, bulky, burly, coarse, fat, massive, obscene, rank, sensual, vulgar
grossly stupid–asinine
grot–fragment, grotto
grotesque – antic, bizarre, fanciful, fantastic, incongruous
grotto – cave, cavern, crypt, den, grot, speos, vault

ground–base, country, earth, establish, initiate, land, milled, premise, root, soil, train

ground (marshy) – bog, marsh, moor, swale

ground (piece of) – acre, farm, lot, plat

ground (piece of marshy)–swale

ground (pleasure) – park, pleasance

ground (raised strip of)–ridge

ground (spongy) – bog, marsh, swale

ground area–terrain

ground beetles (genus of)–amara

ground corn–grist

ground grain – flour, grist, meal

ground grain (chaffy part)–bran

ground squirrel–gopher

ground together–gnashed

groundless – baseless, false, idle, unfounded, unwarranted

grounds–basis

grounds (conscientious) – scruples

grounds (public recreational)–park

groundwork–basis

group–arrange, assemblage, batch, bevy, class, clump, division, flock, herd, sect

group (brilliant)–galaxy

group (nonprofessional) – laity

group (numerical) – octet, trio

group (playing)–eleven, five, nine, side, team, troupe

group (political)–bloc, machine, party, ring

group (singing) – chanters, chorus, duet, octet, quartet, quartette

group (small)–bevy

group (social)–sept, tribe

group (vertebrate) – amnionata, amnionta

group (working) – crew, gang, shift, team

group co-operation – teamwork

group of advanced students –seminar

group of eight–octad, octet, octette

group of five–pentad

group of musicians – band, chorus, orchestra, septet

group of nine–ennead

group of noted persons–galaxy

group of persons – band, chorus, eleven, five, nine, orchestra, team

group of related species–genus

group of related speech–genera

group of seamen – crew, hands

group of seven–heptad, septet, septette

group of singers–choir, chorus, quartet, quartette, trio

group of students–seminar

group of ten–decade, decads

group of three–triad, trine, trio

group of two vowels–digram

group regarded as an individual–unit

grouped–assembled, classed, collected, gathered

grouper (black)–mero

grouping (artistic)–scenery

groups (opposing)–sides

groups (social, of common descent)–clans

grouse–complain, grumble, ptarmigan, repine

grouse (capercaillie courtship performance)–lak

grouse (northern)–ptarmigan

grouse (Scandinavian)–ptarmigan

grouty–cross, sulky, sullen

grove–wood

grove (popular)–alameda

grove of small trees–copse

grow–accrue, augment, bud, come, enlarge, expand, improve, increase, wax

grow dark–darkle

grow dim–blear

grow fat–batten, thrive, wax

grow in length–elongate

grow into slender stalk – spindle

grow more intense–deepen

grow more profound – deepen

grow thin–emaciate

grow tiresome–bore, pall

grow together–accrete

grow uninteresting – bore, pall

grow worse–deteriorate

growing (as plants)–vegetal

growing (living on trees)–epidendral

growing angry–irascent

growing in clusters – racemose

growing in pairs–binate

growing in water–aquatic

growing out–enate

growing under snow–nival

growing wild in field–agrestial

growl–gnar, grumble, mutter, snarl

growl (as a dog)–gnar

grown–expanded, matured

growth – enlargement, expansion, increase, rise, swelling

growth (fungus) – mildew, mold

growth (green)–moss

growth (luxurious)–riot

growth (marine)–seaweed

growth (premature)–precocity

growth (promoting)–nutriment

growth (white on plants)–mildew

growth of wood cut periodically–coppice

grub–dig, drudge, larva, larvae (pl.), plod, root, search, stump

grudge–envy, resentment

grudging sense of inferiority –envy

gruesome – ghastly, horrid, macabre, sordid

gruff–austere, bluff, brusque, deep, harsh, hoarse, morose, rough, severe, sour, surly

grum–glum, morose, sour, surly

grumble–complain, grouse, growl, kick, mumble, mutter, repine

Guam capital–Agana

guanaco–llama

guarantee–avouch, endorse, ensure, insure, security, surety, warrant, warranty

guaranty–pledge, warranty

guarapucu–wahoo

guard–attention, bridle, care, convoy, curb, escort, gaoler, jailer, jailor, keep, keeper, police, protect, protection, protector, sentinel, sentry, shield, tend, watch, watchman

guard (advance)–van

guarded – careful, cautious, circumspect, defended, discreet, protected, wary, watchful

guardian–custodian, defender, keeper, patron, protector, warden

guardian (alert)–Cerberus

guardian (vigilant)–Cerberus

guardian (watchful)–Argus

guardianship–custody

guarding (protecting)–tutelar

guards (line of)–cordon

guariba–monkey

guasa–grouper

Guatemala capital (first) – Ciudad Viega

Guatemala city–Guatemala la Nueva (c.), Quezaltenango, Salama, Totonicapan

Guatemala coin – centavo (cop.), peso (cop., alum.), quetzal (s.)

Guatemala Indian tribe (extinct)–Xinca

Guatemala lake–Amatitland, Atitlan, Dulce, Peten

Guatemala measure – caballeria, cajuela, cuarta, fanega, manzana, vara

Guatemala peak (volcanic)– Fuego

Guatemala port–Champerico, Livingston, San Jose

Guatemala river – Chixoy, Pasion, San Pedro

Guatemala volcano – Agua, Fuego

Guatemala weight–caja

gubbins–fragments, refuse

gudame (Scot.) – grandmother

gudesire (Scot.) – grandfather

Gudrun's (Guthrun) husband–Atli

gue–rogue, sharper

guerdon – recompense, requital, reward

Guernsey coin–double (br.)

guess – conjecture, divine, fancy, presume, surmise, suspect

guest–caller, inmate, lodger, visitor

Guiana (British) coin – bit (s.)

Guiana tree–dali

guide–cicerone, clue, con, direct, govern, lead, marshal, pilot, polestar, rein, steer, tutor, usher

guide (sight-seeing)–cicerone

guide way (knitting machine)–sley

guiding strap–rein

Guido's first note–ut

Guido's high note–ela

Guido's note–alamire, elami

Guido's scale note–alamire

Guido's second note–are

Guido's third note–bmi

guild (merchant)–hanse

guild hall statue (wooden)– gog, magog

guile–craft, deceit, duplicity, treachery

guileless–innocent, naive

guilt – culpability, iniquity, wickedness

guilty–nocent

guilty (to prove)–attaint

Guinea measure–jacktan

guinea pig–cavy

Guinea trees (food)–akees

Guinea weight – aguirage, akey, benda, piso, quinto, seron, uzan

guitar (Oriental)–sitar

gulch–arroyo, coulee, gorge, ravine

gulf (bottomless)–abyss

gull–cheat, deceive, defraud, dupe, kittiwake, mew, mislead, skua, tern, trick

gull (distinguished by small hind toe)–kittiwake

gull (having hind toe, short or rudimentary) – kittiwake

gull (jaeger)–teaser

gull family (pert. to)–larine

gulled–fooled

gullet – esophagus, maw, throat

gullible–credulous

Gulliver's Travels, filthy race of brutes–Yahoo

gully – drain, gorge, gulch, gutter, ravine

gum–chicle, tissue

gum (aromatic)–myrrh

gum (inflammable tree) – resin

gum arabic–acacia, acacin, acacine

gum astringent (used in medicine)–kino

gum resin–elemi, myrrh

gum tree–xylan

gumbo–okra

gummy–adhesive, viscous

gums–ula

gums (pert. to)–gingival

gun (antiaircraft)–ack-ack

gun (artillery large, army slang)–barker

gun (coll.)–gat, rod, tommy

gun (37-mm., army slang)– little poison

gun barrel cleaner–ramrod

gun cavity–bore

gun cock–nab

gunfire (raking) – enfilade, strafe

gunlock pawl–sear

gun range–carry

gun part (wooden)–stock

gun platform–emplacement

gunner–cannoneer

guns (antiaircraft)–archies

gurgling sound–gobble
gurnard (yellow)–dragonet
guru (Ind.)–teacher
gush – outpouring, pour, spurt
gushing–effusive, teeming
gushing flow–jet
guss–dragrope
gusset–gore
gust – blast, gale, squall, storm, wind
gust of wind–berry
gust of wind (violent)–blast
gusto – appreciation, elan, liking, relish, taste, zest
gut–bowels, defile, destroy, disembowel, entrails, eviscerate, gully, intestine, plunder

gutter – brook, channel, groove, gully, watercourse
gutter (Scot.)–siver
gutter (ship's deck)–scupper
guttural sound–burr
guy–chaff, chain, decamp, fellow, guide, person, rod, rope, stay
guy rope–stay, vang
guzzle–debauch, drain, gutter, liquor, throat, tope
gymnast–acrobat, athlete
gymnastic–acrobatical
gymnastic swing–trapeze
gymnastic term (coll.)–kip
Gypsies – Romanies, Rommanies, Roms
gypsum (var.)–selenite

Gypsy – Gitana (fem.), Gitano, Rom, Romany, Rommany
Gypsy book–lil
Gypsy dialect – Romany, Rommany
Gypsy foreman–Rom
Gypsy language – Romany, Rommany
Gypsy letter–lil
Gypsy man–chal
Gypsy paper–lil
Gypsy pocket book–lil
Gypsy woman–chai, chi
gyrate–revolve, rotate, spin, twirl, whirl
gyves–chains, fetters, irons, shackles

H

H (the letter)–aitch, aspirate
haar (Scot.)–fog
habble – brawl, confusion, difficulty, gabble, uproar
habile–able, adroit, clever, expert, skillful
habiliment – apparel, attire, clothing, costume, dress, garb, habit, raiment, vestment
habilitate–clothe, dress, entitle, equip, qualify
habit–array, clothe, custom, dress, guise, habitude, practice, usage, use, wont
habit (bad)–vice
habitat–abode, home, locality, range, reside, station
habitation–domicile, dwelling, home, residence, tenement
habitation (crowded)–warren
habitation (mean)–hovel
habitual–accustomed, common, customary, regular, usual
habituate–accustom, addict, enure, familiarize, frequent, inure, season, settle

habituate (to foreign environment)–acclimate
habitue–frequenter
hacendero–farmer
hache–ax, hatchet
hacienda–establishment, estate
hack–carriage, chop, coach, cough, cut, hew, mangle
hack (literary)–devil
hackberry–oneberry
hackee–chipmunk
hackle–comb, stickleback
hackle (artificial fly making)–shiner
hackneyed–banal, trite
had a presentiment of–boded
had being–was
had courage–dared, durst
had effect–told
had no hope–despaired
had on–wore
had recourse–resorted
haddock (smoked)–finnan
Hades–hell, pit, Sheol, Tartarus
Hades river–Lethe, Styx
haff–lagoon
haft–handle
hag (vixenish)–harridan
haggard – anxious, bony,

gaunt, lank, lean, spare, suffering, thin, untamed, wildeyed
haggard and thin–gaunt
haggle–bargain, chisel, cut, hack, hew, palter, wrangle
Haida memorial post–xat
hail – accost, address, ave, call, greet, health, salutation
hail (nautical)–ahoy
hail and farewell–ave
hair–crine
hair (Angora goat)–mohair
hair (braid of)–pig, pigtail, queue
hair (coarse, stiff) – bristle, shag
hair (cue of)–pig
hair (having thick)–maned
hair (horse)–mane
hair (ornamental tuft of)–plume
hair (pert. to)–pilar
hair (shaggy)–mane
hair (thick fine)–fur
hair band–fillet
haircloth–aba, cilice
hair curler–rat
hairdresser (Fr.)–friseur

hair dye–henna
hair falling out–psilosis
hair fillet–snood
hairline–cerif, serif
hair ointment–pomade
hair on horse's foot–fetlock
hair on intestine–membrane, villus, villi (pl.)
hair on plants–villus, villi (pl.)
hair pad–rat
hair remover–epilatory
hair removing agents–depilatories
hair ribbon–snood
hair roll (back of woman's head)–chignon
hair tufts–beards
hair wave–marcel
hairless–bald, epilose
hair's breadth–ace
hairy–comate, hirsute, pilar, pilose, shaggy
Haitian city–Port-au-Prince
Haitian coin–gourde (s.)
Haitian island (between Porto Rico and Haiti)–Mona
Haitian magic–obi
Haitian sweet potato–batatas
halberd–bill, weapon
halberd-shaped–hastate
halch–embrace, knot, salute
halcyon – bird, kingfisher; calm, peaceful
hale – draw, haul, pull, strong, vigorous
half–moiety, part, partner, semester, semi, term
half (prefix) – demi, hemi, semi
half-breed – mestee, metif, metis, metisse (fem.), mestizo, mestiza (fem.)
half circumference–semicircle
half diameter–radius, radii (pl.)
half-man and half-bull monster–minotaur
half-man and half-horse–centaur
half mask–domino
half mask (usually of silk)–loup
half-moon shape–semilunate

half rotten–dotted
half tune–semitune
halfway between stern and stem–midships
half year's stipend of dead minister (Scot. law)–ann, annat
hall – corridor, entry, hallway, passage, passageway, room
hall (entrance) – atrium, atria (pl.), foyer, hallway
hall (large room)–auditorium, aula, aulae (pl.)
hall (music)–odeon, odeum, odea (pl.)
hall (student's)–burse
hallow – bless, consecrate, dedicate
hallowed place – altar, church, fane, shrine, temple
hallucination–delusion, fantasy
hallucination (desert) – mirage
halma–jump
halo–arc, aura, aureola, aureole, circle, glory, glow, nimb, nimbus
halt–arrest, cease, docked, lame, lameness, limp, limping, mutilated, stand, stop
halting – hesitating, lame, limping, spavined, vacillating
halting place for troops – camp, etape
Hamatic race (one of)–Somal
hameil–domestic, homely
Hamilton's (Alexander) birthplace–Nevis
Hamite–Somal, Somali
hamlet–village
Hamlet's nationality–Danish
Hamlet's sweetheart–Ophelia
hammer – beat, belabor, strike, swinge
hammer (heavy)–jack, maul, sledge
hammer (kind of) – claw, tack

hammer (leaden, Eng.) – madge
hammer (mason's)–peen
hammer (small tilt)–oliver
hammer (small, worked by foot)–oliver
hammer (stone-shaping) – kevel
hammer (wooden heavy)–beetle
hammer (yellow)–skite
hammer down–tamp
hammer end (flat)–poll
hammer head (reverse end)–peen
hammer out–anvil
hamper – basket, burden, clog, confine, cramp, curb, embarrass, encumber, fetter, hanaper, hinder, impede, load, manacle, ped, restrain, restrict, shackle, slow, trammel
hamper (wickerwork)–crate
Ham's son–Cush
hanaper–basket, hamper
hand–craftsman, give, grasp, pass, power, share, transmit, worker, workman
hand (clenched)–fist
hand (pert. to)–chiral
hand used in writing Arabic–neski
handbag – etui, grip, purse, reticule, satchel
handbag (lady's)–reticule
handbag (woman's)–cabas
handball point–ace
hand covering – gantlet, gauntlet, glove, mitt, muff
hand covering (anc. Roman boxer's)–cestus, cesti (pl.)
handicap – advantage, burden, disadvantage, encumber, hinder, impede
handicap (vocal)–lisp, stuttering
handkerchief – neckcloth, neckerchief
handkerchief (loud) – bandana
handle–ansa, control, deal, direct, feel, haft, helve, hilt, knob, manage, paw.

ply, second, touch, treat, use, wield
handle (bench plane)–tote
handle (cannon)–anse
handle (having)–ansate
handle (kettle or pail)–bail
handle (of joiner's plane) toat
handle (pail or kettle)–bail
handle (pitcher)–ansa
handle (printing press) – rounce
handle (pump)–swipe
handle (scythe) – snath, snathe, thole
handle (sword)–haft, hilt
handle (urn)–ansa
handle attacher–bailer
handle awkwardly–fumble
handle carelessly–tweedle
handle roughly–maul
handle rudely–paw
handle-shaped–ansated
handle skillfully (skilfully)– manipulate
handled–pawed, treated
handling–control, management, treatment, use
handlock–handcuff
hand-me-down – cheap, readymade, secondhand
handout–food, meal, snack
hand-picked–eleme, selected
hand-picked (as figs)–eleme
hand-picked, carefully sifted (Turk.)–eleme
hand-shaped–palmate
handsome – dexterous, elegant, limber, manageable, ready
handsome (Scot.)–braw
hand-thrown explosive shell –grenade
handwriting–script
handwriting word (first)– mene
hands–crew
hands on hips and elbows turned out–akimbo
handy – adept, convenient, deft, skillful, versatile
hang–depend, droop, pend, rest, suspend
hang around–loaf, loiter
hang down–droop, lop
hang loosely–dangle, loll, lop

hanger on–loiterer, parasite
hanging (neck, for soldiers) –havelock
hanging of tapestry–tapis
hanging ornaments–bangles, pendants
hanging over on one side– alop
hangings (rich, at back of altar)–dorsals
hangings (stage)–scenery
hangman (public) – Jack Ketch
hank–skein
hank of twine–ran
hankered–longed, yearned
Hannibal's father (var.) – Hamilcar
happen – befall, betide, chance, come, fall, fare, occur, transpire
happen again–recur
happening – episode, event, incident, occurence
happening (actual)–fact
happening (at fixed intervals)–periodic
happily–appropriately, contentedly, fitly, gladly, opportunely, prosperously, successfully, tactfully
happiness–beatitude, blessedness, bliss, felicity, prosperity
happiness (great)–bliss
happy – blessed, blest, content, contented, felicitous, fortunate, glad, lucky, propitious, prosperous, sunny
happy (dial.)–seely
harangue–address, declaim, nag, orate, oration, screed, speech, tirade
harangue (slang)–spiel
harass–agitate, annoy, badger, bait, beset, bother, bully, chafe, distress, disturb, fag, fret, gall, grind, harry, heckle, hector, irritate, jade, molest, nag, perplex, persecute, pester, plague, provoke, tantalize, tease, tire, torment, trouble, try, vex, weary, worry

harass (var.)–gall, haze
harass with questions (Scot.) –targe
harassed with clamor – dinned
harbinger–forerunner, harborer, herald, host, messenger, precursor, presage
harbor–foster, haven, lodging, port, refuge, retreat, shelter
hard – callous, close, cold, complicated, diligent, fit, impenetrable, inflexible, intricate, iron, knotty, mean, onerous, rigorous, robust, stern, stingy, strenuous, stringent, toilsome, unyielding, wearisome
hard drawn–tense
hard finish–enamel
hard question–poser
hard rubber–ebonite
hard, smooth, transparent– glossy
hard substance–adamant
hard twisted cotton–lisle
hard water–ice
harden–cake, enure, freeze, inure, set, steel, temper, toughen
harden (as cement)–set
hardened – callous, frozen, hard, impenetrable, impenitent, impervious, inveterate, obdurate, reprobate, solidified, steeled
hardened insensibility–callous
hardened into a mass–caked
hardened to war–aguerri
hardening of eyeball–glaucoma
hardhead–boche
hardhearted–cruel, mean
hardness (impenetrable) – adamant
hardship–injury, privation, rigor
hardtack (Fr.)–galette
hardwood–ash, mahogany, maple, oak, teak, walnut
hardy–bold, brave, daring, intrepid, lusty, resolute,

robust, rugged, spartan, stout, sturdy, tough
Hardy's character–Tess
Hardy's heroine–Tess
hare (female)–doe
hare (half-grown)–leveret
hare (little chief)–pika
hare (tailless)–pika
hare (young)–leveret
harem–seraglio, zenana
harem room–oda, odah
hark–hearken, hist, listen
harkened – heard, hearken, heeded, listened
harm – damage, evil, grief, hurt, injure, injury, pain, sorrow, wickedness, wrong
harmed–endamaged, injured
harmed (obs.)–baned
harmful – bad, damaging, deleterious, evil, hurtful, nocent, noisome, pernicious, sinister
harmless – innocuous, unharmed, unhurt, uninjured, unoffending
harmonious – accordant, agreeable, compatible, congruous, consonant, melodious, musical, peaceful, symmetrical, tuneful
harmonize – agree, attune, blend, chime, consist, correspond, go, sympathize, tone
harmonize (coll.)–gee
harmony – agreement, concord, cosmos, melody, music, tune, unison, unity
harmony (in)–cooperatively
harmony (to be in)–accord, agree, jibe
harness–gear, tackle
harness part–collar, hame, rein, trace, tug
harness part (to take pull of tugs)–breastband, hames
harness ring (for reins)–terret
harp (Japanese)–koto
harp-shaped–lyrate
harpoon–javelin, spear
harpsicord (old form)–spinet
harpy–Aello, Celeano, Ocypete, Podarge

Harrington (James) **utopia** (imaginary)–Oceana
harrow–disk, distress, harry, lacerate, oppress, torment, wound
harrow spike–tine
harrow tooth–tine
harry–agitate, annoy, hector, hound, plague, plunder, ravage, ravish, sack, vex, violate
Harry's madcap companion (in Merry Wives of Windsor)–Falstaff
harsh–acerb, acrid, acrimonious, asper, bitter, clashing, crude, disagreeing, discordant, drastic, grim, jangling, raspy, relentless, rigorous, severe, stern, strident
harsh (to make less)–mitigate
harsh and bitter–acerb
harsh sound–bray
harshness–crudite, raucity, rigor
hart–stag
hart (three-year-old)–spade
hartebeest–antelope, caama
Harvard prize (scholarship)–Detur
harvest–crop, gather, reap
harvest (goddess of)–Ceres, Ops
harvest home (Scot.)–kern, kirn
harvest sheaf (last, Scot.)–kern
has–owns
has a presentiment–forefeels
has compassion for–pities
has effect–enures
has influence–militates
has recourse to–betakes
has the power–able, can
hash–mince
hashish – bhang, cannabis, hemp
hassock–footstool
hastened–accelerated, expedited, galloped, hied, hurried, precipitated, raced, ran, rushed, sped
hasty–brash, cursory, expeditious, fast, fleet, impet-

uous, quick, rash, speedy, stirabout, swift
hasty pudding–mush, stirabout
hat–beret, bonnet, panama, sombrero, tam
hat (brimless)–fez
hat (coll.)–dicer
hat (English)–bowler
hat (English straw)–Dunstable
hat (French) – beret, chapeau, chapeaux (pl.)
hat (made of fur)–castor
hat (made of pith)–topee, topi
hat (opera)–gibus, topper
hat (silk, slang)–tile
hat (small, brimless)–toque
hat (spongewood)–sola
hat (stiff)–tile
hat (summer)–Panama, sailor, straw
hat (type of ladies')–bolero, caddie, caddy, cooie, duckbill, harlequin
hat crown–poll
hat-making fiber–sola
hatchet–adz, adze
hatchet (aboriginal stone, Australia)–mogo
hate–abhor, abominate, detest, loathe, rancor
hateful – abhorrent, abominable, detestable, disagreeable, disgusting, distasteful, invidious, loathsome, obnoxious, odious, offensive, revolting
hater of mankind–misanthrope
hater of marriage–misogynist
hatred–abhorrence, animosity, aversion, detestation, enmity, malevolence, malignity, odium, rancor, repugnance
hatred (inveterate)–rancor
hatred of women–misogyny
haughtiest–proudest
haughtiness–arrogance
haughty–arrogant, disdainful, high, lofty, proud, scornful

haul–cart, drag, draw, lug, pull, tow, tug

haul down flag–strike

haul up and lash with small rope–trice

hauling charges – cartage, drayage, towage

haunch–hindquarters, hip

haunt–den, dive, frequent, habit, infest, resort

haunt (low)–den, dive

hautboy–oboe

have–own

have (Scot.)–hae

have ambitions–aspire

have benefit of–enjoy

have direction (to)–lie

have effect – enure, inure, militate, tell

have interest in–care

have on–wear

have thoughts of–ideate

have to do with–deal

have weight–militate

haven – bay, harbor, inlet, port, recess

having a backbone – vertebrate

having a beak–rostrate

having a beard–aristate

having a chiseled appearance (Fr.)–cisele

having a handle–ansate

having a rank–generic

having a shield–clypeated

having a stem–petiolate

having a tail–caudate

having a tuft of soft hairs–comose

having a veil (botany)–velate

having a wavy outer edge–repand

having ability–competent

having agreement of all–unanimous

having an account at Oxford buttery–battel

having antlers (as some animals)–horned

having apex rounded with a light notch–retuse

having arisen–up

having beard-like appendage–aristate

having blue color–cyanic

having branches–ramose

having competing claims–corrival

having constant and teasing desire–itch

having curvature in or near middle (her.)–nowy

having ears–aurate

having effect–tell

having equal sides–isosceles

having extraordinary properties–magical

having faith–trusting

having feelers (as an insect) –antennate

having fingers–digitate

having fin-like locomotive organs–pinniped

having flavor–sapid

having foot digits turned inward–intoed, pigeon-toed

having force of a decree–decretive

having form of smooth shallow depression–glenoid

having four feet–quadrupedal

having granulated surfaces–grained

having great dignity–majestic

having great force or impulse–driving

having harmful qualities–innocuous

having knowledge of coming events–prescient

having large nose–nasute

having lateral surfaces–sided

having least intensity of color–palest

having leaves–foliar

having limits–finite

having local application – topical

having long rectangular inset–paneled

having lumps–noduled

having made a will–testate

having more than one husband–polyandry

having most intensity of sound–loudest

having no common measure –incommensurable

having no interest–supine

having no teeth – edental, edentate

having notable history – storied

having nothing to do–otiose

having offensive odor–olid

having offensive smell–olid

having one color – monochromatic

having only one foot–uniped

having organs of hearing–eared

having pendent ornaments–tasseled

having pincer-like claws–chelate

having point of radiation–polar

having power over fire–ignipotent

having quality or power of believing–creditive

having raised surface – ridged

having reference to prior time–retroactively

having risen–up

having rounded appendage–lobate

having rounded divisions–lobate

having same ending – conterminal

having same parents – germane

having saw-like edge – serrate, serrated

having scales–perulate

having scalloped edge – crenate

having second sight – fey, psychic

having sharp turns of direction–quirky

having shoots–twigged

having short flat nose (obs.) camus, camuse

having sides and angles unequal–scalene

having slender tip–aristate

having small depressions (pits)–foveolarious

having small globes–beaded

having small plane surfaces–faceted

having smooth reflecting surface-specular

having stem growing from ground-scapose

having stimulating qualities -inspirational

having susceptibility-alive

having tail-caudate

having taste-sapid

having the least-minimifidian

having thorns-spinate

having three broods in a year-trigoneutic

having three cycles-tricyclic

having three metrical units-trimeter

having three syllables - trisyllabic

having tow-like matted filaments-stupose

having two equal sides-isosceles

having two feet-bipedal, bipede

having two horns-bicorn

having two meanings-ambiguous

having two poles-dipolar

having undivided concern-interested

having unequal sides (as a triangle)-scalene

having wide scope-comprehensive

having wings-alar

havoc-destroy, destruction, devastate, devastation, waste

haw-sloe, hedge, fence, enclosure, messuage, hawthorn

haw (black)-sloe

Hawaiian-Kanaka

Hawaiian banquet - ahaaina

Hawaiian bird - ava, iiwi, ioa, iwa, oo, ooaa

Hawaiian bird (frigate)-iwa

Hawaiian bird (indigenous raptorial)-io

Hawaiian bird (tropical)-oo

Hawaiian bush-olona

Hawaiian canoe-waapa

Hawaiian cat's cradle (game of)-hei

Hawaiian cord-aea

Hawaiian dance-hula

Hawaiian feast-Ahaaina

Hawaiian fern chaff-pulu

Hawaiian food-poi

Hawaiian food fish - lania, uku

Hawaiian food staple-taro

Hawaiian for company-aha

Hawaiian for eating-aina

Hawaiian goddess-Pele

Hawaiian goose-nene

Hawaiian grass (tufted) - emoloa

Hawaiian hawk-io

Hawaiian island - Hawaii, Kahoolawe, Kauai, Lanai, Maui, Molokai, Niihau, Oahu

Hawaiian Islands (former name)-Sandwich

Hawaiian lava (rough)-aa

Hawaiian mahogany-koa

Hawaiian majugua-hau

Hawaiian mohos-oos

Hawaiian octopus-hee

Hawaiian pepper-ava

Hawaiian plant (starch)-pia

Hawaiian precipice-pali

Hawaiian puffin-ao

Hawaiian raven-alala

Hawaiian root (edible)-taro

Hawaiian salutation-aloha

Hawaiian shrub-akia

Hawaiian starch plant-pia

Hawaiian town-Hilo

Hawaiian tree-alani, koa

Hawaiian tree (timber)-koa

Hawaiian tree fiber (silk)-pulu

Hawaiian valley-Manoa

Hawaiian veranda-lanai

Hawaiian wreath-lei

hawk-peddle, canvass, cry, falcon

hawk (fish)-osprey

hawk (fledgling)-eyas

hawk (kind of)-elanet

hawk (large)-io

hawk (male)-tarse, tercel

hawk (young)-eyas

hawk-eyed deity-Ra

hawk-headed deity-Ra

hawk's disease-cray

hawk's nest-aerie

hawk's nostril-nare

hawker-peddler

hawkers (of fruit)-costers

hawking leash-lune

hawser-line, rope

hawser post-bitt, bollard

hawthorn (Eng.)-may

hawthorn berry-haw

hay (dry)-ted

hay (long pile of)-windrow

hay (mowed line of)-swath

hayfork (Eng. dial.)-pikel

hay-spreading machine-tedder

haystack (rounded)-rick

hay storage place-mow, loft

hay sweep-buck

hazard - danger, endanger, imperil, jeopard, jeopardy, peril, risk, venture

hazard (navigation)-fog

hazardous-fortuitous, perilous, precarious, queasy, risky, uncertain, unsafe

hazardous (coll.)-chancy

haze-beat, drizzle, film, fog, frighten, mist, scold

haze (on sea)-glin

hazy-dim, filmy, foggy, indistinct, misty, nebular, obscure, smoky, thick, vague

he (Fr.)-il

he (Latin)-ipse

he remains (stage direction) -manet

he who wept for more worlds to conquer-Alexander

head-aim, chief, lead, nob, pate, poll

head (abbey)-abbot

head (coll.)-nog, noggin

head (convent)-abbess

head (Fr.)-tete

head (hammer)-peen

head (hard)-boche

head (medium proportion)-mesaticephalous

head (side of)-temple

head (top of)-pate, scalp

head and neck covering - hood

head covering - beret, bonnet, cap, fascinator, hair, hat, hood, peruke, scalp, toupee, wig

head of hair–crine
head of nunnery–abbess
head skin–scalp
head yards braced back – abox
headache (nervous) – megrim, migraine
headband (ornamental) – diadem
headdress – bonnet, coife, permanent, tiara, toque
headdress (cape-like, with lapets)–pinner
headdress (18th century widow's)–bandore
headdress (false hair)–periwig, peruke, wig
headdress (liturgical)–miter
headdress (ornamental) – coronet
headgear–beret, berretta, biretta, bonnet, hat, sombrero, tam
heading–caption
headland–cape, Morro, ness, promontory
headland (var.)–nase
headless (Fr.)–etete
headline–caption, heading
headliner–star
headman–ataman
headpiece–beret, beretta, biretta, bonnet, hat, sombrero
headstrong–rash
heal–cure, knit, restore
healer–balm, practitioner
healing–curative
healing (goddess of, Teutonic)–Eir
healing compound–balm
health (nut on)–hypochondriac
health, happiness and prosperity–welfare
health resort–spa
healthful – salubrious, salutary, sanatory, wholesome
healthy–hale, hearty, robust, salubrious, salutary, sane, vigorous, well, wholesome
healthy and strong–robust
heam–afterbirth
heap – accumulate, amass, crowd, lump, multitude, pile, plenty, raff, raft, stack, throng
heap (combustible)–pyre
heap (Scot.)–dess
heap of stones (rounded)–cairn
heap together–cumulate
heaper–piler
hear–attend, feel, hearken, listen, perceive, see
hearer–auditor, disciple
hearing (pert. to)–aural, auricular, otio
hearken–attend, hear, heed
hearsay–report, rumor
heart – affection, center, cheer, cor, core, depths, emotion, essence, feeling, gist, love, middle
heart (Egyptian myth.)–ab
heart (pert. to)–cardiac
heart auricle–atrium, atria (pl.)
heart beat–pulsation, pulse, systole, throb
heart cavity – atrium, atria (pl.)
heart contraction–systole
heart-shaped–cordate
heart stimulant – thialdin, thialdine
heartbreak–grief, sorrow
heartbroken–brokenhearted, grief-stricken, inconsolable
heartburn–cardialgia
hearten – cheer, encourage, inspirit, reassure
hearth–fireside
hearth (goddess of)–Vesta
hearth (goddess of, Italian)–Ops
heartwood (hard tough) – dura, duramen
hearty – cordial, earnest, heavy, real, robust, sincere, stanch, substantial, unfeigned, vigorous, warm
heat – calor, degree, excitement, passion, temperature, warm, warmth
heat (gentle)–tepor
heat (pert. to)–caloric
heat (principle of)–caloric
heat (white)–incandescence
heat measure – calorie, calory, centigrade, fahrenheit, therm, therme
heat of temper–choler
heat, sweeten and spice – mull
heat unit – calorie, calory, therm, therme
heater (water)–boiler, etna
heath–erica, ling, moor
heath scrub–chaparral
heath tree (var.)–brier
heathen–ethnic, gentile, irreligious, pagan
heathen deity–idol
heather–erica
heather mulberry – cloudberry
heating apparatus–boiler, etna, oven, stove
heaume–helmet
heave – hoist, raise, throw, toss
heavenly – angelic, divine, supernal, uranian
heavenly being – angel, seraph
heavenly body–comet, luna, star, sun
heavenly city of God–Sion, Zion
heavens – Elysium, empyrean, ether, Nirvana, Paradise, sky, Valhalla, welkin
heavens (model of)–orrey
heavy – actor, burdensome, leaden, massy, onerous, ponderous, pregnant, villain, weighty
heavy and dull–logy
heavy board–plank
heavy reed–clump
heavy with moisture – sodden
Hebrew–ab, Semite, Semitic
Hebrew abode of the dead–Sheol
Hebrew alphabet–*see* Jewish alphabet
Hebrew ascetic–essene
Hebrew evening (before festival)–ereb
Hebrew God – El, Eloah, Elohim
Hebrew high priest–Eli

Hebrew holiday-Purim

Hebrew incense making spice-stacte

Hebrew instrument (stringed)-asor

Hebrew lawgiver-Moses

Hebrew letter (first)-Alef

Hebrew letter (obs.)-Tsade

Hebrew marriage custom-levirate

Hebrew measure-bath, cab, cor, cubit, epha, ephah, ezba, handbreadth, hin, homer, kaneh, kor, log, omer, qaneh, reed, seah

Hebrew measure (anc.)-hin

Hebrew measure (dry)-cab. epha, ephah

Hebrew month - Tishri, Heshvan, Kislev, Tebet, Shebat, Adar, Veadar, Nisan, Iyar, Sivan, Tammuz, Ab, Elul

Hebrew name for God-El, Eloah, Elohim

Hebrew patriarch - Isaac, Noah

Hebrew plural ending-im

Hebrew priest - Aaron, Levite

Hebrew prophet - Amos, Daniel, Elias, Elijah, Hosea, Jonah, Zechariah

Hebrew prophetess - Deborah

Hebrew proselyte-ger

Hebrew resident (in alien territory)-ger

Hebrew sabbath-Saturday

Hebrew sacred objects-urim

Hebrew scarf-tallith

Hebrew school (for boys)-cheder, heder

Hebrew sect-essene

Hebrew stringed instrument -asor

Hebrew synagogue-yad

Hebrew synagogue pointer-yap

Hebrew teacher-rabbi

Hebrew tribe (stranger received by)-ger

Hebrew trumpet (battor or sacred festival) - shofar, shophar

Hebrew vestment (anc.) - ephod

Hebrew vowel point-tsere

Hebrew weight-bekah, gerah, mina, reba, rebah, shekel, talent, zuzu

Hebrew women's garment-sari

Hebrew youth (who escaped from fiery furnace) - Abednego, Meshach, Shadrach

Hebrides island (one of)-Iona

hecco-woodpecker

heckle-badger, gibe, hackle, harass

hectoliter-vat

hector-browbeat, bully, harass, worry

Hector's slayer-Achilles

Hecuba's and Priam's daughter-Cassandra

Hecuba's and Priam's son-Deiphobus, Hector, Helenus, Paris

heddles of a loom-caam

hedge-bar, boundary, enclose, fence, haw, surround

hedgehog - porcupine, urchin

hedgerow (Eng. prov.)-rew

hedge trimmer-plasher

heed-attend, attention, ear, hear, mind, note, notice, regard

heedful - advertent, attentive, mindful, wary

heedful (arch.)-attend

heedless-careless, inadvertent, inattentive, insouciant, negligent, regardless, remiss

heedless of consequences - desperate

heeds (arch.)-recks

heel-cant, incline, tilt, tip

heel (sword blade)-talon

heel over-careen

heifer-quey

height-altitude, elevation

height (natural)-stature

heighten-elevate, intensify, lifted, raise

heimweh-homesickness

heinous-atrocious, flagrant, hateful, odious

heir-heritor, legatee

Hejaz city-Mecca

helcosis-ulcer

held aloof-refrained

held closely together-tight

held forth-descanted

held in higher estimation-preferred

held up-boost

Helen of Troy's husband-Menelaus

Helen of Troy's mother - Leda

heliacal-solar

helical-helix, spiral

helicoid cyme-bostryx

helixes-spirals

hell bent - determinedly, recklessly

Hellenic character-Beta

Hellenistic school - Pergamene

Hellespont-Dardanelles

Hellespont swimmer (legendary)-Leander

hellier-slater, thatcher, tiler

helluo-glutton, gormandizer

helm-tiller, wheel

helm (position of) - alee, aport

helmet - armet, basinet, casque, galea, heaume, morion, sallet, sconce, topee

helmet (great 13th century) -heaume

helmet (light)-salade, salet, sallet

helmet (pith)-topee, topi

helmet-shaped part of calyx or corolla-galea

helmsman-pilot, steersman

helmsman's director-conner

heloe-bashful, squeamish

Heloise's lover-Abelard

help-abet, aid, alleviate, assist, avail, befriend, benefit, forestall, forward, further, improve, relieve, strengthen, support, sustain

help toward result-conduce

helped up-boosted

helper–aider, apprentice, assistant

helpful – aidant, salutary, useful

helping–aidant, assisting

helping over hard place–tiding

helpless – bewildered, defenseless, destitute, powerless, unaiding, unprotected, unsupplied

helpmate–companion, helper, wife

helpmeet–helpmate, wife

Helsinki native–Finlander

helve–handle, lever

hem–border, edge, margin

hem in (to)–beset

hemi–half

hemmel–hovel, outbuilding, shed, stage

hemp–fennel

hemp (African)–ife

hemp (kind of)–abaca, flax, istle, Manila, sisal

hemp (Manila)–abaca

hemp (Russian)–rine

hemp (short)–tow

hemp (sisal)–sizal

hemp filament–harl

hen (young)–pullet

hence–ergo, so

hence (Latin)–ergo

henchman – attendant, follower, gillie, page, squire, supporter

hend (hende)–civil, clever, comely, dexterous, fair, gentle, gracious, kind, pleasant, skillful

Hengist's brother–Horsa

Henry IV's birthplace–Pau

Henry VII's surname – Tudor

hepar–liver

hepatic–liverworts

heptad–seven

Hera's husband–Zeus

Hera's son–Ares

herald–forerunner, messenger

heraldic bearing–ente, orle, pheon

heraldic cross – patee, patonce, patte, pattee, paty

heraldic devices (bearing)–

altiers, crests, ente, orles, unde

heraldic fillet–orle

heraldic sign–ente

heraldic snake–bisse

heraldic term–cotise

heraldic wreath–torse

heraldry (notch)–dentil

heraldry (red)–gules

herb–mint, sage, thyme

herb (allied to chicory)–endive

herb (apiaceous)–nondo

herb (aromatic) – catnip, clary

herb (aster family)–arnica, boneset, elecampane

herb (bean family)–tare

herb (biennial)–parsley

herb (bitter)–aloe, rue

herb (bog) – steepweed, steepwort

herb (bulbous)–canna

herb (buttercup family) – anemone

herb (chicory-like)–endive

herb (clover-like)–medic

herb (coarse perennial) – pokeweed

herb (cuckoopint)–arum

herb (culinary)–leek

herb (edible)–spinach

herb (European)–borage

herb (forage)–clover

herb (genus)–arum

herb (genus of bog)–abama

herb (goosefoot family) – blite

herb (grass-like)–sedge

herb (honey)–tolaliote

herb (kind of)–iva

herb (medicinal) – arnica, boneset, lovage, senna

herb (medicinal tree) – sumac, sumach

herb (mint family)–hyssop

herb (odd-colored flowered) –stapelia

herb (old world)–woad

herb (pasture)–grass

herb (perennial) – lopweed, madder, pia, yarrow

herb (pink family)–silene

herb (poppy family)–celandine

herb (primrose family) – pimpernel

herb (pungent cultivated)– mustard

herb (pungent, genus of)– asarum

herb (salad)–watercress

herb (seasoning)–marjoram, mint, sage, thyme

herb (senna family)–cassia

herb (stemless evergreen)– galax

herb (taccaceous)–pia

herb (used in soup) – ocra, okra

herb (yellow flowered)–celandine

herb eve–iva

herb Paris (the)–oneberry

herb Peter–cowslip

herb trinity–hepatica, pansy

herb twopence–moneywort

herb verbascum (genus of)– mullein

herb yielding starch–pia

herbage (green)–grass

herbbane–broomrape

herbivorous mammal–tapir

herbs (fabulous, of occult powers)–molies

herbs (genus of)–arum, cassia, inula, psoralea

Hercules stone–loadstone

Hercules' sweetheart–Iole

Hercules' wife–Hebe

herd – aggregation, crowd, drove, flock, guard, rabble, shelter

herdsman–drover, ranchero

here–hither, present

here (Fr.)–ici

hereafter–after, future, later

hereamong–hereabout

hereat–here

hereditary – ancestral, descended, heirship, inheritable, inheritance, patrimonial

hereditary (quality of being) –lineality

hereditary class–caste

heredity–inheritance

heredity factor–gene

herehence–away, henceforth

heretic – dissenter, noncon-

formist, schismatic, sectarian
heretofore–previous
heretofore (arch.)–erewhile
heritage – inheritance, patrimony
heritrix (heretrix)–heiress
herl–barb
Hermes' father–Zeus
Hermes' mother–Maia
Hermes' winged shoes–talaria
Hermetic–alchemist
hermit – anchorite, ascetic, beadsman, eremite, recluse
hermit (religious)–monk
hermitary–cell
hermits (who live on top of pillars)–stylites
hermit's hut–cell
herne–corner, nook
hero–demigod
hero (Babylonian myth.) – Etana
hero (myth.)–Ajax, Ledda
hero (Revolutionary)–Allen
hero (Trojan)–Aeneas
hero (who tried to mount to heaven on an eagle)–Etana
Herodias' daughter–Salome
heroic – courageous, epic, epical, epos, extreme, fearless, gallant, great, intrepid, magnanimous, noble, spartan, valiant
heroic poem–epos, saga
heroic story–saga
heroine–demigoddess
heroine (beautiful fleet-footed)–Atalanta
heroine (Hardy)–Tess
heroine (myth.)–Europa
heroine (Old Testament)–Esther
heroism – bravery, courage, fortitude, unselfishness, valor
heron–egret, herneshaw
heron (flock of)–sedge
heron (small)–bittern
herring (lake)–cisco
herring (round)–shadine
herring (small)–sprat
herring (young)–brit, sprot

herring alec–pickle, sauce
herring barrel (small)–cade
herring family fish–alewife
herring sauce–alec
hesitantly–reluctantly
hesitate–delay, falter, loiter, pause, stall, wait
hesitation of speech – haw, stutter
hesped–eulogy
Hesperides (one of)–Aegle, Arethusa, Erytheia, Erytheis, Hespera, Hestia
hest–behest, bid, command, injunction, pledge, precept, promise
hetaera (hetaira) – mistress, paramour
heterogeneous – dissimilar, diverse, mixed, unlike
hew–chop, cut, hack
hew out–carve
hex–bewitch, jinx
hexameter (dactylic)–epos
hey–ahey
heyrat–kinkajou
Hezekiah's (King) mother–Abi
Hezekiah's kingdom–Judah
hiatus–chasm, gap, opening
Hiawatha's grandmother – Nokomis
Hiawatha's nurse–Nokomis
hibernate–winter
Hibernia–Erin, Ireland
Hibernian–Irish
hickory (species of)–pecan, shellbark
hickory nut–pecan
hickory tree–pecan
hidage–tax
hidalgo–nobleman
hidden – buried, cached, closed, concealed, covered, covert, cryptic, inner, latent, lurk, masked, mysterious, obscure, occult, perdu, screened, secret, secreted
hide–bury, cache, carucate, cloak, conceal, cover, cuticle, cyst, dern, derne, disguise, dissemble, ensconce, mask, pelt, screen, secrete, shroud, skin, suppress, veil

hide (fish, close fitting)–eelskin
hide (to) – cache, lurk, secrete
hide cleaning instrument – slater
hide fleshing tool–slater
hide of small beast–kip
hide worker–tanner
hidebound–bigoted, conventional, illiberal, narrow
hideous – dreadful, fell, frightful, ghastly, grim, grisly, horrid, terrible, terrifying, ugly
hiding (rare)–coverture
hiding place–cache, lair
high–alt, elevated, steep, tall
high-brow–intelligentsia
high-flying–icarian
high-hat (British)–swank
high in pitch–alt
high in value–dear
high note–alt, ela
high pointed hill–tor
high pressure–forceful, importunate, pressing
high priest–Eli
high relish (enjoyment) – gusto
high respect–esteem, honor
high sea–main
high-sounding speech – fustian
high-spirited – fiery, lively, mettlesome
high-strung–excitable, nervous, tense
high temperature–heat
high time–binge, carousal, spree
high-toned (more, slang)–tonier
highborn–noble
higher than–above
highest point–acme, meridian, summit, zenith
highest point (at)–zenith
Highlander–Celt, Gael, Kelt
Highlander's pouch (purse)–sporan, sporran
highly excited–fevered
highly seasoned dish–ragout
highly sensible–prudent
highly strung – excitable, nervous

highly valued–dear

highway–artery, boulevard, course, path, road, street, thoroughfare, turnpike

highway (cross-country) – Lincoln

highwayman – bandit, ladrone, robber, thief

hike – jerk, march, raise, tramp, throw, toss

hilarious – mad, merry, mirthful, noisy

hilarity–cheerfulness, exhilaration, gaiety, glee, jollity, joviality, joyousness, mirth

hill–barrow, heap, mound

hill (broad-topped)–loma

hill (conical)–pap

hill (conspicuous)–butte

hill (craggy, high)–tor

hill (high craggy)–tor

hill (high pointed)–tor

hill (isolated)–butte

hill (Jerusalem)–Olivet

hill (round, Span.)–morro

hill (rounded)–knob

hill (sand)–dene, dune

hill (sand, Eng.)–dene

hill (short of stratified drift) –kame

hill (Span., round)–morro

hill (steep-sided)–butte

hill (western, broad-topped) –loma

hill (wooded, poetic)–holt

hillock–knoll

hills (range of)–ridge

hillside (Scot.)–brae

hillside (steep)–brae, cleeve, cleve, cliff

hilt–handle

hilum (pert. to)–hilar

Himalayan animal (bearlike)–panda

Himalayan bearcat–panda

Himalayan carnivore (raccoon-like)–panda

Himalayan cedar–deodar

Himalayan cypress–Bhutan

Himalayan marmot–pia

Himalayan monk's hood – atees, atis

Himalayan mountain–Everest

Himalayan oxen–yaks

Himalayan peak–Everest

hind – doe, hindquarter, peasant, posterior, rustic, servant

hind (male)–stag

hinder – cramp, bar, block, debar, delay, deter, hamper, impede, posterior, prevent, retard

hindered (arch.)–let

hindering from action – deterrent

hindrance–bar, check, clog, delay, impediment, interruption, obstacle, obstruction, restraint, rub, snag, stop

Hindu (low caste)–Koli

Hindu acrobat–nat

Hindu Aryan language – Hindi

Hindu ascetic–sadh, sadhu, yogi, yogin

Hindu barn–byre

Hindu books (holy)–Veda

Hindu books (pert. to)–vedic

Hindu calendar – Baisakh, Jeth, Asarh, Sawan (Sarawan), Bhadon, Asin (Kuar), Katik (Kartik), Aghan, Pus, Magh, Phagun (Phalgun), Chait

Hindu calendar (division of)–Asin

Hindu carpet–agra

Hindu caste (artisan)–sonar

Hindu caste (low)–palli

Hindu caste (lowest, var.)–soodra

Hindu caste (member of dominant and military)–rajpoot

Hindu caste member–Brahman

Hindu ceremony–sraddha

Hindu chief–sirdar

Hindu city (sacred) – Benares

Hindu coin–ana

Hindu convert (to Islam)–Shaikh

Hindu cymbals–tal

Hindu deification of first to die–yama

Hindu deity–Agni, Brahma,

Brahman, Brama, Deva, Krishna, Maya, Ramachandra, Siva, Vishnu, Yama

Hindu deity (var.)–Shiva

Hindu deity consort–sakti

Hindu demon–asura, bali, rahu

Hindu dialect–tamil

Hindu division (territorial) –Taraf

Hindu doctrine–karma

Hindu dye (red)–alta

Hindu ejaculation (mystic)–om, um

Hindu evil spirit–Mara

Hindu fairs (religious)–melas

Hindu female energy–Shakti, Sakti (var.)

Hindu fire god–Agni

Hindu garment–saree, sari

Hindu gentleman – baboo, babu, sahib

Hindu giant (thousand-armed)–Bana

Hindu glazed pottery–uda

Hindu god–Brahma, Brahman, Brama, Deva, Krishna, Rama, Ramachandra, Shiva, Siva

Hindu god of dead–Yama

Hindu god of love–Kama

Hindu god of spirit–Asura

Hindu god of wisdom–Ganesa, Ganesha

Hindu goddess–Chandi, Devi, Durga, Gauri, Haimavati, Kali, Parvati, Shakti, Uma

Hindu goldsmith–sonar

Hindu guitar–sitar

Hindu hero–Nala

Hindu hero (myth.)–Rama

Hindu holy man – Sadh, Sadhu

Hindu idol worship (waving lighted lantern)–arati

Hindu incarnation–avatar

Hindu instrument – saran, vina

Hindu jackal–kola

Hindu king–rajah

Hindu king (myth.)–Nala

Hindu language (sacred) – Pali

Hindu law author–Manu
Hindu law charitable gift–enam
Hindu lawgiver–Manu
Hindu literature (sacred)–Veda
Hindu loincloth–dhoti
Hindu magician – fakeer, fakir
Hindu margosa–neem
Hindu measure–kos
Hindu measure of distance–yojan
Hindu merchant – banian, banyan
Hindu merchant caste–banian, banyan
Hindu monastery–math
Hindu mountain pass–ghat, ghaut
Hindu musical instrument–daira, saran, sitar, vina
Hindu mystic–Yogi, Yogin
Hindu mystic word–om, um
Hindu mythological hero–Rama
Hindu nursemaid–ayah
Hindu organ of volition – manas
Hindu Paradise–Nirvana
Hindu peasant–ryot
Hindu philosophy–Yuga
Hindu philosophy (form of) –yoga
Hindu philosophy (spiritual darkness)–tamas
Hindu physicist–Raman
Hindu pillar–lat, xat
Hindu pledge (law)–adhi
Hindus pots (for ablution, of brass or copper)–lotas
Hindu prayer rug–asan, asana
Hindu prince–rajah, rana
Hindu princess–ranee, rani
Hindu principle of existence –Tattva
Hindu private apartment–mahal
Hindu pulse–dal
Hindu queen–ranee, rani
Hindu race (sacred)–om
Hindu religious festival – Mela
Hindu religious hero–Rama

Hindu revenue collector – amil, aumil, aumildar
Hindu ruler–raj
Hindu ruler–rajah
Hindu sacred word–om, um
Hindu sage–manu
Hindu savant–swami
Hindu scarf–saree, sari
Hindu scripture (anc.)–Veda
Hindu sect (religious)–Sikh
Hindu series of underworld (myth.)–patala
Hindu serpent (deified) – Naga
Hindu Siva worshiper–Saiva
Hindu slave (female)–dasi
Hindu soldier–sepoy
Hindu sovereignty–raj
Hindu spirit (evil) – asura, mara
Hindu stock (parent)–Aryan
Hindu storehouse–golah
Hindu tenant–ryot
Hindu territorial division–Taraf
Hindu title–rao
Hindu title of respect–miam
Hindu trader–banian, banyan
Hindu treatise explaining scriptures–sastra, shastra
Hindu triad god–Siva
Hindu tribesman – naga, tamil
Hindu tunic–jama, jamah
Hindu viol–ruana, sardina
Hindu weight–ser, tol, tola
Hindu widow (cremate) – suttee
Hindu woman's cremation on husband's pyre–suttee
Hindu woman's foot stain (red dye)–alta
Hindu woman's garment – saree, sari
Hindu word (sacred)–om, um
Hinduism life principle (soul)–atman
Hindustan (poetic)–Ind
Hindustan hill dweller–toda
Hindustan language–Urdu
Hindustani–Urdu
hinge–depend, hang, joint, pintle, stand, turn

hinge recess (for leaf of)–pan
hinge socket–pan
hint – allude, allusion, cue, imply, inkling, insinuate, intimate, intimation, suggest, suggestion
hint to a solution–clue
hip–hop, huckle, limp, miss, skip
hip bone (pert. to)–iliac
hip bone part–ileum, ilium, ilia (pl.)
hire – allowance, charter, compensation, employ, engage, lease, price, rent, reward, salary, stipend, use, wages
hire (for exclusive use)–charter
hireling – esne, mercenary, serf, slave
hirmos–canticle, hymn, troparion
hirondelle–swallow
hirple–hobble, limp
hirsel–flock, herd
hirsute – boorish, coarse, hairy, rough, shaggy, uncouth
hispid (obs.)–strigous
hissing–sibilance, sibilant
historian – annalist, chronicler
historical period–era
historical period (pert. to)–eral
history–account, annals, drama, narrative, record, relation, story
history (personal) – biography, memoir
history (stage of)–era
history of individual development–ontogeny
histrio–actor
histrion–actor
histrionics – acting, theatricals
hit–batted, clout, rap, smite, strike, success, swat, tap
hit (lightly)–bunt, tap
hit aloft–lob
hit or miss–careless, casual, chance, haphazard
hitch–catch, crick, enlist, en-

listment, halt, hindrance, hobble, hop, knot, limp, marry, pull, tie, tug, unite
hitchhiker (nautical)–stowaway
hither–here
hitherto–ago, yet
Hitler follower–Nazi
hoactzin (hoatzin) – anna, bird
hoar–ancient, gray, hoary, venerable
hoard – accumulate, amass, husband, store, supply, treasure, treasury
hoarder–miser, treasurer
hoarfrost–rime
hoarse–discordant, grating, rough
hoarse and rough–raucous
hoarse sound–caw
hoary–aged, ancient, old
hoatzin–anna, bird
hoax–artifice, bam, canard, cheat, deceive, deception, ruse, sham, trick
hoax an opponent–bluff
hob–clown, countryman, elf, fairy, ferret, game, havoc, mark, mischief, peg, pin, rustic, sprite
hobbledehoy–lad, youth
hobbler–boatman, hoveler, laborer, pilot, retainer
hobbling–lame
hobbly–rough, uneven
hobby–avocation, fad, falcon
hobby bird–wryneck
hobgoblin–bogy, bugaboo, imp, Puck, sprite
hobhouchin–owl
hob-like–boorish, clownish
hoblob–boor, lout
hobo–tramp
hock – hamstring, pawn, pledge, thigh
hock (horse's)–ankle
hockey (informal)–shinny
hockey game–bandy
hockey team–seven
hocus–adulterate, cheat, deceive, drug
hocus-pocus – charlatanism, cheat, flimflam, humbug, juggler, quackery, trick, trickster

hod–barrow, scuttle
hodgepodge–hotchpot, medley, mess, mixture, olio, stew
hodgepodge (literary)–cento
hog–pig, swine
hog (gelded male, Eng.)–galt
hog (male)–boar, stag
hog (wild)–boar
hog (young)–shoat, shote
hogfish–scorpene
hog peanut–earthpea
hogshead–barrel, cask
hogshead (two)–pipe
hog side (salted)–flitch
hog thighs (cured)–hams
hoi polloi–masses, mob, populace, rabble
hoist–elevate, heave, hoise, lift, raise
hoist (anchor)–cat
hoisted–hove
hoisting device (large stone)–lewis
hoisting machine – crane, davit, derrick, elevator, gin, jack
hoity-toity–arrogant, flighty, giddy, haughty, irresponsible, proud, thoughtless
hold–contain, detain, entertain, harbor, have, keep, own, retain, seat, stow
hold (naut.)–avast
hold a brief for–advocate, defend
hold a course–tend
hold an opinion–deem
hold and condense–absorb
hold as a belief–suppose
hold back–dam, detain, deter, repress, retard, stem
hold dear–cherish
hold fast–cling
hold forth–continue, exhibit, maintain, offer, propound
hold in check–curb, rein, restrain
hold in custody–intern, jail
hold in hand–assure, promise
hold in mind–entertain
hold in with–retain, secure
hold it (naut.)–avast

hold motionless (for lack of wind)–becalm
hold on–continue, forbear, stop, wait
hold out–continue, endure, exclude, last
hold session–assemble, convene, sit
hold up–check, display, exhibit, halt, lift, raise, rein, rob, robbery, support, sustain
hold up to scorn–pillory
hold water–consistent, sound
holder (record)–binder, file
holder (yarn)–cop
holder of another's property–trustee
holder of certain reward of merit–medalist
holder of claim on another's property–lienor, mortgage
holding (act of)–tenure
holding fast–persistent, tenacious
holding sway–regnant
holds (one who)–possessor
hole–bay, cave, cavern, cavity, cove, cranny, den, dungeon, grotto, hollow, mine, nook, opening, pit, prison, recess, shaft
hole (deep)–abysm, abyss, cave, chasm, pit
hole (mud)–wallow
hole (water) – oasis, oases (pl.)
hole enlarger–reamer
hole for pouring metal into mold–sprue
hole in a mold (pouring)–sprue
hole in an implement–eye
Holi (Hoolee, Hohlee)–festival
Holi powder (red perfume)–abir
holiday–convivial, feria, feriae (pl.), festive, festival, fete, fiesta, jovial, merry, outing, vacation
holiday (pert. to)–ferial
holier–saintlier
holiness–righteousness, sanctity
Holland–Netherlands

Holland checkers–damrod
Holland city (commune)–
Ede, Doorn, Hague, Ley-
den
Holland coin (debased) –
raps
Holland native–Dutch
Holland pottery–delf, delft
Holland radio station–Hil-
versum
Holland seaport–Edam
Holland sovereign house –
Orange
hollow–cavity, concave, depressed, empty, faithless,
gaunt, sepulchral, sinus,
specious, sunken, thin, un-
satisfying, unsound, va-
cant, void, worthless
hollow (long)–groove
hollow (not)–solid
hollow (subterranean)–cavern
hollow-eyed–haggard
hollow of eye–socket
hollowed (like shallow pit)–
glenoid
hollowed out–cavate
holly–ilex, yapon
holly (genus of)–ilex
holm–islet, oak, sea
holm oak–ilex, holly
holm tree–holly
holobaptist–immersionist
holocaust–destruction, sacrifice
holour – debauchee, whore-
monger
holy–devout, hallowed, sacred, sainted
holy herb–vervain
Holy Joe–clergyman
Holy Land–Palestine
Holy Land pilgrim–Palmer
Holy One–Christ, God, Je-
hovah, Supreme Being
holy rood–cross, crucifix
holy seed–wormseed
holy statue–icon
holy water receptacle–stoup
holy water sprinkler–aspergillum
homage – allegiance, fealty,
honor, loyalty, obeisance,
reverence
homage (devoted)–cult

homager–vassal
homard–lobster
hombre–fellow, man
home – abode, domicile,
dwelling, estate, habita-
tion, nest, residence, village
home (animal's)–den
home (cozy)–nest
home (Irish king's)–Tara
home base (in games)–den,
plate
home of Irish kings–Tara
home places–homestead
Home Sweet Home author–
Payne
homeless wanderer–waif
homely – homelike, kindly,
plainly, ugly, unpreten-
tious, unsightly
homemade–domestic, plain,
simple
Homeric hero–Aeneas
Homeric wise man–Nestor
Homer's book–Iliad
Homer's poem–Iliad
Homer's poem (epic)–Odys-
sey
homesickness–nostalgia
homicides–murders
homily – adage, assembly,
communion, converse,
discourse, sermon
homing pigeon instincts –
orientation
hominy (coarse)–samp
homo sapiens–man
homopterous–aphid
Honduras city–Cedros, Gra-
cias, Iriona, Juticalpa, Te-
gucigalpa (c.), Yoro
Honduras coin – centavo,
lempira (ac.), peso (ac.)
Honduras Indian–Lenca
Honduras measure – caba-
lleria, cajuela, manzana,
mecate, milla, tercia, vara
Honduras mountain–Ceiba,
Colon
Honduras port–San Loren-
zo, Truxillo
Honduras river – Aguan,
Chamelicon, Choluteca,
Negro, Patuca, Sulaco,
Ulua
Honduras weight–caja

hone–delay, dress, grumble,
lament, long, oilstone,
pine, whetstone, yearn
honest–candid, chaste, faithful, frank, guileless, ingenuous, open, straight-
forward, upright, virtuous
honesty–equity, fairness, justice, integrity, probity,
trustworthiness, upright-
ness
honey–mel
honeybee (genus of)–apia,
apis
honey buzzard–pern
honeycomb cell–alveolus, alveoli (pl.)
honeyed–mellifluous, sweet
Hong Kong city–Victoria
Hong Kong coin – British
dollar (s.), cent (br.), dollar (s.), Hong Kong dol-
lar (s.)
honor–credit, esteem, fame,
honesty, reputation, re-
spect, reverence, revere
honor (old word)–tir
honor (source of)–credit
honorable – commendable,
creditable, estimable, honorary, meritorious, moral,
reputable, respectable
honorable (most, slang) –
whitest
honorable fame (radiant
beauty)–glory
honorary disc–medal
honorary sobriquet–title
honored–graced
honored with a festival –
feted
hood–babushka, blind, cap-
sheaf, covering, cowl,
hide
hood (academic) hanging
part–liripipe
hood (clerical)–amice
hood (close fitting)–coif
hood (leather stirrup covering)–tapadero, tapidero
hood (medieval)–liripipe
hood (Mexican saddle stirrup)–tapadera
hood (monk's)–atis, cowl
hooded cape–amice
hoodwink – befool, blind,

blinder, blindfold, cover, deceive, delude, fool, hide, mislead, wile

hooey–buncombe, nonsense

hoof–ungula

hoof (part of)–frog

hoof part (under horny covering)–pododerm

hook (iron)–gaff

hook (large)–gaff

hook (medieval fighting)–croc

hook (pointed)–gaff

hook (safety)–clevis

hook (stretching)–tenter

hooked–anchoral

hooked at end–uncinate

hooks (group of, turned backward for fishing) – scrodgill

hooligan–loafer, ruffian

hooly–slow, soft, wary

hoop–bail, circle, circlet

hoop skirt–crinoline

Hoosier poet–Riley

Hoosier State–Indiana

hop – bound, dance, halt, jump, leap, limp, spring

hop back–vat

hop bush–ake, akeake

hop crease–hopscotch

hop kiln–oast, ost

hop stem–bine

hop vine–bine

hope – anticipation, aspire, bay, cherish, desire, expect, expectation, haven, inlet, reliance, trust, wish

hope (almost beyond)–desperate

hope (future)–after hope

hopeful–confident, expectant, sanguine

hopeless–despairing, desperate, despondent, desponding, disconsolate, downcast, forlorn, futile, incurable, ineffectual, irrecoverable, irremediable, irretrievable, useless, vain

hopelessness–despair

hoplite–soldier

hopper–box, chute, dancer, leaper, receptacle

hopper (rock)–penguin

horal–hourly

horde–army, camp, crowd, pack, swarm

hordeolum–sty

horizon (ocean)–sea line

horizontal–flat, level

horn–antler, cornucopia

horn (comb. form)–kera

horn (fog)–siren

horn (huntsman's)–bugle

horn (insect's)–antenna

horn (Latin)–cornu

horn blare–fanfare, tantara

horn of crescent–cusp

horn of plenty–cornucopia

horn player–bugler, trumpeter

horn points–prong

hornbill–bird

hornless–nat

horns–brasses, cornets, cornus, sirens, trumpets, tubas

horny – callous, hard, semiopaque

horny substance on animal's feet–hoofs, hooves

horny tissue (essential ingredient of)–keratin

horrible – dreadful, grisly, hideous, horrid, horrific, shocking, terrible

horror–abhorrence, abomination, detestation, dread, fear, terror

horse – beastband, charger, equine, footrope, jackstay, mare, pacer, saddler, steed

horse (aged)–nag

horse (British slang)–prad

horse (calico)–pinto

horse (certain colored)–bay, chestnut, roan

horse (farm)–dobbin

horse (fast, U.S.)–pelter

horse (genus of)–equus

horse (golden-hued) – palomino

horse (half-wild)–mustang

horse (harness)–pacer, trotter

horse (high-spirited)–stepper

horse (inferior race)–plater

horse (kind of)–Arab, Barb, Belgian, Clydesdale, Galloway, Morgan, Percheron, Shetland, Shire, Suf-

folk; harness, pacer, roadster, saddle, trotter

horse (last pick of)–ruck

horse (never a race winner) –maiden

horse (old)–nag

horse (one-horned fabulous) –monoceros, unicorn

horse (pack)–sumpter

horse (pert. to)–equine

horse (riding)–cob, saddle

horse (riding, driving) – hackney

horse (saddle)–mount

horse (small)–cob, nag, tit

horse (Span., small)–genet, jennet

horse (spirited)–courser

horse (stylish riding)–cob

horse (swift)–courser

horse (thickset)–cob

horse (trotting)–morgan

horse (war)–charger, steed

horse (wheel)–poler

horse (winged)–Pegasus

horse (work, provincial Eng.)–capo

horse (working)–dobbin

horse (worn-out)–harridan

horse (worthless)–shack

horse (young) – colt, filly, foal

horse blanket–manta

horse chestnut–buckeye

horse covering (ornamental, anc.)–caparison

horsefly–botfly

horsefly larva–bot, bott

horsehair–mane

horsekeeper–groom, hostler

horselaugh–guffaw

horse laurel–rhododendron

horseleech (arch.)–farrier

horse lily–spatterdock

horseman – broncobuster, buckaroo, buckayro, cavalryman, centaur, cowboy, equestrian, rider, vaquero

horseman's goad–spur

horsemanship (half-turn) – caracole

horsemen (military)–cavalry

horse measure–hand

horse racing–turf

horse-radish tree – behen, behn
horse-radish tree fruit–ben
horse rope–halter
horseshoe spur–calk
horseshoer–blacksmith, farrier
horseshoer's stool–butteris
horse tackle–harness
horse training place–longe
horse trappings – caparison, harness, tackle
horses (drove of)–atajo
horses (pair matched)–span
horses (team of three arranged as a pair and one in front)–unicorn
horse's ankle–hock
horse's breastplate (med. armor)–peytrel
horse's foot (part of)–fetlock, hoof, pastern
horse's hair–mane
horse's leap – bound, buck, curvet, hurdle
horse's motion of rearing – pesade
horse's pace–amble, canter, lope, trot
horse's pace (peculiar)–amble
horse's shoe spur–calk
horse's tooth–tush
horse's tooth (incisor)–nipper
hory (horry)–dirty, foul, impure
hospice (Oriental) – imaret, maret
hospitable–cordial, friendly, receptive
hospital–infirmary, sanatorium
hospital (foundling, Fr.) – creche
hospital (mobile) – ambulance
hospital doctor–interne
hospitality–xenodochy
host–army, assemble, entertainer, legion, multitude, swarm, throng
host of Absalom captain–Amasa
Host's plate–paten
hostel–hotel, inn, lodgings

hostelry – caravansary, caravanserai, hostel, hotel, inn, tavern
hostile–antagonistic, belligerent, contrary, enemy, malevolent, opposed, unfriendly, unsympathetic
hostile feeling–animus
hostile incursion–raid
hostilities (armed)–war
hostility–animosity, antagonism, bitterness, enmity, hatred, ill will, opposition, rancor, vindictiveness
hostler–groom
hot–burning, eager, fervent, fervid, passionate, peppery, sizzling, torrid
hot (arch.)–calid
hot cakes (army slang) – kneepads
hot tempered–iracund
hot water bottle–pig
hotel–albergo, caravansary, caravanserai, hostel, hostelry, inn, tavern
hotel keeper–host
Hottentot instrument (musical)–gora, gorah
Hottentot tribe – damara, nama
hound (hunting)–harrier
hound (small)–basset, beagle, harrier
hound (small short-legged) –basset
hound (wolf)–alan
hound dog's tail–stern
hounder–dogger
hounds (fresh relay of hunting)–avantlay
hour–time
hour (canonical)–sext
hour (pert. to)–horal
hour (when lights must be put out)–curfew
hourly–horal
hours (devotional)–nones
house – abode, billet, cover, domicile, dwelling, enclose, habitation, home, lodge, quarter, residence, shelter
house (comb. form)–eco
house (dog)–kennel

house (elegant country) – villa
house (large, stately)–mansion, palace
house (like a)–domal
house (lodging)–hotel, inn, tavern
house (Oriental rest)–serai
house (pert. to)–domal
house (pretentious) – mansion, palace
house (small) – cabin, cote, cottage, hut, nest, shack
house (small country)–casino
house (southwestern ranch) –casa
house (Span.)–casa
house (summer, elevated)–belvedere
House of Congress (upper)–Senate
housed–billeted, lodged
housefly (genus of)–musca
household–menage
household (arch.)–meiny
household deity–Lar, Lares, Penates
household god–Lar, Lares, Penates
household linen–napery
household management – menage
housekeeper–matron
houseleek–jobade, jobarbe
house mouse (genus of)–mus
houses (cluster of)–hamlet
housewarming–infare
hove clear–atrip
however–but, though, yet
however (poetic)–tho
howl–bay, cry, ululate, wail, yell
howling of dog–baying, ululation
hoyden–hoiden, tomboy
Hreidmar's son–Fafnir, Otter
hub–center, centre, nave
hub (wheel)–nave
hubbub – ado, clamor, commotion, din, racket, stir, uproar
hubby–husband
hubristic–contemptuous, insolent
hubshi–Negro

huck–bargain, haunch, higgle, hip, hollow, hook, howk
huckle–bend, haggle, stoop
huckleberry family – vacciniaceae
Huckleberry Finn author – Samuel Clemens, Mark Twain
Huckleberry Finn character (Negro)–Jim
huckster – hawker, peddler, retailer
huddle – bustle, confusion, conglomeration, disorder, jumble, miser, skinflint
huddroun–sloven
hue – color, outcry, shout, tinge, tint
hue (of dark) – swart, swarthy
hug–embrace
huge – big, colossal, enormous, giant, gigantic, immense, large, massive, monster, monstrous, titanic, vast
huge appetite (pert. to)–gargantuan
hui – assembly, firm, guild, partnership
huisache – popinac, shrub, wabe, wabi
huissier–bailiff, doorkeeper, usher
huitan–octet, stanza
huitre–oyster
huke–cape, cloak
hulky – clumsy, hulking, large, loutish
hull–covering, husk, strip
hullabaloo – clamor, confusion, din, hubbub, racket
hulled corn–samp
hulver–holly
hulver head–foolish, stupid
hum–buzz, croon, drone
human–mortal
human being – Adamite, creature, man, mortal, person
human bondage–slavery
human race–man, mankind
human trunk–torso
humble–abase, abash, deferent, degrade, demit, disgrace, low, lower, mean, mild, modest, mortify, plain, poor, reverent, simple

humbug–deceive, deception, fraud, guile, hoax, mislead, sham, stratagem, trick
humbug (coll.)–fake
humdrum – commonplace, dull, indifferently, irksome, monotonous, undecidedly
humect–moisten, wet
humid–damp, dank, moist
humiliate–abase, abash, degrade, disgrace, humble, mortify, shame
humiliation – abasement, mortification
humming bird (kind of)–ava, aves (pl.), colibri
humming bird (large)–carib
humming bird (long forked tail)–sheartail
humming bird (topaz)–ava, aves (pl.)
humor (humour)–drollery, gratify, indulge, levity, mood, please, wit
humorist–wag
humorous–capricious, comic, funny, jocular, whimsical
humorous (obs.) – humid, moist, watery
humorously–capriciously, facetiously, jocosely, whimsically
hump – bulge, hummock, hunk, lump, mound
humus–mold, mould
Hun-like tribe (8th and 9th century)–Avars
Hun's legendary king–Etzel
hunch–bend, chilly, crook, frosty, fudge, intuition, lump, shove, thrust
Hunchback of Notre Dame–Quasimodo
hundred (comb. form)–hecto
hundred per cent – entire, genuine, perfect, thoroughgoing, unalloyed, unquestionable

hundred years–centenary
Hundred Years' War battle –Cressy
hundredth of a right angle –grade, grad
hundredweight–cental
hung – dangled, drooped, lopped
hung (bending down) – drooped
Hung Wu dynasty–Ming
Hungarian (dominant) – Magyar
Hungarian capital–Budapest
Hungarian cavalryman – Hussar
Hungarian city – Budapest, Budapesth, Debrecen, Hodmezo-Vasarhely, Kecskemet, Szegedin
Hungarian coin–filler (ac.), filler (br.), korona (ac.), pengo (g., s.)
Hungarian coin (med.) – balas
Hungarian currency–pengo
Hungarian lake – Balaton, Neusiedler See, Platen See
Hungarian measure – ako, antal, hold, huvelyk, itcze, joch, marok, merfold, metze, yoke
Hungarian mountain–Carpathians
Hungarian people–Magyars
Hungarian point – embroidery
Hungarian pretender to throne–Otto
Hungarian river – Danube, Drave, Poprad, Theiss, Vistula
Hungarian turnip–kohlrabi
Hungarian weight–vamfont, vammazsa
Hungarian wine–tokay
hunger–craving, desire, long, want
hungering for honor (humorous)–esurient
hungry – barren, esurient, poor
hunt–chase, follow, hound, pursue, quest, search, seek, track, trail

hunt (goddess of, Italian)–Diana

hunt laboriously (thoroughly)–delve, probe

hunted animals–game, prey

hunter – huntsman, jager, nimrod

hunter (famous)–Nimrod

hunter (mythical)–Orion

hunter (slain by Artemis)–Orion

hunter (stealthy)–stalker

hunter (successful)–nimrod

hunter of Golden Fleece–Jason

hunter's aid–beater

hunting coyotes–wolfing

hunting dog–basset, pointer, setter

hunting expedition–safari, safaris (pl.)

huntsman–venerer

huntsman's horn–bugle

Hur's son–Uri

hurdy-gurdy–rota

hurl–cast, fling, pelt, pitch, throw

hurl (as a dart)–elance

hurled–betossed, cast, flung, pelted, slung, threw, tossed, tost

hurly-burly–confused, confusion, storm, tumult, tumultuous, uproar

huron–grison

hurrah–applause, cheer, encouragement, huzza, joy, shout, triumph

hurr-bur–burdock

hurricane–cyclone

hurricane (tropical)–chubasco

hurries – expedites, hastens, hies, hustles, impels, precipitates, quickens, races, rushes, speeds, urges

hurry – agitation, commotion, dispatch, disturbance, expedition, haste, rush, scud, scurry, speed, tumult

hurst – copse, hill, hillock, grove, wood

hurt – damage, detriment, distress, grieve, harm, impair, injure, injury, maim, mischief, pain

hurt (Scot.)–lesed

hurtful–baneful, destructive, detrimental, disadvantageous, malefic, malign, noisome, noxious, pernicious, prejudicial

hurtle–brandish, clash, collide, fling, jostle

husband–conserve, cultivate, cultivator, economize, eke, husbandman, manager, mate, save, spouse, steward, store, tiller

husband's brother (Irish) – levir

husbandman – carl, cultivator, farmer, tiller

husbandry – cultivation, thrift

hush – allay, appease, calm, hist, soothe, still

hushed – lulled, quiet, silenced, silent, still

husk–leam, rind, shuck

husk (of threshed grain) – straw

Husky–dog, Eskimo

huss–buzz, dogfish, hum

hut – hovel, scale, shanty, shed

hutch–bin, box, car, chest, coffer, coop, hoard, hovel, hut, humped, hunched, shanty

Huzzar uniform jacket–dolman

hyacinth (wild)–camas

hybrid (bovine)–cattalo

hybrid animal–mule

hybrid crossbreed–Husky

hybrid quadruped–mule

hydraulic engine–ram

hydrazoate–azid, azide

hydrobromic acid–bromide

hydrocarbon–butane, retene

hydrocarbon (colorless, gaseous)–ethane

hydrocarbon (gaseous)–ethane, ethene, ethylene

hydrocarbon (oily)–terpene

hydrocarbon (paraffin series)–nonane

hydrocarbon (white crystalline)–idryl, tolan

hydrocarbon radical–amyl

hydrocyanic–prussic

hydrocyclic–alicyclic

hydrogen (arseniurated) – arsin, arsine

hydrogen compound–acide, amine

hydrogen compound (nitrogen)–ammonia

hydrophobia–rabies

hydrophyllia–bracts

hydrous silicate (brownish)–cerite

hydrous sulphate (zinc, iron and manganese)–ilesite

hygienic–sanitary

hymn–canticle, ode, psalm, song

hymn (funeral)–dirge

hymn (patriotic)–America

hymn tune–choral, chorale

hypnotic – narcotic, opiate, soporific

hypnotic compound–trional

hypnotic state–trance

hypnotist (first)–Mesmer

hypocrisy–simulation

hypocrite – cheat, deceiver, dissembler, Levite

hypocritical–false, insincere, sanctimonious, specious

hypocritical profession–pretense

hypocritical talk–cant

hypodermic injection vessel (glass, one dose) – ampoule, ampule

hypothesis–assumption, postulate, supposition, theory

hypothesis (working)–theory

hypothetical–theoretical

hypothetical being–ens, entia (pl.)

hypothetical force–od

hypothetical medium (fill space)–ether

hypothetical structural unit (biology)–id

I

"I" (the big)–ego
I have found it–Eureka
I love (Latin)–amo
Iago's wife–Emelia
Iberian title–senor
ibex–tur
Ibsen character–Ase, Nora
ice (floating sheets of)–floes
ice (Fr.)–glace
ice (glacial)–serac
ice block–serac
ice cream (in a soda)–float
ice cream dish–parfait, sundae, sunday
ice creeper–crampon
ice crystals–frost, snow
ice fragments (afloat)–brash
ice mass–berg, floe
ice mountain–berg
ice tower–serac
iced–frosted, glaced
Icelandic assembly–Althing
Icelandic bishopric – Holar, Skalholt
Icelandic capital–Reikjavik, Reykjavik
Icelandic coin–aurar (br.), eyrir (br.), krona (s.)
Icelandic epic (tale record)–edda
Icelandic giant–Atli
Icelandic legend–saga
Icelandic measure–alin, almenn turma, almud, almude, engjateigur, fathmur, feralin, ferfathmur, ferfet, fermila, ferthumlungur, fet, kornskeppa, korntunna, lina, mila a landi, oltunna, pottur, sjomila, thumlungur, tundagslatta
Icelandic mountain – Jokul, Orafajokul
Icelandic saga–atli, edda
Icelandic story–saga
Icelandic tales giant–Atli
Icelandic volcano – Hecla, Hekla
Icelandic weight – pound, pund, tunna smjors
Icelandic writing–edda

icer–refrigerator
ichneumon (snake killing)–mongoose
icicles (stone)–stalactites
icing (pie)–meringue
icy – chilling, cold, frigid, frosty, gelid
Idaho county–Ada
Idaho senator (former) – Borah
idea – concept, impression, motion, opinion
idea (comb. form)–ideo
idea (fanciful)–conceit
idea (Fr.)–idee
idea (general)–motif
idea (helping)–clue
ideal – conceptual, consummate, fanciful, imaginary, intellectual, mental, pattern, perfect, Utopian
idealist–dreamer, visionary
identical – alike, equal, equivalent, same, self, tantamount
identification mark–brand, earmark
identify–designate, establish, name, prove
identity – exactness, homogeneity, sameness, unity
identity pitch–unison
ideologist–dreamer, theorist, visionary
Ides (9th day before)–Nones
idiasm – idiosyncrasy, peculiarity
idiocy–amentia, anoesia
idiograph–trademark
idiom–phrase
idiom (country)–ruralism
idiosyncrasy–eccentricity
idiot – blockhead, booby, dolt, dullard, dunce, fool, imbecile, oaf, simpleton
idiot (natural)–cretin
idiotic–daft, foolish, senseless
idle–baseless, empty, inactive, indolent, ineffectual, lazy, loaf, loafing, loiter, otiose, slothful, trifling,

unemployed, unfounded, unoccupied, unused, useless, vacant, vain, worthless
idled (abstractedly) – mooned
idleness–delirium, folly, inactivity, inertia, laziness, lightheadedness, silliness, vanity
idler–drone, loafer, loiterer
idol–afgod, god, image, impostor, phantom, satyr
idolater–adorer, Baalite, pagan, worshiper
idolatrous–pagan
idolize–adore
idols (anc. Semitic)–Baal
idyl (idyll)–poem
if–provided
if (Italian)–si
if ever–once
if it be not true–else
if not–else
igneous rock–basalt, peridot, trap
ignite – ardent, fiery, fire, hot, kindle, light
ignited (capable of being easily) – flammable, inflammable
ignited again–relighted
ignition cap–fuse, fuze
ignoble – base, disgraceful, dishonorable, low, mean, shameful, vile
ignorant–illiterate, nescient, unaware, unlettered, untutored
ignore–cut, eliminate, neglect, omit, overlook, snub
Igorot (Igorrote) – Bontok, Kankanai, Nabaloi
Igorot chief–Apo
iguana–lizard, tuatara
Iguvine–Eugubine, Umbrian
ihi–halfbeak, skipper, stitchbird
Ihlat–Sunnites
ijolite–apatite, calcite, titanite

ikary–caviar
ikbal–arrival, prestige, prosperity
ikona–greenhorn, simpleton
ikra–caviar
ileum (comb. form)–ileo
ilex–holly
Ilium–Troy
ill–bad, evil, iniquitous, noxious, poor, sick, wrong
ill (prefix)–mal
ill at ease–awkward
ill-boding–dire
ill-bred–bourgeois
ill feeling–animus
ill-gotten gain–graft, pelf
ill-natured–dour
ill treatment–abuse
ill will–malice
ill-wisher–foe
illegal–foul, illicit, unlawful
illegality–illicitness, unlawfulness
illegally entered–ringer
illegitimate–bastard
illicit–improper, unlawful
illimitable – boundless, infinite, measureless, vast
Illinois city–Alton, Decatur, Paua, Streator
illiterate – ignorant, unlearned, unlettered, unread, untaught, untutored
illuminant–gas, petroleum
illuminate – bright, enlighten, illume, illumine, light, lighten, luminous
illuminate with splendor–irradiate
illusion–chimera, deception, delusion, fallacy, mirage, mockery, phantom
illusive–deceitful, deceptive, false, fantasmal, illusory, unreal
illusory – deceptive, fallacious, illusive
illustrate – adorn, elucidate, exemplify, illuminate, picture
illustrious – celebrated, distinguished, eminent, exalted, glorious, heroic, honorable, noble, noted
illustrious (not)–detestable,

ignoble, iniquitous, nefarious, shameful
ilvaite (mineral)–yenite
image – effigy, god, icon, idol, idolon, ikon, likeness, picture
image (carved)–statue
image (good luck)–alraun
image (mental)–conception, idea, phantasm, recept
image (of something)–phantom
image (sacred)–icon, ikon
image (televised)–video
image seen after sight is gone–photogene
image worshiper–idolator
images (mental)–idola
images (mental, considered collectively)–imagery
images (succession of mental)–reverie
imaginably true–possible
imaginary – fancied, ideal, mythical
imagination–fancy, fantasy
imaginative–dreamy, poetic
imagine – conceive, conjecture, dream, fancy, suppose, think
imbecile–anile, dolt, dotard, driveling, idiot, moron
imbed–cement, embed, inset
imbibe–absorb, drink, imbue, saturate, soak, steep
imbricate–tile
imbrue – defile, drench, moisten, saturate, soak, stain, steep, wet
imbue–dye, impregnate, ingrain, leaven, permeate, steep, tincture, tinge
imbue with bad or good qualities–teach
imbue with creative urge–inspire
imbue with vigor–nerve
imburse–pay, recompense
imidogen compound–imin
imitant – counterfeit, imitation
imitate–ape, copy, dissemble, echo, mime, mimic, mock, pastiche, simulate
imitate the sound of the

thing signified–onomatopoeic, onomatopoetic
imitation–apery, copy, echo, ectype, paste, sham
imitation (fantastic)–travesty
imitative (servilely)–apish
immaculate – clean, pure, spotless, undefiled, unsoiled, unstained, unsullied
immalleable–unyielding
immanent – indwelling, inherent, intrinsic
immaterial–impalpable, insignificant, intangible, slight, trifling, unsubstantial
immatriculate – enroll, matriculate
immature–crude, green, premature, undeveloped, unfinished, unripe, untimely, untried, youthful
immeasurable–boundless, illimitable, immensurable, indefinitely, infinite, unlimited
immediacy in space–here
immediate – direct, instant, next, succeeding
immediately–directly, now
immemorial – ageless, dateless, prehistoric, traditional
immense–enormous, grand, great, huge, immeasurable, infinite, monstrous, prodigious, unmeasured, vast
immerge – dip, immerse, plunge
immerse–bury, dip, douse, engross, plunge, sink, souse
imminent–impending
immobile – fixed, immovable, inert, motionless, moveless, set, stable, stationary
immoderately – excessively, exorbitantly, extremely, inordinately, intemperately
immolation–sacrifice
immoral–bad, corrupt, de-

praved, dissolute, indecent, licentious, vicious

immortal – amaranthine, ceaseless, deathless, divine, endless, enduring, eternal, godlike, incorruptible, undying

immortality – athanasia, deathlessness, everlastingness

immortality (Hindu myth.) –amreeta, amrita

immovable – adamant, fast, firm, fixed, immobile, obdurate, pat, rigid, stationary

immunity–exemption, freedom, unrestraint

immure–imprison, incarcerate, wall

immutable – eternal, firm, unadulterated, invariable

imp–brat, bud, child, cion, demon, devil, flibbertigibbet, graft, offspring, progeny, rogue, scion, shoot, slip

impact – brunt, impulse, pack, shock, slam, stroke, wedge

impair–damage, debase, decrease, deteriorate, enfeeble, harm, hurt, injure, lessen, mar, reduce, spoil, vitiate, weaken, wear

impair (essentially)–ruin

impair by indolence–rust

impaired by use–worn

impairment of character – deterioration

impale – border, confine, edge, encircle, pierce, spike, surround

impalpable–intangible

impar–odd, unequal

impart – communicate, confer, convey, discover, distribute, divulge, lend, reveal, share, tell, yield

impart character to–tone

impart knowledge–enlighten

impart to–lend

impartial–disinterested, dispassionate, equitable, even, fair, just, unbiased

impartiality – disinterestedness, fairness

imparting motion–motor

imparting no knowledge–uninstructive

impassable–impervious, stolid

impassioned–eloquent

impassive – apathetic, calm, impassible, passive, serene, stoic, stolid

impatient – choleric, eager, fretful, irascible, irritable, peevish, petulant, restless, testy

impatiently desirous–eager

impavid–fearless

impeach – accuse, arraign, censure, charge, criminate, discredit, disparage, harm, hinder, impair, impede, indict, prevent

impeccable–faultless

impede – block, encumber, hamper, hinder, let, obstruct, stimy, stymie

impediment – bar, defect, difficulty, encumbrance, hindrance, malady, obstacle, obstruction, rub, snag

impel–drive, incite, induce, influence, move, urge

impel a boat–oar, pole, row, scull

impel forward–forge

impelled–driven

impending – hindering, imminent, menacing, threatening

impenetrable–proof

impenitent–obdurate, unrepentant

imperative–imperious, mandatory, peremptory, pressing

imperceptible–inappreciable, indiscernible, insensible

imperfect – cull, defective, faulty, inadequate, incomplete, second

imperfection – blemish, defect, deficiency, failing, fault, flaw, frailty, shortcoming, vice, weakness

imperfectly–half

imperial – kingly, majestic, regal, royal

imperial cap (sovereignty)–crown

imperial domain – empery, emperies (pl.), empire

imperial organization – empire

imperial palace officer–palatine

imperil – endanger, jeopardize, risk

imperious–arrogant, despotic, dictatorial, domineering, haughty, lordly, overbearing, pressing, tyrannical

imperish–impair, injure

imperishable – enduring, eternal, everlasting, immortal, indestructible, undying

impermanent – ephemeral, fleeting, temporary, transient

impersonate–ape, exemplify, personify, pose, typify

impertinence – impropriety, incivility, insolence, irrelevance, unfitness

impertinence (dial.)–sass

impertinent – disrespectful, ill-bred, impudent, inapposite, inconsequent, officious, rude

imperturbable – cool, impassive, phlegmatic, placid, serene, tranquil

impervious–impassable, impenetrable, tight

impervious to heat – athermancy

impetition – accusation, charge

impetuous – ardent, eager, fervid, forcible, furious, hasty, headlong, heady, hot, precipitate, rash, sharp, vehement, violent

impetuosity (Fr.)–fougee

impetus–impulse, incentive, momentum, stimulus

impi–soldiers

impious–irreligious, irreverent, profane, undutiful

impish–mischievous

implacable – immitigable, unappeasable

implant – enforce, engraft, impress, infix, infuse, inoculate, inset, insinuate, inspire, instill, introduce

implanted (firmly)–rooted

implement–instrument, material, tool, utensil

implement (anc. stone)–eolith, paleolith

implement (baker's spade-like)–peel

implement (braying mortar)–pestle

implement (cleaning) – broom, brush, mop

implement (cutting)–knife, mower, reaper, scissors, scythe, shears

implement (for stirring melted iron in puddling)–rabble

implement (garden) – hoe, mower, rake, sickle, weeder

implement (grasping)–tongs

implement (hide cleaning)–slater

implement (lifting) – lever, pry, tongs

implement (log handling)–peavey, peavy, peevey, peevy

implement (log skidding)–tode

implement (lumberman's)–peavey, peavy, peevey, peevy

implement (printer's inking)–biron

implement (reaping)–mower, reaper, scythe, shears, sickle

implement (shovel-like) – scoop

implement (threshing)–flail

implement (torture)–rack

implement (used with mortar)–pestle

implement (war, offensive)–armory

implement (war, old) – petard

implement (wooden, for

beating clothes while washing)–dolly

implement for holding objects–pliers, tongs, tweezers

implement for pounding – pestle

implement for raising nap on woolen cloth–teasel

implement of war (weapon) –petard

implete–filled, replete

implicate – entwine, interweave, involve

implicit–complete, constructive, tacit

implied–inferential, tacit

implied (opposite of) – expressed

implore–ask, beg, crave, entreat, petition, pray, solicit, supplicate

imply–argue, connote, hint, infold, involve, predicate

impolite – crude, discourteous, disrespectful, rough, rude, uncivil, ungracious, unmannerly

impolitic–undiplomatic, indiscreet, inexpedient, unwise

import–betoken, denote, indicate, meaning, sense

import tax–duty

importance – consequence, moment, prestige

important – consequential, considerable, considerate, grave, influential, material, momentous, pompous, urgent

important (very) – momentous

important occurrence–event

importune–appeal, beg, entreat, plead, urge, woo

impose–burden, command, duty, inflict, levy, obligation, penalty, tax

impose (as necessary result) –entail

impose on another for bed and board (Scot.)–sorn

impose upon–delude, dupe, fool

imposing–commanding, impressive, stately

impossible to pay–bankrupt, insoluble

impost–custom, excise, levy, tariff, task, tax, tribute, weight

impost (additional)–surtax

impost (government)–tax

impost block–dosseret

impostor–charlatan, empiric, mountebank, quack

imposture–deception, delusion, fraud, imposition, trick

impotent–barren, powerless, sterile

impound – appropriate, collect, freeze, reservoir, seize, store

impouring–influx

impoverish–beggar, exhaust, ruin

imprecation – anathema, curse, execration, malediction, oath

impregnable–hard, inexpugnable

impregnate–fructify, infuse, permeate, saturate

impregnate with anise–anisate

impresa – device, emblem, maxim, motto, proverb

impresario – conductor, entrepreneur, manager, projector

impress–bite, enlist, fix, imprint, inculcate, levy, mark, press, print, seal, stamp

impress deeply–engrave

impressed with one's own inferiority–awed

impressed with sense of grandeur–awed

impressed with solemn wonder–awed

impression – idea, mark, stamp

impression (strike off from type)–print

impression in printing (double)–macule

impression made by seal – signet

impressionable – plastic, responsive, sensitive, susceptible

impressive – arresting, grandiose

impressive (gravely) – solemn

imprint–dint, fix, impress, press, stamp

imprison–arrest, confine, detain, immure, incarcerate, jail, limit, restrain

imprison (within walls) – immure

imprisonment – coercion, confinement, durance, duress, restraint

imprisonment (arch.) – duresse

impromptu – extemporaneous, extempore, offhand

improper–amiss, evil, ill, illegal, inaccurate, incorrect, indecent, indecorous, indelicate, unbecoming, unseemly, wrong

impropriety–solecism

improve – advance, ameliorate, amend, augment, better, correct, cultivate, emend, enhance, intensify, meliorate, mend, moise, promote, rectify

improve morally–edified

improvident – negligent, prodigal, thoughtless, thriftless, wasteful

imprudence–hardihood

imprudence (coll.)–brass

imprudent–audacious, bold, brash, brassy, brazen, indiscreet, injudicious, insolent, malapert, pert, rash, reckless, rude, unwary

impudence–indecency, insolence, shamelessness

impudence (coll.)–cheek

impudent (to be, slang)–sassy

impulse–force, impetus, incentive, instigation, motive, urge

impulse (natural)–instinct

impulse (ruinous, blind)–ate

impulsive–impellent, impetuous, quick

impurity–solution

impute – ascribe, attribute, consider, reckon, regard

in–at

in (prefix)–en

in (prefix, before "r")–ir

in a brave manner–fearlessly

in a chamber (law)–incamera

in a flutter–pitapat

in a pile–aheap

in a row – aligned, alined, arow

in a vertical line (naut.)–apeak

in addition–also, too

in addition to–plus

in aerial flight–awing

in an elucidative manner–explanatory

in another direction–away

in any case–ever

in any degree–ever

in as much as–seeing

in behalf of–for, pro

in capacity of–qua

in case–lest

in character of–qua

in company of–with

in current style–alamode

in effect–operative

in excess–over, too

in fact–truly

in favor of (prefix)–pro

in front–aface, ahead

in general favor–popular

in good health – fit, hale, hearty

in good health (dial.)–peart

in good season–betime

in good spirit (coll.)–peart

in great degree–much

in here–consist

in manner of–ala

in manner relating to spring–vernally

in necessary manner–vitally

in no manner–not

in no way–nowise

in place of – for, instead, stead

in private (law)–incamera

in process of development–nascent

in process of settlement – pend

in proper manner–duly

in proportion to–as

in recent times–lately

in regard to–anent

in relation to–anent

in respect to–anent

in same place–ibid

in same place (abbr.)–ib

in so far as it is (Latin)–qua

in spite of–despite, mauger, maugre, over

in state of acting–energic

in style of–ala, alla

in succession–serially, seriatim

in such cases–then

in that case–then

in that way–how

in the back – aft, arear, astern, postern

in the center of–amid

in the future–hence, later

in the future (var.)–hense

in the highest degree–essentially

in the main–generally

in the presence of (Latin)–coran

in the same manner (Scot.)–so-wise

in the same place (abbr.)–ibid

in truth–indeed, verily

in truth (arch.)–certes

in what way–how

in what way (Latin)–quomodo

inability – impotence, incapacity, incompetence

inability to chew–amasesis

inability to name objects correctly–paranomia

inability to read (due to brain illness)–alexia

inability to utter articulate sounds (med.)–alalia

inaccessible – unapproachable, unattainable

inaccurate–defective, faulty, imperfect, loose

inaccurately–inexactly

inaction–idleness, inertness

inaction (temporary) – abeyant

inactive – idle, inert, sedentary

inadequacy – deficiency, insufficiency

inadvertence – carelessness, heedlessness, thoughtlessness

inane–characterless, empty, fatuous, frivolous, silly, trifling

inanimate–dead, inert, lifeless, stolid, unconscious

inappropriate–inept, undue, unsuitable

inattentive–absent, careless, inadvertent, lax, negligent, remiss, unheeding, unmindful

inaugura–accession

inaugurate–auspicate, consecrate, induct, initiate, install, introduce, start

inauspicious – adverse, ominous, sinister, unpropitious

inborn–connate, inbred, inherent, innate, native, natural

inbreak – incursion, inroad, invasion

inbred–innate

Inca's empire–Peru

incalculable – boundless, illimitable, immeasurable, uncertain

incandescence–glow

incandescent particle–spark

incantation – enchantment, magic, sorcery, spell

incapable–disqualified, inefficient, unable, unqualified

incapable of being satisfied–insatiable

incapable of holding–untenable

incapacitate–cripple, disable, disqualify

incapacitate by age–superannuate

incarcerate–confine, imprison

incarnation–avatar, Christ

incase – cover, enclose, surround

incase in cans–can, tin

incautious–careless, heedless, impolitic, imprudent, indiscreet, rash, reckless, unwary

incendiarism–arson

incendiary–firer, inflammatory, seditious

incense – anger, arouse, enrage, incite, instigate, irritate, provoke

incense burner–censer

incense burning place (raised)–altar

incense spice–stacte

incensed–angered, enraged, irate, mad

incentive – encouragement, goad, incitement, inducement, influence, motive, provocation, spark, spur, stimulus

inception – commencement, initiation, intussusception, origin, reception

incessant–ceaseless, constant, continual, unremitting

incessantly–continually, forever, unceasingly

inches (39.37)–meter

inchmeal–gradually

inchpin–sweetbread

incident–accident, casualty, contingency, episode, event, subject

incidental – accessory, accidental, bye, contingent, episodic, fortuitous

incidentally–obiter

incinerate – burn, consume, cremate

incipient – commencing, inaugurate, induct, initial, seat

incipient laugh–smile

incise–carve, cut, engrave

incised (narrowly)–laciniate

incision – cut, gash, laceration, lance

incite–abet, animate, arouse, egg, encourage, fire, goad, prod, provoke, spur, stimulate, sting, tew, urge

inclination–affection, attachment, bent, bias, conatus, fancy, leaning, love, penchant, predilection, prepossession, proclivity, proneness, slant, taste, tendency, trend, urge

inclination (strong) – penchant

inclination downward–dip

incline – bend, bevel, dip, grade, heel, lean, slant, slide, slope, tend, tilt, tip, trend

incline (naut.)–alist

inclined – apt, dip, prone, wont

inclined (beforehand)–predisposed

inclined to lee–sag

inclined to sin–transgressive

inclined walk–ramp

inclose – case, encase, environ, hem, incase, pen

inclose (arch.)–embar

inclose in walls–mure

inclosed in a sac–cysted

inclosed part–interior

inclosure–impalement, sepiment

inclosure (animal) – cage, corral, cote, hutch, kraal, pen, sty

inclosure (Scot.)–ree

include – comprise, contain, embrace, involve

including everything–overall

including much – comprehensive

incoherent–broken, disconnected, illogical, incongruous, inconsequent, inconsistent

income – emolument, gain, interest, proceeds, produce, profit, receipts, return, revenue

income (Fr., yearly)–rente

income derived from wealth –usance

incommensurate– disproportionate, insufficient, unequal

incommode–annoy, disquiet, inconvenience, plague, trouble, vex

incomparable – superlative, surpassing, unrivaled

incompatible – contradictory, inharmonious, irreconcilable, unsympathetic
incompetence–disability, inability, unfitness
incompetent – disqualified, incommensurate, inefficient, inept, unfit, insufficient
incomplete–crude, defective, immature, imperfect, lacking, partially, undone, unfinished
incomprehensible – unconceivable, unimaginable, unreadable, unthinkable
incomprehensibly – mysteriously
incongruity – disagreement, incoherence, inconsistency, inharmony, unsuitableness
incongruous – absurd, alien, inappropriate, inconsistent, inharmonious, unsuitable
incongruous color mixture–motley
inconsequent–illogical, impertinent, inconsecutive, inconsistent, invalid
inconsiderate – improvident, imprudent, incautious, indiscreet, injudicious, neglectful, negligent, rash, unkind
inconsistent – contradictory, discordant, discrepant, dissonant, incoherent
incontestable – certain, indubitable, undeniable
inconvenience – awkwardness, disquiet, disturbance, incommode, uneasiness
inconvenient – annoying, troublesome, unhandy, unreasonable, unsuitable
incorporate – assimilate, blend, fuse, merge, mix, unite
incorporeal–bodiless, spiritual, unsubstantial
incorrect–erroneous, wrong
increase – accelerate, accession, accrue, add, aggra-

vate, aggravation, amplification, enlargement, expand, expansion, extend, extension, gain, heighten, intensification, intensify, multiply, raise, rise, swell, wax
increase by addition access
increase possession of–amass, enrich
increase pressure of fluid–boost
increased in size – grew, waxed
increasing by successive additions–cumulative
increasing in amount–intensive
increasing in loudness (slowly)–crescendo
increasing in value – increment
increment – augmentation, increase
inculcate–implant, impress, infuse, instil, instill
incumbent – impending, threatening
incumbents (political)–ins
incurable – hopeless, irremediable, irreparable, remediless
incurious–apathetic, unconcerned, uninquiring, uninterested
incurred the hostility of–antagonized
incursion–foray, inroad, invasion, raid
incus–anvil
indecency–immodesty, impurity, indecorum, indelicacy, obscenity
indecent – gross, immodest, improper, impure, obscene
indecision–doubt, hesitation, irresolution, uncertainty, vacillation
indecisive–hesitating, irresolute, vacillating
indecorous–coarse, impolite, improper, rude, unbecoming, uncivil, unseemly
indefatigable – perseverance,

tireless, untiring, unwearying
indefensible–inexcusable, insupportable, unpardonable
indefinite – equivocal, inexact, inexplicit, loose, vague
indefinite amount–any
indefinite "one"–an
indefinite pronoun–one
indefinite quantity–any, hatful, some
indehiscent fruit–uva
indehiscent legume–uva
indelible – fast, fixed, ineffaceable, ineradicable, inerasable, inexpungible, permanent
indelicate – coarse, fulsome, gross, impolite, improper, indecorous, offensive, unbecoming, unrefined, unseemly
indemnification–restitution
indemnify–compensate, pay, recoup, reimburse
indent – emboss, inlay, jag, notch, press, stamp, tooth
indentation–crenel, dint, impression, nick, notch, recess
indentation (small)–crenelet
indented–dented, impressed, jagged, milled, notched, sinuous, undulating
indenture–agreement, contract
independence–freedom
independencies–nations
independent–uncoerced, uncontrolled, unrestricted
independent lands–alod, allod
index – file, list, pie, pye, table
India–Hindustan
India (kingdom of)–Inepal, Nepal
India (poetic)–Ind
India (ten million rupees)–crore
India rubber–caoutchouc
Indian–aborigine
Indian (Algonquin) – Ottawa

Indian (American)–Algonquin, Amerind, Apache, Apalachee, Banak, Cherokee, Chickasaw, Choctaw, Comanche, Coree, Cree, Creek, Erie, Hopi, Huron, Iowas, Iroquois, Kania, Kaw, Lenape, Miami, Muskhogean, Narragansett, Navajo, Omaha, Oneida, Osage, Oto, Otoe, Pawnee, Piute, Sac, Sambos, Seminole, Seneca, Sioux, Siwash, Zuñi
Indian (American Delaware)–Lenapes
Indian (Athapascan)–Dene, Tinne
Indian (Iroquoian)–Oneida
Indian (male married)–sannop
Indian (Mexican) – Aztec, Cora, Opata, Otonia
Indian (Nahuatlan)–Aztec
Indian (North Carolina) – Coree
Indian (Shoshonean)–Hopi
Indian (Siouan)–Omaha
Indian (Terra del Fuego)–Agni, Ona
Indian (unfriendly)–hostile
Indian (western)–Piute, Ute
Indian (Yucatan)–Maya
Indian animal (cat-like) – zibet
Indian animal (ox-like)–zebu
Indian antelope–nilgai, nilgau, nilghai, sasin
Indian antelope (large)–nilgai, nilghai
Indian army officer (native)–jemadar
Indian bird (thrush family) –shama
Indian book (sacred)–avesta
Indian brick (pulverized and mixed with lime)–soorkee, soorki, soorky
Indian buck (black)–sasin
Indian buffalo (wild)–arna, arnee
Indian buzzard–tesa
Indian capital–Delhi
Indian carpet–agra

India carriage (one-horse)–ekka
Indian cart (two-wheeled)–tonga
Indian caste (cowherds and dairymen)–ahir
Indian cedar–deodar
Indian chief–raja, rajah, rana, sirdar
Indian chief (American) – sachem
Indian city–Agra, Ahmadabad, Ajmere, Aligarh, Allahabad, Ambala, Amritsar, Bangalore, Bareli, Baroda, Benares, Bhagalpur, Bhopal, Bombay, Calcutta, Calicut, Cawnpur, Dacca, Daman, Darbhangah, Delhi, Gaya, Girot, Gorakhpur, Gwalior, Haidarabad, Howrah, Hyderabad, Indore, Jabalpur, Jaipur, Jodhpur, Jubbulpore, Karachi, Kolhapur, Kurrachee, Lahore, Lucknow, Madras, Madura, Mandalay, Meerut, Mirzapur, Moradabad, Multan, Muttra, Mysore, Nagapatam, Nagpur, Patna, Peshawar, Poona, Puna, Rampur, Rangoon, Rangpur, Rawalpindi, Rewa, Saharanpur, Salem, Shahjahanpur, Sholapur, Simla, Srinagar, Surat, Trichinopoli
Indian city (British)–Agra
Indian city (sacred)–Benares
Indian civet–zibet, zibeth
Indian coasting vessel–doni
Indian coin – anna (ni.), crore (ac.), lac (ac.), lakh (ac.), pice (br.), pie (br.), rupee (s.)
Indian coin (small)–pie
Indian college (Sanskrit) – Tol
Indian corn–maize, samp
Indian council–powwow
Indian country–Nepal
Indian court (supreme) – Sudder
Indian craft–canoe
Indian crane (large)–sarus

Indian crocodile–gavial
Indian cubit measure–hath
Indian dam (irrigating) – anicut
Indian dancer (rope)–nat
Indian deer (barking) – kakar
Indian Delhi province district–Simla
Indian devil tree–dita
Indian dialect–Tamil, Urdu
Indian dignitary–rajah
Indian district–malabar
Indian district (provincial, rural)–Mofussil
Indian division (British) – Sind
Indian dog (tiger-hunting)–dhole
Indian dravidian – Arava, Tamil
Indian dravidian ghost – Bhut
Indian elephant trappings–jhool
Indian elk–sambar
Indian emperor – King of England
Indian fair (religious)–mela
Indian falcon–shaheen, shahin
Indian festival (northwest U.S.)–potlatch
Indian fetich–totem
Indian fig (sacred)–pipal
Indian fig tree–banian
Indian fig tree (sacred)–pipal
Indian fighter–Custer, Miles
Indian fire screen (for cooling air)–tattie
Indian fish (walking)–chenas
Indian flour (wheat)–ata, atta
Indian food (fish)–hilsah
Indian garment–saree, sari
Indian gateway–toran, torana
Indian god–Deva
Indian grass (pasture)–doorba
Indian groom–syce
Indian guardian spirit – totem
Indian gum (tree)–amra

Indian harvest (chief)–rabi
Indian hatchet–tomahawk
Indian health resort–Abu
Indian herb–pia, sesame
Indian hereditary class of society–caste
Indian hero–Rama
Indian holi powder (red perfumed)–abir
Indian honey–tabasheer
Indian horse trappings–jhool
Indian iceroot–goldenseal
Indian idiom–Tamil
Indian irrigation dam–anicut
Indian jewel weight–tola
Indian king's son–shahzada, shahzadah
Indian kingdom–Nepal
Indian knife–dah
Indian land-grant tenant – enamdar
Indian lake–Chilka, Kolair
Indian lake (after inundation)–jheel, jhil
Indian language–Tamil, Urdu
Indian legal claim or right–hak, hakh
Indian lemur (slow moving)–lori
Indian leopard (hunting)–cheetah
Indian loan–dhan
Indian lodge–tepee
Indian macaque–rhesus
Indian madder–aal
Indian mahogany–toon, toona
Indian mail (inland)–dak
Indian man–buck, chief
Indian marsh (after inundation)–jheel, jhil
Indian meal–ata, atta
Indian meal (unsorted)–atta, ata
Indian measure – adhaka, adoulie, ady, amunam, angula, bigha, byee, cahar, cos, covid, covido, crosa, cudava, cumbha, dain, danda, denda, dha, dhan, dhanush, drona, garce, gavyuti, geerah, gireh, guz, hasta, hath, jaob, jow, khahoon, kos,

koss, kunk, lamany, lan, moolum, moot, mushti, niranga, okthabah, palgat, pally, para, parah, parrah, prastha, raik, ropani, salay, seit, taun, teng, tipree, unglee, vitasti, yojan, yojana
Indian medium of exchange –wampum
Indian memorial post–xat
Indian merchant–soudagur
Indian midwife–dhai
Indian millet–durr, durra
Indian millet (var.)–doura
Indian money – anna, lao, wampum
Indian money (bead)–wampum
Indian money (shell bead)–seawan
Indian mountain–Ghats, Himalayas, Hindu-Kush, Neilgherries, Nilghiris, Suleiman, Vindhya
Indian mountain pass–ghat, ghaut
Indian mountain range – ghat, ghaut
Indian mulberry–aal, ach, al
Indian muslin–dorea
Indian myrobalan–chebule
Indian native–Hindu, Tamil
Indian native nurse–ayah
Indian nurse (wet)–dhai
Indian officer (native)–jemadar
Indian ox–gaur
Indian palm–tal
Indian partridge–kyah
Indian partridge (sand)–seesee
Indian pastoral people (one of)–Toda
Indian peace pipe–calumet
Indian peasant–ryot
Indian petty officer–foujdar
Indian pillar–lat, xat
Indian pipe of peace–calumet
Indian plant–chirata
Indian plant (nettle family) –ramie
Indian police station–tana, tanna, thana, thanah

Indian pool (after inundation)–jheel, jhil
Indian porridge (corn) – samp
Indian potato – breadroot, yamp
Indian presidency – Bengal, Bombay, Madras
Indian prince–bana, rajah
Indian prince's court – Durbar
Indian property or wealth–dhan
Indian province (British) – Assam
Indian province natives – Bengalis
Indian queen–Begum
Indian race–Hindu, Tamil
Indian rat–bandicoot
Indian red–almagra
Indian revenue collector – amil
Indian rice–boro
Indian river–Cauvery, Ganges, Godavari, Indus, Kistna, Krishna, Nerbudda, Sind, Sutlej, Tapti, Vindhyas
Indian robes of state–seerpaws
Indian rule–raj
Indian ruler (deputy) – nawab
Indian saffron – turmeric, zedoary
Indian sarsaparilla–nunnari
Indian school (Sanskrit)–Tol
Indian seaport–Bombay
Indian servant (native) – maty
Indian shah's son–shahzada, shahzadah
Indian sheep (wild)–sha
Indian shopkeeper – soudagur
Indian shrine–dagoba
Indian snake charmer's clarinet–been
Indian social standing (hereditary)–caste
Indian soldier (East)–sepoy
Indian sorcery (West)–ob, obe, obi
Indian spirit (great)–Manitou

Indian spirit (guardian)–totem

Indian split pea–dal

Indian state–Assam, Baluchistan, Bastar, Bengal, Berar, Bhutan, Bihar, Bombay, Central India, Central Province, Chitral, Cutch, Gujarat, Gujerat, Haidarabad, Hyderabad, Kashmir, Madras Presidency, Mysore, Nepal, Northwest Frontier, Orissa, Oudh, Presidency, Punjab, Rajputana, Sikkim, Travancore, United Provinces

Indian state (native)–Manipur

Indian state reception (British)–durbar

Indian Sudra low caste–Mal

Indian sugar (crude)–gur

Indian tamarisk (used in basket making)–jhow

Indian tax system–ryotwar

Indian tenant–ryot

Indian timber tree–teak

Indian title – saheb, sahib, sahibah

Indian title (of respect) – mian

Indian title (sir, master) – mian

Indian tongue–Hindu, Tamil

Indian tower–minar

India tower (pyramidal) – sikar, sikara

Indian town (Madras)–Arcot

Indian transportation (mail)–dak

Indian tree–banyan, lin, teak

Indian tree (sacred fig)–pipal

Indian tree gum–amra

Indian tribe (old)–Erie

Indian tribe religious head–elderman

Indian tribes (American)–see Indian

Indian tribesman (anc.)–Aryan

Indian tulip tree–majagua

Indian turmeric–goldenseal

Indian turnip–breadroot

Indian umbrella–chattah

Indian vehicle (light two-wheeled)–tonga

Indian vessel (coasting) – doni

Indian viceroy–nawab

Indian wall of tent–kanat

Indian walnut–candlenut

Indian warrior–brave

Indian water lily–wokas

Indian water vessel–lota

Indian weapon–tomahawk

Indian weaver bird–baya

Indian weight–abucco, adpao, bahar, catty, chittack, chittak, dhan, dhurra, drum, hubba, karsha, kona, myat, masha, maund, moo, pai, pala, pally, pank, peiktha, pice, pouah, raik, rati, ratti, retti, ruay, seer, ser, tank, tical, ticul, tikal, tola, vis, yava

Indian weight unit–ratti

Indian wheat flour–ata, atta

Indian wheat meal–ata, atta

Indian wild dog–dhole

Indian wild sheep–sha

Indian woman–squaw

Indian woman's garment – saree, sari

Indian yam–cush-cush

Indiana town–Ari, Fowler, Marion

indicate – bespeak, connote, declare, denote, designate, disclose, display, evidence, evince, manifest, mark, point, register, reveal, show, signify, specify

indicated – betokened, marked, signed

indicating a chemical group –azo

indicating succession–ordinal

indication – clue, evidence, hint, manifestation, mark, note, omen, proof, sign, signal, token, trace

indicator – annunciator, arrow, gauge, hand, index, indices (pl.), pointer, sign, vane

indicator (circular)–dial

indicator (time)–gnomon

indicia (indicium, sing.)–appearances, indications, marks, signs, tokens

indict–charge, decree, proclaim

indictive – appointed, declared, proclaimed

indifference – apathy, carelessness, coldness, heedlessness, insensibility, lukewarmness, negligence

indifferent – adiaphorous, blase, careless, casual, cold, cool, ill, listless, nonchalant, nonessential, poorly, regardless, sick, uneager

indifferent to pain–stoical

indigence–deficiency, lack, need, penury, poverty, want

indigene–native

indigenous – autochthonous, inborn, inherent, innate, native, natural

indigenous to–endemic

indigent–destitute, free, impecunious, lacking, necessitous, needy, penniless, poor, void, wanting

indign – disgraceful, undeserved, undeserving

indignant–angry, annoyed, exasperated, incensed, irate, wrathful, wroth

indignant at–resents

indignation – anger, contempt, disdain, fury, ire, wrath

indignity–affront

indigo–anil, blue

indigo (natural source)–indican

indigo dye–al

indigo dye (pert. to)–anilic

indigo plant–anil

indigo source (artificial)–isatin

indigo source (natural)–indican, isatin

indirect–circuitous, devious, dishonest, misleading, oblique, roundabout

indirect expense–overhead

indiscreet–careless, foolish, hasty, heedless, imprudent, incautious, inconsiderate, injudicious, rash, silly, undiscerning, unwise, witless

indiscriminate – heterogeneous, mingled, mixed, wholesale

indispensable – basic, essential, exigent, imperative, requisite, vital

indisposed–ailing, disqualified, ill, sick, unsuited

indisposition–ailment, reluctance, unwillingness

indisposition to motion–inertia

indisputable – certain, evident, incontestable, incontrovertible, indubitable, irrefragable, positive, sure, undeniable, unquestionable

indistinct – ambiguous, blurred, dim, indefinite, indistinguishable, obscure, unrefined, vague

indistinct (make or become) –blur

indite – compose, inscribe, pen, write

individual–identical, inseparable, one, selfsame, sole, special

individual (comb. form) – idio

individual (physiological) – bion

individual (selfish)–egoist

individual of genus homo–man

individuality (rare)–seity

individually – distributively, personally, severally

individuals–ones, persons

individuals (living)–bions

individuals (marine, collectively)–merpeople

individuate–inseparable, undivided

Indo-Aryan deity–Indra

Indo-Chinese–Tai, Yao

Indo-Chinese dialect–ao

Indo-Chinese kingdom – Anam, Annam

Indo-Chinese language–aka, ao, hu, sai, tai, thai, wa

Indo-Chinese linguist stock–Tai

Indo-Chinese race–Tai

Indo-Chinese tree–eng, mee

Indo-European–Aryan, Slav

Indo-Iranian–Aryan

Indo-Malayan chevrotain – napu

indolence–scorn, sloth

indolence (listless)–languor

indolent–idle, inactive, inert, lazy, slothful, sluggish

indomitable–intractable, invincible, unconquerable

Indonesian Indian–Ata

Indonesian race – Battak, Bontok, Dyak, Ifugao, Igorot, Lampong, Manobo

Indonesian tribe–Ata

indoor game–gobang

indorsement (official)–visa, vise

indorsement on passport – visa, vise

Indra (Hindu myth.)–Sakka, Sakra

indubitable–evident, incontestable, incontrovertible, irrefragable, sure, undeniable

induced–allured, caused, enticed, impelled, incited, instigated, led, moved, persuaded, urged

inducement – incentive, influence, motive, reason

induct–install, introduce

inductile–inflexible, unyielding

induction – accession, commencement, deduction, entrance, initiation, introduction

indue–assume, clothe, endow, furnish, invest

indulge – gratify, humor, pamper, pet

indulge in recreation–play

indulge in self-esteem–pride

indulge in vanity–pride

indulge to excess–pamper

indulgence to fretfulness – repine

indulgent–compliant, easy, lenient, tolerant

indulger–humorer

indulger in hobbies and whims–faddist

industrial magnate–tycoon

industrious–assiduous, busy, diligent, painstaking, sedulous, zealous

industrious (steadily)–assiduous, indefatigable, sedulous

indwelling–immanence, immanent

inearth–inter

inebriacy – drunkenness, intemperance

inebriate–drunk, intoxicated, stupefied

ineffable–indescribable, inexpressible, unpronounceable, unspeakable, unutterable

ineffaceable–indelible, ineradicable

ineffectual–fruitless, futile, inefficacious, inefficient, unavailing, useless, vain, weak

inefficient–incompetent

inelegant–vulgar

inept–unsuitable, unsuited

inequality–disparity, disproportion, diversity, odds, unevenness

ineradicable–indelible, ineffaceable, lasting, permanent

inerrant–infallible, unerring

inert–apathetic, dead, inactive, lazy, lethargic, lifeless, passive, phlegmatic, slothful, sluggish, stupid, supine, torpid

inert (mentally)–supine

inesculant–inedible

inestimable–incalculable, invaluable, priceless

inevitable–unavoidable

inexorable–inflexible, relentless, unyielding

inexorability–rigor

inexperience – disadvantageous, imprudent, inadvisable, indiscreet, unprofitable, unwise

inexpedient–impolitic

inexperience–naif

inexperienced – amateurish, callow, green, naive, raw

inexplicable – preternatural, supernatural

infallible–certain, indubitable, inerrable, inerrant, sure, unerring

infallibly true–gospel

infamous – base, contemptible, detestable, ignominious, nefarious, odious, shameful

infamy–disgrace, dishonor, reproach

infant–baby, bantling, child

infantryman–musketeer

infantryman (army slang)–gravel agitator

infatuated–mad

infatuation–ate, folly

infatuation (leading men to ruin)–ate

infatuation (transient)–craze

infect – contaminate, defile, poison, pollute, taint

infelicity – misery, misfortune, unhappiness, wretchedness

infer–conclude, construe, deduce, drive, guess, hint, imply, surmise

inference–assumption, conclusion, deduction

inference (derived incidentally)–corollary

inferential – deductive, illative

inferior–bad, baser, humbler, inadequate, less, lesser, lower, mediocre, nether, poor, subordinate, unequal

inferior (law)–petit

inferior adjunct–pendicles

infernal–damnable, demoniacal, devilish, satanic, tartarean

infest – beset, overrun, plague, torment, vex

infidel–agnostic, atheist, deist, freethinker, Kaffir, pagan, skeptic, unbeliever

infidelity–deceit, disloyalty,

faithlessness, incredulity, perfidy, treachery

infinite–boundless, endless, illimitable, interminable, limitless, unlimited

infinitesimal – atomic, minute, small

infinitive (part of)–to

infirm – anile, doddering, fragile, frail, irresolute, vacillating, weak

infirm with age–senile

infirmary–hospital

infirmities (moral)–vices

infirmity – debility, disease, failing, feebleness, frailty, weakness

inflame–arouse, fire, irritate, kindle, madden

inflame with rage–madden

inflammable – combustible, excitable, irascible, irritable, tinder

inflammable mineral substance–bitumen

inflammation of ear–otitis

inflammation of ear (pert. to)–otitic

inflammation of iris–iritis

inflammation of spinal cord –poliomyelitis

inflated–bombastic, dilated, distended, elated, expanded, plethoric, pompous, swollen, turgid

inflect–bend, bow, curve, deflect, modulate

inflection on words (tabulated)–paradigm

inflexible – immovable, implacable, inexorable, relentless, rigid, rigorous, stiff, unbending, uncompromising

inflict–deal, impose

inflict vengeance–wreak

inflow–inst, influx

influence–affect, authority, control, effect, force, induce, infuse, inspire, lead, mastery, move, prestige, sway

influence (corruptly)–bribe

influence (derived from past success)–prestige

influence (political, of special interests)–lobby

influence (protecting)–egis

influence (strong, effecting a change)–leaven

influence by fixed idea–obsess

influence derived from past success–prestige

influenced–biased

influenced (easily)–pliable

influx–illapse, inflow, influence, inpouring

infold – clasp, embrace, envelop, laps, wrap

inform–advise, apprise, communicate, instruct, lighten, notify, tell, train

informal – unceremonious, unconventional

informal conversation–chat

information – datum, data (pl.), knowledge, news, tidings

information (body of condensed)–digest

information at hand–data

information giver–tattletale, telltale

informed–apprised, posted, up, wise

informer – canary, delator, gossip, informant, spy, stool pigeon, teller, telltale, tout

informer (common)–delater, delator

infra–after, below, under

infraction – encroachment, intrusion, transgression, trespass

infrequency–isolation, rareness, rarity, solitude, uncommonness

infrequent–occasional, rare, scarce, seldom, sparse, uncommon

infrequently–rarely, seldom

infrequently encountered – rare

infringe–confute, defeat, destroy, frustrate, refute, trespass

infringement–breach, infraction, nonfulfillment, violation

infuriate–enrage, madden
infuscate–darken, obscure
infuse – implant, insinuate, instill, introduce, steep
infuse slowly–instill
infusion – admixture, affusion, impouring, instillation, tea, tincture
infusion (makes an)–steep
infusion (malt)–wort
ingang–entrance, intestines, porch
ingenious–adroit, clever, daedal, daedalian, dedal, dedalian, deviceful, gifted, intelligent, resourceful, sharp, skillful, smart, subtle, talented, witty
ingenuity–adroitness, inventiveness, originality
ingenuous – artless, candid, frank, freeborn, guileless, innate, innocent, naif, naive, noble, plain, sincere, sophisticated, unreserved
ingenuousness–innocence
ingot (metal)–gad, pig
ingot worker–barman
ingrained–imbued, inhered, innate, inveterate, native, saturated
ingredient–component, element
ingredient (poisonous dye)–analine
ingredient (varnish)–lac, resin, rosin
ingress–entrance, entry
ingrowing nail–acronyx
inhabitant–citizen, denizen, inmate, people, resident, tenant
inhabitant (city)–cit
inhabitant of (suffix)–ese, ite
inhabitant of a city–cit, citizen
inhabited – dwelled, lived, peopled, populated
inhabiting an island–nesiote
inhale–breathe, respire
inharmonious – conflicting, discordant, dissonant, jarring, unmusical
inherent – inborn, imma-

nence, immanent, indispensable, indwelling, infixed, intrinsic, subsistent
inheritance–heredity, legacy
inheritance (restricted)–entailment
inheritance (Scot. law)–annat
inheritance portion–legitime
inheritance seizer–abator
inherited–native
inheritor–heir, legatee
inhibit–check, forbid, hinder, interdict, prohibit, restrain
inhibition–ban, bar, embargo, interdiction, prohibition, restraint
inhuman–barbarous, bestial, brutish, cruel, devilish, diabolical, fell, ferocious, savage
inhumane–brutal, cruel
inhume–bury, deposit, inter
inimical–averse, hostile, unfavorable, unfriendly
iniquity – crime, injustice, sin, vice, wickedness
initiate–admit, inaugurate, inchoate, induct, install, instate, open
initiation–admittance, introduced
injection–enema, hypo
injudicious – impolitic, imprudent, inexpedient
injunction–behest, mandate
injunction (moral)–precept
injure – affront, damage, harm, hurt, impair, lame, maim, mar, slander, tarnish, wound, wrong
injurious–abusive, bad, defamatory, detrimental, evil, harmful, hurtful, mischievous, slanderous
injury–damage, deface, detriment, evil, harm, hurt, ill, impairment, injustice, lesion, loss, mar, trauma, traumata (pl.), wrong
injury (civil)–tort
injury (serious physical, inflicted upon persons) – mayhem
injustice–hardship, imposi-

tion, inequity, iniquity, injury, unfairness, wrong
ink–millrynd
ink (pert. to)–atramental
inkling–hint, intimation, report, rumor
inlaid–champleve, decorated, mosaic
inland sea–Aral
inlay work–champleve, mosaic
inlet – admit, bayou, bight, cove, entrance, firth, inlay, oe, orifice, ria, rias (pl.)
inlet (long narrow)–ria
inlet (narrow from sea) – estuary, fiord, firth, fjord
inlet (of sea)–arm, bay, bayou
inlet (river)–slew
inlet (sheltered)–cove
inlet (sluggish)–bayou, fiord, firth, fjord
inlet (small)–cove
inlets–estero
inn–albergo, hospice, hostel, hostelry, hotel, tavern
inn (arch.)–hostel
inn (Oriental)–serai
inn (slang)–pub
innate – born, congenital, constitutional, hereditary, inborn, inbred, ingrained, instinctive, intrinsic, native
innate abilities–talents
inner–inside, interior, internal, inward
inner (anat.)–ental
innocence–guiltlessness, purity, sinlessness
innocent – artless, guiltless, ingenuous, naive, simpleminded, stainless, unblamable, upright
innocuous – harmless, inoffensive, innocent, innoxious, unoffending
innovation–novelty, novity
innuendo–hint, implication, insinuation, intimation, slur
innumerable–legion, myriad
inodorous – odorless, scentless

inopportune–ill-timed, mal-
apropos, unseasonable,
untimely
inordinate–disorderly, excessive, immoderate, unregu-
lated, unrestrained
inorganic–mineral
inquest – examination, inquiry, investigation, quest,
search
inquire–ask, examine, interrogate, investigate, query,
question
inquirer – searcher, seeker,
zetetic
inquiry–examen, examine,
investigation, query, question, research
inquiry (thorough)–investigation
inquiry for lost goods–tracer
inquisition–examination, investigation, search
inquisitive–curious, meddlesome, meddling, prying
inquisitiveness–curiosity
inquisitor–examiner, tracer
inroad–foray, incursion, invasion, irruption, raid
insane – crazy, daft, loony,
luny, mad
insane propensity to steal–
kleptomania
insanity – alienation, delirium, dementia, derange-
ment, frenzy, madness,
mania
inscribe – blazon, engrave,
etch, stamp, write
inscribed–dedicated
inscribed with Teutonic
characters–runed
inscription–epigraph, legend,
superscription
inscrutable – incomprehensible, inexplorable, myste-
rious, secret, unfathoma-
ble
insculpture–carving, inscription
insect–ant, bee, beetle, bug,
bumblebee, centipede, earwig, emmet, flea, fly,
gnat, katydid, lice, man-
tis, mite, roach, spider,
termite, tick, wasp

insect (adult)–imago
insect (aquatic)–boatman
insect (armed)–stinger
insect (bee-like)–wasp
insect (blood-sucking)–flea
insect (burrowing)–borer
insect (butterfly-like)–moth
insect (carnivorous)–mantis
insect (coleopterous)–beetle
insect (destructive) – scale,
termite
insect (flying)–moth
insect (grotesque)–mantis
insect (hymenopterous)–ant,
bee, gallfly, ichneumons,
sawfly, wasp
insect (immature)–pupa
insect (large green)–katydid
insect (leaf)–aphid
insect (many-legged)–centipede
insect (nocturnal)–moth
insect (obnoxious)–vermin
insect (orthopterous)–mantis
insect (parasitic)–lice, louse
insect (plant-juice sucker)–
aphis
insect (praying)–mantis
insect (small)–aphis, midge,
mite
insect (small black water)–
bullhead
insect (social)–ant
insect (undeveloped)–pupa
insect (winged) – hornet,
wasp, yellow jacket
insect (wingless)–flea
insect (with caudal forceps)
–earwig
insect (worm-like form) –
larva
insect (young)–nit
insect adult (developed) –
imago
insect adult (winged)–imago
insect egg–gnat, nit
insect feelers–palps, tentacles
insect horn–antenna
insect pupa–chrysalis
insect stage–imago, pupa
insect stage (immature)–larva
insect trap–web
insect which sucks plant
juices–aphid
insect wing vein–media

insect's back–nota
insect's sound–chirr
insectivore (small)–tenrec
insecure–dangerous, hazardous, infirm, precarious,
risky, shaky, unsafe, un-
stable, unsure
insensate–blind, brutal, fatuous, foolish, harsh, in-
sensible, unfeeling, un-
touched
insensible–insensate, insensitive
insensibility (state of)–coma
insert–inset, intercalate, interpolate, interpose
insert (triangular) – gore,
wedge
insert scions–graft
insert surreptitiously–foist
insert twig into another tree
–engraft
inserted at edge of eye–in-
ocular
inserted clauses or phrases–
parentheses
insertion–inset
insertion of a day in a calendar–intercalation
insertion of cords in cloth–
shirr
inset (rectangular)–panel
insidious – deceitful, deep,
guileful, treacherous
insight–discernment, ken
insignia–badge, emblem
insignificant–inferior, paltry,
petit, petty, puny, senseless, trivial
insignificant (law)–petit
insignificant obstacles–mole-
hills
insignificant part–iota, tithe
insincere – deceptive, false,
hypocritical
insinuate–allude, hint, ingratiate
insinuate contempt–sneer
insinuation (derogatory) –
innuendo
insipid – dead, flat, jejune,
lifeless, monotonous,
prosy, spiritless, stale,
tame, tasteless, unani-
mated, vapid
insisted–demanded

insnare – benet, enmesh, noose, trap, trapan, trepan, web

insolence (coll.)–nerve

insolence (scornful) – contumely

insolent–abusive, arrogant, contemptuous, contumelious, impudent, overbearing, pert, rude

inspect – examine, grade, scrutinize

inspected and condemned (military)–I.C.

inspection (military)–parade

inspector (leather)–sealer

inspector of making light globes–ager

inspire–animate, encourage, enliven, exalt, fire, motivate, move

inspired (divinely)–entheos

inspiring–pierian

inspiring aversion–repellent

inspiring awe–eerie, eery

inspiring confidence–encouragement

inspiring favorable opinion –prepossessing

inspiring fear–awful

inspiring good opinion–prepossessing

inspiring horror–grisly

inspiring spirit–encouragement

inspirit–animate, elate, encourage, enliven, hearten, inspire, invigorate, quicken, rouse

inspiriting–stirring

instability – changeability, changeable, unsteadiness

install–establish, inaugurate, induct, initiate, seat

installer of vessel's cordage system–rigger

instance–case, example

instant–flash, importunate, importune, minute, moment, pressing, second, solicit, trice, urge, urgent

instead–else, equivalent, substitute

instigate–abet, egg, foment, goad, impel, incite, motivate, move, prod, pro-

voke, spur, stimulate, urge

instigator–abetter, abettor

instill–imbue, impart, inculcate, infuse, insinuate, pervade

instinct – aptitude, impulse, innate, instigation, knack

instinct (homing pigeon) – orientation

instinctive – automatic, inherent, innate, intuitive, involuntary, natural, original, spontaneous

institute–academy, erect, establish, found, inaugurate, initiate, ordain, organize, originate

institute suit–prosecute, sue

institution (educational) – college, school, seminary

institution (maritime underwriters)–veritas

instruct – coach, discipline, educate, enlighten, indoctrinate, inform, show, teach, train

instruct in moral and religious knowledge–edify

instruction – act, practice, teaching, tuition

instruction (prepared)–propaedeutics

instructive–didactic, sermonic

instructor – mentor, preceptor, professor, teacher, trainer, tutor

instrument–agent, contrivance, deed, implement, means, medium, tool, utensil, writ, writing

instrument (anc. musical)–asor, cithern, rocta

instrument (astronomical)–aba

instrument (bandage fastening)–ligator

instrument (bone scraping)–xyster

instrument (brain operating)–trepan, trephine

instrument (brass wind) – helicon

instrument (butcher's) – cleaver, steel

instrument (current regulating)–rheometer

instrument (cutting)–knife, razor, scissors, scythe, shears, sickle

instrument (double pointed) –barb

instrument (drawing)–pantograph

instrument (edged)–cutlery, knife, razor, scissors, scythe, shears, sickle

instrument (egg measuring) –oometer

instrument (electric measuring)–ameter

instrument (for detecting sound transmitted through water) – hydrophone

instrument (for examining eyes)–otoscope

instrument (for extracting roots of numbers, anc.)–mesolabe

instrument (for increasing and concentrating heat)–blowpipe

instrument (for making holes)–awl, stiletto

instrument (for marking musical time)–metronome

instrument (for measuring distance)–odometer

instrument (for measuring hardness)–durometer

instrument (for recording musical work)–ergograph

instrument (for reducing dislocations)–scala

instrument (for regulating electric current)–rheostat

instrument (gripping) – clamp, pincers, tongs, vise

instrument (guitar-like) – bandore

instrument (high temperature)–pyronometer

instrument (hollow metallic)–bell

instrument (ingredient mixer)–stirrer

instrument (lapidary's)–dop

instrument (light-refraction measuring)–refractometer

instrument (lute-like)–asor, bandore
instrument (lyre-like)–rota
instrument (measuring) – meter, ruler, tape, tapeline
instrument (measuring distance in military work) –stadia
instrument (measuring errors in observation)–aberrometer
instrument (meteorological) –barometer, bolide
instrument (musical)–cello, cornet, dulcimer, gong, guitar, ocarina, uke, ukelele, ukulele
instrument (musical, anc.)–asor, cithern, rocta
instrument (nautical) – aba, pelorus, sextant
instrument (navigating) – aba, pelorus, sextant
instrument (negotiable financial)–check, note
instrument (obsolete) – penorcon
instrument (old)–lyre
instrument (old keyed) – spinet
instrument (old musical) – lute
instrument (old stringed)–bandore
instrument (old wind) – shawn
instrument (optical) – periscope, telescope
instrument (part of optical) –alidade
instrument (part of surveying)–alidad, alidade
instrument (percussion) – drum, gong
instrument (picture by wire transmitting) – telegraphoscope
instrument (plate-like musical)–cymbal
instrument (pointed, for graving)–stylet
instrument (pricking)–spur
instrument (rhythm)–drum
instrument (rhythm marking)–castanet

instrument (sealed)–escrow
instrument (seer's sacred)–urim
instrument (17th century, obs.)–theorbo
instrument (small, simple, wind)–horn, ocarina
instrument (stringed)–lute, lyre, rebab, rebec, rebeck, viola, violin
instrument (stringed, anc.)–asor
instrument (surgeon's)–xyster
instrument (surgical)–levator, ligator, scalpel, trocar
instrument (surveying, part of)–alidad, alidade
instrument (two-pronged)–bident
instrument (viol class, earliest known)–rebec
instrument (wind)–bassoon, clarinet, cornet, flageolet, flute, horn, oboe, ocarina, organ, reed, sax, saxophone, trombone, trumpet, tuba
instrument (zither-type stringed, anc.)–psaltery
instrument duet–duo
instrument for affixing dates –dater
instrument for indicating the amount of dust in air –koniscope
instrument for measuring distance traveled–odometer
instrument part (optical) – alidade
instrumental composition – sonata
instrumentality – agency, means
instrumentality for acquisition of knowledge–organon
insubordinate – contumacious, disobedient, mutinous
insubstantial – apparitional, flimsy, frail, solid
insufficient–deficient, inadequate, incommensurate,

scanty, scarce, short, unequal, wanting
insular–islander, nesiote
insulated–isled
insulated (as wire)–taped
insulating substance–balata
insult – affront, contempt, contumely, indignity, offense, outrage, revile, slur
insulting–arrogant, insolent, offensive
insurance – assurance, guaranty, protection, warranty
insurance official – actuary, adjuster
insure jointly with others–coinsure
insurgent – insubordinate, rebel, rebellious
insurmountable–impassable, insuperable, invincible
insurrection–rebellion
intact–undefiled, uninjured, untouched, whole
intangible–impalpable, imperceptible, insubstantial, vague
integer–integral, one, whole
integral–totality, whole
integrity–honesty
integument – coat, covering, investment, testa, testae (pl.)
intellect – genius, intelligence, mind, nous, reason
intellect (highest)–nous
intellect (pert. to)–noetic
intellectual–mental, noetic
intellectual (an)–highbrow
intellectual (coll.)–brainy
intellectual facilities–wits
intelligence – mind, news, sense
intelligent – acute, bright, knowing, rational, sensible, smart, understanding
intelligentsia–intellectuals
intelligible – clear, comprehensible, perspicuous, plain, suprasensuous
intelligibly–simply
intemperate – excessive, extreme, immoderate, inclement, inordinate, in-

violate, pure, severe, undefiled, ungovernable
intemperate speech–tirade
intend–aim, mean
intended for cure–remedial
intense–ardent, deep, great, powerful, strong, vivid
intensify – aggravate, condense, deeper, enhance, increase
intensity (greater)–deeper
intent – design, eager, earnest, intention, purpose, rapt, tense
intention – design, object, purpose, will
intention (malicious) – animus
intentional – deliberate, voluntary
intentions–aims, ends, purposes
intently – attentively, diligently, eagerly, earnestly, fixedly, sedulously, steadfastly
inter–bury, inhume
intercalate–insert
intercede – arbitrate, interpose, intervene, mediate
interchange – alternate, exchange, permute, reciprocate, transposal, vary
intercourse – coition, commerce, communication, connection, conversation, dealing, fellowship
interdict–ban, debar, forbid, inhibit, prohibit
interdiction–ban, veto
interest–attract, behalf, concern, engage, entertain, hold
interested–rapt
interested (was)–cared
interesting talker–conversationalist
interfere–clash, intermeddle, interpose, intervene, meddle, tamper
interim–interval, meantime
interior–inner, inside
interjection–alas, egad, lo
interjection (old)–aroint
interjection (slangy)–aw

interjection (to attract attention)–ahem
interlace – braid, interpolation, intertwine, interweave, weave
interlock–knit, interlace, interrelate, unite
interlope – insert, intermeddle, interpolate, intrude, obtrude
interloper–intruder
interlude (organ, short) – verset
interlude in conflict–truce
intermediary – agent, go-between, interagent, mediator
intermediate–interjacent, intervening, medial, mediate, medium, mesne, middle, napthols, phenylene-diamine, toluidine
interminable * – boundless, endless, eternal, infinite, limitless, unending, unlimited
interminable (period of time)–aeon, eon
intermission – cessation, pause, recess, respite, rest, suspension
intermit–cease, discontinue, interpose, interrupt, stop, suspend
intermittent – alternating, broken, fitful, periodic, recurrent, spasmodic
intermitter–rester
international agreement – pact, treaty
international language–ido, ro
international measure – tonneau-de-jauge
international tennis cup – Davis
international understanding –entente
interpose – intercede, interfere, intervene, mediate
interpose on another's behalf–intercede
interpret – construe, define, elucidate, exegesis, explain, expound, read, rede, translate

interpretation – definition, explanation, rendering, sense, solution, translation
interpretation (mystic, of scriptures)–anagoge
interpreter – exegesist, exponent, gnomon
interrogate – ask, inquire, query, question
interrogative – erotematic, question, who
interrupt – arrest, break, check, hinder, intercept, obstruct, stop, thwart
interrupt course of–intercept
interrupter (electrical) – rheotome
interruption–cessation, gap, hiatus, hindrance, intermission, obstruction, pause, suspension.
intersect – cross, cut, decussate, divide, meet, pierce
interstice – areola, areolas (pl.), areole, areolae (pl.), areolate, chink, crack, crevice, interval
interstice (net)–mesh
intersticed–areolar
interstices (between leaf veins) – areolae, areolas, areoles
interstitial–areola, areolate
intertwine – entangle, interlace, entwine, intertwist, lace, twist
interval – distance, gap, recess, rest, space
interval of rest–intermission, recess, respite, rest
intervene–interpose
intervene to effect reconciliation–mediate
intervening (law)–mesne
intervening space–distance
intervening time–interlude
interweave–braid, enlace, intermix, plait, plat, wattle
interweave (twist together)–braid, mat, raddle
intestinal–enteric
intestine–inner
intestine (comb. form)–entero
intestine (last division of

small)–ile, ileum, ilium, ilia (pl.)

intimacy–association, closeness, connection, familiarity

intimate – confidant, confidential, familiar, friendly, hint, infer, informal, near, sib

intimation – cue, hint, inkling

intimidate – abash, awe, browbeat, bully, cow, daunt, deter, frighten, overawe, terrify

into (prefix)–en

intolerance–bigotry, dogmatism, illiberality, narrowness, prejudice

intolerant–bigoted, dogmatic, impatient, narrow, prejudiced

intolerant person–bigot

intone–chant, sing

intoxicated–drunk

intoxicated (slang)–boiled

intoxicated (slightly)–tosy

intractable – headstrong, indocile, obstinate, perverse, refractory, restive, stubborn, ungovernable, unruly, unteachable, willful

intransitive–neuter

intrant – entering, penetrating

intrepid–courageous, dauntless, doughty, heroic, resolute, valiant

intrepidity – courage, nerve, valor

intricate – complex, complicated, daedal, dedal, difficult, gordian, perplexed

intrigue – cabal, cheating, conspiracy, machination, plot, scheme

intrinsic–essential, genuine, inborn, inbred, indispensable, inherent, inseparable, native, natural, necessary, real, true

intrinsic nature of things–essence

intrinsic value–utility

intrinsically – essentially, really, truly

introduce–preface, present, sponsor, start, usher

introduce as topic of conversation–broach

introduce by a first act–initiate

introduced a serum – inoculated

introduced from foreign country–exotic

introduction–debut, exordium, foreword, isagoge, preamble, preface, preparation, proem

introduction (biblical)–isagogics

introduction of a drama–protasis

introduction of spurious or foreign matter–interpolation

introductory–prefatory, prelusive

introductory line–cue

introit – entrance, introduction

introitus–entrance, opening

intrude – infringe, interfere, interlope, invade

intruder–invader, outsider, trespasser

intrust–commit, consign

intuition–hunch

intuitive–instinctive, noetic

inulase–enzyme

inunction (pert. to)–aliptic

inundate – deluge, drown, flood, overflow, overwhelm, submerge

inured – accustomed, hardened, obdurate, seasoned

inutility – unprofitable, uselessness

invade–overrun, raid, trespass

invader–intruder

invader (early, of England) –Pict

invader (repeller of parachute)–parashootist

invalid–feeble, infirm, null, sickly

invalid (sent out of London) –evacuee, vackie (slang)

invalidate–undo

invalidism (chronic)–valetudinarianism

invaluable–inestimable, precious, priceless, worthless

invariable – constant, unchangeable, unchanging, uniform

invariableness–uniformity

invasion–incursion, inroad, irruption, raid

invective – diatribe, railing, vituperation

invective (violent)–tirade

inveigle–allure, entice, lure, rope

invent–coin, concoct, design, devise, discover, frame, originate

invented (not, abbr.)–nei

inventive – adroit, creative, fertile, ingenious, original

inventor–discoverer, originator

inventor (telegraph)–Morse

inventor (X-ray)–Roentgen

inventor slain by Daedalus–Talos

inventor slain by jealous uncle (Gr. myth.)–Talos

inventory–account, catalog, catalogue, list, register

invert–reverse

invertebrate animal–insect, mollusk

invest – array, clothe, don, dress, endue, envelop, indue, surround, vest, wrap

invest with authority – accredit

invest with ministerial functions–ordain

invest with sovereignty–enthrone

investigate – excuss, probe, pry, scrutinize, search, study

investigation – examen, examination, inquiry, research

investigation of logical difficulty–aporeme

investiture – clothes, clothing, vesture

investiture with citizenship–enfranchisement

investment – clothing, garment, vestment

investments (list of)–portfolio

inveterate – chronic, confirmed, hardened, ingrained, rooted

inveterate strife–feud

invidious–envious, hateful, malignant, odious

invigorate – animate, brace, enliven, exhilarate, nerve, pep, refresh, renew, staminate, stimulate, strengthen, vivify

invigorating – stimulating, tonic

invigoration–renewal

invincible–indomitable

inviolate – incorruptible, inviolable, sacred, undefiled, unstained

invisible – hid, unapparent, undiscernible

invisible emanation – aura, aurae (pl.)

invite–allure, ask, bade, bid, court, entice, request, solicit

invocation – entreaty, plea, prayer, sermon

invoice–bill

invoke–conjure, entreat, solicit, supplicate

involuntary – reluctant, unwilling

involve – entail, implicate, lap, wrap

involve in perplexities – ensnare

involved–complex

involving as a necessary accompaniment–entailing

involving imaginary perfection–Utopian

involving less risk–safer

involving punishment–punitive

inward–entad, inner, interior, internally

iodine (combining form) – iod

iodine (compound of) – iodide

iodine source–kelp

iodoform substitute–aristal

ion (negative)–anion

Iona island coin–obol

Iona monk–Aidan

iota–atom, jot, particle, tittle, whit

Iowa city–Ames, Oskaloosa

ipecac (substance extracted from roots of)–emetine

ipecac plant–evea

irade–decree

Iran–Persia

Iranian city–Amol, Teheran

Iranian poet–Omar

Iraq coin–dinar (g., pap.)

Iraq kingdom capital–Bagdad, Baghdad

irascible – brash, captious, choleric, hasty, hot-tempered, irate, peevish, petulant, quick-tempered, snappish, splenetic, techy, testy, touchy

irascibility–choler, ire

irate – angry, enraged, incensed, irascible

ire–anger, wrath

ireful–angry, iracund, irascible, passionate, wroth

Ireland–Eire, Erin, Irena

Ireland (personified by Edmund Spenser)–Irena

Ireland (used by Aristotle)–Ierne

iridescent–irised, opalescent, opaline, prismatic

iridium (pert. to)–iridic

iridium (symbol for)–ir

iris–rainbow

iris (dark portion of)–uvea

iris (Florentine)–orris

iris (inflammation of)–iritis

iris (kind of)–orrice, orris

iris (part of)–uvea

iris flower (family of)–irid, tileroot

iris layer (pigmented)–uvea

iris of eye (pert. to)–irian

Irish – Celt, Celtic, Erse, Gael, Hibernian

Irish (pert. to)–Celtic, Gaelic

Irish-American composer – Herbert

Irish battle cry–abu

Irish bit–traneen

Irish capital (old)–Tara

Irish cardinal (19th century)–Cullen

Irish cattle–Kerry

Irish cattle (small black)–Kerries

Irish Celts (legendary ancestor of)–Mil, Miledh, Milesius

Irish Chamber of Deputies–Dail

Irish chemist–Boyle

Irish city – Belfast, Cork, Limerick, Tipperary

Irish city (old)–Tara

Irish clan–sept

Irish club–shillalah

Irish coin (debased)–rap

Irish confetti–bricks

Irish county–Mayo

Irish dagger–skean

Irish daisy–dandelion

Irish dividend–assessment

Irish ecclesiastics (early)–erenaches

Irish emblem (national) – shamrock

Irish expletive–arra, arrah

Irish fairies–banshees, shees

Irish fort (hill)–rath

Irish freeman–aire

Irish Free State capital–Dublin

Irish Free State coin – real (ni.)

Irish frock (early, sleeved)–inar

Irish goddess–Dana

Irish groggery (selling illegal liquor)–shebeen

Irish harvesters (wandering)–spalpeens

Irish infantryman (old) – kern

Irish island (off coast)–Aran

Irish island group–Aran

Irish king's home–Tara

Irish lass–colleen

Irish man – paddy, paddies (pl.)

Irish measure–bandle, mile

Irish mountain–Carrantual, Lugnaquilla, Macgillicuddy, Wicklow

Irish name–Sean

Irish novelist–Shaw

Irish parliament–Dail

Irish patriot–Emmet

Irish peasant–kern, kerne

Irish pennants – ravelings, threads

Irish poet–Wilde, Yeats

Irish princess–Iseult

Irish province – Connaught, Leinster, Munster, Ulster

Irish river – Bandon, Bann, Barrow, Blackwater, Boyne, Dee, Foyle, Lee, Liffey, Shannon, Suir

Irish saint (patron)–Patrick

Irish sea god (Gaelic)–Ler

Irish social unit (medieval)–sept

Irish song–rann

Irish spirit–banshee

Irish sweetheart–gra

Irish system of landholding –Rundale

Irish tenants–saers

Irish tribal law (lord of)–Tanist

Irish tribe (descended from common ancestor)–Cinel

Irish tribesman (anc.)–Aire

Irish verse–rann

irk – annoy, bore, nettle, trouble, vex, weary

irksome – burdensome, fatiguing, monotonous, painful, tedious, tedium, tiresome, wearisome

iron–fetter, firmness, handcuff, manacle, power, press, shackle, strength

iron (comb. form)–sidero

iron (dross of)–sinter

iron (lump of)–pig

iron (pert. to)–ferric

iron (smoothing)–goose

iron (tailor's)–goose

iron brown–negro

Iron City–Pittsburgh

iron dog–firedog

iron fence–rail

iron frame (for torch fire)–cresset

iron molder's tool–lifter

iron ore (kind of)–hematite

iron rod (glass handling) – pontee, punty

iron sand (titanic)–iserin

ironclad–armored, monitor

ironer–presser

ironic–satiric

irons (sharp pointed for ice walking)–creepers

irony–sarcasm, satire

Iroquoian Indian – Cayuga, Cherokee, Conestoga, Erie, Huron, Litre, Mohawk, Neuter, Nottoway, Oneida, Onondaga, Seneca, Tionontati, Tuscarora, Wyandot

irregular–abnormal, anomalous, changeable, crooked, desultory, devious, eccentric, erose, erratic, immoderate, intemperate, mutable, rugged, unequal, uneven, unsettled, unsystematic, variable, wild

irregular (strangely)–abnormal

irregular on edge–erose

irregular voter–repeater

irregularity of muscular movement–ataxia

irregularly branched–desma

irregularly shaped mass – lump

irrelevant – inconsequent, unessential, unrelated

irreligious – impious, pagan, profane

irreparable–irretrievable, recovered, regained, remedied

irrepressible (as laughter)–homeric

irresolute – changeable, doubtful, fickle, inconstant, undecided, undetermined, unstable, unsure

irresponsible–carefree, unaccountable, undependable

irretrievable – incurable, irremediable

irreverence in conduct–profanity

irrigate–moisten, sluice, water, wet

irritable–cranky, cross, edgy, fretful, iracund, peevish, snappish, techy, tempery, testy, touchy

irritable (coll.)–onery, onery

irritate–acerbate, anger, annoy, chafe, cross, exasperate, fret, gall, grate, incense, irk, madden, nag, nettle, pique, provoke, rankle, rasp, sting, tease, vex

irritate (coll.)–rile

irritated–sore

irritated (easily)–testy

irritation–itch, pique, temper

irritative–acrid

is able–can

is angered at–resents

is compelled–has

is in agreement–consorts

is in store for–awaits

is not (arch.)–nis

is of use–avails

is possible–may

is present at–attends

is skeptical–doubts

is suitable to–becomes

Isaac's son–Esau, Jacob

Ishmael's mother–Hagar

Ishmael's son–Nebaioth

isinglass–mica

Isis' husband–Osiris

Islam founder–Mahomet

Islamic holy city (containing Mahomet's tomb)–Medina

Islamic pilgrimage object–Caaba, Kaaba, Kaabeh

Islamic supreme being–Allah

island–Bali, cay

island (coastal low)–key

island (coral)–atoll

island (fabled, at earth's center)–Meru

island (Fr.)–ile

island (little)–islet

island (low)–cay, key

island (North Atlantic)–Iceland

island (off Ireland)–Aran

island (pert. to)–insular

island (small)–ait, eyot, eyoty, ilot, isle, islet

island (small, beside large one)–calf

island group–Samoa

island of saints–Erin

islands (sea-studded)–archipelago

isle (river)–ait

Isle of Man (northernmost point of)–Ayre

Isle of Man city–Castletown, Douglas, Peel, Ramsey

Isle of Man judge–Deemster, Dempster

Isle of Man legislature–Tynwald

Isle of Man measure–kishen, kishon

Isle of Man mountain–Snaefell

islet–cay

islot–ilot, islet

ism–tenet

isolate – enisle, isle, seclude, segregate, separate, sequester

isolation – insulation, loneliness, seclusion, segregation, separation, solitude

isomer–metamer

Israel (appellation for)–Jeshuran

Israelite causing Jewish defeat at Ai–Achan

Israelite judge – Elon, Jephthah

Israelite king–Ahab, David, Jehoahaz, Jehoram, Jehu, Jeroboam, Omri, Pekah, Pekahiah, Saul, Solomon

Israelite king (first)–Saul

Israelite king (second)–David

Israelite king (seventh) – Ahab

Israelite lawgiver–Moses

Israelite priest–Eli

Israelite tribe–Aser, Asher, Dan, Reuben

Israelite tribe (priestly) – Levi

issue–arise, child, come, emanate, emerge, emit, escape, flow, offspring, proceed, progeny, son, source, utter

issue (final)–upshot

issue (over)–inflation

issue (rapidly)–gush, spout

issue forth – emanate, gush, sally

issued in installments–serial

issuing of troops (sudden, from besieged place of attack)–sortie

Istanbul Greek quarter–Fanar

Istanbul section (Christian)–Pera

Istanbul suburb–Pera

isthmus–neck

it is (poetic)–tis

it may be–haply

Italian (of certain city)–Roman

Italian affirmative–si

Italian ancient race–Oscan

Italian architectural pictures –ancone

Italian article–el, il

Italian capital–Rome

Italian city – Alba, Alessandria, Ancona, Asti, Bari, Bologna, Bra, Brindisi, Cagliari, Catania, Este, Ferrara, Fiume, Florence, Foggia, Genoa, Leghorn, Lucca, Mantua, Marsala, Massa, Messina, Milan, Modena, Naples, Nola, Ora, Padua, Palermo, Pavia, Perugia, Pisa, Pola, Ravenna, Reggio Nell Emilia, Rome, Sorrento, Spezia, Taranto, Trent, Trieste, Turin, Udine, Venice, Verona

Italian city (anc.) – Ostia, Pompeii

Italian city (Parmesan cheese mfg.)–Lodi

Italian coin–centesimo (br.), lira (s.), lira (ni.), soldo (cop.)

Italian coin (anc.)–tari

Italian coin (anc. silver)–sudo

Italian coin (old)–teston, testone

Italian coin (small) – soldo, soldi (pl.)

Italian commune–Asola

Italian commune (scene of Napoleonic triumph over Austria)–Rivoli

Italian condiment (spicy)–tamara

Italian country (anc.)–Etruria

Italian deity–Faun

Italian department–Apulia, Aruzzi e Molise, Basilicata, Calabria, Campania, Emilia, Liguria, Lombardia (Lombardy), Marca, Piemonte (Piedmont), Roma (Rome), Sardinia, Sicilia (Sicily), Tuscana (Tuscany), Umbria, Venetia

Italian dictator–Mussolini

Italian district (anc.)–Lucania

Italian division (north)–Emilia

Italian dome (var.)–cima

Italian employment agent–padrone

Italian entertainment (public)–ridoto

Italian faction (medieval political)–Neri

Italian family (princely) – Asti, Este

Italian family (violin makers)–Amati

Italian family members (noted)–Cencis

Italian fascist leader (local) –Ras

Italian festival–festa

Italian gallant–Amoroso

Italian goddess–Juno

Italian goddess (anc.)–Diana

Italian goddess of harvest – Ops

Italian goddess of hunt–Diana

Italian guessing game–mora

Italian hamlet–casale

Italian holiday–festa

Italian house–casa

Italian house (summer)–casino

Italian innkeeper–padrone

Italian island–Capri, Elba, Ischia, Leros, Lipari, Sardinia, Sicily

Italian lady–donna, signora

Italian lake–Albano, Bolsena, Como, Garda, Lugano, Maggiore, Trasimene

Italian land (marshy)–ma-
remma
Italian magistrate–podesta
Italian marble (used in statu-
ary)–carrara
Italian measure–barile, boc-
cale, braccio, canna, carat,
giornata, miglio, moggio,
orna, palmo, pie, piede,
polonick, punto, qua-
drato, rubbio, salma, sec-
chio, staio, stero, tavola,
tomolo
Italian medieval faction –
Neri
Italian millet–buda, moha,
mohar
Italian monk–padre
Italian mountain–Alps, Ap-
ennines
Italian musician–Guido
Italian noblewoman – mar-
chesa
Italian opera–Aida, Tosca
Italian opera house–Scala
Italian painter–Reni
Italian pastry dish–ravioli
Italian patriot–Garibaldi
Italian people (anc.)–Sabines
Italian people (anc. East
Rome)–Marsi
Italian physicist–Galvani
Italian poet – Dante, Redi,
Tasso

Italian possession – Dhalak,
Eritrea, Somaliland, Trip-
oli
Italian province–Bari, Istria,
Salerno
Italian race (member of)–
Oscan
Italian region–Carso
Italian resort–Lido
Italian river–Adda, Adige,
Arno, Garigliano, Oglio,
Po, Secchia, Tiber, Ticino,
Trebbia, Volturno
Italian saint–Neri
Italian seaport–Mola, Otran-
to, Pola, Trani
Italian secret society–Camor-
ra, Mafia
Italian summer house – ca-
sino
Italian theologian–Peronne
Italian town–Bra, Este, Gen-
oa
Italian town (anc. southern)
–Elea
Italian town (Piedmont) –
Aosta
Italian tribe (anc. central)–
Aequi
Italian vessel (small coastal
sailing)–trabacolo, trabas-
colo
Italian volcano–Etna, Vesu-
vius

Italian weight – cara, chilo-
grammo, denaro, libbra,
libra, oncia, ottava, pound
Italian wine–Asti
Italian "yes"–si
Italic language–Oscan
Italy (poetic name)–Ausonia
item – article, bit, detail,
scrap, topic
item (recorded)–entry
item (short)–personal
item of property–asset
item of value–asset
iterate–repeat
ithand – constant, diligent,
unintermittent
itinerant – nomadic, peripa-
tetic, traveling, unsettled,
wandering
itinerary–guide, guidebook,
record, roadbook, route
itinerary (royal)–gest
itineration–eyre
Ivanhoe character–Rowena
ivory–dentine
ivory dust and cement–ebu-
rine
ivy (English)–hedera
ivy fiber–rootlet
Izaak Walton–fisherman
izle (Scot.) – ember, soot,
spark

J

jab–poke, punch, stab, thrust
jabber–chat, chatter, gibberish
jabble–agitation, confusion,
dashing, rippling, splashing
jacare–cayman
jacent–prone, recumbent
jack rabbit–hare
jackdaw–daw
jackdaw (old word)–coe
jacket (crocheted)–sontag
jacket (elaborate)–doublet
jacket (knitted)–sontag
jacket (life, Fr. slang)–Mae
West

jacket (loose)–bolero
jacket (man's short)–spencer
jacket (short)–eton, reefer
jacket (sleeveless knitted)–
penelope
jacket (woman's close fitting)–spencer
jackstones–dibs
Jacob's brother–Edom, Esau
Jacob's father-in-law–Laban
Jacob's son–Dan, Gad, Levi,
Reuben
Jacob's son (fifth)–Dan
Jacob's wife–Leah, Rachel
jade–fatigue, tire
jaeger gull–teaser

jager – diamond, hunter,
huntsman
jagged – cutting, erose,
ragged, rough, sharp
jaguar–ounce
jail–imprison, lockup
jail (coll.)–calaboose, clink,
hoosegow, jug
jail (Eng.)–gaol
jail (ship's)–brig
jail sentence (coll.)–rap
jail warden – alcaide, caid,
jailer, jailor, keeper
jalousie–blind, shutter
Jane Eyre author–Bronte
Janizarian chief–dey

Japan (Chinese name for)–Jipun

Japan (Japanese name for)–Niphon, Nipon, Nippon

Japanese–Nip, Nipon, Nipponese, Nisei, Skibby

Japanese aborigine – Aino, Ainu

Japanese aborigine (North)–Aino, Ainu

Japanese admiral–Togo

Japanese airplane–Zero

Japanese-American children (second generation)–Nisei

Japanese apricot–ume

Japanese army first line (two-year service)–geneki

Japanese army levy (annual)–geneki

Japanese army officer–samurai

Japanese art of self-defense–judo, jujitsu, jujutsu

Japanese artistic combinations of lights and darks–notan

Japanese Asiatic protectorate–Manchukuo

Japanese battle cry–banzai

Japanese bay–ise

Japanese boat (raiding)–spit kit

Japanese boxes (set of, worn at girdle)–inro

Japanese Buddha–Amida

Japanese Buddhist festival–Bon

Japanese button (small carved)–netsuke

Japanese capital–Tokio, Tokyo

Japanese capital (anc.)–Nara

Japanese cedar–sugi

Japanese chess–shogi

Japanese circle–maru

Japanese city–Akamagaseki, Fukuoka, Hakodate, Hiroshima, Kagoshima, Kanazawa, Kioto, Kobe, Kumamoto, Kure, Nagasaki, Nagoya, Niigata, Okayama, Osaka, Otaru, Sapporo, Sasebo, Sendai, Tokio, Tokyo, Tokushima, Wakatama, Yokohama, Yokosuka

Japanese coast bay–ise

Japanese coin–rin (ac.), sen (br.), yen (g., s.)

Japanese coin (copper)–sen

Japanese coin (former oval, gold)–oban

Japanese crest (decorative)–mon

Japanese deer–sika

Japanese dextrose–ame

Japanese dog (wild)–tanate

Japanese drama–no

Japanese drink–mate, saki

Japanese emperor–Hirohito

Japanese emperor's title – Tenno

Japanese family badge–mon

Japanese fan–ogi

Japanese festival (Buddhist)–Bon

Japanese fish–tai, tho

Japanese fish (rainbow)–tai

Japanese fish (small)–ayu

Japanese game (of forfeits)–ken

Japanese gateway–torii

Japanese girdle–obi

Japanese girdle ornament – inro

Japanese girdle receptacle–inro

Japanese girl (singing)–geisha

Japanese goldfish–funa

Japanese governor's title (former military)–shogun, tycoon

Japanese herb–udo

Japanese instrument (banjo)–samisen

Japanese island–Hondo, Kiushu, Kiusiu, Kuril, Kurile, Loo-Choo, Niphon, Riu-kiu, Shikoku, Sikok, Yesso

Japanese island (N.E. Kyushu prefecture)–Oita

Japanese lake–Biwa

Japanese magnolia–yulan

Japanese measure–boo, bu, carat, cho, go, hiro, jo, ken, koku, kujira shaku, mo, ri, rin, se, shaku, sho, sun, tan, to, tsubo

Japanese measure (capacity)–go

Japanese measure (length)–ri

Japanese measure (surface)–se

Japanese medicine case–etui, inro

Japanese military governor's title–shogun, tycoon

Japanese monastery–tera

Japanese money–mo, ro

Japanese money of account–mo, rin, yen

Japanese mountain – Fusiyama, Hondo, Kiusiu, Yesso

Japanese musical instrument–samisen

Japanese native–Aino, Ainu

Japanese naval base–Yokosuka

Japanese news agency–Domei

Japanese ornament (girdle)–inro

Japanese outcast–ronin

Japanese outlaw–ronin

Japanese overcoat (straw)–mino

Japanese pagoda–taa

Japanese painting (style of)–kano

Japanese palanquin–kago

Japanese palanquin (bamboo)–cango

Japanese persimmon kaki

Japanese plant (edible shoot)–udo

Japanese plant (fiber) – sugamo

Japanese porgy–tai

Japanese port – Hakodate, Hiogo, Kobe, Nagasaki, Niigata, Osaka, Yokohama

Japanese prefecture–ehime

Japanese province (old)–Ise, Iwaki

Japanese province (pottery making)–Satsuma

Japanese race–Aino, Ainu

Japanese race (member of indigenous)–Aino, Ainu

Japanese rainbow fish–tai

Japanese receptacle (small)–inro

Japanese religion–Buddhism, Shintoism
Japanese religion (primitive) –shinto
Japanese rice cake–ame
Japanese rice flour–ame
Japanese rice paste–ame
Japanese river – Tonegawa, Yalu
Japanese robe–kimono
Japanese salad plant–udo
Japanese samurai (ostracized)–ronin
Japanese sash–obi
Japanese screen (paper) – shoji
Japanese seaport – Osaka, Otaru
Japanese seaweed–nori
Japanese ship name–Maru
Japanese shock troops–tatori
Japanese silkworm (large)–yamamai
Japanese singing girl–geisha
Japanese small fish–ayu
Japanese society (lowest of three classes)–Heimin
Japanese song–uta
Japanese statesman–Abe, Ito
Japanese suicide (by disembowelment) – hara-kiri, hari-kari, hara-kari
Japanese suntree–hinokis
Japanese title–kami
Japanese tree–akeki
Japanese tree (evergreen) – camphor
Japanese tree (timber)–kiaki
Japanese village community –Mura
Japanese volcano–Asamayama, Asame
Japanese weight–carat, catty, fun, hiyak-kin, kati, kin, komma-ichida, kon, kwamme, kwan, mo, momme, niyo, picul, rin, shi
japanner–varnisher
jape–deride, fool, fraud, jeer, jest, jipe, mock, trick
japery–buffoonery, jest, jesting, joke, trickery
Japeth's son (second)–Magog
jar–cruse, jolt, jug, olla, urn
jar (two-handled)–amphora

jar (water)–hydria
jar rubber–lute
jarble–bemire, wet
jardiniere – flowerpot, jar, jug, urn, vase
jargon–argot, cant, idiom, lingo, patter, slang
jargon (adopted for secrecy) –cant
jargon (technical)–cant
Jason's father–Aeson
Jason's friend–Medea
Jason's ship–Argo
Jason's sweetheart–Medea
jauk (Scot.)–dally, trifle
jaunt–journey, ramble, trip
jaunt (pleasure)–ride
jaunty–finical, perky, showy, smart, stylish
Javanese badger–ratel, teledu
Javanese berry (shrub)–cubeb
Javanese capital–Batavia
Javanese carriage–sado
Javanese city–Batavia, Jokjokarta, Samarang, Surabaya, Surakarta
Javanese community (village)–Dessa
Javanese island (east)–Bali
Javanese measure–paal
Javanese mountain badger–teledu
Javanese ox–bantens
Javanese pepper–cubebs
Javanese port–Batavia, Surabaya
Javanese puppet show–wajang, wayang
Javanese skunk–teledu
Javanese squirrel–jelerang
Javanese straw (cheap)–peanit
Javanese tree–upas
Javanese tree (poisonous)–upas
Javanese village community –Dessa
Javanese weight–amat, pond, pound
javelin–dart, spear
javelin (Persian, Turkish)–jeerid, jerid
javelin (short)–dart
jaw–chop, scold, scolding
jaw (pert. to)–malar

jawab–answer, reply
jawbone–maxilla
jay bird (Scot.)–gae
jazz (old-time)–barrelhouse
jazz (primitive heartfelt) – gutbucket
jealous – imagine, mistrust, suspect
jealousy–envy
jeer–flout, hoot, mock, scoff, scout, sneer, taunt
Jeeter Lester's vegetable (favorite)–turnip
Jehiada's wife–Jehoshabeath, Jehosheba
Jehoahaz's mother–Hamutal
Jehoiachin's successor–Salathiel
Jehoshaphat's son–Jehu
Jehovah – Almighty, God, Jah, Lord, Yah
Jehovah prophet–Elias
jehu–driver
Jehu's father–Jehoshaphat
jejune – arid, barren, dry, foodless, hungry, insipid, meager, trite
Jekyll's alter ego–Hyde
jellify–gel, gelatinous, jelly
jelly (kind of)–kisel
jelly (meat)–aspic
jellyfish–medusa
jellyfish (top of)–exumbrella
jemmy – boot, crowbar, dandy, greatcoat, handy, jimmy, neat, spruce
jenna (Moham. religion)–Paradise
jeofail (law)–mistake, oversight
jeopardize – endanger, expose, hazard, imperil, risk
jeopardous–daring, hazardous, perilous, venturesome
jeopardy – danger, menace, peril, risk
Jerahmeel's son–Oren
Jericho woman (who sheltered Joshua's spies)–Rahab
jerk – charqui, jerque, tic, yank
jerkin–coat, gyrfalcon, jacket, salmon, waistcoat
jeroboam (Eng.) – bottle, bowl, goblet

jerry–aware, conscious, German, knowing

Jersey livelong – cudweed, enaena

Jersey tea – checkerberry, wintergreen

Jerusalem–Sion, Zion

Jerusalem (anc. name)–Salem

Jerusalem (poetic)–Ariel

Jerusalem city–Jaffa, Joppa

Jerusalem corn–durra

Jerusalem cucumber–gherkin

Jerusalem Delivered author–Tasso

Jerusalem haddock–opah

Jerusalem hill–Olivet

Jerusalem mosque–Omar

Jerusalem mountain–Olivet

Jerusalem pickle–gherkin

Jerusalem pony–ass

Jerusalem region (beyond Jordan)–Perea

Jerusalem the Golden translator–John Mason Neale

jess–strap

jessamy–dandy, fop

Jessur–daboia, deboya

jest–droll, fool, fun, jape, joke, quip, sport, trifle

jester – buffoon, merry-andrew, mime

Jesuit's bark tree–cinchona

jet – gush, ladle, nozzle, spout, spouting, spurt

jet black–ebon, raven

jetty–mole, pier, wharf

Jew–Semite

Jew (monastic)–Essene

jewel–beryl, diamond, garnet, gem, opal, ornament, ruby

jewel connoisseur–lapidarist

jewel weight–tola

jewelry (artificial)–costume, paste, strass

jewelry (piece of)–bracelet, brooch

Jewish alphabet–(1) Aleph, (2) Beth, (3) Gimel, (4) Daleth, (5) He, (6) Vau, (7) Zayin, (8) Cheth, (9) Teth, (10) Yodh, (11) Caph, (12) Lamedh, (13) Mem, (14) Nun, (15)

Samekh, (16) Ayin, (17) Pe, (18) Sadhe, (19) Koph, (20) Resh, (21) Sin, (22) Shin, (23) Tav

Jewish ascetic–essene

Jewish benedictions (used in daily liturgy)–Shema

Jewish Bible–Tora, Torah

Jewish brotherhood member –Essene

Jewish calendar–(1) Tishri, (2) Heshvan, (3) Kislev, (4) Tebet, (5) Shebat, (6) Adar, Veadar, (7) Nisan, (8) Iyar, (9) Sivan, (10) Tammuz, (11) Ab, (12) Elul

Jewish Day of Atonement–Yom Kippur

Jewish family of patriots–Maccabees

Jewish feast (name of)–Yom

Jewish female demon (folklore)–Lilith

Jewish festival–Purim, Sedar, Seder

Jewish festival (Passover)–Sedar, Seder

Jewish general–Abner

Jewish harp–crembalum

Jewish high priest–Aaron, Annas, Eli, Ezra

Jewish high priest's articles (worn by)–urim

Jewish high priest's miter (part of)–petalon

Jewish high priest's vestments–ephod

Jewish holiday – Tishabov, Tishahbab

Jewish law (body of)–tora, torah

Jewish law (civil)–Talmud

Jewish law body–Talmud

Jewish law book–Talmud

Jewish law ceremonial (unclean)–tref

Jewish lawgiver–Moses

Jewish leader–Moses

Jewish letter–see Jewish alphabet

Jewish liturgy (daily morning)–Shaharith

Jewish measure (anc.) – epha, ephah

Jewish measure (anc. dry)–epha, ephah

Jewish member (sect) – Essene

Jewish monk (anc.)–Essene

Jewish month (old, later called Nisan)–Abib

Jewish month (var.)–Sebat

Jewish months – see Jewish calendar

Jewish New Year–Rosh Hashana

Jewish Passover festival–Sedar, Seder

Jewish plotter–Haman

Jewish prayer book–siddur

Jewish proselyte–ger

Jewish psalm of praise–hallel

Jewish quarter–ghetto

Jewish Sanhedrin president–Nasi

Jewish school for boys–heder

Jewish sect (anc.) – Essene, Pharisee

Jewish sect member–Essene

Jewish spice (anc.)–stacte

Jewish synagogue platform –almemar

Jewish synagogue ram's horn–shofar

Jewish teacher–rabbi

Jewish term of reproach – raca

Jewish title–abba

jew's-harp–crembalum

jib–boom, crane, fleece, gib

jib derrick–spar

jiffy–instant, moment

jiggle–teeter

jimmy – dexterous, handy, jemmy, neat, smart, spruce

jingle–clink, rime, tinkle

jinn (chief of, myth.)–Eblis

jinni (evil)–afreet

jittery (not)–nerveless

Joachim's wife – Susanna, Susannah

job (bad)–botch

job (easy)–sinecure

job (small)–chore

Job's home–Uz

jockey–cheat, cushion, minstrel, outwit, pad, rider, vagabond

jockey (famous)–Earl Sande

jocose–droll, facetious, jocular

jocose (slyly)–dry

jocular–animated, comical, convivial, droll, elated, facetious, festive, frolicsome, funny, gay, gleeful, hilarious, jocund, lively, merry, mirthful, playful, vivacious, waggish, witty

jocular (coarsely)–ribald

jocund–airy, cheerful, gay, jocular, lively, merry, sportive

jog–canter, lope, trot

jogging gait–trot

John (Gaelic)–Ian

John (Scot.)–Ian

John (Spanish)–Juan

John the Baptist's death causer–Herod, Herodias

johnnycake (southern)–pone

join–add, ally, annex, attach, blend, coalesce, compound, conjoin, connect, engage, enter, hitch, incorporate, link, meet, merge, mingle, mix, team, tie, unite, wed, yoke

join battle–joust

join by alliance–ally

join by stitching–suture

join firmly – cement, fuse, knot, splice, weld

join strands–splice

join the colors–enlist

join together–fay, piece

joining of two cords–splice

joining together–syzygy

joins closely–grafts, knits

joint–elbow, hangout, knee, node, resort, seam

joint (arm) – ares, elbow, wrist

joint (articulated)–hinge

joint (bird's wing, small)–alula

joint (grooved)–rabbet

joint (horse's leg)–pastern

joint (right angle)–ell

joint (wood)–tenon

joints (pert. to)–particular, nodal

joke–banter, gag, jape, jest, pun, rally, sport

joke (practical)–hoax

joker–card, wag, wit

jollity–gaiety, hilarity, joviality, merriment, mirth

jolly–jocular, jovial, mellow

jolly boat–yawl

jolt–blow, butt, jar, jounce, knock, shake

Jonah–jinx

Jordan region (beyond) – Perea

Jordan region (east of) – Basham

Joseph's mother–Rachel

josh–banter, chaff, guy

josh (coll.)–guy

josh (English)–spoof

josh (slang)–kid

Joshua tree–yucca

Joshua's associate–Caleb

Joshua's father–Nun

jostle–crowd, elbow, hustle, jolt, push, shove

jot – atom, bit, iota, point, tittle

jouk – cheat, cringe, dart, dodge, duck, evade, fawn, hide, skulk

journal–log, logbook, magazine, paper, periodical, record

journal (keeper of)–diarist

journalist–editor, reporter

journey – excursion, iter, jaunt, peregrination, pilgrimage, tour, travel, trek, trip

journey (adventurous long) –odyssey

journey (extended)–tour

journey (long)–trek

journey (sea)–voyage

journeyed–fared, traveled

journeyer–tourist, traveler

joust–combat, tilt, tournament

jousting field–list

jovial–elated, hilarious, jocular, jolly, joyous, merry

jowl–cheek, chop, dewlap, jaw, jawbone, wattle

joy – delight, ecstasy, exult, exultation, felicity, happiness, hilarity, rapture, rejoice, transport

joy (poetic)–gelid

joyous–blithe, cheerful, festal, gay, glad, jocular, merry, mirthful

jubilant–elated, exulting, triumphant

jubilation–exultation, rejoicing

Judah descendant – Anub, Jerahmeel

Judah's son–Er

Judaism convert–ger

Judas's place of suicide–Aceldama

Judean king – Ahaz, Asa, Herod, Jehoiachin, Jehoram, Jehoshaphat

Judean king (third)–Asa

Judean place–Berea

Judean ruler–Herod

judge – adjudicate, arbiter, critic, criticize, deem, estimate, referee, sentence, suppose, try

judge (inferior rank)–puisne

judge (junior)–puisne

judges (group of)–bench

judge's bench (court)–banc, bancus

judge's chambers–cameras

judgment – award, censure, criticism, decision, doom, opinion, sensibility, taste

judgment (critical)–taste

judgment (settled)–opinion

judicial circuits–cabal

judicial hearing–trial

judicial hearing (second)–retrial

judicial order–writ

judicial safekeeping–custody

judicial writ–elegit, venire

judiciary–bench

judicious–discerning, wise

jug–cruse, ewer, jail, lockup, pitcher, prison

jug (classical archaeology)–ascus, asci (pl.)

jug (small)–ewer, toby

jug (small, in shape of fat man)–toby

jug (water)–tinaja

jug (wide-mouthed)–ewer

juggler–cheat, deceiver, legerdemainist

juggler's trick–sleight

Jugoslavian–*see* Yugoslavian

juice–succulent
juice (evaporated sugar) – sirup, syrup
juice (fruit)–rob
juice (plant)–latex, milk
juice (unfermented grape)–must, stum
juice (woody plant)–sap
juice of sugar (evaporated)–sirup, syrup
juju–amulet, charm, fetish
jujube–ber
Jules Verne character–Nemo
Juliet family name–Capulet
jumble–agitate, botch, disorder, heap, mess, muddle, raff, riffraff, shake, stir
jumble type–pi
jump – hop, leap, scold, spring, vault
jump (dial.)–lep
jump (long, with weights in hands)–halma
jump beyond–overleap
jumped about (playfully)–capered
jumping stick–pogo
junction–meeting, union
junction of branch–axil
junction of two edges–seam, suture
junctures – conjuncture, crises, emergency, exigency, pass, predicament, quandary, strait

June bug–dor
June grass–poa
jungle dweller–beast
junior–puisne
juniper–cade, gorse, savin
Juno's messenger (special)–Iris
junto–cabal, clique, combination, coterie, faction
jupe – bodice, coat, jacket, shirt, skirt, tunic
Jupiter–Jove
Jupiter's daughter–Bura
Jupiter's lover–Io
Jupiter's satellite–Io
Jupiter's son–Castor
jurassic strata–lias
Jurassic system (division of)–Lias
jure – jurisprudence, law, right
juries–panels
jurisdiction–authority, law
jurisdiction (early English law)–soc, soke
jurisdiction (ecclesiastical dignitary)–patriarchy
jurisdiction (feudal) – soc, soke
jurisdiction (suffix)–ric
jurisdiction of a consul–consulate
jurisprudence–law
jury–panel

jury additions–tales
jury influencing (attempt of)–embraceor
jury list–panel, venire
jury summons–venire
just – equal, equitable, fair, legitimate, unbiased, upright, valid
just (to)–tilt
just clear of ground (as an anchor)–atrip
just received–fresh
justice (supreme, 1888)–Lamar
justification–apology
justify – authorize, defend, maintain, sanction, support, warrant
justly–fairly, honestly, truly
justness – accuracy, correctness, exactness, fitness
jute–burlap, gunny, sacking
jute fabric burlap
Jutlander–Dane
jutout–beetle
jutting forth – projecting, protruding, salient
jutting rock–crag, tor
juvenile – actor, immature, undeveloped, young, youthful
juxtaposition – contact, contiguity, nearness, proximity
jynx–charm, spell, wryneck

K

kaama–hartebeest
kae–jackdaw
Kaffir boy (nurse)–umfaan
Kaffir (Kafir) tribe member –Matabele, Pondo, Tembu, Xosa
Kaffir warriors (body of)–Impi
Kaffir weapon (club)–keri, knobkerrie
Kaiser's residence (former) –Doorn
kaka–parrot
kakapo–parrot

kaki–persimmon, stilt
kakkak–bittern
kakke–beriberi
kala–bulbul
kale–cabbage, cole, colewort
kale (variety of)–collard
kales (sea, Eng.)–coles
kali–carpet
kallah–bride
kamerad–surrender
kamias–bilimbi
Kanaka–Hawaiian, Melanesian, Polynesian
kanara–rug, runner

Kanarese sect–Bali
kangaroo (female)–doe
kangaroo (male, large) – boomer
Kansas city – Abilene, Iola, Lyons
Kansas county–Reno
Kansas river–Osage
Kartvelian people–Svane
kasha–mush
Kashmir alphabet–sarada
Kashmir official (native) – pundit
kashyapa–tortoise

katchung–peanut
keek–peep, peeper
keel (after part)–skeg
keel (blossom)–carina, carinae (pl.)
keelbill–ani
keeling–codfish
keen – acrimonious, acute, astute, avid, clever, cute, eager, nice, sharp, shrewd, tart, trenchant
keen relish–gusto
keenly–perspicaciously
keenly desirous–avid
keenness–acumen
keenness of insight–acumen
keenness of mind–acumen
keep – confine, detain, husband, maintain, preserve, restrain, retain, withhold
keep afloat–buoy
keep aloof from–boycott
keep apart–seclude, separate
keep at distance–repel
keep away from–avoid
keep back–bar, dam, detain, reserve
keep back for future use–reserve
keep from progressing–delay
keep going–sustain
keep hidden–secrete
keep in check–restrain
keep off–fend
keep quiet–silence
keep straight–direct
keeper – custodian, guard, warden
keeper (elephant)–mahout
keeper of birdhouse–aviarist
keeper of prison–gaoler, jailer, jailor, turnkey, warden
keeping – care, caretaking, custody, guard, guardianship, maintenance, possession, trust
keeve – haystack, knoll, plume, tub, tuft
kef–dreamy, languor, tranquillity
keg–cask
kelly–derby, hat
kenneled–stabled
Kentucky blue grass–poa
Kentucky city–Paducah

Kentucky college–Berea
kept afloat–buoyed
kept bow on to sea–atry
kept from happening–prevented
Keresan Indian–Sia
kernel–meat, nut
kernel (aromatic seed)–nutmeg
kernel (small bony)–acini
ketch (kind of)–saic
ketch (Levantine)–saic
ketone (crystalline)–deguelin
ketone (saturated)–camphor
ketone (volatile liquid)–acetone
kettle (copper, anc.)–lebes
kettle (large)–caldron
kettle (Spanish silver reduction)–cazo
kettledrum–atabal, attabal, naker, timpano, timpani (pl.)
key–opener, solution
key (feather)–spline
key (piano)–digital
key (telegraph)–tapper
key notch–ward
key tone (music)–tonic
keynote–do, tonic
keynote (music)–tonic
keys (feathered)–fins
Keystone State founder – Penn
kick–boot, object, punt
kick (Scot.)–funk
kick backwards (Scot.)–funk
kid (slang)–guy, hoax, humbug
kid (undressed)–suede
kidang–muntjac
kidcote–prison
kidney (pert. to)–renal
kidneys–reins
Kilauea goddess–Pele
kill – dispatch, murder, slaughter, slay
kill by stoning–lapidate
killed–murdered, slain, slew
killed (as sacrifice)–immolated
killer (of brother)–fratricide
killer (of bull)–matador
killer (of father)–patricide
killer (of mother)–matricide

killer (of sister)–sororicide
killer (snake) – mongoose, mongoos, mongooses (pl.)
killer whale – grampus, orc, orca
kiln–oast, oven, stove, tiler
kiln (brick)–clamp
kiln (hop)–oast, ost
kiln (tobacco)–oast
kiloliter–stere
kind – benign, class, genus, genera (pl.), humane, ilk, order, sort, type
kind (of the same)–homogeneal
kind (varying)–divers
kindle–fire, ignite, inflame, light
kindly – benign, benignant, genial, humane, sympathetic
kindness – benignity, clemency, compassion, favor, generosity, gentleness, goodness, humanity, mildness, tenderness
kindred–kin, kinsfolk, kinsmen, relationship, sib
king–ruler, sovereign
king (checkers)–dam
king (founder of Rome Anglo-Saxon school)–Ine
king (French for)–roi
king (Latin for)–rex
king (march)–Sousa
king (petty)–regulus
king (Spanish for)–rey
king (water)–Neptune
King Arthur's abode–Avalon
King Arthur's court seat–Caerleon
King Arthur's court site–Camelot
King Arthur's father–Uther
King Arthur's fool–Dagonet
King Arthur's lance–ron
King Arthur's queen–Guinever, Guinevere
King Arthur's sword – Excalibur
King Hezekiah's mother–Abi
King of Bashan–Og
king of beasts–lion
king of cheese–Brie

King of Denmark and England–Knut
king of fairies–Oberon
king of gods–Jupiter
king of golden touch–Midas
King of Israel–Ahab, David, Jehoahaz, Jehoram, Jehu, Jeroboam, Omri, Pekah, Pekahiah, Saul, Solomon
King of Judea–Herod
King of Judea (third)–Asa
King of Troy–Priam
King of Visigoths–Alaric
King Saul's uncle–Ner
king slain by Samuel–Agog
king vulture–papa
kingdom–empire, realm
kingdom divided by Spain and France–Navarre
Kingdom of Asia–Nepal
Kingdom of Indo-China – Anam, Annam
kingfish–bagara, opah
kingly – imperial, majestic, regal, royal
kingly symbol–scepter
king's baton–scepter, sceptre
king's murderer–regicide
king's officer (in charge of horse provender)–avener
king's private audience chamber–camarilla
king's representative – viceroy
king's stable officer–avener
king's title–majesty, sire
kings (family of)–dynasty
Kings (three of Cologne)–Gaspar, Melchior, Balthasar
kinkajou–potto
kinship – agnation, affinity, consanguinity, nearness, propinquity
kinship (Mohammedan law)–nasab
kinship on father's side–agnat, agnate, agnation
kinship on mother's side – enate, enatic, enation
kinsman–sib
kinswoman–niece
kiss–buss, osculate
kiss (loud)–smack
kiss (to)–neb
kite (white-tailed)–elanet

kitty (something for)–ante
kiwi (brown)–roa
knack – art, dexterity, ease, facility, gift, skill
knag (Scot.) – barrel, cask, keg
knapsack–bag
knave–cheat, miscreant, rascal, rogue, scoundrel, villain
knave in cards–pam
knave of clubs–pam
knavish–dishonest, rascally, trickish
knead–incorporate, manipulate, massage, mix
knead (Scot.)–elt
knead to softness–malax
knee bone–patella
knee breeches – knickers, smalls
knee cap–patella
knew–wist, wot
knickknack – bauble, gewgaw, gimcrack, toy, trifle
knickknack (esthetic) – artware
knife–bolo, snee, stab, shiv
knife (dissecting)–scalpel
knife (fruit)–corer
knife (large)–bolo, bread, cane, carving, corn, gully, machete, snee
knife (surgical)–scalpel
knife maker–cutler
knight–cavalier
knight (famous)–Galahad
knight (next degree to)–armiger
knight (rare)–eques
knight errant–paladin
Knight of the Round Table –Galahad, Gawain, Kay, Lancelot, Percivale, Tristram
knighthood (paragon of)–paladin
knight paragon–paladin
knight's cloak (mantle)–tabard
knight's lance banner–gonfalon, gonfanon
knight's title–sir
knight's wreath (bearing crest)–orle
knit–bind, cement, conjoin,

connect, consolidate, contract, fasten, join, plait, unite, woven, wrinkle
knitting machine guideway –sley
knitting stitch–purl
knob – boss, bulge, lump, node, nub, protuberance, stud
knobkerrie–bout, club, kiri, stick
knock – beat, bump, dash, hit, pound, rap, tap, thump
knock (old word)–poss
knock (Eng. dial.)–snop
knock (Scot.)–hill, hillock
knock (slang) – criticism, faultfinding
knock down (cut or beat)–fell
knock out–K.O., kayo
knocker (door)–rapper
knocker (door, notched bar) –risp
knocking (sharp)–rapping, rattat
knoll–bunch, clod, hillock, knell, knob, lump, mound
knot – burl, knob, laniard, lanyard, lump, node, protuberance, tangle, tie
knot (hard)–knur
knot (in cotton fiber)–nep
knot (ornamental)–bow
knot (ribbon)–rosette
knot (running)–noose, slip
knot (small)–nodules
knot (the)–dunne
knot (tough)–gnarl
knot (tree trunk)–gnarl
knot in cotton fiber–nep
knot in wood–gnarl, knag, knar
knot in wood (var.)–nur
knots (full of small)–nodulose, nodulous
knotted (as in a drama)–noded
knotted fiber–nep
knotty–difficult, gnarled, intricate, knarred, knarry, knurled, nodal, nodular, perplexing, puzzling
know (arch.)–wot

know (not to, Scot.)–unken
know (Scot.)–ken
know (to)–wis
know again–recognize
know how to–can, experienced
know-it-all–wiseacre
know little–ignoramus
know nothing–agnostic, ignoramus
Know Nothing party member–Sam
knowledge – information, learning, lore, science, wisdom
knowledge (classified and systematized)–science
knowledge (exhibitor of) – pedant

knowledge (pert. to)–gnostic
knowledge (private) – privity
knowledge (Sanskrit)–Veda
knowledge (slight)–inkling
knowledge (superficial) – smatter
knowledge (systemized) – science
knowledge (transmitted orally or by belief)–tradition
knowledge (universal)–pantology
knowledge range–ken
kobird–cuckoo
kobold–gnome, goblin, nis
kokopu (New Zealand) – para

kopecks (100)–ruble
Koran–Ulema
Koran (chapters or sections of)–Suras
Koran register–sijil, sijill
Korea (old name)–Chosen
Korean city – Pingyang, Seoul
Kosher (state of being) – Kashruth
krona (one-hundredth of)–ore
krone (part of)–ore
Krupp works site–Essen
Kurland Peninsula inhabitant–Lett
Kwantung seaport–Dairen
Kyushu prefecture (N. E. Japan)–Oita

L

La Boheme heroine–Mimi
laagte–bottom, valley
Laban's daughter – Leah, Rachel
label – band, fillet, lappet, tag, tassel
labial–lip
labial organ stop–melodia
labor – drudgery, exertion, industry, labour, moil, task, toil, work
labor (hard)–sweat
labor for breath–gasp, pant
labor hard – drudge, moil, strive
labor imposed as an undertaking–taskage
labor organization – union, A.F.L., C.I.O., U.M.W.
labored – difficult, forced, heavy, strained
labored earnestly–strove
labored excessively – overworked
laborer – peon, worker, workman
laborer (farm)–hind
laborers (Oriental)–coolies
laborious–arduous, hard, in-

dustrious, operose, toilsome
Labrador dog – Newfoundland
Labrador tea–ledum
labyrinth–maze
lac–resin
lace–laniard, lanyard
lace (frilled)–ruche
lace (gold and silver)–orris
lace (heavy large pattern)–guipure
lace (make)–tat
lace (point)–alencon
lace (silk)–tulle
lace (silver and gold)–orris
lace frill–jabot
lace material–allover
lace ornament–jabot
lace tag (metal)–aglet, aiglet
lacerate–cut, rend, tear
lachrymal drop–tear
lachrymist–weeper
lachrymose drop–tear
lack–absence, dearth, need, paucity, scarcity, want
lack of delicacy–grossness
lack of difficulty–ease
lack of elusiveness–reserve

lack of energy – anergy, atony
lack of feeling–insensibility
lack of fineness–grossness
lack of interest–apathy
lack of knowledge – ignorance
lack of power–atony
lack of red corpuscles–anemia
lack of tone–atony
lack of vital energy–atony
lackadaisical–sentimental
lackaday–alas
lackey–footman, toady, valet
lacking – barren, destitute, short, shy
lacking cordiality–cool, rude
lacking determination–irresolute
lacking energy–atonic
lacking feeling–insensate
lacking knowledge (one who)–ignoramus
lacking nourishing quality–jejune
lacking refinement – inelegant

lacking steadiness–timorous
lacking that required by good taste–inelegant
lacking tone–atonic
lacking vitality–sapless
lacking zeal–tepid
Laconian capital (anc.) – Sparta
Laconian division (old)–Obe
Laconian subdivision–Obe
Laconian tribe–Obe
laconic–brief, concise, pointed, short, succinct, summary, terse
lacquer–Japan, varnish
lacrimando (music)–lamenting, plaintive
lactarium–dairy
lactate (silver)–actol
lacteal–milky
lacteal fluid–milk
lad–boy, stripling, youth
lad (serving)–gossoon
ladder (British)–run
ladder (scaling)–scalade
lade–bail, dip, drain, draw, load
laden – burdened, fraught, freighted, loaded
ladies' man–beau
lading – burden, cargo, freight, load
lading (ship)–cargo
ladle – dip, dipper, scoop, spoon
ladle (large)–scoop
lady–dame, female, senora
lady (Latin)–domina
lady (young, arch.)–damozel
Lady of Troy–Helen
lady's maid – tirewoman, woman
lady's thumb – peachwort, persicary
lag–linger, loiter
lagarto–alligator
laggard–backward, loiterer, sluggish, straggler
lagnappe – gratuity, pilon, present
laic–layman, secular
laid by for future use–hoarded, saved, stored
laid down–posed

laid out with hope of return –invested
lair–den, lie
lair (animal's)–den
laity (member of)–layman
Laius' son–Oedipus
lake red
Lake (Great)–Erie, Huron, Michigan, Ontario, Superior
lake (mountain, 64 acre)–tarn
Lake Baringo Kenya Negro –Suk
Lake Garda day breeze–ora
lake on which Perry defeated the British–Erie
Lake Tahoe trout–pogy
lakes (Scot.)–lochs
lakes (small)–meres, ponds
lakes (small steep-banked mountain)–tarns
lakhs (100) crore
Lamaism reliquary–Chorten
Lamaism stupa–Chorten
lamb–baahling, ean, yean
Lamb (Charles)–Elia
lamb (pet)–cosset
lamb (used as symbol)–agnus
lamb leg (cooked)–gigot
lambskin leather–suede
Lamb's pen name–Elia
Lamb's sobriquet–Elia
lambent–flickering, radiant, wavering
lame – crippled, disabled, halt, halting
Lamech's son–Jabal
lament – bemoan, bewail, condole, deplore, jeremiad, moan, mourn, plaint, regret, sigh, wail, weep, yammer
lamentation–grief
lamentation (for the dead)–keen
lamentation (utter)–cry
lamina–blade, flake, hinge, layer
lamp (pine knot)–torch
lamp (portable covered) – lantern
lamp (safety)–davy
lamp (spirit)–etna
lampblack–soot

lampstand–candelabra
Lamps of the Lord–Yucca
Lamparas de Dios–Yucca
lampoon – pasquinade, ridicule, satirize
lampoon writer–satirist
lamprey–eel, ramper
lamprey angler–eeler
lamprey catcher–eeler
Lancashire (Eng.) section–Eccles
lance – cut, hurl, lancet, launch, spear, weapon
lance battle–joust
lance head (blunt)–morne
lancer–soldier, spearer
lancet–fleam
land – country, debark, disembark, ground
land (barren)–moor
land (cultivated) – arada, farm, tilth
land (firm) soil
land (grazing) – pasture, range
land (imaginary, of diminutive people)–Lilliput
land (Italian marshy) – maremma
land (jutting piece of)–neck
land (Latin)–ager, terra
land (low rich river, Scot.) –carse
land (Orkney Islands held in fee simple without charter) – odal, odalborn, odaler, odalman, udal
land (parcel of)–acre, farm, lot
land (pasture)–grass
land (plowed)–arada
land (Shetland Islands held in fee simple without charter) – odal, odalborn, odaler, odalman, udal
land (Spanish tilled)–arada
land (tilled, southwest U.S.) –arada
land (tract of arable, in Sussex, Eng.)–laine
land (tracts of undulating)–downs
land (waste)–heath
land (world's northernmost, anc. geog.)–thule
land apart (French)–ile

land between two streams–
daob
land elevation – hill, mountain
land fighting force–army
land held in absolute ownership–allod, alod
land held in fee simple –
odal, odalborn, odaler,
odalman, udal
land measure–acre, ar, are,
mile, perch, rod, rood
land of the sheiks–Arabia
land surveyor–arpenteur
land under cultivation –
farm, orchard, ranch
landholding–tenure
landlocked–Mediterranean
landmark–copa
landscape–scenery
landscape aspect (general)–
scenery
landslide–avalanche
landsman (green)–lubber
landed–alit
landed (possessing)–acred
landed estate – demesne,
manor
landed property–estate
landing place–airplace, airport, dock, pier, wharf
landing stage–stair
lands–acres
lands (independent) – allod,
alod
lane – alley, gullet, path,
throat
lane-alley (narrow, Eng.
dial.)–tewer
language – dialect, speech,
tongue
language (anc.)–Pali
language (Aramaic)–Samar-
itan
language (artificial) – esperanto, ido, ro, volapuk
language (Buddhist sacred)
–Pali
language (international) –
ido, ro
language (most universal)–
(1) Chinese, (2) English,
(3) Russian, (4) Spanish
language (North Caucasian)
–Avar

language (nonmetrical) –
prose
language (pretentious) –
bombast
language (Romance)–Cata-
lan, Italian
language (sacred)–Pali
language (secret, of a class)–
argot
language (Semitic)–Arabic
language (strange)–lingo
language (synthetic)–ro
language (universal)–ido, ro
language expression (peculiar)–idiom
language passages (used in
learning)–chrestomathy
languid – careless, dreamy,
faint, feeble, heedless, indolent, sickly, sluggish,
spiritless, supine, torpid
languish – decline, die,
droop, fail, faint, pine, repine, wilt
languor - dreaminess, dullness, indolence, kef, lassitude, sluggishness, stag-
nation
Laodamia's father–Acastus
Laomedon's son (changed to
grasshopper by Eos)–Ti-
thonus
lap–fold, lick, sip
lap robe–blanket, rug
lapatic–cathartic, laxative
lapicide–stonecutter
lapidary's instrument–dial
lapidate–stone, stoned
lappet (woman's dress)–pan
lapwing–pewit
larboard (naut.)–else, port
larceny – burglary, robbery,
stealage, theft
larceny (petty, Eng. slang)–
scrounging
larch (black)–tamarac
lard – baste, enrich, fatten,
grease
lard (as in cooking)–enarm
lard (Latin)–adeps
larder–cupboard, pantry
larder (obs.)–spence, spense
large – ample, big, bold,
bulky, copious, extensive,
great, immense, liberal,

massy, plentiful, titanic,
weighty
large (indefinitely)–nth
large (very)–giant, gigantic,
huge, vast
large (very, poetic)–enorm
large and stout (of body)–
burly
large antelope–aste
large artery–aorta
large beast (pert. to) – leonine
large fish–opah, swordfish,
tuna
large in scope–general
large knife–bolo, snee
large number–myriad
large number of people
(coll.)–slew
large of body–burly
large pulpit–ambo
large quantity–much, raft
large quantity (slang)–scads
large spoon–ladle
large tub–vat
large volume–tome
larger than life–heroic
largess (largesse) – bounty,
generosity, gift, liberality,
present
lariat–lasso, noose, reata, riata, rope
lariat (Spanish)–reata
laridae (one of)–larid
larigot–flageolet
larrigan–moccasin
larrup–beat, blow, flog
larry–confusion, excitement,
grout, hoe, mortar, noise
larva–grub
larva (botfly)–bot
larva (butterfly, worm-like)
–caterpillar
larva (ch...opod)–atrocha
larva (firefly)–glowworm
larva (fly)–bot
larva (horsefly)–bot
larva (oestrid fly)–bot
larval stage of trematode
worms–cercaria
lascivious–lecherous, libidinous, licentious, salacious
lassie – colleen, girl, lass,
maiden
lassitude–debility, languor
lasso–lariat, reata, riata, rope

last – endure, eventual, extreme, final, latest, rearmost, ultimate
last (but one)–penult
last (the)–omega
Last Days of Pompeii character–Ione, Nydia
Last Days of Pompeii maiden–Ione
last offer of conditions–ultimatum
last used in compounds–yester
lasting – abiding, constant, continual, durable, eternal, permanent, stable, steadfast
lasting but a brief time–ephemeral
lasting for a time only–temporary
latchet (shoe)–tab
late – belated, new, recent, tardy
late (comb. form)–neo
late (too)–belated
Late Latin (abbr.)–L.L.
latent – dormant, potential, quiescent, suspended
later–after, anon, presently, soon, subsequently
later on–anon
later strata–neozoic
lateral – indirect, side, sideward
lath–slat
lathe attachment–setover
lathe operator–turner
lathe spindle (revolving) – mandrel
lather–foam, froth, suds
Latin (thieves)–slang
Latin-American dance–criolla
Latin conjunction–et
Latin connective–et
Latin god–Dei, Deo, Deus
Latin god of commerce – Mercury
Latin goddess–Dea
Latin grammatical case–ablative
Latin poet–Ovid
Latin pronoun–tu
Latinize–Romanize
latite–lava

latitude – breadth, distance, extent, width
latitude degrees–parallels
latrine–privy
latter–final, last, latest
Latter Day Saints–Mormons
lattice–trellis
Latvian–Lett
Latvian capital–Riga
Latvian city – Daugavpils, Dunaburg, Dvinsk, Libau, Libava, Riga
Latvian coin–kapeika (ac.), lat (s.), rublis (ac.), santimas (br.)
Latvian coin (gold)–lat
Latvian measure–deciatine, kanne, krouchka, kroushka, kulmet, lofstelle, pourvete, sagene, stof, stoff, tonnstelle, verchoc, verchok, verst, versta, verste
Latvian monetary unit–lat
Latvian river–Aa
Latvian weight–liespfund
laud – applaud, commend, eulogize, glorify, magnify, praise
laudatory– complimentative, panegyric
laugh–chortle
laugh (incipient)–smile
laugh contemptuously–snort
laugh in coarse manner – fleer
laugh loudly–guffaw, hawhaw, snort
laugh raucously–cackle
laugh to scorn–deride
laughable – amusing, burlesque, comical, diverting, droll, facetious, funny, humorous, ludicrous, merry, odd, queer, ridiculous, sportive, strange, waggish, witty
laughably–risibly
laughing (gay)–riant
laughing bird–loon
laughter–mirth
launder–wash
laurel–bay, daphne
laurel (mountain) – spoonwood
lava–latite, scoria

lava (cool)–aa
lava (fragmentary)–scoria
lava (molten)–aa
lava (powdered)–ashes
lava (rough)–aa, oo
lava (scoriaceous)–aa
lava (smooth)–pahoehoe
lava (stream of)–coulee
lavatory–basin, piscina
lave–bathe, lade, pour, rinse, wash
lavender–purple
laver–basin
Lavinia's father–Latinus
Lavinia's husband–Aeneas
Lavinia's mother–Amata
lavish – bountiful, extravagant, exuberant, free, immoderate, impetuous, luxuriant, profuse, rank, reckless, spend, superabundant, unrestrained, unstinted, wild
lavish (recklessly)–prodigal
lavish fondness–dote
law–act, canon, enactment, equity, justice, rule, statute
law (fundamental, of civil states)–constitution
law (general)–canon
law (intervening)–mesne
law (Latin)–lex
law (logical doctrine of thought)–noetic
law (mosaic)–torah
law (offender against) – criminal, wrongdoer
law (offense against)–delict
law (pert. to)–judiciary, legislative
law (science of) – jurisprudence
law (wrong)–tort
law action–suit
law expert (American international)–Moore
law of Moses–tora, torah
law to revoke–adeem
laws of manu–sutra
lawful–due, legal, licit
lawmaker – legislator, senator, solon
lawsuit–case
lawsuit subject–res

lawyer–attorney, counsellor, counselor
lawyer (petty, tricky)–pettifogger, shyster
lawyer's patron saint–Ives
lawn (cotton)–batiste
lawny–grassy
lax – backward, dissolute, dull, free, inactive, licentious, loose, open, remiss, slack, slow, tardy, unconfined, unrestrained
lay–appease, ascribe, ballad, bet, ditty, hazard, impose, impute, poem, quiet, song, stake, still
lay away – accumulate, amass, cache, hoard, husband, store, treasure
lay bare–denude, strip, uncover
lay down weapons–disarm, surrender
lay flooring–pave
lay hold of–apprehend
lay in sepulcher–entomb
lay in surrounding matter–embed
lay on (upon)–impose
lay out–expend, spend
lay smooth–even
lay up for future use–hive
lay waste – depredate, desolate, devastate, ravage
layer–bed, lamina, stratum, strata (pl.), tier
layer of clay in coal–sloam
layer of earth (between seams of coal)–sloam
layer of iris (pigmented)–uvea
layer of skin–derm
layers (flagstone)–pavers
lazar–leper
lazy–idle, indolent, otiose, slothful
lea–grassland, meadow, pasture
leach – moisten, percolate, wet
lead – con, conduct, direct, escort, guide, head, influence, lode, pilot, usher, van
lead (pig of)–fother

lead (principal ore of)–galena
lead (white)–ceruse, krems
lead a passive existence–vegetate
lead astray – allure, delude, entice, inveigle, lure, pervert
lead color–livid
lead from truth–delude
lead glass–strass
lead glass strips (for stained glass)–cames
lead ore (principal of)–galena
lead sulphide–galena
leader–chief, chieftain, conductor, director, guide, head, sinew, tendon
leader (band) – choragus, choragi (pl.), conductor
leader (choir)–cantor
leader (feminist)–Catt
leading–controlling, directing, foremost, governing, guiding
leading to–inductive
leaf–page, sepal
leaf (appendage of foliage)–ligula
leaf (at base of flower)–bract
leaf (banana)–frond
leaf (corolla)–petal
leaf (depressed at base)–areola
leaf (flower cluster)–bract
leaf (grass)–blade
leaf (large colored blossom)–spathe
leaf (modified in flower cluster)–bract
leaf (palmyra palm) – ola, olay, ole
leaf (part of)–stipel
leaf (tropical)–frond
leaf midrib–pen
leaf of book–folio
leaf of calyx–sepal
leaf rib vein–costa
leaf vein–rib
leaflet – folder, pamphlet, pinna
leaflet (stipule of)–stipel
league – alliance, coalition,

combination, confederation, union
League of Nations city – Geneva
league of states–federation
leagued–federated
Leah's sister–Rachel
leak–crack, crevice, drip, fissure, hole, seep
leal–accurate, correct, faithful, genuine, just, lawful, legal, loyal, observant, real, true
lean and rough–scrag, scraggy
Leander's sweetheart–Hero
leaned–reclined
leaner–poorer, skinnier
leaning – inclination, pronate, tendency
leaning (strong)–penchant
leap – bound, jump, spring, vault
leap (frolicsome)–caper
leap (lightly)–skip
leaping–salient, saltant
leaping (as in a dance)–saltation
leaps out–sallies
learn (old word)–lere
learn thoroughly–master
learned – erudite, lettered, pedants, read, sage, wot
learned (in law)–legist
learned man–professor, pundit, scholar, teacher
learning–art, education, erudition, knowledge, lore, pedantry, scholarship
learning (love of)–philology
learning (ostentatious display of)–pedantry
lease–demise, let, rent, tenure
leasehold right–rental
leash (hawking)–lune
least – little, lowest, minimum, shortest, slightest, smallest
least complicated–simple
least possible amount–grain
least possible particle–minim
leather (Arabian goat) – mocha
leather (artificial)–keratol

leather (bookbinding)–roan
leather (cheap strong)–skiver
leather (convert into) – tan, taw
leather (from calfhide)–kip, vici
leather (from horsehide) – Cordovan
leather (kind of)–calf, Cordovan, kip, suede, vici
leather (lambskin)–suede
leather (old spelling)–leder
leather (piece of)–clout
leather (sheepskin)–roan
leather (slipper)–roan
leather (soft)–suede
leather (soft tawed)–aluta
leather (used for books) – levant
leather (used for gloves) – trank
leatherback–turtle
leather bottle–matara
leather cuirass–lorica
leather fastener – strap, thong
leatherneck–marine
leather splitting tool–skiver
leather strap–latigo
leather strip–thong
leave–allowance, depart, go, liberty, permission, quit, retire, vacate
leave empty–vacate
leave in helpless isolation–maroon
leave nothing to be desired–satisfy
leave of absence–exeat, furlough
leave off–cease
leave out–omit, skip
leave undone–omit
leaven–yeast
leaves–foliage
leaves (calyx)–sepals
leaves (dried for medicine)–senna
leaves (floating)–pads
leaves (grass)–blades
leaves of absence (from college)–exeats
leavetaking – A.W.O.L., adieu, conge, departure, parting

leaving–dross, offal, ort, refuse, relic, remnant, residue
leaving (worthless)–ort
leaving desolate–bereaving
lech – capstone, monument, slab
lecher – debauchee, glutton, gourmand, libertine, parasite
lectern–desk, escritoire
lectern (early Christian) – ambo
lecture – discourse, lection, lesson
lecturer–prelector
lecturer (university)–reader
led in–pioneered
ledge–shelf, sill
ledge (behind altar)–retable
ledge (narrow bank)–berm
lee (opposed to)–stoss
leep–boil, curdle, scald, toast
leer–akin, cheek, contempt, empty, face, flank, lear, lehr, loin, look, lust, unlade, void
lees–dregs
Leeward group island–Nevis
left–gone
left-hand page (abbr.)–vo
left to one's judgment–discretionary
leftist–radical
leg (ornamental chair)–cabriole
leg (part of)–calf, shin
leg (part of hind between thigh and ankle)–crus
leg armor–greave
leg bone–fibula, tibia
leg of lamb (cooked)–gigot
leg piece (medieval armor)–jambeau
legacy–bequest, gift
legacy inheritor–legatee
legal – authorized, lawful, legitimate, licit, valid
legal action–res
legal acts–acta, actus (sing.)
legal case postponed–remanet
legal claim–lien
legal conveyance–deed
legal critic–censor

legal defense–alibi
legal delay–mora
legal order–writ
legal paper–writ
legal pleading–demurrer
legal point–res
legal profession–bar
legal prohibition–estoppel
legal thing–res
legal tribunal–court
legal warning–caveat
legal writ–capias
legal writ (form)–elegit
legal wrong–malum
legate – ambassador, bequeath, envoy
legend–myth, saga
legendary–traditional
legendary of a people–lore
legendary primate (who crowned King Arthur)–Dubric
legislate–act, elect, enact
legislative assembly – diet, senate
legislative enactment – law, statute
legislative group–bloc
legislator–senator, solon
legislator (distinguished) – statesman
legislature–diet, senate
legitimate – cogent, efficacious, genuine, lawful, legal, licit, real, true, valid
legume–bean, lentil, loment, pea, pod
legume (indehiscent)–uva
legume (kind of)–loment
leguminous vegetable–bean, lentil, pea
leisure–freedom, opportunity, time
leisure (at)–otiose
lemur–angwantibo, aye-aye, galago, loris, potto, tarsier
lemur (flying)–colugo
lemur (Madagascar) – aye-aye
lemur (Malagasy)–aye-aye
lemurine (West Africa) – potto
lemurs–makis
lena–procuress
lenad – leucite, nephelite, noselite, sodalite

length of ten meters–deca-meter

length of ¾ inch–digit

length of time–age, eon, era, moment, period

length of 2¼ inches–nail

lengthen – amplify, dilate, eke, elongate, expand, extend, increase, produce, prolong, protract, stretch

lengthen out – protract, stretch

lengthwise – along, longitudinally

lengthy – extended, long, protracted

leniate–alleviate, soften

leniency–charity, mercy

lenient – assuasive, clement, easy, emollient, lax, merciful, mild, relaxing, softening

lenify – alleviate, assuage, mitigate, soften

Leningrad (former name)–Petrograd

lenitive – assuasive, emollient, gentle, mild, mitigant, palliative

lenity–gentleness, humanity, kindness, mercy

lens–anastigmat

lens (kind of)–meniscus

lens (type of)–bifocal, toric

lens exactness – apochromatism

Leo constellation star–Regulus

leonine–lionlike

leopard–panther

leopard (poetic)–pard

leopard (Indian hunting) – cheetah

leopard (snow)–ounce

leper–lazar

leper (Old Testament) – Naaman

leper's cry (anc.)–unclean

Lepotine Alps (highest) – Leone

leprosy–lepra

Les Miserables author–Hugo

less – few, fewer, minus, smaller

less refined–coarser

less than–under

lessen–abate, bate, decrease, impair, peter, reduce, relieve, wane, weaken

lessen in value – depreciate, deteriorate, shrink

lessen the tension–relax

lesser – inferior, minor, smaller

let–allow, hinder, impede, leave, permit, prevent

let bait drop lightly–dap, dib

let down–comedown, drawback, lower, relaxing, slackening

let down tension–relax

let fall–drop, vail

let fall or run out (unintentionally)–spill, spilt

let in–admit, enter, insert

let it stand (printing)–stet

let it stand (music)–sta

lethal–deadly, fatal, mortal

lethargic – comatose, dull, heavy, inert, sleepy

lethargy–coma, sopor, stupor, torpor

letter–communication, epistle, message, note

letter (a)–zed

letter (alphabetic)–ess, jay, kay, wye

letter (Anglo-Saxon) – edh, wen

letter (authorizing)–breve

letter (decorated at beginning of paragraph)–fac

letter (either vowal or consonant)–semiconsonant

letter (first)–initial

letter (short) – billet, line, note

letter (sloping)–italic

letter (two, representing single sound)–digraph

letter carrier (Span.)–correo

letter of challenge–cartel

letter of defiance (challenge) –cartel

letter writer–correspondent

lettuce (kind of)–cos, head, romaine

lettuce (summer)–cos

leucite–lenad

levant–decamp, wager

Levant–East, Orient

Levantine–Orient

Levantine ketch–saic

Levantine river–wady

Levantine ship–saic

Levantine valley–wady

Levantine vessel–saic

Levantine vessel (small, one or two masted)–jerm

levee – bank, dike, embankment, pier, quay, reception

level–demolish, equal, even, flat, flatten, plane, point, raze, smooth

level (common)–par

level (stout, like canthook)–peavey, peavie, peavy

leveler–planer

leveling device–gimbal

lever–peavey, peavie, peavy, pedal, pry, tappet

lever (foot)–pedal, treadle

lever (for turning a rudder) –tiller

lever (weaving machine) – lam

leverage–pry

Levi's descendant–Levite

Levitical–Aaronic

levity – buoyancy, frivolity, gaiety, lightness

levy–fine, tax

levy (government)–tax

levy a tax–stent

lewd–debauched, dissolute, impure, lascivious, lecherous, libidinous, licentious, lustful, obscene, pornographic, salacious, sensual, unchaste

Lewis Carroll character - Alice

Liaatung city–Dairen

liability–debit, debt, obligation

liable – answerable, apt, responsible

liable (not)–exempt

liable to objection – exceptionable

liable to penalty–guilty

liaison–intimacy, intrigue

liar–Ananias, deceiver, fibber, prevaricator, wernard

lias–limestone, rock

lias basic system–Jurassic
lib–castrate, geld, sleep
libation–drink, potation
libel–bill, certificate, circular, declaration, handbill, lampoon, request, roorback, supplication
liberal – bountiful, eclectic, electic, frank, generous, munificent, profuse
Liberal (old)–Whig
liberal gift–largess, largesse
liberate–deliver, emancipate, flee, free, loose, manumit, release, unfetter
liberator–deliverer
Liberian capital–Monrovia
Liberian city – Buchanan, Greenville, Marshall, Monrovia (c.)
Liberian measure–kuba
Liberian Negro people–Vai, Vei
Liberian river–Manna, San Pedro
liberty–ease, freedom, leave, license
liberty of action–play
Libya's children – Agenor, Belus
Libyan city–Tripoli
Libyan measure – barile, bozze, donum, jabia, mattaro, teman
Libyan seaport – Bengazi, Benghazi, Derna
Libyan weight–gorraf, kele, kharouba, termino, uckia
lice (plant)–aphides, aphid (sing.), aphis (sing.)
license–approbate, authority, authorize, bandon, dismiss, freedom, liberty, licence, permit, sanction
licentious – dissolute, lax, loose, profligate, uncontrolled, unrestrained, unruly
lichen–moss
lichen dyestuff–litmus
lichens (genus of)–evernia, usnea
licit–lawful, legal, permitted
lick – conquer, flog, overcome, thrash, vanquish, win

lick up with tongue–lap
licorice–abrin, jequirity
licorice (seed of)–jequirity
lid–bred, cover, hat
lie – deception, equivocate, falsehood, falsity, fib, mendacity, prevarication, rest, untruth
lie abjectly prostrate–grovel
lie at ease–loll
lie face down–pronate
lie hidden–lurk
lie in ambush–lurk
lie in warmth–bask
Liechtenstein monetary unit –rappen
lief – beloved, dear, freely, gladly, leave, permission, precious, willingly
Liege bishop–Hubert
lieu – instead, place, room, stead
lieutenant (slang)–loucy
lieutenant (second, slang)–shavetail
life–animation, energy, existence, vie, vitality, vivacity
life (animal and plant)–bios
life (not endowed with)–inanimate
life (pert. to)–vital
life (prolonger of)–elixir
life (relating to)–biotic, biotical
life (staff of)–bread
life course–career
life insurance (old form) – tontine
life jacket (slang)–Mae West
life-like–realistic
life principle–atman, prana
life principle (theosophy) – prana
lifeless – amort, dead, dull, flat, heavy, inactive, inanimate, inert, jejune, powerless, spiritless, tasteless, torpid, unanimated, vapid
lifetime–aeon, age, day, eon
lift–derrick, elevate, elevator, heave, hoist, jack, pry, raise
lift (quickly)–perk
lift (with effort)–heave

lifting device–capstan, crane, davit, derrick, lever, pry, pump, tongs
lifting device (ship's)–capstan, davit
lifting muscle–erector, levator
ligan (relating to)–flotsam, jetsam
ligature – band, bandage, bond, taenia, tie
light – bright, candle, delicate, easy, fragile, gay, gentle, glim, ignite, lamp, leger, luminous, merry, mild, soft, trifling, trivial
light (act of making)–levitation
light (burning)–cresset
light (burst of)–flash
light (circle of)–aureola, aureole, halo
light (clear yellow)–amber
light (cloud of)–nimbus
light (dazzling)–arc, glare, sun
light (faint)–glim
light (faint unsteady)–glimmer
light (kind of)–arc, incandescent
light (Sanskrit)–dey
light (slang)–glim
light (source of)–moon, sun, taper
light (standard of)–carcel
light (sudden brilliant)–flare
light and airy–ethereal
light and delicate–ethereal
light and fine–leger
light and free–flyaway
light and graceful–airy
light and quick–volant
light coating–film
light dress fabric–paramatta, parramatta
light globe–bulb
lighthouse–beacon, pharos, seamark
lighthouse (to guide seamen)–pharos
light on a beacon–cresset
light refractor–prism
light touches–dabs
light unit – Hefner, lumen, lux, pyr

light up–illume
lighted–alit, illumined
lighten–allay, brighten, clear, ease, illume, illuminate
lighter–barge, scow
lighter (lamp, old-fashioned) –spill
lightness–airiness, buoyancy, flightiness, flippancy, frivolity, gaiety, giddiness, inconstancy, instability, levity, thoughtlessness, unsteadiness, volatility
lightning beetle–firefly
lightning bug–firefly
lightning stone–fulgurite
lightning war (German) – blitzkrieg
lights out–taps
lightsome–agile, airy, cheerful, cheering, fickle, frivolous, gay, graceful, light, merry, nimble, unsteady
ligneous – firewood, wood, woody
lignite–coal
like–admire, as, equal, love, similar
like (suffix)–ar, ic
like a certain fiber–hempy
like a fern–frondous
like a funeral vase–urnal
like a gland–adenose
like a house–domal
like a malt drink–aly
like a palm leaf–frondous
like a stake–palar
like an originator–parental
like better–prefer
like bone–osteal
like gold (rare)–aurate
likeable (very)–oran
likely–apt, probable, prone, verisimilar
likely to be true–probable
likely to crepitate–crackly
liken–compare
likeness–comparison, copy, effigy, image, parable, parallel, photograph, picture, portrait, replica, representation, semblance
likeness (artificial) – imitation
likeness (perfect)–twin
likeness (sculptured)–statue

likening–comparing
likewise–also, ditto, moreover, nor, not, too
liking–comely, delight, fancy, lust, pleasing, sensuality
lilac color–mauve
liliaceous plant–leek, onion
Lilliputian–midget
lilt–air, song, tune
lily (butterfly) – mariposa, sego
lily (corn)–ixia
lily (French)–lis
lily (kind of)–calla, mariposa, sego, water
lily (palm)–ki, ti, tis (pl.)
lily (the)–lis
lily family–liliaceae
lily family (genus of)–bessera
lily family plant–aloe, lotos, lotus, sego, ti, yucca
lily grass–cuckoopint
lily iron–harpoon
Lily Maid of Astolat–Elaine
lily of France–fleur-de-lis
lily of the valley bud–pip
lily of the valley family–convallariaceae
lily of the valley shrub–fetterbush
lily of the valley tree–fetterbush, pepperbush
lily palm–ti
lily-shaped–crinoid
liman–lagoon, marsh
limb – arm, bough, branch, leg, wing
limb (fish)–fin
limb (seal's)–flipper
limb (tree)–bough, branch
limb (upper)–arm
limb flexion (fordible)–anaclasis
limber–flexible, limp, lithe, pliant, supple, yielding
limbo–hell
limestone–ganil
limestone (brittle)–ganil
limestone (kind of)–oolite, pisolite
limestone (soft)–chalk
limestone (soft, friable) – malms
lime tree–linden, tupelo

limey (Eng.)–sailor, soldier
limit–boundary, bourn, confine, restrict, restriction, terminal, termination
limit (comb. form)–ori
limitary–boundary, limit
limitation–stint
limited–astricted, bounded, circumscribed, conditioned, confined, finite, local, narrow, reserved, restricted, scant, scanty
limited estate–entail
limited in size–narrow
limited to a certain area–topopolitan
limited to given area–local
limiting–hedging, relational, restrictive
limits–scants
limits (having definable) – finite
limned – delineated, drawn, portrayed
limp–drooping, flabby, flaccid, inelastic, limber, loose, soft, thin, unsubstantial
limpid–bright, crystal, lucid, pellucid, pure, translucent, transparent
Lincoln's friend (intimate)–Speed
Lincoln's secretary of war–Stanton
Lindbergh's (Mrs.) first name–Anne
linden tree–lime, lin, teil
line–mark, row, rule
line (agonic)–agone
line (barometer)–isobar
line (bounding)–side
line (central)–axis
line (comb. form)–lino
line (cross, fine at top and bottom of letter)–cerif, serif
line (cutting another)–secant
line (fastening) – earing, hawser, painter
line (fine)–etch
line (finishing)–tape
line (geometry)–tangent
line (guiding)–rein
line (hair)–cerif, serif
line (horse race finish)–wire

line (imaginary on earth's surface)–agone

line (light and fine)–leger

line (long slender)–stripe

line (longitudinal)–meridian

line (median valve)–raphe

line (nautical)–marline, ratlin, ratline

line (not forming an angle)–agone

line (oblique)–cant

line (race-starting)–scratch

line (raised)–ridge

line (short, fishhook)–snell

line (showing equal barometric pressure points) – isobar

line (transport)–carrier

line (without an angle) – agone

line joining points on earth's center–isothere

line left by cut–seam

line marking places of equal barometric pressure–isobar

line of dehiscence–suture

line of guards–cordon

line of juncture–seam

line of type (in one piece)–slug

line roof of–ceil

line to fasten reef band–earing

line with boards–wainscot

lines (equidistant)–parallels

lines of juncture–seams

lineage–birth, descent, family, pedigree, progenitor, race, tribe

lineal–racial

lineman–end, center, guard, tackle, wireman

linen (fine)–damask, lawn

linen (household)–napery

linen (Scotch, stout, figured)–dornick

linen (scraped)–lint

ling–burbot, chestnut, fish, heath, heather

linger–dally, dawdle, delay, drag, loiter, remain, tarry, wait

linger about–hover

linger idly–loiter

lingerie – underthings, underwear

lingering–chronic

linget–linseed

lingo–cant, jargon, language, patter, tongue

lingot–ingot, mold

lingua (insect's)–glossae

linguist–polyglot

lingy–heathery, heathy, lazy, limber

linhay–outhouse, shed

lining (well)–stean, steen

link – connect, nexus, tie, torch, unite, yoke

link (to)–catenate

links (number in a chain)–hundred

linseed–flaxseed

lion (noisy)–roarer

lion (young)–cub, lionet

lionlike–leonine

lip–kiss, labium, labellum, rim

lipped–labiate

lips (orchid corolla)–labella

liquefy–dissolve, melt

liquefy (by heat)–fuse, fusile, melt

liquefying by absorbing moisture from air – deliquescence

liqueur–noyau

liqueur (sirupy, Fr.)–creme

liqueur (sweet)–genepi

liquid–fluid, watery

liquid (inflammable, volatile)–alcohol, ether

liquid (light, volatile)–ether

liquid (oily, poisonous, basic)–aniline

liquid (sweet)–sirup, syrup

liquid (thick)–dope

liquid (viscid)–tar

liquid (volatile) – alcohol, ether

liquid part of fats – elain, elaine, olein, oleine

liquid vessel (large)–cistern, tank, vat

liquidate – amortize, discharge, settle

liquor–ale, beer, brew, grog, rum, whisky

liquor (heavy)–rum

liquor (illicitly distilled) – moonshine

liquor (intoxicating)–grog

liquor (spirituous)–dew

liquor bottle cabinet–cellaret

liquor manufacturer–abkari, distiller

liquor server–skinker

liquor shop (Scotch illicit)–shebeen

liquor tax–abkari

liquor vessel–barrel, bottle, decanter, flask, keg

liquors (spirituous, var.) – arak

lirk–crease, wrinkle

lish–active, agile, quick

lisk–flank, groin, loin

liss–assuage, cease, free, lisse, relieve

lissome–agile, flexible, limber, lithe, nimble, supple

list–catalog, catalogue, file, incline, inventory, register, roll, roster, rota, rote, schedule, tabulate, tilt, tip

list (alphabetical) – catalog, catalogue

list (food)–carte, menu

list (prearranged)–slate

list (written)–scrip

list of actors–cast

list of competitors–entry

list of investments–portfolio

listed (referentially) – indexed

listen–attend, harken, hear, hearken

listen furtively–eavesdrop

listen to–heed

listened to that which was not intended for one's ears –overheard

listening–attentive, audient

listening posts (detecting enemy's mines)–ecoutes

lister–lector, reader

listful–attentive

listing – enlistment, enrollment

listless–abject, careless, dull, heedless, languid, sluggish, spiritless, supine, uninteresting

listless (be)–drowse

literary composition–essay

literary composition (art of) –rhetoric
literary composition (formed by selection)–cento
literary drudge–hack
literary fragments–ana, analect
literary hack–devil
literary notes–ana
literary passage selection–excerpt
literary scraps–ana
literature–letters
literature (Hindu sacred, anc.)–Veda
lithe – flexible, limber, lissom, slender, supple, svelte
lithograph (colored) – chromo
Lithuanian–Lett
Lithuanian capital–Kovno
Lithuanian city–Kovno, Memel, Vilna
Lithuanian coin – auksinas (ac.), centas (cop., alum.), fennig (ac.), lit (s.), marka (ac.), ostmark (pap., ac.), skatikas (ac.)
Lithuanian Jew–Litvak
Lithuanian monetary unit–lit, litas, litai (pl.)
litigant–suitor
litigate–contest
litigation – discussion, dispute, suit
litigious – belligerent, contentious
litten–cemetery, churchyard
litter – bed, couch, doolee, dooley, dooli, doolie, dooly, hay, mulch, rubbish, straw, stretcher, young
litter (coffin)–bier
litter of pigs–far, farrow
little – dapper, petit, petite, puny, small, tiny, wee
little (comb. form)–steno
little (indefinitely)–nth
little (musical)–poco
little (Scot.)–sma
little, active and neat–dapper
little by little (music)–poco a poco
little fellow–shaver
little finger–minimus

little flag–banderole
Little Orphan Annie author –Riley
little ring–annulet
little toe–minimus
Little Women's surname – March
liturate–blur, spotted
liturgical form–service
liturgy–rite, ritual
live – breathe, continue, dwell, exist, reside
live by shifts and stratagems –shark
live by sponging–cadge
lively – active, agile, airy, alert, animate, blithe, buoyant, energetic, gay, pert, snappy, sprightly, vif, vivacious, yare
lively (coll.)–peart
lively (dial.)–peart
liver (pert. to)–hepatic
liver fluid–bile
liverwort–agrimony, hepatica
liverwort (genus of)–riccia
lives earlier–preexists
lives in tents (one who)–nomad, scenite
living–alive, animate, benefice, extant, livelihood, subsistence, sustenance
living (ecclesiastical)–benefice
living again–redivivus
living along river bank – riparious
living being–animal
living in currents–lotic
living in rivers–rheophile
living in streams–rheophile
living near the ground–epigeal
living on a shore–littoral
living on same plane – coplanar
Livonian river–Aa
lixivium–lye
lizard–agama, anoli, basilisk, chameleon, eft, iguana, saurian, skink
lizard (beaded)–gila
lizard (brilliant colored) – dragon

lizard (color changing) – chameleon
lizard (comb. form)–sauro
lizard (edible)–iguana
lizard (Egyptian common)– adda
lizard (herbivorous iguanid harmless)–chuckwalla
lizard (insectivorous)–chameleon
lizard (kind of) – agama, anoli, uran
lizard (large stout)–gila
lizard (monitor)–uran, varan
lizard (new world)–ameiva
lizard (North American) – dab, dabb, dhab
lizard (old world)–agama, seps
lizard (Philippine)–ibid
lizard (pleurodont)–skink
lizard (sand)–scink, skink
lizard (serpent)–seps
lizard (small)–eft, gecko
lizard (spiny) – dab, dabb, dhabb
lizard (tropical American)– iguana
lizard (varanoid)–waran
lizard (wall)–gecko
lizard (winged)–dragon
lizard-like animal–eft, salamander
lizard-like mammal – salamander
llama (kind of)–alpaca
load – burden, charge, encumber, freight, lade, oppress, weight
load (small)–jag
loader of vessels–stevedore
loadstone (lodestone)–magnet, magnetite
loaf–idle, loiter, lounge
loafer–idler, lounger
loam (calcareous)–loess
loam (constituent of)–chalk, clay, lime
loam (India, rich black) – regur
loam (kind of)–rab
loam deposit–loess, silt
loam deposit (yellow brown) –loess
loan–borrow, lend

loan (Scot.)–provisions
loanin (Scot.)–lane
loathe – abhor, abominate, detest, dislike, hate
loathsome (more)–viler
lob–box, lugworm, pollack, stair, step, till, vein
lobby–enclosure, foyer, room
lobe–lappet
lobe (ear)–earlap
lobe (posterior of fly wing) –alula, alular
lobe (small)–lobule
lobe (wing of diptera)–alula
lobster (part of)–thorax
lobster claw – chela, chelae (pl.), nipper
lobster eggs–roe
lobster pot–creel, pot
lobster roe–coral
lobster tail (middle lobe of) –telson
lobster trap (floating)–corf, creel
local (not)–general
locale–place, scene, site
locality–habitat, place, position, situs, spot
locality (particular)–endemic
locate–discover, find, situate, spot
located–sited
locatio–leasing, letting
location – place, seat, site, situation, situs, ubiety
location (native)–habitat
locator (forest fire)–alidade
loch–bay, lake
lock – bolt, fastener, hasp, latch, tress
lock of hair–berger, curl, tress
lockjaw–tetanus, trismus
lockman–executioner
lock-stepper (slang)–convict
lockup (slang)–jail
locomotive (heavy)–mogul
locomotive (kind of)–electric, Mallet, mogul
locomotive cowcatcher–pilot
locomotive driver's shelter–cab
locomotive service car – tender
locomotor ataxia–tabes

locus–drug, locality, place, site
locust–cicad, cicada, cicala
locust bird–starling
locust plant–senna
locust tree–acacia, carob
lode–canal, course, deposit, drain, ledge, path, road, vein, waterway
lode cavity (small unfilled)– vug, vugg, vugh
lodestone–magnet, magnetite
lodge–cabin, encamp, hovel, hut, lie, quarter, reside, tent
lodge (soldier's)–billet
lodge doorkeeper–tiler
lodge for safekeeping – deposit
lodger–guest, roomer
lodging – abode, dwelling, habitation, quarters, room, roost
lodging house – dormitory, hotel, inn, tavern
loess–loam, silt
lof–praise
loftiness – eloquence, eminence
lofty–aerial, aerie, aery, Andean, Andesic, arrogant, dignified, elevated, eminent, haughty, majestic, proud, sublime, tall
lofty place–eminence, eyry, peak, pinnacle
lofty pointed summit–peak, pinnacle
log–diary, record
log (first piece out of)–slab
log (revolve a floating)–birl
log (split, with smooth face) –puncheon
log-handling implement – peavey, peavy, peevey, peevy
log noser–sniper
log of wood supporting a mine roof–nog
logrolling–birling
log section (from which shingles are sawed)–spalt
log-skidding implement – todes
log-turning machine–nigger

logarithm inventor–Napier
logarithmic unit–bel
loge–booth, box, stall
loggerhead–blockhead, turtle
logger's boot (felt) – pac, pack
loggia–gallery
logging sled – tode, travois, travoise
logic preposition assumed true–lemma
logic term–ferio, ferison
logical – reasonable, sane, sound, valid
logically consistent–coherent
logion (logia, pl.) – maxim, saying
logograph–anagram, rebus, riddle
Lohengrin heroine–Elsa
Lohengrin's wife–Elsa
loin (pork)–griskin
loiter–dally, dawdle, delay, lag, linger, saunter, tarry
loiterer – drone, idler, laggard, slug, sluggard
Loki's daughter–Hel, Hela
Loki's son–Nare
Loki's wife–Sigyn
loll – dangle, droop, hang, lounge, recline, sprawl
loma (Southwest U.S.)–hill
lombard (16th cent.)–cannon
lomboy (Java)–plum
lomilomi (Hawaiian)–massage, rub, shampoo
lomita (Southwest U.S.)–hill
London district – Alsatia, Soho
London hawker–coster
London porter (Lyon tearoom)–George, Georgina
London roisterer–mun
London stables (royal) – mews
London undertaker–bant
Londoner–Cockney
londres–cigar
lone–single, solitary, unmarried
Lone Star State–Texas
loneliness–dejection, depression, desolation, isolation, solitude

lonely – lonesome, lorn, secluded, sequestered, solitary, unfrequented
lonesome–solitary
long–aspire, lengthy, pine,
prolix, prolonged, pro-
tracted, tedious, thirst,
tiresome, wearisome,
yearn
long abusive speech–tirade
long ago (poetic)–yore
long and slender–reedy
long and uniform in width–
linear
long discourse–descant, philippic, screed, tirade
long drawn out–protracted
long drink (coll.)–swig
long for–aspire, covet, crave,
desire, hope, pine
long inlet–ria
long journey–odyssey, trek
long jump (Greek)–halmo
long life–longevity
long periods–eons
long spear–lance
long suffering–patient
long talk–rigmarole
long wandering–odyssey
long windedness – longilo-
quence
longer of limb and slenderer
–rangier
longing – craving, desire,
wistful
longing (slang)–yen
longshoreman–stevedore
loo (five card, highest
trump)–pam
look–con, gander, ken, pore,
pry, see, seem
look (arch.)–leer
look (furtive)–peep
look (quick)–scry
look (sly)–leer
look after–tend
look askance–leer, ogle
look at – examine, eye, regard, view
look closely–scan
look curiously–pry
look down upon with con-
tempt–despise
look for–expect, seek
look forward to–anticipate
look malignly–gloat, leer

look obliquely–skew
look of derision–fleer
look on with favor–smile
look slyly–leer, ogle, peer
look steadily–gaze
look sullen–lower
looked about in meddlesome
manner–snooped
looked for–sought
looking back–retrospective
looking over (about) – surveying, reconnoitering,
reconnoitring
lookout (ship's)–conner
looks – cons, ganders, kens,
peers, pores, pries, seeks,
seems, sees
looks like–resembles
looks with malignant satisfaction–gloats
loom – appear, auk, guillemot, implement, loon,
machine, puffin, recepta-
cle, tool, vessel, weaver
loom (heddles of)–caam
loom (lower levers of)–lam
loom bar–easer
loom frame–lathe
loom harness–leaf
loom heddle–caam
loom reed–sley
loop–ansa, bride, doubling,
folding, noose, terry
loop (close)–kink
loop (running)–noose
loop and thimble at sail's
corner–clew
loop for lace border–picot
loop for lifting–tab
loop for nap (weaving) –
terry
loop in lace–picot
loop in lariat–honda, hondo,
hondoo, hondou
loop of rope–becket, bight,
noose
loophole–eyelet, oilet, opening, meuse, muse
loose – free, immoral, insecure, lax, movable, re-
laxed, slack, unbound, unconfined, unconventional,
unlash, unleash, unstable,
wobbly
loose ends–dags, tagrags

loose gravel and stones of
earth's surface – erratice,
eratum
loose jointed – lanky, ramshackle, rickety
loose robe (woman's)–kimono, simar
loose shirt (India woolen)–
banian
loosely dressed–discinct
loosen–ease, free, pried, relax, slacken, undo
loosened – eased, freed, relaxed, slackened, undid
looseness–slack
loot–booty, pillage, plunder,
spoils, swag
looter–pillager
lop–cut, trim
lop off – bob, oche, prune,
snathe, sned
lopsided–alop, unbalanced
loquacious – chattering, garrulous, talkative
loquacious (is foolishly) –
prates
loquacity – garrulity, talkativeness
loquacity (excessive)–leresis
lord–aga, agha, earl, governor, Jehovah, Jesus Christ,
liege, marquis, master,
nobleman, peer, prince,
rule, ruler, Saviour, viscount
lord (feudal)–suzerain
lord (superior)–suzerain
lord (supreme)–tsar
lord's attendant (med.) –
thane
Lord's Prayer–Paternoster
lordly – arrogant, despotic,
domineering, masterful,
overbearing, tyrannical,
uppish
lore–advice, counsel, erudition, instruction, lear,
learning, wisdom
lorgnette – eyeglass, opera
glass
lorica–cuirass
lorikeet–parrot
loriot–oriole
loris–lemur
lorn–abandoned, bereft, desolate, forlorn, forsaken

loro–fish, parrot
lose – amit, forfeit, mislay, miss, perish
lose balance–trip
lose by neglect–forfeit
lose courage – despair, despond
lose freshness – fade, wilt, wither
lose luster–tarnish
lose spirit–despond
lose vigor–decline, fag, fail, flag, pine, sag, weaken
loss – damage, destruction, detriment, injury, privation, ruin
loss (having suffered)–reft
loss of commodities by shifting–ullage
loss of eyelashes or eyebrows –madarosis
loss of feeling–anaesthesia, anesthesia
loss of hair–alopecia
loss of memory–amnesia
loss of reason–amentia
loss of sense of smell–anosmia
loss of speech–alalia, aphasia
loss of voice–aphonia
loss of will power–abulia
lost–abandoned, abstracted, confused, defeated, dissipated, forfeited, gone, hidden, irreclaimable, lorn, mislaid, obscured, overthrown, preoccupied, reprobate, ruined, subverted
lost life fluid–bled
lost sap–bled
lost to view–perdu
lot – allotment, apportionment, chance, destiny, doom, fate, fortune, luck, much, plat, portion, share
lot (appointed)–fate
lotebush–buckthorn
lotion–ablution, linament, wash
lotion (obs.)–loture
Lot's father–Haran
Lot's grandson–Moabite
Lot's sister–Milcah
Lot's son–Moab
lots (divination by)–sortilege

lottery (kind of)–raffle
lottery prize–tern
lotus–chinquapin, nelumbo
lotus bird–jacana
lotus tree–sadr
loud – blatant, blustering, boisterous, clamorous, coarse, flashy, gaudy, noisy, obstreperous, showy, tumultuous, turbulent, vehement, vociferous, vulgar
loud-voiced person–stentor
louey–lieutenant
Louis Viaud (pen name)–Pierre Loti
Louise De La Ramee (pen name)–Ouida
Louisiana county–parish
Louisiana court decree–arret
Louisiana court of judgment arret
Louisiana patois–creole
Louisiana town–Begg
lounge–divan, loll, sofa
louse (immature)–nit
louse (plant)–aphis
louse (wood)–slater
lout–bumpkin, clod, lubber, oaf
lout (country)–bumpkin
loutish–awkward, boorish, clownish, rude
lovable–amiable, endearing
love – affection, charity, fancy, fondness, gra, like
love (full of)–amative
love (god of)–Amor, Ares, Bhaga, Cupid, Eros
love (goddess of)–Aphrodite, Athor, Freya, Freyja, Hathor, Venus
love (I, Latin)–amo
love (Irish)–gra
love (Italian)–amore
love (opposite of)–hate
love (parental)–storge
love (pert. to) – amatory, erotic
love (science of)–erotology
love (Scot.)–loe, loo
love affair–amour
love apple–tomato
lovebird–parrot
love deity–Cupid

love feast (Christian primitive)–agape
love intrigue–amour
love knot–amoret
love-making–amour
love of fine arts–virtu
love of woods and forests–nemophily
love poem–erotic
love potion–philter, philtre
love song–madrigal
love story–romance
love to excess–dote
love token–amoret
Lovelace heroine–Lucasta
loveliness–pulchritude
lovely – amiable, amorous, loving, tender
lover–amorist, beau, beaux (pl.), sweetheart
lover (ardent) – Don Juan, Romeo
lover (famous)–Romeo
lover (luxury)–Sybarite
lover of country–Arcadian
lover of Heloise–Abelard
lover of luxury–Sybarite
lovers' meeting place–tryst
lovers of cruelty–sadists
loving – amative, amatory, amorous, erotic
loving (comb. form)–phil, phile
loving cup (kind of)–tig, tyg
loving deeply–enamored
low–bas, base, deep, moo, neap
low (cow's)–moo
low (French)–bas
low dividing wall in Roman circus–spina
low green shrubs (genus of) –erica
low-lived–mean
low-necked–decollete
low note–ut
low-spirited–despondent
low tide–ebb, neap
low tufted plant–moss
lower–abase, base, bemean, degrade, demean, depress, descend, diminish, dip, frown, lessen, meaner, nether, reduce
lower (as a banner)–vail
lower (as a sail)–vail

lower back (pert. to)–lumbar

lower in value–debase, depreciate

lower world–erebus, hades, orcus

lowering – dark, frowning, gloomy, sullen, threatening

lowery–cloudy, gloomy, lowering

lowest–least

lowest class of animal life–ameba, amoeba

lowest deck–orlop

lowest member of pedestal–quadra

lowest point–bottom, nadir

lowest point in planet's orbit –perigee

lowest ranking peer–baron

lowing–bellowing, mugient

lowland–bottom, holm, spit

lowland (river)–bottom, flat

lowland (swampy Indian)–terai

lowly–humble, mean, meek, modest, unpretending

lowness of spirits–blues, megrim, migraine

loxia–wryneck

loxotic–distorted, slanting

loy–slick, spade

loyal – faithful, feal, leal, liege, stanch, staunch, true

loyal (Scot.)–leal

loyalist–patriot, Tory

loyalty–allegiance, constancy, devotion, faithfulness, fealty, homage

Loyolite–Jesuit

lozenge–jujube, pastil, pastille, tablet, troche

lozenge (medicated)–pastil

lubber–boor, churl, drone, gawk, landsman, lout

lubricate–oil

lucban–shaddock

luce–pike

lucent – bright, clear, shining, translucent, transparent

lucern–dog, lynx

lucerne (lucern) – alfalfa, lamp

lucet–pike

lucid–bright, clear, lucent, luminous, pellucid, resplendent, sane, shining, translucent

luck–cess, chance, fortuity, hap

luck (bad) – ambsace, cess, deuce

lucky – canny, fortunate, happy

lucky animal, person or thing–mascot

lucky token–amulet, charm, periapt

lucrative – fat, gainful, paying, productive, profitable, remunerative

lucre–gain, pelf, profit, riches

ludicrous–antic, burlesque, comic, droll, funny, laughable, risible

ludicrous change of speech–pathos

lug – box, carry, ear, hale, hug, tote

lug (to)–hale, haul, tote

lugubrious–doleful, mournful, sad

lugworm–arenicola, lob

luhinga–petticoat

lukewarm–tepid

lukewarm (to make)–tepefy

lumber (inferior)–saps

lumberman–sawyer

lumberman (who marks trees for felling)–scorer

lumberman's half boot–pac

lumberman's sled–tode, travois, travoise

luminary – illumination, light, star

luminous – bright, brilliant, illuminated, lucid, shining, transparent

luminous impression–phosphene

lummox – boor, bumpkin, bungler, lout, yahoo

lump–beat, blob, bulge, clot, cluster, hunk, lob, mass, nodule, protuberance, thresh, wad

lump (dial.)–gob

lump (large)–hunk

lump (small)–nodule

lump of butter (small)–pat

lump of clay–clag, clod

lump of metal–ingot, pig

lumpish–dull, heaviness, inertness, shapelessness, sluggish, stupid

lumpy – choppy, nodular, rough

lumpy jaw–actinomycosis

lunacy – craziness, derangement, insanity, madness, mania, moon

lunar–lunate, satellite

lunar deity–Selena, Selene

lunate bone–lunatum

lunatic – demoniac, insane, mad, moonstruck

lunch–collation

lunch (light)–snack

luncheon–bunch, hunk, repast, tiffin

lundyfoot–snuff

lung sound–rale

lunge–jab, namaycush, stab, thrust

lurch–joll, lunge

lure–allure, bait, decoy, entice, snare, tempt, trap

lurid – dismal, ghastly, gloomy, pale, wan

lurk – hide, skulk, slink, sneak

lurked (obs.)–loted

luscious–creamy, lascivious, rich, sweet, voluptuous, wanton

lush – flexible, intoxicated, limber, luxuriant, mellow, soft, succulent

lushy (slang)–drunk

lusk–idle, skulk

lusory–playful, sportive

lust–desire, passion, virility

luster (lustre) – distinction, gloss, iridescence, polish, sheen, shine, splendor

luster (bronze-like, iridescent)–schiller

luster (having true natural) –naif

luster (obs.)–cave

luster (to lose)–tarnish

lusterless–dead, mat

lustful–lecherous, lewd

lustrous – bright, illustrious,

nitid, orient, radiant, shining, transparent
lustrous (natural)–naif, nitid
lustrous mineral–spar
lute–cement, clay, ring
lute-like instrument – asor, bandore, pandore
Luxemburg measure–fuder
Luxemburg river–Moselle
luxuriant–fertile, lush, opulent, profuse, prolific, rich, teeming
luxuriate–bask
luxuriated–basked, reveled
luxury – elegance, extravagance, gratification, lechery, lust, pleasure, richness, sensuality, voluptuousness
luxury (lover of)–Sybarite
Luzon dialect (northern)–Itaves
Luzon mountain–Iba
Luzon native – Ata, Aeta, Atta

Luzon negrito – Ata, Aeta, Atta
Luzon savage – Ata, Aeta, Atta, Igorot, Igorote
Luzon tribe (Malay) – Aripas, Arupas
lyam–bloodhound, leash
lyard–gray, variegated
lyart–gray, variegated
Lycian city–Myra, Sardis
lydian–effeminate, soft, voluptuous
Lydian king–Croesus, Gyges
lye–lixivium
lye (pert. to)–lixivial
lying (habitual)–mendacity
lying across–transverse
lying at base of mountains–piedmont
lying near point of earth's axis–polar
lying on the back–supine
lying prone–supine
lying story–fudge
lyme–bloodhound, leash

lymphatic–plasmic
lymphatic (innermost coat of)–intima
lymphoid organ–tonsil
lymphoid tissues (masses of)–tonsils
lynx–caracal, lucern
Lyon tearoom porter (London)–George, Georgina
lyre – asor, cithara, harp, kithara
lyre (anc.)–asor
lyre (brilliant blue of the)–vega
lyre (five-stringed)–kissar
lyre (triangular)–trigon
lyre turtle–leatherback
lyric–melic, ode, odic
lyric ode–epode
lyric poem–melic
lyric poem (thirteen-line)–rondeau
lyric poet–odist
lyrical–epodic
lyrichord–harpsichord

M

macabre – eerie, eery, gruesome, weird
macaca–lemur, monkey
macan (Phil. Is.)–rice
Macao coin–avo (br.), pataca
Macao monetary unit–avo
macaw–ara, arara, maracan, parrot
Macbeth's title–Thane
Macbeth's victim–Duncan
maccaboy–snuff
mace–mallet, maul, staff
mace (royal) – scepter, sceptre
mace bearer–beadle
Macedonian people–Albanians, Bulgarians, Greeks, Serbians
macerate–soak, steep, ret
machar–field, plain
machete–bolo, fish
Machiavellian – crafty, cunning, deceitful, guileful

machila–hammock
machin–macaque
machinate – contrive, plan, plot
machination – conspiracy, plot, scheme
machine – auto, automaton, automobile, car, engine
machine (clay-tempering)–malaxator
machine (cloth-stretching)–tenter
machine (cotton-cleaning)–gin
machine (cotton-spinning)–mule
machine (electric current measuring)–meter, metre
machine (for charging with gas)–aerator
machine (for compressing bundles)–baler
machine (for cutting thin slices)–slicer

machine (for flying)–plane
machine (for glazing)–calender
machine (for maturing cloth)–ager
machine (for reducing to small pieces)–crusher
machine (for separating ore)–vanner
machine (for shaping rubber into seamless tubes)–extruder
machine (hay-spreading) – tedder
machine (hay-tying)–baler
machine (hoisting) – crane, davit, derrick, gin, lever, pry, pump, tongs
machine (hummeling) – awner
machine (military catapult)–onager
machine (mixing)–malaxator

machine (planing)–surfacer
machine (planting)–seeder
machine (reckoning)–calculator, tabulator
machine (road-making) –
bulldozer, grader
machine (self-propelling
hauling)–tractor
machine (shaping) – lathe,
shaper
machine (spinning)–jenny
machine (surgical)–scala
machine (textile-cleaning)–
stamper
machine (type of)–rand
machine (war)–ram
machine (weight-lifting) –
gin
machine (which imitates
movements of living crea-
tures)–automaton
machine gun – Gatling,
Hotchkiss, Maxim
machine gun (Eng. slang)–
chatterbox
machine gun place (hidden)
–nest
machine power (energy) –
input
machine tool–lathe
mackerel (chub)–tinker
mackerel (horse)–atule, tunny
mackerel bird – kittiwake,
wryneck
mackerel goose–phalarope
mackerel-like fish – bonito,
cero
mackerel net (seine-like) –
spiller
mackle–blur
mad–angry, crazy, dement-
ed, enraged, frantic, fre-
netic, furious, insane,
irate, rabid, vexed
Madagascar animal–tenrec
Madagascar animal (nocturnal)–aye-aye
Madagascar capital–Tananarive
Madagascar city–Antanana-
rivo (c.), Mojanga, Tama-
tave, Tananarive, Tana-
narivo
Madagascar lemur–aye-aye,
indri

Madagascar mammal – ten-
drac, tenrec
Madagascar palm (fiber) –
raffia
Madagascar tree (northern)
–antankarana
Madagascar tribe – Betsileo,
Betsimasaraka, Hovas,
Malagasy, Sakalava
Madagascar tribe (southern)
–Bara
Madagascar weight – gan-
tang
madam–hussy, mistress, senora
madcap – blood, hotspur,
reckless, wild
madden–craze, enrage, vex
madder (genus of)–rubia
madder (Indian)–al
madder family–Rubiaceae
made – artificial, built, constructed, created, invented, manufactured, pre-
pared, produced, ren-
dered
made a heavy rolling sound
–rumbled
made a rustling sound –
swished
made a scalloped edge –
pinked
made accurate–trued
made afraid – daunted,
frightened
made agent–deputed, depu-
tized
made arrangements –
planned
made asunder–riven
made believe–pretended
made blind–seeled
made callous–hardened
made clear–elucidated
made destitute–bereft
made ductile–tensiled
made fluid by heat–fusile
made foolishly ardent–infatuated
made friendly, hospitable –
socialized
made fun of–derided
made hard–steeled
made headway against –
stemmed
made light of–belittled

made liquid by heat–fusile
made lower–deepened, de-
pressed
made new version of – re-
vised
made obdurate–steeled
made of certain cereal–oaten
made of certain wood – ce-
darn
made of clay–pictile
made of dissimilar compo-
nents–mixed
made of flax–linen
made of grain–cereal
made of silver–argent
made of three parts–threefold
made otherwise–altered
made over – reformed, re-
made, remodeled, re-
vamped
made plain–evidenced
made poor–beggared
made possible–enabled
made public–aired, delated
made ready – geared, pre-
pared
made rigid (as muscles) –
tensed
made sound of sheep–bleat-
ed
made speeches (humorous)–
orated
made strong–steeled
made trim–perked
made uniform–evened
made up–artificial
made up of–consists
made up of distinct parts–
composite
made up one's mind–decid-
ed
made use of–applied
made valid–authenticated
made wealthy–enriched
made whole again–redinte-
grated
Madeira Island wind (sirocco dry, hot)–leste
Madeira wine–bual, malm-
sey, sercial, tinta, tinto,
verdelho
madhouse–asylum
madid–moist, wet
madman – lunatic, maniac,
phrenetic

madness – insanity, lunacy, mania

Madras hemp–sunn

Madras measure – cawney, cawny, manei, mercal, ollock, olluck, para, parah, parrah, puddee

Madras seaport–Calicut

Madras town (India)–Arcot

Madras weight–cash, chinnam, fanam, mangelin, pagoda, pollam, powe, seer, ser, varahan

madrepore–coral

Madrid boulevard–prado

madrigal–lyric, poem

maduro–cigar

Maecenas–patron

maelstrom–whirlpool

maestro–composer, conductor, master, teacher

maestro-di-cappella – choirmaster, kapellmeister

maffle – confuse, muddle, squander

maffler–mumbler

mafflin–simpleton

mafoi–indeed

mafoo (mafu)–groom

mag–chat, chatter, chatterbox, halfpenny, magneto, magpie, titmouse

magadis–flute, monochord

magas–monochord

magazine–depot, ephemeris, periodical, repository, reservoir, storehouse, warehouse

magazine (Fr.)–shop, store

magazine rifle–Mauser

mage – conjurer, magician, magus

magg–steal

maggot – caprice, gentle, grub, larva, mathe, mawk, notion

magi (three wise men) – Balthasar, Gaspar, Melchior

magic–art, conjuration, enchantment, fairy, necromancy, rune, sorcery

magic (act of)–conjuration

magic (goddess of) – Circe, Hecate

magic (white)–turgy

magic art (effect of) – conjured

magic ejaculation – om, selah, sesame, shelah, um

magic lantern–stereopticon

Magic Mountain author – Mann

magic staff (Greek myth.)–caduceus

magic symbol–caract, charm

magic tree–polemoniaceae

magic wand (Greek myth.) –caduceus

magic word–om, selah, sesame, shelah, um

magical – charming, goetic, goety

magician – charlatan, conjurer, enchanter, juggler, mage, magi, magus, mandrake, necromancer, prestidigitator, sorcerer, thaumaturge, wizard

magician (Eng., famous) – Merlin

magician (great)–archimage

magician (of Camelot) – Merlin

magician's assistant – famulus

magician's command–presto

magician's period of retirement to gain control over jinn–chille

magician's running talk – patter

magirics–cookery

magirist–cook

magisterial – arrogant, august, authoritative, dictatorial, dignified, dogmatic, domineering, haughty, imperious, lofty, lordly, overbearing, proud, stately

magistrate – alcade, alcaid, alcaide, alcalde, bailie, edile, judge, syndic

magistrate (Athens, anc.)–archon

magistrate (chief)–doge

magistrate (former)–doge

magistrate's orders (Roman) –acta

magma–dregs, sediment

magma basalt–limburgite

magnanimity (with)–nobly

magnanimous–disinterested, exalted, free, generous, high-minded, honorable, liberal, lofty, noble, unselfish, unstinted

magnate–grandee, lord, millionaire, mogul, noble, rich man

magnate (industrial)–tycoon

magnate (Turkish Pasha) – bashaw

magnesian limestone – dolomite

magnesium (symbol for) – Mg

magnesium silicate–talc

magnesium sulphate – loweite

magnet – loadstone, lodestone

magnet (electric)–solenoid

magnet (spherical) – terella, terrella

magnet pole–red

magnetic–electrical

magnetic flux unit–weber

magnetism (personal) – oomph

magnetized–attract, lure

magnificence – glory, grandeur, splendor

magnificent – grand, lavish, munificent, palatial, regal, splendid, sublime, sumptuous

magnificent display–pomp

magnify–exalt, extol, glorify, increase, laud, overstate, praise

magnitude–bigness, extent, greatness, size

magnitude (three-dimensional)–solid

magnum–bottle

magnum opus–achievement, work

magot–ape, figure

magpie – chatterer, daw, madge, mag, pica, pie, piet, scold

magpie diver–smew

magpie shrike–tanager

magsman–swindler

maguari–stork

magus–magician

Magyar–Hungarian
maha–deer
mahajan–moneylender
mahal – apartments, residence
mahala–squaw
mahogany (India)–toon
mahogany (mottled appearance in)–roe
mahogany (New Zealand)–totara
mahogany (streak in)–roe
mahogany burls–roe
mahogany pine–totara
maholi–lemur
Mahomet–Mohammedan
Mahomet's birthplace–Mecca
Mahomet's flight from Mecca–hegira
Mahomet's son–Ali
Mahomet's son-in-law–Ali
Mahomet's successor–Calif
Mahomet's successor (fourth)–Ali
Mahometan–Islamite, Mussulman (see also Mohammedan)
Mahometan (non)–Kafir
Mahometan Bible–Koran
Mahometan caravansary (pilgrim's)–imaret
Mahometan chief–datto
Mahometan chief (of the jinn)–eblis
Mahometan college (hierarchy)–Ulema
Mahometan dervish–sadite
Mahometan divorce–talak
Mahometan Easter–Eed
Mahometan faith teaching–imam
Mahometan fast days–Ramadan
Mahometan festival–Bairam
Mahometan governor – ameer, amir, emeer, emir
Mahometan minister of state –vizier
Mahometan months – see Mohammedan months
Mahometan power (organizer of)–Omar
Mahometan priests–imams, imans, wahabis

Mahometan prince – ameer, amir, emeer, emir
Mahometan ruler – ameer, amir, emeer, emir
Mahometan spirit–genie
Mahometan student–softa
Mahound – devil, Mohammed
mahout–driver, keeper
mahu–devil
Maia's son–Hermes
maid–girl, maiden, servant, virgin, woman
maid (lady's)–Abigail, tire-woman
Maid of Athens – Theresa Macri
maiden–virgin
maiden changed into heifer –Io
maiden changed to spider–Arachne
maiden duck–shoveler
maidenhair–adiantum
maidenhair tree–ginkgo
maidenhair tree family – ginkgoaceae
maiden lip–stickseed
maidenly – gentle, modest, virgin
maigre (the)–bar
mail–armor, post
mail (coat of)–armor, brinie, brunie, byrnie
mail (improperly addressed) –nix
mail boat–packet
maim – mangle, mayhem, mutilate
main–chief, first, foremost, leading, ocean, prime, principal, sea
main act of a drama–epitasis
main beam–girder, walking
main gauche–dagger
mainland–continent
main part–body
main part of a play–epitasis
main pin–kingbolt
main point – crux, gist, jet, pith
main post–sternpost
mainsheet–rope
main substance–gist
Maine capital–Augusta

Maine city–Bangor, Hiram, Orono, Saco, Skowhegan
Maine Coast Bay–Casco
Maine lake–Sebago
Maine mountain–Kineo
Maine promontory–Kineo
Maine river–Saco
Maine university (seat of)–Orono
mainferre–armor, gauntlet
maintain – assert, claim, defend, hold, keep, retain, sustain
maintain (as true)–avouch
maintained (capable of being)–tenable
maintenance–alimony, defense, livelihood, support, sustenance, upkeep
maintenance for separate support–alimony
maison–house
maison de sante – asylum, hospital, sanatorium
maize–corn
maize (genus of)–zea
maize (Indian)–corn
maja (Span.)–belle
majagua (Hawaiian)–hau
majestic–dignified, elevated, grand, imperial, kingly, lofty, magnificent, noble, regal, royal, splendid, stately, sublime
major–dur, officer
major (music)–ditone, dur
major-domo – bailiff, seneschal, steward
majority–age, greater, most, quorum
make – compel, contrive, create, form, generate, induce, manufacture, produce, render, shape
make a countercharge – recriminate
make a mess of–pie
make accordant–attune
make active–energise, energize
make alcohol undrinkable–denature
make allusion to–mention
make amends–atone, redress
make amends for–atone, redeem

make an address–speak
make anew–recreate
make arrangements–plan
make bare–balden, denude, strip
make believe–feign, pretend, pretense, sham
make beloved–endear
make better–improve, meliorate
make brief note–jot
make buoyant–levitate
make calm – allay, appease, compose, quiet, serene
make certain–assure, ensure
make cheerful–solace
make choice–choose, opt, select
make clean breast – confess, disclose
make clear–elucidate
make content–satisfy
make correct–straighten
make deduction from–rebate
make defenseless – unarm, unarmor
make desolate (with loneliness)–bereave
make destitute–bereave
make different–alter, change
make diminutive–bantamize
make do–eke, improvise
make eccentric–decenter
make edging–tat
make effective–enforce
make enduring–anneal
make equal–equate
make ethereal–aerate
make even – balance, level, slick, square
make evident–evince
make false pretense–sham
make familiar by use–accustom
make fast – belay, secure, snub
make fast (naut.) – batten, belay
make firm – brace, cement, fix
make fit–adapt
make foolish–stultify
make forceful–energize
make full again–refill
make fun of–rib, ridicule, scoff

make glass into sheets–platten
make glossy–sleek
make god of–deify
make good–vindicate
make happy–beatify, felicific
make hard–freeze, steel
make harmonious–attune
make headway – advance, progress
make headway against–stem
make holy–bless
make honorable–ennoble
make ill–ail
make insane – dement, demonize
make insensible to pain – anaesthetic
make into coin–mint
make into law–enact, legislate
make into leather–tan, taw
make into parcel–packet
make known–disclose, discover, divulge, impart, proclaim, reveal, uncover
make known to people in general–publish
make lace–tat, tatt (var.)
make less dense–rarefy, thin
make level–true
make light–illume, jetsam, jettison
make lively–energize
make loud noise (expressing joy)–chortle
make love–coo, court, woo
make lusterless (as paint)–flatten
make merry–disport, laugh
make milder–melt, mitigate, modulate
make moral–ethicize
make more tolerant–liberalized
make muddy by stirring – roil
make multiform–diversify
make neat–groom, tidy
make necessary–entail
make notes–annotate
make of no effect – annul, void
make out–analyze, decode, discern

make out meaning of–decipher, decode, solve
make over–redo, refashion, revamp
make pale–chalk
make pleasing–sweeten
make poetry–poesy
make poignant–sauce
make possible–enable
make precious–endear
make preparation–plan
make prize of–capture
make progress–advance, gain
make public–delate, divulgate, publish
make quiet–allay, soothe
make ready – coach, gear, prepare, prime
make reparation–atone
make requital–repay
make resistance–rebel
make return to–requite
make right–straighten
make rosy (suddenly)–flush
make secure–batten, belay, fasten, fix, nail, pin, snub
make shrill noise–stridulate
make smart–perks
make smooth – buff, iron, scrape, slick
make soggy–sop
make sore–lame
make spiritless–mope
make spruce–smarten
make stiff–bone, lame
make suit to–court
make suitable–adapt
make supremely happy – beatify
make tardy–belate, laten
make thin–attenuate
make three-cornered – triangulate
make trim–perks
make unhappy–embitter
make uniform–unify
make up – build, complete, compose, construct, cosmetic, prepare
make up for–atone, compensate
make-up of a book–format
make-up of an organization –anatomy
make-up of publication–format

make use of–apply, utilize
make use of instrumentally
 –employ
make waste (law)–estrepe
make water–leak, urinate
make watertight–calk, seal
make well–cure, heal
make white–blanch
make whole again–redinte-
 grate
make wine–vint
make worse–aggravate
Maker–Creator
maker (arrow)–fletcher
maker (barrel)–cooper
maker (bundle)–baler
maker (knife)–cutler
maker of earthen vessels –
 potter
maker of pottery–ceramist
makes an infusion–steeps
makes headway against –
 stems
makes more comprehensive
 –widens
maki–lemur
Malabar bark–ochna
Malabar coast canoe–tonee
Malabar palm–talipot
Malacca measure–asta, jum-
 ba
Malacca weight – kip, tam-
 pang
malachite color–bice
maladive – sick, sickly, unhealthy
maladroit – awkward, bun-
 gling, clumsy, unhandy
maladventure – escapade,
 mishap
malady – ailment, disease,
 disorder, illness, sickness
malady (nervous, desire to
 kill)–amok
Malagasy lemur–aye-aye
malagma–plaster, poultice
malanders–eczema
malanga–taro
malaria–miasm, miasma
malarial fever–agie, ague
malarial poison–miasma
Malay and Thailand isthmus
 –Kra
Malay ape–lar
Malay Archipelago island –
 Bali, Borneo

Malay article of apparel–sa-
 rong
Malay buffalo–carabao
Malay buffalo (wild)–sela-
 dang
Malay canoe–prahu, proa
Malay coin (tin or pewter)–
 tra, trah
Malay dagger–creese, crise,
 kreese, kris
Malay disease–amok, amuck
Malay disease (neurotic,
 nervous)–lata, latah
Malay dress–sarong
Malay garment–sarong
Malay gibbon–lar
Malay island–Java
Malay jacket (short)–baju
Malay jumping disease–lata,
 latah
Malay knife – creese, crise,
 kreese, kris
Malay knife (large)–parang
Malay Luzon race – Tagal,
 Tagalog
Malay malady (desire to kill)
 –amok
Malay mammal (deer-like)–
 chevrotain
Malay natives (seafaring) –
 bajau
Malay neurotic disease–lata,
 latah
Malay orangutan–mias
Malay ox (wild)–banteng
Malay palm (feather)–areng,
 arenga, ejoo, gomuti
Malay parrot – lory, lories
 (pl.)
Malay peninsula coin – tra,
 trah
Malay peninsula state – Jo-
 hore
Malay peninsula town (sea-
 coast)–Malacca
Malay pirates–bajau
Malay race (one of)–Bisayan,
 Tagal, Tagalog, Visayan
Malay state–Perak
Malay title of respect–tuan
Malay tree–durian, durion,
 niepa, upas
Malay tree (fiber)–terap
Malay tribe–Aripas
Malay vessel – praam, pra-
 ham, prahu, proa

Malay weight–tael
Malay wild ox–banteng
Malayo-Polynesian language
 –Tagalog
malconduct - maladminis-
 tration
malconformation - dispro-
 portionate, imperfect
malcontent–agitator, discontented, rebellious, uneasy
male–mas
male (gelded)–galt
male (various) - bull, jack,
 rooster, stallion, stud, tom
male being (hundred-eyed)–
 Argus
male bird–rooster, tom
male bovine–bull
male elephant–bull
male falcon–tercel
male figure (used as supporting column)–Atlantes
male figure supporting column–Telamon
male hawk–tercel
male horse–stallion, stud
male mule–jack
male name – see masculine
 name
male of falcon–tercel
male plant–mas
malediction - anathema,
 curse, denunciation, im-
 precation, slander
malefaction–crime, offense
malefactor–criminal, culprit,
 evildoer, felon
malevolence–animosity, bitterness, malignity, pique,
 spite
malevolent–evil, ill-disposed,
 rancorous, spiteful
malfeasant–criminal
malheur–misfortune
malice–animosity, bitterness,
 maliciousness, malignity,
 malevolence, pique, ran-
 cor, spite
malicious–bitter, evil, ill-disposed, rancorous, resentful, sinister, spiteful, unpropitious
malicious destruction of
 property–sabotage
malicious intention–animus
malign – abuse, asperse, ca-

lumniate, evil, libel, slander, virulent

malign monster (myth.) – harpy

malignancy – noxiousness, virulence

malignant–deleterious, evil, felon, felonious, invidious, malicious, poisonous, rebellious, vicious

malignity–hate, heinousness, spite, venom

malikana – duty, fee, payment

maline–net

malkin–cat, drab, hare, mop, scarecrow, slattern, sponge

mall–mallet, walk

mallangong–duckbill

malleable–ductile, soft

mallemuck – albatross, fulmar, petrel

mallet–mace, maul

mallet (chairman's)–gavel

mallet (hatter's)–beater

mallet (heavy wooden) – beetle

mallet (judicial)–gavel

mallet (leaden, covered with woolen cloth)–madge

mallet (paver's)–tup

mallet (presiding officer's)–gavel

mallet (small)–gavel

mallet (wooden) – beetle, mall, maul

mallow–althaea, hock, maw

malm–limestone

malodorous–fetid, noisome, rank

malt (ground used for brewing)–grist

malt froth–barm

malt infusion–wort

malt liquor–brew

malt vinegar (Eng. dial.)–alegar

malt worm–tippler, toper

Malta capital–Valetta

Malta coin–grain (br.)

Malta measure–caffiso, canna, salm, salma

Malta weight – artal, artel, kantar, parto, ratel, rotl, salm, salma

malted wheat beverage – zythem

maltreat–abuse, misuse

malty (slang)–drunk

mammal (arboreal nocturnal)–lemur

mammal (American)–paca

mammal (American marsupial)–opossum

mammal (amphibious)–otter

mammal (aquatic)–dugong, manatee, seal, whale

mammal (aquatic extinct)–rytina

mammal (aquatic herbivorous)–dugong, manatee

mammal (aquatic musteline)–otter

mammal (Asia, deer-like)–chevrotain

mammal (Australian)–kangaroo, koala, tait

mammal (badger-like musteline)–ratel

mammal (bovine)–zebu

mammal (burrowing) – armadillo, badger

mammal (carnivorous)–lion, panda, weasel

mammal (cat-like) – mongoose, ocelot

mammal (cetacean) – dolphin, whale

mammal (desert)–camel

mammal (fish-eating)–otter

mammal (giraffe-like)–okapi

mammal (gnawing)–mouse, rat

mammal (herbivorous) – daman

mammal (highest order of) –primate

mammal (huge)–elephant

mammal (Indian)–zebu

mammal (insectivorous) – bat, tendrac, tenrec

mammal (large)–moose

mammal (large marine) – walrus

mammal (large tropical) – rhino

mammal (Latin) – homo, homines (pl.)

mammal (lemurine)–potto

mammal (long-tongued toothless)–anteater

mammal (lowest order of)–marsupial, marsupialia

mammal (Malay deer-like)–chevrotain

mammal (marine) – seal, walrus, whale

mammal (marine tusked)–walrus

mammal (marsupial, American)–opossum

mammal (mole-like, aquatic)–desman

mammal (musteline)–otter, ratel

mammal (nocturnal) – bat, lemur, ratel, tapir

mammal (nocturnal plantigrade)–raccoon

mammal (northern horned) –reindeer

mammal (ocean)–whale

mammal (omnivorous) – hog, pig, swine

mammal (order of)–edentata

mammal (order of aquatic) –cetacea

mammal (order of gnawing)–rodentia

mammal (order of marine) –cetacea, cete

mammal (Palestine)–daman

mammal (pig-like)–peccary

mammal (ruminant)–alpaca, antelope, bull, camel, cow, deer, llama, sheep

mammal (sea)–seal, whale

mammal (small)–mouse, rat

mammal (small Asia)–panda

mammal (South American) –ai, coati, tapir

mammal (water)–otter

mammal (whose hands differ from feet)–bimana

mammal (worm-eating) – mole

mammal's coat–pelage

mammock – break, scrap, tear

mammoth (genus of extinct)–Dinotherium

man – adult, human, male, mankind, person

man (big, important)–mugwump

man (brass)–Talos

man (brave)–hero

man (brutal, lawless)–ruffian

man (castrated)–spado

man (confirmed to bachelorhood)–celibate

man (cruel)–ogre, ruffian

man (eccentric, old)–codger

man (elderly)–grandfather, grandpa, grandpop, sire

man (end of minstrel show) –bones

man (entire)–ego

man (fabulously rich)–Midas, plutocrat

man (fashionable, about town)–Corinthian

man (hardheaded)–boche

man (important)–nabob

man (iron)–Talus

man (ladies')–beau, beaux (pl.)

man (Latin for)–homo

man (lawless, brutal)–ruffian

man (learned) – pundit, savant, scholar

man (legendary, strong) – Atlas

man (literary)–philologist, scholar

man (lowbred, surly)–churl

man (medicine)–shaman

man (newspaper) – editor, journalist, reporter

man (of all work)–factotum

man (of buffoonery) – mountebank

man (of letters) – erudite, literatus

man (of trickery)–mountebank

man (old) – grandfather, grandpa, grandpop, uncle

man (old clothes)–poco

man (powerful business) – tycoon

man (powerful voiced) – stentor

man (red)–Indian, Ute

man (rich) – capitalist, Midas, nabob, plutocrat

man (rural, aged)–gaffer

man (ultrafashionable) – dandy, dude, fop

man (undercover) – detective, investigator, spy

man (very old)–patriarch

man (very rich) – Croesus, Midas, millionaire, millionnaire

man (wise, old)–nestor

man fungus–earthstar

man-like – android, androides, anthropoid

man of all work–mozo

Man of Destiny–Napoleon Bonaparte

Man of Galilee–Jesus Christ

man of God – ecclesiastic, saint

man of law–attorney, barrister, counsel, lawyer

man of learning–pundit, savant, scholar

man of letters–author, litterateur, scholar

man of motley–fool

Man of Ross–Kyrle

Man of Sorrow–Jesus Christ

man of the woods–orangutan

man of the world–cosmopolite, layman

man of war–frigate, soldier, warrior

man of war's lowest deck–orlop

manservant – garcon, gilly, mozo, syce, valet

man with three wretched comforters–Job

man's fate (goddess of)–Ker

man's name – see masculine name

manacles–fetters, hampers, handcuffs, irons, shackles

manada–drove, flock, herd

manage–boss, contrive, control, dight, direct, engineer, head, lead, man, manipulate, operate, rule, run, wield

manage (with frugality) – husband

manage culinary affairs – cater

manageable–compliant, controllable, docile, ductile,

easy, governable, tame, tractable, wieldy, yare

managed–ran

managed (easily)–docile

management–care, charge, conduct, control, direction, government

management (arch.)–gestion

management (household) – menage

manager – boss, director, entrepreneur, governor, grieve, leader, operator, overseer, steward

manager (business) – entrepreneur

manager (good)–economist

managery – administration, artifice, cunning, frugality, husbandry, management, managership

manas (Hindu)–mind

Manchurian city – Kirin, Mukden, Niuchwang

Manchurian river–Liao

manciple–purveyor, servant, slave, steward

manco–calamanco

mandarin's residence (official)–yamen

mandarin's wife–mandariness

mandate – behest, bidding, charge, command, decree, direction, injunction, order, precept

mandate (sealed)–writ

mandatory–obligatory, preceptive

mandible – beak, chelicera, jaw

mandible part–molar

Mandingan Negroes–Veis

mandrel – arbor, axle, hob, spindle

mandrel (miner's)–pick

mane–hair, juba

manege – academy, school (for horses)

maneuver – artifice, jockey, manipulate

maneuver (aerial)–loop

maneuver (aviation) – Immelmann

maneuver (military)–tactic

maneuver (shrewd)–stratagem

maneuvers (army slang) – G.I. war

maneuvers (skilful)–tactics

manful–brave, courageous, male, noble, resolute

mang–bewildered, frenzied

manga–poncho

mange – eat, fodder, itch, meal

mange (sheep)–scab

manger–banquet, bin, crib, meal, trough

mangle – bruise, calender, cut, hack, ironer, lacerate, mutilate

mango bird–hummingbird, oriole

mango clump–tope

mango fish–threadfin

mango grove–tope

mango tree–tope

mangy – ronion, ronyon, scurvy

manhandle–maul

mania–craze, delirium, frenzy, furor, madness, passion

mania (var.)–furore

manifest–clear, declare, disclose, discover, evident, evince, express, index, indisputable, indubitable, obvious, open, overt, patent, show, unmistakable, visible

manifest (outwardly)–overt

manifest a specified quality–savor

manifest one's self–show

manifest unlikeness – contrast

manifestation – demonstration, disclosure, display, exhibition, phase, revelation

manifestation (with incarnation of Vishnu)–avatar

manifestation of deity Apis–serapis

manifestation of god of lower world–serapis

manifested–demonstrated

manifesting veneration–reverent

manifesto – demonstration, evidence

manikin – dwarf, model, phantom, pygmy

Manila hemp–abaca

Manila hemp plant–abaca, abaka

Manila nut–peanut

manioc–cassava

maniple–handful

manipulate–control, handle, manage, operate, treat, wield, work

manipulate (by deceptive means)–rig

Manitoba Indian–Cree

mankind–Adam

mankind (division of)–race

mankind (hater of)–misanthrope

mankind (pertaining to division of)–racial

manlike–male, manly, mannish, masculine

manly–bold, brave, daring, hardy, noble, resolute, undaunted

manner–air, aspect, fashion, guise, method, mien, mode, trick, way

manner (frenzied) – amok, amuck

manner (meditative) – contemplative

manner (rough, short) – brusque

manner (violent, frenzied)–amuck

manner in which wings are placed–alation

manner of making anything –facture

manner of pronouncing–accent

manner of speaking–grammar

manner of striking a baseball–bunt

mannerism–affectation

mannerly–decorous, moral, nice, politely, seemly

manners (obs.)–lates

manners (pleasant)–amenities

Mannheim gold–brass

mano–hand

manoc–chicken, fowl, rooster

manor–abode, hall, house, mansion

manor house–hall

manor land–demesne

manred–homage, vassalage

manta–blanket, cloak, cloth, wrap

manteel–cape, cloak, mantle

mantegar–ape

mantilla–cape, cloak

mantis–cagn

mantis crab–squilla

mantle–cape, cloak, cope, kittel, robe

mantle (incandescent)–filament

mantle (Jewish burial)–kittel

mantle (priest's)–cope

mantle (woman's long)–capote

manto–cloak, gown, mantle, mantua

mantoid–mantis

mantua–gown, manto, overdress

Mantuan bard–Vergil

Mantuan muse–Vergil

Mantuan swan–Vergil

Manu laws–sutra, sutta

manual–book, clavier, handbook

manual (early Christian)–didache

manual (music)–clavier

manual digit–thumb

manual training system – sloid, slojd, sloyd

manufacture–fabricate, invent, make, produce

manufacturer of liquors–abkari

manumea–toothbill

manumission–freeing, liberation

manumit–free, liberate, release

manurance–control, cultivation, occupation, tenure, tillage, training

manuscript–codex, composition, document, handwriting, writing

manuscript (abbr.)–MS

manuscript (anc.)–codex
manuscript blank space–lacuna
manuscript copier–scribe
manuscript mark (old)–obelus, obeli (pl.)
manuscripts (unpublished)–inedita
many–manifold, multiplied, numerous, various
many (prefix)–poly
many times–often, frequently
mao–peacock
Maori charm (grotesque greenstone)–heitiki
Maori clan–Ati, Hapu
Maori club–patu
Maori club (war)–mere
Maori dance (native posture)–haka
Maori hen–weka
Maori hero–Maui
Maori oven–umu
Maori parson bird–poe, tue, tui
Maori priest–tuhunga
Maori root stock–roi
Maori tree (fuel)–mapau
Maori tribe–Ati, Hapu
Maori war club–mere
Maori weapon (club-like) – patu
map–carte, chart, delineate, design, diagram, embodiment, epitome, explore, image, picture, plat, representation, sketch, survey
map (line of weather)–isobar
map maker – cartographer, charter
map making method (originator of)–Mercator
maple bowl (large drinking)–mazer
maple cup (large drinking)–mazer
maple family–aceraceae
maple genus–acer
maple scale–pulvinaria
maple seed–samara
maple sugar sap (boiled down for transporting)–humbo
maple sugar spout–spile

maple tree (air hole in)–spile hole
maple tree (genus of)–acer
maple-like trees (genus of)–rulac
mar – damage, deface, impair, scar, spoil
marabou–argala, marabout, stork
maranatha–curse
maranon–cashew
marasca–cherry
maraschinos–cherries
marasmus–emaciation, waste
maraud – pillage, plunder, plundering, raid, rove
marble–agate, basalt, cold, dolomite, hard, mig, taw
marble (Belgian, dark red)–rance
marble (Catalonia)–brocatel, brocatelle
marble (choice playing) – alley, taw
marble (dial.)–mib
marble (dull yellow)–brocatel, brocatelle
marble (large colored)–alley
marble (Roman, light colored)–cipolin
marble block (disfiguring place in)–terras
marble-breasted–unfeeling
marble cork wood – tambookie
Marble Faun character–Hilda
marble flower–poppy
marblehead–fulmar
marblehearted – cold, hardhearted
marble slab (decorative) – dalle
marble slab (Fr.)–dalle
marbler–carver, sculptor
marbles (game of)–taw
marbly–cold, rigid
marc–refuse, residue
marcantant–merchant
marcato–accented, emphatic
march – border, boundary, frontier, parade, procession, smallage, trek
march (horsemen's formal)–cavalcade
march (spirited)–quickstep

march in review–parade
March King–Sousa
marched off (in a line)–defiled
marched on–trooped
marching cry–hep
marchland – borderland, frontier
marcid–decayed, emaciating, exhausted, tabetic, weak, withered
marcobrunner–wine
marcor–decay, maramus
Mardi Gras king–Rex
mare–jade, meare, yad, yade, yaud
mare (young)–filly
mare's tail–cirrus
marge – border, edge, margin, shore
margeline–chickweed, pimpernel
margent–border, bordering, brink, edge, margin, marginal
margin–border, brim, brink, edge, rand, rim, side
margin (having notched)–erose
margin (having scalloped edge)–crenate
margin (to straighten)–align
marginal note–annotation, apostil, scholium
marigold–boots, caper, cowslip
marigold (genus of)–tagetes
marigold (marsh) – boots, caper, cowslip
marijuana (coll.)–hay
marijuana cigarette (slang)–reefer
marikina–tamarin
marina–basin, dock, esplanade, promenade
marinade–brine, marinate, pickle
marinal – marine, mariner, nautical, sailor, saline
marine – maritime, naval, oceanic, pelagic
marine (American)–leatherneck, tar
marine (Eng. sailor slang)–jolly

marine animal–jellyfish, orc, polyp

marine animal (genus of)–otaria

marine animal (minute) – coral

marine calcerous skeleton–coral

marine crustacean–barnacle

marine fish–menhaden

marine gastropods (genus of)–conus, murex, terebra

marine growth–seaweed

marine individuals (collectively)–merpeople

marine plant–enalid

marine whale food–brit

mariner–gob, Jacky, sailor, seaman, tar, waterman

mariner's card–chart

mariner's compass points–rhumbs

marionette–puppet

maritime–marine, nautical, naval

marjoram–mint, origan

mark–betoken, brand, denote, identify, impress, imprint, insigne, insignia (pl.), label, line, note, rist, score, stamp, target

mark (aimed at in games)–target, tee

mark (black)–demerit

mark (critical)–obclus

mark (curved)–breve

mark (diacritical)–tilde

mark (distinctive) – badge, cachet

mark (distinguishing)–earmark

mark (fingerprint)–whorl

mark (for identification) – earmark

mark (for omission)–dele

mark (identifying) – earmark

mark (in archery)–target

mark (in curling)–tee

mark (minute)–dot

mark (misconduct)–demerit

mark (of disgrace)–stigma

mark (over vowels)–macron

mark (poor)–demerit

mark (printer's)–caret, dagger, diesis, obelisk

mark (proofreading)–caret, dele

mark (punctuation)–colon, comma, dash, diaeresis, dieresis, period, semicolon

mark (significant)–dot

mark again–restamp

mark by bounds–demarcate

mark denoting "C" pronounced "S"–cedilla

mark denoting long vowel–macron

mark denoting short vowel–breve

mark down–lower

mark in music–slur

mark indelibly–brand

mark of blow–dent, weal, welt

mark of disgrace–stigma

mark of nothing–zero

mark of omission–apostrophe, caret

mark of punctuation–colon, comma, dash, diaeresis, dieresis, period, semicolon

mark of wound–scab, scar

mark on card–pip

mark out–cancel, obliterate

mark out boundaries of–delimit

mark to be equaled–bogey, bogie

mark to restore after deleting–stet

Mark Twain character – Huckleberry Finn, Tom Sawyer, Sellers

Mark Twain's name–Samuel Langhorne Clemens

mark with dots–stipple

mark with figure of cross bars–grill

mark with pointed instrument–scrive

mark with printed design–stamp

mark with ridges–rib

mark with seams–enseam

mark with spots–dapple

marked–designated, distinguished, emphasized, scarred

marked by abrasions–scarred

marked by characteristics (anc.)–primitive

marked by dispute–controversial

marked by maneuvering – tactical

marked by nicety–elegant

marked by two stars–bistellar

marked into small areas – areolated

marked time–dated

marked with colors–variegated

marked with depressions in skin–dimpled

marked with grooves (parallel)–lirate

marked with irregular furrows–rivose

marked with lines – linear, ruled

marked with lines (bot.)–notate

marked with spots–mottled

marked with spots (bot.)–notate

marked with stripes–lineate

marked with zones–zonate

marker – brander, counter, marksman, monitor, recorder, scorer

marker (airplane course) – pylon

marker (air race)–pylon

marker (floating)–buoy

market–mart, rialto, sale

market (sell as bonds)–float

market place–agora, bazaar, emporium, plaza, rialto

market place (Greek)–agora

market place (Oriental)–bazaar

marketable–salable, staple, vendible

markhor–goat

marking (crescent-shaped)–lunula

markings (skin on wrist)–rasceta

marks (boundary)–meres

marks (to restore after deleting)–stets

marks of respect (public)–ovation

marks on skin made by whip
–wales

marks representing signa-
tures–signa

marks time on shipboard–
bell

marks to return after canceling–stets

marksman–shot, sniper

marl–fertilizer, greensand,
manure, overspread

marl (variety of)–marlite

marli–gauze, lace, tulle

marlin – curlew, godwit,
spearfish

marlinespike–fid

marlock–frolic, prank, trick

marmalade–jam, sapote

marmit–kettle, pot

marmoset–sagoin, tamarin

marmoset (black-tailed) –
mico

marmoset (squirrel-like) –
tamarin

marmot – bobac, rodent,
whistler, woodchuck

marmota–arctomys, wood-
chuck

Marner's (Silas) substitute
for stolen gold–Eppie

maroon–isolate

marooner–buccaneer, pirate

Marpessa's abductor–Idas

marquee–canopy, tent

marriage–matrimony, wed-
ding, wedlock

marriage (absence of) –
agamy

marriage (goddess of)–Hera

marriage (nonrecognition
of)–agamy

marriage (pert. to)–hyme-
neal, marital

marriage (second) – deuterogamy, digamy

marriage (to promise)–affiance

marriage broker (Jewish)–
schatchen

marriage forswearer – celibate

marriage notice–banns

marriage of gods–theogamy

marriage portion–dot

married – connubial, es-
poused, wedded, wived

married (many times) – polygamy

married (twice, illegally) –
bigamy

married (twice, legally) –
deuterogamy, digamy

married person – benedict,
husband, spouse, wife

married woman (with more
than one husband)–poly-
androus

marrow–medulla, pith

marrow of bones–medulla

marrow bones–knees

Mars–Ares

Mars (pert. to)–Arean, Mar-
tian

Mars (priests of)–Salii

Mars red–totem

Mars' sons (twin) – Remus,
Romulus

Marseillaise author–Rouget
de l'Isle

Marseilles soap–castile

marsh–bog, everglade, fen,
liman, moor, morass,
swale, swamp

marsh (salt)–salina

marsh bird–stilt

marsh crocodile–goa

marsh elder–iva

marsh fever–helodes

marsh gas–firedamp, meth-
ane

marsh grass–sedge, spart

marsh hawk–harrier

marsh mallow–altea

marsh marigold–boots

marsh shrub–moorwort

marshal–align, aline, array,
direct, farrier, groom,
lead, officer, official, parade, usher

marshal (French)–Ney

marshwort–cranberry

marshy – boggy, fenny,
moorish, morassey, palu-
dine, wet

marshy country (Italy)–maremma

marshy lake–liman

marshy place–slew, slough

marsupial (arboreal)–coala,
koala

marsupial (Australian)–tait

marsupial (bearlike) – coala,
koala

martel–hammer

marten–fisher

marten (genus of)–mustela

martial–warlike, military

Martin Chuzzlewit charac-
ter (doctor)–Bevan

Martinique volcano–Pelee

martyr (first Christian) –
Stephen

marvel – astonish, portent,
wonder

marvelous – improbable,
strange, wondrous

Maryland city–Baltimore

masculine–male, mas

masculine name – Abiel,
Adam, Al, Alan, Alf, Al-
lan, Alva, Amos, Asa,
Ben, Bert, Bertram, Brian,
Cal, Caleb, Carl, Caspar,
Dan, Ed, Elias, Emile,
Eneas, Enos, Ernie, Esme,
Ethan, Evan, Ezra, Fabi-
an, Gerald, Gil, Hal, Hi-
ram, Ian, Ike, Ira, Ivan,
Lem, Len, Lester, Levi,
Lou, Nat, Ned, Olaf, Ole,
Otto, Pat, Peleg, Peter,
Ray, Rene, Rex, Roger,
Roy, Sam, Si, Sid, Stan,
Steven, Ted, Tex, Ugo,
Walter

masculine plant–mas

mash–crush, flirt, ogle

mashal–parable, proverb

masher (potato)–ricer

mask–cloak, conceal, cover,
domino, screen, veil

mask (half)–domino

mask (silk half, Fr.)–loup

mask (topknot on tragic)–
onkos

masked – concealed, larvate,
larvated, obscure

maskery–masquerade

masking–mummery

maslin–brass, mixture, potpourri

mason work (of squared
stones)–ashlar

mason's mixing rod–rab

Masonic doorkeeper–tiler

masonry (hewn stone)–ash-
lar

masonry retaining wall–revetment

mass – body, bulk, lump, magnitude, size, wad

mass (confused)–cot

mass (dial.)–gob

mass (globular)–blob

mass (large floating ice) – berg, floe

mass (overspreading)–pall

mass (pert. to)–molar

mass (roundish)–cob

mass (shaped)–loaf

mass (small)–dab, pat

mass (soft pulpy)–mash

mass (tangled)–mop

mass (unit of)–gram

mass (unshaped) – lump, pulp

mass book–missal

mass mountain–tom

mass of bread–loaf, roll

mass of coal–jud, judd

mass of glass (molten before blowing)–parison

mass of materials (heaped up)–clamp

mass of molten glass (coming from furnace) – parison

mass of nerve center–ganglion

mass of particulars – aggregate

mass vestment–amice

Massachusetts capital – Boston

Massachusetts city–Salem

Massachusetts island – Nantucket

Massachusetts mountain – Tom

massacre–butchery, carnage, pogrom, slaughter

massacre (organized, of helpless people)–pogrom

massage–knead, rub

massager (male)–masseur

massager (female)–masseuse

Massenet's opera–Thais

massive – big, bold, bulky, large, massy, weighty

mast – beechnuts, cue, spar, stick

mast (inclination from perpendicular)–rake

mast crosspiece–fid

master–captain, chief, commander, conquer, humble, lord, man, mian, overcome, padrone, preceptor, rab, rabbi, regulate, rule, subjugate, surmount, tutor, vanquish

master (Indian)–sahib

master in any art–maestro

master of a house–paterfamilias

master of ceremonies – emcee, M.C.

master of the horse (Lat. abbr.)–EM

master stroke–coup

masterful–arrogant, authoritative, commanding, dictatorial, domineering, haughty, lordly, magisterial, overbearing

masterly – arbitrary, domineering, imperious

mastery–control, gree

mastic–adhesive, asa, gummy

masticate–chew

masticatory–chewing, gum

mastiff–burly, massive

mastodon–giant, mammoth

mat–platt, rug

mat (small table)–doily

mat (to)–snarl, tangle

mat grass–nard

matador's sword–estoque

matagasse–butcherbird

match–compare, equal, marriage, marry, pair, peer, pit, tally, vesta

match (English)–lucifer

match (friction)–fusee

match (in politics)–locofoco

match (wax)–vesta

matched – equaled, mated, paired, teamed

matchless–incomparable, inimitable, unequaled, unlike

matchlock–gun

mate–companion, comrade, husband, marry, match, pair, wife

mates – buddies, pairs, partners

matelot–sailor

material–corporeal, essential, fabric, matter, nonspiritual, tangible, weighty

material (clay building) – tapia

material (dress)–surah

material (dyeing)–sumac

material (elastic, from whales)–baleen

material (embroidery) – arrasene

material (fluffy corded) – chenille

material (for making glass) –frit

material (Fr. polishing) – rabat

material (gem-like)–datolite

material (heavy)–tweed

material (insulating)–asbestos, asbestus, okonite

material (lace)–allover

material (mosaic)–tessera

material (plaited for making hats)–sennat

material (polishing made from clay)–rabat

material (ribbed dress)–tricot

material (roll of)–web

material (roofing plant) – thatch

material (silk)–surah, tulle

material (sweet viscid) – honey

material (upholstering) – damask, lampas, mohair, tapestry

material (used in dyeing)–sumac, sumach

material (used in making mortar)–cement, lime

material (used in tanning)–sumac, sumach

material (waste) – refuse, rubbish, trash

material (waste leather) – tanite

material (writing, made of animal skin)–parchment

material universe (pert. to)–cosmic

materials (oyster-bed making)–culches

materiel – apparatus, equipment, supplies

maternal relation–enation
matezite–pinitol
math–monastery, mowing
mathe–grub, maggot
mathematical abbreviation–
Q.E.D.
mathematical arbitrary constant–parameter
mathematical arbitrary number – radix, radices (pl.)
mathematical deduction – analysis
mathematical diagram – graph
mathematical equation–sine
mathematical equation (irrational)–surd
mathematical exercise–problem
mathematical factor–quaternion
mathematical instrument (pert. to)–sectoral
mathematical line–vector
mathematical number–digit, multiplicand
mathematical number (irrational)–surd
mathematical operation–operand
mathematical operation for quaternion–nabla
mathematical operator – nabla, quaternion
mathematical proposition – theorem
mathematical quantity–scalar
mathematical ratio – derivate, pi, sine
mathematical statement which can be proved–theorem
mathematical symbol – faciend, multiplicand, operand
mathematical term – cosine, sine
mathematician (Greek) – Euclid, Euclides
mathematics (branch of) – algebra
mathematics (in a line having both length and direction)–vector

mathemeg–catfish
mathes–mayweed
matie–herring
matin song–aubade
matinee – entertainment, negligee, party, reception, soiree
matipo–mapau
matka (matkah)–seal
matlow (British slang)–sailor
matranee–servant, sweeper
matrass–bottle, flask, tube
matrass (chemical) – bolthead
matriculant–enroller
matriculate–enroll, enter
matrimonial–conjugal, connubial, nuptial, spousal
matrix – gangue, mold, womb
matron–dame, housekeeper, widow, wife
matter–affair, gear, material
matter (alluvial)–geest
matter (celestial)–nebula
matter (coloring, in plant cells)–endochrome
matter (difficult to be settled)–problem
matter (diffused, suspended in the air)–vapor
matter (fatty)–sebum
matter (masses of)–solids
matter (noxious)–miasma
matter (portions of)–bodies
matter (rarefied)–gas
matter (reddish coloring) – eosin
matter (spinal cord, white)–alba
matter (volatile, constituting perfume)–essence
matter (volcanic) – aa, lava, oo
matter in gaseous state–vapor
matter of fact–literal
matter of factness–pragmatism
matter to be observed–notandum
matter to dwell upon–food
matthiola–stock
matting grass–nard
mattress cover–tick

mature – age, develop, develope, digest, grown, mellow, old, ripe, ripen, season
mature (to)–season
matured–adult
maturing – ratheripe, rathripe
maturity–ripeness
matutinal–early, matin
maty (India)–servant
maud–plaid, rug, shawl
maudlin–beery, lachrymose, tearful, tipsy, weeping
maul – beat, beetle, club, mace, mall, mallet, moth, staff
maul (mason's setting) – gavel
maul (small)–mallet
mauled–bunged
maumet – doll, god, guy, idol, image, puppet
maund – basket, beg, begging
Mauritius coin–cent (br.)
Mauritius Islands measure–cash
Mauser–firearm, rifle
mauve–lilac, purple, violet
maux – prostitute, slattern, slipshod
mavis–thrush
maw – craw, crop, mallow, stomach
mawk–maggot
mawkish–sentimental, sickly, squeamish
maxim – adage, aphorism, apophthegm, apothegm, axiom, dict, gnome, motto, precept, proverb, rule, saw, saying, tenet
maxim (concise)–aphorism
maxims – logia, logion (sing.)
maximum–greatest, highest, limit, most
maximum in morals – precepts
maximum of religious teacher)–logion, logia (pl.)
maximus–largest
may–can
may (arch.)–maiden
May (goddess of)–Maia

May apple–mandrake
Maybird–thrush
May blob–marigold
Maybloom–hawthorn
maybush–hawthorn
maycock – maypop, melon,
plover
May curlew–whimbrel
May First (Scot.)–Beltane
mayfish–killifish
Mayflower–arbutus, cuckooflower, hawthorn, mari-
gold, stitchwort
May fly–dun
Mayfowl–whimbrel
May gowan–daisy
Maythorn–hawthorn
May tree–hawthorn
Mayan calendar – haab
(year), uinal (months),
uayeb (days)
Mayan Indian (Mexico) –
Mam
maybe–perhaps, possibility,
uncertainty
mayhap–peradventure, per-
haps
mayor–magistrate
mayor (Fr.)–mairie, maire
mayor (Ger.)–burgomaster
mayor (Span.)–alcade
maze–confound, deception,
delirium, delusion, fancy,
labyrinth, stupefy
mazed – bewildered, lost,
stupefied
Mazhabi–sectarian
mazuma (slang)–money
mead – drink, hydromel,
meadow, metheglin
meadow – field, grassland,
lea, mead
meadow (low)–ing
meadow (piece of)–swale
meadow (poetic)–mead
meadow mouse – arvicole,
vole
meadow saxifrage–seseli
meadow saxifrage (genus
of)–seseli
meadowsweet–spiraea
meager–arid, bare, emaciated, gaunt, jejune, lank,
lenten, meagre, scant,
slim, spare, sparse,
starved, sterile

meal – bucket, dune, feed,
pulverize, repast, sand-
bank, tub
meal (army)–mess
meal (farinaceous)–salep
meal (light) – collation,
snack
meal (old word)–padar
meal (orchid)–salep
meal (sumptuous)–banquet,
feast
meal fragment–ort
mealy–farinaceous, farinose,
friable
mealy back–cicada
mean–average, base, beggarly, denote, disgraceful,
dishonorable, intend, low,
middle, niggardly, paltry,
parsimonious, petty, pur-
port, shameful, sordid,
sorry, wretched
mean (like a person)–snotty
mean (slang)–snide
mean line–bisectrix
mean local time, 75 degrees
west longitude–est
meaning–import, intending,
intent, knowledge, pur-
port, sense, significance,
signification, understanding
meaning (pert. to)–semantic
meaning (real)–spirit
meaning in language (pert.
to)–semantic
meaningless from overuse–
banal
meaningless refrain–derry
meaningless repetition–rote
meanly–humbly, poorly
means–averages, resources
means of communication –
flags, letter, note, phone,
postal, radio, smoke, telegraph, telephone, tomtom
means of livelihood – labor,
profession, trade, voca-
tion, work
means of support – aliment,
maintenance
meant–intended
meantime–interim
measles–rubeola
measurable aspect of duration–time

measure–gage, gauge, inch,
knot, liter, litre, mete,
meter, mile, ounce, pe,
pint, rod, rotl, rule, scale,
tape, time, yard
measure (Annam)–mau
measure (Biblical)–cab, cubit, epha, ephah, hin, homer, kor
measure (Biblical, liquid)–
log
measure (capacity) – cask,
gallon, gill, liter, litre,
orna, pint, quart
measure (capacity, Malta)–
salm
measure (Chinese) – chang,
chih, ching, li, tsun, tu
measure (cloth)–ell
measure (Dutch)–aam, an-
ker
measure (Dutch East India)
–depa, depoh
measure (Egyptian)–ardab,
ardeb
measure (established) –
standard
measure (fish)–vog
measure (Fr., old)–toise
measure (Hebrew)–cab, cu-
bit, epha, ephah, hin, homer, kor, omer
measure (herring, Scot.) –
crans
measure (India) – adoulie,
gaz, guz
measure (India, distance)–
coss, kos
measure (Japanese) – koku,
mo, ri, rin, se, shaku, sho
measure (Jewish, anc.) –
epha, ephah
measure (land)–acre, ar, are,
mile, rod, rood
measure (length)–cubit, micron, mikron, pace, perch
measure (length, anc.
French)–toise
measure (linen yarn)–lea
measure (liquid)–minims
measure (liquid, obs.)–lagen
measure (metric)–are, hectare, hectoliter, hectometer, hectostere, kiliare,
kiloliter, kilometer, liter,
meter, micron

measure (metric, cubic) –
stere
measure (metric land)–are
measure (metric, two feet)–
dipody
measure (metrical foot)–an-
apaest, anapest
measure (nautical)–fathom,
knot
measure (Netherlands)–el
measure (old)–span
measure (old Dutch)–aam
measure (old Dutch wine)–
aam
measure (paper) – page,
quire, ream, sheet
measure (Persian)–gaz, guz
measure (Philippine) – apatan
measure (rayon yarn) – denier
measure (Russian length)–
verst, versta, verste
measure (silk yarn)–denier
measure (smallest liquid)–
minim
measure (superficial)–are
measure (Swiss)–imi, immi
measure (¾ inch)–digit
measure (Tunisia)–saa, saah
measure (Turkey, length)–
draa, pik, dra
measure (2¼ inch, 5.715
cm.)–nail
measure (typographical) –
em, en
measure (wine)–tun
measure (wine, two hogs-
heads)–butt
measure (wire)–mil, stone
measure (work)–erg, ergon
measure (yarn, varying)–lea
measure of heat–calorie, calory, therm
measure of length (old)–ell
measure of length (Port.)–
vara
measure of length (Span.)–
vara
measure of time–day, hour,
minute, moment, month,
second, week, year
measure of weight–bale, carat, pound, ton
measurement (astronomi-
cal)–azimuth

measurement (co-ordinate
geometry)–abscissa
measurement by the ell–el-
nage
measurer – gager, gauger,
ruler, tapeline
measurer (lumber)–scaler
measures (consisting of certain metrical)–anapaestic,
anapestic
measuring device – chain,
meter, ruler, tape, tape-
line, yardstick
measuring instrument – alidade
measuring wheel–odometer,
perambulator
meat–beef, fish, flesh, food,
lamb, mutton, pork
meat (cured) – biltong, bil-
tongue, bultong, ham
meat (cut of) – aitchbone,
icebone
meat (dried) – biltong, bil-
tongue, bultong, jerky
meat (dried, with suet, rai-
sins and sugar, used by
explorers and army) –
pemican, pemmican
meat (fat)–bacon, speck
meat (jerked) – biltong, bil-
tongue, bultong
meat (minced)–rissole
meat (pieces of roasted seasoned)–cabobs
meat (ragout of)–haricot
meat (roasted on a stick)–
cabob, kabob (var.)
meat (spiced, smoked)–pastroma
meat and vegetable dish –
stew
meat and vegetable dish
(naut.)–lobscouse
meat and vegetable dish
(tramp's)–mulligan
meat ball–rissole
meat curer–salter
meat cut–rasher
meat dish–ragout
meat fastening pin–skewer
meat jelly–aspic
meatman–butcher
meat pie–pasty
meat roll–rissole
meat roll (Fr.)–rissole

meat sauce – A1, caper,
gravy, Worcestershire
meat savor (cooked)–nidor
meat smoking place–bucan
meatworks–abattoir, slaughterhouse
meated–fattened, fed
meatus–canal, passage
meatus of ear (external) –
burr
meaty–pithy, solid, substantial
Mecca governor – shereef,
shirif
Mecca governor's wife–she-
reefa, shirifa
Mecca pilgrim's dress – ihram
Mecca shrine–Caaba, Kaaba,
Kaabeh
Mecca (great mosque) stone
building – Caaba, Kaaba,
Kaabeh
mechanic–artificer, artisan,
craftsman, operative, op-
erator, workman
mechanic (branch of)–statics
mechanic (Fr. slang)–erk
mechanical–automatic
mechanical adjustment by
successive trials–tentation
mechanical lever–tappet
mechanical man–robot
mechanical part (moving)–
rotor
mechanical part (stationary)
–stator
mechanics dealing with laws
of motion–dynamics
mechanism–apparatus, gear,
machinery
mechanism (simple)–tool
medal–badge, disk, plaque
medallion–coin, ornament
meddle – dabble, interfere,
nose, tamper
meddler–busybody
meddlesome–officious, pragmatical
Mede–Aryan
Mede's caste (priestly)–magi
media (culture)–agar
medial–intermediate, mean,
middle
Median–Mede, Mesne

Median king–Evi
median line of valve–raphe
Median priestly caste–Magi
mediate–intercede, interpose
mediator–intercessor
medic–median, physician
medical–iatric
medical fluids – sera, serum (sing.)
medical monster–Teras
medical practice (system of) –allopathy, homeopathy, homoeopathy
medical preparation (obs.)– dia
medical prescription–recipe
medicinal berry–cubeb
medicinal compound–iodin, iodine
medicinal dose–pill
medicinal fluid–serum, sera (pl.)
medicinal herb–jalap, senna, tansy
medicinal mixture–hepar
medicinal nut–cola
medicinal plant–aloe, arnica, chirata, cohosh, ergot, ipecac, rue, valerian
medicinal plant leaf–senna
medicinal plant root–licorice
medicinal powder (heavy, yellow)–turpeth
medicinal practice – allopathy, homeopathy, homoeopathy
medicinal remedy–antidote
medicinal root–artar, jalap, orris
medicinal tablet–troche
medicinal tree bark–cartex
medicinal unit–dose, drop
medicine – drug, remedy, tonic
medicine (antiseptic)–iodine
medicine (bracing)–tonic
medicine (goiter)–iodine
medicine (malt)–maltine
medicine (mild)–tisane
medicine (noncuring) – ptisan
medicine (of each)–ana
medicine (pain allaying) – anodyne
medicine (patent)–nostrum

medicine (pert. to)–cnemial, iatrac, iatrical
medicine (quack)–nostrum
medicine (quantity of) – dose, drop
medicine (relieving pain) – paregoric
medicine (science of)–physics
medicine (universal)–panacea
medicine dropper–pipette
medicine man – magician, shaman
mediciner – doctor, physician, sorcerer
medico – physician, student, surgeon
mediety (law)–moiety
medieval automaton–golem
medieval cards (playing) – tarots
medieval club–mace
medieval convention (agreement)–mise
medieval counts–palatines
medieval galley – aesc, bireme, trireme, unireme
medieval galley (large fast sailing) – dromon, dromond
medieval garment–tabard
medieval headdress–abacot
medieval helmet–armet
medieval instrument (stringed)–clavichord
medieval Italian political faction–neri
medieval money of account– ora
medieval prayer book – portas, portass, porthors, porthouse
medieval shield–ecu
medieval ship–nef
medieval tale (short)–lai
medieval trading vessel–nef
medieval vessel–xebec
medieval viol–rebec, rebeck
medieval weapon (with hooked iron head)–oncin
medieval weighing toll – tronage
Medina (Mahomet's time)– Aus

Medina citizen (early Islam convert)–Ansar
mediocre–average, indifferent, mean, medium, middling, ordinary
meditate – brood, cogitate, consider, contemplate, deliberate, muse, ponder, pore, reflect, revolve, study, watch, weigh
meditate (moodily)–brood
meditation–contemplation
meditation (religious)–yoga
meditation of death – thanatopsis
mediterranean – inland, landlocked, midland
Mediterranean (eastern) – Levant
Mediterranean boat – nef, saic, setee, settee, xebec, zebec
Mediterranean cat (civet)– genet
Mediterranean coast (east, pert. to)–Lavantine
Mediterranean colony (Fr.) –Algeria
Mediterranean country native–Italian
Mediterranean fish–remora
Mediterranean fruit–azarole
Mediterranean fruit fly – ceratitis
Mediterranean galley–galiot
Mediterranean island – Candia, Crete, Cyprus, Ebusus, Elba, Ibiza, Iviza, Malta
Mediterranean island (British)–Gozo
Mediterranean island (seized by Nazis)–Crete
Mediterranean sailing vessel –tartan
Mediterranean sea (pert. to) –Levant
Mediterranean shrub – azarole
Mediterranean tree–azarole, carob
Mediterranean tree (evergreen)–carob
Mediterranean vessel – nef, saic, setee, settee, xebec, zebec

Mediterranean vessel (fast, lateen-rigged)–felucca
Mediterranean vessel (lateen-rigged sailing)–mistic, mistico
Mediterranean vessel (sailing)–setee, settee, tartan, xebec, zebec
Mediterranean wind–levanter, mistral, solano
Mediterranean wind (cold)–gregales
Mediterranean wind (cold dry)–mistral
Mediterranean wind (hot)–solano
Mediterranean winds (periodical)–etesan
medium–degree, interagent, intermediary, mean, medial, mediator, organ, psychic
medium (culture)–agar
medley – farrago, hodgepodge, jumble, melange, mingling, mixture, olio, potpourri
medley (musical)–fantasia
medley of familiar airs–fantasia
medrick–gull, tern
medulla–compendium, marrow, pith, summary
Medusa head representation –Gorgoneum
meed–bribe, bribery, desert, merit, recompense, repay, reward
meek–docile, gentle, humble, mild, moderate, pacific, spiritless, yielding
meerkat–monkey
meerschaum–seafoam, sepiolite
meet–assemble, battle, combat, confront, congregate, contact, convene, encounter, equal, face, fulfill, touch
meet again–reencounter
meeting–assembly, conclave, congregation, contact, convention, gathering, intersection, junction, mall, synod, tryst, union

meeting (Anglo-Saxon)–gemot, gemote
meeting (of leaders of a party)–caucus
meeting (private)–conclave
meeting (spiritualist) – seance
meeting by appointment – rendezvous
meeting place–rendezvous
meeting place (Anglo-Saxon)–gemot, gemote
meeting point – focus, foci (pl.)
meets desires of–suits
meg–guinea, halfpenny
megagamete–macrogamete
megalithic chamber–dolmen
megapode–maleo
megapode (mound building)–leipoa
megapodiidae – leipoa, maloe, turkey
megrim–blues
Mekong River tribe–Moi
mel–honey
melancholy – atrabile, blue, dejection, depression, despondency, doleful, downhearted, drear, gloom, glum, hypochondria, mournfulness, sadness, sombre, sorrow
melancholy (to make)–hyp
Melanesian native–Fiji
melange–medley, mixture
melee–affray, fray, ruction, skirmish
melicocca–genip
melicratum – beverage, hydromel, mead
melilotus–clover
meliorate – ameliorate, improve, soften
melisma–cadenza
mell – beetle, hammer, honey, mallet, maul, meddle, mingle, mix
melli (comb. form)–honey
mellow – mature, matured, rich, ripe, soft, tender
melodic–ariose, melodious
melodic outline–melos
melodious – ariose, arioso, dulcet, harmonious, musical, tunable, tuneful

melodist – composer, harmonist, singer
melodramatic – dramatic, sensational
melody – air, aria, charm, harmony, music, strain, tune, tunefulness
melody (Anglo-Indian) – raga
melody (form of)–rosalia
melody (melancholy)–dirge
melody (of a)–plagal
melody characterization – ariosa, arioso
melon–paddymelon, pepo
melon (kind of) – casaba, honeydew, musk, Persian, water
melon-like fruit–gourd
melon pear–pepino
melon shrub–pepino
melon tree–papaya
melongena–eggplant
melos–melody, song
melt – disintegrate, dissolve, fuse, render, run, soften, thaw
melt (partly)–frit
melt down–render
melt ore–smelt
member – branch, district, limb, organ, part, section
member (Arctic race) – Eskimo
member (diplomatic staff)–attache
member (Eastern Caliph's dynasty)–Ommiad
member (Jewish brotherhood)–essene
member (oldest)–dean
member (projecting)–tenon
member (Roman Catholic Society)–Jesuit
member (terminal)–toe
member of boy's organization–scout
member of chapter–capitular
member of crew–hand
member of Know Nothing Party–Sam
member of laity–layman
member of religious sect – Shaker
member of society (for pro-

moting literature)–academist

member of special regiment –grenadier

member of state–citizen

membrane – caul, lemma, skin, striffin, tela

membrane (brain)–tela

membrane (fold of)–plica

membrane (optical)–retina

membrane (tympanic)–eardrum

membrane (web-like)–tela

membrane of eye (pert. to)–retinal

membranous fringe–loma

memento – keepsake, relic, souvenir, token, trophy

memoir–biography, history, narrative, note, record, report

memoir (eulogistic)–eloge

memorable – namable, notable, reminding, reminiscent

memoranda–minutes, notes

memorandum (memoranda, pl.)–note

memorandum (preliminary) –proctol

memorandum book–agenda, diary, tickler

memoria – chapel, church, reliquary, shrine

memorial–commemorative, memoir, memory, mnemonic, monument, recollection, record, remembrance, trophy   '

memorial mound (carved)–totem

memorial mound (stone) – cairn

memorist–prompter

memory–mind, recollection, remembrance, reminiscence

memory (aid)–anamnestic

memory (jog)–remind

memory (loss of)–amnesia, forgetfulness, lethe

memory (painful)–sore

memory (partial loss of) – aphasia

memory (pert. to) – mnemonic, mnesic

memory book–diary, scrapbook

Memphis chief–Evi

Memphis deity–Ptah

Memphis god (chief)–Ra

Memphis god (chief of anc.) –Ptah

men–males, masculines

men (aged rural)–gaffers

men (body of armed)–army posse

men (mechanical)–robots

men (on flying trapezes) – acrobats

men (slang)–bloaks, blokes

men (three wise)–Balthasar, Gaspar, Melchior

men (very old)–pátriarchs

men (wild)–savages

men (wise, of East)–magi

men (womanless) – bachelors, celibates, stags

men of learning – erudites, literati, literatus (sing.)

men's party–smoker, stag

men's section of Greek church–andron

menace–threat, threaten

menace (vehement)–fulmination

menaden's young–sardines

menage – club, household, housekeeping, management, society

menagerie–collection, zoo

menald – speckled, variegated

menaspis–shark

mend – ameliorate, amend, better, darn, emend, fix, heal, improve, knit, moise, repair, sew

mend (as a fracture)–knit

mend (clumsily)–botch

mendacious–false, lying

mendacity – deceit, falsity, lie, lying, untruth

Mendanoan Indonesian–Ata

mender (pots and pans) – tinker

mendicant–beggar, begger

mendicant (religious) – fakeer, fakir

mendole–cackerel

Menelaus' wife–Helen

meng–blend, mingle, mix

menhir–momolith, stone

menial–servant, servile, slavish, varlet

meniscus–lens

mennom (mennon) – minnow

meno (music)–less

mensk–adorn, credit, favor, grace, graciousness, honor, ornament, reverence

mental – intellectual, intelligent

mental alienation–insanity

mental deficient–idiot, imbecile, moron

mental disorder – paranoia, paranomia

mental disturbance – doldrum

mental faculties–wits

mental feeling–emotion

mental image – conception, idea, idolum, idola (pl.), phantasm

mental peculiarity – idiosyncratic

mental perception (sensitive)–tact

mental picture–idea

mental state (condition of)–morale

mental strain–tension

mentality–acumen, endowment

mentally engaged–versant

mentally inert–supine

mention – cite, indication, mind, name, record, speak, statement, trace, vestige

mention by implication – connotate

mention specifically–denote, indicate, name

mentionable–namable

mentor–instructor, teacher

mentum–chin

menu – bill of fare, card, carte

menu (part of)–dessert, entree, salad

Mephistopheles–devil, Satan

mephitis–odor, smell, stench

mephitis (genus of)–polecat

mercantile–commercial

mercature–commerce, trade

mercenary – hack, hireling, sordid, venal, vendible

merchandise – goods, ware, wares

merchant–shopkeeper, storekeeper, trader, vintner

merchant (Hindu)–Seth

merchant (wine, wholesale) –vintner

merchant guild–hanse

Merchant of Bagdad (in the Arabian Nights)–Sindbad

merchant ship (large)–argosy

merchant's confederacy – gild, guild

merciful – benignant, clement, humane, kind, lenient, mild, tender

merciless–cruel, pitiless

mercurous chloride–calomel

Mercury – guide, Hermes, messenger, newspaper

mercury (alchemist's name for)–azoth

mercury subchloride – calomel

Mercury's son–Cupid

Mercury's staff–caduceus

Mercury's winged cap–petasos, petasus

Mercury's winged shoes – talaria

mercy–blithe, charity, clemency, forbearance, grace, indulgence, lenience, leniency, lenity, ruth, tolerance

mere–bound, boundary, divide, landmark, limit, sea

mere (merely)–only

mere handful–wisp

mere taste–sip

merely–absolutely, also, entirely, just, only, purely, quite, scarcely, simply, single, solely, unmixedly, utterly

merganser–smee, smew

merganser (red-breasted) – harle, robin

merge – coalesce, combine, mingle, unite

merge imperceptibly–blend

merged–blended, combined, mingled, unified, united

merger–absorption, amalgamation

mericarp–hemicarp

meridian–culmination, midday, noon

meringue–icing

Merino–sheep, wool

merit–desert, deserve, earn, reward

merit (unusual)–superexcellence

merited–adequate, deserved, fit, suitable, worthy

meriting–worthy

meritorious – deserving, worthy

merkin–mop

merlin–falcon

Merlin's grass–quillwort

mermaid (enticing)–siren

mero–grouper, guasa

meropodite–meros

merriment–amusement, diversion, fun, glee, hilarity, mirth

merrow–mermaid, nymph

merry–blithe, cheerful, gay, glad, gleeful, happy, hilarious, jocose, jocular, jovial, lively, mirthful, sportive, sprightly

merry andrew – buffoon, clown, zany

merry-go-round–carrousel

merrymaking (old form of) –wassail

merryman–buffoon, clown, jester

merry song–lilt

merrythought–wishbone

merrytrotter–seesaw, swing

merrywing – bufflehead, goldeneye

merse–dip, immerse, marsh, plunge

merycism–rumination

mesel–leper, leprosy

meshed fabric–net

meshes (minute, on surface of a plant)–areola, areolas (pl.), areolae (pl.)

mesial plane–meson

mesial plane (toward)–mesad

mesmeric force–od

mesmerism–hypnotism

Mesopotamia–Irak, Iraq

Mesopotamia city – Bagdad, Kerbela, Mosul

Mesopotamia inhabitant (anc.)–Aramean

Mesopotamia river–Tigris

Mesopotamia wind (NW) – shamal

Mesopotamian–Iraqi

mesosperm (bot.)–secundine

mesotasis–base, groundmass

Mesozoic reptile (gigantic)–dinosaur

mesquin–mean, shabby, sordid

mesquita–mosque

mess – batch, bungle, confusion, disorder, litter, meal

mess up–melee, muddle

message – communication, communique, letter, news, note, tidings, wire, word

message (good news)–evangel

message (transoceanic)–cable

messenger – angel, carrier, courier, envoy, herald, minister, page, prophet, sand, toty, totyman

messenger (divine)–apostle

messenger (mounted)–courier, estafet, estafette

messenger of the gods–Hermes

Messina Strait rock–Scylla

messy–disordered, untidy

mestive–mournful

met–measure, measurement, trysted

met (coll.)–contacted

met at appointed place and time–trysted

met in session – assembled, sat

metabolism (constructive) – anabolism

metad–rat

metagnomy–divination

metagnostic–unknowable

metal – copper, gold, iron, lead, potassium, silver, tin, zinc

metal (artificer in)–smith

metal (bars of)–ingots

metal (chunk of)–slug
metal (coarse)–matte
metal (dross)–sprue
metal (gray white)–chrome
metal (heavy)–lead
metal (impure mass formed in smelting)–regulus
metal (lump of)–pig
metal (mass of)–ingot
metal (nonexpanding or noncontracting)–invar
metal (of gold brilliancy)–oroide
metal (perforated)–stencil
metal (rare)–erbium
metal (silver white)–cobalt
metal (slender pointed piece of)–nail
metal (stringed instrument playing)–plectrum
metal (tin-like)–cadmium
metal (to decorate) – damascene, damaskeen
metal (two per cent base)–dross
metal (type, used for spacing)–quad, slug
metal (unrefined)–ore
metal alloy (tin and copper) –pewter
metal bar–gad, ingot
metal bar (on house door)–risp
metal-bearing vein–lode
metal billet–gad
metal cement–solder
metal deposit–lode
metal disc (thin)–paten, patten
metal dross–slag
metal fastener – bolt, brad, cotter, nail, pin, rivet
metal filings–lemel
metal free from contraction and expansion–invar
metal ingot–gad
metal magnetized by electric current–electromagnet
metal money–specie
metal plate (for holding machine parts in place)–gib
metal plates (thin) – lames, lamina
metal rod (used for tamping)–stemmer
metal shaper–swage

metal spike–gad
metal strip to prevent turning–spline
metal substance (soft and waxy)–sodium
metal tag (of a lace)–aglet, aiglet
metal-working tool–swage
metallic content–ory
metallic element–radium
metallic element (bluish white, hard)–gallium
metallic element (low melting)–gallium
metallic element (rare) – cerium, iridium, zinc
metallic element (rare earth group) – lutecium, terbium, yttrium
metalliferous rocks–ore
metamere – somatome, somite
metamerism – segmentation
metamorphose–transform
metaphor–comparison, simile, tralatition, trope
metaphorical (not)–literal
mete–award, boundary, distribute, give, goal
meted–awarded, distributed, doled, gave
meteor–Andromede, Andromedid, fireball, Leonid, Lyraid, Lyrid
meteor (brilliant exploding) –bolide, bolis
meteor (Leo)–Leonid
meteorite (stony) – aerolite, aerolith
meteorite (strong iron) – siderolite
meteorite containing no iron –asiderite
meteorological instrument – barometer, bolide
meteorological phenomenon –snow
meteors (shower of) – andromede, andromedid
meter – cadence, measurer, metre, rhythm
meter (cubic)–stere
meter (millionth of)–micron
meter (square)–centare
meter unit – mora, morae (pl.)

meters (hundred square, of land)–ar, are
meters (ten)–decameter
methane hydrocarbon–paraffin, paraffine
metheglin–beverage, mead
mether–cup
method – course, fashion, manner, means, mode, order, procedure, process, rule, system, way
method of ornamenting textiles–fagoting
method of procedure–manner
Methuselah's father–Enoch
methyl cyanide–nitrile
methyl ethyl ketone - butanone
methyl ketols–acetols
meticulous–careful, fearful, fussy, nice, prim, scrupulous, timid
metier – business, calling, line, occupation, profession
metis–halfbreed, octoroon
metric feet (two, taken together)–dipody
metric foot–anapest, iamb, iambic, iambus
metric land measure–ar, are, decare
metric measure–ar, are, carat, centare, centiare, centiliter, centimeter, centistere, decaliter, decameter, decare, decastere, deciare, deciliter, decimeter, decistere, dekadrachm, dekagram, dekaliter, dekameter, dekiare, dekistere, hectar, hectare, hectoliter, hectometer, hectostere, kiliare, kiloliter, kilometer, kilostere, liter, litre, manzana, megameter, meter, microliter, micromillimeter, micron, miglio, milliare, milliliter, millimeter, millistere, myrialiter, myriameter, myriare, stere, tonne
metric measure (capacity)–myrialiter

metric measure (surface)–decare

metric measure (volume)–decastere

metric table (capacity) – centiliter, decaliter, deciliter, hectoliter, kiloliter, liter, milliliter, stere

metric table (length)–centimeter, decameter, decimeter, hectometer, kilometer, meter, millimeter, myriameter

metric table (weight)–centigram, decagram, decigram, gram, hectogram, kilo, kilogram, millier, milligram, myriagram, quintal, tonneau

metric weight – centigram, decagram, decagramme, decigram, decigramme, gram, gramme, hectogram, hectogramme, kilogram, kilogramme, microgram, millier, milligram, myriagram, quintal

metrical composition–poesy

metrical foot–anapest, iamb, iambic, iambus

metrical foot (accented syllable)–arsis

metrical foot (two long-syllabled)–spondee

metrical foot (two-syllabled) –trochee

metrical stress–ictus

metronome–timer

metronome inventor–Maelzel

metropolis–city

metropolitan–bishops, chief, cit, leading, principal

mettle–ardor, courage, fortitude, nerve, pluck, spirit, spunk

mettlesome–spirited

meuse (muse)–conceal, gap, hole, loophole, lurk, opening

mew – cage, cast, change, concealment, confinement, coop, den, garages, gull, miaow, molt, shed, spicknel, stables

mew (as a cat) – miaul, miaow

mewl–whimper

mews (Scot.)–maas

Mexican (anc.)–Aztec, Maya, Mixtec, Nahau, Toltec, Zapotec

Mexican (mixed blood) – mestizo

Mexican agave (species of)–datil

Mexican asphalt–chapapote

Mexican bedbug–conenose

Mexican beverage (agave juice)–pulque

Mexican beverage (pulque and sugar)–tepache

Mexican bird–jacamar, jacana, tinamou, towhee

Mexican blanket–serape

Mexican brigand–ladrone

Mexican cactus–chaute, mescal

Mexican cake–tamale

Mexican candlewood – ocotillo

Mexican cape–serape

Mexican card game–frog

Mexican cat (spotted)–margay

Mexican cherry tree–capulin

Mexican city – Chihuahua, Colima, Culiacan, Durango, Guadalajara, Hermosillo, Jalapa, Juarez, Leon, Luis Potos, Mazatlan, Merida, Mexico (c.), Monterey, Oaxaca, Orizaba, Puebla, Saltillo, San Luis Potosi, Tampico, Tepic, Vera Cruz, Victoria

Mexican cloak–manta

Mexican coin – azteca (s.), centavo (s.), peso (s.), piaster (s.)

Mexican community–ejidos

Mexican coral drops–bessera

Mexican cornmeal mush – atole

Mexican cottonwood–alamo

Mexican dish–tamal, tamale

Mexican dollar–peso

Mexican dollar (silver) – adobe

Mexican drink (intoxicating)–mescal

Mexican drug–damiana

Mexican dumpling–tamale

Mexican elm–mezcal, ulmaceae

Mexican fever (typhus)–tabardillo

Mexican fiber–istle

Mexican fiber (plant)–sisal, istle, pita

Mexican fish (food)–salema

Mexican grass–henequen

Mexican gruel–atole

Mexican hog–peccary

Mexican house (hut)–jacal

Mexican Indian–Aztec, Cora, Mam, Opata, Otomi, Otonia, Seri, Yaqui

Mexican Indian (Mayan)–Mam

Mexican insect (parasitic)–turicata

Mexican ivy–cobaea

Mexican king (petty)–Cacique

Mexican labor confederation –C.R.O.M.

Mexican laborers (bound in servitude)–peonage

Mexican lake–Chapala

Mexican landmark–senal

Mexican masonry–adobe

Mexican measure–baril, caballeria, carga, cuarteron, cuartillo, fanega, jarra, labor, legua, linea, pie, pulgada, sitio, vara

Mexican money (of account) –cuarto

Mexican mountain – Citlaltepetl, Ixtaccihuatl, Orizaba, Popocatepetl

Mexican mullet–bobo

Mexican name for Americans–gringos

Mexican native (prehistoric) –Toltec

Mexican Noah–Coxcox

Mexican octoroon–albino

Mexican onyx–tecali

Mexican orange–choisya

Mexican peasant–peon

Mexican peninsula–Yucatan

Mexican persimmon – chapote

Mexican pine (resinous) – ocote

Mexican plant–agave, maguey

Mexican plant (century) – tequila

Mexican plant (fiber)–istle, pita, sisal

Mexican plant (soap)–amole

Mexican plant (Spanish bayonet)–datil

Mexican plant (yucca-like)–sotol

Mexican plant fiber–sisal

Mexican porridge–atole

Mexican president–Comacho

Mexican president (former) –Calles

Mexican race–Toltec

Mexican river–Panuco, Tabasco

Mexican rubber tree–ule

Mexican saddle stirrup hood –tapadera, tapadero, tapidero

Mexican sandal – guaracha, guarache, guaracho, huarache, huaracho

Mexican sauce–tabasco

Mexican scarf–tapalo

Mexican shawl–serape

Mexican shrub–chosiva, colima

Mexican sisal–henequen

Mexican state–Colima, Michoacan, Tabasco

Mexican statesman–Juarez

Mexican stirrup cover–tapadera, tapadero, tapidero

Mexican tea–apasote

Mexican thong–romal

Mexican tree (boxwood) – seron

Mexican tree (cherry)–capulin

Mexican tree (rubber)–ule

Mexican tree (small)–colima

Mexican tree (timber)–capulin

Mexican village (Pueblo)–tecali

Mexican volcano – Colima, Jorullo

Mexican weight – adarme, arroba, bag, carga, libra, marco, ochava, onza, quintal, tercio

Mexican yucca (species of)–isote

Mexican (Gulf of) peninsula –Yucatan

mezereon–daphne

mezzanine–entresol

miaow (miaou)–mew

miasma–malaria

miaul–caterwaul, mew

mib–marble

mica – biotite, damourite, glist, hydromica, isinglass, silicate

mica (lithia)–lepidolite

mica (Muscovite)–talc

mice (genus of)–mus

mice (meadow)–voles

miche–conceal, lurk, pilfer, skulk, sneak

micher–pander, sneak, thief, truant

michery–cheating, theft

Michigan motto (I will defend)–Tuebor

Michigan river–Cass

Michigan town – Detroit, Flint

Mick–Irishman

Mickey Mouse inventor – Disney

mico–marmoset

micramock–cowrie

micrander–male

micraner–ant

micro–moth

microbe–germ, organism

microcosm–universe, world

microorganism–germ

microorganism (growing in presence of oxygen) – aerobe

microscopic–minute, small

microscopic algae–diatom

microscopic anatomy – histology

microscopic animal–ameba, amebic, amoeba, amoebic

microscopic life (pert. to)–amoebic

microscopic organism–ameba, amebic, amoeba, amoebic

mid-kidney–mesonephros

mid-Lent Sunday–laetare

midday–noon

midday (pert. to)–meridian

midday intermission–lunch, noon hour, nooning

midday nap–siesta

middle–center, central, centry, intermediator, median, mesial, mesne

middle (comb. form)–mes, meso

middle (law)–mesne

middle (pert. to)–median

Middle Ages (pert. to)–medieval

Middle Ages fur–miniver

middle mast–mainmast

middle post–kingpost

middle rate–mediocre

Middle State – Delaware, New Jersey, New York, Pennsylvania

middle way–halfway, midway

middling–average, fair, mediocre, medium, moderate, ordinary

midge – carriage, fish, fly, gnat, punkie, stout

Midian king–Evi, Reba

midnoon–midday, noon

midshipman–cadet, reefer

Midsummer Night's Dream character–Oberon

Midwestern college–Coe

midwife–accoucheuse, baba, cummer, kimmer

mien – air, appearance, aspect, bearing, carriage, demeanor, deportment, eye, guise, manner, ostent

miff–displease, offend, quarrel, sulkiness, sullenness, tiff

mig–duck, marble

migale–mouse, shrew

migeloid fish of Cuba–bobo

might–ability, arm, efficacy, force, power, strength

mightier–greater, vaster

mighty – efficacious, enormous, extremely, potent, powerful, strong, vast, very, violent

migniard – dainty, delicate, mincing, minion, mistress

mignon – dainty, delicate, graceful, petite, small

mignonette (garden, color of)–reseda

mignonette vine – Madeira, tarweed

migraine – headache, hemicrania

migrate–move, trek

migration–passage, trek

migration (of large numbers)–exode, exodus

migratory – nomadic, peregrine, roving, wandering

migratory cell–leucocyte

migratory thrush–robin

mihrab – chamber, niche, slab

Mikado (court of)–dairi

mikania–willugbaeya

mike (Eng. slang)–loaf, loiter

mike (slang)–microphone

milady – gentlewoman, noblewoman

milarite–silicate

mild–assuasive, benedict, benign, bland, calm, clement, considerate, gentle, gracious, indulgent, kind, lenient, lenitive, moderate, mollifying, soft, soothing, temperate, tranquil

mild offense (law)–delict, delit

milder–decay, molder, tamer

mildew–honeydew

mile (one-eighth)–furlong

mile (sea, of 2029 yards)–naut

Miled's son–Ir

milepost (anc.)–stela, stelae (pl.), stele, steles (pl.)

milestone–stela, stelae (pl.), stele, steles (pl.)

milfoil–yarrow

militant–combating, combative, fighting

military–martial

military advance–anabasis

military assistant–aide

military automobile–jeep

military call (to quarters)–tattoo

military cap–kepi, shako

military chest–funds

military cloak–sagum

military commander – marshal

military commission–brevet

military depot–base

military device–croc

military division–company, corps, platoon, regiment, squad

military division (front)–sector

military engine – onager, robinet

military engine for hurling darts and stones–robinet

military entanglement–abatis

military expedition to recover Holy Land–crusade

military force–legion, troop

military force (liable to call)–reserve

military front part–sector

military hat–helmet, kepi, shako

military hat (stiff)–shako

military horsemen–cavalry, Hussars

military inspection–parade, review

military instrument (wind)–althorn

military maneuver–tactic

military messenger–estafet

military obstruction–abatis

military officer – corporal, sergeant, lieutenant, subaltern, captain, major, colonel, general, brigadier

military operations (series of)–campaign

military order–command

military organization (skeleton)–cadre

military parley signal–chamade

military pit–trou-de-loup

military police–constabulary, gendarmes, M.P.

military punishment–strappado

military quarters–barracks, billets, camp

military rank–colonelcy

military rank (old)–banneret

military salute–salvo

military signal–chamade

military staff officer–aide

military storage place–arsenal

military storehouse–arsenal

military supplies–ordnance

military survey (preliminary)–reconnoiter

military truck–camion

military unit – cadre, company, platoon, regiment, squad, troop

military unit (hindmost)–rear

military unit (leading)–van

military unit framework (skeleton)–cadre

military work (protected)–fort

militate – conflict, contend, debate, fight

milk–drain, elicit, lac, suckle

milk (curdled)–clabber

milk (fermented) – kefir, koumis, koumiss, koumyss, kumiss, kumys

milk (pert. to)–lactary, lacteal, lactic

milk (sour)–whig

milk (thickened part)–curd

milk (watery part)–whey

milk and egg dish–custard

milk coagulator–rennet

milk crust–eczema

milk curdling substance – rennet

milk deodorizing device – aerator

milkfish–awa, sabolo

milk food (used on fasting days)–lacticinia

milk glass–opaline

milk preparation (of casein)–lactarene, lactarine

milk sap–latex

milk selling place–dairy, lactarium

milk separator–creamer

milksop–mollycoddle, sissy

milk strainer (Scot.)–milsey, milsie

milk sugar–lactose

milkweed family–asclepiadaceae

milkweed fluid–latex

milkweed pod down–silk

milk whey–serum, sera (pl.)

milk whey cheese – ziega, zieger

milkwood–paperbark

milkwort family–polygalaceae

milky – effeminate, gentle, mild, tame, timorous

milky iridescence–opaline

milky way–galaxy

mill–beat, comminute, crush, dress, factory, finish, grind, housebreaker, powder, shape, snuffbox, thief, thrash, transform, vanquish

mill (drag stone for pulverizing ore)–arrasta

mill (grain)–quern

mill (small hand grinding) –quern

mill (to)–knurl, nurl

mill beetle–cockroach

mill bill–adz

millclapper–chatterbox

millcourse–millrace

mill end–remnant

millrace (below wheel)–tailrace

millrace (Scot.)–lade

mill run–millrace

mill sail–vane

millstone support–ink, moline, rynd

mill wheel float–ladle

mill wheel water current – millrace

millefleurs–perfume

millenarian–chiliast

millepede–myriapod

millepore–coral

miller–boxer, flycatcher, harrier, moth, pugilist, ray

miller's-thumb – bird, cottidae, goldcrest, titmouse, warbler

millerite–sulphide

millesimal–thousandth

millet–cenchrus

millet (broomcorn)–hirse

millet (Italian)–moha

millet (kind of)–milly

millet (pearl)–bajra, bajree, bajri

millimeter (thousandth part) –micron

millimeter (millionth part) –micromillimeter

millions of millions–trillions

Mills bomb–grenade

milo–grain

milt–spleen

mim–modest, prim, shy

mime–actor, aper, buffoon, clown, copy, imitate, jester, mimic

mimesis–imitation, mimicry

mimic–actor, ape, aper, buffoon, copy, copying, counterfeit, imitate, imitative, mime, mimetic, mock, parrot

mimic (Greek root for) – mimo

mimic thrush–mockingbird

mimicry–apism, mimesis

mimidae–catbird, mockingbird, thrasher

mimmock–dainty, fastidious

mimsey–prim, prudish

min – memory, remember, remembrance, remind, prince, ruler

minar–myna, tower

minaret – lamp, lighthouse, tower

minaway–minuet

mince–chop, cut, hash

minced dish–hash

minced meat–rissole

minced oath–drat, egad

minchery–nunnery

minchiate–tarot

mind–care, intellect, intelligence, memory, obey, reck, remembrance

mind (jubilant state of)–elation

mind (peace of)–ataraxia

mind (pert. to) – mental, phrenic

mind (quality)–nature

mind (state of)–tune

mind picture–imagine

minded – cared, obeyed, tended

minded (feeble)–anile

minds (Scot.)–mins

Mindanao town (Philippine)–Dapa

Mindanao tribe–Ata, Bagobo, Illano, Lutao, Lutayo

Mindanao volcano–Apo

Mindanaon–Ata, Illano, Lutao, Lutayo

mine – cavity, dig, excavation, gallery, my, passage, pit, sap

mine (coal)–rob

mine (Cornish)–bal

mine (deviate from vertical in a)–hade

mine (Spanish)–mio

mine (unsystematically)–gopher

mine basket (ore-conveying) –corf

mine ceiling–astel

mine chisel–gad

mine clearing device–paravane

mine entrance–adit, stulm

mine excavation (staircaselike)–stope

mine floor passage–sill

mine gallery floor–sill

mine guardian (myth.) – gnome

mine level–stope

mine partition (longitudinal)–sollar, soller

mine passageway (horizontal)–stulm

mine platform (shaft)–sollar, soller

mine prop–sprag

mine refuse–rubbish

mine reservoir (shaft bottom, for waste water)– standage, sump

mine run–average, common, unassorted

mine shaft (lowest part) – sump

mine shaft depression–sump

mine signalman – cageman, cager

mine sweeping device–paravane

mine thrower–minenwerfer, minnie

mine trap-door tender–trapper

mine tub (ore-carrying) – corf

mine vein–lode

mine wagon–tram

mine waste–goaf, gob

mine worker (at bottom of shaft)–onsetter

mine worker (loader)–cageman, cager

miner's anemia–ancylostomiasis

miner's basket–corf

miner's chisel–gad

miner's consumption–phthisis

miner's instrument (surveying)–dial

miner's lamp (safety)–davy

miner's worm–hookworm

mineral – apatite, barite, edenite, egeran, epidote, iolite, ore, tin, uraninite

mineral (black) – cerine, graphite, jet, niobite

mineral (black crystallized, found on the island of Elba)–yenite

mineral (black, micaceouslike biotite)–minguetite

mineral (brown) – cerine, egeran

mineral (brown elastic) – elaterite

mineral (calcium and magnesium)–diopside

mineral (calcium carbonate)–calcite, calcspar

mineral (common yellow)–pyrite

mineral (crystalline)–apatite, boracite, elatern, spar

mineral (dark igneous) – minette

mineral (deep red)–garnet

mineral (emerald green)–erinite

mineral (fibrous)–asbestos

mineral (flaky)–mica

mineral (for jewelry)–diopside

mineral (gray white)–trona

mineral (green)–erinite

mineral (hard) – adamant, spinel, spinelle

mineral (kind of)–apatite, ataxite, barite, edenite, egeran, epidote, iolite, iron, ore, tin

mineral (light green)–alalite

mineral (lustrous)–spar

mineral (macrocrystalline)–felsite, felspar, felspath

mineral (magnetic) – loadstone, lodestone

mineral (nonmetallic) – boron, iodine

mineral (nonmetalliferous)–gangue

mineral (pale brass yellow)–pyrite

mineral (pale yellow)–iron

mineral (phosphorus yielding)–apatite

mineral (plaster paris)–gypsum

mineral (potassium sulphate)–misenite

mineral (rare, brittle) – euclase

mineral (real or imaginary hard)–adamant

mineral (reddish brown) – rutile

mineral (salt, potash)–alum

mineral (silicate)–mica

mineral (soap making)–talc

mineral (soft)–talc

mineral (transparent)–mica

mineral (used in gunpowder)–niter

mineral (vitreous)–spar

mineral (waxlike)–ozocerite

mineral (white, colorless)–barite

mineral (with nonmetallic luster)–blendes

mineral (yellow)–topaz

mineral (yellowish green)–epidote

mineral caoutchouc–elaterite

mineral cavity (small unfilled)–voog, vug, vugg, vugh

mineral dark spot–macle

mineral deposit–lode

mineral deposit (alluvial or glacial)–placer

mineral deposit cavity (small unfilled) – voog, vug, vugg, vugh

mineral green–malachite

mineral jelly–vaseline

mineral oil–colza

mineral or vegetable (neither)–animal

mineral pitch–asphalt

mineral pocket–nest

mineral rock–ore

mineral salt–alum

mineral silicate–mica

mineral source of phosphorus–apatite

mineral spring–spa, well

mineral tallow–hatchettine

mineral tar–maltha

mineral used in making gunpowder–niter

mineral water–selter, seltzer

mineral wax–ozocerite

mines (rare)–threats

ming–mention, recount, remember, remind

minge–midge

mingle–amalgamate, associate, blend, coalesce, combine, consolidate, fuse, merge, unite

mingle (imperceptibly) – blend

mingle-mangle – hodgepodge, medley, mixture

mingwort–wormwood

mingy–mean, stingy

minhag (Jewish religion)–conduct, custom, manner

miniate–decorate, luminate, paint, rubricate

minikin – affected, dainty, delicate, elegant, mincing

minim–jot, minute, smallest

minimize – belittle, depreciate, detract, disparage, reduce

minimum–least, lowest

mining chisel–gad

mining excavation–stope

mining hut (over shaft)–coe

mining place–minery, mining

mining shack (over shaft)–coe

mining surveyor–dialer

mining term (deviate from vertical)–hade

minion–dainty, darling, delicate, elegant, favorite, idol, ladylove, lover, mistress, neat, paramour, pretty

minionette–delicate, small

minister – afford, angel, attend, clergyman, curate,

executor, furnish, parson, pastor, preacher, priest, serve, supply
minister (assistant)–curate
Minister of State (first)–Premier
minister's home–manse, parsonage
ministration–service
ministry (home)–interior
minitant–threatening
Minnesota city–Ely
minor–less, lesser, smaller, youth
minor (law)–petit
minor parts–details
minorate–curtail, diminish
minoress–clare
minority–immaturity, nonage
minority (legal)–nonage
Minos' daughter–Ariadne
Minos' wife–Pasiphae
Minotaur's owner–Minos
minster–church, monastery
minstrel–bard, entertainer, gleeman, jongleur, musician, poet, troubador, troubadour
minstrel (Celtic)–bard
minstrel (12th and 13th century)–goliard
ministrel show endman – bones
minstrel show middleman–interlocutor
minstrel show part–olio
minstrel show questioner – interlocutor
mint – aim, attempt, blow, coin, endeavor, feint, hyssop, intend, money, purpose, ramona, venture
mint (European)–hyssop
mint (genus of)–mentha
mint (mountain)–basil
mint (shrubby)–sage
mint (true)–mentha
mint camphor–menthol
mint charge–brassage, seigniorage
mint family–lamiaceae
mint family plant–basil, catnip
mint geranium–costmary
mint herb–dittany

mint hog (Irish)–shilling
mint levy, charged on bullion–brassage, seigniorage
mint sauce (Eng. slang) – money
minuend–diminish, lessen
minuet–dance
minuet (movement used by Beethoven)–scherzo
minus – defect, deficiency, lack, less, subtract
minuscule – diminutive, insignificant, manuscript, petty, small
minute–atomic, circumstantial, draft, instant, jot, little, memorandum, mite, moment, note, petty, record, slight, small, trifling, tiny, tittle, wee
minute (extremely)–atomical
minute (more)–nicer
minute animal–animalcule
minute details–particulars
minute difference–shade
minute distinction of detail –nicety
minute glass–hourglass
minute Jack–timeserver
minute of document (original)–protocol
minute opening–pore
minute organism – monad, spore, zoospore
minute organism (simple)–monad
minute orifice–pore, stoma
minute part–tittle
minute particle–atom, iota, mote
minutely–continual, exactly, unceasing
minutes–record
minutes (court)–acta, actum (sing.)
minutes (pert. to)–minutary
minutes of law court–acta, actum (sing.)
minx–girl, jade
miny–mine
minyan–quorum
mir–chief, head, president
mirabilia–miracles, wonders
mirac (mirach)–abdomen
miracle – anomy, feat, mar-

vel, occurrence, phenomenon, wonder
miracle (scene of Christ's first)–Cana
miracle wheat–Poulard
miraculous – marvelous, supernatural, wonderful
miraculously balanced by hair of Buddha (in Burma)–Kryailteyo Pagoda
mirador – balcony, loggia, oriel, turret, watchtower
mirage–chimera, phenomenon, reflect, serab
Miranda's father–Prospero
mirandous–wondrous
mirate–wonder
mird–attempt, meddle, toy
mire – addle, bog, marsh, moil, mud, ooze, slud, sludder, slush, stall, swamp, wet
mirror–glass, reflect, speculum
mirror iron–spiegeleisen
mirrored–image
mirth–cheerfulness, delight, fun, gaiety, gladness, glee, happiness, hilarity, joy, joyousness, levity, merriment, spleen
mirth (boisterous)–hilarity
mirthful–gay, happy, jolly
miry–boggy, filthy, lutose
mis–amiss, wrong
misadventure–accident, calamity, casualty, disaster, mischance, misfortune, mishap
misaffect–dislike, harm
misanthrope–cynic
misapplied–abused
misapprehend – misunderstand
misbear–misbehave
misbede – abuse, injure, wrong
misbirth–abortion
miscalculate–err, misreckon, overshoot
miscall – abuse, misname, mispronounce, revile
miscarriage – abortion, failure, lapse, mischance, misdeed, misdemeanor, mis-

hap, mismanagement, mistake

mischance – calamity, disaster, misadventure, misfortune

mischief–ate, damage, evil, harm, hurt, ill, wrack

mischief (goddess of)–Ate, Eris

mischievous – arch, elvish, impish, mocking, naughty, roguish, sportive, waggish

mischievous (dangerously)– parlous

misconduct – delinquency, offense, misbehavior, misdemeanor

miscreant – heretic, misbeliever, rascal, villain, wretch

miscue–miss, mistake, slip

misdeed – crime, offense, wrong

misdemeanor – crime, misdeed, misdemeanant, sin

mise–grant, immunity, layout, levy, privilege, treaty

miser–hoarder, hunks, Nabal, niggard, nipper, wretch

miserable – abject, commiserative, disconsolate, forlorn, pitiful, unhappy, wretched

misericord (misericorde) – compassion, dagger, hall, mercy, pity, refectory

miserly–avaricious, churlish, close, covetous, mean, niggardly, parsimonious, penurious, stingy

miserly (most)–meanest

misery – affliction, anguish, avarice, calamity, covetousness, despondency, distress, misfortune, niggardliness, poverty, privation, unhappiness, woe, wretchedness

misfare – misbehave, miscarry, misfortune, mishap

misfeasance–trespass, wrong

misfortune–adversity, calamity, disaster, evil, ill, mischance, mishap, reverse

misfortune (great) – calamity, catastrophe, disaster, holocaust

misgiving – apprehension, qualm

misgo–err, miscarry

mishap – accident, miscarriage, misfortune, slip

Mishna women–Nashim

misinterpret–err, warp

misjudge–err, misconstrue

misky–foggy, misty

mislay–displace, misplace

misle–drizzle, mist, mizzle, rain

mislead–blear, deceive, deception, delude, fool, misbehave, misguide, mismanage

misleading – crooked, fallacious, false, fraudulent

mislippen – delude, disappoint, neglect, suspect

mismanage–blunk, bungle

misplace – displace, mislay, mislocate, misset

misplaced in order of time– anachronistic

misplay–err, error, mismove, renege

misprise (misprize) – contempt, despise, misprision, mistake, scorn, slight, undervalue

misprision–contempt, depreciation, misconduct, misdemeanor, misprize, mistake, misunderstanding, scorn

mispronunciation–cacology

misrepresent–belie, deceive

miss – desiderate, err, fail, lapse, lose, mistress, omit, prostitute, skip, title

miss (pert)–chit

Miss Dombey's suitor (unsuccessful)–Toots

Miss Nancy–Sissy

Miss O'Hara–Scarlett

missel–mistletoe

misshapen – deformed, distorted, monstrous, ugly

missile–arrow, bullet, dart, outcast, shot, spear, weapon

missile weapon–arrow, bola, bolas

missing – absent, lost, out, wanting

mission – charge, commission, delegation, deputation, errand, message

mission (Texas)–Alamo

missionary (first)–apostle

Mississippi (nickname for State of)–Bayou

Mississippi bridge builder– Eads

Mississippi county – Amite, Pontotoc

Mississippi resort–Biloxi

Mississippi university chancellor–Hume

Mississippi Valley tree–catalpa

Mississippi's nickname–Bayou

missive – billet, document, letter, message, missile, note

Missouri gourd–calabazilla

Missouri skylark–pipit

misspelling–cacography

misspend–lose, squander

misstep–fauxpas, slip, trip

mist – bedim, blur, brume, cloud, dim, fog, haze, misle, mystery, obscurity, uncertainty

mistake–blunder, bull, err, erratum, error, folly, inadvertence, misapprehension, misconception, slip

mistake (coll.)–boner, bull

mistake (minor grammatical)–solecism

mistake in date – anachronism

mistake in printing – erratum, errata (pl.)

mistake in rules of syntax– solecism

mistake in writing–erratum, errata (pl.)

mistaken–erroneous, wrong

mistletoe family – loranthaceae

mistonusk–badger

mistook–erred, violated

mistreat–abuse, violate

mistress – amie, governess, ladylove, sweetheart
mistress (kept)–concubine
Mistress of Adriatic–Venice
misty – blurry, cloudy, dim, foggy, hazy, indistinct, obscure, roky, rouky, shadowy, unenlightened, unilluminated, unintelligible, vague
misuse–abuse, maltreat, misemploy, pervert
misuse of words in speech– heterophemy
mite–acaridan, acarus, acari (pl.), smidge, smidgen
mites (small)–acari, acarus (sing.), acarina
miter (mitre) – belt, fillet, frank, girdle, gusset, headband, headdress, tavern, tiara
miter (Jewish high priest, part of)–Petalon
miter flower–cyclamen
mithridate – alexipharmic, antidote, electuary
mitigate–abate, allay, alleviate, appease, diminish, ease, lenitive, lessen, mease, meliorate, moderate, mollify, palliate, relax, relieve, remit, soften, temper, tone
mitigate (Scot.)–mease
mitigates pain–balm
mix – blend, coalesce, cross, jumble, knead, meng, mingle, stir, unite
mix and stir when wet (as clay for bricks)–pug
mix circularly–stir
mix-up–conflict, confusion, melee
mix wine–part
mix with yeast–barm
mixable–miscible
mixed blood (person of)– halfbreed, mestizo, mestiza (fem.), metic, metisse (fem.), octoroon
mixed breed – mongrel, quadroon
mixed type–pi
mixen–dunghill
mixer–bartender

mixhill–dunghill, mixen
mixture–blend, hash, mash, melange, olio, potpourri
mixture (cinnamon, cloves, coriander, anise and fennel seed)–tamara
mixture (confused)–chaos
mixture (cooking)–batter
mixture (flour and butter gravy)–roux
mixture (linseed oil and whiting)–putty
mixture (medicinal)–hepar, prescription
mixture (of impure metallic arsenides)–speiss
mixture (of sand and clay)– loam
mixture (wine, honey and spice)–clary
mizar star (small)–alcor
mizmaze – bewilderment, confusion
mizzle–drizzle, misle, mist, rain
mizzy–bog, quagmire
moa – dinornis, dinornithidae, ratite, ratitae (pl.)
moa (genus of)–apertyx
moab–hat
Moab inhabitants (anc.) – Emims
Moab's descendants – Moabites
moan–bemoan, bewail, complaint, groan, lament, lamentation, wail
moan (as the wind)–sough
moanification – grieving, lamentation, moaning
Moas mountain–Nebo
moat–foss, fosse, trench
mob – clique, dishabille, drove, flock, gang, group, herd, prostitute, set, undress
mob member–rioter
mobile–mob, movable, populace, vision, wandering
mobilanter–turtle
moble–furniture, movables
Moby Dick author–Herman Melville
moccasin–larrigan, pac, pack
moch–moth
mocha–coffee, leather

mochy–damp, misty, moist, muggy
mock – ape, deride, disappoint, fleer, flout, gibe, imitate, jape, mimic, ridicule, sneer, taunt
mock brawn–headcheese
mock cucumber–apple (wild balsam)
mock moon–paraselene
mock nightingale–blackcap, warbler
mock orange–seringa, syringa, syringe
mock ore–sphalerite
mock plane–sycamore
mock sun–parhelion
mockage – imitation, mimicry
mocker – aper, bird, deceiver, mimic, mockingbird, scoffer
mocker nut–hickory
mockery – counterfeit, derision, farce, imitation, mimicry, sarcasm, satire
mocking–derisive, fleering
mocking remark–quip
mode – fad, fashion, form, manner, method, style, vogue
mode (third figure valid)– ferison
mode of expression (local)– vernacular
mode of government – regime
mode of procedure (customary)–order, system
mode of speech–parlance
mode of speech (meaning opposite)–irony
mode of standing – posture, stance
mode of woman's hairdressing–madonna
model–act, archetype, example, ideal, manikin, mannequin, mold, norm, paradigm, paragon, pattern, plan, plot, pose, precedent, shape, template, templet
model for imitation (arch.) –ensample
model of a word–paradigm

model of excellence – paragon

model of perfection – paragon

model of solar system–orrery

moderate – abate, bate, conservative, control, ease, frugal, lessen, lower, reasonable, soften, some, temper, temperate

moderation–abatement, control, diminution, governance, limitation, mitigation, restraint, restriction, temperateness

moderator – arbiter, mediator, umpire

modern–late, latter, neoteric, new, recent

modern (prefix)–neo

modern Syriac script–serta

modernize–renovate

modest–chaste, coy, demure, diffident, humble, reserved, retiring, shy, unpretentious, virtuous

modest (affectedly, Scot.)–mim

modesty – chastity, decency, diffidence, humility, reserve, shyness

modicum of drink–drop

modification – alteration, change, limitation, umlaut, variation

modified within limitation–ranged, varied

modify – alter, assuage, attemper, influence, limit, master, mitigate, moderate, qualify, temper

modifying circumstance – condition

modish – chic, fashionable, stylish

modiste – dressmaker, milliner

modulated – inflected, intoned, regulated, softened, tempered, toned

modulation (voiceless, var.) –inflexion

moggan–stocking

moggy–calf, cat, cow, scarecrow, slattern

mogo–hatchet

moha–millet

Mohammed–Mahomet, Mahound, Mohammedan

Mohammed's birthplace – Mecca

Mohammed's daughter–Fatima

Mohammed's flight from Mecca–hegira

Mohammed's horse – Alborak

Mohammed's son (adopted) –Ali

Mohammed's successor – Calif, Caliph

Mohammedan – Moro, Moslem, Mussulman, Saracen (see Mahometan)

Mohammedan (hostile to crusaders)–Saracen

Mohammedan (orthodox)–Moslem

Mohammedan angel (of death)–Azrael

Mohammedan annual fast–Ramadan

Mohammedan ascetic – fakeer, fakir

Mohammedan ascetic (mystic)–Sufi

Mohammedan Bible – Alcoran, Koran

Mohammedan bier–tabut

Mohammedan book (sacred)–Alcoran, Koran

Mohammedan calendar–(1) Muharram, (2) Safar, (3) Rabia, (4) Rabia II, (5) Jumada, (6) Jumada II, (7) Rajab, (8) Shaban, (9) Ramadan, (10) Shawwal, (11) Zu'lkadah, (12) Zu'lhijjah

Mohammedan calif (caliph) –Abu Bekr, Ali, Omar, Othman

Mohammedan cap–taj

Mohammedan caravansary–imaret

Mohammedan chief – sayid, sidi

Mohammedan chief (Moro) –dato, datto

Mohammedan chief officer–aga, agha

Mohammedan city (sacred) –Mecca, Medina

Mohammedan college of wise men–ulema

Mohammedan commander–aga, agha

Mohammedan court officer–aga, agha

Mohammedan crier (prayer hour)–muezzin

Mohammedan crusade – jehad, jihad

Mohammedan deity–Allah

Mohammedan demon–afrit, eblis, jinnee, jinni

Mohammedan dervish–santon

Mohammedan dervish's cap –taj

Mohammedan devil – Eblis, Shaitan, Sheitan

Mohammedan divorce (at instance of any person other than wife)–mubarat

Mohammedan divorce (by act of husband)–talak

Mohammedan Easter–Eed

Mohammedan era – see Mohammedan calendar

Mohammedan exclamation–bismillah

Mohammedan expounder (of law) – molla, mollah, mufti, mulla, mullah

Mohammedan faith–Islam

Mohammedan fast – Ramadan

Mohammedan fasting month (annual) – Ramadan

Mohammedan festival–Bairam, Eed

Mohammedan garment – izar, jubbah

Mohammedan garment (women's outer)–izar

Mohammedan guide (spiritual)–Pir

Mohammedan hero–Ghazi

Mohammedan hierarchy – ulema

Mohammedan high caste–said, sayid, sayyid, seid

Mohammedan hostile to crusaders–Saracen

Mohammedan house (men's part)–selamlik
Mohammedan imam (last)–Mahdi
Mohammedan infidel – kaffir, kafir
Mohammedan instrument (stringed)–rebab
Mohammedan Javanese – Sassak
Mohammedan judge–cadi
Mohammedan knife (long) –yatagan, yataghan
Mohammedan law expounder–molla, mollah, mufti, mulla, mullah
Mohammedan leader – ameer, amir, emeer, emir
Mohammedan leader of the faithful (last)–Mahdi
Mohammedan lord–sayid
Mohammedan magistrate – cadi
Mohammedan Malay – Sassak
Mohammedan marriage custom (period in which widow may not marry)–iddat
Mohammedan marriage settlement (in favor of wife, antenuptial)–mahr
Mohammedan messiah (Sunni belief)–Mahdi
Mohammedan minister of state–vizier
Mohammedan month – see Mohammedan calendar
Mohammedan month (annual fasting)–Ramadan
Mohammedan mysticism – Sufism
Mohammedan noble–ameer, amir, emeer, emir
Mohammedan noble (non)–kaffir, kafir
Mohammedan nymph – houri
Mohammedan officer (chief)–aga, agha
Mohammedan officer (court)–aga, agha
Mohammedan orthodox – Hanif, Sunnite
Mohammedan prayer (chief,

recited five times daily)–namaz
Mohammedan prayer (ritual)–salat, salawat (pl.)
Mohammedan prayer call – adan, azan
Mohammedan prayer hour (five times daily) – adan, azan
Mohammedan prayer leader –imam, imaum
Mohammedan priest–imam, imaum, wahabee, wahabi, wahhabi
Mohammedan priest (body) –ulema
Mohammedan prince – ameer, amir, emeer, emir, said, seid, sayid, sayyid
Mohammedan princess – begum, tola
Mohammedan professor (sincere to faith)–Hanif
Mohammedan property (undivided, common) – mushaa
Mohammedan reformer – Wahabee, Wahabi, Wahhabi
Mohammedan religion – Islam
Mohammedan religious concept–fana
Mohammedan religious teacher–alim
Mohammedan ruler–ameer, amir, emeer, emir, sultan
Mohammedan ruler (former)–calif, caliph
Mohammedan saint – Pir, Santon
Mohammedan saint's tomb–pir
Mohammedan salutation – salaam, salam
Mohammedan Satan–Eblis
Mohammedan scholars (body of)–ulema
Mohammedan school (early)–Sifatite
Mohammedan school of theology–Hanafi, Hanafite
Mohammedan scripture – Alcoran, Koran
Mohammedan sect – Wahabis

Mohammedan sect (early)–Sifatite
Mohammedan settlement (antenuptial marriage in favor of wife)–mahr
Mohammedan shirt–kamis
Mohammedan shrine (Mecca)–Caaba, Kaaba, Kaabeh
Mohammedan spirit–genie, genii (pl.), jinnee, jinni, jinn (pl.), jinniyeh (fem.)
Mohammedan spirit (evil)–Shaitan, Sheitan
Mohammedan spirit (female)–jinniyeh
Mohammedan stringed instrument–rebab
Mohammedan student (theological)–softa
Mohammedan succession – calif, caliph
Mohammedan sword (short) – yatagan, yataghan
Mohammedan teacher–alim, imam, imaum, molla, mollah, mulla, mullah
Mohammedan theologians (body of)–ulema
Mohammedan title–aga, ali, nawab, nuwab, nuwaub, said, sayid, sayyid
Mohammedan tomb–tabut
Mohammedan tribe – Dervish
Mohammedan unbeliever – kafir, kaffir
Mohammedan veil (women's double) – yashmac, yashmak
Mohammedan weight–miskal
Mohammedan word (sacred)–om, um
Mohammedan wrap (poor women's outer)–izar
Mohammedanism–Islam
mohock–attack, maltreat
moider–bother, distract, encumber, perplex, smother, toil, wander, worry
moieter–roller
moil – confusion, defile, defilement, drudgery, labor, spot, taint, tire, toil, tor-

ment, trouble, turmoil, vexation, weary

moire–watered

moise – improve, mend, thrive

moist–damp, dank, humid, rainy, wet

moisten – bedew, dampen, dew, leach, moil, sparge, sprinkle, wet

moisten hides – sam, samm, sammy

moisture – fog, humidity, liquid, vapor, water

moisture (condensed)–drip

moisture (excess of)–edema

moisture (expose to)–ret

moisture (Scot.)–bree

moisture (to remove)–wipe, wring

mojo – amulet, charm, majagua, Moxo

moke – dolt, donkey, horse, minstrel, Negro, performer

moke (Eng. dialect) – fog, mesh, mist

moke (net-like)–mesh

moki–raft

moko–tattooing

moky–foggy, misty

molar – grinder, grinding, tooth

molarimeter–thermometer

molasses–theriaca, treacle

molave–vitex

mold – cast, die, humus, knead, matrice, matrix, mildew, mould, must, plasm, soil

mold (bottom part)–nowel

mold (core of)–nowel

mold (pouring hole in) – sprue

mold (rare)–plasm

mold again–recast

mold for casting – matrice, matrix

Moldavia (dept. of) – Iasi, Jassy

Moldavian measure–faltche

molder–crumble, rot

molding – astragal, bead, beak, cavetto, conge, cornice, cyma, fascia, fillet, gula, ogee, ogive, ovolo,

reed, reeding, splay, thumb, torus

molding (column above plinth)–torus

molding (concave)–cavetto, scotia

molding (convex)–astragal, ovolo, reed, reeding, torus

molding (convex, beaded, small)–astragal

molding (curved)–ess, nebule

molding (flat, narrow)–reglet

molding (large convex profile)–tore, torus

molding (lowest in base of column)–torus, tori (pl.)

molding (narrow)–reglet

molding (ornamented with disks)–bezantee

molding (rounded convex)–ovolo

molding (rule for)–screed

molding (S-shaped)–ogee

molding (semicircular)–torus, tori (pl.)

molding (square, small) – listel

molding (sunken)–scotia

molding (wave-like)–cyma

molding (with reverse curve)–cyma

moldy–fusty, mucid, musty, stale

mole – burrow, excavate, fault, imperfection, quay

molecast–molehill

mole-colored–taupe

mole gray–taupe

molehead–pierhead

mole-like animal – desman, tape

moleskin color–taupe

moles (genus of)–talpa

molecule component–atom

molest–bother, disturb, harass, incommode, pester, tease

molge–triturus

Molière character–Eraste

Molière comedy–L'Avare

mollify–allay, appease, calm, pacify, relax, sleek, soften, temper

mollitious–luxurious, sensuous, softening

mollusk – chiton, clam, cuttlefish, limpet, mussel, oyster, slug, snail, whelk

mollusk (bivalve) – chama, clam, cockle, mussel, oyster, scallop, spat

mollusk (bivalve, genus of) –anomia

mollusk (edible)–asi, mussel

mollusk (eight-armed) – octopus

mollusk (fresh water)–etheria

mollusk (gastropod) – abalone, slug, snail, whelk

mollusk (genus of)–astarte, buccinum, chama, chiton, murex

mollusk (larval)–veliger

mollusk (marine) – murex, nautilus

mollusk (one shell) – univalve

mollusk (Samoa edible)–asi

mollusk (sea)–abalone

mollusk (shelly concretion) –pearl

mollusk (ten-armed)–squid

mollusk (used for bait)–limpet, squid

mollusk (wrinkled shell) – cockle

mollusk (young)–spat

mollusk shell–cowrie, cowry

mollusk shell concretion – pearl

mollusk teeth–radula

molly–mallemuck, milksop, moll, mollycoddle

mollycoddle – coddle, pamper

molt (moult)–cast, exuviate, mew, mute, shed

molten rock–aa

moly–garlic, herb

momble–jumble, tangle

mome–blockhead, buffoon, critic, fool

moment–avail, instant, minute, point, signification, trice, twinkling, value, weight

moment (critical, decisive)–crisis, crises (pl.)

moment (crucial) – crisis, crises (pl.)

momentary – ephemeral, instantaneous, transient, transitory

momentous – important, influential, weighty

momist–faultfinder

mommy–duck, mammy

momo–owl

momus – critic, faultfinder, ridicule

mon–badge

monachist–monkish

monad–atom, deity, particle, unit, zoospore

monarch – butterfly, czar, despot, dynasty, emperor, ruler, sovereign, tsar, tzar

monarch (absolute) – czar, tsar, tzar

monarch (mighty) – potentate

monastery – abbey, cloister, convent, lamasery

monastery church abbey – minster

monastery head–abbot

monastery room–cell

monastic – monk, monkish, oblate

monastic community (old)–Laura

monastic officer–prior

monastic title–dom

monde–circle, coterie, globe, mound, society

monetary–financial, pecuniary

monetary token–coin

monetary transactions – finance

monetary unit–cash, dollar, frank, lira, maneh, mark, mina, ora, pound

monetary unit (Anglo-Saxon)–ora

money–cash, coin, currency, funds, grig, lucre, maneh, mina, pelf, spondulics, spondulix, wad

money (anc. bronze)–aes

money (Anglo-Saxon)–ora

money (coinage of)–mint

money (coined)–specie

money (found)–trove

money (metal)–coin, specie

money (roll of coin)–rouleau

money (Scotch for)–siller

money (slang)–boodle, jack, rhino, wampum

money (standard bank) – banco

money (sudden oversupply of)–inflation

moneybag–wealth

money bill–fine, penalty, tax

money box–arca, chest, till

money broker–changer

money-changer–saraf, seraf, shroff

money-changing–agio

money coined–specie

money cowrie–shells

money exchange premium–agio

money found–trove

money gained–lucre

money gift–alms, bequest

money given to confirm the hiring of servants (Scot.)–arles

moneylender–pawnbroker

moneylenders (excessive interest)–usurers

money-maker–coiner, counterfeiter, minter

money manual (of exchange values)–cambist

money matters (pert. to) – economics

money paid down–cash, deposit

money paid to avoid a feud–cro

money plant–moneywort

money premium–agio

money sent–remittance

money sorter – saraf, seraf, shroff

money spinner–usurer

money value–banco

moneyed – affluent, rich, wealthy

moneyed corporation–bank

moneyer – banker, coiner, minter

moneyer's weight – blank, droit, mite, perit

mong–barter, crowd, intercourse, mingle, mingling,

mix, mixture, traffic

monger–dealer, trader

mongler–sandpiper

Mongol–see Mongolian

Mongolian – Asian, Buriat, Eleuts, Kalmucks, Khalkhas, Tartar, Tatar

Mongolian caravan leader – bashi

Mongolian city – Kobdo, Ulan Bator Khoto (c.)

Mongolian city (sacred) – Urga

Mongolian coin – mungo (br.), tugrik (s.)

Mongolian conjurer – shaman

Mongolian desert–Gobi

Mongolian ecclesiastic–lama

Mongolian monk–lama

Mongolian priest–shaman

Mongolian religion–Confucianism, Shamanism, Shintoism

Mongolian river–Onon, Pei, Peiho

Mongolian town–Urga

Mongolian weight–lan

Mongoloid–Asian

Mongoloid (Assam)–Garo

Mongoloid (Nepal)–Rais

Mongoloid race (one of) – Lapp

Mongoloid tribe (member of)–Lai, Tartar, Tatar

Mongoloid tribe member (Burma)–Lai

mongoose–lemur, urva

mongoose (Asiatic crab-eating)–urva

mongrel–cur, hybrid

mongrel whitefish–tullibee

monial–nun

moniker–name, nickname

monish–admonish

monition – admonition, advice, caution, citation, indication, instruction, intimation, notice, order, summons, warning

monitor – admonish, catamaran, ibid, inciter, instigator, ironclad, lizard, mentor, nozzle

monitor bug–conenose

Monitor builder–Ericsson

monitor lizard–uran, varan

monitory – admonition, warning

monk – bullfinch, cenobite, fra, friar, padre, saki

monk (anc. father of English language)–Beda

monk (convent community) –cenobite

monk (Eastern Church) – caloyer

monk (English, early)–Beda

monk (Franciscan) – Capuchin

monk (hermit) – anchoret, anchorite

monk (monastic order) – friar

monk (Moslem)–dervish

monk (Spanish)–padre

monk (Tibetan)–lama

monk's-head–dandelion

monkshood (the plant)–aconite

monk's hood–atis, cowl

monk's period of time – monachate

monk's title–fra

monks living in convent community–cenobites

monkey – entellus, langur, lar, mona, nisnas, tota, wanderoo

monkey (Asiatic)–macaque

monkey (Asiatic, long-tailed)–langur

monkey (bonnet)–zati

monkey (caplike hair on head)–entellus

monkey (capuchin)–sai, sapajou

monkey (cebine)–sai

monkey (Central American, howling)–mono

monkey (Ceylon) – maha, toque

monkey (East Indian, long-tailed)–entellus

monkey (genus of spider)– ateles

monkey (grivet)–tota

monkey (howling) – araba, mono, stentor

monkey (Indian)–rhesus

monkey (Indian peninsula) –wanderoo

monkey (kind of) – catar-rhine, mona

monkey (large)–sajou

monkey (long-tailed)–entellus, sai

monkey (Nile, upper)–grivet

monkey (Oriental) – macaque

monkey (proboscis) – kaha, noseape

monkey (small) – apeling, marmoset

monkey (South African) – vervet

monkey (South American)– marmoset, saki, titi

monkey (South American, howling)–araba

monkey (spider)–ateles

monkey (squirrel)–samiri

monkey (tailless)–ape

monkey (West African) – potto

monkey (West African, long-tailed)–patas

monkey bear–koala

monkey board–footboard

monkey bread–baobab

monkey cup–nepenthe

monkey flower–mimulus

monkey godmother–anjana

monkey jug–goglet

monkey-like animal–lemur

monkey-like animal (small, arboreal)–tarsier

monkeynut–peanut

monkeypot–goglet

monkey puzzle–pinon

monkey wheel–gin

monkey wrench–spanner

monkeys (genus of)–cebus

monkey's coconut–coquito

monoceros–sawfish, sword-fish, unicorn

monochord–sonometer

monocle–eyeglass

monocleid (monocleide) – cabinet, desk

monocracy–autocracy

monodist–composer, singer, writer

monogram – character, cipher, outline, sketch

monolith – menhir, monument, pillar, statue

monologize–soliloquize

monomachy–combat, duel

monophone–homophone

monopole–combination, emporium, monopoly

monopoly – charter, control, grant, privilege, right, trust

monostele–prostele

monotonous – dead, drab, dreary, dull, humdrum, tedious, wearisome

monotonous from want of variety–samely

monotonous rhythm – sing-song

monotony – sameness, uniformity, wearisome

monoxylon (monoxyle) – boat, canoe

monster – cerberus, geryon, ogre, teras

monster (classic myth.) – minotaur

monster (comb. form)–terato

monster (eight-headed) – Scylla

monster (fabled) – centaur, sphinx

monster (fabulous) – bucentaur, harpy, kraken

monster (fairy tale)–ogre

monster (female)–gorgon

monster (flame-vomiting)– chimaera, chimera

monster (frightful female)– gorgon

monster (giant)–ogre

monster (greedy, classical)– harpy

monster (half man, half bull)–minotaur

monster (Hercules slew) – Geryon

monster (man-eating)–ogre

monster (many-headed) – hydra

monster (medical)–teras

monster (mythical)–chimaera, chimera, minotaur, ogre

monster (nine-headed)–hydra

monster (serpent) – dragon, ellops

monster (winged)–harpy
monster (with lion's body and woman's head and bust)–sphinx
monster-like–teratoid
monsters with no hind legs–api
monstrous – enormous, extraordinary, gigantic, huge, overpowering, overwhelming, prodigious, strange, stupendous, titanic, unnatural, vast
monstrous (arch.)–enorm
Montague's son–Romeo
Montana city–Butte, Havre, Helena, Kipp, Missoula
Montana river–Teton
montant–mounting, rising
montanto – broadsword, sword
Montenegro coin–florin (s.), para (ac.), perpera (ac.)
montero – forester, huntsman, mountain, ranger
Montezuma cypress – ahuehuete
month (excess of calendar, over lunar)–epact
month following–proximo
month preceding–ultimo
monticle–hill
monticule–hillock, mount
montilla–sherry
Montmorency–sherry
monture–horse, mount
monument – sepulcher, tomb, vault
monument (loose stone) – cairn
monumental stone–menhir
monuments (anc., made of flat stones)–cromlechs
moo–low
mooch – loaf, loiter, pilfer, skulk, sneak, steal, vagrant
moocha–girdle
mood – caprice, disposition, freak, humor, humour, vein, whim
mood (Scot.)–tid
moods (sulky)–pets
moody–capricious, gloomy, pensive, sad, sullen

mool–bury, crumble, earth, grave, mingle, mold, soil
mools–chilblains
moon – Cynthia, Diana, Luna, Phoebe, satelles, satellite
moon (above)–superlunar
moon (areas on)–mare
moon (pert. to)–lunar
moon (poetic)–Dian
moon (the)–Cynthia, Diana, Luna, Phoebe
moonack–woodchuck
moonbeam–ray
moonbill–duck
mooncalf–dolt, mole, monster, monstrosity
mooncreeper – moonflower, moonseed
moon crescent point – cusp, horn
moon delineation – selenograph
moondown–moonset
moonfall–moonset
moon fern–moonwort
moonfish – opah, spadefish, sunfish
moonflower–daisy, oxeye
moonglow–moonlight
moon goddess – Astarte, Diana, Luna, Salena, Selene
moon goddess (Greek)–Artemis, Hecate, Hekate, Selena, Selene
moon goddess (Phoenician) –Tanit, Tanith
moon goddess (Roman) – Luna
moon inhabitant–Selenite
moonlighting – adventure, expedition, moonshining, raid
moon lily–moonflower
moon-mad–lunatic
moonman–gipsy, robber
moon of Uranus–Ariel
moon on fingernails–lunule
moon picture–selenograph
moon point–cusp, horn
moon point (farthest from earth)–apogee
moon point (nearest earth)–perigee
moonraking–woolgathering
moon-shaped–lunate

moon-shaped (half)–semilunate
moonshine – balsamweed, empty, idle, liquor, month, nonsense, sauce, trivial, whiskey
moonsick–lunatic
moonstone–hecatolite
moon valley (narrow)–rille
moon valley (telescopic) – rille
moon's age (at beginning of calendar year)–epact
moon's distance between apogee and perigee–apsis
moonery–madness
moonet–satellite
moonish–capricious, flighty
moony–dreamy, round
Moor – Berber, Moroccan, Moslem, Saracen
moor – anchor, bog, fen, marsh, swale
moor (infertile)–lande
moorberry–cranberry
moorbird–grouse
moor blackbird–ouzel
moorburn – illtemper, quarrel
moor buzzard–harrier
moor cock–blackcock
moor dance–morisco
moor evil–dysentery
moorfowl–grouse
moor game–moorfowl
moor grass–sundew
moor hawk–harrier
moor hen–coot, gallinule
moorish–marshy, swampy
Moorish–Moresque
Moorish garment–jupon
Moorish horse–barb
Moorish judge–cadi
Moorish kettledrum–atabal, tabor
Moorish tabor–atabal
moose–alce, elk
moose (genus of)–alces
moose (the)–eland
mooth–damp, misty, wet
mooting–discussion, gathering, meeting
mop–swab
mop (cannon cleaning) – merkin, moppet
mopish–confused, foolish

moppet–baby, darling, doll

mora – default, delay, footstool, postponement, stool

mora tree–fustic

moral–epimyth, ethic, ethical, good, pure, righteous, upright

moral (treatment of)–ethical

moral excellence–virtue

moral faults–vices

moral injunction–precept

moral obligation–duty

moral poem (short)–dit

moral religious knowledge (to teach)–edify

moral story–apologue

moral taint–stain

morale – confidence, hope, morality, spirit, zeal

moralist (prim)–prig

morality–righteousness, virtue

morality (not involving) – amoral

morally base–depraved, immoral, perverted, vile

morals (description of) – ethography

morass – bog, fen, marsh, swamp

morass weed–hornwort

moration–delay

moray–eel, hamlet

moray (genus of)–muraena

morbid–sick, unhealthy, unwholesome

morbid desire for music – melomania

morbus–disease, illness

morceau–bit, morsel

mordant – biting, burning, caustic, corrosive, keen, pungent, sarcastic, scathing

more – additional, greater, mair, plus

more cunning–slyer, tricky

more difficult–harder

more distant–ulterior

more mature–older, riper

more miserly–closer, meaner, nearer

more precious–dearer

more severe–sterner

more so–yea

more than–above, over

more than enough–too

more than one–many, plural

more than this–yea

more underhanded–slyer

more unusual–rarer

more willingly–rather

moreover – again, also, and, besides, further

morepork (New Zealand)–boobook, ruru

mores – conventions, customs, manners

morgay–dogfish

morglay–sword

morgue–deadhouse, haughtiness, impassivity, stolidity

morindin dye–al

morinel–dotterel

moringa oil–ben

moringa seed–ben

morion–helmet, quartz

morion (armor)–cabasset

mormo – bugbear, shemonster

Mormon–Danite, mandrill

Mormon state–Utah

Mormon tree–poplar

Mormon weed–velvetleaf

morning – aurora, dawn, matin, sunrise

morning (belonging to) – matin

morning (of the)–matin

morning (pert. to) – matin, matutinal, wight

morning clouds–velo

morning coat–cutaway

morning concert–aubade

morning glory–ipomoea, nil

morning glory family–convolvulaceae

morning performance–matinee

morning prayer–matin

morning reception–levee

morning serenade (open air)–aubade

morning service–matin

morning star–Daystar, Jupiter, Lucifer, Mars, Mercury, Saturn, Venus

moro–finch

Moro chief–Dato, Datto

Moro dialect–Sulu

Moro high priest–atli, sarip

Moro island–Mendanoa

Moro knife–barong

Moro tribe (one of)–Sulu

Moro tribe (one of leading)–Lanao

Moro tribe chief–Dato, Datto

Moroccan – Berber, Moor, Moslem

Moroccan capital–Fez, Marrakech, Rabat

Moroccan city–Fez, Morocco, Rabat, Rabbat, Tangier

Moroccan coin – mouzouna (br.), rial (s.)

Moroccan coin (money of account)–okia, okieh

Moroccan district–Riff

Moroccan emperor – Miramamolin, Miramolin

Moroccan government – Maghzen, Makhzan, Makhzen

Moroccan hat–fez

Moroccan head–merganser

Moroccan island–Madeira

Moroccan jaw–scoter

Moroccan measure – fanega, sahh, tomini

Moroccan native – Berber, Moor

Moroccan port – see Moroccan seaport

Moroccan province–Sus

Moroccan quarter (Jews)–El Millah

Moroccan ruler–sultan

Moroccan seaport – Agadir, Ceuta, El Araish, Laraiche, Mogador, Rabat, Rabbat, Tangier

Moroccan (Span.) seaport – Tetuan

Moroccan soldier (native infantry)–askar

Moroccan tribe (privileged)–Maghzen, Makhzan, Makhzen

Moroccan tribesman–Kabyle

Moroccan weight–artal, artel, dirhem, gerbe, kintar, quintal, ratel, rotl

morocco (imitation)–roan

morology–folly, nonsense

moron – dull, sluggish, stupid
morose – crabbed, crusty, dour, embittered, gloomy, glum, grum, moody, sour, splenetic, sullen, surly, unhappy
morose (be)–sulk
morphia–morphine
morphine derivative–heroin
morphon (opposed to)–bion
morro–castle, hill, point
Mors–death
morse–brooch, clasp, walrus
morsel–bite, fragment, morceau, ort, piece, snack
morsel (choice)–titbit
morsing–priming
morsure–bite, biting
mort – abundance, dead, deadly, death, fatal, grease, lard, salmon
mortacious–extremely, very
mortal–deadly, fatal, human
mortally – alamort, deathly, fatally
mortar–bowl, cannon
mortar (fine)–putty
mortar (lime)–putty
mortarboard–cap, hawk
mortar mixer (beater)–rab
mortgage–bond, pledge
mortician–undertaker
mortification – chagrin, humiliation, shame, vexation
mortification (medical) – gangrene
mortify – abase, abash, chagrin, humble, humiliate, shame, spite
mortify (rare)–ashame
mortise (complement of) – tenon
mortise (law)–amortize
mortuary–deadhouse, funeral, morgue, sepulcher
morvin–mallein
mosaic gold–ormolu
Mosaic law–torah
Moscow citadel–Kremlin
Moses' brother–Aaron
Moses' emissary–Caleb
Moses' father-in-law–Jethro
Moses' mountain–Nebo
Moses' sister–Miriam

Moses' wife–Zipporah
mosker–decay, molder
Moslem – Islamic, Mohammedan, Mussulman, Saracen
Moslem (orthodox)–Hanif
Moslem (Turkestan)–Salar
Moslem ablution (before prayer) – widu, wudu, wuzu
Moslem assessor (court) – mufti
Moslem belt–zonar, zonnar
Moslem (East) booth–sook
Moslem cap–taj
Moslem capturer of Jerusalem–Omar
Moslem caste–mopla, moplah
Moslem chief–rais
Moslem cleric – imam, imaum
Moslem college – madrasa, madrasah, madrassah, madrasseh
Moslem college (religious)– ulema
Moslem council–ulema
Moslem court official–hajib
Moslem deity–Allah, Eblis
Moslem devotee–dervish
Moslem exclamation–bismillah
Moslem expounder (official) –mufti
Moslem headgear–fez
Moslem interpreters of Koran (body of)–ulema
Moslem invocation–bismillah
Moslem javelin–jereed
Moslem judge–cadi
Moslem lawyer–mufti
Moslem leader–ameer, amir, emeer, emir
Moslem (East) market–sook
Moslem minister (finance)– dewan
Moslem name–Ali, Hassim
Moslem nymphs–houris
Moslem official–mufti
Moslem orthodox–Hanif
Moslem pilgrimage to Mecca –hadj
Moslem prayer leader – imam, imaum

Moslem priest–imam, imaum
Moslem priests (body of)– ulema
Moslem prince–ameer, amir, emeer, emir, nawab
Moslem pulpit–mimbar
Moslem religion–Islam
Moslem religious college – ulema
Moslem ruler–nawab
Moslem sage–ulema
Moslem scholars (body of)– ulema
Moslem school – madrasa, madrasah, madrassah, madrasseh
Moslem scripture (sacred)– Koran
Moslem sect (North African)–Senousi, Senusi, Senusite, Senussi, Senussian
Moslem shrine (Mecca) – Caaba (var.), Kaaba, Kaabeh
Moslem spirit–genie, genii (pl.), jinnee, jinni, jinn (pl.), jinniyeh (fem.)
Moslem teacher (religious) –alim
Moslem teacher (Shiites, religious)–mujtahid
Moslem theologian–mujtahid
Moslem title–sid
Moslem tradition (bridge of Paradise)–Al Sirat
Moslem tribe (Kartvelian)– Laz, Lazi, Lazes (pl.)
Moslem tribe head–sheik
Moslem tribesman–Moro
Moslem university–madrasa, madrasah, madrassah, madrasseh
Moslem viceroy–nawab
Moslem warrior–Saracen
Moslemism – Mohammedanism
Moslemite–Moslem
mosque (mosk)–masjid
mosque official – imam, imaum
mosque (Great at Mecca) stone building – Caaba, Kaaba, Kaabeh
mosque tower – manarat, minaret, minarete

mosque warden–nazir
mosquito (large, coll.)–galli-
nipper
mosquito bee–angelito, kar-
bi
mosquito fish–gambusia
mosquito hawk–dragonfly,
nighthawk
Mosquito Indian drink (fermented, from cassava or
plantain)–mushla
mosquito larvae–wigglers
mosquito plant–mint, penny-
royal
Mosquito State–Jersey
moss – bog, lichen, morass,
swamp
moss (Ceylon)–agar, agar-
agar
moss (edible) – agar, agar-
agar
moss (kind of)–rag
moss (long)–treebeard
moss (pendulous tree)–treebeard
moss animalcule–bryozoan
mossback–fogey, fogy
mossberry–cranberry
mossbunker–menhaden
moss cheeper–bunting, pipit
moss coral–bryozoan
moss corn–silverweed
moss duck–mallard
moss fruit–sporogonium
moss-grown–antiquated
moss hammer–bittern
mosshead–merganser
moss-like plant–hepatic
moss polyp–bryozoan
moss substance–agar, agar-
agar
mosswort–bryophyte
mossy – abounding, boggy,
covered, downy, dull,
marshy, overgrown, stu-
pid
most–utmost
most important–chief, main
most in want–neediest
most inexperienced–rawest,
rookie, rooky
most keen–sharpest
most miserly–meanest
most noble–Hiram
most northerly land of world
(anc. geog.)–Thule

most sensitive–sorest
most terrible–direst
mot – butt, device, mark,
moat, motto, opinion, word
mote – atom, barrow, emi-
nence, height, hill, iota,
match, particle, speck,
squib, trifle, tumulus
motet–anthem
moth – egger, io, lappet,
miller, tineah, tinean,
tineid, tineidae, tineina
moth (carpet)–tineoidea
moth (clothes)–tinea, tineid,
tineidae
moth (genus of)–tinea
moth (large yellow)–io
moth (Lasiocampidae)–eg-
ger
moth (med.)–chloasma
moth (suborder of)–heteroc-
era
moth (tree)–egger
moth hawk–goatsucker
moth hunter–goatsucker
moth larva (worm-like,
elongated)–caterpillar
moth patch (med.)–chloas-
ma
moth spots (med.)–chloasma
moth wing spot–fenestra
mother (animal's) – dam,
dame
mother (god) – cummer,
kimmer
mother (Great)–Brigantia
mother (Latin)–mater
mother (myth., turned to
stone)–Niobe
mother (pert. to)–maternal
mother (Philippine Island)–
ina
mother (Tagalog)–ina
mother and father (pert. to)
–parental
Mother Carey's chickens –
petrels
Mother Carey's goose–ful-
mar
Mother Carey's hen–petrel
mother church–cathedral
mother city–metropolis
mother gate–bord, tramway
Mother Goose author –
Charles Perrault

Mother Goose character–Bopeep, Simon, Sprat
Mother Goose publisher –
John Newbery
mother house – convent,
monastery
Mother Hubbard – dress,
gown
mother land–fatherland
Mother Maid–Virgin Mary
mother of coal–charcoal
mother of gods–Brigantia,
Rhea
mother of graces–aegle
mother of man–Cybele
mother of pearl–nacre
mother of presidents–Vir-
ginia
mother of states–Virginia
mother of the months–moon
mother turned to stone
(myth.)–Niobe
mother's mark–birthmark
mothered–thick, viscid
motherly–maternal
motion – move, movement,
petition, propose, request,
suggest, unrest
motion (due to)–kinetic
motion (expressive)–gesture
motion (horse's rearing) –
pesade
motion (jerky)–bob, lipe
motion (of body)–gesture
motion (quivering)–tremor
motion (reciprocating)–seesaw
motion (vibratory)–tremor
motion expressing disinter-
est–shrug
motion picture – cinema,
movie, photoplay
motion picture (sound, coll.)
–talky
motion picture arc lamp –
kleig
motion picture machine –
animatograph, cinemato-
graph, cinematographe,
kinetoscope, projector,
theatrograph
motion picture outline–scenario
motion picture show–cine-
ma, movie, photoplay

motion transmitter – belt, cog, gear
motionless–inert, rigid
motionless point (pert. to)–nodal
motivate–impel, incite, induce, move, stimulate
motive–cause, consideration, incentive, incitement, inducement, influence, instigation, sake, spur, stimulus
motive (ostensible)–pretext
motley–checkered, diverse, heterogeneous, mixed, mottled, variegated
motor–engine, kinetic
motor (hand-powered)–baromotor
motor (rotary)–turbine
motor speed control–rheocrat
mottled–dappled, pied, pinto, spotted
mottled appearance in mahogany–roe
mottled appearance in woods –roe
mottled soap–castile, eschwege
motto–aphorism, axiom, device, gnome, maxim, mot, precept
motto (Order of the Garter) –honnisoitquimalypense
mouche–patch
mouchoir–handkerchief
moufflon–sheep
mould–matrix
moulding–see molding
moulrush–pollack
mound – bank, boundary, bounds, bulwark, dam, dene, doon, dun, dune, elevation, embankment, hill, knoll, rampart, tee, tumulus
mound (memorial stone) – cairn
mound (Polynesia)–ahu
mound (sand, Eng.)–dene, dune
mound (Scot.)–toman
mound bird–megapode
Mound City–St. Louis
mound fowl–megapode

mound maker–megapode
mound of light–kohinoor
mound turkey–megapode
mount–arise, ascend, climb, glue, hill, horse, mountain, paste, promontory, rise
mount (polo)–pony
Mount Etna city (at foot of) –Catania
Mount Everest peak (south) –Lhotse
mount horizontal bar–kip
Mount Parnassus fountain–Castalia
mount the ass–bankrupt
mountain–berg
mountain (Asia Minor)–Ida
mountain (Babylonian) – Ararat
mountain (California)–Helena, Shasta, Whitney
mountain (comb. form)–oro
mountain (East Africa) – Pare
mountain (fabled, at earth's center)–Meru
mountain (from which Moses saw Land of Canaan)–Nebo
mountain (Greece)–Ida, Ossa, Psiloriti
mountain (Greek myth., residence of Muses and Apollo)–Helicon
mountain (high)–Alp
mountain (highest)–Everest
mountain (Hindu myth., at earth's center)–Meru
mountain (ice)–berg
mountain (Japan)–Fujiyama
mountain (legendary)–Kaf, Meru, Qaf
mountain (low)–butte
mountain (most beautiful)–Fujiyama
mountain (near ancient Troy)–Ida
mountain (North American, second highest)–Logan
mountain (of earth's center) –Meru
mountain (prefix)–oro
mountain (Scot.)–Ben
mountain (Thessaly)–Ossa, Pelion

mountain (western U.S.) – Helena, Shasta, Whitney
mountain (where Moses first saw promised land)–Nebo
mountain (world's highest) –Everest
mountain (Wyoming)–Moran
mountain andromeda – fetterbush
mountain ash–rowan, rowen
mountain at earth's center–Meru
mountain badger–marmot
mountain balsam–fir
mountain banana–fei
mountain barometer–orometer
mountain beaver–sewellel
mountain blackbird–ouzel
mountain bramble – cloudberry
mountain cat–bobcat, cacomistle, cougar
mountain centaury–bluet
mountain chain–range, Appalachian, Blue Ridge, Rocky, Sierras
mountain cock–capercaillie
mountain colley–ouzel
mountain cowslip–auricula
mountain crest (rugged) – aret, arete
mountain crest (southwest U.S.)–Cumbre
mountain curassow – oreophasis
mountain defile–gap, gate, ghat, ghaut, gorge, pass
mountain depression–col
mountain devil–moloch
mountain dew (Scot.)–whisky
mountain duck – harlequin, sheldrake
mountain finch–brambling
mountain flax–centaury
mountain folks – Cameronians
mountain fringe–fumitory, wormwood
mountain gap–defile, gate, ghat, ghaut, gorge, pass
mountain goat–ibex
mountain ivy–laurel
mountain knapweed–bluet

mountain lake (pool)–tarn
mountain leatherwood–flannelbush
mountain linnet–twite
mountain lion–cougar, puma
mountain magpie – woodpecker
mountain manchineel–poisonwood
mountain mango–fig
mountain mint–basil; calamint
mountain nymph–oread
mountain oak–chestnut
mountain panther – cougar, ounce
mountain parrot–kea
mountain partridge–quail
mountain partridgeberry – snowberry
mountain pass – col, defile, gate, gap, ghat, ghaut, gorge
mountain peak (rocky)–tor
mountain peak (Fr.)–pic
mountain peak (tooth-like)–dent
mountain pheasant–grouse
mountain pool–tarn
mountain quail–partridge
mountain range–ridge
mountain range (acute crest of)–arete
mountain range (between Turkestan and Mongolia) –Alatau
mountain range (myth.) – Kaf, Qaf
mountain range (pert. to)–Andean
mountain raspberry–cloudberry
mountain ridge–aret, arete, sierra
mountain ridge (rugged)–sierra
mountain rose–laurel
mountain snow–neve
mountain spinach–orach, orache
mountain spur–aret, arete
Mountain State–Montana
Mountain States – Arizona, Colorado, Idaho, Mon-

tana, Neveda, New Mexico, Utah, Wyoming
mountain sunset (reflection of)–alpenglow
mountain tallow – hatchettine
Mountain Tartar–Tauli
mountain tea–wintergreen
mountain tobacco–arnica
mountain top–peak, summit
mountain trail marker (stone)–karn
mountained–elevated
mountaineer–Aaron
mountainous–high, rugged
mountainous country–highland
mountains (science of)–orology
mountains (study of)–orography
mountant – ascendant, mounting, raised, rising
mountebank – charlatan, cheat, empiric, gull, impostor, minstrel, pretender, quack
mounted–elevated, raised
mounting – embellishment, equipment, setting
mountings (parts of cannon) –rimbase
moup (moop)–associate, nibble
mourn–bemoan, bewail, deplore, erme, grieve, lament, long, mourning, murmur, rue, sigh, sorrow, wail
mourner (professional) – wailer
mournful–elegiac, elegiacal, plaintive, repine, sad, sorrowful, woebegone
mournful poem–elegy
mourning – crape, drapery, garb, lament, lamentation, sad, sorrow, sorrowing
mourning bride–scabious
mourning dress – sables, weeds
mourning widow–scabious
mouse (European shrew) – erd
mouse (field)–vole

mouse (leaping)–jerboa
mouse (male)–buck
mouse (meadow)–vole
mouse (old world)–jerboa
mouse (shrew)–erd
mouse (small field)–harvest
mouse bird–coly, shrike
mouse deer–chevrotain
mouse-ear – chickweed, hawkweed
mouse hare–pika
mouse hound–weasel
mouse-like–murine
mouse milk–spurge
mouse web–cobweb, gossamer, phlegm
mouser–cat, detective
mousing–inquisitive, prowling, prying, rapacious
mousle–rumple
mousse–dessert, messboy
moutan (Chinese)–peony
mouth–cavity, dupe, impudence, mow, mun, opening, os, ora (pl.), rictus, stoma, stomata (pl.)
mouth (away from)–aboral
mouth (furnace)–bocca
mouth (glass furnace)–bocca
mouth (Greek)–stoma, stomata (pl.)
mouth (Latin)–os, ora (pl.)
mouth (part of)–lip, palate, pharynx, uvula
mouth (pert. to)–oral, rictal, stomatic
mouth (river)–lade
mouth (Spanish)–boca
mouth (toward)–orad
mouth (uttered through the) –oral
mouth (wry)–mop
mouth deformity–harelip
mouth disease medicine–stomatic
mouth of Amazon–Para
mouth of canyon–abra
mouth organ–harmonica
mouthpiece (brass musical instrument)–bocal
mouthpiece (criminal, slang) –lawyer
mouth roof–palate
mouth roof (pert. to)–palatal
mouthful–gulp, lot

mouths–ora, os (sing.)
mouton (in prisons)–spy
movable–mobile
movable fence barrier–bars, gate
movable property–chattels, gear
move – actuate, animate, budge, cause, gee, goad, impel, incite, induce, instigate, kindle, mog, motion, prompt, provoke, rouse, shift, spur, stimulate, stir
move along (slang)–mosey, scram
move apart – diverge, separate
move away (coll.) – mog, scram
move back–ebb, recede, retire, retreat, retrograde
move backward and forward –oscillate, shuttle
move briskly–spank
move clumsily–joll, lumber
move forward – advance, edge
move forward (as if driven) –scud
move from one place to another–migrate
move furtively–slink, sneak
move heavily–lug, trudge
move in circles–purl
move in violent agitation – seethe
move inwardly–enmove
move noisily–bustle
move obliquely–sidle, skew
move on (coll.)–mog, scram
move on wheels–roll, trundle
move out of country–emigrate
move over–edge, joll, sidle
move quickly – dart, dash, fly, hurtle, scud, shot, spank
move quickly (coll.)–scoot
move quickly (with whirling sound)–scur, skirr
move rapidly–career, gallop, hurtle
move rhythmically–dance
move sideways–sidle
move sidewise–slue

move slowly–edge, inch
move slowly and steadily – jog, mog
move smoothly–glide, slip
move spasmodically–twitch
move stealthily–slink, sneak
move swiftly–dart, fly, scoot, scud
move to and fro–flap, wag
move towards each other–converge
move (turn) towards east – orientate
move unsteadily–wabble
move up and down – bob, teeter
move with impetuosity – hurtle
move with light steps–tiptoe
move with measured tread–march
move with short turns – dodge, zigzag
moved–emigrated
moved (easily) – emotional, loped, mobile
moved by entreaty (capable of)–exorable
moved carelessly–rollicked
moved in dancing (to right or left)–chassed
moved swaggeringly – rollicked
moved swiftly–swept
moved while in contact with –slid
moved with difficulty – waded
moved with exertion–hove
movement–action, emotion, impulse, maneuver, motion, rhythm
movement (balanced, measured)–rhythm
movement (causing)–motile
movement (dance) – chasse, pirouette
movement (forward)–progress
movement (involuntary)–reflex
movement (overpowering influence or power)–maelstrom
movement (quick, vibratory)–tremor

movement (rhythmic) – dance, lilt
movement (rolling)–welter
movement (steady)–constant
movement (strong upward) –surge
movement (upward, of a vessel)–scend
movement (without recoil)–deadbeat
movement from point to point–passage
moving – active, affecting, ambulant, astir
moving backward – retrogressive
moving cause–reason
moving force–agent
moving mechanical part – rotor
moving picture – cinema, movie, photoplay
moving stairway–escalator
mow–cornfield, cut, grimace, heap, lay, mass, math, mew, mouth, stack
mowana–baobab
mowie–stackyard
mowing – derision, grimacing, meadowland, mockery
mowing machine – mower, scythe, sickle
mowland – meadowland, mowlot
mowth–mowing
moxie berry–snowberry
moy – affected, demure, gentle, mild
moyen–agency, course, influence, means, property, substance, way
mozo–manservant
mucago–coating, mucilage, mucus
much–abundant, fele, great, high, lot, many, uncommon
mucid–slimy, mucous, musty
mucilage–arabin, gum, mucago
mucilaginous–viscid
muck–dung, manure
muckender–handkerchief

mucker–confusion, disorder, hoarder, mess, muddle
muckle–bother, fret
muckment–dirt, filth, trash
muckmidden–dunghill
muckthrift–miser, niggard
mucor–filthiness, hoariness, moldiness
muculent–moist, slimy, viscous
mud – mire, offscourings, slime
mud (deep)–mire
mud (fix in)–bemire
mud (prairie)–gumbo
mud (sticky)–slime
mud (thick)–slime
mud (viscous)–slime
mud bath–illutation
Mud Cat state–Mississippi
mud dab–flounder
mud dabbler–killifish
mud dauber–wasp
mud devil–hellbender
mud eel–siren
mud lark – gamin, horse (race), magpie, urchin
mud mark–mudflow
mud peep–sandpiper
mud pike–saury
mud puppy–hellbender, salamander
mud rake–claut
mud snipe–woodcock
mud sunfish–warmouth
mud teal–greenwing
mud volcano–salse
mud worm (Samoan)–ipo
mudwort–mudweed
muddier–mirier
muddle–addle, bemuse, bewilder, confound, confuse, daze, disorder, intoxicate, mess, mix, perplex, soss, stir, stupefy
muddled–burbled, confused, fuddled, muzzy, ree, tipsy
muddling (stupefying) – bemusing
muddy – base, besmeared, clouded, confused, dirty, miry, sensual, slaky, slushy, turbid
muddy (covered with clay)–lutose

muddy (turbid) – feculent, roily
muezzin's call to prayer – azan
muff (obs.)–German, Swiss
muffed – crested, irritated, vexed
muffet–whitethroat
muffetee – muffler, wrister, wristlet
muffin–cob, crumpet, gem
muffin (light)–gem
muffin (puffy)–popover
muffle–damp, deaden, dull, envelope, mute, shroud, wrap
muffled – dampened, deadened, dulled, enveloped, gagged, muted, shrouded, wrapped
muffler–mute, scarf, tippet
mufflin–titmouse
mufti – alim, assessor, expounder, official
mufty–whitethroat
mug – cram, drizzle, dupe, face, fool, grimace, mungo, photograph, pulse, sheep, study
mug (ale)–toby
mug (earthenware)–stein
mug (small)–noggin
mug (small, in shape of fat man)–toby
mug house – alehouse, pothouse
mug weed–mugwort
muga–caterpillar
mugger–crocodile, peddler, tinker
mugget (mugwet) – woodruff
muggins–game, simpleton
muggy – damp, humid, moist, moldy, whitethroat
mugwet–woodruff
muir–moor
muishond–weasel, zóril
mujer–wife, woman
mulatto's and white's child –quadroon
mulberry (Indian)–ach, al
mulberry bark (paper)–tapa, tappa
mulberry bird–starling
mulberry dye–al

mulberry family–Moraceae
mulberry fig–sycamore
mulberry tree (comb. form) –mor
mulch–sawdust, straw
mulct–amerce, amercement, blemish, deceive, defect, fine, penalty, punish, scot
mulcter–amercer
mule – chilblain, coble, hinny, hybrid, locomotive, mewl, mool, mute, slipper, tractor
mule (leading in pack train) –cencerro
mule (untrained)–shavetail
mule chair–cacolet
mule driver–skinner
mule killer–mantis
mule skinner–driver
mules (drove of)–atajo
muleteer–peon
mulga–shield, wattle
muliebrile–feminine
muliebrity–effeminacy, femininity, womanhood, womanliness
mulish–hybrid, sterile, stubborn, sullen
mull–cow, crag, crush, dust, failure, grind, heat, mess, mold, muslin, muzzle, ointment, powder, promontory, pulverize, rubbish, snout, snuffbox, spice, squeeze, sweeten
mullein (common)–torch
mullet–liza, puffin
mullet (Central America)–bobo
mullet (Mexican)–bobo
mullet hawk–osprey
mulligan (tramp's slang) – stew
mulligatawny–soup
mulligrubs – blues, colic, sulks
mullock–dirt, litter, refuse, rubbish
mulloway–jewfish
mulmul–muslin
multifarious–manifold
multifold–manifold, many, numerous
multiform–diverse
multiplier (the)–facient

multiply–amplify, breed, increase, magnify

multitude – crowd, horde, host, legion, many, mob, much, shoal, swarm, throng

multitudinously–myriadly

mumble – chavel, chavle, chew, mump, mutter, patter

mummer – actor, buffoon, performer

mummy–corpse

mummy apple–papaya

mump – cheat, displeasure, grimace, mumble, sulks, sullenness

mumper–beggar, impostor, sulker

mumpish–dull, sulky, sullen

mumruffin–titmouse

mun – face, may, mouth, must, shall

munch–chew, eat

munch (as a horse)–champ

mundane – cosmic, earthly, secular, temporal, terrene

mungo–mongoose, Negro

municipality–city, town

municipality (pert. to)–civic

munificence – benevolence, bounty, generosity, liberality

muniment – evidence, furnishing, record, valuables, writings

munity–privilege

muntjac (muntjak)–kidang

mura (Japan) – community, village

mural–painting, wall

murchy–mischief

murder–assassinate, carnage, homicide, kill, slaughter, slay

murderer (English, famous) –Aram

murderer of brother–fratricide

murderer of father–patricide

murderer of a king–regicide

murderer of kings (pert. to) –regicidal

murderer of mother–matricide

murderer of a prophet–vaticide

murderer of sister–sororicide

murderous – bloody, bloodthirsty, gory, sanguinary

mure–gentle, immure, meek, modest, soft, wall

murk–dark, darkness, fog, gloom, mist

murky–dark, dense, foggy, gloomy, impenetrable, obscure, thick

murlin (Ireland) – badderlocks

murmur–babble, complain, curr, fret, hum, mutter, purl, repine, whisper

murmur softly – coo, pur, purl, purr

muscle–brawn, lacert, sinew, teres, thew

muscle (contracting)–agonist

muscle (either of two body) –teres

muscle (expansion)–dilator

muscle (neck)–scalenus

muscle (present in)–inosic, inosinic

muscle (raising)–levator

muscle (round)–teres

muscle (straight)–rectus

muscle (stretching)–tensor

muscle (that draws down an organ)–depressor

muscle (that raises some part)–levator

muscle (turning)–rotator

muscle column–sarcostyle

muscle curve–myogram

muscle segment–myocomma

muscle sugar–inosite, inositol

muscles (triangular) – deltoids

Muscovite–Russ, Russian

Muscovite mica–talc

Muscovite mineral–mica

muscular–brawny, sinewy, strong, thewy, torose, vigorous

muscular contraction (involuntary)–spasm

muscular inability to co-ordinate actions properly in walking–abasia

muscular movement irregularity–ataxia

muscular spasm–tonus

muscular stiffness–crick

muscular stomach–gizzard

muse – cogitate, consider, dream, meditate, mull, ponder, ruminate

Muse of astronomy – Clio, Urania

Muse of bucolic poetry – Thalia

Muse of choral song–Terpsichore

Muse of comedy–Thalia

Muse of dancing–Terpsichore

Muse of eloquence–Calliope

Muse of heroic poetry–Calliope

Muse of history–Clio

Muse of joy–Tara

Muse of lyric (amatory) – Erato

Muse of lyric (sacred)–Polyhymnia, Polymnia

Muse of music–Euterpe

Muse of poetry–Erato

Muse of tragedy–Melpomene

Muses (chief of nine)–Calliope

Muses (number of)–nine

Muses (the)–Calliope, Clio, Erato, Euterpe, Melpomene, Polymnia (Polyhymnia), Terpsichore, Thalia, Urania

Muses' epithet–Pierian

Muses' home–Aonia

Muses' seat of worship–Pieria

musee–museum

museful–meditative, silent, thoughtful

musery–amusement, play

musette – air, bagpipe, gavotte, oboe

museum keeper (chief)–curator

mush–cut, flattery, indent, notch, sentimentality, sepawn, sepon, supawn, suppawn, umbrella

mush (cornmeal)–atole

mushed–confused, crushed

mushroom–agaric, morel

mushroom (edible)–morel
mushroom (kind of)–morel
mushroom (part of)–annulus, basidiospore, basidium, gill, hymenium, sterigma, trama
mushroom (poisonous)–amanita, toadstool
mushroom disease–flock
mushroom part (umbrellashaped)–pileus
mushroom poisoning – mycetism
mushroom stem–stipe
music (a lead in)–presa
music (abrupt)–staccato
music (aftersong in)–epode
music (all voices)–tutti
music (as written)–sta
music (augmented fourth)–tritone
music (be silent)–tacet
music (choral, one performer on each part)–soli
music (clear-cut, disconnected tones)–staccato
music (closing measure) – coda
music (composition for nine) –nonet
music (do)–ut
music (eight successive notes)–ottava
music (finale)–coda
music (flourish)–cadenza
music (form of)–jazz
music (go back)–DC, DS
music (Greek major third)–ditone
music (grow louder)–crescendo
music (half note)–minim
music (half tone)–semitone
music (high in)–alt
music (high vocal part) – canto
music (instrumental duet)–duo
music (it proceeds)–va
music (less)–meno
music (let it stand)–sta
music (little by little)–poco a poco
music (lively)–allegro
music (loud in)–forte
music (low in pitch)–grave

music (major)–dur
music (major key)–dur
music (manual)–clavier
music (mark in)–slur
music (marked emphatic)–marcato
music (marked melodic phrase)–leitmotif, leitmotiv
music (melodious style) – arioso
music (more rapid)–stretta, stretto
music (moving moderately) –andante
music (much)–molto
music (muted)–sorda
music (nature of an aria and recitative)–arioso
music (ninth in)–nona
music (nonconcerted)–solo
music (pert. to)–choral
music (piano, with fast rolling base)–boogie woogie
music (poem set to)–ode
music (quick time)–presto
music (refrain)–epode, tra
music (rhythmic)–swing
music (sextuplet) – sestole, sestolet
music (shake)–trill
music (silent)–tacet
music (slow in)–largo, lento
music (slow, moderately)–andante
music (slow movement) – adagio
music (smooth, connected)–legato
music (so much)–tanto
music (soft) – dulce, piano, zart
music (soprano in)–canto
music (stately)–largo
music (stop playing)–tacet
music (tenor in)–canto
music (third)–tierce
music (32nd note) – demisemiquaver
music (three-chord note) – triad
music (thrice)–ter
music (time in)–tempo
music (trembling effect)–vibrato
music (triplet)–tercet, triole

music (trombone mute)–wawa, wah-wah
music (turn over)–verte
music (twice)–bis
music (very) – assai, molto, tres
music (very fast)–vivo
music (very slow)–molto
music (very soft)–pp
music (vivacity)–brio
music (with bow)–arco
music beat (measured) – pulse
music hall–odeum, odeon, odea (pl.)
music hall (low-class)–gaff
music scale (major)–gamut
music song (simple)–lay
music staff–stave
music syllable–tra
music timing device–metronome
musical–harmonious, lyric, melodious
musical (abrupt)–staccato
musical (closing measure)–coda
musical (exceedingly)–tres
musical (grow louder)–crescendo
musical (less)–meno
musical (lively)–allegro
musical (refrain) – apode, repetend, tra
musical (shake)–trill
musical (silent)–tacet
musical (slow)–largo, lento
musical (slow, moderately)–andante
musical (soft)–dulce, piano, zart
musical (very)–assai, molto, tres
musical (with bow)–arco
musical abridgement–ridotto
musical aftersong–epode
musical and rich–orotund
musical and ringing – orotund
musical arrangement–ridotto
musical ballad–derry
musical bells (set of)–peal
musical bells (set of tuned)–chimb, chimes

musical cadence–melos, plagal

musical canto–passus

musical character–bar, clef,
cleft, clefts, rest

musical character (anc.) –
neume

musical comedy–revue

musical composition – ballade, concerto, fugue, glee,
motet, op, opus, oratorio,
rondo, serenata, sonata,
trio

musical composition (cho-
ral)–motet

musical composition (closing of)–coda

musical   composition
(formed by selection) –
cento

musical composition (melodious style)–arioso

musical composition (nine
instrument)–nonet

musical composition (religious) – anthem, cantata,
motet

musical composition (sa-
cred)–motet

musical composition form–
serenata

musical direction – largo,
presa, tacet, tanto, ter,
tutti

musical direction (silence)–
tacet

musical   direction   (with
bow)–arco

musical disk–record, recording

musical drama–opera

musical ending–coda

musical exercise–etude

musical feature–motif

musical half globe (brass)–
cymbal

musical half tone – minim,
semitone

musical instrument – asor,
bagpipe, bugle, cello, con-
certina, gittern, guitar,
harp, harpsichord, heli-
con, horn, lute, lyre, oboe,
ocarina, organ, rebec, rebeck, rocta, spinet, uke,

ukulele, viol, viola, violin,
violoncello, zither

musical instrument (Afri-
can)–nanga

musical instrument (anc.)–
asor

musical instrument (anc.
Irish)–crut

musical instrument (bass
wind, obs.)–serpent

musical instrument (Biblical)–tabret

musical instrument (dulci-
mer-like)–citole

musical instrument (Egyp-
tian jingling)–sistrum

musical instrument (flute-
like)–flageolet

musical instrument (Greek,
lyre-like)–cithara

musical instrument (guitar-
like)–lute

musical instrument (harpsi-
chord-like)–spinet

musical instrument (Hindu,
anc.)–vina

musical instrument (India,
guitar-like)–vina

musical instrument (India,
viol-like)–ruana

musical instrument (Irish)–
crut

musical instrument (Italian,
trumpet)–tromba

musical instrument (Japa-
nese, three-stringed) –
samisen

musical instrument (lute-
like, 17th cent.)–theorbo

musical instrument (mando-
lin-like)–pandura

musical instrument (medi-
eval guitar-like)–gittern

musical instrument (Nubi-
an)–nanga

musical instrument (saxhorn
family) – althorn, alto-
horn, tuba

musical instrument (six-
stringed)–guitar

musical instrument (Span-
ish, kettledrum-like)–atabal

musical instrument
(stringed, anc.)–bandore,
rebec, rebeck

musical instrument (ten-
stringed)–asor

musical instrument (terra
cotta body)–ocarina

musical instrument (trum-
pet-like)–clarion

musical instrument (wind)–
clarinet, flute

musical instrument pick
(for mandolin, etc.)–plectrum

musical interlude (short)–
verset

musical interval–octave, seventh

musical interval (anc.) – ditone

musical interval (three
tones)–tritone

musical measured beat –
pulse

musical medley–cento, olio

musical nocturne–serenade

musical note–breve

musical note (Guido's scale)
–alt, are, ela, elami, ut

musical note (old)–alt, are,
ela, elami, ut

musical note forerunner
(modern)–neume

musical organization–band,
choir, chorus, orchestra

musical pair–duo

musical passage (conclud-
ing)–coda

musical passage (florid, brilliant style)–bravura

musical performance–recital

musical phrase (marked
melodic) – leitmotif, leitmotiv

musical pieces – duets, duos,
fugues, interludes, prel-
udes, rondos, solos, sona-
tas, trios

musical pipe–reed

musical play–opera, operetta

musical prelude (short) –
verset

musical rattle (jingling)–sistrum

musical refrain–epode, tra

musical refrain (meaning-
less, in old songs)–derry

musical repetition–rondo

musical run–volata

musical scale (major)–gamut
musical scale (whole)–gamut
musical shake–trill
musical show–revue
musical sign–segno
musical sign (of pitch)–clef
musical slur–ligature
musical song (simple)–lay
musical sounds (pert. to)–tonal
musical staff (upright)–bar
musical stage direction–sennet
musical studies–etudes
musical syllable–re, si, tra
musical syllable (meaningless)–tra
musical symbol–presa
musical symbol (early) – neume
musical tempo (irregular)–rubato
musical term–coda, lento
musical theme–tema
musical third–tierce
musical time marker–metronome
musical tones (combination of)–chord
musical work–opera, opus
musical work (abbr.)–op
musical work feature (leading)–motif
musician – bandsman, composer, piper
musicians (group of)–band, duet, nonet, nonetto, orchestra, quartet, quartette, septet, septette, sextet, sextette, trio
musimon–mouflon
musing–meditation, meditative
musing (abstracted)–reverie
musing (listless)–reverie
musk beaver–muskrat
musk cat–civet
musk cavy–hutia
musk cod–fop
musk crowfoot–moschatel
musk cucumber – cassabanana
musk deer–chevrotain
musk hog–peccary

musk lorikeet–parakeet
musk mallow–abelmosk
muskmelon–cantaloupe, casaba
musk milfoil–yarrow
musk okra–abelmosk
musk parakeet–lorikeet
musk poulp (polyp)–octopus
muskrat–desman, shrew
musk shrew–desman
muskellunge–pike
musket – falcon, firearm, flintlock, hawk
musketeer–fusilier, soldier
Musketeers (three)–Aramis, Athos, Porthos
Musketeers' (three) friend–D'Artagnan
muslin – femininity, nainsook, sheeting, shela, shelah, womanhood
muslin (East India)–ban
muslin (Indian) – dorea, doria, gurrah
muslin (striped, Indian) – dorea, doria
muslin (thin)–organdy
muslin bag–tillot
muslin cap (old woman's)–mutch
muslin kail (Scot.)–broth
mussed – confused, crumpled, dirty, disarranged, disordered, messed, rumpled, scrambled, soiled, tousled, wrinkled
mussel (fresh water)–mucket, naiad, naid, unio
mussel (kind of sea)–nerita
mussel (large)–horse
mussel (part of)–byssus
mussel (river)–unio
mussels (genus of)–mytilus
Mussulman – Mohammedan, Moslem, Saracen
must – juice, mold, moldy, musk, ought, refuse, shall, stum
mustang–bronco, pinto
mustard–senvy
mustard (black)–nigra
mustard (pert. to)–brassica
mustard family–brassicaceae
mustard plaster–sinapism
mustard seed alkaloid–sinapic, sinapin, sinapine

mustee–octoroon
musteline carnivore–pekan
muster – assemble, erect, gather, marshal, summon
musty – damp, fusty, hoar, moist, moldy, pungent, rafty, rancid, stale, trite
Mut's husband – Amen, Amon
mutable – alterable, changeful, vacillating, variable
mute–deadener, dumb, muffle, mum, silencer, silent, speechless, surd, voiceless
mute (phonetic)–lene
mute (smooth)–lene
mute (trombone) – wa-wa, wah-wah
mutilate – castrate, cripple, deface, destroy, dismember, geld, hack, injure, maim, mangle, mar
mutilate (as in war)–maim
mutinous – intractable, rebellious, refractory, seditious, turbulent, unruly
mutiny – commotion, insubordination, insurrection, rebellion, revolt, strife, tumult
mutt–cur, mongrel
mutter – growl, grumble, maunder, murmur, patter
mutton–prostitute, sheep
muttonbird – petrel, shearwater
muttonchop–whiskers
muttonfish – eelpout, mojarra, pargo, porgy, sama
mutton ham–sail
mutton leg (roasted)–cabob, gigot
mutton-legger–sail
muttonmonger–pimp
mutual – common, responsive
mutual association – interrelation
mutually agreeing–consentient
mux–botch, mess
muy–greatly, very
muzz–grind, muddle, study
muzzle – clevis, cope, gag, maul, respirator, restrain, sheathe, snout, thrash

muzzle (gun, bell-shaped swell)–tulip
my father is El–Abiel
my lady–madam
mycoid–fungoid
mycose–trehalose
mycosin–chitosan
Mynheer–Dutchman
myriad–innumerable, multitudinous, sea
myriapod–centipede
myrtle–periwinkle
myrtle (New Zealand)–ramarama
myrtle-like shrub – cajeput, cajuput
mysterious–abstruse, arcane, cabalistic, cryptic, dark, esoteric, inexplicable, mystic, occult, recondite, secret, unfathomable
mystery – arcane, arcanum, enigma, rune, secret
mystery (arch.)–craft, trade
mystic – cabalistic, esoteric,

occult, orphic, runic, seer
mystic art–cabala
mystic cry–evoe
mystic doctrine–esoteric
mystic ejaculation–om, um
mystic initiate–epopt
mystic ocean island–Avalon
mystic philosophy–cabala
mystic system–cabala
mystic word–abraxas
mystical–cryptic, enigmatic, furtive, obscure, occult, secret
mystical character (Teutonic)–Eckehart
mystify–becloud, befog, befuddle, confuse, muddle, obfuscate, puzzle
myth – fable, legend, story, tale
myth (half man, half fish)–triton
mythical–fabulous, fancied, imaginary, legendary

mythical aviator–Icarus
mythical being–centaur
mythical being (half man, half bird)–Garuda
mythical bird–roc
mythical character–Pandora
mythical demon (who caused eclipse by swallowing the sun and moon)–Rahu
mythical hero–Ajax, Leda
mythical heroine–Europa
mythical Hindu king–Nala
mythical hunter–Orion
mythical island (Western)–Atlantis
mythical monster–chimera, griffin, ogre
mythical mother (turned to stone)–Niobe
mythical princess–Atalanta
mythical river–Styx
mythical serpent–apepi
mythical woman–Gorgon

N

N (the letter)–en
nab – catch, grab, nibble, seize
Nabal's wife–Abigail
nabob – governor, nawab, viceregent, viceroy
nabob deputy–nawab
nace–ashamed, destitute
nacelle–boat, shelter
nacket–caddie, cake, lunch
nacre – conchiolin, mother-of-pearl, pearl
nadir (opposite of)–zenith
nag – annoy, cobra, heckle, hector, horse, pony, scold, snake, twit
nahoor–bharal, sha, sheep
nahoor sheep–sha, urial
Nahor's brother–Abraham
Nahor's grandchild – Abraham
Nahor's son–Terah
Nahor's wife–Milcah
naiad–mussel, nymph
nail–brad, clout, cut, finish-

ing, hob, spad, spike, stud, unguis, ungula, upholstering, wire
nail (driven slantingly) – toed
nail (headless small)–sprig
nail (heavy)–hob, spike
nail (ingrowing)–acronyx
nail (marking on)–lunule
nail (miner's)–spad
nail (part of)–lunule
nail (shoemaker's small) – sparable
naissance–birth, origin
naive–artless, frank, simple, unphilosophic, unsophisticated, untaught
naked – bare, nude, uncovered
nakoo–gavial
namaycush–togue, trout
name – appellation, cognomen, denomination, designation, dub, entitle, intitle, mention, nemme,

nemne, nom, nomen, reputation, style, term, title
name (added)–agnomen
name (assumed)–alias, pseudonym, sobriquet
name (bad)–caconym
name (derivation of)–eponymy
name (Blackmore heroine's given)–Lorna
name (endearing)–pussy
name (English surname) – cognomen
name (family)–cognomen
name (fictitious) – pseudonym
name (Lamb's pen)–Elia
name (nickname) – cognomen, monica, monicker, moniker, monniker
name (objectionable) – caconym
name (pen)–anonym, pseudonym

name (real, written backwards)–ananym
name (surname given after something)–eponymy
name (to) – nemme, nemn, neven
name (under assumed) – incognito
name (unknown) – anonymous
name (wrongly)–misterm
name based on location of thing named–toponym
name of a thing–noun
name of some–ilk
name or call–clepe
name tablet–facia
named (arch.) – ycleped, yclept
named as agent–deputes
nameless – anonymous, illegitimate, indescribable, unnamable
namely – especially, expressly, famous, noted, specifically, towit, videlicit
names (additional) – agnames
namesake–homonym
nandu–rhea
nanny–nurse
nanny plum–sheepberry
nanoid–dwarfish
nanpie–magpie
naos–cella, shrine, temple
nap–doze, fluff, grasp, nod, pile, seize, siesta, sleep, snooze, steal, wink
nap (afternoon)–siesta
nap (coarse, of cloth)–shag
nap (long)–shag
nap (midday)–siesta
nap-like cloth (woolen) – duffel
nap-raising contrivance – teasle
nape–niddick, nucha, scrag, scruff, turnip
nape of neck–nucha
nape of sheep's neck–scrag
napellus–monkshood
napery–linen
Naphtalite–Enon
naphtha–petroleum
naphthol–alpha, beta

napkin – diaper, kerchief, neckerchief
napkin (small)–doily
Naples biscuit–ladyfinger
Naples island–Capri
napless–threadbare
Napoleon's brother-in-law–Murat
Napoleon's island–Capri
Napoleon's isle (of exile)–Elba
Napoleon's village (where he defeated Blucher) – Ligny
nappy – ale, dish, downy, liquor, shaggy, wooly
napron–apron
napu–chevrotain
nar (Scot.) – near, nearer, nearly
Naraka (Hindu)–hell
narcotic – anodyne, bang, bhang, belladonna, cocaine, heroin, hyoscyamus, junk, morphine, opiate, opium, soporific, stramonium
narcotic distributor (illicit)–doper
narcotic dose–locus
narcotic-using gathering – snowparty
narcotized–doped, opiated
nard–anoint, ointment, rhizomes
nardoo (nardu)–clover
narghile (nargile, narghileh)–hooka, hookah, pipe
nargile–coconut
narial–rhinal
narica–coati
nark – annoy, irritate, spoilsport, spy, stool pigeon, tease
narky–vexed
narr–growl, snarl
narrate–describe, detail, recite, recount, relate, tell
narration – account, detail, discourse, recital, rehearsal, relation, story, tale
narration (acted)–drama
narrative–account, anecdote, conte, epic, fable, history, narration, recital, statement, story, tale

narrative (epic)–saga
narrative (fictitious)–fable
narrative (short)–conte
narrative (symbolic) – allegory
narrative poem–epos
narrator–relator
narrow – closely, mean, niggardly, parsimonious, scant, straighten, strait, strictly
narrow (comb. form) – sten, steno
narrow (very)–linear
narrow down staves–buck
narrow-mindedness–bias
narrow opening–rima, slot
narrow-souled–ungenerous
narrow strip of leather – thong
narrowly incised–laciniate
narrows–strait
narrows (wide)–sound
narsinga–trumpet
nasab – consanguinity, kinship
nasal–rhinal
nasal eminence–glabella
nasal scale–naricorn
nascency – beginning, birth, genesis, origin
naseberry–sapodilla
nashgob–chatter, gossip
nasi–patriarch, prince
nasicornia–rhinoceros
Nassau grouper–hamlet
nast–dirt, filth
nastika–atheist
nastiness – dirty, foul, obscene
nasua–coati
nasus–clypeus
nasutiform–noselike
Nata's wife–Nana
natal–gluteal, native
natator–swimmer
natatorium–bath, natatory, pool
natch–rump
natchbone–aitchbone
nates–buttocks, umbone
nation – caste, class, community, country, people, race, state
national–federal
nationalist–socialist

nations bound by treaties – allies

nation's war vessels–navy

native – aboriginal, indigenous, natal, natural, original, son

native (epirus)–epirote

native (not)–foreign

native (not of indigenous blood)–creole

native (original)–primeval

native (prefix)–un

native agent–comprador

native bear–kaola

native beech–flindosa

native-born–indigenous, native

native cat–dasyure

native cavalryman (India)–sowar

native chief (Hindu)–sirdar

native dog–dingo

native house servant – comprador

native of (suffix)–ite

native of Asia–Arab

native of Madagascar–Hova

native pheasant–leipoa

native plant–indigene

native rabbit–marsupial

native salt–halite

native sloth–kaola

nattle–gnaw, nibble

natty–chic, neat, spruce, tidy

natural–born, common, cretin, inborn, inbred, inherent, innate, normal, ordinary, regular, unassumed, unfeigned, usual

natural (inborn)–innate, native

natural (not) – acquired, alien, artificial, labored, strange

natural color–beige

natural condition–norm

natural features–geography

natural location–situs

natural philosophy–physics

natural singing voice–dipetto

natural state–norm

naturalist (famous)–Muir

naturalize–acclimate, accustom, familiarize

nature – essence, kind, sort, type

nature (concealed)–latency

nature (goddess of)–Nymph

nature (of the same)–homogeneal

nature movies–scenics

nature of thing–essence

nature story writer–Seton

nature worship–physiolatry

nausea–pall, qualm

nauseate–loathe, sicken

nauseous – fulsome, loathsome, sickening, squeamish

nautical–marine, maritime, naval, oceanic

nautical direction–avast, belay

nautical hailing call–ahoy

nautical hook–becket

nautical instrument – aba, compass, pelorus, sextant

nautical instrument (compass-like)–pelorus

nautical line – marline, ratline

nautical measure – cable's length, fathom, knot, renning, seam, sea mile, ton

nautical term – atry, abeam, avast, belay

nautical term (cease)–avast

nautical term (hove clear)–atrip

nautical term (make fast)–belay

nautical term (stop)–avast

nautical unit (of measure)–knot

nautical yearbook–almanac

nautilus (paper)–argonauta

Navaho (Navajo) hut (rude)–hogan

naval–marine, nautical

naval depot–base

naval officer – yeoman, bosun, ensign, lieutenant, commander, captain, admiral

naval officer (line)–mustang

naval station (Fr.)–Brest

naval stores–supplies, pitch, tar, turpentine

nave–fist, hob, hub, nieve

nave (church)–apse, nef

nave of church (pert. to)–apsidal

nave of wheel–hob

navew–rape, turnip

navigate–keel, sail

navigate the air–aviate, fly

navigating instrument–aba, compass, pelorus, sextant

navigator – laborer, navvy, pilot

navvy – excavate, laborer, navigator

navy board–Admiralty

navy line officer–mustang

navy slang (aircraft carrier)–flattop

navy slang (coffee)–mud

navy slang (rumor)–scuttlebutt

navy slang (salt)–seadust

nawab–nabob

nay–denial, deny, flute, negative, never, no, prohibition, refusal, refuse

nay (former spelling)–nai

nayaur–sheep

naysay–denial, refusal

nayword–byword, proverb, watchword

naze–headland, promontory

Nazi–Hitlerite

Nazi dictator–Hitler

nazim–governor, viceroy

nchega–chimpanzee

neal–anneal, deep, temper

neanic–immature, youthful

Neapolitan dance–tarantella, tarantelle

Neapolitan medlar–azarole

near – approach, around, close, dear, handy, nigh

near by–adjacent, anent, beside, gin, handy, nigh, vicinal

Near East–Balkans, Levant

near ocean–maritime

near of kin–germane

near the beginning–early

near the horizon–low

near the middle–central

nearer (former spelling) – nar

nearer (obs.)–ner

nearest–closest, next, proximate

nearly–almost, approximately, closely, similarity

nearness–propinquity

nearsighted–myopic

nearsighted person–myope

neat – adroit, dapper, natty, orderly, prim, tidy, trig, trim

neat (primly)–smug

neat, trim (Scot.)–snod

neathmost (Scot.)–lowest

neb – beak, bill, face, kiss, nose, snout

Nebraska city–Omaha

Nebraska county–Otoe

Nebraska Indian – Omaha, Otoe

nebris–fawnskin

nebula – atmosphere, cloud, mist, sky, vapor

nebulous – clouded, cloudy, hazy, misty, nebulose, vague

nebulous envelope – chevelure, coma

necessarily – indispensably, perforce, unavoidably

necessary – essential, indispensable, needful, requisite, unavoidable, vital

necessary antecedents – prerequisites

necessitate – compel, constrain, entail, force, impel, oblige

necessity – inevitableness, mister, need, urgency

necessity of life – aliment, drink, food

neck–cervix

neck (back of)–nape, nucha, scruff

neck (nape of)–nucha

neck (part of)–gula

neck (part of horse's)–withers

neck (pert. to)–juglar

neck and neck – close, even, tie

neck armor (defending throat)–gorgelet, gorget

neck artery (chief)–carotid

neck chain ornament–lavalier, lavaliere, lavalliere, locket

neck frill–jabot, ruche

neck of land–strake

neck of water (narrow) – strait

neck part of coat–george

neckatee–neckerchief

neckband–collar

neckcloth – barcelona, cravat, muffler, neckerchief

neckerchief – handkerchief, kerchief

neckerchief (flashy)–belcher

necklace – baldric, baldrick, chaplet, riviere, torque

necklace (anc., twisted wire) –torc

necklace of gems (Fr.)–riviere

neckpiece – boa, collar, kerchief, rabat, scarf, stole

necktie–band, scarf, tie

necktie (kind of) – ascot, bow, cravat, four-in-hand, scarf

necromancy – conjuration, enchantment, goety, magic

necropolis–cemetery

necropsy–autopsy

nectar bird–sunbird

nectar of the gods–ambrosia

nedder–adder

neddy–donkey

need – compulsion, extremity, lack, necessity, require, thar, tharf, urgency, want

need (pressing)–exigency

needful–essential, indispensable, integral, necessary, requisite, vital

needing support–dependent

needle (comb. form)–acu

needle (in neutral equilibrium)–astatizer

needle (kind of) – bodkin, darning, obelisk, sail, upholstery

needle (Latin)–acus

needle (slender sewing) – sharp

needle (surgical)–acus

needle bug–ranatra

needlecase–etui, etwee

needlefish–gar

needle gun–Dreyse

needle hole–eye

needle hole (under skin) – seton

needle-like body–spicule

needleman–tailor

needle-pointed – acerate, acerose, acicular

needle-shaped–acerate, acerose, acicular

needle spar–aragonite

needle spike rush–sedge

needlestone–natrolite

needlewoman–seamstress

needlewood–needlebush

needlework (old-time piece) –sampler

needle zeolite–natrolite

needless–unnecessary

neednot–superfluity

needy – distressed, indigent, necessary, penniless, poor, requisite

neel-bhunder – monkey, wanderoo

neem–margosa, neemba

neep–turnip

neer–kidney

nef–clock, nave

nefarious – atrocious, detestable, heinous, horrible, impious, infamous, iniquitous, villainous, wicked

nefas–sinful

nefast–wicked

neftgil–ozocerite

negate–deny, nullify, refute

negation–blankness, denial, empty, ne, not, nullity, refusal

negative – ir, minus, nae, nay, neutral, no, non, nor, not, veto

negative (former)–ne

negative electrode–cathode, kathode

negative ion–anion

negative particle–not

negative pole–cathode, kathode

negative prefix–il, ir, non, un

negative terminal – cathode, kathode

neglect–disregard, fail, failure, inattention, negli-

gent, omit, pretermit, shirk, slight, slip
neglected–undone
neglected (more)–rustier
negligee–undress
negligence – carelessness, inadvertence, inattention, laxness, oversight, remissness
negligent–careless, lash, lax, remiss, supine
negotiate – bargain, deal, transact, treat, treaty
Negrito–Aeta, Ata, Ita
Negrito (African)–Aka, Akka, Bambute, Batwa
Negrito (Dutch New Guinea)–Tapiro
Negrito (Malayan Peninsula)–Ata, Semang
Negrito (Philippine) – Aeta, Ata, Ita
Negro – Beni, Benin, Bini, Ethiopian, Suk; cuffy, cuffee, quashee, quashie
Negro (African)–Dahoman, Jur, Vai, Vei
Negro (aversion to)–negrophobia
Negro (Cape Verde)–Serer
Negro (Gold Coast)–Ga
Negro (Liberian) – Kroo, Krooboy, Krooman, Kru, Kruman
Negro (Niger Delta)–Ebo, Eboe, Ibo
Negro (one friendly to) – negrophil, negrophile
Negro (seven-eighths, and one-eighth white)–sacatra
Negro (South Kordofan) – Nuba
Negro (Southern Nigeria)–Beni, Benin
Negro (Sudan)–Hausa
Negro (Yoruba)–Egba
Negro and Caucasian blood –mulatto
Negro dish (rice and meat)–jambalaya
Negro half-breed – mestee, mustee, sambo
Negro magic–voodoo
Negroid–Aeta, Ata, Bantu, Bechuana, Damara, Ita, Kaffir, Swahili

Negroid (Cape Province) – Pondo, Xosa
Negroid (South African) – Bantu, Bechuana, Damara, Kaffir, Pondo, Swahili, Xosa
neigh–akin, nie, whinny
neighborhood law–venue
neither animal nor vegetable –mineral
neither inferior nor superior –equal
neither masculine nor feminine–neuter
neither right nor wrong – adiaphorous
Neleus' son–Nestor
nemoral–sylvan
neophyte–beginner, catechumen, convert, novice, proselyte, tyro
neoteric–late, modern, new, recent
nep–bryony, catnip
Nepal capital–Katmandu
Nepal city – Katmandu, Khatmandu
Nepal coin–mohar (s.)
Nepal Mongoloid people – Rais
Nepal tribe–Aoul, Gorkhali, Gurkha
Nephele's daughter–Helle
nephesh–soul
nephew–nepote, neve
nephew (Scot.)–nepote
nephew-like–nepotal
nephrite–jade
nephroid–reniform
nepote–grandson, nephew
nepotism – favoritism, patronage
Neptune–ocean, sea
Neptune (Celtic)–Ler
Neptune's emblem–trident
Neptune's scepter–trident
Nereids' mother–Doris
Nereus' daughter–Nereid
Nereus' wife–Doris
nerve – aplomb, audacity, cheek, coolness, courage, pluck, resolution, sinew, tendon
nerve (comb. form)–neuro
nerve (pert. to)–neural
nerve cell–neuron, neurone

nerve cell axon–neurite
nerve center–rete
nerve force–neurism
nerve group–rete, retia (pl.)
nerve inflammation–neuritis
nerve network – rete, retia (pl.)
nerve operation (adhesion freeing)–neurolysis
nerve passage–hilum
nerve root (cranial)–radix
nerve sensory–afferent
nerve sleep–neurohypnotism
nerve tissue gray matter – cinerea
nerve tumor–neurinoma
nerve tumor (form of)–neuroma, neuromatosis
nerves (interlacing)–plexus
nerves (pert. to)–neuro
nerves and muscles (collectively)–neuromusculature
nervous–apprehensive, fearful, highstrung, neurotic, sensitive, timid, timorous, touchy
nervous affection–chorea
nervous disease specialist – neuropathist
nervous disorder–ataxia
nervous malady – aphasia, neuritis
nervous malady (desire to kill)–amok
nervous system (description of)–neurography
nervous system activity – neurosis
nervous system nomenclature–neuronymy
nervous system science – neurology
nervous system syphilis – neurosyphilis
nervous tissue tumor–neurocytoma
nervous twitching–tic
ness–cape, headland, promontory
nest–den, haunt, nide, nidus, nidi (pl.), nye
nest (bird of prey) – aerie, aery, eyrie, eyry
nest (build a)–aerie, nidify
nest (eagle's) – aerie, aery, eyrie, eyry

nest (eggs of insects)–nidus
nest (predatory bird)–aerie, aery, eyrie, eyry
nest (rare)–nid
nest (spider's)–nidus, web
nest (squirrel's)–dray, drey
nest of boxes–inro
nestle–cuddle, nest, pet, pettle, snuggle
nestling–eyas, nest, nidulant, retreat
net–clear, gin, mesh, seine, snare, toil, trap, web, weir
net (fine silk)–maline, tulle
net (fishing) – lam, seine, trammel
net (hair)–snood
net (large bag)–trawl
net (long bag)–fyke
net (opening of)–mesh
net (silk, thin, fine)–tulle
net interstice–mesh
net-like–retiary, reticular
net value–reserve
net-winged–neuropteroid
netheist (rare)–atheist
Netherlands–Dutch
Netherlands city – Ede, Hague, Leiden, Utrecht
Netherlands coin–cent (br.), florin (s.), gulden (s.), rijksdaalder (s.), stiver (ni.)
Netherlands commune – Aalsmeer, Aalten, Amsterdam, Arnhem, Breda, Epe, Gravenhage, Grohingen, Haarlem, Hague, Leiden, Rotterdam, Utrecht
Netherlands inhabitant – Fleming, Frisian
Netherlands inlet – Zuider Zee
Netherlands island – Ameland, Schelling, Texel, Vlieland
Netherlands lake–Haarlem
Netherlands land (enclosed by dykes)–polders
Netherlands measure–aam, ahm, anker, aum, bunder, carat, duim, el, ell, kan, kop, last, leaguer, legger, maatje, mijl, mimgelen, mud, muddle, mutsje,

okshoofd, roede, rood, rope, schepel, steekkan, stoop, streep, vat, vingerhoed, voet, wisse, zak
Netherlands motto – Jemaintiendrai
Netherlands possession–Borneo, Celebes, Curacao, Dutch Guiana, Java, New Guinea, Saba, St. Eustatius, Sumatra, Surinam
Netherlands province–Brabant, Drenthe, Friesland, Gelderland, Groningen, Holland, Limburg, Overijssel, Utrecht, Zeeland
Netherlands river – Ijssel, Kromme, Leck, Maas, Meuse, Rhine, Scheldt, Waal
Netherlands weight–bahar, esterlin, esterling, grein, korrel, last, lood, ons, pond, pound, wichtje
nethermore–lower, nether
netherstock–stocking
netherward–downward
netted–reticulated
netted a profit (rare)–neated
netting–lint, mesh
nettle – fret, irritate, line, pique, provoke, sting, vex
nettle (genus of)–urtica
nettle (original form) – knittle
nettle (sea) – cnida, cnidae (pl.)
nettlebird–whitethroat
nettle cell–nematocyst
nettle creeper–whitethroat
nettle family–Urticaceae
nettle geranium–coleus
nettle potato–queenroot
nettle rash–hives, uredo, urticaria
nettlesome–irritable, irritating
nettlewort–Urticaceae
nettling–irritating, splicing, stinging, vexing
nettling cell–nematocyst
network – cobweb, mesh, moke, plexus, reseau, rete, retia (pl.), reticulum, web
network (nerve)–rete, retia (pl.)

network (of veins)–plexus
neume (music)–pneuma
neurad (opposed to)–hemad, haemad
neural–dorsal
neural (opposed to)–hemal, ventral
neuralgia drug–tonga
neuter – castrate, impartial, neither, neutral
neutral – indifferent, middling, negative, noncombatant
neutral equilibrium (being in)–astatic
neutralize – annul, counteract, counterbalance, countervail, frustrate, nullify, vitiate
Nevada and California lake–Tahoe
Nevada city – Carson, Elko, Reno
Nevada county–Clark, Nye
Nevada Indian–Digger
neve–firn, glacier, nephew
nevel (nevell)–fisticuff
never–nary
never growing old–ageless
"never mind" (Russian exclamation) – nichevo, nitchevo
nevertheless–however, still, yet
nevertheless (arch.)–natheless
new – fresh, late, modern, neoteric, nova, novel, original, recent, untested
new (prefix)–nea
New Brunswick mineral – albutite
new, but yet old–novantique
New England native–Yankee
New England of the West Minnesota
New Guinea capital–Rabaul
New Guinea city–Lae, Rabaul, Soron
New Guinea echidna – nodiak
New Guinea export–copra
New Guinea gulf – Huon, Papua

New Guinea hog (wild) – bene
New Guinea native–Papuan
New Guinea parrot – lory, lories (pl.)
New Guinea port–Lae
New Guinea port of entry– Daru
New Guinea river–Fly
New Guinea section–Buna- gona
New Guinea tribe–Karon
New Guinea wild hog–bene
New Hampshire city – An- trim, Dover, Exeter, Han- over, Keene, Laconia, Nashua
New Hampshire town (col- lege)–Hanover
New Jersey capital–Trenton
New Jersey river–Raritan
New Jersey town – Raritan, Verona
New Mexico county–Mora, Taos
New Mexico Indian–Tano, Taos
New Mexico Indian guessing game–canute
New Mexico river–Gila, Pe- cos
new set–relay
new star–Nova
new word (introduction of) –neologism, neoterism
New York county–Oneida, Oswego, Tioga, Yates
New York governor (form- er)–Dix
New York Indian–Oneida
New York lake–Oneida, Sar- anac
New York river – Harlem, Hudson
New York theater district– Rialto
New York town–Cohoes, El- mira, Goshen, Gotham, Ilion, Olean, Oswego, Owego, Rome, Utica
New York university–Col- gate, Columbia, Cornell
New Zealand aborigine – Maori
New Zealand army man – Anzac

New Zealand birch–notho- fagus
New Zealand bird–apteryx, kaka, kakapo, kea, kulu, moa, morepor, notornis, ruru, titi, weka
New Zealand bird (extinct) –moa
New Zealand bird (ostrich) –moa
New Zealand bird (parson) –poe
New Zealand bird (shore)– wrybill
New Zealand bird (wing- less)–apteryx
New Zealand bur–acaena
New Zealand caterpillar (vegetable)–aweto
New Zealand city – Auck- land, Wellington
New Zealand clan–Ati
New Zealand clay (bluish)– papa
New Zealand club (war) – mere
New Zealand fern rootstock –roi
New Zealand gallinule (ex- tinct)–moho
New Zealand hedge laurel– tarata
New Zealand island–Otea
New Zealand kakapo–par- rot
New Zealand lake–Taupo
New Zealand mahogany pine–totara
New Zealand morepork – boobook, ruru, peho
New Zealand mountain – Aorangi
New Zealand myrtle–rama- rama
New Zealand native–Maori
New Zealand native fort–Pa
New Zealand oak–puriri
New Zealand ostrich–moa
New Zealand owl–ruru
New Zealand palm–nikau
New Zealand parrot–kaka, kakapo, kea
New Zealand parson bird– poe
New Zealand pine (mahog- any)–totara

New Zealand pine (white)– kahikatea
New Zealand ratite (non- existent)–moa
New Zealand reptile (car- nivorous, guana-like)–tua- tara, tuatera
New Zealand rootstock (edi- ble, of fern)–roi
New Zealand sandalwood – santalaceae
New Zealand shark (large) –mako
New Zealand teak–puriri
New Zealand tree–ake, ake- ake, kauri, kaury, mako, makomako, miro, rata, ta- rata, taratah, tawa, titoki, toro, totara
New Zealand tree (ever- green)–tarata, taratah
New Zealand tree (fodder)– mahoe
New Zealand tree (fuel) – mapau
New Zealand tree (medici- nal)–wahahe
New Zealand tree (small coast)–ngaio
New Zealand tree (tea) – manuka
New Zealand tree (timber)– pelu, rata, totara
New Zealand tree (tough wood)–ngaio
New Zealand tribe – Ati, Maori
New Zealand vine (woody) –aka
New Zealand volcano–Rua- pehu
New Zealand wages–utu
New Zealand war club – mere
New Zealand wren (genus of)–xenicus
news–tidings
news (good)–evangel
news agency – (American) AP, INS, International, UP; (British) Reuters; (Dutch E. Indies) Aneta; (German) DNB; (Japa- nese) Domei
news gatherer–reporter
news organization – Aneta,

AP, DNB, Domei, INS, International, Reuters, UP

news supplying agency–syndicate

newspaper – daily, Gazette, Herald, News, sheet, Times, Tribune

newspaper article–item

newspaper file department–morgue

newspaper man–editor, journalist

newspaper parts–ears

newspaper writers – columnist, correspondent, reporter

newspapers (collectively) – press

newsstand–kiosk

newt–ask, axolotl, eft, evet, lizard, salamander, triton

next–adjoining, closest, contiguous, following, nearest, then

next (Scot.)–neist

next to–adjacent, almost, beside, nearly

next to last syllable of a word –penult

nexus–connection, interconnection, link, tie

nib–beak, bill

nibble–browse, gnaw, nab

Nicaragua city–Chinandega, Choluteca, Granada, Leon, Managua (c.), Masaya

Nicaragua coin – centavo (br.), cordoba (s.), peso (s.)

Nicaragua lake–Managua

Nicaragua measure – cabelleria, cahiz, cajuela, estadal, manzana, milla, suerte, tercia, vara

Nicaragua river–Coco, San Juan, Tuma, Wanks

Nicaragua weight–bag, caja, tonelada

nice–agreeable, appetizing, considerate, dainty, delightful, exacting, fastidious, finical, good, hypercritical, particular, pleas-

ing, prudish, queasy, squeamish, tickle

nice discernment–acumen

niche – alcove, apse, covert, nook, recess, retreat, tabernacle

nick–dent, dint, notch, slit

nickel (symbol for)–Ni

nickel alloy–invar

nickel bronze–cupronickel

nickel steel–invar

nickelodeon (record-playing) –juke, jukebox

nickname–agname, cognomen, misapply, misname, monica, monicker, moniker, monniker

nicknaming–prosonomasia

nictate–nictitate, wink

nictitate–wink

nid–bend, bob, nod

niddick–nape

nide–brood, nest

nidge–quiver, shake

nidget–fool, idiot

nidification–nesting

nidus (nidi, pl.)–nest

niepa bark–niota

nieshout–sneezewood

nieve–fist, hand

niffer (Scot.) – bargain, exchange

niff-naff–trifle

Niger Delta Negro – Ebo, Eboe, Ibo, Ijo

Niger river mouth-nun

Nigerian (southern)–Benin

Nigerian capital–Lagos

Nigerian city–Bidi, Ede, Ibadan, Lagos, Ogbomosho, Yakoba

Nigerian native–Aro, Beni, Eboe, Ibo

Nigerian Negro–Aro, Beni, Eboe, Ibo

Nigerian tribesman – Beni, Benin, Edo

niggard – miser, scanty, stingy

niggardly–avaricious, parsimonious, penurious, scant, sordid

niggardly (to be)–scrimp

nigh–adjacent, at, close, contiguous, near, neighboring

nigh (English dial.)–nei

nigh (obs.)–nei

nigh (poetic)–anear

night (goddess of) – Nox, Nyx

night bird – nightingale, shearwater

night blindness–nyctalopia

nightchurr–goatsucker

nightfall–dusk

nightfall (poetic)–een, eve

"Night in Horse" spouse (myth.)–Annar

nightingale (poetic)–philomel

nightjar–potoo

nightmare–incubus, mara

nightmare (Teutonic folklore)–alp

nightshade–belladonna, bittersweet, henbane, morel, morelle

night watchman (Span.) – sereno

Nihilist–anarchist, socialist

nil–nothing

Nile (pert. to)–Nilotic

Nile bird–wryneck

Nile bird (wading)–ibis

Nile boat captain–rais, reis

Nile cargo boat–nuggar

Nile Delta city (anc., pert. to)–Saite

Nile fish – mormyrid, mormyroid, saide

Nile freight boat–baris

Nile island–Roda

Nile (upper) Negro tribe–Madi

Nile plant–lotus

Nile River boat (house) – dahabeah

Nile River dam–Aswan

Nile River falls–Ripon

Nile River tributary–Kagera

Nile River vegetable matter (floating)–sudd

nilgai–antelope

nilgai (male)–nil

Nilgiri tribe (southern India)–Badaga

nim tree–neem, margosa

nimble–active, agile, brisk, deft, fleet, flit, lish, lively, prompt, quick, spry, volant

nimble (dial.)–lish

nimbose–cloudy, stormy
nimbus–atmosphere, aureola, aureole, cloud, gloria, halo, vapor
nimiety–excess, redundancy
nimious–excessive, extravagant
nimmer–thief
nimrod–hunter
nimshi – flighty, fool, half-witted, hasty
Nimshi's son–Jehoshaphat
nincompoop–dolt, fool, simpleton, witling
nine (comb. form)–ennea
nine (composition for) – nonet
nine (group of)–ennead
nine (number)–ennead
nine (poetic)–ninefold
nine-banded armadillo–peba
nine days' devotion–novena
nine-eyes–gunnel, lamprey
nine-headed monster (Greek)–Hydra
nine inches–span
nine-killer–shrike
Nine Power Treaty (signers of) – Belgium, Britain, China, France, Italy, Japan, Netherlands, Portugal, United States
nine-sided plane figure–nonagon
nine-sided polygon–nonagon
nine times (occurring once in every) – enneatic, enneatical
nine times repeated – ninefold
nine worlds – Alfheim, Asgard, Hel, Jotunnheim, Midgard, Muspellsheim, Niflheim, Svartalfaheim, Vanaheim
nine worthies – Alexander, Arthur, Caesar, Charlemagne, David, Godfrey, Hector, Joshua, Judas
ninefold (poetic)–nine
ninepins–kayles, keels, skittle, skittles
nineted–wicked
Nineveh founder (Greek legend)–Ninus

ninny–fool, goose, sammy, simpleton
ninny broth–coffee
ninth (every)–enneatic
ninth day (recurring on) – nonan
ninth day before ides–nones
Ninus' wife–Semiramis
ninut (Eng. dial.)–magpie
niobate–columbate
niobe–funkia, hosta
Niobe's brother–Pelops
Niobe's father–Tantalus
Niobe's husband–Amphion
niobic–columbic
niobite–columbite
nip–benumb, catnip, cheat, check, clamp, clip, compress, draft, dram, pickpocket, seize, sever, sip, squeeze, thief, tipple
nipa palm–atap, attap, drink
nipcheese–miser, purser
nipper – biter, boy, claw, costermonger, cunner, eyeglasses, grab, gripper, handcuffs, incisor, lad, miser, pincenez, pincers, thief, urchin
nipple–mammilla, pap, papilla, teat
nippy–active, biting, brisk, grasping, vigorous
nirmanakaya–unselfish
nis–kobold
nisse–brownie, goblin, kobold
Nisus' daughter–Scylla
nite–abjure, deny, refuse
nitency–brightness, luster
niter (nitre) – peter, petre, potash, saltpeter
nither–blast, debase, humiliate, oppress, shiver, tremble
nithing – coward, dastard, niggard
nitid–bright, lustrous
nitrate–ester, salt
nitric acid–aquafortis
nitrite–azotite
nitrobenzene–mirbane
nitrocotton–guncotton
nitroform–trinitromethane
nitrogen–azote

nitrogen (comb. form)–az, azo
nitrogen (old chemistry name for)–azote
nitrogen and hydrogen compound–ammonia
nitroglycerin–glonion
Niuan's language–Niue
niveau–level
nivenite–uraninite
niveous–snowy
nivosity–snowiness
nix–nobody, nothing, sprite
Njorth's daughter – Freya, Freyja
Njorth's son–Frey, Freyr
no–baal, bail, bale, nae, naw, nay, ne, nit
no (arch.)–ne
no (Australian aboriginal)–baal, bail, bale
no (Eng. prov.)–naw
no (Gay Nineties)–nit
no (Scot.)–nae
no different–identical
no longer in play–dead
no longer visible–lost
no matter what one–any
no one–nix
no points scored (tennis)–love
Noah (Biblical, old style)–Noe
Noah (French)–Noe
Noah's dove–Columba
Noah's grandson–Aram
Noah's great-grandson–Hul
Noah's raven–Corvus
Noah's son–Ham, Shem
Noah's son (eldest)–Shem
Noah's son (var.)–Sem
Noah's wine cup–Crater
Nobel powder–ballistite
Nobel prize winner (literature, 1904)–Mistral
nobility–peerage
noble–aristocratic, dignified, ducal, elevated, eminent, epic, epical, fine, generous, grand, honorable, liberal, manly, renowned, sublime
noble (grand)–epical
noble (Spanish)–grandee
noble pine–pipsissewa
nobleman – baron, barony,

count, duke, earl, grandee, lord, marquess, marquis, peer

nobleness – grandeur, soul, splendor

nobleness of birth–eugeny

noblewoman – baroness, countess, duchess, lady, marchioness, marquise, marquisess, peeress

nobley (obs.)–grandeur, nobility, prowess, splendor

nobody–none, nonetity

Nobody Knows author–Barton

nocturnal – night, nightly, nightwalker, streetwalker

nocturnal animal – coon, opossum, possum

nocturnal bird–owl, owlet

nocturnal carnivore–ratel

nocturnal mammal–bat, lemur

nocturnal signs–zodiacal

nocturne–lullaby, serenade

nod – beck, beckon, bend, bow, wink

nodding–annuent, cernuous, drooping, nutant

noddy – auk, drowsy, fool, foolish, fulmar, hackney, noodle, simpleton, sleepy

node–complication, difficulty, knot, protuberance, swelling

node of a poem–plot

node of a stem–joint

nodule – bump, granule, lump, tubercle

nodule (of one kind of rock in another kind)–nablock

nodule (stone)–auge, geode

nodus – complication, difficulty, knot, node

noeud–bow, knot

nog–block, eggnog, noggin, peg, pin

noggin–cup, mug

noise–blare, chang, clamor, clang, din, outcry, quarrel, report, rout, rumor, shouting, sound, strife, uproar

noise (clattering)–brattle

noise (dull)–klop

noise (explosive)–blast, pop, report

noise (harsh, shrill)–stridor

noise (loud)–bang

noise (loud, confused, Scot.) –chang

noise (metallic)–clang

noise (of disturbed water)– plash, splash

noise (raucous)–bray

noise (respiration)–rale

noise (rustling)–swish

noise (sharp)–click

noise (to)–norate

noise (whirring)–burr

noise of disturbed water – plash, splash

noised – dinned, reported, rumored

noisemaker–horn, rattle

noises about–bruits, reports, rumors

Noise's father–Usnech

noisette–hazel

noisily (to go)–larum

noisome–destructive, fetid, harmful, malodorous, noxious, offensive, pernicious, stinking, unwholesome

noisy – blatant, clamorous, clattery, loud, vociferous

noll–head, noddle

nom–name

nom de plume–pen name, pseudonym

nomad–Arab, roamer, Saracen, scenite, wanderer

nomad (Arabian)–Saracen

nomad (Asiatic)–Arab

nomad people (anc.)–Alani

nomarchy (Greek)–department, nome

nome (Greek)–department, Elis, nomarchy, province

nominal–par, titular, unreal

nominal recognizance (law) –Doe

nominal value–par

nominalist–terminist

nominate–appointment, call, denominate, entitle, name, propose, specify

nominate (Scot.)–leet

nominate for election–propose

nominators – namers, proposers

nonage – immature, neanic, youthful

nonappearance–absence, default

nonaspirate–lene

nonbeing–nonexistence, void

nonbeliever–atheist, pagan

nonchalant–careless, casual, cool, imperturbable, indifferent, insouciant

noncircular rotating piece – cam

noncleric–laic, lay

noncombatant – chaplain, civilian

noncommissioned officer (abbr.)–N.C.O.

noncompliance (obstinate)– recalcitrance

nonconformer of accepted views–heretic

nonconformity–dissent, dissidence, recusance, recusancy

nondependent–independent

nondescript – indescribable, indeterminable

nonessential–adventitious

nonessential (in religion) – adiaphoron

nonfestal–ferial

nonlicit–unlawful

non-Mahometan–Kafir

nonmetallic element–boron, bromin, bromine, iodine, silicon

nonmetallic mineral–spar

nonmetrical language–prose

nonpareil – nonesuch, paragon, peerless

nonplus–perplexed, puzzle, quandary, stump

nonpositive–negative, privative

nonprofessional – amateur, laic, lay

nonprofessional group–laity

nonsense – bah, blah, blah-blah, blather, bosh, bunk, drivel, falderal, folly, frivolity, monkeyshine, moonshine, pah, silliness, stite, triviality, twaddle

nonsense (Eng. dial.)–tosh

nonsense (Scot.)–stite

nonviolence (Hindu)–ahim-sa
none–nae, no, un
none such–model, paragon
noodle – blockhead, ninny, nizey, nizy, simpleton
nook – cant, corner, cove, crevice, cranny, in, niche, recess
noon – dinner, meridian, midday
noonday rest–siesta
noose–bond, halter, laniard, lanyard, loop, snare, tie
noose (old word)–grane
Nootka–aht
nor (former spelling)–ner
norate–gossip, noise
Norbertine – Premonstrant, Premonstratensian
norie–cormorant
norm–model, pattern, rule, standard, type
norma–gauge, model, pattern, rule, standard, template
normal–average, just, mean, natural, par, regular, sane
Normandy capital–Rouen
Normandy capital (anc.) – Caen
Normandy conqueror (early)–Rollo
Normandy departments – Calvados, Eure, Manche, Orne
Normandy duke (Viking)–Rollo
Norn – Skuld, Urth, Verthandi, Wyrd
Norse – mink, Norwegian, Scandinavian
Norse (old)–Icelandic
Norse abode of gods–Asgard
Norse abode of slain heroes–Asgard
Norse alphabet–runic
Norse bard–sagaman, scald, skald
Norse chief deity–Odin
Norse chieftain–Jarl
Norse collection of songs (myth.)–edda
Norse deities (three Vanir) –Frey, Freya, Njorth
Norse deity–*see* Norse god

Norse epic–saga
Norse fate–norn
Norse galley–aesc
Norse giant (myth.)–Fafnir, Jotun, Jotunn, Loke, Loki, Mimer, Mimir
Norse giant (primeval) – Ymer, Ymir
Norse giantess (myth.) – Natt, Norn, Nott
Norse god–Aeger, Aegir, As, Asa, Gymir, Hler, Hlorrithi, Loke, Loki, Odin, Ran, Thor, Ull, Ve, Van, Woden
Norse god (of crops)–Frey, Freyr
Norse god (of discord and mischief)–Loke, Loki
Norse god (of fertility) – Frey, Freyr
Norse god (of justice)–Forsete, Forseti
Norse god (of light and peace)–Balder, Baldr
Norse god (of peace and prosperity)–Frey, Freyr
Norse god (of poetry) – Brage, Bragi, Odin, Othin
Norse god (of sea)–Aeger, Aegir
Norse god (of thunder) – Thor
Norse god (of war)–Odin, Thor, Tyr
Norse god (of watchfulness) – Heimdal, Heimdall, Heimdallr
Norse god (of wisdom) – Odin, Othin
Norse god (supreme)–Odin
Norse goddess–Eir
Norse goddess (drinking from golden beaker) – Saga
Norse goddess (giant) – Norn, Urth, Wyrd
Norse goddess (minor) – Asynjur
Norse goddess (of beauty)–Freya, Freyja
Norse goddess (of death)–Hel, Hela
Norse goddess (of faith)–Norn

Norse goddess (of flowers)–Nanna
Norse goddess (of healing)–Eir
Norse goddess (of love) – Freya, Freyja
Norse goddess (of peace)–Eir
Norse goddess (of sky) – Frigg, Frigga
Norse goddess (of underworld)–Hel, Hela
Norse gods–Aesir
Norse guardian of Asgard–Heimdal, Heimdall, Heimdallr
Norse headman–jarl
Norse king (myth.)–Atli
Norse legend–saga
Norse letters–runes
Norse myth–saga
Norse myths (first man of)–Askr
Norse navigator–Eric
Norse nobleman–jarl
Norse patron saint–Olaf
Norse plateau–fjeld
Norse poem–rune
Norse poem (pert. to)–runic
Norse poet–scald
Norse poetry–rune
Norse queen (underworld)–Hel, Hela
Norse reciter (singer)–scald
Norse saint–Olaf, Olaus
Norse sea serpent–Midgard
Norse sprite (myth.)–alf
Norse tale–saga
Norse toast–skoal
Norse tree (symbolizing universe)–Ygdrasil, Yggdrasill
Norse viking–Rollo
Norse warrior – Baresark, Berserker
Norse watchdog (Hel's) – Garm, Garmr
Norse wolf–Fenrir
Norse work (old)–edda
norsel–band, fillet
North African–Moor, Nilot
North African country–Tunis
North African fruit–date
North African lyre–kissar
North African oasis–wadi

North African region–Nubia
North African sheep (wild)
–aoudad
North American bird–buf-
flehead, cardinal, fulmar,
grackle, killdeer, kingrail
North American continent
discoverer–Cabot
North American Indian–*see*
American Indian
North American Indian
blanket–stroud
North American mountain
(second highest)–Logan
North American orchids –
arethusas
North American rail–sora
North American reindeer –
caribou
North American resident –
Mexican
North American river–Ni-
agara
North American snake
(harmless)–adder
North American thrush –
robin
North American tree–tupelo
North Atlantic island–Ice-
land, Ireland
North Atlantic seagull–skua
North Britain–Scotland
North Briton–Scot
North Carolina cape–Fear,
Hatteras
North Carolina county –
Ashe, Avery
North Carolina Indian–Co-
ree
North Carolina river–Neuse,
Pedee, Tar
North China city–Urga
North Dakota city – Fargo,
Minot
North Dakota county–Traill
North European sea–Baltic
north magnetic pole dis-
coverer–Ross
north pole of magnet (pert.
to)–tactile
North Sea river–Weser
North Star–loadstar, lode-
star, polaris, polestar
North Syrian deity–El
north wind–boreas
northeast bird–hhalarope

Northeast prefecture–Oita
northeaster – gale, storm,
wind
northern–boreal, septentrio-
nal
Northern Bear–Russia
northern constellation–Andromeda, Cor
northern eagle–ern
northern European – Lapp,
Lett
northern horned mammal–
reindeer
northern land (world's most,
anc. name)–Thule
northern ptarmigan–ripa
Northern Rhodesia tribe –
Balokwakwa
northern tree – fir, maple,
pine
northernmost portion of
world (inhabited)–Thule
Northmen galley (armed)–
Aesc
Northmen gods–Aesir
Norwegian bird–rype
Norwegian brownie (folk-
lore)–kobold, nisse
Norwegian capital–Oslo
Norwegian capital (former)
–Christiania, Kristiania
Norwegian city – Bergen,
Christiania (c.), Dram-
men, Kristiania, Oslo,
Stavanger, Trondhjem
Norwegian coin–krone (s.),
ore (br.)
Norwegian composer –
Grieg
Norwegian counties (collec-
tively)–amter
Norwegian county – Fin-
mark, Tromso
Norwegian county (name
for)–fylke
Norwegian dramatist–Ibsen
Norwegian explorer – Nan-
sen, Sars
Norwegian goblin (folklore)
–kobold, nisse
Norwegian governor – amt-
man
Norwegian haddock – rose-
fish
Norwegian henchman of
Quisling–Hirden

Norwegian inlet of sea –
fiord, fjord
Norwegian king – Haakon,
Olaf
Norwegian lake – Miosen
Vand
Norwegian land division –
fylke
Norwegian language–Norse
Norwegian measure – alen,
fathom, fot, kande, korn-
tonde, maal, mal, pot,
skieppe
Norwegian mountain–Gald-
hoepig, Glitretind, Kjo-
len, Skagastolstind, Sogne
Norwegian needlework –
hardanger
Norwegian patron saint –
Olaf, Olaus
Norwegian philologist – Aa-
sen
Norwegian plateau (fjeld)–
Dovre, Hardanger
Norwegian poet–Ibsen
Norwegian police (Nazi) –
Gestapomen
Norwegian river – Ena,
Glommen, Lougen, Oi,
Tana
Norwegian saint (patron)–
Olaf, Olaus
Norwegian sea monster –
kraken
Norwegian tale–edda
Norwegian territorial divi-
sion–amt
Norwegian town–Nes, Oslo
Norwegian traitor–Quisling
Norwegian violinist – Ole
Bull
Norwegian weight–bismer-
pund, lod, mark, pund,
skaalpund
Norwegian writer–Ibsen
nose – conk, muzzle, neb,
proboscis, scent, snout
nose (bee's) – lorum, lora
(pl.)
nose (cartilage in)–septum
nose (flat)–simous
nose (having large)–nasute
nose (long)–proboscis
nose (long, projecting) –
snout
nose (openings of)–nares

nose (partition in)–vomer
nose (pert. to)–nasal
nose (snub)–simous
noseband (horse bridle) – musrol
nosebleed–epistaxis
nosegay – boquet, bouquet, posy
nosegay tree–frangipani
nose glasses–pincenez
nose hole–boccarella
nose inflammation – coryza, rhinitis
nose muscle–nasalio
nose nippers–pince-nez
nosepiece–nasal
nosepinch–pince-nez
nosocomium–hospital
nostalgia–homesickness
nostalgic wistfulness–regret
nostic–paragerontic
nostril – nare, nares, naris, thrill
nostril (pert. to)–narial
nostril-shaped–nariform
not – awnless, beardless, hornless, negation, nothingness, nought, polled, shaven, shorn
not (prefix)–il, im, ir, non, un
not acquired–ungot
not any–no, none
not any (law)–nul
not any (Scot.)–nane
not artificial–natural, real
not at all–nowise
not between poles of a battery–extrapolar
not boastful–diffident, modest, reserved, retiring, shy
not bringing to final conclusion–indecisive
not busy–idle, inactive
not covered–unlined
not discharged (as a debt)–unpaid
not easily abashed (disconcerted)–imperturbable
not easily discovered–inner
not efficient–lame
not either–neither
not existing–tame
not feral–tame
not fixed–unlaid

not forward–diffident, modest, reserved, retiring, shy
not general–local
not genuine–tin
not giving out–inexhaustible
not hard–easy, soft
not having made a will–intestate
not hollow–solid
not in harmony–out
not inclined–unapt
not invented (abbr.)–nei
not involving morality – amoral
not kept in motion – fixed, stabile, stable, static, stationary
not marked with time of origin–undated
not open (as of fruits)–indehiscent
not priced–unlaid
not professional–laic
not qualified–unfit
not raised from main branch by stem–sessile
not ready–unprepared
not regular–unsteady
not running in a stream – stagnant
not separable into parts–indivisible
not so fresh–older, stale
not so good–bad, worse
not so large–smaller
not so much–less
not sound–lame
not straightforward–evasive
not suitable–inept
not thinking logically – unreasoning
not to know (Scot.)–unken
not yet settled–moot
notable – distinguished, extraordinary, historic, memorable, noteworthy, notorious, remarkable
notandum–entry, memorandum, note
notar–notary
notary – notable, notebook, noter, notorious, observer
notation – annotation, etymology, marking, note
notation (coll.)–memo

notator–annotator, noter, recorder
notch–crena, dent, dint, gap, indent, indentation, indenture, jag, nick, score, undercut
notch (heraldry)–dentil
notched – coped, crenated, erose, indented, scored, serrate
notched bar (door knocker)–risp
notched on edge (like a saw)–serrate, serrated
notches–hila, hilum (sing.)
note – billet, character, dispatch, eminence, heed, indication, jot, marginal, mark, memorandum, notice, observation, remark, report, sign, sole, song, sound, token, tone, tune
note (explain by)–gloss
note (explanatory) – scholium
note (half)–minim
note (high accompanying)–overtone
note (high in pitch)–alt
note (little)–chit
note (low, Guido)–ut
note (marginal)–annotation, apostil, apostille, postil
note (musical)–breve, punctus
note (musical half)–minim
note (musical, old)–alamire, are, ela, ut
note (of)–famed
note (prisoner's)–kite
note (short)–chit, memo
note (short, cheerful)–chirp
note (single unvaried)–monotone
note (stem of, music)–filum
note (to) – jot, observe, remark
note (visible)–mark
note contents of–label
note duration of–clock, time
note of scale (Guido's)–alamire, alt, are, ela, ut
note speed of–clock, time
note supplier–annotator
notebook–adversaria, street
notebook (rate)–street

notecase–pocketbook

noted–celebrated, distingue, eminent, famed, famous, prominent, renowned, seen

notes (collection of)–adversaria

notes (succession of)–tiralee

notes (two performed in time of three)–duole

nothing–luke, naught, nihil, nill, nought, zero

nothing but–only, mere

nothing more than–mere

notice–advice, affiche, espial, heed, idea, intelligence, mark, mention, mind, news, note, notion, observe, quote, regard, remark, see, sign

notice (commendatory in book)–blurb

notice (for heroic service)–citation

notice (of death)–obit, obituary

notice (of marriage)–banns, bans

notice (official) – bulletin, edict, proclamation

notice (public)–ad, ban, sign

notify–apprise, cite, declare, page, publish, tell

notion – conception, idea, opinion, theory, view

notion (extravagant)–vagary

notion (fantastic)–bee, maggot

notionable – fanciful, whimsical

notoriety–eclat, publicity

notorious – arrant, famous, flagrant, known

notorious executioner – Jack Ketch

notour–infamous, notorious

notus–southwind

notus (zool. comb. form)–back

notwithstanding – despite, however, mauger, maugre, yet

nought – bad, nil, nothing, useless, wickedness, worthless, wrong, zero

noughty–bad, worthless

noumenal–ontal

noun (common gender) – epicene

noun (indeclinable)–aptote

noun (suffix) – ent, ery, et, ier, ion, ior

noun (suffix of diminutive force)–ole

noun (suffix signifying state, action, quality, degree)–ence

noun (verbal)–gerund

nourish–cultivate, feed, foster, grow, nurse, suckle, supply, support, sustain

nourishing–alible, nutrient, nutritive

nourishment–aliment, food, manna, meats, nutriment, nutritiousness, nutritiveness, pabulum, sustenance

nourishment (spiritual) – manna

nous–mind, reason

Nova Scotia–Acadia, Acadie

Nova Scotia mountain ash–dogberry

Nova Scotians – Acadians, bluenoses

novel–fiction, new, original, strange, unusual

novel by Zola–Nana

novelty–fad, freshness, newness, recentness

novice–abecedarian, apprentice, beginner, learner, neophyte, puny, tiro, tyro, tyrone

novice (in India)–chela

novitiate – apprenticeship, probation

now – forthwith, here, present

now (Scot.)–noo

nowise (former spelling) – navis

nowt – blockhead, bullock, lout, ox, oxen

Nox's brother–Erebus

Nox's daughter (who guarded golden apples) – Hesperides

Nox's husband–Chaos

noxious – baneful, destructive, evil, harmful, hurtful, injurious, insalubri-

ous, miasmatic, nocent, noisome, pernicious, unwholesome

noy–annoy, harm

nozzle (blast furnace air)–tuyere

nozzle (forge)–tew

nozzle (mining, large) – giant

nozzle (to force air to a forge)–tuyere

nuance–shade

nub – hang, knob, knot, knub, lump, neck, protuberance, snag

Nubian harp (small)–nanga

nucha–nape

nuclear network fiber–linin

nucleus (having a)–nucleate

nucleus of a regiment–cadre

nude–bare, denuded, naked, stripped, unclothed

nudge – block, elbow, jog, knub, lump, nog, poke, push

nugatory–ineffectual, invalid, trifling, trivial, vain, worthless

nuisance–annoyance, harm, hurt, injury, pest

nuit–night

nullah (Hindu) – gorge, gully, ravine, watercourse

nullified – abolished, annulled, canceled, counteracted, negated, neutralized, voided

nullify – abolish, abrogate, annul, counteract, negate, neutralize

nullo–game, task

numb – benumbed, clumsy, deadened, helpless, incapable, stupid

number–aggregate, complement, count, digit, enumerate, sum

number (added)–encore

number (cardinal)–primary, one, two, three (etc.)

number (considerable)–several

number (great)–multitude

number (large)–herd, myriad

number (least whole)–unit

number (ordinal)–first, second (etc.)
number (prime)–one, two, three (etc.)
number (pure, math.)–scalar
number (vast)–myriad
number (whole)–integer
number again–renumerate
number consecutively–folio
number expressed in scale of ten–decimal
number four–tetrad
number nine–ennead
number nine (based on) – nonare
number of copies issued at one time–edition
numbers–data
numbers (untold)–myriads
numbers at one's command–repertoire
number's third power–cube
numbles–entrails, inwards
numeral (style of) – Arabic, Roman
numerous – abundant, copious, lots, many, plentiful
Numidian bird (crane) – demoiselle
numskull–dolt, dunce
nun – priestess, smew, titmouse, votaress
nun (Franciscan)–Clare
nun (Latin)–Vesta
nunbird (genus of)–monasa
nun moth–tussock
nun's headdress–wimple
nunciate – announcer, messenger
nuncio – delegate, legate, messenger
nuncupate – declare, dedicate, designate, inscribe, proclaim
nuncupative – oral, unwritten
nunnery–abbey, cloister
nunnery head–abbess
nunni–blesbok
nuphar–nymphaeaceae
nupson–fool, simpleton
nuptial–bridal, marital, matrimonial
nurse – amah, ayah, baba,

bonne, mammy, nanny, norice, nourice
nurse (Oriental) – amah, ayah
nurse (to)–rear, tend
nurse shark–gata
nursed – cradled, fed, nourished, nurtured, suckled, tended
nursery (day)–creche
nurture – breeding, cherish, education, feed, foster, nurse, rear, training
nut – almond, beechnut, betel, Brazil, cashew, chestnut, cola, filbert, hazel, hickory, kola, niggertoe, peanut, pecan; crank, fellow, guy, head, problem, undertaking
nut (African)–cola, kola
nut (brown bitter)–kola
nut (diminutive)–pyrene
nut (edible part)–kernel
nut (former spelling)–nute
nut (hickory)–pecan
nut (ivory)–anta
nut (pert. to)–nucal
nut (walnut family)–butternut
nut bearing–nuciferous
nutbreaker–nutcracker
nut brown–chestnut, hazel, walnut
nutcake (New England) – doughnut
nut coal–anthracite
nut confection–praline
nutcracker–nuthatch
nut dash (printing)–en dash
nut grass–sedge
nuthatch – nutbreaker, nutcracker, nutpecker
nuthatch (tropical)–xenops
nuthatches (genus of, typical)–sitta
nuthook–beadle, constable
nutjobber–nuthatch
nutlet (small hard)–pyrene
nutmeg bird–cowry
nutmeg covering (dried) – mace
nutmeg family – myristicaceae
Nutmeg State–Connecticut

nutpecker–nuthatch
nut quad (printing) – en quad
nuts (collectively)–mast
nuts (fallen to ground) – shack
Nut's daughter–Nephthys
Nut's son–Ra
nutation–nod
nutramin–vitamin
nutria fur bearing animal–coypu
nutrice–nurse
nutrify–nourish
nutriment – aliment, food, nourishment, pabulum
nutritious – alimental, alimentary
nutty (slang)–crackbrained, gaga, piquant, queer, spicy
nuzzle–foster, nestle, nurse
nye–brood, eyas, nest, nide
nymph–dryad, hamadryad, naiad, nereid, oceanid, oread, sylph
nymph (alluring)–siren
nymph (Alpheus pursued)–Arethusa
nymph (any various)–Aegle
nymph (Apollo pursued) – Daphne
nymph (Arcadian)–syrinx
nymph (changed to laurel tree)–Daphne
nymph (changed to sea bird)–Scylla
nymph (fountain)–Naiad
nymph (hills)–Oread
nymph (lake)–Naiad
nymph (Leucippus pursued) –Daphne
nymph (Messina Strait) – Scylla
nymph (Mohammedan Paradise)–houri
nymph (Mt. Ida)–Oenone
nymph (mountain)–Oread
nymph (ocean)–Oceanid
nymph (of the hills)–Oread
nymph (Pan pursued) – Syrinx
nymph (river)–Naiad
nymph (sea) – Galatea, Nereid, Oceanid, siren

nymph (seafarer's menacer) –Scylla
nymph (springs)–Naiad
nymph (tree)–Dryad, Hamadryad
nymph (water) – Hydriad, Naiad, Undine
nymph (who loved Narcissus)–Echo

nymph (wood of Ellis, Gr.) –Arethusa
nymph (woods)–Dryad
nymph (young)–nymphet
nymph of Paradise–houri
nymphaea – Castalia, Castalie, Castaly
nymphs (pert. to)–nymphal, nymphical

nymphs (queen of)–Mab
nyroca–aythya
nyssa–tupelo
nystagmus–tic
Nyx–Nox
Nyx's daughter – Day, Eris, Light
Nyx's father–Chaos

O

oaf – blockhead, dolt, idiot, lout, simpleton
oak (California)–encina
oak (California white) – roble
oak (comb. form)–querci
oak (European)–durmast
oak (evergreen)–holm
oak (fruit of)–acorn
oak (genus of)–quercus
oak (holm)–ilex
oak (Jerusalem)–ambrose
oak (live)–encina
oak (playing cards)–club
oak (Turkey)–cerris
oak (unripe fruit of)–camata
oak (white)–roble
oak bark (rough part)–crut
oak beauty–moth
oak blight–louse
oak family–fagaceae
oak fern–polypody
oak fungus–armillaria
oak tannin (yellow brown)–quercinic, queric
oak web–cockchafer
oam–steam
oar – oarsman, paddle, propel, row, rower, scull
oar (flat part of)–palm, peel
oar (short)–scull
oar blade–palm, peel
oar feather–remex
oar fulcrum–thole
oarlock–rowlock, thole
oar lop–rabbit
oars (collectively)–oarage
oars (having one bank of)–unireme

oars (having three banks of) –trireme
oars (having two banks of)–bireme
oarsman – rower, sculler, stroke
oasis–ojo, wadi, wady
oasis (Central Asia)–merv
oast–kiln, oven
oat ear–wagtail
oaten pipe–oat
oats (genus of)–avena
oats (unthreshed)–oathay
oath–aith, aithe, curse, serment, vow
oath (mild, coll.)–drat
oath (minced)–egad
oath (to take)–swear
obclude–hide
obduction–autopsy
obdurate – adamant, firm, hard, hardhearted, inflexible, insensible, intractable, obstinate, persistent, rough, rugged, stony, stubborn, unbending, unfeeling, unsusceptible, unyielding
obedient–attentive, compliant, docile, duteous, dutiful, submissive, yielding
obedient person–conformer
obedient plant–dragonhead
obeisance–binge, bow, curtsy, deference, fealty, homage, respectful
obeisance (Oriental) – salaam, salam
obeisance (to make a) – conge, congee, salaam, salam

obelisk–needle, pillar
obelisk (reference)–dagger, mark, obelus
Oberon–fairy
Oberon's wife–Titania
obese–corpulent, fat, fleshy, liparous, pursy, stout
obey–ear, hear, heed, mind, yield
obfuscate–bewilder, confuse, dim, perplex
obi–girdle, sash
obit – death, died, notice, obituary, obsequies
obiter–incidentally
object – aim, demur, end, goal, intention, motive, protest
object (bulky, unwieldly) – hulk
object (circular)–trundle
object (cloud-like)–nebula
object (rare)–antique, curio
object (tilted at)–quintain
object (very small)–mite
object captiously–cavil
object of derision–scoff
object of devotion – fetish, idol, totem
object of dread – bogey, bogie, bogy, bugbear
object of greed – lucre, money, wealth
object of Islamic pilgrimage –Caaba, Kaaba, Kaabeh
object of worship–icon, idol, fetish, totem
object to–demur, protest
objection – cavil, exception, protest, quarrel
objection (frivolous)–cavil

objection (petty)–cavil

objectionable – exceptional, offensive

objective – aim, end, goal, motive, purpose, target

objector (conscientious) – c.o., conchie, conchy

objects (floating on sea) – flotsam

objects (used by high priest, Biblical)–Urim

objects (unknowable, whose existence is problematical)–noumena

objurgate – abuse, chide, reprove

oblate (opposite of)–prolate

obligation–agreement, bond, contract, debt, duty, oath, obstriction, onus, promise, vow

obligation (moral)–duty

obligation extension–renewal

obligatory–binding, imposing

oblige – bind, compel, constrain, engage, force, require

obliging – accommodating, agreeable, complaisant, courteous, kind

oblique–bevel, circuitous, inclined, scalene, sidelong, slanting

oblique (mining)–clinic

obliquely – askance, aslant, sideways, sidewise, skew

obliterate–blot, cancel, dele, delete, efface, erase, expunge

obliteration – deletion, erasure, extinction, rasure

obliteration (rare)–rasure

oblivion–forgetfulness, lethe

oblivion (river of)–Lethe

oblong–elongated, rectangular

oblong piece of metal–sow

oblong with rounded ends–elliptic

obloquy – abuse, calumny, reprehension

obnoxious – hateful, objectionable, odious, offensive, rancid

oboe–hautboy

oboe (small, simple) – musette

obscuration–eclipse

obscure – becloud, bedim, cloudy, dark, darkling, dim, eclipse, enigmatic, fog, hazy, indistinct, mirky, misty, murky, mystic, obstruse, remote, shadowy, slur, unknown

obscure (to) – delude, oversile

obscured (least)–clearest

obscurity – dimness, imperspicuous, uncomprehended, unknown

obsecrate – beseech, supplicate

obsequious – compliant, devoted, obedient, servile, slavish, subservient, toadying

observance – act, ceremony, custom, form, practice, rite

observance (religious solemn)–sacrament

observant–attentive, careful, heedful, mindful, regardant, regardful, watchful

observant of duty (scrupulously)–conscientious

observation–espial, remark

observation (casual)–remark

observatory (California) – Lick

observe – behold, celebrate, espy, eye, heed, keep, lo, nark, note, notice, obey, preserve, remark, see, solemnize, witness

observe (furtively) – nark, spy

observe (secretly)–tout

observed–seen

observed (matter to be)–notandum

observer–beholder, eyer, informer, looker-on, nark, onlooker, spectator, stool pigeon, witness

obsidian–iztle, lapis

obsignate–ratify, seal, stamp

obsolete – antiquated, archaic, old, outworn, passe

obstacle – dam, difficulty, hindrance, hurdle, impediment, let, obstruction, snag

obstacle (unsuspected)–snag

obstacles (fill with)–obstruct

obstetrician–accoucheur

obstetrix–midwife

obstinate–assish, balky, determined, dogged, headstrong, mulish, opinionated, perverse, pigheaded, set, stubborn, sullen, tough, willful

obstinate (be)–sulk

obstreperous – clamorous, noisy, unruly, vociferous

obstruct – arrest, bar, barricade, beset, block, check, choke, clog, dam, dit, ditt, embarrass, hamper, hinder, impede, interfere, interrupt, oppose, stop

obstruction–barrier, difficulty, filibuster, hindrance, impediment, snag

obstruction (military) – abatis

obstruction (water) – bar, dam, reef

obtain–achieve, acquire, attain, capture, derive, earn, fang, gain, get, procure, secure, win

obtain (with difficulty)–eke

obtain access–reach

obtain at another's expense–sponge

obtain by intimidation – blackmail

obtain by threats of violence –extort

obtain control of – corner, overcome

obtain equivalent for – recoup

obtest–beseech, supplicate

obtrude – eject, expel, impose, intrude

obtruncate–lop

obtruse fellow–cad

obtrusive – forward, intrusive, pushing

obtund–blunt, dull, quell

obtuse – blunt, crass, dense, dull, stupid

obvelation–concealing, veiling

obverse – complement, converse, counterpart, front

obviate–forestall, preclude

obvious – apparent, clear, conspicuous, evident, gross, manifest, palpable, patent, plain

obvious (not)–inner

obvolute – contorted, convolute, overlapping

oca–oxalis, sorrel

occasion – cause, ceremony, condition, event, excuse, exigency, function, happening, incident, nonce, pretext, sele, time

occasion (present)–nonce

occasion (special)–nonce

occasional – casual, incidental, infrequent, odd, stray

occasional (Scot.)–orra

occasionally–sometimes

occasive–setting, westward

Occident–West

Occident (opposed to)–East, Orient

Occidental – Hesperian, ponent, West, Western

occlude – absorb, close, obstruct

occult – alchemy, concealed, cryptic, hidden, imperceptible, magic, mysterious, mystic, necromancy, recondite, supernatural, supernormal

occult power–magic

occult science–esoterics

occultation – concealment, eclipse

occultism–cabala

occupant–prostitute, tenant

occupation–business, calling, career, employment, job, note, profession, pursuit, tenure, trade, vocation, work

occupation (transient)–avocation, hobby

occupied–busy, engaged, engrossed, filled, held, pervaded, sat

occupied (not)–empty, evacuated, free, idle, untaken, vacant

occupied (wholly)–rapt

occupy–cohabit, employ, engage, engross, expend, fill, hold, oversit, pervade, use

occupying a superior position–dominate

occupying much time or space–extended

occur–appear, befell, betide, clash, happen, meet

occurrence – appearance, event, hap, happening

occurrence (important) – event

occurrence (possible)–eventuality

occurrence (threat of immediate)–imminence

occurring after one's death–posthumous

occurring every eighth day–octan

occurring every fifth year–penteteric

occurring every fourth year (modern reckoning)–penteteric

occurring every third day (obs.)–tartane

occurring occasionally – sporadic

occurring often–frequent

ocean – brim, brine, deep, main, sea

ocean (little)–sealet

ocean (on the)–asea

ocean (pert. to)–pelagic

ocean approach (convenient)–seagate

ocean bottom–bed

ocean mammal–whale

ocean route–lane

oceanic – marine, maritime, pelagic

oceanic tree (timber)–ipil

Oceanid–nymph

Oceanus' daughter – Doris, Oceanid

Oceanus' sister–Tethys

Oceanus' wife–Tethys

ocellus–eye, stemma

ocelot–cat

ocher (Indian red)–almagra

ocher (red)–tiver

ocher (yellow)–sil

ochone (Scot.)–alas

ocilla (one of)–stemma

octahedrite–anatase

octapody–octameter

octave–eight

octave of a church feast–utas

octoate–caprylate

October bird–bobolink

October birthstone–beryl

octopean (rare)–octopus

octopus – polyp, polypus, poulp, poulpe

octopus (Hawaiian)–hee

octopus arm–tentacle

octoroon–metis, metisse

octose–sugar

octroi – concession, grant, privilege, tax

octuple–eightfold

ocuby–rum

ocular–optic, visual

odd–azygous, bizarre, droll, extra, occasional, queer, rare, strange, uneven, unmatched, unpaired, unusual

odd (Scot.)–orra

odd (strikingly)–outre

oddity – peculiarity, queerness, singularity

odds – dispute, dissension, probabilities, quarrel, variance

odds and ends – orts, remnants, scraps

ode–canticle, poem, psalm

ode (choral, var.)–pean

ode (pert. to)–odic

ode (type of)–pindaric

odeon–gallery, hall, odeum, theater

Odin–Wodan, Woden, Wotan

Odin's brother–Ve, Vili

Odin's hall–Valhall, Valhalla

Odin's horse–Sleipner

Odin's son – Balder, Baldr, Tyr, Vali

Odin's wife–Frigg, Frigga

odious–foul, hateful, vile

odium – abhorrence, antipathy, detestation

odor – aroma, fetor, foetor,

fragrance, nidor, nose, odour, perfume, scent, smell, stench
odor (agreeable)–aroma
odor (cooking)–nidor
odor (meat cooking)–fumet, fumette
odor (offensive)–funk, olid
odoriferous principle of violet root–irone, orris
odorous–fragrant, redolent
Odysseus–Ulysses
Odysseus' dog–Argos
Odysseus's wife–Penelope
Odyssey (author of)–Homer
oecist–colonizer
oecodomic–architectural
oeconomus–manager, steward
Oedipus' father–Laius
Oedipus' mother–Jocasta
Oenomaus' daughter – Hippodamia
oestrin–theelin
oestrus–desire, frenzy, fury, impulse, stimulus, sting
of a chamber–cameral
of a class related to things–generic
of a flock–gregal
of a forefather–ancestral
of a reign–regnal
of a river bank–riparian
of a wife–uxorial
of all–ava
of an early origin–ancient
of an epoch–eral
of common gender–epicene
of each (medicine)–ana
of equal regard–comparable
of great importance – momentous
of high standard–sterling
of highest quality–best
of like kind–such
of little importance–trivial
of long standing–old
of musical sound–tonal
of necessity–needs
of no avail–futile
of noble birth (obs.)–gent
of planet's path–orbital
of primary importance–capital
of same family–cognate
of same kind–akin

of same mind–agrees
of same name–ilk
of same parentage–germane
of small importance–petty
of tears–lacrimal
of that class–such
of that kind–such
of the (French for)–des, du
of the age (Latin, abbr.)–aet
of the city–urban
of the cod family–gadoid
of the color of thread–ficelle
of the country–rural
of the ear–aural, otic
of the earth–geal
of the morning–matin
of the mouth–oral
of the new stone age–neolithic
of the Salian Franks–Salic
of the same class–such
of the same name–ilk
of the shoulder–alar
of the sinus–sinal
of the skull–cranial
of the spring–vernal
of the summer–estival
of the sun–solar
of the third degree–cubical
of the throat–gular
of the tongue–glossal
of the tribe of Dan–Danite
of the wrist–carpal
of uniform pitch–level
of winter–hiemal
of yore (poetic)–olden
off–away, begone, distant, doff, remote
offal – carrion, garbage, refuse, rubbish
offend–affront, anger, annoy, cag, displease, insult, miff, mortify, pique, revolt, vex
offender – transgressor, wrongdoer
offender against law–criminal, wrongdoer
offense–crime, delinquency, fault, felony, grief, indignity, insult, malum, mala (pl.), misdemeanor, outrage, resentment, sin, trespass, umbrage
offense (civil)–stellionate

offense (mild law) – delict, delit
offense against law – delict, delictum
offense against right of law–mala
offensive–abusive, attack, attacking, disagreeable, displeasing, distasteful, foul, fulsome, invading, loathsome, opprobrious, repugnant, scurrilous, shocking
offensiveness–odium
offer–bid, overture, proffer, propine, propose, tender
offer (last of conditions)–ultimatum
offered for consideration–proposed
offered for sale – auctioned, vended
offering–gift, oblation, present, sacrifice
offering (as a vow)–corban
offering (religious, obs.) – deodate
offering block (deity's)–aloe
offering resistance to force–renitent
offhand–autoschediastic, extemporary
office – appointment, function, place, position, post, situation, station, wike, wiken
office (relinquish)–demit
office (Roman Curia)–dataria, datary
office (ruler's)–regency
office (staff of)–mace
office of ruler–regency
officeholders–ins, placemen
officer – adjutant, bailiff, command, conduct, constable, direct, general, manage, marshal, policeman, sheriff, tindal
officer (air navigation)–aviator
officer (American naval) – Byrd
officer (army camp head)–commandant
officer (British royal guard) –exon

officer (cabinet) – Hull, Ickes, Morgenthau, Perkins, Stimson
officer (chief congregation, Jewish religion)–parnas
officer (chief executive) – governor, mayor, president, sheriff
officer (church)–elder
officer (church under)–sexton
officer (civil) – bailiff, constable, marshal, police, policeman, sheriff
officer (civil, with limited authority)–magistrate
officer (club)–steward
officer (datary)–dataria
officer (diplomatic)–attache
officer (excise, slang)–revenooer, revenuer
officer (former)–aga
officer (future)–cadet
officer (king's stable) – avener
officer (law) – bailiff, constable, marshal, policeman, sheriff
officer (monastic)–prior
officer (naval)–ensign
officer (naval, petty) – yeoman
officer (parish)–beadle
officer (petty)–yeoman
officer (presiding) – chairman, president, speaker
officer (public)–notary
officer (religious)–prior
officer (royal household) – naperer
officer (ship's) – boatswain, bosun, mate, purser
officer (subordinate)–exon
officer (warrant)–boatswain, bosun
officer (weight and measure certifying)–sealer
officer (yeoman)–exon
officer's assistant–aide
offices of proconsuls – promagistracies
official (despotic subordinate)–satrap
official (government authoritative)–bureaucrat

official (insurance)–actuary, adjuster
official (king's representative)–missus
official (local)–burgess
official (of games) – judge, referee, umpire
official (old administrative) –reeve
official (public)–notary
official (sent by king)–missus
official approval–visa, vise
official command–edict
official declaration – proclamation
official mark–stamp
official order–rescript
official proclamation–ukase
official record – actum, acta (pl.)
officiating–acting, performing
officious – cool, efficacious, formal, impertinent, impudent, official, pert, pragmatical, saucy
officiousness–pragmatism
offshoot–branch, rod, scion
offspring–descendant, fruit, issue, produce, product, progeny, result, seed
offspring (coll.)–brat
oficina – factory, laboratory, office, works
oflete – oblation, offspring, wafer
often–frequently
ogdoad–eight
ogee–gula
ogee molding–talon
ogle–gaze, leer, stare
ogtiern–lord, master, son
oh (German)–ach
O'Hara's (Scarlett) home – Tara
Ohio city–Ada, Akron, Berea, Cadiz, Canton, Columbus, Toledo, Xenia
Ohio county–Erie
oil–aceite, anoint, ben, bribe, grease, oleum
oil (an)–ben
oil (comb. form)–oleo
oil (distilled bone)–olanin

oil (essence of roses)–atar, attar, ottar, otto
oil (essential of orange blossoms)–neroli
oil (fragrant)–atar, attar, ottar, otto
oil (kind of)–asarum
oil (lamp)–lucigen
oil (light, obtained from coal)–photogen
oil (made from butter)–ghee
oil (orange)–neroli
oil (pert. to)–oleic
oil (prefix denoting)–ol
oil (suffix for)–ol
oil (torch)–lucigen
oil (unproductive drilling for)–duster
oil (whale)–sperm
oil of cloves (chief constituent of)–eugenol
oil of orange flowers–neroli
oil of rose petals–atar, attar, ottar, otto
oil of rose petals (var.)–ottar, otto
oil of salt–bittern
oil beetle–meloe
oil beetle (genus of)–meloe
oil berry–olive
oilbird–guacharo
oilcan–oiler
oil cask (small)–rier
oilcloth–linoleum
oil flask (leather)–olpe
oillet–eyelet
oil plant–sesame
oil rock–limestone, shale
oilseed – castorbean, cottonseed, linseed, rapeseed, sesame, teel, til
oilstone–hone, shale, whetstone
oil-tongued–suave
oil tree–candlenut, mahua, mahwa
oil tubes (destitute of)–evittate
oil well (flowing)–gusher
oil-yielding plant–odal
oils (liquid portion of natural essential) – elaeopten, elaeoptene
oily–bland, compliant, glib, oleaginous, oleose, plau-

sible, suave, supple, unctuous

oily ketone–carone, irone

oily liquid–aniline, octane

oily liquid (from coal tar)–cresol

oily solids (from coal tar) cresol

oily tissue–fat

ointment–balm, balsam, cerate, nard, salve, unguent

ointment (dry)–xeromyron, xeromyrum

ointment (fragrant) – balm, balsam, nard

ointment (hair)–pomatum

ointment (healing)–salve

ointment (of ancients)–nard

ointment (oil)–carron

ointment (oil and wax)–cerate

ointment (perfumed) – pomade

ointment (soft oil)–oleamen

ointment (stiff)–xeromyron, xeromyrum

ointment (wax)–cerate

ointment application – embrocation

oisivity–laziness

ojo–oasis

oket–ounce

Oklahoma city–Ada, Alva, Cushing, Enid, Lawton, Sayre

Oklahoma county–Garvin

Oklahoma Indian – Cherokee, Creek, Osage, Pawnee

Oklahoma mountain–Ozark

Oklahoma river–Red

Oklahoma university–Norman

Oklahomans–Okies, Sooners

okra–bendy, gumbo

old–aged, ancient, anile, antiquated, antique, archaic, doddering, infirm, obsolete, senile, venerable

old (arch.)–agy, eld

old (dial.)–ald

old (former spelling)–ald

old (growing)–aging, senescent

old age (pert. to)–geratic, senile

old Arabian coin (gold)–dinar

Old Bay State–Massachusetts

old believers–Raskolnik

old billy–squaw

old boy–alumnus, devil, employer, father, teacher

old clootie–devil

old cloth measure–ell

old coin (Arabian)–dinar

old coin (Persian, gold)–daric

Old Dominion State – Virginia, Va. (abbr.)

old Dutch measure–aam

old exclamation–la

old expletive–egad

Old Faithful–geyser

old fashioned – antique, primitive

Old Franklin State–Tennessee

old French suffix–ison

Old Gentleman (the)–devil

Old Gooseberry–devil

old granny–squaw

Old Harry–devil

Old Hickory–Andrew Jackson

old in experience–veteran

Old Line State–Maryland

old maid–spinster

old man–captain, commander, employer, father, gaffer, geezer, husband, nestor

old man and woman–houseleek

old military rank–banneret

old musical note–ela, ut

Old Nick–devil

Old Noll–Oliver Cromwell

old Norse–Icelandic

Old North State–North Carolina

Old Rosey–Rosecrans

Old Rough and Ready–Taylor

old sailor–salt

old saying – adage, maxim, saw

Old Sol–sun

old songs (refrain in)–fala, falla

Old Testament (abbr.)–AT

Old Testament land of gold –Ophir

Old Testament name of deity–Elohim

Old Testament objects–Urim

Old Three Stars–Grant

old time (poetic)–eld

old time (Scot.)–syne

old timer (coll.)–vet

old timers–stagers

old wife–gammer

old woman–crone, gammer, hag

old womanish–anile

old world ape – catarrhina, catarrhine

old world carnivore–genet

old world dish (of herb juice, etc.)–tansy

old world falcon–saker

old world lizards (genus of) –agama

old world monkey – catarrhina, catarrhine

old world shrubs (genus of) –olax

old world trees (genus of)–olax

olden time (poetic)–eld, yore

older–senior

oldest–stalest

oldest division (European)–Jurassic, Lias

oldest in service–dean

olcaginous–oily, unctuous

oleander–rhododaphne, rhododendron

oleic acid salt–oleate

oleoresin – anime, copaiba, elemi, tolus

oleoresin (fragrant in varnish)–elemi

oleum–oil

oleum (symbol for)–ol

olfact–smell

olfaction–osmesis

olfactory organ–nose

olid–fetid

olinda bug–weevil

olio – hodgepodge, medley, mixture

oliphant–elephant

oliprance–jollity, ostentation, romp, show

olitory–potherb

olive (overripe)–drupe

olive (stuffed)–pimola
olive (stuffed with peppers)
 –pimola
olive (the)–olea
olive (true)–olea
olive enzyme–olease
olive family of shrubs and
 tree (pert. to)–oleaceous
olive family tree–ash
olive tree (genus of)–olea
oliver–hammer
Oliver Twist character–Fa-
 gin
olla–jug, pot
ollapodrida – hash, hodgepodge, medley, olio
oloroso–sherry
olpe–flask, pitcher, vessel
olycook (olykoek) – cruller,
 doughnut
Olympia–heavenly
Olympian–celestial, godlike,
 heavenly
Olympian god–Apollo, Ares,
 Dionysus,   Hephaestus,
 Hercules, Hermes, Posei-
 don, Zeus
Olympian god (of youth)–
 Apollo
Olympian goddess – Aphro-
 dite, Artemis, Athena,
 Demeter, Hera, Hestia
Olympic game site–Elis
omadhaun (omadawn)–fool,
 idiot, simpleton
Oman coin–gaj (ac.), mah-
 mudi (ac.)
Omar Khayyam's country –
 Iran
Omar Khayyam's fish (fa-
 bled)–mah
omega–end, last
omen–abode, augury, fore-
 bode, foreboding, foretoken, portent, presage, sign
omen (evil)–knell
omened (ill)–ominous
omers (ten)–epha
ominous – dour, ferocious,
 grim, inexorable, portentous, sinister
omission–neglect
omission of syllable from
 end of word–apocope
omit–skip
omit (in pronouncing)–elide

omit (in writing)–elide
omitted (from considera-
 tion)–elided
omitting (act of)–elision
omnes (stage direction)–all
omnitude – allness, totality,
 universality
omoplate–scapula
Omphale's son–Agelaus
omphalos–boss, center, hub,
 knob, navel
on – above, ahead, along,
 atop, upon
on account (abbr.)–oa
on all sides–about
on and on–tediously
on behalf of–for
on condition that–if
on dit–report, rumor
on every side–around
on grand scale–epic
on hand–here, present
on high–aloft
on other side–across, over
on sheltered side–alee
on tap–broached
on the hither side of river
 Po–cispadane
on the move–afoot
on the ocean–asea
on the side–apart
on this–hereon, hereupon
on this side (prefix)–cis
on unfriendly terms–outs
on windward side–aweather
onager–ass, catapult
onas (pert. to)–onan
once in a while–occasionally
once more–again, anew, encore
once over–O.O.
once upon a time–formerly
oncorhynchus–salmon
ondoyant–wavy
one – alone, an, individual,
 single, unit, unity, unmarried
one (comb. form) – mono,
 uni
one (French)–un
one (German)–ein
one (indefinite)–an
one (prefix)–mono, uni
one (Scot.)–ain, ae, ane
one accused–defendant

one after another – serially,
 successively
one after the other–serially,
 seriatim
one against–anti
one and all–every
one and one–singly
one appointed to act for
 sheriff–elisor
one before the other (as
 horses)–tandem
one behind the other–tan-
 dem
one born a serf (law)–neif
one by one–apiece, singly
one charged with high mission–apostle
one complaining–grumbler
one curious to know–gossip,
 quidnunc
one devoted to a pursuit–ist
one devoted to his own opinion–bigot
one devoted to monastic life
 –oblate
one devoted to table delicacies–epicure
one discontented with government–malcontent
one easily tricked (obs.)–
 cully
one engaging in marauding
 (Ind.)–lootie
one enrolled–draftee, enrol-
 lee, enroller, entrant, matriculant
one entirely lost (slang) –
 goner
one entitled to bear heraldic
 arms–armiger
one fond of fast driving–
 jehu, speeder
one for whose use a thing is
 done (law)–usee
one gigantic in size and
 power–titan
one given to despondent
 views–pessimist
one given to deviltry (coll.)
 –hellion
one-grained wheat–einkorn
one-hand sign language –
 dactylology
one having gigantic strength
 –titan

one having special information–insider
one having unorthodox
views–heretic
one-horse – inferior, petty,
small
one hundred thousand–lac,
lakh
one in controversy–disputant
one in favor of–for, pro
one in second childhood–
dotard
one instructed in secret system–epopt
one lacking in sense–tomfool
one living at another's expense–parasite
one looked at (humorous)–
staree
one lost entirely (slang) –
goner
one making show of reli-
gious feeling–pietist
one missing–absentee
one next in degree to knight
–armiger
one of a party–ite
one of ancient Persian dynasty–Sassanid
one of ancient race–Iberian,
Mede
one of medieval religious
sect–Anabaptist
one of mixed blood–mestee,
mestizo, metis, mustee,
mulatto, mulatta (fem.)
one of the Bears–Ursa
one of the causes of finite
existence (Buddhism) –
nidana
one of the initiated–epopt
one of the wise men of
Greece–Thales
one of twins–gemel
one of two equal parts–half
one opposed–anti
one owing allegiance to government–citizen
one performer on each part
(music)–soli
one preferred above others–
favorite, favourite, pet
one proposed for office –
nominee
one-sided – biased, bigoted,

partial, unfair, unilateral,
unjust
one skilled in international
diplomacy–diplomat, di-
plomatist
one skilled in military deception–strategist
one skilled in science of government–statesman
one sound–monotone, syl-
labic
one-spot–ace, pip
one supposed to bring good
luck–mascot
one that moves stealthily–
prowler
one that undergoes changes
–mutant
one thousand–mil
one time–former, formerly,
quondam
one to whom property is
willed–devisee
one to whom property title
is transferred–alienee
one to whom secrets are en-
trusted–confidant
one trained to shoot or capture parachutist–parashot
one trillion (prefix)–treg
one under another's care –
patient, protege, protegee
one undergoing change–mu-
tant
one versed in art of memory
–mnemonist
one versed in art of politics–
statesman
one versed in ecclesiastical
law–canonist
one versed in hygiene and
diseases of children–pedi-
atrician
one versed in law–legist
one versed in literature–savant
one versed in science–savant
one versed in science of
wealth and resources –
economist
one who absconds–eloper
one who adheres to certain
theory of matter–atomist
one who appropriates–pre-
emptor
one who attacks – assailant,

assailer
one who believes in all re-
ligions–omnist
one who believes in new
ideas–neo
one who believes in personal
god–deist
one who believes that all
space is full of matter–
plenist
one who bequeaths real estate–devisor
one who beseeches–pleader
one who bestows–granter
one who brings meat to the
table–dapifer
one who brings up to date–
reviser
one who carries (coll.)–toter
one who cherishes–fosterer
one who collects voluntary
taxes–tither
one who colors–dyer
one who conveys property–
alienor
one who defames–slanderer
one who defies–darer
one who differs–anti, dissi-
dent
one who disowns–repudiator
one who displays mere learning–pedant
one who disposes of prop-
erty by will–devisor
one who does (suffix)–ist
one who does professionally
(suffix)–ier
one who dresses skins–tanner
one who endeavors–striver
one who engages to do work
–contractor
one who ensures–securer
one who entertains–host
one who excels–ace
one who exercises power by
his wealth–plutocrat
one who feigns illness–ma-
lingerer
one who fights for noble
cause–crusader
one who forsakes faith principles–apostate
one who forestalls–anticipator

one who forwards goods – consigner, consignor, shipper

one who frustrates a plan–marplot

one who gathers–collector, reaper

one who gives his life for a cause–martyr

one who gives up–abnegator

one who grants by deed–remiser

one who hates his fellow-man–misanthropist

one who holds an office–in, incumbent

one who ignores (Eng.) – goofer

one who inculcates–instiller

one who inflicts retribution –nemesis

one who inspects–examiner

one who institutes suit at court–prosecutor

one who is always after the latest–neo

one who is excessively fond–doter

one who keeps horses for hire–liveryman

one who leads astray–temptress

one who leads into error–deceiver

one who learns by repetition –roter

one who lives by sponging–cadger, parasite

one who loves to excess – doter

one who makes an attack–aggressor

one who makes show of knowledge–pedant

one who manages–gerent

one who maximizes adverse aspects–pessimist

one who misuses his authority–satrap

one who moves rhythmically –dancer

one who offers sympathy–condoler

one who originates–initiator, inventor, producer

one who paginates–pager

one who parades knowledge –pedant

one who performs alone – soloist

one who pillages–ransacker, rifler, sacker

one who plunders–depredator

one who practices palmistry –chiromancer

one who preserves food – canner

one who prevents from entering–hajib

one who produces as new–initiator, inventor, originator

one who pursues wild animals–haha, hunter

one who puts new bottoms in chairs–caner

one who receives property by will–heritor, inheritor

one who removes a nuisance (law)–abator

one who rents property–lessee

one who resists authority–rebel

one who resorts to legal action–prosecutor

one who rules–gerent

one who seeks to undo political progress–reactionary

one who sells provisions to troops–sutler

one who sets free–deliverer

one who shoots from ambush–sniper

one who spoils a plan–marplot

one who stays–bider

one who stirs–agitator

one who summons spirits–evocator

one who takes over transferred property–alinee

one who takes prisoners–captor

one who takes the initiative –leader

one who testifies–deponent

one who tests – examiner, taster

one who transfers property –alienor

one who traps game–snarer

one who upholds doctrine varying from his church's –heretic

one who walks–pedestrian

one who wars about words–logomachist

one who works inefficiently –putterer

one who worships according to prescribed form–ritualist

one who wraps embalmed bodies–cerer

one whose interest is centered in external objects and actions–extrovert

one whose officious interference frustrates a plan – marplot

one wrongfully condemned –calas

one's self (belief in)–solipsism

one's strong point–forte

oneberry–hackberry

onefold – guileless, simple, sincere, single

onegite–amethyst

oneism–egoism, monism

oneness – agreement, aloneness, concord, loneliness, singleness, singularity, undividedness, union, uniqueness, unity

onerous – burden, burdensome, heavy, load, oppressive

onerous (former spelling)–onerose

onfall–attack, onset

onflemed–undismayed

onion–cepa, cibol

onion (genus of)–allium

onion (small)–cibol, eschalot, leek, onionet, scallion, shallot

onion (small inferior)–rareripe

onion (young)–shallot

onion-like herb–chive

onion-like plant–leek

onion-like vegetable – leek, shallot

onions (rope of)–reeves

onkos–topknot

onlepy–only, sole, solitary, unmarried

onlooker–spectator, witness

only – companionless, just, lone, lonely, mere, simple, single, singly, sole, solely

onomasticon – dictionary, lexicon

onset – assault, attack, onslaught

onslaught – assault, attack, onset

Ontario capital–Toronto

onus–burden, charge, duty, load, obligation

onward – along, forth, forward

oont–camel

oop–join, unite

oopak–tea

oorial–sha, urial

ooze–exude, leak, percolate, seep

ooze through pores – transude

oozing moisture–adrip

oozy–miry, muddy, slimy

opah–fish, soko

opah (native name) – kingfish

opal–girasol, girasole, hyalite

opal (colorless)–hyalite

opal (fire)–girasol, girasole

opal (variety of)–cacholong, menilite

opalescent – iridescent, irisated, opaline

opaque–dark, eyeshade, unilluminated

open–ajar, apparent, artless, frank, honest, obvious, overt, patent, patulous, plain, start, straightforward, unbolt, unclose, undissembling, undo, unfurl, unlock, unreserved, unseal, unstop, untie

open (bursting)–dehiscence

open (fully)–wide

open (half)–mid

open (partly)–ajar

open (poetic)–ope

open (wide)–agape

open a keg–unhead

open a way–pioneer

open acknowledgement – avowal

open and bold–glaring

open country–weald, wold

open court–area, patio

open for discussion–moot

open land–heath, moor

open out–deploy

open place in forest–glade

open-shelf cabinet–etagere

open to scorn–derisible

open to view–overt

open wide–gape

openhanded–free

opening – aperture, breach, cleft, door, gap, gate, hiatus, hole, initial, mouth, pore, portal, sinus, start, vent

opening (as a mouth)–os, ora (pl.)

opening (chess)–gambit

opening (from third ventricle to aqueduct of Sylvius) –pyla

opening (in a mold)–ingate

opening (minute)–stoma

opening (narrow) – crevice, rima, slot

opening (nasal)–nare

opening (of ear)–burr

opening (small)–chink, eyelet, lacuna, orifice, pore

opening (small mouth-like) –stoma, stomata (pl.)

opening wide–dehiscent

openings–ora

openwork (decorative)–tracery

opera (Verdi)–Aida

opera glass–lorgnette

opera hat–crush, gibus, topper

opera house–theater

opera singer–diva

opera star–diva

operate–go, manage, run

operatic solo–aria, scena

operatic soprana – Bori, Eames

operating backward – retroactive

operation (tumor) – ancotomy

operation of intelligence only–noesis

operation on skull–trepane

operative–artisan, detective, hand, mechanic

operative (become) – enure, inure

operator – agent, dealer, mountebank, quack, surgeon

operator (airship)–aeronaut, aviator, flier, flyer, pilot

operculum – covering, flap, lid

operose–busy, diligent, laborious

ophidian – reptile, serpent, snake

ophthalmic–ocular

opiate–anodyne, hemp, narcotic, opium, paregoric

opine – conjecture, deem, judge, suppose, think

opinion–esteem, estimation, feeling, idea, impression, judgment, notion, sentiment, view

opinion (religious unorthodox)–heresy

opinion (unorthodox)–heresy

opinion expression (formal) –vote

opinion held in opposition– heresy

opinions (collection of) – symposium

opinions (set of professed)– credo

opium–drug, intoxicant

opium (alkaloid) – codein, codeine, morphine, narcotin, narcotine, papaverin, papaverine

opium (camphorate tincture of)–paregoric

opium (derivative of)–meconic

opium (Egyptian)–thebaine

opium (prepared)–chandoo, chandu

opium (source of)–poppy

opodeldoc–liniment, plaster

opossum–marsupial

opossum (mouse)–marmosa, marmouse

opossum (water) – yapock, yapok

opponent–adversary, antagonist, foe, rival

opportune – convenient, fit, pat, ready, suitable, timely

opportunity–chance, circumstance, opening

oppose – contest, contradict, contravene, face, fight, gainsay, oppugn, pit, resist

oppose (to)–wither

oppose by argument–rebut

oppose by force–rebel

opposed – anti, averse, contested, contrary, coped, fronted, met, pitted, reactionary, resisted, vied, withstood

opposed (persistently)–renitent

opposed against–pitted

opposed to entad–ectad

opposed to lee–stoss

opposed to science–art

opposed to stoss–lee

opposed to zenith–nadir

opposer – antagonist, contester, foe

opposing–resistant

opposite – antagonistic, contradictory, contrary, converse, inverse, polar, repugnant, reverse

opposite (directly)–antipodean

opposite (exact)–antipode

opposite in action–polar

opposite in nature–inverse

opposite middle of ship's side–abeam

opposite to spring tide–neap

opposition–atilt, resistance

opposition (in)–wither

oppress–burden, crush, depress, distress, extinguish, harass, overpower, overwhelm, rape, ravish, suppress

oppress with heat–swelter

oppressive–burdensome, depressing, harsh, onerous, rigorous, severe, tyrannical

oppressor – burdener, czar, nero, tsar, tyrant

opprobrious–abusive, contumelious, disgraceful, insulting, offensive, scurrilous

opprobrium – disgrace, infamy, odium

oppugnacy – antagonism, hostility

oppugnation–attack, opposition

Ops' associate–Consus

Ops' consort–Saturn

Ops' daughter–Ceres

Ops' festival–opalia

opt–choose

optic–eye

optic defect–myopia

optic tube–telescope

optical apparatus – ultramicroscope

optical glass–lens

optical illusion–mirage

optical instrument–alidade, eriometer

optical instrument (distance measuring)–optometer

optical instrument (pert. to) –spectroscope

optical instrument cross wires–reticle

optical instrument part–alidade

optical membrane–retina

optical organ–eye

optimist (opposed to)–pessimist

optimistic–hopeful, roseate, sanguine

optimistic (more)–rosier

option – alternative, choice, refusal

optional – elective, permissive, voluntary

opulence–affluence, amplitude, plenty, profusion, riches, wealth

opulent – affluent, lavish, luxuriant, profuse, rich, wealthy

opus–composition, work

oracle–seer, sibyl

oracular–vatic, vatical

orage–storm, tempest

oral–parol, spoken, verbal, vocal

oral (law)–parol

oral declaration (law)–nuncupative

oral pledge (pert. to)–parole

orange (Chinese)–mandarin, tangerine

orange (genus of)–citrus

orange (heraldry)–tenne

orange (kind of)–bergamot, hedge, mock, Navel, Osage, Valencia

orange (mock)–seringa, syringa, syringe

orange (species of)–mandarin

orangeat–orangeade

orangeberry–cranberry

orangebird–tanager

orange-flower oil–neroli

orangeleaf–karamu

orange-like fruit–bel

orange membrane (between divisions)–zest

orange pekoe–tea

orange red–coral

orange seed–pip

orange-shaped–oblate

orangewood tree–Osage

orangutan–satyr

Oraon–Dravidian

orate – harangue, plead, speak

orate (slang)–spiel

oration–discourse, petition, prayer, speech

oration (funeral)–eloge, encomium, eulogy

oration (panegyrical funeral)–eloge, encomium, eulogy

oration (preacher's)–sermon

orator – petitioner, rhetor, rhetorician, speaker

orator (professional)–rhetor

orator (second-rate)–rhetor

oratorical–eloquent, rhetorical

oratory – chapel, elocution, eloquence

orb–ball, bereft, earth, encircle, enclose, eye, globe, moon, planet, sphere, star, sun, surround

orb bone cavity–eye

orbed–lunar, round

orbit of a planet–ellipse

orbit of planet point–apsis

orbit point–apsis
orbit point (farthest from earth)–apogee
orbs–planets
orc–grampus, whale
orca–whale
orchestra bells–glockenspiel
orchestra circle – parquet, parterre
orchestra part–brass, string, wind, wood
orchestral direction (stop playing)–tacit
orchid–arethusa, lycaste, pogonia
orchid appendage–caudicle
orchid meal–salep
orchid tuber–salep
orchid tuberous root–cullion
orchids (genus of)–listera
ordain–appoint, command, decree, destine, enact, install
ordainer–decreer
ordeal–trial
order – arrangement, array, bid, class, command, cosmos, direct, dispose, edict, enjoin, fiat, genus, genera (pl.), manage, mandate, regulate, rule, sect, system, will
order (in connected)–seriatim
order (in grammer)–taxis
order (including men)–primate
order (judicial)–writ
order (legal)–writ
order (peremptory)–fiat
order (proper)–kilter
order (written)–billet
order for writ–precipe
order of amphibians–anura
order of aquatic mammals–cetacea
order of architecture–Doric, Ionic
order of birds (abandoned)–rasores
order of cucumber (sea) –pedata
order of frogs and toads–anura
order of Greek architecture (pert. to)–Ionic

order of holy beings–hierarchy
order of insects–diptera
order of mammals–edentata
order of mammals (aquatic, including whales)–cetacea
order of mammals (highest)–primate
order of plants–rosaceae
order of protozoans–lobosa
order of sea cucumber–pedata
Order of the Garter motto–Honnisoitquimalypense
order of toads and frogs–anura
order of whales–cete
order of winged insects–diptera
order which includes mites–acarid
ordered–bade
ordered (well)–trim
orderly – methodical, neat, obedient, regular, regularly, shipshape, systematic, tidy, trim
orderly arrangement–series
orders–genera
ordinal–orderly, regular
ordinance – assize, control, direction, edict, law, management, regulation, rite, sacrament
ordinance (Latin) – decretum, decreta (pl.)
ordinance (petty)–bylaw
ordinarily–usually
ordinary–average, common, everyday, habitual, lala, natural, nomic, normal, ruck, so-so, usual, vulgate
ordinary (coll.)–lala
ordinate – methodical, moderate, orderly, regular, temperate
ordnance–armor, guns, petards, torpedoes
ordnance (old piece of)–petard
ordnance (old-time piece)–orgue
ordnance (piece of)–gun
ore–brass, copper, iron, mineral, seaweed, tin
ore (earthy looking)–paco

ore (impure)–speiss
ore (iron, impure) – ocher, ochre
ore (kind of iron)–hematite
ore (lead)–galena
ore (principal of lead)–galena
ore (small bunch of)–squat
ore (tungsten)–cals
ore (worthless)–matte
ore body capping (mining)–hat
ore crushers–dollies
ore deposit in rocks–lode
ore dressing machine–vanner
ore-filled fissure–lode
ore fusing establishment – smelter
ore loading platform–plat
ore mill roller–edgestone
ore refuse (after smelting)–scoria, tailings
ore separator–vanner
ore sluice–trunk
ore vein–lode
ore vein (small)–scrin
ore washing trough–strake
oread–nymph
Oregon capital–Salem
Oregon Indian–Modoc
Oregon mountain–Cascade, Coast, Hood
Oregon river – Columbia, Klamath
Oregon university (seat of)–Eugene
Oregon wind (southwest)–chinook
oreortyx–quail
Orestes' father – Agamemnon
Orestes' friend–Pylades
Orestes' mother–Clytemnestra
Orestes' sister–Electra
Orestes' wife–Hermione
orfevreri–jewelry
organ (auricular)–ear
organ (bird's vocal)–syrinx
organ (bristle-like)–seta
organ (leafless plant) – tendril
organ (lymphoid)–tonsil
organ (mouths of)–ora
organ (of volition, Hindu-

ism)–manas
organ (olfactory)–nose
organ (optical)–eye
organ (plant breathing) – stoma
organ (plant, secreting honey)–nectary
organ (reed)–harmonium
organ (respiratory)–lung
organ (sensory)–ear
organ (small portable, 16th century)–regal
organ (spider's web spinning)–spinneret
organ (vertebrate)–liver
organ cactus–saguaro
organ desk–console
organ fish–drumfish
organ flutter device–tremolo
organ gallery–loft
organ interlude (short) – verset
organ of living bodies – organism
organ of speech–lip, throat, tongue
organ openings–ora
organ part–reed, stop
organ piano–melopiano
organ pipes–flues, reeds
organ pipes (family of) – reeds
organ prelude (short)–verset
organ reed pipe stop – bassoon
organ reed stop–oboe
organ stop–bassoon, diapason, dulciana, oboe, orage, register
organ stop (labial)–melodia
organ stop (of two banks of pipes)–tertian
organ stop (select and adjust)–registrate
organ stop (storm imitating) –orage
organ stop (with string tone)–gamba
organic – instrumental, organlike
organic compound – amin, amine, ketol, ketole, ketone
organic portion of soil–humus

organic radical–ethyl
organic remains (without)–azoic
organical–constitutional, instrumental, mechanical
organism–animal, plant
organism (bacterial)–germ
organism (body of)–soma
organism (in certain plants) –spore
organism (minute)–spore
organism (pelagic, swimming)–nekton
organism (simple minute)–ameba, monad
organism (vegetable)–plant
organism (vegetable, large) –tree
organization – constitution, setup
organization (imperial)–empire
organization (men's patriotic, abbr.)–S.A.R.
organization (political) – bloc, party
organization (World War veteran's)–Fidac
organization into groups – regimentation
organizations (with many branches)–octopuses
organize – arrange, form, regiment
organized body of persons–corps, posse
organology–phrenology
organophone–harmonium
organoscopy–phrenology
orgueil–haughtiness, pride
orgy–carousal, frolic, lark, revelry, romp, shindy, spree, wassail
Oriana's father–Lisuarte
Oriana's lover–Amadis
oribi–antelope
oriel–balcony, bay, corridor, gallery, portico, recess, window
Orient–Asia, East, Levant
orient – bright, eastern, lustrous, oriental, pellucid, resplendent, shining
orient (poetic)–dawn, sunrise
oriental–bright, ortive

Oriental–Chinese, Eastern, Indian, Japanese, Mohammedan
Oriental archangel–Uriel
Oriental beverage–arrack
Oriental building (tower-like)–pagoda
Oriental burden bearer – hamal
Oriental cap–calpack
Oriental caravansary – imaret, khan, serai
Oriental carpet–kali
Oriental cart–araba
Oriental chief–khan
Oriental Christian (under Rome jurisdiction)–Uniat
Oriental coin–dinar, sen, yen
Oriental commander – ameer, amir, emeer, emir, ras
Oriental contrivance (water-raising)–shadoof
Oriental corn–para
Oriental council (of state)–Divan
Oriental covered wagon – araba
Oriental cymbals–zels
Oriental deity–Bel
Oriental destiny–Kismet
Oriental dish (of rice, etc.)–pilau, pilaw
Oriental drum–tomtom
Oriental drum (cavalry) – anacara
Oriental dulcimer–santir
Oriental dwelling–dar
Oriental garment – aba, sarong
Oriental gate–dar
Oriental guitar–sitar
Oriental head covering–turban
Oriental hospice – imaret, maret
Oriental inn–serai
Oriental instrument (musical)–samisen
Oriental kettledrum – anacara
Oriental laborers–coolies
Oriental leader–ameer, amir, emeer, emir
Oriental leathers–shagreens

Oriental litter–doolee, dooley, dooli, doolie, dooly

Oriental manservant–hamal

Oriental market place – bazaar

Oriental measure (Asiatic)–dra, mao

Oriental musical instrument –samisen

Oriental native–Asian

Oriental note–chit

Oriental nurse–amah, ayah

Oriental obeisance–salaam, salam

Oriental pagoda–taa

Oriental palanquin–doolee, dooley, dooli, doolie, dooly

Oriental patent–berat

Oriental people (anc.)–Seres

Oriental periodic wind – monsoon

Oriental pipe (smoking) – narghile, nargile, nargileh

Oriental porter–hamal

Oriental potentate – ameer, amir, emeer, emir

Oriental rest house – khan, serai

Oriental rice paste–ame

Oriental rug (small)–sedjadeh

Oriental ruler – calif, khan, shah, sultan

Oriental sabre–scimitar

Oriental sailor–lascar

Oriental salute–kowtow, saheb, salaam, salam

Oriental salute (var.)–salam

Oriental sash–obi

Oriental sea captain – rais, ras, reis

Oriental servant (female) – amah, ayah

Oriental servant (man) – hamal

Oriental skipper–rais, reis

Oriental smoking apparatus –narghile, nargile, nargileh

Oriental staple food–rice

Oriental structure (towerlike)–pagoda

Oriental tamarisk–atle, atlee

Oriental tambourine–daira

Oriental term of address (to Englishman) – saheb, sahib

Oriental term of address (to Englishwoman)–sahibah

Oriental title – aga, baba, pasha

Oriental tree–atle, atlee

Oriental trousers (women's) shaksheer

Oriental vessel (sailing) – dhow

Oriental wagon (cart)–araba

Oriental wagon (covered)–araba

Oriental weight–abbas, catty, miskal, picul, rotl, tael

Oriental weight (pound) – rotl

orifice – aperture, chimney, hole, inlet, mouth, opening, vent

orifice (brain)–lura

orifice (breathing)–spiracle

orifice (in side of a cask)–bunghole

orifice (minute)–pore, spiracle, stoma, stomata (pl.)

origin – beginning, birth, cause, commencement, genesis, inception, nature, nee, parent, parentage, rise, root, seed, source, start

origin (earliest quality) – mordiality

original–first, fontal, native, novel, primal, primary, primer, primitive, pristine

originals (copies of)–ectypes

originate–arise, breed, coin, create, derive, emanate, generate, invent, open, produce, rise, start

originate (as a word)–coin, etymologize

origination – creation, etymology, invention

originator – contriver, creator, discoverer, inventor, maker

originator (like an)–parental

oriole (European)–loriot

oriole (golden)–loriot, pirol

Orion (star of)–Rigel

Orion's hound–Aratus

Orion's slayer–Artemis

orison–prayer

oristic – definitive, determinate

Orkney Island (largest of)–Pomona

Orkney Island capital–Kirkwall

Orkney Island fisherman's hut–skio

Orkney Island land (held in fee simple without charter)–odal, udal, udalborn, udaler, udalman

Orkney Island supreme court president–foud

Orkney Island tower–broch

orle–bearing, border, chaplet, fillet, wreath

orlean–annatto

orlop–deck

ornament – adorn, amulet, appliquer, brooch, decorate, decoration, embellish, embellishment, finery, gutta, ouch

ornament (apex)–finial

ornament (architectural eggshaped, Fr.)–ove

ornament (Biblical)–Urim

ornament (boat-shaped)–nef

ornament (brilliant)–spang, spangle

ornament (by indenting) – chase

ornament (by setting in wood or ivory)–inlay

ornament (delicate)–tracery

ornament (dress)–jabot

ornament (flashy)–gaud

ornament (former) – stomacher

ornament (gaudy)–tinsel

ornament (hair) – barrette, comb

ornament (hanging) – bangle, pendant, tassel

ornament (head)–tiara

ornament (Japanese girdle) –inro

ornament (mantel)–bibelot

ornament (of vine leaves and grapes)–pampre

ornament (pendant) – bangle, earring, tassel

ornament (personal)–parure
ornament (priest's habit) – Urim
ornament (protuberant) – boss
ornament (rose-shaped) – rosette
ornament (shoulder)–epaulet, epaulette
ornament (silverware)– gadroon, godroon
ornament (style of)–rococo
ornament (terminal)–finial
ornament (tie)–pin
ornament (tufted)–pompon, pompoon
ornament (wall)–plaque
ornament with raised designs–brocade
ornamental – decorative, fancy
ornamental bottle–decanter
ornamental button–stud
ornamental knot–bow
ornamental lace edge–picot
ornamental stand–etagere
ornamental vase–urn
ornamental vessel–urn
ornamental vessel (sailing)–dhow
ornamentation – embellishment
ornamentation (florid style) –rococo
ornamented – chased, engraved, etched, tooled
ornamented (as a book) – tooled
ornamented (excessively) – tawdry
ornamenting metal (black inlay)–niello
ornamenting with raised designs–brocading
ornaments (sets of)–parure
ornate–adorned, decorated, fancy, florid, gay
ornithon–aviary
oro–gold
orotund – bombastic, pompous
orp–fret, weep
orpheum–theater
Orpheus' father–Apollo
Orpheus' mother–Calliope
Orpheus' wife–Eurydice

orphrey–band, embroidery
orpit–fretful
orra–odd, occasional, miscellaneous, unemployed
orris root oil (colorless) – irone
ort – bits, leavings, refuse, remnant, scraps
orthodox – accepted, canonical, customary, standard
orthodox Moslem–hanif
orthographer–speller
ortolan – bird, bobolink, bunting, rail, wheatear
oryx–antelope
os–bone, mouth, opening
oscillate – fluctuate, rock, sway, swing, vary, vibrate, wag, waver, weave
oscine–scopoline
oscitancy – drowsiness, dullness, sluggishness
oscitant – careless, drowsy, gaping, sleepy, sluggish, yawning
oscitate–gape, yawn
osculate–buss, kiss
osculation–kiss
osier–rod, sallow, wand, willow
osier band–withe
Osiris' brother–Set
Osiris' father–Geb, Keb, Seb
Osiris' mother–Nut
Osiris' sister–Isis
Osiris' son–Anubis, Horus
Osiris' wife–Isis
Osmanli–Turk
osmesis–olfaction, smelling
osprey–hawk
ossature–skeleton
osse–attempt, dare, presage, promise, prophesy, recommend
osseous–bone, bony, ossiferous
osseus–osteal
ossified cartilage–bone
ossifrage – eagle, lammergeier, osprey
ossuary – depository, tomb, urn
ostend–exhibit, manifest, reveal
ostensible – apparent, seeming, specious

ostensible (reason or motive)–pretext
ostensive–demonstrative, exhibiting, showing
ostensorium – monstrance, pix, pyx
ostentation–eclat, flare, pageant, parade, portent, presage, show
ostentatious–pompous, pretentious
ostentatious (coll.) – arty, sporty
ostentatious (more, coll.) – louder
ostentatiously fashionable – dashy
osteria–inn, tavern
ostiole – aperture, orifice, pore, stoma, stomata (pl.)
ostler–stableman
ostrich–emu, nandu, rhea
ostrich (three-toed)–rhea
ostrich-like birds–cassowaries, emeus, emus, moas, ratitae, rheas
ostriches (genus of)–rhea
otacust–listener, spy
Otaheite–Tahiti
otalgia–earache
Othello (character in)–Iago
Othello (opera composer) – Verdi
Othello's friend (perfidious) –Iago
Othello's wife–Desdemona
other–else
other (Scot.)–ither
others–rest
otherwise–alias, else, or
otherworldly–fey
Othman's successor–Ali
otiant–idle, reposing, unemployed
otic–auditory, auricular
otidium–otocyst
otiose–idle, indolent, futile, sterile, unemployed
otium–leisure
otkon–demon, okee, oki
otologist–aurist
ottar–attar
ottavino–piccolo
otter–annatto
otter (sea)–kalan
otter sheep–ancon

otters (genus of)–lutra
otto–attar
ottoman–footstool, stool
Ottoman–Turk
Ottoman court–porte
Ottoman Empire–Turkey
Ottoman Empire province–Vilayet
Ottoman Empire subject (non-Moslem)–Raia, Rayah
Ottoman governor–pasha
Ottoman poetry couplet – beyt
Ottomans (leader of) – Osman
oubliette–dungeon
ouch – bezel, brooch, clasp, fibula
ought – bood, cipher, must, naught, should
ought to–should
ouk (Scot.)–week
ounce (sixteenth of)–dram
oundy–curly, waving, wavy
ouphe–elf, goblin
our (French)–notre
ourie–cold, dingy, dreary
ousia – essence, nature, substance
oust – bar, eject, evict, remove
out – absent, away, issued, published
out of–from
out of (prefix)–ec
out of danger–safe
out of date–antiquated, old, passe
out of place–inept
out of style–antiquated, old, passe
out of the way–afield, aside
outage–outlet, vent
outbearing–arrogant
outbraid–upbraid
outbreak–emeute, eruption, insurrection, outcrop, riot, tumult
outbreak (new) – recrudescence
outbreak (noisy)–ruction
outbreak (seditious) – emeute, riot
outbreak (sudden)–spurt

outbreak (violent)–eruption, riot
outbreak of wild emotionalism–hysteria
outbuilding – backhouse, barn, outhouse, privy, shed
outburst (violent)–blast, explosion
outcast – castaway, expatriate, leper, pariah, vagabond
outcast (Japan)–ronin
outcast (social)–pariah
outclass–excel, surpass
outcome–consequence, emanate, issue, outlet, result, sequel, upshot
outcome (final) – consequence, issue, result, upshot
outcraft–excel, outwit, surpass
outcry–alarm, clamor, proclaim, shout, yell
outdate–antiquate, outmode
outdistance – outstrip, surpass
outdo–exceed
outdoor game – badminton, cricket, croquet, polo, tennis
outer–ectad, ectal, exterior, external, outside, utter
outer (opposed to)–ental
outer boundary of plane figure–perimeter
outer covering – coat, hull, jacket, tegument
outer garment–cloak, mackinaw, mackintosh, mantilla, overcoat, paletot
outer layer of roots – exoderm
outer membrane of grain–extine
Outer Mongolia (capital of) –Urga
outermost–extreme, utmost
outer shell of mollusks, oysters, etc.–test
outer skin–epidermis
outfit–equip, kit, organization, rig, suit, unit
outflow–efflux

outflow (continuous)–drain, efflux
outgate – egress, exit, outcome, outlet
outgive–cease, end
outing–excursion, vacation
outknee–bowleg
outlander – alien, foreigner, stranger
outlaw–bandit, fugitive
outlaw (Japan)–ronin
outlay–cost, expenditure
outlet – exit, opening, outcast, vent
outlet (water)–bayou
outline–chart, compendium, configuration, contour, delineate, delineation, draft, map, perimeter, shape, sketch, summary
outline (melodic)–melos
outline (moving picture) – scenario
outline of contour – configuration
outline of play–scenario
outlines–frames
outlive–outlast, survive
outlook – perception, prospect, purview, vista
outmost – extremest, farthest, final, outermost, outward, remote, utmost, utter, uttermost
outpeer–excel, surpass
output – cut, energy, expel, power, production, yield
outraged–abused, affronted, insulted, offended
outrageous–exorbitant, heinous, monstrous
outre–bizarre, extravagant
outrival–eclipse, excel, outvie
outroot–eradicate, extirpate
outside (comb. form)–ecto
outside (prefix)–ect, exo
outspoken – candid, frank, free, unreserved
outstanding – conspicuous, eminent, famed, famous, noted, principal, prominent, uncollected, unpaid
outstretched (Scot.)–stent
outstrip – best, excel, lead, surpass

outtake–deliver, except, exclude, outlet, vent, withdraw

outward–ectad, exterior, external, extrinsic, outer

outward (anat.)–ectad

outward (turn)–evert

outward circle–spiral

outwardly – externally, extrinsically

outwardly manifest–overt

outwit – baffle, balk, best, block, check, checkmate, circumvent, cross, disappoint, foil, frustrate, thwart

outwork–preterit

ouvrier–operative, worker

ouzel (ousel) – blackbird, piet, thrush, whistler

oval – ellipse, ellipsoidal, elliptical

oval figure–ellipse

ovale (French)–egg

ovate (inversely)–obovate

oven–furnace, kiln, oast

oven (glass annealing)–leer, lehr

oven (hop drying)–oast

oven (Maori)–umu

oven (Polynesian)–umu

oven mop–scovel

over – above, again, also, anew, ended, finished, too

over (poetic)–oer

over (prefix)–super, supra, sur

over again–anew

overabundance–excess, surplus

overalls (cowboy, coll.) – chaps

overbearing–arrogant, domineering, haughty, overpowering, snobbish, subduing

overcast – cloudy, darken, dim, gloomy

overcoat – capote, greatcoat, surtout, topcoat, ulster

overcoat (close fitting)–surtout

overcoat (Fr., loose)–paletot

overcoat (heavy) – paletot, ulster

overcoat (loose) – paletot, raglan

overcoat (slang)–benny

overcoat (sleeveless)–inverness

overcoat (soldier's)–capote

overcoat (worn like cloak, Scot.)–slipon

overcome–awe, beat, beaten, conquer, crush, defeat, exceed, outstrip, overbear, overpower, overthrow, overturn, overwhelm, prostrate, vanquish, win

overcrowded–congested

overcrowded state – congestion

overdetailed – prolix, protracted, tiresome, wearisome

overdue payments–bygones

overfeed – agrote, crapulate, glut, overfill, pamper, surfeit

overflow–deluge, inundate, outlet, overrun, spate, teem

overflow with water–awash

overflowing – abundant, copiousness, exuberance, inundation

overflowing with enthusiasm and exhilaration – ebullient

overfond of–dote

overfull–plethoric

overhang – beetle, jut, project, suspend

overhasty–daring, rash

overhaul–examine, renovate

overhead – above, aloft, expense

overhung (ominously) – beetled

overissue–inflation

overlaid with richer material–plated

overlapping–imbricate

overlaps chamfered plank edges to make flush joint –syphers

overloaded–plethoric

overlook – absolve, acquit, condone, excuse, forgive, ignore, miss, skip, supervise

overlord – domineer, tyrannize

overly – careless, negligent, overbearing, supercilious, superficial, too

overmatch–best

overmodest person–prude

overmost – highest, uppermost

overmuch – excess, surplus, too

overnice–fastidious, fussy

overornate–rococo

overparticular – fastidious, fussy

overplus–excess, surplus

overpower – awe, conquer, crush, defeat, master, overbear, overcome, overthrow, overwhelm, rout, subdue, vanquish

overpower by lights–dazzle

overpowered with sudden emotion–enrapt, stunned

overpowering–fierce

overprecise – fastidious, finical, finicky

overreach – cheat, nobble, outwit

overrun–crush, destroy, infest, overwhelm, spread

overscrupulous person – prude

overseer – boss, curator, inspector, manager, superintendent, supervisor

overseer (anc.)–reeve

overseer (spiritual)–pastor

overshadow–darken, eclipse, obscure

overshoe–arctic, galosh, galoshe, gum, rubber

oversight–care, charge, control, direction, inspection, supervision, surveillance, watch

overskirt (puffed)–pannier

overt – apparent, manifest, obvious, open, patent, public

overtake–apprehend, captivate, detect, ensnare

overtaken by darkness–benighted

overthrow–conquer, defeat, demolish, destroy, down, overcome, overturn, prostrate, rout, ruin, ruinate, unhorse, unseat, vanquish, worst
overthrown–fallen, ruined
overtones–partials
overtop – dwarf, excel, obscure, override, surpass, tower, transcend
overture – aperture, offer, opening, prelude, proem, proposal, proposition
overturn – destroy, overthrow, sill, subvert, throw, tip, topple, upset
overwhelm–bury, conquer, crush, defeat, deluge, engross, engulf, oppress, overpower, overthrow, overturn, rout, submerge
overwhelm (by argument)–confute
ovine (female)–ewe
ovoid–egg-like
ovoid-shaped–obovoid
ovule–egg, embryo, seed
ovum–egg, seed, spore
ovum (comb. form)–ova
owe–due, own, possess
ower–debtor
owl (barn)–lulu
owl (short-eared)–momo
owl (young)–owlet, utum
owl-like–strigine
own – acknowledge, admit, have, possess
own (Scot.)–ain
owner–proprietor
owner (plantation)–planter

owner's mark on sheep (Eng.)–smit
ownership–dominium, proprietorship, tenancy, title
ownership of land (absolute)–odal, udal, udaler, udaller, udalman
owning–admits, has
owns–has
ox–steer
ox (Celebes)–anoa
ox (European extinct wild) –urus
ox (forest)–anoa
ox (horned, wild)–reem
ox (India)–gayal
ox (kind of)–yak
ox (Malay Peninsula, wild)– banteng
ox (small)–runt
ox (wild, extinct)–urus
ox (wild, small)–anoa
ox (working)–aver
ox-like–bovine
ox-like quadruped–bison
oxalis plant–oca
oxalyl–carbonyl
oxen–beeves, bisons
oxen (Celebes)–anoas
oxen (forest)–anoas
oxen (Tibet)–yak
oxen (yoke of)–span
oxen harness–yoke
oxeye–boce, dunlin
oxford–shoe
Oxford College account–battel
Oxford officer (var.)–bedel
Oxford scholarship founder –Rhodes
oxide (kind of)–dioxide

oxide of hydrocarbon radical–ether
oxide of iron (red)–rust
oxide of strontium–strontia
oxidize by heat–calcine
oxter–arm, armpit
oxwort–butterbur
oxygen (allotropic form) – ozone
oxygen (binary compound) –oxide
oxygen (kind of)–ozone
oxygen acid – chloric, sulphuris
oxygen compound (binary) –oxide
oxygenate–aerate
oyster–bivalve
oyster (cultivated artificially)–native
oyster (young)–spat
oyster bed–oysterage
oyster bed (artificial)–layer, stew
oyster bed materials (for making)–culches
oyster bird–sanderling
oyster catcher–olive, tirma
oyster eggs–spawn
oyster farm–claire, park
oysterfish–tautog
oyster gatherer–tongman
oyster ova–spawn
oyster rake–tongs
oysterroot–salsify
oyster shell–husk, shuck
oyster shell (outer)–test
oyster spawn–cultch
oyster tree–mangrove
oysters (uncooked)–raws
Ozark State–Missouri

P

P (the letter)–Pee
pa–father, papa
pa (pah) – fort, settlement, stockade
paaauw–bustard
pabulum – aliment, food, fuel, nutriment, support, sustenance
pac (pack)–moccasin

paca–rodent
pacate–appeased, pacified
pacay–angelin, mesquite
pace–gait, lope, rate, speed, step
pachak–costusroot
pachyderm – elephant, rhinoceros

pacific – calm, irenic, irenical, peaceable, peaceful, placid, serene, tranquil
Pacific archipelago – Malay, Samoa, Sulu
Pacific bonito–victorfish
Pacific coast tree–madrona
Pacific island – Carolines, Guam, Marquesas, Sa-

moa, Tasmania, Wake, Yap
Pacific island bird–kagu
Pacific island cloth–tapa
Pacific island natives–Japanese
Pacific island tree–ipil
Pacific islands (group of southwest)–Samoa
Pacific lands (collective name)–Oceania
Pacific shark–mako
Pacific state – California, Oregon, Washington
Pacific "stepping stones" – Aleutians
pacifier–sop
pacify – abate, allay, alleviate, appease, assuage, calm, ease, lull, mitigate, mollify, placate, propitiate, soften, soothe
pack–bundle, embale, flock, horde, load, steve, stow, tamp
pack (carried on back) – knapsack
pack animal (small)–burro, llama
pack horse–sumpter
pack horse bag–kyack, pannier
pack of hounds–kennel
package–bale, bundle, packet, pad, parcel
package (covered with hair) –seroon
package of peppers (East Indies)–robbin
package of wool–fadge
packer–canner, roper
packet–bundle, parcel
packing (clay)–lute
packing plant (for fruit, fish, etc.)–cannery
paco–alpaca
Pacolet–dwarf, horse
pact – agreement, bargain, contract
paction–agreement, bargain, compact
Pactolian–golden
pad–cushion, footpad, highwayman, mat, path, quilt, stuff, tablet, trudge, walk
pad (hair)–rat

pad (horse's saddle) – housing
pad (perfume)–sachet
pad (saddle)–panel
pad (soft)–bolster, cushion
padcloth – housing, saddlecloth
padder – footpad, highwayman
padding–stuffing, wadding
paddle–lumpfish, oar, row, spud, wade
paddlecock–lumpfish
paddock – enclosure, field, frog, garston, park, sledge, toad
paddock pipe–horsetail
paddockstone–greenstone
paddockstool–toadstool
paddy – cushiony, padlike, soft
Paddy–Irishman
Paddy's hurricane–calm
paddywhack – beat, blow, thrashing
Paddywhack–Irishman
Paderewski's compatriot – Pole
padfoot–footpad, barghest
padle (Scot.)–hoe
padou–ferret, ribbon
padre – chaplain, monk, priest
padrona–landlady, mistress
padrone – innkeeper, landlord, master, patron
pagan–ethnic, heathen, idolatrous, paynim
pagan god–idol
page–boy, child, folio, leaf, messenger
page (blank at beginning of book)–flyleaf
page (book)–folio
page (lady's)–escudero
page (left hand)–verso
page (left hand, abbr.)–vo
page (reverse)–verso
page (right hand)–recto
page (title)–rubric
page number–folio
pages (number of)–pagination
pages (number the) – paginate
pages (of)–paginal

pageant–exhibition, parade, pomp, tableau
pageant (natatorial) – aquacade
Pagliacci character–Tonio
Pagliacci composer–Leoncavallo
pagne–loincloth, petticoat
pagoda – summerhouse, taa, temple
pagoda finial–tee
pagoda stone–agalmatolite
pahi–canoe, ship
pahmi–bobac
paho–pahutan
paid – content, discharged, satisfied, settled, yielded
paid attention to – heeded, listened
paid office (without employment)–sinecure
paid out–disbursed, expended, spent
paideutics–pedagogy
paigle–crowfoot, stitchwort, cuckooflower
paik–beat, pommel, strike
pail – beat, bucket, harass, pan, thrash, vessel
pail (Latin) – situla, situlae (pl.)
pain – ache, afflict, agony, agra, disquiet, pang, punishment, suffering, trouble, wound
pain (back)–notalgia
pain (extreme)–torture
pain (persistent)–gnawing
pain (to be in, Scot.)–thraw
pain (violent)–pang, throe
painful–bitter, sore
painful (dial.)–sare
painkiller–anodyne
painstaking – assiduity, assiduous, careful, diligent, laborious
paint – color, limn, rouge, stain
paint (blue)–bice
paint (green)–bice
paint (to, Latin, comb. form)–picto
paint (to, the face)–parget
paint (used on face)–fard
paint (used on lips)–rouge

paint through perforated pattern–stencil
painted pavement (used by Romans)–asarotum
painted vermilion–miniate
painter (surrealist)–Dali
painter's equipment–easel
painter's table–palette
painting–oil
painting (decorative, in gray monochrome)–grisaille
painting (process of) – tempera
painting (sacred)–pieta
painting (soften effect of)–scumble
painting (style of) – fresco, genre
pair – brace, couple, diad, dyad, mate, span, team, two, unite, yoke
pair of horses (harnessed together)–span, team
pair of units (treated as one) –diad, dyad
paired–gemel
paisano – countryman, peasant
pal–accomplice, chum, companion, crony, pard, partner
palace–praetorium, pretorium
palace (French)–palais
palace officer–paladin, palatine
palais–palace
Palamon's rival–Arcite
Palamon's wife–Emelye
palanquin (India) – palkee, palki
palanquin (Japanese)–kago
palanquin (Oriental) – doolee
palanquin bearer–hamal
palas–dhak
palatable – acceptable, pleasing, sapid, savory
palatable (to render)–season
palate (soft) – cion, uxula, velum
palate part–uvula
palatine–paladin, palatial
pale – ashen, ashy, blanch, dim, haggard, lily, ob-

scure, pallid, sickly, stake, wan, white, whitish
pale (ghastly)–lurid
pale yellow–flaxen
Palestine (conquerors of) – Turks
Palestine (part of)–Canaan
Palestine animal–daman
Palestine coin – mil (br.) pound (g.)
Palestine country–Philistia
Palestine district – Gaza, Ghazze, Haifa
Palestine lake–Merom
Palestine landmark–Dan
Palestine mammal (small)–daman
Palestine measure – cubit, donum, sacred
Palestine mountain – Ebal, Gilead
Palestine people (anc.) – Amorite
Palestine plain–Sharon
Palestine port–Acre, Haifa, Jaffa
Palestine river (flowing into Dead Sea)–Jordan
Palestine town–Cana, Gaza, Ghazze, Jerusalem
Palestine village (anc.)–Endor
paletot–overcoat
palfrenier–groom
palimpsest–parchment, tablet
paling – enclosure, fence, fencing, limit, picket, stake
paling board–slab
palisade – cliff, enclose, espalier, fence, fortify, furnish, impalement, stake, surround
pall – cloak, faint, nausea, pale, qualm
pallall–hopscotch
pallet – bed, blanket, headpiece, quilt
palliard–beggar, lecher, rascal, vagabond
palliate – alleviate, cloak, conceal, cover, disguise, extenuate, gloss, hide, mitigate, shelter, soften
pallid–pale, wan, white

pallion–bit, pellet
Pallu's father–Reuben
palm–areca, rattan, talipot
palm (African)–palmyra
palm (Arabian)–doum
palm (areng)–gomuti
palm (betel)–areca, bonga
palm (betel nut) – areca, bonga
palm (book)–taliera, tara
palm (Brazilian)–assai, bacaba, tucum, tucuma
palm (Brazilian feather) – urucuri, urucury
palm (bussu)–troolie, trooly
palm (cabbage)–palmetto
palm (Ceylon)–tala, talipot
palm (climbing)–rattan
palm (dwarf fan, genus of)–sabal
palm (East India)–jaggery, nipa, tokopat
palm (fan)–palmetto
palm (fan-leafed)–talipot
palm (flexible)–rattan
palm (Florida)–royal
palm (fruit)–cocoanut
palm (gingerbread)–doom, doum
palm (kind of)–nipa
palm (Malayan feather) – gomuti
palm (New Zealand)–nikau
palm (nipa)–atap, attap
palm (of hand)–thenar
palm (palmyra)–brab, ola, ole, olla, tal
palm (pinnate-leaved) – nikau
palm (sago)–areng, gomuti, irok
palm (spiny)–grugru
palm fiber–raffia, tal
palm fiber (palmyra)–tal
palm genus–acer, areca, assai, nipa, raphia
palm juice (East India, fermented)–sura
palm juice drink (alcoholic) –nipa
palm leaf–frond, ola, olay, olla
palm leaf (var.)–ola, olay
palm leaf (palmyra)–ola, ole
palm lily–ti

palm of genus calamus–rattan

palm of hand (Latin)–palmus

palm off–foist

palm pith–sago

palm reader–palmist

palm seeds (edible)–nipa

palm starch–sago

palm stem (flexible)–cane, ratan, rattan

palm thatch–nipa

palm tree–coco, nipa, ti

palm tree sap (fermented or not)–toddy

palm tree trunk food–sago

palmed–palmate

palmer–prestidigitator

Palmetto State (abbr.)–S.C.

palmistry–chirognomy, chiromancy

palmistry practicer – chiromancer

palmodic–jerky

palms (genus of)–areca, assai, nipa, raphia, serenoa

palms (pertaining to) – palmaceous

palms down–pronate

palmula–pulvillus

palmyra palm leaf–ola, ole

palmyra palm tree–tal

palmyras–talas

palo blanco–hackberry

palp–feeler, tentacle

palpable – manifest, noticeable, patent, tangible

palpebra–eyelid

palpebrate–wink

palpitant – throbbing, trembling

palsied – paralyzed, shaky, tottering

palter – babble, chatter, equivocate, mumble

paltock–doublet, jacket

paltry–contemptible, despicable, mean, petty, picayune, pitiful, rubbish, trash, trashy, trifling, vile, worthless

pameroon bark–muskwood

pampas–plain

pamper–caress, coddle, cosset, cram, cuddle, glut,

gratify, indulge, pet, posset

pamperer–dandler

pamphagous–omnivorous

pamphlet–tract

pamphlet (religious)–tract

pampinocele–varicocele

pan – acetabulum, basin, brainpan, cranium, criticize, hardpan, lappet, part, portion, ridicule, subsoil, tab, wash

pan (almagating)–tina

pan (frying)–skillet, spider

pan (mining)–tina

Pan's seat of worship–Arcadia

Pan's son–Seilenos, Silenus

panacea – catholicon, cure, nepenthe, panchreston, remedy

panachure–mottling

Panama (old name)–Darien

Panama Canal dam–Gatun

Panama Canal lock–Gatun

Panama city – Aspinwall, Colon, Cristobal, Panama (c.)

Panama coin–balboa (s.)

Panama Indian–Cuna

Panama measure–celemin

Panama redwood–quira

Panama river–Chagres, Sambu, Tuira

Panama rubber–Castilla

panaris – felon, paronychia, Whitlow

panatela–cigar

Panay native–Ati

pancake – fraise, fritter, froise, griddlecake

panda–bearcat, wah

pandemonium – noise, tumult, uproar

pander–cater

pandle–shrimp

Pandora's husband–Epimetheus

panegyric – discourse, eloge, elogy, encomium, eulogy, oration, writing

Panegyric on Cromwell author–Waller

pang–throe, twinge

pangolin–anteater

pangolin (genus of)–manis

pangolin (order of) – pholidota

panhandle–beg

panic – alarm, fear, fray, fright, scare, terror

pannier–basket, dorsel, dorser, dosser, overskirt, ped

panorama–picture, view

pant–beat, gasp, heave, palpitation, pulsate, throb

Pantagruel's father–Gargantua

pantalan–platform, wharf

pantheon–temple

panther – cougar, jaguar, leopard, pard, puma

panther (var.)–painter

panther-like animal–jaguar, ocelot

pantry–ambry, buttery, cupboard, larder, pannier, pantler, spencer

pants–pantaloons, trousers

pants (leather, cowboy's) – chaparajos, chaparejos

panuelo–kerchief, neckcloth

pap–mammilla, nipple, teat

papa–baboon, dad, father, potato, priest, vulture

papal–apostolic

papal book of decrees–decretal

papal court–curia

papal court office – dataria, datary

papal crown–tiara

papal envoy–legate

papal envoy (special mission)–ablegate

papal epistle–decretal

papal letter–bull

papal line–papacy

papal reformer–Gregory

papal seal–bulla

papal veil–fannel, orale

paper (absorbent)–blotter

paper (broken)–casse

paper (coated for medicinal applications)–charta

paper (collection of)–dossier

paper (crisp, thin)–pelure

paper (damaged, imperfect) –retree

paper (fine)–linen, vellum

paper (flat strip of)–tape

paper (gummed pieces)–labels, pasters
paper (imperfect)–retree
paper (large size)–atlas
paper (legal)–writ
paper (official)–document, targe
paper (once folded)–folio
paper (postage stamp)–pelure
paper (small piece of)–scrip
paper (thin)–pelure, tissue
paper (untrimmed edge) – deckle
paper (writing size)–cap
paper case at head of rocket –pot
paper measure–page, quire, ream, sheet
paper nautilus–argonaut
paper size–atlas, cap, copy, crown, demy, folio, imperial, legal, pott
papyrus (Egyptian)–reed
parable–apologue, comparison, fable, myth, similitude, tale
parabola–curve
parachute invader (repeller of)–parashootist
parade – flaunt, flourish, grandeur, magnificence, march, pageantry, pretension, procession, show, splendor
parade (showy) – pageant, pomp
Paradisaic–Edenic
Paradise – Eden, Elysium, Heaven
Paradise (Mohammedan religion)–Jenna
Paradise Lost author–Milton
paragon – model, pattern, type
paragon of knighthood – paladin
paragraph–item
Paraguay city – Asuncion (c.), Ita, Paraguari, Villa Rica
Paraguay coin–peso (pap.)
Paraguay measure – cordel, cuadra, cuarta, fanega, league, legua, line, linea, lino, pie, vara

Paraguay river–Apa, Paraguay, Parana, Tibiquare
Paraguay tea–mate
Paraguay weight–quintal
parallelogram (equilateral with oblique angles) – rhomb
paralysis–palsy, paresis
paralysis (incomplete)–paresis
paralysis (partial)–paretic
paralysis sufferer–paretic
paralyze–benumb, scram
paramount–chief, dominant, pre-eminent, superior, supreme
paramount (lord)–liege
parapet–breastwork, fortification, railing, rampart, wall
parapet (indented)–embattlement
parapet (V-shaped)–redan
paraphrase–translation, version
parasite – bur, sycophant, toady
parasite (coll.) – sponge, sponger
parasite (internal)–entozoa
parasite (plant)–entophyte
parasite (trout)–sug
parasitic fish–remora
parasitic fungi–rust
parasitic worm–trichina
parcel – bundle, fragment, lot, package, packet, part, piece, portion
parcel of ground (law)–solum
parcel out–mete
parch – bristle, burn, roast, scorch, shrivel, toast, torrid
parchment (book cover) – forel, forrel
parchment (fine)–vellum
parchment (kind of)–forel, forrel
parchment (piece of)–membrane
parchment (roll of)–pell
parchment (rolled)–scroll
parchment manuscript–palimpsest
parchment roll–scroll

pard – camelopard, chum, leopard, panther, partner, tiger
pardesi–foreigner, outlander
pardie (parde, pardi, pardy) –certainly, oath, surely, verily
pardo–mulatto
pardon – absolve, amnesty, condone, excuse, forgive, mercy, remit, remission, spare, tolerate
pardon chair–confessional
pardon stall–confessional
pardonable–venial
pare–cut, peel, shave, skin
pared away–resected
parent–father, mother, genitor, begetter, pater
parental affection–storge
parents and children–family
parget–coat, decorate, plaster, whitewash
pariah–outcast
parian–market
pari-mutuel machine–totalizer
Paris bishop (first)–Denis
Paris district–Auteuil
Paris green–insecticide
Paris hat–belltopper
Paris palace (anc.)–Louvre
Paris subway–metro
Paris thug–apache
Paris' father–Priam
Paris' mother–Hecuba
Paris' wife–Oenone
parish lantern–moon
parish officer (English law) –borsholder
paristhmion–tonsil
park (public)–Commons
parlance–conversation, diction, discourse, phraseology
parlay–paroli
parle–parley, talk
parley–confer, discuss, treat
parliament–diet
parlous–cunning, dangerous, keen, risky, shrewd
parnassian–poet
parody–caricature, satire
paroemia–proverb
parol–oral
paronomasia–pun

paroxysm–access, agitation, attack, exacerbation, fit, orgasm, throe

parrot–ara, arara, cockatoo, kea, lorikeet, lory, lovebird, macaw, parakeet, polly, tiriba

parrot (Australia)–lory

parrot (gray)–jako

parrot (kind of)–lory

parrot (large)–kea

parrot (long-tailed)–macaw

parrot (monk)–loro

parrot (New Guinea)–lory

parrot (New Zealand)–kaka, kakapo, kea

parrot (owl)–kakapo

parrot (sheep-killing)–kea

parrot (small)–parakeet

parrot (small, bright-colored)–lovebird

parrot disease–psittacosis

parrot fish–labroidea, scar

parrot-like–arine

parrots (genus of)–psittacus

parrots (genus of New Zealand)–nestor

parry – avoid, evade, fend, thwart, ward

Parsee bible–Avesta

Parsee priest (second rank)–mobed

Parsi–*see* Parsee

parsimonious – avaricious, close, covetous, grasping, illiberal, mercenary, miserly, narrowheartedness, near, niggardly, penurious, sordid, sparing, stingy

parsimonious (coll.)–skimpy

parsley (derivative of)–apiin

parsley camphor–apiole

parsley family–ammiaceae

parsley family (annual of)–dill

parsley fern–brake, tansy

parsley piert–knawel

parsnip (genus of water)–sium

parson – clergyman, guidepost, minister, preacher, rector

parson bird–poe, tue, tui

parson-in-the-pulpit – cuckoopint

parsonage–manse

part–divide, division, fragment, member, piece, portion, role, section, segment, separate, sever, share, sunder, twin

part (anchor)–palm

part (baglike)–sac

part (bird's wing)–alula

part (broad loosely hanging)–flap

part (choice)–elite

part (choicest)–cream, marrow

part (church) – altar, apse, chancel, nave, transept

part (coarse)–dregs

part (coat neck)–george

part (compass)–needle

part (ear)–lobe, tragus

part (essential) – core, gist, pith

part (extra)–spare

part (eye) – areola, cornea, iris, pupil, retina, uvea

part (farthest)–extremity

part (flower) – calyx, petal, sepal, stamen, stem

part (fortress)–redan

part (forward of cannon)–chase

part (greater)–bulk

part (hardest)–brunt

part (head) – crania, pate, scalp

part (individual)–atom

part (infinitesimal)–mite

part (insignificant) – iota, tithe

part (leaf)–stipel

part (leg)–calf, knee, shin

part (long, narrow, upper)–ridge

part (main)–body, trunk

part (mandible)–mola

part (minor)–bit, cog

part (minstrel show)–olio

part (mouth)–lip, palate

part (moving mechanical)–rotor

part (narrow)–neck

part (of a measure)–alidade

part (of step)–nosing, riser, tread

part (of turtles)–calipee

part (optical instrument) – alidade

part (printing press)–platen

part (projecting)–apse, arm, ell, hub, lobe, toe

part (proportional)–quota

part (protuberant) – boss, bulge

part (rifle, anc.)–tige

part (root-like)–radicle

part (saw-like)–serra

part (scaly, of fern)–ramentum, ramenta (pl.)

part (separate)–tmema

part (skull)–inion

part (small)–bit, detail, iota, jot, snippet

part (smallest)–minim, whit

part (solo accessory)–obbligato

part (stationary mechanical)–stator

part (temples enclosed)–cella

part (tenth)–tithe

part (theater)–balcony, box, foyer, gallery, loge, niggerheaven, orchestra, parquet, parterre, stage

part (twenty-fourth)–carat

part (typewriter)–platen

part (unpaid)–arrear

part (uppermost)–peak, top, topside, upside

part (wing-like)–ala, alae

part (worked with feet) – pedal, treadle

part of (to be)–inhere

part of anchor–palm

part of church–altar, apse, chancel, nave, transept

part of circle–arc, degree, segment

part of eye–areola, cornea, iris, pupil, retina, uvea

part of flower–calyx, petal, sepal, stamen, stem

part of fort–redan

part of framework – strut, truss

part of infinitive–to

part of mouth–lip, palate

part of play–act, scene

part of ship – bow, bridge, brig, deck, helm, keel, mast, rudder, stern, wheel

part of tree–bole, branch, leaf, root, trunk
part played–role
part stories–serials
part to hold other parts in place–gib
part with for money–sell
part worked with feet–pedal, treadle
parts (final, coll.)–shanks
parts (newspaper)–ears, editorials, items, pages
parts of medicine (equal of each)–ana
partage–part, portion, share
partake–participate, share
partake of reality–ar, are
partan–crab
parted–apportioned, cloven, divided, separated, severed
parten–impart, partake
partial – biased, fractional, incomplete, one-sided, predisposed, prejudiced, unfair
partial (prefix)–semi
partiality–bias, inclination, partisanship, predilection
partially burned brick–bur
participant – entrant, partaker, participating, participator, partisan, sharer, sharing
participate in–compete, enter, partake
participator–partaker, party
participle ending–ing
particle–ace, atom, iota, jot, mite, mote, shred, tittle, whit
particle (electrically charged) –proton
particle (fine icy)–sleet
particle (incandescent) – spark
particle (least possible)–minim
particle (minute) – atom, molecule, mote
particle (negative)–nor, not
particle (negatively charged) –anion
particle (small)–iota, jot
particle (small spherical) – globule
particle of fire–arc

parti-colored–piebald, pied, motley, variegated
particular – circumstantial, detail, especial, fastidious, item, nice, precise, special
particular (over)–fussy
particular (too)–overminute
particular place (pert. to)– local
particular strain of mind or disposition–vein
particularize and complete– detailed
partisan–adherent, follower, halbred, partizan, pike, staff, truncheon
partisan (fanatical)–zealot
partition–distribute, divide, screen, separation, septum, septa (pl.), severance, wall
partition (to)–scantle
partitioned–septate
partless–nonparticipant
partly colored–piebald, pied, variegated
partly illuminated–penumbra
partly open–ajar
partner–accomplice, ally, associate, coadjutor, colleague, confederate, husband, mate, pal, participant, sharer, wife
partridge – chukar, chukor, francolin, seesee, tinamou, titar, yutu
partridge (India small sand) –seesee
partridge flock–covey
party–association, combination, company, detachment, drum, faction, fiesta, reception, sect, side, tea
party (evening)–soiree
party (men's)–smoker, stag
party deserter–bolter
party man–partisan
party member–democrat
par value–face, nominal
parulis–gumboil
parvenue – parvenu (masc.), snob, upstart
Pasch–Easter, Passover

Pasch Day–Easter, Good Friday
Pasch egg–Easter
Pascha–Easter, Passover
paschal – celebration, lamb, Passover, supper
pasear – airing, promenade, walk
pasha (famous)–Enver
pasha's territory – pachalic, pashalic, pashalik
Pasiphae's children – Ariadne, Phaedra
Pasiphae's husband–Minos
pasquilant–lampooner
pasquinade – lampoon, pasquil, satire, squib
pass – canto, elapse, lane, lapse, pace, passage, passus, permission, permit, step, ticket
pass (Alpine)–col
pass (as time)–elapse, spend
pass (mountain)–col, defile, ghat
pass (narrow)–defile
pass (sudden)–lunge
pass a rope through–reeve
pass along (mouth to mouth)–bandy
pass away – die, disappear, perish, surrender, transfer, vanish
pass between mountain peaks–col
pass by – disregard, forego, ignore, omit, overlook, skip
pass by (to)–cote
pass judgment upon – sentence
pass off in vapor–evaporate
pass over–cross, disregard, elapse, excuse, ignore, omit, overlook, skip, transfer, traverse
pass over comprehensively–sweep
pass over lightly–skim
pass over quickly–scud
pass over smoothly–elide
pass rope through opening–reeve
pass slowly–drag
pass through – cross, pene-

trate, permeate, pervade, pierce, traverse

pass through cringle–reeve

pass time idly–loaf

pass up–decline, disregard, reject

pass without touching–clear

passable–admissible, mediocre, moderate, navigable, navigated, so-so, tolerable, traveled, traversed

passado (fencing)–thrust

passage–adit, aisle, allee, alley, atrium, atria (pl.), egress, exit, gang, hall, journey, transit, travel, voyage

passage (air)–flue

passage (between transept and deanery)–slype

passage (brain)–iter

passage (covered)–pawn

passage (mine)–stope

passage (mine floor)–sill

passage (musical, concluding)–coda

passage (narrow)–aisle, alley, defile, pass, slype, strait

passage (one end closed)–impasse

passage (river)–ford

passage of time–hiatus

passage out–egress, exit

passage where tide meets river current–estuary

passageway – aisle, avenue, corridor, gangway, hall, lane, lumen, ramp, slip

passageway (arched)–arcade

passageway (connecting two bodies of water)–strait

passageway (underground)–tunnel

passageway (vaulted)–arcade

passageway cover – canopy, caponier

passant – ephemeral, excelling, surpassing, transitory

passe–aged, antiquated, obsolete, superannuated

passed–elapsed, wended

passed around–doubled

passed from one condition into another–became

passed from one state into another–became

passed into use–enured

passed over swiftly–fleeted

passed through pores–permeated, transuded

passenger – fare, traveler, wayfarer

passenger (stagecoach, unbooked)–cad

passenger vehicle–bus, cab, car, omnibus, taxi, train

passerine bird – finch, sparrow

passes away–elapses

passing–cursory, departing, elapsing, ephemeral, fleeting, transitory

passing through–permeate

passion–affliction, emotion, feeling, ire, lust, martyrdom

passion flower–maypop

passion flower family–passifloraceae

passion for doing great things–megalomania

passion for music (inordinate) – melomane, melomania

passionate–ardent, emotional, irascible

passive – apathetic, inert, stoic, stolid

Passover (pert. to)–paschal

Passover (the)–Pasch

Passover festival–Seder

passport–conge

passport endorsement–visa, vise

past–ago, by, since, yore

past (immediate)–yesterday

past events (pert. to)–historic

past tense–preterite

past time–yore

paste–glue, pap, stick

paste (rice)–ame

paste (taro)–poi

pastime–amusement, diversion, game, hobby, sport

pastor – guardian, keeper, shepherd

pastor and teacher–rabbi

pastoral–drama, poem, romance, rural

pastoral (pert. to)–agrestic

pastoral cantata–serenata

pastoral crook (shepherd's)–pedum

pastoral oboe–musette

pastoral pipe–oat, reed

pastoral poem–bucolic

pastoral staff–pedum

pastoral staff (eccl.)–crosier

pastry–napoleon, pie, strudel, tart

pastry (June)–shortcake

pasture (summer) – agostadero

pastry shell (cup)–dariole

pasturage–eatage, herbage

pasture – grass, graze, lea, meadow

pasture (for hire)–agist

pasture (god of)–Pan

pasture (low)–ing

pasture bird–plover, sparrow

pasture grass–grama

pasture land – grass, lea, meadow

pasture land (piece of)–ham

pasturer–grazier, herdsman

pasty cement–mastic

pat–blow, fixed, immovable, impel, tap, throw

Patagonian cavy–mara

Patagonian deity–Setebos

Patagonian rodent – cavy, mara

patamar–courier, messenger

patand–base, plinth

patch–clump, cover, mend, parcel

patch (to)–bodge, vamp

patch of cloth–clout

patch of darkness–shadow

patch on printed page (pale)–friar

patch up–cobble, revamp

patch up (clumsily)–clout

patch up metal–solder

patcher (humorous)–sartor

patches (white and pale on printed page)–friars

patchwork – scraps, fragments, jumble, hodgepodge

pate–badger, crown, pasty, patty, pie, top

patella–dish, kneecap, kneepan, pan, vase

paten–disc, disk, dish, plate, vessel

paten (priest who bore) – patener

patent–accessible, archives, available, license, manifest, university

patent (notice of)–caveat

patent (Oriental)–berat

pater–father

paternity – father, fatherhood, fatherliness

path–lane, line, track, trail way

path (along side of a canal) –towpath

path (narrow at top or bottom of slope) – berm, berme, roddin, rodding

path (Southwest U.S.)– comino

path of a moving point – locus

path of celestial body–orbit

path of planet–orbit

paths of points moving according to mathematical law–loci

paths of points moving by law–loci

pathetic–affecting, sad, stirring, teary

pathic – catamite, passive, suffering

pathological–morbid

pathway (deer)–run

pathway (sheep) – roddin, rodding

patience – acquiescence, endurance, forbearance, fortitude, resignation, submission

patient – calm, compose, meek

patio–court, courtyard

patriarch–Noah

patrimonial–hereditary

patrimony–heritage

patriot (Roman)–Cato

patriotic–national

patriotic organization (abbr.)–G.A.R.

patriotic song–America

patriotism (exaggerated) – chauvinism

patrocinium–patronage, protection

patron–customer, guardian, guest, protector, supporter

patron (stock exchange) – buyer, seller, trader

patron (who fosters the arts) –Maecenas

patron saint (England) – George

patron saint (female)–Cecilia

patron saint (Irish)–Patrick

patron saint (lawyer's)–Ives

patron saint (musician's) – Cecilia

patron saint (sailor's)–Elmo

patronage – assistance, defend, encouragement, favor, support

patronage and care–auspices, favor

patronizing–condescending, deigning, revealing

patrons (group of)–clientele

patten – clog, skate, snowshoe

pattern – archetype, design, exemplar, ideal, model, norm, paradigm, precedent, template, templet

pattern (cross bar)–plaid

pattern (flower bed) – parterre

pattern (of separate objects) –seme

pattern (perfect)–ideal

Patti subdivision–Dheri

patulous – distended, expanded, open, spreading

pau – completed, consumed, finished

paucity–dearth, exiguity, insufficiency, lack, scarcity

paughty – haughty, pert, saucy

paunch–belly, disembowel, eviscerate, potbelly, rumen

pauper–beggar

pauraque–goatsucker

pause – breath, cease, halt, hesitate, hover, intermission, intermit, interruption, lull, respite, rest, selah, stance, stop, tarry, wait

paut – finger, paw, poke, stamp

pavan–dance

pave–cover, lay, path

pave the way–facilitate, prepare

pavement–tile

pavid–fearful, timid

pavilion–canopy, tent

paving block–paver, sett

paving slab (marble)–dalle

paving stone–paver, sett

pavior's hammer–reel, tup

pavis–cover, protect, shield

paw–forefoot, gaum, patte, pattee, paty, pud

pawl–bolt, detent, dog, pallet, tongue, trip

pawl (gunlock)–sear

pawl (Ind.)–tent

pawn – chessman, counter, gage, guaranty, hock, peacock, pledge

pawnie–peacock

pawpaw–bushwhacker, papaw, papaya

pay – ante, compensate, defray, fee, indemnify, meet, recompense, reimburse, remunerate, repay, requite, reward, salary, satisfy, tip, wage

pay attention to–heed, listen

pay for–aby, abye

pay in heavy penalty–smart

pay one's share–ante

pay out–disburse, distribute, expend, spend

pay the penalty–aby, abye

Payaguas Indian–Agaz

paymaster–purser

payment–chastisement, compensation, cro, defrayal, dues, fee, mail, punishment, recompense, requital, return

payment (immediate)–cash

payment upon delivery (abbr.)–COD

payments (obligatory)–dues

payong–umbrella

pea (chick)–cicer, gram

pea (heath)–carmele

pea (India split)–dal

pea (old style)–pease (pl.)

pea (pigeon)–arhar, dal

pea (Siberian, everlasting)–
  peavetchling
pea dove–zenaida
pea family–fabaceae
pea finch–chaffinch
pea flour–Erbswurst
pea sausage–Erbswurst
pea seeds–pulse
pea-shaped–pisiform
pea vine–earthpea
peaberry–coffeeberry
peabird–oriole, wryneck
peace – amity, harmony,
  quiet, serenity, tranquility
peace (goddess of)–Irene
peace (Latin)–pax
peace of mind (perfect) –
  ataraxia
peace pipe–calumet
peace pledge–Frankpledge
peaceable–amicable, harmonious, pacific, quiet, silent, still, tranquil, undisturbed
peaceful–calm, irene, irenic,
  pacific, placid, serene
peach – accuse, betray, impeach, indict, inform
peach (Australian) – quan-
  dang, quandong, quan-
  tong
peach (kind of)–clingstone,
  Crawford, Elberta, free-
  stone, nectarine
peach (origination of) –
  China
peach family–amygdalaceae
peach grafted on quince
  (obs.)–melocoton
peach stone–putamen
peachwort–persicary
peacock–mao, pawn
peacock (female)–peahen
peacock (genus of)–pavo
peacock (pert. to)–pavonine
peacock bittern–sun
peacock butterfly–io
peacock fan–flabellum
peacock feather fiber–marl
peacock fish–wrasse
peacock flower–poinciana
peacock heron–bittern
peacock ore–bornite, chal-
  copyrite
peacock tail spot (circular)–
  eye

peafowl–peacock, peahen
peage (peag) – pedage, tax,
  toll, wampum
peak–acme, apex, dolt, headland, promontory, shrink,
  simpleton, slink, sneak,
  steal, summit, top
peak (French)–pic
peak (mountain toothlike)–
  dent
peak (unconquered)–Ever-
  est
peal–appeal, clap, resound,
  ring, shovel, summons,
  toll
peal of thunder–clap
Peale Island (Japanese name
  for)–Habe
peanut – earthnut, goober,
  mani, pinda, pindal
peanut (hog)–earthpea
pear (alligator)–avocado
pear (autumn, late)–bosc
pear (prickly)–nopal, opuntia, tuna
pear cider–erry
pear-like fruit–avocado
pear-shaped vessel (nesting
  together)–aludel
pear squash–chayote
pearl–gem, margarite, onion
pearl (imitation)–olivet
pearl (of great luster)–orient
pearlbird–barbet
pearl eye–cataract
pearl moss–carrageen
pearl opal–cacholong
pearlweed–sagina
pearlwort–sagina
peart–active, brisk, frisky
peasant–boor, clown, countryman, hind, knave, rascal, rustic, serf, swain
peasant (Egypt)–fellah
peasant (England)–churl
peasant (farm holding)–cot-
  man
peasant (India)–ryot
peasant (Irish)–kern, kerne
peasant (Russian, rich)–kulak
peasant (Scotland) – cottar,
  cotter
peasant (Syria)–fellah
peasant cottager–cottar, cotter

peasant crop sharer–metayer
peasant-like–base, clownish,
  rude
pease–appease, pacify, quiet,
  reconcile
pease brose–pottage
pease crow–tern
peashooter – beanshooter,
  blowgun, slingshot
peat–darling, favorite, minion, pet, turf
peat bog–cess, moss
peat cutter (Scot.)–piner
peat spade–slane
peatwood–loosestrife
peau–skin
peba–armadillo
pebble–crystal, quartz, stone
peccadillo–fault
peccant–offender, sinner
peccary–tagassu, tayassu
peccary (genus of)–tayassu
peccation–sinning
pech–breath, breathe, pant,
  sigh
pecht – fairy, gnome, pict,
  pygmy
peck–dab, dot, food, hole,
  jerk, kiss, pitch, prick,
  stroke, throw
peck at–attack, carp, harass,
  nag, tease, twit
pectase–enzyme
peculiar–curious, eccentric,
  odd, singular, special,
  strange, unique
peculiar (comb. form)–idio
peculiar (more)–verier
peculiar expression – idiom,
  idioma, idiome
peculiarity – kink, oddity,
  oddness, quirk, trait
peculiarity of phrase–idiom
pecuniary–financial
pedagogue–pedant, school-
  master, teacher, tutor
pedal–lever, treadle
pedal (piano, soft)–celeste
pedal covering – moccasin,
  sandal, shoe, slipper
pedant–dorbel, pedagogue,
  prig, schoolmaster, tutor
peddle–hawk, piddle, retail,
  sell
peddler–coster, costermonger, hawker

peddler (earthenware) – mugger

peddler (itinerant) – chapman

peddler's French–gibberish, jargon

pedestal–anta, base, foundation, support

pedestal (part of)–die

pedestal face–dado

pedestal member (lowest)–plinth, quadra

pedestal rest–plinth

pedestrian–walker

pedestrian (slang)–ped

pedicel–footstalk, peduncle, stalk, stem

pedicle of umbel–ray

pedigree – descent, lineage, stemma

pedum–crook, staff

peduncle–scape, stalk, stem

peek – chirp, glance, peep, pry

peekaboo–bopeep

peel – palisade, pare, rind, shovel, skin, slipe, stake, stockade, strip

peel off – decorticate, harl, pare

peeler–corer, crab, hustler, pillager, policeman

peep–cheep, chirp, peer, pry, pule, skey, squeak

peep-bo–bopeep, peekaboo

peep hawk–kestrel

peephole–crevice, hole

peep show–raree

peeper–eye, pryer, spy

peepeye–peekaboo

peeping (impertinent)–pry

peer – baron, duke, earl, equal, feere, fere, gaze, marquis, match, mate, noble, nobleman, stare, viscount

peer (curiously)–pry

peer (Scot.) – stime, tyme, thane

Peer Gynt's mother–Ase

peer's title (abbr.)–vis

peesoreh–meminna

peesweep – greenfinch, lapwing, pewit

peetweet–sandpiper

peevish – captious, choleric, cross, crusty, fretful, irascible, irritable, pettish, petulant, snappish, spleeny, splenetic, techy, testy, touchy, waspish

peg–drink, hob, nob, pin, pretext, reason, support

peg (iron)–piton

peg (shoe)–cleat

peg (small)–nog

peg (wood)–spill

pega (pagador)–remora

pegall–basket

Pego native–Mon

Pegu ironwood–acle

peho–morepork

peignoir–negligee

peise–balance, blow, force, impact, measure, oppress, poise, weight

pelagic–marine, oceanic

Peleg's son–Reu

Peleus' father–Aeacus

Peleus' son–Pelides

pelf – booty, despoil, gain, lucre, money, pilfer, refuse, riches, rob, rubbish, spoil, trash

Pelias' nephew–Jason

Pelias' son–Acastus

Pelican State–Louisiana

pell–fur, hasten, hide, hurry, pelt, skin

pellar–conjurer, wizard

pellet–ball, bullet, granule, pill

pellicle–film, scum

pellock–porpoise

pellucid–bright, clear, limpid, translucent, transparent

pelmet–valance

Pelops' father–Tantalus

Pelops' son–Atreus, Thyestes

Pelops' wife–Hippodamia

pelota–jai alai

pelt–fell, push, refuse, rubbish, skin, stone, strike, thrust, woolfell

pelt (animal) – fur, pelage, skin

pelt (dressed)–fur

pelt with rocks–stone

peltry–furs, hides, skins

peludo–armadillo

pelvis bone–ilium, ilia (pl.), ischium, pubes

pen–bolt, coop, cot, fasten, hutch, indite, quill, sty, write

pen (sponge-holding)–kraal

pen-like–styloid

penman–calligrapher, scribe, writer

penmanship (style of) – hand

pen name–anonym, nom de plume, pseudonym

pen point–neb, nib

pen point (short, blunt) – stub

pen text–ronde

penned–wrote

penned in–stied

penalize–fine, mulct

penalty–disadvantage, fine, forfeit, hardship, loss, punishment

penalty (pecuniary)–fine

penance – contrition, penitence, punishment, repentance, sorrow

Penang Islands weight – catty, picul

penchant – attraction, bent, inclination, leaning, liking

pendant–aglet, aiglet, bob, tail

pendant (ornamental)–aglet, aiglet

Pendennis' heroine–Laura

pendent–hanging, lop, pend, pendulous, support

pendent cone of lime–stalactite

pendulous throat skin of animals–dewlap

Penelope's father–Icarius

Penelope's father-in-law – Laertes

Penelope's husband – Odysseus

Penelope's suitor–Agelaus

penetrate–bore, enter, gore, perforate, permeate, pierce, stab

penetrate (as through a crowd)–elbow, needle

penetrated or worked (easily)–mellow

penetrating – acute, discerning, pervading, sagacious, sharp, shrill, subtle

penetration–acumen, acuteness, discernment, discrimination, insight, sharpness

penetration in perception – acumen

Peneus' daughter–Daphne

penguin–auk, Johnny

penguin breeding place – penguinery, rookery

peninsula–chersonese, neck, penile

penitent–contrite, repentant

penitential discipline – penance

penitential period–Lent

pennant–banderole, banner, fane, flag, pinion, whip

pennate – feathered, penniform, winged

pennies (collective)–pence

pennon – banner, flag, pennant, pinion, wing

Pennsylvania borough – Homestead, Sayre

Pennsylvania city–Lebanon, Reading, Sharon

Pennsylvania county – Venango

Pennsylvania town – Erie, Ono, York

penny–copper, saltee

penny (Dutch)–stiver

penologist (famous)–Lawes

penology (branch of)–criminology

pensive – contemplative, dreamy, meditative, musing, reflective, sober, thoughtful, wistful

pentastitch – poem, stanza, strophe

Pentheus' grandfather–Cadmus

Pentheus' mother–Agave

penthouse – lean-to, pentice, roof, shed

penury – destitution, indigence, poverty, privation, scantiness, want

peon – attendant, constable, laborer, messenger, policeman, serf, soldier

peon (in chess)–pawn

peony–piny

peony (genus of)–paeonia

people – demos, folk, kin, laity, nation, populace, race, Rais

people (anc.)–Medes

people (long experienced)–stagers

people (lowest class of) – canaille

people (of earliest culture)–Grecians

people (of rank)–aristocracy, aristocrat

people (of the)–ethnic

people (old fashioned) – antediluvians

people (pert. to) – demotic, laic

people (Spanish common)–gente

people (the)–Amerind, citizenry, laity, populace, public, Rais

people (the common) – demos

people (the common, Chinook jargon)–tilikum, tillicum

people (wild romping young)–rantipoles

people of good position – gentry

people subject to one government–nation

peopled (Hindu)–abad

peopled village–abad

peoples–races

pep – dash, energy, go, initiative, liveliness, quicken, stimulate, vim

pepper (Australian shrubby species)–kava, kavakava

pepper (climbing)–betel

pepper (Guinea)–capsicum

pepper (Malay)–siri, sirih

pepper (mild)–paprica, paprika

pepper (species of) – ava, betel

pepper (Turkish) – paprica, paprika

pepper beverage–kava, kavakava

peppery – choleric, pungent, passionate, piquant, spirited, fiery, stinging

peract–perform

perambulate – promenade, ramble, stroll, traverse, walk

perceive–apprehend, behold, descry, discern, discriminate, distinguish, divine, notice, observe, see, sense

perceive directly–know

perceive the flavor of–taste

perceived (by eye)–ocular

perceived (by the sense) – sensate

percentage of assessment – ratal

perceptible–cognizable, discernible, perceivable, tactile, tangible

perceptible (hardly)–faint

perceptible (not)–intangible

perceptible by touch–tactile

perception – acumen, consciousness, discernment, seeing, sense

perception (delicate)–tact

perception (nice)–tact, taste

perceptive faculties–senses

perch–alight, bar, fish, peg, pole, rod, roost, settle, sit, staff, weapon

perch (European)–barse

perch (pike)–sauger

perched–lit, sat

Percheron–horse

perchers–Insessores

percolate–exude, filter, ooze, seep, sift, silt, strain

percolate slowly–ooze, seep

percolate through ashes – leach

percolation–seepage

percussion instrument–bells, castanets, cymbals, drum, glockenspiel, gong, tambourine, traps, triangle

perdition–damnation, ruin

perdrigon–plum

peregrinate–sojourn, travel

peregrine–alien, exotic, foreign, pilgrim, strange

perempt – defeat, destroy, quash

peremptory – absolute, arbitrary, authoritative, conclusive, decisive, express, positive

perennial–continual, enduring, permanent, perpetual, unceasing

perennial (climbing) – liana, liane

perennial (climbing woody) –liana, liane

perennial flower–peony

perennial grasses (genus of) –elymus

perennial herbs (genus of)– geum

perennial weed–toadflax

perfect–blameless, complete, consummate, entire, finished, holy, ideal, improve, pure, righteous, satisfying, spheral

perfect (comb. form)–teleo

perfection–acme, excellence

perfection (standard of) – acme, ideal

perfection (type of) – paragon

perfection of womanhood– Eimer, Emer

perfectly – altogether, completely, correctly, flawlessly, ideally, quite, rightly, thoroughly, utterly

perfecto–cigar

perficient – actual, effective, effectual

perfidious – disaffected, disloyal, faithless, treacherous

perfidy–disloyalty, faithlessness, treachery, treason

perforate–bore, dock, penetrate, pierce, pounce, punch, riddle

perforated block–nut

perforated nozzle–rose

perforated sphere–bead

perforation – aperture, bore, eyelet, hole, piercing, punching

perform–achieve, act, do, effect, enact, execute, exert, perpetrate, play, transact

perform awkwardly–thumb

performance – act, action, completion, consummation, exploit, test, work

performance (clumsy)–bungle

performance (daytime) – matinee

performance (first) – premiere

performance (notable)–feat

performance (unreasonably difficult of) – impracticable

performance for one–solo

performance of duty – feasance

performed again–reenacted

performed alone–soloed

performer – actor, doer, shine, thespian, worker

performer (sleight of hand) –magician, prestidigitator

perfume–aroma, atar, attar, essence, nose, scent, smell

perfume (from flowers) – atar, attar

perfume (medicated) – pastil, pastile, pastille

perfume (musky)–civet

perfume (Oriental)–myrrh

perfume (strong scented) – musk

perfume (to)–cense, incense

perfume (var.)–atar

perfume (violet)–irone

perfume base–musk

perfume in return–reincense

perfume-making substance– civet

perfume obtained from rasse –dedes

perfume substance (found in whales)–ambergris

perfume with burning spice –cense, incense

perfumed–scented

perfumed cherry–mahaleb

perfumy–fragrant, scented

pergola – arbor, balcony, bower, colonnade, trellis

perhaps–belike, contingent, doubtful, maybe, perchance, possibly, probably

perhaps (arch.)–belike, mayhap

peri–elf, fairy

periapt–amulet, charm

pericarp–pod

pericarp (fleshy)–berry

periculum – danger, peril, risk

perigee (opposed to)–apogee

peril–danger, hazard, jeopardy, menace, risk

perilous–dangerous, hazardous

perilous (least)–safest

perilously inadequate–icarian

perimeter – boundary, outline, periphery

period–age, conclusion, cycle, day, dot, duration, epoch, era, stop, term, termination, time, year

period (banting)–fast

period (brief)–moment

period (coll.)–spell

period (five-year)–pentad

period (geological)–eocene, neocene

period (historical)–era

period (long)–eon

period (penitential)–Lent

period (pert. to history)–eral

period (playing) – chukkar, chukker, half, hand, inning, quarter, set

period (preholiday)–eve

period (statutory) – limitation

period (ten-year)–decade

period (tertiary) – eocene, neocene

period (vacation, appointed by law)–justitium

period (vast)–cycle

period (well-defined)–stage

period allotted for possession –lease

period of dryness–drought

period of five years–pentad

period of fifty days – quinquagesima

period of great prosperity– golden

period of holding–tenure

period of instruction–session

period of permissive delay– moratorium

period of probation–novitiate

period of recovery–convalescence

period of recreation – holiday, vacation

period of reduced prices – sale

period of rising prices–boom

period of time – aeon, age, century, decade, eon, epoch, era

period of time (great)–age

period of time (interminable)–aeon, eon

period of time (limited) – span

period of time (pert. to)–eral

period of work–shift, spell, turn, watch

periodic–annual, eral, etesian, intermittent, seasonal

periodic (annual, as winds) –etesian

periodic motion of sea–tide

periodic wind–monsoon, oe

periodic windstorm–oe

periodical – etesian, magazine, review

periodical (annual)–etesian

periods (fortunate)–ups

peripheral–external

periphery – areola, border, brim, circumference, perimeter, rim

perique–tobacco

perish–die, ruin

perish (gradually)–fade

peristyle–colonnade, peripteral

perite–skilled

peritomy–circumcision

peritroch–embryo, larva

periwig–periwinkle, peruke, wig

periwinkle–myrtle

perjink–neat, nice, precise

perjure–aperjurer, forswear

perk – percolate, perquisite, preen, prink, smarten

perkin–cider

permanent – abiding, constant, continuing, enduring, fixed, lasting, stable

permeable to liquor–porous

permeate–imbue, pervade

permeating–pervasive

permirific–wondrous

permission – authorization, consent, grace, leave, license, sufferance

permission (authoritative)–license

permit – allow, authorize, consent, grant, leave, let, leve, permission, pompano, suffer, tolerate, warrant

permit by not preventing–tolerate

permitted by law–legal

permitted to live–reprieved, spared

permutate – change, interchange

pern–buzzard

pernicious–baleful, baneful, deadly, deleterious, fatal, harmful, hurtful, malign, noisome, noxious, ruinous, villainous, wicked

pernicious (anything)–bane

perniciously–evilly

pernio–chilblain

peronate–mealy, wooly

perorate–declaim, harangue

perpendicular – sheer, sine, upright, vertical

perpendicular (math.)–apothem, binormal

perpetrate – commit, perform

perpetual–constant, continual, continuous, endless, eternal, everlasting, forever, unceasing, unending

perpetually–ever

perplex – bewilder, complicate, confuse, entangle, obfuscate, puzzle

perplexes–amazes, confuses

perplexing–carking

perplexity – anxiety, bewilderment, complication, confusion, distraction, fog, tangle, were

perquod–whereby

perse – directly, essentially, intrinsically, itself

persecute–afflict, annoy, harass, harry, hound, oppress

persecution (flies from)–refugee

Persephone's father–Zeus

Persephone's husband – Hades, Pluto

Persephone's mother – Demeter

Perseus (star of)–Atik

Perseus (star of, variable)–Algol

Perseus' father–Zeus

Perseus' mother–Danae

perseverance–constancy, patience, persistence, pertinacity, steadfastness, steadiness

persevere–insist, persist

Persia–Iran

Persian – Iranian, Iranic, Perse

Persian (anc.)–Mede

Persian apple–citron

Persian assembly (national) –Majlis, Mejlis

Persian bed–divan, sofa

Persian bird (song)–bulbul

Persian blinds–persiennes

Persian book of scriptures–Koran

Persian books (Avesta) – Gathas, Vendidad, Vispered, Yashts, Yasna

Persian books (sacred religious)–Avesta

Persian capital–Teheran

Persian carpet (famous, 15th to 17th century)–Isfahan, Ispahan

Persian caste (priestly) – magi

Persian cat–Angora

Persian chief–mir

Persian chief's wife (first)–bibi

Persian city–Balfroosh, Hamadan, Ispahan, Kasvin, Kerman, Kom, Meshed, Niriz, Resht, Shiraz, Tabreez, Tabriz, Tauris, Teheran (c.), Yezd

Persian civil officer–khan

Persian coin – ashrafi (g.), dinar (ac.), kran (g.), kran (s.), daric, pahlavi (g.), pul (cop.), rial (s.),

shahee, shahi (ni.), stater, toman (g.)
Persian coin (anc.)–daric
Persian coin (former)–bisti
Persian coin (gold)–toman
Persian coin (obs.)–asar
Persian coin (silver)–kran
Persian coin (silver, obs.)–larin
Persian country (anc. North)–Elam
Persian deer–fallow, maral
Persian deity (supreme) – Ormazd
Persian demigod–Yima
Persian demon (drought)–Apaosha
Persian diadem–taj
Persian dinars (twenty) – bisti
Persian door–dar
Persian dynasty–sassanidae
Persian dynasty (anc.)–seljuk
Persian elf–peri
Persian fairy–elf, fay, peri
Persian fay–peri
Persian fire worshipper – Parsee, Parsi
Persian gateway–dar
Persian gazelle–cora
Persian god (of light) – Mithras
Persian governor (anc.)–satrap
Persian grass–millet
Persian Gulf kingdom (anc.)–Chaldea
Persian Gulf port–Bushire
Persian Gulf wind (northwest)–shamal
Persian Gulf wind (southeast)–sharki, shurgee
Persian gum–tragacanth
Persian hat–fez, turban
Persian idiom–persism
Persian javelin–jeerid, jerid
Persian javelin (horseman's) –jeerid, jerid
Persian king–shah, Xerxes
Persian Koran student–hafiz
Persian lake–Urumiah
Persian language (anc.) – Pahlavi, Zend
Persian language (3rd to 9th century)–Pahlavi, Pehlevi

Persian lynx–caracal
Persian measure – artaba, cane, capicha, charac, chebel, chenica, collothun, colluthun, farsakh, farsang, foot, gareh, gariba, ghalva, guz, jerib, kafiz, makuk, mansion, mishara, mou, ouroub, parasang, piamaneh, qasab, sabbitha, stathmos, zar, zer
Persian measure (of length) –zar
Persian money – dinar, lari, pul, stater
Persian mountain – Ararat, Demavend, Elburz, Hindu Kush
Persian mystic–sufi
Persian myth–mah
Persian natives (agricultural)–tai
Persian New Year's Day – Nowroze
Persian nightingale–bulbul
Persian nymph–houri
Persian oil center–Abadan
Persian people (agricultural) –tai
Persian people (anc.)–Medes
Persian poet–Omar, Saadi
Persian port–Bushire
Persian priest–magi
Persian priestly caste–magi
Persian prince–satrap
Persian province (eastern)–Ariana
Persian religion founder – Zoroaster
Persian religious doctrine–babiism, babism
Persian river – Euphrates, Karun, Kizil Uzen, Safid Rud, White
Persian rose–gul
Persian rug (kind of)–senna
Persian ruler – atabeg, atabek, shah, sultan
Persian screen–purdah
Persian seat (draped)–musnud
Persian sect – Shiah, Shiite, Sunnee, Sunni, Sunnite
Persian shahi (two-fifths of) –bisti

Persian song bird–bulbul
Persian spirit (evil) – ahriman
Persian tapestry (embroidered)–susanee
Persian tick (venomous) – miana bug
Persian title – mir, mirza, shah
Persian town dwellers–Sart
Persian traders–Sart
Persian tribe–nomad
Persian tribe (Kurd)–Mukri
Persian vessel (water)–aftaba
Persian water vessel–aftaba
Persian water wheel–noria
Persian weight – abbas, abbassi, artal, artel, batman, dirhem, dram, dung, gandum, karwar, maund, miscal, miskal, nakhod, pinar, ratel, rotl, saddirham, sang, seer, ser, tcheirek, zar, zer
Persian wheel (water)–noria
Persian wise men–magi
Persian woman's garment–chedar
Persian writings (religious) –Avesta
persiennes–blinds
persiflage–banter, raillery
persimmon family – ebenaceae, ebony
persimmon (Mexican)–chapote
persist–persevere
persistent – determined, indefatigable, persevering
persistently opposed – recalcitrant, renitent
person – being, individual, one, soul, urf, wight
person (adroit)–adept
person (baptized, early church)–illuminato, illuminatus, illuminati (pl.)
person (bigoted)–prude
person (callow, who tries to show off, coll.)–smarty
person (canonized)–saint
person (charitable)–samaritan
person (clumsy) – bungler, lummox, oaf, staup

person (conceited)–prig
person (crazed) – maniac, psychopath
person (crazy, coll.)–nut
person (credulous)–Simon
person (crotchety)–crank
person (cruel)–fiend
person (destitute)–pauper
person (disgruntled, coll.)–sorehead
person (dishonorable) – rotter
person (dissolute)–roue
person (drunken)–lush
person (dull) – blockhead, dolt, dorbel, stock
person (dull-witted)–dunce, moron
person (dwarfish)–shurf
person (educated)–erudite, literatus, literati (pl.), savant, scholar, student
person (elusive, coll.) – eel, snake
person (enlightened) – illuminato, illuminati (pl.)
person (erudite)–savant
person (extraordinary) – expert, genius, oner
person (fabulously rich) – Midas
person (foolish) – buffoon, clown, idiot, simpleton, zany
person (French descent) – Creole
person (frugal)–saver, stinter
person (garrulous)–sieve
person (gigantic)–titan
person (gloomy)–killjoy
person (grotesque) – golliwogg
person (guilty)–culprit
person (hallowed)–saint
person (held as pledge) – hostage
person (highly skilled)–artisan, master
person (huge)–giant, monster, titan
person (ill)–invalid, patient
person (ill-mannered)–boor
person (ill-tempered)–crab
person (immature)–bud

person (impatient) – fidget, hotspur
person (important)–mogul, personage
person (indefinite, unnamed)–so and so
person (indifferent to pleasure or pain)–stoic
person (inquisitive)–peeper, pryer
person (insignificant)–shurf
person (insignificant pusillanimous)–twerp
person (intermediate between introvert and extrovert)–ambivert
person (intolerant)–bigot
person (jealous)–envier
person (keen, irritable)–tartar
person (lazy) – drone, sluggard
person (learned) – erudit, erudite, highbrow, pedant, pundit, savant, scholar
person (lightheaded) – beehead
person (loud-voiced) – stentor
person (low-bred)–cad
person (made to take blame of others)–goat, scapegoat
person (marked by certain number, slang)–oner
person (married)–husband, spouse, wife
person (mean)–sneak
person (miserly)–curmudgeon, skinflint
person (mixed blood)–mestee, mestizo, metis, mulatto, mulatta (fem.), mustee
person (narrow-minded) – bigot
person (niggardly)–miser
person (non-Jewish)–Aryan, gentile
person (not easily classified)–nondescript
person (of courage and fortitude)–spartan
person (of distinction)–notable

person (of great intellectual powers)–genius
person (of long experience) –stager
person (of low habits)–yahoo
person (of mixed blood) – mestee, mestizo, metis, mulatto, mulatta (fem.), mustee
person (of rank)–magnate
person (of skill) – artisan, master, talent
person (old fashioned)–fogy
person (old, infirm)–senile
person (oppressed) – persecutee
person (overbearing)–cad
person (overmodest)–prude
person (oversensitive to propriety)–prude
person (pedantic)–prude
person (perfidious)–traitor
person (pernicious)–pest
person (powerful voiced) – stentor
person (practical in cunning)–stager
person (presuming)–cad
person (pretentious)–mogul
person (prim)–prude
person (punctilious)–prig
person (rapacious)–harpy
person (ravenous)–harpy
person (reckless)–daredevil, madcap
person (reticent)–clam
person (rude)–boor, yahoo
person (salaried)–employee, payee
person (scatterbrained) – madcap
person (self-centered) – egoist, egotist
person (selfish)–egoist, egotist
person (self-righteous) – pharisee
person (senile)–doter
person (sharp-eyed)–Argus
person (short, pudgy)–roly-poly
person (sick)–aegrotant
person (silly)–boob
person (skilled)–artisan, artist, mechanic

person (slipshod)–sloven
person (sly, knowing)–coon
person (small insignificant) –sprat
person (stunted)–urf
person (stupid) – ass, dolt, gump, moron, stock
person (supercilious)–snob
person (treacherous) – serpent, snake
person (trivial)–peppercorn
person (uncouth)–lout
person (underhanded) – sneak
person (unduly conceited)–snob
person (unimportant)–lightweight
person (unique)–oner
person (unknown)–stranger
person (unknown, Fr.)–inconnu, inconnue (fem.)
person (unmannerly)–cad
person (unmarried)–bachelor, celibate, maiden, spinster
person (unthankful) – ingrate
person (untidy)–sloven
person (unwelcome) – intruder
person (unwieldy, bulky) – hulk
person (valorous)–hero
person (very rich) – multi-millionaire, plutocrat
person (vexatious)–pest
person (violent intractable tempered)–tartar
person (wealthy) – millionaire, millionnaire, nabob, plutocrat
person (whose interest is centered in external objects and action) – extrovert
person (with nervous disorders)–neurotic
person (with self-centered emotions)–introvert
person (witty) – comedian, comedien, comedienne (fem.), punster, wag
person (worthless, dial.) – losel
person (writ serving)–elisor

person acting for another–alternate, proxy
person appointed by court to act for sheriff–elisor
person beyond recall (coll.)–goner
person bringing bad luck–jinx, jonah
person bringing good luck–mascot
person charged with high mission–apostle
person deranged on one subject–monomaniac
person given as pledge – hostage
person of color–negro
person of mixed breed–mestee, mestizo, metis, mulatto, mulatta (fem.), mustee
person proposed for office–nominee
person regarded merely as biological specimen – organism
person who brings good fortune–mascot
person without rank – roturier
persons–ones
persons (from whom family is descended)–stirpes
persons (group of) – army, assembly, association, band, chorus, company, orchestra, team, troupe
persons (organized body of) –corps, posse
persons (set of, who meet familiarly)–coterie
persons who can read and write–literates
personage – bearing, image, portrait, stature
personage (great)–mogul
personal (comb. form)–idio
personal appearance – presence
personal history–memoir
personal interest–self
personal ornament–parure
personal ownership of land–demesne
personality–ego

personate–enact, feign, simulate
personification of truth–Una
perspicacity–acumen, acuteness, discernment, penetration
perspicuity – translucency, transparency
perspiration (pert. to) – sudoric
persuade–coax, convince, induce, influence, suasion, sway, urge
persuade by argument–convince
persuade by artifice (flattery)–inveigle
persuaded (easily)–pliable
persuasive–eloquent, impelling
pert – comely, exquisite, handsome, lively, officious, saucy, sprightly
pert (coll.)–sassy
pert girl–minx
pert girl or woman–chit
pertain – accessory, adjunct, appendage, appertain, attribute, function, relate
pertaining to (suffix)–ar, ic
pertaining to a bull–taurine
pertaining to a marsh–paludine
pertaining to a point of concentration–focal
pertaining to a point of the moon's orbit–apogean
pertaining to a word (reading same forward and backward)–palindromic
pertaining to acid found in grapes–racemic
pertaining to act of rising–ortive
pertaining to aeronautics – aero
pertaining to age–eral, eval
pertaining to agricultural and rural affairs–georgic
pertaining to agriculture – georgic
pertaining to Ailanthus trees –Ailantine
pertaining to air–aural
pertaining to air navigation –aeronautic

pertaining to anatomical passage–meatal

pertaining to ancestral type–ataristic

pertaining to ancient city of Nile delta–Saite

pertaining to ancient Greek people–Ionian

pertaining to ancient Greeks –classical

pertaining to ancient Romans–classical

pertaining to ancient Troy–Iliac

pertaining to animals–zooid

pertaining to animal life–zoologic

pertaining to ankle–tarsal

pertaining to antimony–stibial

pertaining to anything remote–forane

pertaining to apostle–petrine

pertaining to apple acid – malic

pertaining to apple juice – malic

pertaining to apples–malic, malo

pertaining to area–areal

pertaining to aretium – aretine

pertaining to Argolis green valley–Nemean

pertaining to aria–ariose

pertaining to arid division of Austral zone–sonoran

pertaining to Arius–Arian

pertaining to arm bone–ulnar

pertaining to armpit–axillar

pertaining to army–martial

pertaining to arrow–sagittal

pertaining to art of extracting metal from ores – metallurgical

pertaining to Asiatic (old)–Chaldean

pertaining to Asiatic mountain–Altaic

pertaining to assessment – ratal

pertaining to Athens–Attic

pertaining to Austral zone arid division–sonoran

pertaining to authorized doctrine–dogmatical

pertaining to axle–axial

pertaining to back – dorsal, lumbar, tergal

pertaining to back of hip – gluteal

pertaining to backbone – spinal

pertaining to bath–balneal

pertaining to bees – apian, apiarian

pertaining to birds – avian, avine, ornithic

pertaining to birth–natal

pertaining to birth seniority –primogenitive

pertaining to birthmark – naevoid

pertaining to bishop's headdress–mitral

pertaining to blood–haemal, hemal, hemic

pertaining to bodies at rest–static

pertaining to bodily motion –gestic

pertaining to bodily structure–anatomic

pertaining to body–somal

pertaining to body of land–continental

pertaining to boron–boric

pertaining to both ears–binaural

pertaining to both sexes–epicene

pertaining to branch of mathematics – trigonometric

pertaining to branches – ramous

pertaining to breadmaking–panary

pertaining to breastbone – sternal

pertaining to bristles–setal

pertaining to building interior–indoor

pertaining to bunch–comal

pertaining to cadmus – cadmean

pertaining to calf of leg – sural

pertaining to camera–cameral

pertaining to canonical hours–matinal

pertaining to Carthage–Punic

pertaining to carving–glyphic, glyptic

pertaining to case–casal

pertaining to cavity lined with crystal–geodic

pertaining to Celts–Erse

pertaining to center of attraction–polar

pertaining to central line – axile

pertaining to central point–focal

pertaining to certain element–selenic

pertaining to certain group of strata–erian

pertaining to certain lineage –racial

pertaining to chair of state–thronal

pertaining to chamber–cameral

pertaining to chamber of state property management–cameral

pertaining to character of sound–tonal

pertaining to cheek–malar

pertaining to choir–choral

pertaining to church part – apsidal

pertaining to citizenship – civic

pertaining to city–civic, urban

pertaining to civilization of Egypt–Tasian

pertaining to clan–tribal

pertaining to clay–bolar

pertaining to coal–coaly

pertaining to cod family – gadoid

pertaining to coinage–monetary

pertaining to coins – numismatical

pertaining to colors – chromatic

pertaining to common people–demotic

pertaining to conduct–moral

pertaining to conic section–parabolic

pertaining to construction–tectonic

pertaining to cork–suberic

pertaining to Cornwall–Cornish

pertaining to cough–tussive

pertaining to council – cameral

pertaining to council of state property management – cameral

pertaining to country – pastoral, rural, rustic

pertaining to country of British Isles–Welsh

pertaining to court – aulic, judiciary

pertaining to crown–coronal

pertaining to crown of head –coronal

pertaining to currency – monetary

pertaining to cyanogen – cyanic

pertaining to dance motion–gestic

pertaining to dancing–terpsichorean

pertaining to daughter–filial

pertaining to dawn–eoan

pertaining to day (neither feast nor fast)–ferial

pertaining to death register –necrologic

pertaining to debtors' joint obligation–correal

pertaining to description of books–bibliographic

pertaining to desert wastes–eremic

pertaining to deserts–eremic

pertaining to diaphragm – phrenic

pertaining to diaphragm of eye–irian

pertaining to dissenting chapel–pantile

pertaining to distance north or south of equator–latitudinal

pertaining to division of mankind–racial

pertaining to dog–canine

pertaining to dog star – canicular

pertaining to dogma–levitical

pertaining to dominant brown race–Malayan

pertaining to doves–columbine

pertaining to downward motion of air–katabatic

pertaining to dowry–dotal

pertaining to dream–oneiric, oneirotic

pertaining to ducks–anatine

pertaining to Dutch theologian–Arminian

pertaining to dwelling–residential

pertaining to ear–aural, auricular, otic

pertaining to ear inflammation–otitic

pertaining to earliest stage of human culture–eolithic

pertaining to earliest tertiary period–eocene

pertaining to early churchman–patristic

pertaining to early Dutch theologian and scholar – Erasmian

pertaining to early school of philosophy–eleatic

pertaining to early theologian–Arian

pertaining to earth–geal, telluric, terra

pertaining to earthquake – seismic

pertaining to east–eoan

pertaining to East Indian island–Malayan

pertaining to eating–dietary

pertaining to Egyptian goddess–isiac

pertaining to elm family – ulmaceous

pertaining to emission of rays–radiative

pertaining to England–Anglican

pertaining to engraving – glyptic

pertaining to epoch–eral

pertaining to Erastus' teachings–Erastian

pertaining to essence–basic

pertaining to Ethiopian religion–Coptic

pertaining to European mountain range–Alpine

pertaining to eye–optic

pertaining to eye part – corneal

pertaining to fallow deer – damine

pertaining to fashion–modal

pertaining to father – paternal

pertaining to father and mother–parental

pertaining to fats–sebacic

pertaining to fatty or oily substance–adipic

pertaining to feet–pedal

pertaining to feudal service–banal

pertaining to fields–agrarian

pertaining to fine arts–aesthetic

pertaining to fingers–digital

pertaining to first principles –elemental

pertaining to fissure–rimal

pertaining to flat surface – areal

pertaining to flood–diluwan

pertaining to flowers–floral

pertaining to foot–pedal

pertaining to fore part–frontal

pertaining to forearm–cubital

pertaining to forearm bone–ulnar

pertaining to forehead–metopic

pertaining to form of architecture–Doric

pertaining to former Spanish kingdom–Leonese

pertaining to fungus spawn–mycelial

pertaining to furniture–mobiliary

pertaining to France–Gallic

pertaining to Franks–Salic

pertaining to frogs–anuran, ranine

pertaining to funeral – exequial

pertaining to funeral music –threnodial

pertaining to fungus spores– telial

pertaining to gambling–aleatory

pertaining to genesis of anything–genic

pertaining to Gentiles – ethnic

pertaining to geological age –eocene

pertaining to geological stage–achen

pertaining to German state –Bavarian

pertaining to gold–auric

pertaining to gospel – evangelic

pertaining to government– political

pertaining to government conduct–political

pertaining to grain–oaten

pertaining to grammatical form–tamas

pertaining to grandparents– aval

pertaining to great misfortune–catastrophic

pertaining to Greek architecture (oldest)–Doric

pertaining to Greek division –Nomic

pertaining to Greek epic poet–Homerical

pertaining to Greek island– Cretan, Delian

pertaining to Greek philosopher–Eleatic, Platonic

pertaining to Greek race (anc.)–Aeolic

pertaining to Greek school of philosophy–Elian

pertaining to Greek valley (anc.)–Nemean

pertaining to group of European peoples–Celtic

pertaining to group of minerals–salic

pertaining to growth of plants–vegetal

pertaining to gull family – larine

pertaining to gums–gingival

pertaining to hair–pilar

pertaining to halo–coronal

pertaining to hands–chiral, manual

pertaining to head–cephalic

pertaining to head of state– gubernatorial

pertaining to hearing–aural, auricular, otic

pertaining to heart–cardiac

pertaining to heat–caloric

pertaining to high ranking title of nobility–ducal

pertaining to hilum–hilar

pertaining to Hindu books– Vedic

pertaining to Hindu writings–Tantric

pertaining to hipbone–iliac

pertaining to historical period–eral

pertaining to history–bibliographic

pertaining to holiday–ferial

pertaining to honey–melaginous

pertaining to horse–equine

pertaining to hours–horal

pertaining to house–domal

pertaining to huge appetite– gargantuan

pertaining to hypothetical force–odic

pertaining to indigo dye – anilic

pertaining to infernal regions–avernal

pertaining to infusorian family–vorticelloid

pertaining to inion–inial

pertaining to ink–atramental

pertaining to insects–entomologic

pertaining to intellect–noetic

pertaining to inunction – aliptic

pertaining to iridium–iridic

pertaining to iris of eye – irian

pertaining to Irish – Celtic, Gaelic

pertaining to iron–ferric

pertaining to islands–insular

pertaining to Isle of Man– Manx

pertaining to jaw–malar

pertaining to joints–articular, nodal

pertaining to kidney–renal

pertaining to knowledge - gnostic

pertaining to language of ancient Crete–Minoan

pertaining to large beast – leonine

pertaining to large body of land–continental

pertaining to laughter–risorial

pertaining to law–judiciary

pertaining to layers–stratal

pertaining to leg–crural

pertaining to leg bone–fibular

pertaining to life–vital

pertaining to line–filar

pertaining to lips–labial

pertaining to liver–hepatic

pertaining to lockjaw–tetanic

pertaining to love–amatory, erotic, erotical

pertaining to lower back – lumbar

pertaining to lye–lixivial

pertaining to male line–agnatic

pertaining to marriage – hymeneal, marital

pertaining to Mars–Arean

pertaining to marsh – paludine

pertaining to mass–molar

pertaining to material universe–cosmic

pertaining to mathematical instrument–sectoral

pertaining to meaning in language–Semantic

pertaining to mechanical printing of pictures–photomechanical

pertaining to medicine – iatric, iatrical

pertaining to Mediterranean coast (east)–Levantine

pertaining to Mediterranean sea–Levant

pertaining to medulla oblongata–bulbar

pertaining to membrane of eye–retinal

pertaining to memory – mnemonic, mnesic, mnestic

pertaining to meteorological instrument–barometric

pertaining to method–modal

pertaining to microscopic animal ilfe–amoebic

pertaining to midday – meridian

pertaining to middle ages – medieval

pertaining to milk–lactary, lacteal

pertaining to mind–mental, phrenic

pertaining to minute particle of matter–molecular

pertaining to minutes–minutary

pertaining to monasteries – monastic

pertaining to money matters –economic

pertaining to moon–lunar

pertaining to morning–matin, matinal, matutinal, wight

pertaining to Moses–Mosaic

pertaining to mother – maternal

pertaining to mother and father–parental

pertaining to motion–kinetic

pertaining to motionless point–nodal

pertaining to motions of bodies–kinematic

pertaining to mountain–Alpine

pertaining to mountain range–Andean

pertaining to mouth – oral, oscular, stomatic

pertaining to mouth roof–palatal

pertaining to municipality–civic

pertaining to murderer of kings–regicidal

pertaining to muses – Aionian

pertaining to music–choral

pertaining to mustard family–cruciferous

pertaining to natural anatomical passage–meatal

pertaining to nave of church –apsidal

pertaining to navigation – nautical

pertaining to neck–jugular

pertaining to nephew–nepotal

pertaining to nerve–neural, neuro

pertaining to nervous system–neural

pertaining to neuritis–neuritic

pertaining to night–nocturnal

pertaining to Nile–Nilotic

pertaining to non-Christian nations–ethnic

pertaining to Norse poem–runic

pertaining to Norsemen – runic

pertaining to north pole of magnet–red, tactile

pertaining to north wind – boreal

pertaining to nose – nasal, rhinal

pertaining to nostrils–narial

pertaining to nut–nucal

pertaining to nymphs – nymphal, nymphical

pertaining to ocean–pelagic

pertaining to ode–odic

pertaining to oil–oleic

pertaining to old age–geratic, senile

pertaining to old poetry – runic

pertaining to olive family of shrubs and trees – oleaceous

pertaining to onas–onan

pertaining to order of Greek architecture–Ionic

pertaining to oscine birds – timaline

pertaining to pages–paginal

pertaining to palms–palmaceous

pertaining to part of hand–palmar

pertaining to particular place–local

pertaining to Passover–Paschal

pertaining to past events – historic

pertaining to peacock–pavonine

pertaining to people–demotic, laic

pertaining to period of decline–decadent

pertaining to period of time –eral

pertaining to perspiration – sudoric

pertaining to petal–petaline

pertaining to physiological process–digestive

pertaining to pigs–porcine

pertaining to plane surfaces –areal

pertaining to plants–vegetal

pertaining to plants (seedless)–agamic

pertaining to pleasure – hedonic

pertaining to poetry–iambic

pertaining to point of earth's axis–polar

pertaining to poison–arsenious

pertaining to portraiture – iconic

pertaining to pottery–ceramic, keramic (var.)

pertaining to priests–sacerdotal

pertaining to prophecy–vaticinal

pertaining to public–cameral

pertaining to public prayer and worship–liturgic, liturgical

pertaining to punishment–penal, punitive

pertaining to queen–reginal

pertaining to radiant energy –actinic

pertaining to rainbow–iridal

pertaining to rainfall–hyetal

pertaining to raising vegetables–olericultural

pertaining to reason–noetic

pertaining to Red Sea colony –Eritrean

pertaining to region rarely visited by earthquakes – peneseismic

pertaining to regions near equator–tropical

pertaining to religious doctrine–Babiism, Babism

pertaining to Rhine–Rhenish

pertaining to rise and fall of sea–tidal

pertaining to river–amnic

pertaining to river bank – riparian

pertaining to robbery on high seas–piratic

pertaining to rock–petrean

pertaining to rock layers – stratal

pertaining to Roman Catholic–papal

pertaining to roof of mouth –palatal

pertaining to room of state property management – cameral

pertaining to rounded appendage–lobar

pertaining to royal court – aulic

pertaining to runes–runic

pertaining to rural affairs and agriculture–georgic

pertaining to rural life–pastoral

pertaining to Salian Franks –Salic

pertaining to salvation–soterial, soterical

pertaining to sarcasm–ironical

pertaining to Scandinavian (anc.)–runic

pertaining to school of philosophy–eleatic

pertaining to science of mind –psychological

pertaining to Scotch Highlander–Gaelic

pertaining to sculpture – glyphic

pertaining to sea – marine, pelagric, thalassic

pertaining to seacoast–littoral

pertaining to seam–sutural

pertaining to seed plant – herbal

pertaining to semeion–semic

pertaining to sense–sensory

pertaining to sense of taste–gustatory

pertaining to sepulchral mound–tumular

pertaining to shin–cnemial

pertaining to ship's sails – velic

pertaining to shoulder–alar, scapular

pertaining to sign–semic

pertaining to singing birds–oscine

pertaining to sinus – sinal, sinusal

pertaining to six–senary

pertaining to skin–cuticular, deric, dermal

pertaining to skull–inial

pertaining to small dermal bone–scutellar

pertaining to social group of people–tribal

pertaining to soda ash–alkaline

pertaining to soft palate – velar

pertaining to sole of the foot –plantar

pertaining to son–filial

pertaining to son of Miled–Irian

pertaining to song–melic

pertaining to sound–tonal

pertaining to South American country–Chilean

pertaining to space–areal

pertaining to space between a bird's eye and bill–loral

pertaining to Spanish Toledo–Toletan

pertaining to Spice Islands–Molucca

pertaining to spores of fungus–telial

pertaining to spring–vernal

pertaining to star cluster – nebular

pertaining to stars – astral, sidereal, stellar

pertaining to state–statal

pertaining to state affairs–pragmatic

pertaining to state of hostility–feudal

pertaining to stomach–gastric

pertaining to storks–pelargic

pertaining to subgroup of minerals–mitic

pertaining to suborder of dinosaurs–sauropodous

pertaining to summer–aestival, estival, festival

pertaining to sun–heliac, solar

pertaining to Sunday – dominical

pertaining to surface of anything–facial

pertaining to swelling–ensue

pertaining to swimming – natatory

pertaining to syllable second before last – antepenultimate

pertaining to symbol of clan relationship–totemic

pertaining to tail–caudal

pertaining to tailor–sartorial

pertaining to teaching–pedagogic

pertaining to tears–lacrimal

pertaining to teeth–dental, molar

pertaining to tempo–agogic

pertaining to the body (as a whole)–systemic

pertaining to the earth – planetary

pertaining to the plague – loimic

pertaining to the present – modern

pertaining to the rule–rutic

pertaining to the side–lateral

pertaining to theologian (early)–Arian

pertaining to thigh–crural

pertaining to thorax–pectoral

pertaining to thornlike process–spinal

pertaining to thread–filar

pertaining to throat–gular, jugular

pertaining to throat part – glottal

pertaining to tibia–cnemial

pertaining to tile–tegular
pertaining to tin–stranic
pertaining to tissue–telar
pertaining to tithes–decimal
pertaining to titmice–parine
pertaining to toes–digital
pertaining to tone–tonal
pertaining to tongue–glossal, lingual
pertaining to tortoises-–chelonian
pertaining to touch–tactile
pertaining to town – civic, urban
pertaining to traprock–trappose
pertaining to travel–viatic
pertaining to trees–arboreal
pertaining to Troy (anc.)–Iliac, Trojan
pertaining to tuft–comal
pertaining to Turanian people–Akkad
pertaining to type of poem–odic
pertaining to union of states –federal
pertaining to unit of electrical resistance–ohmic
pertaining to us–our
pertaining to vascular system –haemal, hemal, hemic
pertaining to Venice–Venetian
pertaining to verse stress – ictic
pertaining to vessel–vasal
pertaining to vinegar–acetic
pertaining to voltaic pole – anodal
pertaining to vowel sounds –vocalic
pertaining to Vulcan–Mulcibirian
pertaining to walls–mural, parietal
pertaining to warm climates –tropical
pertaining to warships–naval
pertaining to wax–ceral
pertaining to wedlock–marital
pertaining to weekdays–ferial

pertaining to weight–baric, ponderal
pertaining to West Indies – Antillean
pertaining to whales–cetic
pertaining to wheels–rotal
pertaining to wife–uxorial
pertaining to winds–eolian
pertaining to wine–vinic
pertaining to wine making–oenopoetic
pertaining to wings–alary
pertaining to winter–hiemal
pertaining to woman's marriage portion–dotal
pertaining to womanhood–muliebral
pertaining to woods–sylvan
pertaining to wrist–carpal
pertenencia (Latin America) –claim, concession
Perth (Scotland) district – Atholl
pertinacious – adhering, determined, firm, inflexible, obstinate, stubborn, tenacious, unyielding
pertinacity–obstinacy, persistency
pertinency–relevance
pertinent–adapted, applicable, apposite, appurtenance, apropos, apt, felicitous, fit, germane, pat, proper, relative, relevant, telling
pertinent (to be)–apply
pertinentia–fixtures, things
pertness–sauciness
perturb–agitate, confusion, derange, disorder, disturb, trouble
perturbation–agitation, confusion, irregularity
pertusion–perforation
pertussis–cough, whooping cough
Peru–see Peruvian
peruke–periwig, wig
perukier–wigmaker
perula–mentum
peruse–con, read
perused–conned, examined, handled, inspected, read, scanned, surveyed

Peruvian Andes tableland–puna
Peruvian animal – alpaca, llama
Peruvian bark–cinchona
Peruvian bark tree–cinchona
Peruvian capital–Lima
Peruvian chieftain – Inca, Inka
Peruvian city – Arequipa, Callao, Cuzco, Ica, Lima (c.), Paita
Peruvian coin–centavo (br.), dinero (s.), libra (g.), sol (s.)
Peruvian department–Cusco, Cuzco, Ica, Lima, Piura, Tacna, Yca
Peruvian empire (early) – Inca, Ynca
Peruvian goddess–Mama
Peruvian Indian–Inca, Inka
Peruvian inn–tambo
Peruvian king (petty) – cacique
Peruvian lake–Titicaca
Peruvian llama–alpaca, paco
Peruvian measure–celemin, fanegada, galon, topo, vara
Peruvian native (northeast) –Peba
Peruvian plant–oca
Peruvian plant (climbing)–ulluco
Peruvian plant root–ratanay, ratanhia, ratany, rhatany
Peruvian port–Callao
Peruvian province–Tagna
Peruvian river – Apurimac, Huallaga, Maranon, Paucartambo, Santa, Ucayale, Urubamba
Peruvian rodent–chinchilla
Peruvian ruler–Inca, Inka .
Peruvian seaport–Callao
Peruvian tinamou–yutu
Peruvian tuber–oca
Peruvian volcano–Misti
Peruvian weight – libra, quintal
Peruvian wood sorrel–oca
pervade–fill, penetrate, permeate, traverse
pervading – prevalent, universal

perverse – awk, awry, contrary, forward, froward, petulant, wayward, wilful, wogh
perverse fool–ass
perversion of taste–malacia
pervert – apostate, divert, overturn, renegade, ruin, upset
pervious–accessible, permeable
pervulgate–publish
pesante (music)–heavy, impressive
peshkash–offering, present, tax, tribute
peskar – accountant, agent, minister, steward
pesky – pestering, plaguy, vexatious
pess–hassock
pessimist–cynic
pessoner–boat, fishmonger, ship
pest – bane, epidemic, nuisance, pestilence, plague
pest (farm)–ragweed
pest (lawn)–dandelion
pester – annoy, devil, rib, tease, torment, worry
pestilence–disease
pestilent – annoying, contagious, deadly, infectious, mischievous, poisonous, troublesome
pestle (kind of)–muller
pesvalgus–clubfoot
pet–caress, cosset, darling, dear, favorite, fondle, humor, indulge, pamper, tiff
pet lamb–cade, cosset
petal (orchid)–labellum
petal (pert. to)–petaline
petals–ala, alae
petals (flower, collectively)–corolla
petals (having)–petalous
petals (without)–apetalous
petard–firecracker
peteman – cracksman, safeblower
Peter the Great's father – Alexis
peterman – burglar, fisherman, thief

petiole – leafstalk, mesopodium, peduncle, stalk, stem
petit – insignificant, little, mean, small
petite–demure, little, small
petition–apply, ask, beg, entreat, plea, plead, pray, prayer, request, solicit, sue, supplicate
petition in chancery–relator
petitioner–orator
petitor–applicant, seeker
peto–wahoo
petrified body–fossil
petrifying–deadening, hardening, petrescent
petroleum (derivative of)–butane, naphtha
petroleum by-product – butane, deisel, propane, propylene
petroleum product–naphtha
petroleum product (between gasoline and cymogene)–rhigolene
petrosal–hard, petrous, stony
petted–cade, pettish, piqued
petticoat–fustanella, jupon, kilt, kirtle, undercoat, underskirt, waistcoat
petticoat (tropical, native, short)–pagne
petticoat (women's outer, arch.)–kirtle
petticoat tails–shortcake, teacake
pettifogger–attorney, lawyer
pettish – fretful, irritable, peevish
pettle–cherish, cuddle, indulge, nestle, potter
petty–diminutive, frivolous, inconsiderable, inferior, insignificant, mean, minor, nugatory, orra, paltry, small, subordinate, trifling, unimportant
petty captain–centurion
petty fern–spleenwort
petty larceny (Eng. slang)–scrounging
petty morel – nightshade, spikenard
petty mugget–woodruff
petty mullein–cowslip

petty objection–cavil
petty prince–satrap
petty rice–quinoa
petty trader–monger
petty whin–restharrow
petulance – insolence, peevishness, pertness, pettishness, sauciness, wantonness
petulance (fit of)–huff
petulant – contrary, cross, forward, fretful, immodest, insolent, peevish, pert, querulous, saucy, short, wanton, wayward, wilful
petulant (more)–testier
pezzo–bit, piece
pfefferkuchen–gingerbread
Phaedra's father–Minos
Phaedra's husband–Theseus
phaeton–carriage
phalacrocorax–coot, cormorant
phalacrosis – alopecia, baldness
phalanger (Tasmania)–tapoa
phalera–boss, cameo, disk
phantasm–delusion, dream, fancy, fantasy, ghost, idola, idolum, specter, spirit
phantasmal – illusive, spectral, transitory, unreal
phantom – eidolon, eidola (pl.), ghost
phantom being–fairy
Pharaoh–Rameses
Pharaoh's ancestor–Ra
Pharaoh's chicken–vulture
Pharaoh's fig–sycamore
Pharaoh's hen–vulture
Pharaoh's mouse – ichneumon
phare–lighthouse, pharos
pharmaceutical preparation (obs.)–dia
pharmaceutical weight – obole, obolus
pharos–beacon, chandelier, cloak, lighthouse
phase–aspect, passover, stage
phase of the moon–horning
phasm – apparition, appearance, meteor, phantom
pheasant – cheer, kallege, monal, pukras, tragopan

pheasant (Asiatic)–tragopan
pheasant brood – nid, nide, nye
pheasant cuckoo–coucal
pheasant duck – merganser, pintail
pheasant finch–waxbill
pheasants (flock of) – nid, nide, nye
Phenician–*see* Phoenician
phenol derivative–anol
phenomenal–extraordinary, unusual
phenomenon (contradictory) –paradox
phenomenon (in atmosphere)–meteor
phenomenon (meteorological)–snow
phenomenon (optical) – mirage
phenomenon (winter) – snowfall
phial–bottle, bowl, cup, vessel, vial
philabeg–kilt
philander – flirt, flirtation, lover
philanthropist–altruist, benefactor, donor, humanitarian
philanthropy – almsgiving, charity
philippic–tirade
Philippine aborigine – Aeta, Ata, Ita
Philippine ant (white)–anai, anay
Philippine archipelago–Sulu
Philippine boat–balsa, banca
Philippine-Borneo sea–Sulu
Philippine breadfruit – casmansi, rima
Philippine buffalo–timarau, timerau
Philippine canoe–banca
Philippine capital–Manila
Philippine capital (summer) –Baguio
Philippine chair (on two poles, carried by four men)–talabon
Philippine chief native–Ilocano, Iloco, Ilokano
Philippine christianized tribe – Bicol, Bikol, Bisayan,

Tagal, Tagalog, Vicol, Visayan
Philippine city–Albay, Aparri, Baguio, Cavite, Dagupan, Davao, Manila (c.)
Philippine civil governor – Taft
Philippine cloth fiber–pineapple
Philippine coin – centavo (br.), peso (s.)
Philippine dagger–itac
Philippine dialect – Ibanag, Tagal, Tagalog
Philippine director of health –Heiser
Philippine district–Lepanto
Philippine drink (alcoholic) –beno
Philippine drink (fermented rice)–bubud
Philippine dugout–banca
Philippine dwarf race–Aeta
Philippine dyewood tree – tua, tui
Philippine fabric (fine)–pina
Philippine farmer–tao
Philippine fennel–anis
Philippine fern–nito
Philippine fetish–anito
Philippine fiber (cloth) – pineapple
Philippine food (staple) – baha, taro
Philippine fort–Corregidor, Gota
Philippine governor (civil)– Taft
Philippine governor general –Ide
Philippine headmen–dattos
Philippine hemp – abaca, manila
Philippine house–bahay
Philippine idol–anito
Philippine Igorots division of a town–iato
Philippine island –Bohol, Cebu, Leyte, Luzon, Mindanao, Mindora, Negros, Palawan, Panay, Paragua, Samar
Philippine island (largest)– Luzon
Philippine island group–Sulu

Philippine Islands (discoverer of)–Magellan
Philippine knife–bolo
Philippine language–Moro, Tagal, Tagalog
Philippine liquor–beno, vino
Philippine litter–talabon
Philippine Luzon savage – Aeta, Ata, Igorot, Igorrote
Philippine mango (used for pickles)–pahutan
Philippine mango (wild) – bauno
Philippine market day (weekly)–tiangue
Philippine measure–apatan, balita, braza, caban, cavan, chupa, ganta, loan, quinon
Philippine Mohammedan – Moro
Philippine Moslem–Moro
Philippine mountain–Apo, Iba, Mayon
Philippine mudfish–dalag
Philippine muskmelon–atimon
Philippine narra–asana
Philippine native–Aeta, Ata, Ita, Moro, Sulu, Tao
Philippine native (chief) – Ilocano, Iloco, Ilokano
Philippine native (subject to forty days' work, annually)–polista
Philippine negrito – Aeta, Ata, Ati, Ita
Philippine parrot (green) – cagit
Philippine patriot–rizal
Philippine peasant–Lao, Tao
Philippine plant–abaca
Philippine port–Cebu
Philippine priest (Moro) – pandita
Philippine province – Abra, Albay, Iloilo
Philippine race (dwarf) – Aeta
Philippine reptile–python
Philippine rice (inferior) – paga
Philippine rice field embankment–pilapil
Philippine river–Abra, Agno, Pasig

Philippine road–daan
Philippine sash–tapis
Philippine savage–Ata, Atta, Igorot, Igorrote
Philippine sea–Sulu
Philippine shirt–baro
Philippine shrub–alem, anilao
Philippine slave–alipin
Philippine soldiers' barracks –cuartel
Philippine stream (wide)–ilog
Philippine sweetsop–ates
Philippine termite – anai, anay
Philippine town–agoa
Philippine town division – Ato
Philippine trader (Chinese)–sangley
Philippine tree–acle, anam, ates, balinghasay, dao, dita, iba, ipil, ligas, mambong, tua, tui
Philippine tree (dyewood)–tua, tui
Philippine tree (forest)–dita
Philippine tree (hard valuable wood)–tindalo
Philippine tree (hardwood) –macaasim
Philippine tree (large) – mambong
Philippine tree (timber) – yacal
Philippine tree (timber, dark pigment)–molave
Philippine tree bark (used for rope)–aga, agamid
Philippine tribe – Igorot, Igorrote
Philippine tribe (christianized)–Bicol, Bikol, Bisayan, Tagal, Tagalog, Vicol, Visayan
Philippine tribesman–Moro
Philippine turnip (sweet)–cincoma
Philippine vehicle (two-wheeled, box-like) – carromata
Philippine volcano – Apo, Mayo
Philippine ward division – ato

Philippine water buffalo – carabao
Philippine water jar–bango
Philippine weapon–bolo
Philippine weight – catty, chinanta, fardo, lachsa, picul, punto, quilate
Philippine white ant–anai, anay
Philippino–Filipino, Moro
Philistine city–Gath
Philistine deity–Dagan
Philistine god–Baal, Dagon
Phillips Academy seat–Andover
Philomela's father–Pandion
Philomela's sister–Procne
philosopher–Socrates
philosopher (18th century)–Kant
philosopher (French) – Renan
philosopher (German)–Kant
philosopher (grave)–sage
philosopher (Greek) – Nestor, Plato
philosopher (one of the seven sages)–Solon
Philosopher of Ferney–Voltaire
philosophical–rational, temperate, unruffled, wise
philosophy (adherent of certain)–dualist
philosophy (sublimated) – transcendentalism
philosophy (system of ascetic)–yoga
philosophy of law–jurisprudence
philosophy school (follower) –eleatics
phlegm–mucus
phlegmasia–inflammation
phlegmatic – inert, mucous, viscous, watery
phloem–bast
phlogistic – burning, fiery, heated, impassioned, inflammatory
Phocis king's son–Pylades
phoebe–peewee, pewee, pewit
Phoebus–Sol
Phoenician capital (anc.) – Tyre

Phoenician city–Sidon, Tyre
Phoenician colony–Carthage
Phoenician deity–Baal
Phoenician god–Baal
Phoenician goddess (of love) –Astarte
Phoenician seaport–Sidon
phonetic notation system – romic
phony – counterfeit, fake, faked
phosphate mineral–apatite
phosphate of lime–apatite
phosphorous compound source (mineral)–apatite
photo bath–toner
photo developer–amidol
photo printing–ozotype
photograph–heliograph, pictorial, portrait
photograph (to)–mug
photograph developer–ortol
photographed – filmed, pictured
photographic bath – developer, reducer, toner
photographic negative (flexible)–film
photography inventor–Talbot
photography inventor (Fr.) –Niepce
photology–optics, photics
photometric unit–pyr, rad
photometric unit (proposed) –rad
phrase (catch)–slogan
phrase (descriptive)–epithet
phrase (peculiarity of) – idiom
phrase (pithy)–epigram
phrased–worded
phraseology–parlance, wording
phratries–clans
Phrixos' father–Athamus
Phrixos' mother–Nephele
Phrixos' sister–Helle
Phrygian deity (youth and vegetation)–Attis
Phrygian enthusiast – Montanist
Phrygian king–Midas
phyletic–phylogenetic, racial
phyma–nodule, tumor
physic–cathartic, purge

physical – bodily, corporeal, material, natural
physical unit–erg
physician – doctor, galen, medi
physician (comb. form) – iatro
physician (Fr.)–Galen, Laveran
physician (quack)–medicaster
physicist–Galvani, naturalist
physicist (famous)–Faraday
physiognomy–face, mug
physiological process (pert. to)–digestive
piacle–crime, guilt, offense, piaculum, sin
pian–frambesia, framboesia, yaws
piano–quietly, softly
piano (dumb keyboard) – digitorium, digitoria (pl.)
piano (early)–spinet
piano (forerunner of)–spinet
piano (small)–spinet
piano (small upright) – pianette
piano duet (upper part) – primo
piano key–digital
piaster (120th of)–asper
piation–atoning, expiating
piatti–cymbals
piazza–gallery, porch, portico, veranda
pic–picayune
pic (French)–peak
picacho–butte, hill
picador–debater, jester, wit
picadura–tobacco
pical–vitiated
picaro – knave, rogue, sharper, vagabond
picaroon – brigand, corsair, pirate, rascal, rogue, thief
pick–choose, cull, diamond, elect, gaff, pickax, plectrum, pluck, select, sort
pick (mining, dial.)–beele
pick (the)–elite
pick flaws–cavil
pick out carefully – assort, cull, sort
pickax–mattock, pick
pickax (mining)–bede

picked – adorned, dainty, fastidious, peaked, piked, pointed, spiny, spruce, stripped, trim
pickerel (genus of)–esox
picket–enclose, fasten, fence, fortify, pale, peg, post, stake, tern
picket (fence)–pale, paling
pickle–achar, brine, dawdle, nibble, peck, piddle, pilfer, trifle, vitriol
pickle (fish)–alec
pickled–drunk, soused, soust
pickled in vinegar – marinated
pickpocket (slang)–dip
pickpocket's helper–bulker
picnic–gipsy, gypsy, junket, outing
pict–depict, paint
picture – chromo, chromolithograph, copy, image, likeness, oil, painting, pastel, portrait, porture, print, tableau
picture (changeable) – diorama
picture (crayon)–pastel
picture (kind of)–etching
picture (living)–tableau
picture (mounted on paper in a scroll)–makimono
picture (moving) – cinema, movie
picture (outdoor)–exterior
picture (positive)–print
picture (sea)–marine
picture (vivid)–tableau
picture border–mat
picture cast by lens–image
picture house–cinema, movie
picture play–cinema, movie, photoplay
picture puzzle–rebus
picture stand–easel
picture-viewing instrument–alethoscope
picturesque–scenic, scenical
picuda–barracuda
piddle – pick, play, putter, toy, trifle
pie–chaos, confusion, jumble, magpie, mess
pie (small)–patty
pie dish–coffin

pie icing–meringue
piebald – heterogeneous, mixed, mongrel, motley, pied, pinto, variegated
piece–bit, crumb, part, portion, scrap, shred
piece (armor)–tace, tasse
piece (broad thick)–slab
piece (eccentric)–cam
piece (fastening)–gib
piece (flat)–slab
piece (horizontal over door) –lintel
piece (large thin)–sheet
piece (long)–length
piece (long narrow) – slat, strip
piece (neck) – boa, collar, kerchief, rabat, scarf, stole
piece (nose)–nasal
piece (rotating)–cam, rotor
piece (short blunt)–stub
piece (short dramatic)–skit
piece (side)–rib, stave
piece (small)–bit, bite, chip, driblet, morsel, mot, shippet
piece (small flat)–flake
piece (small, Fr.)–morceau
piece (split off) – slivers, splinter, splint
piece (tapering)–gore, gusset
piece (thin)–slice
piece (thin tapering)–shim
piece (triangular) – gore, gusset, miter, mitre, wedge
piece (upright door)–jamb
piece for strengthening a statue–tenon
piece holding other piece in place–gib
piece of baked clay–tile
piece of metal (oblong)–sow
piece of money–coin
piece of skilled needlework –sampler
piece of work–chore, job
piece of work (variegated)– mosaic, pane
piece of work (with black inlay)–niello
piece that fits into mortise– tenon

piece to prevent slipping–cleat

piece used to make tight fit –shim

pieced out (laboriously) – eked

pieces (antiaircraft) – pom-pom

pieces (to)–apart

pieces of eight (Span.) – escudo

pieces of meat (roasted seasoned)–cabob

pieces of waste silk–noil

piecing–joining, mending, patching

piecing out–eking

pied–piebald, variegated

pied animal–piebald, pinto

pied antelope–bontebok

pied diver–smew

pied monk–Bernardine, Cistercian

Piedmont (Italy) town – Aosta

pielet–tart

pier – breakwater, dock, groin, landing, mole, quay, wharf

pier (architectural)–anta

pier (architectural, treated as pilaster)–anta

pierce – bore, enter, gore, penetrate, probe, puncture, riddle, spear, spike, stab, sting

Pierce (C.S., philosophic doctrine)–pragmaticism

pierce with a stake–empale, impale

pierced–lanced, perforated, punctured

piercing – clearly, keen, searching, sharply, shrill, shrilly, spearing, spiking, tart, thorn

piercing (act of)–pertusion

piet–chatterbox, chattering, magpie, ouzel, piebald

pietoso–compassionate, sympathetic

piety–compassion, devotion, holiness, pity, religion, reverence

piewipe–lapwing

pig – bacon, casting, crock,

dogboat, far, farrow, hog, pork, pressman, sixpence, swine

pig (female)–sow

pig (iron)–ingot

pig (last of litter)–runt

pig (little)–piggie, piggy

pig (male)–boar

pig (guinea)–cavy

pig (Scot.)–crock

pig (young)–farrow, shoat, shote

pig (young female)–gilt

pig (young, Scot.)–grice

pig bed–sty

pig deer–babiroussa, babirusa

pig hickory–pignut

pig iron ballast–kentledge

pig-like animal–babiroussa, babirusa, babirussa, peccary

pig of lead–fother

pig potato–cowbane

pig rat–bandicoot

pig yoke–quadrant, sextant

pigdan–spittoon

pigs (genus of)–sus

pigs (litter of)–farrow

pigs (pert. to)–porcine

pigs and whistles – fragments, wreckage

pig's-eye–trillium

pig's feet–pettitoes

pig's whisper–grunt, instant

pigeon–coward, dove, dupe, fleece, gull, pluck, sweetheart

pigeon (African, long-tailed) –namaqua

pigeon (Australian, large)– wonga, wonga-wonga

pigeon (Cape)–pintado

pigeon (carrier) – homer, homing, scandaroon

pigeon (clay)–bird

pigeon (domestic) – nun, ruff, trumpeter

pigeon (domestic variety)– spot

pigeon (European wild) – turtledove

pigeon (extinct)–dodo

pigeon (homing) – scandaroon

pigeon (kind of) – carrier,

fantail, homer, homing, jacobin, nun, pouter, trumpeter, tumbler, turbit

pigeon (large domestic) – runt

pigeon (long-tailed, African)–namaqua

pigeon (pouter)–cropper

pigeon (short broad-beaked) –barb

pigeon (small)–isabel

pigeon (young)–piper

pigeon call–coo

pigeon feed (salt, meal, lime)–saltcat

pigeon grass–foxtail

pigeon house – columbary, dovecot

pigeon-livered–gentle, meek, mild

pigeon pea–cajanus, dal

pigeon pox–sorehead

pigeon woodpecker–flicker

pigeonberry – coffeeberry, Juneberry, pokeweed

pigeonhearted – chickenhearted, cowardly, timid

pigeonman–messenger

pigeonry–dovecot

pigeons (genus of)–columba

pigeons (genus of crowned) –goura

pigeon's-blood–garnet

piggery (Scot.)–crockery

piggish–filthy, greedy, mean, selfish, stubborn

pigheaded – obstinate, perverse, stubborn

pigment–color, ocher, ochre, paint

pigment (anthracene)–alizarin, alizarine

pigment (arsenic, yellow)– orpiment

pigment (black)–sepia, tar

pigment (black amorphous) –melanin

pigment (blue, dark)–smalt

pigment (blue-green)–bice

pigment (brown)–bister, bistre, umber

pigment (brown, rich)–sepia

pigment (brownish)–sienna

pigment (calico printing)– canarin, canarine

pigment (coal tar)–aniline
pigment (cuttlefish)–sepia
pigment (dark brown)–bister, bistre, melanin, umber
pigment (deep blue)–smalt
pigment (madder root) – rubiate
pigment (orange red)–realgar
pigment (oxide of lead) – massicot
pigment (red, in certain feathers)–turacin
pigment (yellow) – etiolin, ocher, ochre
pigment (yellow, earthy) – ocher, ochre
pigment (yellow, formed by plants grown in the dark) –etiolin
pigmy–chimpanzee, dwarf, dwarfish, elf, gnome, minim, pixy, pygmy, short
pignorate – pawned, pignoratitious, pledged
pignus (civil law) – pawn, pledge
pigpen–sty
pigsconce–pighead
pigskin–football, saddle
pigsney–darling, dear, sweetheart
pigstick–butcher
pigsticker–butcher, pocketknife, sled, sword
pigtail–queue
pigwash–hogwash, swill
pika–rodent
pike–beacon, cairn, fish, ged, gedd, luce, pick, pickax, poulaine, tower
pike (Scot.)–ged, gedd
pike (walleyed)–dore
pike-like fish–gar, luce, robalito, robalo
pike perch–dory, sauger
pike squirrel–chinchilla
piked shoe–crakow
pikel (pikle)–hayfork, pitchfork
pikelet–crumpet
piker – coward, quitter, shirker, thief, tightwad, tramp, vagrant
pilar–downy, hairy

pilaster – anta, antae (pl.), column
pilaster-like abutment of arch–alette
pile–breakwater, heap, mole, mow, nap, pier, pillar, shag, spile, stack
pile (burning)–pyre
pile (Scot.)–dass, dess
pile defense work–estacade
pile driver–fistuca
pile driver falling weight– tup
pile of hay–mow, rick, stack
pile up–amass, heap, stack
pilfered – cabbaged, filched, looted, purloined, robbed, snitched, stole
pilgrim – crusader, peregrinator, sojourner, traveler, wanderer, wayfarer
Pilgrim settler–Puritan
Pilgrim to Holy Land–Palmer
Pilgrim's bottle – ampulla, costrel
Pilgrim's dress (Mecca, peculiar)–ihram
Pilgrim's father–Alden
Pilgrim's Progress author– John Bunyan
Pilgrim's Progress character –Demas
pill–ball, bolus, creek, decorticate, pare, peel, pellet, pilule, pitcher, pool, strip
pill (large)–bolus
pill (little)–pilule
pill bug–slater
pillage – booty, depredate, despoil, flay, foray, harry, loot, plunder, prey, rapine, ravage, sack, spoil, spoliation, strip
pillaging–predatory
pillar – column, shaft, support
pillar (antique)–stela, stelae (pl.), steles (pl.)
pillar (bearing an inscription)–stela, stelae (pl.), stele, steles (pl.)
pillar (Buddhist temple)–lat
pillar (capital of)–chapter
pillar (carved)–totem pole
pillar (little)–pillaret

pillar (lofty)–obelisk
pillar (sculptured) – stela, stelae (pl.), stele, steles (pl.)
pillar (tapering four-sided)– obelisk
pillar (with figure set before it)–osiride
pillar-like–stelar
pillar of air course–pylon
pillar of Buddhist temple– lat
Pillar of Fire church leader– Alma White
pillar projecting from wall– pilaster
pillar saint–stylite
pillar stone–cornerstone
pillarist–stylite
Pillars of Hercules (location of)–Abila (Africa), Calpe (Europe), Gibraltar
pillbox–brougham, cap, fortification, shelter
pillion (clerical)–cap, hat
pilliver–pillow, pillowcase
pillory–stock, trone
pillow–block, cushion, pad, support
pillow cover–sham
pilm–dust
pilot–clergyman, cowcatcher, director, guide, helmsman, lead, leader, preacher, steer
pilot (expert)–ace
pilot (sky) – clergyman, preacher
pilot bird–plover
pilot fish–remora, romero
pilot snake–copperhead
pilot weed–rosinweed
pilot whale–blackfish
piltock–coalfish
pilum–javelin, pestle
Piman Indian–Opata
pimento–allspice, paprika
pin–affix, axle, badge, bolt, brooch, confine, enclose, fasten, gudgeon, join, peg, pen, secure, spindle, transfix
pin (axletree)–linchpin
pin (carpentry)–dowel
pin (connecting)–dowel

pin (fastening) – cotter, linchpin
pin (fulcrum for oar)–thole
pin (iron quoit)–hob
pin (jackstraw) – spilikin, spillikin
pin (looped head)–eyebolt
pin (meat fastening)–skewer
pin (metallic) – bolt, cotter, rivet
pin (of a dial)–style
pin (pivot)–pintle
pin (quoits)–hob
pin (sailmaker's wooden)–fid
pin (ship's)–belaying
pin (small)–lill
pin (supporting)–nog
pin (used in certain games) –skittle
pin (with looped head)–eyebolt
pin (wooden) – dowel, fid, nog, peg, spile, stake, trenail
pin fastening–dowel
pin grass–alfilaria
pin point–dot
pinafore–apron
pinag–lake
pinax – catalogue, picture, plaque, scheme, table, tablet
pinbone–hipbone
pince-nez–eyeglasses
pincers – chela, forceps, pliers, tew
pincers (small)–pliers
pinch – arrest, confine, contract, cramp, extort, nip, raid, rob, snatch, snitch, squeeze, steal, stint, straiten, tweak, twince
pinch (sharp)–tweak
pinch bar–lever, pry
pinch pennies – niggardly, stint
pinchem–titmouse
pinda–peanut
pine – flag, grieve, lament, languish, repine, waste, wither, yearn
pine (Australian) – kauri, kaury
pine (fir)–balsam

pine (low-growing)–pinon
pine (mahogany)–totara
pine (Polynesia)–ara
pine (textile screw) – ara, pandan
pine bark aphid–phylloxera
pine family–pinaceae
pine gum–sandarac
pine knot–dovekie
pine leaf–needle
pine linnet–siskin
pine siskin–finch
pine tar derivative–retene
pine tar extract–retene
pine tree (family of) – fir, larch, spruce
pine tree exudation – resin, rosin
Pine Tree State–Maine
pine tulip–pipsissewa
pineapple – anana, ananas (pl.), nana, pina
pineapple (gangster's slang) –bomb
pineapple family – bromeliaceae
pineapple segment–pip
pineapple weed–marigold
pinguescent–fattening
pinguid–fat, fatty, rich, unctuous
pinguitude–fatness, obesity, oiliness
pink – adorn, coral, deck, decorate, grayling, minnow, pierce, rose, salmon, stab
pink eye–conjunctivitis
pink family–caryophyllaceae
pink needle–alfilaria
pink pill–cure-all
pinkeen–minnow
pinkster flower – azalea, honeysuckle
pinna – auricle, feather, fin, leaflet, wing
pinnace – boat, procuress, prostitute, tender, woman
pinnacle–acme, apex, crown, epi, finial, needle, peak, summit, top
pinnacle (ice)–serac
pinnacle (rock)–needle
pinnacle (rocky)–tor
pinnacle (slender)–epi
pinnacle (T-shaped)–tee

pinnacle of ice (in a glacier) –serac
pinnate–featherlike
pint (quarter)–gi, gill
pintado – cero, chintz, fish, pigeon
pintail duck–smee
pinto–calico, mottled, painted, piebald, pied
pinwing–penguin
pion–dig, excavate
pioneer–colonist, digger, excavator, miner, settler
pious–devout, godly, loyal, reverential
pip–cheep, chirp, paip, peep, seed, speck, spot
pipe – duct, hooka, hookah, main, reed, tube
pipe (clay)–TD
pipe (clay, long-stemmed)–straw
pipe (discharging) – outlet, spout
pipe (flanged end of)–taft
pipe (form of)–tubular
pipe (Indian peace)–calumet
pipe (Oriental smoking) – nargile
pipe (pastoral)–reed
pipe (rain water)–leader
pipe (rustic)–reed
pipe (shepherd's) – larigot, oat, reed
pipe (short tobacco)–dudeen
pipe (smoke)–tewel
pipe (steam)–riser
pipe connection – cross, elbow, ell, "T," tee, "Y"
pipe ends (flanged)–tafts
pipefish–earl, snacot
pipe of peace–calumet
pipe player–fifer, shepherd
pipe wrench–Stillson
pipettes–droppers, tasters
pipit–titlark
pips (three)–treys
piquant – racy, sharp, spicy, stinging, tart, zesty
piquantly forward–saucy
pique–annoy, displease, displeasure, fret, goad, grudge, irritate, irritation, nettle, offend, offense, provoke, resentment, sting

piquet tricks (winning of all)–capot

pirate – buccaneer, corsair, freebooter, picaroon, robber

pirate flag–Roger

piratical–predatory

pirogue–canoe

pirol–oriole

Pisa king–Oenomaus

piscary–fishery

piscation–fishery, fishing

piscator–angler, fisherman

piscina–fishpond, reservoir, tank

pishogue – sorcery, spell, witchcraft

pismire–ant, emmet

piste–path, spoor, track, trail

pistil (simple flower)–carpel

pistle–epistle, story, tale

pistol (anc.)–dag

pistol (automatic, slang)–gat

pistol (coll.)–gat, rod

pistol (large, short-barreled) –derringer

pistol (old time)–dag

pistol case–holster

piston–plunger

pit–cavity, cockpit, excavation, grave, hole, mine, pool, waterhole, well

pit (anatomy)–fossa

pit (fodder)–silo

pit (theater)–parquet

pit for baking (Hawaii) – imu

pitch–encamp, fling, heave, hurl, key, resin, send, tar, throw, tone, toss

pitch (below)–flat

pitch (cobbler's, obs.)–code

pitch (highest, three string) –paranete

pitch (identity)–unison

pitch (mineral)–bitumen

pitch color–piceous

pitchblende (derivative of)– radium, uranium

pitched (high)–shrill

pitcher–carafe, ewer, gorge, olpe

pitcher (Irish liquor)–cruiskeen, cruisken

pitcher (small)–toby

pitcher (wide-mouthed) – ewer

pitcher (wine) – oenochoe, olpe

pitcher and catcher–battery

pitcher plant – cephalotus, nepenthe, sarracenia

pitcher-shaped–urceolate

pitcher-shaped vessel – aiguiere

pitcher's motions–windup

piteous – compassionate, devout, pious, pitiable, pitiful, pitying, tender

pitfall – danger, difficulty, lure, snare, trap

pith – essence, gist, jet, kernel, marrow, meat, nub, nucleus, pulp

pith helmet–topee

pith of matter–gist

pith tree–ambatch

pithy–crisp, laconic, meaty, terse

pithy phrase–epigram

pithy saying–mot

pithy sentence–motto

pitiable – lamentable, miserable, piteous, sad, sorrowful, woeful

pitiful–contemptible, despicable, mean, pathetic, piteous

pitiless – cruel, merciless, ruthless

pitpit–guitguit

pittance–alms, bequest, dole, gift

pitted–stoned

pitted like a honeycomb–alveolate

pity–clemency, commiseration, compassion, condolence, mercy, remorse, repentance, ruth, sympathy, yearn

pivot–slew, slue, turn

pivot (bearing)–toe

pivot pin–pintle

pivotal–polar

pivotal point–crux

pixy (pixie)–fairy, sprite

Pizarro (yielders to)–Incas

placard–affiche, bill, manifesto, post, poster, proclamation

placate – appease, conciliate, pacify, sooth

place–demesne, deposit, lieu, locale, location, locus, loci (pl.), posit, position, post, put, seat, set, site, situation, situs, spot, stead

place (burial) – catacomb, cemetery, graveyard, necropolis

place (camping)–etape

place (for keeping fish) – aquarium

place (from which a jury is taken)–venue

place (hallowed) – altar, church, fane, shrine, synagogue, temple

place (halting of troops) – etape

place (hiding)–mew

place (high)–eminence

place (horse training)–longe

place (incense burning)–altar

place (intermediate, for souls)–limbo

place (landing) – airport, dock, pier, wharf

place (market)–agora, rialto

place (meeting)–tryst

place (of confinement) – limbo, mew

place (of nether darkness)– erebus

place (of restraint)–limbo

place (of worship) – altar, chapel, church, shrine

place (open in forest)–glade

place (provision keeping) – larder

place (public amusement)– casino, midway, park

place (raised)–ridge

place (resting) – bed, chair, couch, grave, lair

place (retired)–cranny, den, nook

place (stopping) – hostelry, hotel, inn, rest

place (suitable)–niche

place (to)–deposit, put, set

place (trading) – market, mart

place (wet and marshy) – slew, slough

place (where an action has occurred)–venue
place (wrestling)–palaestra
place another has had–stead
place apart–isolate
place aside–sequestered
place away for future reference–file
place before–appose
place between–insert, interpose
place by itself–isolate
place confidence in–believe, trust
place end for end–reverse
place for keeping animals–barn, menagerie, pasture, zoo
place for keeping fish – aquarium
place in (rare)–innest
place in a row–align, aline, allign
place in bondage–enslave
place in charge–entrust
place in common fund–pool
place in comparison–parallel
place in funeral vase–inurn
place in order–arrange, systematize
place in position for use–instal, install
place interpretation on–construe
place of action–arena, scene
place of assembly–agora
place of bliss–Eden, paradise
place of concealment – den, mew, prison
place of confinement – asylum, cage, calaboose, coop, corral, dungeon, gaol, jail, pen, penitentiary, prison, stir
place of confinement (U.S. warship)–brig
place of confusion–Babel
place of content–Arcadia
place of contrasting color–spot
place of exchange–mart
place of exit–egress
place of neglect (oblivion)–limbo

place of nether darkness – Erebus
place of origin – cradle, source
place of preparation–laboratory
place of protection–shrine
place of refuge–ark, haven, port
place of resort–purlieu
place of safety–haven, port
place of seal–LS
place of simplicity–Arcadia
place of sleep – bed, berth, couch, doss, hammock, pallet
place of trial–venue
place of utter darkness – Erebus
place of worship–altar, chapel, church, fane, shrine, synagogue, temple
place one inside another – nest
place opposite–appose
place or bring near–appose
place over–superimpose
place side by side–collocate, juxtapose
place under legal impediment–estop
place under restraint–intern
place under severe strain – tax
place value upon – appraise, evaluate, inventory
place where boats must be carried–portage
place where candles are kept –chandlery
place where things are united–joint, seam
place where trial is held–venue
place where troops are stationed–base, camp, field, fort, post
placed–deposited, paid, put
placed alone–enisled, isolated
placed apart–enisle
placed apart as one's share–allotted
placed cargo aboard ship–laded, steeved, stowed
placed in arbor–embowered

placed in cipher–coded
placed in lodgings–billeted, roomed
placed in or at middle–centric
placed in same age–contemporize
placed in vase–urned
placed near–apposed
placed on mound–teed
placer in proximity–apposer
places–demesnes, loci
places (bryophyte cultivating) – mosseries, mossery (sing.)
places (frequented) – dives, haunts, resorts
places (sacred)–altars, chapels, churches, fanes, shrines, synagogues, temples
places (sleeping) – beds, berths, bunks, couches, hammocks, pallets
places (uncultivated) – deserts, wilds
places (uninhabited)–wilds
places of great suffering – gethsemanes
places rubbed out–erasures
placid – calm, gentle, peaceful, quiet, serene, undisturbed, unruffled
pladaroma–tumor
plage – beach, country, region, transept, zone
plagiarism–piracy
plagiarist–stealer, thief
plagiarize – crib, purloin, steal
plague – dun, harass, harry, hector, infestation, nuisance, pest, pestilence, scourge, tease, torment, twit, vex, worry
plague carrier–rat
plaguy–harassing, tormenting, troublesome, vexing
plaid (Scot.)–tartan
plaid (shepherd's gray) – maud
plain – apparent, artless, blunt, clear, distinct, downright, evident, frank, genuine, heath, legible, lenten, moor, ob-

vious, prairie, primitive, unadorned, unaffected, undisguised

plain (among grassy hills)–camas

plain (Arctic)–tundra

plain (elevated)–mesa

plain (European, southeast) –steppe

plain (Florida) – savanna, savannah

plain (grassy)–lea

plain (Italian)–campagna

plain (Russian)–steppe, tundra

plain (small grassy, among hills)–camas

plain (South Africa)–veldt

plain (Spanish-American)–llano, vega

plain (treeless) – savanna, savannah, steppe

plain (vast)–steppe

plain English – straightforward

plain-hearted – artless, sincere

plain-spoken–blunt

plains–downs

plains (treeless) – llanos, pampas, steppes

plaint – bewail, complaint, lament

plaintail–escolar

plaintiff–orator, suer

plaintive – complaining, cross, discontented, elegiac, fretful, lamenting, melancholy, peevish, pettish, petulant, repining, sorrowful

plait – braid, fold, knit, weave, wimple

plaited rope yarns cord–sennit

plaited straw (for hat making)–sennit

plan – arrange, design, devise, diagram, draft, engineer, ettle, form, frame, intend, map, method, outline, plat, plot, project, scheme

plan (architectural)–epure

plan (frustrator of)–marplot

plan (mechanical)–diagram

plan (preliminary)–idea

plan in detail–layout

plan of future procedure – program

plan of townsite–plat

plan secretly–conspire

plan to do–intend

plan tree–sycamore

planate–flattened, plane

planch (planche) – board, floor, plank, slab

plancher–bed, ceiling, floor, pallet, plank, planking, platform

plancier–soffit

plane – airplane, even, flat, level, surface

plane (kind of) – block, grooving, iron, jack, router, tounging

plane (outer boundary of)–perimeter

plane block–stock

plane figure with four angles–tetragon

plane figure's outer boundary–perimeter

plane handle–toat, tote

plane handle (bench)–tote

plane handle (joiner's)–toat

plane surfaces (pert. to) – areal

plane tree–chinar

plane trees (genus of)–platanus

planet–Earth, Jupiter, Mars, Mercury, Neptune, Pluto, Saturn, star, Uranus, Venus, wanderer

planet (brightest)–Venus

planet (large)–Saturn

planet (minor)–satellite

planet (recent)–Pluto

planet (red)–Mars

planet (red lighted)–Mars

planet (ringed)–Saturn

planet (small)–asteroid

planet's orbit–ellipse

planeta–cloak

planetarian–astrologer

planetarium–orrery

planeticose–wandering

plangor–lamentation, wail

plank – board, deal, gravestone, slab, stone

plank (placed beneath an object)–shole

plank (pontoon bridge floor)–chess

plank (used as a prop)–shole

plank down–pay

planking (curved ship's) – sny

planking breadth–strake

planned beforehand – prepense

planner–architect, designer, engineer, projector

plant–ache, alyssum, arum, clote, clover, decoy, detective, herb, rape, seed, shrub, sow, spy, trap, tree, wort

plant (abnormally modified)–ecad

plant (acid juice)–ribes

plant (aconite)–bikh

plant (adapted to dry climate)–xerophyte

plant (African) – argel, arghel

plant (agave)–aloe, pita

plant (alismaceae)–alismad

plant (Alpine)–edelweiss

plant (amaryllis family) – agave

plant (ambrosia genus)–ragweed

plant (American century) – aloe

plant (ammoniac)–oshac

plant (anise)–dill

plant (any climbing)–liana, liane

plant (apiaceous)–ache

plant (aquatic, northwest U.S.)–sugamo

plant (Arabian narcotic) – kat

plant (aralia elata)–fatsia

plant (aromatic) – alecost, anise, basil, lavender, mint, nard, tansy, thyme

plant (aromatic seasoning)–tarragon

plant (arum family)–aroid, calla, taro

plant (Asiatic fiber)–ramie

plant (Asiatic oil)–odal

plant (aster family) – fleabane

plant (Australia) – correa, hakea

plant (Australian clover-like)–calomba

plant (bean family)–licorice, liquorice, lupine

plant (bell-shaped flower)–gloxinia

plant (berry)–currant

plant (bitter)–rue

plant (blue dye yielding)–woad

plant (box)–buxus

plant (brassica) – cole, rape, turnip

plant (broom)–spart

plant (broomcorn millet) – hirse

plant (bryophytic) moss

plant (bud of)–cion

plant (burdock)–clite

plant (burning bush) – wahoo

plant (butter and egg)–ramstead, ranstead, ransted

plant (cabbage family)–rape

plant (cactus family)–cereus, dildo, mescal

plant (cactus-like) – xerophyte

plant (canary broom) – genista

plant (canna)–achira

plant (caoutchouc)–rubber, ule

plant (cassia genus)–senna

plant (catchfly)–silene

plant (catnip family)–nep, nepeta

plant (celery-like)–udo

plant (century)–agave, aloe, maguey

plant (cherry laurel) – cerasus

plant (China)–ramie

plant (class of)–alga, algae (pl.)

plant (climbing)–vetch

plant (climbing, woody stem)–liana, liane

plant (clover-like)–calomba, medic

plant (common century) – pita

plant (creeping)–ipecac

plant (crocus family)–irid

plant (crossbred)–hybrid

plant (crowfoot family) – peony

plant (cruciferous)–alyssum, cress

plant (cryptogamous)–moss

plant (cyperaceous)–sedge

plant (delicate twining) – smilax

plant (dill)–anet

plant (dipsacus genus)–teasel

plant (dock-like)–sorrel

plant (dogwood)–cornus

plant (drug)–aloe

plant (dwarf)–cumin

plant (dye) – anil, madder, weld, woad, woald, wold, would

plant (East India) – benne, madder, rea, sesame, sola, sunn

plant (East Indian fiber)–ambary, da

plant (Egyptian aromatic)–cumin

plant (elephant's ear)–taro

plant (embryo)–plantule

plant (erica genus)–heath

plant (Euphorbia genus) – spurge

plant (European) – azarole, sneezewort

plant (European mint)–lavender

plant (evergreen, linked to a season)–mistletoe

plant (everlasting)–orpine

plant (fanaceous)–ers

plant (fern)–tara

plant (fiber) – aloe, flax, hemp, pita, ramie, sisal

plant (floating)–frogbit

plant (flourishing in dry region)–xerad

plant (flowering)–acanthus, arum, bareta, barreta, candytuft, calla, canna, coreopsis, geranium, lobelia, monkshood, orpin, pavonia, petunia, pulsatilla, rhodora, snapdragon, tamarix, yucca

plant (flowering moss-like)–orpine

plant (flowering water)–lotus

plant (flowerless) – fern, lichen, thallogen

plant (for tanning) – alder, sumac, sumach

plant (forage)–rape

plant (fragrant)–angelica

plant (fragrant root)–orris

plant (furze)–gorse, ulex

plant (garden)–aster, lettuce

plant (garden blue-flowered)–harebell

plant (garden succulent) – lettuce

plant (garlic, wild)–moly

plant (genus of amaryllis family)–agave

plant (genus of ambrosia)–ragweed

plant (genus of anthemis)–camomile, chamomile

plant (genus of araceae) – arum

plant (genus of eryngium)–eringo, eryngo

plant (genus of Eurasian mints)–nepeta

plant (genus of geum) – avens

plant (genus of grasses) – avena

plant (genus of isatis)–woad

plant (genus of lychnis) – campion

plant (genus of nepeta cataria)–catmint

plant (genus of palezoic fossil)–calamites

plant (genus of ulex)–furze

plant (grass cloth) – ramee, ramie

plant (grassland) – baccar, bacchar

plant (grass-like)–sedge

plant (growing from inside) endogen, endogenae (pl.)

plant (growing on rock) – lichen

plant (growing on sea bottom)–enalid

plant (growing wild)–agrestal, agrestial

plant (growth on)–gall

plant (habitat)–ecad

plant (having grape-like leaves)–salal
plant (having sour juice) – sorrel
plant (haw, black)–sloe
plant (Hawaiian)–olona
plant (heather family) – erica, ling
plant (hemp)–carl
plant (herbaceous)–sesame
plant (holly) – yapon, yaupon, youpon, yupon
plant (hop, vine stem)–bine
plant (house)–aphis, calla
plant (indigo)–anil
plant (interior chaff of)–palea, palet
plant (ipecac)–evea
plant (iris family)–irid, ixia
plant (Japanese) – aucuba, tea
plant (Japanese quince)–cydonia
plant (joint of)–node
plant (lacking pigment or chromatophores)–albino
plant (leafy stemmed)–daisy
plant (leguminous) – lentil, senna
plant (lilac)–syringa
plant (lilaceous)–aloe, leek, onion
plant (lily family)–aloe, lotos, lotus, sego, yucca
plant (linen producing) – flax
plant (low, tufted)–moss
plant (main axis of)–stalk
plant (male)–mas
plant (mallow family) – altea, escoba
plant (manioc) – cassava, tapioca
plant (marine)–enalid
plant (marine skeleton) – coral
plant (marsh)–fern
plant (masculine)–mas
plant (medicinal) – aconite, aloe, arnica, boneset, camomile, catnep, catnip, gentian, herb, ipecac, lobelia
plant (Mexican)–chia, sabidilla, slavia, sotol

plant (Mexican cactus, button-like)–chaute
plant (mint family) – basil, catnep, catnip, hyssop
plant (monkshood)–aconite
plant (moss-like, small) – hepatic
plant (mustard family) – alyssum, cress, woad
plant (nep)–catnep, catnip
plant (New Zealand)–tara
plant (nightshade family) – tomato
plant (North American) – garrya
plant (noxious)–weed
plant (of lily family)–aloe, lotos, lotus, sego, yucca
plant (of mint family)–basil, catnep, catnip, hyssop
plant (oil yielding)–odal
plant (oily seed)–sesame
plant (old world)–lotus
plant (one-seeded fruit) – olacaceae
plant (Oriental fiber)–ramie
plant (oxalis)–oca
plant (packing for fruit, fish, etc.)–cannery
plant (painful to skin) – smartweed
plant (pansy, wild)–heartsease
plant (parsley, Eng. wild)–eltrot
plant (parsley family)–anise, dill
plant (part of)–stipel
plant (pepper)–ava
plant (perennial)–carex, sedum
plant (perennial suffrutescent)–rue
plant (Peru)–oca, rhatany
plant (Philippine)–aga, agamid, alem
plant (pigment lacking)–albino
plant (pitcher) – chrysamphora, darlingtonia
plant (poisonous) – datura, oleander
plant (poisonous to cattle)–loco
plant (poisonous to fowls)–henbane

plant (Polynesian)–taro
plant (poppy family)–celandine
plant (pore of a)–lenticel
plant (potato-like)–oca
plant (prickly)–brier, cactus, nettle, teasel
plant (primrose)–auricula
plant (pungent)–pepper
plant (ramie)–rhea
plant (red pepper)–chilli
plant (rock)–lichen
plant (rockrose)–cistus
plant (rose family)–avens
plant (sage)–salvia
plant (salad) – celery, cress, endive, lettuce, romaine, watercress
plant (satin pod)–honesty
plant (sedge family)–carex
plant (sensitive)–mimosa
plant (silene)–campion
plant (silk)–floss
plant (small aromatic)–dittany
plant (snake bite antidote)–guaco
plant (snake root) – seneca, senega
plant (soap)–amole
plant (solanaceous)–tobacco
plant (South African)–aloe
plant (South American) – tillandsia
plant (Spanish pepper family)–aji
plant (starch)–arum
plant (starch producing) – pia, taro
plant (strawberry)–frasier
plant (succulent)–aloe, herb
plant (summer)–savory, savoury
plant (supposed to cause forgetfulness when eaten)–lotus
plant (sweet scented)–yerba
plant (symbol of Ireland)–shamrock
plant (Syrian aromatic) – cumin
plant (Tahitian food)–taro
plant (tansy)–tanacetum
plant (tapioca)–cassava
plant (taro root)–eddo

plant (tendril climbing) – creeper

plant (thorny)–briar, thistle

plant (three-leaved)–clover, shamrock

plant (trifolium) – clover, shamrock

plant (tropical) – agave, arum, mangrove, palm, taro

plant (tropical American genus)–hamelia

plant (tropical American mallow)–altea

plant (tropical flowering)–zamia

plant (tropical with edible root)–dasheen

plant (tropical woody vine) –redwithe

plant (troublesome)–weed

plant (true heath)–erica

plant (trumpet)–bignonia

plant (twining)–smilax

plant (urticaceous)–nettle

plant (used to flavor vinegar)–tarragon

plant (valerian genus)–nard

plant (verbenaceous) – lantana

plant (vetch family)–ers

plant (water, flowering) – lotos, lotus

plant (water side)–sedge

plant (which grows by addition to outside)–exogen

plant (white blossom)–calla

plant (wild carrot)–hilltrot

plant (with aromatic odor)–tansy

plant (with aromatic seed)–cumin

plant (with dark foliage and small berries)–sabine, savin, savine

plant (without woody stem) –herb

plant (woody, climbing)–liana, liane

plant (woody vine genus)–vitis

plant (yielding cosmetic dye)–alhenna, henna

plant (yielding white juice) –milkweed

plant (young creeping) – vinelet

plant (yucca-like)–sotol

plant animal–zoophyte

plant apoplexy–esca

plant appendage–stipule

plant body in higher plants–cormus

plant breathing organ – stoma, stomata (pl.)

plant broom–spart

plant calyx leaf–sepal

plant capsule–pod

plant cells' coloring matter–endochrome

plant coloring matter (green)–chlorophyl, chlorophyll, clorofil

plant cuticle ingredient–cutin

plant deeply and firmly – radicate

plant disease–blister, ergot, smut

plant exudation–gum, resin, rosin, sap

plant fiber–istle

plant formation changes – seres

plant fungus (rye)–ergot

plant genus–arum

plant geography – phytogeography

plant head (prickly)–bur

plant hemp–jute

plant insulin–glucokinin

plant juice–latex, milk, sap

plant lice–aphids

plant lice (genus of)–aphis

plant life–flora, vegetation

plant louse–aphid

plant modified by abnormal environment–ecad

plant of cabbage family – rape

plant of genus erica–heather

plant of gourd family–melon

plant of mustard family – cress

plant of nettle family–hemp

plant opening – stoma, stomata (pl.)

plant organs (minute breathing) – stomata, stoma (sing.)

plant organs (secreting honey)–nectary

plant receptacle–torus

plant root – radix, radices (pl.)

plant root (principal) – taproot

plant sap (in certain plants) –milk

plant scale – ramentum, ramenta

plant seaweed (leaf of) – frond

plant secretion – laap, laarp, lerp

plant seed leaf–cotyledon

plant seed organ–pistil

plant shoot–cion

plant shoots (food)–asparagus

plant stalk–haulm

plant stem–bine

plant stem joint–node

plant that dies after flowering–herb

plant trees–forest

plant used to raise nap on woolen cloth–teaser

plant weed (kind of)–dock

plant with purple flowers–gerardia

plants–flora, seeds, sows

plants (containing chlorophyl)–algae, alga (sing.)

plants (division of) – archichlamydeae

plants (genus of) – arum, canna, cola, datura, syringa

plants (leafy stemmed and axillary violet flowers)–gloxinias

plants (pert. to seedless) – agamic

plants (used for fodder) – deerweed

plants (woody, obs.)–treen

plants of area–flora

plants which add exterior ring annually–exogens

plantain–banana

plantain eater–touraco

plantain family–plantaginaceae

plantation conifer–pinetum

plantation of trees – forest, orchard
planters (government by)–plantocracy
plantigrade carnivore – panda
planting stick–dibble
plantling–plantlet
plaque–brooch, medal
plash–pool, puddle
plasm–matrix, mold
plaster–salve, teer
plaster (coarse)–grout, parget
plaster (used in painting)–gesso
plaster of Paris–gesso
plaster stone–gypsum
plastered – mortared, smeared
plasterer–mason
plasterwork (decorative) – parget
plastic–ductile, fictile, gesso, waxen
plastic (used for sizing cotton)–viscose
plastic clay–pug
plastosome–mitochondrium
plat–absolute, braid, chart, directly, flat, flatly, interweave, level, map, plain, plait, plan, plateau, straight, straightforward, tableland
platanist–susu
plate–disc, dish, gib
plate (communion)–paten
plate (eucharist)–paten
plate (eucharistic bread) – paten
plate (graduated)–dial
plate (insect, bony)–scutum
plate (numbered)–disc
plate (perforated)–dod
plate (roofing)–pantile, tile
plate (sacred)–paten
plate (shaped like ship)–nef
plate (soap frame)–sess
plate (steel armor)–taces
plate (storage battery)–grid
plate (thin) – lamina, laminae (pl.), paten
plate (used in communion service)–paten

plate armor (for thigh) – cuish
plate bone–scapula
plate for The Host–paten
plateholder–cassette
plate mark–hallmark
plate of glass–slide
plateau–dish, mesa, plaque, salver
plated–laminated, overlaid
platform – chart, dais, estrade, kang, map, plan, stage
platform (at top of ship's mast)–foretop
platform (gun) – barbette, emplacement
platform (in a fort) – barbette, emplacement
platform (mine)–sollar, soller
platform (nautical)–foretop, maintop
platform (part of)–plank
platform (raised)–dais
platform (reloading, British)–staith
platform (ship boarding) – gangplank
platform (speaker's) – tribune
platform (wheeled)–float
platic–imperfect
plating (protective)–armor
platinum (comb. form) – platin, platino
platinum (crude)–platina
platinum wire (looped)–oese
platitude – commonplace, commonplaceness, staleness, triteness
platoid–broad, flat
platonic body–cube, dodecahedron, hexahedron, icosahedron, octahedron, tetrahedron
platoon–coterie, set, squad, volley
Platoon School–Gary
platter–dish, grail, plate
platter-shaped–scutellate
platyfish–moonfish
plaudit – acclamation, applause, approbation, approval, encomium

plausible–applausive, credible, ostensible, plauditory, specious
plausible excuse–alibi
play–amusement, dally, disport, diversion, drama, fun, game, pantomime, recreation, romp, sport
play (exhibit a)–stage
play (part in)–role
play (stupid)–boner
play (without words)–pantomime
play above pitch–sharp
play at tenpins–bowl
play badly–strum
play boisterously–romp
play carelessly–strum
play for time–stall
play into each other's hands –collude
play mean tricks–shab
play outline–scenario
play pranks upon–haze
play slower – ritard, ritardando
play the bagpipe–skirl
play the bagpipe (coll.) – doodle
play the buffoon–droll
play the coquette–flirt
play tricks of levity–frolic
play tricks on–hoax
play truant–miche
play unskillfully on stringed instrument–strum
play upon words–pun
play without dialogue–pantomime
playa–beach
playboy – buffoon, clown, fool
played–executed, performed
played leading part–starred
played out–exhausted, finished, tired
player – actor, gambler, gamester, thespian
player (bagpipe)–piper
player (card cutting)–pone
player (itinerant) – stroller, troubadour
player (piano)–pianola
player (poor, slang)–dub
player (principal)–star

player at duck on a rock – tenter

player on words–punster

playful – humorous, jocular, lusory, sportive

playhouse–theater

playing cards (14th century)–tarots

playlet–skit

playman–gambler, gamester

playock–plaything

playsome–playful, sportive, wanton

plaything–bauble, die, toy

playwright–dramatist

plea–appeal, entreaty, prayer, pretense

plea (defendant's)–nolo contendre

plea (legal)–abater

plead – appealed, beg, entreat, sue

plead for–solicit

pleader–advocate, entreater, intercessor, suer

pleading–advocacy, imploring, intercession, litigation, suppliant, supplication

pleading (legal)–demurrer

pleasant – agreeable, amusing, diverting, gay, humorous, laughable, merry, pleasing, sportive, sprightly, sweet

pleasant (coll.)–nice

pleasant in sound–euphonic

pleasant manners–amenities

pleasant to peruse–readable

pleasantness–amenity

pleasantness (acts of)–amenities

please–appease, arride, content, delight, gratify, placate, satisfy, suit

pleased – contented, fain, glad, gratified, happy

pleases greatly–delights

pleaseship–litigation

pleasing–agreeable, amiable, desirable, lief, nice, pleasant, sooth

pleasing (rare)–sooth

pleasing aspect of nature – scenery

pleasing to eye (Scot.) – eesome

pleasurable – gratifying, hedonic, pleasant

pleasure – delight, enjoyment, gratification, gree, joy, will

pleasure (pert. to)–hedonic

pleasure ground – park, pleasance

pleasure seeker–epicure

pleasureful – delightful, pleasing

pleating attachment (for sewing machine)–plicator

plebeian – common, illbred, lowborn, ordinary, vulgar

plebiscite – decree, referendum, vote

pleck–enclosure, speck, spot, stain

plectrum – malleus, tongue, uvula

pledge – bet, engage, gage, gate, mortgage, oath, parole, pawn, plight, promise, seal, troth, vow, wage

pledge (conveying)–promissory

pledge (Hindu law)–adhi

pledge (legally)–bond

pledge faith–troth

pledged to marry–engaged, troth

pledges–earnests

pledget–compress, swab

Pleiad of Alexandria–Apollonius, Aratus, Callimachus, Homer, Lycophron, Nicander, Theocritus

plenary–absolute, complete, entire, full, perfect, unqualified

plenipotentiary–envoy

plenteous–abundant, bounteous, bountiful, copious, generous, liberal, plentiful, plenty

plentiful–abounding, abundant, ample, bounteous, bountiful, copious, fruitful, full, liberal, opulent, profuse, prolific, rich, rife

plentifully – abounding, galore

plenty–abundance, complete-

ness, copiousness, enough, fullness, perfection, plenitude

plenty (in)–galore

plenty (poetic)–enow

pleon–abdomen, telson

pleonasm – fullness, redundancy

plethora–excess, glut, superabundance

plethoric – bombastic, inflated, overfull, overloaded, turgid

plexiform–complicated

plexiform arrangement–rete

plexus–network, rete, retia (pl.)

pliable – flexible, limber, limp, plastic, pliant, supple

pliant–bending, compliant, flexible, pliable, tensile, willowy, workable, yielding

plicate–fold, pleat

plight–braid, condition, embrace, fold, plait, position, predicament, status

plinth (any width, flat)–orlo

plod–dig, drudge, mog, toil, tore, trudge

plodder–drudge, grub

plot–brew, burn, cabal, conspiracy, conspire, design, frame, intrigue, machination, map, pack, plan, project, scald, scheme, scorch, secret

plot of ground–grave, lot, terrain

plotted–charted, conspired, hatched, lineated

plotter – agitator, conspirator, contriver, planner, schemer

plotter against existing government–Jacobin

plotter against Jews–Haman

ploughshare–colter, coulter

plouk (plook)–knob, pimple

plounce–flounder, plunge

plousicracy–plutocracy

plover – courtesan, drome, dupe, sandy

plover (American) – kildee, killdee, killdeer, piping

plover (crab)–drome
plover (crested)–lapwing
plover (Old World)–dotterel, lapwing
plover (ring)–sandy
plow–break, furrow, rove, till
plow (deep furrow)–miner
plow (kind of) – breaker, moldboard, prairiebreaker, rotary, shovel, snow, stirring, sulky, turnplow
plow (subsoil)–mole
plowfish–ray
plowgang–oxgang
plow handle–hale, stilt
plowhead – beam, cleves, frame
plow into ridges (by turning two furrows together) – rove
plow knife–colter, coulter
plowland (equivalent to) – carucate
plowman–countryman, husband, rustic
plowman's command – gee, haw
plowman's spikenard – cinnamonroot
plowman's wort–fleabane
plowmell–mallet
plow part (bottom)–slade
plowshare–colter, coulter
plowshare bone–vomer
plow sole–slade
plow spade–plowstaff
plowed–broken, furrowed, tilled
plowed land–arada
pluck–fleece, gather, jerk, nerve, pick, plunder, pull, rob, strip, tug, twitch
pluck off–avulse, pug
plucky–adhesive, brave, courageous, game, resolute, spirited, spunky, sticky
plug – blow, bung, knock, peg, punch, stopper, stopple, tampeon, tampion, tampon, tampoon, tap
plug (cannon muzzle)–tampeon, tampion
plug (doggedly)–slog
plug (medical)–clot, embolus

plug (slender)–spill
plug (small)–spile
plug (water)–hydrant
plug bib–spigot
plugboard–switchboard
plug cock–spigot
plug hat–gibus, tile, topper
plug-ugly – rowdy, ruffian, tough
plug up–calk, caulk
plum–drupe, prune
plum (bitter)–sloe
plum (coco)–icaco
plum (dried)–prune
plum (European, small wild)–bullace
plum (half domesticated)–bullace
plum (Java)–jambool, jambul
plum (kind of) – damson, gage, greengage
plum cake–baba
plum colored–puce
plum curculio–weevil
plum duff–pudding
plum family–amygdalaceae
plum-like fruit–sloe
plum weevil–curculio
plumage–feathers
plumage (downy, of young birds)–floccus
plumage (soft)–down
plumb–absolute, complete, delve, downright, plummet, vertical
plumbage–leadwork
plumbean–leaden
plumbeous – dull, heavy, leaden, stupid
plume–aigret, egret, crest, feather, panache, pride
plume (head)–aigret, egret
plume (helmet)–crest
plume (military)–panache
plume (small) – plumelet, plumet
plumicorn (obs.)–egrette
plummet – criterion, fall, lead, test
plump–blunt, chubby, dilate, distend, drop, dull, fall, fat, obese, plop, rude, sink, tidy
plump and rosy–buxom
plump and round–chubby

plunder–boodle, boot, booty, depredate, despoil, loot, maraud, pelf, prey, rapine, ravage, raven, reave, rifle, rob, sack, spoliate, spoils, strip
plunder (arch.)–reave
plunder (by stealth)–poach
plunder (by violence)–raid, raven
plundered–reft
plunderer – looter, pillager, robber, spoiler, stealer, thief
plundering–predatory
plunge–bet, dip, dive, douse, drive, gamble, plumb, pool, risk, sink, souse, thrust
plunge into–clap, dive, immerge, immerse, merse
plunger – diver, gambler, risker, speculator
plunk–drive, drop, plump, pull, push, sink, throw
plunther (rare) – flounder, plod
plural ending–es
plural marriage–polygamy
plurality – majority, multitude
Pluto's mother-in-law – Demeter
Plutus' father–Iasion
Plutus' mother–Demeter
ply – bend, fold, handle, mold, plait, urge, wield
pneuma–breath, breathing, neume, soul, spirit
pneumonia (type of)–bronchial, lobar
Po tributary–Adda
poach–drive, encroach, force, poke, push, ram, stir, thrust, trespass
poacher – lurcher, stalker, widgeon
poblacht (Irish)–republic
Pocahontas' name–Powhatan, Rebecca Rolfe (after marriage)
pocket – bag, cly, conceal, confine, enclose, poke, pouch, sack
pocket (small)–fob
pocket (watch)–fob

pocket (water)–tinaja
pocketbook – bag, pouch, purse, wallet
pocketbook (gypsy)–lil
pocketbook (small) – fob, purse
pod–bag, belly, kid, legume, pouch, sac, shuck
pod (locust)–carob
Poe heroine–Lenore
Poe's poem–Lenore
poem–ballade, lay, ode, sonnet, verse
poem (bucolic)–eclogue
poem (descriptive of rural life)–idyll
poem (division of long) – canto
poem (epic)–epopee, epos
poem (famous)–Iliad
poem (fourteen lines)–sonnet
poem (French)–dit
poem (heroic)–epos, saga
poem (Icelandic)–edda
poem (idyll)–eclogue
poem (imitation of)–parody
poem (irregular, wild)–dithyramb
poem (long narrative)–epic
poem (love)–erotics
poem (lyric) – dithyramb, ode, rondel
poem (mournful)–elegy
poem (mystic)–rune
poem (narrative)–ballad, lay
poem (Norse, old)–rune
poem (of lamentation) – elegy
poem (part of)–epode, refrain
poem (past part)–epode
poem (pastoral)–idyl, idyll
poem (religious) – hymn, psalm
poem (sacred)–hymn, psalm
poem (satirical)–iambic
poem (short)–dit, sonnet
poem (short, exalted)–ode
poem (short, rural subject)–eclogue
poem (short, usually satirical)–dit
poem (six stanzas)–sestina
poem (song)–hymn, lyric

poem (wild irregular strain)–dithyramb
poem part–epode, refrain
poems (collection of)–sylva
Poems of Ossian (hero of)–Fingal
poesy–verse
poet–bard, dreamer, lyrist, odist, rimer
poet (German)–Heine
poet (inferior)–rimer
poet (poor)–rimer
poetaster–rimer, versifier
poetic–lyric, odic
poetic contraction–oer, tis
poetic foot–iamb, iambus
poetic foot (three syllables)–anapest
poetic inspiration (spring)–pierian
poetic unit–feet, foot
poetry (arch.)–poesy
poetry (designating a type)–iambic
poetry (god of, myth.) – Bragi
poetry (goddess of)–Erato
poetry (inspiring to)–helicon
poetry (line of)–stich
poetry (medieval lyric)–lai
poetry (muse of amatory)–Erato
poetry (muse of bucolic) – Thalia
poetry (muse of heroic)–Calliope
poetry (muse of lyric)–Erato
poetry (narrative)–epos
poetry (pert. to)–iambic
poetry (rhythmic break in lines)–cesura
poetry (style of)–epic
poetry (unconnected in) – rhapsodic
poetry measure–feet, foot
pogoniate–bearded
pogonip–fog
pogrom–massacre
poignant–acute, bitter, biting, cutting, pungent
point–aim, apex, apices (pl.), cape, dot, focus, foci (pl.), focuses (pl.), gist, jot, peak, promontory
point (antler)–prong

point (backward projecting)–barb
point (carbon in arc lamp)–crayon
point (cardinal)–east, north, south, west
point (central) – focus, foci (pl.)
point (crucial)–crux
point (double of a curve, geom.)–acnode
point (double, with two real tangents)–crunode
point (essential)–crux
point (farthest)–apogee
point (farthest from earth)–apogee
point (finishing)–tape
point (handball)–ace
point (highest)–acme, apex, apogee, maximum, maxima (pl.), meridian, peak, zenith
point (in law)–res
point (in orbit nearest earth)–perigee
point (in orbit of moon)–perigee
point (legal)–res
point (lowest)–bottom, nadir
point (main)–gist
point (main of action)–gist
point (meeting)–focus, foci (pl.)
point (one's strong)–forte
point (path of moving, according to law)–locus
point (pen)–neb, nib
point (pivotal)–crux
point (projecting)–jab
point (salient)–feature
point (scoring)–ace, run
point (sharp)–barb
point (single)–ace
point (small apical)–apicula, apiculae (pl.), apiculus, apiculi (pl.)
point (starting)–tee
point (turning)–crisis, crises (pl.)
point (uniplanar)–unode
point (utmost)–extreme
point (vibrationless)–node
point (where curve crosses itself)–crunode

point at stake–issue
point at which there is no vibration–node
point beyond which no progress can be made–end
point-blank – blunt, direct, unqualified
point device–completely, exact, particular, perfectly, precise
point directly above focus of earthquake–epicenter
point draftsman–engraver
point exactly overhead – zenith
point in debate–issue
point in orbit farthest from earth–apogee
point in orbit of planet – apsis
point of an orbit–syzygy
point of compass–airt, airth
point of concentration–focus
point of crescent moon–cusp
point of culmination–apex
point of debate–issue
point of dispute–issue
point of geometric curve (double)–acnode
point of land–spit
point of no vibration–node
point of time–date
point of view–angle, slant
point opposite zenith–nadir
point out–indicate
point out the way–direct
point under discussion–issue
point where leaf branches– axil
point won on serve–ace
pointed–aimed, conspicuous, marked, peaked, pertinent, piercing, poignant, stinging, terse
pointed (as a leaf)–apiculate
pointed (sharp)–acuate, aculeate
pointed arch–ogive
pointed end–cusp
pointed instrument–prod
pointed instrument (for graving)–stylet
pointed rod–goad
pointed tool–awl, gad, gimlet
pointed tool (mining)–gad

pointer–tip
pointer (gauge)–arm
pointer (teacher's)–fescue
pointer on sun dial–gnomon
pointers – indices, index (sing.)
pointless – dull, inane, insipid, silly, stupid, vapid, witless
pointleted–apiculate
points–apices, apex (sing.), foci, focuses, focus (sing.)
points of earth's axis (pert. to)–polar
pointsman–flanker, switchman
poise–aplomb, balance, ballast, bearing, carriage, carry, counterbalance, counterpoise, equilibrium, equipoise, librate, maintain, stability, support, suspend, weigh
poise (as a golf ball)–tee
poison–atter, bane, corrupt, fig, gall, pervert, ptomaines, venin, venom, virus, vitiate
poison (animal origin)–venom
poison (ant) – formicicide, formicide
poison (arrow)–curare, curari, inee, urali
poison (deadly) – arsenic, bane, inee
poison (extracted from species of aconite)–nabee
poison (for hexapods)–insecticide
poison (malarial)–miasma
poison (pert. to)–arsenious
poison (potent vegetable)– abrin
poison (upas tree gum)–antiar
poison (virulent)–bikh
poison ash – sumac, torchwood
poison daisy–mayweed
poison dogwood–sumac
poison fish – scorpion, toadfish, weever
poison fish (Japan)–fugu
poison flag–iris
poison flower–bittersweet

poison ivy–sumac
poison producing–septic
poison rhubarb–butterbur
poison tobacco–henbane
poison wood–manchineel
poisonous – corrupting, destructive, malignant, noxious, toxic, venene, venomous, virulent
poisonous alkaloid–coniine, conin, conine
poisonous element–arsenic
poisonous fungus–amanita
poisonous gas–arsine, mustard
poisonous herb (European)– henbane
poisonous lizard–gila
poisonous protein–abrin
poisonous protein (in castor oil bean)–ricin
poisonous substance–arsenic
poissarde–fishwife
poisson–fish
poisson bleu (Alaska)–catfish, grayling
poitrel – breastplate, stomacher
poke–bag, bore, jab, jog, nudge, prod, sack, thrust, tobacco, wallet
poke around–probe, root
pokeful–bagful
poker–beadle, bugbear, hobgoblin, pochard, rod
poker (eldest hand)–age
poker (form of)–draw, stud
poker drawing–pyrography
poker painting–pyrography
poker picture–pyrogravure
poker stake–ante, pot
pokeweed–pocan
pokeweed family–phytolaccaceae
pokey (poky)–dowdy, dull, mean, narrow, shabby, slow, tedious
Poland (poetic name)–Sarmatia
Poland (rare name for)–Polonia
polar–Arctic
polar exploration base–Etah
polar plant–rosinweed
pole–bar, mast, rod, spar, staff

pole (as a symbol)–totem
pole (boat-propelling)–poy
pole (ceremonial)–totem
pole (clothes)–prop
pole (fish-handling)–pew
pole (Indian memorial)–xat
pole (large)–mast
pole (lure, for birds)–stool
pole (negative)–cathode
pole (positive)–anode
pole (small)–sprit
pole (Spanish-American) – palo
pole (terminal)–electrode
pole (throwing, in Gaelic games)–caber
pole (vehicle)–thill
pole (well)–sweep
polecat – fitchet, fitchew, skunk, zoril
polecat (Eur.)–fitchet, fitchew
polecat (genus of)–putorius
polecat (South African) – musang
pole fluke–flounder
polehead–tadpole
pole horse–wheeler
pole of magnet–red
polestar–lodestar
pole strip–template
pole sweat–poleburn
polemic–controversial
polenta–porridge
Poles (derived from) – Demas
police chief office–marshalcy
policeman–bobbie, constable, cop, copper, officer, peeler
policeman (state)–trooper
policeman's badge–buzzer, shield
policeman's club–espantoon
policy – administration, management, sagacity, shrewdness, wisdom, wit
polish–burnish, culture, elegance, furbish, levigate, refinement, rub, shine
polish and cut (as precious stones)–lapidate
polish by friction–scour
Polish cake–baba
Polish capital–Warsaw
Polish city–Beuthen, Bialystok, Bielostok, Byelostok,

Brest, Cracow, Gleiwitz, Grodno, Krakow, Lemberg, Litovsk, Lodz, Lublin, Posen, Warsaw
Polish coin–ducat (g.), fennig (ac.), grosz (br.), halerz (ac.), korona (ac.), marka (ac.), zloty (ni.)
Polish composer and pianist –Chopin
Polish dance – cracovienne, krakowiak, mazurka, polonaise
Polish king (one-time) – Conti
Polish measure–cal, cwierc, garniec, korzec, kwarta, kwarterka, linja, lokiec, mila, morg, morga, pret, sazen, stopa, vloka, wloka
Polish monetary unit–zloty
Polish port–Gdynia
Polish premier (former) – Paderewski
Polish president (first)–Pilsudski
Polish river–Dnieper, Dniester, Dwina, Niemen, Pripet, San, South Bug, Vistula
Polish weight–centner, funt, kamian, lut, skrupul, uncya
polished – elegant, refined, scoured
polisher–burnisher, glazer
polishing–limation
polishing material – rabat, rabbat
polishing material (from potter's clay)–rabat, rabbat
polissoir wheel–lap
polite–civil, courteous, cultivated, debonair, debonaire, debonnaire, genteel, gentle, polished, refined, smooth, urban, urbane
politic–diplomatic, discreet, politique, provident, wary
political boss–cacique
political district – borough, canton, city, county, parish, state, ward
political division – borough, city, county, district, hun-

dred, parish, state, ward
political division (ruled by prince)–palatinate
political faction–bloc
political gathering–caucus, rally
political group – bloc, machine, party, ring
political hanger-on–heeler
political incumbents–ins
political influence of special interest–lobby
political mass meeting (coll.) –rally
political party (old)–Tory, Whig
political science–policy
politically successful (the)–ins
politician – intriguer, schemer, statesman
politician (petty)–politicaster
politicious–crafty, politic
polizei–police
poll – clip, despoil, fleece, shear
pollan–whitefish
pollen–flour, meal
pollen-bearing part of stamens–anther
pollen brush (of bees)–scopa, scopae (pl.)
pollenization (form of) – xenia
pollent–powerful
poller – barber, extortioner, plunderer, taxgatherer
pollex–dactylopodite, thumb
pollicitation – promise, proposal
pollinoid–spermatium
polliwog–tadpole
pollute–befoul, contaminate, corrupt, debauch, defile, desecrate, profane, ravish, soil, taint
pollution – contamination, defilement, desecration, impurity, uncleanness
Pollux's brother (twin)–Castor
Pollux's mother–Leda
polo cart–dogcart
polo game division–chucker, chukker

polo mount–pony
polo stick–mallet
Polonius' daughter–Ophelia
polony–sausage
polt–club, knock, thump
poltfoot–clubfoot
poltroon coward, cowardly, craven, dastard, dastardly, idle, lazy
polverine–pearlash, potash
polyandrium–cemetery
polybunous – hill, mound, multituberculate
polychromatic–multicolored
polygamy (illegal)–bigamy
polygon (certain)–ngon
polygon (nine-sided)–nonagon
polyhedron (of 24 congruent faces)–triakisoctahedron
polylogy–garrulity
polymny–song
Polynesian–Kanaka, Maori
Polynesian chestnut–rata
Polynesian cloth–tapa
Polynesian dragon–ati
Polynesian god of forests – Tane
Polynesian goddess of volcanoes–Pele
Polynesian herb–pia
Polynesian island–Fiji, Phoenix, Samoa, Tokelau
Polynesian loin cloth–pareu
Polynesian memorial–ahu
Polynesian native – Malay, Maori
Polynesian oven (native earth baking)–umu
Polynesian pepper plant – avas
Polynesian pine (screw) – ara, hala
Polynesian skirt–pareu
Polynesian sling–ma
Polynesian tree–ahia, ti
Polynesian tree (chestnut)–rata
Polynesian tribe–Ati
Polynesian wages–utu
Polynesian yam – ube, ubi, uve, uvi
polyp (hydrozoan)–hydra
polyp skeleton–coral
polyp skeleton (forming islands)–coral

polyphone–lute
polytropic–versatile
polyzoan (colony forming)–retepore
pomace of grapes–rapes
pome (fruit)–apple, pear
pomelo–grapefruit
Pomerania island – Rugen, Usedom
Pomerania river–Oder
Pomeranian dog's tail – plume
pomme de terre–potato
pomp – ceremonial, cortege, display, grandeur, magnificence, ostentation, pageant, pageantry, parade, pride, spectacle, state
pompano–alewife
pompous–budge, grandiose, ostentatious, stilted
pond–Atlantic, lagoon, pool
pond (frog) – ranarium, ranaria (pl.)
pond (glass plant)–aquarium, aquaria (pl.)
pond (shallow sea)–lagoon
pond (small)–aquarium, lagoon
pond crow–coot
pond dogwood–buttonbush
pond duck–mallard
pond hen–coot
ponder – appraise, brood, cogitate, consider, evaluate, meditate, mull, muse, opine, pore, reflect, weigh
ponderous – bulky, heavy, important, momentous, weighty
pongee (kind of ribbed) – shantung
poniard–dagger, dike, kill, pierce
ponica–gardener
pont–bridge, caisson, ferry, ferryboat, float, pontoon
pontoon bridge floor plank–chess
pony–nag
pony (native-bred, India) – tattoo
pony (small hardy) – Shetland
pony (student's)–cab, crib

pooch–dog
pook–pluck, pull
pooka–goblin, specter
pool – alberca, car, carr, game, lagoon, linn, meer, mere, plashet, pond, pot, puddle, reservoir, stake
pool (above waterfall)–lin
pool (dirty)–puddle
pool (mountain)–tarn
pool (small)–plash
pool (supplementary, in games)–kitty
pool (swimming)–natatorium, tank
pool (var.)–meer
pool ball–cue, ringer, spot
poon tree–keena
poon tree (Singhalese) – domba
poor–hapless, impecunious, imperfect, impoverished, indigent, infertile, insufficient, mean, needy, unfortunate, unlucky, unsatisfactory
poor creature–pilgarlic
poor-do–scrapple
poorhouse–almshouse, workhouse
poor Jan's leaf–houseleek
poor joe–heron
poor John–cod, hake
poor man's pepper – peppergrass, stonecrop
poor man's remedy–valerian
poor man's soap–hardhack
poor man's weatherglass – pimpernel
poor player (slang)–dub
poor soap–hardhack
poor soldier–friarbird
poor-spirited–base, cowardly
poorer–needier, worse
poorer quality–culls, inferior, seconds
poorest – neediest, seediest, worst
poorly – abjectly, badly, defectively, ill, inadequately, indigently, shabbily, ungenerously
popadam–wafer
popdock–foxglove
pope–bishop, bullfinch, puffin, ruff, shrike, weevil

Pope (first)–Peter
Pope (former)–Gregory
Popes (name of)–Pius, Ratti, Urban
Pope's cathedral–Lateran
Pope's collar–orale
Pope's court officer–datary
Pope's crown–tiara
Pope's headdress – miter, mitre
Pope's palace–Vatican
Pope's scarf–fanon
Pope's triple crown–tiara
Pope's veil–orale
popeler–seagull, spoonbill
popinac–huisache
popinjay–parrot
poplar–abele, alamo, aspen, cottonwood
poplar (Asia Minor)–bahan, garab
poplar (balsam)–tacamahac
poplar (Fr., black)–liar
poplar (genus of)–alamo
poplar (Lombardy)–populus
poplar (white)–abele, bolle
poppy–foxglove, papaver
poppy (corn)–canker, ponceau
poppy seed (opium)–maw
poppies (genus of)–papaver
populace–demos, mass, mob, plebs
popular – demotic, favorite, lay, nontechnical, pop, proletarian, simple, well-liked
popular success–hit
population study–larithmics
porcelain (kind of) – Dresden, Haviland, Limoges, Sevres
porcelain (soft)–frit
porcelain clay–kaolin, kaoline
porcelain ware–china
porcelain ware (fine) – Limoges
porch–colonnade, door, entrance, gallery, harbor, loggia, portico, stoa, stoae (pl.), stoop, veranda
porch (Eng. church)–galilee
porcine animal–hog, pig
porcupine–hedgehog
porcupine (Canada)–urson

porcupine anteater–echidna
porcupine disease–ichthyosis
porcupine grass–stipa
porcupine quill–pen
pore–con, gaze, opening, orifice, ponder, stare, stoma, stomata (pl.), study
pore (minute)–ostiole, stoma, stomata (pl.)
pore of woody plant–lenticel
porgy–pagrus, scup
porgy (red)–tai
pork chop–griskin
pork loin–griskin
pork steak–griskin
porker–hog, swine
porkfish–sisi
porky–porcupine
porphyry (granite)–elvan
porpoise–dolphin, seahog
porpoise (fresh water)–inia
porpoise (genus of) – inia, phocaena
porpoise (Scot.)–pellock
porr – cram, kick, poke, poker, push, stir, thrust
porrect–present, tender
porret–leek, scallion
porridge–atole, grout, gruel, oatmeal, polenta, pottage, samp
porridge (corn)–samp
porridge (maize meal)–atole
porridge (Scot.)–brose
port–harbor, harbour, haven, larboard, wine
Port India coin–rupia (s.)
portable–movable, mobile
portable altar–superaltar
portable prayer book–portas, portass, porthors, porthouse
portal–door, entrance, gate
portance–carriage, demeanor
portator – bearer, carrier, messenger
portcullis–bar, herse, shut
porte (decree of)–irade
porte-bonheur – amulet, charm
portefeuille–portfolio
portemonnaie – pocketbook, purse
portend – augur, betoken, bode, forebode, foretell, predict, presage, prophesy

portent–forewarning, omen, ostent, prodigy, sign
portentous–dire, fatal, fateful, ominous, sinister
porter – attendant, carrier, doorkeeper
porter (Oriental)–hamal
Porter's (Sydney) nickname –O'Henry
portia tree–bendy
Portia's maid–Nerissa
portico–colonnade, stoa
portico (covered athletic) - xyst, xystus
portico (enclosed space of)–pteroma, pteromata (pl.)
portico (Greek)–stoa, stoae (pl.)
portico (long open) – xyst, xystus
portico (Roman)–atrium
portion–allotment, bit, dab, dole, dunt, half, moiety, parcel, part, piece, quantity, section, segment, share, whack
portion (coll.)–cut
portion (inheritance) – legitime
portion (of curve)–arc, segment
portion (sectional)–pane
portion (small detachable)–coupon
portion (widow's)–dower
portion (woman's marriage) –dowry
portion of a curve–arc, segment
portion of territory–canton
portly–corpulent, imposing, stately, stout
portmanteau – bag, cloak, mantle, telescope, valise
portoise–gunwale, portlast
Porto Rico–*see* Puerto Rico
portpass–passport
portrait–copy, image, likeness, picture, similitude
portrait on fifty-dollar bill–Grant
portrait on five-dollar bill–Lincoln
portrait on five-hundred-dollar bill–McKinley

portrait on five-thousand-dollar bill–Madison
portrait on one-dollar bill–Washington
portrait on one-hundred-dollar bill–Franklin
portrait on one-hundred-thousand-dollar bill–Wilson
portrait on one-thousand-dollar bill–Cleveland
portrait on ten-dollar bill–Hamilton
portrait on ten-thousand-dollar bill–Chase
portrait on twenty-dollar bill–Jackson
portrait on two-dollar bill–Jefferson
portrait sitting–seance
portraiture (pert. to)–iconic
portray–act, delineate, depict, describe, draw, fashion, form, frame, image, limn, paint, picture
portrayal – act, delineation, description, portrait, process
portrayed (vividly)–graphic
portreeve–bailiff, mayor
portsalut–goal, haven
Portuguese city–Braga, Braganca, Coimbra, Guarda, Lisbon (c.), Oporto
Portuguese coin – centavo (br.), conto (ac.), escudo (g., s.), dobra (g.), real
Portuguese coin (copper, 1811–33)–pataco
Portuguese coin (copper, 16th century)–patacao
Portuguese coin (gold, 1640 to 1732)–moidore
Portuguese coin (incorrect English)–rei, reis (pl.)
Portuguese coin (old)–indio
Portuguese coin (silver) – testao, tostao
Portuguese colony–Angola, Cape de Verde, Goa, Guinea, Macao, Principe, Sao Thome, Timor
Portuguese colony (in India) –Goa
Portuguese dollar–ataca
Portuguese harbor–Aveiro,

Faro, Figueira, Lisbon, Oporto, Setubal, Vianna
Portuguese island–Angola, Azores, Madeira, Principe, Sao Thome
Portuguese lady–dona
Portuguese legislature–cortes
Portuguese measure – alqueire, alquier, bota, braca, canada, covado, estadio, fanga, ferrado, geira, legoa, linha, meio, milha, moio, oitava, palmo, pe, pipa, pollegada, quartilho, quarto, selamin, tonelada, vara
Portuguese money – dobra, johannes, peca, rei
Portuguese money of account–escudo
Portuguese money of account (former)–real, reis (pl.)
Portuguese mountain–Serra d'Estrella
Portuguese navigator–Gama
Portuguese ounce–onca
Portuguese province–Alemtejo, Algarve, Azores, Beira, Estremadura, Madeira, Minho, Traz-os-Montes
Portuguese river – Douro, Duero, Guadiana, Minho, Mondego, Sado, Tagus
Portuguese saint–Sao
Portuguese seaport–Oporto, Ovar
Portuguese territory (India) Goa
Portuguese title–dom, dona
Portuguese weight–arratel, arroba, escropulo, grao, libra, oitava, onca, quintal
porwigle–tadpole
posada–hotel, inn
posaune–trombone
pose–attitude, model, position, posture, sit, stance
Poseidon's father–Cronus
Poseidon's mother–Rhea
Poseidon's son–Triton
Poseidon's wife–Amphitrite
poser–problem, puzzle
posh – elegant, luxurious, smart, spruce
position – attitude, coign,

coigne, job, lie, pose, posture, rank, site, situs, stance, stand
position (fencing)–septime
position (golf)–stance
position (inclined)–alist
position (location) – place, seat, site
position (relative)–standing
position (secure)–footing
position (social)–caste
position (vertical, as anchor) –apeak
position (vertical, naut.) – apeak
position affording no escape –impasse
position of affairs–status
position of the helm–alee, aport
position with no responsibility–sinecure
positive–plus, sure, thetic
positive electron–positron
positive saying – dictum, dicta (pl.)
positive school–Lombrosian
positive terminal–anode
positivism–certainty, Comtism, confidence, dogmatism
positure–arrangement, configuration, disposition, posture
posnet–saucepan
poss – beat, dash, drive, knock, pound, push, stamp, thrust
possess – have, inhabit, occupy, own
possessed (poetic)–hadst
possessed by an evil spirit–demoniac
possesses (arch.)–hath
possessing consciousness of feeling–sentient
possessing feeling–souled
possessing flavor–sapid
possessing full power–plenipotent
possessing landed property–acred
possessing savor–sapid
possessing special abilities - talented
possession – control, hold,

mastery, ownership, property
possession (law)–seisin
possession (not in)–devoid
possession (prefix)–ose
possession of more than one husband at the same time –polyandry
posset – coagulate, curdle, pamper, turn
possible–feasible, likely, potential, practicable
possible (not)–potential
possibly–maybe, perhaps
post–dak, dawk, enter, mail, newel, office, pillar, placard, place, position, station, sternpost
post (boat or dock, wooden or metal)–bollard
post (door)–alette
post (hawser)–bitt, bollard
post (Indian carved memorial)–totem, xat
post (listening, detecting enemy's mines)–ecoute
post (memorial carved) – totem
post (metal, on dock or boat)–bollard
post (shipboard)–bitt
post (stair)–newel
post (totem)–xat
post (vertical)–bitt
post (wooden)–stock
post (wooden, on dock or boat)–bollard
post at back of ship–sternpost
post boat–packet
post box–mailbox
postboy–courier, postilion
post chaise–jack
post croaker–spot
post dance (army slang) – struggle
post horses–stagers
post office (Span.)–correo
post service–mail
postage stamp paper–pelure
postage stamp space (triangle)–spandrel
postal service–mail
poster–bill, billposter, placard, sticker

posthumous reputation – memory
postimpressionistic artists – cubists
postpone–adjourn, defer, delay, procrastinate, prolong, remit, wait
postpone discussion (to future time)–table
postpone indefinitely – pigeonhole, shelve
postponement–reprieve, respite
posture–attitude, pose, position, stance
posture of defense–guard
pot (bulging)–olla
pot (earthen)–crock, olla
pot (goldsmith's melting)–cruset
pot (pear-shaped)–aludel
pot ball–dumpling
pot hat–bowler, derby
pot lead–graphite
pot-rustler–cook
pot-sick–tipsy
pot-walloper–scullion
pot wheel–noria
potash–niter, nitre
potash (crude)–salin, saline
potash feldspar–orthoclase
potassium aluminum sulphate–alum
potassium carbonate–potash
potassium compound–alum
potassium dichromate – chrome
potassium sulphate–alum
potate–liquefied
potation – beverage, draft, drink
potato–spud, tuber, yam
potato (sweet musical)–ocarina
potato (the)–papa
potato beetle–hardback
potato bogle (Scot.) – scarecrow
potato disease–pox
potato family–solanaceae
potato masher (kind of) – ricer
potato moss–pondgrass
potato pea–groundnut
potatoes (French method of preparing)–lyonnaise

potator–tippler
potbank–pottery
potboiler – book, painting, potwaller
potdar – assayer, cashier, weigher
pote – crimp, kick, poke, poker, push, stir, thrust
potence–cross, gallows, gibbet
potency–elan, vis
potent – able, cogent, effective, efficacious, efficient, forcible, mighty, powerful, puissant, strong
potentate–monarch, prince, ruler, sovereign
potentate (Eastern)–ameer, amir, emeer, emir
potentate (Oriental)–ameer, amir, emeer, emir
potential–influential, latent, mighty
potential energy–ergal
poter–drinker, toper
potgun – braggart, pistol, popgun, rumor
pothead–blackfish, dullard
pother–ado, bother, bustle, disturbance, fluster, fuss, harass, perplex, perturbation, row, stir, trouble, worry
potherb–greens, mint, spinach
pothery – choking, stifling, sultry
pothole–tinaja
pothouse–alehouse, low, pottery, tavern, vulgar
potiche–vase
potion – dose, draft, drink, drug
potion (love)–philter, philtre
potlatch–feast, gift
potomania–dipsomania
potong–crown, wreath
potpie–fricassee
potpourri – anthology, medley, mixture, olio
potrero–farm, pasture
potshot – assail, attack, drunkard, drunkenness
pottage–soup

pottage (in which beef is boiled)–brewis
pottah – certificate, deed, lease
potter – dawdle, meddle, poke, pry, push, saunter, tamper, trifle
potter's clay–argil
potter's wheel–disk, jigger, lathe, palet, pallet, throw
pottery–ceramics, delftware, Delft
pottery (black)–basalt
pottery (broken) – shard, sherd
pottery (decorated by means of stamps)–sigillate
pottery (fragment of) – shard, sherd
pottery (French for)–keramos
pottery (glass-like)–vitreous
pottery (glaze on)–enamel
pottery (glazed, colored) – Delft
pottery (glazed, richly colored)–Majolica
pottery (Greek for)–keramikos
pottery (pert. to)–ceramic
pottery (red)–aretine
pottery (Renaissance Italian) –Majolica
pottery (term in coating) – slip
pottery box (clay for firing)– sagger
pottery clay–kaolin, kaoline
pottery fragment – shard, sherd
pottery maker–ceramist
pottery mineral–feldspar
potty – crazy, foolish, haughty, supercilious
poucey – dirty, dusty, rubbishy
pouch – bag, bursa, cyst, mailbag, pod, purse, sac, sack, silicle
pouch (girdle)–gipser
pouch (Highlander's)–sporran
pouch (large flat)–gipser
pouch (large, of skin)–sporran
pouch bone–marsupial

pouch dog–thylacine
pouch-like part–sac
pouch marmot–spermophile
poulp (poulpe)–octopus
poultry – chickens, ducks, fowl, geese, guinea, pheasants, pigeons, turkeys
poultry (dish of)–galantine
poultry disease–pip, roup
pounamu–greenstone, jade, nephrite
pounce upon (coll.)–nab
pound–beat, ding, enclosure, hammer, maul, pond, thump
pound (gently)–tamp
pound down–hammer, tamp
pounder–pestle
pounds (one hundred, avoirdupois)–cental
pour copiously–stream
pour down–rain
pour forth–gush, well
pour in by drops–instill
pour molten metal–teem
pour off–decant, drain
pour oil upon–anoint
pour out–decant
pour out (as a drink offering)–libate
pour out (copiously)–gush, spout
pour sacrificial liquid–libate
pouring hole (in mold) – sprue
poustie–dominion, power
pout–catfish, eelpout, mop, moue, pique, sulk, sulkiness
poverty – destitution, illth, indigence, lack, need, penury, want
poverty (abject)–penury
powder–cosmetic, dust, pollen, pulverize
powder (antiseptic)–aristol, formin
powder (astringent)–boral
powder (dermatologist's) – boral
powder (earthy white)–yttria
powder (fine, formed in flowers)–pollen
powder (fine, white)–boral

powder (goa)–araroba
powder (Holi festival)–abir
powder (India)–abir
powder (insecticide) – hellebore
powder (polishing)–tripoli
powder (skin)–boral
powder (smokeless)–cordite, poudre
powder (stamping)–pounce
powder (used in making chocolate)–pinola
powder (white, crystalline, used as an antiseptic) – formin
powder (yellowish gray, medicinal)–tannigen
powder (yellowish white, amorphous) – ethylhydrocupreine
powder bag–sachet
powder base (soft)–talc
powder heater–sinterer
powdered (her.)–seme
powdered antimony–kohl
power – ability, arm, art, dint, efficacy, efficiency, energy, force, gift, iron, might, potency, puissance, strength, sway, vigor, vis
power (capability)–potency
power (civil)–state
power (controlling)–dominator
power (degree of)–potence
power (great resisting)–wiry
power (inherent)–energy
power (Latin for)–vis, vires (pl.)
power (occult)–magic
power (persuasive)–rhetoric
power (sovereign)–throne
power (staying)–stamina
power (superior) – prepotency
power (third)–cube
power device (hydraulic) – telemotor
power hammer face (striking)–trip
power of attorney – agent, procurator
power of mind–wits
power of resistance–stamina
power of vision–eyesight
power to excite feelings and

gain affections – magnetism

power to persuade–force

power to produce effects–efficacy

powerful – cogent, effective, effectual, efficacious, efficient, forcible, intense, mighty, potent, puissant, strong

powerful (mighty, in battle) –armipotent

powerful (more)–stronger

powerful businessman–magnate, tycoon

powers (intellectual)–wits

pownie (Scot.)–peacock

powwow – assembly, ceremony, conference, congress, conjurer, meeting, priest

poyou–armadillo

prabble – chatter, quarrel, squabble

practic – artful, cunning, difficult, experienced, practical, practiced, shrewd, skilled

practical–available, feasible, possible, pragmatic, pragmatical, usable, utilitarian, workable, working

practical (rare)–utile

practical example–praxis

practical joke – hoax, humbug

practically–virtually

practice – come, custom, do, drill, exercise, habit, intrigue, perform, plot, rehearse, scheme, train, ure

practice (customarily)–use

practice (established)–canon

practice (formerly)–rite

practice (playful sword) – fence

practice (specific)–praxis

practice diligently – addict, ply

practice fraud–shark

practice of government after manner of father – paternalism

practice of propagating plants by snipping – cuttage

practice the sol-fa–intonate

practice witchcraft–hex

practiced – drilled, experienced, rehearsed, veteran

practiced economy–scraped, scrimped

practiced exercises–drilled

practiced in or on water – aquatic

practicer of palmistry–chiromancer

practicer of shifts or evasions –tergiversator

practices (corrupt)–abuses

prad (Eng. slang)–horse

prado – boulevard, promenade

pragmatic – conceited, dogmatic, meddling, officious, opinionated, skilled, systematic

pragmatical – commonplace, dogmatic, officious

Prague–Praha

prairie–bay, camas, cammas, llano, plain, quamash, steppe

prairie (small)–prairillon

prairie anemone – pasqueflower

prairie antelope–pronghorn

prairie apple–breadroot

prairie artichoke–sunflower

prairie berry–trompillo

prairie breaker–plow

prairie chicken–grouse

prairie crocus–pasqueflower

prairie dog–marmot

prairie dog weed–marigold

prairie moneywort – loosestrife

prairie mud–gumbo

prairie pigeon–plover

prairie potato–breadroot

prairie schooner – wagon (covered)

Prairie State–Illinois

prairie trees (clump of) – motte

prairie turnip–breadroot

prairie weed–cinquefoil

prairie wolf–coyote

praise – acclaim, adulation, applaud, applause, approbation, bless, celebrate, commend, commenda-

tion, encomium, eulogize, eulogy, extol, glorify, honor, laud, magnify, panegyric, plaudit

praise (acts of)–commendations

praise (high)–encomium

praise (insincere, slang) – bull

praise (insincerely)–flatter

praise (warm)–encomium

praise (continually)–chants

praise highly–extol

praise of another's felicity–macarism

Praise Ye The Lord–Alleluia

praiseworthy–laudable

Prakrit dialect – Bahlika, Dakshinatya

prance–caper, cavort, swagger

prance (elaborately, coll.) – cavort

prank – antic, caper, escapade, fold, frolic, jig, monkeyshine, pleat, shine, trick

prank (mischievous) – escapade

prank (roguish, obs.)–prat

prat – beat, buttock, prank, spank, trick

prate – babble, chat, chatter, gab, talk

prate (rare)–blate

prattle – babble, blather, blether, chat, gab, prate, talk

prawn–crustacean

prawn (comb. form)–caris

pray–ask, beg, devotion, entreat, implore, request, sue, supplicate

praya – beach, bund, road, strand

prayer – appeal, ave, bene, orison, petition, plea, suit, supplication

prayer (arch.)–orison

prayer (devotional)–orison

prayer (evening)–angelus

prayer (Lord's)–paternoster

prayer (morning)–matin

prayer (of invocation)–ave

prayer (short)–collect

prayer bead–rosary

prayer book–missal
prayer call (Mohammedan) –adan, azan
prayer cloak–tallith
prayer shawl–orale
prayer tower–minaret
praying (act of)–precation
praying cricket–mantis
praying figure–orant
praying insect–mantis
prays (one who)–precant
preach (obs.)–sermonize
preacher–clergyman, homilist, minister, parson, pulpiteer, rector
preacher's oration – homily, sermon
preamble – introduction, preface, prelude, proem
prebellum–antewar
precarious – assumed, dubious, insecure, uncertain, unsettled, unstable
preceded – introduced, led, prefaced
preceded (in time)–anteceded, antedated
precedence–lead, pas, priority
precedence (right of)–pas
precedent–model, standard, usage
preceding (in time) – antecedent
preceding all others – first, lead
preceding by threes–ternary
precept–adage, axiom, command, commandment, direction, doctrine, law, lesson, mandate, maxim, order, principle, rule, tora, torah
precept (Brahmanism) – sutra
precept (Hebrew)–tora, torah
precept (mandatory)–writ
preceptor–instructor, teacher, tutor
precinct – ambit, boundary, district, environs
precious – costly, dear, rare, valuable, valued
precious (more)–dearer
precious stone–agate, beryl, diamond, emerald, gem, keas, naif, opal, pearl, ruby, sapphire, sard, topaz
precious stone (mentioned in Bible)–ligure
precipice – bluff, cliff, crag, declivity, linn, pali
precipitate – abrupt, hasty, heady, impetuous, rash, sudden
precipitation – acceleration, hastening, mist, rain
precipitation (gelatinous) – gel
precipitation (icy) – hail, sleet, snow
precipitous – abrupt, hasty, precipitate, rash, steep, sudden
precipitous rock–scar, steep
precis – abstract, epitome, summarize, summary
precise – accurate, ceremonious, correct, definite, exact, overnice, particular, prim, punctilious, scrupulous
precise (too)–overminute
preciseness – exactness, definiteness, strictness
precisian (conceited) – pedant
precision–accuracy, definiteness, exactness, nicety
preclude – avert, bar, close, debar, estop, hinder, impede, prevent, stop
preclude (law)–estop
preconceive–foreknow, ideate
precourse–forerun, herald
predatory–pillaging, piratical, plundering
predatory raid–foray
predestine – appoint, decree, determine, doom, fate, foreordain, ordain
predetermine – bias, destine, prejudice, preordain, prepossess
predicament – condition, dilemma, plight, quandary, scrape, situation, state
predicator–preacher, predictor, prophet, seer

predict – augur, bode, dope, forecast, foretell, omen, presage, prognosticate, prophesy, weird
prediction–augury, foreboding, prognostication, prophecy
predilection–bias, predisposition, preference, propensity
predominant – controlling, hegemonic, outstanding, reigning, ruling, superior
predominant idea–motive
predomination–prevalence
pree–prove, taste, try
preeminent–excellent, only, outstanding, ranking, star, superior
preemption–monopoly
preen–bodkin, brooch, clasp, pin, plume, sew, stitch
preface – exordium, foreword, front, herald, introduction, preamble, proem, prologue
prefect–director, magistrate, minister, officer, official, praefect, president
prefect (China)–Fu
prefect (Jesuit school)–dean
prefecture (Greek)–eparchy
prefecture (northeast)–Oita
prefer–choose, elect, select
preferably–rather
prefigure–foreshadow, foretell, ideate, type
prefix denoting—
    about–amb
    above–super, supra, sur
    across–dia, tran
    again–re
    against–anti, para
    ahead–pre
    alongside–para
    apart–dia, dis, se
    around–peri
    Austrian name–Von
    away–aph, apo
    back–re
    backward–retro
    bad–mal
    before – ante, prae, pre, pro
    between–dia, inter, meta
    black–atra

prefix denoting—cont.
chemical–para
Chinese–chino, sino
clear (biol.)–delo
dawn–eo
definite (biol.)–delo
difficult–dys
distant–tel, tele
double–di
down–de
earth–geo
equal–iso
equally–equi
evil–mal
false–pseudo
far–tel, tele
fictitious–pseudo
for–pro
former–ex
from–de
from away–apo
German name–Von
good–eu
half–demi, hemi, semi
ill–mal
in–en
in favor of–pro
into–en
many–multi, poly
modern–neo
mountain–oro
nail–helo
native–un
negative–il, ir, non, un
new–neo
not–il, im, ir, non, un
oil–ol
on this side–cis
one–mono, uni
one trillion–treg
out of–ect
outside–ect
over–super, supra, sur
partial–semi
possession–ose
priority–pre
relation to pharynx–lemo
reversal–di
separation–di, dis
shoulder–humero
son of–ap
ten–deca
this side of–cis
three–tri
thrice–ter, tri
through–dia

together–com, con, syn
toward–ob, oc
trice–ter, tri
twice–bi, di
two–bi
twofold–di
under–sub
upon–ep, epi
upward–ana, ano
very much–eri
well–eu
with–col, com, pro, syn
within–eso, intra
without–ect, ecto, se
wood–xylo
wrong–mis
prehistoric continent–Atlantis
prehistoric tool–eolith
preholiday period–eve
prejudiced–biased, bigoted, partial
prejudicial – disadvantageous, injurious
prelate–chief, head, superior
prelate (highest rank) – primate
prelector – lecturer, praelector, professor, reader
preliminary–antecedent, entrance, introduction, introductory, precedent, preface, prelude, preparatory, previous, prior, proemial, threshold
preliminary memorandum – protocol
preliminary plan–idea
prelude–introduction, overture, preface, proem
prelude (organ short)–verset
prelude (short vocal)–ritornel, ritornelle
premature – precocious, untimely
premature growth – precocity
premier – chief, leading, principal
premium–agio, bonus, prize, recompense, reward
premium (exchange)–agio
premonition – forewarning, information, notice, presentiment, warning

preoccupied – absent, absorbed, engrossed, filled
preparation (medical, pharmaceutical, obs.)–dia
preparation (sugar in candy)–fondant
preparation (wax)–cerate
preparation that burns without flame–punk
preparation of a corpse for internment–pollincture
prepare – adjust, arrange, equip, fit, fix, get, make ready, pave
prepare (old word)–yark
prepare by boiling–decoct
prepare copy for publication –edit
prepare for melting (as glass)–frit
prepare for printing–edit
prepare golf ball for drive–tee
prepare skins for gloves–taw
prepare with seasoning – marinate
prepared – adapted, armed, equipped, groomed, ready
prepared for a contest – trained
prepared instruction – propaedeutics
prepared sizes (of coal) – broken, chestnut, egg, stove
prepared skins–tawed
prepares flax–rets
prepares leather–tans
preponderous–weighty
prepose–preface, prefix
preposition – at, by, in, off, onto, out, over, to, upon, with
preposition (arch.)–unto
preposition (out)–ex
preposition (Scot.)–tae
prepossession – bent, bias, inclination, predilection, predisposition
presage – augury, betide, bode, foretell, omen, osse, portend, predict, preindicate, prognostic, sign, token
presbyter (4th century)–Arius

presbyter (old word) – prester
prescribe – control, guide,
limit, order, set
prescribing punishment –
penal
prescription (medical)–recipe
present – benefaction, boon,
bounty, donate, donation,
gift, give, grant, gratuity,
here, introduce, largess,
nonce, now, offer
present (from pupil to teacher)–minerval
present (to foreign ambassador)–xenium
present (to guest or stranger)–xenium
present day – contemporary,
current
present for acceptance – tender
present occasion–nonce
present time – nonce, now,
today
presently – anon, forthwith,
immediately, soon
presents in brief–sums
presents without warrant or
solicitation–obtrude
preservation – conservation,
safeguard,   safekeeping,
saving
preservative – alcohol, salt,
spice, vinegar
preserve – can, conserve,
corn, cure, defend, guard,
jam, jelly, keep, retain,
secure, shield, spare, store,
sustain, tin, uphold
preserve (fruit)–compote
preserve (grape)–uvate
preserve by drying–desiccate
preserve in brine–corn, cure,
salt
preserve in sugar–candy
preserved human in twilight
of gods–Lif
president – governor, head,
ruler, sovereign
president (Confederacy) –
Davis
President (U.S.)–(1, 1789–
97) George Washington;
(2, 1797–1801) John

Adams;   (3, 1801–09)
Thomas   Jefferson;   (4,
1809–17) James Madi-
son; (5, 1817–25) James
Monroe; (6, 1825–29)
John Quincy Adams; (7,
1829–37) Andrew Jack-
son; (8, 1837–41) Martin
Van Buren; (9, 1841)
William Henry Harrison;
(10, 1841–45) John Ty-
ler; (11, 1845–49) James
K. Polk; (12, 1849–50)
Zachary   Taylor;   (13,
1850–53) Millard Fill-
more; (14, 1853–57)
Franklin Pierce; (15,
1857–61) James Buchan-
an; (16, 1861–65) Abra-
ham Lincoln; (17, 1865–
69) Andrew Johnson;
(18, 1869–77) Ulysses S.
Grant;   (19,   1877–81)
Rutherford B. Hayes; (20,
1881) James A. Garfield;
(21, 1881–85) Chester A.
Arthur; (22, 1885–89)
Grover   Cleveland;   (23,
1889–93) Benjamin Har-
rison; (24, 1893–97) Gro-
ver Cleveland; (25, 1897–
1901) William McKinley;
(26, 1901–09) Theodore
Roosevelt; (27, 1909–13)
William H. Taft; (28,
1913–21) Woodrow Wil-
son; (29, 1921–23) War-
ren G. Harding; (30,
1923–29) Calvin Cool-
idge; (31, 1929–33) Her-
bert Hoover; (32, 1933–)
Franklin D. Roosevelt
presidente–headman, mayor
presiding officer–chairman,
speaker
press – compress, cram,
crowd, force, impress,
iron, squeeze, urge
press (bookbinder)–smasher
press corrector–proofreader
press critic (official)–censor
press for payment–dun
press forward–drive
pressed amber–amberoid
pressed cheese–cheddar

pressed grape residue–marc,
mark
pressed together – compact,
crowded, dense, serried
presses closely and painfully
–mash
presses together (firmly) –
impacts, serry
pressing – exacting, exigent,
importunate, urgent
pressing into a mass–kneading
pressing need–exigency
pressure – compression, constraint, exigency, force,
squeeze, stress
pressure (one of dyne) –
barad
pressure (resisting)–renitent
pressure boiler–autoclave
pressure cooker–autoclave
pressure measuring instrument–piezometer
pressure of necessity–urgency
pressure unit–barad
prest – advance, enlist, hasten, hire, lend, loan, prepared, prompt, quick,
quickly, readily, ready,
soon
prester – hurricane, serpent,
vein, whirlwind
prestezza – celerity, quickness
prestidigitator – cheat, conjurer, juggler, magician
prestige–deception, illusion,
influence, sorcery
presto–immediately, instantaneous, passing, quickly,
suddenly
presumably–probably
presume–impose, suppose
presumption – audacity, impudence, insolence
presumptive – apriori, arrogant
presumptuous – arrogant,
foolhardy,   forward,
haughty, venturesome
pretend–act, assume, claim,
feign, profess, sham, simulate
pretend to attack–feint

pretended – intended, ostensible, proposed

pretended omission–paralepsis, paralipsis

pretender–charlatan, claimant, cowan, idol, impostor, quack, seemer, snob

pretender (boastful, unscrupulous)–mountebank

pretender (Scot.)–cowan

pretender (vulgar)–snob

pretender to inspiration–eolist

pretense–affectation, appearance, artifice, cloak, cover, excuse, fabrication, feint, ostentation, pretext, ruse, sham, show, stalking-horse, study, subterfuge, tinsel

pretense (false)–flam

pretensions (false)–mountebank

pretentious – ostentatious, pompous, showy

pretentious (coll.)–arty

pretermit – intermit, interrupt, neglect, omit, suspend

pretext–cover, deception, excuse, flam, plea, pretence, pretense, semblance, trick

prettikin–feat, trick

pretty – attractive, bonnie, bonny, clever, comely, ingenious, knickknack, toy

pretty (attractive, small, coll.)–cute

prevail – frequent, induce, predominate, prevalent, succeed, triumph, win

prevail in–obtain

prevail upon – fold, induce, persuade

prevail without restraint – rage

prevailed – succeeded, triumphed, urged, won

prevailing – common, current, extensive, general, predominant, predominantly, prevalent, rife, widespread

prevalent–dominant, efficacious, influential, potent,

powerful, rife, successful, victorious

prevaricate–evade, lie, quibble, shuffle

prevene–anticipate, forestall, prevent

prevent–avert, circumvent, debar, deter, forestall, frustrate, preclude, warn

prevent by authority–debar

prevent legally–estop

preventative–deterrent

preventative for scurvy–antiscorbutic

previous – before, earlier, foregoing, former, preceding, premature, prior, untimely, unwarranted

previous to church council–antenicene

previously (arch.)–erst

previously mentioned–aforesaid, said

prey – booty, plunder, quarry, spoil

prey (living on)–raptorial

prey upon–raven, ravin, ravine

Priam's and Hecuba's daughter – Cassandra, Creusa, Polyxena

Priam's and Hecuba's son–Deiphobus, Hector, Helenus, Paris, Polydorus, Troilus

Priam's servant–Agelaus

Priam's wife–Hecuba

price – charge, cost, estimation, excellence, expense, fare, preciousness, rate, value, worth

price for keeping goods in warehouse–storage

prick painfully–sting

pricked – dotted, pinked, pointed, punctured

prickle – acantha, aculeus, pierce, prod, seta, tingle

prickle (slender, straight) – seta

prickly (like a hedgehog)–echinate

prickly flower–burr

prickly pear–nopal, opuntia, tuna

prickly plant–thistle

prickly sensation–tingle

prickly shrub–briar

pries into another's affairs–snoops

priest – abbe, cleric, clerk, druid, father, oratorian, padre

priest (British order, anc.)–druid

priest (French)–pere

priest (high)–Eli

priest (high, who trained Samuel)–Eli

priest (Jewish)–Cohen, Kohen

priest (Maori)–tuhunga

priest (newly ordained) – priesteen

priest (old word)–prester

priest (parish)–father, papa

priest (Spanish)–padre

priest (Tibetan)–lama

priest (young) – priesteen, priestling

priest in the pulpit–cuckoopint

priestess–vestal

priestly–sacerdotal

priestly cap–biretta

priestly Israel tribe–Levi

priestly vestment–alb, ephod

priests (pert. to)–sacerdotal

priest's assistant–acolyte

priest's collar (white)–amice

priest's garment (working)–scapular

priest's habit ornament – Urim

priest's hood–cuckoopint

priest's mantle–cope

priest's neckpiece – amice, stole

priest's ornament–Urim

priest's scarf–maniple, rabat

priest's surplice–ephod

priest's vestment–alb, cope, ephod, scapular

prig – bargain, beg, buck, dandy, entreat, filch, fog, haggle, pan, pilfer, pilferer, pitcher, plead, prink, purist, steal, thief, tinker

priggish–prim

prill – button, nugget, rill, stream

prim – decorous, demure,

neat, precise, prudish, smelt

prima donna–diva

primal – elemental, first, original, primary, primitive

primary – elemental, first, fundamental, initial, primal, prime, primeval, primitive, primordial, pristine

primary cortex–periblem

primate – ape, lemur, marmoset, monkey

prime – first, original, primary, primeval, primitive

prime minister–premier

prime number – eleven, seven

primer (child's)–hornbook

primeval deity–Titan

primitive – aboriginal, ancient, antiquated, first, priscan, pristine

primitive art products–artifacts

primness–neatness, niceness, preciseness, stiffness

primp–dress, preen, prink

primrose–cowslip, rimula

primrose family – primulaceae

prince – dynasty, monarch, sovereign

prince (diminutive)–princekin

prince (little)–princeling

prince (petty) – princelet, princeling, satrap

Prince Charlie's name (last) –Stuart

prince of apostate angels–Eblis

prince of Apostles–St. Paul, St. Peter

prince of darkness – Ahriman, devil, Satan

prince of demons – Beelzebub, devil

prince of destruction–Tamerlane

prince of evil–Satan

prince of liars–Pinto

Prince of Peace–Jesus Christ

prince of the church–cardinal

prince of the ode–Ronsard

prince of the power of the air–Satan

prince of the sonnet – Joachim de Bellay

prince of this world–Satan

prince of Tunis–bey

prince's allowance – appenage

prince's pine–pipsissewa

princedom – jurisdiction, rank, sovereignty

princely – kingly, magnificent, munificent, noble, regal

princely Italian family–Este

princess (loved by Zeus) – Europa

princess (Mohammedan) – begum

princess (mythological)–Atalanta

princess of Argos–Danae

princess of Tyre–Dido

principal – arch, captain, chief, foremost, head, important, leader, leading, main, major, outstanding, primary, prime, top

principal (of school) – preceptor

principal meal (Roman, anc.)–cena

principality (independent)–Monaco

principle–prana, tenet

principle (active tobacco) – nicotine

principle (dogmatic) – dictum, dicta (pl.)

principle (established)–canon

principle (governing)–hinge

principle (Hindu, female)–Sakti

principle (life, theosophy) – prana, tenet

principle (tobacco, active) – nicotine

principle (vital)–anima, soul

principle of key in music–tonality

principle of science (basic)–logic

principles (general)–generalia, generalities

principles (summary of) – creed

princox–coxcomb

prink – bedeck, deck, dress, glance, preen, primp, wink

print – engrave, impress, stamp

printed defamation–libel

printed fabric–percale

printed within text of page–letin

printed work (few sheets unbound)–pamphlet

printer–lithographer, typographer

printer's aid–devil

printer's dauber–biron

printer's direction (let it stand)–stet

printer's faux pas–pies

printer's hand roller–brayer

printer's implement–biron

printer's ink pad–dabber

printer's ink spreader–brayer

printer's inking department –biron

printer's manuscript–copy

printer's mark–caret, dash, stet, tilde

printer's measure – em, empen, en, pica

printer's photoengraving – heliotypography

printer's term–stet

printing (blurred appearance in)–macul

printing cylinder–rounce

printing direction–stet

printing error – erratum, errata (pl.)

printing for the blind – braille

printing form–die

printing hand instrument – brayer

printing mark – diesis, ellipses

printing measure–agate, em, empen, en

printing metal block–quad

printing mistake – erratum, errata (pl.)

printing necessity–ink

printing plate (short for)–stereo
printing press handle–rounce
printing press part – frisket, platen, rounce
printing process–lithograph
printing process of engraving–cerotype
printing system for blind–braille
prion–petrel
prior – antecedent, before, fore, former, preceding, previous
prior time–past
prior to–before, ere
priory–cloister
priscan–primitive
Priscian – grammar, grammarian
Priscilla's (Mullen) husband –John Alden
Priscilla's lover–Miles Standish
prismatic–iridescent
prison – Bridewell, brig, clink, gaol, guardhouse, jail, jug, keep, kidcote, penitentiary, quod
prison (federal) – Alcatraz, Atlanta
prison (Fr., former)–Bastille
prison (German university student's)–carcer
prison (guarded from one central point)–panopticon
prison (naval)–brig
prison (Roman, anc.)–carcer
prison (slang) – big house, cooler, hoosegow, limbo, quod, rock, stir
prison (Spanish)–carcel
prison courtyard–quad
prison keeper–gaoler, guard, jailer, jailor, keeper, turnkey, warden
prison spy–mouton
prisoner–captive
Prisoner of the Vatican – Pope
Prisoner of Zenda author–Anthony Hope
prisoner's pledge of honor–parole
pristine – original, primary, primitive

pritch–offense, pique
privacy – retreat, seclusion, solitude
privacy of life or condition–privity
private–confidential, esoteric
private entrance–postern
Private Life of Helen of Troy author–Erskine
privateer – caper, corsair, Kidd, pirate
privately–aside, secret, unofficial
privation–loss, misery, want
privilege–advantage, charter, concession, favor, right, use
privilege (legal)–easement
privilege (old English law) –soc
privilege (special)–charter
privilege of jurisdiction–soc
prix–prize
prize–award, esteem, premium, purse, stake, treasure, value
prize (Harvard scholarship) –Detur
prize (lottery)–tern
prize (race)–medal, plate
prize contended for in contests–cup, medal
prize fight–bout, contest, go
prize fight patron's desire–K.O.
prize ring–arena
pro–for
probabilities – chances, conclusions, credibility, likelihoods, likeliness, odds
probe–examine, instrument, scrutinize, search
probe (slender) – seeker, tracer
probe (surgical)–stylet, tent
probity – honesty, rectitude, uprightness
problem – crux, knot, nut, question, riddle, situation
problem (perplexing)–crux, knot
problem (subsidiary)–rider
proboscis–nose, snout, trunk
proboscis monkey–noseape
procaccia–carrier, post

procacious – insolent, pert, petulant
procavia–hyracoidea, hyrax
procedure – continuance, order, process, step, system
procedure (orderly)–method, system
procedure (secret)–stealth
proceed–advance, arise, continue, derive, emanate, fare, go, issue, move, originate, pass, progress, wend
proceed hastily–speed
proceed leisurely (slang) – mosy
proceed on one's way–wend
proceed rapidly–gallop
proceeded on–wended
proceeding–conduct, course, measure, procedure, step, transaction
proceeding (from the earth) –telluric
proceeding (from the sun)–solar
proceeding (recorded) – actum, acta (pl.)
proceeding by threes – ternary
proceedings–acta, doings
proceedings (court)–trial
proceeds–goes, income, profits, returns
proceeds (it, music)–va
procerity–height, tallness
process – advance, cook, course, lapse, mandate, notice, order, procedure, progress, sterilize, summons, writ
process (bear-like, small) – rostrulum
process (elementary mathematical)–division
process (fish wing-like)–fin
process (of development) – nascent
process (small pointed)–awn
process for coloring fabrics–batik
process in organism–meiosis, miosis
process in steel making – Bessemer
process of adjustment–pend

process of decision (be in)–pend

process of electroplating metal (with steel or iron) –acierage

process of making steel–cementation

process of promoting growth –nutrition

process of scraping (rare)–raison

process of transferring pictures–decalcomania

process used in surveying–triangulation

procession–cortege, file, formation, parade

prochein–nearest, next

proclaim – announce, blaze, declare, herald, promulgate, publish, tout, voice

proclaim (aloud)–roar

proclaim (formally) – enounce

proclamation – blaze, edict, notice, publication, ukase

proclamation (official)–promulgation

proclamation (public) – banns, bans

proclamation (wedding) – banns, bans

proclivity–bent, disposition, inclination, leaning, propensity

Procne's husband–Tereus

procrastinate – defer, delay, postpone, soldier, stall

procrastination–delay, dilatoriness

procrastinator–deferrer, delayer

procreant–fruitful, generating, producing

procreated–begat, begot, engendered, sired

procurator (Judean)–Pilate

procure–acquire, bring, contrive, effect, gain, get, obtain

prod–egg, goad, jab, poke, urge

prodigal – extravagant, lavish, spender, spendthrift, squanderer, squandering

prodigality – extravagance, waste

prodigious–amazing, astonishing, enormous, extraordinary, huge, monstrous, portentous, tremendous

prodigy – marvel, miracle, omen, sign, wonder

prodition–betrayal, treason

produce–carry, cause, create, effect, engender, exhibit, generate, make, originate, show, stage, yield

produce an audible effect–sound

produce an effect–act

produce an idea–ideate

produce copy of–type

produced by action of intense heat–igneous

produced by igneous action–volcanic

produced by the wind–aeolian, eolian

produced in a kitchen garden–olitory

produced regularly–staple

producer–farmer, manufacturer, parent

producing illusions–phantasmagorial

producing poison–septic

producing small particles of fire–sparking

product–fruit

product (new)–creation

product (petroleum, between gasoline and cymogene)–rhigolene

product of cotton fiber used as sizing–viscose

production – fruit, performance, produce, work

production (carefully wrought)–elaboration

production (remarkable) – creation

production (successful)–hit

productive–creative, fertile, fruitful, generative, rich

productive of sound vibrations–sonorous

products (chemical, of organs)–hormones

products (impure metallic)–mattes

products of primitive art–artifacts

proem – foreword, introduction, preamble, preface, prelude

profane–desecrate, godless, temporal, ungodly, unhallowed, unholy, unsanctified, wicked, worldly

professed – acknowledged, avowed, claimed, declared, ostensible

profession – calling, metier, occupation, trade

profession (French)–metier

professional–expert, finished, hired, paid, skilled, trained

professional (non)–laic, lay

proffer – bid, give, offer, tender

proficient–adept, apt, expert, skilled, versed

profile–contour, form, representation

profit – avail, benefit, boot, gain, interest, mend, net, return

profitable – beneficial, helpful, lucrative, paying, repaying, useful

profligate – abandoned, corrupt, depraved, reprobate, spender, vicious

profound – deep, far-reaching, recondite, unfathomable

profuse–bountiful, extravagant, galore, lavish, liberal, munificent, overflowing, prodigal, wasteful

profuse (recklessly)–prodigal

profuse talk–palaver

progenitor–ancestor, forefather, parent, sire

progenitor of giants (Norse myth.)–Ymir

progenitors (immediate) – parents

progeny–children, daughter, descendants, family, issue, offspring, race, seed, son

prognostic – forecast, omen, portent, presage, prophecy, sign, token

prognosticate–betoken, bode,

forebode, foreshow, foretell, foretoken, presage, predict, prophesy
prognosticator–diviner, seer
program – bulletin, card, edict, notice, outline, proclamation, prospectus, syllabus
programma – decree, edict, preface, prolegomenon
progress – advance, course, expedition, fare, journey, march, tour, wend
progress (clumsily)–scramble
progress (intelligently planned and directed) – telesia, telesis
progress (laboriously)–plod, wade
progress hindered by lack of wind–becalm
progression (degree of) – stage
progressive – advancing, enterprising, forward, onward
prohibit – bar, bid, debar, estop, forbid, hinder, interdict, prevent, stop, taboo, tabu, veto
prohibited–illegal, illicit, unlawful
prohibition – ban, estoppel, interdicting
prohibition (legal)–estoppel
prohibitionist–dry
project – abut, beetle, contrive, design, device, idea, intention, jet, jut, pattern, plan, proposal, protrude, scheme, shoot
projectile–missile, shot
projectile (cigar-shaped explosive)–torpedo
projectile (explosive)–bomb, bullet, cartridge, shell
projectile (high explosive)–bomb
projectile (lead)–bullet
projectile curve–parabola
projecting–beetle, salient
projecting arm from moving part–tappet
projecting member – socle, tenon

projecting part–apse
projecting pedestal–socle
projecting point–jag
projection–arm, bulge, hob, lee, lobe, protuberance, tappet, toe
projection (cam wheel)–lobe
projection (coastal) – cape, headland, ness
projection (curved, hooking)–barb
projection (rounded)–lobel, lobule, teeth
projection (sharp, of an object)–fang
projection (wall)–redan
projection on piece of timber–tenon
projet–draft, plan
prolific–fecund, fertile, fruitful, generative, reproductive
prolix – diffuse, prolonged, protracted, tiresome, verbose, wearisome, wordy
prolocutor – mouthpiece, speaker, spokesman
prolonged–chronic, continued, delayed, extended, lengthened, postponed, protracted
promenade–alameda, mall, marina, pasear, walk
promenade (Spanish)–pasear
promenade (tree-lined) – Alameda
Prometheus' father–Iapetus
Prometheus' mother–Clymene
prominence – cusp, distinction, eminence, prestige, salience
prominent–celebrated, conspicuous, distinctive, distinguished, manifest, marked, noticeable, obvious, salient
promise–assurance, betroth, declaration, engage, parole, pledge, plight, vow
promise (good)–hope
promise (or vow, old word)–hote
promise (solemn)–oath, vow
promise by vow–votive
promise marriage–affiance

promontory – cape, headland, mount, ness, point, scaw, skaw
promontory (var.)–nase
promote – advance, dignify, elevate, exalt, help, nurse, patronize, prefer
promoter–agent
promoter (business)–ad
promotion–advance, brevet, preferment
promotion of Christianity–irenics
prompt–alert, animate, cue, expeditious, punctual, ready, remind
prompt (arch.)–yare
prompter–aid, readier
promptest–readiest
promptly (Scot.)–tite
promulgate – declare, proclaim, publish
prone–apt, bent, flat, prostrate
prone (face downward) – prostrate
prone (face upward)–supine
prone to servile imitation–apish
prong–fork, nib, peg, tang, tine, tooth
prong (antler)–tine
prong (fork)–tine
prong buck – pronghorn, springbok
prong key–spanner
pronoun–he, it, itself, my, myself, them, they, this, thou, thy, we, ye, you, your
pronoun (demonstrative) – this
pronoun (intensive)–itself, myself
pronoun (interrogative) – who
pronoun (old)–thine, thy, ye
pronoun (possessive) – her, his, mine, my, ones, our, ours, their, your
pronoun (substantive)–who
pronounce–announce, articulate, declare, deliver, enunciate, speak, utter
pronounce holy–bless

pronounce with hissing sound–assibilate

pronouncement – announcement, declaration

pronouncement (public) – manifesto

pronto – promptly, quick, quickly

pronunciation (correct)–orthoepy

pronunciation (dialectic) – burr

pronunciation mark–dieresis, tilde

pronunciation mark (Span.) –tilde

proof – confirmation, evidence, outcome, result, test, verification

proofreader's direction–stet

proofreader's mark – caret, dele, stet

proofreader's mark (small letter)–l.c.

prop – fulcrum, leg, nog, shore, shorer, sprag, staff, support

prop (mine)–sprag

prop (Scot.)–stell

propagate – breed, diffuse, generate, increase, multiply

propago–bulblet, layer

propel – drive, impel, pole, project, row, urge

propeller – driver, fan, oar, screw, vane

propeller (air)–fan

propeller (ship's)–screw

propelling device–gun

propensity–bent, inclination, proclivity, proneness

proper–appropriate, chaste, decent, excellent, fine, fit, honest, meet, prim, respectable, suitable

proper (is)–beseem, fit

proper (stiffly)–prim

proper condition (coll.) – kilter

proper order–kilter

proper sense of dignity – pride

proper sense of worth–pride

properly–correctly, decently,

fitly, rightly, strictly, suitably

property – attribute, bona, characteristic, estate, gear, goods, holding, possessions, realty, wealth

property (act to regain) – repleven, replevin

property (bride's to husband)–dos

property (entirely one's own)–alodium

property (item of)–asset

property (landed)–estate

property (law)–res

property (movable)–chattel, gear

property (one who takes over transferred)–alienee

property (personal)–chattel, gear

property (Roman law)–bona

property (stolen)–loot, lucre, pelf, spoil

property (suit for)–trover

property (wanton destruction of)–sabotage

property (woman's absolute, Hindu)–stridhan, stridhana, stridhanum

property of emitting light without sensible heat – phosphorescence

property of matter–inertia

property right–lien

property transferrer–alienor

prophecy–oracle, utterance

prophecy (pert. to)–vaticinal

prophesied – doped, forecasted, foretold, predicted

prophesies–dopes, forecasts, foretells, predicts

prophesy – augur, foreshow, foretell, osse, predict, preindicate, presage, prognosticate

prophet–mantis, oracle, seer, soothsayer

prophet (biblical) – Amos, Elijah, Hosea, Syrus

prophet (carried to heaven in chariot of fire)–Elias, Elijah

prophet (minor) – Amos, Hosea

prophet (Mormon) – John Smith

prophet (Moslem)–Mohammed

prophet (of the restoration)–Malachi

prophet (Old Testament)–Hosea

prophet (pert. to)–vatic, vatical

prophetess–Sibyl

prophetic – fateful, mantic, oracular, vatic

prophetic sign–omen

prophetical–vatic, vatical

propinquity–kinship, nearness, neighborhood, proximity, relationship

propitiate–conciliate, pacify

propitiation–atonement, expiation, reconciliation, satisfaction

propitious – advantageous, auspicious, benign, favorable, happy, lucky, opportune, promising, prosperous

proponent of penny postage –Hill

proportion–prorate, rate, ratio

proportion to (in)–ratio

proportional amount–rate

proportionately–adequately

proportioned suitably–commensurable

proposal–bid, feeler, motion, proposition, suggestion

proposal (tentative)–feeler

propose a health–toast

proposed for consideration–suggested

proposed for debate–mooted

proposed international language–ido, od, ro

proposition – corollary, porism, project, undertaking

proposition (antecedent) – premise

proposition (tentative) – feeler

proposition assumed to be true logic–lemma

proposition founded on experience–empirema

proposition leading to a conclusion–premise
propped up–shored
proprietary right–interest
proprietor–owner
propriety–decency, decorum,
possessorship
propugnaculum – bulwark,
defense, fortress
propugnator–defender, vindicator
prorogue–adjourn, defer, extend, postpone, prolong,
protract
prosaic – drab, flat, humdrum, insipid, matter-of-
fact, prolix, prosy, stupid,
tedious, tiresome, unex-
citing, unimaginative
proscribe–ban, interdict, ostracize, outlaw, prohibit
proscribing (act of)–outlawry
prosecute – enforce, pursue,
sue, urge
prosecute at law–sue
prosecutor–relator
proselyte–convert
proselyte (Judea)–ger
proseuche (proseucha)–oratory, synagogue
Prosimiae (Prosimian)–Le-
muroidea
prospect – applicant, buyer,
candidate,   contestant,
customer, outlook, scene,
view, vista
prosper–cheve, fare, flourish,
speed, succeed, thrive
prosperity–boom, hap, success, thrift, ups, weal, welfare, well-being
prosperous – auspicious, fortunate, flourishing, lucky,
palmy, sonsie, sonsy, successful, thriving
prosperous periods–ups
prosperous state–weal
prostitute – corrupt, drab,
harlot, infamous, street-
walker, venal, whore
prostrate – flat, flattened,
helpless, prone, recum-
bent, supine
prostrating–felling

prosy–dry, dull, jejune, pro-
siac, tedious
protagonist–contender, hero,
leader, principal
protasis–introduction, maxim, proposition
protect – arm, cherish, defend, guard, police, pre-
serve, save, screen, shelter,
shield
protect against loss–insure
protect with covering –
sheath
protected–aproned, guarded,
shielded
protecting a person or thing
–tutelar, tutelary
protecting covering–armor
protecting influence–aegis
protection–aegis, apron, armor, bib, defense, egis,
fort, guard, lee, parapet,
preservation, safety, se-
curity, shelter
protection (for neck from
sun)–havelock
protective coat–armor
protective covering–apron,
armor, bib, shell
protective ditch–moat
protective garment – apron,
bib, smock
protective influence – aegis,
egis
protective slope–glacis
protector–defender, guardian, patron
protector of vineyards and
gardens–Priapus
protege–ward
proteid (bacteria destroying)
–alexin
proteid (of bean family) –
legumelin
proteid body–albumin
proteida family – necturus,
proteus, typhlomolge
protein (granular)–aleurone
protein (in castor oil bean)–
ricin
protein (in cereal seeds) –
edestin
protein (in milk)–casein
protein (in muscles) – crea-
tine
protein (in seeds)–prolamin

protein (in wheat, rye, etc.)–
mucedin
protein (of the blood)–fibrin
protein (of the egg)–albumin
proteins (group of)–globu-
lin
protest – assert, asseverate,
aver, declare, deny, stipulate
protest (kindly)–expostula-
tion
protest (slang)–beef, holler
protest against–testify
Proteus–Olm
protogonous–primal
protograph–holograph
protoplasmic – archetypal,
primordial
protoplasmic body (outer
layer)–ectoplasm
protoplasmic cell–ameba
protoplasmic substance–gel
protozoans (order of)–lobosa
protozoans (parasitic)–ameba, amoeba, amoebida
protract–continue, elongate,
extend, lengthen, prolong,
spin
protracted–extended, long,
spun
protrude–bulge, exsert, jut,
project
protuberance – boss, bulge,
bump, hump, knot, lobe,
node, nub, projection,
snag, wen
protuberance (at base of
bird's bill)–cere
protuberance (at base of
skull)–inion
protuberance (aural)–lobe
protuberance (knob-like) –
caput
protuberance (occipital)–inion
protuberance (rounded) –
umbo
protuberance (skin)–mole,
wart
protuberance (skull) – inia,
inial, inion
protuberant–bottled, prominent, swelling
protuberant (regularly)–convex

protuberant part–boss, bulge

proud–arrogant, conceited, elated, gratified, haughty, imposing, impressive, independent, lofty, noble, supercilious, vain, valiant

prove – ascertain, confirm, demonstrate, establish, evince, justify, manifest, test, try, verify

prove (as a will)–nurse, probate

proved to be false–refuted

provender – fodder, food, hay, provisions

proverb – adage, aphorism, axiom, maxim, saw, saying

proverbial – aphoristic, sententious

provide–cater, furnish, stock, store, supply ,

provide food–cater, ration

provide force–man

provide free entertainment–treat

provide meals for – cater, mess

provide with weathercock–vane

provided–afforded, boden, if, sobeit, supplied

provided that–if, so

provident – frugal, prudent thrifty

province – area, arena, district, domain, nome, range, shire, tract

province (imperial palace officer's)–palatinate

province (metropolitan) – eparch

provincial – crude, insular, narrow, rude, uncultured, unsophisticated

provincial dialect–patois

provision–board, fare, food, stock, store

provision seller (to troops)–sutler

provisional – aeolian, tentative

provisionally–conditionally

provisions–cates, food, terms, viands

provisions (in general)–cate, chow

provisions (search for)–forage

proviso–clause, salvo

provoke–anger, bate, challenge, exasperate, incite, invite, invoke, irritate, nettle, spur, start, stir, summon, vex

provoking laughter–risible

prow–beak, benefit, brave, courage, duty, gallant, good, honor, prowess, stem, valiant

prow (ship's, obs.)–steven

prow (ship's, poetic)–prore

proximate – closest, direct, immediate, nearest, next

proximity–adjacence, closeness, nearness, nighness, vicinity

proxy–agency, agent, deputy, proctor, procurator, substitute

prudence – calculation, caution, circumspection, foresight, forethought, sagacity

prudent – canny, cautious, circumspect, considerate, discreet, economical, frugal, provident, wary, wise

prudish–prim

prune – anoint, clip, cut, dress, lop, plum, plume, preen, purge, simpleton, tonsure, trim

prune (imperfectly ripened) –frog

prune (var.)–rasee

prune-like fruit–myrobalan

Prussian bay–Danzig, Kiel, Pomeranian

Prussian cathedral city–Essen

Prussian cavalryman–uhlan, ulan

Prussian city–Aachen, Berlin (c.), Breslau, Charlottenburg, Cologne, Dusseldorf, Essen, Frankfort, Hanover, Kiel, Konigsberg, Magdeburg, Stettin

Prussian district–Stettin

Prussian government (Rhine province)–Aachen

Prussian haff – Friche, Kurische, Pommerische

Prussian island–Frisian, Rugen, Usedom, Wollin

Prussian lagoons–haffs

Prussian lancer–uhlan, ulan

Prussian measure – fuder, fuss, meile, morgen, oxhoft, rute, scheffel, zoll

Prussian mountain – Harz, Riesengebirge, Schneekoppe, Sudetic

Prussian province – Berlin, Brandenburg, Hanover, Hesse-Nassau, Hohenzollern, Pomerania, Posen, Prussia (East, West), Rhineland, Saxony, Schleswig-Holstein, Silesia, Westphalia

Prussian resort–Ems

Prussian river–Alle, Eder, Elbe, Ems, Memel, Niemen, Oder, Passarge, Pregel, Saar, Vistula, Weichsel, Weser

Prussian seaport – Emden, Kiel

Prussian university town – Halle

Prussian watering place – Ems

Prussian weight – mark, quentchen

prussic acid discoverer – Scheele

pry–lever, mouse, nose

prying–curious, inquisitive, peeping, peering

psalm (after matin)–laud

Psalm (98th)–Cantate

Psalm (95th)–Venite

psalm (opening communion, Anglican Church) – introit

psalm (penitential, most commonly used)–Miserere

psalmist–cantor, precentor

Psalms (book of)–Psalter

Psalms (Old Testament) – Psalter

psalterium–lyra, manyplies, omasum

psammite–sandstone

pseudo – counterfeit, false, feigned, pretender, sham, spurious
pseudologist–liar
pseudology–falsehood, lying
pseudonym–alias, anonym, anonyme
psittaceous–parrotlike
psychic emanation – aura, aurae (pl.)
psychologist (Fr.)–Binet
psychotic–insane, mad
ptarmigan (northern)–ripa
pteroid–fernlike, winglike
ptisan–tea, tisane
Ptolemy's astronomy work–almagest
pubble–fat, plump
public–inn, open, state
public (not) – hidden, personal, private, secret
public (pert. to)–cameral
public building – capitol, hotel, inn
public conveyance–bus, cab, car, jinricksha, jinrikisha, omnibus, ricksha, rickshaw, taxi, train, tram
public demand–cry
public display (practice of making)–exhibitionism
public edict–ban
public entertainment (18th century)–ridotto
public esteem–repute
public hangman–Jack Ketch
public life course–career
public notice – ad, notice, sign
public office–post
public official–notary
public park–commons
public performer–artiste
public proclamation–edict
public recreation grounds – park
public service–utility
public square – commons, plaza
public storehouse–etape
public tract–commons, parc, park
public vehicle–bus, cab, car, omnibus, jinricksha, jinrikisha, ricksha, rickshaw, taxi, train, tram

public walk–alameda, esplanade, mall, promenade
public warehouse–etape
public way–highway, road
publication – notification, proclamation, promulgation
publication (condensed) – tabloid
publication (make-up of) – format
publication (periodical) – bulletin
publication (preliminary) – prodromus
publication article (prominent)–feature
publicist – journalist, solon, writer
publish–blazon, delate, disseminate, divulge, edit, issue, print, vent
publish abroad–promulge
publish far and wide–blazon
publish without authority–pirate, plagiarize
published after death of author–posthumous
publisher–journalist, issuer, printer
publisher's inscription at end of book–colophon
publisher's summary of a book–blurb
pucker–contract, purse
puckered–bullate
puckfist–puffball
puckneedle–alfilaria
pud–forefoot, hand, paw
pudding–dessert, duff, mush
pudding (hasty)–mush
pudding (paste with fruit)–roly-poly
puddle–plash, plashet, plud, pond, pool, swamp
puddock – buzzard, enclosure, kite, toad
pudgy and short–roly-poly
Pueblo Indian–Hopi
Pueblo Indian ceremonial chamber–kiva
puerile – babyish, childish, juvenile, trivial, weak, youthful
Puerto Principe–Camaguey

Puerto Rico (conqueror of) –Miles
Puerto Rico bark–mabi
Puerto Rico beverage–mabi
Puerto Rico capital – San Juan
Puerto Rico city–Ponce
Puerto Rico dove (ground)–rola
Puerto Rico fish–sama
Puerto Rico harbor–Arecibo, Mayaguez, Ponce, San Juan de Porto Rico
Puerto Rico island–Mona
Puerto Rico measure–caballeria, cuerda
Puerto Rico porkfish–sisi
Puerto Rico tree (fustic) – mora
puff–blow, chug, flan, gust, pant, waff
puff (in hair dress)–pouf
puff (Scot., var.)–pegh
puff of wind (Scot.)–flam
puff out–blub
puff up–elate
puffbird–barbet
pug–bargeman, chaff, dog, elf, harlot, hobgoblin, mistress, puck, pugilist, refuse, sprite
pug dog's tail–twist
pug-nosed–camus
pugging–grasping, thieving
puggy (Scot.)–monkey
pugilist–boxer, fighter
pugilist's handler–second
pugilistic–fistic
pugnacious – belligerent, quarrelsome
puisne–feeble, judge, junior, later, petty, puny, subordinate, subsequent, unskilled
puissance – force, might, power, strength
puissant – forcible, mighty, potent, powerful
puke–vomit
pulchritude – beauty, loveliness
pule–cheep, peep, whimper, whine
pulicat–bandanna
puling – babyish, childish, delicate, sickly, whining

pull – arrest, drag, draw, haul, lug, tow, tweak, yank
pull (naut.)–heave
pull (with force)–lug, tug
pull after–tow
pull apart–rend, tear
pull away – remove, withdraw, wrest
pull down – demolish, destroy
pull laboriously–lug, tug
pull off–avulse, pug
pull one's freight – depart, leave
pull one's leg–deceive, hoax, hoodwink
pull out–extract
pull suddenly–yank
pull up–elate, trice
pulled (naut.)–hove
pullet (sterilized)–poullard
pulley–sheave
pulley (grooved)–fusee, fuzee
pulley block end–arse
pulley block part–arse
pulley groove–gorge
pulley wheel–sheave
Pullman–sleeper
pulp–pap
pulp (fruit)–pap
pulp (pressed fruit)–marc
pulpit–desk, platform, scaffold, stage
pulpit (Christian early) – ambo
pulpit (early)–ambo
pulpit (early church)–bema
pulpit (large)–ambo
pulpit (raised, large)–ambo
pulpy dregs–magma
pulpy fruit – pome, sidder, siddow, uva
pulpy state–mash
pulsate–beat, throb
pulsation – ictus, moving, throbbing, vibrating
pulsation (of an artery)–ictus
pulsative–beating, pulsatile, throbbing
pulsatory – rhythmic, systaltic, throbbing
pulse–battuta, sphygmus
pulverize – atomize, bray, crush, grind, mull, triturate
pulverize (by grinding) – comminute, triturate
pulverize (thoroughly)–triturate
pulverize (to smooth powder) levigate
pulverulent–dusty
puma–cougar
pummel–batter, beat, hammer, maul, thump
pump (hydraulic)–ram
pump (vacuum) – pulsometer
pump (windmill)–gin
pump handle–sweep, swipe
pumper (vinegar)–racker
pumpernickel–bread
pumpkin head – blockhead, dolt
pumpkin seed–sunfish
pun – assonance, paragram, paronomasia
punch – beverage, douse, drink, paste, perforate, pierce, poke, prod, puncture
punch (etcher's)–mattoir
Punch (first editor of)–Lemon
punch (spiced)–negus
punch house–inn, tavern
puncheon–cask, dagger, die, punch, stamp
puncher – cowboy, cowpuncher, perforator
punching (act of)–pertusion
punctilious–exact, nice, precise, scrupulous
punctuation mark – colon, dash, dot, period, semicolon
pundit – Brahman, nestor, teacher
pung–sleigh
pungent – acrid, keen, peppery, piercing, piquant, poignant, racy, sharp, smart, tart
pungent herbs (genus of) – asarum
punish – castigate, chasten, chastise, correct, discipline, wreak
punish by a pecuniary penalty–fine, mulct
punish by cutting off from church membership – excommunicate
punish by exacting money–fine
punish by fine–amerce
punish corporally–spank
punishment–fine, penalty
punishment (law)–peine
punishment (pert. to) – penal, punitive
punitive–penal
punk–touchwood
punk (coll.) – prostitute, strumpet
punk (tinder)–amadou
punk (vegetable)–amadou
puny – frail, petty, puisne, sickly, weak
pupa of an insect–chrysalis
pupil – learner, neophyte, scholar, son, tyro
puppet–doll
puppet (moved by strings)–neuropast
puppy or cub–whelp
purchasable–corrupt, venal
purchase back–redeem
purchaser–buyer, customer, patron, vendee
purchaser of an estate (Fr. and Can. law)–acquereur
purchasing agent–buyer
pure – candid, chaste, clean, downright, filtered, neat, pute, refined, sheer, stainless, uncorrupted, undefiled, unqualified, utter, vestal
purgative–cathartic
purgative tuberous root – jalap
purified by washing–elutriated
purified wool fat – lanolin, lanoline
purify – clean, cleanse, epurate, filter, lustrate, purge, refine, renovate, spurge
purifying–depurant
purl–frill, murmur
purloin – filch, finger, steal, swipe
purple (delicate)–mauve

purple (obtained from chloride of gold)–cassius
purple (seller of Bible) – Lydia
purple (shade of)–tyrian
purple coneflower – echinacea
purple copper ore–bornite
purple dye–cassius
purple ragwort–jacoby
purplish brown–puce
purplish brown pigment – uda
purplish color–amaranth
purplish red–lake
purport – feck, gist, import, intent, meaning, sense, substance, tenor
purport (general)–tenor
purpose–aim, avail, end, intent, intention, main, motive, plan, sake
purpose (beforehand) – predesign
purpose (denoting)–telic
purpose (final)–goal
purpose (special)–sake
purpose (without)–idly
purpose intended–end
purposive–telic
purse–bag, cly, pocketbook, portemonnaie, pouch, pucker, wallet
purser – boucher, bursar, cashier, paymaster
pursue–chase, follow, run
pursue (as game)–hunt
pursue zigzag course–tack
pursuer of wild game–hunter, huntress
pursuit–chase, occupation
purvey–cater
purveyor of untruth (Biblical, well-known)–Ananias
push–ping, press, prod, propel, shove, thrust
push (coll.)–elbow, go
push (old word)–por, porr, poss
push along–prod
push around–regiment
push gently–nudge
push up (coll.)–boost
push with long stick–pole

push with the head – bunt, butt
pusillanimous – cowardly, tame, timid
put–deposit, place, set
put an end to (law)–quash
put another in place of–relieve
put apart–sever
put back – demote, replace, restore
put before–apposed
put down–depress
put down by force–suppress
put forth–exert
put forth great effort–exert, struggle
put in–insert
put in (coll.)–ante
put in forgotten place–mislay
put in holy place–enshrine
put in motion–arouse
put in opposition–pit
put in order–arrange, organize, settle, systematize, trim
put in order (Scot.)–mense
put in relation–correlate
put in same rank–coordinate
put in scabbard–sheathe
put in shape–trim
put in vigorous action–exert
put into case–sheathe
put into ecstasy–entrance
put into rhythm–meter, metre
put into words–express, state
put new point on pen–renib
put new soles on shoes–resole, retap
put off–doff, haft
put on–apply, don, endue
put on a short allowance–scrimp
put on decorative touches (coll.)–titivated
put on the alert (poetic) – alarum
put out – anger, evict, oust, retire
put out of action–disable
put out of joint–dislocate
put to flight–rout
put to severe strain–tax
put to trouble–discommode

put to use–apply
put to wrong use–misapply
put together–add
put up stake–ante
put up with – bear, endure, stand, stomach, tolerate
put with–add
puts a false appearance on–belie
puts on–dons, indues
putrefaction–decay, rot
puttee–gaiter
puzzle – anagram, cap, conundrum, crux, enigma, griph, griphus, nonplus, perplex, rebus, riddle
puzzle (monkey)–pinon
puzzle (picture)–rebus
puzzle (word)–charade
puzzled–posed
puzzling–paradoxical
pygarg–addax
Pygmalion's sister–Dido
Pygmalion's statue (ivory)–Galatea
pygmy–atomy, dwarf, minim, short
pygmy musk deer – chevrotain
pygostyle–vomer
pyic–purulent
pyknic–fat, stout, squatness
pylon–gateway, post, tower
Pylos king–Nestor
pyosis–suppuration
pyramid (builder of largest of three great) – Cheops, Khufu
pyramid (largest of three great)–Cheops
pyramid (Mexican, site of)–Cholula
pyramidal–enormous, huge, imposing
pyramids (site of three great)–Giza
pyre–bier
Pyrenees bandit–Miquelet
Pyrenees mountain peak – Aneto
Pyrenees republic–Andorra
Pyrenees resort (famous winter)–Pau
pyriform–pear-shaped
pyrotechnics–fireworks
pyroxene – augite, diopside,

hedenbergite, schefferite
Pythagoras' birthplace – Samos

Pythias' friend–Damon
python (slayer of the)–Apollo

pythonic–oracular
pyx (pix) – binnacle, box, chest, ciborium, coffer

Q

quabird–heron
quack – charlatan, empiric, faker, impostor, mountebank, pretender
quack doctor–crocus
quack medicine–nostrum
quadra–fillet, listel, plinth, podium
quadragesimal – forty, lent, lenten
quadrangle–tetragon
quadrant – farthing, fourth, gill, instrument
quadrate – agree, balanced, correspond, correspondent, ideal, perfect, square, squared, suit
quadrilaterals–tessara
quadrumane–ape
quadruped–ass, bull, bullock, burro, calf, colt, cow, donkey, horse, jennie, mule
quadruped (burrowing) – badger
quadruped (carnivorous) – lion, panda, tiger
quadruped (flesh-eating) – cat
quadruped (hybrid)–mule
quadruped (young)–foal
quaff–drink
quag–quake, quiver
quaggy – boggy, queachy, spongy
quagmire – bog, fen, lair, marsh, morass, swamp
quail – bird, blench, bobwhite, coagulate, colin, courtesan, cow, cower, curdle, flinch, massena, quake, shake, shrink, tremble, tremor, turnix
quail (American)–bobwhite, colin
quail (button)–turnix
quail (flock of)–bevy
quail (genus of)–coturnix

quail hawk–falcon
quail snipe–dowitcher
quaint–odd, proud, strange
quake–earthquake, quiver, shake, shiver, shudder, tremble, tremor, vibrate, waver
Quaker–Friend
Quaker (famous)–Penn
Quaker City–Philadelphia
Quaker colonizer–Penn
Quaker poet–Barton, Whittier
Quaker's founder – George Fox
quaking–quivering, shivering, trembling, trepid
quaking (rare)–trepid
qualified–able, adapted, capable, conditional, enabled, equipped, fitted, prepared, restrained, restricted, tempered
qualify – abate, adapt, assuage, diminish, enable, equip, fit, mitigate, prepare, restrain, restrict, soften, temper
quality – attribute, caliber, rate, strain, trait
quality (active)–agent
quality (artistic)–virtu
quality (color)–tone
quality (distinctive) – specialty, talent, tang
quality (exciting pity and sympathy)–pathos
quality (highest)–pathos
quality (model of noble) – hero
quality (peculiar and characteristic)–property
quality (poorer)–inferior
quality (rich)–mellow
quality (structural)–texture
quality (to improve)–enrich

quality (without ethical) – amoral
quality of being hereditary–lineality
quality of tone–timbre
qualm–compunction, faintness, misgiving, nausea, regret, scruple
quamash – camas, camass, cammas
quandary–dilemma, predicament
quannet–file
quant–pole, punt
quantity–amount, any, bulk, degree, extent, hatful, lot, number, size, some, sum
quantity (fixed)–constant
quantity (great)–sea, store
quantity (irrational)–surd
quantity (large)–gob, hatful, mass, much, oceans, raff, raft, scad
quantity (mathematical, irrational)–surd
quantity (minute) – atom, dram, iota, mill
quantity (of matter)–mass
quantity (per unit of time)–rate
quantity (small)–any, capful, drop, handful
quantity (standard)–unit
quantity (very small)–ace
quantity (visual representation of varying)–graph
quantity produced at one time–batch
quantity with magnitude but not direction–scalar
quap – heave, palpitate, quaver, throb
Quapaw tribe Indian–Ozark
quar–block, choke, curdle, fill
quarentene–furlong, rood
quark–caw, croak, quawk

quarl (quarle)–brick, curdle, jellyfish, medusa, tile
quarred–curdled, soured
quarrel – affray, argument, bicker, broil, chisel, diamond, flite, flyte, gnarr, misunderstanding, row, scene, scrap, spat, squabble, tiff, tile, wrangle
quarrel (hereditary)–feud
quarrel (in words)–jangle
quarrel (noisy)–fracas
quarrel (petty)–miff, tiff
quarrel (small)–spat
quarrelsome – belligerent, choleric, contentious, irascible, irritable, litigious, petulant, pugnacious
quarry–delf, game, prey
quart–fourth, health, measure, schooner
quart (one-eighth of)–gill
quarter (low)–dive, slum
quarter acre–rood
quarter note–crotchet
quarter pint–gill
quarter ripsaw–handsaw
quartered in lodgings–billeted, roomed
quarters (military)–barracks, billets, camp
quarters (officers of British warship)–gunroom
quarters (sleeping) – dormitory
quarter (soldier's)–barracks, billets
quarters (winter)–hibernacle
quartodeciman – paschalist, paschite
quartz–onyx, silica
quartz (blood-red brownish) –sinople
quartz (green)–prase
quartz (hard variety)–flint
quartz (kind of) – onyx, prase, sard, silica
quartz (leek green)–prase
quartz (opaque)–jasper
quartz (ruby red)–rubasse
quartz (variety of) – agate, amethyst, citrine, flint, jasper, prase, topaz
quartz (very hard)–flint
quartz flint–silex
quartzite–itabarite

quash – abate, annul, cass, crush, overthrow, shake, shatter
quaternion turning factor – versor
quaver–quiver, shake, tremble, tremolo, trill, vibrate
quawk–caw, heron, screech
quay – embankment, levee, pier, quell, subdue, wall, wharf
queach–thicket
queachy – boggy, bushy, marshy, swampy
quean – harlot, hussy, jade, slut, wench
queasy – delicate, hazardous, nauseated, ticklish, troubled, uncertain, unsettled
Quebec town–Sorel
Quebec vehicle (two-wheeled)–caleche
quebracho – aspidosperma, macaglia
quebradilla–brooklet
quebrith–sulphur
qued–bad, evil
queechy–feeble, sickly, small
queen (pert. to)–reginal
Queen Anne's lace–carrot
Queen Anne's pocket melon –dudaim
Queen City–Cincinnati
Queen City of the Lakes– Buffalo
queen of fairies–Mab
queen of gods–Hera, Juno
queen of Greek gods–Hera
Queen of Hearts–Elizabeth
queen of heaven – Mary, moon
Queen of Isles–Albion
queen of night–moon
Queen of Palmyra–Zenobia
Queen of Roman gods–Juno
Queen of Sheba–Balkis
queen of spades (in solo)– basta
Queen of the Adriatic–Venice
Queen of the Antilles–Cuba
Queen of the East–Zenobia
queen of the fairies – Mab, Titania
queen of the tides–moon

queene (faerie)–Gloriana
queened pawn (chess)–fers
queenly–reginal
queen's arm–musket
queen's-balm–alyssum
queensberry–cloudberry
queen's-delight–queenroot
queen's-flower–bloodwood
queen's-gilliflower – damewort
queen's-herb–tobacco
queen's-Julyflower – damewort
queer–counterfeit, odd, peculiar, questionable, rum, sham, singular, spurious, strange, suspicious
queer chap (slang)–galoot
queersome – abnormal, odd, strange
queest–ringdove
questing–bundling
queet–ankle, coot
queeve–bend, turn, twist
quell–allay, calm, crush, destroy, overpower, quash, quiet, reduce, repress, soothe, stifle, subdue, suppress
quench – allay, assuage, check, cool, damp, extinguish, overwhelm, slake, stifle, still, subdue, suppress
quenelle–dumpling
querent – complainant, inquirer, plaintiff
querido–darling, dear
querken–choke, stifle
querl–coil, twist
quern–mill
quernstone–millstone
querulist–complainer
querulous – complaining, fretful, peevish, plaintive
query – inquire, inquiry, question
quest – adventure, ask, inquest, search, seek
quest of perfection–ideal
question–ask, dispute, doubt, inquire, inquiry, interpellate, interrogation, query, quiz, scout
question (essential)–crux

question (formally) – interpellate
question (hard)–poser
question (mark indicating a) –erotema, eroteme
question (puzzling)–riddle
question seriously–catechise
questionable–debatable, disputable, doubtful, dubious, problematical, uncertain
quet–guillemot
quetch–go, move, stir
quethe–bequeath, call, clamor, cry, say, speak, tell, testament, will
quetzal–trogon
queue–cue, pigtail
quey–heifer
quiapo–lettuce
quiaquia–cigarfish
quib–gibe, quibble, quip
quibble – carp, cavil, cheat, evade, pun, shuffle
quick – agile, deft, expeditious, fast, fleet, nimble, prompt, rapid, sprightly, swift
quick (Mexican)–pronto
quick (skillfully)–deft
quick anatomy–vivisection
quick and light–volant
quick throw–flirt
quick time (music)–presto
quick to learn–apt
quicken–animate, expedite, hurry, incite, refresh, reinvigorate, resuscitate, revive, sharpen
quickly–apace, fast, presto, promptly, pronto, rapidly, soon, speedily, vigorous
quickness–acidity, acuteness, agility, briskness, celerity, dispatch, expedition, fleetness, haste, promptness, pungency, rapidity, sharpness
quickness (mental)–nous
quickness of discernment – acumen
quickness of mental perception–acumen
quicksand–syrt, syrtis
quickset–hawthorn, hedge, thicket

quicksilver–mercury
quicksilver container–flask
quid–cud, fid, guinea, sovereign
quidam–somebody
quiddany–jelly, sirup
quiddit–quibble, subtlety
quiddle–dawdle, trifle
quidnunc–gossip
quiescent–latent, motionless, quiet, static
quiet–calm, halcyon, hush, lull, peace, peaceable, pet, reposeful, restful, silence, smooth, sober, soothe, still, tranquil, undisturbed, unmolested, unruffled
quiet please–Sh
quieted – allayed, calmed, hushed, sobered, stilled
quietive–sedative
quietude–repose, rest, tranquillity
quietus–death
quietus (Eng. law) – discharge, release
quiff–puff, whiff
quilkin–frog, toad
quill – bobbin, cop, pen, spindle
quill (for winding silk)–cop
quill (porcupine)–pen
quill (wing)–remex, remiges (pl.)
quill feather (bird's wing)–remex, remiges (pl.)
quilt–caddow, comfortable, counterpane, coverlet, duvet, flog, gulp, swallow
quilt (down)–duvet
quin–scallop
quink–brant
quinnet–wedge
quinoa–pigweed
quinoline (derivative of) – analgen
quinse–carve
quintal–hundredweight
quintessence–col, elite, elixir
quip – gibe, gimcrack, jest, oddity, sally, taunt
quip (smart)–mot
quires (twenty)–ream
quirk – clock, deviation, flourish, twist, turn

quirl–bend, coil, twist
quirt–whip
quirt (Mexican)–romal
quis–woodcock
quisby – bankrupt, idler, queer
quit–abandon, cease, clear, discontinue, leave, liberate, release, relieve, relinquish, renounce, resign, stop
quit (office, etc.)–abdicate
quitclaim–acquit, release, relinquishment
quite – all, completely, entirely, positively, really, stark, totally, truly, wholly
quite some–considerable
quittance–departure, recompense, repay, repayment, requital, requite, return
quitter–coward, welsher
quitter (slang)–piker
quitting–departure
quiver–case, quake, quaver, sheath, shiver, tremble, tremor, vibrate
quiver (Scot.)–thirl, tirl
quiver leaf–aspen
quivering – aspen, palpitation, tremulous
qui vive (on the)–agog, alert
quixotic–utopian, visionary
quiz–banter, chaff, examination, mock, ridicule
quizzical–amusing, bantering, eccentric, odd, teasing
quizzing glass – eyeglass, monocle
quod–jug, prison
quoddies–herring
quodlibet–debate, subtlety
quodlibet (music)–fantasia, medley
quoit–disc, discus
quoit mark (aimed at)–tee
quoit pin–hob
quomodo – how, manner, means
quondam–former, formerly, sometime
quop–throb
quota – part, proportion, share

quotation – cital, citation, memorandum, passage
quotation (developed into short essay)–chria
quotation (short, prefixed to an essay)–motto

quotation mark–guillemet
quote – adduce, cite, name, reference, repeat
quotennial–annual
quoth–said, spoke

quotha–forsooth, indeed
quotidian – commonplace, daily, everyday, recurring
quotity – collection, group, quota

R

Ra (sun god)–Aten, Chepera, Harmachis, Horus, Khepera, Re, Shu, Sokaris, Tem, Tum
Ra's father–Nut
Ra's son–Khonsu
Ra's wife–Mut
raad–catfish
raash (raasch)–catfish
rab–beater, master, teacher
raband–ropeband
rabat–plane
rabatine–collar
rabato (rebato)–collar, piccadill, ruff
rabban–Gamaliel
rabbet–channel, groove, recess
rabbi–amora, amoraim, lord, master, sabaraim, saboraim, tannaim, teacher
rabbi's assistant–cantor
rabbit–bunny, cony, coney, conies (pl.), coneys (pl.), hare, novice, rodent, tyro
rabbit (Eur.)–cony, coney, coneys (pl.), conies (pl.)
rabbit (female)–doe
rabbit (genus of)–lepus
rabbit (male)–buck
rabbit (South American, small)–tapeti
rabbit (swamp, U.S.)–tapeti
rabbit (young)–starter
rabbit breeding pen–warren
rabbit burrow–clapper
rabbit-ear–toadflax
rabbit fish–chimaera
rabbit flower–toadflax
rabbit-foot–talisman
rabbit fur–cony, coney, lapin
rabbit-like animal – marot, pika
rabbit-meat–archangel

rabbit-mouthed–harelipped
rabbit net–hay
rabbitroot–sarsaparilla
rabbit shelter–hutch
rabbitskin (two months old)–rack
rabbit tobacco–balsamweed
rabbit vine–groundnut
rabbit's fur–scut
rabbit's tail–scut
rabbit's tail (Scot.)–fud
rabbitry–warren
rabble–bobtail, canaille, confusion, herd, mob, raff, ragtag, riffraff, rout, tumult
rabble rouser–ragtag
Rabelaisian character–Badebec
rabid – fanatical, frantic, frenzied, furious, raging, virulent
rabies – hydrophobia, lyssa, lytta
raccoon (animal allied to)–coati
raccoon-like animal–panda
raccoon-like mammal–coati
race – breed, caste, contest, course, cut, family, lane, line, nation, passageway, people, run, running, rush, scratch, slit, sort, speed, stem, strain
race (ancient)–Mede
race (comb. form)–geno
race (conquered by Rome)–Sabine
race (family)–ilk, stirps
race (fast)–sprint
race (half man and half horse)–centaur
race (human)–man
race (mill)–lade

race (northern France) – Walloons
race (one of ancient)–Hittite
race (one of wandering)–gypsy
race (prehistoric)–Aryans
race (rowing)–regatta
race (running)–relay
race (science of)–ethnology
race (short)–bicker, sprint
race (ski obstacle)–slalom
race (type of)–relay, sprint
race (undivided)–holethnos
race (water)–arroyo
raceabout–roadster, sloop
race board–gangplank
race course–circus, heat
race course marker – meta, pylon
race forecaster–dopester
race gait (long)–lope
race ginger–gingerroot
race horse–mantis
race horse (cheap)–plater
race horse (never winning)–maiden
race track tipster–tout
racer–miler
Rachel's father–Laban
Rachel's sister–Leah
rachis–spine
racial strain–breed
rack – agonize, excruciate, gin, skin, wrench
rack (barrel)–jib
rack (corn)–crib
rack (floating)–vapor
rack (plate)–creel
racket–bat, bustle, clamor, din, noise, outcry, scheme
rackety–exciting, noisy, turbulent
rackle–clank, clatter, rattle
racy – brisk, exhilarating,

fresh, lively, piquant, pungent, smart, spicy, spirited, stirring, zestful

rad–afraid, eager, elated, exhilarated, quick, ready

raddle–beat, branch, cheat, fence, hedge, hurdle, rod, thrash, wheedle

radial–quadrant, ray

radiance – beaming, beamy, brilliancy, brilliant, effulgence, glare, glitter, glowing, lambent, luster, nitor, shining, splendor

radiant–beaming, beamy, effulgent, lambent, sheen

radiant (Scot.)–lambent

radiate – diffuse, emanate, emit, illuminate, irradiate, shine

radiating–emanant, stellate

radical – capital, cardinal, drastic, fundamental, red, ultra

radical (acetic acid)–acetyl

radical (alcohol)–amyl

radical (electrolytic)–ion

radical (hydrocarbon)–amyl

radical (univalent, aromatic) –aryl

radical expression–surd

radicated–established, rooted

radicel–rootlet

radices–roots

radio (portable) – walkie-talkie

radio antenna–aerial

radio frequency–audio

radio interference–static

radio operator (army slang) –dit-da artist

radio rays (directed)–beams

radio receiver (generating currents interfering with another set)–blooper

radio tube (kind of)–diode

radish (French)–radis

radium (source of)–uranite

radium discoverer–Curie

radium emanation – niton, radon

radix–etymon, radical, root

raff – heap, jumble, litter, rake, riffraff, rubbish, sweep, trash

raffish–disreputable, frowsy,

low, unkempt, worthless

raffle – crumple, lottery, plucking, plundering, rabble, riffraff, serrate, stripping

raft–catamaran, float, rafter, spar

raft (long narrow)–catamaran

raft (Philippine)–balsa

raft-breasted (ornithology)– ratite

raft duck–bluebill, scaup

rafty–damp, musty, rancid, stale

rag–farthing, fog, hoarfrost, mist, remnant, tatter; chiffonier, chiffonnier

rag wool–mungo, shoddy

rage–chafe, fad, fret, fume, furor, fury, passion, rant, rese, storm, tear, vehemence, wrath

rage (var.)–furore

ragged – jagged, rough, shaggy, shreddy, tattered, uneven

ragged edge–jag

raging – acharne, ferocious, grim, rabid

raglan–overcoat

ragout of beef–goulash

ragout of game (partly roasted)–salmi, salmis

ragout of meat–haricot

raid – foray, incursion, inroad, invasion, tala

raid (predatory)–foray

rail–banter, bar, cloak, coot, crake, dress, garment, jest, revile, scoff, scold, sora

rail (altar)–septum

rail (American shortbill) – sora

rail at–jaw, reproach, revile, scold

railbird–clocker, crake, sora, spectator

railing (protective) – balustrade, parapet

raillery–banter, chaff, ridicule, sport

raillery (playful)–badinage

railly – jacket, jest, mock, rally, ridicule

railroad bolter of splices to rails–strapper

railroad flare signal–fusee

railroad signal–semaphore

railroad sleeper–tie

railroad switch–frog

railroad tie–sleeper

railroad torpedo–detonator

rails (pert. to)–ralline

railway freight charge–haulage

raiment – apparel, clothe, clothing, dress, garb, garments, vesture

raiment (ecclesiastical)–amice

rain – dag, misle, mizzle, serein, shower

rain (fine)–mist

rain (fine after sunset)–serein

rain (heavy or sudden fall of)–deluge, plash

rain (icy)–sleet

rain (light)–mist

rain (short)–shower

rainbow–arc, iris

rainbow (goddess of)–Iris

rainbow (pert. to)–iridal

rainbow chaser–doctrinaire, visionary

rainbow flower–iris

rain cloud–nimbus

rain cloud (heavy dark) – nimbus

raincoat – mackintosh, poncho, slicker

raincoat (Japanese)–mino

rainfowl – channelbill, cuckoo, woodpecker

rain gauge–hyetometer, pluviometer, udometer

rain gauge (self-registering) – hyetometrograph, pluviograph

rain glass–barometer

rain leader–downspout

rainspout (Scot.)–rone

rainstorm (heavy) – plash, spate

rainstorm (sudden)–downpour, shower, spate

rainstorm (violent)–deluge, spate

rain unit–inch

rainworm–earthworm, nematode
rainy–showery, wet
rais (reis) – captain, chief, head
raise – breed, collect, cultivate, elevate, end, enhance, exalt, gather, heave, heighten, hoist, leaven, lift, lighten, muster, present, rear, remove, rouse, stir, trice, uplift
raise (coll.)–boost
raise a nap – tease, teasel, teasle, teazel, teazle
raise by tillage–cultivate
raise high–exalt
raise nap on woolen cloth–tease, teasel, teasle, teazel, teazle
raise to third power–cube
raise upright–rear
raised–bred, elevated, hefted, hoisted, hove, leavened, lifted, reared
raised (Fr.)–enleve
raised up–buoyed, elevated, promoted
raised uproar–rioted
raised with a bar–levered
raises (slang)–ups
raises the spirits–elates
raises troops – conscripts, drafts, levies
raising vegetables (pert. to)–olericultural
raja (rajah)–chief, dignitary, king, prince
rajah's consort–ranee, rani
rajah's wife–ranee, rani
Rajmahal creeper–jiti
rakan–arhat, lohan
rake – debauchee, groove, path, raff, roue, rut, track
rake (with shot)–enfilade
rakehell–debauched, debauchee, dissolute, profligate, rake
rakh – grassland, hay, hayfield
rallidae–coots, crakes, gallinules, rails, wekas
rally–assemble, banter, reunite, ridicule
rallying cry–slogan
ralph–raven

ram–buck, butt, collide, hit, pun, rancid, sheep, tup
ram (castrated)–wether
ram (the)–Aries
ram cat–male, tom
ram down–tamp
ram into–crash
ram-like–arientine
Ram's Horn (Hebrew) – Shofar, Shophar
Rama's bride–Sita
ramage–frenzied, rough, unruly, untamed, wild
ramage hawk–brancher
ramass–collect, gather
ramberge–galley
ramble–gad, jaunt, prowl, range, roam, rove, wander
rambling–devious
rambunctious – rampageous, uncontrollable, unruly, wild
ramentum–palea, palet
ramex–hernia, varicocele
ramgunshoch–harsh, rough
ramhead–clodpate, cuckold, lever
ramie–rhea
ramie plant–rhea
ramification – arm, branch, branching, divergence, offshoot, ramus
rammack – clamber, gawk, romp, scamp
rammel–brushwood, undergrowth
Ramona author – Helen Hunt Jackson
ramp – bound, crawl, creep, cuckoopint, dupery, gradient, impetuous, platform, rage, rampage, rob, storm, swindle, unruly, walk
ramp (curving)–helic-line
rampart – bulwark, mound, parapet, redan
rampart (detached)–ravelin
rampart (palisaded)–vallum
rampart (part of)–spur
rampart (raised work)–agger
rampart (V-shaped)–redan
ran – coursed, fled, flowed, managed, operated, sped, trotted

ran aground–stranded
ran away–eloped, fled
ran out–petered, spilled
ran out (coll.)–petered
ran out unintentionally – spilt
ranarian–croaking, froggy
rance–marble, prop, support
rancel (ransel) – ransack, search
ranch house (southwestern) –casa
rancid – musty, obnoxious, offensive, rank, unpleasant
rancor – animosity, enmity, hatred, ire, malice, rankle, spite
rand–border, edge, margin, rant, ridge, storm
random–accidental, aimless, casual, chance, fortuitous, haphazard, stray
random cut–slash
randy – beggar, canvass, carousal, coarse, disorderly, festivity, frolic, revel, unmanageable, virago
rang loudly–clanged
rang mournfully – knelled, tolled
rang slowly–tolled
range – align, ally, area, arrange, classify, compass, gamut, line, roam, scope
range finder – mekometer, telemeter
range finder (British field service)–trekometer
range of hills or mountains–ridge
range of knowledge–ken
range of stables–mews
ranger–sieve
rangle–straggle, stray, wander, wrangle
rank – absolute, caste, class, degree, downright, estate, file, flagrant, glaring, grade, luxuriant, order, palpable, position, rancid, range, rate, row, tier
rank (exalted)–eminence
rank (military, old)–banneret
rank (noble)–patriciate

rank (social)–caste
rank of holy beings – hierarchy
rank rider–highwayman
rankle–fester
rankwise–arow
rann–stanza, strain, verse
rannel–jade, prostitute
ransack – rake, rifle, sack, search
ransom–expiate, redeem
ransom from bondage – redeem
rant – bombast, declaim, rage, rail, rave, steven
rantipole–rakish, termagant, unruly, wild
rantock–goosander
ranty–excited, riotous, wild
ranula–cyst
rap–grab, knap, knock, sentence, snatch, steal, tirl
rapacious–greedy, ravening, ravenous, voracious
rapacity–appetite, ravin
rapid–fast, fleet, quick, swift
rapid (more, music)–stretta, stretto
rapidity – fleetness, haste, quickness, speed
rapidly–apace
rapids–dalles, rifts
rapier–bilbo, sword, verdun
rapine – pillage, plunder, spoliation
rapport–accord, agreement, harmony
rapt–absorbed, enraptured
rapture – bliss, delight, ecstasy, exultation, transport
rare – infrequent, odd, raw, scarce, seldom, uncommon, unusual
rare metallic element–yttrium
rare object–antique, curio
rarefied matter–gas
rarefies–attenuates, dilutes
rarely–seldom
rarity–tenuity, thinness
ras–cape, headland, prince
rasa–amrita, essence, flavor, fluid, sap, taste
rasant–grazing, sweeping

rascal – cad, knave, miscreant, rogue, scamp
rascally – knavish, mischievous, roguish
rase – cut, rub, scrape, scratch, tear
rash – careless, desperate, hasty, headstrong, heady, heedless, icarian, impetuous, incautious, indiscreet, mad, scamp, thoughtless, unwary
rash (nettle)–hives
rash (skin)–exanthema
rashness–acrisy, temerity
rasion – erasing, filing, rasping, scraping, shaving
rasores–columbae, gallinae
rasp–belch, eruct, file, grate, raspberry, rub, scrape
rasping – grating, harsh, irritating, raucous, scraping
raspings (of ivory)–scobs
rassasy–satiate
rasse–civet
rasure–cut, erasing, erasure, obliteration, scraping, scratch, shave
rat–adviser, councilor, counselor, deserter, ratton, rottan, rut, scratch, track, wart
rat hare–pika
rat-like rodent–vole
rat pineapple–pinguin
rat poison–ratsbane
ratafia–curacao, curacoa, noyau
ratchet – bobbin, click, detent, pawl
ratchet (catch of)–pawl
ratchet detent–pawl
rate – account, appraise, assess, estimate, evaluate, fare, pace, price, reprove, value
rate (to)–classify
rate of exchange–agio, batta
rate of motion (to make vessel answer helm) – steerageway
rate of movement–tempo
ratero–pickpocket, thief
ratfish–chimaera
rath (ratha) – car, chariot, temple

rathe–betimes, eager, quick, quickly, soon, speedily, speedy
rather – before, earlier, ere, erer, immediately, liever, quickly
rather than–ere
ratification–amen, confirmation, logic, reasoning, sanction
ratify – amen, approve, authorize, confirm, roborate, sanction, seal, verify
ratify (obs.)–enseal
ratio – portion, proportion, ration, share
ratio (geometrical)–pi
ratio (mathematical) – pi, sine
ratio (trigonometric)–cosine
ratiocination – logic, reasoning
ration–allotment, allowance, calculation, relation, share
rational–intelligent, logical, reasonable, sane, sensible, sober
ratite bird–cassowary, emeu, emu, moa, ostrich
ratoon–shoot, spring, sprout, stalk
rattan – cane, palm, switch, whip
rattan (tough)–sega
ratteen–mahogany
rattle–agitate, annoy, assail, chatter, clack, clatter, confuse, disconcert, rale, rick, tirl
rattle (crier's)–clapper
rattle (gourd-like orchestra) –maracas
rattle (respiratory)–rale
rattlemouse–bat
rattlenut–chinquapin
rattlepate–ass
rattleroot–bugbane
rattlesnake–crotalus, crotalidae (pl.), sistrurus
rattlesnake (pygmy)–massasaugas
rattlesnake bean–cedron
rattlesnake bite–rue
rattlesnake fern–sporangia
rattlesnake herb–baneberry
rattlesnake leaf–plantain

rattlesnake pilot – copperhead

rattletop–bugbane

rattletrap–gewgaws, knick-knacks, ramshackle, rickety

ratton–rat

ratwa–muntjac

raucous – harsh, hoarse, strident

raucous noise–bray

rauk–poke, scratch, stir, vapor

raun–roe, spawn

raupo–cattail, mace

ravage – desolation, despoilment, destroy, devastate, loot, overrun, pillage, plunder, ruin, sack, spoil, waste

rave – declaim, rage, rant, storm

ravel–fray, separate, unravel, untwist, unweave, unwind

ravel (vertical)–runner

ravelin–demilune

raven–consume, devour, obtain, ravish, seize

Raven (The) author–Poe

Raven character–Lenore

Raven God (the)–Odin

ravener – glutton, ravisher, robber

ravening – devouring, mad, preying, rabid, rabies, rapacious, voracious

ravenous–greedy, rapacious, voracious

ravenousness–edacity, voracity

ravine–arroyo, clough, coulee, dell, gap, gorge, gulch, gulley, lin, linn

ravine (deep)–gorge

ravine (narrow, deep)–chine

ravine (steep sides)–barranca

ravine (through which a stream flows) – wadi, wady

ravish – corrupt, deflower, delight, despoil, enrapture, entrance, plunder, rob, transport, violate

raw–crude, inclement, inex-

perienced, natural, uncooked, unprepared, unprocessed, unskilled

rawbones–death, skeleton

raw flesh (eating of)–omophagia

rawhide whip–knout, quirt, thong

rawness–crudite

raw sugar–cassonade

rax–reach, strain, stretch

ray – arrangement, array, beam, besmear, defile, dress, order, raiment, skate, soil

ray (flat-bodied)–skate

ray (thornback)–dorn

ray (X-ray tube source)–target

raya (East Indian) – broadbill

rayed–striped

raylike–radial

raze–cut, demolish, destroy, dismantle, efface, erase, obliterate, prostrate, ruin, scrape, shave

razee–abridge, cut, prune

razoo–racket, racketing

razor (kind of)–rattler

razor (to sharpen) – hone, strop

razorback–hog, ridge, roustabout

razorbill–skimmer

razorbilled auk–murre

razor clam–solen

razor stone–novaculite

razor strap–strop

razz–banter, chaff, ridicule, tease

razzia–foray, raid

rea–turmeric

reach–achieve, attain, come, extend, gain, hawk, possess, retch, span, spit, stretch, vomit

reach (Scot.)–ryke

reach across–span

reach an ambition–attain

reach first base on a hit – single

reach for applause or favor–captation

reach high point–culminate

reach out–stretch

reach up–aspire

reached under–subtended

reacquire–regain

reaction (vivid)–kick

reactionary in politics–tory

read – advise, con, counsel, decipher, declare, describe, discern, foresee, foretell, guess, interpret, peruse, relate, solve, stomach, tell

read (here and there) – browse

read carefully–con

read metrically–scan

read rapidly–skim

read with profound attention–pore

readable–legible

readdressed–redirected

reader – elocutionist, lector, license, lister, pocketbook, primer, proofreader, reciter

reader (Eastern Church) – anagnost, anagnostes

reader (elementary)–primer

reader (here and there) – browser

reader (historical term for)–lector

reader and writer–literate

readily understood – clear, lucid

readiness–alacrity, art, facility, preparedness, promptness

readiness (cheerful)–alacrity

readiness of speech – facundity

reading–lection, perusal

reading desk–escritoire, lectern

reading desk (early form)–ambo

reading desk (large)–ambo

ready – apt, bain, cheerful, eager, facile, fit, free, here, point, prepared, prompt, quick, ripe, skillful, unhesitating, willing, yare

real–authentic, existent, factual, genuine, real, sincere, veritable

real (substantial)–tangible

real being–entity

real estate–freehold, hereditaments, lands, property, realty, tenements

real estate (held in absolute independence) – alod, allod

real government (in exile)–defacto

real name (written backwards)–ananym

realistic–vivid

reality–realism, sooth

realize – accomplish, conceive, convert, get, know

realized (coll.)–sensed

realm – country, demesne, department, division, domain, empire, kingdom, province, region

realm (great)–empire

realm of darkness (Polynesian myth)–Po

realm of perfection (imaginary)–Utopia

ream–bore, countersink, enlarge

reamy–creamy, frothy

reanimate – rally, reinvigorate, renascent, revive

rear – aft, arriere, back, behind, breed, build, construct, elevate, erect, establish, lift, posterior, raise, stern, train

rear (French)–arriere

rear (toward the)–abaft

rearhorse–mantis

rearing (as a horse)–pesade, stend

rearrange – readjust, reordinate, sort

reason – argument, cause, ground, motive, ratiocinate, sense, think, understanding

reason (higher)–nous

reason (Latin)–causa

reason (ostensible)–pretext

reason (pert. to)–noetic

reason (want of)–amentia

reason offered in proof–argument

reason why–cause, motive

reasonable – equitable, fair,

just, logical, moderate, plausible, rational, sane

reasoning (basis of)–premise

reasoning (delusive)–fallacy

reasoning (exact)–logic

reassert–claim, maintain

reassumes title to–revests

reata–lariat, lasso, riata

reave – burst, plunder, split, tear

reb–rebel

rebate – abatement, check, deduction, diminish, reduce, weaken

rebato (rabato) – collar, piccadill, ruff

rebel – insurgent, red, renounce, revolt, rise

rebellion–insurrection, mutiny, revolt, revolution

rebellious – contumacious, insubordinate, insurgent, refractory

rebirth – reincarnation, renaissance, revival

reboant–rebellowing, reverberating

rebound – bounce, carom, carrom, recoil, re-echo, resound, reverberate, ricochet, stot

rebounding–springy

rebozo–scarf

rebuff – chide, censure, lesson, reprimand, reprove, scold, slap, snub, repulse

rebuke–chide, criticize, reprehend, reprimand, reprove

rebuke (stinging)–nip

rebuking–lecturing

recalcitrant–obstinate, rebel, rebellious, refractory, renitent

recall – annul, encore, recollect, remember, remind, reminisce, retract, revoke, withdraw

recant – abjure, contradict, disavow, renounce, repudiate, retract, revoke, withdraw

recapitulate – argument, essay, repeat, restate, sum, summarize

recapture–recall, recover, regain, retake

recede–depart, deviate, ebb, retire, retreat, retrograde

receipt–acquit, formula, recipe

receipts (the, coll.)–take

receive–accept, derive, greet, obtain, procure, reset, take

receive a reward–reap

receive confession–shrive

receive stolen property–reset

receiver – catcher, donee, treasurer

receiver of income–pernor

receiver of income from stock, lands, etc.–rentier

receiver of profits–pernor

receiver of stolen property–fence

receiving set–radio

recension–enumeration, examination, review, reviewing, revising

recent – current, fresh, late, new

recent in origin–neoteric

recently–lately

recently acquired–new

receptacle – basket, bin, can, carton, case, container, etui, hanaper, holder, pan, tray

receptacle (bark, for butter)–ruskin

receptacle (coal)–bin

receptacle (coffee and tea)–canister

receptacle (document)–hanaper

receptacle (for oil in orange vine)–cyst

receptacle (grain)–bin, elevator

receptacle (holy water) – stoup

receptacle (large)–bin

receptacle (ore assayer's)–sebilla

receptacle (plant)–torus

receptacle (shallow) – pan, tray

receptacle (stonecutter's) – sebilla

receptacle (vote, Latin)–situla, situlae (pl.)

reception – accueil, admission, entertainment, levee, receipt, salon, soiree, tea

reception (cordial)–welcome

reception (court)–levee

reception (fashionable) – salon

reception (morning)–levee

reception hall–atrium, atria (pl.)

reception room–salon

receptive–acceptant

receptor – basin, dispositor, receiver

recess–ala, alcove, apse, bay, crypt, intermission, niche, nook, sinus

recess (hinge leaf)–pan

recess (semicircular)–apse

recess (small)–ala

recess (wall)–alcove, niche

recharge–reload

recidivation–apostasy, backsliding, relapse

recipe – formula, prescription, receipt

recipient–donee, legatee, receiver, receiving, receptive

recipient (rightful, future)–heir

recipient of bequest–legatee

recipient of gifts–donee

reciprocal – convertible, correlative, interchangeable, mutual

recision – canceling, repeal, rescinding

recit–recital, story, tale

recital–enumeration, narrative, recitation, rehearsal, story, tale

recital (second time)–iteration

recitation–oral, reading

recite – enumerate, narrate, recapitulate, recount, rehearse, relate, repeat, tell

recite in monotone–intone

recite in singing tone–intone

recite metrically–scan

recite musically–chant

recite oratorically–declaim

recite rhetorically–declaim

recite to music – chant, intone

reciter–relater

reck – care, concern, deem, estimate, heed

reckless–careless, desperate, heedless, hotheaded, hotspur, imprudent, inconsiderate, indifferent, madcap, neglectful, perdu, perdue, rash, regardless, thoughtless

recklessly–desperately

reckon – calculate, compute, connumerate, consider, count, date, deem, enumerate, estimate, impute, include, number, regard, repute, suppose, tell, think

reckon in–include

reckoning–account, calculation, counting, esteem, estimation, score, shot

reckoning machine–calculator, tabulator

reckoning table–abacus

reclaim – ransom, recall, recover, redeem, regenerate, restore, revoke, tame, train

reclaim from barbarism–civilize

recline–incline, lay, lean, lie, rest, sit

reclining–lolling, recumbent

recluse–anchoret, anchorite, cloistered, eremite, hermit, hidden, monk, nun, secret, sequestered, solitary

recluse (religious)–eremite, nun

recognize–acknowledge, admit, consent, know

recognize worth of–appreciate

recoil – funk, rebound, retreat, shrink, shy, withdraw, wonde

recollect – recall, remember

recollection–memory, mind

recommence–resume

recommence ascending by turning on full power – zoom

recommend–advocate, commit, consign, denote, entrust

recommended–touted

recommitted – recommended, remanded

recompense–compensate, indemnify, meed, pay, premium, reciprocate, reimburse, remunerate, repay, requite, reward

recompense for homicide (Brehon Law)–eric

recompense for killing (Scot. law)–cro

recompense for murder (Welsh law)–galanas

recompense of a manslayer (Germanic law)–wergild

reconcile – atone, conciliate, harmonize, pacify, propitiate, reunite, wean

reconciliator–intermediator

recondite–abstract, abstruse, concealed, cryptic, dark, deep, esoteric, hidden, mystic, occult

reconnaissance – examination, survey

reconnoiter–examine, scout, survey

reconstruct–rebuild, remodel

record – agenda, annal, archive, chronicle, chronology, diary, enter, entry, estreat, file, history, legend, log, memoir, memorial, postea, register, score, tab, transcribe, transcript

record (criminal investigation)–dossier

record (formal)–register

record (historic)–rotulet

record (informal, coll.) – memo

record (of events, Latin) – fasti

record (of past events)–history

record (of single event)–annal

record (official)–actum, acta (pl.)

record (pictorial)–graph

record (year's)–annal, calendar
record holder–binder, file
record keeper–registrar
record of an event–annal
record of document (original)–protocol
record of earth's tremor – seismogram
record of ship's voyage–log
recorded proceeding–actum, acta (pl.)
recorder (archive) – cartulary, chartulary
recorder (official)–registrar
recoup–compensate, indemnify, reimburse
recouple–reyoke
recourse – recur, recurrence, resort, retreat, return, revert
recount–enumerate, narrate, reckon, rehearse, relate, repeat, retail, tell
recover – get, reclaim, recoup, recruit, recuperate, regain, repossess, resume, retake, retrieve, upset
recovery – reclamation, reformation, restoration, retrieval, return, salvage
recreation–diversion, meal, play, refreshment, renewal, sport
recreation (period of)–holiday, vacation
recreational contest–game
recrement – dross, refuse, scoria
recruit–assemble, gather, refresh, reinforce, restore, revive, strengthen
recruit (new) – inductee, rookie
rect–erect, right, straight
rectangle (equilateral) – square
rectify – adjust, amend, better, correct, emend, emendate, reform, regulate, remedy, right
rector–chief, clergyman, director, governor, leader, proctor, proproctor, ruler
rectory–parsonage
reculade–retreat

recumbent – idle, inactive, leaning, lying, reclining, reposing, resting
recuperate–recoup, recover, regain, reimburse, rest
recur–reappear, reoccur, repeat, return
recurred constantly–persisted
recurrence – reappearance, return
recurrent effect of past experience–mneme
recurring continually – constant
recurring ninth day–nonan
recurring seventh day – septan
recurring third day–tertian
red–bloodshot, bloodstained, cerise, coral, inflamed, rosy, ruddy, scarlet
red (bright)–cherry
red (brilliant)–titian
red (color) – lake, magenta, nacarat, puce
red (dark brownish) – maroon
red (deep)–garnet
red (deep purplish)–claret
red (eureka)–puce
red (heraldry)–gules
red adder–copperhead
red ape–orangutan
Red Army–Russians
red arsenic–realgar
red-backed sandpiper–dunlin
red bearcat–panda
red bell–columbine
red-bellied snipe–dowitcher
red belly–grouper
red benjamin–birthroot
redbird–bullfinch, tanager
redbird cactus–jewbush
red blotch–adustiosis
red-box – bureaucratic, official
red bream–rosefish
redbuck–impala
red bug–chigger
redcap–porter
red cap (Turkish)–tarboosh
red cedar–flindosa, juniper, sabine, savin, savine
red cell–erythrocyte

red chalk–ruddle
red cobalt–erythrite
red cohosh–baneberry
red color (antique)–canna
red copper ore–cuprite
red cosmetic–henna
red crooner–gurnard
Redcross Knight's wife–Una
red curlew–godwit, ibis
red dace–redfin
red daisy–hawkweed
red dead nettle–archangel
red deer–hart, roe, stag
red dye–aal, chay, choy, eosin, lac
red dye (orange, crystalline) –morindin
red dye (synthetic) – aurin, aurine
redeye–rudd, sunfish
red faced–blowzed
red fender–terrapin
red fever–erysipelas
redfinch–linnet
red fir–Douglas
red grouse–ptarmigan
red gum–eucalyptus, strophulus
redhead – finch, pochard, woodpecker
red hickory – mockernut, pignut
red hind–grouper
red honeysuckle–sulla
red horse–sucker
red Indian trophy–scalp
redknees–smartweed
red lane (coll.)–esophagus
red lead ore–crocoite
red Madeira wine–Tinto
red man – Indian, Oto, redskin, Ute
red manganese arsenate–sarkinite
red-minded–radical
red ocher–tiver
red orpiment–realgar
red perch–rosefish
red pigment (used by painters)–roset
red rag (coll.)–tongue
red rock decay–laterite
Red Sea–Erythrean
Red Sea colony (pert. to)–Eritrean
Red Sea gulf–Aqaba

Red Sea port city – Leningrad
redshank–clee
redshirt – anarchist, revolutionist
red shrike–minivet
red skin substance–rubefacient
red stone–ruby
red-streaked spider–katipo
red stuff–crocus, rouge
redtop (grass)–fiorin
red viper–copperhead
red vision–erythropia
red vitriol–bieberite, botryogen, colcothar
red-wat – bloodstained, bloody
red water tree–sassy
red whortleberry–cranberry
red willow–cornel, osier
redwing–blackbird, thrush
redwood–Sequoia
redwood (Scot.)–mad, furious
red zinc ore–zincite
redact–edit, revise
redacteur–editor
redactor–editor
redargue – accuse, convict, reproach, reprove
redden – blush, flush, ribric, rubicund, rud, rudd, rugious
reddish blue – damascene, smalt
reddish brown–auburn, bay, chestnut, roan, russet, sorrel
reddish brown dye–henna
reddish color–coral
reddish dye–annatto
reddish orange color–henna
reddish yellow – amber, orange
reddition–restitution, restoration, surrender, translation
rede – advice, counsel, explain, interpret, predict, relate
redeem–liberate, ransom, reclaim, recover, regain, repurchase
redeem from captivity–ransom

redeemer–savior, saviour
redient–returning
redintegrate–renew, restore
redness–erubescent
redolence–aroma, fragrance, scent, sweetness
redolent – aromatic, balmy, fragrant, impregnated, odorous
redouble – ingeminate, re-echo, repeat, repetition
redouble attack in fencing–reprise
redound–conduce, resound, return, reverberate
redress – amend, correct, emend, relieve, remedy, reparation
reduce – abase, abate, abridge, bant, bate, conquer, curtail, cut, deplete, diminish, humble, lessen, lower, minimize, pare, razee, subdue, subjugate
reduce (by cutting down) – razee
reduce by paring–scale
reduce in density–thin
reduce in flesh–emaciate
reduce in rank–demote
reduce to a mean–average
reduce to ashes–cremate
reduce to average–equate
reduce to charcoal–char
reduce to common measure–commensurate
reduce to common plane – level
reduce to fine spray–atomize
reduce to human bondage–enslave
reduce to lower grade – degrade, demote
reduce to mean time–equate
reduce to powder – grind, pulverize
reducent–diluter
reduction – allowance, discount, rebate
reduction in value–depreciation
reduction to a definite level–standardization
reduction to greater compactness–condensation

redundant – copious, excessive, exuberant, lavish, overflowing, pleonastic, superabundant, superfluous, verbose
ree – arikara, channel, coalyard, crazy, dam, drunk, enclosure, fuddled, harbor, riddle, river, sheepfold, sift, wild
re-echo – resound, reverberate
reechy–rancid
reed (loom)–sley
reed (weaver's)–sley
reedbird–bobolink, warbler
reedbuck–bohor, nagor
reed mace–cattail, matreed
reed pheasant–reedling
reef–bar, cay, cayo, eruption, itch, key, lode, mange, shoal, shorten, vein
reef (coral)–key
reef (low)–cay, cayo
reef (submerged sand)–bar
reefer–midshipman, miner, oyster
reek – equip, rig, seaweed, smoke, steam
reel – dance, lurch, spool, stagger, titubate, totter, windlass
reel (used in dyeing)–wince
reel (yarn)–swift
reel of a fishing rod (Scot.)–pirn
reel off a story (Scot.) – scrieve
reem (King James Bible) – unicorn
re-enact–relive
re-encourage–reman
re-enlist (army slang)–reup
reese–scorch
reeshie–beat, clatter, rustle
reest – balk, moldboard, plowshare
re-establish–reseat
reeve – enclosure, pucker, sheepfold, twist, wind, wrinkle
refactory–rebel
refectory (monastery, hist.)–frater
refer – allude, appertain,

ascribe, attribute, charge, cite, impute, recur, relate, return

refer to–consult, mention

refer to repeatedly–harp

referee – arbiter, judge, umpire

referee's decision (slang) – nod

reference – allusion, connection, pertinence, recommendance, recommendation, regard, relation, relevance, respect

reference book – atlas, dictionary, encyclopedia, handbook, syllabus

reference table–index

referendum–mandate, plebiscite

referring–relative

referring to tropical fever–calentural

refine or purify–sublimate

refined – chaste, clarifies, cleansed, courteous, cultivated, elegant, fastidious, highbred, nice, pure, purified, smelted, urbane

refined ore–smelted, steel

refined spirit–elixir, grace

refinement – clarification, cultivation, delicacy, elegance, gentility, polish, purification

refinery (ore)–smelter

refining cup–cupel

reflect – cogitate, consider, deflect, divert, meditate, mirror, muse, ponder, ruminate, think

reflected sound–echo

reflecting – reverberatory, thoughtful

reflection – cogitation, consideration, contemplation, meditation, musing, rumination, thinking

reflects profoundly–pores

reflex – bent, reflected, turned

reflow–ebb, reflux

reflux – ebb, ebbing, reflow, refluence, returning

refont–recast

reform – amend, better,

emend, mend, rebuild, reclaim, rectify, reformation, regenerate, remass, renew, repair, restore

reformado–volunteer

reformer–amender, Luther, reformado, reviser

reformer (counter)–papist

refraction (pert. to)–anaclastic

refractor (light)–prism

refractory – contumacious, froward, intractable, obstinate, perverse, stubborn, ungovernable, unmanageable, unruly, unyielding

refrain – abstain, avoid, check, chorus, curb, epode, forbear, govern, restrain, shun

refrain from – abstain, restrain, shunned, withhold

refrain from the use of–boycott

refrain from using–spare

refrain in music–epode

refrain of a song–bob

refresco–drink, refreshment

refresh–cheer, dew, freshen, invigorate, reanimate, recreate, refreshment, reinvigorate, renovate, revive

refresh by rest–repose

refresh with water–slake

refreshing–balmy, heartening, invigorating

refrigerant–ammonia, cooler, cooling, ice, refreshing

refrigerate – chill, cool, freeze, ice

refrigerator–icer

refuge–ark, asylum, covert, haven, hospital, protection, retreat, sanctuary, shelter

refugee–emigre, exile

refulgence – brilliancy, radiance, splendor

refund – rebate, reimburse, repay

refurbish–brighten, freshen, renew, renovate, vamp

refusal–declination, nay, rejection

refuse – balk, chaff, culm, debris, decline, deny, dross, junk, litter, lumber, marc, offal, ort, reject, renege, renig, trash, waste, withhold

refuse (anthracite coal) – culm

refuse (coffee berry)–triage

refuse (flax, used as fuel)–pob

refuse (grape)–marc

refuse (melting of metal)–scoria

refuse (mine)–attle

refuse (sugar cane, dry) – bagasse

refuse assent to–veto

refuse matter (from grapes) –marc

refuse politely–decline

refuse to accept–reject

refuse to acknowledge–disavow, repudiate

refuse to comply (obstinately)–recalcitrant

refuse to proceed–balk

refutation–confutation, disproof, rebuttal

refute–deny, disprove, meet, overthrow, rebut, refuge

regain–retrieve, recover

regain (as a loss)–recoup

regal – channel, groove, imperial, kingly, majestic, royal, splendid, stately

regal chair–throne

regale–dine, entertain, feast, fete, treat

regard–adjudge, air, appearance, aspect, behold, consider, deem, esteem, estimate, estimation, honor, look, mind, observe, rate, remark, repute, respect, reverse, sake, treat, view

regard as object of interest–lionize

regard for another's wishes–deference

regard highly–admire

regard too highly–overrate

regard with approval – admire

regard with deference and respect–honor

regard with delight–admire
regard with honor and deference–respect
regard with veneration – revere
regardful – attentive, mindful, thoughtful
regardful of others–altruistic
regardless–inattentive, indifferent, neglectful, negligent, unconcerned, unobservant
regatta–race
regency–dominion, government, rule
regenerate–reborn, reclaim, recreate, redeem, reform, renew, renovate, restore, revive
regeneration–recreation, reformation, renewal, revival
regent–governing, governor, regnant, ruler, ruling
regent diamond–Pitt
regimen – administration, government, regulation, rule, system
regiment (framework of)–cadre
regina–queen
region–area, climate, clime, country, demesne, district, kingdom, province, realm, tract, zone
region (beyond Jordan)–Perea
region (blissful)–Eden
region (desert)–waste
region (desert of shifting sand)–erg
region (east of Jordan) – Basham
region (indefinite extent) – tract
region (India)–des
region (infernal)–Tartarus
region (noted for conflicts)–cockpit
region (poetic)–clime, gay
region (wooded)–wold
region (woodless)–weald
region of dead (Egyptian myth.)–Amenti
region of fabulous riches – Eldorado

region of nether darkness – Erebus
region of rustic simplicity and contentment (poetic) –Arcady
region on opposite side of earth–Antipodes
region where Solomon obtained gold and gems – Ophir
register–annal, archives, catalogue, chronicle, enlist, enrol, enroll, entry, list, matriculate, record, recorder, registrar, roll, schedule
register (legal)–docket
register of deaths–necrology
register opposition–protest
registering apparatus – recorder
registrar–recorder
regius–king, royal
regle–govern, rule
regret – compunction, deplore, grief, penitence, remorse, repent, repentance, repine, rew, rue, ruth, sorrow, sorry
regret (profoundly)–deplore
regretful – repentant, repining, sorry
regular – constant, correct, even, isometric, normal, ordered, ordinary, ordinate, standard, stated, systematic, typical, uniform
regular grouping of accents –rhythms
regularly–correctly, duly, orderly, properly, symmetrically
regularly bulging–convex
regularly produced–staple
regulate – adjust, arrange, control, direct, dispose, govern, methodize, order, rule, set
regulate by test (var.)–standardize
regulate pitch of–key
regulating body of clock – pendulum
regulating box–rheostat
regulation – control, direc-

tion, disposal, law, order, precept, rule, system
regulation (subordinate to a constitution)–bylaw
regulator (current)–rheometer
regulator (electric current)–rheostat
regulus–king, matte, ruler
rehabilitate–reinstall, restore
rehash–rechauffe, restate
rehearse – describe, detail, enumerate, mention, narrate, recapitulate, recite, recount, relate, repeat, say, speak, tell
rehoboam–bowl, flagon, hat, jeroboam
reif–plunder, robbery
reign – dominion, empire, guide, kingdom, realm, rule, sovereignty, sway
reigning beauty–belle
reimbue with courage – reman
reimburse–indemnify, pay, refund, repay, replace
reimkennar (Scot.)–sorcerer, sorceress
Reims (former name)–Remi
rein–check, control, curb, direct, kidney, stop
reina–rockfish
reindeer (American) – caribou
reinfluence–reimpel
reinforce – back, brace, reman, strengthen, support
reinforcement (annular plate)–sput
reit–seaweed, sedge
reiterate–drum, harp, recapitulate, rehearse, repeat
reject–decline, disallow, discard, dismiss, disown, refel, refuse, repel, repudiate, spurn
reject (disdainfully)–spurn
reject (law)–recuse
rejectamenta–excrement, refuse, rejects, rubbish, wrack
rejection of fundamentals–belief, heresy
rejoice–cheer, delight, gladden

rejoin–answer, respond

rejoinder – answer, replication, reply, response

relache–intermission, relaxation

relapse–lapse, sink, subside

relate – appertain, describe, detail, narrate, pertain, recite, recount, rehearse, report, tell

relate in detail–recount

related–akin, described, german, kin, narrated, pertained, recounted, told

related (on father's side)–agnate, agnation

related (on mother's side)–cognate, enate, enatic, enation

related by blood–cognate, sib

relater–narrator, reciter

relating to–*see also* pertaining to

relating to bread–panary

relating to Chinese–Sinitic

relating to country–praedial, predial

relating to dancing–gestic

relating to doctrine of design –teleological

relating to eye–optic

relating to grandparents – aval

relating to Hindu literature–Vedic

relating to holly genus–ilicic

relating to land – praedial, predial

relating to life–vital

relating to one's self–personal

relating to Osmium–Osmic

relating to realities–factual

relating to science of motion –kinematic

relating to soft palate–velar

relating to Sufism–Sufistic

relating to vascular system fluid–hemic

relation–account, kin, narration, recital, rehearsal, relationship, status, tale, telling

relation (blood)–sib

relation (fixed)–ratio

relation (friendly)–amity

relation (Hindu law)–rishtadar

relation (local)–ubiety

relation of likeness–analogy

relation to pharynx (prefix) –lemo

relationship – affinity, consanguinity, kinship

relationship (blood) – consanguinity, kinsman, relative

relationship (inharmonious) –outs

relative – allied, apposite, comparative, eme, kin, kindred, kinsfolk, nephew, niece, pertinent, uncle

relative (material)–enate

relative amount–degree

relative position–standing

relative to Roman language –Latinic

relatives (favoritism shown to)–nepotism

relax – abate, divert, ease, loose, mitigate, remit, rest, unbend

relaxation – abatement, diversion, ease, recreation, remission, rest, slackening

relaxing tension–slackening, slacking

relay–relieve

relay (India)–dak, dawk

relay of fresh hounds (hunting)–avantlay

relay of mounts (Span.)–remuda

release–acquittance, deliver, discharge, drop, exempt, free, freedom, liberate, liberation, loosen, relinquish, remise, trip, undo, unloose, untie

release (as a prisoner)–remit

release (as a prisoner on his own)–parole

release (as claim)–remise

release (conditional)–parole

release from captivity–unpen

release from liability – exempt

release from restraint – undam, unleash

release from slavery–manumit

relegate–banish, commit, deport, dismiss, exile, remove

relevant–germane, pertinent

reliable–tried, trustworthy, trusty

reliable (not) – capricious, fickle, untrustworthy

reliance–confidence, dependence, hope, trust

relic–antique, curio

relic cabinet–atagere, etagere, whatnot

relict–widow

relied–confided, counted, depended, reckoned, reposed, trusted

relief–aid, alleviation, assistance, bot, bote, comfort, deliverance, dole, ease, easement, help, indemnification, mitigation, redress, remedy, succor

relief (ornamental work in) –fret

relieve–aid, allay, assist, assuage, diminish, ease, free, help, lighten, redress, remedy, remove, spell, succor, support, sustain, unloose

relieve (coll.)–spell

relieve from fatigue or depression–refresh

relieved from active service (honorably)–emeritus

religion (barbaric)–voodooism

religion (primitive)–voodoo

religion (secluded and devoted to)–monastic

religious–conscientious, devotional, devout, exact, fervent, godly, holy, pious, rigid, scrupulous, spiritual, zealous

religious (formally)–pharasaic

religious assembly – congregation

religious belief–deism

religious brotherhood–sodality

religious composition–motet

religious denomination–cult, sect

religious devotee – fakir, monk, nun
religious devotion–novena
religious discourse–homily, sermon
religious division–schism
religious expedition (militant)–crusade
religious fair (India)–mela
religious feeling (one who makes show of)–pietist
religious festival–Purim
religious house – convent, monastery
religious leaflet–tract
religious mendicant–servite
religious musical composition–anthem
religious observance – fast, Purim
religious offering (obs.) – deodate
religious order (member of) –marist
religious poem–psalm
religious rite–cult
religious rites (classical antiquity)–sacra
religious sect (one of)–Mormon
religious sect (who dance as they worship)–Shakers
religious system of observance–cult
religious usage–ritus
religious worship (system of)–cult, cultus
relinquish–abandon, desert, forgo, forsake, leave, renounce, resign, surrender, waive, yield
relinquish sovereign power–abdicate
relinquish throne–abdicate
relinquish voluntarily – remise, waive
relinquishment - renunciation, surrender
reliquary – apse, apsis, arca, arcae (pl.), box, casket, chest, shrine
reliquary (lamaism)–chorten
reliquiae–relics
relish–achar, canape, degust, degustate, flavor, gust, gusto, savor, seasoning, tang, taste, zest
relish (keen)–gusto
relish (salty)–caviar
relishable–sapid
relucent–radiant, refulgent, shining
reluctance – aversion, disinclination, indisposition
reluctance unit–rel
reluctant–averse, loath, loth
reluctant (not)–ready
reluctant in giving–chary
reluctate–oppose, repel, repudiate
rely–cleave, confide, count, hold, reckon, repose, trust
rely upon–lippen, trust
remain–abide, bide, continue, endure, lie, reside, rest, stay, tarry, thole
remainder – balance, leavings, remnant, residual, residue, residuum, rest, stub, stump, surplus
remaining–left, over, remnant, residual, staying
remaining in place–ledger, leger
remaining stationary–static, waiting
remains–ashes, corpse, ruins, stays
remains (geologic)–fossils
remanent–enduring, lasting, permanent, remainder, remains, remnant, residue
remark – annotation, comment, gloss, heed, note, notice, observation, observe, regard, say
remark (amusing, coll.)–gag
remark (clever)–mot
remark (commonplace) – platitude
remark (mocking) – quip, sarcasm
remark (smarting)–stinger
remark (witless)–boner
remark (witty)–quip
remarkable–notable, observable, strange, unusual, wonderful
reme–scream, shout
remede–redress, remedy
remedial–panacean

remedied–cured, redressed
remediless – cureless, hopeless, irremediable, irreparable, irretrievable
remedy–aid, amend, assistance, bot, bote, cure, gain, help, medicine, relief
remedy (alkaline)–antacid
remedy (counteractive)–antidote
remedy (cure-all)–elixir
remedy (dysentery) – sulfaguanidine
remedy (gout)–lycetol
remedy (mysterious) – arcanorum, arcanum
remedy (quack)–nostrum
remedy (soothing)–balm
remedy (universal)–panacea
remedy for rheumatism – salacetol, salol
remember–recall, recollect, remind, reminisce
remembrance – memento, memorial, memory, minnie, recollecting, souvenir, token, trophy
remind–recall, remember
reminder–memento, memo
reminder (derisive)–twit
reminiscence – act, experience, fact, memory, power, recollection
reminiscence (noteworthy)–memorabilia
remise–giving, granting, release, remission, replace, respite, return, surrender
remiss – careless, dilatory, heedless, inattentive, lax, neglectful, negligent, slack, thoughtless
remissful – careless, lenient, merciful, remiss
remissness (law)–laches
remit–abrogate, cancel, excuse, forgive, liberate, pardon, release, resign, surrender, suspend
remnant – dreg, fragment, left, ort, relic, remainder, remains, rest, scrap, stub, suggestion, trace
remnant of combustion–ash
remodel–recast, reconstruct
remoisten–redamp

remolade – dressing, ointment, sauce

remonstrate – expostulate,
protest

remora (West Indies)–pega,
pegador

remord–afflict, censure, rebuke, remorse, taint

remorse–compassion, com-
punction, distress, peni-
tence, pity, regret, repent-
ent

remorseful – compassionate,
penitent, pitiable, pitiful,
sorry

remorseless–implacable, pitiless, relentless, unmerci-
ful, unpitying, unrelent-
ing

remote–alien, distant, elenge,
far, forane, foreign, off,
secluded, vague

remote (more)–ulterior

remote (most)–ultima

remoter–ulterior

remotest–endmost

remove–abstract, assassinate,
change, dele, delete, de-
pose, dismiss, displace,
eliminate, eradicate, erase,
extract, remble, rid, transfer, translate, void, weed

remove (afar off)–eloign

remove (as clothes) – doff,
strip

remove bark from–ross, scale

remove beyond jurisdiction
(law)–eloin

remove cover–uncap

remove forcibly–evict, expel,
rend

remove foreign substance
from wool–garnett

remove from office–depose,
recall

remove from point of origin
–distal

remove legally–eloign, eloin,
oust

remove mast from base
(naut.)–unstep

remove moisture–dehydrate,
dry, wring

remove seed from flax –
ribble

remove seed part–picul

remove seeds–gin, pit

remove stalk from–strig

remove to another–translate

remove to inferior position–
relegate

removed–apart, betook, distant, remote, separated,
took

removed blubber from –
flensed

removed from high position
–deposed

remover–carrier, contractor,
drayman, eradicator, por-
ter, scavenger, solvent

remunerate – compensate,
pay, recompense, reim-
burse, repay, requite, reward, satisfy

remuneration–pay, payment,
recompense, reimburse-
ment, satisfaction

Remus' brother–Romulus

Remus' slayer–Romulus

renable – eloquent, fluent,
glib, ready

renascence–rebirth, revival

rencounter – action, clash,
collision, combat, conflict,
duel, flight

rend–break, cleave, fracture,
rip, rupture, split, tear

rend asunder–rive

render – clarify, deliver, extract, give, make, melt,
pay, present, put, requite,
return, translate, transmit

render (as lard)–try

render accessible–open

render agreeable–dulcify

render choleric–enrage

render dull–hebetate

render enduring–anneal

render fertile–enrich

render free from bacteria –
sterilize

render harsh–hoarsen

render impotent–annul

render ineffective–vitiate

render knotty–gnarl

render like chalcedony–agat-
ize

render muddy–roil

render oblique–splay

render obscure–darkle

render of no force or effect–
annul, invalidate, void

render sharp–acuminate

render stupid–hebetate

render suitable–adapt, prepare

render turbid–roil

render unconscious–stun

render undrinkable (as alcohol)–denature

render unstable–unhinge

rendered capable of absorption–activated

rendered divine–deified

rendezvous – appointment,
meeting, refuge, retreat,
tryst

rendition–delivery, interpretation, performance, sur-
render, translation

renegade–apostate, deserter,
pervert, rat, rebel, traitor,
turncoat

renegade (slang)–rat

renege–decline, deny, desert,
renounce, revoke

renew – invigorate, redintegrate, refresh, regenerate,
renovate, restore, resume,
revive, revamp

renew wine (with must) –
stum

renewal–renovation

renitent – opposed, recalcitrant

renky–lanky, large, robust

rennet – apple, coagulate,
curdle, lab

rennet ferment–rennin

rennin–enzyme

renomme – celebrated, re-
nowned

renommist – braggart, re-
nowner, swaggerer

renounce–abandon, abjure,
abnegate, cede, deny, de-
sert, disown, forego, forgo, forsake, forswear, recant, reject, relinquish,
renay, renege, repudiate,
resign, retract, surrender,
waive

renounce on oath–adjure

renovate–regenerate, renew,
restore, resume, revive

renown–glory, reputation

renowned – celebrated, distinguished, eminent, famed, famous, illustrious, noted

rent–hire, hole, lease, let, pay, revenue, reward, rupture, share, slit, slitted, split, tear, toll, tore, tribute

rent asunder–rived

rent paid (English law)–tac

rent paid in oats–avenage

rentee–lessee, tenant

renter of property – lessee, tenant

renting contract–lease

renunciation–abandonment, abjuration, denial, disavowal, disclaimer, rejection, relinquishment

repaid in kind–retaliated

repair–amend, correct, darn, fix, mend, remedy, renew, restore

repair sails–wearied

reparation–amende, amends, indemnity, recompense, redress, requital, restitution, reward

reparation for injuries–damages

repartee–reply, retort, riposte

repast – feast, feed, meal, treat

repast (light)–collation, tea

repatriate–banish, exile, expatriate

repays – avenges, compensates, meeds, recompenses, refunds, reimburses, remunerates, requites, restores, returns

repeal – abolish, abrogate, annul, appeal, cancel, emend, recall, renounce, rescind, retract, reverse

repeat–duplicate, echo, iterate, rame, recur, restate

repeat a sound–echo

repeat mechanically–parrot

repeat noisily–din

repeat part of circulating decimal–repetend

repeat performance–encore

repeatedly altered–varied

repeating from memory – rote

repel – disgust, oppose, rebuff, refuse, repulse, resist, revolt

repellent – harsh, repulsive, revolting

repent of–regret, rue

repentance – compunction, contrition, penitence, regret, ruth, shame

repenter of sins–penitent

repertory – calendar, catalogue, collection, index, list, magazine, storehouse, treasury

repetition–encore, iterance, iteration, recapitulation, reiteration, troll

repetition (demand for)–encore

repetition (mechanical)–rote

repetition (monotonous) – rote

repetition (music, quavering)–tremolo

repetition (musical)–rondo

repetition (unnecessary) – tautology

repetition of a note (quavering)–tremolo

repetition of homologous parts–merism

repetition of same words – tautology

repetition of slight sounds–patter

repetition of sound–echo

repetitive–redundant

repine – complain, fret, grumble

replace–reset, restore, stead, stet, supersede, supplant

replant (hort.)–reset

replant with trees–reforest

replate–retin

replenish–feed, fill, store

replete–bloated, filled, full, gorged, sated, surfeited

replica–bis, copy, duplicate, facsimile

replies–answers, rebuts, rejoinders, rejoins, responds, responses, retorts

reply (abbr.)–ans.

reply (quick)–riposte

reply (witty)–repartee

reply of ancient god to inquiry–oracle

report–bruit, describe, hearsay, narration, narrative, pop, recital, recite, rumor, state, story

report (absurd)–canard

report (common)–cry

report (false) – rumor, rumour, slander

report (false, vicious) – canard

report (official, of British Parliament)–hansard

report (popular)–rumor

report (unverified)–rumor, rumour

report following flash of lightning–thunder

report of proceedings–cahier

reporter–newsman

reporter (young)–cub

reporter's symbol (for end of story)–thirty

repose – deposit, ease, lie, peace, place, quietness, recline, relaxation, rely, rest, sit, sleep

repository–depository, museum, vault

repository (document)–file

repository (sacred)–ark

reposoir–altar

reprance–recaper

reprehensible – blamable, blameworthy, censurable, culpable, reprovable

reprehension – blame, censure, reprimand, reproof

represent–denote, depict, enact, portray, typify

represent (vividly)–depict

representation – avowal, delineation, depiction, enactment, exhibition, icon, idol, portraiture, portrayal, profession, reproduction, show

representation (favorable)–recommendation

representation (graphic) – chart

representation (mental) – image

representation (Medusa's head)–gorgoneum

representation (small scale)–miniature

representation (var.)–ikon

representation by characters –notation

representation in miniature–model

representation of scene–tableau

representation of solar system–orrery

representation of stars (conventional)–etoile

representation of the planets and sun–orrery

representative – agent, ambassador, delegate, envoy, exponent, illustrative, legate, symbolic, typical

representative (legal, coll.)–attorneydom

representative (people's) – tribune

representative example–type

representative part–sample

repress–check, crush, curb, overpower, quell, restrain, stifle, stop, suppress

reprimand – censure, chide, rebuke, reprove, slate

reprisal–requital, revenue

reproach – abuse, blame, chide, condemn, dishonor, disrepute, invective, opprobrium, revile, shend, taunt, twit, upbraid, vilification, vilify

reproach (abusively)–revile

reproach (Jewish term for)–raca

reproach (keen)–sarcasm

reprobate–abandon, disown, hardened, reject, reprehend, reprehensible

reproduce–copy, duplicate, multiply, propagate

reproduction–copy, counterpart, likeness, replica

reproduction (exact)–copy

reproduction of original–ectype

reproductive organ (of flowerless plant)–spore

reproof–admonition, blame-

worthy, censurable, chiding, confutation, rebuke, refutation, reprehensible, reprehension, reprimand

reproof (severe)–roast

reprove – admonish, berate, blame, censure, chide, correct, objurgate, rate, rebuke, reprehend, reprimand, reproach, scold, upbraid

reproving–admonitive

reptile – lizard, serpent, snake, worm

reptile (aquatic)–crocodile

reptile (edible)–turtle

reptile (extinct)–predentate

reptile (flying, extinct)–pterodactyl, pterosaur, pterosauria

reptile (hard-shelled) – tortoise, turtle

reptile (large)–alligator, boa, crocodile

reptile (Mesozoic)–dinosaur

reptile (prehistoric) – dinosaur

reptile scale (hard, on head) –scute

reptilian–saurian

republic (imaginary, ideal)–Oceania

repudiate–abjure, disavow, discard, disown, reject, renounce

repugnance–abhorrence, antipathy, disgust, loathing, reluctance

repugnance (extreme)–odium

repugnant–adverse, incompatible, inimical, irreconcilable, odious, opposed, repellent, repulsive

repulse – denial, rebuff, refusal, rejection, repel

repulsion (Scot.)–ug

repulsive – disgusting, fulsome, loathly, offensive, repellent, ugly, vile

repulsiveness–odium

reputable – creditable, respectable, worthy

reputation – consideration, distinction, fame, glory, honor, lose, name, renown

repute–credit, esteem, honor, regard, revere, word

reputed–putative

request–appeal, ask, beg, demand, entreat, entreaty, petition, plea, pray, solicit, suit, supplication

request (authoritative) – behest

request (formal)–rogation

request (strong)–demand

requiescence–repose

requin–man-eater, shark

require–ask, claim, compel, demand, enjoin, entail, exact, force, mister, necessitate, need

requirement–need, requisite

requiring expiation – piacular, sinful

requisition – application, demand, order

requital – payment, recompense, reprisal, retaliation, retribution, revenge, reward, vengeance

requite–avenge, compensate, pay, recompense, repay, retaliate, return, revenge, reward, satisfy

reredos–screen, wall

reree–cattail

reremouse–bat

res–matter, point, thing

rescind – abolish, abrogate, annul, cancel, repeal, revoke

rescue–deliver, delivery, extricate, free, liberate, ransom, reclaim, recover, redeem, release, save

rese – hurry, impulse, onset, quake, rashness, rush, shake, tremble

resecure–renail, respike

resemblance–affinity, agreement, analogy, likeness, semblance, similarity, similitude

resemblance of properties or relations–analogy

resembling–alike, like

resembling a comb–pectinal

resembling a goose–anserine

resembling a horse–equoid

resembling a seed–ovular

resembling a star–stellated
resembling a wall–mural
resembling bark–cortical
resembling feldspar–gneissy
resembling gypsum–alabastrine
resembling man–android
resembling minute animals–animalcular
resembling rind–cortical
resembling salt–haloid
resembling sea salt – halid, halide
resembling serpent family – elapine
resembling snakes–viperine
resembling tuft of hair–crinite
resentment–animosity, choler, displeasure, dudgeon, enmity, hatred, indignation, ire, malice, malignity, pique, rancor, spite, umbrage
reserve–coldness, constraint, diffidence, distance, fund, keep, limitation, restraint, retention, reticence, save, shyness, spare, withhold
reserve in speech–reticence
reserved–aloof, incommunicative, kept, reticent, sedate, staid, taken
reservoir – reserve, store, sump, supply
reservoir (lamp)–font
reshape–recast
resiance–abode, residence
reside – abide, dwell, live, lodge, remain, room, sojourn, stay
residence–abode, domicile, dwelling, habitation, home, seat, sojourn, stay
residence (ecclesiastical) – deanery
residence (foreign service)–consulate
residence (regal)–palace
residencia (Span.) – court, trial
resident of a city–cit, citizen
residual – remainder, remnant, residuum
residue–ash, ashes, balance, dreg, leavings, relics, remainder, remains, rest, silt, slag
residue (coal)–coke
residue (insoluble)–marc
residue (pressed grape) – marc
residue (pulpy, left in cider making)–pomace
residuum – hangover, leavings, remainder
resign – abandon, abdicate, cede, demit, quit, relinquish, renounce, submit, surrender, yield
resignation – abdication, demit, endurance, patience, relinquishment, renunciation
resigned – acquiescent, contented, uncomplaining
resilient–elastic
resilient support – garter, spring
resin–amber, anime, copal, dammar, lac, mastic, rosin, tolu
resin (agalloch wood)–aloe
resin (aromatic)–balm, elemi
resin (aromatic gum)–myrrh
resin (brittle aromatic) – sandarac
resin (Chian turpentine)–alk
resin (copal, soft variety)–anime, animi
resin (dark brown, bitter)–labdanum, ladanum
resin (dark brown, elastic mineral)–elaterite
resin (fossil)–amber, retinite
resin (fossilized)–amber
resin (fragrant)–elemi
resin (fragrant gum)–frankincense
resin (gum) – elemi, loban, myrrh
resin (gummy)–myrrh
resin (hard)–rosin
resin (hemp)–charas
resin (incense)–sandarac
resin (kind of)–alk, anime, animi
resin (medicinal)–aroiera
resin (mentioned in Bible)–bdellium
resin (mineral, elastic)–elaterite

resin (oleo, fragrant in varnish)–elemi
resin (pale yellow fossilized) –amber
resin (reddish brown) – myrrh
resin (translucent)–sandarac
resin (tropical)–copal
resin (turpentine from pine trees)–galipot
resin (used in making colorless varnish)–dammar
resin (yellowish)–amber
resin (yellowish brown) – myrrh
resink–redip
resinous substance – copal, gum, lac
resinous substance (purified form)–shellac
resist–fend, oppose, prevent, repel, wither, withstand
resist authority–rebel, repel
resist successfully–withstand
resistance–hostility, opposition, rebuff, renitence
resistance box–rheostat
resistance frame–rheostat
resistance to attack–defence, defense
resistant (stubbornly)–obdurate
resisting – antagonistic, hostile, opposing, oppugnant
resisting power–wiry
resisting pressure–renitent
resisting pressure bar–strut
resolute–bold, constant, decided, determined, firm, fixed, inflexible, persevering, positive, steadfast, stern, unshaken
resolution–analysis, decision, disentanglement, firm, fortitude, nerve, perseverance, persevering, purpose, resolve, resolved, separation, steadfastness, steady, strength
resolution (fixed)–determination
resolve–conclude, decide, determine, purpose, reduce
resolve into constituent elements–analyze

resolve into grammatical elements–parse
resolved–determined
resonance–sonority
resonant–resounding, reverberant, ringing, sonorous, sounding, vibrant
resort–betake, dive, haunt, recourse, refuge, resource, spa
resort (dancing)–casino
resort (health)–spa
resort for help–recourse
resort to–betake
resort to underhand methods – fainaigue, fenagle, finagle
resorted–betook
resounded–echoed, pealed, rang, reverberated
resounding–reverberatory
resourceful–sharp
resources – assets, contrivances, expedients, funds, means, money, resorts
resources (accumulations of) –fund
resources (available pecuniary)–funds
respect–awe, concern, defer, deference, esteem, heed, homage, honor, observe, regard, revere, reverence, venerate
respect (fearful)–awe
respectable–decent, estimable, honorable, reputable
respectful–careful, civil, deferential, duteous, heedful
respectful (deeply)–reverent
respective–attentive, careful, heedful, regardful
respiration (audible)–sigh
respiration (normal) – eupnoea
respiratory rattle–rale
respire–breathe
respite–delay, interval, leisure, opportunity, pause, postpone, rest, suspension
resplendent – brilliant, radiant, refulgent, shining, splendid
respond–accord, answer, correspond, echo, react, reply, response, retort

respond to stimulus–react, reaction
response – answer, chorus, echo, refrain, reply
responsibility – accountability, care, charge, onus, reliability, trustworthiness
responsible – accountable, amenable, answerable, liable, reliable, trustworthy
responsive–answering, sensitive, sympathetic
respublica – commonweal, commonwealth, republic, state
respue–reject
rest–balance, calm, cessation, establish, found, intermission, interval, lair, lay, leisure, lodgment, pause, peace, peacefulness, prop, quiet, quietness, refresh, relax, remainder, remains, remnant, renew, reposal, repose, respite, seat, set, sit, slip, stay, stillness, stop, support, surplus
rest (being at)–otiose
rest (brief intervals of) – respite
rest (foot)–hassock, rail
rest (in reading) – caesura, cesura
rest (musket)–gaffle
rest house (oriental)–serai
restaurant – automat, cafe, cafeteria, diner, tearoom
restaurant (small)–diner
rested (obs.)–slep
resting–abed, dormant, quiescent
resting place (for cattle) – lairage
restitution – compensation, recompense, reparation, return
restless–inquiet, reposeless, restive, roving, sleepless, uneasy, unsettled, wandering
restoration–recovery, redintegration, re-establishment, renovation, repair, reparation, return, revival
restorative–acopon, anodyne
restore–cure, heal, rebuild,

reconstruct, recover, redeem, redintegrate, re-establish, refund, rehabilitate, reinstate, renew, repay, replace, revive
restore after cancelling–stet
restore certainty–reassurance
restore confidence to–reassure
restore courage to–reassure
restore to former position–reinstate
restore to health–cure, heal
restore to proper position – right
restrain–arrest, bate, bridle, check, confine, control, cramp, dam, detention, deter, inhibit, limit, rein, restrict, stay, stint, tether, withhold
restrain by fear–overawe
restrain by wier–dam
restrain from free action – cramp
restrain in words and actions –reserved
restrain through fear–deter
restraint–abridgement, bit, check, confinement, constraint, curb, deprivation, force, repression, reserve, reticence, stop, trammel
restraint (personal)–durance
restraint of princes–embargo
restrict–bound, censor, coerce, confine, curb, limit, modify, repress, scant, stint
restrict (narrowly)–cramp
restrict to scant allowance–stint
restricted–local, narrow
restriction–constriction, limitation, qualification, regulation, reservation, stint, tightening
resty – quiet, rancid, reasty, restive, sluggish
result – achievement, aftermath, conclusion, consequence, effect, end, ensue, event, eventuate, follow, fruit, issue, proceed, redound, rise, sequel, spring, terminate

result (additive)–sum
result (natural)–accrue
result of supply and demand
–price
resulted in–caused
resulting from luck–aleatory
results (graceful acceptance
of)–sportsmanship
resume – epitomize, recommence, reiterate, renew,
reoccupy, summarize
resuscitate–restore, revivify,
revive
ret–expose, soak, steep
retable – gradin, gradine,
ledge, predella, shelf
retailer of wine (Eng.) –
cooper
retain – hold, keep, maintain, preserve, save
retainer–vassal
retainer (humble)–menial
retainer (legal)–fee
retainer (servile)–minion
retaining–retentive
retaining wall–revetment
retaliate–avenge
retaliation–punishment, reprisal, requital, retribution
retaliation (malicious) – revenge
retaliation (under Mosaic
law)–talion
retard–belate, deaden, defer,
delay, detain, impede, obstruct, postpone, slow,
trash
retard in development–overage
retardant–obstacle, remora
retch–expand, extend, gag,
hawk, reach, spit, stretch,
vomit
rete–net, network, plexus
retention–holding, keeping,
maintenance
rethe – ardent, cruel, fierce,
severe
reticence–reserve, secretiveness, silence
reticle–bag, etui
reticulated–netted
reticule–bag, etui, workbag
retinaculum–frenum

retinue – entourage, escort,
service, suite, train
retinue (arch.)–meiny
retinue members–retainers
retinue of wives–harem
retired–abed, departed, dis-
appeared, left, pensioned,
receded, recessed, re-
served, retreated, secluded, sequestered, solitary,
vanished, withdrew
retired from active service–
emeritus
retired list–pensioners
retirement – departure, retreat, seclusion, solitude,
withdrawal
retiring – diffident, modest,
reserved, shy, unobtrusive
retort – answer, mot, repartee, reply, ripost, riposte
retort (sharp)–quip
retouch–refeel
retraction (formal) – pali-
node
retracts – abjures, disowns,
recants, repudiates, re-
scinds
retrad–backward, posterior-
ly
retral–backward, posterior,
retrograde
retreat–asylum, den, departure, lair, nest, privacy,
refuge, retiral, retire, retirement, rout, seclusion,
shelter, solitude, with-
drawal
retreat (secluded)–nook
retreat march to sea (Greek)
–katabasis
retreat (underground dug-
out)–abri
retrench – abridge, curtail,
diminish, economize, in-
tercept, lessen, reduce
retrenchment–abridgement,
curtailment, cut, diminu-
tion, lessening
retribution – nemesis, pay,
recompense, requital, re-
turn, reward, vengeance
retrieve–recover, regain
retrograde–backward, decadent, rearward, recede,
retral, slow

retund – attenuate, blunt,
dull, refute, subdue
return – answer, recur, regress, render, repay, re-
ply, report, requite, re-
spond, restore, revert
return evil for evil–retaliate,
revenge
return in high curve (tennis)
–lob
return like for like–retaliate
Return of the Native author
–Thomas Hardy
return thrust–ripost, riposte
return to first theme (music)
–reprise
reune–reunion, reunite
reup (army slang)–re-enlist
reus–defendant
reveal–bare, bid, communicate, disclose, discover, divulge, evidence, exhibit,
impart, jamb, open, tell,
uncover, unveil, wray
reveal in trust–confide
reveal unintentionally – betray
revealed to few–secret
reveille–call, levet, signal
revel–carousal, carouse, conviviality, delight, feast,
festival, joy, merrymak-
ing, orgy, revelry, riot,
spree, wake, watch
revel (wildly)–carouse
revelant – clear, intelligible,
manifest
revelation – disclosure, discovery, manifestation
revelry – carnival, carousal,
joy, riot
revenant–apparition, ghost,
recurring, specter
revendicate–reclaim, recover
revenge – avenge, requital,
require, retaliate
Revenge (The) author–Ten-
nyson
revenue – income, profit, return, yield
revenue (bishop's first year)
–annat, annate
reverberate – echo, re-echo,
resound, ring
reverberation – echo, reflection, repercussion

reverberatory – echoing, resounding

revere – adore, esteem, honor, regard, repute, respect, venerate

revered animal–totem

reverence – adoration, awe, deference, dread, honor, respect, veneration, worship

reverent–devout, respectful

reverie–dream, vision

reversal (prefix)–di

reverse–contrary, converse, invert, opposite, overturn, repeal, revoke, upset

reverse end of hammerhead –peen

reverse the order–transpose

reversion of land title (law)–escheat

reversionary additions – annuity

revert – advert, antistrophe, return

revert to prior condition – react

revest – attire, clothe, dress, robe

review – criticism, critique, edit, examination, inspection, resume

reviewer–critic

revile–abuse, debase, rail, reproach, vilify

revile (abusively)–rail

revince–refute

revise–correct, emend, readjust, redact

revision – correction, re-examination, revisal, revise

revival – quickening, reanimation, rebirth, renaissance, resurrection

revive – enliven, rally, rekindle, renew, restore, resuscitate, rouse

revive wine–stum

revocate – recall, repress, revoke

revocation – recantation, repeal, retraction, reversal, withdrawal

revoke – abolish, abrogate, annul, cancel, countermand, recall, recant, re-

nege, renig, repeal, retract

revoke (as a grant)–adeem

revoke (at cards)–fainaigue, fenagle, finagle, renege, renig

revoke a legacy–adeem

revoke a legal grant–adeem

revolt – mutiny, rebel, sedition, uprising

revolting – disgusting, hideous, nauseating, offensive, repellent, shocking

revolution–circuit, cycle, disorder, gyre, rebellion, rotation, turn

revolutionary–new

Revolutionary hero – Allen, Revere

revolutions per minute–revs, RPM

revolve – circle, deliberate, gyrate, meditate, ponder, roll, rotate, spin, turn, wheel, whirl

revolve (cause to)–trundle

revolve (rapidly) – spin, whirl

revolve in thought–con

revolving–rotary

revolving chimney cover – cowl

revolving part–rotor

revolving storm–cyclone

revue–burlesque

reward – bonus, compensation, guerdon, meed, merit, pay, remunerate, remuneration, retribution, utu, yield

reward (well-deserved) – meed

reward to a dog (entrails of hare)–hallow

rewarding–beneficial, helpful, profitable, remunerative

rezai–coverlet

rhamn–buckthorn

rhapontic–rhubarb

rhea–emu

rhema–verb, term, word

rhenium (symbol for)–re

rheoscope–galvanoscope

rheotome–interrupter

rhetoric digression–ecbole

rhetorical–oratorical

rhetorical figure of speech–aporia

rheumatism remedy–solacetol, salol

rheumatism weed – pipsissewa

rhexis (med.)–rupture

rhine (Eng. dial.) – ditch, drain, runnel

Rhine (pert. to)–Rhenish

Rhine affluent–Ruhr

Rhine Maidens' magic hoard –Rheingold, Rhinegold

Rhine nymph–Lorelei

Rhine (Prussian) province government–aachen

Rhine siren–Lorelei

Rhine tributary–Ruhr

Rhine wine–Moselle

Rhinegold character–Erda

rhino–cash, money, rhinoceros

rhinoceros–abada

rhinoceros (black)–borele

rhinoceros (hornbill)–topan

rhinoceros (two-horned) – keitloa

rhinoceros bird–beefeater

rhizopods (genus of) – ameba, amebas (pl.), amoeba, amoebae (pl.)

rhoda–rose

Rhode Island founder–Roger Williams

Rhodes festival–Chelidonia

Rhodesia (northern) tribe – Balokwakwa

rhododaphne–oleander

rhoeadales–poppy

rhomb–lozenge

rhomboid–parallelogram

rhombus–lozenge

Rhone tributary–Isere

rhubarb–pieplant, yawweed

rhubarb (cultivated) – rhapontic

rhubarb (genus of)–rheum

rhus tree–sumac, sumach

rhus yielding tree – sumac, sumach

rhymester (mechanical) – tintinnabulum

rhyptic–detergent

rhythm–cadence, meter, metre

rhythm instrument–drum

rhythmic–poetic
rhythmic movement–lilt
rhythmic music–swing
rhythmic swing–lilt
rhythmical – cadenced, cadent, measured
rhythmical break in poetry–caesura
ria–creek, inlet
rial – excellent, great, king, magnificent, noble, prince, royal, splendid
rialto – exchange, market, mart
riant–bright, gay, laughing, smiling
riata–lariat, lasso
rib–costa, costae (pl.)
rib (Gothic vault)–lierne
rib (of leaves)–vein
rib (vaulting)–lierne
rib grass–ribwort
ribs (pert. to)–costal
ribs (without)–decostate
ribald–attelan, blasphemous, coarse, low, obscene, scurrilous
riband–ribbon
ribbed–corded
ribble row–rigmarole, string
ribbon–bow, fillet
ribbon (knot of)–rosette
ribbon (silk, thin)–taste
ribbon (silk, used on embroidered girdle)–corse
ribbon (used in vestments)–corse
ribbon (worn as a badge)–cordon
ribbon-like–taenioid
ribbon-shaped–taenioid
ribbon worm–nemertine
ribwort–plantain
rice (boiled with meat, etc.)–pilau, pilaw
rice (cooked with meat, gravy, or cheese)–risotto
rice (feeding on) – oryzivorous
rice (inferior)–paga
rice (second or third grade)–chit
ricebird–bobolink, bunting, gallinule, sparrow
rice bunting–bobolink

rice drink (Philippine fermented)–bubud
rice-field rail–sora
rice hen–gallinule
rice husks–shood, shud
rice paste–ame
rice rail–sora
rice refuse–shood, shud
rich – abundant, affluent, bountiful, copious, creamy, fat, luxuriant, mighty, moneyed, opime, opulent, potent, powerful, wealthy
rich (Eng. slang)–oofy, oofier
rich and musical–orotund
rich man–capitalist, Croesus, magnate, Midas, millionaire, millionnaire, nabob, plutocrat
rich man (parable) – Dives, nabob, plutocrat
richard–plutocrat
richdom–richness, wealth
riche – authority, realm, reign, rule
riches–affluence, lucre, opulence, wealth
riches (demon of) – Mammon
riches personified – Mammon
rick – chatter, heap, noise, pile, rattle, scold, sprain, stack, twist, wrench
rickety – crazy, ramshackle, shaky, tottering, unsound, unstable, weak
rickle–heap, jingle, pile, rattle, rick, stack
rickmatic – affair, business, concern
ricochet–carom, rebound
rid–clear, deliver, disencumber, empty, free, remove, rescue
rid oneself of–doff
ridder–sieve
riddle – conundrum, crux, enigma, perforate, perplex, puzzle, rebus, separate, sieve
riddle (to)–ree, sift
riddlemeree–rigmarole
riddler–screener, sift

ride – carrousel, excursion, journey, merry-go-round
ride shanks' mare (slang)–walk
ride the goat–initiate
ride the line–herd
ride to hounds–hunt
rideau–mound, ridge
rident–laughing, riant, smiling
rider–allonge, endorsement, freebooter, highwayman, knight, mosstrooper, performer
Rider Haggard's novel–She
ridge–aas, chine, crest, rib, weal
ridge (anatomical) – ruga, rugae (pl.)
ridge (between two furrows)–porcate
ridge (broad top mountain)–loma
ridge (circular on shells) – pilae (pl.)
ridge (coral)–reef
ridge (glacial drift) – eskar, esker, kame, oesar, os, osar (pl.)
ridge (glacial sand)–os, osar (pl.)
ridge (long low stony)–rand
ridge (mountain)–aret, arete
ridge (mountain rugged) – sierra
ridge (narrow)–eskar, esker
ridge (narrow, raised)–wale
ridge (raised by a stroke)–wheal, whelk
ridge (rising above surface) –wale
ridge (short)–kame
ridge (short, of stratified drift)–kame
ridge (small) – stria, striae (pl.)
ridge (steep-sided, with sharp summit)–hogback
ridge (subglacial sand) – os, osar (pl.)
ridge oak–blackjack
ridge of gravelly drift (geol.)–eskar, esker
ridge of mountains–sierra
ridge protecting military camp–rideau

ridges (glacial) – eskars, eskers, kames, oesar, osar

ridges (one of, encircling cattle's horn)–ring

ridges of drift (geol.)–osar

ridgeling–cryptorchid

ridicule – asteism, banter, burlesque, chaff, deride, derision, gibe, irony, jeer, mock, mockery, pan, quiz, raillery, sarcasm, satire, sneer, taunt, twit

ridicule (coll.)–guy, pan

ridiculous–absurd, amusing, farcical, laughable, ludicrous, outrageous, preposterous

ridiculous failure–fiasco

riding knot–slipknot

riding school–manege

riding whip–crop, quirt

rife – abounding, plentiful, prevailing, prevalent, replete

riff–diaphragm, midriff, riffle, ripple

riffraff–mean, mob, rabble, refuse, rubbish, sweepings, trashy

rifle – carbine, despoil, firearm, pillage, plunder, ransack, reeve, rob, steal

rifle (cavalryman's)–carbine

rifle (French)–chassepot

rifle (magazine, of great range)–Mauser

rifle (old form of)–tige

rifle (short)–carbine

rifle accessory (old fashioned)–ramrod

rifle ball–minie

rifle part (old)–tige

rifle pin–tige

rifler–hawk, robber

rift–cleave, divide, lag, rive, split

rig–clothe, dress, equip, fit

rig (sailing vessel)–lateen

Riga Gulf island–Oesel

rigging (part of)–spar

right – appropriate, becoming, correct, dexter, equitable, fair, faultless, fit, prerogative, proper, suitable, true, upright

right (constitutional) – franchise

right (just)–pat

right (law)–droit

right (legal, India) – hak, hakh

right (proprietory)–interest

right (turn)–gee

right angle (hundredth of)– grad, grade

right-angled–orthogonal

right down – complete, positively, thorough, thoroughly, very

right hand (on)–dexter

right hand page–recto

right nor wrong (neither)– adiaphorous

right of a husband in wife's property–curtesy

right of belligerent to requisition ships and goods – angary

right of belligerent to use neutral's property–angary

right of first choice accorded eldest (English law) – esnecy

right of ownership–title

right of precedence–pas

right of using another's property–easement

right side (on)–dexter

right to choice–option

right to pasture–eatage

righteous – blameless, equitable, godly, guiltless, moral, pious, upright, virtuous, worthy

righteousness–equity, godliness, holiness, rectitude, uprightness

rightful – appropriate, equitable, honest, just, lawful, legal, proper, true

rigid – austere, firm, rigorous, set, severe, stern, stiff, stringent, tense, unbending, unyielding

rigid in self-denial and devotion–ascetic

rignum–horsemint

rigol – channel, circle, furrow, groove, ring

rigor – asperity, fury, harshness, inflexibility, rigid-

ness, rigour, severity, violence

rigor in conduct–austerity

rigorous – accurate, austere, exact, harsh, inclement, inexorable, inflexible, puritanic, relentless, rigid, severe, strict

rikk–tambourine

rile–anger, irritate, roil, turbidity, vex

riley–irritated, turbid, vexed

rill – brook, course, rivulet, runnel, streamlet

rill (small)–rillock

rim – border, boundary, brim, brink, edge, enclose, horizon, lip, margin, perimeter, shield, tire, verge

rim (external)–flange

rim (projecting) – brim, flange

rim (wheel) – felloe, felly, fellies (pl.)

rim of horseshoes–web

rim of a shield–orle

rima – aperture, breadfruit, cleft, fissure

rimash–hackberry

rimate–fissured

rime–aperture, chink, crack, fissure, hoar, hoarfrost, rent

rime cold giant – Ymer, Ymir

rimed–iced

rimple–fold, ripple, rumple, wrinkle

rimption–abundance, lot

Rinaldo's steed – bajardo, bayard

rind – bark, cortex, crust, husk, peel, skin

rind (fruit)–epicarp

rind (Scot.)–hoarfrost

rindle – brook, rivulet, runnel

ring – arena, band, chime, circle, clique, coterie, encircle, encompass, group, hoop, knell, peal, rim, ring, set, surround, toll

ring (anchor)–tore, toroid

ring (as a bell)–chime, knell, peal, toll

ring (bridle rein)–terret
ring (finger)–hoop
ring (for training horses)–
longe
ring (fruit jar)–lute
ring (gate fastening)–hank
ring (gem setting) – bezel,
chaton
ring (guiding, for bridle
rein)–terret
ring (harness pad)–terret
ring (horse training)–longe
ring (little)–annulet
ring (metal, for arm or neck
ornament)–bee
ring (of rope)–grommet
ring (packing)–lute
ring (rubber fruit jar)–lute
ring around sun–corona
ring carrier–go-between
ringdove–cushat
ring dropper–sharper
ringeye–white-eye
ring finger–third
ring harmoniously–chime
Ring of the Nibelung's
smith–Mime
ring ouzel–thrush
ring-shaped–annular
ring slowly–toll
ring-tailed cat–cacomistle
ringworm–milleped, mille-
pede, serpigo, tinea
ringworm infection–tinea
ringed boa–aboma
ringed worm–annelid
ringing – orotund, resounding
ringing (a)–clangor
ringing and musical – orotund
ringing of two or more bells
–clam
ringle-eye–walleye
ringlet – circle, curl, lock,
ring, tress
ringy–resonant, vibrant
rink–circle, course, encircle,
encounter, hero, man,
race, ring, warrior
rinner–runner
rinse–absterge, cleanse, sind,
wash
rinse (Scot.)–sind
rinthereout – rintherout,
tramp, vagabond, vagrant

rio–coffee, river, stream
Rio Grande Indian–Tao
riot–brawl, carousal, clamor,
din, disorder, dispute, excess, quarrel, revelry, tumult, uproar
riot (Russian)–pogrom
riotous–profligate, seditious,
tumultuous, unrestrained,
wanton
riotous jollity–saturnalian
riotously–ariot, roaringly
rip – debauchee, laceration,
rend, rent, tear
rip (slang)–hag, harridan
rip-roarious – boisterous, hilarious
ripe – finished, fit, mature,
ready
ripe (early)–rareripe
ripe (Eng. dial.) – plunder,
rifle, rob
ripe (rare) – riverbank, seashore
ripen–addle, age, complete,
develop, digest, mature,
mellow, perfect
ripening fruit (early)–rareripe
riposte – repartee, reply, retort, ripost, thrust
rippet (Scot. dial.)–quarrel,
romp, uproar
ripping–admirable, remarkable
ripping iron–ravehook
rippit–fight
ripple – acker, cut, dimple,
fret, graze, purl, riff,
scratch, tear, wavelet
ripple against–lap
ripple grass–ribwort
ripple plantain–ribwort
ripply–purly
rise–arise, ascend, ascension,
attain, begin, beginning,
climb, elevation, emerge,
eminence, flourish, grow,
growth, increase, levitate,
mount, reach, rebel,
spring, start, surge, thrive,
tower, well
rise (hawk's, after prey) –
mounty
rise again (as from dead)–
resurge, resurrected

rise and fall–heave
rise and fall (tumultuously)
–welter
rise and fall of sea (pert. to)
–tidal
rise by buoyance–levitate
rise gradually–loom
rise high–tower
rise of ship–scend
rise threateningly–loom
rise up–rear, rebel
rises – ascends, begins,
climbs, flourishes, grows,
increases, levitates, looms,
springs, starts, surges,
thrives, towers
risible–funny
rising – advancing, ascending, arist, elevated, emer-
gent, growing, surgent
rising (act of)–ascension, ortive
rising and falling – surging,
tidal
rising and falling (periodically)–tidal
rising by degrees–gradient
risk–chance, danger, disadvantage, expose, gamble,
hazard, injury, peril,
plight, venture
risp–file, rasp, rub, scratch,
tirl
risper–caterpillar
risque – hazardous, risky,
risquee
rissle–pole, staff, stick
rist – ascent, engrave, increase, insurrection,
mark, resurrection,
scratch, wound
risus–laugh, laughter
rit–cut, pierce, rip, scratch,
slit, split, tear
ritardando – rallentando, re-
tarding
rite – ceremony, form, observance, solemnity
rites (religious)–cults
rites (religious classical, antiquity)–sacra
Ritter–knight
ritual – ceremonial, ceremony, cult, form, liturgy,
rite
ritus–custom, usage

ritzy–ultrafashionable
rivage – bank, coast, duty, shore
rival – antagonist, compete, competitor, emulate, emulator, even, match, opponent, peer, vie
rivalry competition, emulation, feud
rive – bank, cleft, lacerate, rent, rift, rip, shore, split, tear
rivel–shrink, shrivel, wrinkle
river–ea, rio, run, stream
river (Africa)–Tana
river (ascending from the sea, as fish for breeding)–anadromous
river (Bavaria)–Eger, Isar
river (Belgium)–Yser
river (Bohemia)–Iser, Elbe
river (Bolivia)–Beni
river (Brazil)–Tapajos
river (Chile)–Biobio, Loa
river (China)–Hwang, Wei
river (crossed by Caesar) – Rubicon
river (Dutch) – Eem, Maas, Meuse
river (encircling lower region)–Styx
river (England) – Tees, Trent
river (English dial.)–ea
river (France)–Isere, Meuse, Oise, Rhone
river (Germany)–Alle, Elbe, Hunte, Oder
river (Hades) – Acheron, Lethe, Styx
river (in East)–wadi, wady
river (India)–Kistna
river (Italy) – Arno, Nera, Po, Tevere, Teverone, Tiber
river (Latvia)–Aa
river (Levant)–wadi, wady
river (little) – brook, creek, riverlet, rivulet, streamlet
river (lower world)–Acheron, Lethe, Styx
river (name of)–Aar, Amur, Apo, Arno, Avon, Dee, Eder, Exe, Ob, Oise, Po, Rhine, Rhone

river (Netherlands) – Eem, Maas, Meuse
river (North Carolina) – Neuse
river (pert. to)–amnic, riverine, rivery
river (Poland) – Bug, Seret, Vistula
river (Portugal)–Tagus
river (Prussia)–Alle
river (Rumania)–Sereth, Siret
river (Scotland)–Dee
river (Siam)–Menam
river (Siberia)–Amur, Lena, Ob
river (small branch in delta) –bayou
river (Switzerland) – Aar, Reuss
river (Turkey) – Mesta, Sarus, Seihun, Seyhan
river (Tuscany)–Arno
river (Umbria)–Tevere
river (underworld)–Acheron, Lethe, Styx
river (winding part of)–ess
river (Yorkshire)–Ure
river arm (narrow at lower end)–estuary
riverbank–levee, ripa, ripe
riverbank (pert. to)–riparian
river bed–channel
river bed (dry except in rainy season)–wadi, wady
river boat–ark
river bottom–bed
river bottom land–holm
river channel – alveus, alvei (pl.), bed
river dog–hellbender
river dragon–crocodile
river duck–teal
river fall–shoot
river flatboat–ark
river horse–hippo, hippopotamus
river inlet–slew, slough
river island–ait
river isle–ait
river mouth–delta, estuary, lade
river mussel–unio
river nymph–naiad, nais
river of forgetfulness–Lethe

river of Hades – Acheron, Lethe, Styx
river of oblivion–Lethe
river of underworld – Acheron, Lethe, Styx
river on which Annie Laurie lived–Nith
river passage–ford
river rat–thief
river region (immediately adjoining)–riverine
river shore–bank
river siren–Lorelei
River Thames (at Oxford)–Isis
river thief (among sailors)–ackman
riverweed family – podostemaceae
riviere–necklace
rivose–brook, channel, gutter
rivulet–bourn, brook, burn, rill, runlet, runnel, streamlet
rix–reed, rush
rixatrix–scold, virago
rixy–tern
roach–cockroach
road – agger, expedition, highway, incursion, iter, passage, pavement, raid, way
road (impassable)–impasse
road (one outlet)–cul-de-sac
road agent–highwayman
road goose–brant
roadhouse–inn
road-making machine–bulldozer
roadman–canvasser, drummer, peddler, salesman
road runner–cuckoo
road scraper–harl
roadtrack–roadstead
roadweed–plantain
roam – err, gad, ramble, range, rove, stroll, wander
roam about idly–gad
roam stealthily–prowl
roanoke (Va.)–wampum
roar – bell, bellow, brool, steven
roar (boar)–fream
roar (deer)–bell

roar of surf–rote

roaring – aroar, disorderly, riotous

roaring game (Scot.) – curling

roaring Meg–cannon

roast – assate, banter, criticize, parch, ridicule

roast (by a fire)–torrefy, torrify

roasted (Spanish)–asado(a)

roasted meat (India)–cabob

roasted meat (on skewer)–cabob

roasted seasoned pieces of meat–cabobs

roasting ear–corn

roasting stick–spit

rob–loot, pelf, pilfer, plunder, ravish, reave, steal, touch

Rob Roy–canoe

robbed – looted, pilfered, pinched, reaved, reft, rubato, snatched, snitched, stole

robber – bandit, brigand, burglar, depredator, despoiler, pillager, reaver, rifler, thief, yegg, yegg-man

robber (grave)–ghoul, goul

robber (high sea)–pirate

robber (highway)–footpad, ladrone

robber (India, murderous)–dacoit

robber (privateer)–corsair

robber (sea)–corsair, pirate, privateer

robbery – burglary, depredation, larceny, pillage, piracy, plunder, reif, spoliation, theft

robbery (to commit)–burgle

robbery on high seas (pert. to)–piratic

robe – array, costume, dress, garment, invest, mantle, tunic

robe (bishop's)–chimer

robe (camel's hair)–aba

robe (light loose) – camis, camus, cymar

robe (loose, light, outer) – simar

robe (reaching to ankles) – talar

robe (women's loose) – cymar, simar

robin–bumpkin, lout, toxalbumin, trimming

Robin Bluestring – Robert Walpole

Robin Goodfellow (Eng. dial.)–Hobgoblin, Puck

Robin Hood's chaplain – Tuck

Robin Hood's follower – John

Robin Hood's sweetheart – Marian

robin runaway–dewdrop

robin sandpiper–dowitcher

robin snipe–dowitcher

robinet–cannon, chaffinch

Robinson Crusoe's man–Friday

roborate – corroborate, strengthen, ratify

roborean – oaken, stout, strong

robot–automaton

robust–hale, hardy, hearty, lusty, muscular, sinewy, sound, stout, strong, sturdy, vigorous, wally

roc–simurg, simurgh

rocca–donion, fortress, hold, keep

rock – cliff, diamond, lull, peak, promontory, quiet, shake, stone, teeter

rock (bare)–scar

rock (black)–basalt

rock (brittle)–shale

rock (broken discarded, mining)–attle

rock (cartilaginous)–lytta

rock (chain of, lying on surface of water)–reef

rock (coarse, fragmental) – psephite

rock (crystal ingredient) – silica

rock (crystalline) – gneiss, greisen, phanerite, schist

rock (decay of)–geest, laterite

rock (decomposed)–gossan

rock (dense, composed of

quartz and albite) – adinole

rock (discarded, broken)–attle

rock (eruptive, grayish)–andesite

rock (finely broken)–sand

rock (fissile)–shale

rock (fluid)–lava

rock (formed by geyser deposit)–sinter

rock (fragmental, coarse) – psephite

rock (fragments of)–scree

rock (granite-like)–gneiss

rock (granular)–oolite

rock (granular, composed of aegrite, acmite, quartz, and albite)–rockallite

rock (granular, crystalline igneous)–diorite

rock (gray)–slate

rock (igneous)–basalt, peridot, trap

rock (igneous protuberant)–boss

rock (jutting)–crag, tor

rock (kind of)–agate, basalt, dolomite, egeran, porphyry, schist, shake, slate, trap, tufa

rock (laminar structure) – schist

rock (laminated, Eng.) – shaul

rock (metalliferous)–ore

rock (metamorphic, laminated or foliated)–gneiss

rock (mica bearing)–domite

rock (molten)–aa, lava

rock (opposite Charybdis whirlpool)–Scylla

rock (part of)–ore

rock (porous)–tufa, tuff

rock (rough)–crag

rock (rounded)–rognon

rock (schistose, metamorphic)–epidosite

rock (science of)–petrology

rock (Scot. var.)–stane

rock (slate-like)–shale

rock (small round grains, cemented together) – oolite

rock (steep, rugged)–crag

rock (stratified)–shale

rock (suffix of)–ite, yte
rock (volcanic)–basalt, domite, latite, tufa
rock and gravel (carried and deposited by a glacier)–moraine
rockaway–carriage
Rockaway–Indian
rock badger–cony
rock bass–red-eye
rockbell–columbine
rockbird–murre, sandpiper
rock blackbird–ouzel
rock boring tool–trepan
rock-bottom–cheapest, lowest
rock brake–polypody
rock breaker–crusher
rockcist–rockcistus, rockrose
rock cook–wrasse
rock debris (at base of cliff)–talus
rock dove–guillemot, rockpigeon
rock eel–gunnel
rock falcon–merlin
rockfish (Cal.)–reina, rena
rock flint–chert
rockfoil–saxifrage
rock formation (slaty, cleavable)–schist
rock fragments (loose)–detritus
rock geranium–alumroot
rock goat–ibex
rock grouse–ptarmigan
rock gurnet–fortescue
rock hawk–falcon
rock hind–grouper
rock hopper–penguin
rock kangaroo–wallaby
rock kelp–rockweed
rock layers (pert. to)–stratal
rock ledge spots (moist) – sipes
rock lobster–crayfish
rock moss–lichen
rock native–snapper
rock nodule (cavity in) – geode
rock oak – California, chestnut, chinquapin
rock oil–petroleum
rock opossum–wallaby
rock pinnacle–scar

rock plover–sandpiper, turnstone
rock rabbit–hyrax
rockrose–rockcist, rockcistus
rockrose family–cistaceae
rock samphire–glasswort
rock snake–krait, python
rockstaff–distaff
rock starling–ouzel
rock strata (fold, arch.)–anticline
rock sucker–lamprey
rock tar–petroleum
rock tripe–lichen
rockweed–tang
rocket (thin roofing)–slate
rocket head (paper case) – pot
rocky–cliffy, hard, obdurate, shaky, unfeeling, weak
rocky decay–geest
Rocky Ford–muskmelon
rocky mountain (surrounded by ice sheet)–nunatak
Rocky Mountain park–Estes
Rocky Mountain range–Teton
rocky pinnacle–tor
rod–baton, perch, pole, staff, wand
rod (arc lamp)–carbon
rod (connecting wheels) – axle
rod (fibrous)–lytta
rod (flat)–ferule
rod (for holding meat)–spit
rod (interfermometer)–etalon
rod (knitting)–needle
rod (mason's mixing)–rab
rod (meat holding)–spit
rod (mechanical driving) – piston
rod (metal, used for tamping)–stemmer
rod (pointed)–goad, spit
rod (punishing)–ferule
rod (roasting)–spit
rod (rotating)–spindle
rod (short)–toggle
rod (16½ ft.)–perch, pole
rod (supporting)–rib
rod (thread twisting)–spindle
rod (used in basketry)–osier
rod-like–rhabdo

rodd–crossbow
rodden (Scot.)–rowan
rode goose–brant
rodent–agouti, agoutis (pl.) agouty, agouties (pl.), aguti, cony, hare, hutia, jutia, leveret, marmot, mouse, murine, paca, pika, rabbit, rat, utia
rodent (allied to guinea pig) –paca
rodent (aquatic) – beaver, muskrat
rodent (Belgian)–leporide
rodent (burrowing) – marmot, sewellel
rodent (bushy-tailed)–marmot
rodent (Eur.)–cony, lerot
rodent (fur bearing)–beaver
rodent (gnawing)–mole
rodent (hare family)–rabbit
rodent (jumping)–jerboa
rodent (large, South American)–capibara, capybara
rodent (mouse-like)–vole
rodent (nocturnal jumping) –jerboa
rodent (rabbit-like)–pika
rodent (rat-like)–vole
rodent (short-tailed) – hare, rabbit, vole
rodent (South American) – agouti, agouty, chinchilla, coypu, degu, mara, paca
rodent (South American, aquatic)–coypu
rodent (South American, large)–capibara, capybara
rodent (with stiff sharp spines)–porcupine
rodents (genus of) – lepus, mus
rodents (pert. to)–rosorial
rodeo–roundup
rodge (Eng.)–gadwall
rodomontade–bluster, boast, boastful, boasting, brag, braggart, bragging, empty, rant
rodster–angler
roe–deer, hind, ra
roe (lobster)–coral
roestone–oolite
rog–jumble, pull, shake, stir
rogan–bowl

rogation–litany, petition, request, supplication
rogation flower–milkwort
rogative–supplication
roggle–shake
rogue–beggar, cheat, corsair, imp, kite, knave, picaroon, pirate, rascal, scamp, tramp, vagabond, vagrant, villain, wag
rogue (former spelling) – roge
rogue (tricky)–shark
roguish – arch, espiegle, knavish, mischievous, sly, waggish
roguishly–slily, slyly
roid – frolicsome, riotous, rough, severe, unmanageable
roil – annoy, disturb, fidget, foul, irritate, muddy, roam, romp, ruffle, vex, wander
roister – bluster, boorish, brag, bully, rude, swagger, violent
roister (street of Queen Anne's reign)–Mun
rojo–Indian, redskin
roka–mafura
roke – fog, mist, moisture, smoke, steam, stir, vapor
roker–ray, rockling, thornback
roky – damp, foggy, hoarse, misty, smoky
role–character, duty, office, part
roll–list, rota, rotate, scroll, trill, troll, wind, wrap
roll (cloth)–bolt
roll (minced meat)–rissole
roll (parchment)–pell, scroll
roll (ship's)–seel
roll (spiced meat)–sausage
roll of butter–pat
roll of cloth–bolt
roll of coins put up in paper –rouleau
roll of fish (fried, obs.)–rissole
roll of hair–chignon, rat
roll of meat (fried, obs.)–rissole

roll of military officers – cadre
roll of parchment – pell, scroll
roll of tobacco–cigar, segar
roll on casters–trundle
roll on small wheels–trundle
roll tightly–furl
roll to one side–lurch
roll up–furl
roller–canary, caster, pigeon
roller (Chinese)–sirgang
roller (little, rare)–rowlet
roller (type-blackening) – inker
roller (typewriter)–platen
rolling movement–welter
rolling stock–cabooses, locomotives, motor cars
rolling weed–tumbleweed
rollix–frolic, play, rollick
romaine–cos
romal–thong
Roman–brave, frugal, honest, Italian, Latin, simple
Roman adviser to king – Egeria
Roman afterpiece (comic) – exode
Roman alcove – tablinum, tablina (pl.)
Roman apostle–Neri
Roman army civil barracks–canaba
Roman army wing–ala
Roman assembly (anc.)–comitia, curiata
Roman augur–auspex
Roman author–Pliny, Varro
Roman awning–velarium
Roman basilica–lateran
Roman biographer–Nepos
Roman bishop–Pope
Roman board member (anc.) –duumvir
Roman booth–taberna
Roman bowl–patina
Roman boxing glove (early) –cestus
Roman boy (freeborn, attendant at religious ceremonies)–camillus
Roman broker–Cocio
Roman bronze–aes
Roman building (church)–aedes

Roman calendar – calends, kalends
Roman calendar–Januarius, Februarius, Martius, Aprilis, Junius, Quintilis, Sextilis, September, October, November, December, Mercedonius (intercalary)
Roman case (small, leather or metal)–bulla
Roman cathedral church – lateran
Roman Catholic church (pert. to)–papal
Roman Catholic ecclesiastic –Rosmini
Roman Catholic priest–sacerdos
Roman Catholic society member–Jesuit
Roman Catholic title–abbe
Roman chariot (anc.)–essed, esseda, essede
Roman church (cathedral)–lateran
Roman circus arena wall (law)–spina
Roman circus column (anc.) –meta
Roman cistern (receiving water through compluvium)–impluvium, impluvia (pl.)
Roman citadel–arx
Roman citizens (anc.) – Aerarians
Roman clan–gens
Roman cloak (anc.)–abolla, planeta
Roman cloak (capelike, soldier's)–sagum
Roman cloak (military) – sagum
Roman coin–aes, as, asses (pl.), semis, sesterce
Roman coin (anc.)–semis, sesterce
Roman coin (copper)–aes, as, asses (pl.)
Roman coin (gold)–solidu
Roman coin (old settlement) –dinder
Roman comedy writer–Terence

Roman commander (military)–proconsul
Roman concert hall–odeum, odea (pl.)
Roman conjunction–et
Roman conquered race–Sabine
Roman copper–aes
Roman court–atrium, atria (pl.)
Roman court (Pope's)–Curia
Roman cuirass–lorica
Roman Cupid–Eros
Roman Curia office–datary, dataria
Roman date–ide, ides, none, nones
Roman date (time reckoning)–calends, ides, nones
Roman day (festival)–feria, feriae (pl.)
Roman deities (class of)–faun
Roman deity–di (pl.), faun, Jove, Lar, Lares (pl.), Mors (see also Roman god)
Roman device (used in boxing)–cest, cestus
Roman Diana–Artemis
Roman dictator – Cincinnatus, Sulla
Roman dish (earthenware saucer-like) – patera, paterae (pl.)
Roman dish (sacrificial) – patera, paterae
Roman diviner–auspex
Roman diviner (anc. official)–augur
Roman divinity (chief, anc.)–Jove
Roman division (political)–curia
Roman division (senate) – curia
Roman earthwork–agger
Roman emperor – Constantine, Gaiba, Nero, Nerva, Otho, Otto, Tiberius, Titus
Roman Empire country district–Pagus
Roman Empire member (anc.)–Laeti
Roman Empress–Eudocia

Roman entrance hall–atrium, atria (pl.)
Roman Eros–Cupid
Roman farce–exode
Roman farmer (tenant) – colonus
Roman Fates–Decuma, Morta, Nona
Roman Fates (any of three)–Parca, Parcae (pl.)
Roman festival (of Jupiter)–feria, feriae (pl.)
Roman festival day – feria, feriae (pl.)
Roman fever–malaria
Roman fish sauce–garum
Roman foot covering (antiquity)–udo
Roman founder (legendary)–Romulus
Roman galley (three-banked)–trireme
Roman galley (two-banked)–bireme
Roman garment–palla, stola, toga, togae (pl.), tunic
Roman garment (matron's)–stola, stole
Roman general – Antony, Marius, Scipio, Sulla, Titus
Roman general's cloak (military) – paludament, paludamentum
Roman ghosts–lemures
Roman girl (freeborn, attendant at sacrifice) – camilla
Roman gladiator–retiarius
Roman gladiator trainer – lanista
Roman god (chief) – Jove, Jupiter
Roman god (domestic)–Lar, Lares
Roman god (household) – Lar, Lares, Penates
Roman god (of animal life)–Faunus
Roman god (of dreams) – Morpheus
Roman god (of festive joy)–Comus
Roman god (of fire)–Vulcan
Roman god (of Hades)–Dis, Dispater, Pluto

Roman god (of love)–Amor, Cupid
Roman god (of lower world)–Pluto
Roman god (of mirth)–Comus
Roman god (of seas)–Neptune
Roman god (of sleep)–Morpheus
Roman god (of spirits)–Lar, Lares
Roman god (of underworld)–Dis, Dispater, Pluto
Roman god (of war)–Mars, Quirinus
Roman god (of world of dead)–Orcus
Roman god (rural)–Faunus
Roman god (sun)–Sol
Roman god (supreme)–Jove, Jupiter
Roman god (tutelary)–Lar, Lares (pl.)
Roman god (two-faced) – Janus
Roman god (underworld)–Dis, Dispater, Pluto
Roman gods–di
Roman gods (of lower world)–manes
Roman goddess – Annona, Caca, Ceres, dea, Diana, Juno, Lua, Minerva, Nox, Ops, Venus, Vesta
Roman goddess (agriculture)–Ceres, Ops
Roman goddess (night) – Nox
Roman goddess (obscure)–Caca
Roman goddess (of agriculture)–Ceres, Ops
Roman goddess (religion, anc.)–Maia
Roman goddess of beauty – Venus
Roman goddess of birth – Parca
Roman goddess of burials–Libitina
Roman goddess of childbirth–Lucina
Roman goddess of corpses–Libitina
Roman goddess of crops – Annona

Roman goddess of dawn – Aurora

Roman goddess of earth – Lua, Tellus

Roman goddess of fertility–Annona

Roman goddess of handicrafts–Minerva

Roman goddess of harvests–Ops

Roman goddess of health–Minerva

Roman goddess of hearth–Vesta

Roman goddess of horses–Epona

Roman goddess of love–Venus

Roman goddess of moon – Luna, Phoebus

Roman goddess of nursing mothers–Rumina

Roman goddess of peace – Pax

Roman goddess of strife – Discordia

Roman goddess of victory in war–Vacuna

Roman goddess of war–Juno

Roman goddess of womanhood–Juno

Roman governor–proconsul

Roman guard–lictor

Roman Hades–Orcus

Roman hairpin (old)–acus

Roman hall (concert)–odeum, odea (pl.)

Roman helmet–galea, galeae

Roman highway–iter, itero (pl.)

Roman highway (famous paved)–Appian

Roman hills–Aventine, Caelian, Capitoline, Esquiline, Palatine, Quirinal, Viminal

Roman historian–Livy, Nepos

Roman holiday–feria, feriae (pl.)

Roman house god – Lar, Lares, Penate

Roman house rooms (principal)–atria, atrium (sing.)

Roman javelin (foot soldier's)–pile, pilum

Roman judge–aedile, edile

Roman king (anc.)–Romulus (735–716 B.C.); Numa Pompilius (715–676); Tullus Hostilius (674–642); Ancus Martius (642–618); L. Tarquinius Priscus (617–578); Servius Tullius (578–534); Tarquinius Superbus (534–509)

Roman king (first)–Romulus

Roman king (legendary) – Numa

Roman king's adviser–Egeria

Roman lake–Nemi

Roman land (anc. public)–ager

Roman lands (public, acquired by war conquests) –ager

Roman language (anc.) – Latin

Roman language (relative to)–Latinic

Roman law–cern

Roman law (divine, Latin) –fas

Roman magistrate – aedile, censor, edile, praetor, pretor, tribune

Roman maiden (betrayer of citadel to Sabines)–Tarpeia

Roman market day–nundine

Roman matron's garment – stola, stole

Roman meal (principal) – cena, coena

Roman male lineage–gens

Roman measure – acetabulum, actus, actus major, actus simplex, amphora, centuria, clima, congius, cubit, cubitus, culeus, cyathus, decempeda, digitus, dolium, gradus, hemina, heredium, juger, jugerum, miglio, mile, milliarium, modius, pace, palmipes, palmus, passus, pes, quadrant, quartarius, Roman foot, Roman mile, Roman pace, saltus, scrupulum, scrupulus, sextarius, stadion, stadium, uncia, urn, urna, versus

Roman military cloak–sagum

Roman military machine – terebra

Roman military unit–legion

Roman military unit (anc.)–maniple

Roman money–aes

Roman month date (anc., first)–calends, kalends

Roman month dates – calends, ide, ides, none

Roman naturalist–Pliny

Roman nun–vestal

Roman nymph (fountain)–Egeria

Roman officer (fasces bearer) –lictor

Roman official–aedile, edile, tribune

Roman official (priestly) – augur

Roman orator–Cicero, Pliny

Roman ornament (hung around neck)–bulla

Roman palace–lateran

Roman palace troops (anc.)–palatines

Roman papal chancery–dataria

Roman patriot–Cato

Roman pax–Irene

Roman people (anc.)–patricians, plebeians

Roman people (conquered) –Sabines

Roman philosopher–Seneca

Roman poet–Ovid

Roman poet (satirical)–Juvenal

Roman port (anc.)–Ostia

Roman pounds–as, librae, libra (sing.)

Roman praenomen – Caius, Gaius, Titus

Roman priest (anc.)–epulo

Roman priest (in service of a god)–flamen

Roman priest (of the Faunus)–luperci

Roman priestess–vestal

Roman procurator (in Judea)–Felix

Roman province (conquered)–Dacia

Roman provisions (free to citizens)–annona

Roman public land (anc.)–ager

Roman public office (one of three)–triumvir

Roman race (conquered) – Sabine

Roman race course marker–.meta

Roman ram (battering) – aries

Roman recess–tablinum, tablina (pl.)

Roman recess (small)–ala

Roman religious law–fas

Roman religious rite (anc.)–sacra

Roman right to pass over land of another–via

Roman river–Tiber

Roman road–iter, itero (pl.), itinera (pl.)

Roman road (famous, great, paved)–Appian

Roman roof opening (square, for catching water for impluvium)–compluvium, compluvia (pl.)

Roman room–atrium, atria (pl.)

Roman room (anc.)–tablinum, tablina (pl.)

Roman room (small)–ala

Roman sacred marriage – confarreation

Roman sacrificial vessel–patera

Roman saint–Neri

Roman sauce (fish)–garum

Roman scholar–Varro

Roman seat–sella

Roman senate division–curia

Roman serf (female)–colona

Roman serf (male)–colonus

Roman seven hills – Aventine, Caelian, Capitoline, Esquiline, Palatine, Quirinal, Viminal

Roman shelter (temporary) taberna

Roman shield (leather-covered)–scutum, scuta (pl.)

Roman shop–taberna

Roman slave (whose life was saved by befriending a lion)–Androcles

Roman sock (felt or fur)–udo

Roman soldiers (body of ancient)–cohort

Roman soldier's protection–testudo

Roman spirit–Lar, Lares

Roman spirits (of the dead)–lemures, manes

Roman statesman – Caesar, Cato, Seneca

Roman statesman (orator)–Cicero

Roman street (famous)–Corso

Roman tablet (writing)–diptych

Roman tank (receiving water through compluvium)–impluvium

Roman temple–cella, naos

Roman tenant farmer–colonus

Roman tenant farmer (female)–colona

Roman tent–taberna

Roman theatre–odeum

Roman trainer (gladiator)–lanista

Roman travesty–exode

Roman triumvirate (first, 60 B.C.) – Caesar, Crassus, Pompey

Roman triumvirate (second, 43 B.C.)–Antony, Lepidus, Octavius

Roman tyrant–Nero

Roman vase (costly jasper)–murrine

Roman vase or jar (for wine, honey, etc.)–amphora

Roman vestment–toga

Roman virgin (religious) – vestal

Roman warship–bireme, trireme

Roman way (famous)–Appian

Roman weight–as, bes, dodrans, duella, pood, scrupulum, scrupulus, sextula, sicilicum, solidus, uncia

Roman weight (anc.) – as,

asses (pl.), bes, dodrans, libra

Roman wine shop–taberna

Roman wing (army)–ala

Roman woman's garment – stola, stole, stolae (pl.)

Roman world of the dead–Orcus

Roman writer–Varro

Roman writer (comedy) – Terence

Roman writing tablet–diptych

romance – falsehood, fancy, fantasy, fiction, novel, romanza, sentiment

romance language–Catalan

Romanese – gypsies, Walachian

romantic–extravagant, fabulous, fantastic, fictitious, idealistic, imaginary, sentimental, unreal

Romany tongue–Romanes

rome (obs.)–bellow, groan, growl, roar

Rome–see Roman

romping girl–hoiden, hoyden, tomboy

Romulus' brother–Remus

Romulus' father–Mars

rond–border, rand, shred

rondure–plumpness, roundness

rone–brushwood, thicket

ronin–outcast, outlaw

rood–cross, crucifix

rood goose–brant

roodebok–impala

roof (comb. form)–stego

roof (having two slopes on all sides)–mansard

roof (kind of) – cupola, dome, flat, gable, gambrel, hip, jerkinhead, mansard, nave, penthouse, pyramidal

roof (rounded)–dome

roof (tapering)–spire

roof (thatched) – chappar, chopper

roof (truncated)–hip

roof border–eave

roof covering (straw-like)–thatch

roof covering of brain ventri-
cles–telachorioidea
roof of mouth–palate
roof timber (sloping)–rafter
roof tool–zax
roof with thin boards–sark
roofing material – copper,
paper, shakes, shingles,
slate, tile, tin
roofing plate–tile
roofing tile–pantile
roofing tin–terne
rook–castle, cheat, crow, defraud
rook's cry–caw
rooker–sharper, swindler
rookie (rooky) – beginner,
novice, recruit
rooky – disheveled, foggy,
rascally, roky, swindling,
untidy
rool–crumple, ruffle
room – apartment, aula,
chamber, lodge, place,
scope, seat, space
room (children's)–nursery
room (convent reception)–
parlatory
room (dining)–cenacle, dinette, refectory
room (drawing)–parlor
room (entrance)–hall
room (for keeping pitchers,
table linen, etc.)–ewery,
ewry
room (harem)–oda, odah
room (large) – auditorium,
aula, hall, theater
room (monastery)–cell
room (principal house)–ben
room (prison) – cell, dungeon, hole, solitary, tank
room (provision)–cupboard,
larder, pantry
room (public)–auditorium,
casino, hall, theater
room (Pueblo Indian cere-
monial)–kiva
room (Roman house, anc.)–
atrium, atria (pl.)
room (round, large) – ro-
tunda
room (ship's) – brig, cabin,
salon
room (sleeping) – barrack,

bedroom, dormer, dormi-
tory, lodge
room (small)–cell, den
room (small side)–ala
room (storage)–attic, cellar,
shed, storeroom
room (supping)–cenacle
room (washing)–laundry
room for action (coll.)–leeway
room for table linen and
towels–ewery, ewry
room in tower (bell)–belfry
room to move–leeway
roomy – commodious, spa-
cious
roon–border, darling, shred,
treasure
roorback–falsehood, lie
roosa–boast, praise, vaunt
roost–jouk, lodging, perch,
pole, support
rooster – chanticleer, cock,
percher
root – cheer, radical, radix,
radices (pl.), tuber
root (cranial nerve)–radix
root (edible)–beet, eddo, oca,
parsnip, rutabaga, taro,
turnip, yam
root (garden, edible)–radish
root (kind of)–bulb
root (medicinal)–ipecac
root (plant) – radix, radices
(pl.)
root (stringy, used by Indians for sewing canoes)–
watap
root (taro)–eddo
root (used as tonic)–atis
root (used in cough remedy)
–senega, seneka
root (violet, aromatic principle of)–irone
root bark (for tea making)–
sassafras
root out–eradicate, extirpate,
stub
root stalk (edible)–taro
root stock (bot.)–rhizome
root stock (edible)–yam
root stock (pungent)–ginger
root stock (used for food by
Maoris)–roi
root word–etymon
rootlet–radicel, radicle

roove–rivet
rope – bind, cord, cordage,
fasten, lariat, lasso, line,
tie
rope (boat-fastening)–hawser, painter
rope (boat's anchor, light)–
rode
rope (confining)–tether
rope (dancer's)–poy
rope (flag-raising)–halyard
rope (for fastening ship's
tackle)–lanyard
rope (for guiding horses)–
longe
rope (for hoisting ship's
yard)–tye
rope (for training horses)–
longe
rope (guiding)–longe
rope (gun carriage) – pro-
longe
rope (guy)–stay, vang
rope (heavy)–cable, hawser
rope (horsehair)–lariat
rope (ship's)–halyard, hawser, painter, ratline, tye
rope (ship's ladder)–ratline
rope (ship's short fastening)
–lanyard
rope (ship's towing)–hawser
rope (short cart, Scot.) –
wanty
rope (straw, twisted by
hand) – soogan, sougan,
sugan, sugann
rope (throwing)–lariat, lasso, reata, riata
rope (towing, obs.)–tew
rope (two-strand)–marline
rope (yard-hoisting, naut.)–
tye
rope collar (sliding, naut.)–
parral, parrel
rope fiber–coir, cotton, flax,
istle, jute, Manila, sisal
rope loop – becket, bight,
noose
rope loop (naut.) – parral,
parrel
ropemaker's tool–loper
rope of onions–reeve
rope securing device – bitt,
cleat
rope slack–slatch
rope splicer's tool–fid

rope storeroom (ship's)–lazaret, lazarette, lazaretto
rope threaded thru block – reeved
ropery–roguery
roral–dewy
roric–dewy
ros (the)–rus
rosary–chaplet, garland
rosary beads–ave
roscid–dewy
rose–flower, hove
rose (Christmas)–hellebore
rose (dog)–canker
rose (former spelling)–ris
rose (garden)–delta
rose (genus of)–rosa
rosebush (poetic)–rosier
rosebush fruit–hip
Rose City–Portland
rose cross–Rosicrucian
rose family–rosaceae
rose family plant–avens
rose high–surged
rose into prominence – loomed
rosemary (obs.)–rosmarine
rose parakeet–rosella
rose petal oil–atar, attar, ottar, otto
rose pogonia–snakemouth
rose rash–roseola
rose red dye–eosin, eosine, rhodamin, rhodamine
rose-shaped ornament – rosette
rose threateningly–loomed
rose up–ascended, loomed
roses (collection of live) – rosetum
roses (essential oil of)–atar, attar, ottar, otto
Rosenmiller's organ – epoophoron
rosettes (arranged in form of)–rosular, rosulate
rosety (rosetty)–resinous
rosilla–sneezeweed
rosin (Scot.)–roset, rozet
ross–rubbish, waste
Rossini's opera–Semiramide
roster–list, rota, slate
rosy – blooming, blushing, flushed, pink, red, rosaceous, roseate
rosy tint–blush

rot–corrupt, decay, decompose, putrefy, spoil
rot by exposure–ret
rot grass–butterwort, flukewort
rota–court, list, roll, roster
rotary motion (pert. to) – rotal
rotary motor–turbine
rotate–gyrate, revolve, roll, rotiform, spin, trundle, turn, wheel
rotated a plane in coincidence with another plane –rabatte
rotating part–rotor
rotating piece–cam
rotation – revolution, spin, turn
rotator–muscle
rotche–dovekie
rote–condition, course, custom, practice, routine, system
rotella–buckler, shield
rotge–rotche
roti–roast, roasted
rotor–stator
rotor of centrifugal pump–impeller
rott goose–brant
rottan–rat
rotten – decayed, depraved, fetid, offensive, putrefied, putrescent, putrid, undermined, unsound, unstable
rotten (half)–doted
rotter – blackguard, shirker, slacker
rotund – chubby, plump, roly-poly, round, rounded, spherical, stout
Rotwelsch–argot
roud–spawn
roue–debauchee, rake
rouge–blush, flush, redden
rough–approximate, boorish, broken, choppy, coarse, crude, hard, harsh, hoarse, imperfect, incomplete, inequal, inexact, jarring, rude, ruffled, rugged, seamy, severe, shaggy, stern, tumultuous, turbulent
rough (to become)–coarsen

rough and hoarse–raucous
rough and lean – scrag, scraggy
Rough and Ready (Old) – Taylor
rough cloth–terry
rough hair–shag
rough in tone–husky
rough music (Eng.)–charivari
roughneck – boor, rowdy, tough
rough rock–crag
rough to touch–asperate
rough with bristles–hispid
roughen (to)–chap, shag
roughened–coarse
rougher–coarser
roughly–brusquely, coarsely, harshly, rudely, severely, unevenly
roughness (slight sea)–lipper
roughsome – rough, rustic, uncouth
rouky (Scot.)–foggy, misty, roky
roulade–arpeggio, division, flourish, run
roulette (bet in)–bas
rounceval–giant, termagant, virago
round–bout, circle, circular, curved, cylindrical, globular, orbed, rotund, spherical
round (regularly traversed)–beat
roundabout–about, approximately, circuitous, circumlocution, dance, devious, indirect
roundabout course–detour
round and plump–chubby
round and tapering–conic, conical
round bone–hipbone
round building–rotunda
round clam–quahog
round dance–ray, roundelay
round dance (rustic)–hay
round hand–ronda
roundhead (northwest U.S.) –Swede
round meal–oatmeal
round of applause–plaudit
round protuberance–umbo

round robin–angler, cigar-fish, pancake

round room–rotunda

Round Table knight–Galahad, Kay

roundtail–hardtail

round timber–spar

roundup–rodeo

rounded (irregularly)–gibbous

rounded convex molding – ovolo

rounded projection – crena, crenae (pl.), tooth

rounded ver (her.)–pomey

roup–auction, clamor, cold, hoarseness, shouting

rouse–disturb, excite, raise, start, stimulate, stir, upset, wake, waken

rouse into quick action–hie

rouse to action–bestir

rouse to vigilance–alarm

rouser (rabble) – demagog, demagogue

rousette–dogfish, shark

roust – bellow, bellowing, roar, roaring, tumult

rout–bellow, bray, debacle, defeat, discomfit, disperse, low, overpower, overthrow, roar, snort, stampede, vanquish

route – circuit, course, line, path, way

route (circuitous)–detour

routh–abundance, abundant, plentiful, plenty

routier (Fr.) – adventurer, brigand

routine–course, round, system, troll

routine (wearisome)–grind, rut, treadmill

rove – part, ramble, range, roam, straggle, stray, stroll, swerve, wander, washer

rove in quest of plunder–maraud

rove on the wing–flit

rover–marauder, nomad

rover (high sea)–corsair, pirate

roving in quest of knightly adventure–errantry

row–air, brawl, broil, file, fuss, line, oar, paddle, propel, quarrel, spat, tier

row (coll.)–quarrel, ruction, spat

row (form in a)–align, aline

rowan tree–sorb

rowboat–canoe, gig, randan, skiff

rowboat (flatbottom)–dory

rowboat (Scot., flatbottom river)–cobil, coble

rowboat (small)–cog, skif, skiff, skift

rowdy – larrikin, rough, tough

rowel–spur

rowen–aftermath, field

rower–oarsman

rowing (style of) – randan, sculling

rox–decay, rot

roxy–decayed, softened

roy–king

royal–basil, imperial, kingly, majestic, real, regal, rial, stag, stately, true

royal agaric–mushroom

Royal Air Force (abbr.) – R.A.F.

royal bay–laurel

royal blue–smalt

Royal Canadian Mounted Police (coll.)–Mountie

royal color (British)–flag

royal court (pert. to)–aulic

royal mace–scepter, sceptre

royal martyr–Charles

royal maundy–alms

royal metal (old name)–gold

royal muscadine–grape

royal officer (household) – naperer

royal rights–regalia

royal rock snake–python

royal stables–mews

royal standard (British) – emblem, flag

royal stars–Aldebaran, Antares, Fomalhaut, Regulus

royalist fugitive (during French Revolution)–emigre

royally befurred–ermined

royet – mischievous, romping, unruly, wild

rub–burnish, chafe, fret, irritate, massage, polish, scour, smear, smooth, triturate

rub away–abrade

rub down–comb, curry

rub elbows with–associate, fraternize

rub off–abrade, erase, obliterate

rub out–arase, cancel, efface, erase, expunge, obliterate

rub out (U.S. slang)–kill

rub with something soft – wipe

Rubaiyat author–Omar

rubbed–abraded, worn

rubbed with cleansing agent –soaped

rubber (hard)–ebonite

rubber check (bank's notation)–N.S.F.

Rubber City–Akron

rubber plant (genus of) – ficus

rubber shoe–galosh, galoshe

rubber tree – caucho, caoutchouc, ule

rubbish–debris, dross, junk, ross, trash, trumpery, waste

rubbish (mine)–attle

rubbish (tin streamers) – stent

rubbishly–paltry

rubble – chalk, foolishness, nonsense, rubbish, trash

rubedity–redness, ruddiness

rubellite–tourmaline

rubeola–measles

rubescent–erubescent, flushing, red, reddening

rubiator–bully, rake, rascal

rubicund – florid, red, redness, ruby, ruddy

rubicundity–redness, ruddiness

rubious–red, ruby

rubric–red, redden

rubrics (book of)–ordo

ruby colored gem–spinel

ruby spinel–balas

ruck–cower, crease, crouch, heap, pile, rick, sit, squat, stack, wrinkle

rucksey–bend, stoop, yield

ruckus–ado, ruction, rumpus, uproar

ruction – fight, outbreak, quarrel, uproar

rudd–complexion, hue, redden, redness

rudd (blue variety)–azurine

rudder edge (forward) – bearding

rude–barbarous, boisterous, clumsy, coarse, curt, discourteous, impertinent, impolite, inclement, insolent, makeshift, rough, rowdy, rugged, turbulent, uncivilized, uncouth, unskilled, vulgar

rudiment–element

rudimentary–elemental, initial

rudimentary digit–dewclaw

rue–afflict, bitterness, compassion, disappointment, grieve, rake, regret, repent, repentance, sorrow

rue (common)–ruta

rue (French)–street

ruff (female)–ree, reeve

ruff (support for)–rabato, rebato

ruffer–napper

ruffian – assassin, cutthroat, cuttle, desperado, pander, paramour, pimp, rowdy, thug

ruffle – agitate, disarrange, dishevel, disorder, disturb, flounce, fret, frill, irritate, nettle, roil, tousle, vex

ruffle (lace)–jabot

ruffler – boaster, braggart, swaggerer

ruga–fold, wrinkle

rugged–asper, hardy, irregular, robust, rough, strong, sturdy, vigorous

ruggle–pull, shake, tug

ruin–bane, blast, defeat, demolish, desolation, destroy, doom, downfall, fate, havoc, loss, perdition, spoil, subversion, subvert, wrack, wreck

ruin (cause of)–bane

ruinate – demolish, destroy, overthrow, ruin, subvert

ruined – dilapidated, gone, spoiled, undone

ruinous–baneful, deadly, decayed, demolished, destructive, pernicious, subversive, tumbledown

ruins–remains

rukh–forest, jungle

rule–canon, counsel, direction, dominate, govern, guide, influence, law, manage, maxim, method, norm, order, persuade, precept, principle, regency, regimen, reign, sway

rule (accepted, established)–standard

rule (authoritative)–law

rule (dictatorial) – totalitarianism

rule (liturgical)–fabric

rule (supreme)–reign

Rule Britannia composer – Arne

rule for molding–screed

rule of conduct–law, precept

rule of conduct (general)–maxim

ruler–ameer, amir, dynast, dynasty, emeer, emir, emperor, ferule, governor, lord, min, monarch, prince, regent

ruler (absolute)–tyrant

ruler (oppressive)–tsar, tyrant

ruler (Oriental)–sultan

ruler (petty)–satrap

ruler (powerful)–potentate

ruler (religious body)–hierarch

ruler (supreme)–autocrat

ruler (temporary)–regent

ruler (vicarious)–regent

ruler's domain (absolute)–empery

rules (system of)–code

ruling–law, regnant, statute

rull–trundle, wheel

rullion–sandal, shoe

rum (distilled from sugar cane)–taffia, tafia

rum shop–barroom, saloon

rumal–kerchief

Rumanian capitol–Bucharest

Rumanian city–Arad, Bacau, Braila, Brasov, Bucharest, Bucurest, Bukharest, Cernauti, Constanta, Craiova, Cronstadt, Czernovitz, Czernowitz, Focsani, Galati, Galatz, Grosswardein, Iasi, Irongate, Jassy, Kishenef, Klausenburg, Kolsovar, Kronstadt, Nagyvarad, Ploesti, Severin, Temesvar, Timisoara, Turnu

Rumanian coin–ban (cop., ac.), leu (s.), ley (s.), lei (pl.)

Rumanian conservative–Boyar

Rumanian king (ex)–Carol

Rumanian monarch (former)–Carol

Rumanian money unit–leu, lei (pl.), ley

Rumanian premier–Antonescu

Rumanian queen (ex) – Marie

Rumanian river–Alt, Aluta, Arges, Jiu, Schyl, Sereth, Siret

Rumanian river port–Galati, Galatz

Rumanian unit of currency–ban, bani (pl.)

rumbo–grog

rumen–chew, cud, paunch, stomach

rumen (part good for food)–tripe

ruminant–alpaca, antelope, bull, camel, cow, deer, goat, llama, moose, sheep, steer, yak

ruminant (chamois and similar)–antelope

ruminant (deer-like) – antelope

ruminant (female, hollow-horned, coll.)–nannygoat

ruminant (long-haired)–yak

ruminant (long-necked) – giraffe

ruminant animal–see ruminant

ruminants (division of)–ungulata

ruminants (genus of)–bas
ruminant's cud–rumen
ruminant's food–cud
ruminant's stomach (first)–rumen
ruminant's stomach (fourth) –abomasum, read, reed
ruminant's stomach (fourth, Scot.)–roddikin
ruminant's stomach (second)–reticulum
ruminant's stomach (third) –omasum
ruminate – chew, consider, meditate, muse, ponder, reflect
rumor–bruit, Fama, hearsay, noise, norate, report
rumor (marine slang)–scuttlebutt
rumor (navy slang)–scuttlebutt
rumor (personified)–Fama
rumor (to, coll.)–norate
rump bone–sacrum
rump fed–pampered
rumpad–highway
rumpade–rob
rumple – crinkle, crumple, muss, touse, tousle, wrinkle
rumpus–confusion, disturbance, fracas, hubbub, row
rumtytoo – commonplace, ordinary
run – blend, charge, discharge, elapse, extend, flow, fly, function, go, hurry, liquefy, manage, operate, roulade, speed, sprint, stream, stretch, suppurate, tend
run (in great haste)–scuttle
run about–gad
run after–chase, pursue
run aground – founder, strand
run along edge of–skirt
run at cards–tenace
run at top speed–sprint
run away – bolt, decamp, elope, escape, flee
run away from one's duties –elope
run away in panic–stampede
run before the wind–scud

run between ports–ply
run down–dilapidated, exhausted
run in haste–scuttle
run off–elope, flee, impress, print
run out – elapse, exhaust, lapse, squander, waste
run out (coll.)–peter
run over–exceed, overflow
run quickly – dart, scamper, scoot
run rapidly–career, charge, gallop
run swiftly–scud, sprint
run through–inspect, pervade, pierce, transfix
run up–enlarge, grow, increase, rise
runagate–fugitive, renegade, runaway, vagabond, wanderer
rundle – ball, circle, coil, round, rung, sphere, step, stream
rundlet–barrel
rune–mystery, secret
runes (pert. to)–runic
rung–girdled, round, stair, step, tread
rung of ladder–rundle, step
rung of rope ladder–ratline
runnel (Eng. dial.)–rhine
runner – messenger, miler, smuggler, sprinter
runner (distance)–miler
runner (snow)–skee, ski
running–cursive, smuggling
running about–ado
running knot–noose
running race–relay, sprint
runt–pygmy
runt of a brood–wrig
runway–file, ramp
rupa–body
rupee (¹⁄₁₆ of)–anna
rupees (1,000)–lac
rupees (100,000)–lac, lakh
rupees (ten million)–crore
rupia–eruption
ruption – bursting, ruction, rupture
ruptuary–plebeian, roturier
rupture – breach, break, burst, disruption, hernia, rent, rhexis

rural–agrestic, bucolic, pastoral, rustic
rural game–dib
rural life (pert. to)–pastoral
rural poem–georgic
rural scenes–pastorals
ruralize–rusticate
Rusa deer (resembling)–Rusine
ruse – artifice, deceit, fall, fraud, slip, stratagem, trick, wile
rush – brook, cattail, haste, press, runlet, scoot, scud, stampede, surge
rush (kind of)–sprat, sprot
rush family–juncaceae
rush hour–peak
rush nut–chufa
rush out–sally
rush toad–natterjack
rushee (prize)–nugget
rusk–biscuit, bread
rusma–quicklime
Russ–Russian
Russia (former name)–Muscovy
Russia (founder of)–Ivan
Russian – Muscovite, Russ, Slav
Russian (Little) – Russene, Ruthene
Russian antelope–saiga
Russian assembly–rada
Russian assembly (administrative)–zemstvo
Russian assembly (former)–duma
Russian association (labor)–artel
Russian bank–game (card)
Russian base (Black Sea fleet)–Sevastopol
Russian bast–raffia
Russian beer–kvass
Russian beverage (alcoholic) –kvass
Russian birch rod (used in prison)–plet
Russian bondman–serf
Russian braid–soutache
Russian cactus–thistle
Russian calendar (used to 1918)–Julian
Russian cap (peasant's)–aska
Russian capital (alternate)–

Kuibishev
Russian carriage–drosky, tarantas, troika
Russian carriage (four-wheeled)–tarantas
Russian carriage (low, open, four-wheeled)–drosky
Russian carriage (three-horse)–troika
Russian cart–telega
Russian cathedral–sobor
Russian chess champion – Alekhine
Russian church conclave – sobor
Russian church synod–sobor
Russian citadel–Kremlin
Russian city–Archangel, Astrakhan, Bataisk, Cheliabinsk, Ekaterinburg, Ekaterinodar, Gomel, Ivanovo, Kalinin, Kasan, Kazan, Kertch, Kostroma, Minsk, Moscow, Moskva, Nizhnii, Novgorod, Novorossiisk, Omsk, Orel, Orenburg, Pensa, Penza, Perm, Petrograd, Pskov, Rost-on-the-Don, Rostov, Saint Petersburg, Samara, Saratof, Sebastopol, Sevastopol, Simferopol, Smolensk, Taganrog, Tashkend, Tsaritsyn, Tula, Tver, Ufa, Vitebsk, Vladikavkas, Vladimir, Vladivostok, Voronezh, Voznesensk, Yaroslaf, Yekaterinburg
Russian cloak (fur)–shuba
Russian coin – chervonets (g.), copeck, kopeck (cop.), poltinnik (s.), ruble (s.)
Russian commune–mir
Russian composer (Jewish)–Rubinstein
Russian convict shelter – etape
Russian cooperative society–artel
Russian cossack–Tatar
Russian council–duma, soviet
Russian council (assembly)–soviet

Russian council (political)–rada
Russian currency unit – chervonetz
Russian czar–Ivan
Russian decree–ukase
Russian desert–tundra
Russian despot–czar, tsar
Russian dictator (former) – Lenin
Russian diet–duma
Russian district–Karelia
Russian dog (shaggy, long haired)–owtchah
Russian dress (peasant woman's national)–sarafan
Russian duke – knais, knez, knyaz
Russian edict–ukase
Russian emperor–Ivan, czar, tsar, tzar
Russian empress (former) – czarina, tsarina
Russian exclamation (it doesn't matter, or, never mind)–nichevo, nitchevo
Russian fur (new-born lamb)–karakul, karakule
Russian general–Timoshenko
Russian government–Soviet
Russian government (southeast)–Astrakhan
Russian governmental form –orel
Russian grand duke–Nicholas
Russian grass–fescue
Russian guild (labor)–artel
Russian gulf–Azov
Russian hemp–rine
Russian hides of leather – jufti, jufts (pl.)
Russian horse (small, steppes)–tarpan
Russian hut (log)–isba
Russian imperial order – ukase
Russian inhabitant (western)–Lett
Russian instrument–balalaika
Russian instrument (rudimentary Balkan) – gusla, gusle
Russian isthmus–Karelia

Russian Jewish composer – Rubinstein
Russian labor union–artel
Russian lake – Aral, Ilmen, Onega, Sego
Russian landed proprietor – boyar, boyard
Russian language–Russ
Russian Lapland capital – Kola
Russian leader–Lenin, Stalin
Russian leather–bulgar
Russian leather (untanned) –shagreen
Russian legal assembly–rada
Russian liquor (alcoholic, made from rye)–vodka
Russian man (old)–starets
Russian marten fur origination–opossum
Russian massacre–pogrom
Russian measure – arshin, arsheen, botchka, boutylka, charka, chetverik, chetvert, chkalik, dessiatine, duim, duime, fass, foute, fut, garnetz, korec, krouchka, kroushka, last, last margin, ligne, liniya, lof, loof, osmin, osmina, pajak, paletz, polugarnetz, poluosmina, sagene, stof, stoff, stoof, tchast, vedro, verchoc, verchok, verst, versta, verste
Russian measure (of distance)–verst
Russian mile–verst
Russian monetary unit – ruble
Russian monk – Rasputin, starets
Russian mountain–Ural
Russian muskrat–desman
Russian name–Igor
Russian news agency–Tass
Russian novelist–Tolstoi
Russian order (aristocratic member)–boyar, boyard
Russian order (imperial) – ukase
Russian overcoat (fur) – shuba
Russian parliament–duma
Russian peasant–kulak, muzhik, muzjik

Russian peasant's cap–aska
Russian peninsula – Crimea, Kola
Russian peninsula (south)– Crimea
Russian people (northern Little Russia)–Russniak
Russian plain–steppe
Russian poet – Aleksandr Sergyeevich Pushkin
Russian prairie–steppe
Russian prince–knais, knez, knyaz
Russian prison camp–etape
Russian prison stockade – etape
Russian province – Amur, Tula
Russian riot–pogrom
Russian river–Amur, Dnieper, Don, Donets, Ili, Kara, Lena, Neva, Ob, Onega, Orel, Ros, Sura, Ufa, Ural
Russian rod (birch, used in prison)–plet
Russian salt lake–Elton
Russian saltwort–thistle
Russian sea–Aral, Azov
Russian sea (inland)–Azov
Russian seaport–Archangel, Eisk
Russian secret police–cheka, N.K.V.D., O.G.P.U.
Russian secret police (succeeding cheka)–gay-pay-oo, gaypoo
Russian sheep (broad-tailed) karakul, karakule
Russian shelter (convict) – etape
Russian society (cooperative)–artel
Russian soldiers–reds
Russian soup (cabbage) – shchi, shtchee, stchi

Russian sovereign–czar, tsar
Russian stockade–etape
Russian storehouse–etape
Russian tea urn–samovar
Russian teacher–starets
Russian team (three horses abreast)–troika
Russian town – Kola, Riga, Uman
Russian trade union–artel
Russian Turkestan sea–Aral
Russian turnip–rutabaga
Russian Ukraine council – rada
Russian unit of measure – sagenes
Russian vehicle (drawn by three horses)–troika
Russian village–mir
Russian viol (primitive, three-stringed)–gudok
Russian violinist–Elman
Russian wagon (springless)– telega
Russian watering place–Ems
Russian weight – berkovets, berkowitz, dola, dolia, funt, kamian, last, lot, packen, pound, tcharik, tscharik, yakman, zolotnik
Russian whip – knout, plet, plete
Russian wolfhound–alan
Russian women's dress (national peasant)–sarafan
Russians (division of Little) –Russine
russud–forage, grain
rust–aerugo, erode
rust of plants–blight
rust on bronze and copper– patina
rustic – artless, awkward, boorish, bucolic, carl,

carle, coarse, Corydon, Damon, honest, pastoral, plain, rough, rube, rude, rural, sylvan, unpolished, yokel
rustic (poetic)–carl
rustic (young)–plowboy
rustic (youthful)–swain
rustic life description (artless)–idyl, idyll
rustic lover–swain
rustic maiden–Thestylis
rustic peasant–boor
rustic pipe–reed
rustic poet–carl
Rustum's son (Persian legend)–Sohrab
rut – furrow, groove, track, wrinkle
rut (cartwheel)–rit
rutabaga–turnip
rutate–caprate
ruth–grief, regret, remorse, repentance, sadness, sorrow
Ruth's husband–Boaz
Ruth's mother-in-law – Naomi
Ruthenia county–Ung
ruthful–pitiful, tender
ruthless – cruel, pitiless, savage
ruthless invader–hun
rutyl–capryl
ruvid–harsh, rough
rye (arch.)–ree, rie
rye (genus of cultivated) – secale
rye (spurred)–ergot
rye disease–ergot
ryke (Scot.)–reach
ryot (India) – cultivator, peasant
rytina–hydrodamalis

S

S-curve–ogee
S-shaped–sigmoid
S-shaped molding–ogee

saal–hall, room
sabalo–milkfish, tarpon
sabana–plain, plateau

sabbat–assembly
sabbatism–intermission, rest
saber (dagger-like, double

curved) – yatagan, yata-
ghan
saber (Oriental) – scimitar,
scimiter
sabino (Mex.)–ahuehuete
sabio–priest, sage
sable–black, ebon, pellet
sable (Alaska)–skunk
sable (American) – marten
sabot–disk, shoe
sabotage – destroy, destruction, waste
sabre–see saber
sabretache–case, pocket
sabuline–arenaceous, sandy
sabulosity–grittiness, sandiness
sabulous–arenaceous, gritty,
sandy
saburrate–ballast
saburration–arenation
sabutan–fiber, straw
sac – bursa, cavity, cyst,
pouch, saccus
sac (abnormally developed)
–cyst
sac (biological)–saccus, sacci
(pl.)
sac (little)–sacculus
sac (poisonous)–cyst
sac (spore)–ascus, asci (pl.)
sac-like cavity–bursa
sacalait–killfish, warmouth
saccadic–jerky, twitching
saccharine – sweet, sweeten-
ing
saccharine compound – inosite, inositol
saccos–tunicle, vestment
sacerdocy–priesthood
sacerdos–priest
sachet–bag, pouch, reticule
sack – bag, bursa, bursae
(pl.), desolate, loot, pillage, plunder, poke,
pouch, purse, ravage
sack (jute)–burlap, gunny
sack (spore)–ascus, asci (pl.)
sacrament house – ambry,
tabernacle
sacrarium – chapel, oratory,
sanctuary, shrine
sacred–blessed, consecrated,
divine, holy, sacrosanct
sacred (comb. form)–hiero
sacred (not)–profane

sacred bean–lotus
sacred bean family–nelum-
bonaceae
sacred beetle–scarabaeus
sacred bird–ibis
sacred bo tree–pipal
sacred book–Bible, Koran
sacred bull–apis, zebu
sacred cantata–motet
sacred chest–arca, ark
sacred chest (utensil)–cist
sacred composition – motet,
oratorio
sacred disease–epilepsy
sacred Egyptian bird–ibis
sacred extracts–catena
sacred fig–pipal
sacred Hindu language–Pali
sacred Hindu word–om, um
sacred image–icon, ikon
sacred instrument–urim
sacred interdiction – taboo,
tabu
sacred language (Hindu) –
Pali
sacred malady–epilepsy
sacred picture–icon, ikon
sacred scriptures–Koran
sacred song – chant, hymn,
psalm
sacred things (traffic in) –
simony
sacred tongue–Pali
sacred utensil room–sacristy
sacred weed–vervain
sacred wine vessel–ama
sacred word–om, um
sacred writ–scriptures
sacredness–inviolability
sacrifice – immolate, loss,
oblation, offering, privation, victim
sacrifice (great)–hecatomb
sacrifice (of a thousand
oxen)–chiliomb
sacrificer of cause or principle–martyr
sacrificial grain–ador
sacrilege–profanation
sacrosanct–holy, sacred
sad – bad, cheerless, dejected, deplorable, depressed,
despondent, distressing,
doleful, dull, dusky, melancholy, pathetic, pensive,

solemn, somber, sorrow-
ful, wicked
sad (French)–triste
sad tree–hursinghar
saddle (elephant)–howdah
saddle (light)–pilch, pillion
saddle (pack)–aparejo
saddle (place behind)–croup
saddle (raised part of) –
crutch
saddle (rear part of)–cantle
saddleback–hill, ridge
saddlebag–pannier
saddle blanket – corona, til-
pah
saddle boot–gambado
saddlebow–arson, pommel
saddlecloth–housing, panel,
shabrack
saddle corncrusher–quern
saddle cover–pilch
saddle cushion–pillion
saddle flap (side)–skirt
saddle girth–cinch
saddle horse–mount
saddle pad–panel
saddle pommel–tore
saddle rock–oyster
saddle side flap–skirt
saddle strap–girth, latigo
saddler–cobbler, horse, lorimer, loriner, seal, shoe-
maker
sadness – dejection, dolor,
gloominess, melancholy,
sorrow, sorrowfulness,
unhappiness
safari – caravan, expedition,
journey
safe–chest, closet, cupboard,
secure, sure, unharmed,
unhurt, vault
safe-conduct–convoy, cowle,
guard, pass, protection
safeguard – convoy, defense,
escort, pass, passport, protect, protection, safety
safekeeping–storage
safe retreat–haven, port, refuge
safety–assurance, security
safety lamp (miner's)–Davy
safety rail–guardrail
saffron–crocus, yellow
saffron plant–crocus
saftly (Scot.)–softly

sag–drift, droop, reed, rush, sedge, sink, slump

saga – recital, seeress, story, witch

saga (narrator of)–sagaman

saga (Norse myth.)–edda

sagaciate–fare, thrive

sagacious–argute, astute, discerning, farsighted, judicious, penetrative, perspicacious, politic, sage, sapient, shrewd, wise

sagacity – acuteness, discernment, judiciousness, penetration, quickness, shrewdness, wisdom

sage–counselor, discerning, judicious, mint, philosopher, salvia, sapient, shrewd, solon, wise

sage (Greek, early)–Thales

sage (holy)–Rishi

sage (wild)–clary

sage cheese–Cheddar

sage cock–grouse

sage hen–grouse

sage of Bethlehem – spearmint

Sage of Chelsea – Thomas Carlyle

Sage of Concord – Ralph Waldo Emerson

Sage of Ferney–Voltaire

Sage of Monticello–Thomas Jefferson

Sage of Pylon–Nestor

Sagebrush State–Nevada

sagene–network, seine

saginate–fatten, pamper

sagitta – Arrow, keystone, otholith

sagittarius–archer, bowman

sago palm–coontie

sago plant–cuckoopint

sago tree–coontie

sagoin–marmoset

saguaro–cactus

saguing–banana

Sahara nomad–Taureg

said–stated, uttered

said to be–reputed

sail–jib, navigate

sail (after edge of)–leech

sail (center of)–bunt

sail (four-sided)–lugsail

sail (lower corner of)–clew

sail (next to lowermost, on square-rigged ship)–topsail

sail (poetic)–keel

sail (principal) -mainsail

sail (storm)–trysail

sail (triangle)–lateen

sail (windmill)–awn

sail corner loop and thimble –clew

sail fast–scud

sail in (slang)–barge

sail line–earing

sail rope–sheet

sail yard (Scot.)–ra

sailboat – caravel, caravelle, sloop, yawl

sailing–asea

sailing ship–bark, brig, frigate, schooner, sloop, vessel

sailing vessel–bark, barkentine, barquentine, frigate, schooner, ship, sloop, yawl

sailing vessel (light, var.)–spynace

sailing vessel's rig–lateen

sailor (in charge of ship's boat)–coxswain

sailor (Oriental)–lascar

sailor (Pacific)–toty

sailor's associate at meals – messmate

sailor's mess tub–kid

sailor's patron saint–Elmo

sailor's song – barcarole, chantey, chanty

sails (ends supporting) – yardarms

saindoux–grease, lard

saint (abbr.)–St.

saint (English patron) – George

saint (female, abbr.)–Ste.

saint (lawyer's)–Ives

saint (lover's)–Valentine

saint (patron)–Patrick

saint (patron of children)– Nicholas

saint (Portuguese)–Sao

saint (sailor's)–Elmo

Saint Barnabas' prayer–Ave Maria

Saint Helena hemlock (water)–jellica

Saint Kitts (B.W.I.) island– Nevis

Saint Martin's feast – Martinmas

saint, whose festival is on July 26–Anne

saintlier–holier

Sais City native–Saite

salacious – lecherous, lewd, lustful

salad plant–celery, cress, endive, lettuce, romaine, watercress

salad vegetable–endive

salamander – axolotl, caudata, eft, newt, urodela, urodele

salamander (aquatic)–newt, triton

salamander (Mexican)–axolotl

salary–allowance, compensation, emolument, fee, hire, honorarium, pay, recompense, remuneration, reward, stipend, wages

salary (meager)–pittance

sale–auction, deal

sale (illegal, of products in war period)–black market

salesman – drummer, representative, solicitor

salesman (sidewalk)–pitchman

salesman (traveling)–agent, drummer, representative

salient–bounding, extended, jumping, leaping, line, prominent, trench

salient (her.)–cabre

salient angle formed by meeting of two surfaces– arris

salient point–feature

saline drop–tear

saline solution–brine

sallies–sorties

sally–start

sally against besiegers–sortie

sally forth–issue

salmagundi–hash, potpourri

salmon–lax

salmon (after spawning) – kelt

salmon (blue back)–nerka

salmon (dog)–keta
salmon (female) – baggit, raun
salmon (genus of) – oncorhynchus
salmon (hump back)–haddo
salmon (newly hatched, Brit.)–pink
salmon (silver)–coho
salmon (small)–grilse, peal
salmon (young) – fog, par, parr, smolt
salmon-catching enclosure – yair, yare
salmon trout–sewen
salmonoid fish–ahyu, powan
salmonoid fish (large) – nelma
Salonika campaign hero (1918)–Kosca Pecanac
saloon – apartment, bar, coach, hall, room
saloon (Span.)–cantina
saloop–sassafras
salt–brine, cure, sailor, sal
salt (acetic acid)–acetate
salt (alkaline)–borax
salt (anisic acid)–anisate
salt (arabic acid)–arabate
salt (astringent)–alum
salt (astringent, mineral) – alum
salt (auric acid)–aurate
salt (block or rock)–pig
salt (boric acid)–borate
salt (capric acid)–rutate
salt (casein)–caseate
salt (chemical)–bromate, sal
salt (coll.)–tar
salt (crenic acid)–crenate
salt (crystalline)–analgene
salt (crystalline acid) – racemate
salt (ethereal)–ester
salt (French)–sel
salt (hydrobromic acid) – bromide
salt (iodic acid)–iodate
salt (malic acid)–malamate, malate
salt (mineral)–alum
salt (navy slang)–seadust
salt (nitric acid)–nitrate
salt (oleic acid)–oleate
salt (oxalic acid)–oxalate
salt (resembling)–haloid

salt (soluble)–alkali
salt (toluic acid)–toluate
salt (uric acid)–urate
salt (vinegar)–acetate
salt-covered plain (Span.) – salada
salt lake–salina
salt marsh–salina
saltpeter–niter, nitre
salt pit–vat
salt pond–salina
salt solution–brine
salt water–brine
salt water fish–porgies
saltworks–salina, saltern
salted–corned, cured
salted (Philippine Is.)–alat
salty–briny, salic, saline
saltatory variation–mutant
salutary – curative, healthy, medicinal, restorative
salutation – ave, hail, hello, hi, howdy
salutation (ceremonial) – salaam, salam
salutation (drinking)–skoal
salutation (Hawaiian) – aloha
salutation (nocturnal, musical)–serenade
salutation (Oriental) – kotow, salaam, salam
salutation (parting) – Mizpah, Mizpeh
salute–greet, hail
salvage–rescue, save
salvation (pert. to)–soterial, soterical
salve–anoint, cerate, flattery, ointment
salver–tray
Salween River town–Paan
Samaria deity–Nibhaz
Samaritan people (anc.) – Assyrians, Israelites
Sambar deer–maha
same – ditto, identic, identical, ilk, one
same (arch.)–ilk
same (the)–ditto, ibid, idem, ilk, self
same (the, abbr.)–id
same place (in)–ibid
sameness – identicalness, invariableness, monotony, oneness

sameness (wearisome) – monotony
Samian Sage–Pythagoras
samlet–par, parr
Samoan capital–Apia
Samoan city–Apia
Samoan food fish–sesele
Samoan mollusk (edible) – asi
Samoan mudworm–ipo
Samoan owl (barn)–lulu
Samoan seaport–Apia
Samoan warrior–Toa
samovar–urn
sample–example, specimen, swatch
sampleman – demonstrator, taster
Sampson–see Samson
Samson's birthplace–Zorah
Samson's death city–Gaza
Samuel Lover's hero's name –Rory
Samuel's mentor (keeper of) –Eli
Samuel's son–Abiah
San Francisco military post–Presidio
sanative–curing, healing
sanatorium–spa
sanctimonious–holy, sacred, saintly
sanction – amen, approval, approve, authority, authorization, authorize, countenance, endorse, endorsement, permit, ratification, ratify, support
sanction (authoritative)–fiat
sanction (officially) – approbate
sanctuary – abbey, cloister, convent, fane, haven, holy, monastery, priory, retreat, shelter
sanctuary (criminal)–alsatia
sanctuary (innermost)–naos
sanctum–den, office, retreat, study
sand–grit, nerve
sand (full of fine)–arenulous
sand (mass of, cemented on sea bottom)–paar
sand (submerged bank)–bar
sand (sugar)–niter
sand and clay mixture–loam

sand eel–grig, launce
sand formation–dene, dune
sand hill–dene, dune
sand hill (Eng.)–dene
sand mound–dene, dune
sandpiper–canderling, dunlin, knot, ruff, terek
sandpiper (female) – ree, reeve
sand ridge–dene, dune
sand spurries–tissas
sandstone (siliceous, in Eng. coal measure)–ganister
sandstone block (large)–sarsen
sandstone blocks on English chalk downs–sarsens
sandiness–arenosity
sandy–arenose, arenous
sandy waste–desert
sandal–slipper, sock
sandal (made of untanned leather)–rullion
sandal (winged)–talaria
sane–lucid, rational, sensible
sang–chanted
sanguinary – bloodthirsty, bloody, cruel, gory, murderous
sanguine – hopeful, optimistic
sanity–reason
Sanskrit dialect–Pali
Sanskrit division of literature–Sruti
Sanskrit epic character–Sita
Sanskrit soul–atman
Santa Barbara island – Catalina
Santa Claus' reindeer–Blitzen, Comet, Cupid, Dancer, Dasher, Donder, Prancer, Vixen
sap–mine, undermine
sap (dried)–gum
sap (French)–seve
sap (poisonous)–upas
sapodilla–zapote
saponified–soaped
sapor–taste
sapper–digger, miner
Sarah's slave–Hagar
sarcasm–gibe, irony, ironies (pl.), ridicule, satire, taunt
sarcasm (pert. to)–ironical

sarcasm (subtle)–irony
sarcastic–dry, ironic, sardonic, satiric
sarcastic (subtly)–ironic
sarcastic remark–taunt
Sardinia sheep (wild) – moufflon, mouflon
Sarmatia people (anc.) – Roxolani
sartor–tailor
sash–belt, girdle, obi
sash (around waist) – cummerbund, kummerbund
sash (broad)–girdle, obi
sash (colored silk, Scot.) – benn
sashes (window)–casements
sassafras tea–saloop
sassafras tree–ague
Satan–eblis, Mephistopheles
satchel–case, valise
satchel (small)–cabas
sate–cloy, glut, gorge, satiate, surfeit
sated with pleasure–blase
satellite – follower, luna, moon
satellite of Jupiter – (I) Io, (II) Europa, (III) Ganymede, (IV) Callisto
satellite of Saturn (fifth)–Rhea
satiate – cloy, glut, gorge, pall, sate, surfeit
satin (imitation)–sateen, satinet, satinette
satire–irony, lampoon, parody
satire (malicious)–lampoon
satiric–abusive, bitter, caustic, cutting, ironic, ironical, poignant, reproachful, sarcastic
satirical (slyly)–dry
satirical writing–lampoon
satisfaction – amends, atonement, compensation, content, contentment, gratification, indemnification, pleasure, propitiation, recompense, remuneration
satisfaction (obs.)–assethe
satisfaction made for killing a man (anc. Scot. law)–cro

satisfactory–adequate, expiatory, pat, satisfying
satisfied–content, sated
satisfied (highly)–proud
satisfier of appetite–sater
satisfy–assuage, compensate, content, do, fill, gratify, pay, please, sate, satiate, suit
satisfy by evidence–convince
saturate–drench, imbue, impregnate, permeate, ret, seethe, soak, sop, souse, steep
saturated–sodden
Saturn's rings (part of)–ansae
satyr–faun
sauce–alec, caper, gravy
sauce (anchovy)–alec
sauce (fish)–alec, garum
sauce (herring)–alec
sauce (salad)–dressing
sauce (sharp)–alec
sauce (spicy) – catchup, catsup, ketchup
saucepan–casserole
saucy – bold, forward, impudent, malapert, officious, pert
Saul of Tarsus–Paul
Saul's concubine–Rizpah
Saul's daughter–Michal
Saul's meeting place with witch–Endor
Saul's wife–Ahinoam
Saul's witch's home–Endor
Sault Sainte Marie (abbr.)–Soo
saunter–lag, loiter, ramble, range, roam, rove, stray, stroll, wander
saurian–lizard
sausage–bologna, salame, salami (pl.)
sausage (kind of)–bologna, rollejee, rolliche, rollichie
sausage (summer) – salame, salami (pl.)
savage–atrocious, barbarian, brute, brutish, cruel, feral, ferine, ferocious, fierce, Indian, merciless, pitiless, rude, uncivilized, wild, yahoo
savage (Luzon)–att, atta

savage who eats human flesh –cannibal
savant–sage, scientist
save – but, conserve, economize, redeem, rescue, salvage, scrimp
save from evil fate–rescue
Savior–Redeemer
savor – flavor, odor, sapor, savour, smack, smell, taste, zest
savor (cooked meat)–nidor
savory – agreeable, appetizing, delightful, piquant, sapid, savoury, tasty
savory meat jelly–aspic
Savoy prince–Humbert
saw – adage, dict, maxim, noticed, proverb, saying
saw (comb-making)–stadda
saw (cross cut)–briar
saw (log-squaring)–edger
saw (surgeon's) – trepan, trephine
saw (surgical crown)–trepan
sawdust–scobs
saw for squaring logs–edger
saw-like edge (having)–serate, serrate, serrated
saw-like part–serra
sawmill gate–sash
saw suddenly–beheld
saw tines–teeth
saw tooth–tine
saw wildly–rave
saw with grain–rip
saxhorn–tuba
saxifrage (genus of)–seseli
saxifrage (meadow)–seseli
Saxon chief–Horsa
Saxon king (western warlike)–Ine
Saxon lady (of royal descent)–Rowena
Saxon serf–esne
Saxon warrior–thane
Saxony capital–Dresden
say–aver, remark, state, utter
say a blessing–bensh
say again or differently–restate
say from memory–recite
say further–add
say or do again–reiterate, repeat

saying – adage, aphorism, apothegm, axiom, byword, maxim, phrase, proverb, saw, quip
saying (collection of pithy)–gnomology
saying (distinguishing the adherents of a party or sect)–shibboleth
saying (dogmatic) – dictum, dicta (pl.)
saying (instructive) – apothegm
saying (obs.)–dit, enigma
saying (religious teacher's)–logia
saying (short pithy) – apothegm
saying (witty)–mot
scab–ratter, scoundrel
scabbard–holster, sheath
scabbard tip (metal sword)–crampit
scaddle – cruel, fierce, mischievous, nervous, noxious, skittish, thievish, timid
scads–oodles
scaff–beg, food, rabble, riffraff, sponge
scaffie (Scot.)–scavenger
scaffolding–staging
scalawag (scallawag) – scamp, scapegrace
scale – ascend, climb, compare, gamut, husk, hut, lamina, measure, peel, rate, shed, size, weight
scale (chaffy)–rament
scale (chaffy inner, of grass flower)–palea
scale (chaffy, on flowers) – palea
scale (cornstalk, outside) – shive
scale (diatonic)–gamut
scale (external large)–scute
scale (large)–scute
scale (major)–gamut
scale (musical, whole)–gamut
scale (note of diatonic)–sol
scale (on grand)–epic
scale (second note of) – supertonic

scale (zoology, comb. form) –cten
scale-like–leprose
scaled off–flaked
scaler (boiler tube)–sooter
scallop–crena, mollusk
scalloped (minutely)–crenulate
scalloped with notches–crenate
scam–scorch, spot, stain
scamp – cheat, imp, knave, rascal, rogue, scalawag
scamp (Irish)–spalpeen
scamper–race
scamper (coll.)–skedaddle
scan – contemplate, eye, peruse, scrutinize
scance – blame, comment, glance, glitter, shine
scandal – calumny, defamation, detraction, gossip, odium, shame, slander
scandal monger (Eng. dial.) –clat
scandent–climbing
Scandinavian–Dane, Norse, Norseman, Norwegian, Swede
Scandinavian (anc.)–Norseman
Scandinavian (pert. to, anc.) –runic
Scandinavian bard–sagaman
Scandinavian brownie–nis
Scandinavian character (myth.)–Atli
Scandinavian division (territory)–amt
Scandinavian dwarf–troll
Scandinavian giant–troll
Scandinavian heroes' abode (immortal)–Valhalla
Scandinavian king (myth.)–Atli
Scandinavian kobold–nis
Scandinavian legend–saga
Scandinavian literature–edda
Scandinavian measure–alen
Scandinavian minstrel–scald
Scandinavian money unit – krone
Scandinavian myth–saga
Scandinavian navigator – Eric

Scandinavían ptarmigan – ripa
Scandinavian rulers (of Russian slaves)–Ros, Varangians
Scandinavian tale–saga
Scandinavian vessel–aesc
scant–chary, parsimonious, slight, sparing
scanty – meager, meagre, scrimpy, sparse
scapegrace–scalawag, scallawag, scamp
scar–cicatrice, cicatrix, seam
scarce–deficient, rare, scanty, short, uncommon
scarcely–hardly
scarcely enough–scant
scarcity–dearth, famine, infrequency, insufficiency, rareness, rarity, want
scare–affright, alarm, frighten, panic, startle, terrify
scare (war, Br. slang)–flap
scarecrow (deer frightening)–sewel
scarf–ascot, fascinator, muffler, sash, tippet
scarf (broad)–shawl
scarf (clerical)–orale, stole
scarf (feather)–boa
scarf (head)–fascinator
scarf (long, decorative)–sari
scarf (Mexican)–tapalo
scarf (neck)–ascot, boa
scarf (papal)–orale
scarf (Pope's)–fanon
scarf (wooly) – cloud, fascinator
scarf (silk)–dopatta, muffler
scarlet–red
Scarlett O'Hara's home – Tara
scarp–cliff, declivity, descent
scarves–cravats, ties
scarves (neck)–ascots, ascot (sing.)
scary – eerie, eery, ghostly, uncanny, weird
scat (scatt)–beat, burst, scatter, smash, tax, tribute
scatch–crutch, stilt
scathe–damage, harm, hurt, injury, misfortune
scatter–deal, diffuse, dispel, disperse, disseminate,

shower, sow, spray, spread, strew, ted
scatter (Scot.)–skail
scatter over–bestrew
scatter water–splash
scattered – dealt, dispersed, separated, sparse
scattering–dissemination
scatty–showery
scaw–headland, promontory
scene–site, view
scene (last)–finale
scene (opera)–scena
scene of action – arena, sphere, stage
scene of confusion–babel
scene of first miracle–Cana
scene of large-scale commando raid–Dieppe
scenic – panoramic, picturesque
scenic enigma–charade
scenic view–scape
scent – aroma, fragrance, nairn, nose, odor, smell, spoor
scent of cooking meat–nidor
scented–nosed
scented (agreeably) – odoriferous
scepter – baton, mace, rod, sceptre, staff
scepter (reformed spelling)–staf
schedule–calendar, card, catalog, catalogue, inventory, list, slate, table, tabulate, timetable
schedule of duties–tariff
scheme–concoct, conspiracy, contrive, device, devise, machination, plan, plot, purpose
scheme (factious)–cabal
scheme (reacting against originator)–boomerang
scheme (regular)–system
scheme (secret) – cabal, cabala, cabbala
scheme for–complot
schism – breach, division, rent, separation, split
schismatic–heretic
schist (argillaceous)–slate
scholar – disciple, learner,

pedant, philologist, pupil, savant, student
scholar (erudite)–savant
scholarly–academic, erudite, learned, scholastic
scholarship–education, erudition, foundation, instruction, knowledge, learning
school – cult, drill, educate, instruct, sect, seminar, seminary, teach, train
school (French)–ecole
school (French secondary)–lycee
school (in which students live)–convent
school (riding)–manege
school (wrestling)–palaestra, palestra
schoolbook–primer, reader, speller
school head–scholarch
schoolmaster – caji, domine, dominie, pedagog, pedagogue
school of art (modern)–dada
school of philosophy (early Christian)–gnostic
school of seals–pod
school of whales–gam, pod
school task–assignment, lesson
school term–semester
schooner – boat, glass, measure, vessel
schooner (three-masted) – tern
schooner (two-masted, square-rigged)–brig
science–knowledge, ology
science (ear)–otology
science (moral conduct) – ethics
science (occult)–esoterics
science (skilled in)–ists
science (treating life of forest trees)–silvics
science of breeding–eugenics
science of children's disease–paediatrics, pediatrics
science of elasticity (in solids)–elaterics
science of government–politics
science of healing–latrology

science of interpretation – exegesis

science of kissing–philematology

science of law–jurisprudence

science of life–biology

science of light–optics

science of mind (pert. to)–psychologically

science of moral duty–ethics

science of preserving health –hygiene

science of pure thought–noetics

science of reality–philosophy

science of reasoning–logic

science of recording genealogies–heraldry

science of rocks-petrology

science of sound–acoustics

science of thinking–logic

science of versification–prosody

science of virtues–aretaics

sciences (the)–arts

scientific–technical

scimitar (scimiter) – saber, snee

scintilla–atom

scintillate – coruscate, flash, gleam, glitter, spark, twinkle

scoff – deride, fleer, flout, gibe, gird, jeer, mock, rail, sneer

scog–shelter

scogger (worsted and footless)–stocking

scoke–pokeweed

scold – berate, carp, chide, nag, rail, rate, rebuke, reprove

scold (coll.)–slate

scold vehemently–berate

scolding woman–shrew

sconce – candlestick, head, lantern, screen, shelter, skull

scoop–bail, beat, bucket, excavate, hollow, lade, ladle, shovel, spoon

scoop (broad)–shovel

scope – ambit, area, arena, domain, latitude, range, reach

scorch – char, parch, sear, singe

score–account, arrange, berate, goal, judge, notch, obligation, orchestrate, rate, run, scold, scratch, tab, tally, twenty

score (cribbage)–peg

score (standard, estimated) –bogey, bogie, bogy

scorer–marker

scoria (volcano)–lava, slag

scoring points – aces, goals, runs, tallies

scorn – contemn, contempt, contumely, deride, derision, despise, disdain

scornful – contemptuous, contumelious, derisive, insolent

Scorpio's star (brightest) – Antares

scorpion–alacran, arachnid

scorpion (water)–nepa

Scot–Caledonian, Gael

Scot's peer–Thane

Scotch accent (peculiar rough)–birr

Scotch alder tree–arn

Scotch attendant–gillie

Scotch basket–corf

Scotch beret – tam, tamoshanter

Scotch bird–gae

Scotch blessing – rebuke, scolding

Scotch blood money–cro

Scotch bluebell–harebell

Scotch bonnets–mushroom

Scotch brandy (with honey and oatmeal)–athole

Scotch brier–rose

Scotch broth–soup

Scotch bull (young)–stot

Scotch bushel–fou

Scotch cake–scone

Scotch cap–tam, tamoshanter

Scotch chemist (author) – Ure

Scotch chief (school)–dux

Scotch child–bairn

Scotch church–kirk

Scotch city–Aberdeen, Ayr, Dublin, Dundee, Edinburgh (c.), Glasgow, Greenock, Inverness, Kilmarnock, Leith, Paisley, Perth, St. Andrews, Stirling

Scotch cloth (homespun) – kelt

Scotch coin–demy

Scotch county–nairn

Scotch court officer–macer

Scotch cuddy–draper, peddler

Scotch cup (drinking)–tass

Scotch curlies–kale

Scotch dagger (anc.)–skean

Scotch dance–reel

Scotch dance (grave, old fashioned)–ecossaise

Scotch dipper–bufflehead

Scotch district–Rinns

Scotch district (former) – Breadalbane, Galloway, Lothian, Tweeddale

Scotch district (Perth) – Atholl

Scotch dramatist–Barrie

Scotch drinking cup–tass

Scotch duck–bufflehead

Scotch elder–tobacco

Scotch elm–wychelm

Scotch explorer–Rae

Scotch fiddle–itch, scab

Scotch fine (early)–cro

Scotch fingering–yarn

Scotch firth – Clyde, Cromarty, Forth, Linnhe, Loch, Lorn, Moray, Tay

Scotch for lake–loch

Scotch for money–siller

Scotch for one–ae, ane

Scotch fort (anc. roofed)–dune

Scotch fort (circular)–roundabout

Scotch Gaelic–Erse

Scotch goblet–tass

Scotch griddle cake–scone

Scotch hands–paddles

Scotch heath–heather

Scotch herring measure – crans

Scotch highland marauder–cateran

Scotch highland soldier – cateran

Scotch Highlander–Gael

Scotch Highlander (pert. to)
–Gaelic
Scotch Highlander's knife–
skeandhu
Scotch Highlander's lan-
guage–Erse
Scotch Highlander's sword–
claymore
Scotch hillside–brae
Scotch homespun cloth–kelt
Scotch hopper–hopscotch
Scotch island–Arran, Heb-
rides, Iona, Orkney, Shet-
land, Skye
Scotch island (west)–Arran
Scotch kale–borecole
Scotch king (anc.)–Robert
Scotch lake–loch
Scotch land (low, rich river)
–carses
Scotch landholder (histori-
cal)–thane
Scotch landowner – laird,
thane
Scotch language–Erse
Scotch leader (school)–dux
Scotch linens (stout figured)
–dornicks
Scotch lovage–parsley
Scotch machine (weighing)
–trone
Scotchman (jocular)–Mac
Scotch manservant – gillie,
gilly
Scotch marauder–cateran
Scotch mark off–rit
Scotch measure – auchlet,
boll, chalder, choppin,
cop, davach, davoch, fall,
firlot, lippie, lippy, mile,
mutchkin, particate, peck,
pint, rood, rope, shaft-
ment, shaftmont, stim-
part, stimpert
Scotch mercury–foxglove
Scotch monk–culdee
Scotch mountain–Ben Nevis,
Grampians
Scotch musical instrument–
bagpipe
Scotch name (good)–Ian
Scotch native (old)–Pict
Scotch one–ae, ane, tae
Scotch painter–Allan
Scotch payment for killing
(anc.)–cro

Scotch peasant–crofter
Scotch peasant (rent-paying)
–cottar
Scotch peninsula (south-
west)–Rinns
Scotch petticoats (short) –
kilts
Scotch poet–Burns
Scotch porridge–brose
Scotch proprietor–laird
Scotch race (old)–Pict
Scotch ridge of hill–run
Scotch rifles (first battalion)
–Cameronians
Scotch river–Afton, Annan,
Ayr, Clyde, Dee, Deveron,
Don, Doon, Esk, Find
Horn, Forth, Nith, Spey,
Tay, Tweed
Scotch rope (short cart) –
wanty
Scotch scholar–Nicoll
Scotch scurvy grass–seabells
Scotch seaport–Leith
Scotch shawl (shepherd's
gray plaid)–maud
Scotch teal–bufflehead
Scotch title–laird
Scotch to–tae
Scotch toad–taed
Scotch toe–tae
Scotch tone–tae
Scotch topaz–cairngorm
Scotch tourist resort–Oban
Scotch tribal payments–cro
Scotch tribesman (anc.)–Pict
Scotch uncle–eme
Scotch waistcoat (under) –
fecket
Scotch water place–Oban
Scotch water spirits–kelpies
Scotch weighing machine–
trone
Scotch weight–boll, bushel,
drop, trone weight
Scotch wheat cake–scone
Scotch whiskey (with honey
and oatmeal)–athole
Scotch woodcock–eggs
scoter–coot
Scotland–Caledonia
Scottish–see Scotch
Scott's character (in The
Pirate)–Norna
Scott's hero (Marmion) –
Lochinvar

Scott's novel–Ivanhoe
scoundrel–cad, cheat, knave,
miscreant, villain
scoundrel (arch.)–varlet
scoup – leap, run, scamper,
skip
scourge – affliction, bane,
chastise, flog, infliction,
lash, punish, punishment,
swinge, switch, whip
scout–emissary, flout, lookout, reconnoiter, scoff,
spy, watchman
scow (small)–garvey
scowl–frown, glower, lower
scraggy (coll.)–weedy
scrap – chip, cutting, end,
fight, fragment, ort,
quarrel, refuse, remnant
scrape–grate, row, rub
scrape (raspingly, obs.) –
gride
scrape the ground (golf) –
sclaff
scraped–shaven
scraped together–raked
scraper – abrader, barber,
fiddler, rasper, strigil
scraper (wood)–harl
scraping (act of)–rasure
scraps (slang and dial.) –
scran
scratch – cancel, expunge,
itch, mar, rake, rist, score
scratch (dial.)–rit
scratch (mark, wound)–rist
scratch (Scot.)–rit
scratch with nails–claw
scrawm – climb, scramble,
scratch, scrawl
scrawny – lean, rawboned,
scranny, thin
scrawny (coll.)–poor
scream–cry, screech, shriek
scree–peeble, stone, talus
screech–cry, outcry, scream,
shriek, ululate
screed – fragment, rend,
shred, tear, tirade
screen – conceal, curtain,
hide, partition, protect,
shade, shelter, sift
screen (altar)–reredos
screen (architectural)–spier
screen (fixed)–spier
screen (of tapestry)–arra

screen (ornamental, behind altar)–reredos

screen from light–shade

screw-like–spirod

screw thread–worm

scribble – scrabble, scratch, scrawl

scribe – author, journalist, penman, writer

scride–crawl, creep

scriggle – curlicue, squirm, twist, wriggle

scrimp–scant, stint

scrine–bookcase, chest, reliquary, shrine

scrip – bag, list, schedule, wallet, writing

script writing (with heavy, nearly upright strokes)–ronde

scriptural–plastic

scripture–Bible, writ

scripture (Latin version) – Itala

scripture part–lesson

Scriptures (The)–Oracles

scrivener–amanuensis, notary, scribe, writer

scroll – draft, engross, inscribe, record, roll, spiral, volute

scrolling (absent-minded drawing)–doodling

scrub–clean, cleanse, drudge, dwarf, inferior, mean, mop, paltry, rub, runt, scour, wash

scruff–dandruff, dross, nape, refuse, scum

scruple–demur, qualm

scrupulous – conscientious, exact, proper, punctilious

scrutinize–eye, probe, pry, scan

scry–cry, glance, look, shout, sift

scud–skim

scuffle–melee, shuffle, struggle, tussle

scuffle along–shamble

scug – pretense, protection, schoolboy, shade, shadow, shelter, squirrel

sculch–cultch, refuse

sculduddery – grossness, obscenity

scull–basket, gull, oar, propel, rowboat, scullion, shoal

scullion–base, menial, servant

scullog (scullogue)–farmer, rustic

sculp–carve, engrave

sculptor (obs.)–imager

sculptor's tool–graver

sculpture–carve, engrave

sculpture (piece of)–statue

sculptured–graven

scum – dross, foam, froth, impurities, refuse, scoria, spume

scum on surface of molten metal–dross

scurrility–abuse

scurrilous – abusive, foul-mouthed, gross, indecent, insulting, low, opprobrious, scurrile, vile, vulgar

scurry–flurry, hie, scamper, scuttle

scurry (coll.)–skelter

scurry off–scoot

scurvy – contemptible, discourteous, mean

scurvy preventative – antiscorbutic

scuttle – basket, cuttlefish, dish, hatchway, hod, octopus, platter, run, scoot, scurry, shovel, sink

scuttle (coal)–hod

Scylla's love–Minos

scythe (Scot.)–sy

scythe (whole sweep of) – swath

scythe handle–snath, snathe, thole

sea – brine, ocean, swell, wave

sea (Antarctic)–Ross

sea (arm of)–bayou, estuary, firth, gulf, meer

sea (between Arabia and Africa)–Red

sea (between West Indies and Central America) – Caribbean

sea (comb. form)–mer

sea (connected with Black Sea)–Azov

sea (French)–mer

sea (inland)–Aral

sea (pert. to)–marine, pelagic, thalassic

sea (the)–meer, mere

sea air (coll.)–ozone

sea animal–inia

sea bird albatross, ern, erne, gull, petrel, shearwater, smew, solan, tern

sea bird (predaceous)–yager

sea biscuit–hardtack

sea biscuit (French)–galette

seaboard–coast, tidewater

sea bottom–bed

sea bottom plant–enalid

sea cow–dugong, hippopotamus, manatee, sirenian, walrus

sea cow (Steller's)–rytina

sea cucumber–trepang

sea cucumber (order of) – pedata

sea demigod–triton

sea dew–rosmarine

sea diving hazard–bends

sea duck – eider, scooter, scoter

sea dwelling–marine

sea eagle–ern, erne, tern

sea eel–conger

seafarer–mariner, navigator, sailor, seaman, tar

sea foam–meerschaum, sepiolite

seafolk – mariners, navigators, sailors, seamen

sea god–Neptune, Proteus

sea goddess–Doris

sea gull–cob, mew

sea gull (black-backed)–cob

sea gull (old word)–gore

sea hog–porpoise

sea inlet–arm, bay, bayou

sea interspersed with small islands–archipelago

sea kales (Eng.)–coles

sea lettuce–laver

sea mammal–seal, whale

seaman–gob, mariner, sailor, tar

seaman's chapel–bethel

seamen (group of) – crew, hands

sea mile (of 2029 yards)–naut

sea nymph–Galatea, nereid, oceanid, siren

sea otter–kalan

sea picture–marine

seaplane–supermarine

sea robber–buccaneer, corsair, pirate, privateer

sea roughness (slight)–lipper

sea shell–conch

seashore–coast

seashore silicate–sand

sea slug–trepan

sea spray–spindrift, spoondrift

sea swell–surf

sea term–ahoy, avast, belay, trice

sea undulation (long)–swell

sea unicorn–narwhal

sea urchin–repkie

sea urchin's rock hole–geode

sea wave–breaker

seaweed – agar, agar-agar, alg, alga, algae (pl.), desmid, desmidian, dulse, kelp, ore, sargasso

seaweed (edible)–agar, agar-agar, dulse, laver

seaweed (edible purple) – laver

seaweed (purple)–laver, nori

seaweed (red)–dulse

seaweed (var. of)–oreweek

seaweed ashes–kelp, varec

seaweed extract–agar

seaweeds–algae, ores

seaweeds (genus of)–alaria

seaweedy–algous

sea wolf–pirate, privateer

sea worm (eunicoid)–sao

seal – attest, authenticate, cachet, close, confine, confirm, fasten, fix, imprison, leather, ratify, secure, shut, signet, validate

seal (Antarctic)–Ross seal, Ross's

seal (arch.)–sigil

seal (eared)–otary

seal (fur)–ursal

seal (large, bearded)–makluk

seal (papal letter)–bulla

seal (place of, abbr.)–LS

seal (young)–pup, saddler

seal with wax–cere

seal's (fur) breeding ground –rookery

seal's limb–flipper

sealed instrument–escrow

sealer (bottler)–capper

seam – burden, crevice, groove, horseload, interstice, line, load, packsaddle, ridge, suture

seam (as of coal)–streak

seam (irregular, naut.)–fash

seam (natural, constituting flaw in stone)–dry

seamed–lined

seamstitch–purl

search–frisk, hunt, inquire, investigate, probe, quest, ransack, scrutinize, seek, survey

search (as a trail)–quest

search (obs.)–sphere

search (thoroughly) – comb, ransack

search (uncertainly)–grope

search for (by feeling) – grope

search for fish–fish

search for provisions–forage

search out–ferret

search thoroughly–probe

searcher (disorderly) – rummager

searchlight (Fr. slang)–Paul Pry

season–fall, salt, spice, tide, time

season (right, Scot.)–tid

season (French Lenten) – Careme

season (Scot.)–sele

season for use–age

season highly–devil

season with hot sauce–devil

seasonable–apropos, opportune, suitable, timely

seasoned (more)–riper

seasoning – allspice, cloves, condiment, mustard, paprika, pepper, spice, thyme

seasoning herb – marjoram, sage

seasons (the)–Horae

seasons (goddess of)–Horae

season's shearing–clip

seat–bench, chair, establish, install, pew, settee, settle, stool

seat (backless)–stool

seat (chancel)–sedile, sedilia (pl.)

seat (church) – pew, sedile, sedilia (pl.)

seat (Latin)–sella

seat (outdoor)–exedra

seat of consciousness–ego

seat of justice–banc

seat on elephant's back – howdah

seat worm–pinworm

secern–discriminate, distinguish, separate

secluded – aloof, apart, debarred, expelled, hidden, isolated, private, recessed, remote, retiring, screened

seclusion–aloofness, privacy, retirement, solitude

second – abet, aid, assist, back, echo, encourage, reinforce, support, sustain

second childhood–dotage

second childhood (in)–dotage, dotard

second copy–redraft

second crop–rowen

second growth crop–rowen

second sight (having)–fey, psychic

second team–scrubs, Yannigans

secondary – bye, inferior, minor, subordinate

secondary color – green, orange, purple

secondary importance–bye

secondary school–prep

secondhand – two-handed, used

secondhand auction–resale

secrecy – concealment, hiding, privacy, privity, reticence

secret–arcanum, arcana (pl.), clandestine, concealed, covert, esoteric, inner, mystery, occult, private, privy, retired, surreptitious, underhand, unknown

secret agent–emissary, spy

secret language–argot, dialect, jargon

secret movement–stealth

secret place–cache, cranny

secretary–amanuensis, desk

Secretary of Treasury (first) –Hamilton

secretion (alimentary canal of whales, used in perfumes)–ambergris

secretion (from inflamed tissues)–pus

secretion (from shrubs)–lerp

secretion (gland)–hormone

secretion (resinous insect)–lac

secretiveness–reticence

secretly–aside, inly

secretory organ–gland

secrets (keeper of)–confidant

sect–clan, class, cult, order, party, school

sect (anc. ascetic)–essene

sect (anc. religious)–alogi

sect (religious)–Baptist, Congregational, Episcopal, Lutheran, Methodist, Mormon, Presbyterian, Quaker

sectarian–heretic

section–part, piece, segment, signature, subdivision, tmema

section (body, main)–torso

section (conic)–parabola

section of three folio sheets–ternary, ternion

secular – earthly, laic, lay, profane, temporal, worldly

secure–dependable, easy, ensure, fast, fasten, firm, get, nail, obtain, procure, safe, spike, stable, tape, undisturbed

secure (as a sail)–trice

secure aid of–enlist

secure position–footing

security–bail, defense, gage, guard, guarantee, pledge, protection, shelter

sedate–calm, decorous, demure, dispassionate, proper, quiet, serene, serious, settled, sober, staid, unruffled

sedative – chloral, lenitive, palliative, paregoric, remedy, soothing

sedative hypnotic–barbital

sediment – dregs, grounds, lee, silt

sediment (fine earthly)–silt

seditious–factious, insurrectionary, turbulent

seduce–allure, debauch, decoy, entice, inveigle, mislead, tempt

seducer (gay)–Lothario

seduction – charm, corruption, debauchment, lure, temptation

sedulous – assiduous, busy, diligent, industrious, laborious, persevering, persistent, unremitting, untiring, unwearied

see–descry, detect, discern, discover, perceive, understand, witness

see below (Latin abbr.)–vi

see unexpectedly–espy

see visions in crystal–scry

seeing–viewing

seeing actually–ocular

seed–egg, ovule, pip, sperm

seed (aromatic)–anise

seed (bean-like, for soups)–lentil

seed (edible)–bean, pea

seed (food)–lentil

seed (fragrant)–anise, aniseed

seed (lemon)–pip

seed (lens-shaped)–lentil

seed (Moringa)–ben

seed (oak)–acorn

seed (opium poppy)–maw

seed (skin of)–tunica

seed (small, apple-like)–pip

seed (small bony) – acinus, acini (pl.)

seed (tropical tree)–ben

seed (winged)–samara

seed albumen–endosperm

seed appendage–aril

seed cells (plant)–cysts

seed coat–aril

seed coating – pod, testa, testae (pl.)

seed coating (external)–testa

seed coating (internal)–tegman

seed container–legume, loment, pod

seed container (prickly)–bur

seed covering – aril, arillus, testa

seed covering (outer)–testa

seed enclosing soft fruit – drupe

seed expansion–ala

seed plants (pert. to)–herbal

seed vessel–carpel, legume

seed vessel (dehiscent)–pod

seed which ripens underground–peanut

seeded–rowed

seedlet–spore

seeds – eggs, ovules, pips, sperms

seeds (used in cocoa and chocolate)–cacao

seeds (used for perfume and coffee)–abelmosk

seek–beg, endeavor, essay, hunt, pursue, search, solicit

seeker – probe, pursuer, tracer, zetetic

seeker (pleasure) – epicure, hedonist

seem–appear, look

seeming contradiction–paradox

seeming truth–verisimilitude

seemingly–quasi

seemingly true–paradox

seemliness–decorum

seemly–decent, decorous, fit, proper

seep–leak, ooze, percolate

seep through–ooze

seep through (as liquid) – leak

seep through pores–exude

seep through small openings –transude

seer – forecaster, Nostradamus, oracle, predictor, prophet, scryer, soothsayer

seeress–prophetess, sibyl

seesaw–crossruff, teeter, tilter

seethe–boil, stew, teem

segment – cantle, part, section, tmema

segment (corresponding part of, zool.)–isomere
segment (pineapple)–pip
segment of curve–arc
segment-shaped–toric
seize–annex, apprehend, arrest, bind, capture, catch, cly, collar, confiscate, fasten, grab, grasp, grip, nab, net, snatch, take, trap, wrest
seize (coll.)–nab
seize (slang)–cop
seize and hold–catch
seize and hold (without right)–usurp
seize forcibly (without right) –usurped
seize illegally–usurp
seize suddenly–nab, snatch
seize with mouth (those who)–biters
seized by violence–ravened, ravin
seizing–raptorial
seizure–arrest, manucapture
seladang–animal
select–choose, elect, exclusive, name, pick
select and adjust organ stops –registrate
select group–elite
selection–choice
selection (literary)–analect
selections rendered – program
selenium compound–selenid
self–ego
self (comb. form meaning) –auto
self (French)–soi
self (love and thought of)– egoism
self (Scot.)–sel
self-acting–automatic
self-confidence – aplomb, poise
self-contradictory statement –paradox
self-esteem – concept, pride, vanity
self-evidence (to assume) – postulate
self-evident–clear
self-evident truth – axiom, truism

self-examination–introspective
self-important (slang) – chesty
self-possessed–cooler
self-possession–aplomb, poise
self-reproach–remorse
self-righteous–Pharisaic
selfsameness–identity
self-satisfied–jaunty, smug
self-worship–autolatry
selfish grudging–envy
selfish individual–egoist
sell–auction, vend
sell (as securities)–negotiate
sell direct to consumer–retail
seller–dealer, peddler, tradesman, vender, vendor
seller of purple (Biblical)– Lydia
selling place–market, mart, shop, shoppe, store
semblable – alike, apparent, like, ostensible, resembling, seeming, similar, suitable
semblance – aspect, countenance, face, guise, pretext, resemblance, similarity
semeion (pert. to)–semic
semen–seed
semester–period, term
semidiameter – radius, radii (pl.)
semidiameter of circle–radius, radii (pl.)
Semiramis' husband–Ninus
Semite – Arab, Aramaean, Assyrian, Babylonian, Jew, Phoenician
Semitic deity (anc.)–Baal
Semitic dialect–Geez
Semitic god (any false god) –Baal
Semitic god (evil)–Moloch
Semitic language–Arabian, Egyptian, Iraqui, Palestinian, Syrian
Semitic language (group of) –Aramaic, Eramic
Semitic people (anc.)–Moabites
Semitic tribe (nomadic) – Shagia, Shaigia, Shaikiyeh
Semitic weight (anc.)–mina

senate – assembly, boule, council, legislature
send–convey, dispatch, forward, issue, propel, ship, transmit
send back – remand, remit, return
send by public carrier–ship
send by several different persons–relay
send forth–emit
send out–emit, shoot
send out rays–radiate
send to an address–deliver
send to obscurity–relegate
sending out–emissive
Senegal timber–cailcedra
Senegambian gazelle–korin
senile person–doter
senility–dotage
senior–dean, elder, superior
senior (Fr.) – aine, ainee (fem.)
sensation (deprive of)–benumb
sensation of cold–rhigosis
sensational–emotional, lurid, melodramatic
sense–feel, meaning, sane
sense (pert. to)–sensory
sense of beautiful–tasteful
sense of personal dignity – pride
sense of sight–vision
sense of taste–palate
sensed–felt
senseless–foolish, idiotic, inanity, insensate, irrational, stupid, unfeeling, unintelligent, unwise
sensible – aware, cognizant, privy, rational, reasonable, responsive, sane, sensitive, sound, susceptible
sensible (highly)–prudent
sensitive–acute, impressionable, receptive, responsive, sore, susceptible, tender, touchy
sensitive (delicately)–nice
sensitiveness (fine)–delicacy
sensory organ–ear
sent back – remanded, returned
sent by public carrier – shipped

sent on way–sped
sent out–exported
sent payment–remitted
sentence – adjudge, axiom, decide, decision, decree, determination, judgment, maxim, saw
sentence (part of)–phrase
sentence (pithy)–motto
sentence (subordinate part) –clause
sentence expressing a guiding principle–motto
sententious–concise, terse
sentient–conscious, feeling, sensible
sentient creature–animal
sentiment (exaggerated) – lyrics
sentimental – lackadaisical, romantic, schmaltz, schmalz
sentimental (over)–maudlin
sentimental (weakly) – mawkish
sentinel–guard, sentry, vedette, watchman
sentinel (mounted)–vedette
sepad – believe, suppose, think
separate–cleave, detach, discrete, dissociate, distinct, diverse, divide, isolate, part, segregate, sever, shed, single, sleave, sort, space, sunder, winnow
separate (as in distillation) –fractionate
separate (as threads)–sleave, sley
separate and divide (as thread filaments)–sleave
separate from–aloof
separate from others–isolate
separate into classes again– reassort
separate metal from ore – smelt
separated forcibly–rifted
separation (act of)–secessions
separation (prefix)–di, dis
separation (seclusion) – sequestration
separation of elements of compound word–tmesis

separation of parts of compound word–tmesis
sepia–color, cuttlebone, cuttlefish, dun, pigment
sepiment–defense, enclosure, hedge
sept–clan, seven, tribe
sepulcher–repository, sepulchre, tomb, vault
sepulchral–charnel, funeral, gloomy
sequence–series, succession
sequence (whole)–gamut
sequence of events (customary)–course
sequential – following, processive, succeeding
sequestered–isolated, lonely, private, retired, secluded, separated, solitary, unfrequented, withdrew
seraglio–harem
Serb–Slav
Serbian coin (silver)–dinar
Serbian revolutionary–Chetnik
sere–cere, claw, effete, sear, talon, withered, worn, yellow
serenade (burlesque nuptial) –charivari
serenade (mock)–charivari
serenade (opposite of)–aubade
serene–calm, collected, cool, peaceful, placid, quiet, tranquil
serf–esne, helot, peon, slave, thrall, vassal, villein
serf (anc. Spartan)–helot
series–sequence, set
series (closely connected) – catena
series (connected)–suite
series (in a)–gamut, seriatim
series of events–epos
series of heroic events–epos
series of meetings–session
series of races–regatta
series of reasons–rationale
series of rings–coil
series of rooms–suite
series of syllogisms–sorites
series of travels–odyssey
serious – capital, earnest,

grave, important, sedate, sober, solemn, staid
serious (comb. form)–serio
serious and composed–demure
serious and modest–demure
seriousness–gravity
sermon–discourse, harangue, homily, preach, talk
sermon (Biblical, poetic) – psalm
sermon's starting point–text
seron–crate, hamper, pannier
seroon–bale, package
serpent–adder, asp, racer, snake
serpent (fabulous, at whom looks were fatal)–basilisk
serpent (large)–aboma, boa, python
serpent (sky, Vedic myth.)– ahi
serpent monster–ellops
serpents (suborder of)–asinea
serpent's poison tooth–fang
serpentine–snaky
serrate–notched, toothed
serried – compact, crowded, dense
serum (like)–serous
servant–boots, butler, chela, cook, domestic, maid, menial, vassal
servant (body)–valet
servant (Cambridge college) –gyp
servant (female) – cook, maid, nurse
servant (house) – domestic, maid
servant (man)–garcon, gilly, mozo, syce, valet
servant of God–bishop
servant's dress–livery
servant's uniform (dress) – livery
serve – advance, aid, assist, bestead, cater, forward, further, help, succor, wait
serve a purpose–avail
serve as accomplice–abet
serve as an escort–squire
serve food–cater, wait
serve food to soldiers–mess

server–tray
server (priest's)–acolyte
Servian coin (silver)–dinar
Servian prince–Cral
service – aid, attendance, benefit, employ, favor, help, kindness, mass, ministration, ministry, rite, servitude
service (church)–mass, rite
service (church, afternoon or evening)–evensong
service (early Christian, at midnight or daybreak)–nocturn
service (ecclesiastical)–matin
service (morning)–matin
service (postal)–mail
service (public)–utility
service (to be of)–avail
service trees (the)–sorbs
servile – abject, menial, obsequious, slavish, subservient, sycophantic, truckling
servile (meanly)–parasitic
servile favorite–minion
servile retainer–minion
servilely imitative–apish
serving of sweetmeats–dessert
serving to assuage pain–anodyne
serving to complete–complementary
serving to discourage–deterrent
serving to increase–additive
serving to instruct–docent
sesame–benne, te, teel, til
sess–heap, pile
session (spiritualistic) – seance
set–adjust, coagulate, collection, confirm, coterie, define, designate, determined, group, laid, lay, obstinate, pose, posit, post, series, settle, solidify, stabilize, staid, stand, station, stiffen
set (exclusive)–elect, elite
set about–began
set afloat–launch
set apart–allocate, elect, ex-

empt, isolate, reserve, segregate, separate, sequester
set aside–annul, discard, dismiss, except, exclude, overrule, reject, void
set aside for special purpose –earmark
set at defiance–beard
set at intervals–spaced
set back–check, hinder, loss, recess, relapse
set bounds to–determine
set erect–cock
set fire to–ignite, inflame, irritate, kindle
set firmly–cement, embed, imbed, posit
set forth–adorn, commend, decorate, manifest, promote, promulgate, propone, publish
set forth (interpret)–explain, expose, expound, translate
set forth (publicly) – announce, enounce
set free–emancipate, liberate, release, unloose
set in a groove–dadoe
set in a row – align, aline, range, tier
set in columns–tabular
set in from margin–indent
set in opposition–pit
set in order–adjust, alined, arrange
set in position–plant
set in something solid–cement, embed, imbed
set into groove–dadoe
set of eight–ogdoad
set of jeweled ornaments – parure
set of laws–code, statutes
set of opinions–credo
set of organ pipes–stop
set of persons who meet familiarly–coterie
set of rules–code
set of sheets (paper)–quire
set on end–upended
set out–adorn, allot, assign, embellish, exhibit, extol, issue, plant, proclaim, promulgate, publish, start
set right–corrected
set tax–impose, impost

set thickly–stud
set time–dated
set-to–bout, go
set up–build, elevate, erect, establish, exalt, hoist, raise, stable
set with stiff bristles–strigose
Set's sister–Nephthys
Set's wife–Nephthys
Seth's father–Adam
Seth's son–Enos
setting–locale, scene
settle–agree, arrange, assign, clarify, clear, colonize, confirm, decide, designate, determine, locate, lodge, nest, order, pay, purify, quiet, regulate, root, seat, secure, solve, soothe, strengthen, tranquilize
settle for in advance–prepay
settle property on a person– entail
settle snugly–ensconce
settle upon–endow
settled–sedate
settled course of procedure– rut
settled in advance–predetermined
settled snugly (method) – policy
settlement – camp, colony, hamlet
settlement (Eskimo)–etah
settlement (property at marriage)–dos
settler–colonist, planter
settler (early)–pioneer
settler (early American) – Puritan
settler (metic)–immigrant
settler on government property before opening–sooner
settlings – adjustings, dregs, sediments
seven (group of) – heptad, septet
seventy-year-old person–septuagenarian
sever – cleave, cut, detach, disjoin, dissociate, disunite, divide, except, ex-

empt, part, rend, segregate, separate

several–distinct, divers, sundry

severe – austere, bad, biting, bitter, censorious, chaste, condign, cruel, hard, harsh, intense, keen, restrained, rigid, serious, simple, sober, solemn, sore, stern, strenuous, strict, stringent, tart, trying

severe (barbarously)–draconian

severe (become less)–relent

severe (more)–sterner

severely–sharply

severity–austerity, bitterness, cruelty, difficulty, exactness, hardness, harshness, rigor, rigorousness, solemnity, sternness, stiffness, strictness, violence

Seville cathedral tower–Giralda

sew–baste, needle, stitch

sew loosely–baste

sewer opening–manhole

sewing (act of)–suture

sewing machine inventor – Elias Howe

sewing machine part (for pleating)–plicator

sex–gender

sexton–sacrist, sacristan, underofficer

sextuplet (music) – sestole, sestolet

Seychelles Islands measure–cash

sha–oorial, urial

shab–rubbers, scab

shabbiness–seediness

shabby–contemptible, dowdy, scurvy, threadbare, worn

shabby (coll.)–seedy

shabrag–ragamuffin

shack–hibernate, husk, hut, plug, shanty, stubble, tramp, vagabond

shackle – band, bind, bond chain, fetter, hobble, iron, manacle, restrain, ring, tie

shackled–bound, curbed, fet-

tered, gyved, hampered, hindered, hobbled, ironed, manacled, restrained, tied, trammeled

shackler–ironer

shad–allice, alose, alosa (pl.)

shad (genus of)–alosa

shade–dull, eclipse, nuance, parasol, protect, shadow, shield, sprite, tinge, tint, tone, veil

shade (European)–aloses

shade (overhanging) – awning, canopy

shade of difference (in color)–nuance

shaded walk – alameda, arcade, mall

shades of feeling–nuances

shading–shadowing

shadow–attend, cloud, darken, dim, dog, follow, shade, tail

shadow (complete)–umbra

shadow (partial)–penumbra

shadow (to, slang)–dog, tail

shady – dark, shadowy, underhand

shaft – arrow, column, obelisk, rod, stalk, stem, tole, tongue, trunk

shaft (coal mine)–pit

shaft (column)–fust, scape

shaft (square, pyramidal top)–obelisk

shaft (wagon)–thill

shaft (wheel)–axle

shaft of column–shank, tige

shaft of feather–scape

shaft of wagon–thill

shaft part–orlo

shag–blackguard, chase, cormorant, follow, hair, mane, nap, pile, rascal, tobacco

shaggy – furry, hirsute, nappy, rough, unkempt, unpolished, villous

shagrag – ragged, rascally, unkempt

shake – agitate, dither, dodder, enfeeble, jar, jolt, quiver, rock, stir, sway, swing, tremble, vibrate, wag, weaken

shake (dial.)–tose

shake (slight)–jog

shake together in confusion –hustle

Shakespeare's wife–Anne

Shakespearean actor – Modjeska, Sothern, Ward

Shakespearean character – Iago, Iras, Oberon

Shakespearean forest – Arden

Shakespearean hero–Romeo

Shakespearean heroine – Juliet, Portia

Shakespearean king–Lear

Shakespearean play–Cymbeline, Macbeth

Shakespearean scene (in Hamlet)–Elsinore

Shakespearean villain–Iago

shaky – insecure, wabbly, wobbly

shale–metal

shale (indurated)–slate

shall–must, obliged

shallow–cursory, depthless, frivolous, shoal, superficial, trivial

shallow place–shoal

sham – chemisette, counterfeit, deceit, dummy, fake, false, feigned, fraud, hoax, humbug, imitation, imposture, mock, pretended, pretense, substitute

Shamash's consort–Ai, Aya

shame – abash, disgrace, humiliate, impropriety, mortify

shameful – degrading, dishonorable, disreputable, flagrant, ignominious, improper, infamous, mean, outrageous, scandalous

shamefully–disgracefully

shameless–arrant, audacious, brazen, immodest, impudent, unblushing

shammer–afer

shank – crus, crura (pl.), gamb, gambe

shape – bend, contour, fashion, figure, form, frame, incline, model, mold

shape roughly with broad chisel–boast

shaped–tooled
shaped (differently) – variform
shaped (halbred)–hastate
shaped (handled)–ansated
shaped (shield)–peltate, scutate
shaped like a comb–pectinate
shaped like a strap–lorate
shaped like a thong–lorate
shaped like an urn–urceolate
shaped with an ax–hewn
shapeless – amorphous, contorted, deformed, distorted, misshapen
shapely – gainly, neat, symmetrical
shapes (fantastic, in gardening)–topiary
share – enter, lot, part, partake, participate, portion, quota, ration
share (allotted)–allowance
share (fixed)–ration
share (proportional)–quota
share (slang)–cut
sharecropper–metayer
Shari River (Cameroon) people–Sara
shark–gata
shark (small)–dogfish, tope
sharp–acerb, acid, acrid, acrimonious, acute, alert, astute, bitter, brisk, caustic, crisp, cutting, discerning, edged, harsh, incisive, keen, nipping, penetrant, poignant, pointed, pungent, sagacious, sarcastic, steep, tart, trenchant
sharp (disagreeably)–waspish
sharp (make)–cacuminate
sharp (Scot.)–snelly
sharp and harsh–acerb
sharp answer–retort
sharp blow–slap
sharp cornered–angular
sharp edge (architecture) – arris
sharp flavor–tang
sharp pain–pang
sharp pointed–acute
sharp-sighted–astute

sharp sound–ping
sharp taste–tang
sharp-witted – intelligent, shrewd
sharpen – cacuminate, edge, enhance, grind, hone, intensify, nib, point, quicken, whet
sharpen a sickle–ted
sharpened–acuate
sharpener – edger, hone, strop
sharper – cheat, deceiver, keener, rogue, swindler, trickster
sharpness–poignancy
sharpshoot–snipe
sharpshooter (aerial)–bombardier
shatter – blast, break, crash, smash, splinter, split
shave–pare
shave (close)–ace
shave the head–tonsure
shaveling–monk, priest
shavetail–lieutenant, mule
shawl (camel's hair) – cashmere
shawl (kind of)–paisley
shawl (prayer)–orale
shawl (Scotch shepherd's gray plaid)–maud
shawl (Spanish)–serape
Shawnee Indian chief – Tecumseh, Tecumtha
She (of D'Urbervilles)–Tess
she cat–grimalkin
She launched ships–Helen
She who let all human ills escape from box–Pandora
She who stopped to pick up golden apples–Atalanta
sheaf–bundle, cluster, omer
sheaf (last of harvest, Scot.)–kern
shear–clip, cut
shear off–snip
sheatfish–som
sheath–case, glove, scabbard
sheath (book)–forel
sheath (cover with)–glove
sheath (flower protecting)–spathe
sheathe–cover, ocrea, plate, scabbard, sheath, spathe
sheathe (internally)–ceil

sheathes again–replates
sheave–pulley, wheel
shebang – concern, contrivance, establishment, outfit
shed – cote, cottage, diffuse, effuse, hut, lair, molt, radiate, scale, shelter, slough, spill
shed (French)–abri
shed freely–poured
shed light–glow
shedding (act of)–ecdysis
shedding of skin–ecdysis
sheen–luster
sheen (having)–lustrous
sheep (after first shearing)–shearhog
sheep (Asiatic, large, wild, bighorn)–argal, argali
sheep (breed of) – Cheviot, Corriedale, Cotswold, Dorset, Horn, Hampshire Down, Leicester, Lincoln, Merino, Oxford Down, Romney, Shropshire, Southdown, Suffolk
sheep (castrated male) – wether
sheep (female)–ewe
sheep (fine-wooled white)–Merino
sheep (genus of)–ovis
sheep (male) – ram, tup, wether
sheep (male, unshorn, eight to nine months old) – heder
sheep (Nahoor)–sha
sheep (Napaul)–Nahoor
sheep (North Africa, wild)–aoudad
sheep (past its first year)–teg
sheep (Sardinia, wild) – moufflon, mouflon
sheep (second year)–teg
sheep (two years old) – bident, gimmer, teg
sheep (unshorn, old) – tag, teg
sheep (wild)–aoudad, argal, argali, sha, urial
sheep (wild, India)–sha
sheep (yearling)–shearhog, tag, teg

sheep (yearling female)–sheder

sheep (young)–lamb

sheep brand (Eng.)–smit

sheep disease–coe, gid, rot

sheepfold–cot, cote

sheep-killing parrot–kea

sheep-like–ovine

sheep shelter–fold

sheepskin (tanned with bark)–basil

sheepskin leather–roan

sheep's coat–fleece

sheep's cry–baa, bleat

sheep's head (used for food) –jemmy

sheep's head broth–powsowdy

sheep's kidney extract–renes

sheep's sound–bleat

sheer – diaphanous, deviation, mere, perpendicular, pure, steep, swerve, thin, transparent, turn, undiluted, unmixed

sheet–rope, shroud

sheet (news)–daily, paper

Sheik's land–Arabia

shelf–ledge, mantel, sill

shelf (above altar)–retable

shelf (above fireplace)–mantel

shell – boat, bomb, capsule, carapace, conch, covering, crust, crusta, crustae (pl.), exterior, grenade, husk, pod, shuck

shell (animal, various)–carapace

shell (carved in relief) – cameo

shell (cone, richly colored)– admiral

shell (ear)–abalone

shell (hard)–lorica

shell (imperfect)–dud

shell (mollusk)–testa, testae (pl.)

shell (oyster)–shuck

shell (pastry-filled)–dariole

shell (top, used in making buttons)–troca

shell (tun fossil)–dolite

shell (unexploded)–dud

shell (zool.)–test

shell casing (metal)–gaine

shellfire (curtain of) – barrage

shellfish (small)–limpet

shell of a minute seaweed– frustule

shell seafood (large) – abalone

shellac–lac

shelter – asylum, burrow, cote, cover, coverture, defense, haven, house, lee, port, protect, protection, quarters, retreat, roof, sanctuary, screen, security, shield, tent

shelter (airplane and balloon)–hangar

shelter (animal)–cote

shelter (blimp)–hangar

shelter (bulletproof) – mantelet

shelter (fortified)–pillbox

shelter (French)–abri

shelter (prov. Eng.)–skug

shelter (rabbit)–hutch

shelter (sheep)–cote

shelter (temporary)–camp

shelter (wayfarer's)–hospice

sheltered closely–snug

sheltered side–leeward

sheltered side (on)–alee

shelves–ledges, mantels, pigeonholes, platforms, retires, tables

Shem (descendant of)–Semite

shend–destroy, harm, injure, mar, ruin, spoil

shepherd–feeder, pastor

shepherds (band of) – pastoureau, pastoureaux (pl.)

shepherd's pipe–reed

sherbet–ice

sheriff's aides–posses

sheriff's deputy–bailiff

sheriff's (or coroner's) deputy–elisor

sheriff's force–posse

sheriff's jurisdiction – bailiwick

sheriff's successor, if disqualified–elisor

sherry (fragrant variety) – oloroso

sherry wine–zeres

Shetland Island land (held

in fee simple without charter)–odal, udal, udalborn, udaler, udalman

Shetland Island supreme court president–foud

Shetland viol (two-stringed) –gue

shield–aegis, boss, ecu, egis, pavis, protector, shelter, target, umbo

shield (arch.)–targe

shield (boss)–umbo

shield (division of heraldry) –ente

shield (emblem)–impresa

shield (for protection) – aegis, egis

shield (linear, furrowed lichen)–lirelle

shield (medieval)–ecu, targe

shield (Middle Ages)–pavis

shield (part of) – boss, ente, umbo

shield (rim of)–orle

shield (round, carried by medieval foot soldier) – rondache

shield (small circular) – target

shield (small, medieval triangular)–ecu

shield base (her.)–pointe

shield bearer–escudero

shield border–bordure

shield part (protuberant) – umbo

shield-shaped – peltate, scutate

shift – artifice, change, device, eddy, move, mutation, ruse, shunt, stir, subterfuge, transposition, veer

shift for oneself–fend, rustle

shift of service–tour

shift suddenly (as a boat)– jibe

shifty–tricky

shim–washer

shin–cnemis

shin bone–tibia

shindy–carousal, frolic, lark, orgy, revel, romp, spree, wassail, wince

shine – beam, excel, glisten,

glister, gloss, radiate, ray, star

shine brightly (Scot.)–beek
shine out–ray
shine upon–irradiate
shingle (tool for splitting)–prower
shining – aglow, beaming, glary, glistening, glossy, glowing, irradiating, lucent, lustrous, nitid, refulgent, splendid
shining bright–lucid
Shinto deity temple – Jinja, Jinsha
Shinto gateway temple–torii
Shinto temple–sha
Shinto temple entrance–torii
shiny – bright, luminous, radiant, sleek, unclouded
ship – lade, send, steamer, vessel
ship (across middle)–beam
ship (Argonaut's)–Argo
ship (auxiliary)–tender
ship (deserted)–derelict
ship (former sailing) – caravel
ship (having upper deck cut away)–razee
ship (kind of)–xebec
ship (large merchant) – argosy
ship (Levantine)–saic
ship (medieval)–nef
ship (middle part)–waist
ship (mythical Greek)–argo
ship (pert. to)–bridge, brig, keel
ship (poetic)–keel
ship (richly laden)–argosy
ship (sailing)–bark, barkentine, barque, barquentine, brig, frigate, schooner, sloop
ship (small)–pinnace
ship (small, sailing)–cutter
ship (three-masted) – bark, barque
ship (three-oar bank) – trireme
ship (two-masted) – brig, schooner
ship (two-oar bank)–bireme
ship (unseaworthy)–hulk

ship boarding platform – gangplank
ship bow–prow
shipbuilding cross timber – rib
ship capacity–tonnage
ship channel–gat, strait
ship crane–davit
ship deck – main, poop, upper
ship deck (lowest)–orlop
ship deserter–rat
ship device used in mine area–paravane
ship form clock–nef
ship internal unit capacity–ton
ship knee–sternson
ship of desert–camel
ship of refuge–ark
ship on which Argonauts sailed–Argo
ship part–keel, rudder
ship prison–brig
ship record–log
ship side (opposite middle)–abeam
ship structure frame (unfinished)–carcass
ship table frame–fiddle
ship tender–pinnace
ship timber - bitt, keel, rib, spar
ship upward movement – scend
ship window–port
shipworm–borer, teredo
shipwright (launching slide marker)–wayman
ship yard-hoisting rope–tye
ships (company of)–armada, fleet
ship's boat–dingey, dinghy, dingy, dory, life, pinnace, tender
ship's body–hull
ship's burden–cargo
ship's cargo invoice – manifest
ship's carpenter–Chips
ship's compass housing–binnacle
ship's curved planking–sny
ship's employee–steward
ship's jail–brig

ship's lifting device–capstan. davit
ship's log screwlike part – rotator
ship's movement (lateral) – leeway
ship's officer–boatswain, bosun, mate, purser, steward
ship's prow (poetic)–prore
ship's rope–halyard, hawser, painter, ratline
ship's station–berth
ship's tiller–helm
ship's voyage record–log
shipment–cargo
shipping center–seaport
shire in Scotland–Ayr
shirk–avoid, duck, evade
shirk one's duty–slack
shirt (arch.)–sark
shirt (hair)–cilice
shirt (light, loose, var.) – kamis
shirtwaist–blouse
shiver–quake, quiver, shake, shudder, tremble, vibrate
shiver (fit of)–ague
shivering–aquiver, tremor
shoal–bank, reef
shoal (long narrow, extending from shore)–spit
shock – appal, brunt, collision, concussion, disgust, horrify, impact, jar, startle, terrify
shock (sudden)–jolt, shake
shock absorbers–snubbers
shocking–disgusting, ghastly, horrible, lurid, offensive
shocks to reality–sobers
shod–soled
shoe–boot
shoe (baby's)–bootee
shoe (dancing)–pump
shoe (flexible steel)–solleret
shoe (heavy) – brogan, brogue
shoe (kind of)–moyle
shoe (made of untanned leather)–rullion
shoe (mule, flat) – planch, planche
shoe (put new soles on) – retap

shoe (rider's steel)–solleret
shoe (soft soled)–sneaker
shoe (winged)–talaria (pl.)
shoe (wooden)–patten, sabot
shoe (wooden, thin soled)–
patten
shoe form–last, tree
shoe grip–cleat
shoelace–lacet, latchet
shoe latchet–tab
shoemaker (Latin)–sutor
shoemaker's awl (Scot.)–elsin
shoemaker's knife–butt
shoe part–cap, rand, vamp,
welt
shoeshine–bootblack
shoe sole (narrow part) –
shank
shoe stretcher–tree
Shogun title–tycoon
shone–eradiated, glowed
shoneen (Anglo-Irish)–snob,
toady
shook–trembled
shoot–plant, scion, vimen
shoot (detached)–scion
shoot (fleshy underground)
–tuber
shoot (flexible)–bine
shoot (grafting)–scion
shoot (new)–sprout
shoot (short, thickened, underground)–tuber
shoot (slender)–spear, stolon
shoot (small)–sprig
shoot (small tree)–spray
shoot (twining)–bine
shoot a bullet into–plug
shoot for grafting–scion
shoot forth rays of light –
eradiate, irradiate
shoot from ambush–snipe
shoot game–pot
shoot of plant–cion
shoot out–dart
shooting match (Fr.)–tir
shooting matches–skeets
shooting objective–target
shooting star–comet, meteor
shop (grog)–saloon
shop (large)–emporium
shore – bank, beach, coast,
prop, strand, support
shore (arch.)–rivage
shore bird–ree

shore recess – bay, bayou,
cove, inlet
short – abridged, brief, curt,
summary
short (comparatively) – curtate
short and pointed–terse
short and pudgy–rolypoly
short and stout – stocky,
thickset
short and stout (dial.) –
bunty
short and to the point–terse
short blunt end–stub
short stop–cessation, delay,
interval, pause, respite,
stop
shortage (financial)–deficit
shorten–abbreviate, abridge,
condense, curtail, reef
shorten by cutting–bob, lop
shortening – Crisco, lard,
Snowdrift, Spry
shortening of a syllable (for
metric purpose)–systole
shortest–least
shortsightedness–myopia
Shoshone Indian – Hopi,
Otoe, Utah, Ute
shot (billiard)–carom, masse
shot size–BB, BBB, DE, FF,
TT
shoulder (comb. form)–omo
shoulder (pert. to)–scapular
shoulder (prefix)–humero
shoulder (road)–berm
shoulder angle of bastion –
epaule
shoulder armor–epauliere
shoulder blade–scapula
shoulder of a road–berm
shoulder ornament–epaulet,
epaulette
shout – acclaim, call, cry,
hoop, hoot, root, yell
shout (loud, inarticulate) –
hoot
shout applause–cheer
shouting–clamor
shove–drive, elbow, propel,
push, shunt, thrust
shovel–spade
shovel (baker's)–peel
shovel (frit, sand, turned up
at edge)–strockle
shovel (long handle)–skeet

show – betoken, cinema,
demonstrate, display, di-
vulge, escort, evidence,
evince, exhibit, indicate,
lead, manifest, movie,
prove, reveal, revue
show (cheap street)–raree
show (deceptive)–gloss
show (empty)–farce
show (false)–tinsel
show (medieval)–pageant
show (musical)–revue
show (peep)–raree
show (pompous)–cavalcade,
display, exhibition, pag-
eant, pageantry, parade
show (ridiculous)–farce
show (street, cheap)–raree
show (superficial)–veneer
show appreciation–applaud,
clap
show clearly–evince
show deference–bow
show disapproval of – boo,
hiss
show displeasure–pout
show emotion–emote
show feeling–emote
show how–instruct, teach
show in clear fashion–evince
show irresolution–waver
show of mere learning (one
who makes)–pedant
show ostentatiously–flaunt
show plainly–evince
show response to treatment
–react
show to a seat–conduct, usher
show to be false–belie, disprove
show up–appear
shower–bath, rain
shower (sudden, heavy) –
deluge, sump
showing care–regardful
showing envy–invidious
showing former life–zootic
showing good judgment –
astute, sensible
showing narrow structural
bands or lines–striate
showing qualification–adap-
tive
showy – arty, flashy, garish,
gaudy, gorgeous, loud,

ostentatious, pompous, splendid, striking, sumptuous

showy (not)–lenten

shred–rag, sliver, snip

shrew–outcast, satan, scoundrel, termagant, villain

shrew (European)–erd

shrew (ill-tempered)–vixen

shrew (squirrel)–tana

shrewd–acute, artful, astute, canny, clever, crafty, cunning, discerning, foxy, knowing, penetrating, perspicacious, sagacious, sage, sapient, sharp, sly, smart, subtile, wily

shrewd (slang)–cagy

shrewdness–acumen

shriek – holler, outcry, scream, yell

shrill – highpitched, keen, penetrating, sharp, squeak

shrine–altar, box, case, chapel, chest, naos, patt, receptacle, reliquary, temple, tomb

shrine (Mecca)–caaba, kaaba

shrine (small)–reliquary

shrink – blench, contract, cringe, dwindle, flinch, quail, recoil, shrivel, wince

shrink (arch.)–rivel

shrink (in terror)–cringe

shrinking–sly

shrivel–parch, shrink, wither

shrivel with heat–parch

shroud–cerecloth, cerement, cloak, conceal, curtain, hide, screen, sheet, veil

Shrove Tuesday–Mardigras

shrub – barberry, buckeye, bush, lilac, oleaster, sumac

shrub (allied to poison ivy)–sumac

shrub (aromatic)–thyme

shrub (bean family)–ulex

shrub (botany)–frutex

shrub (bushy)–cade

shrub (evergreen) – box, heath, ilex, jasmine, juni-

per, laurel, mistletoe, salal, savin, titi

shrub (flowering) – azalea, laurel, lilac, oleaster, spiraea, spirea, syringa

shrub (flowering evergreen)–oleander

shrub (flowering fragrant)–mignonette

shrub (genus of) – azalea, itea, lantana, olea, rosa

shrub (green)–lilac

shrub (hardy)–heather

shrub (juniper-like)–retem

shrub (leaves containing pilocarpine)–jaborandi

shrub (maritime strong-scented)–batis

shrub (mint family, flowering)–rosemary

shrub (olive)–olea

shrub (order of cone-bearing)–gnetales

shrub (parasitic)–mistletoe

shrub (pink, flowered)–rhodora

shrub (poisonous) – sumac, sumach

shrub (prickly)–bramble

shrub (rosy flower)–myrtle

shrub (small evergreen) – moss

shrub (spiny)–gorse

shrub (spiny, bean family)–whin

shrub (synthetic rubber) – guayule

shrub (tea-like)–cocas

shrub (thick)–tod

shrub (thorny)–hawthorn

shrub (tropical)–henna, lantana, olacad

shrub (tropical, bright-flowered)–lantana

shrub (used in dyeing and tanning)–sumac, sumach

shrub (western)–salal

shrub (with large pith)–elder

shrub (yielding seeds used in perfume)–abelmosk

shrubs–sidas

shrunk gradually–dwindled

shrunken – atrophied, lank, shriveled

shudder (Chaucer way of saying)–agrise

shuffle – equivocate, juggle, mix, quibble, shift

shun–avoid, eschew, evade

shun (arch.)–evite

shut in–bottled, confine, embar, enclose, fenced, hem, hemmed, impound, invalid, surrounded

shut out–bar, exclude, lockout, occlude, preclude

shut up – close, conclude, confine, enclose, end, imprison, pent, terminate

shutter–blind, jalousie

shuttle (sewing machine) – looper

shy–aloof, bashful, coy, demure, diffident, modest, retiring, shamefaced, sheepish, shrinking, throw, timid, unassuming, unobtrusive, unostentatious

shy (affectedly)–coy, mim

shy (affectedly, Scot.)–mim

shy (coquettishly)–coy

shy in sudden alarm–boggle

Shylock's coin–ducat

shyness – bashfulness, coyness, diffidence, reserve, timidity

sialidae–alder, hellgrammite

Siam–Thai, Thailand

Siamese–Tai, Thai

Siamese capital – Bangkok, Bankok

Siamese capital of province–Muang

Siamese city–Bangkok, Puket

Siamese coin – at (pewter), att (pewter), baht (s.), fuang (s.), pynung, salung (s.), satang (br.), tical (s.)

Siamese coin (bean-shaped)–tical

Siamese demon–nat

Siamese dynasty–eng

Siamese land measure–rai

Siamese measure–anukabiet, chai meu, chang awn, kabiet, kam meu, kanahn, ken, keup, kwien, laang, ngan, nmu, rai, roeneng, sat, sen, sesti, sok, tanan, tang, wa, wah, yot, yote

Siamese measure (length) – wa

Siamese native–Tai

Siamese race–Tai

Siamese river–Menam

Siamese spirit–nat

Siamese tribesman–Tai

Siamese twins' names–Eng (right), Chang (left)

Siamese weight–baht, catty, chang, coyan, fuang, hap, haph, klam, klom, pai, picul, salung, sompay, tamlung, tical

Siberian antelope–saiga

Siberian Arctic gulf–Ob

Siberian blizzard (violent)– buran

Siberian carnivore–sable

Siberian city – Barnaul, Blagovestchensk, Chita, Irkutsk, Krasnoyarsk, Omsk, Tomsk, Vladivostok

Siberian fishers–giliaks

Siberian fur (gray squirrel)– calabar

Siberian gulf–Ob

Siberian hunters–giliaks

Siberian Mongolian people (obs.)–yakoots

Siberian Mongoloid–Tartar, Tatar

Siberian mountains–Altai

Siberian people (nomadic steppe)–kirgizes

Siberian plain – steppe, tundra

Siberian prison sleeping platform–nare

Siberian river–Amur, Lena, Maya, Ob, Olenek, Om, Onon

Siberian sheep-like antelope –saiga

sibilant sound–hiss, kiss

sibilate–hiss

sibyl–seeress

sicarian–assassin

siccaneous–dry, unwatered

siccity–aridity, dryness

sice–six

Sicily cape–Boeo, Faro, Passaro

Sicily city–Alcamo, Caltanissetta, Catania, Girgenti, Messina, Modica, Palermo, Ragusa, Trapani

Sicily city (anc.)–Aetna

Sicily harbor–Palermo

Sicily measure – caffiso, salma

Sicily mountain–Etna

Sicily name (anc.) – Trinacria

Sicily river – Belice, Platani, Salso, Simeto

Sicily town (anc.)–Bidis

Sicily volcano–Etna

sick (be)–ail

sick (mortally)–alamort

sick person – aegrotant, patient

sick unto death–alamort

sicken – impair, impoverish, surfeit, tire, weaken, weary

sickly–ailing, diseased, faint, feeble, infirm, unhealthy, weakly

side–flank, lateral

side (away from wind)–alee, lee

side (ditch)–escarp

side (hog, salted)–flitch

side (pert. to)–lateral

side (triangle)–leg

side by side–parallel

sideboard (Fr.)–dressoir

side-kick–assistant, pal, partner

sidelong – lateral, oblique, obliquely, slanting, sloping

sidelong glance–leer, skew

side of cavity–wall

side of head–temple

side of triangle–leg

sidepiece–rib

sideshow–attraction

sideslip–skid

side-step–duck, evade

side view–profile

sidewalk salesman – pitchman

sideways–askance

sidewise–lateral

sidereal – astral, starry, stellar

Sidi's wife (Arabian Nights) –Amine

sidle–edge

siege (former spelling)–sige

Siegfried's slayer–Hagen

Sierra Nevada fog (dense winter)–pogonip

siesta–nap, rest

sieve–filter, screen, sift, sifter, strain, strainer

sieve (coarse)–riddle

sieve (flour)–bolter

sieves (dial.)–tems

sift – bolt, filter, riddle, screen, sieve, winnow

sifter–sieve, strainer

sigh – bemoan, bewail, deplore, grieve, lament, mourn, sob, yearn

sighs (prov. Eng.)–sithes

sight – behold, descry, discern, display, espy, exhibition, gaze, scene, vision

sight (imaginary)–vision

sight (offensive to)–eyesore

sight along an object (to see if level)–bone

sighted (sharp)–astute

sightedness (short)–myopia

sigil–seal, signet

sign–emblem, engage, hire, insigne, insignia (pl.), intone, motion, notice, omen, portent, presage, signal, subscribe, symbol, token, trace, underwrite, vestige

sign (briefly)–initial

sign (diacritical)–tilde

sign (illuminated)–neon

sign (importunate)–omen

sign (pert. to)–semic

sign (prophetic)–omen

sign (spiritual)–sacrament

sign (Zodiac third)–Gemini

sign of an idea (visible)–emblem, symbol

sign of approaching cold – sniffle

sign of command–beck

sign of full house–S.R.O.

sign of infinitive–to

sign of Zodiac – Aquarius, Aries, Cancer, Capricornus, Gemini, Leo, Libra, Pisces, Sagittarius, Scorpio, Taurus, Virgo

signs (arbitrary, representing words)–logograms

signs of Zodiac (number of) –twelve

signal–alarm, communicate, conspicuous, cue, eminent, extraordinary, flag, memorable, notable, notify, prominent, remarkable, semaphore, striking, warning

signal (aviator's)–roger

signal (danger, arch.)–alarum

signal (marine)–S.O.S.

signal (railroad)–fusee, semaphore

signal (warning)–alarm, tocsin

signal blaze–flare

signal for exit (var.)–senet

signal of assent–aye

signal of dissent–nay

signal system–code

signal to act–cue

signal to speak–cue

signal which precedes taps– tattoo

signal with flags–wigwag

signature–mark, sign, stamp

signature of approval – visa, vise

signet – impression, mark, seal, stamp

signet (arch.)–sigil

significance – import, meaning, purport

significance (mystical)–anagoge

significance (with) – meaningly

significant – indicative, meaningful, ominous, portentous, sinister

signification–meaning, sense

signified – denoted, indicated, meant, purported

signify–betoken, declare, denote, imply, import, intimate, manifest, matter, mean, sign, signal, utter

signum–cross, sign, "X"

sike – brook, ditch, drain,

gully, ravine, rill, stream, trench

silage–fodder

silanga–bay, channel

Silas Marner's substitute for stolen gold–Eppie

sile – betray, cheat, conceal, cover, deceive, drip, drop, fall, filter, flow, fry, glide, pass, pour, sieve, sink, skim, spawn, strain, strainer, stream, subside

silence – confute, eliminate, gag, hush, muffle, mute, noiselessness, preclude, quiet, secrecy, silentness, still, stillness, suppress

silence (by force)–gag

silence (musical direction)– tacet

silence (sudden)–hush

silent–mum, mute, reserved, reticent, speechless, still, tacit, taciturn, uncommunicative

silent (habitually)–taciturn

silent (inclined to keep)–reticent

silent (music)–tacet

silent but understood–tacit

silica–silex

silicate (hydrous, brownish)–cerite

silicate (mineral)–mica

silicate (transparent)–mica

silicate (white)–wellsite

silicate (white zinc) – calamine

silicate of calcium, aluminum and iron–epidote

silicon derivative–monox

silk (artificial)–rayon

silk (black)–crape

silk (castor)–eri, eria

silk (fine untwisted)–floss

silk (gold, interwoven) – samite

silk (heavy)–crin

silk (kind of) – China, eri, eria, taffeta, taffety, tulle

silk (not twisted)–sleave

silk (pieces of waste)–noil

silk (rich)–mantua

silk (smooth, glossy)–taffeta, taffety

silk (thin, glossy)–alamode

silk (thin, woven)–sarsenet

silk (twill woven)–almas

silk (twilled)–tobine

silk (unspun)–sleave

silk (untwisted)–sleave

silk (upholstery, former) – tabaret

silk (waste)–noil

silk fabric–surah

silk fabric (corded)–ottoman

silk fabric (heavy, interwoven with gold)–samite

silk fabric (Middle Ages, light, thin)–sendal

silk fiber (coarse) – tussah, tusseh

silk filling–tram, trame

silk material–surah

silk net (fine)–tulle

silk thread (formed from two or more in velvet, (Fr.)–tram, trame

silk treatment (to make rustle)–scroot

silk tube–cop

silk twister–thrower

silken – ingratiating, seric, silklike, silky, sleek, smooth, suave

silkworm – eri, eria, erias (pl.), sina

silkworm (castor oil plant feeder)–eri

silkworm (Oriental)–tussah, tusseh, tusser, tussore

silkworm cocoon–clew

silky – delicate, glossy, ingratiating, quiet, sericeous, smooth

silly – anile, asinine, brainless, daft, dense, fond, foolish, inane, indiscreet, mad, shallow, simple

silly (fantastically)–apish

silly (Scot.)–dottle

silly (stupidly)–fatuous

silver (containing)–lunar

silver (in ingots)–sycee

silver alloy–billow

silver and gold braid–orris

silver and gold lace–orris

silver coin (old)–tester

silver lactate–actol

silver oak–flannelbush

silver plover (Scot.)–knot

silver symbol–Ag

silver thaw–glaze, rime
silver thistle–acanthus
silver-white metal–cobalt
silverware – dishes, ornaments, tableware, vases
silverware ornament – gadroon, godroon
silverweed–tansy
silvery–argent
silvery white (as plumage)–frosted
simian – ape, apelike, monkey
similar–akin, alike, analogic, analogous, homogeneous, like, such, uniform
similarity–analogy, approximation, homogeneity, likeness, resemblance
simper–smirk
simple–artless, dorian, easy, elementary, ingenuous, innocent, mere, naive, oafish, unsophisticated
simple minute organism – ameba, amoeba, monad
simple song–ballad
simple, stylish and well-dressed–tailored
simple sugar–ketose
simpleton–daw, dolt, dunce, fool, gander, goose, idiot, ninny, oaf, Simon, zany, zannies (pl.)
simpleton (slang) – boob, simp
simpleton (South Africa) – ikona
simpletons–geese
simplicity–homeliness, humbleness, ingenuousness, innocence, modesty, naivete, purity, simpleness, unaffectedness
simplify – clarify, elucidate, expound, interpret
simply–alone, barely, merely, solely
simulated – acted, aped, assumed, feigned, pretended, shammed
simurgh (simurg)–roc
sin – crime, deviation, err, evil, misdemeanor, offense, transgression, wickedness, wrong

sin or offense–peccancy
Sinai mountain–Horeb
since–ago, as, ergo, gone, hence, therefore, whereas
since (Scot.)–syne
sincere–earnest, frank, unaffected, unfeigned, unvarnished, upright
Sinclair Lewis character – Babbitt
sind–drench, quench, rinse
Sindbad's bird–roc
sindico – assignee, receiver, trustee
sinew – muscle, nerve, tendon, thew
sinewy–fibrose, wiry
sinful – bad, evil, iniquitous, unrighteous, vicious, wicked
sing–carol, celebrate, chant, croon, hum, hymn, intone, lilt, warble
sing above pitch–sharps
sing in gay manner–lilt
sing in jovial manner–trollol
sing in Swiss manner–yodel
sing off key–flat
sing or whistle–tweedle
sing shrilly–pipe
sing slower – ritard, ritardando
sing softly–croon
sing with closed lips–hum
sing with trills–roulade
singe–scorch, sear
singer – cantor, chanteuse, crooner, minstrel
singer (falsetto tenor)–tenorino
singer (male choir) – songman
singer (opera)–diva
Singhalese tree (poon) – domba
singing (suitable for)–melic
singing birds (pert. to)–oscine
singing organization–choir, chorus
single – alone, lone, sole, unal, unique, unmarried
single (comb. form)–uni
single thing–unit
single unvaried tones–monotones

singleness–unity
singly–once
singular–eccentric, extraordinary, fantastic, odd, peculiar, rare, remarkable, strange, unexampled, unprecedented
singularity–uniqueness, odd, queer
sinister–ominous, portentous
sink–cave, decline, decrease, depress, descend, drain, droop, drop, ebb, fall, lower, sag, settle
sink down–bog
sink under prospect of danger–quail
sinuous–circuitous, wavy
Siouan Indian–Kaw, Omaha, Oto, Otoe, Tutelo
sip–lap, sup
siren–charmer, circe, lurer
siren (Rhine)–Lorelei
siren (river)–Lorelei
sisal hemp–sizal
sissy–mollycoddle
sister of charity–nun
sisterhood–sorority
sisterly–sororal
sit–isle, press, roost, squat, weigh
sit indolently–loll
site – locale, locate, place, scene, seat, venue
site (anc.)–ruin
site of crime (law)–venue
sitting–seance, seat, session
sitting (as statues)–sedent
sitting (court)–session
sitting (portrait)–seance
Sitting Bull's O.K.–ugh
situated – case, lie, located, plight, seat, station
situated (be)–lie
situated at back–postern
situated at base–basal
situated at bottom–basal
situated between folds–interplical
situated on right hand–dexter
situated toward the back – astern, posterior
situation – place, position, post, site, state

situation (approximate) – whereabouts

situation (calling for immediate action)–emergency

situation (difficult) – dilemma, predicament, quandary, scrape

situation (favorable) – vantage

situation (involving choice) –dilemma

situation (Latin)–situs

situation (perplexing)–strait

situation (unpleasant)–predicament

situation in which one is hopelessly doomed – rattrap

situations with three difficult choices–trilemmas

Siva's consort–Devi, Uma

Siva's wife–Sati

six (pert. to)–senary

sixfoldly–sextuply

six-line stanza–sestet

sixty sixties (Babylonian numeral)–saros

size – adjust, arrange, area, bulk, classify, grade, magnitude

size (hosiery, between standard and outsize)–pope

size (paper)–cap, pott

sizzle–siss

skate–ray

skate blade–runner

skate without taking feet off ice–scull

skating arena–rink

skean–dagger, dirk

skeeg–flog, lash, slap

skeel–bucket, pail, tub

skeesicks–rascal, skinflint

skein–hank

skein (120 yards)–rap

skelder – cheat, panhandle, vagrant

skeleton (internal marine animal)–sponge

skeleton (part of)–ilium

skeleton (polyp)–coral

skeleton (zoophyte)–coral

skelp–beat, kick, slap, strike

skeptic (sceptic) – doubter, infidel, unbeliever

sketch–apercu, delineation, design, draft, draw, limn, map, outline, plan, trace

sketch (humorous)–skit

sketch (offhand)–jot

sketch (preliminary)–draft

skewer–pin, rod, truss

ski race (obstacle)–slalom

skid – clog, shoe, sideslip, slide, slip, trig

skiff–boat, canoe, rowboat, skiff, skift

skiing term–slalom

skill–ability, address, adeptness, adroitness, aptness, art, cleverness, deftness, dexterity, facility, finesse, knack, mastery, proficiency, readiness

skill (delicate)–finesse

skill in language–rhetoric

skilled in government science–statesman

skillful – adept, adroit, apt, clever, deft, dexterous, handy, proficient, tactical

skim over–skirr

skin–bark, cuticle, fell, flay, hide, peel, pelt, rind

skin (beaver)–plew

skin (burning sensation of) –uredo

skin (comb. form) – derm, derma

skin (covering head)–scalp

skin (deep layer)–cutis

skin (folds of, under animal's neck)–dewlaps

skin (fruit)–epicard

skin (hardened)–callous, callus

skin (inner part of animal, of which leather is made) –dermas

skin (layer of)–derm, derma

skin (on gobbler's throat)–tar

skin (pert. to) – cuticular, dermal, epidermal

skin (resembling)–dermoid

skin (squirrel, used in ancient kingly costumes) – vair

skin (the)–cutis

skin (thin)–pellicle, striffen

skin (to dress)–taw

skin (true)–derm, derma

skin (vascular)–derm

skin ailment (eruption) – acne

skin decoration–tattoo

skin disease–acne, eczema, hives, psora, tetter

skin disease (animal) – mange

skin disease (fungus)–tinea

skin drying frame–herse

skin protuberance – mole, wart

skin removing tool–parer

skinflint–miser, niggard

skink–adda, lizard

skinned (dark)–swarthy

skinned (thick)–pachyderm

skinny–emaciated, lean, thin

skip – bound, caper, elide, leap, omit

skip over–elide

skip over water–dap

skipper of East Indian boat–serang

skirl–pipe

skirmish–brush, melee

skirt (medieval, armor) – tace, tasse

skirt (short)–kilt

skirt (steel, reaching to knees)–lamboys

skittles–ninepins

skoal–toast

skulk–dodge, hedge, lurk

skull–cranium, crania (pl.)

skull (back part)–occiput

skull (obs.)–crany

skull (of the)–cranial

skull cap–calotte

skull cap (felt)–pileus

skull part–inion

skull protuberance–inia

skulls (part of)–inia

skunk–polecat

skunk-like animal–civet

sky–firmament, heavens

sky (god of)–Anu

sky (the)–welkin

sky (unclouded)–azure

sky blue–celeste

skylarks (genus of)–alauda

skylight (Fr.)–abatjour

sky serpent (Vedic myth.)·· ahi

slab (grave) – stela, stelae (pl.), stele, steles (pl.)

slab (marble, decorative)–dalle

slab (marble paving)–dalle

slab (sculptured) – stela, stelae (pl.), stele, steles (pl.)

slab (sculptured in doric frieze)–metope

slab (upright)–stela, stelae (pl.), stele, steles (pl.)

slab-like–stelene

slab of marble (Fr.)–dalle

slack–abated, careless, dilatory, diminished, inactive, lax, loose, relaxed, slow, tardy

slacken–relax

slackening bar in a loom–easer

slackening of relations between nations (Fr.)–detente

slag – dross, scoria, scoriae (pl.)

slaggy–cindery

slain – assassinated, dead, killed

slain in battle–fallen

slam–bang, vole

slander–asperse, belie, defame, derogate, libel, malign

slander (printed)–libel

slanders–defames, scandals, traduces

slang–argot, cant

slant – bevel, cant, hypotenuse, occasion, opportunity, skew, slope

slanting–beveled, oblique

slap–blow, buffet, clap, cuff, rebuff, skelp, slight, snub, strike

slashed – cut, lashed, scourged, slittered

slate (breaking into slabs for splitting)–sculp

slate (suitable to write on) –grapholite

slate measuring tool–scantle

slate roof–rag

slate roof tool–zax

slater–hellier

slattern – careless, idler,

sloppy, slovenly, slut, trifler, trollop

slaughter–butcher, butchery, carnage, kill, killing, massacre, murder, slay

slaughter (great)–hecatomb

slaughterhouse–abattoir

Slav–Croat

Slav (Central Europe) – Czech

slave–bondman, bondslave, boor, captive, chattel, chela, drudge, esne, helot, peon, serf, thrall, vassal

slave (born, hist.)–neif

slave (fugitive)–marooner

slave (harem, female)–odalisk

slave (land)–peon, serf

slave (The Tempest) – Caliban

slave attendant (warrior) – thane, thegn

Slave Coast negro–Ewe

slaves (advocate of freeing) –emancipationist

slavery – bond, captivity, drudge, enslavement, enthrallment, service, servitude, vassalage

slavey–drudge, maid, servant

Slavic race (one of)–Croat, Sorb

Slavic tribe member–Serb

slay – butcher, kill, knock, murder, slaughter, smite, strike

sled–pung

sled (box)–pung

sled (logger's)–tode

sled (long, flatbottomed, light)–toboggan

sled (lumberman's)–travois

sledge (kind of)–drag

sleek (to make)–preened

sleep – doze, drowse, nap, slumber

sleep (coll.)–snooze

sleep (deep)–lethargic, sopor

sleep (English slang)–doss

sleep (lethargic)–sopor

sleep (light)–doze, drowse

sleep (profound)–sopor

sleep inducer – opiate, sedative

sleeper–drone, Pullman, reposer, rester, slumberer, tie

sleepiness–drowsiness, somnolence

sleeping–dormant, dormient, inactive, latent, quiescent

sleeping place – bed, berth, bunk, couch, pallet

sleeping place (English slang)–doss

sleeping quarters–dormitory

sleeve (leg of mutton)–gigot

sleeveless garment–aba

sleigh (box)–pung

sleigh (one-horse)–cutter

sleight-of-hand performer – mage, magician, prestidigitator

slender–gaunt, gracile, lank, lean, leger, lissom, slim, svelte, thin

slender (graceful woman)–sylph

slender (obs.)–leger

slender and long–reedy

slender and thin–lanky

slender pinnacle – epi, epis (pl.)

slender plug–spile, spill

slenderness–tenuity

sleuth hound (extinct)–talbot

slice – cut, shiver, sliver, splinter

slice (thick)–rasher, shave, slab, sliver

slice (with motions)–saw

slice into dried strips–jerk

slick up–preen

slid–skidded, slipped

slide–avalanche, glide, scoot, skid, slip

slide (dial.)–slither

slide sideways–skid

slight – contempt, cut, delicate, disdain, disregard, flimsy, fragile, ignore, indignity, leger, minor, neglect, nominal, scorn, shallow, small, snub, unsubstantial

slight (extremely) – imperceptible

slight convexity of a part–camber

slight intentionally–snub
slight sound–peep
slighter–remoter
slightest–barest
slighting remark–slur
slightly sour–acescent
slightly tapering–terete
slim–lean, slender, svelte
slime–mud, ooze
slip–lapse, pew, skid, slide
slip (to, rare)–illapse
slip away (as time)–elapse
slip away (dial.)–slither
slip by–elapse
slipe–blow, innuendo, pare, peel, sled, sleigh, slice, split, strip
slipped (dial.)–rused
slipper (blanket)–neap
slipper (kind of) – moyle, mule, sandal
slipper (open work)–sandal
slipper (quarterless)–mule
slippery–eely
slit–kerf, slash
sliver–splinter
sloe–haw
slogan–cry, motto, phrase
slope–bevel, declivity, dip, lie, ramp, scarp, slant, talus
slope (downward)–declivity
slope (gentle)–glacis
slope (steep)–bank
slope for exercising horse's haunches–calade
sloping earth bank–terrace
slot in shaft–spline
sloth–ai, ais, unau
sloth (three-toed)–ai
sloth (two-toed)–unau
sloth and surliness–acedia
slothful–inactive, indolent, lazy, sluggish
slough off–molt
slovenly–careless, disorderly, messy, slattern, sloppy, untidy
slow–dilatory, hinder, inactive, inert, lingering, poky, retard, slacken
slow (moderately, music)–andante
slow (music)–lento
slow (very, music)–molto
slow in action–deliberate

slow up–decline, lag, retard
slow witted–dull, stupid
slowness (rare)–lentor
slowpokes–dawdlers, snails
slug–blow, drink, drone, hit, sluggard, snail
slug (a)–limax
slug (sea)–trepang
slugs (genus of)–arion
slugger–hitter, mauler
sluggish – dronish, drowsy, inactive, indolent, inert, logy, slow, supine, torpid
sluggish (slang)–dopey
sluggishness–languor, stagnancy, torpidity, torpor
sluice–race
slumber – doze, drowse, repose, sleep
slump–depression, drop, fall
slur–aspersion, calumniate, calumny, disgrace, disparage, insult, reproach, stigma, traduce
slur over–elide
slush–mire
slushy–miry
slut–bitch, harlot, jade, slattern
sly – crafty, cunning, foxy, snaky, sneaky, subtle, underhand
sly (former spelling) – sle, slee, slye
sly (playfully)–arch
sly one (a)–puss
sly trick–ruse
slyly spiteful–catty
slyness–craft
smack–boat, cutter, hit, savor, sloop, taste, vessel
smack (coll.)–buss
smaik–scoundrel, rascal
small – diminutive, little, miniature, minute, thumbnail, tiny, wee
small (comb. form)–lepto
small (delicately)–mignon
small (French)–petite
small (law)–petit
small (neat, active)–dapper
small (pretty, attractive, coll.)–cute
small (Scot.)–sma, wee

small (very)–minute, picayune, tiny, wee
small amount – modicum, morsel
small area – areola, areloae (pl.)
small bit of food–morsel
small bottle–phial, vial
small bunch–wisp
small case (handbag)–etui
small chunk–dab, pat, wad
small distance–step
small field–croft
small fish–ide, ides
small insect–midge
small island–ait, isle
small lake–mere, pond
small opening–orifice, pore
small part–detail, iota, snippet
small particle–atom, molecule, mote
small piece – chip, driblet, mot, speck
small piece (Fr.)–morceau
small piece (part of)–snippet
small piece of something–tate
small quantity–drop, handful
small spar–sprit
small spark–sparklet
small Sumatra deer–napu
small surrounding area – areola, areolae (pl.)
small talk–babble, chitchat, prattle
small task–chore
small tower–minaret, turret
small unfilled cavity of ore deposit–vug
small wild ox–anoa
smaller (comb. form)–mio
smallest–least
smallest part–minim, whit
smallness of number or quantity–paucity
smallpox–variola
smart – acute, clever, competent, natty, nifty, pungent, shrewd, spruce, sting, trig, wise
smart in appearance–natty, posh
smarten–spruce
smash–break, crush, shatter

smear – bedaub, dab, daub, defile, plaster, pollute, rub, smirch, smudge

smear with mud–slime

smear with white of eggs–glair

smell – aroma, fragrance, odor, perfume, reek, scent, sniff

smell (offensive)–olid

smelling (ill)–noisome

smelling salts–hartshorn

smelt (young)–prim

smelting by-product–slag

smile–grin

smile (affected)–smirk

smile in silly manner–simper

smiling–riant

smiling broadly–agrin

Smiling Jack–sergeant

smirch – begrime, blacken, blemish, blot, blotch, discolor, smear, smutch, stain, sully, taint, tarnish

smirk–leer, simper, smicker

smit – smirch, smut, spot, stain, tarnish

smithy – blacksmith, forge, smithery

smock–chemise, philander, shift, woman

smock (light, loose, var.)–kamis

smoke–cure, reek

smoke (a) – cheroot, cigar, cigaret, cigarette, cubeb, pipe, segar

smoke (Scot.)–smook

smoke (wisp of)–floc

smoke flue–stack

smokeless powder–poudre

smokestack–funnel

smolder (smoulder)–choke, smoke, smother, smudge, suffocate

smooth – clear, comb, ease, even, glossy, iron, lene, level, mangle, pave, plane, press, sleek

smooth (coll.)–slick

smooth (phonetics)–lene

smooth and glossy–sleek

smooth and soft–furry, silky, soapy

smooth and soothing–bland

smooth and sweetly–mellifluently

smooth and white–alabastrine

smooth feathers–preen

smooth, hard, transparent – glassy

smooth oneself–preen

smooth phonetically–lene

smooth-spoken–glib

smooth-tongued–glib

smoothing iron–goose, sad-iron

smoothly–sweetly

smot–brand, mark, stain

smother – choke, overlie, stifle, suffocate

smudge – begrime, blot, smear, smut, smutch, soil, stain

smudge (sooty)–smut

smuggler–runner

smur–drizzle, mist, smurr

Smyrna figs–elemes

snail–gastropod, slug

snails (genus of)–mitra

snails (genus of large)–triton

snake–adder, asp, cobra, ess, racer, rattler, reptile, viper

snake (black)–racer, lora

snake (hooded)–cobra

snake (heraldic)–bisse

snake (large)–aboma, boa, bom, boma

snake (large, var.)–bom

snake (spitting)–ringhals

snake (tree)–lora

snake (U.S. poisonous)–copperhead, coral, cottonmouth, moccasin, rattler, rattlesnake

snake (venomous) – elapid, elapidae (pl.), elapinae (pl.), krait, mamba

snake dance exponents–Taus

snake expert–herpetologist

snake killer–mongoos, mongoose, mongooses (pl.)

snake-like–colubrine

snakes (genus of)–ophidia

snap–break, crackle

snap with fingers–fillip

snapper (black fin)–sesis

snappish–edgy

snare–bag, benet, entoil, gin, mesh, net, trap, trapan, trepan

snare (hidden)–pitfall

snarl–complication, confuse, gnar, gnarl, gnarr, growl, tangle

snarl (as a dog)–arr

snarl (dial.)–yirr

snatch – catch, grab, gripe, pluck, seize, wrest

sneak–lurk, slink

sneak (prying)–snoop

sneaking – contemptible, cowardly, craven, dastardly, furtive, hidden, mean, niggardly, paltry, poor, secret, sly, stealthy, surreptitious, underhand

sneer–flout, gibe, jeer, scoff

snell – active, acute, biting, eager, keen, piercing, pungent, quick, swift

snicker–titter

sniff–nose

snifter – dram, excellent, good, sniff, snivel, snort

snirl–gnarl, snare, tangle, wrinkle

snirt–sneer, snicker, snort

snitch–betray, inform, pilfer, pinch, steal

snod–cunning, neat, plausible, smooth, snug, trim, trimmed

snood–fillet, snell

snoop–nose

snooze–doze, drowse, nap, snoozle

snoozle–cuddle, doze, nuzzle, sleep, snooze, snuggle

snoring–stertor, stertorous

snotty–contemptible, dirty, nasty, offensive, offish, snooty, supercilious

snow (glacial)–neve

snow (granular)–neve

snow (half melted)–slush

snow (mountain)–neve

snow field (glacial)–neve

snow mass (sliding) – avalanche

snow ridges (wavelike, formed by wind) – sastrugi, zastrugi

snow runner–ski, skee (var.)

snowshoe–pac, skee, ski

snow slope sliding descent–glissade

snowy–nival

snubbed–ignored, neglected, quelled, repressed, slighted

snuff (darker, ranker)–rappee

snuff (kind of) – Copenhagen, Maccaboy

snuff (West Indies)–Maccaboy

snuff box–tabatiere

snuff box (Scot.)–mull

snug – close, comfortable, compact, cozy, neat, trim

snuggle–cuddle, nestle

snugly (var.)–cosily

so – ergo, hence, therefore, thus

so (Latin)–sic

so (Scot.)–sae, sic

so be it–amen

so far–yet

so may it be–amen

soak–dip, macerate, ret, saturate, sog, sop, souse, steep

soak (thoroughly)–saturate

soak (to)–buck

soak flax–ret

soak in liquid–seethe

soak through–ooze

soap–lather

soap frame bar–sess

soap frame part–sess

soapmaker's frame–sess

soapmaking substance–lye

soap plant–amole

soapstone–steatities, talc

soapstone (full of)–talcose

soapstoner–talcer

soapsuds froth–lather

soapweed–yucca

soar–aspire, float, fly, plane, rise

soaring in spirit–essorant

sob–weep, whimper

sober–abstemious, abstinent, calm, chasten, cool, collected, earnest, moderate, quiet, regular, sedate, serious, solemn, somber, staid, steady, subdue, temper, unimpassioned

sobriety–abstinence, moderation, restraint, soberness, temperance

sobriquet – appellation, byname, epithet, nickname

sobriquet (honorary)–title

sociable–accessible, affable, communicative, companionable, familiar, friendly, gregarious, informal

social career (beginning of)–debut

social class–caste, estate, sept

social division–caste, tribe

social function – reception, tea

social gathering–bee, party, reunion, tea

social gathering for men – smoker, stag

social graces (faculties acquired)–accomplishments

social group–coterie, sept

social group of people (pert. to)–tribal

social groups of common descent–clans

social insect–bee

social outcast–leper, pariah

social person–host, hostess, mixer

social set–coterie

social standing–estate

social system–regime

social unit–clan, sept

social worker (expert)–clinician

socialist – anarchist, bolshevist, collectivist, communist, nationalist, nihilist

socialist (extreme)–Red

society–alliance, association, companionship, company, confederation, partnership, union

society (Chinese)–Tong

society (high)–elite

society (secret)–lodge

society bud (coll.)–deb

Society Island tree–aitoa

society member (for promoting literature)–academist

sock (short)–anklet

sockdolager (coll.)–oner

socket (eye)–orbit

socket (hinge)–pan

Socrates' wife – Xanthippe, Xantippe

sod–glebe, sward, turf

sod (piece of)–divot

soda ash (pert. to)–alkaline

sodium–natrium

sodium (symbol for)–Na

sodium carbonate – borax, salsoda, soda, trona

sodium carbonate (hydrous)–natron

sodium chloride – sal, salt, tar

sodium chloride (lump of)–saltcat

sodium chloride (symbol for)–NaCl

sodium compound–soda

sodium tetraborate–borax

sofa – chesterfield, couch, davenport, divan, lounge, settee

sofa (small)–settee

soft–bland, clement, compassionate, downy, dreamy, ductile, flexible, gently, lightly, limp, mushy, peacefully, placid, quietly, silken, squashy, sympathetic, temperate, tender, tractable, tranquil

soft (music)–dulce, piano

soft (Scot.)–saft

soft (smooth, glossy)–silken

soft and pliable–waxen

soft and smooth–furry, silky, soapy

soft and sweet–dolce, dulcet

soft and tender–mellow

soft and wet–mushy, squashy

soft, dry and friable–mealy

soft food–pap

soft in texture–supple

soft mass–pulp

soft palate–cion, uvula, vela (pl.)

soften – allay, appease, assuage, enervate, enfeeble, melt, mitigate, modulate, mollify, pacify, relax, relent, soothe, tranquilize, weaken

soften by kneading–malax

soften by soaking–macerate

soften by steeping–macerate

soften in temper–relent

softening-emulsive
softens - lenitive, mitigates, relents, tempers
softest-gentlest
softhearted-tender
softheartedness-pity
softly-low, sotto
soggy-soaked, sodden, watery
soil - bedaub, begrime, bemire, besmear, bespatter, contaminate, daub, dirt, dirty, earth, glebe, land, pollute, spot, stain, sully, tarnish
soil (character of)-lair
soil (goddess of fruitful) - Demeter
soil (kind of)-clay
soil (organic portion) - humus
soil (poetic)-glebe
soil or sod (poetic)-glebe
soiled-dirty
soils-moils
sojourn - abidance, abide, bide, reside
sojourn (rare)-abode
solace (to)-allay, alleviate, assuage, comfort, console, soothe
solacing-dulcet
solan-gannet
solar disk-aten, aton
solar system member-planet
solar system representation-orrery
solar system working models -orreries
solar year (excess of)-epact
soldering flux-resin, rosin
soldering piece-lug
soldier - poilu, private, trooper, warrior, Zouave
soldier (carrying pointed weapon)-lancer
soldier (cavalryman) - dragoon, lancer, trooper
soldier (cavalry, furnishing own horse)-silladar
soldier (Celtic foot) - kern, kerne
soldier (common)-private
soldier (ex)-vet, veteran
soldier (experienced) - trooper, vet, veteran

soldier (French)-poilu
soldier (French digging) - sapper
soldier (girl)-WAC
soldier (light cavalry)-lancer
soldier (married, army slang)-shacktman
soldier (old, coll.)-vet, veteran
soldier (permanent army)-regular
soldier (slang)-galoot
soldier (very young, army slang)-chicken
soldier employed in digging mines-sapper
soldiers-men
soldiers (armored)-panzer
soldiers (body of)-brigade, company, platoon, troop
soldiers (captured)-losses
soldiers (killed)-losses
soldiers (wounded)-losses
soldier's drinking flask-canteen
soldier's overcoat-capote
soldier's quarters-barracks, billets
soldier's vacation-furlough, leave
sole-alone, desolate, fish, isolated, lonely, only, single, solitary, unmarried
sole (plow)-slade
solecism-barbarism, impropriety
solemn - ceremonial, devotional, devout, earnest, formal, grave, reverential, ritual, sad, serious, sober
sol-fa syllables-fi
solicit - ask, beg, beseech, campaign, canvass, court, crave, entreat, implore, importune, invite, request, supplicate
solicit (coll.)-tout
solicit (slang)-panhandle
solicit individually-canvass
solicitor at law (abbr.)-SL
solicitor of patronage (noisy)-barker
solicitor's chambers-inns
solicitude - anxiety, apprehension, care, carefulness, coda, concern, heed

solid - cone, cube, dependable, estimable, firm, full, homogeneous, inflexible, level, responsible, sound, sterling, stiff, trustworthy, uniform
solid (comb. form)-stereo
solid (geometrical)-prism
solid (seven-faced) - heptahedra
solid (tapering)-cone
solid (with six sides)-cube
solidified-cemented
solidify-compact, crystallize, gel, harden, set
solidity - compactness, dependability, firmness, hardness, solidness, stability
solidum-dado
soliloquy - discourse, monologue, poem
solitary-alone, desolate, individual, lone, lonely, lonesome, recluse, single
solitary (comb. form) - eremo
solitude - isolation, loneliness, seclusion, solitariness
solo-air, alone, aria, strain
solution - analysis, answer, disentanglement, key
solution (alkaline, strong) - lye
solution (antiseptic) - eusol, iodin, iodine, phenol
solution (disinfectant) - iodin, iodine
solution (saline)-brine
solution (strength of)-titer
Somaliland (British) city - Berbera (c.)
Somaliland (Italian) city - Mogdisho (c.)
Somaliland (Italian) coin - besa (cop.)
Somaliland measure - caba, chela, cubito, darat, tabla, top
Somaliland weight-parsalah
Somalis Proper-Asha
somber (sombre) - depressing, grave, melancholy
some-any, one, several
somersault-flip

something consecrated – sa-
scrum
something extra – bonus,
bounty, lagnappe, la-
gniappe, lanyap, premi-
um
something found–trove
something frightful – bugbear
something illogical–alogism
something inserted–gore, inset, wedge
something out of normal –
freak, malformation,
monstrosity
something poisonous–upas
something similar–analogue
something small–atom, dot,
iota, jot, tittle, whit
something superfluous–lux-
us
something to be learned –
lesson
something unexplained –
mystery
something whose weight is
borne–ponderant
sometime–once
somewhat–rather
somewhat like–similar
somnus–sleep
son (as in Welsh names)–ap
son (favorite)–Absalom
son (pert. to)–filial
son (state of being)–sonship
son (youngest)–cadet
son-in-law–gener
son of (Scot.)–Mac
son of a gun (slang)–fellow,
rogue, wretch
Son of God–Savior, Saviour
son of Jacob–Levi
son of Judah–Er
Son of Middle Border author
–Garland
son of Odin–Ve
son of Seth–Enos
sonance–sound, tune
sonant–oral
song – aria, canticle, carol,
chant, chantey, chanty,
ditty, lay, noel, shantey,
shanty, tune
song (after)–epode
song (boat)–barcarole, bar-

carolle, chantey, chanty,
shantey, shanty
song (college)–glee
song (depressing folk)–blues
song (erstwhile, popular) –
cucaracha
song (evening) – serenade,
vesper
song (folk)–blues
song (funeral)–dirge, elegy,
threnody
song (German)–lied
song (gondolier)–barcarole,
barcarolle
song (merry)–lilt
song (morning)–matin
song (mourning)–dirge
song (night)–serenade, vesper
song (obscure)–rune
song (of joy)–paean, pean
song (of lament)–threnody
song (of love)–madrigal
song (of praise) – carol,
paean, pean
song (patriotic)–America
song (pert. to)–melic
song (religious) – anthem,
chant, hymn, psalm
song (sacred) – anthem,
chant, hymn, polymny,
psalm
song (sailor's) – barcarole,
barcarolle, chantey,
chanty, shantey, shanty
song (simple)–ballad
songbird–robin
song-hit words–lyrics
song-like–lyrical
song thrush–mavie, mavis
sonnet–poem, song, verse
sonnet (first eight lines of)–
octet
sonnet (last six lines of) –
sestet
sonsie (sonsy) – buxom,
comely, comfortable,
happy, lucky, plentiful,
prosperous
sontag–cape, jacket
soodle–saunter, stroll
soon – anon, early, erelong,
immediately, promptly,
quickly, shortly, speedily
soon to occur–early
sooner (obs.)–erst

Sooner State–Oklahoma
sooner than–ere
soot–smut
soot-charged gaseous product of combustion–smoke
soot from mercury furnace
flue–stup
soothe–allay, assuage, calm,
compose, lull, mitigate,
pacify, pet, quiet, solace,
tranquilize
soother–balm, flatterer, lull-
er
soothing–appeasing, balmy,
calming, demulcent, dul-
cet, lenitive, sedative,
tranquilizing
soothing substance–balsam
soothsayer–augur, seer
sophistical–captious
soporific – narcotic, opiate,
somniferous
soprano–singer, treble
soprano (operatic) – Alda,
Eames
sora–rail
sorcerer–mage, magi, magician, wizard
sorceress–sibyl, witch
sorceress (myth.)–Circe
sorceress (snaky-haired) –
Gorgon
sorcery–magic, necromancy,
witchcraft
sorcery (African) – obe,
obeah, obi
sorcery (degraded form) –
voodoo
sorcery (form of) – obe,
obeah, obi
sordid – base, contemptible,
despicable, filthy, gross,
ignoble, low, mean, me-
nial, servile, slatternly,
sluttish, vile
sore (Scot.)–sair
soreness – ache, irritability,
painfulness, vexation
sorghum (grain)–durra
sorority–club, fraternity, sisterhood, society
sorrel (derived from)–oxalic
sorrel (South American
wood)–oca
sorrel (wood)–oca, oxalis
sorrow–adversity, affliction,

calamity, distress, dolor, grief, lament, misery, mourn, rue, sigh, tribulation, weal, woe, wretchedness

sorrow (arch.)–teen

sorrow for sin–contrition

sorrowful–disconsolate, dismal, distressing, doleful, drear, dreary, mournful, rueful, sadly, unhappy

sorry–afflicted, chagrin, contrite, disappointed, grievous, hurt, mortified, painful, pitiful, regret, regretful, vexed, wretched

sort–character, classify, cull, grade, ilk, kind, nature, rank, variety

sortie–foray, sally

sottish – doltish, drunken, dull, senseless, stupid

soud – fasten, join, solder, strengthen, unite

soudagur – merchant, shopkeeper

soul–pneuma, spirit

soul (beatified)–saint

soul (dwelling place of)–Po

soul (Egyptian religion)–ba

soul (Sanskrit)–atman

soul (the)–ba

souls (in other bodies)–reincarnation

sound – cry, flawless, hale, intact, noise, perfect, plumb, reliable, robust, sane, scrutinize, stable, sturdy, test, tone, valid, whole

sound (addition of meaningless at end of word)–paragoge

sound (adventitious)–rale

sound (agree in final)–rimes

sound (atonic)–surd

sound (automobile horn) – honk

sound (beating drum)–rataplan

sound (breathing)–snore

sound (dashing)–swash

sound (exclamatory blow-like)–bam

sound (explosion)–report

sound (fixed)–toned

sound (flogging, slang)–larrup

sound (gurgling)–gobble

sound (harsh)–bray, cacophony, creak

sound (harsh, ringing) – twang

sound (harsh, whistling, respiratory)–stridor

sound (hoarse)–bray, caw

sound (insect's)–chirr

sound (light, repeated)–pitapat

sound (long, loud)–peal

sound (loud, brazen)–blare

sound (low, monotonous) – drone, hum

sound (low, prolonged) – moan

sound (metallic) – clang, ping, ting

sound (metallic sharp)–tinkle

sound (morbid, respiratory) –rale

sound (murmuring)–groan

sound (murmuring low) – purr

sound (nasal)–snore

sound (nasal, whistling) – stridor

sound (of musical)–tonal

sound (open, vocal)–vowel

sound (pert. to)–tonal

sound (ringing metallic) – clang

sound (shallow)–lagoon

sound (sharp nasal)–twang

sound (shrill)–reedy

sound (sibilant)–hiss

sound (simple, open, vocal)– vowel

sound (slight tinkling) – clink

sound (small)–peep

sound (small, made by leaves)–rustle

sound (smart)–pop

sound (soft and clear) – silvery

sound (splashing)–swash

sound (tinkling)–tink

sound (to)–toot

sound (trumpet)–clarion

sound (vibrating)–twang

sound (vocal, short, catching)–hiccough, hiccup

sound (warning) – alarm, alarum, tocsin

sound (whirring)–birr

sound (whizzing) – ping, swish

sound (without)–asonant

sound (yelping)–yip

sound (accompanying respiration–rale

sound discordantly – bray, jangle, jar

sound due to rapid motion–whirr

sound loudly–blare

sound of bell–ding

sound of bullet passing through air–zip

sound of contempt–bah, boo

sound of disapproval – boo, hiss

sound of plucked banjo string–tum

sound of rising birds–whirr

sound of surf–rote

sound reasoning–logic

sounded – blew, clanged, rang, tooted

sounded (one)–syllabic

sounded loudly–blared

sounded vibrantly–rung

sounding–plangent, sonant

sounding (high)–bombastic

soundness of mind–sanity

sounds (adventitious)–rales

sounds (sobbing)–yoops

sounds (succession of)–peal

sounds (vocal symbols) – sonant

sounds having melody–music

sounds having rhythm–music

soup–broth, consomme

soup (thick)–pottage, puree

soup (thick meat or fish)– bisk, bisque

soup dish (bowl)–tureen

soup-fin shark–topes

soup ingredient – noodles, okra

soupçon – portion, suggestion, suspicion, taste

sour–acerb, acetose, acetous, acid, acidify, acrid, astringent, bitter, embitter, tart, wry

sour (bitter, harsh) – acerb, acetic, acid, tart

sour (in temper)–crabbed

sour (slightly)–acescent

sour and harsh (to taste)–acerb, tart

source – beginning, font, fount, fountainhead, origin, parent, rise, root, seed, wellspring

source (primary)–germ

source of caoutchouc–ule

source of honor–credit

source of income–revenue

source of iodine–kelp

source of metal (basic)–ore

source of natural indigo–indican

soured–acidulated

sourish–acidulous

south (French)–sud

South Africa Republic coin–pond (g.)

South African–Boer

South African animal (small)–das

South African animal (grazing) disease–nenta

South African antelope – eland, gnu, oribi, peele, rhebok, sassaby

South African antelope (extinct)–blaubok

South African antelope (maned)–gnu

South African apricot (salted, dried)–mebos, meebos

South African armadillo – para

South African ass–quagga

South African camp–laager

South African city–Durban, Germiston, Johannesburg

South African coin – cent (br.), florin (s.), rand (g.)

South African colonist–Boer

South African cony–das

South African council–Raad

South African dialect–Taal

South African diamond–jager

South African Dutch–Boer, Taal

South African Dutch dialect –Taal

South African Dutch colonist–Boer

South African Dutch descent –Boer

South African farmer–Boer

South African fox–asse, caama

South African grass country –veld, veldt

South African grassland – veld, veldt

South African grazing animal disease–nenta

South African gully–donga

South African hill–kop

South African hillock–kopje

South African hut (grass)–rondavel, rondawel

South African mountain – kop

South African negroid tribe –Bantus, Bechuanas, Damaras, Kaffirs, Pondo, Swahilis, Xosa

South African pass (mountain)–nek

South African plant–aloe

South African province – Transvaal

South African race–Hottentot, Namas

South African reedbuck – reitboc, reitbok

South African rodent–ratel

South African shrub–protea

South African snake (small harmless)–eggeater

South African stream (underground)–aar

South African tableland (dry)–karoo

South African term (contempt for Britisher)–Rouinek

South African tree–assagai

South African tribe – Bantu, Zulu

South African village–kraal

South African warrior–impi

South American – Chilean, Brazilian

South American aborigine–Arawak

South American animal–ai, anteater, llama, paca, sloth, tapir

South American animal (burrowing)–armadillo

South American animal (leopard-like)–jaguar

South American armadillo–apar

South American armadillo (small burrowing)–pichiciago

South American arrow poison–curara, curare, curari

South American balsam – tolu

South American beast of burden–llama

South American bird – agami, arara, barbet, bellbird, boatbill, chaja, guacharo, guan, myna, mynah, oilbird, puffbird, rara, tinamou

South American bird (crane-like)–seriema

South American bird (game)–tinamou

South American bird (hawk)–caracara

South American bird (weaver)–taha

South American blanket – serape

South American brocket – pita

South American cameloid – llama, ruminant

South American coin – centavo

South American country – Argentina, Brazil, Chile, Colombia, Patagonia, Peru

South American country (pert. to)–Chilean

South American district (most southern) – Patagonia

South American dog (wild) –agouara

South American drink–assai

South American dwellers (plain)–llanero

South American equine – quagga

South American estuary – Para, Plata

South American fiber (silky seed tree)–yachan

South American fish–paru

South American fish (large, fresh water) arapaima

South American fish (pike-like)–arapaima

South American fox–asse

South American fumarole (oven-shaped)–hornito

South American genus of prickly herbs–loasa

South American hare–tapeti

South American fish (small) –scalare

South American hawk–caracara

South American herdsman–llanero

South American Indian – Carib, Ona

South American Indian tribe –Ges

South American knives (heavy)–machettes

South American language – Ona

South American lapwing – terutero

South American liberator – Bolivar

South American limestone– tosca

South American mammal – alpaca, llama, tapir

South American mammal (nocturnal arboreal)–kinkajou

South American marmoset– tamarin

South American monkey – acari, ouakari, sai, saki, titi

South American monkey (small)–titi

South American monkey (titi)–orabassu

South American mountains –Andes

South American native (north)–Carib

South American opossum – sarigue

South American ostrich – rhea

South American oxalis–oca

South American palm–assai

South American parrot–macaw

South American plains (treeless)–llanos, pampas

South American plains dweller–llanero

South American plainsman– llanero

South American plant–crassula, ipecac

South American plant (creeping)–ipecac

South American plant (medicinal)–ipecac

South American plant root– ipecac

South American rabbit–tapeti

South American range of mountains–Andes

South American republic – Argentina, Chile, Colombia

South American river–Acre, Amazon, Apa, Para, Plata

South American rodent – agouti, chinchilla, coypu, degu, mara, paca

South American rodent (aquatic)–coypu

South American rodent (large) – capibara, capybara

South American root–oca

South American rubber tree –para

South American ruminant– alpaca, llama

South American shrub–coca

South American shrub dried leaves–coca

South American snake (large)–anaconda

South American snake (tree)–lora

South American stock (linguist)–Ona

South American tapir–danta

South American timber tree –fotui, pekea

South American tinamou – tataupa

South American toucan (brilliant)–aracari

South American tree–cacao

South American tree snake– lora

South American tribe–Ona

South American trumpeter– agami

South American tuber–oca

South American vulture – condor

South American weapon (missile)–bola, bolas

South American wild cat – eyra

South American wind (pampas)–pampero

South American wood sorrel –oca

South Carolina fort (former)–Sumter

South Dakota capital–Pierre

South Dakota Indian–Brule

South European plant–anise

South India tribe–Tamil

South Kordofan Negro–Nuba

South Pacific island–Tonga

South Pole bird – penguin, skua

South ruling class (member of)–planter

South Sea (pert. to)–Samoan

South Sea canoe–proa

South Sea island (nicknamed Tincan)–Naifou

South Sea island drink (fermented)–ava

South Sea island food–taros

South Sea islander – Maori, Samoan

South Sea plant–taro

South Sea staple–taro

South wind–auster, notus

South Wind author – Douglas

southeast wind–eurus

Southeastern Asia country– Siam, Thailand

southern–austral

Southern agriculturist – planter

Southern California Indians –Seris

Southern dish–hoecake

Southern Europe gecko–tarente
Southern France–Midi
Southern johnnycake–pone
Southern Nigeria negro – Beni, Benin
Southern river–Pedee
Southern Russia peninsula– Crimea
Southwark inn (Chaucer's tales)–Tabard
Southwest Pacific islands (group of)–Samoa
southwest wind–afer
Southwestern country paths –camino
Southwestern ranch house – casa
Southwestern river–Gila
Southwestern U.S. lands (cultivated)–arada
souvenir–keepsake, memento, memory, recollection, relic, remembrancer, reminder
sovereign – independent, liege, monarch, potentate, prince, ruler
sovereign authority–dominion
sovereign power–throne
sovereign prerogative claim –seigniorage
sovereignty – diadem, empire, realm, scepter, sceptre
Soviet administrative committee–presidium
Soviet government farm – sovkhos, sovkhose, sovkhoz
Soviet hero–Lenin, Stalin
Soviet police–Ogpu
Soviet Republic (part of) – Bokhara
sow–broadcast, disseminate, implant, plant, scatter, seed
soy bean–soja
space–area, arrange, gap, interval, range, rank, room, void
space (architectural triangular)–pediment
space (between eyes and bills

in reptiles, birds, fish) – lore, lora (pl.)
space (empty)–blank, inane, vacuum, void
space (included)–contents
space (on surface)–area
space (open building)–area
space (pert. to)–areal
space (portion of)–place
space (small, between veins of leaves)–areola
space (storage)–attic, cellar, shed, storeroom, warehouse
space (triangle on postage stamp)–spandrel
space between two points – distance
space occupied–volume
space of time–interval
space theory–plenism
spacious – ample, capacious, comprehensive, expansive, roomy
spack–forward, intelligent, knowing
spad–nail
spade (Irish peat-digging)–slane
spade (peat-digging)–slane
spade (turf)–slane
spae–divine, foretell
Spain (anc. name)–Iberia
spale – chip, lath, shaving, splinter
span–bridge, extend, reach, spread, stretch, team
spangle–aiglet, glitter, sparkle
Spanish "an"–un, una
Spanish article–el, la, las, los, un, una
Spanish bassoon mouthpiece –tudel
Spanish bayonet–yucca
Spanish belle (lower class)– maja
Spanish boat (dispatch) – aviso
Spanish brandy–aguardiente
Spanish cape (coast)–Trafalgar
Spanish card game–monte
Spanish champion–Cid
Spanish chaperone–duenna
Spanish city–Barcelona, Bil-

bao, Cadiz, Cartagena, Carthagena, Cordoba, Cordova, Gijon, Granada, Irun, Jerez de la Frontiera, Madrid (c.), Malaga, Murcia, Ronda, Santander, Saragossa, Seville, Siero, Toledo, Valencia, Valladolid, Xeres, Zaragoza
Spanish city (cathedral) – Saragossa
Spanish cloak–capa, manta, mantle
Spanish coast cape–Trafalgar
Spanish coat (shepherd's sheepskin) – zamarra, zamarro
Spanish coin–Alfonso (g.), centimo (br.), peseta (s.), piaster (s.)
Spanish coin (anc. gold) – dobla
Spanish coin (obs., copper)– ochavo
Spanish coin (old) – dobla, pistole
Spanish conqueror–Pizarro
Spanish dance–bolero, fandango, gitano, tango
Spanish dance (lively)–saraband
Spanish dandy (lower class) –majo
Spanish dish–posole
Spanish dispatch boat–aviso
Spanish district–Xeres
Spanish dollar–duro
Spanish epic–Cid
Spanish explorer–Mendoza
Spanish fabric (silk)–tiraz
Spanish fleet (old)–armada
Spanish foreign minister – Suner
Spanish game–jai-alai, omber, pelota
Spanish game (like tennis)– pelota
Spanish gentleman – caballero, cavalier, senor
Spanish gold–oro
Spanish grass–esparto, spart
Spanish Guinea seaport – Bata

Spanish head covering–man-
tilla
Spanish hero–Cid
Spanish holiday–fiesta
Spanish horse (small)–genet
Spanish hotel–posada
Spanish house–casa
Spanish inn–posada
Spanish instrument (percus-
sion)–castanet
Spanish jar (wide-mouthed)
–olla
Spanish judge–alcalde
Spanish justice of peace–en-
trada
Spanish kettle (silver reduc-
ing)–cazo
Spanish king (former)–Ara-
gon
Spanish king (last)–Alphon-
so
Spanish lady–dona, senora
Spanish language (one of)–
Catalan
Spanish lariat–reata, riata
Spanish legislature–cortes
Spanish linen cloth–croa
Spanish man–don
Spanish measure–aranzada,
aroba, azumbre, braza,
caballeria, cafiz, cahiz,
cantara, celemin, codo,
copa, cordel, cuarta, cuar-
teron, cuartilla, cuartillo,
dedo, estadal, estado,
fanega, fanegada, league,
legua, linea, medio, milla,
moyo, palmo, paso, pie,
pulgada, racion, sesma,
vara, yugada
Spanish measure (length)–
vara
Spanish monk–padre
Spanish Morocco seaport –
Tetuan
Spanish mountain–Asturian,
Cantabrian, Guadarrama,
La Maladetta, Mulaha-
cem, Pic de Netou, Pyre-
nees, Sierra de Toledo,
Sierra Morena
Spanish native (northeast)–
Catalan
Spanish nobleman – don,
grandee
Spanish painter–Goya

Spanish palace–Escorial
Spanish paprika fruit – pi-
miento
Spanish peninsula–Iberia
Spanish people (common)–
Gente
Spanish plant (pepper fami-
ly)–aji
Spanish porridge–atole
Spanish port–Palos
Spanish possessive–mia
Spanish promenade–paseo
Spanish pronunciation mark
–tilde
Spanish province–Alava, Al-
bacete, Alicante, Almeria,
Avila, Badajoz, Balearic Is-
lands, Barcelona, Burgos,
Caceres, Cadiz, Castellon
de la Plana, Ciudad Real,
Cordova, Coruna, Cuenca,
Gerona, Granada, Gua-
dalajara, Guipuscoa, Huel-
va, Huesca, Jaen, Leon,
Lerida, Logrono, Lugo,
Madrid, Malaga, Murcia,
Navarra, Orense, Oviedo,
Palencia, Pontevedra, Sal-
amanca, Santander, Sara-
gossa, Segovia, Seville,
Soria, Tarragona, Teruel,
Toledo, Valencia, Valla-
dolid, Vizcaya, Zamora
Spanish province (anc.)–An-
dalusia, Aravarre, Asturi-
as, Basque, Castile, Estre-
madura, Galicia, Leon
Spanish province natives –
Leonese
Spanish queen (last)–Ena
Spanish raisin–pasa
Spanish river–Duro, Ebro,
Guadalquivir, Guadiana,
Tagus
Spanish room–sala
Spanish seaport–Palos
Spanish shawl–manta, serape
Spanish sherry–Xeres
Spanish silk fabric–tiraz
Spanish slaughterhouse –
matadero
Spanish soldier (used as es-
cort)–miquelet
Spanish "the" – el, la, las
(pl.), los (pl.)
Spanish title–don, senor

Spanish Toledo (pert. to)–
Toletan
Spanish town in Gerona –
Olot
Spanish trail–camino
Spanish weight – adarme,
arienzo, arroba, caracter,
castellano, dinero, drac-
ma, escrupulo, frail,
grano, libra, marco,
ochava, onza, quilate,
quintal, tomin, tonelada
Spanish wind (east coast)–
solano
Spanish American arbor –
ramada
Spanish American biscuit –
panal
Spanish American crow
(carrion)–aura
Spanish American game –
pelota
Spanish American garment–
serape
Spanish American measure
(length)–vara
Spanish American shawl –
manta
spar–boom, box, gaff, mast,
rung, sprit, yard
spar (cargo stowing)–steve
spar (small)–sprit
spar (upright)–mast
spare–frugal, lanky, meager,
parsimony, scanty, thin
sparing–chary, frugal, merciful, reticent, saving,
scanty, scrimping, stinting
sparked – arced, spotted,
streaked, variegated
sparkle – coruscate, flash,
glint, glisten, glitter, radiate, scintillate, shine
sparkling (with luster)–brilliant
sparoid fish–sar
Spartan army (main divi-
sion)–mora
Spartan bondman–helot
Spartan commander (mili-
tary unit)–lochage
Spartan dog–bloodhound
Spartan king–Menelaus
Spartan magistrate (anc.) –
ephor

Spartan method of cipher writing–scytale
Spartan serf (anc.)–helot
spasmodic–excitable, fitful, snatchy
spasmodic disease–tetanus
spasmodic twitch–tic
spat–dispute, gaiter, legging, quarrel, row, slap
spate – flood, freshet, gush, waterspout
spatial–areal
spatter–dabble, splash
spatter water–splash
spawn (fish)–roe
speak–articulate, chat, discourse, orate, pronounce, say, talk, tell, utter
speak affectedly–mimp
speak against–opposed
speak from memory–recite
speak ill of absent–backbite
speak imperfectly – lisp, stutter
speak in undertone – murmur
speak of–call, mention
speak of boastfully–vaunt
speak offhand–extemporize
speak profusely–palaver
speak rapidly–patter
speak rhetorically–declaim
speak slightingly–disparage
speak slowly–drawl
speak softly–whisper
speak sullenly–murmur
speak thoughtlessly–blat
speak to first–accost
speak under breath–mumble, mutter
speak with exaggeration – enlarge
speak with guttural articulation–bur
speaker – lecturer, sayer, talker
speaker (drawling)–drone
speaker (eloquent) – orator, spellbinder
speaker (sibilant)–lisper
speaker (tedious)–proser
speaker of many languages–linguist, polyglot
speaker's hammer–gavel
speaking (style of)–staccato
speaking with facility–fluent

speaking without preparation–extemporizing
spear–javelin, lance
spear (anc.)–fram, framea
spear (barbed)–angon, gaff
spear (fish)–gig
spear (hardwood, slender)–assagai, assegai
spear (three-pronged fish)–trident
spear (two-pronged)–bident
spear-shaped–hastate
special–concrete, extraordinary, individual, noteworthy, particular, peculiar, specific, uncommon
special ability–talent
special edition–extra
specialist (city planning) – urbanist
species–kind, sort, variety
specific passages–transits
specific uses–applications
specify – designate, name, stipulate
specify singly–enumerate
specimen–example, model, pattern, sample
specimen (additional biological)–cotype
specimen (finest)–pearl
specious–colorable, ostensible, plausible
speck–bit, blemish, blot, dot, mite, mote, nit, particle, spot, whit
speck of dust–mote
spectacle–display, exhibition, pageant, representation, show, sight
spectacles–glasses
spectator–beholder, looker-on, observer, onlooker, witness
specter (spectre) – ghost, phantom, spook, wraith
spectral – ghostly, ghosty, spooky
speculate–consider, contemplate, deliberate, meditate, philosophy, ponder, ruminate, theorize
sped – darted, dashed, galloped, hastened, hied, raced

speech – address, harangue, oration, utterance
speech (bit of acidulous)–vinegar
speech (conversational form) –colloquialism
speech (declamatory)–tirade
speech (figure of)–trope
speech (inelegant)–slang
speech (intemperate)–tirade
speech (long abusive)–tirade
speech (pompous in)–magniloquent
speech (prolonged)–tirade
speech (to make, slang) – spiel
speech (vehement) – harangue
speech (vitriolic)–tirade
speech (voiceless element)–spirate, surd
speech part – adjective, adverb, conjunction
speechify–orate
speechless–dumb, mute, silent
speechmaking (to please constituents)–buncombe, bunkum
speed–accelerate, assist, celerity, dispatch, expedite, expedition, facilitate, haste, hie, hurry, quickness, rapidity, velocity
speed (great)–posthaste
speed (put on sudden)–spurt
speed (undue)–haste
speed rate–tempo
speed upward–zoom
speedily – apace, betimes, expeditiously, promptly, quickly, rapidly
spell – charm, enchantment, glamour, magic, sorcery
spell (brief)–snap
spell in character of another alphabet–transliterate
spell of weather (sudden)–snap
spellbinder–orator, spieler
spelling event (former) – evenment
spend – disburse, dissipate, exhaust, expend, lavish, pass
spend foolishly–squander

spendthrift–prodigal, profligate, waster, wastrel
Spenserian character–Una
spent–effete, exhausted, lavished, paid, squandered, wasted, weary
speos–cave, grotto, temple, tomb
spermaceti (substance from) –cetin
sphere – arena, ball, field, globe, jurisdiction, orb, scope
sphere of action–domain
sphere of influence–domain
sphere of life–world
sphere of operation–theater
sphere of thought–domain
spherical–globular, rotund
spherical (nearly)–obrotund
spherical (rare)–orbic
sphericity–rotundity, roundness
sphinx (land of)–Egypt
spice (kind of)–clove, mace, nutmeg
spice (pungent)–pepper
spice (sweet)–stacte
spice moderately–season
spices–aromatics
spiciest–raciest
spicule–sclerite
spicule (star-shaped)–aster
spicy–racy
spider–arachnid, cob, pan, tripod, trivet
spider (black widow)–pokomoo
spider (garden)–epeira
spider (old word for)–attercop
spider (venomous)–tarantula
spider (web-spinning)–retiary
spider crab–maian
spider crab (genus of)–maia
spider monkeys (genus of)–ateles
spider nest–nidus, web
spider web (old word for)–attercop
spider web (resembling) – arachnoid
spiders (genus of)–agalena
spider's organ (web spinning)–spinneret

spieler–barker
spiff–bonus, gratuity, PM, premium
spiffy–excellent, fine, neat, smart, splendid
spigot – dossil, spile, spout, tap
spike–ear, nail, tine
spike (brad-shaped)–brob
spike (cereal)–ear
spike (grain)–ear
spike (wooden)–trenail
spike hole–spile
spike of flowers–ament
spikelet–spinule
spikenard–nard
spile–pin, plug, spigot, spill, spout, stake, tube
spill liquid–slop
spill over–slop
spin–gyrate, rotate, twirl
spin (Scot.)–birl
spinach (mountain)–orach, orache
spinal cord–myelon
spinal cord (white matter of)–alba
spindle–axis, axle, xeres
spindle (for holding lathe work)–mandrel
spindling–leggy
spine – backbone, chine, thorn
spine (needle-like)–acicula
spine (slender)–awn
spine bone – sacrum, sacra (pl.)
spinel (ruby)–balas
spinet–harpsichord
spinnaker–sail
spinner–narrator, spider, top
spinning–rotary, whirling
spinning a web–telarian
spinning device–distaff
spiracles – apertures, orifices, pores, vents
spiral–coil, corkscrew, helical
spiral form (having)–helix
spire – coil, curl, steeple, twist, whorl
spire finial–epi, epis (pl.)
spire ornament–finial
spirit – action, animation, bravery, cheerfulness, dash, elan, enterprise,

fairy, fire, ghost, life, metal, mettle, morale, pluck, pneuma, shade, soul, vim
spirit (ancestral)–mane
spirit (animating)–animus
spirit (animation)–dash
spirit (avenging)–alecto, ate, erinys, megaera, tisiphine
spirit (coll.)–gimp
spirit (dead friend, Cambodian rel.)–arac
spirit (disembodied)–soul
spirit (evil)–demon, devil
spirit (female)–banshee
spirit (female water) – Undine
spirit (full of)–mettlesome
spirit (good)–Eudaemon
spirit (household)–lar
spirit (impish, Eng. folklore)–Po
spirit (in The Tempest) – Ariel
spirit (little)–imp
spirit (malignant)–demon
spirit (mischievous)–imp
spirit (moving)–soul
spirit (of man, Egypt rel.)–akh
spirit (of the air)–Ariel
spirit (of the people)–ethos
spirit (powerful, under mortal's control)–genie
spirit (refined)–elixir, grace
spirit (Roman, of dead) – manes
spirit (Siam worshipped) – nat
spirit (unyielding)–game
spirit (water)–Ariel
spirit lamp–etna
spirit of avarice–mammon
spirit of mockery–momus
spirit of people actuating manners and customs – ethos
spirit of the air–Ariel
spirited – audacious, brisk, eager, gamy, mettlesome, spunky
spirited and stylish–dashing
spiritless – dejected, depressed, vapid
spirits (dwelling place of)–Po

spirits (low)–gloomy
spirits of the dead–manes
spiritual–churchly, devout, disembodied, holy, immaterial, internal, platonic, pure, unworldly
spiritual apathy (in monasteries)–acedia
spiritual beings–angels, seraphs
spiritual content–peace
spiritual darkness (Hindu philosophy)–tamas
spiritual torpor (in monasteries)–acedia
spiritualistic meeting–seance
spital – hospital, lazaretto, refuge
spite–animosity, enmity, malevolence, malice, pique, venom
spiteful – annoying, irritating, malicious, malignant, mean, troublesome
spiteful (slyly)–catty
splash–spatter
splash gently upon–lap
splashboard–fender
splay – adorn, carve, dislocate, display, expand, spread
splendid–brilliant, fine, glorious, gorgeous, grand, illustrious, magnificent, regal, shining, showy, sumptuous
splendid (cheaply)–tinny
splendid (Scot.)–braw
splendor – display, eclat, glory, gorgeousness, grandeur, luster, pomp, radiance, resplendence, showiness
splendor (ceremonial)–pageantry
splint (armor)–tasse
splint (steel armor) – tace, tasse
splinter–sliver
split – burst, cleave, cleft, cloven, divided, rend, rifted, rive, rupture, tear, wedge
split pea (India)–dal
spoil (law)–estrepe
spoiled – addled, bad,

botched, decayed, marred, molded, pampered, pillaged, preyed, tainted
spoiled by age–musty
spoiler of plans–marplot
spoils – booty, loot, prey, swag
spoke–uttered
spoke monotonously–droned
spoke slightingly of–disparaged
spoken–oral
spoken (law)–parol
spoken (smooth)–glib, oily
spoken rhetorically – declaimed
spoliation–rapine
sponge (fresh water)–badiaga
sponge (type of)–rhagon
sponge (young)–ascon
sponge out–erase
sponge tree–huisache
sponger–cadger
spontaneous–instinctive, involuntary, self-acting
spontoon – club, espantoon, pantoon, pike, spantoon, truncheon
spoof – deceive, deception, fool, guy, hoax, swindle
spook – apparition, ghost, hobgoblin, specter, spirit
spool on which to wind thread–reel
spoon (cuplike)–ladle
spoon (long handle)–ladle
spoon-shaped–cochlear
spore capsule – ascus, asci (pl.)
spore sac–ascus, asci (pl.)
sport–amusement, diversion, entertainment, frolic, fun, game, mirth, pastime, play, racing, recreation, toy
sport (cheap, slang)–piker
sport (winter)–skiing
sportive – gay, frolicsome, lusory, merry, playful
sportsman's cry–soho
spot–asperse, blemish, blot, discolor, disgrace, flaw, fleck, locality, macula, macule, point, site, speck, splotch, stain, taint

spot (comb. form)–spil
spot (decayed fruit)–blet
spot (fertile) – oasis, oases (pl.)
spot (rain, Scot.)–rone
spot (secluded)–alcove
spot (small)–dot
spot (sun)–lucule
spot (to)–freckle
spot (verdant)–oasis, oases (pl.)
spot in mineral (dark) – macle
spot in wood (archery) – wems
spot on playing card–pip
spots (moist, in rock ledge) –sipes
spotted – dappled, mottled, stained, sullied, tarnished
spotted (finely, as a dog)–ticked
spotted with drop-like spots –guttate
spouse–consort, mate, wife
spouse (night, in Norse myth.)–annar
spout–dale, declaim, gush, jet, jut, rant, spigot, spurt, squirt
spout (short, open)–lip
spout for drawing sap–spile
sprat (Scot.)–garvie
spray (sea)–spindrift, spoondrift
sprayer–atomizer
spread – broadcast, diverge, scatter, strew, ted, unfurl, widen
spread by report (to)–norate
spread by rumor–noise
spread defamation–libel
spread loosely–ted
spread on thick–slather
spread out – deploy, fan, open, span
spread out battle line–deploy
spread outward–flare
spreading–dissemination
spreading of light beyond its proper boundaries – halation
spree–carousal, frolic, lark, orgy, romp, shindy, wassail

sprig – active, scion, shoot, smart, spruce, trim, twig

sprightliness–animation

sprightly–alive, blithe, briskly, incorporeal, lively, pert, spiritedly

sprightly wit (Fr.) esprit

spring–arise, font, hop, leap, spa, vault, well

spring (eruptive, boiling) – geyser

spring (old word for)–ver

spring (pert. to)–vernal

spring (short)–hop

spring (surrounded by rank grass, southwest U.S.)–ojo

spring back–rebound, recoil

spring-like–vernal

spring suddenly–bounce

spring tide (opposite of) – neap

spring up–arise

springboard–alcade

springe – agile, ensnare, snare, supple

springing again into vigor–renascent

springing back–elastic

springs (warm)–thermae

springy–elastic, resilient

springy (not)–inelastic

sprinkle–dot, sparge, spray, water, wet

sprinkle (dial.)–deg

sprinkle (rare)–affuse

sprinkle with dirty water or mud–bespatter

sprinkle with flour–dredge

sprinkle with grit–sand

sprinkle with powder–dust

sprinkle (her.)–seme

sprinkler (holy water)–aspergillum

sprinkling (art)–seme

sprint–race

sprite–apparition, Ariel, elf, fairy, fay, ghost, gnome, goblin, hob, imp, peri, pixie

sprite (female water)–nixie

sprite (in The Tempest) – Ariel

sprite (water) – naiad, nix, nixie

sprite-like–elfish

sprout–bud, burgeon, germinate, shoot, spire

sprout (arch.)–cion

sprout (bamboo pickled) – achar

sprout artificially–malt

spruce–dapper, finical, natty, neat, smart, smug, titivate, trig, trim

spruce (to make)–smarten

spruce in appearance–natty, posh

sprung a leak (as a vessel)–bilged

spry – active, agile, brisk, nimble, vigorous

spry (Scot.)–smart, spruce

spud – dagger, drill, knife, potato, reamer, shovel

spume–foam, froth, scum

spunky–game, mettlesome, plucky, quick, spirited

spur–calcar, drive, egg, excite, goad, incite, instigate, move, press, rowel, stimulate, urge

spur (gamecock) – gablock, gaff

spur (horseshoe)–calk

spur (mountain)–arete

spur on–stimulate

spur wheel–rowel

spurge–milkweed

spurious – adulterate, artificial, bogus, counterfeit, false, fictitious, forced, sham, snide, superficial, supposititious

spurl–scramble, sprawl

spurn–contemn, disdain, reject, scorn

spurries (sand)–tissas

spurt–gush, jet, jut

spy–behold, descry, discover, emissary, espy, examine, informer, note, search, sneak, snoop, snooper, watch

spy (clothing, slang)–keek

spy (prison)–mouton

squab – cushion, fledgling, nestling, piper

squabble–bicker, brawl, contend, jangle, quarrel, wrangle

squad–posse, team

squalid–dirty, filthy, foul, mean, poor, repellent, repulsive, sordid

squally–gusty

squalor–filthiness, miserable, squalidness

squander–disperse, dissipate, lavish, misspend, scatter, waste

squanderer–loser, wastrel

square–even, honest, parallelogram, quadrate, settle

square (public) – common, plaza

square shaft (pyramidal top) –obelisk

squarely and sharply–smack

squares (in checker pattern) –panes

squaring tool–edger

squash – beat, crush, press, squeeze, suppress

squash (summer)–pattypan

squat – dumpy, pudgy, squatty, stubby, thickset

squatter–nester

squeamish – dainty, nice, overnice, prudish, scrupulous

squeeze–compress, constrict, crowd, crush, hug, jam, press, wring

squeezer (fruit)–reamer

squelch – crush, disconcert, quash, quell, suppress

squib–lampoon, pipe, skit, speech, tube, writing

squiffed (slang) – drunk, intoxicated

squire–escort

squirm – twist, wiggle, wriggle, writhe

squirm about–wiggle

squirrel (African ground)–xerus

squirrel (American red) – chickaree

squirrel (European ground) –sisel

squirrel (European short-tailed)–sisel

squirrel (ground)–gopher

squirrel (large, handsome)–jelerang

squirrel skin (used in an-

cient kingly costumes) –
vair
squirrel shrew–tana
squirrel's nest–dray, drey
stab – gore, knife, knive,
lunge, pierce, pink, pon-
iard, puncture, thrust
stability – constancy, firmness, immovability, im-
mutability, indissolubility,
permanence, stableness,
steadfastness, steadiness
stabilize–poise, regulate
stable–barn, confirmed, constant, durable, established,
firm, fixed, lasting, permanent, solid, sound,
stall, steadfast, steady,
strong
stableman–hostler, ostler
stables (London royal) –
mews
stables (range of)–mews
stables (royal)–mews
stack – heap, mound, pile,
rick
stack (hay)–rick
stack of grain–rick, shock
staff–baton, mace, pole, rod,
stave
staff (heavy)–mace
staff (magician's)–rhabdos
staff (marshal's)–baton
staff (member of)–attache
staff (mountain climbing)–
alpenstock
staff (music)–stave
staff (pastoral)–crosier, cro-
zier, pedum, peda (pl.)
staff (sovereign's) – scepter,
sceptre
staff bearer–macer
staff member (diplomatic)–
attache
staff of office–mace, scepter,
sceptre
staff officers–aides
stag–hart
stag (eight-year-old)–royal
stag (that has cast antlers)–
pollard
stag (three-year-old)–spade
stag (twelve-point)–royal
stage – dais, degree, phase,
platform, rostrum

stage (declining, of disease)
–catabasis
stage (insect, immature) –
larva
stage (landing)–stair
stage (part of)–proscenium
stage a comeback–rally
stage dialogue–patter
stage direction–all, enter, exeunt, exit, omnes, sennet,
solus
stage direction (alone)–solus
stage direction (he or she remains)–manet
stage extra–supe, super
stage in a series–stair
stage in development–phase
stage of disease (declining)–
catabasis
stage of insect's development
–imago
stage parentheses–aside
stage signal–sennet
stage speech (to audience)–
aside
stage whisper–aside
stagger – lurch, reel, stun,
sway, titubate, totter
staggering–areel
staggers (blind)–gid
stagnant – dull, foul, inert,
stale, standing, still, un-
progressive
stagnate–dull, inert, motionless, rot
stagnation–torpor
staid – decorous, demure,
grave, sedate, sober, steadfast
stain – blemish, blot, contaminate, corrupt, dis-
color, discoloration, disgrace, dishonor, dye, in-
famy, maculate, paint,
pollution, smear, smudge,
soil, sully, taint, tint
stained (by partial decay)–
doty
stained glass (lead pieces for
holding)–cames
stainer–dyer
stainless–pure
stair–degree, stage, step
stair (upright part)–riser
staircase (spiral)–caracole
stair post–newel

stairway (moving)–escalator
stake – ante, bet, chance,
gamble, hazard, pale, peg,
pile, pin, post, risk, wager
stake (for roasting meat) –
spit
stake (large)–spile
stake (pointed)–pale, picket,
sowel
stake (sword practicing)–pel
stake (tinsmith's)–teest
stale–old, trite
stale (insipid)–vapid
staleness–triteness
stalk – axis, hunt, pedicel,
peduncle, reconnoiter,
stem, stipe
stalk (flower)–petiole
stalk (pea, strawberry, etc.)
–risp
stalk (short)–stipe
stalk (slender) – pedicel,
spear
stalk (strawberry, pea, etc.)
–risp
stalk (zoology)–stipes
stalk of grain–straw
stalk of grain (Scot.)–ressum
stalker–hunter
stalkless–sessile
stalks of grain (dry)–hay
stall – check, confederate,
loge, manger, mire,
stable, stop
stall (finger)–cot
stall (market)–booth
stalwart – brave, resolute,
stout, strong, sturdy, valiant
stam–stalk, stump, trunk
stammer–hesitate, stutter
stamp–distinguish, impress,
imprint, mark, print
stamp (ornamental)–seal
stamp battery block (iron)–
vol
stamp border (ornamental,
enclosing main design)–
tresure
stamp design on–tool
stampede–debacle, rout
stamping form–die
stamps – impresses, postage,
prints
stance – pose, position, posture, station

stanch – allay, check, extinguish, quell, quench, stem, stop

stanchion – bar, brace, post, prop, support, upright

stanchion (iron)–piton

stand – arise, attitude, bear, booth, endure, sustain, tolerate, tripod

stand (bric-a-brac)–atagere, etagere

stand (coffin)–bier

stand (framework)–rack

stand (glass, to protect table) –coaster

stand (ornament) – atagere, etagere

stand (pulpit-like)–ambo

stand (three-legged) – teapoy, tripod, trivet

stand (with shelves) – atagere, etagere

stand against–resist

stand by–aid

stand cost of–treat

stand for–represent

stand in–substitute

stand in some respect–relate

stand on end–upend

stand the cost of entertaining–treat

standard – criterion, mark, norm

standard (flag)–vexillum

standard (in battle) – oriflamb, oriflamme

standard copy–model

standard of chemical strength–titer

standard of excellence–ideal

standard of light–carcel

standard of perfection–ideal

standard quantity–unit

standard work–classic

standardize–calibrate

standing–status

standing (mode of)–stance

standing (social)–estate

standing out clearly – eminent

standing room only (abbr.)– S.R.O.

standstill–deadlock

stannum–tin

stanza–verse

stanza (eight lines)–octave

stanza (eight lines on two rimes)–triolet

stanza (six lines)–sestet

star–Almak, Deneb

star (athletic)–ace, Ruth

star (between Lyra and Pegasus)–Cygnus

star (blaze)–Nova

star (bright)–Vega

star (brightest)–sun

star (brightest in Aquila) – Altair

star (brightest in constellation)–Cor

star (brightest in the Swan) –Deneb

star (brilliant blue)–Vega

star (brilliant, temporarily) –Nova

star (constellation)–Ara, Argo, Aries, Capella, Cor, Leo, Nova, Vega

star (conventional)–etoile

star (dog)–Sept, Septi, Sirius

star (dog, var.)–Sopt

star (evening)–Evestar, Hesperus

star (evil, emanating from, astrology)–sideral

star (feather)–Comatula

star (first magnitude)–Deneb, Rigel

star (fixed)–Alkes, Vega

star (genus of feather)–antedon

star (guiding)–lodestar

star (in Aquila constellation)–Deneb

star (in Cetus)–Mira

star (in Cygnus)–Albireo

star (in Geminorum constellation)–Wasat

star (in Leo constellation)– Regulus

star (in Orion)–Rigel, Saiph

star (in Taurus)–Pleiad

star (in the Dragon)–Adib, Arc, Etamin

star (in the Lyre)–Vega

star (in the Whale)–Mira

star (in Virgo)–Spica

star (large)–Rigel

star (morning) – Daystar, Jupiter, Mars, Mercury, Saturn, Venus

star (new)–Nova

star (shooting) – comet, meteor

star (short existing bright)– Nova

star (six-pointed)–pentacle

star (six-pointed, Fr.) – estoile, etoile

star (theatrical)–hero, heroine, lead

star (variable)–Mira, Nova

star (variable, in Perseus) – Algol

star (with Mizar, small)–Alcor

star cluster–nebula

star facet–pane

starfish–asteria

star-like–astral, stellar, stellate

star-shaped–astroid, stellate

star-shaped figure – aster, estoile, etoile

starwort–aster

starry–astral

stars (Northern group of)– Draco

stars (pert. to)–astral, sideral, sidereal

starch–fecula, sago

starch (dry granulated) – sago

starch (kind of) – cassava, sago

starch (old word)–amyl

starch (potato)–farina

starch-like substance in plant roots–inuzin

starchy–mealy

stare–gaze

staring–agape, gazing

stark–bare, tense, unadorned

starling (crested)–pastor

starling (rose colored) – pastor

starling (thrush-like)–sali

start – begin, commence, dash, jerk, origin, originate, twitch

start (hunting)–dig

start aside–dodge

started aside suddenly–shied

started from bottom (anchor, etc., naut.)–atrip

starting line (race)–scratch

starting point (sermon)–text

startle – alarm, electrify,

fright, frighten, rouse, scare, shock, surprise
startling–rousing
starve–atrophy, famish
stash–end, stop
stashie–banter, clamor, frolic, quarrel
state – affirm, allege, assert, case, circumstance, condition, declare, express, mode, plight, predicament, situation, status
state (agitated) – perturbation
State (Centennial) – Colorado
state (disordered)–clutter
state (disturbed)–unrest
state (formally)–propound
state (French)–etat
state (hypnotic)–trance
state (ideal)–Utopia
state (mental)–morale
state (of a)–statal
State (Old Dominion)–Virginia
state (overcrowded)–congestion
state (pert. to)–statal
state (ultimate)–end
state affairs (pert. to)–pragmatic
state again–reassert
state as a fact–posit
state differently–reword
state formally – enounce, enunciate, pronounce, utter
state meaning of–define
state of affairs–case, pass
state of being–plethora
state of being a layman – laicality
state of being a peon–peonage
state of being a son–sonship
state of being a woman – muliebrity
state of being artless–naivete
state of being awakened – arousal
state of being behindhand–arrear
state of being beyond natural laws – supernaturalistic

state of being cast out – elimination
state of being complete – plenitude
state of being confined – internment
state of being drawn–traction
state of being free from error–inerrancy
state of being married twice illegally–bigamy
state of being married twice legally–digamy
state of being neither more nor less–equality
state of being passive–stolidity
state of being poison–toxicity
state of being satisfied–contentedness
state of being settled–sedentariness
state of being voiced–sonancy
state of being worse–pejority
state of being wrong – errancy
state of disorder–mess
state of dissension–scission
state of disuse–desuetude
state of ecstasy (rapture)–trance
state of excitement–nerves
state of feeling–mood
state of happiness–paradise
state of having grooves–striation
state of health–condition
state of hostility (pert. to)–feudal
state of insensibility–coma
state of mind–attitude, humor, mood, morale
state of mind (as of soldiers)–morale
state of needing attention – disrepair
state of unconsciousness – coma, faint
state office–secretariat
state on oath–depose
state policeman–trooper

state positively–allege, assert, asseverate, aver
state secret–arcanum, arcana (pl.)
state treasury–fisc
state with conviction–affirm, aver, avouch, declare
state without proof–allege
stately – august, grand, haughty, imperial, imposing, kingly, magnificent, majestic, queenly, regal, royal
statement – assertion, bill, expression, presentation, recitation
statement (abridged)–summary
statement (appended, of supplementary details) – schedule
statement (authoritative) – dictum, dicta (pl.)
statement (brief)–remark
statement (concise)–precis
statement (condensed) – abridgment, resume, summary
statement (contradictory, that is possibly true) – paradox
statement (defamatory) – libel
statement (dogmatic) – dictum, dicta (pl.)
statement (equivocal) – prevarication
statement (introductory) – foreword, preface, prelude, proem
statement (mathematical, which may be proved)–theorem
statement (prefatory) – prolog, prologue
statement (seemingly contradictory)–paradox
statement (self-contradictory)–paradox
statement (slanderous)–libel
statement assumed true – premise
statement of account (final)–audit
statement of belief – credo, creed

statement of particulars–bill

states (prosperous)–ups

states leagued by treaties – allies

states under control of stronger ones – protectorates

statesman–Ito

statesmen–politicians

station–depot, dignity, place, position, post, rank, seat

station (abbr.)–sta

station (caravan)–serai

station (ship's)–berth

station (supply)–depot

station (temporary surveying)–stadia

station (trading)–post

stationary–set

stationary mechanical part–stator

stationed (is)–lies

statue–bust, image

statue (gigantic)–Colossus

statue (heroic style) – Telamon

statue (holy) – icon, ikon, ikono

statue (large wooden)–gog

statue (small)–figurine

statue (that came to life)–Galatea

statue (undraped)–nude

statue (wooden, anc.)–gog

statue (wooden, in London Guild Hall)–Magog

statue base–plinth

statue by Pygmalion–Galatea

statue trunk–torso

statute – act, decree, edict, law, ordinance, regulation

statute (division of)–title

statute (volume of)–codex, codices (pl.)

stave – cudgel, lag, staff, stick

stave (bishop's pastoral) – baculus, baculi (pl.)

stave (cask)–lag

staves (Hindu, five-foot, bamboo)–lathis

stay–arrest, guy, leg, remain, rib

stay for–wait

stay lace (tag of)–aglet, aiglet

stead–lieu

steadfast – firm, stable, staunch, true

steadily industrious – sedulous

steadiness (physical)–nerve

steady–constant, equable, incessant, invariable, stable, steadfast, uniform

steady movement–constant

steak (pork)–griskin

steal – cly, embezzle, filch, nim, peculate, pilfer, purloin

steal (dial.)–nim

steal (slang)–snitch, swipe

steal along furtively–slink

steal cattle (slang)–rustle

stealer (cattle)–abigeus

stealthy – catty, feline, furtive, secret

steam–reek, smoke, vapor

steam pipe–riser

steamer (passenger)–liner

steamer cabin–texas

steaming–aboil

steamship routes (transocean)–lanes

steatite–talc

steed–horse

steed (winged)–Pegasus

steel – harden, inure, strengthen

steel armor plate–tace, tasse

steelmaking process–cementation

steep – abrupt, clifty, elevated, high, hilly, infuse, lofty, macerate, perpendicular, precipitous, ret, seethe, sharp, sheer, soak, tall

steep (to)–buck

steep descent (declivity) – scarp

steep flax–ret

steep in softening solution (leather)–bate

steeper–teapot

steeple–spire, tower

steer – con, control, direct, govern, guide, manage, pilot

steer (dial.)–stot

steer into wind–luf

steer wildly–yaw, yew (var.)

steering apparatus – helm, rudder, wheel

steers (one who)–helmsman, pilot

steeve – lade, pack, store, stuff

stein–mug

stellar–astral, starry

Steller's sea cow–rytina

stem – check, dam, prow, root, shaft, stalk, stanch

stem (bulblike)–corm

stem (central cylinder)–stele

stem (climbing)–bine

stem (enlarged underground)–tuber

stem (hop)–bine

stem (inner part of)–pith

stem (little twining)–tendril

stem (mushroom)–stipe

stem (pea, strawberry, etc.) –risp

stem (pithy jointed)–cane

stem (short bulblike)–drub

stem (short, thickened, underground)–tuber

stem (tall coarse grass)–reed

stem (twining)–bine

stem (underground thickened)–tuber

stem (zoology)–stipes

stem joint–node

stem of plant–bine

stem of twining plant–bine

stemless–sessile

stemless herb (evergreen)–galax

stench–odor, smell, stink

stenographer (of 60 B.C.)–Tiro

step–pace, rung, stair, stride, tread

step (clumsy)–staup

step (dance)–chasse, pas

step (for getting over fence or wall)–stile

step (ladder)–rung

step (proud gait)–strut

step (stately)–stalk

step-like arrangement of body of troops–echelon

steps (flight of outdoor) – perron

stereotyped–trite

sterile–arid, barren, unfruitful

stern–austere, dour, gloomy,
grim, hard, hardhearted,
harsh, rigorous, severe,
strict, sullen, unfeeling,
unkind

sternness–rigor

sternutative–errhine

sternward–abaft, aft, astern

stevedore–stower

Stevenson (R.L.) character–
Hyde

stew – imbue, olio, steep,
worry

steward–foreman, waiter

steward (farm)–granger

steward of king's household
–dapifer

Stewart sovereigns (last of)
–Anne

Stewart's badge (National
Scot emblem)–clauran

stewed fruit–compote

stick–adhere, cane, cleave,
cling, cohere, glue, gum,
paste, stab, stave

stick (jumping)–pogo

stick (magic)–wand

stick (music) – baton, bow,
clarinet, drumstick, fife,
flute

stick (polo)–mallet

stick (radiating fan)–brin

stick (slender)–wand

stick (straight)–rod

stick (tan vat stirring) –
pooler

stick (walking)–cane, staff,
stilt

stick fast–cleave

stick-like insects (genus of)
–emesa

stick together–cement, cohere

sticker – bur, burr, label,
paster

sticker for formality–tapist

sticking together–cohesive

stickler for perfect English–
purist

sticky–adhesive, viscid

sticky stuff (coll.)–goo

stiff–cadaver, corpse, hard,
harsh, proper, rigid, rigorous, severe, stark,

taut, tense, unbending

stiff (not)–limber, limp

stiff-necked – contumacious,
obstinate, stubborn

stiffened–starched

stiffness–rigidity, starchiness

stiffness (spasmodic muscular)–crick

stifle–choke, muffle, smother, strangle, suffocate,
throttle

stigma–blemish, blot, brand,
odium, slur, stain, taint

stigmatize–brand, denounce

still–allay, calm, check, even,
hushed, inactive, inert,
lull, mum, pacify, quiet,
restrain, silence, silent,
soothe, subdue, suppress,
tranquil, yet

still open to discussion–moot

still water (within coral island)–lagoon

stillness – calmness, silence,
taciturnity

stimulant–bracer, tonic

stimulant (aromatic)–sassafras

stimulant (heart)–digitalis,
thialdin, thialdine

stimulate–elate, encourage,
enliven, excite, filip, fillip,
goad, impel, incite, in-
spire, instigate, irritate,
jog, pep, quicken, rouse,
stir, urge, whet

stimulator–inciter

stimulus–motive, sting, spur

sting–bite, smart, tingle

sting of conscience – compunction

stingy – avaricious, close,
covetous, miserly, near,
niggardly, parsimonious,
selfish

stint–duty

stipend – allowance, ann,
compensation, pay, pen-
sion, wages

stipendiary–salaried

stipulation–agreement, contract, covenant, detail,
proviso

stipulation (conditional) –
proviso

stipule of leaflet–stipel

stir–ado, agitate, animate,
arouse, awaken, budge,
bustle, commotion, excite,
flurry, fuss, hubbub,
hurry, jail, move, penitentiary, pother, prison, provoke, roil, rouse

stir (great)–bustle

stir colors in calico printing
–teer

stir the fire–stoke

stir together (dial.)–stodge

stir up – agitate, arouse,
awake, excite, foment, incite, mix, roil, rouse

stir up (as colors)–teer

stirring – animating, bus-
tling, exciting, inspir-
ing, quickening, rousing,
stimulating

stirrup hood (Mexican saddle)–tapadera

stitch–hem, sew

stitch (seam)–purl

stitchbird–ihi

stitcher–seamer, sewer

stithy–anvil, forge, smithery,
smithy

stoat–ermine, weasel

stoat (in winter dress)–ermine

stob – gibbet, pierce, post,
stab, stake, stub

stocah–idler, menial

stock–capital, fund, hoard,
race, store, strain, supply

stock (middle American lin-
guistic)–Yuma

stock (preliminary)–scrip

stock abundantly–replenish

stock certificate (preliminary)–scrip

stock exchange–bourse

stock exchange patron –
buyer, seller, trader

stock of food–foray

stock of goods–line

stocking (French)–bas

stocky–stub

stoke–coal, fire, fuel

stoker–fireman, firer, greaser

stoker (glassworks)–teaser

stole (deacon's)–orarion

stole away–slunk

stolid – dull, impassive, passive

stomach (animal)–craw
stomach (beast's)–maw
stomach (bird's second)–gizzard
stomach (pert. to)–gastric
stomach (ruminant's) – rumen
stomach (ruminant's first)–rumen
stomach (ruminant's fourth)–abomasum, read, reed
stomach (ruminant's fourth, Scot.)–roddikin
stomach (ruminant's second)–reticulum
stomach (ruminant's third)–omasum
stomach ache (acute)–colic
stomach acidity–acor
stomata–pores
stone–diamond, gem, lapis, rock
stone (Biblical)–ezel
stone (broken, used in making roads)–metal
stone (carved)–cameo
stone (eagle)–etite
stone (famous) – Blarney, Cullinan, Excelsior, Kohinoor, Kohinur, Orloff, Sancy
stone (flat)–flag, slab
stone (fruit)–putamen, paip
stone (god of)–idol
stone (grave) – stela, stelae (pl.), stele, steles (pl.), marker, monument
stone (hewn, squared)–ashlar
stone (hollow, lined with crystals)–geode
stone (last of horizontal course)–closer
stone (mocha)–agate
stone (monumental)–menhir
stone (oil)–hone
stone (orange red)–sard
stone (precious)–beryl, diamond, gem, keas, opal, pearl, peridot, sapphire, topaz
stone (precious, mentioned in Bible)–ligure
stone (semiprecious)–onyx, sard

stone (sepulchral) – stela, stelae (pl.), stele, steles (pl.)
stone (sharpening) – hone, oil, whet
stone (squared)–ashlar
stone (thin, flat)–slab, slat
stone (undressed)–rubble
stone (upright, rough) – menhir
stone (which served as clue to Egyptian hieroglyphics)–Rosetta
stone (writing)–slate
Stone Age tool–celt
stone chip–spall
stonecrop (genus of)–sedum
stonecutter–jadder
stonecutter's disease–silicosis
stonecutter's wooden receptacle–sebilla
stone for hammering leather –lapstone
stone fragment–spall
stone fruit–drupe
stone heap (rounded)–cairn
stone of arch (top)–keystone
stone tool (anc.) – eolith, paleolith
stone used in making road (broken)–metal
stone weapon (old)–celt
stoneworker–mason
stones (heap of)–cairn
stones (single, shaped into pillars)–monoliths
stoning (to death)–lapidate
stony–inexorable, inflexible, relentless, rigid, uncompassionate, unyielding
stooge–foil
stool–seat, taboret
stool (three-legged)–tripod
stop – arrest, avast, block, cease, check, choke, close, delay, desist, detain, discontinue, end, halt, ho, preclude, prevent, quit, stay, stem
stop (momentarily)–pause
stop (naut.)–avast
stop (organ) – gemshorn, organ, posaune
stop (unintentionally)–stall
stop from fermenting–stum
stop seams in boat–calk

stop up–clog, plug
stop watch–timer
stop with clay–pug
stoppage (temporary)–delay
stoppage of debate–cloture
stopped unintentionally – stalled
stopped up–obturated
stopper–bung, cork, plug
storage battery plate–grid
storage bin–elevator, granary, loft, mow
storage place–attic, bin, cellar, closet, cupboard, elevator, granary, shed
storage place (military)–arsenal
storage room (small)–closet
store – accumulation, bin, cache, deposit, fund, mass, save, shop, stock, stow, supply
store (hidden)–cache
store fodder–ensile
store in silo–ensile
storehouse – barn, depot, etape
storehouse (military) – arsenal, depot
storehouse (public) – depot, etape
storehouse (rural) – barn, crib, mow, shed, silo
storekeeper – grocer, merchant
stores fodder–ensiles, silage
stories (following)–sequels
stories (presented in installment form)–serials
stork (adjutant)–marabou
stork (wood)–ibis
storklike–pelargic
storm – agitation, calamity, eruption, fume, gale, gust, rage, rave, tempest, upheaval
storm (gentle)–rain
storm (god of evil)–Zu
storm (occidental)–wester
storm (terrific) – cyclone, gale, hurricane, tempest, tornado
storm (violent)–tornado
storm (wind)–gale
storm at sea–gale
stormed–blew, raved

stormy–agitated, furious, inclement, riotous, tumultuous

story–anecdote, fable, floor, parable, tale, tier, yarn

story (adventure, coll.)–yarn

story (allegorical, teaching truth)–parable

story (exclusive)–beat, scoop

story (extravagant, absurd)–canard

story (Fr., short)–conte

story (heroic)–saga

story (love)–romance

story (made up)–fudge

story (medieval)–saga

story (part of)–serial

story (past)–legend

story (popular type)–mystery

story (type of short)–novella

storyteller–raconteur

storyteller (anc.)–Aesop

stout – bold, brave, bulky, burly, corpulent, courageous, fat, fleshy, forcible, hardy, obese, plump, powerful, resolute, rotund

stout and short – stocky, thickset

stove – etna, heater, plate, range

stove (alcohol)–etna

stove (small)–etna

stove part–firebox, griddle, oven

stow – cram, crowd, mass, pack, store

stow cargo – steeve, steve (var.)

stow in vessel's hold–steeve

Stowe (Harriet Beecher) child heroine–Eva

straddle–astride, bestride

straggle – meander, rove, stray, wander

straight–direct, erect, honest, straightforward

straight (coll.)–spang

straight batted ball–liner

straight course–beeline

straight edge–ruler

straight line (cutting curves)–secant

straight line (whose curves

continually approach but never meet)–asymptote

straighten–align, aline, level, plumb

straightener–aliner

straightforward–candid, direct, frank, honest

straightway–anon

strain – dash, filter, shade, stress, strive, tax, tension, touch, vein

strain (great)–tax

strain (laboriously)–tug

strain (sift, Scot.)–sye

strain by pulling or tugging –overheave

strain to high pitch–tense

strained–intense, taut, tense

strainer–filter, sieve

strainer (Eng. prov.)–sile

strainer (of cloth)–tamis

strainer (of wool)–tamis

strainer (woolen cloth)–tamis

strains (subject to severe)–taxes

strait – difficult, distressful, narrow, neck, need, rigorous, scrupulous, strict

strait (wide)–channel

strait between Labrador and Newfoundland–Belleisle

straiten–scant

Straits Settlements city – Georgetown, Malacca, Singapore

Straits Settlements coin – cent (cop.), dollars (s.), Straits dollar (s.)

Straits Settlements measure –chupak, gantang, para, parah, parrah, pau, pipe, tun

Straits Settlements native state–Johore, Negri Sembalan, Pahang, Perak, Selangor, Sungei Ujong

Straits Settlements weight–bedur, bhara, catty, chee, hoon, koyan, picul, saga, tahil

strand–beach, shore

strange – alien, curious, eccentric, eerie, erratic, extraordinary, novel, odd, outlandish, peculiar, pre-

ternatural, quaint, queer, rare, singular, uncommon, unusual

strange (comb. form)–xeno

strange (Scot.)–unco

strange language–lingo

strangely irregular – abnormal

stranger–alien, foreigner

stranger (Hebrew law, early)–ger

strangle – choke, garrote, stifle, suffocate

strap–laniard, lanyard, latigo, thong, whip

strap (African rawhide) – riem

strap (bridle, to fasten to bit) –rein

strap (for holding a shield on arm)–enarme

strap (leading)–leash

strap (oxhide)–reim

strap (short, of leather or silk)–jess

strap-shaped–ligular, lorate

strapped–belted

strass–paste

strata–layers

strata (later)–neozoic

stratagem – artifice, device, finesse, ruse, trick, wile

stratagem (sudden, unexpected)–coup

strategy – artifice, intrigue, maneuver

stratum–bed, layer

stratum (thin)–seam

straw (half rotten)–mulch

straw (plaited hatmaking)–sennit

straw (used in making hats) –sabutan

straw color–flaxen

stray–err, gad, range, rove, swerve, wander

straying from right–aberrant

streak–strain, vein

streak (different colored) – vein

streak (narrow)–stria, striae (pl.)

streak (regular)–stripe

streaked – brindle, brindled, striped

stream–burn, current, flow, river, rivulet, run, runnel

stream (diminutive)–brook, race, rillet, rivulet, run, streamlet

stream (dry bed)–arroyo

stream (small)–brook, rill, rillet, runlet

stream (South African underground)–aar

stream (violent)–torrent

streamer (small)–guidon

streamlet–brook, rill, rillet, rivulet, runlet

streamline curve of minimum resistance – lissoneoid

street – avenue, boulevard, road, roadway, thoroughfare

street (broad)–avenue, boulevard, highway

street (narrow, short)–alley

street arab (Fr.)–gamin

street roister (Queen Anne's reign)–mun

street urchin–arab, gamin

strength–brawn, endurance, energy, firmness, lustiness, might, potency, power, robustness, stamina, sthenia, stoutness, vigor

strength (regain)–rally

strength of a solution–titer

strengthen–brace, confirm, deepen, encourage, fortify, invigorate, nerve, prop, reinforce, roborate, toughen

strengthening–roborant

strenuous–energetic, severe, vigorous

strepent–loud, noisy

streperous–boisterous, harsh, loud, noisily, noisy, turbulent

stress – accent, labor, pressure, strain

stress (mechanical)–erossure

stress (metrical)–ictus

stress (voice)–accent, arsis

stretch – distend, enlarge, exaggerate, expand, extend, hang

stretch injuriously–sprain

stretch the neck–crane

stretched out–craned, porrect

stretched tight–taut, tense

stretched while drying (as cloth)–tentered

stretcher litter, racker

strew – disseminate, scatter, spread

strewing (art)–seme

strewing (heraldry)–seme

strewn (heraldry)–seme

strewn with scattered articles–littered

stria–channel, fillet, furrow, groove, hollow, line, stripe

stricken–smitten, wounded

strickle–pattern, template

strict–ascetic, austere, exact, forbidding, hard, harsh, inexorable, inflexible, puritanic, relentless, rigid, rigorous, scrupulous, severe, stern, straitlaced, stringent, uncompromising

strict (not)–lax

strict disciplinarian – martinet

strict discipline–regimentation

strictest–severest

strictly true (anything)–fact

strictness–rigor

strictness in conforming to law–legalism

stride – advance, bestride, progress, stalk, step, straddle, walk

strident–grating, shrill

strife – altercation, contest, quarrel, struggle

strife (civil)–stasis

strife (inveterate)–feud

strife about mere words – logomachy

strike–bump, hit, impinge, pat, rap, slap, smite, swat

strike (dial.)–lam

strike (Scot.)–strick

strike a baseball (without swinging a bat)–bunt

strike a mean–average

strike and rebound–carom, carrom (var.)

strike heavily–slog

strike heavily (slang)–bash, lam, ram, slug

strike out–cancel, dele, delete, elide, erase, fan

strike violently–ram

strike with fist–plug

strike with head–butt

strike with violence–slam

strikebreaker–scab

striker – assistant, helper, smiter

striking–arresting, noticeable, remarkable, salient, surprising

striking effect–eclat

string–cord, twine

string (fastening) – lacet, lachet

string (rawhide)–snare

string course–guidon

string instrument – banjo, fiddle, guitar, harp, lute, lyre, mandolin, piano, uke, ukulele, viola, violin, zither

string instrument (old) – psaltery

string of beads – necklace, rosary

stringed instrument bridge–magas

stringent–restrictive, rigid, ropy, severe, strict, tense

stringiness–ropiness

strings–cords, twines

stringy–fibrous, filamentous, gluey, ropy, sinewy, viscid

strip–bare, belt, denude, deprive, dismantle, dispossess, divest, peel, shred, skin, uncloak, uncover, unrig

strip (inside, along ship's gunwale)–inwale

strip (long for drawing curves)–spline

strip (metal, to prevent turning)–spline

strip (metal type separating)–lead

strip (narrow)–reeve, tape

strip (narrow wood)–lath, slat, stave

strip (raised)–ridge

strip (to prevent slipping)–cleat

strip (wooden)–lath, slat

strip (wooden, separating printing)–reglet

strip blubber from whale–flense

strip of leather – latigo, thong, welt

strip off equipment–dismantle

strip off skin–flay

strip off surface–flay

strip on boat (lengthwise)–gunwale

strip tease dancer–ecdysiast

strips (grooved lead for fastening stained glass)–cames

strips (lead for holding stained glass)–cames

strips of wood (curved) – staves

stripe – bar, chevron, sort, streak, strip, type, weal, welt

stripe (encircling)–zone

striped–banded, barred, lineate, streaked

striped longitudinally–vittate

stripling–boy, lad, youth

stripped of property by trickery – buncoed, bunkoed, fleeced

strive–aim, contend, endeavor, labor, strain, struggle, toil, try, tug

strive after–seek

strive for–aim

strive to equal or excel – emulate, rival, strain

strive to overtake–ensue

strive with–vie

strobile (carpellate)–cone

strobile (staminate)–cone

strobilophyta–cone

strockle–shovel

stroil – capability, dexterity, power

stroke – beat, blow, caress, fondle, pat, pet, rub, shot, trait

stroke (measured, regular)–pulse

stroke (short, quick)–flip

stroke (sudden)–coup

stroke of letter (cross) – ceriph, serif

stroke of work--chare

stroll–ramble, range, roam, saunter, stray, wander

strolled (here and there) – rambled

stroller – beggar, peddler, saunterer, tramp, vagrant

strong – able, firm, hardy, lusty, muscular, robust, sinewy, sound, stalwart, stout, sturdy, vigorous, wiry

strong (Hebrew)–elon

strong (very) – intense, potent

strong and healthy–robust

strong and vibrant–resonant

strongbox–chest, safe, vault

strong cloth–scrim

stronghold – citadel, fort, hold, keep

strong man (Biblical) – Sampson, Samson

strong man (legendary) – Atlas

strong point (one's)–forte

strong upward movement–surge

strongly–stably

strove desperately–agonized

strow – confusion, disturbance, strife, turmoil

stroygood–spendthrift, wastrel

strub–despoil, rob, strip

strubbly–unkempt, untidy

struck–smitten, smote

struck (was)–smitten

struck an attitude–posed

struck out – deled, deleted, elided, erased, fanned

struck with small missiles–pelted

struck with sudden fear – alarmed

structural member (curved) –arch

structural quality–texture

structure–building, composition, constitution, edifice, frame, make-up

structure (abnormal) – malformation

structure (calcareous)–coral

structure (conical)–pyramid

structure (crown-like)–corona

structure (filamentous)–hair

structure (floating)–raft

structure (high)–tower

structure (human)–physique

structure (light, open)–kiosk

structure (light, ornamental) kiosk

structure (monumental) – pylon

structure (Oriental, tower-like)–pagoda

structure (original)–isogen

structure (raised)–altar, dais, platform, stage

structure (sheltering)–cot

structure (supporting)–pier

structure (tent-like)–tabernacle

structure on roof (small)–cupola, dormer

structure over obstacles and depressions–bridge

structure projecting into water–jettee, jetty, jiti

struggle – contend, contention, contest, cope, difficulty, effort, endeavor, labor, strife, strike, strive, tug, vie, wade, wrestle

struggle (confused)–scuffle

struggle (eager, unceremonious)–scramble

struggle (physical)–scuffle, tussle

struggle (playful)–tussle

struggle (spiritual)–Peniel

struggled–striven

struggles–throes

strumpet – belie, debauch, harlot, prostitute, slander

strumpet (worn out)–harridan

strung–beaded

strung (highly)–nervous

stub–coupon, squat, stocky, stump, thickset

stubborn – coarse, determined, fixed, hardy, headstrong, mulish, obstinate, perverse, pigheaded, rough, rude, set, starkish, sturdy, tough, unyielding

stuck–cohered
stud–boss
stud for shoe sole–hobnail
stud with jewels–engem
stud with radiating bodies–enstar
student – disciple, learner, pupil, scholar
student (college) – senior, junior, soph, sophomore, freshman
student (French)–eleve
student (girl, co-educational)–coed
student of Arabic literature–Arabist
student of birds–ornithologist
student of English school–Etonian
student of proverbs–paroemiologist
student of relics–archaeologist
student of reptiles–herpetologist
student of spiders–arachnologist
students (group of advanced)–seminar
students (group of, studying together)–class
student's hall–burse
studied–designed, planned, pored, premeditated, reasoned
studied hard (coll.)–boned
studies–pores, reads
studies (chosen by students)–electives
studio–atelier
studious–scholarly
study – analyse, analyze, bone, con, den, grind, peruse, pore, scan
study (advanced course of)–seminar
study (musical)–etude
study (optional college curriculum)–elective
study closely–examine
study course–seminar
study hard–bone
study of bird's eggs–oology
study of human generations–anthropogenesis

study of insect's habits – entomology
study of population–larithmics
study of punishment for crime–penology
study of sacred edifices – naology
study of sacred images–iconology
study of words–etymology
stuff–cram, element, fabric, material, matter, pad, principle, ram, substance, wad
stuff (var.)–steve
stuff (sticky, coll.)–goo
stuff full (Eng. dial.)–stodge
stuffing (prepared with)–marinate
stuggy–short, stodgy, sturdy, thickset
stulm–adit, entrance
stumble – blunder, chance, falter, happen, lurch, trip
stump–stab, stub
stump (projecting)–snag
stun – astound, benumb, daze, deaden, stupefy
stun (momentarily)–bowl
stung–smarted
stunted – blunted, checked, curtailed, dwarfed, undersized
stupa (lamaism)–chorten
stupefied – doped, drugged, shocked, sotted, stunned
stupefy – bedaze, besot, bewilder, confuse, daze, dope, drug, dull, muddle, numb, stun
stupefying (muddling)–bemusing
stupid–asinine, blunt, brainless, clod, crass, dense, doltish, dumb, inane, oafish, obtuse, simple, stolid, witless
stupid (grossly)–asinine
stupidity–crassness
stupidity (excessive) – idiotism
stupor–coma, lethargy, sopor
sturdy–determined, hardy, lusty, stable, stalwart,

steady, stout, strong, vigorous
sturdy and stout–burly
sturgeon (small)–sterlet
sturgeon roe–caviar
sturt – annoy, disturbance, startle, stir, strife, trouble, vex
stutter–stammer
sty–enclosure, ladder, pen, stair, steps, stile
style–alamode, diction, fashion, mode, phrase, vogue
style (artistic)–gusto
style (emphasizing at expense of thought)–rhetorical
style of architecture–Doric, Ionic
style of dress (coll.)–get-up
style of painting–genre
style of penmanship–hand
style of performance–execution
styled–named, termed
stylet–poniard, stiletto
stylet (surgical)–trocar
stylish–alamode, chic, jaunty, modish, nifty, smart
stylish (coll.)–tony
styptic–alum
suant – agreeable, demure, equable, even, grave, placid, quiet, regular, smooth, steady
suave–bland, fulsome, mannered, oily, smug, unctuous, urbane
subdivide–mince
subdivision of rocks–range
subdue–allay, conquer, cow, disarm, overpower, quell, repress, sober, subjugate, suppress, surmount, tame
subdue (arch.)–amate
subdue (ignominiously) – squelch
subdued – conquered, soft, subjugated
subgroup of mineral (pert. to)–mitic
subject–inferior, subjugate, submit, subordinate, text, theme, topic, vassal
subject of discourse–theme

subject of disease–case, patient
subject of lawsuit–res
subject of verb–noun
subject to abuse–revile
subject to argument–moot
subject to authority–master
subject to change–mutable
subject to control–rulable
subject to dislike–aversion
subject to fits of depression–moody
subject to great strain–tax
subject to ill treatment–misuse
subject to mistakes–erratic
subject to some action–treat
subject to taxation–rateable
subjoin–add, affix, attach
subjugation–conquest
sublime–exalted, expletive, grand, lofty, majestic, noble
sublimity – grandeur, magnificence, majesty
submarine–boat, sub, submersible
submarine (eye of) – periscope
submerge–sink
submerge one's self–plunge
submission–compliance, deference, surrender
submission (passive) – non-resistance
submission to arbitrament of destiny–fatalism
submissive–compliant, dutiful, humble, meek, obedient, resigned
submissive to control–obedient
submissive to wife–uxorious
submissively–tamely
submit–bow, defer, moderate, obey, soften, stoop, succumb, surrender, temper, yield
submit an animal to medical treatment–vet
submit for consideration – remit
submultiplies–parts
subordinate – assistant, collateral, inferior, secondary, subservient

subordinate (obs.)–servient
subordinate activity–parergon
subordinate adjunct – appendage
subordinate officer–exon
subordinately–secondarily
subsequent–ensuing, following, later
subsequent to birth – postnatal
subsequently–later
subside–abate, bate, ebb, fall, lull, relapse, sink
subsidiary – auxiliary, supplementary, tributary
subsist–be, live
subsoil–sole
subsoil (hard)–pan
subsoil plow–mole
substance – actuality, affluence, aliment, essence, gist, hardness, import, material, matter, meaning, meat, solidness, sum, wealth
substance (adhering) – cement, glue, paste
substance (aeriform)–gas
substance (amber colored)–resin, rosin
substance (amorphous)–resin, rosin
substance (amorphous in rocks)–ferrite
substance (antitoxic)–serum
substance (apples crushed by grinding)–pomace
substance (aromatic) – balsam
substance (basic derived from ammonia) – amin, amine
substance (bitter, crystalline)–amarine
substance (bitter, crystalline in aloes)–aloin
substance (bitter resinous)–aloes
substance (bitter, white) – linin
substance (brittle, transparent)–glass
substance (brown, containing sulphur)–hepar

substance (capable of absorbing)–fomes
substance (capable of expansion)–dilatants
substance (chemical)–iridol, linin
substance (chemical, reaction securing)–reagent
substance (cleansing)–clarifiant
substance (containing sulphur)–hepar
substance (corrosive) – caustic
substance (derived from Ceylon moss)–agar, agar-agar
substance (derived from fat and oil)–adipic
substance (dissolved)–solute
substance (electrical)–ion
substance (elementary) – metal
substance (extracted from ipecac root)–emitine
substance (fatty from sheep wool)–suint
substance (ferment)–activator
substance (finely powdered)–flour
substance (flat-like)–lipoid
substance (flocculent)–wool
substance (food)–protein
substance (fruit jellying) – pectin
substance (fusible)–metal
substance (gaseous)–argon
substance (gelatinous)–agar
substance (greasy, from sheep wool)–suint
substance (hard)–adamant
substance (hard animal) – bone
substance (hard, creamy, white)–ivory
substance (in cubeb)–cubebin
substance (inflammable) – tinder
substance (inflammable mineral)–bitumen
substance (inorganic)–mineral
substance (made from tar)–cresol

substance (main)–gist
substance (milk curdling) – rennet
substance (neutralizing acid)–alkali
substance (nonsolid) fluid
substance (obtained from parsley)–apiin
substance (oily)–lanolin
substance (perfume from whales)–ambergris
substance (poisonous) – arsenic
substance (powdered)–flour
substance (protoplasmic) – gel
substance (related to cellulose)–lignin
substance (resinous) – copal, gum, lac
substance (resinous, purified)–shellac
substance (secreted by a scale insect)–lac
substance (simple)–element
substance (soap making) – lye
substance (sour)–acid, vinegar
substance (stabilizing)–ballast
substance (starch-like in plant roots)–inulin
substance (steadying) – ballast
substance (sticky) – glue, gum, paste
substance (unctuous)–oil
substance (used in making perfume)–civet
substance (used in pigment) sienna
substance (used in tanning) –sumac
substance (used to curdle milk)–rennet
substance (used to detect other substance)–reagent
substance (used to make sole leather heavy)–splate
substance (used to nurture bacteria)–agar
substance (very light)–cork
substance (viscous)–grease
substance (wax)–cerin
substance (waxy)–paraffin

substance (waxy, basis of cork)–suberin
substance (which dissolves other substance) – resolvent
substance (white, crystalline)–alanine, elaterin
substance (white nerve) – alba
substance (white, starchlike, tasteless)–inulin
substance (wood ash) – potash
substance (wood, distilled)–tar
substance (zymogen activating)–kinase
substance obtained from animal tissue (transparent)–gelatine
substance used in medicine as a hypnotic–ural
substance used to give weight to sole leather – splate
substantial – actual, bodily, corporeal, solid, stable, sturdy, tangible
substantive–noun, pronoun; firm, sound
substitute – deputy, exchange, proxy, surrogate, vicar
substitute (German for)–ersatz
substitute (poor)–apology
substitute (sugar)–honey
substitute for Lamb's name–Elia
substitute in office – deputy, vicar, vicegerent
substitutes–alternates, commutes, replaces, reserves
substructure – foundation, podium
subterfuge – artifice, blind, evasion, prevarication, refuge, ruse
subtile – delicate, elusive, rarefied, tenuous, wily
subtle–acute, aura, sly
subtle (more)–nice
subtle invisible emanation–aura
subtle sarcasm–irony
subtlety–delicacy, slyness

subtracting–deducting
suburb–environ
subvert – overthrow, overturn, ruin, uproot, upset
subvert (by digging)–sap
subway–tube, tunnel, underground
succade–confection, preserve
succeed–achieve, ensue, follow, prosper, replace
succeeding–following, next
success – elate, fortune, go, hit, luck, outcome, prosperity
success (popular)–hit
successful – flourishing, fortunate, lucky, prosperous, thriving
succession–sequence, series
succession of chords – cadence
succession of kings of one family–dynasty
succession of related things–series
succession of sounds (rhythmic)–music
succession of things–series
successive–consecutive, serial
successively–arow
successor–follower, heir
successor (law)–heres
successor of clan chieftains–tanist
successor of deceased person (universal law)–heres
succin–amber
succinct – brief, compendious, compressed, concise, curt, hasty, laconic, short, summary, terse
succor (succour)–aid, assistance, comfort, deliver, help, relief, relieve, rescue, sustain
succor (carried by Alpine dogs)–brandy
succulent–juicy, lush, pappy, tasty, tender, uva
succulent plant–aloe, cactus
succumb–die, submit, yield
such (Scot.)–sic
such (var.)–sic
Sudan antelope–oterop
Sudan gazelle–dama
Sudan language–Ga

Sudan millet beer–dolo
Sudan Negro–Hausa
Sudan people–Dazas
Sudan stockade (improvised)–zereba
Sudanese–Fulah
sudden–abrupt, hasty, headlong, impetuous, precipitate, speedy, swift, unexpected
sudden and brilliant–meteoric
sudden fear–consternation
sudden issuing of troops from besieged place for an attack–sortie
sudden shock–jolt
sudden stroke–coup
sudden thrust–jab, lunge
suddenly – precipitately, presto
sudor – exudation, perspiration, sweat
Sudra caste (India, low) – mal
Sudra caste member (India) –palli
sue – beg, entreat, petition, plea, plead, request, woo
suet–tallow
Suez Canal builder–Lesseps
suffer – admit, allow, bear, dree, endure, let, permit, submit, tolerate, undergo
suffer (Scot.)–dree
suffer distress–gripe
suffer from heat–swelter
suffer great affliction–groan
suffer remorse–rue
suffer ruin–wreck
sufferance – endurance, misery, pain, permission
sufferer–victim
sufferer (paralysis)–paretic
sufferer (reliever of)–Samaritan
suffering–pain
suffering (extreme)–agony
suffering (long)–patient
suffice–answer, do, serve
sufficiency–competency, fill
sufficient–adequate, ample, due, enough, good, plenty, responsible, valid
sufficient (be)–do

sufficient (poetic)–enow
sufficiently – capable, duly, qualified
suffix (chemical)–ene
suffix for or denoting—
  abundance–ose
  act–ure
  adherent–ite
  adjective–ent, ial, ian, ic, il, ile, ive
  agent–ator
  alcohol–ol
  and ten–teen
  being–ure
  causing–fic
  chemical – ac, ane, idin, ile, ine, ion, ol, ole, ose
  condition–ile
  derivative nouns–ac
  diminutive – cle, el, ette, ole, ule
  disease–itis
  doer–ator
  enzyme–ase
  follower–ite
  forming adjectives from verbs–ent
  full of–ose
  fullness–ose
  hydrocarbons–ene
  inhabitant of–ese, ite
  jurisdiction–ric
  law–ee
  like–ar, ic
  making–fic
  noun–ac, ent, ery, et, ia, ial, ic, ier, orium
  noun (of diminutive force)–ole
  numeral forming–eth
  office–ate
  oil–ol
  old French–ison
  one of a party–ite
  one who does–ist
  one who does professionally–ier
  ordinal numbers–eth, th
  participal–ing
  pertaining to–ac, ar, ic
  possession–ose
  profession–eer
  quality–ness
  resident of–ite
  superlative–est
superlative degree–est

  those who do professionally–iers
  three parts–tri
  times ten–ty
  used in forming certain numerals–eth
  vocation–ier
suffocate–asphyxiate, choke, extinguish, smother, stifle
suffrage – franchise, petition, prayer, supplication, voice, vote
sufisin (relating to)–sufistic
sugar–bribe, doctor, sweeten
sugar (beet)–saccharose
sugar (burnt)–caramel
sugar (cane)–saccharose, sucrose
sugar (crude)–gur, piloncillo
sugar (group of)–biose, disaccharide
sugar (malt)–maltose
sugar (simple)–glucid, glucide, ketose, monosaccharide, ose
sugar (without)–sec
sugar cane disease–sereh
sugar cane pulp–bagasse
sugar cane refuse (dry)–bagasse
sugar cane stalk (shoot) – ratoon
sugar containing three molecules of carbon–triose
sugar preparation (in candy) –fondant
sugar sand–niter
sugar substitute–honey
sugar-yielding vegetable – beet
sugarless–sec
suggest–allude, hint, imply, insinuate, inspire, move, prompt, propose
suggest in addition to primary meeting–connotes
suggest indirectly–hint
suggestion – hint, idea, intimation, proposal, soupçon, trace
suggestion (indirect)–hint
suidae–hogs, swine
suit – accommodate, answer, attire, become, befit, cards, clothes, comport,

costume, dress, fit, habit, match, petition, prayer, retinue, serve, tally, wooing
suit (starter of)–relator
suit (to)–become, fit
suit at law–litigation
suit for property–trover
suitability–propriety
suitable – accordant, agreeable, apposite, appropriate, apt, compatible, competent, congruent, congruous, consistent, consonant, correspondent, due, fit, meet, pat
suitable (exactly)–pat
suitable (not)–inept
suitable place–niche
suitably proportioned–commensurable
suite (member of)–attache
suite of attendants–retinue
suited–adapted
suited to song–lyric
suitor–wooer
sulk–mope, pet, pout
sullen – austere, churlish, cross, crusty, cynical, dour, fretful, gloomy, glum, gruff, harsh, moody, morose, peevish, petulant, pouty, sour, spiteful, sulky, surly
sully – bespatter, blemish, contaminate, corrupt, defile, disdain, foul, pollute, smear, smirch, stain, taint
sully (deeply)–grime
sulpharsenate of copper–enargite
sulphate (aluminum)–alum
sulphate (barium)–barite
sulphate (hydrous of iron, zinc and manganese)–ilesite
sulphate (magnesium) – loweite
sulphate (potassium)–alum
sulphide (calcium)–hepar
sulphides (crude mixture) – mattes
sulphur–brimstone
sulphur alloy (black metallic)–niello
Sultan's daughter–Sultana

Sultan's decree–irade
Sultan's mother–Sultana
Sultan's sister–Sultana
Sultan's wife–Sultana
sultry–hot, humid, sweltering, torrid
sum – add, aggregate, amount, loot, number, quantity, total, whole
sum (unexpended)–savings
sum of particulars – aggregate
sum total–entirety
sum up–perorate, tot
Sumatra animal–tana
Sumatra ape–orang
Sumatra city – Achin, Bencoolen, Bonkulin, Indrapoor, Jambi, Padang, Palembang
Sumatra measure–paal
Sumatra raft (bamboo, large)–rakit
Sumatra ramie fiber–caloee
Sumatra river – Indragiri, Jambi, Musi, Rokan
Sumatra squirrel shrew – tana
Sumatra wildcat–balu
sumless – incalculable, inestimable, uncountable
summaries – recapitulations, resumes
summarize–epitomize, precis
summary–abridgement, abstract, breviate, brief, compendious, compendium, digest, epitome, medulla, precis, resume, short, succinct
summary (concise)–precis
summary of book (publisher's)–blurb
summary of knowledge–encyclopaedia
summary of principles – creed
summary of speech–notes
summer (French)–ete
summer (of the)–estival
summer (pert. to)–estival
summer house (elevated) – belvedere
summer recreational resort–camp

summer tendency–lethargy
summing up (recapitulating)–counting
summit–apex, crest, crown, height, peak, pinnacle, top
summit (lofty, pointed) – pinnacle
summon–call, cite, demand, page
summon by name–page
summon forth–evoke
summon in public place – page
summon together–muster
summon up–rally
sun–sol, star
sun (comb. form)–helio
sun (part of)–corona
sun (pert. to)–solar
sun (poetic name)–daystar
sun (the)–Phoebus
sun-baked brick–adobe
sunburnt–adust
sun clock–sundial
sun crosses equator (time of) –equinox
sundial arm–gnomon
sundial part–gnomon
sundial pin–gnomon
sundial plate (vertical)–gnomon
sun disk–aten, aton
sun disk (myth.)–aton
sundown–eve
sun god – Apollo, Baal, Ra, Tem
sun god (Cymric) – Lleu, Llew
sun path (among the stars)–ecliptic
sun path (around celestial sphere)–ecliptic
sun ring–corona
sun satellites–planets
sunset (poetic)–een
sunshade–parasol, visor, vizor
sunspot – macula, maculae (pl.)
sunspot (small)–facula, faculae (pl.)
Sunda Isles (one of)–Bali
sundang–bolo, knife
sunder–dissever, divide, divorce, rend, sever

sundry – divers, frequent, manifold, multifarious, multiplied, numerous, several, various

sung by choir–choral

sunken fence – aha, haha, hawhaw

sup–dine, eat

supawn – hasty pudding, mush

superabundance – exuberance, flood, plethora

superabundant – excessive, exuberant, lavish, luxuriant, overflowing, profuse, rank

superannuate–retire

superb–elegant, grand, lordly, majestic, noble, rich, stately, sumptuous

supercilious–arbitrary, arrogant, contemptuous, hypercritical, overbearing, proud

supercilious person–snob

superfamily (comprising true bees)–apina

superficial–cursory, external, glib, shallow, slight, surface

superficial (not)–thorough

superficial knowledge–smatter

superfluity – excess, overset, redundancy, superabundance

superfluous – redundant, needless, spare, useless

superintend–oversee

superintendent (museum) – curator

superior – above, excellent, over, preeminent, ranking, senior, upper

superior to all others–paramount

superiority (excess)–preponderance

superiority (in rank)–priority, seniority

superlative–best

superlative (absolute) – elative

supermarine–seaplane

supernatural–magic, miraculous, preternatural

supernatural event–miracle

superscribe–address, direct

supersede–overide, replace

superstition (degraded form)–voodoo

superstitious (profoundly)– fetishistic

supervene–happen

supervise – inspect, oversee, perusal, peruse, read, revise, superintend

supine – abject, careless, drowsy, inattentive, indolent, listless, servile, sluggish, thoughtless

supplant–displace, eradicate, extirpate, overthrow, remove, replace, supersede, uproot

supple – agile, compliant, flexible, lissom, lissome, lithe, nimble, pliant, yielding

supple twig–withe

supplement–add

supplicate – appeal, beg, beseech, crave, entreat, implore, importune, petition, plead, pray, solicit

supplication – craving, entreaty, petition, plea, prayer, rogative, solicitation

supplication (solemn form)– litany

supplied with medicine – dosed, prescribed

supplies (hidden)–hoards

supplies (military) – ordnance

supplies with resolution – nerves

supply – administer, cater, contribute, give, provide, stock, store, yield

supply (dial.)–plenish

supply (extra)–reserve, reservoir

supply (hidden) – cache, hoard

supply equivalent for – replace

supply food–cater

supply of horses (fresh)–relay

supply provisions–purvey

supply station–depot

supply with carbon dioxide –aerate

supply with fuel–stoke

supply with funds–endow

supplying food–alimental

support – abet, aid, arm, back, bolster, brace, cleat, fulcrum, leg, limb, peg, pillar, prop, reinforce, rib, second, shore, stay, strut, underlie

support (coffin)–bier

support (curved)–rib

support (millstone)–rynd

support (movable)–trestle

support (poor)–reed

support (resilient)–spring

support (Scot.)–stell

support (three-legged) – easel, tripod, trivet

support (trestle tree)–bibb

support (upper millstone)– rynd

support (upright)–stanchion

support (upright rail) – baluster

support (wedge-shaped) – cleat

support at side of cannon barrel–trunnion

support for a glass–coaster

support with firmness–brace

supported–based

supported by strong evidence–probable

supporters – allies, bracers, garters, suspenders

supporters (of party in power)–ministerialists

supporting–auxiliary

supporting bar–fid

supporting rod–rib

supporting timber–spile

suppose – assume, conclude, conjecture, consider, deem, judge, opine, presume, repute

suppose (arch.)–trow, ween, wis

suppose (poetic)–wis

supposed emanation–aura

supposed to be–reputed

supposedly wise–sapient

suppositions – conjectures, hypotheses, ifs, theories

suppress – crush, kill, oppress, overpower, quash, quell, repress, smother, stifle

suppress in pronouncing – elide

suppression of sound in pronouncing–elision

suprarenal–adrenal

suprarenal gland–paranephros

supremacy–mastery

supreme–foremost, greatest, paramount, peerless, preeminent

supreme being – allah, creator, monad

Supreme Court Justice (early)–Iredell

Supreme Court Justice (1888)–Lamar

supreme ruler–autocrat

surcease – cessation, end, relief, respite, stop

surd mutes (one of)–Tenuis

sure – assured, certain, confident, incontestable, infallible, positive

sure (dial.)–sho

sure (not)–uncertain

sure (to be)–indeed

surety – backer, bail, engager, sponsor

surf roar–rote

surf sound upon shore–rote

surface – exterior, face, outside, pave

surface (artificial)–rink

surface (downy)–nap

surface (flat)–area

surface (geometrical) – nappe, tore

surface (outer)–periphery

surface (plane)–area

surface (small)–facet

surface (small plane)–facet

surface a street–pave

surface between triglyph channels–meros

surface margin–side

surface of anything (pert. to)–facial

surface of water–ryme

surfaces described by a conic section–tores

surfeit – cloy, sate, satiate, satisfy

surfeited–complete, overate, replete

surfeited with pleasure – blase

surge – billow, swell, tide, wave

surge of emotion–thrill

surgeon's instrument – lancet, probe, trepan, tweezer

surgeon's instrument case – tweezer

surgeon's saw – trapan, trepan, trephine

surgeon's stylet–trocar

surgery (cut off)–resect

surgical compress–stupe

surgical counterirritant – seton

surgical crown saw–trepan

surgical hooks (sharp-pointed)–tenacula

surgical instrument – lancet, levator, scalpel, trepan, trocar

surgical instrument (ligation)–ligator

surgical knife–scalpel

surgical lancet–fleam

surgical machine–scala

surgical probe–stylet

surgical saw – trepan, trephine

surgical stylet–trocar

surgical thread–seton

surgical treatment – operation

Surinam measure–ketting

Surinam toad–pipa, pipal

surly–glum, grum, grumpy, morose

surmise–assumption, conjecture, guess, imagine, presume, supposition, suspicion

surmount – conquer, overcome, pass, subdue, top, transcend

surmounted (as a crisis) – tided

surmounting–atop

surmounts–tides

surname–agnomen, appellation, cognomen

surnames indicating relation to father–patronymics

surpass–better, cap, exceed, excel, outdo, outreach, outstrip, outvie, top

surpass (obs.)–cote

surpass in equitation – outride

surpass in status–outrank

surpassed–outsoared

surpassing–transcendent

surpassing excellence–inimitability

surplice (short)–cotta

surplus–excess, overplus, redundancy, reserve, rest

surprise – amaze, amazement, astonish, astound, bewilder, confound, dumfound, overwhelm, perplex, shock, startle, wonder

surprising–amazing, astonishing, extraordinary, striking, unexpected

surrender–cede, cession, dedition, relinquish, remittal, yield

surrender by deed–remise

surrender of property – divestiture

surround–beset, encircle, enclose, environ, gird, hem, incase, invest

surround with water–isle

surrounded–amid, bounded, encircled, encompassed, flooded

surrounding – about, enveloping, hemming, setting

surrounding by eye – perioptic

surrounding by the pole – circumpolar

survey–delineate, determine, examination, examine, reconnaissance, regard, review, scan, scrutinize, study

survey (critical)–review

survey (general)–review

survey (military preliminary)–reconnoiter

survey carefully–traverse

surveying (process of) – triangulation

surveying instrument–transit

surveying instrument (part of)–alidad, alidada, alidade

surveyor (land)–arpenteur

surveyor (mine)–dialer

surveyor's helper – lineman, poleman

surveyor's rod carrier – rodman

survival–relic

survival of past age–relic

survivor–relict

susceptibility – affectibility, emotion, feeling, sense, sentimentality

susceptible – easy, impressionable, receptive, responsive, sensible, sensitive, softhearted, tenderhearted

suslik–sisel, spermophile

suspect–disbelieve, discredit, distrust, doubt, fancy, guess, mistrust

suspend – dangle, debar, expel, hang, intermit, oust, pensile, remit

suspended–debarred, hung, inactive, inoperative, latent, pendent

suspenders – galluses, supporters

suspenders (Eng.)–braces

suspense–anxiety, apprehension, uncertainty

suspension – delay, failure, intermission, interruption, stop

suspension (temporary) – abeyant

suspicion – askance, diffidence, distrust, doubt, jealousy, mistrust, soupçon

suspicion (slang) – leary, leery

Sussex land measure–wist

Sussex tract of land (arable) –laine

sustain – bear, buoy, carry, continue, feed, maintain, prolong, prop, uphold

sustenance – aliment, food, living, meat, nourishment, provisions, subsistence, viands

suture–seam

svelte–lissom, lissome, lithe, slender, slim

swab–lout, lubber, mop

swabbing device – mop, sponge

swack – beat, strike, thrash, whack

swaddle with bandages – swathe

swag–boodle, booty, bundle, plunder, sag, sink, spoils

swagger – boast, brag, dashing, domineer, prance, roister, strut, stylish, swell, ultrafashionable

swain – admirer, boy, countryman, gallant, lover, peasant, rustic, suitor, youth

swallow – absorb, consume, englut, engulf, gulp, imbibe, ingest

swallow (European)–martin

swallow (greedily)–engorge

swallow (sea)–tern

swallow (small)–martin

swallow again–resorb

swallow up–absorb

swamp – bog, deluge, everglade, fen, marsh, mire, moor, morass, overwhelm, quagmire, slough, slue

swamp earth (black)–muck

swampish–miry

swampland tract–everglades

swan (female)–pen

swan (genus of) – cygnus, olor

swan (male)–cob

Swan (upper course of) – Avon

swan (young)–cygnet

Swan star (brightest)–Deneb

Swann's Way author–Proust

swap – barter, exchange, trade

sward–greensward, sod, turf

sward land–lea

swarm–crowd, flock, horde, multitude, throng

swarm of young fish–fry

swarming–alive

swarthy–dark, dun, dusky

swashbuckler – bravo, dare-

devil, Drawcansir, gascon, swaggerer

swastika–Fylfot, Gammadion

swat–bat, hit, strike

sway – ascendancy, bias, direct, empire, influence, oscillate, power, rock, rule, shake, sovereignty, swing, totter, wave

sway (suddenly)–lurch

swaying–pensile

sways from side to side (in walking)–waddles

swear off from–eschew

swearing (false)–perjury

sweat through pores – transude

Swedish city – Falkoping, Falun, Goteborg, Gottenburg, Jonkoping, Malmo, Norrkoping, Stockholm (c.), Upsala

Swedish clover–alsike

Swedish coin–krona (s.), ore (br.)

Swedish dance–polska

Swedish division (territorial)–Eire, Laen, Lan

Swedish government – Blekinge, Christianstad, Elfsborg, Gefleborg, Gotland, Gottenborgoch Bohus, Halland, Jemtland, Jonkoping, Kalmar, Kopparberg, Kronoberg, Malmohus, Norrbotten, Orebro, Oster Gotland, Skaraborg, Sodermanland, Stockholm, Upsala, Wermland, Westerbotten, Westernorrland, Westmanland

Swedish gulf–Bothnia

Swedish hero–Wasa

Swedish island – Gothland, Oeland

Swedish king–Wasa

Swedish lake – Asnen, Hielmar, Malar, Siljan, Vatter, Wener, Wennen, Wetter

Swedish legislature–Riksdag

Swedish measure – aln, am, carat, famn, fathom, fjarding, foder, fot, jumfru, kanna, kappe, kappland, kollast, koltunna, last, linje, mil, nymil, oxhuvud, ref, spann, stang, stop, tum, tunland, tunnland, tunna

Swedish mountain–Sarjek

Swedish Nightingale–Jennie Lind

Swedish parliament – Riksdag

Swedish province (administrative)–Lan

Swedish religion (of state)–Lutheran

Swedish river – Gota, Kalix, Klar, Lainio, Ljungan, Ljusne, Lulea, Pitea, Ranea, Tornea, Umea, Windel

Swedish soprano – Jennie Lind

Swedish territorial division–amt

Swedish weight – ass, carat, centner, last, lispound, lispund, lod, mark, nylast, ort, pund, ship pound, skalpund, skeppund, sten, untz

Swedish writer–Lagerlof

sweep–oar, surge

sweep (hay)–buck

sweet – agreeable, aromatic, dulcet, gentle, honeyed, luscious, melodious, musical, pleasant, schmalz, schmaltz, spicy, sugary

sweet (Chaucer spelling) – sote

sweet (divinely)–ambrosial

sweet and delicious – nectarine

sweet and fair–bonny

sweet and soft–dolce

sweet cake–eclair

sweet drink–nectar

sweet potato–batata, yam

sweet potato (musical)–ocarina

sweet to ear–dulcet

sweet to taste–dulcet

sweet wine–lunel

sweetbread–burr

sweetbread (calf's) – risdeveau

sweetbrier–eglantine

sweeten–candy, cleanse, disinfect, edulcorate, freshen, mitigate, mollify, perfume, purify, sugar

sweetened drink–julep, toddy

sweetheart – enamorata, inamorata, lass, leman, lover

sweetheart (Scot.)–jo

sweethearts (Irish)–gras

sweetly and smoothly–mellifluently

sweetmeat–comfit

sweetmeat (after meals) – cake, candy, caramel, confection, dessert, pastry

sweetness–fragrance

Sweet's system of phonetic notations–Romic

sweetsop–ates

swell–augmentation, billow, bulge, dilate, distend, enlargement, expand, grow, growth, inflate, prominence, rise, surge

swell (bell-shaped, of gun muzzle)–tulip

swell (long rolling)–seagate

swell (ocean)–billow, roller, sea

swell (slang)–nob

swelled heads–egos

swelled out–podded

swelling–edema

swelling (pert. to)–ensue

swerve – deflect, deviate, sheer, veer

sweven–dream, sleep, vision

swift–fast, fleet, racy, rapid, speedy

swift footed–aliped

swiftly–apace, fast

swiftness–celerity, haste

swimmer (legendary Hellespont)–Leander

swimming–naiant, natant

swimming (pert. to) – natatory

swimming birds–natatores

swimming pool–natatorium, tank

swindle – cheat, defraud, dupe, fake, gip, gyp, sell, trepan

swindle (slang)–gip, gyp

swindler – gip, gyp, knave, rogue, sharper

swindler (coll.)–biter

swine–hog, pig, sow

swine (genus of)–sus

swine (white)–Cheshire

swine butcher's shop – porkery

swine-like–porcine

swing – dangle, hang, oscillate, shake, suspend, sway

swing (gymnastic)–trapeze

swing (rhythmical)–lilt

swing (staccato)–mugging

swingtree–whippletree

swinish – beastly, gross, sensual

swink – drudgery, labor, slave, toil

swinker–laborer

swipe – draft, drink, gulp, handle, lever, swape, swath, sweep

swire–neck, throat

swirl – curve, eddy, twist, whirl

swirly–knotted, twisted

Swiss (obs.)–Muff

Swiss administrative district –canton

Swiss ax (two-headed, ice)–piolet

Swiss cabin–chalet

Swiss canton – Aargau, Appenzell, Basel, Bern, Freiburg, St. Gall (Sankt Gallen), Geneva (Geneve, Genf), Glarus (Glaris), Grisons (Graubunden), Lucerne (Luzern), Neuchatel, (Neuenberg), Schaffhausen (Schaffhouse), Schwyz (Schwytz), Solothurn (Soleure), Thurgau, Ticino (Tessin), Unterwalden, Uri, Valais (Wallis), Vaud (Waadt), Zug, Zurich

Swiss capital–Bern, Berne

Swiss city–Bale, Basel, Basle, Bern, Berne, Faizabad, Farukhabad, Fribourg, Fyzabad, Geneva, Lausanne, Locarno, Lucerne.

Montreux, Neuchatel, Schwyz, Sion, St. Gallen, Winterthur, Zurich
Swiss coin – centime (br.), franc (s.)
Swiss commune–Aarau
Swiss cottage–chalet
Swiss dialect–ladin
Swiss district–canton
Swiss herdsman's hut–chalet
Swiss hero (legendary)–Tell
Swiss lake–Uri
Swiss language – French, German, Italian, Romansch
Swiss legislative chamber – grosserat, grossrat, grossrath
Swiss mathematician–Euler
Swiss measure – aune, elle, fuss, holzklafter, immi, juchart, klafter, lieue, ligne, linie, maass, moule, muid, perche, pied, pot, pouce, quarteron, saum, schuh, setier, staab, strich, toise, viertel, zoll
Swiss measure (old)–saum
Swiss mountain – Alps, Blanc, Jura, Rigi, St. Gothard
Swiss musical composer – Raff
Swiss people – French, German, Italian, Rhaetian, Romansch
Swiss pine–arolla
Swiss river – Aar, Aare, Doubs, Inn, Reuss, Rhone
Swiss sled–luger
Swiss theologian–Hess
Swiss valley–Aar
Swiss warble–yodel
Swiss weight – centner, pfund, quintal, zugthierlast, zugtierlast
Swiss and German lake – Constance
switch–beat, change, divert, flog, shift, shunt, strike, whip
switchback (aquatic)–chute
switchboard section–panel
switchman–shunter
Switzerland–*see* Swiss

Switzerland (poetic) – Helvetia
swollen – bulbous, tumid, turgid
swoon–faint, syncope
swoop down–pounce
swooping–souse
sword (anc.)–estoc
sword (cavalry)–saber, sabre
sword (curved) – scimitar, simitar
sword (dueling) – saber, sabre
sword (fencing) – epee, foil, rapier
sword (fine) – Damascus, Damask, Toledo
sword (French fencing) – epee
sword (kind of)–creese, cutlass, epee, estoc, rapier, saber, sabre
sword (Scot.)–gully
sword (short)–parang
sword (straight, two-edged) –pata
sword (two-handed) – espada, espadon
Sword blade heel–talon
sword handle–haft, hilt
sword-like–xiphoid
sword play practice–fence
sword practice (playful) – fence
sword scabbard tip (metal)–crampit
sword-shaped–ensate, gladiate, xyphoid
sword used by sheik–pata
swordfish–espada, espadon
swordsman–fencer
swordsman (expert)–epeeist
swordsman's dummy–pel
swore–cursed, curst
sworn to secrecy–tiled
sybil–seer, seeress
syce–groom
sycophant–flatterer, informer, parasite, spaniel, talebearer, toady
sycophantic – obedient, servile, slavish
syllable (accented, of a foot) –arsis, arses (pl.)
syllable (bobization)–ni

syllable (last of a word) – ultima
syllable (meaningless, musical)–tra
syllable (musical)–si
syllable (mystic)–om, um
syllable (next to last)–penult
syllable (short)–mora
syllable (singing)–tra
syllable (solmization)–si
syllable (unaccented)–lene
syllable (wanting at end) – catalectic
syllable (word)–penult
syllable of hesitation–er
syllable second before last (pert. to) – antepenultimate
syllable shortening–systole
syllabled (three)–trisyllabic
syllabus – compendium, synopsis, synopses (pl.)
syllogism–epicheirena
syllogism (series of)–sorite
sylvan – forest, forestlike, woody, wooded
sylvan deity–Pan, Satyr
sylvan deity (myth.)–Satyr
sylvan demigod–Satyr
symbol–emblem, figure, image, letter, sign, token, type
symbol (graphic of any sort) –character
symbol (tribal)–totem
symbol (victory)–palm
symbol denoting third-class ship–AE
symbol for agent–Agt
symbol for argent–Ag
symbol for arsenic–As
symbol for calcium–Ca
symbol for cerium–Ce
symbol for chlorine–Cl
symbol for chromium–Cr
symbol for cobalt–Co
symbol for copper–Cu
symbol for erbium–Eb
symbol for faithful dead – orant
symbol for gas (Adamsite)–DM
symbol for gas (brombenzyl)–CA
symbol for gas (chloracetophenone)–Cn, CNS

symbol for gas (chlorine)–Cl

symbol for gas (chlorpicrin) PS

symbol for gas (diphenyl-chlorarsine)–DA

symbol for gas (diphosgene) –DP

symbol for gas (ethyldi-chlorasine)–ED

symbol for gas (HC mixture)–HC

symbol for gas (Lewisite)–MI

symbol for gas (mustard)–HS

symbol for gas (phosgene)–CG

symbol for gas (sulphur trioxide)–FS

symbol for gas (thermit)–TH

symbol for gas (titanium tetrachloride)–FM

symbol for gas (white phosphorous)–WP

symbol for glucinum–Gl

symbol for gold–Au

symbol for iridium–Ir

symbol for iron–Fe

symbol for lead–Pb

symbol for lutecium–Lu

symbol for magnesium–Mg

symbol for neon–Ne

symbol for nickel–Ni

symbol for oleum–Ol

symbol for radium–Ra

symbol for rhenium–Re

symbol for rhodium–Rh

symbol for ruthen–Ru

symbol for ruthenium–Ru

symbol for samarium – Sa, Sm

symbol for selenium–Se

symbol for silicon–Si

symbol for silver–Ag, Ar

symbol for sodium–Na

symbol for tantalum–Ta

symbol for tellurium–Te

symbol for terbium–Tb

symbol for thallium–Tl

symbol for thorium–Th

symbol for tin–Sn

symbol for xenon–Xe

symbol for yttrium–Yt

symbol in Greek antiquity–egis

symbol of bondage–yoke

symbol of comedy–sock

symbol of France–lily

symbol of peace–dove

symbol of power – scepter, sceptre

symbol of victory–palm

symbol on which mathematical problem is done–operand

symmetry–conformity, congruity, consistency, proportion

symmetry (lack of)–disproportion

sympathetic–congenial, tender

sympathetically – compassionately, piteously

sympathy–agreement, commiseration, condolence, interest, pity, tenderness

symptom–indication, mark, note, sign, token

synchronized–synk

syncopated–rag

synonym – antonym, homonym

synonymous – equivalent, like, similar

synopsis – abridgement, abstract, compendium, conspectus, epitome, summary, syllabus

syntactical deviation – synesis

synthesis – combination, incorporation

Syriac script (modern)–Serta

Syrian–Druse

Syrian bishop–abba

Syrian capital (anc.)–Antioch

Syrian church plan–triconch

Syrian city–Aleppo, Alexandretta, Beirout, Beirut, Beyrout, Damascus, Homs

Syrian coin–piaster (ni., br.), pound (ac., pap.)

Syrian county–Lebanon

Syrian deity–El, Resheph

Syrian deity (North)–El

Syrian fanatic–Druse

Syrian goat–angora

Syrian god (of riches)–Mammon

Syrian grass–Johnson

Syrian harbor–Alexandretta, Beyrout

Syrian lake–Merom, Tiberias

Syrian mallow–okra

Syrian measure–garava, makuk

Syrian mountain – Carmel, Libanus

Syrian nomad–saracen

Syrian peasant–fellah

Syrian port–Acre

Syrian province–Aleppo

Syrian religious sect–Druse

Syrian river–Jordan, Orontes

Syrian seaport–Acre

Syrian vilayet–Aleppo

Syrian weight–artal, artel, cola, ratel, rotl, talent

Syrian wind (hot, dry)–simoon

syrup (corn)–glucose, Karo

syrup (date)–dhebbus

syrup (flavoring)–orgeat

syrup (grape juice, evaporated)–sapa

syrup (light-colored, uncrystallizable)–glucose

Syryenian language–Kami, Komi

system – arrangement, hypothesis, method, order, philosophy, religion, theory, universe

system (governmental, prevailing)–regime

system (mystic)–cabala

system (numbering) – decimal

system (phonetic notation)–Romic

system (religious)–cult, cultus

system (solar member of)–planet

system of accepted rules of conduct–codes

system of eating–dietary

system of lines in the focus of an optical instrument–reticle
system of management–regime
system of manual training–sloid, sloyd
system of signals–code

system of weights–avoirdupois, troy
system of worship of a deity –cult
systematic–methodical, neat, orderly
systematic body of law–code
systematical–regimental

systematize – catalog, catalogue, codify, regiment
systematized – arranged, methodize, organized
systematized (as law, coll.)–coded
systematized knowledge–science

T

tab – eartab, flap, latchet, strip, tag
tab (on woman's dress)–pan
tab (shoelace)–aglet
tabard–cape, cloak, jacket, mantle
tabby–cat
tabby's tonic–catnip
table–board, lamina, panel, plate, repast, slab, tablet
table (communion)–altar
table (small)–stand
table cover–tapis
table dish–tureen
tableland–mesa, plateau
table linen–napery
table philosophy (those excelling in)–deipnosophists
tablet–pad, slab
tablet (having antipyretic properties)–aspirin
tablet (medicine)–troche
tablet (sculptured) – stela, stelae (pl.), stele, steles (pl.)
tablet (upright)–stela, stelae (pl.), stele, steles (pl.)
tablet (writing)–pad, slate
taboo (opposed to)–noa
tabulation (of the year) – calendar
taccaceous herb–pia
taccada–fanflower
tache–blemish, spot, stain
tacit–implied, noiseless, silent, unspoken, wordless
taciturn – reserved, reticent, silent
taciturn (heavy disposition) –saturnine
tack–clothes, gear, tackle
tack (glazier's)–brad

tack (to)–jibe
tack (two-pointed)–staple
tack to windward–trip
tackle–equipment, gear, harness, rigging
tackle (strong)–cat
tackle (using single and double block)–burton
tact – address, delicacy, discernment
tadpole–polliwog
tag–flap, game, label, strip, tab
tag (metal)–tab
tag (metal of lace)–aglet, aiglet
tag (small)–tab
tag of stay lace–aglet, aiglet
Tagalog (to learn)–aral
Tagalog child–bata
Tagalog children–Anacs
Tagalog for mother–Ina
Tagalog peasant–Tao
Tagalog race (one of)–Ita
Tahiti (old name)–Otaheite
Tahitian capital–Papeete
Tahitian coronation robe – maro
Tahitian god (national) – Oro
Tahitian robe–maro
Tahitian supreme god–Taaroa
Tai race (branch of)–Lao
tail–appendage, back, cue, end, follow, last, rear, shadow
tail (comet)–streamer
tail (having a)–caudate
tail (hound dog's)–stern
tail (rabbit's)–scut
tail (pert. to)–caudal

tail (Pomeranian dog's) – plume
tail (pug dog's)–twist
tail (short)–scut
tailless–anurous, ecaudate
tailor–draper, sartor
tailor (pert. to)–sartorial
tailor's goose–flatiron
taint–contaminate, corrupt, defile, deprave, pollute, vitiate
taint (moral)–stain
Taj Mahal (site of)–Agra
take–accept, atone, doff, receive
take a chair–sit
take a direction–steer
take as one's own – adopt, borrow
take away–adeem, adempt, deduct, deprive, detract, remove, subtract
take away (as legacy) – adeem, adempt
take away (law) – adeem, adempt
take away by force–rebel
take away publicly–recant, retract
take back–recant, retract
take by stratagem–trap
take care – beware, mind, nurse, watch
take care of–nurse, tend
take cognizance of – note, notice
take delight–revel
take evening meal–dine, sup
take for granted – assume, presume
take form–deduct, deprive.

derived, detract, divest,
subtract
take great delight–revel
take heed (arch.)–reck
take in–include
take in sail–reef
take into custody – apprehend, arrest
take legal possession of –
seise, seize
take liberties–presume
take meals for pay–board
take no notice of–disregard
take notice–NB
take off–doff
take offense of–resent
take on again–reassume
take on cargo–lade
take one's way–wend
take out–dele, delete, efface,
elide
take out curves and bends–
straighten
take out of pawn–redeem
take place of–supersede, supplant
take pleasure in–enjoy, fancy
take shelter–nestle
take some of–partake
take turns–alternate
take umbrage at–resent
take up again–renew, re-
sume
take up weapons–arm
taker of court action–suer
taker of income or profits–
pernor
takes in and feeds cattle –
agists
takes rise–emanates
taking everything into account–overall
taking in all–inclusive
taking out–elision
talc–soapstone, steatite
tale–anecdote, fable, legend,
story, yarn
tale (fanciful)–romance
tale (fictitious)–romance
tale (figurative)–allegory
tale (French short medieval)
–lai
tale (heroic)–gest
tale (medieval, short)–lai
tale (tall)–yarn
tale (traditional)–saga

tale of adventure–gest
tale of chivalry–romance
tale of daring–saga
tale of fatality–tragedy
tale of sorrow–jeremiad
tale of woe–jeremiad
talebearer–gossip, newsmon-
ger, scandalmonger, tat-
tler
talent – ability, accomplishment, flair, genius, gift
talent (one's special)–forte
talent sale (mercenary) –
venality
talented–able, gifted
talesman–juror, narrator
taliera–tara
talisman – amulet, charm,
tara
talisman (beetle-like)–scarab
talk–colloquy, converse, discourse, parlance, speak
talk (arch.)–parle
talk (coll.)–chin, gab
talk (deliriously)–rave
talk (familiar, coll.)–confab
talk (fatuously)–babble
talk (flattering)–palaver
talk (fluent)–verbose, voluble
talk (hypocritical)–cant
talk (inconsiderately loud)–
blate
talk (long, meaningless) –
rigmarole
talk (prolix and rambling)–
rigmarolery
talk (running)–patter
talk (silly)–twaddle
talk (slang) – chatter, gab,
spiel
talk (small)–chitchat, prattle
talk (Spanish)–palabra
talk about–discuss, gossip
talk enthusiastically–rave
talk foolishly–blather, drivel,
drooz
talk idly (glibly) – chatter,
gab, prate, tattle, twaddle
talk indiscreetly–blab
talk indistinctly–sputter
talk nonsense (coll.)–gas
talk profusely–palaver
talk rapidly–sputter
talk slowly–drawl
talk to no purpose–blat

talk wildly–rave
talk with passion–rave
talkative–garrulous, verbose,
voluble
talkativeness–fluent, garrulous, glib, loquacious, loquacity, voluble
talked idly (slang)–gassed
talked together–conversed
talker (interesting)–conversationalist
talker (tedious)–proser
talker (voluble, coll.)–spieler
tall–high, lofty
tall (very)–skyhigh
tall coarse grass stem–reed
tallet–attic, hayloft
talliar–watchman
tallow–suet
tallow sediment–greaves
tally–check, count, goal, run,
score
tally (coll.)–tab
Talmud commentary – Ge-
mara
talon–claw
talus–scree
tam–beret
tamarisk (Oriental) – atle,
atlee
tamarisk salt tree–atle, atlee
tamas–dullness, ignorance,
inertia
tamasha–commotion, excitement, fuss, pageant, spectacle
tambourine–timbrel
tambourine (Oriental)–daira
tambourine playing vibrant
effect–travale
tame–docile, domesticated,
gentle, subdue, tractable
Tamil–Dravidian
tamis–sieve, strainer, tammy
tamper–meddle
tampon – drumstick, plug,
tympan
tampon (nasal)–rhinobyon
tan–brown, dun, taw
tan (derived from)–tanic
tan or brown – ecru, em-
brown, imbrown
Tanganyika (Africa) moun-
tain–Meru
tangible–palpable, tactile

Tangiers measure – kula, mudd

tangle–ensnare, entrap, involve, kink, mat, ravel, sleave, snare, snarl

tangle of thread–snarl

tangled mass–mop

tank–cistern, pool, reservoir, vat

tankard–facer

tankard (anc.)–hanap

tankard (large)–pottle

tanker–oiler

tanned – brown, sunburnt, tawny

tannic acid salt–tannate

tanning and dyeing material–sumac, sumach

tanning and dyeing shrub–sumac, sumach

tantalize–harass, taunt, tease, torment

tantalum (symbol for)–Ta

Tantalus' daughter–Niobe

Tantalus' father–Zeus

Tantalus' son–Pelops

tantamount – equivalent, identical

tantara–fanfare

tantrum–rage

tap–faucet, hob, plug, rap, spigot

tap down–tamp

tape (lamp)–wick

taper–candle, ream

taper (timber in ship building)–snape

tapering (slightly)–terete

tapering blades–spires

tapering cylindrical–conic

tapering four-sided pillar – obelisk

tapering piece–gore, gusset, miter

tapering solid–cone

tapestry–arras, tapis

tapestry (famous)–bayeux

tapestry (for back of throne or chair)–dorser, dosser, dossier, dossiere

tapestry (French city)–arras

tapestry (hanging of)–tapis

tapestry (kind of)–gobelin

tapestry (rich hanging)–dosser

tapestry screen–arras

tapeworm – taenia, taeniae (pl.)

tapeworm (embryonic form) –oncosphere

tapioca-like food–salep

tapirus Americanus–anta

tapster–skinker

Tapuyan – Botocudo, Caingang, Camacan, Cayapo, Chavante, Coroado, Ge, Ges, Gesan, Goyana, Timbra

Tapuyan Indian–Ges

tar–sailor, salt, seaman

tar (by-product of)–cresol

tarboosh–fez

tardy–behindhand, belated, lag, lagging, late, remiss, slow

target–bull's-eye, butt, mark, object, tee

target center–eye

target center (archery)–clout

tariff – charge, duty, rate, schedule

tariff favorer–protectionist

tarnish–cloud, dim, dull, obscure, smirch, spot, stain

tarnish (stain)–dim, sully

taro–dasheen

taro (West Indian) – coco, tania

taro paste–poi

taro root–eddo, eddoes (pl.)

taro root (ground)–poi

taro root dish–poi

tarred a vessel's bottom – payed

tarried–dallied, lingered, remained, waited

tarry–abide, lag, linger, stay

tarsus (fore, of water bugs)–pala

tart–acrid, astringent, pungent, severe, sharp, sour

tartan–plaid

Tartar–see Tatar

tartar (crude)–argol

task–assignment, chore, employment, job, stint, toil

task (assigned)–stent, stint

task (definite, prescribed)–stent, stint

task (easy, slang)–snap

task (fixed)–stent, stint

task (household)–chore

task (small)–chore

Tasmanian animal (bearlike, burrowing)–wombat

Tasmanian phalanger–tapoa

taste–palate, sample, sapor, savor, sip, smack, soupçon, tang

taste (decided)–penchant

taste (penetrating)–tang

taste (savor)–sapor, savor

taste (sharp)–acid, tang

taste (slight)–sip

taste (unripened fruit)–prose

taste combined with aptitude –flair

taste of liquid (small)–sip

tasted (Span.)–sipt

tasteless–dull, flat, inartistic, insipid, savorless, vapid

tasting like malt (obs.) – corny

tasty – sapid, savory, toothsome

Tatar country principality–Khanate

Tatar lancer–Uhlan

Tatar militiaman – Uhlan, Ulan (var.)

Tatar ruler's dominion – Khanate

Tatar tribe (old) – Alani, Alans

Tatar tribe (one of)–Hun

tatter–rag, ribbon

tattle–blab, chatter, gossip, prate

tattler–gossip, telltale

taunt – deride, gibe, mock, ridicule, tease, twit

taunt (obs.)–check

Taurus group of stars–Pleiades

taut–tense, tight

tauten–tense

tautological–redundant

tave – labor, rage, sprawl, struggle, toss

tavern–hotel, inn, saloon

tavern (Eng. slang)–pub

tawdry–cheap, gaudy, showy

tawny – brindled, dusky, tanned

tawny colored–olive

tax–assess, assessment, cess, duty, impost, levy, license,

rate, scat, scatt, scot, stent,
toll, tollage, tribute
tax (church)–tithe
tax (feudal)–tailage
tax (homicide, anc.)–cro
tax (old)–soc
tax (road)–toll
tax (Shetland Island)–scat
tax (tribal, anc.)–cro
tax (voluntary)–tithe
tax on liquors–abkari
tax rate–assessment
taxation (degree of)–ratal
taxed–levied
taxi (two-seated, Eng. slang)
–jixie
taxing–tailaging
tea–function, reception
tea (black)–oopack, oopak
tea (inferior, black)–bohea
tea (kind of) – black, cha,
green, hyson, oolong, pe-
koe
tea (kind of Asia, rolled)–
cha
tea (rolled)–cha
tea and coffee constituent–
caffeine
tea cake–scone
tea container–canister
tea plant–thea
tea receptacle–canister
tea sassafras–saloop
tea tester–taster
tea urn–samovar
teach – direct, enlighten,
guide, instruct, school,
show, train, tutor
teach (publicly)–preach
teacher–doctor, edifier, educator, instructor, peda-
gogue, pedant, preceptor,
pundit, reader, tutor
teacher (private)–tutor
teacher (Russia)–starets
teacher (university)–regent
teacher (wise)–mentor
teacher and pastor–rabbi
teacher of eloquence (anc.)–
rhetor
teaching–docent, instruction,
precept
teaching (pert. to)–pedagogic
teaching of a fable–moral

team (second)–scrubs, Yannigans
teamed with–paired, yoked
teamster–carter
tear–cleave, lacerate, rend,
rent, rip, rive, split
tear apart–rend
tear down–rase, raze
tear into shreds–tatter
tear up by the roots–arache
teardrop design (in lace)–
larme
tearful–lacrimal, watery
tears (pert. to)–lacrimal
tears (poetic)–rheum
tease–aggravate, devil, guy,
harass, heckle, nag,
plague, tantalize, taunt,
torment, twit
tease (persistently)–tantalize
tease (slang)–rag
tease wool–tum
tease wool (before carding)
–toom
teaser–carder, curler, gull,
pesterer, sniper, willow,
willower
technology of agriculture –
agrotechny
techy–fretful, irascible, irritable, peevish, touchy
tedious–boring, displeasing,
dry, dull, irksome, laborious, noxious, prolix, prosy,
wearisome
tedium–boredom, ennui
teem–abound
teem (Scot.)–empty
teeming–abounding, crowd-
ing, full, pouring, prolific,
replete
teen–affliction, anger, damage, distress, grief, harm,
hate, injure, injury, irritate, pain, provoke, sor-
row, vex, vexation
teeny – fretful, malicious,
peevish, small, tiny, wee
teer–daub, plaster
teeter–jiggle, sandpiper, seesaw, waver
teeter board–seesaw
teeth–canines
teeth (false)–denture
teeth (large)–buck
teeth (long)–fangs

teeth (long, pointed)–tushes
teeth (outer covering of)–
enamel
teeth (pert. to)–dental, molar
teeth (projecting beyond
others)–snags
teeth (serpent's)–fangs
teeth coating–enamel
teetotaler – abstainer, dry,
nonuser
tegula–tile
tegument–coat, cover
tela–tissue
telegraph (coll.)–wire
telegraph cable–wire
telegraph inventor–Morse
telegraph key–tapper
telegraphic communication
(lengthy)–lettergram
telephone–buzz, call, dial,
phone
Telephus' mother–Auge
telescope–collapse, glass
television subject (suitable)–
telegenic
tell–acquaint, communicate,
impart, inform, narrate,
recite, recount, rehearse,
relate, repeat, report, reveal, say, utter
teller – describer, informer,
narrator
telling–effective, pertinent
telltale–blab, informer, talebearer, tattler
telltruth–frankness, honesty
telluride (lead)–altaite
tellurium (symbol for)–Te
temerity–rashness, venture-
someness
temper–adjust, animus, anneal, assuage, dander, disposition, humor, mitigate,
moderate, mollify, mood,
season, soften
temper (hastiness of)–choler
temper (heat of)–choler
temper (mildness of)–lenity
temper clay–puddle
temper of mind–mood
temperament – disposition,
mood
temperate–abstemious, calm,
cool, moderate, sober

tempered–annealed, moderated, mollified

tempered (even)–sedate

tempest–agitation, commotion, gale, storm, tumult, turmoil, wind

Tempest (The) character – Miranda

Tempest (The) character (slave)–Caliban

Tempest (The) spirit–Ariel

tempestuous–galey, stormy, turbulent, violent

temple–fane, naos, speos

temple (anc.)–cella, cellae

Temple (as Seven Pagodas in Madras)–Rath, Ratha

temple (poetic)–fane

temple (Shinto)–sha

temple basin–laver

temple sanctuary–penetralia

tempo–pace, time

temporal – carnal, earthly, laic, secular, temporary

temporarily–nonce

tempt–allure, entice, lure

tempter–baiter

temptress – Delilah, mermaid, siren

ten (number)–decad

ten (prefix)–deca

ten ares–decare

ten commandments – decalogue

ten dollars (slang)–sawbuck

ten-sided figure–decagon

ten-twenty-thirty – show, theater

ten-year periods – decades, decenniad, decennium

tenfold–decuple, denary

tens of thousands–myriads

tenth of a cent–mill

tenth part–tithe

tenacious of purpose–persistent

tenaciously–doggedly

tenant–leaser, lessee, renter

tenant (feudal)–vassal

tenant (free, Eng.)–dreng, drengh

tend – attend, care, serve, wait

tend in certain direction – lead

tend the fire–stoke

tend to–mind, nurse

tend toward any object – gravitate

tend toward one point–converge

tendency–bent, bias, course, drift, inclination, leaning, proclivity, propensity, tide, trend

tendency (structural, bot.)–peloria

tendency (summer)–lethargy

tender – bid, effeminate, fond, gentle, humane, kind, merciful, offer, pitiful, proffer, sensitive, soft, softhearted, sore

tender (ship's)–pinnace

tender feeling–sentiment

tending to arouse the feelings–emotive

tending to check–repressive

tending to clear from alleged guilt–exculpatory

tending to control–regulatory

tending to develop in detail –elaborative

tending to drive away–repellent

tending to evade–elusory

tending to heal–sanative

tending to rip–lacerative

tending to tear–lacerative

tending to wear away–abrasive

tending toward an end–telic

tendon – aponeurosis, aponeuroses (pl.), chord, sinew

tendon (comb. form)–teno

tendril–branch, cirrus, sprig

tenet–belief, canon, creed, doctrine, dogma

tenet contrary to received opinion–paradox

Tennessee governor (first)–Sevier

Tennessee national park – Shiloh

tennis (no points scored)–love

tennis games (series of)–set

tennis points–aces

tennis racket–bat

tennis score–deuce, love

tennis stroke–cut, lob

tennis term–ace, advantage, deuce, fault, let, lob, love, receive, serve, volley

Tennyson character–Elaine, Enid

Tennyson heroine–Enid

Tennyson "In Memoriam" subject–Hallam

tenon–cog

tenor–holding, tendency

tense–intense, intent, rapt, rigid, strained, taut, tight

tense (past)–preterite

tensile–ductile, tensible

tension–strain, stress

tent (general's, anc. Roman) –praetorium, pretorium

tent (Indian)–tepee

tent (large, rounded top)–pavilion

tentacle–feeler, palp

tentative–provisional, temporary

tentative proposition–feeler

tenterhooks (on)–agog

tenuous–delicate, rare, slender, subtile, thin

tenure–lease

tenures (husband's in dead wife's lands)–curtesies

tepid–lukewarm, warm

teras–monster

tergiversate–lie

term–name, word

term (college year)–semester

term (connotation of a)–intent

term (fencing)–touche

term (glacial)–stoss

term (grammatical)–phrase

term (in logic)–ferio, ferison

term (school)–semester

term (sea)–ahoy, avast, belay

term of address–milady, sir, sirrah

term of life–sands

termagant–Amazon, boisterous, furious, quarrelsome, scolding, shrew, tumultuous, turbulent, virago

termed–styled

terminal–end, finish, limital

terminal (battery) -- anode, electrode

terminal (electric) – anode, electrode
terminal (positive)–anode
terminal ornament–finial
terminal pole–electrode
terminate–cease, close, complete, conclude, end, expire, halt
terminating in a trefoil (heraldry)–botone
terminating in animal's head (heraldry)–anserated
termination – amen, close, conclusion, ending, outcome, result, terminus
terminus–depot, end
termite (Philippine) – anai, anay
ternary – threefold, trinity, triple
terns (genus of)–sterna
terpsichorean–dancer
terrace–balcony, colonnade, gallery, portico
terrace (natural)–mesa
terrain–environment, milieu, region, tract
terrapin–turtle
terrapin (fresh water) – emyd, emydea, emydidae, emydinae, emys
terrapin (obs.)–emyde
terrene – earthly, earthy, mundane, terrestrial, worldly
terrestrial – earthly, earthy, mundane, worldly
terrible – appalling, dire, dread, fearful, frightful, horrible, terrifying, tragic
terrier (kind of)–fox, Irish, Scottish, Sealyham, Skye, Welsh
terrific–appalling, excessive, exciting, extreme, terrible, tremendous
terrified–aghast, awed
terrifier–haunter
terrify–alarm, appal, appall, awe, daunt, dismay, scare
terrifying–horrid
territorial division (Fr.)–arrondissement, canton, commune, department

territory (imperial palace officer's)–palatinate
territory governed by bans–banat
territory portion–canton
territory under a Pasha – Pashalic
terror – alarm, dread, fear, panic
terror (amazed)–consternation
terrorized–appalled, awed
terrorsome–alarming
terse – compact, concise, laconic, pithy, pointed, succinct
tertiary period–neocene
tessellated–mosaic
test–assay, criterion, examination, examine, experiment, proof, prove, sample, taste, trial, try
test (severe)–ordeal
test in fineness and weight–pyx
test ore–assay
test value–assay
testament (old)–Job
testator–legator
tester–prover
testified under oath – deponed
testifier–deponent, witness
testify–depone, depose
testimonial–certificate, evidence, warrant
testimony–attest, attestation, evidence, witness
testing–sampling, tasting
testy–fretful, irascible, peevish, petulant, snappish
tetragon–quadrangle, rhombus, square
Teuton–German
Teuton (ancient)–Goth
Teutonic alphabet character –rune
Teutonic deities–Nornir
Teutonic demigoddess – Norn
Teutonic fate–Norn
Teutonic god–Er, Hel, Tyr
Teutonic god (pantheon)–Balder, Odin, Thor, Tyr
Teutonic god (poetry)–Bragi
Teutonic god (sky)–Tyr

Teutonic god (war)–Tyr
Teutonic goddess–Eir, Hel
Teutonic goddess (fate) – Norn
Teutonic goddess (healing)–Eir
Teutonic gods (chief pantheon)–Aesir
Teutonic homicide–morth
Teutonic law (old)–Salic
Teutonic nightmare (folklore)–alp
Teutonic pantheon god–As
Teutonic sprite–nis
Teutonic tribe (one of)–Lombard
Teutonic war god–Tyr
Teutonic water nymph–nis
Texas broncho–mustang
Texas citadel–Alamo
Texas city – Abilene, Cuero, Dallas, Denison, Laredo, Odessa, Paris
Texas cottonwood–alamo
Texas county–Starr
Texas fortress–Alamo
Texas itch–mange, scabies
Texas mission–Alamo
Texas river–Pecos, Red
Texas shrine–Alamo
text (as of an opera)–libretto
text (pen)–ronde
text (set to music)–oratorio
text variation–lection
textile cleaning machine – stamper
textile screw pine–ara
textile worker – spinner, warper
textiles–mercery
texture–fabric, grain, textile, wale, web
texture (as cloth)–wale
texture (slight, flimsy)–cobweb
texture (thin and membranous)–scarious
texture of fabric–warp, woof
Thackeray's tale country (imaginary)–Paflagonia
Thailand–Siam
Thailand and Malay isthmus –Kra
thallus of lichens bud (brood)–soredium, soredia (pl.)

thane's estate–manor
thankless person–ingrate
that from which anything springs–germ
that is (abbr.)–eg, ie
that is to say–namely
that may be disregarded–negligible
that may split–fissile
that which brings back–restorer
that which can dissolve – solvent
that which corresponds with some other thing – analogue
that which displeases – offense
that which does not exist–nonent
that which follows–sequel
that which foreshadows – prefiguration, prototype
that which furnishes proof–evidence
that which gives relief–balm, easement
that which goes before–antecedent, precedence, precedent
that which is possible–potential
that which is retained in the mind–retent
that which is unavoidable–inevitability
that which lays waste–desolater
that which makes a thing go–operant
that which must be done–duty
that which one does best–forte
that which one holds as true –belief
that which perplexes–besetter
that which plagues–teaser
that which renders feeble–enervator
that which rouses compassion and sympathy–pathos
that which serves to ornament–decor

that which soothes and heals –balm
that which supplies strength –sinew
"That's for thought"–pansies
thatch (palm)–nipa
thatched–reeded
thatcher–hellier
thaumaturgy – legerdemain, magic
the (French)–la, le, les (pl.)
the (Italian)–il
the (Spanish)–el
the end–omega, thirty
The Harbor (author of) – Poole
the "I" (big)–ego
The Man Nobody Knows (author of)–Barton
The Newcomes painter (fawning portrait)–Smee
The Ocritus' shepherd – Corydon
the reason–nous
the same–ditto, idem
"The Terrible" ruler–Ivan
The Thinker (sculptor of)–Rodin
theater–arena
theater (Greek)–odeon, odeum
theater (low-class)–gaff
theater (part of) – balcony, box, foyer, gallery, loge, niggerheaven, orchestra, parquet, parterre, pit, stage
theater box–loge
theater floor (lower) – parquet
theatrical–dramatic, stagy
theatrical company–troupe
theatrical profession–stage
theatrical sign (full house)–S.R.O.
theatrical spectacle–pageant
theatrical star–hero, heroine, lead
Theban prince–Oedipus
Thebes district–Thebiad
Thebes king–Amphion, Laius, Pentheus
Thebes queen–Jocasta
Thebes queen changed by Zeus to stone–Niobe

thee (Eng. prov.)–tha
thee (of, French)–des
theft – burglary, larceny, robbery
theft (literary or artistic)–piracy, plagiarism
theft-like–piratic
theme–matter, motif, subject, text, topic
theme (musical)–tema
theme (title of)–lemma
Themis' daughter–Astraea
theodolite (with auxiliary arm)–alidade
theologian–divine
theologian (early)–Arius
theologian (follower of early)–Arian
theologian (pert. to)–Arian
theology (branch of)–irenics
theology branch dealing with Christian unity–irenics
theoretical or nominal–platonic
theorize–speculate
theory–contemplation, doctrine, hypothesis, ism, speculation
theory (space)–plenism
theosophy (system of) – cabala
there–thither, yonder
therefore – accordingly, as, consequently, ergo, hence, since, wherefore
therefore (Latin)–ergo
therewith (dial.)–mit
thermometer (high temperature)–pyrometer
thermostat for high temperature–pyrostat
Thesaurus compiler–Roget
these (Eng. dial.)–theasum
these (French)–ces
theses–acts, dissertations, essays
Theseus' wife–Phaedra
thesis–act, dissertation, essay
thespian – actor, actress, player
Thessaly mountain – Ida, Osa, Ossa, Pelion, Psiloriti
they go out–exeunt
thick – broad, close, coarse,

dense, gross, shaggy, solid
thick and short–squat
thick and sticky (become)–gum
thick soup–pottage, puree
thicken – clot, congeal, deepen, gel, harden, incrassate, intensify, stiffen
thicket–bosk, coppice, copse, grove, spinney
thicket (dense tree)–chaparral
thicket (Eng.)–spinney
thicket (low-growing)–coppice
thicket (southern India) – shola
thicket (tree)–coppice
thickheaded–dense, doltish, stupid
thickness – consistency, diameter, layer, ply
thickset–stocky, stout
thick-skinned–pachyderm
thief–burglar, larcener, larcenist, robber
thief (cattle)–rustler
thief (petty)–pickpocket
thief (river, among sailors)–ackman
thieves' Latin–slang
thigh–meros
thigh (animal's)–ham
thigh (pert. to)–crural
thigh plate armor–cuish
thighbone–femur, lemora
thin – bony, dilute, gaunt, haggard, lank, lanky, lathy, lean, meager, rare, slinky, spare, sparse, washy, watery, weak
thin (as fine fabrics)–sheer
thin and delicate–araneous
thin and haggard–gaunt
thin and slender–lanky, lean
thin and vibrant–reedy
thin and weak–watery
thin and withered–wizen
thin out–peter
thin plate of bone covering inner ear–tegmen
thin plate of metal–leaf
thin scale (plate)–lamina
thin tapering piece–shim
thing–article, object

thing (extraordinary)–oner
thing (huge)–monster
thing (indefinite, unnamed)–so and so
thing (law)–res
thing (nonexisting)–nonentity
thing (not easily classified)–nondescript
thing (of little value)–trifle, trinket
thing (of little worth)–stiver
thing (single)–unit
thing (unique)–oner
thing (unsubstantial)–puff
thing done – actum, actus, acta (pl.)
thingamajigs–gadgets
things–gear
things (between extremes or limits)–intermediates
things (invariable) – constants
things (Latin)–res
things (little)–inconsequentials, smalls
things accomplished – acta, actus (sing.)
things added–addenda, additaments
things allied in origin or nature–cognates
things brought into existence–creations
things done – acta, actus (sing.), acts
things for sale–merchandise, wares
things given–data
things known by reasoning and not by senses – noumena, noumenon (sing.)
things left out–omissions
things lost–losses
things suitable for eating–esculents
things that move jerkily from side to side–wagglers
things to be done–agenda, agendum (sing.)
things to be learned–lessons
things which dishearten–discouragements
things which follow–sequels

things which inspire great fear–terrors
things widely separated–extremes
think–believe, contemplate, deem, imagine, meditate, muse, opine, reflect, suppose
think (arch.) – trow, ween, wis
think logically–reason
thinkers (religious free) – latitudinarians
thinly metallic–tinny
thinly scattered–sparse
thinner–rarer
thinness–rarity, tenuity
third (comb. form)–trit
third (music)–tierce
third figure mood (valid)–ferison
third formation (of the) – tertiary
third in number–tertiary
third power of number–cube
thirsty–dry
thirty (French)–trente
this (former spelling)–yis
this spring's eternal–hope
this way–here
thistle (star)–caltrop
thistle-like plants (genus of)–carlina
thither–hence, yonder
thither (arch.)–yon
Thomas Hardy heroine – Tess
Thomas Moore character – Lalla
Thomas' opera–Mignon
thong – laniard, lanyard, strap
thong (javelin casting) – amentum, amenta (pl.)
thong (leather)–leash
thong (Mexican)–romal
thong-shaped–lorate
Thor's wife–Sif
thorax (pert. to)–pectoral
thorn – acantha, briar, brier, spine
thorn (comb. form)–spini
thorn (small)–spinule
thorn-like process (pert. to)–spinal
thorns (full of)–briery

thorny–acanthoid, spinal
thorough – exhaustive, full, intensive
thorough-going–radical
thoroughly–intensive
thoroughly established–certain, set, sure
those (Spanish)–los
those devoted to some habit –addicts
those having permits–licensees
those in office–ins
those in second childhood–dotards
those keeping daily records–diarists
those lacking consciousness–insensibles
those of non-Jewish faith – gentiles
those outside any profession –laity
those produced–creatures
those pursuing the same goal–rivals
those who are ungrateful–ingrates
those who argue–reasoners
those who can be brought to terms–transigents
those who can read and write–literates
those who destroy–spoilers
those who do professionally (suffix)–iers
those who exceed common order of nature–preternaturalists
those who fill or stop up (naut.)–stokers
those who halt–apprehenders, arresters
those who inherit–heirs, legatees
those who lay out with hope of return–investors
those who live at expense of others – moochers, parasites, spongers
those who mark by cutting–engravers
those who operate on lowering market–bears
those who operate on rising market–bulls

those who place away for reference–filers
those who ratify by hand–signers
those who reproach abusively–revilers
those who ridicule–deriders
those who seize–captors
those who take abruptly – snatchers
those who verify–corroborators
those who work together–collaborators
those with longing desires–cravers
those with permits–licensees
thou (prov. Eng.)–tha
thought – care, cerebration, cogitated, consideration, deemed, deliberation, idea, opined, opinion, ratiocination, reflection, view
thought (merry)–wishbone
thought form–ideate
thought reader–telepath
thoughtful – considerate, meditative, pensive, reflective, ruminative, solicitous
thoughtless–inattentive, inconsiderate, rash
thoughtlessly–inconsiderate
thousand (comb. form) – mille
thousand years – millenary, millennium
thousandth of an inch–mil
thrall – bondage, bondman, esne, serf, slave, slavery
thrash–beat, belabor, belam, cane, drub, swinge, twist
thrashing – beating, drubbing, milling
thread–fiber, filament, line, raveling, ravelling, reeve
thread (ball of)–clew, clue
thread (comb. form)–nem
thread (conical roll of)–cop
thread (cross, in weaving)–weft, woof
thread (division of, in weaving machine)–beer
thread (formed on spindle)–cop

thread (hard)–lisle
thread (kind of) – cotton, linen, lisle, silk
thread (knotted part)–sleave
thread (leading to solution of mystery)–clue
thread (linen tape)–inkle
thread (loose)–lint
thread (metal)–wire
thread (screw)–worm
thread (silk and wool)–arrasene
thread (silk, formed from two or more in velvet, Fr.)–trame
thread (to)–reeve
thread (warp)–stamen
thread (wool and silk)–arrasene
thread again–relace
thread cell–cnida
thread in weaving shuttle–weft
thread-like–filar, filose
thread passed through skin–seton
threadbare–sere
threads (fine, comb. form)–byss
threads that cross warp–filler, weft, woof
threaten–menace
threatening–lowery
three (combination of) – triplet
three (group in)–ternary
three (group of)–triad, trine, trio
three (old form)–tre
three (prefix)–tri
three (set of)–trio
three-card monte – montebank
three-dimensional–bruit, cubic
threefold – tern, ternal, treble, trinal, trine, triple
threefold (comb. form)–ter
three-headed goddess–Hecate
three-hundredth anniversary –tercentennial
three in one–trinity, triune
three kings of Cologne–Balthasar, Gaspar, Melchior

three-legged stand – tripod, trivet
three-lined–trilinear
three-masted vessel–schooner, xebec
Three Musketeers – Aramis, Athos, Porthos
Three Musketeers' friend – D'Artagnan
3.1416–pi
three-seeded–trispermous
three-sided figure – triangle, trigon
three-styled (bot.) – trystylous
three-toed sloth–ai
threnody–dirge
threshed grain husks–straw
threshing tool–flail
threshold–eve, limen, sill
threw–flung
threw (naut.)–heaved, hove
threw about – sloshed, thrashed
threw into confusion–rioted, stampeded
threw with force–bunged
thrice (Latin)–ter
thrice (music)–ter
thrice (prefix)–ter, tri
thrift–economy, husbandry, providence
thriftless – extravagant, improvident, lavish, prodigal, wasteful
thrifty–careful, economical, frugal, saving, sparing
thrill (nervous)–tremor
thrive – batten, fatten, flourish, grow, moise, prosper, succeed
thrive (to)–batten
throat (esophagus, comb. form)–lemo
throat (pert. to)–gular, jugular
throat (upper)–gula
throat affection (inflammatory)–angina
throat part–glottis
throb – beat, palpitate, pant, pulsate, vibrate
throb (rhythmically)–drum
throes–pangs
throne (bishop's)–apse
throne (bishop's official)–see

throng – crew, multitude, swarm
throng (dense)–press
throttle – choke, garrote, strangle
through–by, per
through (prefix)–dia
throw – cast, chuck, fling, heave, hurl, peg, pitch, shy, sling, toss
throw (force)–inject
throw (naut.)–heave
throw (quick)–flirt
throw at quoits – leaner, ringer
throw into confusion – demoralize, stampede
throw into disorder–derange
throw into ecstasy–enrapt
throw light upon–illume
throw lightly–toss
throw of double one at dice–ambsace
throw of six at dice – sise, sises (pl.)
throw off the track–derail
throw out–eject, evict, lade
throw out of order–derange
throw over–jilt
throw overboard (as goods)–jettison
throw slowly–lob
throw underhand–lob
throw water upon–douse
throwing rope–lariat, lasso, reata, riata
throwing things out of window (act of)–defenestration
thrush–mavis
thrush (European song) – mavis
thrush (golden)–oriole
thrush (kind of)–veery
thrush (large)–missel, robin
thrush (song)–mavie, mavis
thrush (song, Scot.)–throstle
thrush (Wilson's)–veery
thrushes (tawny)–veeries
thrust–gird, jab, lunge, poke
thrust (abrupt)–jab
thrust (fencing)–estocade
thrust (return)–reposte
thrust (sarcastic)–gird
thrust (sudden)–lunge

thrust (suddenly) – jab, lunge, pop
thrust (verbal, coll.)–dig
thrust in–interpose, obtrude
thrust one's self in–intrude
thrust out–protrude
thrust out of way–detude
thug–assassin, cuttle, ruffian
thumb–pollex
thumb (lady's)–peachwort
thump – bang, beat, blow, knock, pound
thump (Scot.)–clour
thunder–bronte
thunderpeal–clap
thunder-smitten goddess – Semele
thunder witch–baba
thundered forth – fulmination
thunge–bang, thump
thurible–censer
Thursday (god of)–Thor
thus–hence, sic, so
thus (Latin)–sic
thwack–bang, crush, defeat, thrash, whack
thwart–balk, cross, foil, frustrate, parry, prevent, spite
thy (prov. Eng.)–tha
thymus–gland
Tibert (arch.)–cat
Tibetan antelope–sus
Tibetan banner (processional)–tanka
Tibetan beast of burden–yak
Tibetan beer (rice)–chang
Tibetan capital–Lassa, Lhasa
Tibetan city (sacred)–Lassa, Lhasa
Tibetan coin–tanga (s.)
Tibetan deer–shou
Tibetan food (chief cereal) –tsamba
Tibetan gazelle–goa
Tibetan goat fleece (under)–pashm
Tibetan lama (grand)–Dalai
Tibetan monk–lama
Tibetan ox (wild)–yak
Tibetan priest–lama
Tibetan river–Indus
Tibetan sheep (wild) – nayaur
Tibetan urial–sha
Tibetan wildcat–manul

tibia–cnemis
Tiburon Island Indian–Seri
tick–acarid, acaridan, beat, mite
tick (venomous) – pajahuello, pajaroello
ticket–ballot, certificate, license, tag
ticket (complimentary) – comp, pass
ticket (written)–billet
ticket dealer–scalper
tickle–titillate
tidal bore–eagre
tidal creek (Span.)–estero
tidal current (strong)–tiderace
tidal flow–eagre
tidal wave–aigre, eagre
tidbit–goody
tide (low)–neap
tide (lowest of high)–neap
tidings–news, rumors, word
tidings (divine)–message
tidings (glad)–gospel
tidy – antimacassar, meet (obs.), natty, neat, shipshape, trig
tie–ascot, bind, cravat, draw, enlace, knot, link, sleeper, tether, ty
tie (as a bale of goods)–trice
tie (made to imitate a cravat)–teck
tie (puff)–ascot
tie (ready tied four-in-hand) –teck
tie (uniting)–bond
tie off (naut.)–belay
tie ornament–pin
tie securely–trammel
tie up–bind, truss
tied tightly–bound, lashed
tier–row
Tierra del Fuego Indian – Agni, Ona
tiff–drink, outburst, quarrel, sip, spat
tiger (young)–cub
tiger-hunting dog (India)–dhole
tight–closefisted, stingy, taut, tense
tight (making)–tensing
tighten–frap
tighten strings of drum–frap

tightwad–fist
Tigris River city (anc.)–Nineveh
til–sesame
tile–slate, tegula
tile (curved)–pantile
tile (malting floor)–pament, pamment
tile (used in a game)–domino
tile-like–slaty
tiler–doorkeeper, hellier
till – box, casket, cultivate, drawer, farm, plow, tray
tillable–arable
tillage–culture
tilled land (southwest U.S.) –arada
tiller – cultivator, farmer, hoer, rancher
tiller (ship's)–helm
tilt–cant, careen, heel, incline, joust, list, tip, tournament
tilt hammer (worked by foot)–oliver
tilting match–joust
timber–log, wood
timber (bolted to row of piles)–wale
timber (cross, Span. naut.)–bao
timber (curved, in a ship)–sternson
timber (cut)–lumber
timber (floor)–joist
timber (foundation)–sill
timber (horizontal rafter supporting)–purlin
timber (horizontal supporting)–stringer
timber (house foundation)–sill
timber (long upright)–mast
timber (roof)–rafter
timber (ship's lowest)–keel
timber (slightly convexed)–camber
timber (sloping)–rafter
timber (standing)–forest
timber (supporting) – spile, stud
timber (upright)–puncheon
timber (used aboard ship)–rib, spar

timber (vessel's vertical) – bitt
timber bend (upward)–sny
timber end (wedge-shaped) –tenon
timber taper (shipbuilding) –snape
timber tree–ash, birch, cedar, fir, mahogany, maple, pine, redwood, walnut
timber used aboard ship – spar
timber wolf–lobo
timbre–clang, coronet, crest, miter, tone
timbrel – drum, tabor, tambourine
time – hour, minute, moment, period, second, tempo
time (division of)–age, day, decade, minute, moment, month, second, week, year
time (fast)–Lent
time (geological, antedating life)–azoic
time (having reference to prior)–retroactively
time (interminable period of)–aeon, eon
time (intervening)–interim, meantime, meanwhile
time (long ago)–yore
time (pass idly)–loaf
time (preceded in) – antedated
time (present)–nonce
time (right, Scot.)–tid
time (spare)–leisure
time (to come)–tabor
time (waste)–dally, idle
time allowed for note payment–usance
time being–once
time clock–recorder
time granted–delay, frist, reprieve, stay
time measure – aeon, age, century, day, decade, eon, era, fortnight, hour, minute, month, second, week, year
time of highest strength, vigor and bloom–heyday

time or season (right, Scot.)
—tid
timeless – ageless, dateless,
eternal, interminable, premature, undated, unend-
ing, untimely
timely—early, opportune, opportunity, pat, prompt,
seasonably, soon
timepiece – chronometer,
clock, dial, horologue,
sunwatch, watch
times (olden, poetic)—eld
times (preceding)—yesterday
times (prosperous)—ups
times ten (suffix)—ty
timid—afraid, bashful, cowardly, fainthearted, fearful, mousy, pavid, pusil-
lanimous, retiring, shrinking, shy, timorous
timid (apprehensive)—nervous
timidity—fear
timish—fashionable, modish
timon—cynic, helm, misan-
thropy, rudder
timor—dread
Timor coin—avo (br.), pataca
timorous – afraid, fearful,
hesitant, shrinking, timid
timpani—kettledrums
tin—can, stannic, stannum
tin (extracted from slag)—
prillion
tin (Magyar)—cin
tin (pert. to)—stannic
tin (roofing)—terne
tin (symbol for)—Sn
tin and copper alloy—pewter
tin foil (mirror)—tain
tincture—myrrh
tincture deeply—imbue
tincture of opium (camphorated)—paregoric
tinder (punk)—amadou
tinder (vegetable)—amadou
tine—prong, spike, tooth
tinea—ringworm
tines (saw)—teeth
tinge—color, dye, stain
tinge deeply—imbue
tinges (shades)—casts
tingle—ring, tinkle
tinkle—clink, dingle

tinsmith's stake—teest
tint—color, hue, tinge
tint (color graduation)—nuance
tint (rosy)—blush
tinter—dyer
tintype—ferrotype
tiny – atomic, diminutive,
minute, small, teeny, wee
tip—apex, cant, careen, cue,
end, fee, gratuity, heel,
hint, lean, list, overthrow,
overturn, point, slant, tilt,
top
tip (as a vessel)—heel
tip (metal sword scabbard)
—crampit
tip (slender bristle-like) –
arista, aristae (pl.)
tip end of thing—neb
tip of tongue—corona
tip to one side—alist, careen,
list
tip up and over—cant
tippet—cape, hood, liripipe,
muffler, scarf
tippet (clerical)—amice
tipping up—atilt
tipple—bib
tippled—beered, drank
tippler—winer
tipster—tout
tipsy (Scot.)—ree
tirade—philippic, screed
tire—attire, bore, dress, exhaust, fatigue, jade, lag,
weary
tired – exhausted, fatigued,
weary
tired (poetic)—aweary
tireless – indefatigable, untiring, unwearying
tiresome—annoying, boring,
dry, dull, irksome, irritating, tame, tedious, wearisome
tissue—tela
tissue (anatomical)—tela
tissue (animal)—gelatine
tissue (botanical in process
of formation)—meristem
tissue (brain)—tela
tissue (connecting) – ligament, stroma, stromata
(pl.), tendon
tissue (fatty)—suet

tissue (horny, essential ingredient of)—keratin
tissue (mass of nerve)—ganglion
tissue (oily)—fat
tissue (oral)—gum
tissue (pert. to)—telar
tissue (thread-like)—fiber
tissue-like—telar
tissues (masses of lymphoid)
—tonsils
Titan (female)—Dione
Titan's mother—Ge
Titania's husband—Oberon
titanite—sphere
tithe—teind, tenth
tithing—denary
titlark—pipit
title – appellation, caption,
claim, dame, deed, epi-
thet, heading, madame,
name, sir, squire
title (anc.)—lars
title (clerical)—abba
title (knight's)—sir
title (Oriental)—aga, baba
title (pert. to)—tegular
title (ranking knight's)—banneret
title added to superiors by
Brahmans—aya
title of Athena—Alea
title of courtesy—madam, sir
title of honor—Dan
title of respect—madam, milady, sir
titmice—tomtits
titmice (pert. to)—parine
titmouse (blue)—nun
tittered—giggled, snickered,
teeheed
titubate—reel, stagger, totter,
unsteady, vacillating
to (arch.)—unto
to (opposite of)—fro
to (Scot.)—tae
to a conclusion—out
to a point on—onto
to an end—out
to apprehend by insight—in-
tuit
to be (Latin)—esse
to be (part of)—am, been
to be an essential part—inhere
to be available—enure
to be blue—mope

to be carried along–drift
to be certain–know
to be composed–consist
to be insubordinate–rebel
to be interlaced–ramify
to be miserly (coll.)–skimp
to be of importance–matter
to be of use–avail
to be of value–avail
to be on one's guard–beware
to be patient–bear
to be sure–indeed
to become–enure
to become aware of–learn
to benefit (poetic)–vail
to cut (after phrases with snick)–snee
to cut something from–shear
to do–bustle
to do again–repeat
to do bidding of–obey
to draft (frame)–redact
to drag one's self along – slather
to enjoy genial influence – bask
to extinguish by means of sinking fund–amortize
to face–revet
to get clear from–escape
to give grudgingly – scant, stint
to go at once (slang)–scram
to have relation to something–pertain
to hold up–support, sustain
to impart knowledge – enlighten
to inner point–into
to keep in order–regulate
to make fun of–deride
to make love to–woo
to one side–abeam
to position in–into
to remove bark from–peel, ross, scale
to seize and possess by force –usurp
to set in type–print
to sound–toot
to study factors of–analyze
to succeed to–heir
to such a degree–even
to suffer (Scot.)–dree
to take pride–glory
to take root–rhizome

to taper ship's timbers–snape
to that time–until
to the death–alamort
to the degree that–until
to the left–aport, haw
to the opposite side–across
to the rear–astern
to the time that–until
to this–hereto
to this place–here, hither
to thread–reeve
to victor (used in Irish battle cry)–aboo
to which–whereto
toad–amphibian, anuran
toad (Surinam)–pipa
toadfish–sapos, slimers
toadflax (yellow)–ramstead, ranstead, ransted
toads (zoological order of)–anura
toady–sycophant, truckler
toast–brown, parch, pledge, roast, skoal, tan
toasted bread (small pieces of)–sippet
tobacco (chew of)–cud, quid
tobacco (coarse)–caporal
tobacco (Cuban, fine)–capa
tobacco (kind of)–caporal, shag
tobacco (small piece of)–fig
tobacco disease–walloon
tobacco holder – humidor, pipe
tobacco left in pipe–dottel, dottle
tobacco principle (active) – nicotine
tobacco roll–cigar, segar
toboggan–coaster, sled
toby–cigar, jug, mug, pitcher
tocsin–alarm, alarum
to-do–ado, bustle, commotion, stir
toe (little)–minimus
toe (Scot.)–tae
toes (pert. to)–digital
together (prefix) – co, com, syn
together with–and
toggery–dress, haberdashery, harness, set, trappings
toil–drudge, drudgery, employment, labor, moil, oc-

cupation, plod, slave, snare, task, work
toilet case–etui, etwee
toilsome–laborious
token–emblem, medal, signal
token (lucky)–amulet
token of right–ticket
token of victory–palm
told–bidden, counted, narrated, related, reported
told privately–auricular
told stories (coll.)–yarned
told tales–tattled
told without authority – humored
tolerable (coll.)–so-so
tolerably (Scot.)–geyan
tolerant–forebearing, indulgent, patient
tolerate–abide, allow, bear, endure, permit, stand
toll–custom, duty, impost, knell, tax
tomato relish–catsup, ketchup
tomato sauce (savory)–catsup, ketchup
tomb – catacomb, grave, speos, vault
tomb (box-shaped)–cist
tomb (containing three chambers or cists)–tritaph
tomb (empty)–cenotaph
tomboy–hoiden, hoyden
tomboys (Scot.)–megs
tomcat–gib
tome–atlas, volume
tomorrow–manana
tonality (lacking)–atonal
tone–accent, inflection, modulation, note, sound
tone (lacking)–atonic
tone (sharp nasal)–tang
tone (single, unvaried) – monotone
tone (single, vibrant)–twang
tone (unvarying)–monotone
tone color–timbre
toneless–atony
Tonga island–Ono
tongue–language
tongue (classical)–Latin
tongue (coll.)–lingo
tongue (pert. to)–lingual
tongue (pivoted)–pawl

tongue (sacred)–Pali
tongue (tip of)–corona
tongue (wagon)–neap, pole
tongued–prated
tonic–bracer, roborant
tonic (bitter)–boneset
tonic (tabby's)–catnip
tonic leaf–coca
toning down–modulation
Tonka bean tree wood–camara
too – also, likewise, over, overly
too (Scot.)–tae
too late–belated, tardy
too small to be seen–inappreciable
took away–removed
took away (arch.)–reft
took care of – minded, nursed, tended
took first–preempted
took from–detracted
took ill–resented
took intense satisfaction in–reveled
took level of wall–boned
took out – deled, deleted, eliminated, scratched
took part again–reentered
took part of–enacted, sided
took place of–superseded
took up again–resumed
tool–implement
tool (abrading)–file
tool (ancient stone) – celt, eolith
tool (boring) – auger, awl, bit, gimlet, reamer
tool (braying)–pestle
tool (brick-making)–lute
tool (butcher's) – cleaver, saw, steel
tool (carpenter's)–hammer, level, plane, pliers, saw, square
tool (clamping)–vise
tool (cooper's)–howel
tool (cutting)–adz, adze, ax, axe, chisel, knife, plane, razor, saw, shears
tool (cutting, with bevel)–chisel
tool (edged)–adze, ax, axe, chisel, knife, razor
tool (engraving)–burin

tool (excavating)–pick, pickax, shovel
tool (fluted, for sampling cheese or butter)–taster
tool (gem-cutting)–slicer
tool (hide-fleshing)–slater
tool (hole-piercing) – awl, punch
tool (iron molder's)–lifter
tool (log-handling)–peavey, peavy, peevey, peevy,
tool (machinist's)–tap
tool (pointed)–awl, fid, gad, gimlet
tool (prehistoric) – eolith, paleolith
tool (rock-boring)–trepan
tool (roofing)–zax
tool (rope maker's)–loper
tool (rope splicer's)–fid
tool (sculptor's)–graver
tool (shingle-splitting) – frower
tool (smoothing) – file, sleeker
tool (squaring)–edger
tool (taplike cutting)–hob
tool (threshing)–flail
tool (weaver's)–sley
tool (widening)–reamer
tool (wood-decorating) – grainer
tool (wood-engraving) – scauper
tool (woodworker's marking)–scriber
tool (woodworking) – adz, adze
tool handle end–butt
tool temperer–hardener
toosh (Scot.)–gown, nightgown
toot – elevation, eminence, fool, gaze, peep, pry, sprout, spy, whistle
toot (Scot.)–drink, draft
toot (U.S. slang)–carousal, spree
tooth–cog, cuspid, fang, incisor, molar, point, projection, tine, tusk
tooth (canine)–laniary
tooth (double)–molar
tooth (fore)–biter, cutter
tooth (gear wheel)–dent
tooth (grinding)–molar

tooth (harrow)–tine
tooth (large)–fang
tooth (long)–fang, tusk
tooth (projecting)–jag, snag, tusk
tooth (wheel)–cog
tooth covering–enamel
tooth decay–caries
tooth drawer–dentist
tooth edge–dentate
tooth facing–enamel
tooth of gear wheel–dent
tooth puller–dentist
toothed (not)–edental
toothed irregularly–erose
toothed on edge–serrated
toothless–edental
top–acme, apex, cap, crest, crown, fid, pinnacle, ridge, summit, tip
top (ornamental)–finial
top of altar–mensa
top of head–pate, scalp
top of wooden stand (tilemaking)–criss
topaz humming bird–ani, ava, avas (pl.), aves (pl.)
tope – butt, clump, drink, grove, orchard, shark, stupa
topechee (obs.)–artilleryman
topee (topi)–cap, hat
toper–drunkard, shark, sot
topi – antelope, cap, hat, topee
topic – application, remedy, subject, text, theme
topic of discourse–theme
topical–local
topknot on tragic mask – onkos
topmost–apical, uppermost
topnotcher–ace, hero, star
topple–fall, overthrow, somersault, tilt, tip, tumble
torch–flambeau, flambeaux (pl.), flare, fusee, lamp
torment–afflict, bait, devil, harass, harrow, harry, pain, pester, plague, rack, rib, tantalize, tease, torture, vex
torment for sport–bait
torn–lacerated, ripped
torn asunder–riven

tornado – thunderstorm, twister, whirlwind
Tornado Junction–Trinidad
torpedo (railroad) – detonator
torpid–apathetic, dormant, dull, inert, numb, stupid
torpor – apathy, dormancy, lethargy, sluggishness
torpor (spiritual)–acedia
torrent–current, downpour, flood, spate
tortilla cooking vessel – comales
tortoise (marsh)–elodian
torture–distress, pain, rack, torment
tory–reactionary
toss–cast, fling, flip, flirt, heave, hurl, throw
toss about–thrash, thresh
toss carelessly–flip
toss together confusedly – scramble
tosspot–drunkard, sot, toper
total–absolute, add, all, complete, entire, perfect, sum, utter, whole
total (sum)–entirety
totally–quite
totem post–xat
toto–baby
totter–titubate
tottering–faltering, shaky
toucan–aracari
touch – abut, contact, feel, meet, tag, tap, trait
touch (light)–dab
touch (pert. to)–tactile
touch (to, Scot.)–tig
touch at boundary line–abut
touched–met
touchier–techier
touching–affecting, contacting, meeting, moving, pathetic
touching a single point – tangent
touchwood–amadou, punk, punkwood, sponk, spunk
touchy – irascible, irritable, sensitive, sore, ticklish
tough–hardy, leathery, obstinate, robust, rowdy, ruffian, stubborn, wiry
tough and lean–scrag

tough and sinewy–wiry
toughen–harden, temper
toughen and harden–temper
Toulouse magistrate (medieval municipal)–Capitoul
toupee–periwig, wig
toured–journeyed
tourmaline–schorl
tourmaline (red)–rubellite
tournament–battle, contest, encounter, joust, trial
tout–tipster
tow rope (obs.)–tew
tow rope (ship's)–hawser
toward (prefix)–ob
toward any place – anywhither
toward body center–entad
toward bow of boat–afore
toward center–entad
toward left side of boat–aport
toward mesial plane–mesad
toward mouth–orad
toward shore–landward
toward stern – abaft, aft, astern
toward the front–anterior
toward the head water–upriver, upstream
toward the left–aport, haw
toward the ocean–seaward
toward the rear–abaft, aft, astern, backwards
toward the surface–ectad
towel (little)–napkin
tower–elevate, exalt, pylon, spire, steeple, uplift
tower (anc.)–Babel
tower (bell)–belfry, campanile
tower (castle's chief, anc.)–donjon
tower (church)–belfry, spire, steeple
tower (famous) – London, Pisa
tower (glacier ice)–serac
tower (ice)–serac
tower (India)–Minar
tower (mosque)–minaret
tower (Oriental)–minaret
tower (principal, castle) – donjon
tower (small)–turret
tower (watch)–mirador

tower for supporting telegraph wires–pylon
tower of ice–serac
towering – Alpine, high, steep
town (imaginary)–Podunk
town (pert. to)–civic, urban
township (abbr.)–TP
township (Attic)–Deme
townsman–cit, citizen
toy–dally, doll, knickknack, play, rattle, teddybear, teetotum, top
toy (child's)–teetotum
toyed–dallied
toys (trundling)–hooples
trace – derive, hint, mark, shade, sign, sketch, thought, tinge, trail, vestige
trace back–refer
trace by scent–nose
trace course of–deduce
tracer (slender) – probe, seeker
tracing – cardiogram, copy, ergogram
track – follow, path, trail, way
track (animal)–spoor
track (deer)–slot
track (sunken)–rut
track (wild beast's)–spoor
track race–relay
tracking–slotting, trailing
tracks (fossil worm)–nereites
tract – area, brochure, dissertation, district, essay, exposition, leaflet, pamphlet, quarter, region, treatise
tract (arid)–barren, desert
tract (boggy ground)–morass
tract (English sandy)–dene
tract (grassland)–prairie
tract (public)–parc, park
tract (swampland) – Everglades
tract (triangular)–gore
tract (undulating) – downs, wold
tract (vast treeless) – llano, prairie, steppe
tract (wasteland) – desert,

everglades, fen, heath, moor, morass, swamp

tract inclosed within foreign territory–enclave

tract of ground (ornamental)–park

tract of land–estate, range

tract of land (covered with stones)–pedregel

tract of wasteland–heath

tractable – docile, ductile, governable, malleable, pliant

tractableness–amenability

tractacility–ductility

trade–barter, business, buy, craft, deal, exchange, metier, practice, profession, sell, swap

trade combination–merger

trademark–brand

trader – merchant, shopkeeper, tradesman

trader (army)–sutler

trader (petty)–monger

trading association–hanse

trading post (army, abbr.)–P.X.

trading station–post

tradition–legend

tradition (unproved)–myth

traditional–legendary

traditional tale–saga

traduce–asperse, belie, defame, slander

traffic – barter, commerce, trade

traffic (mercantile)–trade

traffic in sacred things–simony

trafficked–traded

tragic–calamitous, dire

trail – follow, path, route, spoor, train, track

trail (marked)–blazed

trail (mountain)–pass

trail (Spanish)–camino

trail (wild animal's)–spoor

trail along–draggle

trail blazer–pioneer

trail marker (above timber) –cairn

train – breed, coach, direct, discipline, drill, educate, focus, rehearse, retinue, school, suite

train (desert)–caravan

train (making all stops) – accommodation, local

train (speedy)–flier, streamliner

train men–crew

train mentally–educate

trained mechanic–artisan

trait – characteristic, peculiarity

trait (well defined)–streak

traitor–Judas

traject – course, ferry, passage, route, way

tram–trolley

tramp – bum, hike, hobo, step, tread, vagabond, vagrant, walk

tramp (coll.)–vag

trample–tread

trance–daze, coma, raptus, stupor

trance (mystic)–amentia

tranchant – cutting, sharp, trenchant

tranquil–calm, easy, pacific, still

tranquil ease (live a life of) –vegetate

tranquility–kef, peace

tranquilize – appease, calm, compose, pacify, quiet, serene, settle, soothe, still

transact–negotiate, treat

transaction–action, deal, discharge, performance, proceeding, sale

transaction (business)–deal, proposition

transaction (commercial) – business

transcend–exceed, excel, outstrip, surpass

transcendant–above

transcribe–copy

transcript–copy, duplicate

transfer–cede, change, conveyance, deed, removal, remove, shift, transport

transfer of ownership or title –alienation

transfer of property–disposal

transfer to another–depute

transferring crown to successor–demise

transferror of property–alienor

transfigure – metamorphose, transform

transfix–impale, pierce, pin, spear

transfix with anything sharp –impale

transform–alter, assimilate, change, convert, metamorphose, transfigure, transmogrify, transmute, turn

transformation – metamorphosis

transgress–err, sin

transgress the command of –disobey

transgression – crime, fault, infringement, misdeed, offense, sin, trespass

transgressor–offender, sinner

transient – ephemeral, evanescent, fleeting, fugitive, migratory, momentary, transitory

transient occupation–avocation, hobby

transit–passage

transition – change, conversion, passage, shift

transitional–transitive

transitory–evanescent, fleeting, temporal, temporary, transient

translate–construe, decode, interpret, read, rede, render, transfer

translation – interpretation, paraphrase, pony, rendition, version

translator (oral)–interpreter

translucent – limpid, transparent

transmission from parents to children–heredity

transmit – convey, devolve, forward, render, send, transfer

transmitted generation to generation–hereditary

transmute – convert, transform

transparency in air (lack of) –haze

transparent – bright, clear,

crystal, diaphanous, laky, lucent, lucid, luminous, lustrous, pelucid, shining, translucent

transparent (not)–opaque

transparent (smooth, hard) –glassy

transport–banish, boat, carry, convey, ecstasy, rapt

transport (equine)–horsecar

transport (flatbottom, horse) –palander

transported with delight – enraptured, rapt

transpose–reverse, translate

Transvaal District (gold mining)–Rand

Transvaal policeman–zarp

trap–catch, corner, deadfall, enmesh, ensnare, gin, pitfall, snare, tree, web

trap (eel-catching)–eelpot

trap (fish)–eelpot, weir

trap (insect)–web

trap (lobster)–creel, pot

trap (old word)–grane

trap (pert. to)–trappose

trap door–drop

trapan – deceiver, entrap, lure, swindle, trick, trickster

trapper–snarer

trappings – apparatus, gear, paraphernalia, tack

trappings (horse)–caparison

trappings (theatrical stage)– properties, props, scenery

trash–dirt, refuse, rubbish, rubble

trashy – cheap, rubbishy, toshy, useless, worthless

trauma – injury, shock, wound

Travancore coin – chakram (s.), chuckrum (s.), fanam (s.)

travel – fare, peregrinate, ride, sojourn, traverse, wend

travel across snow–mush

travel along ground (as an airplane)–taxi

travel along shore–coast

travel by land–overland

travel by wagon–trek

travel from place to place– itinerate

traveler–farer

traveler (itinerant)–tourist

travelers (company of)–caravan

traveling salesman – agent, drummer, representative

traverse – athwart, cross, deny, pass

travesty–caricature, parody, satire

travesty (writer of)–parodist

tray–salver, server

tray (type)–font

treacherous – betray, disaffected, faithless, false, insidious, machiavellian, perfidious, plotting, punic, traitorous, unreliable, unstable, untrustworthy

treachery – deceit, perfidy, treason

treacle–molasses

treacle water–cordial

treacle wort–pennycress

tread–step

tread (circular)–volt

tread heavily–trample

tread under foot–trample

treadle–chalaza, pedal

treason–sedition

treasonable–perfidious, traitorous, treacherous

treasure – cherish, prize, riches, store, value, wealth

treasurer (college)–bursar, bursaries, bursary

treasuring up–pursing

treasury–chest, purse, repository, storehouse

treat–dose, handle, repast, use

treat (each one paying his own check)–Dutch

treat as overlooked or forgotten–condone

treat by surgery–operate

treat improperly–misuse

treat maliciously–spite

treat royally–regale

treat silk to make rustle – scroop

treat tenderly–coddle, pamper

treat with contempt–flout

treat with deference–respect

treat with derision–scout

treat with distinction–honor

treat with iodine–iodate

treat with ridicule–scout

treated with pine product– resined

treating of love–erotic

treating of morals–ethical

treatise–thesis, theses (pl.), tract

treatise (elementary)–grammar

treatise (short)–tract

treatise on forest trees–silva

treatment–usage

treatment (bad)–misusage

treatment (bomb) – fireworks, jet

treatment (compassionate)– mercy

treatment (cruel)–severity

treatment (ill)–abuse

treaty–agreement, arrangement, capitulation, cartel, contract, convention, entente, mise, pact, understanding

treaty (preliminary draft) – proctol

treaty-bound nations–allies

treble–latten, soprano, three, threefold, triple

treble clef–gee

tree–arar, ash, ebo, eboe, fir, locust, mahogany, maple, oak, pine

tree (alder, Scot.)–arn

tree (allspice)–pimento

tree (ament bearing)–alder

tree (American)–oneberry

tree (American gum)–tupelo

tree (American tropical) – papaw, pawpaw

tree (apple)–malus

tree (apple family)–papaw, pawpaw, sorb

tree (Australian wattle) – boree

tree (basswood)–linden

tree (betel nut)–areca

tree (bignoniaceous)–catalpa

tree (buckwheat) – teetee, titi

tree (candlenut)–ama

tree (caoutchouc) – rubber, ule
tree (caucho yielding)–ule
tree (Central American) – ebo, eboe
tree (chocolate)–cacao
tree (cinnamon family)–cassia
tree (common timber)–ash, fir, pine, redwood
tree (cone bearing)–conifer
tree (coniferous)–cedar, fir, larch, yew
tree (devil)–dita
tree (drupe bearing)–bito
tree (dwarf)–scrub
tree (dye-stuff yielding)–annatto
tree (East Indian)–ach
tree (eucalyptus)–yate
tree (European mountain ash)–rowan
tree (evergreen) – balsam, carob, cedar, fir, juniper, larch, madrona, madrono, pine, yew
tree (evergreen, fruit)–avocado, lemon, orange
tree (evergreen, willowy foliaged)–carob, carobe, tawa
tree (fabaceous)–agati
tree (flowering)–titis
tree (flowering, small)–oleaster
tree (fruit-yielding)–bearer
tree (graceful, with short deciduous leaves)–larch
tree (guinea food)–akee
tree (gum)–balta, eucalyptus
tree (hardwood)–mahogany, maple, narra, poon, walnut
tree (hickory)–pecan
tree (holly)–ilex
tree (horse-radish)–behen
tree (hybrid citrus)–tangelo
tree (India)–banyan
tree (juniper)–cade
tree (kind of magnolia)–yulan
tree (large, mimosaceous) – siris
tree (laurel)–bay
tree (lime)–tilicetum
tree (linden)–lime, lin, teil

tree (lotus)–sadr
tree (mafurra)–elcaja
tree (mango)–topes
tree (marmalade) – mamie, sapote
tree (mastwood)–poon
tree (Mexican rubber)–ule
tree (mimosaceous)–siris
tree (New Zealand medicinal)–wahahe
tree (northern)–pine
tree (nut-bearing)–cola
tree (oil-producing)–ben
tree (oil-yielding seed)–tung
tree (olive family)–ash
tree (orange-like)–osage
tree (order of cone-bearing) –gnetales
tree (Pacific Coast)–madrona, madrono
tree (Pacific timber)–ipil
tree (palm)–arengs, coco, ti
tree (Palmyra palm)–tal
tree (part of)–bole, branch, leaf, trunk
tree (Philippine)–dao, dita, ligas, tua, tui
tree (pinaceous)–cedar, fir
tree (pine family)–cedar, fir
tree (plantain)–pala
tree (pod-bearing)–catalpa
tree (poisonous)–upas
tree (poon)–dilo, keena
tree (Puerto Rico fustic) – mora
tree (rain)–genisaro, saman, zaman, zamang
tree (red, yellow, white flowered)–agati
tree (rowan)–sorb
tree (rubber) – caoutchouc, caucho, seringa, ule
tree (rutaceous)–lime
tree (salt)–atle, atlee
tree (sandarac)–arar
tree (sapodilla)–sapota, sapote, zapote
tree (Scotch alder)–arn
tree (service)–sorb
tree (shade)–catalpa
tree (small)–alder, seedling
tree (snake bite antidote yielding)–cedron
tree (softwood)–balsa, linde
tree (southern U.S.)–titi
tree (stunted)–scrub

tree (tamarisk, salt)–atle, atlee
tree (timber)–ash, birch, cedar, fir, mahogany, maple, narra, pine, redwood
tree (timber of Pacific)–ipil
tree (tropical) – anubing, cacao, nepal, palm
tree (tropical American) – dali
tree (tropical fruit)–banana, tamarind
tree (tropical timber) – dagame, icica
tree (tulip)–poplar
tree (turpentine yielding)–terebinth
tree (wattle)–boree
tree (willow)–osier
tree (with quivering leaves) –aspen
tree bark (exterior)–ross
tree bark (used as cloth)–tapa
tree bark (used for tanning) –alder
tree bearing samara–ash
tree branches (cut off) – brushwood
tree dwelling–nest
tree exudation – gum, lac, resin, rosin, sap, tar
tree growth (cut periodically)–coppice
tree growth (small)–copse
tree gum–xylan
tree heath–brier
tree limb–bough, branch
tree nail–nog
tree of genus alnus–alder
tree of oak family–alder
tree snake–gimp, lora
tree sprout–sprig
tree trunk–bole, stock
tree trunk (16 feet)–caber
tree used to make victor's crown–laurel
tree with soft white wood–lin
tree with streaked wood – baria
tree yielding caucho–ule
treeless plain–llano, pampas, prairie, steppe
trees (felled, used as barriers)–abattis

trees (genus of)–olea
trees (genus of maple-like) –rulac
trees (grove of small)–copse
trees (olive)–olea
trees (pert. to)–arboreal
trees (plantation of)–forest, orchard
trees (service)–sorbs
trefoil–clover
tregetour–juggler, magician
trek – expedition, journey, migrate, migration
trellis–arbor, lattice, lattice-work, pergola
trellis (architectural) – pergola
trematode worms (larval stage)–cercaria
tremble–falter, quake, quiver, shake, shiver, shudder, totter, trepidate, vibrate
tremble (shake) – dodder, quaver, quiver
tremble with fear–shudder
trembling – aspen, dither, fearful, quaking, shaking, vibrating
tremendous – awful, frightful, horrible, momentous, monstrous, terrific
tremor – quake, quiver, shake, tremble, vibration
tremulous – aspen, palpitating, palsied, quavering, shaking, vibratory
trench – ditch, encroach, excavation, infringe, trespass
trench (Scot.)–gaw
trench diggers–sappers
trench extension–sap
trench line (extended)–salient
trench maker–sapper
trenchant – biting, cutting, sharp
trend–direction, drift, movement, revolve, skirt, strike, swing, tendency, turn, vein
trend (general)–tone
trend of thought–tenor
trepan – deceiver, entrap,

lure, snare, stratagem, swindle, trick, trickster
trepidation–agitation, confusion, consternation, dismay, disturbance
trespass – breach, encroach, entrench, infringe, infringement, invade, offense, transgression, trench
tress–curl, ringlet
triad–three, trine, trinity
trial–bout, case, contest, examination, experiment, go, test
trial (place of)–venue
trial (severe)–ordeal
triangle–trigon
triangle (equilateral) – square
triangle (side of)–leg
triangle (three acute angles) –oxygon
triangle (two equal sides) – isosceles
triangle (unequal sides) – scalene
triangle side–leg
triangular muscles–deltoids
triangular piece – gore, gusset, miter, mitre, wedge
tribal symbol–totem
tribe–clan, group, race, sept
tribe (head of)–chief, patriarch
tribe (Israel, priestly)–Levi
tribe (which migrated to Europe from Asia)–Aryan
tribe members (five nations) –Senecas
tribe of Israel–Dan, Reuben
tribulation–distress, sorrow, suffering, trial
tribunal – banc, bar, bench, court, forum
tribunal (legal)–court
tributary–auxiliary, contributory, feeder, subordinate
tribute–allegiance, allot, assign, attribute, bestow, contribute, duty, encomium, grant, gratitude, impost, levy, pay, pension, praise, rental, respect, retribution, scat, tariff, tax

tribute (enthusiastic popular)–ovation
tributes (Gael.)–cains
tricar–tricycle
trice – haul, instant, lash, pull, secure, snatch
trice (prefix)–ter, tri
trick – artifice, cheat, deceit, deception, defraud, delude, delusion, finesse, flam, fob, fraud, imposture, ruse, subterfuge, wile
trick (beguiling)–wile
trick (clever)–feat, stunt
trick (sly)–ruse
trickery – artifice, cheating, chicanery, deception, duplicity, fraud
trickery (intentional)–deceit
trickle – distil, distill, drip, dripple
tricks (knavish)–roguery
trickster–cheater, rogue
tricky–sly, snide
tricky (slang)–snide
tried – faithful, proved, reliable, tested, trustworthy
tried (Scot.)–ettled
tries – attempts, contests, essays, tests
tries (Scot.)–ettles
trifle – bagatelle, bit, dally, dawdle, doit, fig, nothing, palter, potter, toy, triviality
trifle (insignificant)–fico
trifle (Irish)–traneen
trifle (mere)–straw
trifle fault–peccadillo
trifler–palterer
trifles–dallies, palters, toys
trifles away time–dallies
trifling – badinage, insignificant, mere, petty, trivial
trig–methodical, natty, neat, precise, smart, spruce, stiff, trim
trigonometric ratio – cosine, sine
trigonometrical figure–sine
trigonometrical function – cosine, sine, tangent
trigonometry of the globe–spherics

trill – move, quaver, shake, vibrate, warble
trill (form of)–mordent
trim–adorn, crop, embellish, lop, natty, neat, ornament, petite, preen, prune, shear, trig
trim (neat, Scot.)–snod
trim a coin–nig
trim off–bob, lop
trimmed with embroidery – paneled
trimming – braid, fringe, gimp, lace, ruche, ruching
trimming (band)–braid
trimming (braid)–lacet
trimming (dress) – ruche, ruching
trimming (showy)–falbala
trimming up–ornamenting, sprucing
trinity–triad, triune
trinket – gaud, gewgaw, knickknack, ornament, toy
trip–cruise, excursion, journey, stumble, tour, voyage
trip (purposeful)–errand
trip hammer operator–tilter
tripe (mixed with minced meat)–rolpens
triple–treble, trine
triple (a, music)–tercet
tripletail–sama
triplets (one of)–trin
tripod–easel, trivet
tripod (cooking vessel, var.) –trevet
tripod (six-footed)–cat
trisaccharide–triose
trismus–lockjaw, tetanus
trist – sad, sorrowful, trust, tryst
Tristan's lover–Iseult
triste – depressing, dismal, dull, sad
Tristram Shandy author – Sterne
trisulphide (arsenic) – orpiment
trite – banal, betide, hackneyed, stale, stereotyped, threadbare, vapid
triton–eft, newt, salamander

triumph–achieve, conquest, prevail, victory, win
triumphs over–defeats
trivial–banal, common, commonplace, doggerel, nominal, ordinary, paltry, petty, piperly, small, trifling, trite
trod – footpath, footstep, path, track
trog–bargain, barter
trogger–paddler, vagrant
Trojan–Dardan
Trojan hero–Eneas, Paris
Trojan king–Priam
Trojan mountain–Ida
Trojan prince – Eneas, Hector, Paris
Trojan prince (itinerant) – Aeneas, Eneas
Trojan war hero–Palamedes
Trojan warrior (bravest) – Agenor
trolley – barrow, cart, handcart, sledge, tram, truck
trolley car–tram, tramcar
trombone (medieval)–sackbut
trombone mute – wahwah, wawa
troop (light, one of body of) –chasseur
troop arrangement–echelon
troop body (arrangement of) –echelon
troop encampment–etape
troop formation–line
troop step-like arrangement –echelon
trooper (light horse)–hussar
troops (German armored)– Panzer
troops (line of attacking) – wave
troops (mounted)–cavalry
troops (sally of, from besieged fort)–sortie
trophy – laurels, memorial, palm, prize, reward
tropical American animal – coati, potto
tropical American animal (piglike)–peccary
tropical American herbs (genus of)–evea, ruellia

tropical American shrubs (genus of)–evea, ruellia
tropical American tree – sapota
tropical American tree (boxwood)–seron
tropical American tree (softwood)–balsa
tropical American wildcat–eyra
tropical animal (allied to raccoon)–coati
tropical arum plant–taro
tropical Atlantic fish–salema
tropical bird–ani, tody
tropical bird (black)–ani
tropical bird (brilliant) – jacamar, jalap
tropical chlorosis (med.) – ancylostomiasis
tropical cuckoo–ani
tropical fish–toro
tropical fruit–banana, date, guava, mango, papaw, papaya
tropical herb–aloe, sida
tropical herbs (genus of) – tacca
tropical lizard–agama
tropical plant–agave, arum, taro
tropical resin–copal
tropical rodent–agouti
tropical shrub – alacad, gardenia, lantana
tropical shrubs (genus of)– urena
tropical timber tree–icica
tropical tree – assai, banana, coco, date, guava, palm, pawpaw, sweetsop, tamarind
tropical tree (fruit)–banana, date, guava, tamarind
tropical trees (genus of) – helicteres
tropical wildcat–eyra
tropical woody vine – cowhage
trot–hurry, jog, run
trotting horse–morgan
trottoir–footpath, pavement, sidewalk
troubadour–minstrel
trouble – ado, adversity, affliction, ail, annoy, anxi-

ety, bother, concern, disorder, disquiet, distress, disturbance, effort, fuss, grieve, irk, matter, misfortune, molest, perplexity, perturb, perturbation, sorrow, stir, worry
trouble grievously–afflict
troubled (deeply)–distressed
troublemaker–agitator, gossiper
troublesome – annoying, bothersome, burdensome, difficult, distressing, disturbing, oppressive, vexatious, wearisome
trough–channel, chute, conduit, dale, gutter
trough (inclined) – chute, sluice
trough for cooling ingots – bosh
trout (green and black salmon)–sewen
trout (salmon)–sewen
trout (young sea) – grilse, peal
trout shad–squeteague
troutlet–fingerling
trovatore–troubadour
trove–treasure
trow–believe, boat, catamaran, expect, hope, think, trust
trowing–belief, creed, opinion
Troy–see also Trojan
Troy (anc.) – Ilion, Ilium, Troas
Troy (besieger of)–Ajax
Troy (defender of)–Aeneas
Troy (founder of)–Ilus
Troy (lady from)–Helen
Troy (pert. to anc.) – Iliac, Trojan
troy weight – grain, ounce, pennyweight, pound
truce – armistice, cessation, intermission
truce (French)–treve
truck – barter, dray, exchange, lorry, peddle, traffic, vegetables
truck (for heavy loads)–lorry
truck (low horse)–lorry

truck (military)–lorry
truck (railway)–bogie
truckle–fawn, toady
truculent – barbarous, cruel, destructive, ferocious, fierce, ruthless, savage, scathing
trudge–plod, tramp
true – authentic, devoted, faithful, germane, lawful, precise, pure, real, reliable, steadfast, unerring, unfaltering
true (infallibly)–gospel
true (poetic)–leal
true (strictly)–fact
true copy–estreat
true skin–derm, derma
true to fact–literal
true to fact (not)–figurative
truehearted (Scot.)–leal
truest–veriest
truffle–tuber
trug–basket, caul, cawl, pail, prostitute, trough, wench
truism – axiom, commonplace
truism (insipid)–platitude
trull – demon, fiend, giant, girl, lass, wench
truly – accurately, exactly, justly, properly, rightly, verily, yea
trump–ruff
trump in five-card loo (highest)–pam
trumpet–clarion, horn
trumpet (kind of)–clarion
trumpet blare–fanfare, tantara
trumpet call (stage, obs.)–sennet
trumpet creeper–tecoma
trumpet forth–blare
trumpeter (golden-breasted)–agami
truncheon – baton, club, cudgel, staff
trunk – body, bole, box, chest, coffer, pool, tank, torso
trunk (felled tree)–log
trunk (main arterial)–aorta, aortae (pl.)
trunk (redwood)–bole
trunk (statue)–torso

trunk (tree)–bole, stock
trunkfish–toro
truss–bind, fasten, tie
trust – believe, confide, confidence, credit, depend, dependence, reliance, rely, syndicate
trust (repeatedly)–dartle
trustee–fiduciary
trustee of personal property–bailee
trustful – confiding, reliant, unquestioning
trustworthy – reliable, safe, solid
truth – fact, sooth, veracity, verisimilitude, verity
truth (arch.)–sooth
truth (fundamental)–principle
truth (goddess of)–Maat
truth (in, arch.)–certes
truth (self-evident)–axiom
truthful – honest, veracious, veridic, veridical
truthfulness–accuracy, honesty, veracity
try – attempt, endeavor, essay, test, trial
try (Scot.)–ettle
try out–test, trial
tsar – autocrat, czar, despot, Ivan, tzar
tsetse fly (genus of)–glossina
T-shaped–tau
tub (brewing)–vat
tub (large)–vat
tub (sailor's mess)–kid
tub (small)–bowie
tub (wooden, large, dial.)–soe
tuba (bass)–helicon
Tubalcain's father–Lamech
tube–conduit, cop, cylinder, hose, pipe
tube (an electron)–bulb
tube (bent)–siphon
tube (electron)–bulb
tube (flexible)–hose
tube (fluid)–duct, hose, pipe
tube (for depositing concrete under water)–tremie
tube (glass, used in blowpipe analysis)–matrass
tube (insulated)–spaghetti
tube (priming)–auget

tube (radio)–diode
tube (silk winding)–cop
tuber–oca, root, taro, yam
tuber (dried species of orchids)–salep, saul
tuber (edible)–beet, oca, potato, taro, uva, yam
tuber (fleshy)–bulb
tuber (like tapioca)–salep
tubular – cylindrical, pipy, round
tucker–bib, fatigue, tire
Tuesday (French)–Mardi
Tuesday (god of)–Tiu, Tyr
Tuesday (Shrove) – Mardi-gras
tufa–toph, tophe
tufa (volcanic)–trass
tuft–coma, comae (pl.), crest
tuft (decorative)–doss
tuft (hairy seed) – coma, comae (pl.)
tuft of feather–crest
tuft of hair–beard
tuft of hairs (on horse's hoof)–fetlock
tuft of soft hairs (bot.) – comose
tug–drag, draw, haul, pull
tulip (seeding)–breeder
tumble fall, precipitate, somersault, spill, stumble
tumbled down–toppled
tumbler–acrobat, cart, dunker, glass, gymnast, tippler, tumbrel, vessel
tumbril–cart
tumeric–rea
tumeric (turmeric)–olena
tumor–edema
tumor (small)–wen
tumor (small, hard)–ganglion
tumor on brain–glioma
tumult–babble, babel, bluster, brawl, bustle, confusion, disorder, disturbance, ferment, hubbub, noise, riot, turbulence, uproar
tumult (seditious) – emeute, outbreak
tumultuous – agitated, boisterous, confused, disorderly, disturbed, lawless, noisy, riotous, violent

tun–cask, jar, tub, vat
tun shell fossil–dolite
tune–aria, song
tune (bagpipe)–port
tune (elaborate)–aria
tune (hymn)–chorale
tune (lively)–lilt
tune (to)–key
tune musical instrument – string
tune out a radio station–detune
tuned correctly–keyed
tunefulness–melody
tungstate (iron manganese) –cal
tungsten (source of)–cal
tungsten ore–cal
tunicate (floating)–salpa
tunicate (free swimming) – salpa
Tunis ruler's title–bey, dey
Tunisian capacity measure–saa, saah, sah
Tunisian cape–Bon
Tunisian city–Bizerte, Ferryville, Gabes, Gafsa, Grombalia, Korba, Korbous, Mateur, Nabeul, Sfax, Susa, Tebourba, Tunis (c.), Zaghouan
Tunisian coin–saah
Tunisian gulf–Gabes
Tunisian island–Jebado
Tunisian measure – cafiz, mettar, millerole, whiba
Tunisian measure (capacity) –saa, saah, sah
Tunisian pasha–bey, dey
Tunisian ruler–bey, dey
Tunisian seaport – Bizerte, Sfax
Tunisian weight–artal, artel, kantar, ratel, rotl, uckia
tunnel – bore, burrow, drift, subway
tunnel (coal)–adit
Turanian people (pert. to)–Akkad
turban – entree, fillet, headdress, seerband
turbid – feculent, muddy, roily
turbine wheel–rotor
turbulence – agitation, commotion, disturbance, im-

petuosity, rioting, tumultuousness, unruliness, uproar
turbulent – loud, stormy, wild
turf–grass, sod, sward
turf (Scot.)–fale
turf dislodged in golfing – divot
turgid – bloated, bombastic, grandiloquent, grandiose, inflated, magniloquent, swollen, tumid
Turk–Ottoman, Tatar
Turk (distinguished)–aga
Turkestan–Ili
Turkestan city – Andijan, Kokand, Samarkand
Turkestan highland–pamir
Turkestan moslem–salar
Turkestan mountain range–Alai
Turkestan people–Sart
Turkestan people (highest civilized)–Usbeg, Usbek, Uzbeg
Turkestan range–Alai
Turkestan regiment–alai
Turkestan river–Ili
Turkestan sea–Aral
Turkestan town dweller – Sart
turkey (genus of)–meleagris
turkey (young)–poult
turkey buzzard–aura
Turkic people member (East Turkestan)–Tatar, Uigur
Turkic tribesman – Tartar, Tatar
Turkish–Osmanli
Turkish caliph (fourth)–Ali
Turkish camp (palisadoed)–palanka
Turkish cap–fez
Turkish cap (large)–calpac
Turkish capital–Ankara
Turkish carpet (misnomer) –seljuk
Turkish cavalryman–spahi
Turkish ceremony (outbreak of war)–alay
Turkish chief–aga
Turkish city – Adana, Adrianople, Afyonkarahisar, Ankara, Broussa, Brusa, Constantinople, Dar-

danelles, Diyarbekir, Edirne, Elaziz, Erzurum, Eskisehir, Homs, Istanbul, Izmir, Kayseri, Konya, Marash, Samsun, Scutari, Sivas, Skutari, Smyrna, Stamboul, Uskudar
Turkish city (anc.)–Edessa
Turkish city (Asiatic)–Adana
Turkish coin–altilik (s.), asper (ac.), beshlik (alum.), lira (g.), medjidie (s.), piaster (ni.), pound (g.)
Turkish coin (silver)–rebia
Turkish commander – aga, sirdar
Turkish counsel (of state)–divan
Turkish court–porte
Turkish decree–irade
Turkish dignitary–pasha
Turkish district–cilicia
Turkish dynasty member – Seljuk
Turkish flag–alem
Turkish general–kamal
Turkish government (old)–porte
Turkish governor–bey, mudir, pasha
Turkish grandee–bashaw
Turkish gulf–Cos
Turkish horde member – Tartar, Tatar
Turkish hospice–imaret
Turkish Imperial standard–alem, toug
Turkish inn–imaret
Turkish javelin–jeered, jerid
Turkish judge–cadi
Turkish landowner–aga
Turkish liquor–raki
Turkish magistrate – aga, cadi
Turkish man-of-war – caravel, cater
Turkish measure – arsheen, arshin, berri, chinik, djerib, donum, fortin, halebi, hatt, khat, kile, kileh, nocktat, oka, oke, parmack, parmak, pik, pik halebi, zira, zirai
Turkish measure (linear) – pic, pik

Turkish military camp–ordu
Turkish minister (of state)–vizier
Turkish money (of account) –asper
Turkish money unit–asper
Turkish mosque (principal, central)–jami
Turkish mountain–Ararat
Turkish name–Ali
Turkish native (anc.)–Edessan
Turkish oak–cerris
Turkish officer–aga
Turkish official – ameer, amir, emeer, emir, osmanli
Turkish official (military)–pasha
Turkish patent–berat
Turkish prayer rug–melas
Turkish president–Inonu
Turkish province–Angora
Turkish province (anc.) – Sert, Siirt
Turkish regiment–alai
Turkish reservist–redif
Turkish river–Mesta, Sarus, Seihun, Seyhan
Turkish rug (prayer)–melas
Turkish ruler–president
Turkish saber (short) – obolus
Turkish sailing vessel–saic
Turkish seaport–Enos
Turkish soldier–nizam
Turkish soldier (turbulent cruel)–bashi, bazouk
Turkish standard (Imperial) –alem, toug
Turkish statue–tanzimat
Turkish sultan–Ahmed, Saladin, Selim
Turkish sultan (1389–1403) –Ilderim
Turkish sultan (1789–1807) –Selim
Turkish sultan's title – calif, caliph
Turkish sword – yatagan, yataghan
Turkish tambourine–daira
Turkish tax–avania
Turkish title – aga, ali, ameer, amir, baba, bey, emeer, emir, pasha

Turkish title (commander)–aga, pacha, pasha
Turkish title (of dignity)–ameer, amir, emeer, emir
Turkish title (of respect) –baba
Turkish town–bir
Turkish tribe (one of)–Tartar, Tatar
Turkish veil (double)–yashmac, yashmak
Turkish vessel (flatbottomed)–mahone
Turkish vessel (sailing)–saic
Turkish vilayet–adana
Turkish war (religious) – crescentade
Turkish weight–artal, artel, batman, cequi, cheke, dirhem, drachma, dram, kantar, kerat, kile, kileh, maund, miskal, oka, oke, quintal, ratel, rotl, yusdrum
Turkish wheat (parched, crushed)–bulgur
Turkish woman's dress bodice–jelick
Turkish zither–canum
Turkoman tribe–Ersar, Viddhal
turmeric–olena, rea
turmoil–ado, confusion, disquiet, ferment, perturbation, tumult
turn–bend, gyrate, pivot, revolve, roll, rotate, spin, swivel, wheel
turn (off side)–gee
turn (old word for)–kyr
turn and twist–slew, slue
turn apostate–renege
turn aside–avert, deflect, depart, diverge, divert, shunt, slew, slue, swerve
turn away–divert, repel
turn back – coward, reflect, repel, revert
turn down–veto
turn for help–resort
turn from one direction to another–vert
turn front wheels–cramp
turn inside out–evert, invert
turn into bone–ossify
turn into steel–acierate

turn inward – introre, introvert

turn of duty–spell

turn off–shunt

turn off to the side–gee

turn on axis–rotate

turn on pivot–swivel

turn out–evert, evict, oust

turn out neatly–trig

turn out to be–prove

turn outward–evert, splay

turn over–keel, spill

turn over (music)–verte

turn over new leaf–reform

turn quickly–slew, slue, veer

turn sharply–swerve, veer

turn to left–haw, port

turn to off side–gee

turn to right–gee, starboard

turn up–appear, keel

turncoat–renegade

turned aside–diverged

turned back (bot.)–evolute

turned back or unfolded – evolute

turned backward–retroverse

turned off–diverged

turned outward–everted, extrorse

turned over at edge–evolute

turned to one side – awry, skew

turned up at end–retrousse

turning – rotary, rotating, whirling

turning backward–inversion

turning point – crisis, crises (pl.)

turning spirally (from right to left)–sinistrorse

turnip (kind of)–rutabaga

turnips (large)–rutabagas

turnips (Scot.)–neeps

turns (full of)–quirky

turns (series of short) – zigzag

turns (univalve shell) – whorls

turns of duty–spells

turnstile–stile

turpentine distillate – resin, rosin

turpentine-yielding tree – terebinth

turpid–cowardly, low, vile

turret–tower

turtle (edible)–terrapin

turtle (fresh water) – emyd, emydea, emydian, emydidae, emydinea

turtle (large)–arrau

turtle (largest sea)–leatherback

turtle (marine, large) – loggerhead

turtle (snapping) – shagtail, torup

turtle part (attached to lower shell)–pee

turtle shell–carapace

Tuscan island (off coast) – Elba

Tuscan wine (dry red)–chianti

Tuscany city (Italy university)–Pisa

Tuscany commune–Greve

Tuscany river–Arno

tusk–fang, tooth

tusk dentia–ivory

tusks (animal's)–ivory

tussle – scuffle, struggle, wrestle

tutelage–nurture, oversight, teaching, tutorage, tutorship

tutelary god–Lar, Lare

tutor – coach, ground, instruct, mentor, pedagog, pedagogue, preceptor, school, teacher

tuyere (furnace)–tewel

twaddle – drivel, gabble, prate, prattle

twaddle (slang)–rot

tweezers–pincers

Twelfth Night character – Olivia

Twelfth Night character (shipwrecked lady)–Viola

Twelfth Night countess – Olivia

twenty-fourth part–carat

twice (Latin)–bis

twice (music)–bis

twice (prefix)–bi, di

twig–shoot, sprig, wattle

twig (flexible, used as band) –withe

twig (pliable, for weaving)–osier

twig (Scot.)–reis

twig (supple)–wattle, withe

twig (willow)–sallow

twigs (brush of)–besom

twigs (consisting of)–osier

twigs (excessive, developing)–plica

twigs (interwoven)–wattles

twilight – crepuscule, dusk, gloaming

Twilight of the Gods–Ragnarok

twilled–corded, reedy, ridgy, sedgy

twin – couple, dual, gemel, pair, two

twin crystal–macle

twine–coil, infold, wrap

twinge of conscience–pang, qualm

twining–viny

twining part–tendril

twining plant stem–bine

twining shoot–bine

twinkle–wink

twins (one of)–gemel

twirl–spin, whirl

twirl (dial.)–querl

twist–contort, cue, curl, distort, slew, slue, spin, tweak, warp, wrest

twist (full of)–quirky

twist (in pain)–writhe

twist (Scot.)–pirl, tirl

twist (spirally)–twine

twist (violently)–wring

twist about–slew, slue

twist and turn around–slew, slue

twist out of shape–contort

twisted – cued, kinky, warped, wrested, wry

twisted (spirally)–torse

twisted (violently)–wrung

twisted about–writhed

twisted to one side–skew

twisting–curling, wresting

twists–screws

twit–blame, reproach, ridicule, taunt, upbraid

twitch (spasmodic)–tic

twitch up–snare

twitching–tic, tweaking

two (poetic)–twain

two (prefix)–bi

two (Scot.)–twa

two-edged and sharp–ancipital

twofold–binary, dual, duple, duplex

twofold (prefix)–di

two-footed animal – biped, bipedal

two-forked–bifurcated

two-handed (circus slang)–secondhand, used

two-headedness – dicephalism

two-horse chariot–biga

two-lined verse–dimster

two metrical feet (taken together)–dipody

two of a kind–couple, pair

two-pronged–bifurcate

two-pronged instrument–bident

two spot–deuce

two-toed sloth–unau

two-wheeled cart (India) – tonga

tyke (little)–shaver

tylopod–camel

Tyndareus' wife–Leda

type – genre, kind, model, norm, pattern, sort, species, standard

type (bold style)–text

type (collection of)–font

type (complete assortment of)–font

type (composed)–metal

type (conventional)–ionic

type (disarranged)–pied

type (general)–average

type (jumbled)–pi, pied

type (kind of)–agate, canon, elite, ionic, italic, pearl, pica, Roman, ronde, ruby

type (large size)–canon

type (line of, in one piece)–slug

type (mixed)–pi

type (perfect)–ideal

type (printing)–agate

type (sloping)–italic

type (style of)–agate, canon, elite, ionic, italic, pearl, pica, Roman, ronde, ruby, runic

type blanks used in spacing–quads

type collection–font

type face (projection of) – kern, kirn

type measure–em, en, pica

type metal (block of, used for spacing)–quad

type metal (piece of)–quadrat

type of curve–memniscate

type of ode–pindaric

type of perfection–paragon

type of poem (pert. to)–odic

type row–line

typesetting (process of) – composition

type size–agate, canon, elite, pearl, pica, ruby

type spacing piece–quad

type squares–ems

type stroke–serif

type tray–font, galley

typewriter bar–spacer

typewriter cylinder–platen

typewriter part–platen

typewriter roller–platen

typical – emblematic, prefigurative, regular, typal

typical example–norm

typographer–printer

Tyr–Er

Tyr (god of war)–Er

tyrannical–despotic

tyrannize–domineer

tyrant – czar, despot, Ivan, tsar, tzar

tyrant (classic)–Nero

Tyre god (Teutonic)–Er

Tyre king–Hiram

Tyrian princess–Dido

tyro–abecedarian, beginner, novice, pupil, tiro

Tyrol mountain–Dolomites

Tyrolean dialect–Ladin

U

ubiquity–everywhere, omnipresence

Uchean Indian–Yuchi

ugly – crabbed, cranky, ill-favored, loathsome, unlovely, unsightly

Ugrian tribe member (anc.) –Avar

ukase – edict, order, proclamation

Ukrainian assembly–rada

Ukrainian city – Berditchef, Cherson, Ekaterinoslaf, Elizavetgrad, Kharkof, Kherson, Kiev, Kremenchug, Kursk, Lugansk,

Nikolaief, Odessa, Poltava, Yekaterinoslav, Zhitomir, Zhitomis

Ukrainian coin–grivna (ac.), schagiv (ac.)

Ukrainian legislative bodies –radas

Ukrainian seaport–Odessa

ullage–shortage, shrinkage

ulna (end of)–ancon

ulnus tree (genus of)–elm

ulster–overcoat

ulterior – further, remoter, succeeding

ultimate–conclusive, eventu-

al, eventful, final, last, maximum

ultimate end (Gr.)–telus

ultimate statement–end

ultra – extreme, extremist, fanatical, radical, uncompromising

ululate – hoot, howl, wail, yelp

Ulysses' father–Laertes

Ulysses' son–Telegonus

Ulysses' wife–Penelope

umbrage–pique

umbrage (take)–resent

umbrella (large, heavy) – gamp

umbrette–omber
Umbria river–Tevere
umpire–arbiter
unable–cannot, helpless, impotent, incapable, incompetent, unqualified
unable to rise to occasion–resourceless
unaboat–catboat
unaccompanied–alone, solo
unaccountable–inexplicable, irresponsible, mysterious, strange, unfathomable
unadorned–bald, plain, stark
unadulterated–pure
unaffected–artless, sincere
unanimously–solidly
unapt – backward, dull, inapt, slow
unaroused–dormant
unaspirated–lene
unaspirated syllables–lenes
unassumed–natural
unassuming–diffident, modest, shy, unostentatious
unattached–free, loose
unbalanced – deranged, lopsided, one-sided, uneven
unbelievable – fantastic, incredible
unbeliever–doubter, infidel, pagan, skeptic
unbend–loosen, relax, rest, slacken, thaw
unbending – inexorable, inflexible, resolute, rigid, stern, unyielding
unbiased–fair, impartial, unprejudiced
unbind– absolve, deliver, dissolve, free, loosen, release, undo, unfasten, untie
unbleached–beige, ecru
unbolt–explain, open, unbar, unfasten, unpin
unbound–free, loose, unconfined, unfastened
unbounded – limitless, unchecked, uncontrolled, unrestrained
unbridled – free, licentious, loose, unrestrained
unbroken – continuous, entire, intact, undug, unplowed, untamed, whole

unburden–ease, relieve, unload
uncanny–eerie, eery, ghostly, mysterious, strange, unnatural, weird
unceremonious–abrupt, informal
unceremonious dismissal – conge
uncertain–changeable, fitful, indefinite, indeterminate, precarious, problematical, unsteady, untrustworthy, vague, variable
uncertainty–doubt
unchanging – steadfast, uniform
unchecked – free, loose, rampant, unbridled
unchristian–barbarous, heathen, pagan, uncivilized
unchristian nation (pert. to) –ethnic
uncivil–barbarous, discourteous, indecorous, rude, savage, ungracious
uncivilized–barbarous, feral, ferine, rude, savage, wild
uncle (Dutch)–eme
uncle (Scot.)–eme
uncle (So. African)–oom
Uncle Remus creator–Harris
Uncle Tom's Cabin author–Harriet Beecher Stowe
unclean – dirty, filthy, foul, impure, unwholesome
unclean (Jewish law)–tref
unclose (poetic)–ope
uncommon–exceptional, extraordinary, infrequent, odd, rare, scarce, unaccustomed, unusual, unwonted
uncommunicative–reserved
uncomplaining–stoical
uncompromising–inflexible, rigid, strict, unbending, unyielding
unconcealed–bare, open
unconcerned–apathetic, disinterested, indifferent
unconfined–loose
unconfused–calm, clear
unconscious – asleep, ignorant, insensible, out, unaware

unconstrained–easy, natural, spontaneous, unrestrained
unconstraint–ease
uncontrollable – intractable, unmanageable, wild
uncontrolled–free, irregular, loose, unregulated, unrestrained, wild
unconventional – casual, informal, unceremonious
unconventional (strikingly)–outre
uncooked–raw
uncouth–awkward, boorish, ignorant, rude, ungainly
uncouth person–lout
uncover (Scot.)–tirl
uncovered – bald, bare, exposed, nude, open, revealed
unctuous – fatty, gushing, oily, oleaginous, pinguid, plastic, suave
unctuous fluid–oil
unctuously complacent – smug
uncultivated–fallow, wild
uncultured–rude, unrefined
undamaged–intact
undaunted–bold, brave, courageous, fearless, intrepid
undeceive–disabuse
undecided–doubtful, irresolute, pend, pending, problematical, unresolved, unsettled
undefiled–pure
undemonstrative–calm, cold, cool, reserved, restrained
undeniable – incontestable, indisputable, true
undependable–irresponsible
under–below
under (naut.)–alow
under (poetic)–neath
under (prefix)–sub
under care of another–protege
undercover–secret, surreptitious
undercover man–detective, spy
underestimate – minimize, underrate, undervalue
underfong – circumvent, en-

snare, entrap, receive, sustain, undertake

undergo–bear, endure, pass, shirt

undergraduate–coed

underground worker–miner, mucker, pitman, sapper

underhand – clandestine, fraudulent, secret, sly, surreptitiously, unfairly, unobtrusively

underhanded person–sneak

underhandedly – secretly, shadily, slily, slyly

underling–inferior, menial, subordinate

undermine–drain, enfeeble, erode, sap, subvert, weaken

underneath–below

underofficer–aide

undersea boat–sub, submarine, submersible, u-boat

undershirt (Eng.)–vest

undershrub (evergreen, hard)–heather

understand – apprehend, comprehend, conceive, discern, explain, grasp, interpret, know, perceive, realize, reason, see

understand (slang) – sabby, sabe, savey, savvey, savvy

understanding – agreement, compact, concept, entente, intelligence, penetration, perception, reason, sense, treaty

understanding (international)–entente

understanding (wrong) – misinterpretation

understanding between governments–entente

understood–tacit

understood (easily)–lucid

understood (readily)–clear, lucid

understood only by special initiated–esoteric

undertake–assume, attempt, contract, covenant, dare, endeavor, engage, try

undertaken (provisionally)–tentative

undertaker – mortician, rebuker, sponsor, surety

undertaker (London)–bant

undertaking – enterprise, task, venture

undertaking (planned)–project

undertone–aside

underwater chamber (construction)–caisson

underwear–lingerie

underworld–Hades, Sheol

underworld (god of) – dia, dis (pl.)

undetermined–vague

undeveloped insect–pupa

undiluted–neat, pure

undisclosed–secret, ulterior

undiscovered thing–secret

undisguised–bald

undivided – continuous, entire, intact, unbroken, whole

undoing–destruction, downfall, overthrow

undomesticated – feral, ferine, wild

undressed kid–suede

undressed stone–rubble

undue–exorbitant, extreme, improper, inappropriate, unsuitable, unwarranted

undulating – aripple, fluctuating, rolling, waving, wavy

undulation (long, sea)–swell

undulatory–wavy

unearth – discover, exhume, expose, uncover

unearthly – appalling, eerie, eery, outlandish, preposterous, preternatural, supernatural, terrific, weird

uneasiness of conscience – scruple

uneasy – awkward, constrained, difficult, inquiet, restive, restless, stiff, troublesome, worried

unemployed – idle, inactive, leisured, otiose

unemployment–idleness, inactivity

unenclosed–fenceless

unencumbered–free

unending–endless, timeless

unequal–irregular, uneven, variable

unequal (comb. form)–aniso

unequaled – matchless, surpassing, unmatched, unparalleled, unrivaled

unequivocal – categorical, clear, plain, sincere

unerring–certain, infallible, sure, true, unfailing

uneven – erose, irregular, odd, rough, rugged

unexpected–inopinate

unexpectedly–suddenly, unaware

unexpended sums–reserves, savings, surplus

unexpired–alive

unexploded shell–dud

unexpress–casual, informal

unexpressed–tacit

unface–unmask

unfaded–fresh

unfair–dishonest, disingenuous, foul, uneven, unfavorable, unjust

unfaithful–inaccurate, recreant, untrustworthy

unfaithful (proves to be)–betray

unfamiliar–new, strange

unfasten – detach, free, loosen, open, unbar, undo, unfix, unlock, unpin, untie

unfavorable–adverse, averse, bad, contrary, ill, repulsive

unfavorably–averse, hardly

unfeeling–callous, cruel, insensate, insensible, insensitive, insusceptible, stolid, stony, unimpressionable

unfeigned – genuine, real, sincere

unfertile–arid, barren

unfettered–free

unfilled–blank, empty

unfinished–sketchy

unfit – incompetent, inept, unsuitable

unfitness–ineptitude

unfledged – callow, immature

unflinching – stanch, steadfast, unwavering, unyielding

unfold – divulge, evolute, evolve, expand, open, spread, unfurl

unfold (poetic)–ope

unfolding development – evolution

unforced – natural, voluntary, willingly

unfortunate – hapless, ill, poor, unlucky

unfounded–baseless, groundless, idle, vain

unfrequently–lonely, seldom

unfriendly–hostile, inimical

unfruitful–barren, infertile, sterile, unproductive, unprofitable

unfurl–expand, spread, unroll

ungainly–awkward, clumsy, uncouth

ungentle – discourteous, harsh, rough, rude

ungovernable–irrepressible, licentious, unbridled, unruly, wild

ungulate–hoofed, tapir

ungulate (odd-toed)–tapir

unhallow – desecrate, profane, unholy

unhamper–free

unhappy–dejected, miserable, sad, wretched

unharness–ungear, unhitch

unhealthy – sick, unwholesome

unhealthy color–sallow

unheard of – strange, unknown

unheeding–deaf, disregard

unhesitating–ready

unicorn (sea)–narwhale

unicorn fish–unie

uniform–consistent, equable, even, invariable, regular, unvarying

uniform (servant's)–livery

uniformity – consistency, equality, evenness, homogeneity

unify–consolidate, integrate, merge

unimaginative–dull, literal, prosaic

unimpaired–entire, intact

unimpeded–free

unimportant (most)–least

unimpressed–unawed

uninformed–ignorant

uninhabited–deserted, desolate, empty, vacant

unintelligent – brute, ignorant, stupid, unwise

unintentionally – inadvertently

uninteresting–arid, boring, drab, dry, humdrum, insipid, prolix, prosaic, stupid, tedious, tiresome, unexciting

uninterrupted–continuous

union–A.F.L., artel, coalition, C.I.O.

union (addition) – annexation

union (political, between Austria and Germany)–Anschluss

Union general–Sherman

union of different things–amalgam

Union of South Africa city –Cape Town, Durban, Germiston, Johannesburg

union of states–empire

union of workers – artel, A.F.L., C.I.O.

unions–coalitions, combinations, junctions, mergers, unities

unique – alone, matchless, new, notable, novel, one, rare, single, sole, special

unison – accord, agreement, concord, concordant, harmony

unit–ace, item, monad, one

unit (biological)–idant

unit (electric)–ampere, coulomb, es, farad, henry, joule, ohm, rel, volt, watt

unit (electric capacity) – farad

unit (electric current)–ampere

unit (electric energy)–joule

unit (electric force)–volt

unit (electric inductance) – henry

unit (electric intensity)–ampere

unit (electric light) – volt, watt

unit (electric power)–watt

unit (electric pressure) – barad

unit (electric reluctance)–rel

unit (electric resistance) – ohm

unit (electric, smallest positive)–proton

unit (electromagnetic)–farad

unit (electromotive force)–volt

unit (heat)–calorie, calory, therm, therme

unit (hypothetical structural, of biology)–id

unit (indestructible)–monad

unit (light)–lumen, lux

unit (light energy)–rad

unit (light intensity)–pyr

unit (local government) – township

unit (logarithmic)–bel

unit (military) – brigade, platoon, regiment

unit (money)–lira

unit (photometric)–pyr, rad

unit (photometric, proposed)–rad

unit (physical)–erg

unit (pressure)–barad

unit (reluctance)–rel

unit (Scot.)–ane

unit (social)–clan, sept

unit (thermal)–calory

unit (wire measure)–mil

unit (work)–ergon

unit of conductivity–mho

unit of discourse–word

unit of electrical resistance (pert. to)–ohmic

unit of energy–erg

unit of force–dyne, kinit, tonal

unit of light–lux, pyr

unit of light intensity–pyr

unit of light measurement–lumen

unit of light velocity–velo

unit of linen yarn size–lea

unit of magnetic flux–weber

unit of matter–monad

unit of measure–are, meter, metre, pint, rod, stere
unit of power (abbr.)–H.P.
unit of pressure–barad
unit of rayon yarn size–denier
unit of reluctance–rel
unit of resistance–ohm
unit of silk yarn size–denier
unit of speed (proposed)–velo
unit of tale–rees
unit of velocity–kin, velo
unit of weight–carat, pound
unit of work–erg, ergon, ergons, joule, kilerg
unite–adhere, ally, amalgamate, coalesce, combine, connect, consolidate, fuse, incorporate, join, link, merge, seam
unite by freezing–regelate
unite by interweaving – pleach
unite by joints–articulate
unite by treaty–ally
unite by weaving–spliced
unite closely–fay
unite firmly–cement, knit
unite in effect of consonance –harmonize
unite more closely–concentrate
united – added, allied, banded, cemented, coalesced, cohered, combined, concerted, corporate, corporated, federated, knit, linked, meld, merged, one, spliced, tied, wed, weld
united into leagues – federated
United States–see also American
United States Army car (little squad)–jeep
United States cape (most westerly)–Alva
United States capitals–Ala., Montgomery; Ariz., Phoenix; Ark., Little Rock; Calif., Sacramento; Colo., Denver; Conn., Hartford; Dela., Dover; Fla., Tallahassee; Ga., Atlanta; Ida-

ho, Boise; Ill., Springfield; Ind., Indianapolis; Iowa, Des Moines; Kan., Topeka; Ky., Frankfort; La., Baton Rouge; Maine, Augusta; Md., Annapolis; Mass., Boston; Mich., Lansing; Minn., St. Paul; Miss., Jackson; Mo., Jefferson City; Mont., Helena; Neb., Lincoln; Nev., Carson City; N.H., Concord; N.J., Trenton; N.M., Santa Fe; N.Y., Albany; N.C., Raleigh; N.D., Bismarck; Ohio, Columbus; Okla., Oklahoma City; Ore., Salem; Penn., Harrisburg; R.I., Providence; S.C., Columbia; S.D., Pierre; Tenn., Nashville; Texas, Austin; Utah, Salt Lake City; Vt., Montpelier; Va., Richmond; Wash., Olympia; W.Va., Charleston; Wisc., Madison; Wyo., Cheyenne
United States coin – cent (br.), dime (s.), dollar (g., s.), eagle (g.), half dollar (s.), half eagle (g.), mil (ac.), nickel (cop., ni.), penny (br.), quarter (s.)
United States general (killed by Indians)–Custer
United States general and senator–Adair
United States measure–acre, barrel, basket, block, board foot, bolt, bushel, carat, chain, cord, decillion, drum, fathom, fluid dram, fluid ounce, foot, gallon, gill, hand, hank, heer, hogshead, inch, iron, labor, last, lea, league, line, link, mil, mile, minim, nail, ounce, pace, palm, peck, perch, pint, pipe, point, pole, pool, pottle, prime, quadrant, quart, quarter, rod, roll, sack, section, skein, span, spindle, square,

standard, stran, strand, tablespoonful, teaspoonful, thread, ton, township, tub, typp, vara, vat, Winchester bushel, wineglassful, yard
United States naval commander–Stark
United States Pacific fleet commander – Chester Nimitz
United States president–see Presidents
United States weight – bag, barrel, bushel, carat, denier, flask, grain, hundredweight, keg, kip, long ton, metric carat, ounce, pound, quarter, quintal, ton, troy ounce, troy pound
united vigorously (in common cause)–rallied
uniting closely–welding
uniting vitally–grafting
unity – accord, agreement, concord, conjunction, harmony, oneness, singleness, union
unity by treaty–ally
univalent–monad
universal–all, catholic, cosmic, general, total, whole
universal (general)–catholic
universal knowledge – pantology
universal language–ido, rɔ
universal remedy–panacea
universal successor of deceased person (law)–heres
universe – cosmos, system, world
universe (controlling principle)–logos
unkempt – disarrayed, disheveled, rough, ruffled, shaggy, squalid, tousled, unpolished
unkind–cruel, harsh, severe
unkind (harsh)–ill
unknit–ravel
unknowable–mystic
unknowable objects whose existence is problematic–noumena

unknown – incognito, strange, unfamiliar
unknown (Fr.) – inconnu (masc.), inconnue (fem.)
unknown person–stranger
unlawful – illegal, illegitimate, illicit, irregular
unleashed – free, loose, released
unless (law)–nisi
unlike – dislike, dissimilar, diverse, improbable, irregular, uneven
unlikelihood – improbability
unlikeness–dissimilarity
unload – discharge, dump, empty, lighten, liquidate
unman–crush, unnerve
unmannerly – boorish, discourteously, rude, uncivilly
unmannerly person–cad
unmarried person–bachelor, celibate, maiden
unmerchantable – unsalable, unsaleable
unmetered writing–prose
unmethodical–desultory
unmistakable – apparent, open, patent
unmitigated–arrant, mere, sheer
unmixed–pure
unmounted–afoot, unset
unmoved – apathetic, calm, firm, serene, unshaken
unmoved by pity–obdurate
unmoving–inert
unnatural–abnormal, artificial, eerie, eery, strange
unnecessary–fuss, needless, useless
unobtrusive–modest, retiring
unoccupied–empty, idle, vacant
unoriginal – secondhand, trite
unorthodox–heretical
unostentatious–lenten, modest, quiet, restrained
unpaid–arrear, due
unparalleled–alone, inimitable, peerless, unequal, unique, unmatched

unpleasant–disagreeable, displeasing, offensive
unpleasant (most)–worst
unplowed edge of field – rand
unpolished–crude, impolite, rough, rugged
unpopular–hated
unpopularity–odium
unprecedented–new, novel, unexampled
unprejudiced–dispassionate, impartial
unprepared–raw, unfit
unprepossessing–ugly
unpretentious–modest, simple
unprincipled–perfidious, unscrupulous
unproductive–barren, sterile
unprofessional–amateur, laical, lay
unprofitable–barren, useless
unpublished manuscript (Latin)–inedita
unpunctuality–lateness
unqualified–plenary, unfit
unqualified (most)–merest
unquestionable – decided, evident, indisputable
unravel – disengage, disentangle, feaze, solve, unlace
unreal–fanciful, imaginary, unsubstantial, visionary
unreasonable–absurd, excessive, exorbitant, extravagant, immoderate, irrational, mad, senseless
unreasonably venturesome–audacious, heedless, rash, reckless, temerarious
unrecognized–unsung
unrefined – coarse, crass, crude, loud, uncultivated
unrelaxed–taut, tense
unrelenting–grim, hard, inexorable, iron, rigorous, severe, stern, unyielding
unreliable – irresponsible, undependable, untrustworthy
unrest – disquiet, motion, restlessness
unrestrained–free, lax, riot-

ous, unbridled, wanton, wild
unrestricted–free
unrevealed–latent
unripe fruit taste–ascerb
unruffled–calm, placid, sedate, serene
unruly – disorderly, lawless, obstinate, refractory, ungovernable
unsafe – exposed, insecure, unreliable
unsatisfactory–lame
unsavory–insipid, tasteless
unscrupulous–unprincipled, untrustworthy
unscrupulous villain–miscreant
unseal–disclose, open
unseal (poetic)–ope
unseemly – improper, indecent, unbecoming
unseen – inexperienced, unskilled, viewless
unsettled – deranged, disturbed, moot, unoccupied, unquieted
unshorn–tag, teg
unshorn sheep (second year) –tag, teg
unsightly–ugly
unskillful–awkward, inept, inexperienced
unsoiled–clean
unsophisticated–genuine, ingenuous, innocent, naif, naive, pure, simple
unspoiled–fresh
unspoken – ineffable, oral, silent, tacit, unuttered
unstable–fickle, fluctuating, irregular, labile, plastic, scandy, ticklish, unsettled, unsteady, vacillating
unsteady–flickering, fluctuating, irregular, rickety, shaky, titubate, vacillating
unsubdued–unbowed, wild
unsubstantial–aerial, flimsy, gaseous, papery, shadowy, slim, visionary
unsuitable – inappropriate, inapt, inept, unbecoming, unfit
unsullied–pure

unsweetened–sec, sour

unswerving in allegiance – loyal

unsymmetrical – disproportional, irregular

untainted–incorrupt

untamed–feral, savage, wild

untangle–disentangle, sleav, sleave, sleeve

unthankful person–ingrate

unthinking–casual, heedless, impetuous, inconsiderate, rash, thoughtless

untidy–careless, messy, slovenly

untidy person–sloven

untie – disengage, free, loosen, unlash

untiring–indefatigable, sedulous

untrained – amateurish, green, indocile, wild

untrained for hardship–soft

untrammeled – free, loose, unlimited

untransferable–inalienable

untraversed–untrod

untried – green, inexperienced, new

untrue–disloyal, false

untrustworthy – dishonest, perfidious, slippery, tricky

untruth–disloyalty, faithlessness, falsehood, lie, treachery

unused–new

unusual–quaint, queer, tall, uncommon, unique

unusual (more)–rarer

unutterable–ineffable, inexpressible, unspeakable

unverified report–rumor

unwarranted–undue

unwavering–constant, firm, solid, steadfast

unwelcome person–intruder

unwholesome – evil, immoral, noisome, noxious

unwieldy–awkward, bulky, clumsy, cumbersome, ponderous, ungainly, unmanageable

unwieldy object–hulk

unwieldy person–hulk

unwilling – averse, loath, loth, reluctant

unwilling (be)–disincline

unwilling to prosecute–nolle prosequi

unwinder–raveler

unworldly–eerie, eery, naive, spiritual, unearthly, weird

unworthy of an adult–puerile

unwrinkled (Scot.)–brent

unyielding–adamant, determined, firm, hard, inexorable, iron, obdurate, obstinate, rigid, set, stern, stiff, stubborn, uncompromising

up to–until

up to date – fashionable, modern, new

up to this time–hereto

upbraid – blame, chide, reproach, reprove, score, twit

upheave–lift, rear, rise

upheld – abetted, aided, backed, defended, encouraged, maintained, supported, sustained

uphold–abet, aid, back, defend, encourage, maintain, support, sustain

upkeep–cost, maintenance, repair

upland (hilly)–coteau

upland (sloping)–wold

uplift–elevation, erect, upheaval

uplifts in spirit–elates

upon–above, atop, on

upon (law)–sur

upon (prefix)–ep, epi

upon that–thereat

upon which–whereat

upper air–ether

upper end–apex, head, tip

upper house of Congress–Senate

upright – equitable, erect, honest, honorable, just, moral, righteous, square, true, vertical, virtuous

upright slab – stela, stelae (pl.), stele, steles (pl.)

uprightness – honesty, rectitude

upriser–rebel

uprising – increasing, insurgency, riot

uproar–bustle, clamor, confusion, hurly-burly, insurrection, pandemonium, riot, rout, tumult, turmoil

uproar (arch.)–tintamarre

upset – capsize, discompose, disconcert, disturb, overthrow, overturn, subvert

upshot–conclusion, consummation, end, issue, result, sequel, termination

upstart–parvenu, parvenue, snob

upward (prefix)–ana

upward movement of ships –scend

uraeus–asp

Uranus (moon of)–Ariel

Uranus' children (any of twelve)–Titan

Uranus' daughter–Rhea

Uranus' mother–Ge

Uranus' satellite–Oberon

urao–trona

urbane–civil, courteous, polite, suave

urchin – arab, brat, gamin, imp, tad

urchin (street)–arab, gamin

urease (biochem.)–urase

urge – animate, coax, constrain, dehort, drive, dun, egg, filip, fillip, goad, impel, importune, incite, induce, instigate, press, spur, stimulate

urge (importunately)–dun

urge forward–impel

urge persistently–importune

urge repeatedly–ding

urge strongly–exhort

urge to action–hie

urgent–clamant, critical, exigent, importunate, pressing

urial–oorial, sha

uric acid salt–urate

urine (used as cosmetic) – lotium

urn–jardiniere, vase

urn (copper)–samovar

urn (obs.)–urna

urn (small)–vaselet

urn (stone)–steen

urn-shaped–urceolate
ursine (young)–cub
ursine baboon–chacma
ursoid–bear-like
urson (Canada)–porcupine
ursuk–seal
urubu–vulture
Uruguay city – Durazno, Florida, Maldonado, Melo, Minas, Montevideo (c.), Paysandu
Uruguay coin – centesimo (cop., ni.), peso (s.)
Uruguay estuary–Plata
Uruguay lake–Merim
Uruguay measure – cuadra, suerte, vara
Uruguay river – Cebollary, Malo, Negro, Tacaurembo, Ulimar, Uruguay
Uruguay weight–quintal
us (pert. to)–our
usage–custom, employment, habit, method, practice, treatment, use
usage (religious)–ritus
use–avail, employ, treat, vail
use (figurative)–trope
use (frugally)–stint
use (specific)–application
use abusive language–rail
use experimentally–try
use of (poetry)–vail
use of new words–neology
use of unnecessary words–pleonasm
use one's ability–exert
use or employ–wield
use subterfuge–chicane
use up – consume, deplete, eat, exhaust
used–secondhand
used in bowling game–ninepins
used in flight–volar
used in provincial forms of speech–dialetic

used sparingly–tasted
useful–advantageous, beneficial, helpful, practical, utile
useful to promote–subservient
usefulness – profit, utility, value
usefulness (of a purpose)–avail
useless–bootless, fruitless, futile, idle, ineffectual, inefficient, inutile, null, unserviceable
uselessness–futility
user–availer
user of an advantage–availer
uses–utilities
usher (theater)–page
using speech–oral
Usnech's son–Noise
U.S.S.R.–see Russia
usual–average
usurer–loaner, shark
usurp – arrogate, assume, seize
Utah mountain range – Uinta, Wasatch
Utah state flower–sego
utensil–implement, instrument, tool, vessel
utensil (cleaning) – broom, brush, Hoover, mop, sweeper
utensil (cleaning, for small arms)–ramrod
utensil with rough surface for rasping–grater
utilitarian – economic, matter-of-fact, practical, useful
utility–avail, benefit, profit, service, use
utilize–use
utmost–best
utmost limits–extreme

Utopian – chimerical, ideal, visionary
utter–abnormal, absolute, assert, complete, deliver, entire, enunciate, express, extreme, issue, pass, peremptory, say, sheer, speak, total, unusual, vent, voice
utter (poetic)–spake
utter affectedly–mince
utter brokenly–gasp
utter harshly–bray
utter heedlessly (coll.)–blat
utter in devotion–pray
utter needlessly–blat
utter publicly–enounce
utter softly – breathe, murmur, whisper
utter want–destitution, indigency
utter with effort–heave
utter without vocal sound–spirate, surd
utterance (dogmatic) – dictum, dicta (pl.)
utterance (gushing)–effusion
utterance (parenthetical) – aside
utterance (rhythmic) – cadence
utterance (uninflected) – monotone
utterance (wise)–oracle
utterance of vocal sound – phonation, phonesis
utterance with local sound–sonance
uttered musically–warbled
uttered with breath but not voice–spirate
uttered with vocal sound–sonant
uttered without voice – spirate
uttered words (arch.)–spake
utterly–stark

V

vacant – blank, empty, expressionless, idle, inane, unencumbered, unfilled, untenanted, void

vacate – abandon, abdicate, empty, evacuate, leave, quit, void

vacation – intermission, outing, recess, rest
vacation (soldier's) – furlough, leave

vacation between court sessions–nonterm
vacation period (appointed by law)–justitum
vacation place–beach, forest, lake, mountains, park, resort, spa
vaccinate–inoculate
vaccination discoverer–Jenner
vaccine–serum, sera (pl.)
vacillate – fluctuate, flutter, oscillate, seesaw, teeter, totter, waver
vacillating–fluctuating, hesitating, titubate, wavering
vacillations–hesitancies, indecisions, uncertainties
vacuate–empty, evacuate
vacuous–blank, dull, empty, unfilled, unintelligent, void
vacuum–void
vacuum (opposite of)–plenum
vacuum pump–pulsometer
vade–depart, leave
vag–vagabond, vagrant
vagabond–vag, vagrant
vagabond (slang)–bum, hobo, tramp
vagary–caper, caprice, fancy
vagrant–rogue, truant, vagabond, wanderer
vague–ambiguous, confused, dark, dreamy, hazy, indefinite, indeterminate, indistinct, loose, obscure, shadowy, unfixed, unsettled
vain–futile, idle, nugatory, overweening, trivial, unavailing, unimportant, unrewarded, vainglorious
Vaishnavas deity (supreme) –Vishnu
Vaisya cast–Aroras
valance – drape, drapery, hanging
valance (short)–pelmet
vale–dell, valley
valediction–adieu, farewell
Valhalla maiden (warrior conducting)–Valkyrie
Vali's mother–Rind, Rindr
valiant–brave, courageous,

heroic, intrepid, stalwart, steadfast, stouthearted
valid–binding, cogent, efficacious, just, lawful, legal, sufficient, weighty
valise (coll.)–grip
valley–basin, dale, dell, glen, vale
valley (circular)–rincon
valley (deep)–canyon
valley (levant)–wady
valley (moon, narrow)–rille
valley (narrow)–dingle, glen
valley (open, western America)–canada
valley (poetic)–vale
valley (retired)–dell
valley (small)–gully
valley (small circular, southwest U.S.)–rincon
valley of the moon–rille
valley where David killed Goliath–Elah
valonia oak's fruit (immature)–camata
valor–bravery, courage
valorous (more)–brave
valorous person–hero
valuable–dear, precious
value–appraise, esteem, estimate, price, prize, use, worth
value (equal)–parity
value (established)–par
value (intrinsic)–utility
value (nominal)–par
value for taxation–assess
value highly–endear, treasure
value reduction – depreciation
valued – appraised, assessed, assized, inventoried
valueless – depreciated, strawy
valve (wind instrument) – piston
vamoose–decamp, depart
vamp–hose, sock
vampire (female)–lamia
van–front, lead
Vancouver Island Indian – Sooke
vandal–hun
vandalize–mar
vane–weathercock

vanish–die, disappear, fade, flee, melt
vanish gradually–evanesce
vanity – egoism, hollowness, pride
vanity box–dorine, etui
vanity box (Fr., small)–dorine
vanquish – beat, best, conquer, defeat, overcome, subdue, surmount
vapid – dull, inane, insipid, spiritless, stale
vapor – fume, gas, halitus, mist, smoke, steam
vapor (mass of floating) – cloud
vaporizable (readily) – volatile
vaporize easily–volatile
variable–capricious, changeable, fickle, fitful, inconstant, shifting, uncertain, unstable, unsteady
variable (exceedingly)–protean
variance (at)–out
variant (exceedingly)–protean
varied – alter, changed, diverse, diversified, several, various
variegated – dappled, enamelled, mottled, pied
variegation–diversity
variety–class, diversity, kind, sort, species
various – different, diverse, manifold, several, sundry
varnish (kind of) – japan, spar
varnish ingredient – lac, resin, rosin
varnisher–japanner
vary–alter, change, deviate, dissent, diverge, diversify, range, shift
vas–duct, pledge, surety, vessel
vascular system fluid (pert. to)–haemal, hemic
vase–jar, jardiniere, urn
vase (anc., used as cinerary urn)–deinos
vase (classical, arch.)–ascus, asci (pl.)

vase (ornamental)–urn

vassal–bondman, dependent, esne, liege, man, serf, servant, servile, slave, subservient

vast–broad, cosmic, enormous, extensive, gigantic, great, huge, immense, large, mighty, untold

vast age–eon, era

vast expanse–desert, empire, ocean

vast number–myriad

vast period–cycle

vastness–magnitude

vat–barrel, cistern, tub, vessel

vat (bleaching, large)–kier

vat (brewer's)–keeve

vat (brewer's fermenting)–tun

vat (cistern)–bac

vat (dyeing)–pit

vat (fermenting)–gyle

vat (large)–keeve, kieve

vaticanism–curialism

vaudeville act–skit, turn

vaudeville piece (act)–skit

vault – bound, crypt, groin, leap, over

vault (church)–crypt

vaulted–domed

vaunt–boast, brag

vaunt oneself–brag

veal cut–cutlet

Vedic fire god–Agni

Vedic goddess who releases from sin–Aditi

Vedic ritual text – Sakha, Shaka

Vedic sky serpent–ahi

veer – alter, careen, change, shift, swerve, turn, yaw

vegetable–beet, cabbage, carrot, eggplant, lettuce, okra, peascod, peasecod, radish, rhubarb, rutabaga, spinach, turnip

vegetable (any green)–sabzi

vegetable (carbonized)–lignite

vegetable (esculent)–legume

vegetable (leafy)–chard

vegetable (leguminous)–lentil, pea

vegetable (onion-like)–leak, scallion, shallot

vegetable (pungent)–onion

vegetable (salad)–chard, endive, lettuce, romaine

vegetable (succulent)–onion

vegetable and meat dish – ragout

vegetable animal feed–herbage

vegetable condiment–spice

vegetable dealer – greengrocer, huckster

vegetable exudation–lac, resin

vegetable ferment–yeast

vegetable growth (rich in)–lush

vegetable oil–macassar

vegetable poison–abrin

vegetable punk or tinder – amadou

vegetable tinder or punk – amadou

vegetables (goddess of)–Ceres

vegetables (raised for market)–truck

vegetation (goddess of) – Ceres

vehemence–ardor, fury, impetuosity, ire, rage, violence

vehement – angry, ardent, fervid, fiery, heated, hot, impetuous, intense

vehemently–amain

vehicle – auto, automobile, bus, cab, car, carriage, cart, sled, taxi, van, wagon

vehicle (air, coll.)–aero

vehicle (child's)–scooter

vehicle (clumsy)–ark

vehicle (covered) – caravan, van

vehicle (for oil colors)–megilp

vehicle (four-wheeled)–landau

vehicle (light passenger) – minibus

vehicle (on runners)–cutter, sled, sledge, sleigh

vehicle (one-horse)–hansom, shay

vehicle (public) – bus, cab, hack, hansom, taxi

vehicle (snow)–cutter, sled, sledge, sleigh

vehicle (two-wheeled)–cart, sulky

vehicle (war)–jeep, tank

vehicle (wheeled)–auto, automobile, bus, cab, car, carriage, cart, taxi, van, wagon

vehicle (wheelless) – sled, sleigh

vehicle (winter)–sled, sleigh

vehicle shaft–thill

vehicle used for hauling – dray, lorry, tractor, truck, van

veil – caul, cover, curtain, dim, mask, screen, soften, velum

veil (papal)–fannel, orale

veil (pope's)–orale

veil (striped, papal)–orale

veil (white silk)–orale

veil of gauze–volet

veiled – covered, curtained, masked, shrouded

veiling (semitransparent, heavy)–voile

veiling material–tulle

vein – cavity, channel, crevice, dash, fissure, lode, shade, smack, spice, streak, tang, tinge, touch, wave

vein (anatomy)–vena

vein (inflammation of a)–phlebitis

vein (metal bearing)–lode

vein (small ore)–hilo

vein (unstratified)–lode

vein of leaf–rib

veined like quarry stone – marbled

veinless (in leaves)–avenous

vellein–esne

velo acceleration (one per second)–celo

veloce – dashing, direction, rapid

velocious–fast, speedy

velocity – celerity, pace, quickness, rapidity, speed, swiftness

velocity (unit of)–kin, velo

velocity of one foot per second–velo

velvet-like fabric – panne, velure

venal – corrupt, hireling, mercenary, salable, saleable, vendible

vend–sell

vender–*see* vendor

vendeuse–saleswoman

vendible–marketable, venal

vendor–alienor, seller, vender

vendor of foods–viander

vendue–sale

venerable – august, classic, hoar, hoary, old, sage

venerate–adore, respect, revere, reverence

veneration – awe, devotion, respect

Venetian (medieval, in China)–Polo

Venetian beach–Lido

Venetian boat–gondola

Venetian bridge (famous marble)–Rialto

Venetian coin (old)–ducat, sequin

Venetian island–Rialto

Venetian magistrate (anc., chief)–doge

Venetian measure (wine) – anfora

Venetian painter–Titian

Venetian red color–siena

Venetian resort–Lido

Venetian ruler (former) – doge

Venetian state barge–bucentaur

Venezuelan capital–Caracas

Venezuelan city–Barcelona, Barquisimeto, Caracas (c.), Guanare, Maracaibo, Valencia

Venezuelan coin – bolivar (s.), centimo, fuerte (s.), medio (s.), morocota (g.), real (s.)

Venezuelan Indian–Carib

Venezuelan Indian (western)–Timotex

Venezuelan lake–Maracaibo, Tacarigua

Venezuelan measure – estadel, fanega, galon, milla

Venezuelan mountain – Andes, Concha, Cuneva, Icutu, Imutaca, Pacaraima, Parima, Roraima, Sierra-Nevada-de-Merida

Venezuelan plains–llanos

Venezuelan port – Ciudad Bolivar, La Guayra, Maracaibo, Puerto-Cabello

Venezuelan river – Apure, Arausa, Cuara, Orinoco, Ventuar

Venezuelan snake (tree) – lora

Venezuelan weight – bag, libra

vengeance–punishment, requital, retribution, revenge

vengeance (goddess of) – Ara, Ate, Nemesis

venial – excusable, pardonable

Venice (pert. to)–Venetian

Venice of the North–Stockholm

vennel – alley, gutter, lane, sewer

venom–poison, virus

venomous – baneful, deadly, envenomed, malicious, poisonous, rancorous, toxic, virulent

venomous snake–krait

vent–aperture, fissure, hole, opening, outlet, release, utter

vent in earth's surface–volcano

ventilate–air

ventose – cup, flatulent, windy

ventral–sternal

venture–brave, chance, danger, dare, enterprise, hap, hazard, risk, stake, try

ventured–durst

venturesome – bold, brave, dangerous, daring, heroic, risky

venturesome (unreasonable) –temerarious

Venus' son–Cupid

Venus' sweetheart–Adonis

vera (third of span)–pie

veracity–truth

veranda–gallery, loggia, piazza, porch, portico, verandah

verb (auxiliary) – had, has, may, would

verb (auxiliary, denoting future tense)–shall

verb (old auxiliary)–shalt

verb expressing future time –shall

verb form table–paradigm

verbal–oral

verbal thrust (coll.)–dig

verbiage–chatter, diction, redundancy, talk, verbosity, wordiness

verbiage (pompous)–fustian

verbose–prolix, wordy

verbosity–redundancy

verboten–forbidden, prohibited

verd – freshness, green, greenness

verdant – green, raw, unsophisticated

Verde (Cape island)–Sal

Verdi's opera–Aida

verdict – finding, opinion, word

verge – border, boundary, edge, limit, marge, margin, prink

Vergil–*see* Virgil

verging upon impropriety–risque

verified – checked, proved, supported

verify – affirm, back, check, confirm, maintain, prove, second, substantiate, support

verify again–recheck

verily–amen, certainly, confidently, really, truly

veritable – actual, gospel, real, true

verity–reality, truth

vermilion–red

vermin–bedbugs, fleas, flies, lice, mice, rats, weasels

Vermont city–Barre

Vern hero–Nemo

verse – canto, lyric, rime, stanza, stave, stich

verse (eight feet)–octameter
verse (form of)–sonnet
verse (four measure) – tetrameter
verse (fourteen lines) – sonnet
verse (Homeric)–epic, epopee
verse (imaginary, arch.) – poesy
verse (Irish)–rann
verse (kind of)–iambic, ionic
verse (one foot only) – monometer
verse (opposite of)–prose
verse (pert. to)–ictic
verse (romance form of) – sestina
verse (satiric)–iambic
verse (scripture)–text
verse (trivial)–jingle
verse (two lines)–dimeter
verse (two metric feet)–dimeter
verse form–triolet
verse of scripture–text
verse writer (sad)–eulogist
versed – acquainted, conversant, familiar
versed (arch.)–beseen
versification–rhyme
versification (form of)–sonnet, triolet
versified–rimed
versifier–poet, rimer
versifier (female)–poetess
version – paraphrase, rendition, translation
version (revised, abbr.)–R.V.
version of the Bible (revised)–Apocrypha
verso (abbr.)–vo
vert (rounded, her.)–pomey
vertebra (first neck)–atlas
vertebral–spinal
vertebrate (abbr.)–vert
vertebrate (division of) – somite
vertebrate (feathered)–bird
vertebrate group–amnionata
vertebrates (class of)–aves
vertical – apeak, erect, perpendicular, plumb, sheer, upright
· vertical line (naut.)–apeak

vertical position (as an anchor)–apeak
vertical position (naut.) – apeak
verticil–whorl
verticillate–whorled
vertigo (Latin) – dinus, dini (pl.)
verve – animation, elan, enthusiasm, pep, spirit, vivacity
very–so
very (comb. form)–eri
very (French)–tres
very (musical)–molto
very cold–gelid
very large (poetic)–enorm
very much (comb. form)–eri
very person mentioned–self
very thin (like fabric)–sheer
vesicate–blister
vesicle (air in algae)–aerocyst
vessel – barrel, boat, bottle, bowl, craft, cup, firkin, hogshead, kettle, liner, mug, pot, receptacle, ship, steamer, stein, utensil, vas
vessel (ablution)–washbasin
vessel (airtight cooking)–autoclave
vessel (anat.)–vas
vessel (anc.) – caravel, galleon, nef
vessel (anc., oar-propelled)– galley
vessel (anc. wine) – ama, amula
vessel (Arabian, lateen sail)– dhow
vessel (archaeological wine) –stamnos
vessel (armored) – cruiser, ironsides
vessel (baptismal)–font, piscina
vessel (brewing)–vat
vessel (broad-mouthed)–jar
vessel (burning oil)–cresset
vessel (chemical)–aludel
vessel (chemist's)–beaker
vessel (church wine)–ama
vessel (coast guard)–cutter
vessel (coasting) – dhow, trader

vessel (Columbus type)–caravel
vessel (communion)–pyx
vessel (condiment dispensing)–caster
vessel (cooking)–etna
vessel (cylindrical glass)–bocal
vessel (dairy)–separator
vessel (dehiscent seed)–pod
vessel (distilling)–retort
vessel (drinking) – beaker, cup, dipper, glass, goblet, jorum, mug, noggin, rumkin, schooner, stein, tankard
vessel (druggist's earthen)– gallipot
vessel (drying)–drain
vessel (eucharistic, wine) – ama
vessel (famous war)–Maine, Monitor
vessel (fishing) – smack, trawler
vessel (glass, cylindrical) – bocal
vessel (glass, pear-shaped)– aludel
vessel (glass, wide-mouthed) –beaker
vessel (hollow, metallic) – bell
vessel (incense)–censer
vessel (jug-like, inclosed in wickerwork)–demijohn
vessel (large)–ark
vessel (leather oil)–olpe
vessel (Levantine)–saic
vessel (light)–canoe
vessel (light sailing, var.)– catboat, ketch, yawl
vessel (liquid heating)–boiler, etna, kettle
vessel (liquid holding)–bottle, bucket, cruse, decanter, demijohn, ewer, jug, pitcher
vessel (liquor)–bottle, flagon, flask
vessel (long-handled)–ladle
vessel (Malayan)–proa
vessel (medieval)–nef
vessel (Mediterranean sailing)–xebec, zebec

vessel (Mediterranean, two or three masted)–polacre

vessel (metallic)–can, drum, pan, pot, tank, tub

vessel (narrow sterned) – pink

vessel (naval armored)–ironsides

vessel (oil) – cruet, cruse, tanker

vessel (one dose, hypodermic injection) – ampoule, ampule

vessel (one-masted) – dhow, sloop

vessel (operating under letter of marque)–privateer

vessel (Oriental)–saic

vessel (ornamental) – urn, vase

vessel (overflow catching)–drip

vessel (pear-shaped, glass) – aludel

vessel (pert. to)–vasal

vessel (river or coast trading)–picard

vessel (sailing) – bark, brig, caravel, frigate, ketch, lugger, schooner, ship, sloop, yawl

vessel (seed)–carpel, legume, pod

vessel (simple, one-sided seed)–carpel

vessel (small)–phial, vial

vessel (small coastal)–hoy

vessel (small coasting) – dhow

vessel (swift sailing)–proa

vessel (three-masted)–xebec, zebec

vessel (toward left side of)–aport

vessel (trading, medieval)–nef

vessel (tubular, branching)–artery

vessel (Turkish sailing)–saic

vessel (twin-hulled) – catamaran

vessel (two-masted) – brig, ketch, schooner

vessel (upward movement of)–scend

vessel (used in chemical sublimation)–aludel

vessel (war) – cruiser, destroyer, dreadnaught, flattop, sub, submarine

vessel (war, with flush decks)–corvette

vessel (water)–bottle, bucket, cruse, decanter, ewer, jug, pitcher, stamnos

vessel (wide-mouthed) – ewer, olla

vessel (wine cooling)–psykter

vessel (with upper deck cut away)–razee

vessel (wooden war) – corvette

vessel for holding pottery while firing–saggar, saggard, sagger

vessel's curved planking–sny

vessel's lack of being full – ullage

vessel's timber (vertical) – bitt, bollard, mast, stick

vest (Eng.)–waistcoat

vestibule – chamber, entry, hall, passage, vestible

vestige–footstep, trace, track

vestiture – clothing, dress, garb

vestment–alb, amice, chasuble, clothing, dress, garb, garment, robe, stole

vestment (bishop's)–dalmatic

vestment (bishop's distinctive)–omophorion

vestment (ecclesiastical) – cope, fanon, orale, stole

vestment (Greek church, alb-like)–saccos

vestment (linen)–alb

vestment (mass)–amice

vestment (priestly) – alb, ephod, orale

vestment (scarf-like)–orale

vestment (white)–alb

vetch–ers, tare

vetch (bitter)–ers

vetch (common)–tare

vetch (plant of family)–ers

vetch-like–ers

vetch seed–tare

veteran – experienced, practiced, seasoned

veto–interdiction, negative, prohibit, vetoes (pl.)

vex – agitate, anger, annoy, bother, chagrin, despite, displease, disturb, fret, fuss, gall, harass, harry, irk, irritate, miff, nettle, perplex, pother, provoke, rile, roil, ruffle, spite, tease, torment

vex (coll.)–rile

vexation–chafe, chagrin, fatigue, irritation, mortification, thorn, trouble, weariness

vexation (annoying)–harassment

vexation (coll.)–pesky

vexatious – afflictive, annoying, disturbed, pestilent, thorny

vexillum–banner, cross, flag, standard

via – along, away, begone, way

viaduct–bridge, trestle

vial–bottle, caster, phial

vial (small) – ampoule, ampul

viameter–odometer, parambulator

viand–fare, food, provisions, victuals

viand (choice)–cate

viand (dainty)–cate

viander–host

viaticals – baggage, impedimenta

viaticum–money, supplies

viator–traveler, wayfarer

vibrant–alive, pulsing, resonant, resounding, sonorous, thrilling, vibrating, vigorous

vibrate–brandish, fluctuate, quake, quaver, quiver, resonate, swing, thrill, throb, waver

vibrate (abnormally)–shimmy

vibrate (Scot.) – dirl, thirl, tirl

vibration–oscillation, quiver, tremor

vibration (rattling)–jar
vibrationless point–node
vicar–deputy, proxy, substitute, vicegerent
vicarage–rectorate
vicarious ruler–regent
vice – blemish, corruption, crime, defect, depravity, evil, fault, iniquity, sin, wickedness
Vichy West African port – Dakar
vicious – bad, corrupt, depraved, evil, foul, ill, immoral, impure, mean, noxious, obstinate, profligate, wicked
vicissitude – change, mutation
victim – dupe, gull, prey, sucker
victor–conqueror, vanquisher, winner
victorious – triumphant, unbeaten, winning
victory–conquest, triumph
victory (goddess of)–Nike
victory symbol–palm
victuals – food, meat, nourishment, viands
vie – compete, contend, contest, cope, emulate, stake, strive, wager
vie with – contest, emulate, run
Vienna–Wien
view – aspect, contemplate, examine, eye, opinion, survey, vista
view (extended)–panorama
view (long narrow)–vista
view opposed to annulling of establishment – antidisestablishmentarianism
vigil – sleeplessness, wake, wakefulness, watchman
vigil before a church festival –eve
vigilant – alert, attentive, aware, cautious, observant, wakeful, wary, watchful
vigor–energy, potency, power, strength
vigor (constitutional)–nerve

vigor (lose) – decline, fag, fail, flag, sag, weaken
vigor (Scot.)–vir
vigor (slang)–pep
vigorous–able, eager, effective, efficacious, energetic, forceful, hale, hardy, lusty, potent, robust, strenuous, strong, vehement, zealous
vigorous (spirited)–racy
vile – base, cheap, corrupt, debased, depraved, disgusting, evil, filthy, foul, impure, loathsome, odious, repulsive, sinful, sordid, unclean, vicious, wicked
vilify–abuse, asperse, calumniate, debase, degrade, malign, reproach, revile, slander, traduce
vilipend – belittle, calumniatory, disparage, slanderous
village–dorp, hamlet, thorp, thorpe
village (Russian)–mir
villain–boor, heavy, scoundrel, serf
villain (unscrupulous)–miscreant
villain's nemesis–hero
villication–nit, tic, twitching
vim – energy, force, spirit, vigor
vim (coll.)–gimp
vincaminor–myrtle
vindicate – absolve, acquit, assert, avenge, claim, clear, defend, exculpate, excuse, exonerate, justify, maintain
vindictive–revengeful
vindictive (maliciously) – punitive, revengeful, vengeful
vindictiveness–revenge
vine (climbing) – cupseed, ivy, liane
vine (creeping)–trailer
vine (crowfoot family)–clematis
vine (hop)–bine
vinegar–acetum, acid
vinegar (dregs of)–mother
vinegar (ester of)–acetate

vinegar (made from ale) – alegar
vinegar (malt, Eng. dial.)–alegar
vinegar (pert. to)–acetic
vinegar (pharm.)–acetum
"Vinegar Joe" (army slang) –Stillwell
vinegar pumpers–rackers
vinegar salt–acetate
vinegary – acetose, crabbed, unamiable
vineyard–cru
vinny–moldy
vinous–winy
viol (large)–lirone
violate – abuse, debauch, defile, deflower, dishonor, invade, mistreat, outrage, pollute, ravage, ravish, transgress, wrong
violate the sanctity of–desecrate
violence – assault, force, infringement, outrage, profanation, unjust
violence (to reduce)–mollify
violent – acute, extreme, fierce, great, intense, loud, savage, sharp, stormy, tempestuous, turbulent, vivid
violent outbreak – eruption, riot
violent pain–pang, throe
violently–amain
violently distracted–frantic
violet–mauve
violet perfume–irone
violet root–orrisroot
violet root (aromatic principle of)–irone
violet tip–butterfly
violin–fiddle
violin (anc.)–Rocta
violin (bass)–violoncello
violin (earliest form)–rebec
violin (famed for beauty of tone and design) – Strad, Stradivarius
violin (fine old, coll.)–Strad
violin (rare old)–Amati
violin (small)–kit
violin (tenor)–alto
violin bar–fret

violin city (famous) – Cremona
violin forerunner–rebec
violin maker (anc.)–Amati
violin piano–harmonichord
violinist (famous) – Elman, Ole Bull
violinist (Norwegian) – Ole Bull
viper–adder, snake
viper (Eastern venomous)–cerastes
vir–activity, vigor
virago – scold, termagant, vixen, woman
viren–green
virga–twig, wand
Virgil's Aeneid character – Amata
Virgil's birthplace–Mantua
Virgil's epic–Aeneid
Virgil's goatherd (Eclogue III)–Damon
Virgil's hero (great epic) – Aeneas, Eneas
Virgil's poem–Aeneid
Virgil's shepherd (Eclogue VII)–Corydon
Virgin Island coin–bit (ac.), daler (s.), franc (s.)
Virginia date plum–persimmon
Virginia goat's rue–catgut
Virginia Indian chief–Werowance
Virginia mountain–Cedar
Virginia quail–bobwhite
Virginia river – Dan, James, Potomac, Rapidan
Virginia snakeroot – birthwort, sangrel
Virginia willow–itea, iva
Virginia willow (genus of)–itea
virginity – celibacy, maidenhood, spinsterhood
virgularian–searod
virile–forceful, male, manly, masculine, masterful
virl–ferrule, ring
virose – fetid, malodorous, poisonous, virulent
virtu (article of)–curio
virtual–constructive
virtually–morally, practically

virtue – chastity, goodness, purity
virtue (tested, confirmed) – probity
virtuous–brave, chaste, efficacious, moral, potent, pure, valiant, valorous
virulent – deadly, noxious, poisonous, rabid
visage – countenance, face, look
viscid–adhering, glutinous, sticking, sticky, viscous, waxy
viscid liquid–tar
viscous–mucous, sizy
viscous substance–grease
vise (part of)–jaw
Vishnu avatar–Rama
Vishnu's bearer–Garuda
Vishnu's incarnation–Rama
Vishnu's vehicle–Garuda
visible–discernible, manifest, obvious, perceivable, seen
visible (no longer)–lost
Visigoth king–Alaric
vision – dream, eye, fancy, imagine
vision (defective)–anopia
vision (illusory)–mirage
visionary – chimerical, delusive, dreamer, dreamy, fantastic, ideal, idealist, imaginative, impractical, quixotic, romantic, unreal, utopian, wild
visionary (poetic)–aery
visioned–dreamed, dreamt
visit – call, inspection, see, visitation
visit (coll.)–chat
visit habitually–haunt
visit poor neighborhoods – slum
visitor – caller, company, guest, visitant
visitor (celestial)–comet
visne–neighbor, venue, vicinage
vison–mink
vista – panorama, prospect, scene, view
visual–ocular, optic, perceptible
visualize–envisage, imagine, picture

vital – animate, basic, exigent, imperative, indispensable, live, necessary, requisite
vitality – animation, liveliness, sap, vigor
vitality lacking–sapless
vitamin (vitamine)–thiamin
vitamin B–thiamin
vitamin B2–riboflavin
vitiate – contaminate, corrupt, debase, deprave, pervert, poison, pollute, spoil, taint
vitiated–contaminated, corrupt, defective, ineffective, invalidated, pical
vitiosity – depravity, viciousness
vitium–defect, fault
vitrella–retinophore
vitreous mineral–spar
vitreous silver–argentite
vitriolic – biting, caustic, scathing, virulent
vituperate – abuse, berate, censure, curse
vituperative–abusive, opprobrious, railing, reviling, scolding, scurrilous
vivacious – active, airy, animated, gay, lighthearted, lively, merry, spirited, sportive
vivacity – animation, ardor, fire, verve, zeal, zest
vivid–animated, clear, colorful, distinct, dramatic, fresh, glowing, graphic, lively, rich, spirited, striking, strong, vigorous
vivid description writer–imager
vivre – barrulet, cotise, dancette
vivres–foodstuff, provisions
vix–scarcely
vixen – scold, shrew, termagant
viz–namely, to wit, videlicet
vizard–mask, visor
voar (Scot.)–spring
vocabulary–diction, dictionary, lexicon, wordbook
vocabulist–lexicographer
vocal chink–glottis

vocal composition–aria, song

vocal composition (extended)–cantata

vocal expression–utterance

vocal handicap–lisp, stuttering

vocal sound–sonant, symbol

vocal sound (open)–vowel

vocalist – alto, basso, coloratura, singer, songster, soprano, tenor

vocation–call, calling, career

vocation (manual)–trade

vocation (suffix of)–ier

vociferation–clamor, outcry

vociferous–bawling, blatant, brawling, clamorous, loud, noisy, turbulent

voe–bay, creek, inlet

vogie–elated, merry, proud, vain

vogue – custom, fashion, mode, practice, style

vogue (French)–ton

voice – articulation, choice, expression, opinion, tongue, utterance, wish

voice (harsh)–hoarse

voice (Latin)–vox

voice (loss of)–anaudia

voice above natural–falsetto

voice box–larynx

voice stress–arsis

voiced–sonant

voiceless – atonic, spirate, surd

voiceless consonant–lene

voiceless modulation (var.)–inflexion

void – devoid, egest, emptiness, empty, lack, null, nullify, vacant, want

void of interest–jejune

void of satisfaction–jejune

void of sense–inane

void of space–inane

volage – fickle, fleeting, flighty, giddy, light, volatile

volaille–fowl, poultry

volant–light, nimble, quick

volatile–airy, buoyant, capricious, changeable, fickle, gaseous, lively, vaporous

volatile alkali–ammonia

volatile flux–smear

volatile liquid–alcohol, ether

volatile matter constituting perfume–essence

volatilized–evaporated

volcanic glass froth (hardened)–pumice

volcanic matter–lava

volcanic rock – dacite, tephrite, trass

volcanic scoria–slag

volcanic tufa (light, occurring on the Rhine)–trass

volcano–Etna, Pelee

volcano (mud)–salse

volcano (scoria of)–slag

volcano deposit (used in cement)–trass

volcano mouth–crater

volcano outlet–crater

volery–aviary, cage

volet–veil

volga–entil

volge–crowd, mob

volition–choice, determination, will

volley–barrage

volt (kind of, var.)–repolon

voluble – fluent, garrulous, glib, talkative

voluble talker (coll.)–spieler

volume – aggregate, book, bulk, mass, mo, tome

volume (large)–tome

volume (ponderous)–tome

voluntary – deliberate, elective, intentional, willingly

volunteer–offer, proffer

vomit–puke, spew

voodoo – fetish, magic, obe, obi

Vor Tigerns wife (British legend)–Rowena

voracious – gluttonous, greedy, immoderate, insatiable, rapacious, ravening, ravenous

voracity–edacity

vortex–eddy, whirlpool

vortex of cone–apex

votary – adherent, devotee, enthusiast, zealot

votary (art) – aesthete, esthete

vote (popular)–plebiscite

vote of the people–referendum

voter–balloter, elector, poller

voter (against)–anti, nay

voter (irregular)–repeater

votes (elicit)–poll

voting–balloting, polling

vouch–affirm, assertion, attest, attestation

vouch for officially–accredit

vouchsafe – assure, condescend, deign, guarantee

voussoir–keystone

voussoir (projection in)–ear

vow – asseveration, consecrate, dedicate, devote, oath, pledge, promise, swear

vow (dial.)–vum

vow (or promise, old word)–hote

vowel (change of)–umlaut

vowel change in German – umlaut

vowels (group of two) – digram

voyage – cruise, excursion, expedition, journey, pilgrimage, trip

voyaging–asea

vrother–anger, provoke

Vulcan epithet (Roman rel.)–Mulciber

Vulcan's consort–Maia

vulcanite (black)–ebonite

vulcanite (kind of)–ebonite

vulcanize–cure

vulgar–coarse, common, obscene, profane

vulgar fellow–cad

vulgar fellow (humorous)–pleb

vulgarian–snob

vulgarity – commonness, slang

vulpine – artful, crafty, cunning, fox, foxy

vult – aspect, countenance, expression, mien

vulture–condor

vulture (American black) – urubu

vulture (black)–urubu

vulture (king)–papa

vulture (large)–condor

W

waag–grivet
waapa–canoe
wabber–daman
wabbly–waveringly, wobbly
wabby–loon
wabe–huisache
wabi–huisache
wack–clammy, damp
wacker – alert, wakeful, watchful
wad–cram, pad, ram, stuff
waddie–cowboy
wade–ford
wader – crane, heron, ibis, rail, sandpiper, snipe
wadi–channel, oasis, ravine, river, valley, wady
wading bird–crane, heron, ibis, rail, sandpiper, snipe, wader
wading through–fords
wady–see wadi
waeg–kittiwake
waeness–sadness
wafer–biscuit, cake, snap
waff–flap, flutter, wag, wave
waffle (thin crisp)–gaufre
wag – farceur, joker, oscillate, wit
wag (coll.)–card
wage–attempt, bet, contend, employ, hire, risk, venture
wage earners–proletariat
wager–bet, sport, stake
wages–compensation, emolument, hire, pay, salary, stipend
waggish – jesting, parlous, roguish, sportive
Wagnerian character–Erda
Wagnerian goddess–Erda
Wagnerian heroine – Eva, Senta
Wagnerian operatic character–Wotan
wagon–aroba, cart
wagon (arch.)–wain
wagon (covered)–van
wagon (for heavy loads)–dray
wagon (low, sideless)–rolley

wagon (mine)–tram
wagon (Oriental cart)–araba
wagon (Oriental, covered)–araba
wagon (platform)–lorry
wagon (Russian)–telega
wagon (small coal)–tram
wagon (springless bullock)–tongas
wagon body (front)–buck
wagonload–fother
wagon pole–neap
wagon shaft–thill
wagon tongue–neap, pole
wahine – mistress, wife, woman
wahoo–buckthorn, elm, fish, guarapucu, nonsense, peto, tommyrot
waif – arab, castaway, flag, stray, vagrant, wanderer
wailing – lamenting, moaning, mourning, weeping
wainscot–ceil, line, lining, partition
waise (Scot.)–mud
waist–bodice, corsage, undergarment
waist (fitted)–basque
waistcoat–vest
waistcoat (Scot., under) – fecket
waists (in dressmaking) – tailles
wait–attend, bide, dally, defer, linger, observe, postpone, remain, tarry, watch
wait for–bide
wait on–cater, serve
waiter – attendant, garçon, salver, servant, server, servitor
waiter (seagoing)–messboy, messman
waive – abandon, desert, leave, reject, relinquish, vacate
waka–canoe
Wakashan Indian–Nootka
wake–arouse, awaken, rouse, stir, vigil, waken, watch

Wake (Robin painted) – Sarah
Wake Island (Japanese new name for)–Ottori
Wales–see also Welsh
Wales city–Bangor, Cardiff, Carnarvon, Hereford, Holyhead, Kidderminster, Pembroke, Rhondda, Swansea, Worcester
Wales emblem (floral)–leek
Wales language–Cymraeg
Wales measure – cover, lestrad, listred
Wales port–Cardiff
Wales river – Dee, Severn, Teifi, Teme, Wye
Wales town (north coppersmelting)–Amlwch
walk–allee, ambulate, hike, mog, pace, path, step, tramp, tread
walk (bordered by limes)–tilicetum
walk (inclined)–ramp
walk (pompous)–strut
walk (public) – alameda, esplanade, mall, promenade
walk (shaded)–alameda, arcade, mall
walk (taken for health) – constitutional
walk about–perambulate
walk clumsily–lumber
walk foppishly–mince
walk heavily–plod, stump
walk leisurely–amble, stroll
walk on–tread
walk pompously–strut
walk proudly (with high steps)–prance
walk slowly–mog
walk the floor–pace
walk trudgingly–tramp
walk unsteadily–reel, toddle
walk wearily – plod, tramp, trudge
walk with difficulty–hobble, limp, wade
walk without lifting feet–scuff, shuffle
walking stick–cane, staff

wall – defense, enclose, enclosure, encompass, fence,
parapet, rampart
wall (dividing) – septum,
septa (pl.)
wall (end)–gable
wall (fortification)–bastion
wall (fortress)–escarp
wall (inner, at foot of rampart)–escarp
wall (masonry retaining)–
revetment
wall (ornamented lower
part)–dado
wall (piece of, between two
openings)–pier
wall (retaining)–revetment
wall (terrace)–podium
wall (upper part of end)–
gable
wall border–dado
wall bracket–corbel
wall end–gable
wall lining–wainscot
wall ornament–plaque
wall projection–redan
wall recess–alcove, niche
wall up–immure
walls (pert. to)–mural, parietal
wallaba tree–apa
waller (Eng.)–saltmaker
wallet–bag, knapsack, pack,
pocketbook, poke, purse,
sack
wallet (arch.)–scrip
wallow – fade, flounder,
grovel, insipid, nauseous,
tasteless, welter, wither
walrus–morse
walrus (obs.)–rosmarine
walrus flock–pod
wamble – quiver, shake,
twist, wriggle
wame–belly, hollow, room,
stomach, womb
wamefu–bellyful
wamfle–flap
wampum–beads, peag, peage
wampum (slang)–money
wampum (Virginia region)
–roanoke
wan – dark, dim, dusky,
gloomy, languid, lurid,
lusterless, pale, pallid,
sickly

wand–baton, osier, pole, rod,
staff, switch
wand (magic)–rod
wander – digress, err, gad,
itinerate, meander, pere-
grinate, ramble, range,
roam, rove, stray
wander about–divagate
wander abstractedly–moon
wander aimlessly–meander
wander from subject–digress
wander in winding course–
scamander
wanderer–Arab, gypsy, itinerant, nomad, peregrina-
tor, ranger, roamer, rover,
straggler, truant
wanderer (coll.)–vag
wanderer (dark-skinned) –
Gypsy
wanderer (homeless)–waif
wanderer from duty–truant
wandering–aberrant, astray,
deviating, errant, itinerant, nomadic, perambu-
lant, peregrination, straying
wandering (anat.)–vagus
wandering (long)–odyssey
Wandering Jew author–Sue
wane–decline, decrease, fail,
peter, sink
wanga–sorcery, spell, voodoo
wangle – adjust, extricate,
manipulate, totter, wig-
gle, wriggle
wangrace–gruel, wickedness
wanhope–misfortune, mishap
wanion–plague, vengeance
wankle–feeble, fickle, irresolute, sickly, unstable,
unsteady
want – absence, dearth, deficient, desire, lack, miss,
poverty
want (utter)–destitution
want of desire–inappetence
want of good sense–folly
want of power–atony
wanting – absent, deficient,
destitute, devoid, lacking,
missing, needy
wanting confidence – dis-
trustful
wanting in energy–atonic

wapiti–elk, stag
war–battle, conflict
war (German for)–krieg
war (German whirlwind)–
blitzkrieg
war (religious)–jehad, jihad
war alarm (Brit. slang)–flap
War and Peace author–Tol-
stoy
war club–mace
warfare – conflict, contest,
hostilities, struggle
warfare (German lightning)
–blitzkrieg
war fleet–armada
war god–Ira, Mars
war god (Babylonian)–Ira
war god (Celtic sky)–Coel
war god (Greek)–Ares
war god (Norse)–Tyr
war goddess–Bella
war hawk–bailiff, jingo
war horse–charger, steed
warlike–belligerent, hostile,
martial, militant, military
war machine–ram, tank
war measure (restrictive) –
blockade
war on words–logomachy
warplane – Airacobra,
Avenger, Boulton-Paul
Defiant, Catalina, Cor-
sair, Hurricane, Kitty-
hawk, Liberator, Mitch-
el, Mustang, Seagull,
Spad, Spitfire, Thunder-
bolt, Typhoon, War-
hawk, Wildcat
war scare (Brit. slang)–flap
warship–cruiser, destroyer,
dreadnaught, sub, subma-
rine
warship (anc.)–onebank
warship (anc., having three
banks of oars)–trireme
warship (anc., having two
banks of oars)–bireme
warship (medieval) – dro-
mond
warship (pert. to)–naval
warship deck (partial)–orlop
war vehicle–jeep, tank
war vessel–cruiser, destroyer,
dreadnaught, sub, subma-
rine

war vessel (with flush decks) –corvet, corvette

warble–carol, sing, trill, yodel

warbler – blackcap, bluethroat, singer, songster, whitethroat, wren

warbler (large beaked) – grosbeak

ward (Fr.)–arrondissement

ward off–avert, fend, forfend, guard, parry, prevent, repel

warden–alcaid, alcaide, custodian, gatekeeper, guard, guardian, jailer, jailor, keeper, sexton, watchman

warden (jail, var.) – alcaid, alcaide, caid

warden (mosque)–nazir

warding off attack–repellent

wardrobe – apparel, closet, clothespress, room

ware – aware, careful, cautious, cognizant, commodities, conscious, heedful, merchandise, prudent, sage, seaweed, shrewd, vigilant, wary

ware (porcelain)–china

warehouse–depot, storage

warehouse (public)–etape

warehouse fee–storage

wariness–stealth

warm–ardent, clement, cordial, eager, enthusiastic, hearty, heat, heated, keen, mild, responsive, tepid, toast

warm (arch.)–calid

warm (moderately)–tepid

warm (very)–torrid

warm bath–therm, therme, thermae (pl.)

warm by friction–chafe

warm by heating apparatus –stove

warm praise–encomium

warm spring–therm, therme, thermae (pl.)

warm thoroughly–toast

warmhearted–friendly, generous, hearty, kind, kindly, sympathetic

warmth–animation, ardency, ardor, earnestness,

elan, excitement, fervency, geniality, glow, heat, vehemence

warn – admonish, apprise, caution, counsel, notify, reprehend

warn (arch.)–rede

warning – admonition, admonitive, beware, caveat, signal, threat

warning (legal)–caveat

warning signal–alarm

warning sound–alarm, alarum, bell, siren, tocsin

warp–distort, sway, swerve

warp (cross threads)–woof

warp yarn–abb

warps–biases

warrant–ensure, guarantee, justify, permit

warranting objection–exceptionable

warrior (female)–Amazon

warrior (Trojan bravest) – Agenor

warriors (Zulu)–impi

Warsaw suburb–Praga

warth–coast, meadow, shore, wardage

wary – canny, careful, cautious, chary, watchful

was able–could

was aware–knew

was discontented–repined

was in store for–awaited

was inclined–cared

was interested–cared

was on view–appeared

was present at–attended

was proper to–beseemed

was solicitous – cared, considerate

was sorry for–rued

was the matter with–ailed

wash – bathe, cleanse, lap, launder, lave, rinse

wash basin (with necessary fittings)–lavabo

wash by draining–leach

wash for a still–sperge

wash for gold–pan

wash lightly–rinse

wash out–elute, erase

wash the hair–shampoo

wash thoroughly–scour

wash vigorously in liquid– slosh

wash with rubbing – scour, scrub

wash with water (to extract soluble substance)–leach

washer (copper boat)–rove

washer (iron axletree)–clove

washes – bathes, cleanses, laps, launders, laves, rinses, soaps

washing (act of)–ablution

washing away–abluent

Washington city – Everett, Olympia, Seattle, Spokane, Tacoma

Washington fort–Lewis

Washington sound–Puget

Washington volcano – Rainier

Washington wind (southwest)–chinook

wasp–hornet

wasp (one of a family of)– vespid

waspish–choleric, irascible, irritable, peevish, petulant, slender, snappish, spiteful, testy

wassail–carousal, frolic, lark, orgy, romp, shindy

waste–chips, clinkers, decrement, demolish, desolation, destruction, devastation, diminution, dissipate, dissipation, dross, eat, exhaust, expend, fritter, havoc, junk, lavish, loss, prodigality, ravage, refuse, rind, ross, rubbish, sack, slag, ted, trash, wear

waste (broken mine)–gob

waste (sandy) – desert, Sahara

waste allowance–tret

waste away – atrophy, fail, molder, tabid

waste matter–clinkers, dross, ort, slag

waste time – dawdle, idle, loiter

wasteful–destructive, extravagant, improvident, thriftless

wasteful (excessive)–extravagant

wasteland – desert, ever-glades, heath, marsh, moor, morass

wasting – awaste, devastating, enfeebling

watch – eye, guard, heed, mark, mind, observe, police, sentry, tend, time, vigil

watch (stop)–timer

watch- and clockmaker – horologist

watch face covering–crystal

watch for–await

watch pocket–fob

watchful–alert, aware, circumspect, heedful, observant, open-eyed, vigilant

watchful (observant) – regardful

watchman – gatekeeper, guard, sentinel, sentry

watchtower–beacon, mirador

watchword (guard's)–parole

watchworks arrangement – caliper

watchworks mechanism – escapement

water–agua, aqua, eau, irrigate, sprinkle

water (baptismal)–laver

water (congealed)–ice

water (fen)–suds

water (French) – eau, eaux (pl.)

water (hard)–ice

water (Latin)–aqua

water (mineral)–selter, seltzer, Shasta, Vichy

water (reddish with iron)–riddam

water (rough)–eddy, rapids, sea

water (sea)–brine

water (soapy)–suds

water (Spanish)–agua

water (still, within coral island)–lagoon

water (surface of)–ryme

water apportioner (in ditches)–divisor

water bird–coot, diver, loon

water bottle–carafe

water channel below mill wheel–tailrace

water cooler–icer, olla

watercourse–arroyo, brook, creek, gully, river, stream, wadi, wady

water cow–manatee

water crake–ouzel, rail

water cress–brooklime

water cress (Eng. dial.) – ekers

water crowfoot (Eng.)–reit

water cure (Med.)–hydropathy, hydrotherapeutics

water current–race

water deerlet–chevrotain

water drain–sewer, sump

water eagle–osprey

water elephant – hippopotamus

water excursion–row, sail

waterfall–cachoeira, cascade, cataract, lin, linn, lyn, Niagara, oe, Victoria, Yosemite

waterfall (Scot.)–lin, linn

waterfowl–coot, diver, loon

water grampus – hellgrammite

water hole–oasis, oases (pl.)

water ice–sherbet

water jug–olla, tinaja

water lily–lotos, lotus

water meter (kind of)–venturi

water nymph – hydriad, naiad, Undine

water passage (artificial) – canal, sluice

water passage (narrow) – strait

water pit (mine waste) – sump

water plant (flowering) – lotos, lotus

water plug–cock, faucet, hydrant, spigot, tap

water pocket–tinaja

water raising apparatus – noria, pump, siphon

water raising contrivance (Oriental)–shadoof

water scorpion (genus of)–nepa

water spirit–Ariel

water spirit (female)–Undine

water spirit (Scot.)–kelpie

waterspout–spate

waterspout (ornamental) – gargoyle

water sprite – naiad, nix, nixie

water sprite (var.)–nys

water vessel (Indian)–lota

waterway (artificial)–canal, sluice

water wheel – naria, noria, sakia, sakieh, sakiyeh

water wheel (Persian)–noria

watered appearance–moire

watering place–oasis, spa

waters of oblivion–lethe

watery–aqueous

wattle–rod, wand, withe

wattle (bird)–lappet

wattle tree–boree

wave–billow, breaker, comber, eagre, float, flourish, flutter, roller, sea, surge, undulate

wave (different colored) – vein

wave (large) – billow, breaker, decuman, sea, surge

wave (tidal)–eager, eagre

wave (upward motion) – scend

wave to and fro–flap, wag

wavelet–ripple

waver–falter, fluctuate, hesitate, reel, sway, totter

wavering–irresolute

waves (breaking)–surf

waving (wavy) – unde, undee, undulating

wavy–curly, undulated

wavy (heraldry)–onde, unde, undee, undy

wax–cere, grow, sere

wax (comb. form)–cer

wax ointment–cerate

wax preparation–cerate

waxed–cerate, cered, grew, increased

waxen–cerated

waxy substance–cerin

way–alley, avenue, highway, lane, milky, path, road, route, street

way (roundabout)–detour
way (sloping)–ramp
way of departure–exit
waylay–ambush
we (Latin)–nos
weak–debilitated, decrepit, feeble, infirm, nerveless, puny, thin, washy, watery
weak and thin–watery
weak point–foible
weaken – debilitate, dilute, enervate, impair, lessen, reduce, sap, thin, tire, undermine, unnerve
weakness–debility, decrepitude, feebleness, foible, frailty, impotence, infirmity, infirmness, powerlessness
weakness (personal)–foible
wealth – abundance, affluence, assets, fortune, opulence, possessions, property, treasure
wealth (god of)–Plutus
wealthy–affluent, rich
wealthy (Eng. slang)–oofier, oofy
wealthy man – capitalist, croesus, nabob, plutocrat
weapon–arm, carbine, dagger, derringer, gun, knife, lance, pistol, snee, spear, stiletto, revolver
weapon (anc.)–celt
weapon (cavalry)–lance
weapon (cutlass-like)–bolo
weapon (fencing)–epee, foil, rapier, sword
weapon (Filipino)–bolo
weapon (halberd-like) – glave
weapon (medieval)–pike
weapon (missile)–arrow, artillery, bolas, dart, shaft
weapon (old)–blunderbuss, crossbow, halberd, poleax
weapon (Philippine)–bolo
weapon (prehistoric) – celt, eolith
weapon (primitive)–lance, spear
weapon (three-pronged) – trident
weapons (quantities of) – stores

weapons (storage place for) –arsenal
wear at edge–fray
wear away–abrade, corrode, erode
wear away by friction – abrade
wear off–abrade
wear ostentatiously–sport
wear out–tire
wearies – bores, fatigues, jades, tires
weariness–lassitude, tedium
wearing a girdle–belted
wearisome–boring, tedious
weary – bore, fag, fatigue, irk, jade, pall, tire
weasel–stoat
weasel (English)–vare
weasel (family of)–ermine, ferret, marten
weasel (prized)–ermine
weasel (small)–cane
weasel (white furred) – ermine
weasel (winter name) – ermine
weasel-like animal (fish feeding)–otter
weasel-like carnivore–ferret
weather condition–climate
weather map (line of)–isobar
weathercock–vane
weave–devise, entwine, fashion, interlace, lace, plait, spin
weave into network–wattle
weave raised patterns–brocade
weave together – interlace, intertwine, intertwist, interwind
weaver bird (India)–baya
weaver's reeds–sleys
weaver's tools–sleys
weaving (threads arranged for)–sleyed
weaving machine thread (division of)–beer
weazen–shrink, shrivel
web – membrane, ply, tela, texture, trap
web-footed–palmate
web-like–lacy, telar
web-like membrane–tela

web spinning–telary
webbed–palmate
wed–espouse, marry
wedding anniversary (first) –paper
wedding anniversary (second)–straw
wedding anniversary (third) –candy
wedding anniversary (fourth)–leather
wedding anniversary (fifth) –wooden
wedding anniversary (seventh)–floral
wedding anniversary (tenth) –tin
wedding anniversary (twelfth)–linen
wedding anniversary (fifteenth)–crystal
weeding anniversary (twentieth)–china
wedding anniversary (twenty-fifth)–silver
wedding anniversary (thirtieth)–pearl
wedding anniversary (thirty-fifth)–coral
wedding anniversary (fortieth)–emerald
wedding anniversary (forty-fifth)–ruby
wedding anniversary (fiftieth)–golden
wedding anniversary (seventy-fifth)–diamond
wedding proclamation – banns
wede–shiveled
wedge (circle)–sector
wedge in–jam
wedge-shaped–cuneal, cuneate
wedlock – ceremony, marriage, matrimony
wedlock (pert. to)–marital
Wednesday (god of name)– Woden
wee–bit, little, small, tiny
weed–darnel, mallows, milk, plantain, spurge, tare
weed (Biblical)–tare
weed (common) – plantain, purslane, ragweed
weed (knot)–allseed

weed (perennial)–toadflax

weed (poisonous)–loco

weed (stinging)–nettle

weed (tropical)–sida

weed (troublesome) – purslane

weekday (neither festival or fast)–feria

weekdays (pert. to)–ferial

weekly–aweek

weel – basket, eddy, pool, whirlpool

weem (Scot.)–cave, cavern, pit

ween–believe, conceive, expectation, imagine, opinion, suppose, think

weep–boohoo, cry, lapwing, leak, percolate, sob

Weeping Philosopher–Heraclitus

weeping sinew–ganglion

weevil (bean)–lota

weevil (cotton)–boll

weigh–consider, poise, ponder, scale, tare

weigh in mind (deliberately)–ponder

weighed down–loaded, sat

weighing machine–balance, scale

weighing machine (Scot.)–trone

weight–burden, encumber, load, oppress

weight (anc.)–mina

weight (gem)–carat

weight (hundred)–cental

weight (hundred, abbr.) – CWT

weight (India)–rati, ratti

weight (jewel)–tola

weight (less package or container)–net

weight (of)–baric

weight (of container)–tare

weight (of container and contents)–gross

weight (Oriental) – picul, tael

weight (pert. to) – baric, ponderal

weight (pile driver's falling) –tup

weight (small)–mite

weight (small balance) – rider

weight (wool)–tod

weight allowance – scalage, tare

weight allowance for container–tare

weight of vessel's cubical content–tonnage

weight or effect (having)–militate

weight or force (little) – lightly

weight-raising machine (anc.)–trispast

weight system–avoirdupois, metric, troy

weight-testing officer–sealer

weighty – bulky, corpulent, heavy, impressive, large, massive, massy, momentous, onerous, ponderous, serious

weir–bank, dam, levee

weird–awesome, eerie, eery, ghostly, uncanny, unearthly

weird sisters–Fates

welcome–acceptable, accueil, adopt, agreeable, desirable, greet, greeting, salutation

weld–consolidate, unite

welfare–weal

welkin–air, atmosphere

welkin (arch.)–air, sky

well–excellently, expertly

well (flowing oil)–gusher

well (gushing water)–artesian

well (Isaac's servants dug)–esek

well (land draining)–sump

well (prefix for)–eu

well (Scot.)–aweel

well-being–comfort, happiness, weal

wellborn–eugenic

Well Born (the)–Federalists

well-bred – cultivated, cultured, genteel, pedigreed, polite, refined, thoroughbred

well eye (Scot.)–pool, source

well-formed–shapely

well-grounded–valid

well-heeled – armed, moneyed, rich

well-known – eminent, famous

well-liked–popular

well lining–stean, steen

Welch–see also Wales

Welsh drake–gadwall

Welsh god (legendary, of underworld)–Bran

Welsh instrument (small reed)–pibcorn

Welshman (a)–Taffy

Welsh onion–cibol

Welsh rabbit–rarebit

welter–grovel, wallow

wench – girl, maiden, servant, strumpet

went – alley, course, crossroad, departed, journey, lane, passageway, proceeded, progress, road

went astray–miscarried

went away–departed, left

went before–anteceded, led, preceded

went down – fell, sagged, sank

went first–led

went over again–retraced

went swiftly–ran, scooted, sped

went up–arose, rose

wenzel–jack, knave

wergild–cro

Wergild (Irish)–Eric

West African British territory–Nigeria

West African capital (French)–Dakar

West African French city–Dakar

West African gazelle–kudu, mhorr, mohr, oryx

West African lemur–kinkajou, potto

West African lemurine–potto

West African monkey (small, geonon)–mona

West African mortar–swish

West African reedbuck–nagor

West African river–Geba

West Indian barricuda–picudilla

West Indian bird (tiny) – tody

West Indian cabbage tree–acapu

West Indian clingfish–testar

West Indian ebony – cocuswood

West Indian evergreen tree –sapodilla

West Indian fish–paru

West Indian fish (food) – sesi

West Indian fleas–chigoes

West Indian fruit–papaw, pawpaw

West Indian herb–ocra

West Indian island–Aruba, Cuba, Haiti

West Indian island (British) –Bahama

West Indian king (petty)–Cacique

West Indian liquor–taffia

West Indian liquor (distilled from sweet potatoes) – mobbie, mobby

West Indian magic–ob, obe, obi

West Indian native–Creole

West Indian Negro – ebo, eboe

West Indian owl–mucaro

West Indian pear–tuna

West Indian region–Malabar

West Indian republic–Haiti

West Indian rodent–agouti

West Indian shrub–anil, joewood

West Indian sorcery–ob, obe, obi

West Indian snuff–Maccaboy

West Indian spirit (distilled from sugar cane)–tafia, taffia

West Indian taro–tania

West Indian tortoise (fresh water)–hicatee

West Indian tree – balata, genip, ramoon, yacca

West Indian tree (tallow)–cera

West Indian tree (timber)–acana

West Indian treewood–galba

West Indian volcano–Pelee

West Indies (pert. to)–Antillean

West Point freshman–pleb, plebe

West Saxon king (warlike) –Ine

western America valley – canada

western hill (broad top) – loma

western U.S. mountain – Helena, Shasta, Whitney

western U.S. timber wolf–lobo

western Venezuela Indian–Timote

wet–damp, dampen, humid, moist, moisten, rainy, soak, watery

wet (moisten)–leach

wet (very)–soggy, soppy

wet and soft – mushy, squashy

wet thoroughly – drench, souse

whale (gray)–ripsack

whale (killer)–grampus, orc, orca

whale (kind of)–orc, orca, sperm

whale (order of)–cete, cetic

whale (school of)–gam, pod

whale (small)–grampus

whale (the)–cetacea, cete

whale (var.)–ceta

whale (white)–beluga

whaleboat steersmen–slewers

whalebone–baleen

whale carcass–kreng

whale fat–spermaceti

whale genus–areta, cete

whale killer (genus of)–orca

whale oil cask–rier

whale secretion (from alimentary canal, used in perfumes)–ambergris

whale (genus of)–areta, cete

whale (pert. to)–cetic

whales (school of)–gam, pod

whale's star (variable) – Muse

whaling ship's visit–gam

wharf–dock, landing, pier, quay

what wonders has God

wrought (Arabic)–Mashallah

whatnot–atagere, etagere

whaup – fuss, lout, outcry, pod, scoundrel

wheal–pustule, stripe, suppurate, whelk

wheat (German)–spelt

wheat (loose-eared)–spelt

wheat beverage (malted) – zythem

wheat chaff–bran

wheaten flour–atta

wheedle–cajole, coax, flatter

wheel–bicycle, cog, roll

wheel (coll.)–bike

wheel (for executing criminals)–rat

wheel (gem grinding)–skive

wheel (grooved, pulley) – sheave

wheel (heraldic spinning)–torn

wheel (monkey)–gin

wheel (small)–caster

wheel (spike)–rowel

wheel (spur)–rowel

wheel (toothed)–gear, pinion

wheel (turbine)–rotor

wheel (water)–naria, noria, sakia, sakieh, sakiyeh

wheel (water-raising)–noria

wheel animalcule–rotifer

wheel bar–axle

wheelbarrow–hod

wheel hub–nave

wheel part – felloe, rim, spoke, tire

wheel piece (projecting) – cam

wheel rim–felloe, felly

wheel-shaped – rotate, rotiform

wheel stopper–trig

wheel tooth–cog

wheeler–poler

wheels (logging, pair of)–katydid

wheels (pert. to)–rotal

wheen–division, few, group, several

wheerikins–posteriors

wheetle–chirp, whistle

when–as, until

where Caesar defeated Mark Antony–Actium
where Hannibal defeated the Romans–Cannae
where Japanese defeated the Russians–Mukden
where Ney defeated the Austrians–Ulm
Where The Blue author – Morley
whereness–ubiety
whet–grind, point, quicken, rouse, sharpen
whether–if
whetter–edger, tippler
whey (milk) – serum, sera (pl.)
which–that
which (for)–forwhat, wherefore
which (on)–onwhat, whereupon
which (to) – thereunto, towhat
which (with) – wherewith, withwhat
which was to be shown (abbr.)–qed
whicker – bleat, neigh, snigger, whinny
whid–fib, frisk, lie, whisk
whiff–gust, puff, waft
while–as, yet
whim – caprice, fad, freak, megrim, migraine, vagary, whimsey
whimper – mewl, moan, pule, sniffle, sob, weep, whine
whimsical–capricious, dish, eccentric, fad, fanciful, fantastic, grotesque, notional, odd, queer
whimsy – caprice, craze, fancy, freak, whim
whin–furze, gorse
whine – pule, snivel, whimper
whinny–neigh
whip–beat, cats, crop, flog, knout, lace, lash, quirt, scourge, strap, swinge, tan
whip (Cossack)–knout
whip (having three lashes

tipped with lead balls)–plet, plete
whip (knotted flogging) – cat, knout
whip (riding)–crop, quirt
whip (three lashes, tipped with lead)–plet, plete
whip handle–crop
whip socket–snead
whir–commotion, hurry
whirl–eddy, gyrate, revolve, rotate, spin, twirl
whirl (be in)–reel
whirl (Scot.)–tirl
whirlpool–eddy, gorce, vortex, vortices (pl.)
whirlpool (noted) – maelstrom
whirlwind–cyclone
whirlwind (Faroe Island) – oe
whisk–tuft, wisp
whiskers–beard
whiskey–see whisky
whisky – flighty, lively, whitethroat
whisky (glass of Scotch) – rubdown
whisky (Irish, illicit)–poteen
whisky (privately made) – poteen
whisky (slang)–corn
whisky and soda–stinger
whisper–buzz, murmur
whist – mute, quiet, silence, silent, silently, still
whist hand with no card over nine–Yarborough
whisterpoop–buffet
whistle–pipe, toot
whistle duck–goldeneye
whistle pig–woodchuck
whistle wing–goldeneye
whit–bit, bodle, iota, jot
white–pale, pallid, wan
white (deadly)–ashy
white (grayish)–ashen, hoar
white (poor)–Yahoo
white amber–spermaceti
white and purple–orpin
white and shining–pearly
white and smooth–ivorine
white ant – anai, anay, termite
white antimony–valentinite
white appearance–pallor

whitebelly – grouse, pigeon, widgeon
white boy–favorite
white cell–leucocyte
white chub–spawneater
white collars – bookkeepers, clerks, salesmen
white crow–vulture
white elephant (land of) – Siam
whitefish–beluga, vendace
white flag–cowardice, truce, yielding
white garnet–leucite
white gentian–feverroot
white grouse–ptarmigan
white heat–incandescence
white horse nettle–trompillo
White Indian–Cuna
White Indian hemp – milkweed
white iron pyrites–marcasite
white jade–alabaster
white lead–ceruse
white lead ore–cerussite
white leprosy–leucoderma
white-livered–cowardly, feeble, pusillanimous
white matter of brain and spinal cord–vole
white merganser–smew
white mica–muscovite
white monk–Cistercian
White Mountain (second highest)–Adams
white mule–gin, whisky
white mundic–arsenopyrite
white neb–rook
white nerve substance–alba
white nun–smew
white oak–roble
white of egg–glair
white partridge–ptarmigan
white plague–consumption, phthisis, tuberculosis
white plantain–pussytoe
whitepot–pudding
white pudding – sausage, whitehass
white pyrite–marcasite
white sanicle–snakeroot
whitesark–surplice
whiteside–goldeneye
white snipe–avocet, sanderling
whitestone–granulite

White Sunday–Whitsunday
white vestment–alb
white vine–bryony
white walnut – butternut, shagbark
whiteweed–daisy
white whale–beluga
white widgeon–smew
whitewing – chaffinch, sail, scoter, sweeper
white with age–hoar
whiten – blanch, blanche, bleach, etiolate
whiter–paler
whither–where
whiting–chalk
whitster–bleacher
whittaw–saddler
whitten–rowan
whitter–chatter, chirp, murmur, twitter, whimper
whitterick–curlew
Whittier's poem title – Ichabod
whittle–cut
whittle (slang)–peach
who (German)–wer
who (Scotch)–wha
whole–all, complete, entire, entirety, intact, perfect, sum, total, uneaten
whole (discrete)–sum
whole (organized)–system
whole-chested–loyal
whole cradle–platform
whole-footed–frank, ingenuous, intimate
wholehearted–complete, devoted, earnest, sincere, unmitigated, unreserved
whole number–integer
whole-skinned–unhurt, unscathed
wholesome – favorable, healthful, healthy, hearty, propitious, robust, salubrious, sound, vigorous
whole-souled – devoted, noble, sincere, zealous
wholly–completely, entirely, entirety, exclusively, fully, solely, thoroughly, totally
wholly (comb. form)–toto
wholly engaged–absorbed
wholly engrossed–rapt
whone–few, little

whoop–cheer, express, hoot, utter
whooping cough–pertussis
whop–beat, bump, fall, flop, knock, strike, stroke
whore–courtesan, drab, harlot, prostitute, strumpet, wench
whorl–spire
whulter (Scot.)–whopper
whute–whistle
wicked – atrocious, bad, criminal, depraved, evil, flagitious, flagrant, guilty, heinous, ill, irreligious, nefarious, profane, sinful, ungodly, unholy, unjust, unrighteous, vicious, vile
wickedness – evil, iniquity, maliciousness, sin
wicker basket (fish catching)–pot
wicker basket (provision) – hamper, pannier
wicker cradle–bassinet
wicker sides (in cricket)–ons
widbin – dogwood, honeysuckle, woodbine
widdifow – rascal, rascally, scamp
widdle – struggle, waddle, wriggle
widdrim–confusion, excitement, madness
wide–ample, broad, distended, expanded, loose, roomy
wide-awake–alert, hat, keen, knowing, tern
wide extent–expanse
widely–abroad, afar
widely accepted–prevalent
widen – broaden, dilate, enlarge, expand, extend, ream, spread
widespread – extensive, general, prevalent, rife, sweeping
widespread (not)–local
widgeon – goose, simpleton, smee
widow–relict
widow fish–viuva
widow man–widower
widow monkey–titi
widow's coin–mite

widow's mite – lepton, lepta (pl.)
widow's portion–dower
widow's right (Scot. law) – terce
widow's weeds–mourning
widower–relict
width – breadth, diameter, girth
wield – brandish, control, cope, deal, handle, manage, ply, power
wield (with address)–manage
wier–see weir
wife – helpmate, helpmeet, mate, spouse
wig–peruke, toupee
wig (coll.) – censure, jasey, rebuke, reprimand, scold
wight – active, brave, loud, nimble, powerful, rough, strong, swift, valiant
wigwag–signal
wigwam–teepee, tepee
wild – aberrant, barbarian, barbarous, bestial, chimerical, feral, ferine, irrational, mad, obstreperous, riotous, savage, tumultuous, uncertain, uncontrollable, uninhabited, unruly, untilled
wild alder–goutweed
wild allspice–spicebush
wild ananas–pinguin
wild animal–antelope, bear, deer, lion, lynx, moose, onager, polecat, tiger
wild arum–cuckoopint
wild ass–kiang, onager
wild bachelor button–milkwort
wild banana – papaw, pawpaw
wild broom–deerweed
wild buffalo–arna, arnee
wildcat–eyra, ocelot, serval
wildcat (chestnut-colored)–eyra
wildcat (tawny)–panther
wild cattle (genus of)–bos
wild celadine–jewelweed
wild China tree–soapberry
wild coffee–feverroot
wild crocus–pasqueflower

wild donkey–onager
wild fancy–vagary
wild flower–anemone, bluet, sage
wild fowl's flight–skein
wild goat–markhoor, tahr
wild gourd–calabazilla
wild headlong flight–stampede
wild hog–boar
wild hop–bryony
wild hyacinth–camas
wild India buffalo–arna, arnee
wild Irishman–tumatakura
wild jalap–manroot
wild kale–charlock
wild masterwort–goutweed
wild mulberry–yawweed
wild musk–alfilaria
wild mustard–charlock
wild navew–rutabaga
wild ox (large)–yak
wild ox (small)–anoa
wild passionflower–maypop
wild pineapple–pinguin
wild plum–sloe
wild potato–manroot
wild pumpkin–calabazilla
wild sage–clary
wild sago–coontie
wild sheep – aoudad, argal, argali, sha, urial
wild succory–chicory
wild sweet potato–manroot
wild talk–raving
wild turnip–rutabaga
Wild West Show–Rodeo
wildebeest–gnu
wilderness–desert
wile–art, artifice, deceit, entice, guile, ruse, stratagem, trick, trickery
wilier–craftier
Wilkes Island (Japanese new name for)–Ashi
will – demise, inclination, testament, volition
will (a)–testament
will power – determination, purpose, resoluteness
will power (loss of)–abulia
will to live (Buddhism) – Tanha
willful – heady, impetuous,

intentional, mad, rash, voluntary, wayward
willful firing–arson
willing–agreeable, desirous, disposed, free, minded, ready, unforced
willing (more)–rather, readier
willing to do something – prone
willingly–fain, lief, readily
willow–osier, teaser
willow (species of)–osier
willow (Virginia)–itea, iva
willow tree–osier
willow twig–sallow
willowy–osier
wilsome – desolate, dreary, violent, wild, willful
Wilson's thrush–veery
wilt–droop, flag, languish
wily – artful, astute, canny, crafty, cunning, foxy, shrewd, sly, smart, subtle
wimick–cry, whimper
win – achieve, obtain, triumph
win by guile–inveigle
win over from hostility–conciliate
wince – cringe, flinch, reel, shrink, start
wind–air, blast, breeze, coil, crank, dotterel, flaw, gale, gust, meander, storm, tempest, wrap
wind (Adriatic)–bora
wind (blast of)–gust
wind (cold mountain gusts)–williwaws
wind (comb. form)–anemo
wind (desert)–simoon, sirocco
wind (East)–eurus
wind (fierce)–buster
wind (god of)–Aeolus, Eolus
wind (gust of)–berry
wind (hot)–sirocco
wind (Mediterranean, hot, moist, southeast)–sirocco
wind (Mediterranean periodical)–etesian
wind (north)–boreas
wind (North Adriatic, violent)–bora

wind (northerly, cold)–bora
wind (Oregon and Washington, southwest) – chinook
wind (Oriental, periodic) – monsoon
wind (south)–auster
wind (southeast)–eurus
wind (southwest)–afer
wind (Spain, East Coast) – solano
wind (violent gust of)–blast
wind and storm (god of) – Adad
wind around a cleat (naut.)–belay
wind gauge–vane
wind indicator–vane
wind instrument – clarinet, cornet, fife, flute, hautboy, horn, oboe, organ, sax, tuba
wind spirally–coil, fake
wind with marline–marl
windflower–anemone
winding – meandrous, sinuous, spiral
winding (a)–sinuosity
windlass–winch
windlass (ship's)–capstan
windlass (vertical)–capstan
windmill blade–vane
windmill sail–awn
winds (strong southwest South American) – pampero
winds of commerce–trades
windstorm–gale
windstorm (periodic)–oe
windstorm (violent) – cyclone, gale, hurricane, typhoon
windup–coil, end, finish
window (bay)–oriel
window (dormer)–gable, lucarne
window (kind of)–bay, casement, dormer, oriel
window (ship's)–port
window arrangement–fenestration
window frame–sash
window projecting from wall–bay, oriel
window recess–exedra
window worker–glazier

wine (Baden)–Rulander
wine (Bordeaux)–claret
wine (excellent quality) – vintage
wine (Fr., rich, sweet)–muscatel
wine (French for)–vin
wine (kind of) – Burgundy, canary, claret, Madeira, Medoc, muscatel, port, sherry, tokay
wine (light)–canary
wine (light-bodied)–claret
wine (palm)–taree
wine (pert. to)–vinic
wine (red)–claret
wine (rich, sweet)–muscatel
wine (still)–pontac, pontacq
wine (Tag.)–alac
wine (Tuscan, dry, red) – chianti
wine (variety of French) – hermitage
wine (white) – malaga, sauterne
wine (white grape)–Riesling
wine and honey–mulse
wine aversionist – oenophobist
wine bottle–decanter
wine bottle (large) – magnum
wine cask–tun
wine cask (large)–pipe
wine cask deposit–tartar
wine cup–ama, chalice
wine drink–negus
wine, honey and spice mixture–clary
wine list–card
wine lover–oenophilist
wine making (pert. to) – oenopoetic
wine measure (old Dutch)– aam, aum
wine merchant (wholesale)– vintner
wine miracle (scene of) – Cana
wine pitcher–oenochoe, olpe
wine preparation (for doctors)–mosto
wine residue (from pressing)–marc
wine strength (Fr.)–seve
wine vessel–ama, chalice

wine vessel (anc.) – ama, amula
wine vessel (eucharistic) – ama, amula
wing–ala, alae (pl.), ell, fly, pinion
wing (bird)–pinion
wing (church)–aisle
wing (disposition of) – alation
wing (false)–alula
wing (part of bird's)–alula
wing-footed–aliped
wing-footed animal–aliped
wing god (var.)–Eolus
wing-like–alar, alary
wing-like part–ala, alae (pl.)
wing-like part of plane–aileron
wing quill – remex, remiges (pl.)
wing-shaped – alar, alary, alate, aliform
wing tip (auxiliary, of airplane)–aileron
winged – alar, alary, alate, alated
winged (her.)–aile
winged child–cherub
winged fruit–samara
winged horse–Pegasus
winged monster–harpy
winged seed–samara
wingless–apteral
wings–alae, pinions
wings (arrangement of) – alation
wings (disposal of)–alation
wings (having)–alate
wings (without)–apteral
wink – blink, nictate, nictitate
wink (Eng. dial.) – periwinkle
wink-a-peep–eyes
winkel–shop, store
winking – nap, nictation, sleep, slumbering
winkle–periwinkle, twinkle
winner – breadwinner, reaper, victor
winning–acquisition, attractive, captivating, charming, gaining, victory, winsome
winninish–ouananiche

winnow–fan, separate, sift
winsome – attractive, captivating, charming
winter–hibernate, snow
winter (pert. to)–hiemal
winter-like–brumal
winter quarters–hibernacle
winter sport–skiing
Winter's Tale character – Perdita
Winter's Tale Queen's attendant–Emilia
wire (bacteriologist's)–oese
wire (conducting)–coil
wire (looped platinum)–oese
wire (platinum)–oese
wire (thick)–cable
wire (used by bacteriologists)–oese
wire measure–mil, stone
wireless–radio
wires (cross, in optical instrument)–reticle
wiry–hardy, sinewy, tough
wis–imagine, suppose, think
Wisconsin city – Kenosha, Madison, Oshkosh, Racine, Sparta
Wisconsin Indian–Sac
wisdom – discretion, erudition, knowledge, learning, sagacity, sapience
wisdom (god of)–Nabu, Nebo
wisdom (goddess of) – Athena
wise – circumspect, enlightened, erudite, expedient, learned, politic, profound, provident, sagacious, sage, sane, sapient
wise (supposedly)–sapient
wise (worldly) – sophisticated
wise counselor–nestor
wise man–sage, solon
wise men–Magi
wise men (the three) – Balthasar, Gaspar, Melchior
Wise Men of East–Magi
wise old man–nestor
wise saying–adage
wisely–sagely, sapiently
wiser–sager, saner
wish–care, desire, hope, petition, request

wish undone–rue
wisp (dial.)–wase
wisp of smoke–floc
wistfulness (nostalgic) – regret
wit–humor, wag
wit (cutting)–satire
wit (sprightly, Fr.)–esprit
witch–hag, lamia, sorceress
witch (thunder)–Baba
witch's cat–Grimalkin
witchcraft–sorcery
witchcraft (goddess of) – Hecate
witcheries–sorceries
with (prefix)–com, pro
with a crook or bend–akimbo
with celerity–rapidly
with force–amain
with full force–amain
with might–amain
with refinement–delicately
with sails furled and helm lashed–ahull
with three times the number or quantity–trebly
with two axes–biaxially
withdraw – absent, detract, recall, recant, recede, refrain, retire, retract, retreat, retrogade, secede, subside
withdraw from active duty–retire
withdraw from association–secede
withdraw from federation–secede
withdraw soldiers from a city–evacuate
withdrawal – departure, regress, retiral, retreat
withdrew–retired
wither–age, die, fade, sear, sere, shrink, shrivel, wilt, wizen
withered–sapless, sere
withered (bot.)–marcesant
withes–wattles
withheld – checked, curbed, denied, detained, refrained, repressed, reserved, restrained
withhold – curb, deny, repress, reserve

within–in, inly
within (comb. form)–endo, ent, ento, eso
within (prefix)–eso, intra
within the time of–during
without–sans, sine
without (comb. form)–ect
without (French)–sans
without (Latin)–sine
without (prefix)–ect, ecto, se
without action–deedless
without appointing day to assemble–sine die
without beginning or end–eternal
without cover–lidless
without day–sine die
without delay–summary
without deliberation – headlong
without doubt–sine dubio
without ethical quality – amoral
without exception – universally
without feet–apod, apodal
without fluid–aneroid
without friends–lorn
without funds – bankrupt, broke
without heed–inadvertently
without interest–barren
without kindred–lorn
without knowledge – ignorant
without limits of duration – ageless
without mate–odd
without natural covering – bald
without personal interest – disinterestedly
without place–endo, eso
without qualification – categorical
without reason–needless
without rule or government –anarchic
without substance–inane
without support–dependent, legless
without teeth – edentate, toothless
without this–sine hoc
without wings–apteral

withstand–bear, endure, resist
withstood–opposed
witless–foolish, heedless, indiscreet
witless (inane)–stupid
witness – attest, beheld, behold, beholder, observe, observer, onlooker, see, spectator, subscribe, testor
witness (law)–teste
witnessing clause to a writ–teste
witticism – jest, joke, mot, sally
witting – information, intelligence, judgment, knowledge, tidings
witty – clever, facetious, knowing, wise
witty (arch.)–facete
witty answer–repartee
witty person – comedian, wag
witty saying–mot
wizard – conjurer, genius, magician, prodigy, sage, sorcerer
wizard (anc.)–Merlin
Wizard's home (comic opera)–Oz
wlo fringe, hem
woad–dyestuff
woe–bale, bane, grief, misery, sorrow
woebegone–dejected, dispirited, melancholy, unhappy
woeful – afflicted, direful, sad, wretched
wold–forest, plain, wood
wolf (prairie)–coyote
wolf (western U.S. timber)–lobo
wolfhound–alan
wolfish–lupine
wolflike–lupine
wolframite–cal
woman (alluring)–siren
woman (Arabic)–bint
woman (attractive, slang) – looker
woman (beautiful, very) – peri
woman (beautiful, young)–Musidora

woman (bewitching)–siren
woman (bored, Fr.) – ennuyee
woman (borne more than one child)–multipara
woman (dignified, elderly)–dowager
woman (dowdyish)–frump
woman (dowdy, old) – frump
woman (evil, old)–hellcat
woman (famous western) – Montez
woman (fascinating) – charmer, siren
woman (gossipy)–cat
woman (graceful)–sylph
woman (gypsy)–romni
woman (humble, old) – crone
woman (ill-tempered) – vixen
woman (learned) – blue, pundita
woman (literary)–blue
woman (loose)–drab, harlot, prostitute, streetwalker, trollop, whore
woman (motherly)–matron
woman (mythical)–gorgon
woman (noisy)–termagant
woman (of affected modesty)–prude
woman (of heroic spirit) – heroine
woman (old)–baba, crone, grimalkin
woman (old, coll.)–gammer
woman (old unmarried) – spinster
woman (pedantic)–blue
woman (poor, old, withered)–crone
woman (pretty)–peri
woman (rare)–maness
woman (scolding)–shrew
woman (sent out of London) – evacuee, vackie (slang)
woman (shrewish)–virago
woman (slender)–sylph
woman (slovenly)–trollop
woman (spiteful)–cat
woman (staid)–matron
woman (stately) – lady, matron

woman (Thomson's Seasons)–Musidora
woman (ugly, old) – crone, hag
woman (unmarried, cohabiting with a man)–concubine
woman (untidy)–slattern
woman (very pretty)–peri
woman (vexatious)–shrew
woman (violent, hot-tempered)–termagant
woman (vixenish)–harridan, shrew, virago
woman (weeping)–Niobe
woman (who acts as adviser)–egeria
woman (young, unmarried) – damosel, damosella, damoysell, damozel, damozell
woman entertainer–hostess
woman hater–misogynist
woman who has made a will –testatrix
woman's club–ebell, sorosis
woman's domain–distaff
woman's marriage portion (pert. to)–dotal
woman's organization (abbr.)–DAR, WAC
woman's organization (religious)–sisterhood
woman's organization (U.S. Service) – Marines, Spars, WACS, Waves
womanhood (perfection of) –eimer, emer
womanless party – smoker, stag
women (brave)–heroines
women (hatred of)–misogyny
women (in general)–distaff
women of rank–dames
women's apartment (harem)–oda, odah
wonder–admiration, amazement, astonishment, awe, marvel, surprise, wonderment
wonderful–amazing, astonishing, extraordinary, marvelous, wondrous
wonderful (slang)–corking
wont–habit, use

woo–court, spark, sue
wood (aromatic)–cedar
wood (black)–ebony
wood (block of)–nog
wood (comb. form)–xylo
wood (curved strip)–stave
wood (elastic, tough)–ash
wood (fragrant)–aloes, cedar
wood (genip tree)–lana
wood (god of)–idol
wood (goddess of the)–Diana
wood (hard) – ash, mahogany, maple, walnut
wood (hard, dark red)–rata
wood (hard, for cabinet work)–zante
wood (hard light)–poon
wood (hard, light-colored)–maple
wood (lighter than cork) – balsa
wood (of the vera)–venesia
wood (open space in)–glade
wood (readily takes fire) – punk, sponk, touchwood
wood (sandarac tree)–alerce, alerse
wood (small)–grove
wood (square block of)–nog
wood (stick of)–billet
wood (thin strip of)–batten, lath, slat, stave
wood (tonka bean tree) – camara
wood (touch) – punk, punkwood, sponk, spunk
wood (used in flutes)–kokra
wood (West Indian tree) – galba
wood ash substance–potash
wood bundles–fagots
wood clearing–glade
wood deity–faun
wood distilled substance–tar
wood god–Seilenos, Seilenoi (pl.), Silen, Silenus, Sileni (pl.)
wood growth (cut periodically)–coppice
wood imperfectly burned (in charcoal pit)–brae
wood knot – gnarl, knag, knar, nur
wood nymph–dryad

wood pigeon–cushat
wood sorrel–oca, oxalis
wood stork–ibis
wood strip–lath, slat, stave
wood strip (curved)–stave
wood strip (used for spacing in printing posters)–reglet
wood used in making bows–yew
wood used in masts (hard)–poon
wood used in masts (hard, light)–ash
woodchopper–axeman, logger, woodsman
woodchuck–marmot
woodcock (Virginia)–pewee
woodcutter–axeman, logger, sawyer, woodsman
woodland–forest
woodland deity–faun, Pan, satyr
woodland godling (Greek myth.)–Silenus
woodpecker–chab
woodpecker (golden winged)–flicker
woodpecker (green)–yaffle, yaffler
woodpeckers (genus of)–picus, pici (pl.)
woodworking tool – adz, adze
wooden block–nog
wooden container – barrel, box, case
wooden joint–tenon
wooden pin–dowel, fid, nog, peg, spile
wooden shoe–patten, sabot
wooden stand (tile making top of)–criss
wooden tub (large, dial.) – soe
woods (growth of, cut periodically)–coppice
woods (pert. to)–sylvan
woody–xyloid
woody fiber (rope making)–bast
woody plant juice–sap
woody plants (obs.)–treen
woody vines (genus of) – hedera
wooed–courted

wooer–suitor
woof–filling, weft
woof (web)–abb
wool–fleece
wool (carded)–teased
wool (colored)–beige
wool (kind of) – alpaca, angora, llama, merino
wool (mixed of varied hues) –tum
wool (or flax combing implement)–teaser
wool (reclaimed)–shoddy
wool (resembling)–lanose
wool (spun)–yarn
wool (taken from dead sheep)–mortling
wool (waste)–noil
wool blemish–mote
wool fat (purified)–lanolin, lanoline
wool fiber–nep
wool fiber cluster–nep
wool grease–lanolin
woolen cloth – cassimere, flannel, serge, tamine
woolen cloth (kind of)–tamine
woolen cloth (naplike)–duffel
woolen goods waste–mungo
woolen stuff (thick)–ratteen
wooly – fleecy, lanate, lanated, lanose
word (catch)–cue
word (containing all vowels in sequence)–caesious
word (distinguishing the adherents of a party or sect) –shibboleth
word (figurative use of) – trope
word (first of handwriting on wall)–mene, tekel, upharsin
word (imitative) – onomatope
word (longest in dictionary) –honnisoitquimalypense
word (most widely used)–amen
word (mysterious, in Psalms)–selah, shelah
word (negative, connecting) –nor

word (not containing vowels A, E, I, O, U) – rhythm, syzygy
word (old love song)–amoret
word (only one ending in eny)–deny
word (reading same backward and forward, pert. to)–palindromic
word (sacred) – om, selah, sesame, shelah, um
word (terminal)–amen, finis
word (that is same backward or forward)–palindrome
word (used for another in figure of speech) – metonym
word (used in epitaphs)–hicjacet
word coiner–neologist
word denoting maker of old violin–fecit
word expressing relation between subject and predicate–copula
word for opening doors – sesame
word for word–literal
word group (expressing complete thought) – sentence
word having same sound but different meaning – homomorph
word introducing an alternative–whether
word inventor–coiner
word of action–verb
word of approval–bravo
word of definite mention – the
word of honor–parole
word of lamentation–alas
word of mouth (done by)–parol
word of reproach–raca
word of reproof–tut
word of solemn assent – amen
word of sorrow–alas
word rhyming with another –clewed
word spelled like another

of different sound and meaning–heteronym

word syllable–penult

word that is the name of a thing–noun

word used–term

word used in limited sense–term

word used in special sense–term

word which predicates something–verb

wordiness–verbiage

words–terms

words (author's original) – text

words (law)–parols

words (song hit)–lyrics

words (use of new)–neology

words (war on)–logomachy

wordy–prolix, verbose

wore–ate, sported

wore away – corroded, eroded

wore ostentatiously–sported

work – drudgery, ferment, function, labor, operate, opus, toil

work (defensive)–fort

work (defensive, isolated)–sconce

work (defensive, of stakes)–estacade

work (diligently)–peg, ply

work (divine)–theurgy

work (inlay)–mosaic

work (musical)–opera, opus

work (ornamental, resembling foliage)–leafwork

work (piece of)–job

work (piece of, with black inlay)–niello

work (skilled mechanical)–sloid, slojd, sloyd

work agreement–code, contract, pact

work at steadily–ply

work clay–puddle

work composed of selections –cento

work diligently – drill, drudge, peg

work for–serve

work hard – drudge, labor, moil, peg, toil

work hard (Scot.)–tew

work horse (Prov. Eng.) – capo

work insidiously–worm

work into a mass–knead

work of acknowledged excellence–classic

work over – elaborate, revamp

work out–solve

work out in detail–elaborate

work resembling a hodgepodge–cento

work slavishly–drudge

work steadily–drudge, ply

work together–cooperate

work too hard–overdo

work unit–ergon

work with–cooperate

work with hands–knead

workman–artificer, artisan, craftsman, laborer, mechanic, operative, operator, wright

workman (organ pipe voicer)–toner

workman (unskilled) – coolie, laborer, peon

workman-like – adept, deft, proficient, skillful

workman's bench–siege

workshop – factory, mill, plant

workshop (artist's)–atelier

workshop (experimental) – lab, laboratory

worked or penetrated (easily)–mellow

worked out (completely) – matured

worked out with care–elaborate

worked up–het, irate

worker (dock)–stevedore

worker (fellow)–confrere

worker (fine)–artisan

worker (hide)–tanner

worker (ingot)–barman

worker (itinerant)–hobo

worker (metal)–smith

worker (ornamental)–enameler

worker (railroad, who bolts splices to rails)–strapper

worker (shoe)–cobbler, laster

worker (skilled)–artisan

worker (social, expert)–clinician

worker (stone)–mason, slater

worker (submarine)–diver

worker (textile) – spinner, warper

worker (underground) – miner, sapper

worker (window)–glazier

workers (gang of)–crew

worker's union–artel

working (not)–idle, off

working together (act of)–collaboration

works of mercy–alms

world–cosmos, universe

world (lower)–Erebus, Hades, Orcus

world (universe in miniature)–microcosm

world of fairies–faerie

World War debts–trillions

World War veteran organization–Fidac

world-wide–global, pandemic

worldly – earthen, earthly, carnal, mundane, secular, sensual, sophisticated

world's speech–volapuk

worm–eri, ess

worm (aquatic)–leech

worm (arrow)–sagitta

worm (caddis)–cadew

worm (class of)–annelid

worm (earth)–annelid, ipomoea

worm (edible mud)–ipo

worm (eye-infecting)–loa

worm (fresh water)–naid

worm (kind of)–cadew, ipomoea, nemertina, nemertinea, nemertini

worm (measuring)–looper

worm (mud)–ipo

worm (ribbon) – nemertina, nemertine, nemertinea, nemertini

worm (ring)–tinea

worm (Samoan mud)–ipo

worm (sea)–sao

worm (ship)–borer, teredo

worm (sigmate)–ess

worm (silk)–eri, eria (pl.)

worm (soft, thick)–grub

worm (voracious)–sao
worm-like–vermian
worm track (petrified)–helminthite
worms (order of marine) – achaeta
worms (trematode larval stage)–cercaria
worn – commonplace, exhausted, hackneyed, sere, stale, trite, used, weakened
worn and gaunt–haggard
worn by friction–attrited
worn off–abraded
worn out – effete, haggard, jaded, passe, seedy
worried – anxious, cared, fearful, fretted, perturbed, stewed, troubled
worry – bedevil, bother, brood, care, faze, fret, harass, perturb, pester, pother, stew, trouble
worry (annoying) – harassment
worry at persistently–nag
worship – adore, adoration, honor, respect, revere, reverence
worship (form of)–ritual
worship (house of)–chapel, church, tabernacle, temple
worship of a god–theolatry
worship of but one god – monolatry
worship of the mob–mobolatry
worshiper–adorer, votary
worshiper (image)–iconolater
worshiper (sun)–heliolater
worshiper of god of wood or stone–idolist
worshiper of one god–monolater
worshipful liturgical petition–preces
worst – bad, beat, disagreeable, evil, harmful, inferior, pernicious, unfortunate, unpleasant
worsted cloth–serge, tamine
worsted ribbed fabric–whipcord

worth – desert, deserving, merit, price, value
worth having–desirable
worthless – base, mean, ort, trashy, undeserving, unworthy, useless, valueless, vile
worthless (Bible)–raca
worthless (Jewish Bible) – raca
worthless (slang)–N.G.
worthless anything–rap
worthless bit–ort
worthless leavings–ort
worthwhile (most)–best
worthy–competent, deserving, estimable, meriting, qualified, valuable
worthy of belief–credible
wough–harm, wrong
wound–damage, detriment, distress, grieve, harm, hurt, injury, pain, rist, scar, sting, trauma
wound (dagger)–stab
wound (dressing for)–pledget
wound about – twined, wrapped
wove–spun
woven–fabricated, spun
woven container–basket
wrangle – altercate, altercation, argue, bicker, bickering, brawl, controversy, debate, dispute, quarrel, spar
wrangler–antagonist, herdsman, opponent
wrap–blanket, cloak, covering, envelop, rug, swathe, wind
wrap (knitted)–afghan
wrap (to)–cere
wrap about a staff–furl
wrap around oneself–roll
wrap in bandage–swathe
wrap up in monks hood–encowl
wrapper – envelope, undershirt, undervest
wrapper (embalmed body)–cerer
wrapping (for dead) – cerement

wrast–disposed, strain, twist, wrest
wrath–anger, fury, ire, passion
wrathful–furious, incensed, irate, ireful, malignant, passionate, raging
wreath – anadem, corona, coronet, festoon, garland, lei, orle
wreath (heraldic)–torse
wreath (knight's, bearing crest)–orle
wreath (poetic)–anadem
wreath of honor–laurel
wreathe together–entwine
wreathed–twined
wreck – demolish, destroy, disable, ruin, smash
wreck (human)–derelict
wreckage (floating on the sea)–driftage, flotsam
wrench – crescent, monkey, pipe, pull, spanner, Stillson, tear, twist, wrest
wrench (monkey)–spanner
wrench (pipe)–Stillson
wrench inventor–Stillson
wrest – extort, rend, turn, wrench
wrest by undue illegal power –extort
wrestle–tug, tussle
wrestling place–palaestra
wretch–dog, rapscallion
wretchedness – meanness, misery, paltriness, poorness
wriggle–squirm, writhe
wriggling–eely
wrinkle–contract, corrugate, corrugation, crease, crimp, pucker, ridge, rimple, ripple, ruga, rugae (pl.) rumple, seam
wrinkle (arch.)–rivel
wrinkled – rugate, rugose, rugous
wrinkled and curled–rugate, savoyed
wrinkles–rugae
wrist–carpus
wrist (of the)–carpal
wrist (pert. to)–carpal
wrist band (ornamental) – bracelet

wrist bone–carpus, ulna
writ (bringing defendant into court)–process
writ (execution)–outre
writ (issued out of chancery or superior court)–certiorari
writ (judicial)–elegit, venire
writ (legal)–capias, elegit
writ (of execution)–elegit
writ (U.S. Federal Court)–certiorari
writ for additional jurors–tales
writ for summoning a jury–venire
writ of execution (authorizing levy on goods)–fierifacias
write–indite, pen
write carelessly – scrawl, scribble
write down–indite, record
write in large hand–engross
write on front of draft–enface
writer – author, columnist, novelist, penman, scribe
writer (depicting real things)–realist
writer (hack)–penster
writer (nature story)–Seton
writer (poor)–hack
writer and reader–literate
writer of explanatory notes –annotater
writer of religious poems–hymnist

writer of sensational plays–dramatist
writer of travesty–parodist
writhing–eely
writing (mounted on paper, in a scroll)–makimono
writing (piece of, abbr.) – MS
writing (script, with heavy, nearly upright strokes)–ronde
writing (unmetered)–prose
writing characters (anc., wedge-shaped) – cuneiform
writing in alternate–boustrophedon
writing in cipher–crytography
writing instrument (pointed)–stylus
writing master–stylist
writing material (of animal skins)–parchment
writing tablet–pad, slate
writings (collective)–literature
writings (sacred)–Bible, Koran, psalms, scriptures, Talmud
written agreement–cartel
written characters–script
wrong–amiss, awry, erroneous, false, faulty, immoral, incorrect, iniquitous, injustice, mistaken, off, out, sinful, tort, unfit, wicked

wrong (civil)–tort
wrong (law)–tort
wrong (legal)–malum
wrong (prefix)–mis
wrong (public)–crime
wrong (Scot.)–agley
wrong nor right (neither)–adiaphorous
wrongdoer–criminal, sinner
wrongly used–misapplied
wrote carelessly – scrawled, scribbled
wroth – angry, exasperated, incensed, irate, wrathful
wrought – decorated, elaborated, fashioned, formed, ornamented, worked
wrought out (carefully) – elaborate
wrought up–agog, eager, excited
wryneck–loxia, torticollis
Wurttemberg city – Esslingen, Heilbronn, Ulm
Wurttemberg lake – Constance
Wurttemberg measure–ecklein, fuder, fuss, imi, juchart, rute, simri, tagwerk, vierling, viertelein
Wurttemberg river–Danube, Neckar
Wyoming city–Laramie
Wyoming mountain–Moran, Teton
Wyoming river–Teton
Wyoming town–Cody

X

xanthic–yellow
xebec–boat, vessel
xenagogue–guide
xenagogy–guidebook
xenium–gift, present
xenon (chem. symbol)–Xe
Xenophon's historical work –Anabasis

Xenophon's history – Anabasis
xeres–sherry
xeromyron–ointment
xerotic–dry
xibalba–underworld
Xingu River Indian–Aneto
Xmas–Christmas

X-ray inventor–Roentgen
X-ray source–target
xylate–ester, salt
xylograph – engraving, impression, print
xyloid–ligneous, woody
xylophone–gigelira
xyrid–iris

Y

yacht–boat, sail, ship
yaffle–armful, handful
yahoo–bumpkin, lout
Yale–Eli
yam (kind of)–ube, uve
yank–jerk, pull, Yankee
yap – bumpkin, greenhorn, yelp
yard – confine, enclose, enclosure, spar, store
yard (sail, Scot.)–rae
yard (sixteenth of)–nail
yard hoisting rope (naut.)–tye
yarm–scream, wail, whine, yell
yarn–crewel, story, tale
yarn (ball of)–clew, clue
yarn (conical mass of)–cop
yarn (for wood)–abb
yarn (quantity)–hank, skein
yarn (warp)–abb
yarn (worsted, slackly twisted)–crewel
yarn holder–cop
yarn measure–lea
yarn of wool–abb
yarn pieces, for fastening sails–ropebands
yarn size (linen)–lea
yarn size (rayon)–denier
yarn size (silk)–denier
yaw–deviate, swerve, turn, veer
yawn–gape
yawn (Scot.)–gant
yawning–agape
ye shall (Scot.)–ye'se
year book (astronomical)–almanac
year division–season
yearly recurring–etesian
years (hundred)–centenary
years (thousand)–millennium
year's record–annal, calendar
yearn–crave, long, pine, sigh
yearn (coll.)–yen
yearning – anxious, eager, longing, tenderness
yeast–ferment, leaven
yeast (brewer's)–barm

yed–fib, lie, quarrel, wrangle
yeder–great, prompt, quick, vehement
yegg – burglar, safebreaker, yeggman
yell (shrilly)–scream
yelling–clamorous, strident
yellow (golden)–gilt
yellow bugle–iva
yellow color (gold, her.)–or
yellow crystalline compound –malarin
yellow dyestuff–morin
yellow gray–drab
yellow gurnard–dragonet
yellow herb–iva
yellow ocher–sil
yellow to red pigment–orpin
yellowhammer–skite, yite
yellowish – amber, golden, lutescent, xanthic
yellowish gray powder (medicinal)–tannigen
yellowish red–nacarat, sandy
yellowish red dyestuff–annatto, annotto, arnatto, orlean
Yellowstone Park attraction –geyser, Old Faithful
yelp–ululate, yip
yeme – govern, guard, heed, observe, regard
Yemen town (fortified) – Damar
yemschik – coachman, postboy, postilion
yeoman–assistant, attendant, butler, clerk, freeholder, retainer, subordinate
yeoman of guard officer – exon
yeoman officer–exon
yep – active, alert, bold, smart, vigorous
yercum (bark yielding) – madar, mudar
yes–aye, yea
yes (Eng. dial.)–iss
yes (German)–ja
yes (Italian)–si
yes (Spanish)–si
yew (former spelling)–ew

yield–accede, afford, bend, cede, comply, defer, give, net, relent, render, soften, stoop, submit, succumb, surrender, vail, waive
yield (former spelling)–elde
yielders to Pizarro–Incas
yielding–compliant, flexible, manageable, soft, submissive, supple, tractable
yielding (respectful)–deference
yielding little–penurious
yielding to a demand, desire, proposal–compliance
yields assent–accedes
yogi–ascetic, fakeer, fakir
yoke–associate, couple, join, link, marry
yoke (as oxen)–inspan
yokel–bumpkin, clod, lout, plowboy, rustic
yonder (poetic)–yon
yore (of, poetic)–olden
yorker (cricket)–tice
Yorkshire river–Ure
younger daughter (Fr.) – cadette
younger sister (Fr.)–cadette
youngster–boy, child, colt, cub, filly, lad, shaver, tad, tike, tot
younker–gallant, gentleman, knight, nobleman
your (arch.)–thy
youth–gossoon
youth (goddess of)–Hebe
youth (Scot.)–callant
youth beloved by Venus – Adonis
youthful – boyish, callow, juvenile, puerile, young
yttrium (chemical symbol)–Yt
Yucatan port–Sisal
Yugoslavian capital – Belgrade
Yugoslavian city–Banjaluka, Belgrade, Bitolj, Cattaro, Maribor, Morava, Mostar, Nis, Prilep, Sarajevo,

Skoplje, Spalato, Subotica, Subotitsa, Vardar, Zagreb
Yugoslavian coin – dinar (cop., ni.), para (ac.)
Yugoslavian commune–Stip
Yugoslavian measure–akov, dan oranja, donum, khvat,

lanaz, motyka, oka, palaze, ralico, ralo, rif, stopa
Yugoslavian monarch–Peter
Yugoslavian money–dinar
Yugoslavian organization (death scorning) – Comitadji

Yugoslavian region–Bosnia
Yugoslavian river–Danube, Drava, Drina, Morava, Sava, Vardar
Yugoslavian weight – dramm, oka, oke, satlijk, tovar, wagon

Z

"Z" (English letter)–zed
"Z" (old form)–izzard, zed
Zambales language–Tino
Zambales Province capital (P.I.)–Iba
Zamindar chief of peons – Mirdaha
Zamindar village overseer–Mirdaha
zanja–arroyo, canal, gully
Zanzibar native–Swahili
Zanzibar sultan's title–sayid
Zanzibar weight–farsalah
zeal–ardor, eagerness, fervor
zealot–devotee, fanatic, votary
zealous – ardent, devoted, earnest, fervid, warm
zebrawood–araroba
zeekoe–hippopotamus
zenana–harem, seraglio
zenith – acme, culmination, peak, summit
zero–cipher, nothing
zest–gusto, relish, tang
Zeus (the avenger)–Alastor
Zeus' beloved princess–Europa
Zeus' brother–Hades
Zeus' daughter – Astraea,

Athena, Despoina, Kore, Persephassa, Persephone, Proserpina, Proserpine
Zeus' epithet–soter
Zeus' mother–Rhea
Zeus' sister–Hera
Zeus' son – Ares, Hermes, Lasus, Perseus
Zeus' sweetheart–Io
Zeus' wife–Danae, Hera
Zeus' wife (first)–Metis
zinc (crude) – tutenag, tutenague
zing – energy, enthusiasm, spirit, vim
zingaro–gypsy
Zobeide's sister (half) – Amina
zodiac sign–(1) Aries (ram); (2) Taurus (bull); (3) Gemini (twins); (4) Cancer (crab); (5) Leo (lion); (6) Virgo (virgin); (7) Libra (balance); (8) Scorpio (scorpion); (9) Sagittarius (archer); (10) Capricornus (goat); (11) Aquarius (water bearer); (12) Pisces (fishes)
zodiac sign (ruler of ten degrees)–Decan

zodiac signs (number of)– twelve
Zola's (Emile) novel – Assommoir, Nana
zone – area, band, belt, region, tract
zone marked–zonate
zones (succession of geological)–assise
zoological family (comprising frogs)–ranidae
zoological group–cnidaria
zoological order (frogs, etc.) –anura
zoological suffix–iid
zoophyte skeleton–coral
Zoroaster's works–Avesta
Zoroastrian–Parsee
Zoroastrian scripture (anc.)– Avesta
Zouave (nickname for)–Zuzu
zounds–egad
zuisan–widgeon
Zulu army–impi
Zulu boy (nurse)–umfaan
Zulu regiment–impi
Zulu spear–assegai
zygon–bench, thwart